Connect™ Accounting

Instructors...

Q Want to **streamline** lesson planning, student progress reporting, and assignment grading? (Less time planning means more time teaching...)

Need to **collect data and generate reports** required by accreditation organizations, such as AACSB and AICPA? (Say goodbye to manually tracking student learning outcomes...)

Want an **instant view** of student or class performance relative to learning objectives? (No more wondering if students understand...)

A With **McGraw-Hill Connect™ Accounting,**

INSTRUCTORS GET

- The ability to **post assignments** and other communication between students and instructors.

- Simple **assignment management**, allowing you to spend more time teaching.

- **Auto-graded homework.**

- **Customized course gradebook** where grades are automatically posted.

- **Online testing capability.**

- A **progress-tracking** function that allows you to easily assign materials that conform to AACSB and AICPA standards.

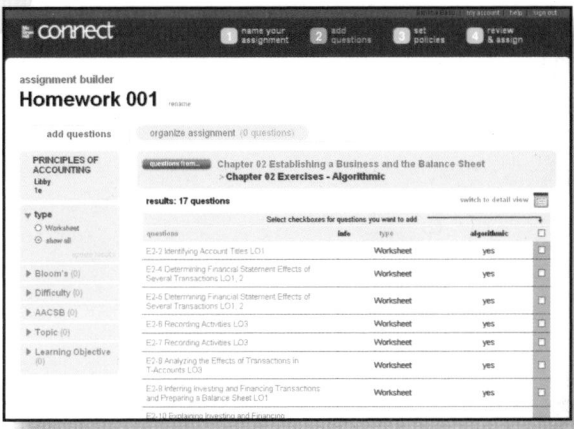

Want an online, **searchable version** of your textbook?

Wish your textbook could be available online while you're doing your homework?

Connect™ Plus Accounting eBook

If your instructor has chosen to use *Connect™ Plus Accounting*, you have an affordable and searchable online version of your book integrated with your other online homework tools.

Connect™ Plus Accounting eBook offers features like:

- topic search
- adjustable text size
- jump to page number
- print by section

Want to get more **value** from your textbook purchase?

Think learning accounting should be a little bit more **interesting**?

Check out the companion website for this textbook www.mhhe.com/wildFA5e

We put it there for you. Go online for test tips and practice problems whenever you study. The companion website for this book includes **quizzes, PowerPoints, and Internet activities** to help you study. Get more from your textbook – use the Online Learning Center.

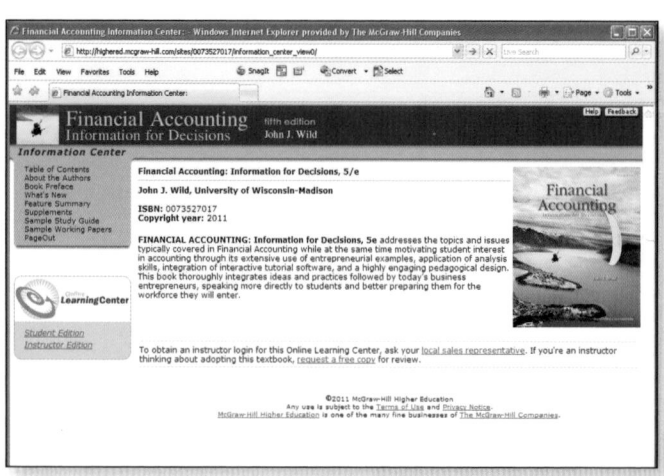

5 edition

Financial Accounting
Information for Decisions

John J. Wild

University of Wisconsin at Madison

McGraw-Hill Irwin

To my wife **Gail** and children, **Kimberly, Jonathan, Stephanie,** and **Trevor.**

 **McGraw-Hill Irwin**

FINANCIAL ACCOUNTING: INFORMATION FOR DECISIONS
Published by McGraw-Hill/Irwin, a business unit of The McGraw-Hill Companies, Inc., 1221 Avenue of the Americas, New York, NY, 10020. Copyright © 2011, 2008, 2005, 2003, 2000 by The McGraw-Hill Companies, Inc. All rights reserved. No part of this publication may be reproduced or distributed in any form or by any means, or stored in a database or retrieval system, without the prior written consent of The McGraw-Hill Companies, Inc., including, but not limited to, in any network or other electronic storage or transmission, or broadcast for distance learning.

Some ancillaries, including electronic and print components, may not be available to customers outside the United States.

This book is printed on acid-free paper.

1 2 3 4 5 6 7 8 9 0 DOW/DOW 1 0 9 8 7 6 5 4 3 2 1 0

ISBN   978-0-07-352701-7
MHID   0-07-352701-7

Vice president and editor-in-chief: *Brent Gordon*
Editorial director: *Stewart Mattson*
Publisher: *Tim Vertovec*
Senior sponsoring editor: *Dana L. Woo*
Director of development: *Ann Torbert*
Senior development editor: *Christina A. Sanders*
Vice president and director of marketing: *Robin J. Zwettler*
Marketing director: *Sankha Basu*
Marketing manager: *Kathleen Klehr*
Vice president of editing, design and production: *Sesha Bolisetty*
Managing editor: *Lori Koetters*
Lead production supervisor: *Carol A. Bielski*
Lead designer: *Matthew Baldwin*
Senior photo research coordinator: *Lori Kramer*
Photo researcher: *Sarah Evertson*
Lead media project manager: *Brian Nacik*
Cover design: *Matthew Baldwin*
Interior design: *Matthew Baldwin*
Cover image: © *Getty Images*
Typeface: *10.5/12 Times Roman*
Compositor: *Aptara®, Inc.*
Printer: *R. R. Donnelley*

Library of Congress Cataloging-in-Publication Data
Wild, John J.
    Financial accounting : information for decisions / John J. Wild.—5th ed.
        p. cm.
    Includes index.
    ISBN-13: 978-0-07-352701-7 (alk. paper)
    ISBN-10: 0-07-352701-7 (alk. paper)
    1. Accounting. I. Title.
HF5635.W695 2011
657—dc22
                                                    2009043318

www.mhhe.com

Dear Friends/Colleagues,

These are exciting times in accounting education. Technology advancements are enhancing our instructional capabilities, international accounting standards are on the horizon, and our students and their skills are in demand. This new edition of *Financial Accounting* reflects these exciting developments through several key revisions. Our new *Connect Plus* offers an innovative way for students to learn and assess their accounting skills. Our new *Global View* section at the end of each chapter promotes international accounting skills suited to our increasingly global accounting system. And, specific chapter-by-chapter learning enhancements further expand the instructional model of our best-selling accounting textbook.

These changes are in many ways due to your teaching commitment and constructive feedback. I thank each of you who provided suggestions and ideas to enrich this textbook. As teachers, we know how important it is to select the right book for our course. This new edition reflects the advice and wisdom of many dedicated reviewers, focus group participants, students, and instructors. Together, we have created the most readable, concise, current, accurate, and innovative accounting book available today.

Throughout the writing process, we steered this book in the manner you directed. This path of development enhanced this book's technology and content and guided its clear and concise writing. Reviewers, instructors, and students say this book's leading-edge technology caters to different learning styles and helps students better understand accounting. *Connect Plus* offers new features to improve student learning and to assist in the assessment of that learning. Our *iPod* content lets students study on the go, while our enhanced *Algorithmic Test Bank* provides an infinite variety of exam problems. You and your students will find all these tools easy to apply.

I owe the success of this book to colleagues, such as you, who graciously took time to help us focus on the changing needs of today's instructors and students. I feel fortunate to have witnessed our profession's extraordinary devotion to teaching. Your feedback and suggestions are reflected in everything I write. Please accept my heartfelt thanks for your dedication in helping today's students understand and appreciate accounting.

With kindest regards,

John J. Wild

John J. Wild is a distinguished professor of accounting at the University of Wisconsin at Madison. He previously held appointments at Michigan State University and the University of Manchester in England. He received his BBA, MS, and PhD from the University of Wisconsin.

Professor Wild teaches accounting courses at both the undergraduate and graduate levels. He has received numerous teaching honors, including the Mabel W. Chipman Excellence-in-Teaching Award, the departmental Excellence-in-Teaching Award, and the Teaching Excellence Award from the 2003 and 2005 business graduates at the University of Wisconsin. He also received the Beta Alpha Psi and Roland F. Salmonson Excellence-in-Teaching Award from Michigan State University. Professor Wild has received several research honors and is a past KPMG Peat Marwick National Fellow and is a recipient of fellowships from the American Accounting Association and the Ernst and Young Foundation.

Professor Wild is an active member of the American Accounting Association and its sections. He has served on several committees of these organizations, including the Outstanding Accounting Educator Award, Wildman Award, National Program Advisory, Publications, and Research Committees. Professor Wild is author of several books, including *Fundamental Accounting Principles, Managerial Accounting,* and *College Accounting,* each published by McGraw-Hill/Irwin. His research articles on accounting and analysis appear in *The Accounting Review, Journal of Accounting Research, Journal of Accounting and Economics, Contemporary Accounting Research, Journal of Accounting, Auditing and Finance, Journal of Accounting and Public Policy,* and other journals. He is past associate editor of Contemporary Accounting Research and has served on several editorial boards including The Accounting Review.

Professor Wild, his wife, and their four children enjoy travel, music, sports, and community activities.

Financial Accounting, 5e

This book helps **students achieve new heights** in their education by providing leading accounting content that engages students with enhanced learning tools and innovative technology.

One of the greatest challenges students confront in a financial accounting course is seeing its relevance. This book tackles this issue head on with **engaging content** and a **motivating style**. Students are motivated when content is **clear and relevant**. This book leads the pack in captivating students. Its chapter-opening features showcase dynamic, successful, entrepreneurial individuals and companies guaranteed to **interest and excite readers**. This edition's featured companies (Best Buy, RadioShack, GOME, and Apple) engage students with their annual reports, which are great vehicles for learning financial statements.

This book also delivers **innovative technology** to help students achieve success. **Connect Accounting™** provides students with instant grading feedback for assignments that are completed online. **Connect Accounting Plus™** integrates an online version of the textbook with our popular Connect system. An enhanced **algorithmic test bank** in Connect offers infinite variations of numerical text bank questions. This book also offers accounting students portable **iPod-ready content**. Each of these tools is user-friendly and encourages our students to better learn financial accounting.

We're confident you'll agree that Wild's *Financial Accounting* **(FA) will help you and your students achieve new heights**.

Innovative Content

FA content continues to set the standard in the financial accounting course. Take a look at Chapters 1, 2, and 3 and you'll see how *FA* leads with the best coverage of the accounting cycle. We are the first book to cover equity transactions the way most instructors teach it and students learn it–by introducing the separate equity accounts upfront and not waiting until a chapter or two later. Chapter 2 has the time-tested 4-step approach to analyzing transactions: [1] Identify, [2] Analyze, [3] Record, and [4] Post. Chapter 3 offers a new 3-step process to simplify adjusting accounts (see excerpt to the side). *FA* also motivates students with engaging chapter openers. Students identify with them and can even picture themselves as future entrepreneurs who successfully use accounting methods.

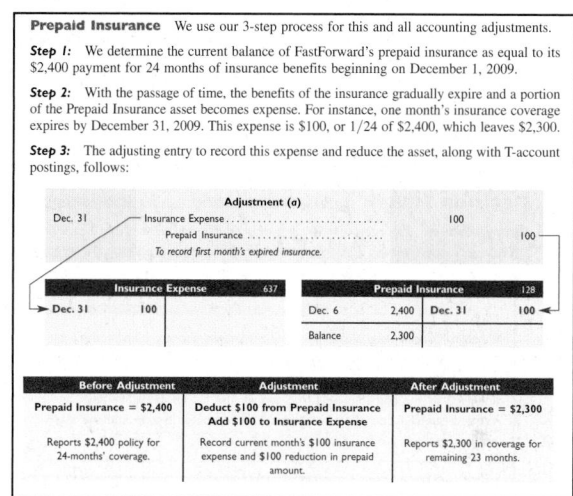

International Coverage

A Global View section has been added to the end of each chapter to highlight international accounting practices, including the similarities and differences for financial reporting under IFRS versus U.S. GAAP. Many chapters also include IFRS boxes showcasing relevant international accounting concepts.

Income Statement Presentation

We explained that net income, profit, and earnings refer to the same (*bottom line*) item. However, IFRS tends to use the term *profit* more than any other term, whereas U.S. statements tend to use *net income* more than any other term. Both U.S. GAAP and IFRS income statements begin with the net sales or net revenues (*top line*) item. Further, for merchandisers and manufacturers, this is followed by cost of goods sold. The presentation is similar for the remaining items with a few differences.

- U.S. GAAP offers little guidance about the presentation or order of expenses. IFRS requires separate disclosures for financing costs (interest expense), income tax expense, and some other special items.
- Both systems require separate disclosure of items when their size, nature, or frequency are important for proper interpretation.
- IFRS permits expenses to be presented by their function or their nature. U.S. GAAP provides no direction but the SEC requires presentation by function.
- Neither U.S. GAAP nor IFRS define *operating* income; this means classification of expenses into operating or nonoperating reflects management discretion.
- IFRS permits alternative measures of income on the income statement; U.S. GAAP prohibits disclosure of alternative income measures in financial statements.

State-of-the-Art Technology

FA offers the most advanced and comprehensive technology on the market in a seamless, easy-to-use platform. As students learn in different ways, *FA* provides a technology smorgasbord that helps students learn more effectively and efficiently. Connect Accounting, eBook options, and iPod content are some of the options. Connect Accounting Plus takes learning to another level by integrating an online version of the book with all the power of Connect. Technology offerings follow:

- Connect Accounting
- Connect Accounting Plus
- iPod content
- Algorithmic Test Bank
- Online Learning Center
- ALEKS for Accounting Cycle and Financial Accounting

What tools drive student learning

Business Decision Relevance

Whether we prepare, analyze, or apply accounting information, one skill remains essential: decision making. To help develop good decision-making habits and to illustrate the relevance of accounting, *FA* 5e uses a unique pedagogical framework called the Decision Center. This framework consists of a variety of approaches and subject areas, giving students insight into every aspect of business decision making. Answers to Decision Maker and Ethics boxes are at the end of each chapter.

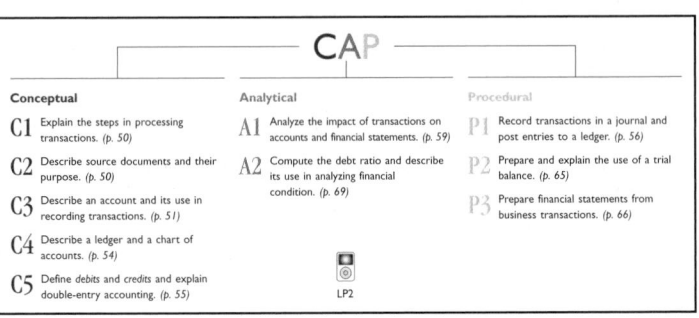

Decision Analysis	Profit Margin and Current Ratio

A2 Compute profit margin and describe its use in analyzing company performance.

Profit Margin

A useful measure of a company's operating results is the ratio of its net income to net sales. This ratio is called **profit margin**, or *return on sales*, and is computed as in Exhibit 3.22.

EXHIBIT 3.22
Profit Margin

$$\text{Profit margin} = \frac{\text{Net income}}{\text{Net sales}}$$

This ratio is interpreted as reflecting the percent of profit in each dollar of sales. To illustrate how we compute and use profit margin, let's look at the results of Limited Brands, Inc., in Exhibit 3.23 for its fiscal years 2006 through 2009.

Decision Maker

Entrepreneur You purchase a batch of products on terms of 3/10, n/90, but your company ha limited cash and you must borrow funds at an 11% annual rate if you are to pay within the discount period. Do you take advantage of the purchase discount? [Answer—p. 182]

Decision Ethics

Credit Manager As a new credit manager, you are being trained by the outgoing manager. She explains that the system prepares checks for amounts net of favorable cash discounts, and the chec dated the last day of the discount period. She also tells you that checks are not mailed until five day adding that "the company gets free use of cash for an extra five days, and our department looks bet When a supplier complains, we blame the computer system and the mailroom." Do you continue th payment policy? [Answer—p. 182]

Decision Insight

SOX: Asset Control Long-term assets must be safeguarded against theft, misuse, and other damages. Controls take many forms depending on the asset, including use of security tags, the legal monitoring of rights infringements, and approvals of all asset disposals. A study reports that 44% of employees in operations and service areas witnessed the wasting, mismanaging, or abusing of assets in the past year (KPMG 2009). Another 21% in general management and administration observed stealing or misappropriation of assets.

IFRS

Adjusting with IFRS Revenue and expense recognition are key to recording accounting adjustments. IFRS tends to be more *principles-based relative* to U.S. GAAP, which is viewed as more *rules-based*. A principles-based system depends heavily on control procedures to reduce the potential for fraud or misconduct. Failure in judgment led to improper accounting adjustments at **Fannie Mae, Xerox, WorldCom,** and others. A KPMG 2009 survey of accounting and finance employees found that 13% of them had witnessed falsification or manipulation of accounting data within the past year. Internal controls and SOX processes are directed at curtailing such behavior.

CAP Learning Model

The Conceptual/Analytical/Procedural (CAP) Model allows courses to be specially designed to meet your teaching needs or those of a diverse faculty. This model identifies learning objectives, textual materials, assignments, and test items by C, A, or P, allowing different instructors to teach from the same materials, yet easily customize their courses toward a conceptual, analytical, or procedural approach (or a combination thereof) based on personal preferences.

CAP

Conceptual

C1 Explain the steps in processing transactions. (p. 50)

C2 Describe source documents and their purpose. (p. 50)

C3 Describe an account and its use in recording transactions. (p. 51)

C4 Describe a ledger and a chart of accounts. (p. 54)

C5 Define *debits* and *credits* and explain double-entry accounting. (p. 55)

Analytical

A1 Analyze the impact of transactions on accounts and financial statements. (p. 59)

A2 Compute the debt ratio and describe its use in analyzing financial condition. (p. 69)

LP2

Procedural

P1 Record transactions in a journal and post entries to a ledger. (p. 56)

P2 Prepare and explain the use of a trial balance. (p. 65)

P3 Prepare financial statements from business transactions. (p. 66)

Global View

This section explains international accounting practices regarding the material covered in that chapter. This section is purposefully located at the end of each chapter so that each instructor can decide what emphasis, if at all, is to be assigned to it. The aim of this Global View section is to describe financial accounting practices and to identify the similarities and differences between International Financial Reporting Standards (IFRS) and U.S. GAAP. As we move toward global convergence in accounting practices, and as we witness the likely conversion of U.S. GAAP to IFRS, the importance of student familiarity with international accounting grows. This innovative section helps us begin down that path of learning and teaching international accounting practices.

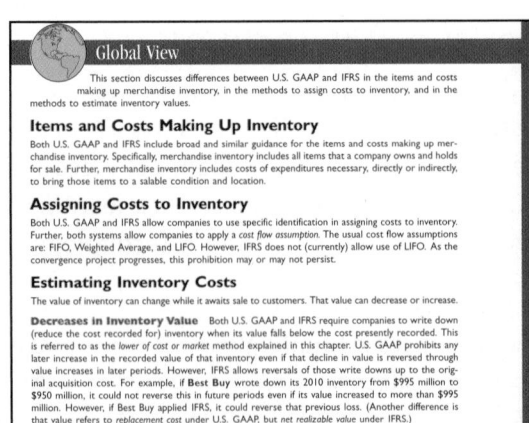

Global View

A2 This section discusses differences between U.S. GAAP and IFRS in the items and costs making up merchandise inventory, in the methods to assign costs to inventory, and in the methods to estimate inventory values.

Items and Costs Making Up Inventory
Both U.S. GAAP and IFRS include broad and similar guidance for the items and costs making up merchandise inventory. Specifically, merchandise inventory includes all items that a company owns and holds for sale. Further, merchandise inventory includes costs of expenditures necessary, directly or indirectly, to bring those items to a salable condition and location.

Assigning Costs to Inventory
Both U.S. GAAP and IFRS allow companies to use specific identification in assigning costs to inventory. Further, both systems allow companies to apply a *cost flow assumption*. The usual cost flow assumptions are: FIFO, Weighted Average, and LIFO. However, IFRS does not (currently) allow use of LIFO. As the convergence project progresses, this prohibition may or may not persist.

Estimating Inventory Costs
The value of inventory can change while it awaits sale to customers. That value can decrease or increase.

Decreases in Inventory Value Both U.S. GAAP and IFRS require companies to write down (reduce the cost recorded for) inventory when its value falls below the cost presently recorded. This is referred to as the *lower of cost or market* method explained in this chapter. U.S. GAAP prohibits any later increase in the recorded value of that inventory even if that decline in value is reversed through value increases in later periods. However, IFRS allows reversals of those write downs up to the original acquisition cost. For example, if **Best Buy** wrote down its 2010 inventory from $995 million to $950 million, it could not reverse this in future periods even if its value increased to more than $995 million. However, if Best Buy applied IFRS, it could reverse that previous loss. (Another difference is that value refers to *replacement cost* under U.S. GAAP, but *net realizable value* under IFRS.)

Increases in Inventory Value Neither U.S. GAAP nor IFRS allow inventory to be adjusted upward beyond the original cost. (One exception is that IFRS requires agricultural assets such as animals, forests, and plants to be measured at fair value less point-of-sale costs.)

Visual Aid Flow Chart

This feature provides a handy textual/visual guide at the start of every chapter. Students can now begin their reading with a clear understanding of what they will learn and when, allowing them to stay more focused and organized along the way.

l statements report on the financial performance and
on of an organization. Knowledge of their preparation,
ation, and analysis is important. A main goal of this
is to illustrate how transactions are recorded, how

they are reflected in financial statements, and how they
impact analysis of financial statements. Debits and credits
introduced and identified as a tool in helping analyze and
process transactions.

Analyzing and Recording Transactions

Analyzing and Recording Process	**Analyzing and Processing Transactions**	**Trial Balance**
• Source documents	• General ledger	• Trial balance preparation
• The account and its analysis	• Double-entry accounting	• Search for and correction of errors
• Types of accounts	• Journalizing and posting	• Trial balance use
	• An Illustration	

Quick Check

These short question/answer features reinforce the material immediately preceding them. They allow the reader to pause and reflect on the topics described, then receive immediate feedback before going on to new topics. Answers are provided at the end of each chapter.

Quick Check
Answers—p. 401

4. Why does a creditor prefer a note payable to a past-due account payable?
5. A company pays its one employee $3,000 per month. This company's FUTA rate is 0.8% on the first $7,000 earned; its SUTA rate is 4.0% on the first $7,000; its Social Security tax rate is 6.2% of the first $106,800; and its Medicare tax rate is 1.45% of all amounts earned. The entry to record this company's March payroll includes what amount for total payroll taxes expense?
6. Identify whether the employer or employee or both incurs each of the following: (a) FICA taxes, (b) FUTA taxes, (c) SUTA taxes, and (d) withheld income taxes.

Marginal Annotations

These annotations provide additional hints, tips, and examples to help students more fully understand the concepts and retain what they have learned. The annotations also include notes on global implications of accounting and further examples.

Point: A sale of a note receivable is often a contingent liability. It becomes a liability if the original signer of the note fails to pay it at maturity.

ing issue is whether the defendant sh
a contingent liability in its notes while
is that a potential claim is recorded in
the amount can be reasonably estimat
or is less than probable but reasonably
ample, includes the following note in
tigations and proceedings and claims are

Debt Guarantees Sometimes a
supplier, customer, or another co

FastForward Case

FastForward is a continuing case in Chapters 1-3 that takes students through the Accounting Cycle. The FastForward icon is placed in the margin when this case is discussed.

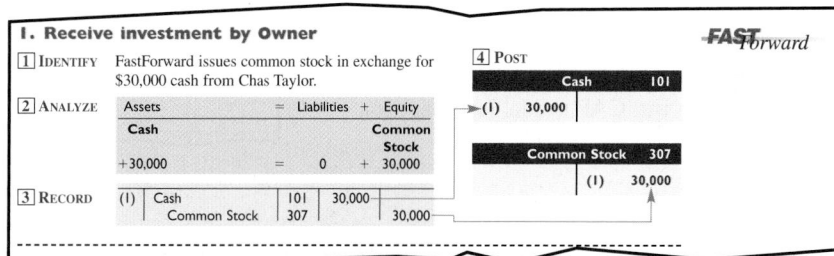

Once a student has finished reading the chapter, how well he or she retains the material can depend greatly on the questions, exercises, and problems that reinforce it. This book leads the way in comprehensive, accurate assignments.

Demonstration Problems present
both a problem and a complete solution, allowing students to review the entire problem-solving process and achieve success.

Chapter Summaries provide students with
a review organized by learning objectives. Chapter Summaries are a component of the CAP model (see page vi), which recaps each conceptual, analytical, and procedural objective.

Key Terms appear in bold in the text and in a list at the end of the
chapter with page numbers indicating their location. The book also includes a complete Glossary of Key Terms.

Multiple Choice Questions quickly test
chapter knowledge before a student moves on to complete Quick Studies, Exercises, and Problems. Additional multiple choice quizzes are available on the textbook Website.

Quick Study assignments are short
exercises that often focus on one learning objective. All are included in Connect. There are usually 8-10 Quick Study assignments per chapter.

Exercises are one of this book's many
strengths and a competitive advantage. There are about 10-15 per chapter and all are included in Connect. Several have real world data and many include at least one addressing international accounting and IFRS.

Problem Sets A & B
are proven problems that can be assigned as homework or for in-class projects. All problems are coded according to the CAP model (see page vi), and Set A is included in Connect.

Demonstration Problem

Clayco Company completes the following selected transactions dur...

July 14 Writes off a $750 account receivable arising from a sale
        months ago. (Clayco Company uses the allowance metho...
     30 Clayco Company receives a $1,000, 90-day, 10% note i...
        Sumrell Company (the merchandise cost $600).
Aug. 15 Receives $2,000 cash plus a $10,000 note from JT Co. in
        for $12,000 (its cost is $8,000). The note is dated August
        in 120 days.
Nov. 1 Completed a $200 credit card sale with a 4% fee (the co...
        ceived immediately from the credit card company.
      3 Sumrell Company refuses to pay the note that was due...
        Prepare the journal entry to charge the dishonored not...
        Company's accounts receivable.
      5 Completed a $500 credit card sale with a 5% fee (the cost
        the credit card company is received on Nov. 9.
     15 Received the full amount of $750 from Briggs Company
        July 14. Record the bad debts recovery.
Dec. 13 Received payment of principal plus interest from JT for the ...

Solution to Demonstration Problem

July 14	Allowance for Doubtful Accounts	750	
	Accounts Receivable—Briggs Co.		750
	Wrote off an uncollectible account.		
July 30	Notes Receivable—Sumrell Co.	1,000	
	Sales		1,000
	Sold merchandise for a 90-day, 10% note.		
July 30	Cost of Goods Sold	600	
	Merchandise Inventory		600
	To record the cost of July 30 sale.		
Aug. 15	Cash	2,000	
	Notes Receivable—JT Co.	10,000	
	Sales		12,000
	Sold merchandise to customer for $2,000 cash and $10,000 note.		
Aug. 15	Cost of Goods Sold	8,000	
	Merchandise Inventory		8,000
	To record the cost of Aug 15 sale.		
Nov. 1	Cash	192	
	Credit Card Expense		

Key Terms

Accounts receivable (p. 296)	Direct write-off method (p. 300)	Payee of the note (p. 307)
Accounts receivable turnover (p. 312)	Interest (p. 307)	Principal of a note (p. 307)
Aging of accounts receivable (p. 304)	Maker of the note (p. 307)	Promissory note (or note) (p. 306)
Allowance for doubtful accounts (p. 301)	Matching principle (p. 300)	Realizable value (p. 301)
Allowance method (p. 301)	Materiality constraint (p. 301)	
Bad debts (p. 300)	Maturity date of a note (p. 307)	

Multiple Choice Quiz   Answers on p. 329   ...hhe.com/wildFA5e

Additional Quiz Questions are available at the book's Website.

1. A company's Accounts Receivable balance at its December 31 year-end is $125,650, and its Allowance for Doubtful Accounts has a credit balance of $328 before year-end adjustment. Its net sales are $572,300. It estimates that 4% of outstanding accounts receivable are uncollectible. What amount of Bad Debts Expense is recorded at December 31?
   a. $5,354
   b. $328
   c. $5,026
   d. $4,698
   e. $34,338

2. A company's Accounts Receivable balance at its December 31 year-end is $489,300, and its Allowance for Doubtful Accounts

3. Total interest to be earned on a $7,500, 5%, 90-day note
   a. $93.75
   b. $375.00
   c. $1,125.00
   d. $31.25
   e. $125.00

4. A company receives a $9,000, 8%, 60-day note. The matur value of the note is
   a. $120
   b. $9,000
   c. $9,120
   d. $720
   e. $9,720

---

connect Available with Connect Accounting

Prepare journal entries for the following credit card sales transactions (the company uses the perpetual inventory system).

1. Sold $16,000 of merchandise, that cost $7,000, on MasterCard credit cards. The net cash receipts from sales are immediately deposited in the seller's bank account. MasterCard charges a 4% fee.

2. Sold $18,000 of merchandise, that cost $7,800, on an assortment of credit cards. Net cash receipts are received 5 days later, and a 3% fee is charged.

QUICK STUDY

QS 7-1
Credit card sales

C1

Available with Connect Accounting connect

EXERCISES

Exercise 7-1
Accounting for credit card sales

C1

Hue Company uses the perpetual inventory system and allows customers to use two credit cards in charging purchases. With the Omni Bank Card, Hue receives an immediate credit to its account when it deposits sales receipts. Omni assesses a 4% service charge for credit card sales. The second credit card that Hue accepts is the Continental Card. Hue sends its accumulated receipts to Continental on a weekly basis and is paid by Continental about a week later. Continental assesses a 2.5% charge on sales for using its card. Prepare journal entries to record the following selected credit card transactions of Hue Company.

Apr. 8 Sold merchandise for $5,600 (that had cost $4,138) and accepted the customer's Omni Bank Card. The Omni receipts are immediately deposited in Hue's bank account.
     12 Sold merchandise for $6,000 (that had cost $4,400) and accepted the customer's Continental Card. Transferred $6,000 of credit card receipts to Continental, requesting payment.
     20 Received Continental's check for the April 12 billing, less the service charge.

PROBLEM SET A

Problem 7-1A
Sales on account and credit card sales

C1

...stomers can use either of two ...on its credit card and credits ...ted. Bantay deposits the Zisa ...rds, Bantay accumulates the ...ccess deducts a 2.5% service ...the following transactions in ...l at the gross price.)

...dia Bullaro.
...s who used their Zisa cards.
...who used their Access cards.

PROBLEM SET B

Problem 7-1B
Sales on account and credit card sales

C1

...mers can use either of ...ce charge for sales on ...t card receipts are de- ...day. When customers ...mits them to Aztec for ...f being billed. Marbus ...n/30; and all sales are

...pen.
...used their Commerce

Beyond the Numbers exercises ask

students to use accounting figures and understand their meaning. Students also learn how accounting applies to a variety of business situations. These creative and fun exercises are all new or updated, and are divided into sections:

- Reporting in Action
- Comparative Analysis
- Ethics Challenge
- Communicating in Practice
- Taking It To The Net
- Teamwork in Action
- Hitting the Road
- Entrepreneurial Decision
- Global Decision

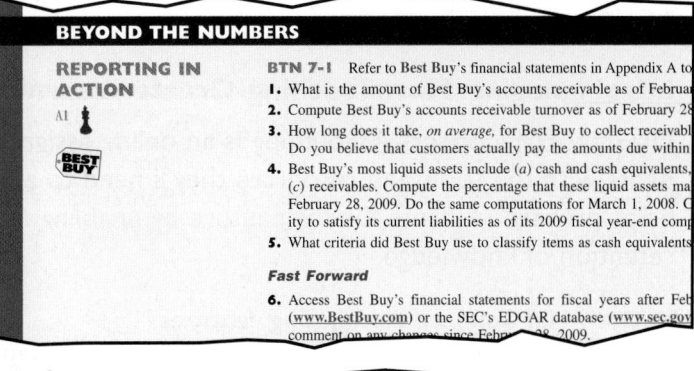

BEYOND THE NUMBERS

REPORTING IN ACTION

A1

BEST BUY

BTN 7-1 Refer to Best Buy's financial statements in Appendix A to
1. What is the amount of Best Buy's accounts receivable as of Februar
2. Compute Best Buy's accounts receivable turnover as of February 28
3. How long does it take, *on average*, for Best Buy to collect receivabl
   Do you believe that customers actually pay the amounts due within
4. Best Buy's most liquid assets include (*a*) cash and cash equivalents,
   (*c*) receivables. Compute the percentage that these liquid assets ma
   February 28, 2009. Do the same computations for March 1, 2008. C
   ity to satisfy its current liabilities as of its 2009 fiscal year-end com
5. What criteria did Best Buy use to classify items as cash equivalents

Fast Forward

6. Access Best Buy's financial statements for fiscal years after Feb
   (www.BestBuy.com) or the SEC's EDGAR database (www.sec.gov
   comment on any changes since February 28, 2009.

Serial Problem uses a continuous running

case study to illustrate chapter concepts in a familiar context. The Serial Problem can be followed continuously from the first chapter or picked up at any later point in the book; enough information is provided to ensure students can get right to work.

SERIAL PROBLEM

Success Systems

*(This serial problem began in Chapter 1 and continues through most of the boo
segments were not completed, the serial problem can begin at this point. It is help
to use the Working Papers that accompany the book.)*

SP 7 Adriana Lopez, owner of Success Systems, realizes that she needs to be
debts expense. Assume that Success Systems has total revenues of $43,853 during
of 2010, and that the Accounts Receivable balance on March 31, 2010, is $22,72

Required

1. Prepare the adjusting entry needed for Success Systems to recognize bad de
   31, 2010, under each of the following independent assumptions (assume a ze
   in the Allowance for Doubtful Accounts at March 31).
   a. Bad debts are estimated to be 1% of total revenues. (Round amounts to th
   b. Bad debts are estimated to be 2% of accounts receivable. (Round amounts
2. Assume that Success Systems' Accounts Receivable balance at June 30, 201
   one account of $100 has been written off against the Allowance for Doubtful

Check (2) Bad Debts Expense, $51

The End of the Chapter Is Only the Beginning

Our valuable and proven assignments aren't just confined to the book. From problems that require technological solutions to materials found exclusively online, this book's end-of-chapter material is fully integrated with its technology package.

connect™

- Quick Studies, Exercises, and Problems available on Connect (see page x) are marked with an icon.

- Online Learning Center (OLC) includes Interactive Quizzes, Excel template assignments, and more.

eXcel
mhhe.com/wildFA5e

- Problems supported with Microsoft Excel template assignments are marked with an icon.

- Material that receives additional coverage (slide shows, videos, audio, etc.) available in iPod ready format are marked with an icon.

Put Away Your Red Pen

We pride ourselves on the accuracy of this book's assignment materials. Independent research reports that instructors and reviewers point to the accuracy of this book's assignment materials as one of its key competitive advantages.

The authors extend a special thanks to accuracy checkers Barbara Schnathorst, The Write Solution, Inc.; Helen Roybark, Radford University; Beth Woods, CPA, Accuracy Counts; David Krug, Johnson Community College; ANSR Source; Yvonne Phang, Borough of Manhattan Community College; and Marilyn Sagrillo, University of Wisconsin - Green Bay. Also to Jeannie Folk, College of DuPage, for creation of the online quizzes and Personal Learning Plan.

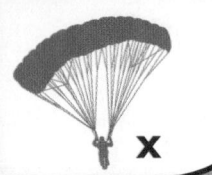

Using technology to

McGraw-Hill Connect Accounting

Less Managing. More Teaching. Greater Learning.

McGraw-Hill Connect Accounting is an online assignment and assessment solution that connects students with the tools and resources they'll need to achieve success. McGraw-Hill Connect Accounting helps prepare students for their future by enabling faster learning, more efficient studying, and higher retention of knowledge.

McGraw-Hill Connect Accounting features

Connect Accounting offers a number of powerful tools and features to make managing assignments easier, so faculty can spend more time teaching. With Connect Accounting, students can engage with their coursework anytime and anywhere, making the learning process more accessible and efficient. Connect Accounting offers you the features described below.

Simple assignment management

With Connect Accounting, creating assignments is easier than ever, so you can spend more time teaching and less time managing. The assignment management function enables you to:

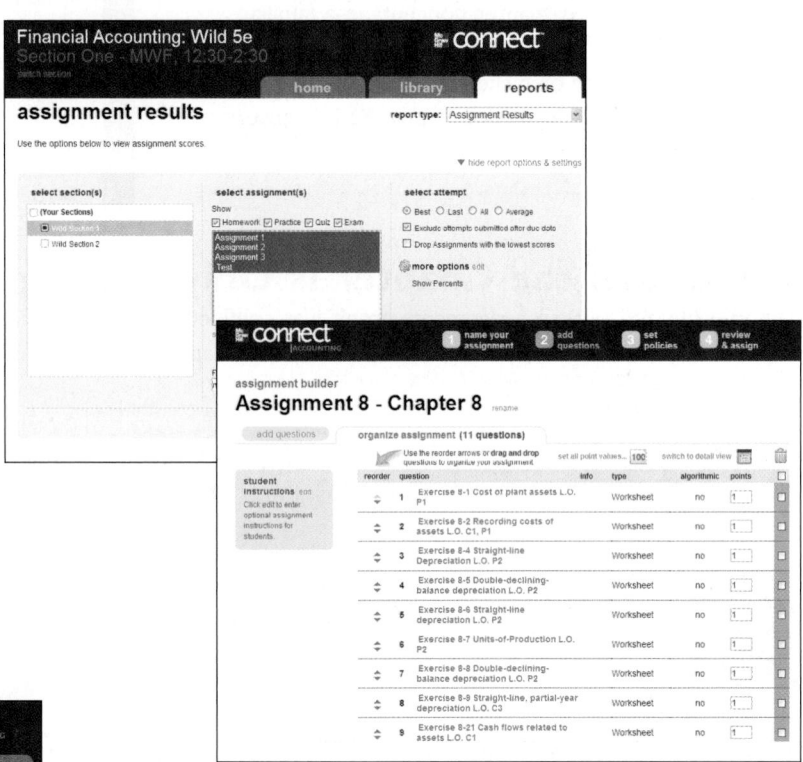

- Create and deliver assignments easily with selectable end-of-chapter questions and test bank items.
- Streamline lesson planning, student progress reporting, and assignment grading to make classroom management more efficient than ever.
- Go paperless with the eBook and online submission and grading of student assignments.

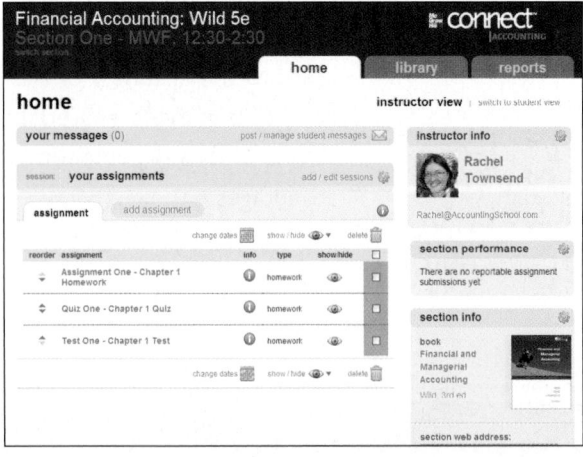

Smart grading

When it comes to studying, time is precious. Connect Accounting helps students learn more efficiently by providing feedback and practice material when they need it, where they need it. When it comes to teaching, your time also is precious. The grading function enables you to:

- Have assignments scored automatically, giving students immediate feedback on their work and side-by-side comparisons with correct answers.
- Access and review each response; manually change grades or leave comments for students to review.
- Reinforce classroom concepts with practice tests and instant quizzes.

Student study center

The Connect Accounting Student Study Center is the place for students to access additional resources.
The Student Study Center:

- Offers students quick access to lectures, practice materials, eBooks, and more.
- Provides instant practice material and study questions, easily accessible on the go.
- Gives students access to the Personal Learning Plan described below.

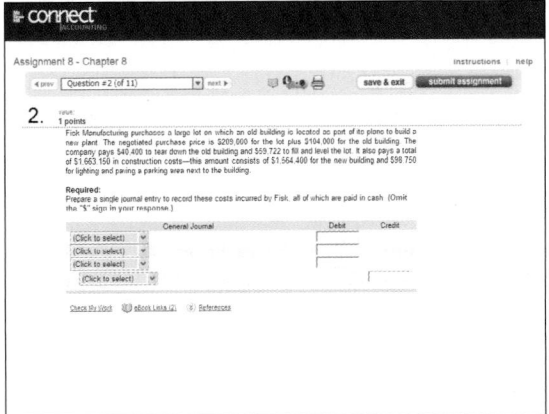
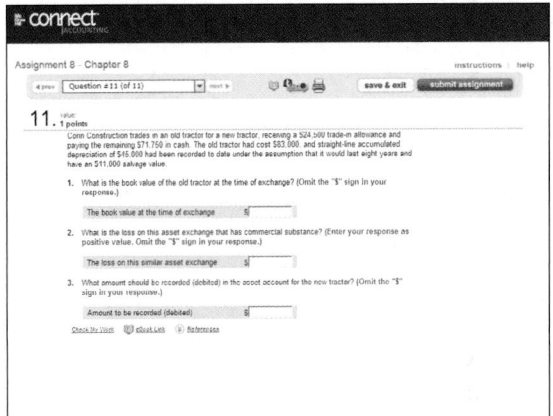

Personal Learning Plan

The Personal Learning Plan (PLP) connects each student to the learning resources needed for success in the course. For each chapter, students:

- Take a practice test to initiate the Personal Learning Plan.
- Immediately upon completing the practice test, see how their performance compares to chapter learning objectives within chapters.
- Receive a Personal Learning Plan that recommends specific readings from the text, supplemental study material, and practice work that will improve their understanding and mastery of each learning objective.

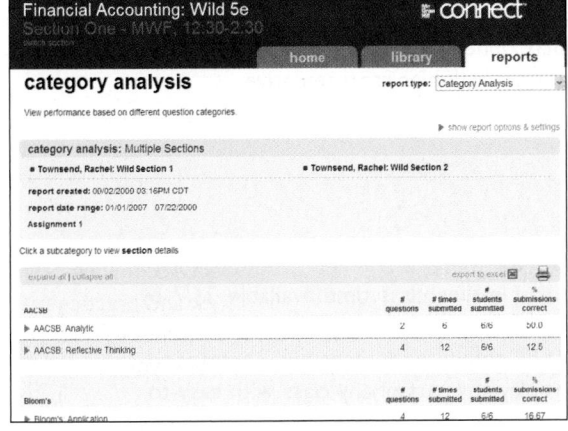

Student progress tracking

Connect Accounting keeps instructors informed about how each student, section, and class is performing, allowing for more productive use of lecture and office hours. The progress-tracking function enables you to:

- View scored work immediately and track individual or group performance with assignment and grade reports.
- Access an instant view of student or class performance relative to learning objectives.
- Collect data and generate reports required by many accreditation organizations, such as AACSB and AICPA.

Lecture capture

Increase the attention paid to lecture discussion by decreasing the attention paid to note taking. For an additional charge, lecture capture offers new ways for students to focus on the in-class discussion, knowing they can revisit important topics later. For more information on lecture capture capabilities in Connect, see the discussion of Tegrity on the following page.

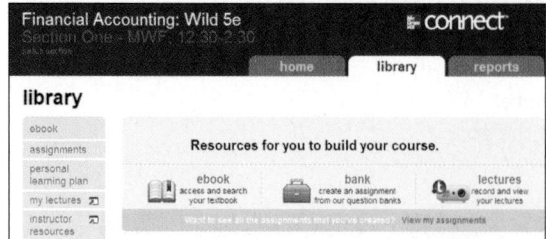

Instructor library

The Connect Accounting Instructor Library is your repository for additional resources to improve student engagement in and out of class. You can select and use any asset that enhances your lecture. The Connect Accounting Instructor Library includes the Solutions Manual, Instructor's Resource Manual, Test Bank, and PowerPoint lecture slides.

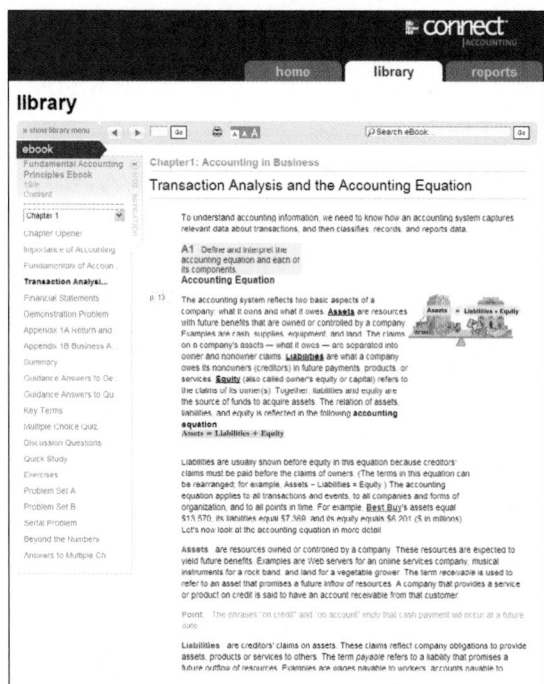

McGraw-Hill Connect Plus Accounting

McGraw-Hill reinvents the textbook learning experience for the modern student with Connect Plus Accounting. A seamless integration of an eBook and Connect Accounting, Connect Plus Accounting provides all of the Connect Accounting features plus the following:

- An integrated eBook, allowing for anytime, anywhere access to the textbook.
- Dynamic links between the problems or questions you assign to your students and the location in the eBook where that problem or question is covered.
- A powerful search function to pinpoint and connect key concepts in a snap.

In short, Connect Accounting offers you and your students powerful tools and features that optimize your time and energies, enabling you to focus on course content, teaching, and student learning. Connect Accounting also offers a wealth of content resources for both instructors and students. This state-of-the-art, thoroughly tested system supports you in preparing students for the world that awaits.

For information about Connect, go to www.mcgrawhillconnect.com, or contact your local McGraw-Hill sales representative.

Tegrity Campus: Lectures 24/7

Tegrity Campus is a service that makes class time available 24/7 by automatically capturing every lecture. With a simple one-click start-and-stop process, you capture all computer screens and corresponding audio in a format that is easily searchable, frame by frame. Students can replay any part of any class with easy-to-use browser-based viewing on a PC or Mac, an iPod, or other mobile device. Educators know that the more students can see, hear, and experience class resources, the better they learn. In fact, studies prove it. Tegrity Campus's unique search feature helps students efficiently find what they need, when they need it, across an entire semester of class recordings. Help turn your students' study time into learning moments immediately supported by your lecture. With Tegrity Campus, you also increase intent listening and class participation by easing students' concerns about note taking. Lecture Capture will make it more likely you will see students' faces, not the tops of their heads.

To learn more about Tegrity, watch a 2-minute Flash demo at http://tegritycampus.mhhe.com.

Assurance of Learning Ready

Many educational institutions today are focused on the notion of assurance of learning, an important element of some accreditation standards. *Financial Accounting* is designed specifically to support your assurance of learning initiatives with a simple, yet powerful solution. Each test bank question for *Financial Accounting* maps to a specific chapter learning outcome/objective listed in the text. You can use our test bank software, EZ Test and EZ Test Online, or in Connect Accounting to easily query for learning outcomes/objectives that directly relate to the learning objectives for your course. You can then use the reporting features of EZ Test to aggregate student results in similar fashion, making the collection and presentation of assurance of learning data simple and easy.

AACSB Statement

The McGraw-Hill Companies is a proud corporate member of AACSB International. Understanding the importance and value of AACSB accreditation, *Financial Accounting*, 5th edition recognizes the curricula guidelines detailed in the AACSB standards for business accreditation by connecting selected questions in the test bank to the six general knowledge and skill guidelines in the AACSB standards. The statements contained in *Financial Accounting*, 5th edition are provided only as a guide for the users of this textbook. The AACSB leaves content coverage and assessment within the purview of individual schools, the mission of the school, and the faculty. While *Financial Accounting*, 5th edition and the teaching package make no claim of any specific AACSB qualification or evaluation, we have within *Financial Accounting*, 5th edition labeled selected questions according to the six general knowledge and skills areas.

McGraw-Hill Customer Care Contact Information

At McGraw-Hill, we understand that getting the most from new technology can be challenging. That's why our services don't stop after you purchase our products. You can e-mail our Product Specialists 24 hours a day to get product training online. Or you can search our knowledge bank of Frequently Asked Questions on our support Website. For Customer Support, call 800-331-5094 or visit www.mhhe.com/support. One of our Technical Support Analysts will be able to assist you in a timely fashion.

How Can Text-Related Web Resources Enrich My Course?

Online Learning Center (OLC)

We offer an Online Learning Center (OLC) that follows *Financial Accounting* chapter by chapter. It doesn't require any building or maintenance on your part. It's ready to go the moment you and your students type in the URL: **www.mhhe.com/wildFA5e**.

As students study and learn from *Financial Accounting*, they can visit the Student Edition of the OLC Website to work with a multitude of helpful tools:

- Generic Template Working Papers
- Chapter Learning Objectives
- Interactive Chapter Quizzes

- PowerPoint® Presentations
- Narrated PowerPoint® Presentations
- Video Library

- Excel Template Assignments
- iPod Content

A secured Instructor Edition stores essential course materials to save you prep time before class. Everything you need to run a lively classroom and an efficient course is included. All resources available to students, plus . . .

- Instructor's Manual
- Solutions Manual

- Solutions to Excel Template Assignments
- Test Bank

The OLC Website also serves as a doorway to other technology solutions, like course management systems.

Teaching and Learning Supplements

Instructor

Instructor's Resource CD-ROM

ISBN13: 9780077268961
ISBN10: 0077268962

This is your all-in-one resource. It allows you to create custom presentations from your own materials or from the following text-specific materials provided in the CD's asset library:

- Instructor's Resource Manual
  Written by Christine Schalow, University of Wisconsin-Stevens Point.
  This manual contains (for each chapter) a Lecture Outline, a chart linking all assignment materials to Learning Objectives, a list of relevant active learning activities, and additional visuals with transparency masters.

- Solutions Manual
  Written by John J. Wild, University of Wisconsin.
- Test Bank, Computerized Test Bank
  Revised by Laurie Hays, Western Michigan University.
- PowerPoint® Presentations
  Prepared by Helen Roybark, Radford University.
  Presentations allow for revision of lecture slides, and includes a viewer, allowing screens to be shown with or without the software.
- Link to PageOut

Student

Excel Working Papers CD

ISBN13: 9780077268916
ISBN10: 0077268911

Written by John J. Wild, University of Wisconsin

Working Papers delivered in Excel spreadsheets. These Excel Working Papers are available on CD-ROM and can be bundled with the printed Working Papers; see your representative for information.

Working Papers

ISBN13: 9780077268992
ISBN10: 0077268997

Written by John J. Wild, University of Wisconsin.

Study Guide

ISBN13: 9780077268985
ISBN10: 0077268989

Written by April Mohr, Jefferson Community and Technical College, SW.

Covers each chapter and appendix with reviews of the learning objectives, outlines of the chapters, summaries of chapter materials, and additional problems with solutions.

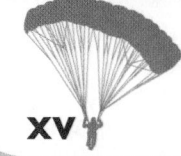

CourseSmart

CourseSmart is a new way to find and buy eTextbooks. CourseSmart has the largest selection of eTextbooks available anywhere, offering thousands of the most commonly adopted textbooks from a wide variety of higher education publishers. CourseSmart eTextbooks are available in one standard online reader with full text search, notes, and highlighting, and email tools for sharing between classmates. Visit **www.CourseSmart.com** for more information on ordering.

How Can Students Study on the Go Using Their iPod?

iPod Content

Harness the power of one of the most popular technology tools students use today–the Apple iPod. Our innovative approach allows students to download audio and video presentations right into their iPod and take learning materials with them wherever they go. Students just need to visit the Online Learning Center at **www.mhhe.com/wild-FA5e** to download our iPod content. For each chapter of the book they will be able to download audio narrated lecture presentations and financial accounting videos for use on various versions of iPods. iPod Touch users can even access self-quizzes.

It makes review and study time as easy as putting on headphones.

How Can McGraw-Hill Help Me Teach My Course Online?

ALEKS®

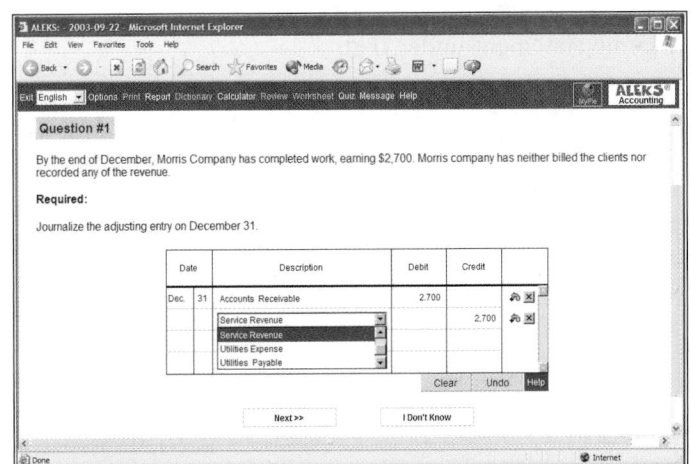

ALEKS® for the Accounting Cycle and ALEKS® for Financial Accounting

Available from McGraw-Hill over the World Wide Web, ALEKS (Assessment and LEarning in Knowledge Spaces) provides precise assessment and individualized instruction in the fundamental skills your students need to succeed in accounting.

ALEKS motivates your students because ALEKS can tell what a student knows, doesn't know, and is most ready to learn next. ALEKS does this using the ALEKS Assessment and Knowledge Space Theory as an artificial intelligence engine to exactly identify a student's knowledge of accounting. When students focus on precisely what they are ready to learn, they build the confidence and learning momentum that fuel success.

To learn more about adding ALEKS to your principles course, visit www.business.aleks.com.

Enhancements for FA 5e

This edition's revisions are driven by feedback from instructors and students. Many of the revisions are summarized here. Feedback suggests that this is the book instructors want to teach from and students want to learn from. General revisions include:

- Revised and updated assignments throughout
- Updated ratio analyses for each chapter
- New content and assignments on International Financial Reporting Standards (IFRS) in each chapter
- New and revised entrepreneurial elements
- Revised serial problem through nearly all chapters
- New art program, visual graphics, and text layout
- New Best Buy annual report financial data with comparisons to RadioShack, GOME (Chinese retailer), and Apple with new assignments
- New graphics added to each chapter's analysis section
- New iPod content integrated and referenced in book

Chapter 1

Facebook NEW opener with new entrepreneurial assignment

Revised section on accounting principles and assumptions

New section on international accounting practices and regulatory bodies

New visual layout on building blocks for GAAP

New graphic listing recent publicized accounting scandals

Transaction analysis with expanded accounting equation

Updated compensation data in exhibit

New discussion of conceptual framework linked to IFRS

New presentation of condensed income statement under IFRS

Chapter 2

SPANX NEW opener with new entrepreneurial assignment

New 4-step process to learn accounting for transactions: Identify, Analyze, Record, and Post

New sequential art layout for visualizing transaction accounting

New arrow lines link journal entries to the ledger

New material on financial statements related to IFRS

New presentation of simplified balance sheet under IFRS

Chapter 3

PopCap Games NEW opener with new entrepreneurial assignment

New 3-step process for accounting adjustments: (1) Determine what is, (2) Determine what should be, (3) Record adjustment

New summary tables show the accounting adjustment AND account balances before and after adjustment

New adjustment tables for prepaid expenses, including insurance, supplies, and depreciation

New adjustment tables for unearned revenue, accrued expenses, and accrued revenues

New graphic for learning the 4-step closing process

New presentation of classified balance sheet under IFRS

New discussion of different measurements for assets and liabilities under IFRS

Chapter 4

Heritage Link Brands NEW opener with new entrepreneurial assignment

Enhanced discussions on purchase allowances and purchase returns

Revised discussions on sales returns and sales allowances

Streamlined 4-step process for merchandisers' closing entries

New material on income statement formats for U.S. GAAP vis-à-vis IFRS

Chapter 5

Beauty Encounter NEW opener with new entrepreneurial assignment

Specific Identification explanation revised for additional clarity

New explanation added to First-in, First-Out

Enhanced explanation to Last-in, First-Out

New description of weighted average

Enhanced explanations for LCM

New material on inventory measurements for U.S. GAAP vis-à-vis IFRS

Illustration of inventory errors is revised and enhanced

Revised exhibit on inventory errors for balance sheet

Appendix 5A, enhanced discussion of periodic inventory

Appendix 5A, expanded explanations of periodic FIFO, LIFO, and weighted average

Chapter 6

Dylan's Candy Bar NEW opener with new entrepreneurial assignment

New material added on Sarbanes-Oxley and internal controls required

New section on cash management

Additional description of electronic funds transfer

Enhanced explanation of bank reconciliation with new assignments

New discussion of internal controls for IFRS conversion

Chapter 7

Under Armor NEW opener with new entrepreneurial assignment

Reorganized sections on valuing accounts receivable

Enhanced explanation of recovering a bad debt

New material on assessing the direct write-off method

Reorganized section on estimating bad debts using percent of receivables

New enhanced summary Exhibit 7.13 on methods to estimate bad debts

Added new exercises on bad debts estimation

New discussion of recognition and valuation of receivables under IFRS

Chapter 8

Sambazon NEW opener with new entrepreneurial assignment

Enhanced explanations on declining-balance and impairments

New description of ordinary repairs and its journal entry

Reorganized discussion of betterments and extraordinary repairs

New material on depreciation estimates for U.S. GAAP vis-à-vis IFRS

Enhanced illustration for depletion including journal entry

Reorganized section on types of intangibles

Enhanced material related to franchises, licenses, trademarks and other intangibles

Enhanced explanation of exchanging plant assets

New discussion of asset valuation and measurement under IFRS

Chapter 9

Noodles & Company NEW opener with new entrepreneurial assignment

Updated real world examples including those for Univision, Six Flags, AMF, and K2

New material on measuring liabilities for U.S. GAAP vis-à-vis IFRS

Updated tax illustrations and assignments using the most recent rates

New section on "Who Pays What Payroll Taxes and Benefits"

Chapter 10

Feed Granola NEW opener with new entrepreneurial assignment

Enhanced graphic and explanation of determining bond discount and premium

Revised bond illustration to use a 4-period bond

Streamlined bond illustration to show entire amortization process from issuance to maturity

Streamlined bond illustration for effective interest amortization

New material on valuing bonds and notes under IFRS

Added new assignments that require accounting for bonds when provided an amortization table

Chapter 11

Inogen NEW opener with new entrepreneurial assignment

New info graphic on subcategories of authorized stock

Updated many real world examples

New info graphic on stock splits

New material on preferred stock classification under IFRS

Additional explanation on closing process for corporations

Updated statement of stockholders' equity

Chapter 12

Jungle Jim's NEW opener with new entrepreneurial assignment

Updated graphics for operating, investing and financing cash flows

Enhanced steps 1 through 5 for preparing the statement of cash flows

Simplified summary in Exhibit 12.12 for indirect adjustments

Updated real world examples and graphics including that for Harley, Starbucks, and Nike

New info on indirect vs direct method under IFRS

New discussion on operating, investing, or financing presentation of cash flows for dividends and interest under IFRS

Chapter 13

The Motley Fool UPDATED opener with new entrepreneurial assignment

New Best Buy, RadioShack, and GOME data throughout chapter, exhibits, and illustrations with comparative analysis

Enhanced presentation on comparative financial statements

New discussion of ratio and other analyses when financial statements are prepared under IFRS

Acknowledgments

John J. Wild and McGraw-Hill/Irwin would like to recognize the following instructors for their valuable feedback and involvement in the development of *Financial Accounting* 5e. We are thankful for their suggestions, counsel, and encouragement.

James Aitken, Central Michigan University

Sylvia Allen, Los Angeles Valley College

Sheryl Alley, Ball State University

Mark Anderson, University of Texas, Dallas

Jack Aschkenazi, American Intercontinental University

Sheila Ammons, Austin Community College

Courtney Baillie, Nebraska Wesleyan University

Kashi Balachandran, New York University

Fred Barbee, University of Alaska Anchorage

Richard Barnhart, Grand Rapids Community College

Mary Barnum, Grand Rapids Community College

Progyan Basu, University of Maryland-College Park

Joe Beams, University of New Orleans

Terry W. Bechtel, Northwestern State University of Louisiana

Gerard L. Berardino, Community College of Allegheny County-Boyce Campus

Swati Bhandarkar, University of Georgia

Jaswinder Bhangal, Chabot College

David Borjarsky, California State University-Long Beach

Anna Marie Boulware, St. Charles Community College

Charles Boxell, Owens Community College

Jerry Braun, Daytona State College

Mia Breen, DeAnza College

Phil Brown, Harding University

Donna Chadwick, Sinclair Community College

Barbara Chaney, University of Montana

Kwang-Hyun Chung, Pace University

Marilyn Ciolino, Delgado Community College

Norman H. Colter, University of New Mexico-Alburquerque

Dori Danko, Grand Valley State University

Howard Davidoff, Brooklyn College

Peggy DeJong, Kirkwood Community College

Rosemond Desir, Colorado State University

Bettye Rogers Desselle, Prairie View A&M University

Terry Elliott, Morehead State University-Ashland

Carol Flowers, Orange Coast College

Mike Foland, Southwestern Illinois College

Jeannie Folk, College of DuPage

Mitch Franklin, Syracuse University

Virginia Fullwood, Texas A&M University

Hubert Gill, University of North Florida

Saturnino Gonzalez Jr., El Paso Community College

Sherry Gordon, Palomar College

Coby Harmon, University of California, Santa Barbara

Tracey Hawkins, University of Cincinnati, Clermont College

Laurie Hays, Western Michigan University

Roger G. Hehman, Raymond Walters College

Steven Hornik, University of Central Florida

Margaret Houston, Wright State University

Tom Hrubec, Franklin University

Constance Hylton, George Mason University

Christie W. Johnson, Montana State University

Vern Jorgensen, Southwestern Community College

Roann Kopel, Eastern Illinois University

Barbara Kren, Marquette University

Jerry Kreuze, Western Michigan University

David Krug, Johnson County Community College

Michael Lawrence, Portland Community College

Miriam Lefkowitz, Brooklyn College

Beixin Lin, Montclair State University

Wesley Linkovich, University of South Florida

Contributing Author

The authors and book team wish to thank Marilyn Sagrillo for her excellent contributions.

Marilyn Sagrillo is an associate professor at the University of Wisconsin at Green Bay. She received her BA and MS from Northern Illinois University and her PhD from the University of Wisconsin at Madison. Her scholarly articles have been published in *Accounting Enquiries, Journal of Accounting Case Research*, and the *Missouri Society of CPAs Casebook*. She is a member of the American Accounting Association and the Institute of Management Accountants. She previously received the UWGB Founder's Association Faculty Award for Excellence in Teaching. Professor Sagrillo is an active volunteer for the Midwest Renewable Energy Association. She also enjoys reading, traveling, and hiking.

Sonja Lolland, Sierra College

James M. Lukawitz, University of Memphis

Chris Lyons, Fort Lewis College

James P. Makofske, Fresno City College

Stacie Mayes, Rose State College

Lynn Mazzola, Nassau Community College

Diana McCabe, Black Hawk College

Suzanne McCaffrey, University of Mississippi

Kevin McNelis, New Mexico State University-Las Cruces

Jeanne Miller, Cypress College

Tim Mills, Eastern Illinois University

April Mohr, Jefferson Community and Technical College, SW

Arabian Morgan, Orange Coast College

Joseph W. Morris, Christopher Newport University

Audrey S. Morrison, Pensacola Junior College

Matt Muller, Adirondack Community College

Kathleen Munter, Pima Community College

Karen Nunez, Elon University

Ash Patel, Normandale Community College

Reed Peoples, Austin Community College

Karin Petruska, Youngstown State University

Yvonne Phang, Borough of Manhattan Community College

Eric Primuth, Cuyahoga Community College Western-Parma

James E. Racic, Lakeland Community College

Usha Ramanujam, Portland Community College

Lawrence A. Roman, Cuyahoga Community College

Barbara Roper, Chicago State University

Lou Rosamilia, Hudson Valley Community College

Helen Roybark, Radford University

Marilyn Sagrillo, University of Wisconsin-Green Bay

Robert W. Saubert, Radford University

Christine Schalow, University of Wisconsin-Stevens Point

Albert Schepanski, University of Iowa

Debra Schmidt, Cerritos College

Richard Schroeder, University of North Carolina at Charlotte

Joann Segovia, Winona State University

Randall Serrett, University of Houston-Downtown

Vicki Shipley, Ball State University

Nancy Snow, University of Toledo

Dennis Stovall, Grand Valley State University

Gracelyn V. Stuart-Tuggle, Palm Beach Community College-South

Dominique Svarc, Harper College

Diane Tanner, University of North Florida

Janet Tarase, Lorain County Community College

Linda Tarrago, Hillsborough Community College

Steve Teeter, Utah Valley State College

Paula Tigerman, Black Hawk College

Karen Varnell, Tarleton State University

Stephen J. Walsh, Clark College

William J. Walsh, Syracuse University

James Weglin, North Seattle Community College

Dave Welch, Franklin University

Jane Wiese, Valencia Community College

Scott Williams, County College of Morris

John Windler, University of Nebraska at Omaha

Karen Wisnewski, County College of Morris

Ken Wright, Indiana University Purdue University, Indianapolis

Lorraine Wright, North Carolina State University

Peter Woodlock, Youngstown State University

Marjorie Yuschak, Rutgers University

Judith Zander, Grossmont College

In addition to the helpful and generous colleagues listed above, I thank the entire McGraw-Hill/Irwin *Financial Accounting* 5e team, including Stewart Mattson, Tim Vertovec, Steve Schuetz, Dana Woo, Christina Sanders, Aaron Downey of Matrix Productions, Lori Koetters, Matthew Baldwin, Carol Bielski, and Brian Nacik. I also thank the great marketing and sales support staff, including Kathleen Klehr, Sankha Basu, and Abbey Woodward. Many talented educators and professionals worked hard to create the supplements for this book, and for their efforts I'm grateful. Finally, many more people I either did not meet or whose efforts I did not personally witness nevertheless helped to make this book everything that it is, and I thank them all.

John J. Wild

Brief Contents

*These appendixes are available as pdf files from the Website

Contents

*These appendixes are available as pdf files from the Website

Financial Accounting

Information for Decisions

1

Introducing Accounting in Business

"We are really just focused on our mission: helping people share information" —Mark Zuckerberg

A Look at This Chapter

Accounting is crucial in our information age. In this chapter, we discuss the importance of accounting to different types of organizations and describe its many users and uses. We explain that ethics are essential to accounting. We also explain business transactions and how they are reflected in financial statements.

A Look Ahead

Chapter 2 describes and analyzes business transactions. We explain the analysis and recording of transactions, the ledger and trial balance, and the double-entry system. More generally, Chapters 2 and 3 show (via the accounting cycle) how financial statements reflect business activities.

*A **Decision Feature** launches each chapter showing the relevance of accounting for a real entrepreneur. An **Entrepreneurial Decision** problem at the end of the assignments returns to this feature with a mini-case.*

Accounting for Facebook

PALO ALTO, CA—"Open Society" conjures up philosophical thoughts and political ideologies. However, for Mark Zuckerberg, his vision of an open society "is to give people the power to share and make the world more open and connected." That vision led Mark to create **Facebook** (**Facebook.com**) from his college dorm room a few short years ago. Today, Facebook is the highest-profile social networking site. Along the way, Mark had to learn accounting and the details of preparing and interpreting financial statements to make his vision a reality.

"It's all been very interesting," recalls Mark. Important questions involving business formation, transaction analysis, and financial reporting had to be answered. Mark answered them expertly and in the process has set his company apart. "I'm here to build something for the long term," declares Mark. "Anything else is a distraction."

Information is the focus—both within Facebook and within its accounting records. Mark recalls that when he launched his business, there were "all these reasons why they could not aggregate this [personal] information." He took a similar tactic in addressing accounting information needs. "There's an intense focus on . . . information, as both an ideal and a practical strategy to get things done," insists Mark. This includes using accounting information to make important business decisions.

While Facebook is the language of social networking, accounting is the language of business networking. "As a company we are very focused on what we are building," says Mark. "We are adding a certain amount of value to people's lives if we build a very good product." That product value is reflected in its financial statements, which are based on transaction analysis and accounting concepts.

Facebook's success is reflected in its accounting books. Its revenues continue to grow and exhibit what people call the monetizing of social networking. "Social Ads are doing pretty well," asserts Mark. "We are happy with how we are doing in terms of numbers of advertisers, and revenue." Facebook also tracks its expenses and asset purchases. "We expect to achieve . . . profitability next year," states Mark. "It means we will be able to fund all of our operations and server purchases from the cash we generate." This is saying a lot as Facebook's operating expenditures must support nearly 1 billion photo uploads and 8 million video uploads per day.

Mark emphasizes that his financial house must be in order for Facebook to realize its full potential—and that potential is in his sights. "We believe really deeply that if people are sharing more, then the world will be a more open place where people can understand what is going on with the people around them."

[Sources: *Facebook Website*, January 2010; *CNN*, October 2008; *Mercury News*, April 2009; *VentureBeat*, March 2008; *FastCompany.com*, May 2007; *Wired*, June 2009]

Learning Objectives are classified as conceptual, analytical, or procedural.

CAP

Conceptual

C1 Explain the purpose and importance of accounting in the information age. *(p. 4)*

C2 Identify users and uses of accounting. *(p. 5)*

C3 Identify opportunities in accounting and related fields. *(p. 6)*

C4 Explain why ethics are crucial to accounting. *(p. 8)*

C5 Explain generally accepted accounting principles and define and apply several accounting principles. *(p. 8)*

C6 *Appendix 1B*—Identify and describe the three major activities of organizations. *(p. 26)*

Analytical

A1 Define and interpret the accounting equation and each of its components. *(p. 14)*

A2 Analyze business transactions using the accounting equation. *(p. 15)*

A3 Compute and interpret return on assets. *(p. 22)*

A4 *Appendix 1A*—Explain the relation between return and risk. *(p. 26)*

Procedural

P1 Identify and prepare basic financial statements and explain how they interrelate. *(p. 19)*

LP1

Today's world is one of information—its preparation, communication, analysis, and use. Accounting is at the core of this information age. Knowledge of accounting gives us career opportunities and the insight to take advantage of them. This book introduces concepts, procedures, and analyses that help us make better decisions, including career choices. In this chapter we describe accounting, the users and uses of accounting information, the forms and activities of organizations, and several accounting principles. We also introduce transaction analysis and financial statements.

Introducing Accounting in Business

Importance of Accounting	Fundamentals of Accounting	Transaction Analysis	Financial Statements
• Accounting information users • Opportunities in accounting	• Ethics—key concept • Generally accepted accounting principles • International accounting standards	• Accounting equation • Transaction analysis—illustrated	• Income statement • Statement of retained earnings • Balance sheet • Statement of cash flows

Importance of Accounting

C1 Explain the purpose and importance of accounting in the information age.

Video1.1

Real company names are printed in bold magenta.

Why is accounting so popular on campuses? Why are there so many accounting jobs for graduates? Why is accounting so important to companies? Why do politicians and business leaders focus on accounting regulations? The answer is that we live in an information age, where that information, and its reliability, impacts the financial well-being of us all.

Accounting is an information and measurement system that identifies, records, and communicates relevant, reliable, and comparable information about an organization's business activities. *Identifying* business activities requires selecting transactions and events relevant to an organization. Examples are the sale of iPods by **Apple** and the receipt of ticket money by **TicketMaster**. *Recording* business activities requires keeping a chronological log of transactions and events measured in dollars and classified and summarized in a useful format. *Communicating* business activities requires preparing accounting reports such as financial statements. It also requires analyzing and interpreting such reports. (The financial statements and notes of **Best Buy** are shown in Appendix A of this book. This appendix also shows the financial statements of **RadioShack**, **Apple**, and **GOME**.) Exhibit 1.1 summarizes accounting activities.

We must guard against a narrow view of accounting. Our most common contact with accounting is through credit approvals, checking accounts, tax forms, and payroll. These experiences are limited and tend to focus on the recordkeeping parts of accounting. **Recordkeeping,** or **bookkeeping,** is the recording of transactions and events, either manually or electronically. This is just one part of accounting. Accounting also identifies and communicates information on transactions and events, and it includes the crucial processes of analysis and interpretation.

EXHIBIT 1.1

Accounting Activities

Identifying	Recording	Communicating
Select transactions and events	Input, measure, and classify	Prepare, analyze, and interpret

Technology is a key part of modern business and plays a major role in accounting. Technology reduces the time, effort, and cost of recordkeeping while improving clerical accuracy. Some small organizations continue to perform various accounting tasks manually, but even they are impacted by technology. As technology has changed the way we store, process, and summarize masses of data, accounting has been freed to expand. Consulting, planning, and other financial services are now closely linked to accounting. These services require sorting through data, interpreting their meaning, identifying key factors, and analyzing their implications.

Users of Accounting Information

Accounting is often called the *language of business* because all organizations set up an accounting information system to communicate data to help people make better decisions. Exhibit 1.2 shows that the accounting information system serves many kinds of users (this is a partial listing) who can be divided into two groups: external users and internal users.

External users

- Lenders
- Shareholders
- Governments
- Consumer groups
- External auditors
- Customers

Internal users

- Officers
- Managers
- Internal auditors
- Sales executives
- Budget officers
- Controllers

EXHIBIT 1.2

Users of Accounting Information

External Information Users   **External users** of accounting information are *not* directly involved in running the organization. They include shareholders (investors), lenders, directors, customers, suppliers, regulators, lawyers, brokers, and the press. External users have limited access to an organization's information. Yet their business decisions depend on information that is reliable, relevant, and comparable.

C2 Identify users and uses of accounting.

Financial accounting is the area of accounting aimed at serving external users by providing them with *general-purpose financial statements*. The term *general-purpose* refers to the broad range of purposes for which external users rely on these statements.

Each external user has special information needs depending on the types of decisions to be made. *Lenders* (creditors) loan money or other resources to an organization. Banks, savings and loans, co-ops, and mortgage and finance companies are lenders. Lenders look for information to help them assess whether an organization is likely to repay its loans with interest. *Shareholders* (investors) are the owners of a corporation. They use accounting reports in deciding whether to buy, hold, or sell stock. Shareholders typically elect a *board of directors* to oversee their interests in an organization. Since directors are responsible to shareholders, their information needs are similar. *External* (independent) *auditors* examine financial statements to verify that they are prepared according to generally accepted accounting principles. *Nonexecutive employees* and *labor unions* use financial statements to judge the fairness of wages, assess job prospects, and bargain for better wages. *Regulators* often have legal authority over certain activities of organizations. For example, the Internal Revenue Service (IRS) and other tax authorities require organizations to file accounting reports in computing taxes. Other regulators include utility boards that use accounting information to set utility rates and securities regulators that require reports for companies that sell their stock to the public.

Accounting serves the needs of many other external users. *Voters, legislators,* and *government officials* use accounting information to monitor and evaluate government receipts and expenses. *Contributors* to nonprofit organizations use accounting information to evaluate the use and impact of their donations. *Suppliers* use accounting information to judge the soundness of a customer before making sales on credit, and *customers* use financial reports to assess the staying power of potential suppliers.

Internal Information Users   **Internal users** of accounting information are those directly involved in managing and operating an organization. They use the information to help improve the efficiency and effectiveness of an organization. **Managerial accounting** is the area of accounting that serves the decision-making needs of internal users. Internal reports are not subject to the same rules as external reports and instead are designed with the special needs of internal users in mind.

There are several types of internal users, and many are managers of key operating activities. *Research and development managers* need information about projected costs and revenues of any proposed changes in products and services. *Purchasing managers* need to know what, when, and how much to purchase. *Human resource managers* need information about employees' payroll, benefits, performance, and compensation. *Production managers* depend on information to monitor costs and ensure quality. *Distribution managers* need reports for timely, accurate, and efficient delivery of products and services. *Marketing managers* use reports about sales and costs to target consumers, set prices, and monitor consumer needs, tastes, and price concerns. *Service managers* require information on the costs and benefits of looking after products and services. Decisions of these and other internal users depend on accounting reports.

Both internal and external users rely on internal controls to monitor and control company activities. *Internal controls* are procedures set up to protect company property and equipment, ensure reliable accounting reports, promote efficiency, and encourage adherence to company policies. Examples are good records, physical controls (locks, passwords, guards), and independent reviews.

Decision Insight boxes highlight relevant items from practice.

Decision Insight

Virtuous Returns   Virtue is not always its own reward. Compare the S&P 500 with the Domini Social Index (DSI), which covers 400 companies that have especially good records of social responsibility. We see that returns for companies with socially responsible behavior are at least as high as those of the S&P 500.

Copyright © 2009 by KLD Research & Analytics, Inc. The "Domini 400 Social Index" is a service mark of KLD Research & Analytics.

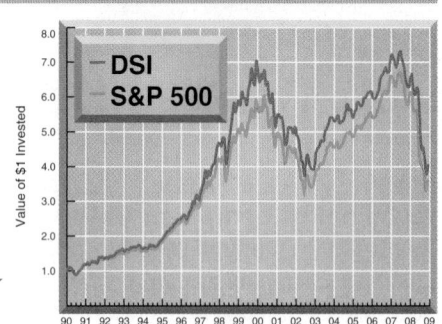

Graphical displays are often used to illustrate key points.

Opportunities in Accounting

C3   Identify opportunities in accounting and related fields.

Accounting information affects many aspects of our lives. When we earn money, pay taxes, invest savings, budget earnings, and plan for the future, we are influenced by accounting. Accounting has four broad areas of opportunities: financial, managerial, taxation, and accounting-related. Exhibit 1.3 lists selected opportunities in each area.

EXHIBIT 1.3

Accounting Opportunities

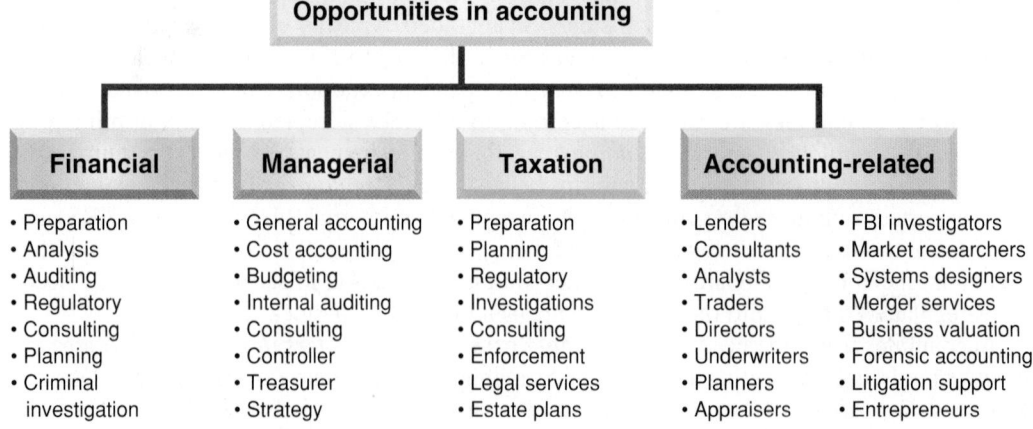

Opportunities in accounting

Financial	Managerial	Taxation	Accounting-related	
• Preparation	• General accounting	• Preparation	• Lenders	• FBI investigators
• Analysis	• Cost accounting	• Planning	• Consultants	• Market researchers
• Auditing	• Budgeting	• Regulatory	• Analysts	• Systems designers
• Regulatory	• Internal auditing	• Investigations	• Traders	• Merger services
• Consulting	• Consulting	• Consulting	• Directors	• Business valuation
• Planning	• Controller	• Enforcement	• Underwriters	• Forensic accounting
• Criminal investigation	• Treasurer	• Legal services	• Planners	• Litigation support
	• Strategy	• Estate plans	• Appraisers	• Entrepreneurs

The majority of accounting opportunities are in *private accounting,* as employees working for businesses—providing services such as auditing and tax advice to a vast range of businesses, as shown in Exhibit 1.4. *Public accounting* offers the next largest number of opportunities. Still other opportunities exist in government and not-for-profit agencies, including business regulation and investigation of law violations.

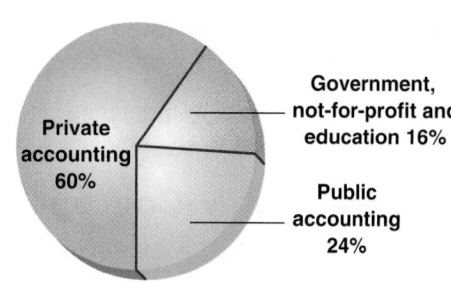

EXHIBIT 1.4

Accounting Jobs by Area

Accounting specialists are highly regarded. Their professional standing often is denoted by a certificate. Certified public accountants (CPAs) must meet education and experience requirements, pass an examination, and exhibit ethical character. Many accounting specialists hold certificates in addition to or instead of the CPA. Two of the most common are the certificate in management accounting (CMA) and the certified internal auditor (CIA). Employers also look for specialists with designations such as certified bookkeeper (CB), certified payroll professional (CPP), personal financial specialist (PFS), certified fraud examiner (CFE), and certified forensic accountant (CrFA).

Point: The largest accounting firms are Deloitte & Touche, Ernst & Young, PricewaterhouseCoopers, and KPMG.

Individuals with accounting knowledge are always in demand as they can help with financial analysis, strategic planning, e-commerce, product feasibility analysis, information technology, and financial management. Benefit packages can include flexible work schedules, telecommuting options, career path alternatives, casual work environments, extended vacation time, and child and elder care.

Demand for accounting specialists is strong. Exhibit 1.5 reports average annual salaries for several accounting positions. Salary variation depends on location, company size, professional designation, experience, and other factors. For example, salaries for chief financial officers (CFO) range from under $75,000 to more than $1 million per year. Likewise, salaries for bookkeepers range from under $30,000 to more than $80,000.

Point: Census Bureau (2009) reports that for workers 18 and over, higher education yields higher average pay:

Advanced degree	$80,977
Bachelor's degree	57,181
High school degree	31,286
No high school degree	21,484

Field	Title (experience)	2009 Salary	2014 Estimate*
Public Accounting	Partner	$190,000	$242,500
	Manager (6–8 years)	94,500	120,500
	Senior (3–5 years)	72,000	92,000
	Junior (0–2 years)	51,500	65,500
Private Accounting	CFO	232,000	296,000
	Controller/Treasurer	147,500	188,000
	Manager (6–8 years)	87,500	111,500
	Senior (3–5 years)	72,500	92,500
	Junior (0–2 years)	49,000	62,500
Recordkeeping	Full-charge bookkeeper	57,500	73,500
	Accounts manager	51,000	65,000
	Payroll manager	54,500	69,500
	Accounting clerk (0–2 years)	37,500	48,000

* Estimates assume a 5% compounded annual increase over current levels.

EXHIBIT 1.5

Accounting Salaries for Selected Fields

Point: For updated salary information: www.AICPA.org Abbott-Langer.com Kforce.com

Quick Check
Answers—p. 28

1. What is the purpose of accounting?
2. What is the relation between accounting and recordkeeping?
3. Identify some advantages of technology for accounting.
4. Who are the internal and external users of accounting information?
5. Identify at least five types of managers who are internal users of accounting information.
6. What are internal controls and why are they important?

Quick Check is a chance to stop and reflect on key points.

Fundamentals of Accounting

Accounting is guided by principles, standards, concepts, and assumptions. This section describes several of these key fundamentals of accounting.

Ethics—A Key Concept

C4 Explain why ethics are crucial to accounting.

The goal of accounting is to provide useful information for decisions. For information to be useful, it must be trusted. This demands ethics in accounting. **Ethics** are beliefs that distinguish right from wrong. They are accepted standards of good and bad behavior.

Point: Sarbanes-Oxley Act requires each issuer of securities to disclose whether it has adopted a code of ethics for its senior financial officers and the contents of that code.

Identifying the ethical path is sometimes difficult. The preferred path is a course of action that avoids casting doubt on one's decisions. For example, accounting users are less likely to trust an auditor's report if the auditor's pay depends on the success of the client's business. To avoid such concerns, ethics rules are often set. For example, auditors are banned from direct investment in their client and cannot accept pay that depends on figures in the client's reports. Exhibit 1.6 gives guidelines for making ethical decisions.

EXHIBIT 1.6

Guidelines for Ethical Decision Making

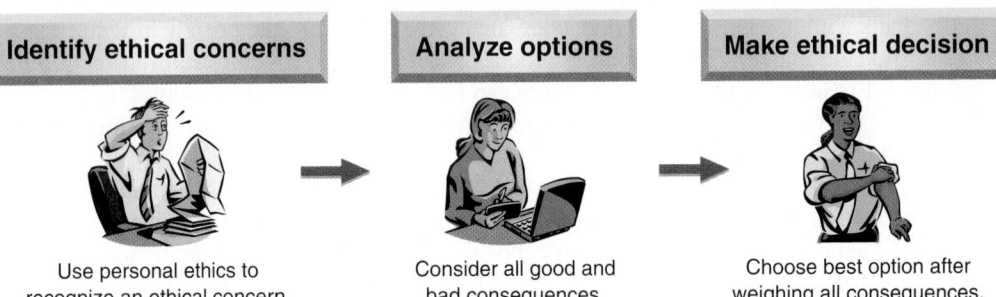

Identify ethical concerns	Analyze options	Make ethical decision
Use personal ethics to recognize an ethical concern.	Consider all good and bad consequences.	Choose best option after weighing all consequences.

Providers of accounting information often face ethical choices as they prepare financial reports. These choices can affect the price a buyer pays and the wages paid to workers. They can even affect the success of products and services. Misleading information can lead to a wrongful closing of a division that harms workers, customers, and suppliers. There is an old saying: *Good ethics are good business.*

Point: The American Institute of Certified Public Accountants' *Code of Professional Conduct* is available at **www.AICPA.org**.

Some people extend ethics to *social responsibility,* which refers to a concern for the impact of actions on society. An organization's social responsibility can include donations to hospitals, colleges, community programs, and law enforcement. It also can include programs to reduce pollution, increase product safety, improve worker conditions, and support continuing education. These programs are not limited to large companies. For example, many small businesses offer discounts to students and senior citizens. Still others help sponsor events such as the Special Olympics and summer reading programs.

Decision Insight

They Fought the Law   Our economic and social welfare depends on reliable accounting. Some individuals forgot that and are now paying their dues. They include Bernard Madoff (in photo) of **Madoff Investment Securities**, convicted of falsifying securities records; Bernard Ebbers of **WorldCom**, convicted of an $11 billion accounting scandal; Andrew Fastow of **Enron**, guilty of hiding debt and inflating income; and Ramalinga Raju of **Satyam Computers**, accused of overstating assets by $1.5 billion.

C5 Explain generally accepted accounting principles and define and apply several accounting principles.

Generally Accepted Accounting Principles

Financial accounting practice is governed by concepts and rules known as **generally accepted accounting principles (GAAP)**. To use and interpret financial statements effectively, we need to understand these principles, which can change over time in response to the demands of users.

GAAP aims to make information in financial statements *relevant, reliable,* and *comparable.* Relevant information affects the decisions of its users. Reliable information is trusted by users. Comparable information is helpful in contrasting organizations.

In the United States, the **Securities and Exchange Commission (SEC),** a government agency, has the legal authority to set GAAP. The SEC also oversees proper use of GAAP by companies that raise money from the public through issuances of their stock and debt. Those companies that issue their stock on U.S. exchanges include both *U.S. SEC registrants* (companies incorporated in the United States.) and *non-U.S. SEC registrants* (companies incorporated under non-U.S. laws). The SEC has largely delegated the task of setting U.S. GAAP to the **Financial Accounting Standards Board (FASB),** which is a private-sector group that sets both broad and specific principles.

Point: State ethics codes require CPAs who audit financial statements to disclose areas where those statements fail to comply with GAAP. If CPAs fail to report noncompliance, they can lose their licenses and be subject to criminal and civil actions and fines.

International Standards

In today's global economy, there is increased demand by external users for comparability in accounting reports. This demand often arises when companies wish to raise money from lenders and investors in different countries. To that end, the **International Accounting Standards Board (IASB),** an independent group (consisting of 16 individuals from many countries), issues **International Financial Reporting Standards (IFRS)** that identify preferred accounting practices.

If standards are harmonized, one company can potentially use a single set of financial statements in all financial markets. Differences between U.S. GAAP and IFRS are slowly fading as the FASB and IASB pursue a *convergence* process aimed to achieve a single set of accounting standards for global use. More than 115 countries now require or permit companies to prepare financial reports following IFRS. Further, non-U.S. SEC registrants can use IFRS in financial reports filed with the SEC (with no reconciliation to U.S. GAAP). This means there are *two* sets of accepted accounting principles in the United States: (1) U.S. GAAP for U.S. SEC registrants and (2) either IFRS or U.S. GAAP for non-U.S. SEC registrants.

The convergence process continues and, in late 2008, the SEC set a roadmap for use of IFRS by publicly-traded U.S. companies. This roadmap proposes that large U.S. companies adopt IFRS by 2014, with mid-size and small companies following in 2015 and 2016, respectively. Early adoption is permitted for large multinationals that meet certain criteria. For updates on this roadmap, we can check with the AICPA (**IFRS.com**), FASB (**FASB.org**), and IASB (**IASB.org.uk**).

> **IFRS**
>
> Like the FASB, the IASB uses a conceptual framework to aid in revising or drafting new standards. However, unlike the FASB, the IASB's conceptual framework is used as a reference when specific guidance is lacking. The IASB also requires that transactions be accounted for according to their substance (not only their legal form), and that financial statements give a fair presentation, whereas the FASB narrows that scope to fair presentation in accordance with U.S. GAAP.

Conceptual Framework and Convergence

The FASB and IASB are attempting to converge and enhance the **conceptual framework** that guides standard setting. The framework consists broadly of the following:

- **Objectives**—to provide information useful to investors, creditors, and others.
- **Qualitative Characteristics**—to require information that is relevant, reliable, and comparable.
- **Elements**—to define items that financial statements can contain

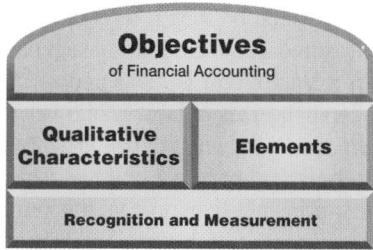

■ **Recognition and Measurement**—to set criteria that an item must meet for it to be recognized as an element; and how to measure that element.

For updates on this joint FASB and IASB conceptual framework convergence we can check with **FASB.org** or **IASB.org.uk** Websites. We must remember that U.S. GAAP and IFRS are two similar, but not identical, systems. However, their similarities greatly outweigh any differences. The remainder of this section describes key principles and assumptions of accounting.

Decision Insight

Principles and Scruples   Auditors, directors, and lawyers are using principles to improve accounting reports. Examples include accounting restatements at **Navistar**, financial restatements at **Nortel**, accounting reviews at **Echostar**, and expense adjustments at **Electronic Data Systems**. Principles-based accounting has led accounting firms to drop clients deemed too risky. Examples include **Grant Thornton's** resignation as auditor of **Fremont General** due to alleged failures in providing information when promised, and **Ernst and Young's** resignation as auditor of **Catalina Marketing** due to alleged accounting errors.

Principles and Assumptions of Accounting   Accounting principles (and assumptions) are of two types. *General principles* are the basic assumptions, concepts, and guidelines for preparing financial statements. *Specific principles* are detailed rules used in reporting business transactions and events. General principles stem from long-used accounting practices. Specific principles arise more often from the rulings of authoritative groups.

EXHIBIT 1.7

Building Blocks for GAAP

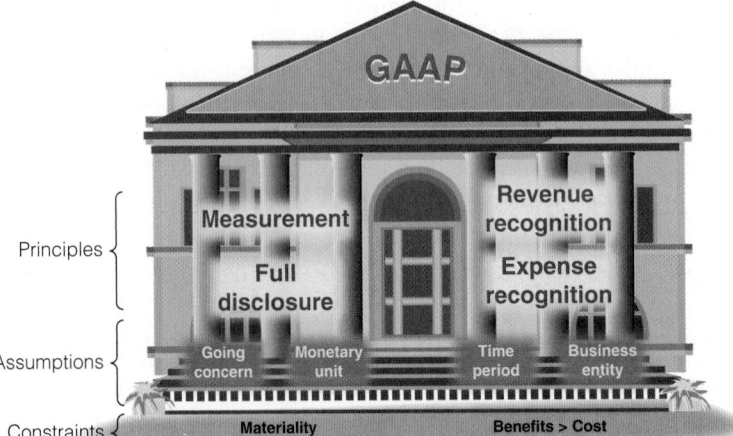

We need to understand both general and specific principles to effectively use accounting information. Several general principles are described in this section that are relied on in later chapters. General principles (in red font with yellow shading) and assumptions (in yellow font with purple shading) are portrayed as building blocks of GAAP in Exhibit 1.7. The specific principles are described as we encounter them in the book.

Accounting Principles   General principles consist of at least four basic principles, four assumptions, and two constraints.

The **measurement principle,** also called the **cost principle,** generally means that accounting information is based on actual cost (with a potential for subsequent adjustments to market). Cost is measured on a cash or equal-to-cash basis. This means if cash is given for a service, its cost is measured as the amount of cash paid. If something besides cash is exchanged (such as a car traded for a truck), cost is measured as the cash value of what is given up or received. The cost principle emphasizes reliability and verifiability, and information based on cost is considered objective. *Objectivity* means that information is supported by independent, unbiased evidence; it demands more than a person's opinion. To illustrate, suppose a company pays $5,000 for equipment. The cost principle requires that this purchase be recorded at a cost of $5,000. It makes no difference if the owner thinks this equipment is worth $7,000. Later in the book we introduce *fair value* measures.

Point: The cost principle is also called the *historical cost principle.*

Revenue (sales) is the amount received from selling products and services. The **revenue recognition principle** provides guidance on when a company must recognize revenue. To *recognize* means to record it. If revenue is recognized too early, a company would look more profitable than it is. If revenue is recognized too late, a company would look less profitable than it is.

Three concepts are important to revenue recognition. (1) *Revenue is recognized when earned.* The earnings process is normally complete when services are performed or a seller transfers ownership of products to the buyer. (2) *Proceeds from selling products and services need not be in cash.* A common noncash proceed received by a seller is a customer's promise to pay at a future date, called *credit sales.* (3) *Revenue is measured by the cash received plus the cash value of any other items received.*

The **expense recognition principle,** also called the **matching principle,** prescribes that a company record its expenses incurred to generate the revenue reported. The principles of matching and revenue recognition are key to modern accounting.

The **full disclosure principle** requires a company to report the details behind financial statements that would impact users' decisions. Those disclosures are often in footnotes to the statements.

Example: When a bookstore sells a textbook on credit is its earnings process complete? *Answer:* A bookstore can record sales for these books minus an amount expected for returns.

Decision Insight

Revenues for the **San Diego Chargers** football team include ticket sales, television and cable broadcasts, radio rights, concessions, and advertising. Revenues from ticket sales are earned when the Chargers play each game. Advance ticket sales are not revenues; instead, they represent a liability until the Chargers play the game for which the ticket was sold. At that point, the liability is removed and revenues are reported.

Accounting Assumptions   There are four accounting assumptions: the going concern assumption, the monetary unit assumption, the time period assumption, and the business entity assumption.

The **going concern assumption** means that accounting information reflects a presumption that the business will continue operating instead of being closed or sold. This implies, for example, that property is reported at cost instead of, say, liquidation values that assume closure.

The **monetary unit assumption** means that we can express transactions and events in monetary, or money, units. Money is the common denominator in business. Examples of monetary units are the dollar in the United States, Canada, Australia, and Singapore; and the peso in Mexico, the Philippines, and Chile. The monetary unit a company uses in its accounting reports usually depends on the country where it operates, but many companies today are expressing reports in more than one monetary unit.

Point: For currency conversion: xe.com

The **time period assumption** presumes that the life of a company can be divided into time periods, such as months and years, and that useful reports can be prepared for those periods.

The **business entity assumption** means that a business is accounted for separately from other business entities, including its owner. The reason for this assumption is that separate information about each business is necessary for good decisions. A business entity can take one of three legal forms: *proprietorship, partnership,* or *corporation.*

Point: Abuse of the entity assumption was a main culprit in **Enron's** collapse.

1. A **sole proprietorship,** or simply **proprietorship,** is a business owned by one person. No special legal requirements must be met to start a proprietorship. It is a separate entity for accounting purposes, but it is *not* a separate legal entity from its owner. This means, for example, that a court can order an owner to sell personal belongings to pay a proprietorship's debt. This *unlimited liability* of a proprietorship is a disadvantage. However, an advantage is that a proprietorship's income is not subject to a business income tax but is instead reported and taxed on the owner's personal income tax return. Proprietorship characteristics are summarized in Exhibit 1.8, including those for partnerships and corporations.

2. A **partnership** is a business owned by two or more people, called *partners.* Like a proprietorship, no special legal requirements must be met in starting a partnership. The only requirement is an agreement between partners to run a business together. The agreement can be either oral or written and usually indicates how income and losses are to be shared.

EXHIBIT 1.8

Characteristics of Businesses

Characteristic	Proprietorship	Partnership	Corporation
Business entity	yes	yes	yes
Legal entity	no	no	yes
Limited liability	no*	no*	yes
Unlimited life	no	no	yes
Business taxed	no	no	yes
One owner allowed	yes	no	yes

* Proprietorships and partnerships that are set up as LLCs provide limited liability.

A partnership, like a proprietorship, is *not* legally separate from its owners. This means that each partner's share of profits is reported and taxed on that partner's tax return. It also means *unlimited liability* for its partners. However, at least three types of partnerships limit liability. A *limited partnership* (*LP*) includes a general partner(s) with unlimited liability and a limited partner(s) with liability restricted to the amount invested. A *limited liability partnership* (*LLP*) restricts partners' liabilities to their own acts and the acts of individuals under their control. This protects an innocent partner from the negligence of another partner, yet all partners remain responsible for partnership debts. A *limited liability company* (*LLC*), offers the limited liability of a corporation and the tax treatment of a partnership (and proprietorship). Most proprietorships and partnerships are now organized as LLCs.

3. A **corporation** is a business legally separate from its owners, meaning it is responsible for its own acts and its own debts. Separate legal status means that a corporation can conduct business with the rights, duties, and responsibilities of a person. A corporation acts through its managers, who are its legal agents. Separate legal status also means that its owners, who are called **shareholders** (or **stockholders**), are not personally liable for corporate acts and debts. This limited liability is its main advantage. A main disadvantage is what's called *double taxation*—meaning that (1) the corporation income is taxed and (2) any distribution of income to its owners through dividends is taxed as part of the owners' personal income, usually at the 15% rate. (For lower income taxpayers, the dividend tax is less than 15%, and in some cases zero.) An *S corporation,* a corporation with special characteristics, does not owe corporate income tax. Owners of S corporations report their share of corporate income with their personal income. Ownership of all corporations is divided into units called **shares** or **stock.** When a corporation issues only one class of stock, we call it **common stock** (or *capital stock*).

Point: Proprietorships and partnerships are usually managed by their owners. In a corporation, the owners (shareholders) elect a board of directors who appoint managers to run the business.

Decision Ethics boxes are role-playing exercises that stress ethics in accounting and business.

♟ Decision Ethics

Entrepreneur   You and a friend develop a new design for in-line skates that improves speed by 25% to 30%. You plan to form a business to manufacture and market those skates. You and your friend want to minimize taxes, but your prime concern is potential lawsuits from individuals who might be injured on these skates. What form of organization do you set up? [Answer—p. 28]

Accounting Constraints   There are two basic constraints on financial reporting. The **materiality constraint** prescribes that only information that would influence the decisions of a reasonable person need be disclosed. This constraint looks at both the importance and relative size of an amount. The **cost-benefit constraint** prescribes that only information with benefits of disclosure greater than the costs of providing it need be disclosed.

Sarbanes–Oxley (SOX)

Congress passed the **Sarbanes–Oxley Act,** also called *SOX,* to help curb financial abuses at companies that issue their stock to the public. SOX requires that these public companies apply both accounting oversight and stringent internal controls. The desired results include more transparency, accountability, and truthfulness in reporting transactions.

Compliance with SOX requires documentation and verification of internal controls and increased emphasis on internal control effectiveness. Failure to comply can yield financial

Point: An **audit** examines whether financial statements are prepared using GAAP. It does *not* attest to absolute accuracy of the statements.

penalties, stock market delisting, and criminal prosecution of executives. Management must issue a report stating that internal controls are effective. CEOs and CFOs who knowingly sign off on bogus accounting reports risk millions of dollars in fines and years in prison. **Auditors** also must verify the effectiveness of internal controls.

A listing of some of the more publicized accounting scandals in recent years follows.

Point: *BusinessWeek* reports that external audit costs run about $35,000 for start-ups, up from $15,000 pre-SOX.

Company	Alleged Accounting Abuses
Enron	Inflated income, hid debt, and bribed officials
WorldCom	Understated expenses to inflate income and hid debt
Fannie Mae	Inflated income
Adelphia Communications	Understated expenses to inflate income and hid debt
AOL Time Warner	Inflated revenues and income
Xerox	Inflated income
Bristol-Myers Squibb	Inflated revenues and income
Nortel Networks	Understated expenses to inflate income
Global Crossing	Inflated revenues and income
Tyco	Hid debt, and CEO evaded taxes
Halliburton	Inflated revenues and income
Qwest Communications	Inflated revenues and income

To reduce the risk of accounting fraud, companies set up *governance systems*. A company's governance system includes its owners, managers, employees, board of directors, and other important stakeholders, who work together to reduce the risk of accounting fraud and increase confidence in accounting reports.

The impact of SOX regulations for accounting and business is discussed throughout this book. Ethics and investor confidence are key to company success. Lack of confidence in accounting numbers impacts company value as evidenced by huge stock price declines for **Enron**, **WorldCom**, **Tyco**, and **ImClone** after accounting misconduct was uncovered.

Decision Insight

SOX   Economic Downturn, Fraud Upturn?
Executives polled show that 80% believe that the economic downturn has or will have a significant impact on fraud control in their companies (Deloitte 2008). The top three responses to the question "What activity would best counter this increased fraud risk?" are tallied in the graphic here.

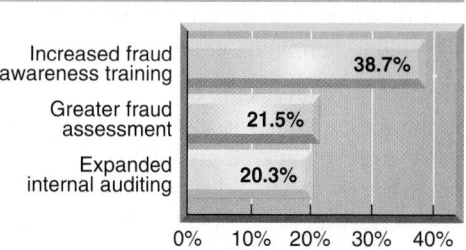

Quick Check
Answers—pp. 28–29

 7. What three-step guidelines can help people make ethical decisions?
 8. Why are ethics and social responsibility valuable to organizations?
 9. Why are ethics crucial in accounting?
10. Who sets U.S. accounting rules?
11. How are U.S. companies affected by international accounting standards?
12. How are the objectivity concept and cost principle related?
13. Why is the business entity assumption important?
14. Why is the revenue recognition principle important?
15. What are the three basic forms of business organization?
16. Identify the owners of corporations and the terminology for ownership units.

Transaction Analysis and the Accounting Equation

A1 Define and interpret the accounting equation and each of its components.

To understand accounting information, we need to know how an accounting system captures relevant data about transactions, and then classifies, records, and reports data.

Accounting Equation

The accounting system reflects two basic aspects of a company: what it owns and what it owes. **Assets** are resources with future benefits that are owned or controlled by a company. Examples are cash, supplies, equipment, and land. The claims on a company's assets—what it owes—are separated into owner and nonowner claims. **Liabilities** are what a company owes its nonowners (creditors) in future payments, products, or services. **Equity** (also called owners' equity or capital) refers to the claims of its owner(s). Together, liabilities and equity are the source of funds to acquire assets. The relation of assets, liabilities, and equity is reflected in the following **accounting equation:**

$$\text{Assets} = \text{Liabilities} + \text{Equity}$$

Liabilities are usually shown before equity in this equation because creditors' claims must be paid before the claims of owners. (The terms in this equation can be rearranged; for example, Assets − Liabilities = Equity.) The accounting equation applies to all transactions and events, to all companies and forms of organization, and to all points in time. For example, **Best Buy**'s assets equal $15,826, its liabilities equal $11,183, and its equity equals $4,643 ($ in millions). Let's now look at the accounting equation in more detail.

Assets   Assets are resources owned or controlled by a company. These resources are expected to yield future benefits. Examples are Web servers for an online services company, musical instruments for a rock band, and land for a vegetable grower. The term *receivable* is used to refer to an asset that promises a future inflow of resources. A company that provides a service or product on credit is said to have an account receivable from that customer.

Liabilities   Liabilities are creditors' claims on assets. These claims reflect company obligations to provide assets, products or services to others. The term *payable* refers to a liability that promises a future outflow of resources. Examples are wages payable to workers, accounts payable to suppliers, notes payable to banks, and taxes payable to the government.

Equity   Equity is the owner's claim on assets. Equity is equal to assets minus liabilities. This is the reason equity is also called *net assets* or *residual equity*.

A corporation's equity—often called stockholders' or shareholders' equity—has two parts: contributed capital and retained earnings. **Contributed capital** refers to the amount that stockholders invest in the company—included under the title **common stock. Retained earnings** refer to **income** (revenues less expenses) that is *not* distributed to its stockholders. The distribution of assets to stockholders is called **dividends,** which reduce retained earnings. **Revenues** increase retained earnings (via net income) and are resources generated from a company's earnings activities. Examples are consulting services provided, sales of products, facilities rented to others, and commissions from services. **Expenses** decrease retained earnings and are the cost of assets or services used to earn revenues. Examples are costs of employee time, use of supplies, and advertising, utilities, and insurance services from others. In sum, retained earnings is the accumulated revenues less the accumulated expenses and dividends since the company began. This breakdown of equity yields the following **expanded accounting equation:**

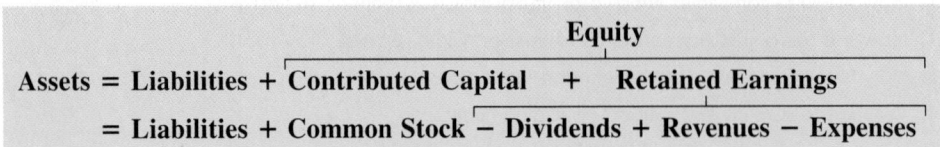

$$
\begin{array}{c}
\overbrace{\hspace{10cm}}^{\textstyle \text{Equity}}\\
\text{Assets} = \text{Liabilities} + \overbrace{\text{Contributed Capital} \quad + \quad \text{Retained Earnings}}\\
= \text{Liabilities} + \text{Common Stock} \underbrace{- \text{Dividends} + \text{Revenues} - \text{Expenses}}
\end{array}
$$

Net income occurs when revenues exceed expenses. Net income increases equity. A **net loss** occurs when expenses exceed revenues, which decreases equity.

Videos 1.1 & 1.2

Point: The phrases "on credit" and "on account" imply that cash payment will occur at a future date.

*Key **terms** are printed in bold and defined again in the end-of-book **glossary.***

Decision Insight

Web Info   Most organizations maintain Websites that include accounting data—see **Best Buy** (**BestBuy.com**) as an example. The SEC keeps an online database called **EDGAR** (**www.sec.gov/edgar.shtml**), which has accounting information for thousands of companies that issue stock to the public (EDGAR is being upgraded and renamed **IDEA**). Information services such as **Finance.Google.com** and **Finance.Yahoo.com** offer additional online data and analysis.

Transaction Analysis

Business activities can be described in terms of transactions and events. **External transactions** are exchanges of value between two entities, which yield changes in the accounting equation. **Internal transactions** are exchanges within an entity; they can also affect the accounting equation. An example is a company's use of its supplies, which are reported as expenses when used. **Events** refer to happenings that affect an entity's accounting equation *and* can be reliably measured. They include business events such as changes in the market value of certain assets and liabilities, and natural events such as floods and fires that destroy assets and create losses. They do not include, for example, the signing of service or product contracts, which by themselves do not impact the accounting equation.

A2   Analyze business transactions using the accounting equation.

This section uses the accounting equation to analyze 11 selected transactions and events of FastForward, a start-up consulting (service) business, in its first month of operations. Remember that each transaction and event leaves the equation in balance and that assets *always* equal the sum of liabilities and equity.

Transaction 1: Investment by Owner   On December 1, Chas Taylor forms a consulting business, named FastForward and set up as a corporation, that focuses on assessing the performance of footwear and accessories. Taylor owns and manages the business. The marketing plan for the business is to focus primarily on publishing online reviews and consulting with clubs, athletes, and others who place orders for footwear and accessories with manufacturers. Taylor personally invests $30,000 cash in the new company and deposits the cash in a bank account opened under the name of FastForward. After this transaction, the cash (an asset) and the stockholders' equity each equal $30,000. The source of increase in equity is the owner's investment (stock issuance), which is included in the column titled Common Stock. The effect of this transaction on FastForward is reflected in the accounting equation as follows:

Point: There are 3 basic types of company operations: (1) **Services**—providing customer services for profit, (2) **Merchandisers**—buying products and re-selling them for profit, and (3) **Manufacturers**—creating products and selling them for profit.

	Assets	=	Liabilities	+	Equity
	Cash	=			Common Stock
(1)	+$30,000	=			+$30,000

Transaction 2: Purchase Supplies for Cash   FastForward uses $2,500 of its cash to buy supplies of brand name footwear for performance testing over the next few months. This transaction is an exchange of cash, an asset, for another kind of asset, supplies. It merely changes the form of assets from cash to supplies. The decrease in cash is exactly equal to the increase in supplies. The supplies of footwear are assets because of the expected future benefits from the test results of their performance. This transaction is reflected in the accounting equation as follows:

	Assets			=	Liabilities	+	Equity
	Cash	+	Supplies	=			Common Stock
Old Bal.	$30,000			=			$30,000
(2)	−2,500	+	$2,500				
New Bal.	$27,500	+	$ 2,500	=			$30,000
		$30,000				$30,000	

Transaction 3: Purchase Equipment for Cash   FastForward spends $26,000 to acquire equipment for testing footwear. Like transaction 2, transaction 3 is an exchange of one asset, cash, for another asset, equipment. The equipment is an asset because of its expected future benefits from testing footwear. This purchase changes the makeup of assets but does not change the asset total. The accounting equation remains in balance.

	Assets					=	Liabilities	+	Equity
	Cash	+	Supplies	+	Equipment	=			Common Stock
Old Bal.	$27,500	+	$2,500			=			$30,000
(3)	−26,000			+	$26,000				
New Bal.	$ 1,500	+	$2,500	+	$ 26,000	=			$30,000
			$30,000					$30,000	

Example: If FastForward pays $500 cash in transaction 4, how does this partial payment affect the liability to CalTech? What is FastForward's cash balance? *Answers:* The liability to CalTech is reduced to $6,600 and the cash balance is reduced to $1,000.

Transaction 4: Purchase Supplies on Credit   Taylor decides more supplies of footwear and accessories are needed. These additional supplies total $7,100, but as we see from the accounting equation in transaction 3, FastForward has only $1,500 in cash. Taylor arranges to purchase them on credit from CalTech Supply Company. Thus, FastForward acquires supplies in exchange for a promise to pay for them later. This purchase increases assets by $7,100 in supplies, and liabilities (called *accounts payable* to CalTech Supply) increase by the same amount. The effects of this purchase follow:

	Assets					=	Liabilities	+	Equity
	Cash	+	Supplies	+	Equipment	=	Accounts Payable	+	Common Stock
Old Bal.	$1,500	+	$2,500	+	$26,000	=			$30,000
(4)		+	7,100				+$7,100		
New Bal.	$1,500	+	$9,600	+	$26,000	=	$ 7,100	+	$30,000
			$37,100					$37,100	

Transaction 5: Provide Services for Cash   FastForward earns revenues by selling online ad space to manufacturers and by consulting with clients about test results on footwear and accessories. It earns net income only if its revenues are greater than its expenses incurred in earning them. In one of its first jobs, FastForward provides consulting services to a power-walking club and immediately collects $4,200 cash. The accounting equation reflects this increase in cash of $4,200 and in equity of $4,200. This increase in equity is identified in the far right column under Revenues because the cash received is earned by providing consulting services.

	Assets					=	Liabilities	+	Equity		
	Cash	+	Supplies	+	Equipment	=	Accounts Payable	+	Common Stock	+	Revenues
Old Bal.	$1,500	+	$9,600	+	$26,000	=	$7,100	+	$30,000		
(5)	+4,200									+	$4,200
New Bal.	$5,700	+	$9,600	+	$26,000	=	$7,100	+	$30,000	+	$ 4,200
			$41,300						$41,300		

Transactions 6 and 7: Payment of Expenses in Cash   FastForward pays $1,000 rent to the landlord of the building where its facilities are located. Paying this amount allows FastForward to occupy the space for the month of December. The rental payment is reflected in the following accounting equation as transaction 6. FastForward also pays the biweekly $700 salary of the company's only employee. This is reflected in the accounting equation as transaction 7. Both transactions 6 and 7 are December expenses for FastForward. The costs of both rent and salary are expenses, as opposed to assets, because their benefits are used in December (they have no future benefits after December). These transactions also use up an asset (cash) in carrying out FastForward's operations. The accounting equation shows that both transactions reduce cash and equity. The far right column identifies these decreases as Expenses.

By definition, increases in expenses yield decreases in equity.

	Assets					=	Liabilities	+			Equity			
	Cash	+	Supplies	+	Equipment	=	Accounts Payable	+	Common Stock	+	Revenues	–	Expenses
Old Bal.	$5,700	+	$9,600	+	$26,000	=	$7,100	+	$30,000	+	$4,200		
(6)	–1,000											–	$1,000
Bal.	4,700	+	9,600	+	26,000	=	7,100	+	30,000	+	4,200	–	1,000
(7)	– 700											–	700
New Bal.	$4,000	+	$9,600	+	$26,000	=	$7,100	+	$30,000	+	$4,200	–	$ 1,700
			$39,600						$39,600				

Transaction 8: Provide Services and Facilities for Credit   FastForward provides consulting services of $1,600 and rents its test facilities for $300 to a podiatric services center. The rental involves allowing members to try recommended footwear and accessories at FastForward's testing area. The center is billed for the $1,900 total. This transaction results in a new asset, called *accounts receivable,* from this client. It also yields an increase in equity from the two revenue components reflected in the Revenues column of the accounting equation:

	Assets								=	Liabilities	+			Equity			
	Cash	+	Accounts Receivable	+	Supplies	+	Equipment	=	Accounts Payable	+	Common Stock	+	Revenues	–	Expenses
Old Bal.	$4,000	+		+	$9,600	+	$26,000	=	$7,100	+	$30,000	+	$4,200	–	$1,700
(8)		+	$1,900									+	1,600		
												+	300		
New Bal.	$4,000	+	$ 1,900	+	$9,600	+	$26,000	=	$7,100	+	$30,000	+	$6,100	–	$1,700
			$41,500								$41,500				

Transaction 9: Receipt of Cash from Accounts Receivable   The client in transaction 8 (the podiatric center) pays $1,900 to FastForward 10 days after it is billed for consulting services. This transaction 9 does not change the total amount of assets and does not affect liabilities or equity. It converts the receivable (an asset) to cash (another asset). It does not create new revenue. Revenue was recognized when FastForward rendered the services in transaction 8, not when the cash is now collected. This emphasis on the earnings process instead of cash flows is a goal of the revenue recognition principle and yields useful information to users. The new balances follow:

Point: Receipt of cash is not always a revenue.

	Assets								=	Liabilities	+			Equity			
	Cash	+	Accounts Receivable	+	Supplies	+	Equipment	=	Accounts Payable	+	Common Stock	+	Revenues	–	Expenses
Old Bal.	$4,000	+	$1,900	+	$9,600	+	$26,000	=	$7,100	+	$30,000	+	$6,100	–	$1,700
(9)	+1,900	–	1,900												
New Bal.	$5,900	+	$ 0	+	$9,600	+	$26,000	=	$7,100	+	$30,000	+	$6,100	–	$1,700
			$41,500								$41,500				

Transaction 10: Payment of Accounts Payable   FastForward pays CalTech Supply $900 cash as partial payment for its earlier $7,100 purchase of supplies (transaction 4), leaving $6,200 unpaid. The accounting equation shows that this transaction decreases FastForward's cash by $900 and decreases its liability to CalTech Supply by $900. Equity does not change. This event does not create an expense even though cash flows out of FastForward (instead the expense is recorded when FastForward derives the benefits from these supplies).

Assets					=	Liabilities	+	Equity			
	Cash	+	Accounts Receivable	+ Supplies	+ Equipment	=	Accounts Payable	+	Common Stock	+ Revenues	− Expenses
Old Bal.	$5,900	+	$ 0	+ $9,600	+ $26,000	=	$7,100	+	$30,000	+ $6,100	− $1,700
(10)	− 900						− 900				
New Bal.	$5,000	+	$ 0	+ $9,600	+ $26,000	=	$6,200	+	$30,000	+ $6,100	− $1,700
			$40,600						$40,600		

Transaction 11: Payment of Cash Dividend   FastForward declares and pays a $200 cash dividend to its owner. Dividends (decreases in equity) are not reported as expenses because they are not part of the company's earnings process. Since dividends are not company expenses, they are not used in computing net income.

By definition, increases in dividends yield decreases in equity.

Assets					=	Liabilities	+	Equity			
	Cash	+	Accounts Receivable	+ Supplies	+ Equipment	=	Accounts Payable	+ Common Stock	− Dividends	+ Revenues	− Expenses
Old Bal.	$5,000	+	$ 0	+ $9,600	+ $26,000	=	$6,200	+ $30,000		+ $6,100	− $1,700
(11)	− 200								− $200		
New Bal.	$4,800	+	$ 0	+ $9,600	+ $26,000	=	$6,200	+ $30,000	− $200	+ $6,100	− $1,700
			$40,400						$40,400		

Summary of Transactions

We summarize in Exhibit 1.9 the effects of these 11 transactions of FastForward using the accounting equation. First, we see that the accounting equation remains in balance after each

EXHIBIT 1.9

Summary of Transactions Using the Accounting Equation

	Assets					=	Liabilities	+	Equity			
	Cash	+	Accounts Receivable	+ Supplies	+ Equipment	=	Accounts Payable	+ Common Stock	− Dividends	+ Revenues	− Expenses
(1)	$30,000					=		$30,000			
(2)	− 2,500			+ $2,500							
Bal.	27,500			+ 2,500		=		30,000			
(3)	−26,000				+ $26,000						
Bal.	1,500			+ 2,500	+ 26,000	=		30,000			
(4)				+ 7,100			+$7,100				
Bal.	1,500			+ 9,600	+ 26,000	=	7,100	+ 30,000			
(5)	+ 4,200									+ $4,200	
Bal.	5,700			+ 9,600	+ 26,000	=	7,100	+ 30,000		+ 4,200	
(6)	− 1,000										− $1,000
Bal.	4,700			+ 9,600	+ 26,000	=	7,100	+ 30,000		+ 4,200	− 1,000
(7)	− 700										− 700
Bal.	4,000			+ 9,600	+ 26,000	=	7,100	+ 30,000		+ 4,200	− 1,700
(8)		+	$1,900							+ 1,600	
										+ 300	
Bal.	4,000	+	1,900	+ 9,600	+ 26,000	=	7,100	+ 30,000		+ 6,100	− 1,700
(9)	+ 1,900	−	1,900								
Bal.	5,900	+	0	+ 9,600	+ 26,000	=	7,100	+ 30,000		+ 6,100	− 1,700
(10)	− 900						− 900				
Bal.	5,000	+	0	+ 9,600	+ 26,000	=	6,200	+ 30,000		+ 6,100	− 1,700
(11)	− 200								− $200		
Bal.	$ 4,800	+	$ 0	+ $9,600	+ $26,000	=	$ 6,200	+ $30,000	− $200	+ $6,100	− $1,700

transaction. Second, transactions can be analyzed by their effects on components of the accounting equation. For example, in transactions 2, 3, and 9, one asset increased while another asset decreased by equal amounts.

Point: Knowing how financial statements are prepared improves our analysis of them. We develop the skills for analysis of financial statements throughout the book. Chapter 13 focuses on financial statement analysis.

Quick Check
Answers—p. 29

17. When is the accounting equation in balance, and what does that mean?
18. How can a transaction not affect any liability and equity accounts?
19. Describe a transaction increasing equity and one decreasing it.
20. Identify a transaction that decreases both assets and liabilities.

Financial Statements

This section introduces us to how financial statements are prepared from the analysis of business transactions. The four financial statements and their purposes are:

1. **Income statement**—describes a company's revenues and expenses along with the resulting net income or loss over a period of time due to earnings activities.
2. **Statement of retained earnings**—explains changes in retained earnings from net income (or loss) and from any dividends over a period of time.
3. **Balance sheet**—describes a company's financial position (types and amounts of assets, liabilities, and equity) at a point in time.
4. **Statement of cash flows**—identifies cash inflows (receipts) and cash outflows (payments) over a period of time.

We prepare these financial statements, in this order, using the 11 selected transactions of FastForward. (These statements are technically called *unadjusted*—we explain this in Chapters 2 and 3.)

P1 Identify and prepare basic financial statements and explain how they interrelate.

Video1.1

Income Statement

FastForward's income statement for December is shown at the top of Exhibit 1.10. Information about revenues and expenses is conveniently taken from the Equity columns of Exhibit 1.9. Revenues are reported first on the income statement. They include consulting revenues of $5,800 from transactions 5 and 8 and rental revenue of $300 from transaction 8. Expenses are reported after revenues. (For convenience in this chapter, we list larger amounts first, but we can sort expenses in different ways.) Rent and salary expenses are from transactions 6 and 7. Expenses reflect the costs to generate the revenues reported. Net income (or loss) is reported at the bottom of the statement and is the amount earned in December. Stockholders' investments and dividends are *not* part of income.

Point: Net income is sometimes called *earnings* or *profit*.

Statement of Retained Earnings

The statement of retained earnings reports information about how retained earnings changes over the reporting period. This statement shows beginning retained earnings, events that increase it (net income), and events that decrease it (dividends and net loss). Ending retained earnings is computed in this statement and is carried over and reported on the balance sheet. FastForward's statement of retained earnings is the second report in Exhibit 1.10. The beginning balance is measured as of the start of business on December 1. It is zero because FastForward did not exist before then. An existing business reports the beginning balance equal to that as of the end of the prior reporting period (such as from November 30). FastForward's statement shows the $4,400 of net income earned during the period. This links the income statement to the statement of retained earnings (see line ①). The statement also reports the $200 cash dividend and FastForward's end-of-period retained earnings balance.

Point: The statement of retained earnings is also called the *statement of changes in retained earnings*. Note: Beg. Retained Earnings + Net Income − Dividends = End. Retained Earnings

EXHIBIT 1.10

Financial Statements and
Their Links

Point: A statement's heading identifies
the company, the statement title, and
the date or time period.

Point: Arrow lines show how the
statements are linked. ① Net income
is used to compute equity. ② Retained
earnings is used to prepare the balance
sheet. ③ Cash from the balance sheet
is used to reconcile the statement of
cash flows.

Point: The income statement, the
statement of retained earnings, and the
statement of cash flows are prepared
for a *period* of time. The balance sheet
is prepared as of a *point* in time.

Point: A single ruled line denotes an
addition or subtraction. Final totals are
double underlined. Negative amounts
are often in parentheses.

FASTFORWARD
Income Statement
For Month Ended December 31, 2009

Revenues		
Consulting revenue ($4,200 + $1,600)	$ 5,800	
Rental revenue	300	
Total revenues		$ 6,100
Expenses		
Rent expense	1,000	
Salaries expense	700	
Total expenses		1,700
Net income		$ 4,400

FASTFORWARD
Statement of Retained Earnings
For Month Ended December 31, 2009

Retained earnings, December 1, 2009		$ 0
Plus: Net income		4,400
		4,400
Less: Dividends		200
Retained earnings, December 31, 2009		$ 4,200

FASTFORWARD
Balance Sheet
December 31, 2009

Assets		Liabilities	
Cash	$ 4,800	Accounts payable	$ 6,200
Supplies	9,600	Total liabilities	6,200
Equipment	26,000	**Equity**	
		Common stock	30,000
		Retained earnings	4,200
		Total equity	34,200
Total assets	$ 40,400	Total liabilities and equity	$ 40,400

FASTFORWARD
Statement of Cash Flows
For Month Ended December 31, 2009

Cash flows from operating activities		
Cash received from clients ($4,200 + $1,900)	$ 6,100	
Cash paid for supplies ($2,500 + $900)	(3,400)	
Cash paid for rent	(1,000)	
Cash paid to employee	(700)	
Net cash provided by operating activities		$ 1,000
Cash flows from investing activities		
Purchase of equipment	(26,000)	
Net cash used by investing activities		(26,000)
Cash flows from financing activities		
Investments by stockholder	30,000	
Dividends to stockholder	(200)	
Net cash provided by financing activities		29,800
Net increase in cash		$ 4,800
Cash balance, December 1, 2009		0
Cash balance, December 31, 2009		$ 4,800

Balance Sheet

FastForward's balance sheet is the third report in Exhibit 1.10. This statement refers to FastForward's financial condition at the close of business on December 31. The left side of the balance sheet lists FastForward's assets: cash, supplies, and equipment. The upper right side of the balance sheet shows that FastForward owes $6,200 to creditors. Any other liabilities (such as a bank loan) would be listed here. The equity (capital) balance is $34,200. Line ② shows the link between the ending balance of the statement of retained earnings and the retained earnings balance on the balance sheet. (This presentation of the balance sheet is called the *account form:* assets on the left and liabilities and equity on the right. Another presentation is the *report form:* assets on top, followed by liabilities and then equity at the bottom. Either presentation is acceptable.) As always, we see the accounting equation applies: Assets of $40,400 = Liabilities of $6,200 + Equity of $34,200.

Decision Maker boxes are role-playing exercises that stress the relevance of accounting.

Decision Maker

Retailer   You open a wholesale business selling entertainment equipment to retail outlets. You find that most of your customers demand to buy on credit. How can you use the balance sheets of these customers to help you decide which ones to extend credit to? [Answer—p. 28]

Statement of Cash Flows

FastForward's statement of cash flows is the final report in Exhibit 1.10. The first section reports cash flows from *operating activities*. It shows the $6,100 cash received from clients and the $5,100 cash paid for supplies, rent, and employee salaries. Outflows are in parentheses to denote subtraction. Net cash provided by operating activities for December is $1,000. If cash paid exceeded the $5,100 cash received, we would call it "cash used by operating activities." The second section reports *investing activities,* which involve buying and selling assets such as land and equipment that are held for *long-term use* (typically more than one year). The only investing activity is the $26,000 purchase of equipment. The third section shows cash flows from *financing activities,* which include the *long-term* borrowing and repaying of cash from lenders and the cash investments from, and dividends to, stockholders. FastForward reports $30,000 from the owner's initial investment and the $200 cash dividend. The net cash effect of all financing transactions is a $29,800 cash inflow. The final part of the statement shows FastForward increased its cash balance by $4,800 in December. Since it started with no cash, the ending balance is also $4,800—see line ③. We see that cash flow measures are different from income statement (*accrual*) numbers, which is common.

Point: Statement of cash flows has three main sections: operating, investing, and financing.

Point: Payment for supplies is an operating activity because supplies are expected to be used up in short-term operations (typically less than one year).

Point: Investing activities refer to long-term asset investments by the company, *not* to owner investments.

Quick Check

Answers—p. 29

21. Explain the link between the income statement and the statement of retained earnings.

22. Describe the link between the balance sheet and the statement of retained earnings.

23. Discuss the three major sections of the statement of cash flows.

Global View

Financial accounting according to U.S. GAAP is similar, but not identical, to IFRS. Throughout the book we use this last section to identify major similarities and differences between IFRS and U.S. GAAP for the materials in each chapter. In this chapter, we discuss basic principles, transaction analysis, and financial statement formulation.

Basic Principles   Both U.S. GAAP and IFRS include broad and similar guidance for financial accounting. However, neither system specifies particular account names nor the detail required. (A typical *chart of accounts* is shown near the end of this book.) IFRS does require certain minimum line items in the balance sheet and other minimum disclosures that U.S. GAAP does not. On the other hand, U.S. GAAP requires disclosures for the current and prior two years for the income statement, statement of cash flows, and statement of retained earnings (equity), while IFRS requires disclosures for the current and prior year. Again, the basic principles behind these two systems are similar.

Transaction Analysis   Both U.S. GAAP and IFRS would apply transaction analysis identically as shown in this chapter. Although some variations exist in revenue and expense recognition and other principles, all of the transactions in this chapter are accounted for identically under these two systems. It is often said that U.S. GAAP is more *rules-based* whereas IFRS is more *principles-based*. The main difference on the rules versus principles focus is with the approach in deciding how to account for certain transactions. Under U.S. GAAP, the approach is more focused on the accounting rules; under IFRS, the approach is more focused on a review of the situation. This difference typically impacts advanced topics beyond the introductory course.

Financial Statements   Both U.S. GAAP and IFRS prepare the same four basic financial statements. To illustrate, a condensed version of **GOME**'s income statement follows (numbers are in Renminbi thousands). GOME is a leader in the consumer electronics and household appliances retail sector in China. Similar condensed versions can be prepared for the other three statements.

GOME
Income Statement (in RMB 000s)
For Year Ended December 31, 2008

Revenue	45,889,257
Cost of sales	41,381,223
Selling, administrative, and other expenses	2,974,185
Taxes	435,156
Net income	1,098,693

Decision Analysis (a section at the end of each chapter) introduces and explains ratios helpful in decision making using real company data. Instructors can skip this section and cover all ratios in Chapter 13.

Decision Analysis   Return on Assets

A *Decision Analysis* section at the end of each chapter is devoted to financial statement analysis. We organize financial statement analysis into four areas: (1) liquidity and efficiency, (2) solvency, (3) profitability, and (4) market prospects—Chapter 13 has a ratio listing with definitions and groupings by area. When analyzing ratios, we need benchmarks to identify good, bad, or average levels. Common benchmarks include the company's prior levels and those of its competitors.

A3 Compute and interpret return on assets.

This chapter presents a profitability measure: return on assets. Return on assets is useful in evaluating management, analyzing and forecasting profits, and planning activities. **Dell** has its marketing department compute return on assets for *every* order. **Return on assets (ROA),** also called *return on investment (ROI)*, is defined in Exhibit 1.11.

EXHIBIT I.II

Return on Assets

$$\text{Return on assets} = \frac{\text{Net income}}{\text{Average total assets}}$$

Net income is from the annual income statement, and average total assets is computed by adding the beginning and ending amounts for that same period and dividing by 2. To illustrate, **Best Buy** reports net income of $1,003 million in 2009. At the beginning of fiscal 2009, its total assets are $12,758 million and at the end of fiscal 2009, they total $15,826 million. Best Buy's return on assets for 2009 is:

$$\text{Return on assets} = \frac{\$1,003 \text{ million}}{(\$12,758 \text{ million} + \$15,826 \text{ million})/2} = 7.0\%$$

Is a 7.0% return on assets good or bad for Best Buy? To help answer this question, we compare (bench-mark) Best Buy's return with its prior performance, the returns of competitors (such as **RadioShack, Conn's,** and **Rex Stores**), and the returns from alternative investments. Best Buy's return for each of the prior five years is in the second column of Exhibit 1.12, which ranges from 7.0% to 10.8%.

	Return on Assets	
Fiscal Year	**Best Buy**	**Industry**
2009	7.0%	2.5%
2008	10.7	3.4
2007	10.8	3.5
2006	10.3	3.3
2005	10.4	3.2

EXHIBIT 1.12

Best Buy and Industry Returns

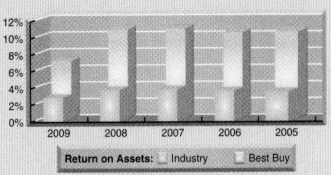

Best Buy shows a fairly stable pattern of good returns that reflect its productive use of assets. There is a decline in its 2009 return reflecting the recessionary period. We compare Best Buy's return to the normal return for similar merchandisers of electronic products (third column). Industry averages are available from services such as **Dun & Bradstreet's** *Industry Norms and Key Ratios* and **Robert Morris Associates'** *Annual Statement Studies*. When compared to the industry, Best Buy performs well.

*Each **Decision Analysis** section ends with a role-playing scenario to show the usefulness of ratios.*

Decision Maker

Business Owner You own a small winter ski resort that earns a 21% return on its assets. An opportunity to purchase a winter ski equipment manufacturer is offered to you. This manufacturer earns a 19% return on its assets. The industry return for this manufacturer is 14%. Do you purchase this manufacturer?
[Answer—p. 28]

*—The **Demonstration Problem** is a review of key chapter content. The Planning the Solution offers strategies in solving the problem.*

Demonstration Problem

After several months of planning, Jasmine Worthy started a haircutting business called Expressions. The following events occurred during its first month of business.

a. On August 1, Worthy invested $3,000 cash and $15,000 of equipment in Expressions in exchange for its common stock.

b. On August 2, Expressions paid $600 cash for furniture for the shop.

c. On August 3, Expressions paid $500 cash to rent space in a strip mall for August.

d. On August 4, it purchased $1,200 of equipment on credit for the shop (using a long-term note payable).

e. On August 5, Expressions opened for business. Cash received from haircutting services in the first week and a half of business (ended August 15) was $825.

f. On August 15, it provided $100 of haircutting services on account.

g. On August 17, it received a $100 check for services previously rendered on account.

h. On August 17, it paid $125 cash to an assistant for hours worked during the grand opening.

i. Cash received from services provided during the second half of August was $930.

j. On August 31, it paid a $400 installment toward principal on the note payable entered into on August 4.

k. On August 31, it paid $900 cash dividends to Worthy.

24   Chapter 1   Introducing Accounting in Business

Required

1. Arrange the following asset, liability, and equity titles in a table similar to the one in Exhibit 1.9: Cash; Accounts Receivable; Furniture; Store Equipment; Note Payable; Common Stock; Dividends; Revenues; and Expenses. Show the effects of each transaction using the accounting equation.

2. Prepare an income statement for August.

3. Prepare a statement of retained earnings for August.

4. Prepare a balance sheet as of August 31.

5. Prepare a statement of cash flows for August.

6. Determine the return on assets ratio for August.

Planning the Solution

- Set up a table like Exhibit 1.9 with the appropriate columns for accounts.
- Analyze each transaction and show its effects as increases or decreases in the appropriate columns. Be sure the accounting equation remains in balance after each transaction.
- Prepare the income statement, and identify revenues and expenses. List those items on the statement, compute the difference, and label the result as *net income* or *net loss*.
- Use information in the Equity columns to prepare the statement of retained earnings.
- Use information in the last row of the transactions table to prepare the balance sheet.
- Prepare the statement of cash flows; include all events listed in the Cash column of the transactions table. Classify each cash flow as operating, investing, or financing.
- Calculate return on assets by dividing net income by average assets.

Solution to Demonstration Problem

1.

	Assets							=	Liabilities	+		Equity				
	Cash	+	Accounts Receivable	+	Furniture	+	Store Equipment	=	Note Payable	+	Common Stock	−	Dividends	+	Revenues	−	Expenses
a.	$3,000						$15,000				$18,000						
b.	− 600			+	$600												
Bal.	2,400	+		+	600	+	15,000	=			18,000						
c.	− 500															−	$500
Bal.	1,900	+		+	600	+	15,000	=			18,000					−	500
d.						+	1,200		+$1,200								
Bal.	1,900	+		+	600	+	16,200	=	1,200	+	18,000					−	500
e.	+ 825													+	$ 825		
Bal.	2,725	+		+	600	+	16,200	=	1,200	+	18,000			+	825	−	500
f.		+	$100											+	100		
Bal.	2,725	+	100	+	600	+	16,200	=	1,200	+	18,000			+	925	−	500
g.	+ 100	−	100														
Bal.	2,825	+	0	+	600	+	16,200	=	1,200	+	18,000			+	925	−	500
h.	− 125															−	125
Bal.	2,700	+	0	+	600	+	16,200	=	1,200	+	18,000			+	925	−	625
i.	+ 930													+	930		
Bal.	3,630	+	0	+	600	+	16,200	=	1,200	+	18,000			+	1,855	−	625
j.	− 400								− 400								
Bal.	3,230	+	0	+	600	+	16,200	=	800	+	18,000			+	1,855	−	625
k.	− 900											−	$900				
Bal.	$ 2,330	+	0	+	$600	+	$ 16,200	=	$ 800	+	$ 18,000	−	$900	+	$1,855	−	$625

2.

EXPRESSIONS
Income Statement
For Month Ended August 31

Revenues		
Haircutting services revenue		$1,855
Expenses		
Rent expense	$500	
Wages expense	125	
Total expenses		625
Net Income		$1,230

3.

EXPRESSIONS
Statement of Retained Earnings
For Month Ended August 31

Retained earnings, August 1*	$ 0
Plus: Net income	1,230
	1,230
Less: Dividend to owner	900
Retained earnings, August 31	$ 330

* If Expressions had been an existing business from a prior period, the beginning retained earnings balance would equal the retained earnings balance from the end of the prior period.

4.

EXPRESSIONS
Balance Sheet
August 31

Assets		**Liabilities**	
Cash	$ 2,330	Note payable	$ 800
Furniture	600	**Equity**	
Store equipment	16,200	Common stock	18,000
		Retained earnings	330
Total assets	$19,130	Total liabilities and equity	$19,130

5.

EXPRESSIONS
Statement of Cash Flows
For Month Ended August 31

Cash flows from operating activities		
Cash received from customers	$1,855	
Cash paid for rent	(500)	
Cash paid for wages	(125)	
Net cash provided by operating activities		$1,230
Cash flows from investing activities		
Cash paid for furniture		(600)
Cash flows from financing activities		
Cash from stock issuance	3,000	
Cash paid for dividend	(900)	
Partial repayment of (long-term) note payable	(400)	
Net cash provided by financing activities		1,700
Net increase in cash................................		$2,330
Cash balance, August 1		0
Cash balance, August 31		$2,330

6. Return on assets $= \dfrac{\text{Net income}}{\text{Average assets}} = \dfrac{\$1,230}{(\$18,000^* + \$19,130)/2} = \dfrac{\$1,230}{\$18,565} = \underline{\underline{6.63\%}}$

* Uses the initial \$18,000 investment as the beginning balance for the *start-up period only.*

APPENDIX

1A Return and Risk Analysis

A4 Explain the relation between return and risk.

This appendix explains return and risk analysis and its role in business and accounting.

Net income is often linked to **return.** Return on assets (ROA) is stated in ratio form as income divided by assets invested. For example, banks report return from a savings account in the form of an interest return such as 4%. If we invest in a savings account or in U.S. Treasury bills, we expect a return of around 2% to 7%. We could also invest in a company's stock, or even start our own business. How do we decide among these investment options? The answer depends on our trade-off between return and risk.

Risk is the uncertainty about the return we will earn. All business investments involve risk, but some investments involve more risk than others. The lower the risk of an investment, the lower is our expected return. The reason that savings accounts pay such a low return is the low risk of not being repaid with interest (the government guarantees most savings accounts from default). If we buy a share of eBay or any other company, we might obtain a large return. However, we have no guarantee of any return; there is even the risk of loss.

EXHIBIT 1A.1

Average Returns for Bonds with Different Risks

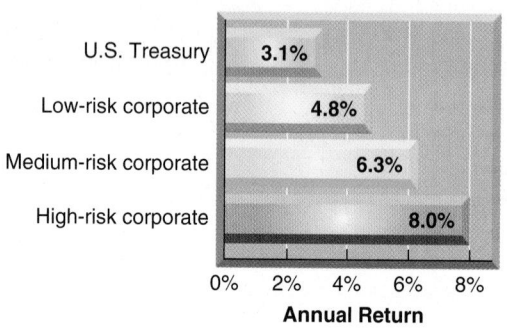

The bar graph in Exhibit 1A.1 shows recent returns for 30-year bonds with different risks. *Bonds* are written promises by organizations to repay amounts loaned with interest. U.S. Treasury bonds provide a low expected return, but they also offer low risk since they are backed by the U.S. government. High-risk corporate bonds offer a much larger potential return but with much higher risk.

The trade-off between return and risk is a normal part of business. Higher risk implies higher, but riskier, expected returns. To help us make better decisions, we use accounting information to assess both return and risk.

APPENDIX

1B Business Activities and the Accounting Equation

C6 Identify and describe the three major activities of organizations.

This appendix explains how the accounting equation is derived from business activities.

There are three major types of business activities: financing, investing, and operating. Each of these requires planning. *Planning* involves defining an organization's ideas, goals, and actions. Most public corporations use the *Management Discussion and Analysis* section in their annual reports to communicate plans. However, planning is not cast in stone. This adds *risk* to both setting plans and analyzing them.

Financing   *Financing activities* provide the means organizations use to pay for resources such as land, buildings, and equipment to carry out plans. Organizations are careful in acquiring and managing financing activities because they can determine success or failure. The two sources of financing are owner and nonowner. *Owner financing* refers to resources contributed by the owner along with any income the owner leaves in the organization. *Nonowner* (or *creditor*) *financing* refers to resources contributed by creditors (lenders). *Financial management* is the task of planning how to obtain these resources and to set the right mix between owner and creditor financing.

Point: Management must understand accounting data to set financial goals, make financing and investing decisions, and evaluate operating performance.

Investing   *Investing activities* are the acquiring and disposing of resources (assets) that an organization uses to acquire and sell its products or services. Assets are funded by an organization's financing. Organizations differ on the amount and makeup of assets. Some require land and factories to operate. Others need only an office. Determining the amount and type of assets for operations is called *asset management*.

Invested amounts are referred to as *assets*. Financing is made up of creditor and owner financing, which hold claims on assets. Creditors' claims are called *liabilities,* and the owner's claim is called *equity.* This basic equality is called the *accounting equation* and can be written as: Assets = Liabilities + Equity.

Point: Investing (assets) and financing (liabilities plus equity) totals are *always* equal.

Operating   *Operating activities* involve using resources to research, develop, purchase, produce, distribute, and market products and services. Sales and revenues are the inflow of assets from selling products and services. Costs and expenses are the outflow of assets to support operating activities. *Strategic management* is the process of determining the right mix of operating activities for the type of organization, its plans, and its market.

Exhibit 1B.1 summarizes business activities. Planning is part of each activity and gives them meaning and focus. Investing (assets) and financing (liabilities and equity) are set opposite each other to stress their balance. Operating activities are below investing and financing activities to show that operating activities are the result of investing and financing.

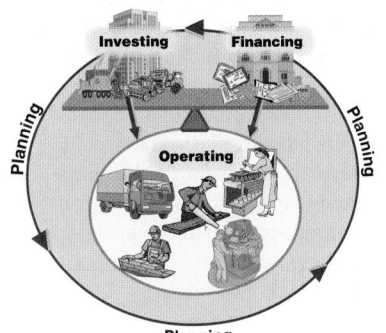

EXHIBIT 1B.1

Activities of Organizations

---

*A **Summary** organized by learning objectives concludes each chapter.*

Summary

C1   **Explain the purpose and importance of accounting in the information age.** Accounting is an information and measurement system that aims to identify, record, and communicate relevant, reliable, and comparable information about business activities. It helps assess opportunities, products, investments, and social and community responsibilities.

C2   **Identify users and uses of accounting.** Users of accounting are both internal and external. Some users and uses of accounting include (a) managers in controlling, monitoring, and planning; (b) lenders for measuring the risk and return of loans; (c) shareholders for assessing the return and risk of stock; (d) directors for overseeing management; and (e) employees for judging employment opportunities.

C3   **Identify opportunities in accounting and related fields.** Opportunities in accounting include financial, managerial, and tax accounting. They also include accounting-related fields such as lending, consulting, managing, and planning.

C4   **Explain why ethics are crucial to accounting.** The goal of accounting is to provide useful information for decision making. For information to be useful, it must be trusted. This demands ethical behavior in accounting.

C5   **Explain generally accepted accounting principles and define and apply several accounting principles.** Generally accepted accounting principles are a common set of standards applied by accountants. Accounting principles aid in producing relevant, reliable, and comparable information. Four principles underlying financial statements were introduced: cost, revenue recognition, matching, and full disclosure. Financial statements also reflect four assumptions: going concern, monetary unit, time period, and business entity.

C6^B   **Identify and describe the three major activities of organizations.** Organizations carry out three major activities: financing, investing, and operating. Financing is the means used to pay for resources such as land, buildings, and machines. Investing refers to the buying and selling of resources used in acquiring and selling products and services. Operating activities are those necessary for carrying out the organization's plans.

A1   **Define and interpret the accounting equation and each of its components.** The accounting equation is: Assets = Liabilities + Equity. Assets are resources owned by a company. Liabilities are creditors' claims on assets. Equity is the owner's claim on assets (*the residual*). The expanded accounting equation is: Assets = Liabilities + [Common Stock − Dividends + Revenues − Expenses].

A2 **Analyze business transactions using the accounting equation.** A *transaction* is an exchange of economic consideration between two parties. Examples include exchanges of products, services, money, and rights to collect money. Transactions always have at least two effects on one or more components of the accounting equation. This equation is always in balance.

A3 **Compute and interpret return on assets.** Return on assets is computed as net income divided by average assets. For example, if we have an average balance of $100 in a savings account

and it earns $5 interest for the year, the return on assets is $5/$100, or 5%.

A4^A **Explain the relation between return and risk.** *Return* refers to income, and *risk* is the uncertainty about the return we hope to make. All investments involve risk. The lower the risk of an investment, the lower is its expected return. Higher risk implies higher, but riskier, expected return.

P1 **Identify and prepare basic financial statements and explain how they interrelate.** Four financial statements report on an organization's activities: balance sheet, income statement, statement of retained earnings, and statement of cash flows.

Guidance Answers to **Decision Maker** and **Decision Ethics**

Entrepreneur   (p. 12) You should probably form the business as a corporation if potential lawsuits are of prime concern. The corporate form of organization protects your personal property from lawsuits directed at the business and places only the corporation's resources at risk. A downside of the corporate form is double taxation: The corporation must pay taxes on its income, and you normally must pay taxes on any money distributed to you from the business (even though the corporation already paid taxes on this money). You should also examine the ethical and socially responsible aspects of starting a business in which you anticipate injuries to others. Formation as an LLC or S corp. should also be explored.

Retailer   (p. 21) You can use the accounting equation (Assets = Liabilities + Equity) to help identify risky customers to whom you

would likely not want to extend credit. A balance sheet provides amounts for each of these key components. The lower a customer's equity is relative to liabilities, the less likely you would be to extend credit. A low equity means the business has little value that does not already have creditor claims to it.

Business Owner   (p. 23) The 19% return on assets for the manufacturer exceeds the 14% industry return (and many others). This is a positive factor for a potential purchase. Also, the purchase of this manufacturer is an opportunity to spread your risk over two businesses as opposed to one. Still, you should hesitate to purchase a business whose return of 19% is lower than your current resort's return of 21%. You are probably better off directing efforts to increase investment in your resort, assuming you can continue to earn a 21% return.

Guidance Answers to **Quick Checks**

1. Accounting is an information and measurement system that identifies, records, and communicates relevant information to help people make better decisions.

2. Recordkeeping, also called *bookkeeping,* is the recording of financial transactions and events, either manually or electronically. Recordkeeping is essential to data reliability; but accounting is this and much more. Accounting includes identifying, measuring, recording, reporting, and analyzing business events and transactions.

3. Technology offers increased accuracy, speed, efficiency, and convenience in accounting.

4. External users of accounting include lenders, shareholders, directors, customers, suppliers, regulators, lawyers, brokers, and the press. Internal users of accounting include managers, officers, and other internal decision makers involved with strategic and operating decisions.

5. Internal users (managers) include those from research and development, purchasing, human resources, production, distribution, marketing, and servicing.

6. Internal controls are procedures set up to protect assets, ensure reliable accounting reports, promote efficiency, and encourage

adherence to company policies. Internal controls are crucial for relevant and reliable information.

7. Ethical guidelines are threefold: (1) identify ethical concerns using personal ethics, (2) analyze options considering all good and bad consequences, and (3) make ethical decisions after weighing all consequences.

8. Ethics and social responsibility yield good behavior, and they often result in higher income and a better working environment.

9. For accounting to provide useful information for decisions, it must be trusted. Trust requires ethics in accounting.

10. Two major participants in setting rules include the SEC and the FASB. (*Note:* Accounting rules reflect society's needs, not those of accountants or any other single constituency.)

11. Most U.S. companies are not directly affected by international accounting standards. International standards are put forth as preferred accounting practices. However, stock exchanges and other parties are increasing the pressure to narrow differences in worldwide accounting practices. International accounting standards are playing an important role in that process.

12. The objectivity concept and cost principle are related in that most users consider information based on cost as objective. Information prepared using both is considered highly reliable and often relevant.

13. Users desire information about the performance of a specific entity. If information is mixed between two or more entities, its usefulness decreases.

14. The revenue recognition principle gives preparers guidelines on when to recognize (record) revenue. This is important; for example, if revenue is recognized too early, the statements report revenue sooner than they should and the business looks more profitable than it is. The reverse is also true.

15. The three basic forms of business organization are sole proprietorships, partnerships, and corporations.

16. Owners of corporations are called *shareholders* (or *stockholders*). Corporate ownership is divided into units called *shares* (or *stock*). The most basic of corporate shares is common stock (or capital stock).

17. The accounting equation is: Assets = Liabilities + Equity. This equation is always in balance, both before and after each transaction.

18. A transaction that changes the makeup of assets would not affect liability and equity accounts. FastForward's transactions 2 and 3 are examples. Each exchanges one asset for another.

19. Earning revenue by performing services, as in FastForward's transaction 5, increases equity (and assets). Incurring expenses while servicing clients, such as in transactions 6 and 7, decreases equity (and assets). Other examples include owner investments (stock issuances) that increase equity and dividends that decrease equity.

20. Paying a liability with an asset reduces both asset and liability totals. One example is FastForward's transaction 10 that reduces a payable by paying cash.

21. An income statement reports a company's revenues and expenses along with the resulting net income or loss. A statement of retained earnings shows changes in retained earnings, including that from net income or loss. Both statements report transactions occurring over a period of time.

22. The balance sheet describes a company's financial position (assets, liabilities, and equity) at a point in time. The retained earnings amount in the balance sheet is obtained from the statement of retained earnings.

23. Cash flows from operating activities report cash receipts and payments from the primary business the company engages in. Cash flows from investing activities involve cash transactions from buying and selling long-term assets. Cash flows from financing activities include long-term cash borrowings and repayments to lenders and the cash investments from and dividends to the stockholders.

Key Terms

Accounting (p. 4)
Accounting equation (p. 14)
Assets (p. 14)
Auditors (p. 13)
Balance sheet (p. 19)
Bookkeeping (p. 4)
Business entity assumption (p. 11)
Common stock (p. 12)
Conceptual framework (p. 9)
Contributed capital (p. 14)
Corporation (p. 12)
Cost-benefit constraint (p. 12)
Cost principle (p. 10)
Dividends (p. 14)
Equity (p. 14)
Ethics (p. 8)
Events (p. 15)
Expanded accounting equation (p. 14)
Expense recognition principle (p. 11)
Expenses (p. 14)
External transactions (p. 15)
External users (p. 5)

Financial accounting (p. 5)
Financial Accounting Standards Board (FASB) (p. 9)
Full disclosure principle (p. 11)
Generally Accepted Accounting Principles (GAAP) (p. 8)
Going concern assumption (p. 11)
Income (p. 14)
Income statement (p. 19)
Internal transactions (p. 15)
Internal users (p. 6)
International Accounting Standards Board (IASB) (p. 9)
International Financial Reporting Standards (IFRS) (p. 9)
Liabilities (p. 14)
Managerial accounting (p. 6)
Matching principle (p. 11)
Materiality constraint (p. 12)
Measurement principle (p. 10)
Monetary unit assumption (p. 11)
Net income (p. 14)

Net loss (p. 14)
Partnership (p. 11)
Proprietorship (p. 11)
Recordkeeping (p. 4)
Retained earnings (p. 14)
Return (p. 26)
Return on assets (p. 22)
Revenue recognition principle (p. 11)
Revenues (p. 14)
Risk (p. 26)
Sarbanes–Oxley Act (p. 12)
Securities and Exchange Commission (SEC) (p. 9)
Shareholders (p. 12)
Shares (p. 12)
Sole proprietorship (p. 11)
Statement of cash flows (p. 19)
Statement of retained earnings (p. 19)
Stock (p. 12)
Stockholders (p. 12)
Time period assumption (p. 11)

Multiple Choice Quiz   Answers on p. 47   mhhe.com/wildFA5e

Additional Quiz Questions are available at the book's Website.

1. A building is offered for sale at $500,000 but is currently assessed at $400,000. The purchaser of the building believes the building is worth $475,000, but ultimately purchases the building for $450,000. The purchaser records the building at:
  a. $50,000
  b. $400,000
  c. $450,000
  d. $475,000
  e. $500,000

2. On December 30, 2010, KPMG signs a $150,000 contract to provide accounting services to one of its clients in 2011. KPMG has a December 31 year-end. Which accounting principle or assumption requires KPMG to record the accounting services revenue from this client in 2011 and not 2010?
  a. Business entity assumption
  b. Revenue recognition principle
  c. Monetary unit assumption
  d. Cost principle
  e. Going-concern assumption

3. If the assets of a company increase by $100,000 during the year and its liabilities increase by $35,000 during the same year, then the change in equity of the company during the year must have been:
  a. An increase of $135,000.
  b. A decrease of $135,000.
  c. A decrease of $65,000.
  d. An increase of $65,000.
  e. An increase of $100,000.

4. Brunswick borrows $50,000 cash from Third National Bank. How does this transaction affect the accounting equation for Brunswick?
  a. Assets increase by $50,000; liabilities increase by $50,000; no effect on equity.
  b. Assets increase by $50,000; no effect on liabilities; equity increases by $50,000.
  c. Assets increase by $50,000; liabilities decrease by $50,000; no effect on equity.
  d. No effect on assets; liabilities increase by $50,000; equity increases by $50,000.
  e. No effect on assets; liabilities increase by $50,000; equity decreases by $50,000.

5. Geek Squad performs services for a customer and bills the customer for $500. How would Geek Squad record this transaction?
  a. Accounts receivable increase by $500; revenues increase by $500.
  b. Cash increases by $500; revenues increase by $500.
  c. Accounts receivable increase by $500; revenues decrease by $500.
  d. Accounts receivable increase by $500; accounts payable increase by $500.
  e. Accounts payable increase by $500; revenues increase by $500.

Superscript letter ^{A} $(^B)$ denotes assignments based on Appendix 1A (1B).

Discussion Questions

1. What is the purpose of accounting in society?

2. Technology is increasingly used to process accounting data. Why then must we study and understand accounting?

3. Identify four kinds of external users and describe how they use accounting information.

4. What are at least three questions business owners and managers might be able to answer by looking at accounting information?

5. Identify three actual businesses that offer services and three actual businesses that offer products.

6. Describe the internal role of accounting for organizations.

7. Identify three types of services typically offered by accounting professionals.

8. What type of accounting information might be useful to the marketing managers of a business?

9. Why is accounting described as a service activity?

10. What are some accounting-related professions?

11. How do ethics rules affect auditors' choice of clients?

12. What work do tax accounting professionals perform in addition to preparing tax returns?

13. What does the concept of *objectivity* imply for information reported in financial statements? Why?

14. A business reports its own office stationery on the balance sheet at its $400 cost, although it cannot be sold for more than $10 as scrap paper. Which accounting principle and/or assumption justifies this treatment?

15. Why is the revenue recognition principle needed? What does it demand?

16. Describe the three basic forms of business organization and their key characteristics.

17. Define (*a*) *assets*, (*b*) *liabilities*, (*c*) *equity*, and (*d*) *net assets*.

18. What events or transactions change equity?

19. Identify the two main categories of accounting principles.

20. What do accountants mean by the term *revenue?*

21. Define *net income* and explain its computation.

22. Identify the four basic financial statements of a business.

23. What information is reported in an income statement?

24. Give two examples of expenses a business might incur.

25. What is the purpose of the statement of retained earnings?

26. What information is reported in a balance sheet?

27. The statement of cash flows reports on what major activities?

28. Define and explain return on assets.

29.^A Define return and risk. Discuss the trade-off between them.

30.^BDescribe the three major business activities in organizations.

31.^BExplain why investing (assets) and financing (liabilities and equity) totals are always equal.

32. Refer to the financial statements of **Best Buy** in Appendix A near the end of the book. To what level

of significance are dollar amounts rounded? What time period does its income statement cover?

33. Identify the dollar amounts of **Radio-Shack**'s 2008 assets, liabilities, and equity as reported in its statements in Appendix A near the end of the book.

34. Refer to **GOME**'s balance sheet in Appendix A near the end of the book. Confirm that its total assets equal its total liabilities plus total equity.

35. Access the SEC EDGAR database (**www.SEC.gov**) and retrieve **Apple**'s 2008 10-K (filed November 5, 2008). Identify its auditor. What responsibility does its independent auditor claim regarding Apple's financial statements?

Denotes Discussion Questions that involve decision making.

Connect Accounting repeats assignments on the Connect Website, which allows instructors to monitor, promote, and assess student learning. It can be used in practice, homework, or exam mode.

Quick Study exercises give readers a brief test of key elements.

CONNECT™ Available with Connect Accounting

Identify the following users as either external users (E) or internal users (I).

a. Shareholders   **d.** FBI and IRS   **g.** Customers   **j.** Business press

b. Lenders   **e.** Consumer group   **h.** Suppliers   **k.** Managers

c. Controllers   **f.** Sales staff   **i.** Brokers   **l.** District attorney

QUICK STUDY

QS 1-1

Identifying accounting users

C2

Reading and interpreting accounting reports requires some knowledge of accounting terminology. (*a*) Identify the meaning of these accounting-related acronyms: GAAP, SEC, FASB and IASB. (*b*) Briefly explain the importance of the knowledge base or organization that is referred to for each of the accounting-related acronyms.

QS 1-2

Identifying accounting terms

C1

There are many job opportunities for those with accounting knowledge. Identify at least three main areas of opportunities for accounting professionals. For each area, identify at least three job possibilities linked to accounting.

QS 1-3

Accounting opportunities

C3

An important responsibility of many accounting professionals is to design and implement internal control procedures for organizations. Explain the purpose of internal control procedures. Provide two examples of internal controls applied by companies.

QS 1-4

Explaining internal control

C1

Identify which accounting principle or assumption best describes each of the following practices:

a. In December 2009, Ace Landscaping received a customer's order and cash prepayment to install sod at a new house that would not be ready for installation until March 2010. Ace should record the revenue from the customer order in March 2010, not in December 2009.

b. If $51,000 cash is paid to buy land, the land is reported on the buyer's balance sheet at $51,000.

c. Jay Keren owns both Sailing Passions and Dockside Supplies. In preparing financial statements for Dockside Supplies, Keren makes sure that the expense transactions of Sailing Passions are kept separate from Dockside's statements.

QS 1-5

Identifying accounting principles

C5

This icon highlights assignments that enhance decision-making skills.

Accounting professionals must sometimes choose between two or more acceptable methods of accounting for business transactions and events. Explain why these situations can involve difficult matters of ethical concern.

QS 1-6

Identifying ethical concerns

C4

QS 1-7

Applying the accounting equation

A1

Use the accounting equation to compute the missing financial statement amounts (a), (b), and (c).

Company	Assets	=	Liabilities	+	Equity
1	$375,000		$ (a)		$250,000
2	$ (b)		$90,000		$160,000
3	$185,000		$60,000		$ (c)

QS 1-8

Applying the accounting equation

A1

a. Total assets of Charter Company equal $500,000 and its equity is $320,000. What is the amount of its liabilities?

b. Total assets of Golfland equal $900,000 and its liabilities and equity amounts are equal to each other. What is the amount of its liabilities? What is the amount of its equity?

QS 1-9

Identifying and computing assets, liabilities, and equity

A2

Use **Apple**'s September 30, 2008, financial statements, in Appendix A near the end of the book, to answer the following:

a. Identify the dollar amounts of Apple's 2008 (1) assets, (2) liabilities, and (3) equity.

b. Using Apple's amounts from part a, verify that Assets = Liabilities + Equity.

QS 1-10

Identifying transactions and events

A2

Accounting provides information about an organization's business transactions and events that both affect the accounting equation and can be reliably measured. Identify at least two examples of both (a) business transactions and (b) business events that meet these requirements.

QS 1-11

Identifying items with financial statements

P1

Indicate in which financial statement each item would most likely appear: income statement (I), balance sheet (B), statement of retained earnings (RE), or statement of cash flows (CF).

a. Equipment   **d.** Net decrease (or increase) in cash   **g.** Assets

b. Expenses   **e.** Revenues   **h.** Cash from operating activities

c. Liabilities   **f.** Total liabilities and equity   **i.** Dividends

---

QS 1-12

Computing and interpreting return on assets

A3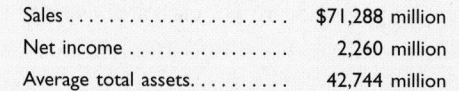

In a recent year's financial statements, **Home Depot** reported the following results. Compute and interpret Home Depot's return on assets (assume competitors average a 5% return on assets).

Sales	$71,288 million
Net income	2,260 million
Average total assets.	42,744 million

QS 1-13

International accounting standards

C5

This icon highlights assignments that focus on IFRS-related content.

Answer each of the following questions related to international accounting standards.

a. The International Accounting Standards Board (IASB) issues preferred accounting practices that are referred to as what?

b. The FASB and IASB are working on a convergence process for what purpose?

c. The SEC has proposed a roadmap for use of IFRS by U.S. companies. What is the proposed adoption date for large U.S. companies to adopt IFRS?

Available with Connect Accounting **connect**

EXERCISES

Exercise 1-1

Identifying accounting users and uses

C2

Much of accounting is directed at servicing the information needs of those users that are external to an organization. (a) Identify at least three external users of accounting information and indicate two questions they might seek to answer through their use of accounting information. (b) Identify at least three internal users of accounting information and describe how each might use accounting information in their jobs.

Many accounting professionals work in one of the following three areas:

A. Financial accounting   **B.** Managerial accounting   **C.** Tax accounting

Identify the area of accounting that is most involved in each of the following responsibilities:

_____ **1.** Investigating violations of tax laws.   _____ **5.** Internal auditing.

_____ **2.** Planning transactions to minimize taxes.   _____ **6.** External auditing.

_____ **3.** Preparing external financial statements.   _____ **7.** Cost accounting.

_____ **4.** Reviewing reports for SEC compliance.   _____ **8.** Budgeting.

Exercise 1-2
Describing accounting responsibilities

C2   C3

Assume the following role and describe a situation in which ethical considerations play an important part in guiding your decisions and actions:

a. You are an accounting professional with audit clients that are competitors in business.

b. You are an accounting professional preparing tax returns for clients.

c. You are a manager with responsibility for several employees.

d. You are a student in an introductory accounting course.

Exercise 1-3
Identifying ethical concerns

C4

Match each of the numbered descriptions with the principle or assumption it best reflects. Enter the letter for the appropriate principle or assumption in the blank space next to each description.

A. General accounting principle   **E.** Specific accounting principle

B. Cost principle   **F.** Full disclosure principle

C. Business entity assumption   **G.** Going concern assumption

D. Revenue recognition principle   **H.** Matching principle

_____ **1.** Usually created by a pronouncement from an authoritative body.

_____ **2.** Financial statements reflect the assumption that the business continues operating.

_____ **3.** Derived from long-used and generally accepted accounting practices.

_____ **4.** Every business is accounted for separately from its owner or owners.

_____ **5.** Revenue is recorded only when the earnings process is complete.

_____ **6.** Information is based on actual costs incurred in transactions.

_____ **7.** A company reports details behind financial statements that would impact users' decisions.

_____ **8.** A company records the expenses incurred to generate the revenues reported.

Exercise 1-4
Identifying accounting principles and assumptions

C5

The following describe several different business organizations. Determine whether the description refers to a sole proprietorship, partnership, or corporation.

a. Wallingford is owned by Gary Malone, who is personally liable for the company's debts.

b. Ava Fong and Elijah Logan own Financial Services, a financial services provider. Neither Fong nor Logan has personal responsibility for the debts of Financial Services.

c. IBC Services does not have separate legal existence apart from the one person who owns it.

d. Computing Services pays its own income taxes and has two owners.

e. Ownership of Zander Company is divided into 1,000 shares of stock.

f. Emma Bailey and Dylan Kay own Speedy Packages, a courier service. Both are personally liable for the debts of the business.

g. Physio Products does not pay income taxes and has one owner.

Exercise 1-5
Distinguishing business organizations

C5

Determine the missing amount from each of the separate situations *a*, *b*, and *c* below.

	Assets	=	Liabilities	+	Equity
a.	?	=	$164,000	+	$16,000
b.	$ 90,000	=	$ 39,000	+	?
c.	$201,000	=	?	+	$62,000

Exercise 1-6
Using the accounting equation

A1

Match each of the numbered descriptions with the term or phrase it best reflects. Indicate your answer by writing the letter for the term or phrase in the blank provided.

A. Audit   **C.** Ethics   **E.** SEC   **G.** Net income

B. GAAP   **D.** Tax accounting   **F.** Public accountants   **H.** IASB

Exercise 1-7
Learning the language of business

C1–C4

_____ **1.** An accounting area that includes planning future transactions to minimize taxes paid.

_____ **2.** Amount a business earns after paying all expenses and costs associated with its sales and revenues.

_____ **3.** Principles that determine whether an action is right or wrong.

_____ **4.** Accounting professionals who provide services to many clients.

_____ **5.** An examination of an organization's accounting system and records that adds credibility to financial statements.

Exercise 1-8
Using the accounting equation
A1 A2

Check (c) Beg. equity, $73,000

Answer the following questions. (*Hint:* Use the accounting equation.)

a. Office Supplies has assets equal to $137,000 and liabilities equal to $110,000 at year-end. What is the total equity for Office Supplies at year-end?

b. At the beginning of the year, Addison Company's assets are $259,000 and its equity is $194,250. During the year, assets increase $80,000 and liabilities increase $52,643. What is the equity at the end of the year?

c. At the beginning of the year, Quasar Company's liabilities equal $57,000. During the year, assets increase by $60,000, and at year-end assets equal $190,000. Liabilities decrease $16,000 during the year. What are the beginning and ending amounts of equity?

Exercise 1-9
Identifying effects of transactions on the accounting equation
A1 A2

Provide an example of a transaction that creates the described effects for the separate cases *a* through *g*.

a. Increases an asset and increases a liability.

b. Decreases a liability and increases a liability.

c. Decreases an asset and decreases a liability.

d. Increases an asset and decreases an asset.

e. Increases a liability and decreases equity.

f. Increases an asset and increases equity.

g. Decreases an asset and decreases equity.

Exercise 1-10
Analysis using the accounting equation
A1 A2

Zen began a new consulting firm on January 5. The accounting equation showed the following balances after each of the company's first five transactions. Analyze the accounting equation for each transaction and describe each of the five transactions with their amounts.

			Assets							=	Liabilities	+		Equity		
Trans-action	Cash	+	Accounts Receiv-able	+	Office Sup-plies	+	Office Furni-ture	=	Accounts Payable	+	Common Stock	+	Revenues
a.	$20,000	+	$ 0	+	$ 0	+	$ 0	=	$ 0	+	$20,000	+	$ 0
b.	18,000	+	0	+	3,000	+	0	=	1,000	+	20,000	+	0
c.	10,000	+	0	+	3,000	+	8,000	=	1,000	+	20,000	+	0
d.	10,000	+	6,000	+	3,000	+	8,000	=	1,000	+	20,000	+	6,000
e.	11,000	+	6,000	+	3,000	+	8,000	=	1,000	+	20,000	+	7,000

Exercise 1-11
Identifying effects of transactions on accounting equation
A1 A2

The following table shows the effects of five transactions (*a* through *e*) on the assets, liabilities, and equity of Trista's Boutique. Write short descriptions of the probable nature of each transaction.

	Cash	+	Accounts Receivable	+	Office Supplies	+	Land	=	Accounts Payable	+	Common Stock	+	Revenues
	$ 21,000	+	$ 0	+	$3,000	+	$ 19,000	=	$ 0	+	$43,000	+	$ 0
a.	− 4,000					+	4,000						
b.				+	1,000				+1,000				
c.		+	1,900									+	1,900
d.	− 1,000								−1,000				
e.	+ 1,900	−	1,900										
	$ 17,900	+	$ 0	+	$4,000	+	$ 23,000	=	$ 0	+	$43,000	+	$1,900

Leora Diamond began a professional practice on June 1 and plans to prepare financial statements at the end of each month. During June, Diamond (the owner) completed these transactions:

a. Owner invested $70,000 cash in the company along with equipment that had a $20,000 market value in exchange for common stock.

b. The company paid $2,000 cash for rent of office space for the month.

c. The company purchased $25,000 of additional equipment on credit (payment due within 30 days).

d. The company completed work for a client and immediately collected the $3,000 cash earned.

e. The company completed work for a client and sent a bill for $9,500 to be received within 30 days.

f. The company purchased additional equipment for $5,000 cash.

g. The company paid an assistant $3,500 cash as wages for the month.

h. The company collected $6,500 cash as a partial payment for the amount owed by the client in transaction *e*.

i. The company paid $25,000 cash to settle the liability created in transaction *c*.

j. The company paid $1,500 cash dividends to the owner.

Required

Create a table like the one in Exhibit 1.9, using the following headings for columns: Cash; Accounts Receivable; Equipment; Accounts Payable; Common Stock; Dividends; Revenues; and Expenses. Then use additions and subtractions to show the effects of the transactions on individual items of the accounting equation. Show new balances after each transaction.

Exercise 1-12
Identifying effects of transactions using the accounting equation
A1 A2

Check Net income, $7,000

On October 1, Keisha King organized Real Answers, a new consulting firm. On October 31, the company's records show the following items and amounts. Use this information to prepare an October income statement for the business.

Cash	$11,500	Cash dividends	$ 2,000
Accounts receivable	12,000	Consulting fees earned	14,000
Office supplies	24,437	Rent expense	2,520
Land	46,000	Salaries expense	5,600
Office equipment	18,000	Telephone expense	760
Accounts payable	25,037	Miscellaneous expenses	580
Common stock	84,360		

Exercise 1-13
Preparing an income statement
P1

Check Net income, $4,540

Use the information in Exercise 1-13 to prepare an October statement of retained earnings for Real Answers.

Exercise 1-14
Preparing a statement of retained earnings P1

Check Retained earnings, $2,540

Use the information in Exercise 1-13 (if completed, you can also use your solution to Exercise 1-14) to prepare an October 31 balance sheet for Real Answers.

Exercise 1-15
Preparing a balance sheet P1

Use the information in Exercise 1-13 to prepare an October 31 statement of cash flows for Real Answers. Also assume the following:

a. The owner's initial investment consists of $38,360 cash and $46,000 in land in exchange for common stock.

b. The company's $18,000 equipment purchase is paid in cash.

c. The accounts payable balance of $25,037 consists of the $24,437 office supplies purchase and $600 in employee salaries yet to be paid.

d. The company's rent, telephone, and miscellaneous expenses are paid in cash.

e. $2,000 has been collected on the $14,000 consulting fees earned.

Exercise 1-16
Preparing a statement of cash flows
P1

Check Net increase in cash, $11,500

Exercise 1-17

Identifying sections of the statement of cash flows

P1

Indicate the section where each of the following would appear on the statement of cash flows.

O. Cash flows from operating activity

I. Cash flows from investing activity

F. Cash flows from financing activity

_____ **1.** Cash paid for rent   _____ **5.** Cash paid for advertising

_____ **2.** Cash paid on an account payable   _____ **6.** Cash paid for wages

_____ **3.** Cash received from stock issued   _____ **7.** Cash paid for dividends

_____ **4.** Cash received from clients   _____ **8.** Cash purchase of equipment

Exercise 1-18

Analysis of return on assets

A3

Iowa Group reports net income of $36,000 for 2010. At the beginning of 2010, Iowa Group had $135,000 in assets. By the end of 2010, assets had grown to $185,000. What is Iowa Group's 2010 return on assets? How would you assess its performance if competitors average a 10% return on assets?

Exercise 1-19[B]

Identifying business activities

C6

Match each transaction or event to one of the following activities of an organization: financing activities (F), investing activities (I), or operating activities (O).

a. _____ An organization purchases equipment.

b. _____ An organization advertises a new product.

c. _____ The organization borrows money from a bank.

d. _____ An owner contributes resources to the business in exchange for stock.

e. _____ An organization sells some of its land.

Exercise 1-20

Preparing an income statement and statement of retained earnings for a global company

P1

Nintendo Company reports the following income statement accounts for the year ended March 31, 2008. (Japanese Yen in millions.)

Net sales	¥1,672,423	Selling, general and administrative expenses	¥ 212,840
Cost of sales	972,362	Other expenses	229,879

a. Use this information to prepare Nintendo's income statement for the year ended March 31, 2008.

b. Use the information above along with the following additional information to prepare Nintendo's statement of retained earnings for the year ended March 31, 2008. (Japanese Yen in millions.)

Cash dividends for year ended March 31, 2008	¥ 97,205
Retained earnings, March 31, 2007	1,220,293

Problem Set B located at the end of Problem Set A is provided for each problem to reinforce the learning process.

Available with Connect Accounting **connect**

PROBLEM SET A

The following financial statement information is from five separate companies:

Problem 1-1A

Computing missing information using accounting knowledge

A1   A2

	Company A	Company B	Company C	Company D	Company E
December 31, 2010					
Assets	$33,000	$25,740	$21,120	$58,740	$90,090
Liabilities	27,060	18,018	11,404	40,530	?
December 31, 2011					
Assets	36,000	25,920	?	65,520	99,360
Liabilities	?	17,625	11,818	31,449	78,494
During year 2011					
Stock issuances	6,000	1,400	9,750	?	6,500
Net income (loss)	7,760	?	(1,289)	8,861	7,348
Cash dividends	3,500	2,000	5,875	0	11,000

Required

1. Answer the following questions about Company A:
   a. What is the amount of equity on December 31, 2010?
   b. What is the amount of equity on December 31, 2011?
   c. What is the amount of liabilities on December 31, 2011?

2. Answer the following questions about Company B:
   a. What is the amount of equity on December 31, 2010?
   b. What is the amount of equity on December 31, 2011?
   c. What is net income for year 2011?

3. Calculate the amount of assets for Company C on December 31, 2011.

4. Calculate the amount of stock issuances for Company D during year 2011.

5. Calculate the amount of liabilities for Company E on December 31, 2010.

Check   (1*b*) $16,200

(2*c*) $1,173

(3) $24,120

Identify how each of the following separate transactions affects financial statements. For the balance sheet, identify how each transaction affects total assets, total liabilities, and total equity. For the income statement, identify how each transaction affects net income. For the statement of cash flows, identify how each transaction affects cash flows from operating activities, cash flows from financing activities, and cash flows from investing activities. For increases, place a "+" in the column or columns. For decreases, place a "−" in the column or columns. If both an increase and a decrease occur, place a "+/−" in the column or columns. The first transaction is completed as an example.

Problem 1-2A
Identifying effects of transactions on financial statements

A1   A2

		Balance Sheet			Income Statement	Statement of Cash Flows		
	Transaction	**Total Assets**	**Total Liab.**	**Total Equity**	**Net Income**	**Operating Activities**	**Financing Activities**	**Investing Activities**
1	Owner invests cash for stock	+		+			+	
2	Receives cash for services provided							
3	Pays cash for employee wages							
4	Incurs legal costs on credit							
5	Borrows cash by signing long-term note payable							
6	Buys land by signing note payable							
7	Provides services on credit							
8	Buys office equipment for cash							
9	Collects cash on receivable from (7)							
10	Pays cash dividend							

The following is selected financial information for Elko Energy Company for the year ended December 31, 2010: revenues, $66,000; expenses, $51,348; net income, $14,652.

Problem 1-3A
Preparing an income statement

P1

Required

Prepare the 2010 calendar-year income statement for Elko Energy Company.

The following is selected financial information for Amity Company as of December 31, 2010: liabilities, $54,244; equity, $87,756; assets, $142,000.

Problem 1-4A
Preparing a balance sheet

P1

Required

Prepare the balance sheet for Amity Company as of December 31, 2010.

Problem 1-5A

Preparing a statement of
cash flows

P1

Check Cash balance, Dec. 31, 2010,
$4,850

Following is selected financial information of Fortune Co. for the year ended December 31, 2010.

Cash used by investing activities	$(3,250)
Net increase in cash	750
Cash used by financing activities	(4,050)
Cash from operating activities	8,050
Cash, December 31, 2009	4,100

Required

Prepare the 2010 statement of cash flows for Fortune Company.

Problem 1-6A

Preparing a statement of
retained earnings

P1

Following is selected financial information for Atlee Co. for the year ended December 31, 2010.

Retained earnings, Dec. 31, 2010	$16,750	Cash dividends	$ 2,000
Net income	7,750	Retained earnings, Dec. 31, 2009	11,000

Required

Prepare the 2010 statement of retained earnings for Atlee Company.

Problem 1-7A

Analyzing transactions and
preparing financial statements

C5 A2 P1

mhhe.com/wildFA5e

Check (2) Ending balances: Cash,
$46,350; Expenses, $5,395

(3) Net income, $7,205;
Total assets, $48,290

Holden Graham started The Graham Co., a new business that began operations on May 1. The Graham Co. completed the following transactions during its first month of operations.

May	1	H. Graham invested $43,000 cash in the company in exchange for common stock.
	1	The company rented a furnished office and paid $2,200 cash for May's rent.
	3	The company purchased $1,940 of office equipment on credit.
	5	The company paid $750 cash for this month's cleaning services.
	8	The company provided consulting services for a client and immediately collected $5,800 cash.
	12	The company provided $2,800 of consulting services for a client on credit.
	15	The company paid $850 cash for an assistant's salary for the first half of this month.
	20	The company received $2,800 cash payment for the services provided on May 12.
	22	The company provided $4,000 of consulting services on credit.
	25	The company received $4,000 cash payment for the services provided on May 22.
	26	The company paid $1,940 cash for the office equipment purchased on May 3.
	27	The company purchased $85 of advertising in this month's (May) local paper on credit; cash payment is due June 1.
	28	The company paid $850 cash for an assistant's salary for the second half of this month.
	30	The company paid $400 cash for this month's telephone bill.
	30	The company paid $260 cash for this month's utilities.
	31	The company paid $2,000 cash for dividends.

Required

1. Arrange the following asset, liability, and equity titles in a table like Exhibit 1.9: Cash; Accounts Receivable; Office Equipment; Accounts Payable; Common Stock; Dividends; Revenues; and Expenses.

2. Show effects of the transactions on the accounts of the accounting equation by recording increases and decreases in the appropriate columns. Do not determine new account balances after each transaction. Determine the final total for each account and verify that the equation is in balance.

3. Prepare an income statement for May, a statement of retained earnings for May, a May 31 balance sheet, and a statement of cash flows for May.

Problem 1-8A

Analyzing transactions and
preparing financial statements

C5 A2 P1

mhhe.com/wildFA5e

Helga Anderson started a new business and completed these transactions during December.

Dec.	1	Helga Anderson transferred $68,800 cash from a personal savings account to a checking account in the name of Anderson Electric in exchange for common stock.
	2	The company rented office space and paid $1,800 cash for the December rent.
	3	The company purchased $13,000 of electrical equipment by paying $4,800 cash and agreeing to pay the $8,200 balance in 30 days.
	5	The company purchased office supplies by paying $1,000 cash.
	6	The company completed electrical work and immediately collected $1,600 cash for these services.

8   The company purchased $2,680 of office equipment on credit.
15   The company completed electrical work on credit in the amount of $6,000.
18   The company purchased $360 of office supplies on credit.
20   The company paid $2,680 cash for the office equipment purchased on December 8.
24   The company billed a client $1,000 for electrical work completed; the balance is due in 30 days.
28   The company received $6,000 cash for the work completed on December 15.
29   The company paid the assistant's salary of $1,500 cash for this month.
30   The company paid $570 cash for this month's utility bill.
31   The company paid $900 cash for dividends.

Required

1. Arrange the following asset, liability, and equity titles in a table like Exhibit 1.9: Cash; Accounts Receivable; Office Supplies; Office Equipment; Electrical Equipment; Accounts Payable; Common Stock; Dividends; Revenues; and Expenses.

2. Use additions and subtractions to show the effects of each transaction on the accounts in the accounting equation. Show new balances after each transaction.

Check (2) Ending balances: Cash, $63,150, Accounts Payable, $8,560

3. Use the increases and decreases in the columns of the table from part 2 to prepare an income statement, a statement of retained earnings, and a statement of cash flows—each of these for the current month. Also prepare a balance sheet as of the end of the month.

(3) Net income, $4,730; Total assets, $81,190

Analysis Component

4. Assume that the owner investment transaction on December 1 was $49,000 cash instead of $68,800 and that Anderson Electric obtained another $19,800 in cash by borrowing it from a bank. Explain the effect of this change on total assets, total liabilities, and total equity.

Inez Lopez started Wiz Consulting, a new business, and completed the following transactions during its first year of operations.

Problem 1-9A
Analyzing effects of transactions
C5 P1 A1 A2

a. I. Lopez invests $67,000 cash and office equipment valued at $11,000 in exchange for common stock.
b. The company purchased a $144,000 building to use as an office. Wiz paid $15,000 in cash and signed a note payable promising to pay the $129,000 balance over the next ten years.
c. The company purchased office equipment for $12,000 cash.
d. The company purchased $1,000 of office supplies and $1,700 of office equipment on credit.
e. The company paid a local newspaper $460 cash for printing an announcement of the office's opening.
f. The company completed a financial plan for a client and billed that client $2,400 for the service.
g. The company designed a financial plan for another client and immediately collected a $4,000 cash fee.
h. The company paid $3,025 cash for dividends.
i. The company received $1,800 cash as partial payment from the client described in transaction f.
j. The company made a partial payment of $500 cash on the equipment purchased in transaction d.
k. The company paid $1,800 cash for the office secretary's wages for this period.

Required

1. Create a table like the one in Exhibit 1.9, using the following headings for the columns: Cash; Accounts Receivable; Office Supplies; Office Equipment; Building; Accounts Payable; Notes Payable; Common Stock; Dividends; Revenues; and Expenses.

2. Use additions and subtractions within the table created in part 1 to show the dollar effects of each transaction on individual items of the accounting equation. Show new balances after each transaction.

Check (2) Ending balances: Cash, $40,015; Expenses, $2,260; Notes Payable, $129,000

3. Once you have completed the table, determine the company's net income.

(3) Net income, $4,140

Coca-Cola and PepsiCo both produce and market beverages that are direct competitors. Key financial figures (in $ millions) for these businesses over the past year follow.

Problem 1-10A
Computing and interpreting return on assets

A3

Key Figures ($ millions)	Coca-Cola	PepsiCo
Sales	$24,088	$35,187
Net income	5,080	5,642
Average assets	29,695	30,829

Check (1a) 17.1%; (1b) 18.3%

Required

1. Compute return on assets for (a) Coca-Cola and (b) PepsiCo.

2. Which company is more successful in its total amount of sales to consumers?

3. Which company is more successful in returning net income from its assets invested?

Analysis Component

4. Write a one-paragraph memorandum explaining which company you would invest your money in and why. (Limit your explanation to the information provided.)

Problem 1-11A

Determining expenses, liabilities, equity, and return on assets

A1   A3

Notaro manufactures, markets, and sells cellular telephones. The average total assets for Notaro is $250,000. In its most recent year, Notaro reported net income of $64,000 on revenues of $468,000.

Required

1. What is Notaro's return on assets?

2. Does return on assets seem satisfactory for Notaro given that its competitors average a 9.5% return on assets?

Check (3) $404,000

(4) $250,000

3. What are total expenses for Notaro in its most recent year?

4. What is the average total amount of liabilities plus equity for Notaro?

Problem 1-12A^A

Identifying risk and return

A4

All business decisions involve aspects of risk and return.

Required

Identify both the risk and the return in each of the following activities:

1. Investing $10,000 in Yahoo! stock.

2. Placing a $2,500 bet on your favorite sports team.

3. Investing $2,000 in a 5% savings account.

4. Taking out a $7,500 college loan to earn an accounting degree.

Problem 1-13A^B

Describing organizational activities

C6

A start-up company often engages in the following transactions in its first year of operations. Classify those transactions in one of the three major categories of an organization's business activities.

F. Financing   **I.** Investing   **O.** Operating

_____ **1.** Purchasing equipment.   _____ **5.** Owner investing land in business.

_____ **2.** Selling and distributing products.   _____ **6.** Purchasing a building.

_____ **3.** Paying for advertising.   _____ **7.** Purchasing land.

_____ **4.** Paying employee wages.   _____ **8.** Borrowing cash from a bank.

Problem 1-14A^B

Describing organizational activities   C6

An organization undertakes various activities in pursuit of business success. Identify an organization's three major business activities, and describe each activity.

PROBLEM SET B

The following financial statement information is from five separate companies.

Problem 1-1B

Computing missing information using accounting knowledge

A1   A2

	Company V	Company W	Company X	Company Y	Company Z
December 31, 2010					
Assets	$36,000	$ 28,080	$23,040	$64,080	$ 98,280
Liabilities	29,520	19,656	12,441	44,215	?
December 31, 2011					
Assets	39,000	28,080	26,130	?	107,640
Liabilities	21,450	?	12,803	34,070	85,035
During year 2011					
Stock issuances	6,000	1,400	?	7,000	6,500
Net income or (loss)	?	1,162	(1,147)	10,045	7,449
Cash dividends	3,500	2,000	5,875	0	11,000

Required

1. Answer the following questions about Company V:
   a. What is the amount of equity on December 31, 2010?
   b. What is the amount of equity on December 31, 2011?
   c. What is the net income or loss for the year 2011?
2. Answer the following questions about Company W:
   a. What is the amount of equity on December 31, 2010?
   b. What is the amount of equity on December 31, 2011?
   c. What is the amount of liabilities on December 31, 2011?
3. Calculate the amount of stock issuances for Company X during 2011.
4. Calculate the amount of assets for Company Y on December 31, 2011.
5. Calculate the amount of liabilities for Company Z on December 31, 2010.

Check (1*b*) $17,550

(2*c*) $19,094

(4) $70,980

Identify how each of the following separate transactions affects financial statements. For the balance sheet, identify how each transaction affects total assets, total liabilities, and total equity. For the income statement, identify how each transaction affects net income. For the statement of cash flows, identify how each transaction affects cash flows from operating activities, cash flows from financing activities, and cash flows from investing activities. For increases, place a "+" in the column or columns. For decreases, place a "−" in the column or columns. If both an increase and a decrease occur, place "+/−" in the column or columns. The first transaction is completed as an example.

Problem 1-2B
Identifying effects of transactions on financial statements
A1   A2   ♟

	Transaction	Total Assets	Total Liab.	Total Equity	Net Income	Operating Activities	Financing Activities	Investing Activities
		Balance Sheet			**Income Statement**		**Statement of Cash Flows**	
1	Owner invests cash for stock	+		+			+	
2	Buys building by signing note payable							
3	Pays cash for salaries incurred							
4	Provides services for cash							
5	Pays cash for rent incurred							
6	Incurs utilities costs on credit							
7	Buys store equipment for cash							
8	Provides services on credit							
9	Collects cash on receivable from (8)							
10	Pays cash dividend							

Selected financial information for Onshore Co. for the year ended December 31, 2010, follows.

Revenues	$69,000	Expenses	$53,682	Net income	$15,318

Problem 1-3B
Preparing an income statement
P1

Required

Prepare the 2010 income statement for Onshore Company.

The following is selected financial information for NuTech Company as of December 31, 2010.

Liabilities	$46,222	Equity	$74,778	Assets	$121,000

Problem 1-4B
Preparing a balance sheet
P1

Required

Prepare the balance sheet for NuTech Company as of December 31, 2010.

Problem 1-5B

Preparing a statement of
cash flows

P1

Selected financial information of HalfLife Co. for the year ended December 31, 2010, follows.

Cash used by investing activities	$(3,750)
Net increase in cash	250
Cash used by financing activities	(4,550)
Cash from operating activities	8,550
Cash, December 31, 2009	3,700

Required

Prepare the 2010 statement of cash flows for HalfLife Company.

Problem 1-6B

Preparing a statement of
retained earnings

P1

Following is selected financial information of Act First for the year ended December 31, 2010.

Retained earnings, Dec. 31, 2010	$10,500	Cash dividends	$ 2,000
Net income	7,000	Retained earnings, Dec. 31, 2009	5,500

Required

Prepare the 2010 statement of retained earnings for Act First.

Problem 1-7B

Analyzing transactions and
preparing financial statements

C5   A2   P1

Nikolas Benton launched a new business, Benton's Maintenance Co., that began operations on June 1. The following transactions were completed by the company during that first month.

June   1   N. Benton invested $41,000 cash in the company in exchange for common stock.
     2   The company rented a furnished office and paid $2,200 cash for June's rent.
     4   The company purchased $1,860 of equipment on credit.
     6   The company paid $780 cash for this month's advertising of the opening of the business.
     8   The company completed maintenance services for a customer and immediately collected $5,700 cash.
    14   The company completed $2,400 of maintenance services for City Center on credit.
    16   The company paid $810 cash for an assistant's salary for the first half of the month.
    20   The company received $2,400 cash payment for services completed for City Center on June 14.
    24   The company completed $3,300 of maintenance services for Build-It Coop on credit.
    25   The company received $3,300 cash payment from Build-It Coop for the work completed on June 24.
    26   The company made payment of $1,860 cash for the equipment purchased on June 4.
    27   The company purchased $80 of product advertising in this month's (June) local newspaper on credit; cash payment is due July 1.
    28   The company paid $810 cash for an assistant's salary for the second half of this month.
    29   The company paid $1,600 cash for dividends.
    30   The company paid $250 cash for this month's telephone bill.
    30   The company paid $300 cash for this month's utilities.

Required

1. Arrange the following asset, liability, and equity titles in a table like Exhibit 1.9: Cash; Accounts Receivable; Equipment; Accounts Payable; Common Stock; Dividends; Revenues; and Expenses.

Check   (2) Ending balances: Cash, $43,790; Expenses, $5,230

2. Show the effects of the transactions on the accounts of the accounting equation by recording increases and decreases in the appropriate columns. Do not determine new account balances after each transaction. Determine the final total for each account and verify that the equation is in balance.

       (3) Net income, $6,170; Total assets, $45,650

3. Prepare a June income statement, a June statement of retained earnings, a June 30 balance sheet, and a June statement of cash flows.

Problem 1-8B

Analyzing transactions and
preparing financial statements

C5   A2   P1

Truro Excavating Co., owned by Raul Truro, began operations in July and completed these transactions during that first month of operations.

July   1   R. Truro invested $68,600 cash in the company in exchange for common stock.
     2   The company rented office space and paid $1,300 cash for the July rent.

3 The company purchased excavating equipment for $14,600 by paying $6,400 cash and agreeing to pay the $8,200 balance in 30 days.
6 The company purchased office supplies for $900 cash.
8 The company completed work for a customer and immediately collected $2,000 cash for the work.
10 The company purchased $2,720 of office equipment on credit.
15 The company completed work for a customer on credit in the amount of $4,300.
17 The company purchased $350 of office supplies on credit.
23 The company paid $2,720 cash for the office equipment purchased on July 10.
25 The company billed a customer $1,000 for work completed; the balance is due in 30 days.
28 The company received $4,300 cash for the work completed on July 15.
30 The company paid an assistant's salary of $1,900 cash for this month.
31 The company paid $590 cash for this month's utility bill.
31 The company paid $900 cash for dividends.

Required

1. Arrange the following asset, liability, and equity titles in a table like Exhibit 1.9: Cash; Accounts Receivable; Office Supplies; Office Equipment; Excavating Equipment; Accounts Payable; Common Stock; Dividends; Revenues; and Expenses.
2. Use additions and subtractions to show the effects of each transaction on the accounts in the accounting equation. Show new balances after each transaction.
3. Use the increases and decreases in the columns of the table from part 2 to prepare an income statement, a statement of retained earnings, and a statement of cash flows—each of these for the current month. Also prepare a balance sheet as of the end of the month.

Check (2) Ending balances: Cash, $60,190; Accounts Payable, $8,550

(3) Net income, $3,510; Total assets, $79,760

Analysis Component

4. Assume that the $14,600 purchase of excavating equipment on July 3 was financed from an owner investment of another $14,600 cash in the business in exchange for more common stock (instead of the purchase conditions described in the transaction). Explain the effect of this change on total assets, total liabilities, and total equity.

Nico Mitchell started a new business, Financial Management, and completed the following transactions during its first year of operations.

Problem 1-9B
Analyzing effects of transactions

C5 P1 A1 A2

a. N. Mitchell invests $70,000 cash and office equipment valued at $12,000 in exchange for common stock.
b. The company purchased a $141,000 building to use as an office. It paid $15,000 in cash and signed a note payable promising to pay the $126,000 balance over the next ten years.
c. The company purchased office equipment for $11,000 cash.
d. The company purchased $600 of office supplies and $1,300 of office equipment on credit.
e. The company paid a local newspaper $500 cash for printing an announcement of the office's opening.
f. The company completed a financial plan for a client and billed that client $2,400 for the service.
g. The company designed a financial plan for another client and immediately collected a $4,000 cash fee.
h. The company paid $3,325 cash for dividends.
i. The company received $1,750 cash as a partial payment from the client described in transaction f.
j. The company made a partial payment of $700 cash on the equipment purchased in transaction d.
k. The company paid $1,750 cash for the office secretary's wages.

Required

1. Create a table like the one in Exhibit 1.9, using the following headings for the columns: Cash; Accounts Receivable; Office Supplies; Office Equipment; Building; Accounts Payable; Notes Payable; Common Stock; Dividends; Revenues; and Expenses.
2. Use additions and subtractions within the table created in part 1 to show the dollar effects of each transaction on individual items of the accounting equation. Show new balances after each transaction.
3. Once you have completed the table, determine the company's net income.

Check (2) Ending balances: Cash, $43,475; Expenses, $2,250; Notes Payable, $126,000

(3) Net income, $4,150

Problem 1-10B
Computing and interpreting
return on assets

A3

AT&T and **Verizon** produce and market telecommunications products and are competitors. Key financial figures (in $ millions) for these businesses over the past year follow.

Key Figures ($ millions)	AT&T	Verizon
Sales	$ 63,055	$ 84,144
Net income	7,356	6,197
Average assets	208,133	178,467

Required

Check   (1a) 3.5%; (1b) 3.5%

1. Compute return on assets for (a) AT&T and (b) Verizon.

2. Which company is more successful in the total amount of sales to consumers?

3. Which company is more successful in returning net income from its assets invested?

Analysis Component

4. Write a one-paragraph memorandum explaining which company you would invest your money in and why. (Limit your explanation to the information provided.)

Problem 1-11B
Determining expenses, liabilities,
equity, and return on assets

A1 A3

Carbondale Company manufactures, markets, and sells ATV and snowmobile equipment and accessories. The average total assets for Carbondale is $243,000. In its most recent year, Carbondale reported net income of $62,500 on revenues of $473,000.

Required

1. What is Carbondale Company's return on assets?

2. Does return on assets seem satisfactory for Carbondale given that its competitors average a 10% return on assets?

Check   (3) $410,500

(4) $243,000

3. What are the total expenses for Carbondale Company in its most recent year?

4. What is the average total amount of liabilities plus equity for Carbondale Company?

Problem 1-12B^A
Identifying risk and return

A4

All business decisions involve aspects of risk and return.

Required

Identify both the risk and the return in each of the following activities:

1. Investing $20,000 in Nike stock.

2. Placing a $250 bet on a horse running in the Kentucky Derby.

3. Stashing $500 cash under your mattress.

4. Investing $35,000 in U.S. Savings Bonds.

Problem 1-13B^B
Describing organizational
activities

C6

A start-up company often engages in the following activities during its first year of operations. Classify each of the following activities into one of the three major activities of an organization.

F. Financing   **I.** Investing   **O.** Operating

_____ **1.** Supervising workers.	_____ **5.** Providing client services.
_____ **2.** Owner investing money in business.	_____ **6.** Obtaining a bank loan.
_____ **3.** Renting office space.	_____ **7.** Purchasing machinery.
_____ **4.** Paying utilities expenses.	_____ **8.** Research for its products.

Problem 1-14B^B
Describing organizational
activities   C6

Identify in outline format the three major business activities of an organization. For each of these activities, identify at least two specific transactions or events normally undertaken by the business's owners or its managers.

This serial problem starts in this chapter and continues throughout most chapters of the book. It is most readily solved if you use the Working Papers that accompany this book.

SERIAL PROBLEM

Success Systems

SP 1   On October 1, 2009, Adriana Lopez launched a computer services company, **Success Systems,** that is organized as a corporation and provides consulting services, computer system installations, and custom program development. Lopez adopts the calendar year for reporting purposes and expects to prepare the company's first set of financial statements on December 31, 2009.

Required

Create a table like the one in Exhibit 1.9 using the following headings for columns: Cash; Accounts Receivable; Computer Supplies; Computer System; Office Equipment; Accounts Payable; Common Stock; Dividends; Revenues; and Expenses. Then use additions and subtractions within the table created to show the dollar effects for each of the following October transactions for Success Systems on the individual items of the accounting equation. Show new balances after each transaction.

Oct. 1   Adriana Lopez invested $55,000 cash, a $20,000 computer system, and $8,000 of office equipment in the company in exchange for common stock.

3   The company purchased $1,420 of computer supplies on credit from Harris Office Products.

6   The company billed Easy Leasing $4,800 for services performed in installing a new Web server.

8   The company paid $1,420 cash for the computer supplies purchased from Harris Office Products on October 3.

10   The company hired Lyn Addie as a part-time assistant for $125 per day, as needed.

12   The company billed Easy Leasing another $1,400 for services performed.

15   The company received $4,800 cash from Easy Leasing as partial payment toward its account.

17   The company paid $805 cash to repair computer equipment damaged when moving it.

20   The company paid $1,940 cash for an advertisement in the local newspaper.

22   The company received $1,400 cash from Easy Leasing toward its account.

28   The company billed IFM Company $5,208 for services performed.

31   The company paid $875 cash for Lyn Addie's wages for seven days of work this month.

31   The company paid $3,600 cash for dividends.

Check Ending balances: Cash, $52,560; Revenues, $11,408; Expenses, $3,620

Beyond the Numbers (BTN) *is a special problem section aimed to refine communication, conceptual, analysis, and research skills. It includes many activities helpful in developing an active learning environment.*

BEYOND THE NUMBERS

BTN 1-1   Key financial figures for **Best Buy**'s fiscal year ended February 28, 2009, follow.

Key Figure	In Millions
Liabilities + Equity	$15,826
Net income	1,003
Revenues	45,015

REPORTING IN ACTION

A1   A3   A4

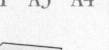

Required

1. What is the total amount of assets invested in Best Buy?

2. What is Best Buy's return on assets? Its assets at March 1, 2008, equal $12,758 (in millions).

Check (2) 7.0%

3. How much are total expenses for Best Buy for the year ended February 28, 2009?

4. Does Best Buy's return on assets seem satisfactory if competitors average a 3.7% return?

Fast Forward

5. Access Best Buy's financial statements (Form 10-K) for fiscal years ending after February 28, 2009, from its Website (**BestBuy.com**) or from the SEC Website (**www.SEC.gov**) and compute its return on assets for those fiscal years. Compare the February 28, 2009, fiscal year-end return on assets to any subsequent years' returns you are able to compute, and interpret the results.

BTN 1-2   Key comparative figures ($ millions) for both **Best Buy** and **RadioShack** follow.

Key Figure	Best Buy	RadioShack
Liabilities + Equity	$15,826	$2,283.5
Net income	1,003	192.4
Revenues and sales	45,015	4,224.5

COMPARATIVE ANALYSIS

A1   A3   A4

Required

1. What is the total amount of assets invested in (*a*) Best Buy and (*b*) RadioShack?

2. What is the return on assets for (*a*) Best Buy and (*b*) RadioShack? Best Buy's beginning-year assets equal $12,758 (in millions) and RadioShack's beginning-year assets equal $1,989.6 (in millions).

Check (2b) 9.0%

3. How much are expenses for (*a*) Best Buy and (*b*) RadioShack?

4. Is return on assets satisfactory for (*a*) Best Buy and (*b*) RadioShack? (Assume competitors average a 3.7% return.)

5. What can you conclude about Best Buy and RadioShack from these computations?

ETHICS CHALLENGE

C4 C5

BTN 1-3   Liz Thorne works in a public accounting firm and hopes to eventually be a partner. The management of Allnet Company invites Thorne to prepare a bid to audit Allnet's financial statements. In discussing the audit fee, Allnet's management suggests a fee range in which the amount depends on the reported profit of Allnet. The higher its profit, the higher will be the audit fee paid to Thorne's firm.

Required

1. Identify the parties potentially affected by this audit and the fee plan proposed.

2. What are the ethical factors in this situation? Explain.

3. Would you recommend that Thorne accept this audit fee arrangement? Why or why not?

4. Describe some ethical considerations guiding your recommendation.

COMMUNICATING IN PRACTICE

A1 C2

BTN 1-4   Refer to this chapter's opening feature about **Facebook.**® Assume that Mark Zuckerberg desires to expand his online services to meet people's demands. He decides to meet with his banker to discuss a loan to allow Facebook to expand.

Required

1. Prepare a half-page report outlining the information you would request from Mark Zuckerberg if you were the loan officer.

2. Indicate whether the information you request and your loan decision are affected by the form of business organization for Facebook.

TAKING IT TO THE NET

A3

BTN 1-5   Visit the EDGAR database at (www.SEC.gov). Access the Form 10-K report of **Rocky Mountain Chocolate Factory** (ticker RMCF) filed on May 26, 2009, covering its 2009 fiscal year.

Required

1. Item 6 of the 10-K report provides comparative financial highlights of RMCF for the years 2005–2009. How would you describe the revenue trend for RMCF over this five-year period?

2. Has RMCF been profitable (see net income) over this five-year period? Support your answer.

TEAMWORK IN ACTION

C1

BTN 1-6   Teamwork is important in today's business world. Successful teams schedule convenient meetings, maintain regular communications, and cooperate with and support their members. This assignment aims to establish support/learning teams, initiate discussions, and set meeting times.

Required

1. Form teams and open a team discussion to determine a regular time and place for your team to meet between each scheduled class meeting. Notify your instructor via a memorandum or e-mail message as to when and where your team will hold regularly scheduled meetings.

2. Develop a list of telephone numbers and/or e-mail addresses of your teammates.

ENTREPRENEURIAL DECISION

A1 A2

BTN 1-7   Refer to this chapter's opening feature about **Facebook**. Assume that Mark Zuckerberg decides to open a new Website devoted to social networking for accountants and those studying accounting. This new company will be called AccountBook.

Required

1. AccountBook obtains a $500,000 loan and Mark Zuckerberg contributes $250,000 of his own assets in exchange for common stock in the new company.

a. What is the new company's total amount of liabilities plus equity?

b. What is the new company's total amount of assets?

2. If the new company earns $80,000 in net income in the first year of operation, compute its return on asset (assume average assets equal $750,000). Assess its performance if competitors average a 10% return.

Check (2) 10.7%

BTN 1-8 You are to interview a local business owner. (This can be a friend or relative.) Opening lines of communication with members of the business community can provide personal benefits of business networking. If you do not know the owner, you should call ahead to introduce yourself and explain your position as a student and your assignment requirements. You should request a thirty minute appointment for a face-to-face or phone interview to discuss the form of organization and operations of the business. Be prepared to make a good impression.

HITTING THE ROAD

C2

Required

1. Identify and describe the main operating activities and the form of organization for this business.
2. Determine and explain why the owner(s) chose this particular form of organization.
3. Identify any special advantages and/or disadvantages the owner(s) experiences in operating with this form of business organization.

BTN 1-9 GOME (www.GOME.com.hk) is the leading chain retailer of consumer electronic products and household appliances in China, and it competes to some extent with both **Best Buy** and **RadioShack**. Key financial figures for GOME follow.

GLOBAL DECISION

A1 A3 A4

Key Figure*	Renminbi (RMB) in Thousands
Average assets	28,666,299
Net income	1,048,160
Revenues	45,889,257
Return on assets	3.7%

* Figures prepared in accordance with International Financial Reporting Standards.

Required

1. Identify any concerns you have in comparing GOME's income and revenue figures to those of Best Buy and RadioShack (in BTN 1-2) for purposes of making business decisions.
2. Identify any concerns you have in comparing GOME's return on assets ratio to those of Best Buy and RadioShack (computed for BTN 1-2) for purposes of making business decisions.

ANSWERS TO MULTIPLE CHOICE QUIZ

1. c; $450,000 is the actual cost incurred.
2. b; revenue is recorded when earned.
3. d;

Assets	=	Liabilities	+	Equity
+$100,000	=	+35,000	+	?

Change in equity = $100,000 − $35,000 = $65,000

4. a
5. a

Analyzing and Recording Transactions

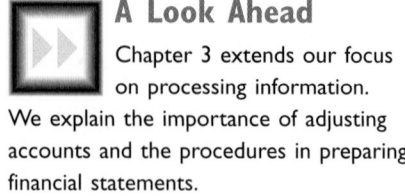

"It has been a dream come true"   —Sara Blakely

◀◀ **A Look Back**

Chapter 1 defined accounting and introduced financial statements. We described forms of organizations and identified users and uses of accounting. We defined the accounting equation and applied it to transaction analysis.

◀▶ **A Look at This Chapter**

This chapter focuses on the accounting process. We describe transactions and source documents, and we explain the analysis and recording of transactions. The accounting equation, T-account, general ledger, trial balance, and debits and credits are key tools in the accounting process.

▶▶ **A Look Ahead**

Chapter 3 extends our focus on processing information. We explain the importance of adjusting accounts and the procedures in preparing financial statements.

The Bottom Line

ATLANTA—"Working as a sales trainer by day and performing stand-up comedy at night, I didn't know the first thing about the pantyhose industry," admits Sara Blakely. "Except, I dreaded wearing most pantyhose." One night Sara cut the feet out of her pantyhose to wear with white pants and open-toed shoes, and at that moment, Sara knew she had a unique idea. Sara took $5,000 in savings and launched **SPANX** (Spanx.com), a manufacturer of footless pantyhose, slimming intimates, hosiery, and other women's apparel.

To pursue her business ambitions, Sara studied business activities and learned the value of accounting information. She established recordkeeping processes, transaction analysis, inventory accounting, and financial statement reporting. I had to get a handle on my financial situation, says Sara, as I wanted to remain self-funded. To this day, Sara remains self-funded and has a reliable accounting system to help her make good business decisions.

I had to account for product costs, office expenses, supplier payments, patent fees, and other expenses, says Sara. At the same time, Sara expanded sales and struggled to stay profitable. "I had no money to advertise, so I hit the road," laughs Sara. "For the entire first year, I did in-store rallies . . . staying all day introducing customers to Spanx."

In her first three months, Sara sold over 50,000 pairs of footless pantyhose. Today, just seven short years from her launch, Sara reports over $150 million in retail sales. "We are still a small company of women," claims Sara, "obsessed with inventing and improving comfortable undergarments." Sara continues to track and account for all revenues and expenses. She maintains that success requires proper accounting for and analysis of the financial side.

The bigger message of SPANX, says Sara, is promoting comfort and confidence for women. Insists Sara, "We believe all women deserve the opportunity to make the most of their assets!"

[Sources: *SPANX Website,* January 2010; *Entrepreneur,* May 2007; *Smart Money,* September 2002; *TV Guide,* July 2007; *Financial Times,* 2006; *ABC Television,* 2007; *Reuters,* February 2009]

CAP

Conceptual

C1 Explain the steps in processing transactions. *(p. 50)*

C2 Describe source documents and their purpose. *(p. 50)*

C3 Describe an account and its use in recording transactions. *(p. 51)*

C4 Describe a ledger and a chart of accounts. *(p. 54)*

C5 Define *debits* and *credits* and explain double-entry accounting. *(p. 55)*

Analytical

A1 Analyze the impact of transactions on accounts and financial statements. *(p. 59)*

A2 Compute the debt ratio and describe its use in analyzing financial condition. *(p. 69)*

Procedural

P1 Record transactions in a journal and post entries to a ledger. *(p. 56)*

P2 Prepare and explain the use of a trial balance. *(p. 65)*

P3 Prepare financial statements from business transactions. *(p. 66)*

LP2

Financial statements report on the financial performance and condition of an organization. Knowledge of their preparation, organization, and analysis is important. A main goal of this chapter is to illustrate how transactions are recorded, how they are reflected in financial statements, and how they impact analysis of financial statements. Debits and credits are introduced and identified as a tool in helping analyze and process transactions.

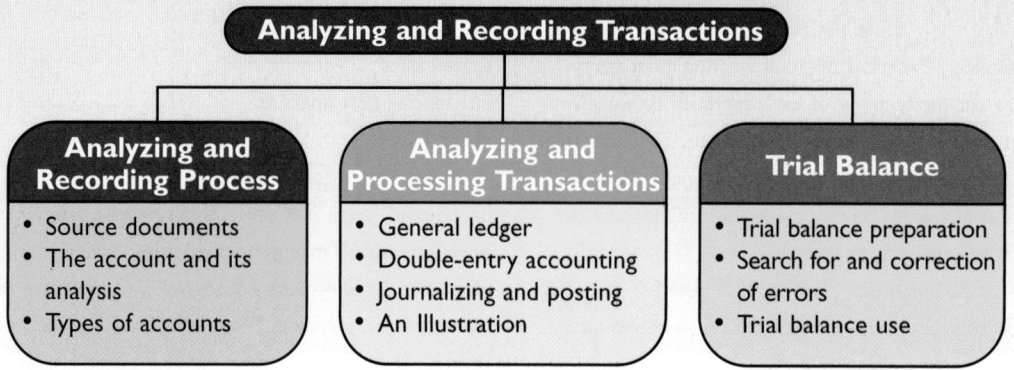

Analyzing and Recording Transactions

Analyzing and Recording Process	Analyzing and Processing Transactions	Trial Balance
• Source documents • The account and its analysis • Types of accounts	• General ledger • Double-entry accounting • Journalizing and posting • An Illustration	• Trial balance preparation • Search for and correction of errors • Trial balance use

Analyzing and Recording Process

C1 Explain the steps in processing transactions.

The accounting process identifies business transactions and events, analyzes and records their effects, and summarizes and presents information in reports and financial statements. These reports and statements are used for making investing, lending, and other business decisions. The steps in the accounting process that focus on *analyzing and recording* transactions and events are shown in Exhibit 2.1.

EXHIBIT 2.1

The Analyzing and Recording Process

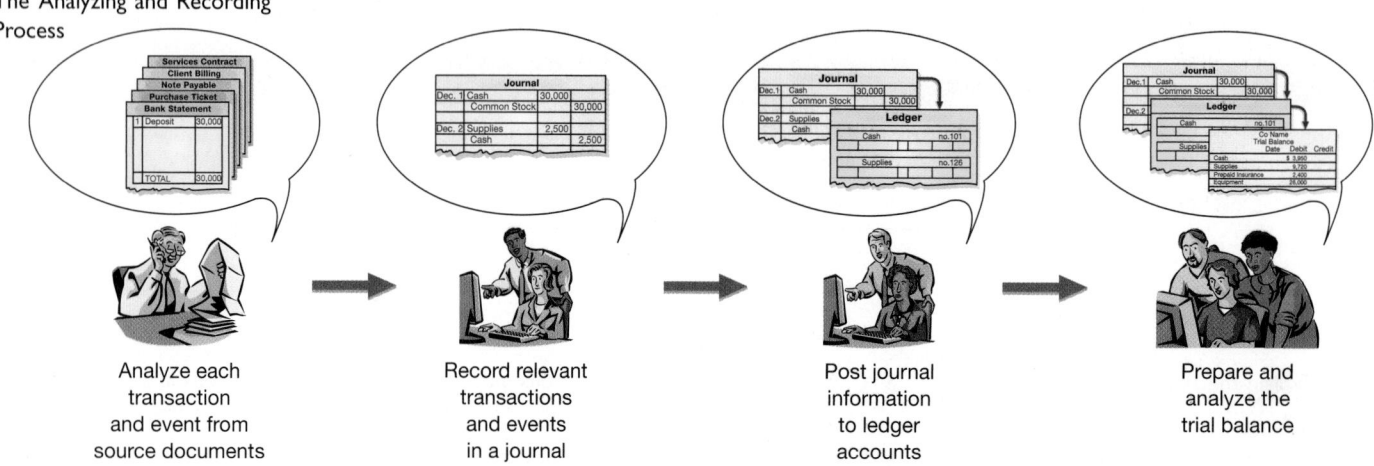

Analyze each transaction and event from source documents → Record relevant transactions and events in a journal → Post journal information to ledger accounts → Prepare and analyze the trial balance

Business transactions and events are the starting points. Relying on source documents, the transactions and events are analyzed using the accounting equation to understand how they affect company performance and financial position. These effects are recorded in accounting records, informally referred to as the *accounting books,* or simply the *books*. Additional steps such as posting and then preparing a trial balance help summarize and classify the effects of transactions and events. Ultimately, the accounting process provides information in useful reports or financial statements to decision makers.

Source Documents

C2 Describe source documents and their purpose.

Source documents identify and describe transactions and events entering the accounting process. They are the sources of accounting information and can be in either hard copy or electronic form. Examples are sales tickets, checks, purchase orders, bills from suppliers, employee earnings records, and bank statements. To illustrate, when an item is purchased on credit, the seller usually prepares at least two copies of a sales invoice. One copy is given to the buyer. Another copy, often sent electronically, results in an entry in the seller's information system to record the sale. Sellers use invoices for recording sales and for control; buyers use them for recording purchases and for monitoring purchasing activity. Many cash registers record information for each sale on a tape or electronic file locked inside the register. This record can be used as a source document for recording sales in the accounting records. Source documents, especially if obtained from outside the organization, provide objective and reliable evidence about transactions and events and their amounts.

Point: To ensure that all sales are rung up on the register, most sellers require customers to have their receipts to exchange or return purchased items.

Decision Ethics

Cashier   Your manager requires that you, as cashier, immediately enter each sale. Recently, lunch hour traffic has increased and the assistant manager asks you to avoid delays by taking customers' cash and making change without entering sales. The assistant manager says she will add up cash and enter sales after lunch. She says that, in this way, the register will always match the cash amount when the manager arrives at three o'clock. What do you do? [Answer—p. 74]

The Account and Its Analysis

An **account** is a record of increases and decreases in a specific asset, liability, equity, revenue, or expense item. Information from an account is analyzed, summarized, and presented in reports and financial statements. The **general ledger,** or simply **ledger,** is a record containing all accounts used by a company. The ledger is often in electronic form. While most companies' ledgers contain similar accounts, a company often uses one or more unique accounts because of its type of operations. Accounts are arranged into three general categories (based on the accounting equation), as shown in Exhibit 2.2.

C3 Describe an account and its use in recording transactions.

EXHIBIT 2.2

Accounts Organized by the Accounting Equation

Asset Accounts   Assets are resources owned or controlled by a company and that have expected future benefits. Most accounting systems include (at a minimum) separate accounts for the assets described here.

A *Cash* account reflects a company's cash balance. All increases and decreases in cash are recorded in the Cash account. It includes money and any medium of exchange that a bank accepts for deposit (coins, checks, money orders, and checking account balances).

Accounts receivable are held by a seller and refer to promises of payment from customers to sellers. These transactions are often called *credit sales* or *sales on account* (or *on credit*). Accounts receivable are increased by credit sales and are decreased by customer payments. A company needs a separate record for each customer, but for now, we use the simpler practice of recording all increases and decreases in receivables in a single account called Accounts Receivable.

Point: Customers and others who owe a company are called its **debtors.**

A *note receivable,* or promissory note, is a written promise of another entity to pay a definite sum of money on a specified future date to the holder of the note. A company holding a promissory note signed by another entity has an asset that is recorded in a Note (or Notes) Receivable account.

Prepaid accounts (also called *prepaid expenses*) are assets that represent prepayments of future expenses (*not* current expenses). When the expenses are later incurred, the amounts in prepaid accounts are transferred to expense accounts. Common examples of prepaid accounts include prepaid insurance, prepaid rent, and prepaid services (such as club memberships). Prepaid accounts expire with the passage of time (such as with rent) or through use (such as with prepaid meal tickets). When financial statements are prepared, prepaid accounts are adjusted so that (1) all expired and used prepaid accounts are recorded as regular expenses and (2) all unexpired and unused prepaid accounts are recorded as assets (reflecting future use in

Point: A college parking fee is a prepaid account from the student's standpoint. At the beginning of the term, it represents an asset that entitles a student to park on or near campus. The benefits of the parking fee expire as the term progresses. At term-end, prepaid parking (asset) equals zero as it has been entirely recorded as parking expense.

future periods). To illustrate, when an insurance fee, called a *premium,* is paid in advance, the cost is typically recorded in the asset account Prepaid Insurance. Over time, the expiring portion of the insurance cost is removed from this asset account and reported in expenses on the income statement. Any unexpired portion remains in Prepaid Insurance and is reported on the balance sheet as an asset. (An exception exists for prepaid accounts that will expire or be used before the end of the current accounting period when financial statements are prepared. In this case, the prepayments *can* be recorded immediately as expenses.)

Supplies are assets until they are used. When they are used up, their costs are reported as expenses. The costs of unused supplies are recorded in a Supplies asset account. Supplies are often grouped by purpose—for example office supplies and store supplies. *Office supplies* include stationery, paper, toner, and pens. *Store supplies* include packaging materials, plastic and paper bags, gift boxes and cartons, and cleaning materials. The costs of these unused supplies can be recorded in an Office Supplies or a Store Supplies asset account. When supplies are used, their costs are transferred from the asset accounts to expense accounts.

Equipment is an asset. When equipment is used and gets worn down, its cost is gradually reported as an expense (called depreciation). Equipment is often grouped by its purpose—for example, office equipment and store equipment. *Office equipment* includes computers, printers, desks, chairs, and shelves. Costs incurred for these items are recorded in an Office Equipment asset account. The Store Equipment account includes the costs of assets used in a store such as counters, showcases, ladders, hoists, and cash registers.

Buildings such as stores, offices, warehouses, and factories are assets because they provide expected future benefits to those who control or own them. Their costs are recorded in a Buildings asset account. When several buildings are owned, separate accounts are sometimes kept for each of them.

The cost of *land* owned by a business is recorded in a Land account. The cost of buildings located on the land is separately recorded in one or more building accounts.

Decision Insight

Women Entrepreneurs   The Center for Women's Business Research reports that women-owned businesses, such as **SPANX**, are growing and that they:

- Total approximately 11 million and employ nearly 20 million workers.
- Generate $2.5 trillion in annual sales and tend to embrace technology.
- Are philanthropic—70% of owners volunteer at least once per month.
- Are more likely funded by individual investors (73%) than venture firms (15%).

Liability Accounts   Liabilities are claims (by creditors) against assets, which means they are obligations to transfer assets or provide products or services to others. **Creditors** are individuals and organizations that have rights to receive payments from a company. If a company fails to pay its obligations, the law gives creditors a right to force the sale of that company's assets to obtain the money to meet creditors' claims. When assets are sold under these conditions, creditors are paid first, but only up to the amount of their claims. Any remaining money, the residual, goes to the owners of the company. Creditors often use a balance sheet to help decide whether to loan money to a company. A loan is less risky if the borrower's liabilities are small in comparison to assets because this means there are more resources than claims on resources. Common liability accounts are described here.

Accounts payable refer to oral or implied promises to pay later, which usually arise from purchases of merchandise. Payables can also arise from purchases of supplies, equipment, and services. Accounting systems keep separate records about each creditor. We describe these individual records in Chapter 4.

A *note payable* refers to a formal promise, usually denoted by the signing of a promissory note, to pay a future amount. It is recorded in either a short-term Note Payable account or a long-term Note Payable account, depending on when it must be repaid. We explain details of short- and long-term classification in Chapter 3.

Unearned revenue refers to a liability that is settled in the future when a company delivers its products or services. When customers pay in advance for products or services (before revenue is earned), the revenue recognition principle requires that the seller consider this payment as unearned revenue. Examples of unearned revenue include magazine subscriptions collected in advance by a publisher, sales of gift certificates by stores, and season ticket sales by sports teams. The seller would record these in liability accounts such as Unearned Subscriptions, Unearned Store Sales, and Unearned Ticket Revenue. When products and services are later delivered, the earned portion of the unearned revenue is transferred to revenue accounts such as Subscription Fees, Store Sales, and Ticket Sales.[1]

Accrued liabilities are amounts owed that are not yet paid. Examples are wages payable, taxes payable, and interest payable. These are often recorded in separate liability accounts by the same title. If they are not large in amount, one or more ledger accounts can be added and reported as a single amount on the balance sheet. (Financial statements often have amounts reported that are a summation of several ledger accounts.)

Point: If a subscription is canceled, the publisher is expected to refund the unused portion to the subscriber.

Decision Insight

Revenue Spread   The **Chicago Bears** have *Unearned Revenues* of about $60 million in advance ticket sales. When the team plays its home games, it settles this liability to its ticket holders and then transfers the amount earned to *Ticket Revenues.*

Equity Accounts   The owner's claim on a corporation's assets is called *equity, stockholders' equity,* or *shareholders' equity.* Equity is the owners' *residual interest* in the assets of a business after deducting liabilities. Equity is impacted by four types of accounts: common stock, dividends, revenues, and expenses. We show this visually in Exhibit 2.3 by expanding the accounting equation. (As Chapter 1 explains, the accounts for dividends, revenues, and expenses are reflected in the retained earnings account, and that account is reported in the balance sheet.)

Point: Equity is also called *net assets.*

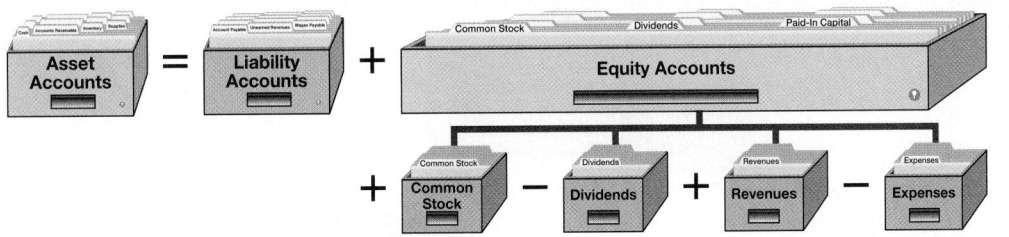

EXHIBIT 2.3

Expanded Accounting Equation

When an owner invests in a company in exchange for common stock, the invested amount is recorded in an account titled **Common Stock.** Any further owner investments are recorded in this account. When the company pays any cash dividends it decreases both the company's assets and its total equity. Dividends are not expenses of the business. They are simply the opposite of owner investments. A **Dividends** account is used in recording asset distributions to stockholders (owners).

Revenues and expenses also impact equity. Examples of revenue accounts are Sales, Commissions Earned, Professional Fees Revenue, Rent Revenue, and Interest Revenue. *Revenues increase equity* and result from products and services provided to customers. Examples of expense accounts are Advertising Expense, Store Supplies Expense, Office Salaries Expense, Office Supplies Expense, Rent Expense, Utilities Expense, and Insurance Expense. *Expenses decrease equity* and result from assets and services used in a company's operations. The variety of revenues and expenses can be seen by looking at the *chart of accounts* that follows the

Point: The Dividends account is sometimes referred to as a *contra equity* account because it reduces the normal balance of equity.

Point: The withdrawal of assets by the owners of a corporation is called a *dividend.*

---

[1] In practice, account titles vary. As one example, Subscription Fees is sometimes called Subscription Fees Revenue, Subscription Fees Earned, or Earned Subscription Fees. As another example, Rent Earned is sometimes called Rent Revenue, Rental Revenue, or Earned Rent Revenue. We must use good judgment when reading financial statements because titles can differ even within the same industry. For example, product sales are called *revenue* at **Best Buy,** but *net sales and operating revenues* at **RadioShack.** Generally, the term *revenues* or *fees* is more commonly used with service businesses, and *net sales* or *sales* with product businesses.

index at the back of this book. (Different companies sometimes use different account titles than those in this book's chart of accounts. For example, some might use Interest Revenue instead of Interest Earned, or Rental Expense instead of Rent Expense. It is important only that an account title describe the item it represents.)

Decision Insight

Sporting Accounts   The **San Antonio Spurs** and the **Cleveland Cavaliers** have the following major revenue and expense accounts:

Revenues	Expenses
Basketball ticket sales	Team salaries
TV & radio broadcast fees	Game costs
Advertising revenues	NBA franchise costs
Basketball playoff receipts	Promotional costs

Analyzing and Processing Transactions

This section explains several tools and processes that comprise an accounting system. These include a ledger, T-account, debits and credits, double-entry accounting, journalizing, and posting.

Ledger and Chart of Accounts

C4   Describe a ledger and a chart of accounts.

The collection of all accounts and their balances for an information system is called a *ledger* (or *general ledger*). If accounts are in files on a hard drive, the sum of those files is the ledger. If the accounts are pages in a file, that file is the ledger. A company's size and diversity of operations affect the number of accounts needed. A small company can get by with as few as 20 or 30 accounts; a large company can require several thousand. The **chart of accounts** is a list of all ledger accounts and includes an identification number assigned to each account. A small business might use the following numbering system for its accounts:

101–199	Asset accounts
201–299	Liability accounts
301–399	Equity accounts
401–499	Revenue accounts
501–699	Expense accounts

These numbers provide a three-digit code that is useful in recordkeeping. In this case, the first digit assigned to asset accounts is a 1, the first digit assigned to liability accounts is a 2, and so on. The second and third digits relate to the accounts' subcategories. Exhibit 2.4 shows a partial chart of accounts for FastForward, the focus company of Chapter 1. (Please review the more complete chart of accounts that follows the index at the back of this book.)

EXHIBIT 2.4

Partial Chart of Accounts for FastForward

Account Number	Account Name	Account Number	Account Name
101	Cash	318	Retained earnings
106	Accounts receivable	319	Dividends
126	Supplies	403	Consulting revenue
128	Prepaid insurance	406	Rental revenue
167	Equipment	622	Salaries expense
201	Accounts payable	637	Insurance expense
236	Unearned consulting revenue	640	Rent expense
		652	Supplies expense
307	Common stock	690	Utilities expense

Debits and Credits

A **T-account** represents a ledger account and is a tool used to understand the effects of one or more transactions. Its name comes from its shape like the letter T. The layout of a T-account, shown in Exhibit 2.5, is (1) the account title on top, (2) a left, or debit side, and (3) a right, or credit, side.

The left side of an account is called the **debit** side, often abbreviated *Dr*. The right side is called the **credit** side, abbreviated *Cr*.[2] To enter amounts on the left side of an account is to *debit* the account. To enter amounts on the right side is to *credit* the account. Do not make the error of thinking that the terms *debit* and *credit* mean increase or decrease. Whether a debit or a credit is an increase or decrease depends on the account. For an account where a debit is an increase, the credit is a decrease; for an account where a debit is a decrease, the credit is an increase. The difference between total debits and total credits for an account, including any beginning balance, is the **account balance.** When the sum of debits exceeds the sum of credits, the account has a *debit balance*. It has a *credit balance* when the sum of credits exceeds the sum of debits. When the sum of debits equals the sum of credits, the account has a *zero balance*.

Account Title	
(Left side)	(Right side)
Debit	**Credit**

C5 Define *debits* and *credits* and explain double-entry accounting.

EXHIBIT 2.5

The T-Account

Point: Think of *debit* and *credit* as accounting directions for left and right.

Double-Entry Accounting

Double-entry accounting requires that for each transaction:

■ At least two accounts are involved, with at least one debit and one credit.

■ The total amount debited must equal the total amount credited.

■ The accounting equation must not be violated.

This means the sum of the debits for all entries must equal the sum of the credits for all entries, and the sum of debit account balances in the ledger must equal the sum of credit account balances.

The system for recording debits and credits follows from the usual accounting equation—see Exhibit 2.6. Two points are important here. First, like any simple mathematical relation, net increases or decreases on one side have equal net effects on the other side. For example, a net increase in assets must be accompanied by an identical net increase on the liabilities and

"Total debits equal total credits for each entry."

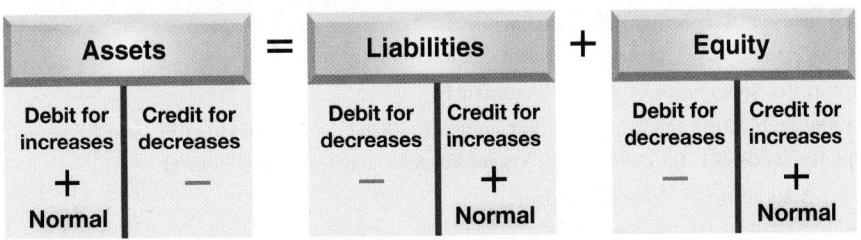

EXHIBIT 2.6

Debits and Credits in the Accounting Equation

equity side. Recall that some transactions affect only one side of the equation, meaning that two or more accounts on one side are affected, but their net effect on this one side is zero. Second, the left side is the *normal balance* side for assets, and the right side is the *normal balance* side for liabilities and equity. This matches their layout in the accounting equation where assets are on the left side of this equation, and liabilities and equity are on the right.

Recall that equity increases from revenues and stock issuances and it decreases from expenses and dividends. These important equity relations are conveyed by expanding the accounting equation to include debits and credits in double-entry form as shown in Exhibit 2.7.

Increases (credits) to common stock and revenues *increase* equity; increases (debits) to dividends and expenses *decrease* equity. The normal balance of each account (asset, liability,

---

[2] These abbreviations are remnants of 18th-century English recordkeeping practices where the terms *debitor* and *creditor* were used instead of *debit* and *credit*. The abbreviations use the first and last letters of these terms, just as we still do for Saint (St.) and Doctor (Dr.).

EXHIBIT 2.7

Debit and Credit Effects for Component Accounts

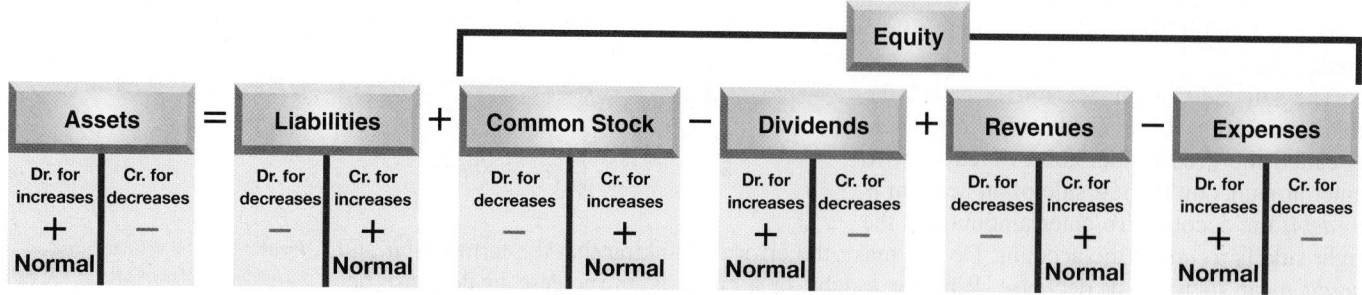

common stock, dividends, revenue, or expense) refers to the left or right (debit or credit) side where *increases* are recorded. Understanding these diagrams and rules is required to prepare, analyze, and interpret financial statements.

The T-account for FastForward's Cash account, reflecting its first 11 transactions (from Exhibit 1.9), is shown in Exhibit 2.8. The total increases in its Cash account are $36,100, the total decreases are $31,300, and the account's debit balance is $4,800. (We illustrate use of T-accounts later in this chapter.)

EXHIBIT 2.8

Computing the Balance for a T-Account

Cash			
Receive investment by owner for stock	30,000	Purchase of supplies	2,500
Consulting services revenue earned	4,200	Purchase of equipment	26,000
Collection of account receivable	1,900	Payment of rent	1,000
		Payment of salary	700
		Payment of account payable	900
		Payment of cash dividend	200
Balance	4,800		

Quick Check   Answers—p. 75

1. Identify examples of accounting source documents.
2. Explain the importance of source documents.
3. Identify each of the following as either an asset, a liability, or equity: (*a*) Prepaid Rent, (*b*) Unearned Fees, (*c*) Building, (*d*) Wages Payable, and (*e*) Office Supplies.
4. What is an account? What is a ledger?
5. What determines the number and types of accounts a company uses?
6. Does *debit* always mean increase and *credit* always mean decrease?
7. Describe a chart of accounts.

Journalizing and Posting Transactions

P1 Record transactions in a journal and post entries to a ledger.

Processing transactions is a crucial part of accounting. The four usual steps of this process are depicted in Exhibit 2.9. Steps 1 and 2—involving transaction analysis and double-entry accounting—were introduced in prior sections. This section extends that discussion and focuses on steps 3 and 4 of the accounting process. Step 3 is to record each transaction chronologically in a journal. A **journal** gives a complete record of each transaction in one place. It also shows debits and credits for each transaction. The process of recording transactions in a journal is called **journalizing.** Step 4 is to transfer (or *post*) entries from the journal to the ledger. The process of transferring journal entry information to the ledger is called **posting.**

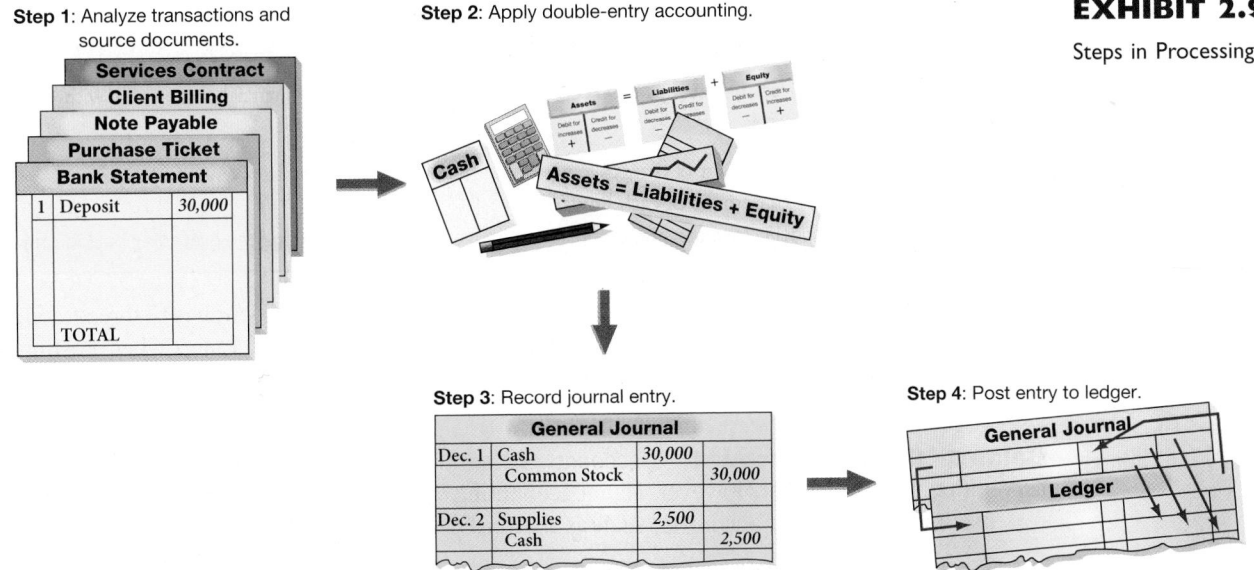

Step 1: Analyze transactions and source documents.

Step 2: Apply double-entry accounting.

Step 3: Record journal entry.

Step 4: Post entry to ledger.

EXHIBIT 2.9

Steps in Processing Transactions

Journalizing Transactions   The process of journalizing transactions requires an understanding of a journal. While companies can use various journals, every company uses a **general journal.** It can be used to record any transaction and includes the following information about each transaction: (1) date of transaction, (2) titles of affected accounts, (3) dollar amount of each debit and credit, and (4) explanation of the transaction. Exhibit 2.10 shows how the first two transactions of FastForward are recorded in a general journal. This process is similar for manual and computerized systems. Computerized journals are often designed to look like a manual journal page, and also include error-checking routines that ensure debits equal credits for each entry. Shortcuts allow recordkeepers to select account names and numbers from pull-down menus.

| GENERAL JOURNAL | | | | Page 1 |
Date	Account Titles and Explanation	PR	Debit	Credit
2009 Dec. 1	Cash		30,000	
	Common Stock			30,000
	Receive investment by owner.			
Dec. 2	Supplies		2,500	
	Cash			2,500
	Purchase supplies for cash.			

EXHIBIT 2.10

Partial General Journal for FastForward

To record entries in a general journal, apply these steps; refer to the entries in Exhibit 2.10 when reviewing these steps. ① Date the transaction: Enter the year at the top of the first column and the month and day on the first line of each journal entry. ② Enter titles of accounts debited and then enter amounts in the Debit column on the same line. Account titles are taken from the chart of accounts and are aligned with the left margin of the Account Titles and Explanation column. ③ Enter titles of accounts credited and then enter amounts in the Credit column on the same line. Account titles are from the chart of accounts and are indented from the left margin of the Account Titles and Explanation column to distinguish them from debited accounts. ④ Enter a brief explanation of the transaction on the line below the entry (it often references a source document). This explanation is indented about half as far as the credited account titles to avoid confusing it with accounts, and it is italicized.

Point: There are no exact rules for writing journal entry explanations. An explanation should be short yet describe why an entry is made.

IFRS

IFRS requires that companies report the following four basic financial statements with explanatory notes:

—Balance sheet   —Statement of changes in equity (or statement of recognized revenue and expense)

—Income statement   —Statement of cash flows

IFRS does not prescribe specific formats; and comparative information is required for the preceding period only.

A blank line is left between each journal entry for clarity. When a transaction is first recorded, the **posting reference (PR) column** is left blank (in a manual system). Later, when posting entries to the ledger, the identification numbers of the individual ledger accounts are entered in the PR column.

Balance Column Account   T-accounts are simple and direct means to show how the accounting process works. However, actual accounting systems need more structure and therefore use **balance column accounts,** such as that in Exhibit 2.11.

EXHIBIT 2.11

Cash Account in Balance Column Format

Cash					Account No. 101
Date	Explanation	PR	Debit	Credit	Balance
2009 Dec. 1		G1	30,000		30,000
Dec. 2		G1		2,500	27,500
Dec. 3		G1		26,000	1,500
Dec. 10		G1	4,200		5,700

The balance column account format is similar to a T-account in having columns for debits and credits. It is different in including transaction date and explanation columns. It also has a column with the balance of the account after each entry is recorded. To illustrate, FastForward's Cash account in Exhibit 2.11 is debited on December 1 for the $30,000 owner investment, yielding a $30,000 debit balance. The account is credited on December 2 for $2,500, yielding a $27,500 debit balance. On December 3, it is credited again, this time for $26,000, and its

Point: Explanations are typically included in ledger accounts only for unusual transactions or events.

EXHIBIT 2.12

Posting an Entry to the Ledger

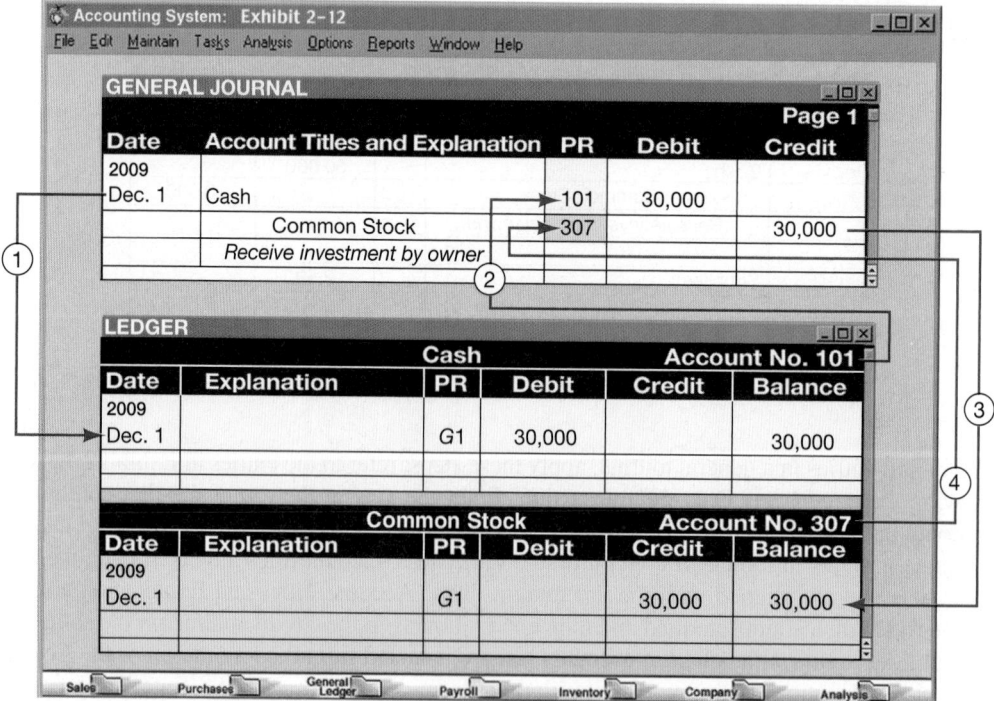

Point: The fundamental concepts of a manual (pencil-and-paper) system are identical to those of a computerized information system.

Key: ① Identify debit account in Ledger: enter date, journal page, amount, and balance.
     ② Enter the debit account number from the Ledger in the PR column of the journal.
     ③ Identify credit account in Ledger: enter date, journal page, amount, and balance.
     ④ Enter the credit account number from the Ledger in the PR column of the journal.

debit balance is reduced to $1,500. The Cash account is debited for $4,200 on December 10, and its debit balance increases to $5,700; and so on.

The heading of the Balance column does not show whether it is a debit or credit balance. Instead, an account is assumed to have a *normal balance*. Unusual events can sometimes temporarily give an account an abnormal balance. An *abnormal balance* refers to a balance on the side where decreases are recorded. For example, a customer might mistakenly overpay a bill. This gives that customer's account receivable an abnormal (credit) balance. An abnormal balance is often identified by circling it or by entering it in red or some other unusual color. A zero balance for an account is usually shown by writing zeros or a dash in the Balance column to avoid confusion between a zero balance and one omitted in error.

Posting Journal Entries   Step 4 of processing transactions is to post journal entries to ledger accounts (see Exhibit 2.9). To ensure that the ledger is up-to-date, entries are posted as soon as possible. This might be daily, weekly, or when time permits. All entries must be posted to the ledger before financial statements are prepared to ensure that account balances are up-to-date. When entries are posted to the ledger, the debits in journal entries are transferred into ledger accounts as debits, and credits are transferred into ledger accounts as credits. Exhibit 2.12 shows the *four steps to post a journal entry*. First, identify the ledger account that is debited in the entry; then, in the ledger, enter the entry date, the journal and page in its PR column, the debit amount, and the new balance of the ledger account. (The letter *G* shows it came from the General Journal.) Second, enter the ledger account number in the PR column of the journal. Steps three and four repeat the first two steps for credit entries and amounts. The posting process creates a link between the ledger and the journal entry. This link is a useful cross-reference for tracing an amount from one record to another.

Point: Computerized systems often provide a code beside a balance such as *dr.* or *cr.* to identify its balance. Posting is automatic and immediate with accounting software.

Point: A journal is often referred to as the *book of original entry.* The ledger is referred to as the *book of final entry* because financial statements are prepared from it.

Analyzing Transactions—An Illustration

We return to the activities of FastForward to show how double-entry accounting is useful in analyzing and processing transactions. Analysis of each transaction follows the four steps of Exhibit 2.9. Step 1: review the transaction and any source documents. Step 2: analyze the transaction using the accounting equation. Step 3: use double-entry accounting to record the transaction in journal entry form. Step 4: post the entry (for simplicity, we use T-accounts to represent ledger accounts). Study each transaction thoroughly before proceeding to the next. The first 11 transactions are from Chapter 1, and we analyze five additional December transactions of FastForward (numbered 12 through 16) that were omitted earlier.

A1   Analyze the impact of transactions on accounts and financial statements.

FAST~Forward~

1. Receive investment by Owner

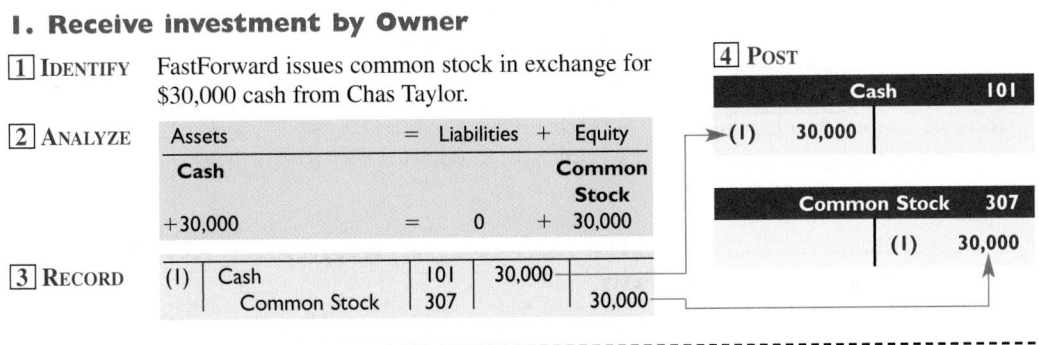

2. Purchase Supplies for Cash

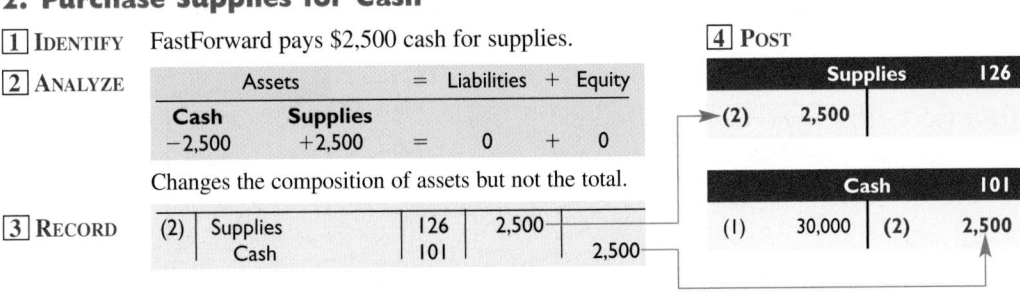

3. Purchase Equipment for Cash

1 IDENTIFY   FastForward pays $26,000 cash for equipment.

2 ANALYZE

Assets		=	Liabilities	+	Equity
Cash	**Equipment**				
−26,000	+26,000	=	0	+	0

Changes the composition of assets but not the total.

3 RECORD

(3)	Equipment	167	26,000	
	Cash	101		26,000

4 POST

Equipment		167
(3)	26,000	

Cash		101
(1)	30,000	(2)	2,500
		(3)	26,000

---

4. Purchase Supplies on Credit

1 IDENTIFY   FastForward purchases $7,100 of supplies on credit from a supplier.

2 ANALYZE

Assets	=	Liabilities	+	Equity
Supplies		**Accounts Payable**		
+7,100	=	+7,100	+	0

3 RECORD

(4)	Supplies	126	7,100	
	Accounts Payable	201		7,100

4 POST

Supplies		126
(2)	2,500	
(4)	7,100	

Accounts Payable		201
		(4)	7,100

---

5. Provide Services for Cash

1 IDENTIFY   FastForward provides consulting services and immediately collects $4,200 cash.

2 ANALYZE

Assets	=	Liabilities	+	Equity
Cash				**Consulting Revenue**
+4,200	=	0		+4,200

3 RECORD

(5)	Cash	101	4,200	
	Consulting Revenue	403		4,200

4 POST

Cash		101
(1)	30,000	(2)	2,500
(5)	4,200	(3)	26,000

Consulting Revenue		403
		(5)	4,200

---

6. Payment of Expense in Cash

1 IDENTIFY   FastForward pays $1,000 cash for December rent.

2 ANALYZE

Assets	=	Liabilities	+	Equity
Cash				**Rent Expense**
−1,000	=	0		−1,000

3 RECORD

(6)	Rent Expense	640	1,000	
	Cash	101		1,000

4 POST

Rent Expense		640
(6)	1,000	

Cash		101
(1)	30,000	(2)	2,500
(5)	4,200	(3)	26,000
		(6)	1,000

---

7. Payment of Expense in Cash

1 IDENTIFY   FastForward pays $700 cash for employee salary.

2 ANALYZE

Assets	=	Liabilities	+	Equity
Cash				**Salaries Expense**
−700	=	0		−700

3 RECORD

(7)	Salaries Expense	622	700	
	Cash	101		700

4 POST

Salaries Expense		622
(7)	700	

Cash		101
(1)	30,000	(2)	2,500
(5)	4,200	(3)	26,000
		(6)	1,000
		(7)	700

Point: *Salary* usually refers to compensation for an employee who receives a fixed amount for a given time period, whereas *wages* usually refers to compensation based on time worked.

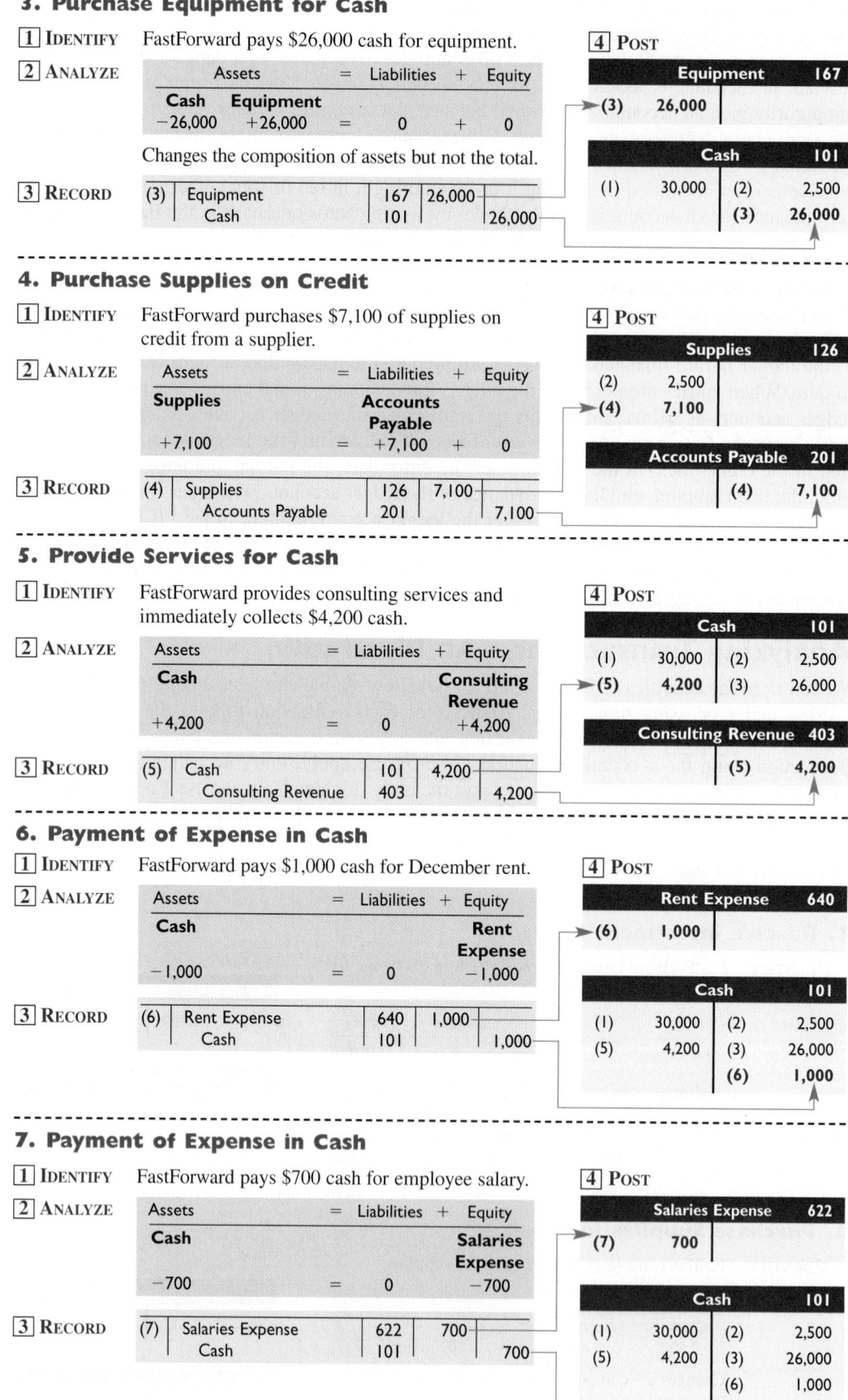

8. Provide Consulting and Rental Services on Credit

1 IDENTIFY FastForward provides consulting services of $1,600 and rents its test facilities for $300. The customer is billed $1,900 for these services.

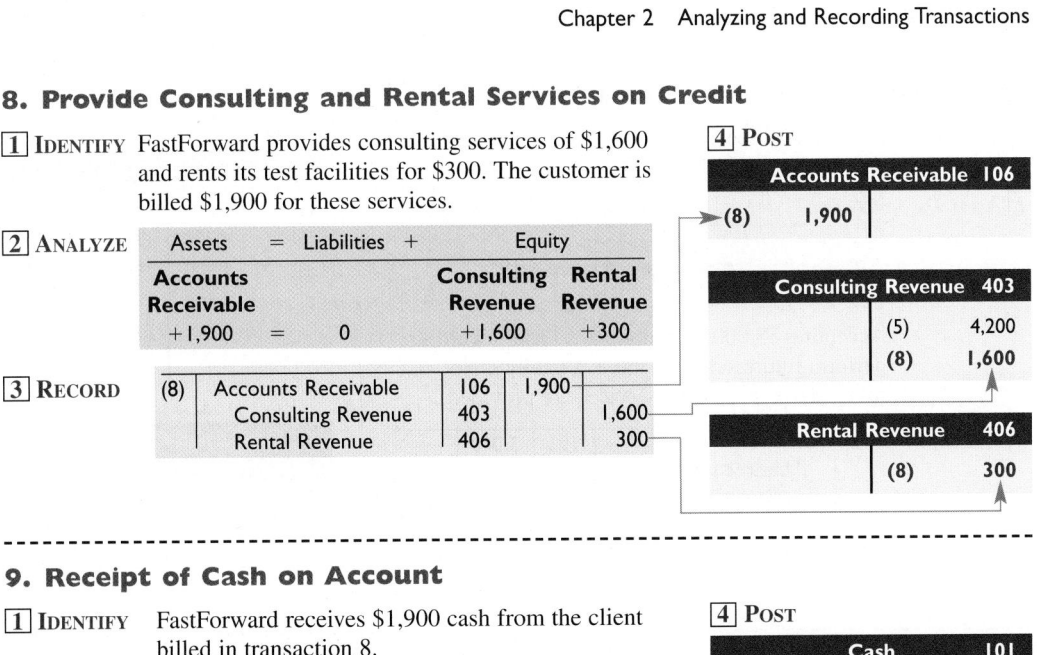

Point: Transaction 8 is a **compound journal entry,** which affects three or more accounts.

9. Receipt of Cash on Account

1 IDENTIFY FastForward receives $1,900 cash from the client billed in transaction 8.

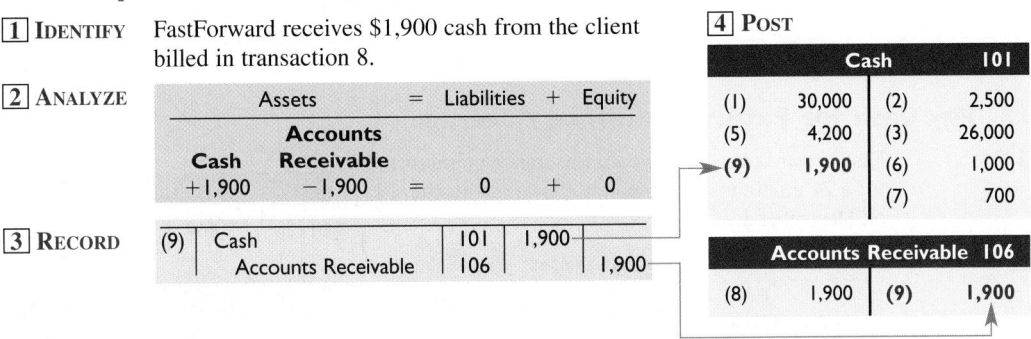

Point: The *revenue recognition principle* requires revenue to be recognized when earned, which is when the company provides products and services to a customer. This is not necessarily the same time that the customer pays. A customer can pay before or after products or services are provided.

10. Partial Payment of Accounts Payable

1 IDENTIFY FastForward pays CalTech Supply $900 cash toward the payable of transaction 4.

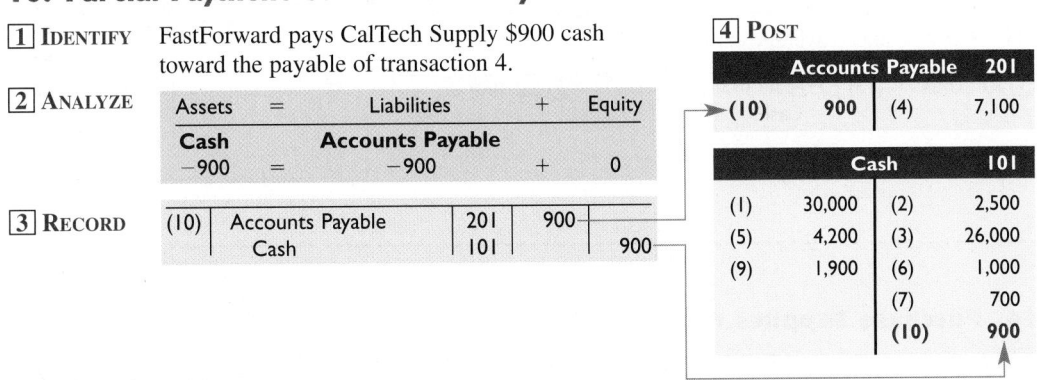

11. Payment of Cash Dividend

1 IDENTIFY FastForward pays $200 cash for dividends.

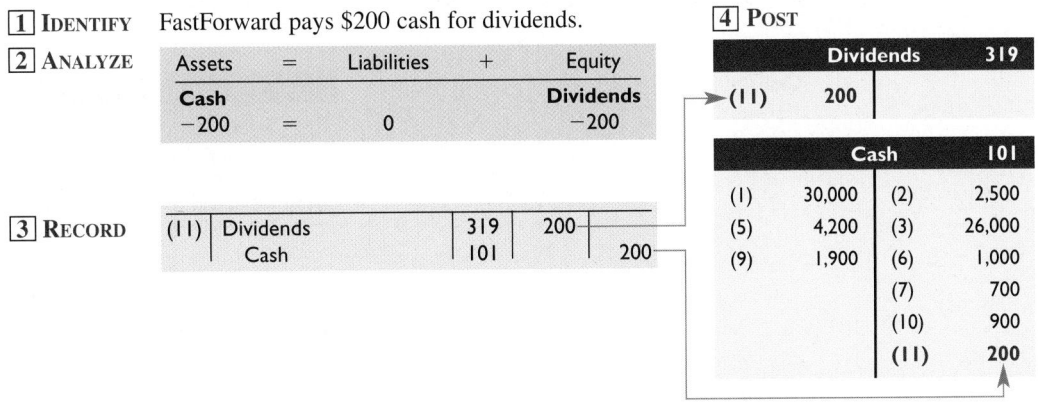

12. Receipt of Cash for Future Services

Point: Luca Pacioli, a 15th-century monk, is considered a pioneer in accounting and the first to devise double-entry accounting.

1 IDENTIFY   FastForward receives $3,000 cash in advance of providing consulting services to a customer.

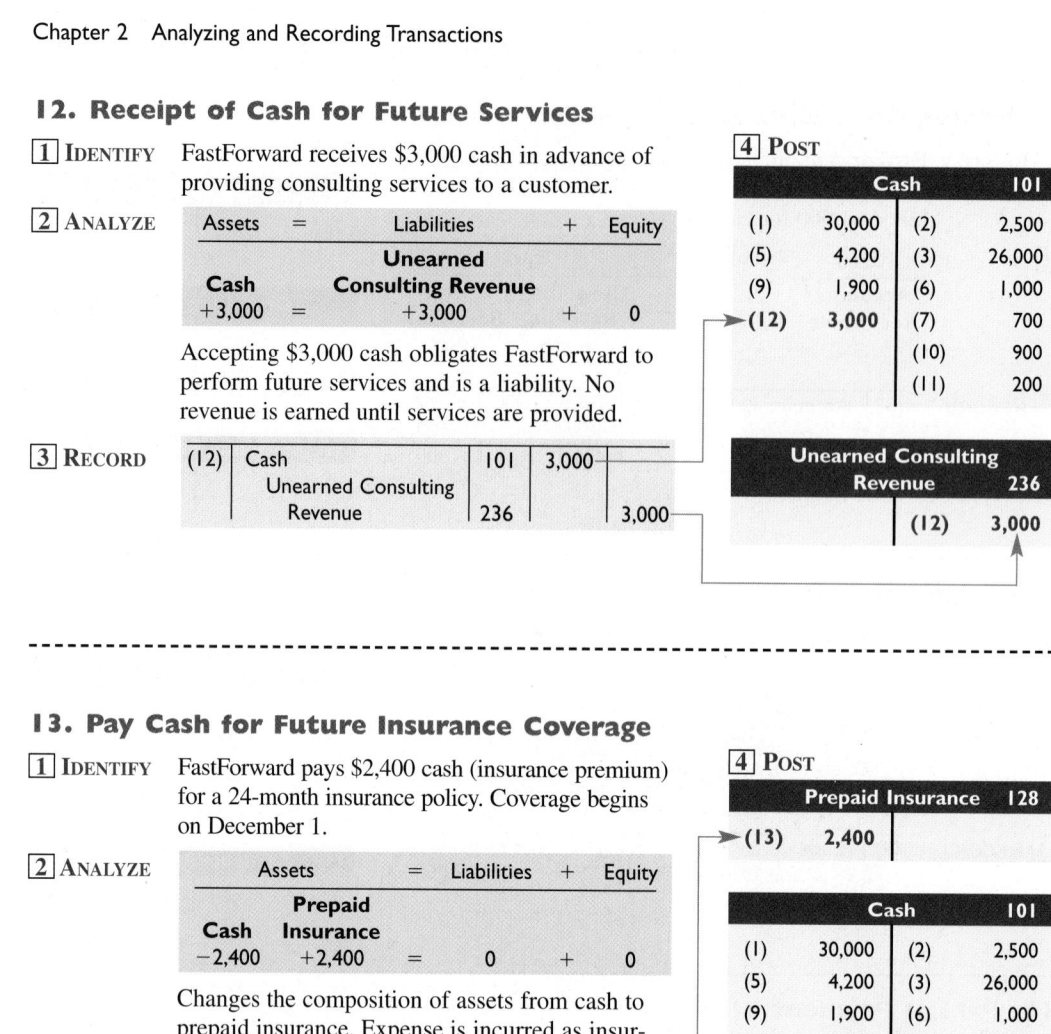

Accepting $3,000 cash obligates FastForward to perform future services and is a liability. No revenue is earned until services are provided.

13. Pay Cash for Future Insurance Coverage

1 IDENTIFY   FastForward pays $2,400 cash (insurance premium) for a 24-month insurance policy. Coverage begins on December 1.

Changes the composition of assets from cash to prepaid insurance. Expense is incurred as insurance coverage expires.

14. Purchase Supplies for Cash

1 IDENTIFY   FastForward pays $120 cash for supplies.

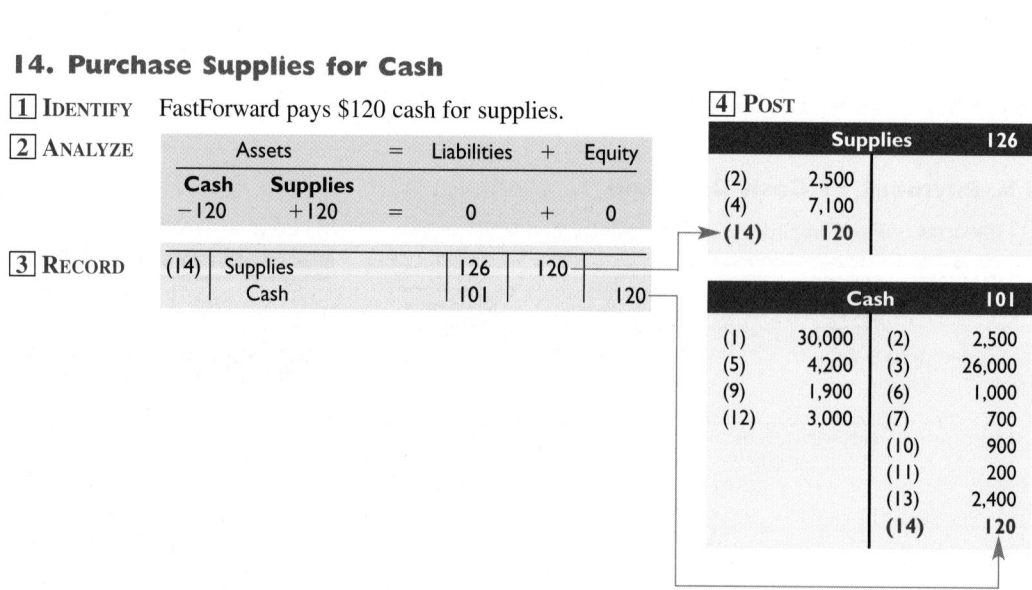

15. Payment of Expense in Cash

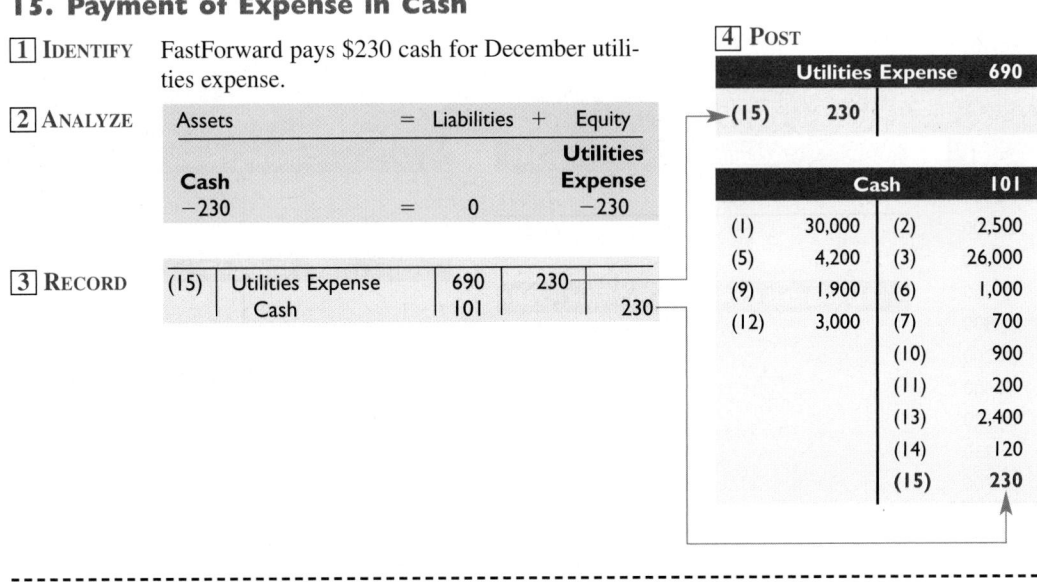

Point: We could merge transactions 15 and 16 into one *compound entry.*

16. Payment of Expense in Cash

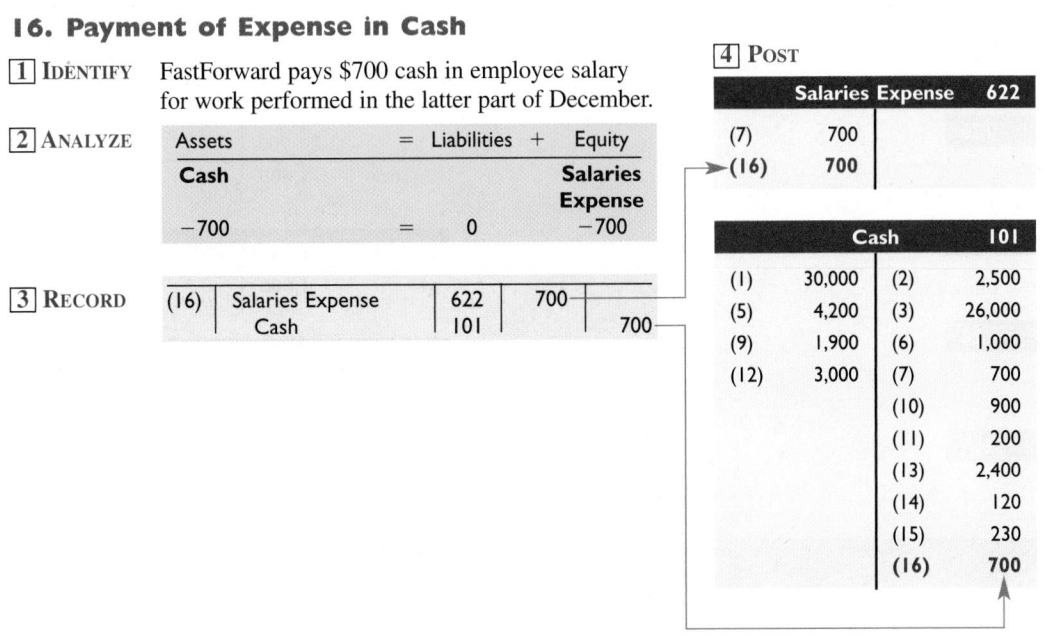

Accounting Equation Analysis

Exhibit 2.13 shows the ledger accounts (in T-account form) of FastForward after all 16 transactions are recorded and posted and the balances are computed. The accounts are grouped into three major columns corresponding to the accounting equation: assets, liabilities, and equity. Note several important points. First, as with each transaction, the totals for the three columns must obey the accounting equation. Specifically, assets equal $42,470 ($4,350 + $0 + $9,720 + $2,400 + $26,000); liabilities equal $9,200 ($6,200 + $3,000); and equity equals $33,270 ($30,000 − $200 + $5,800 + $300 − $1,400 − $1,000 − $230). These numbers prove the accounting equation: Assets of $42,470 = Liabilities of $9,200 + Equity of $33,270. Second, the common stock, dividends, revenue, and expense accounts reflect the transactions that change equity. The latter three account categories underlie the statement of retained earnings. Third, the revenue and expense account balances will be summarized and reported in the income statement. Fourth, increases and decreases in the cash account make up the elements reported in the statement of cash flows.

Debit and Credit Rules		
	Increase	
Accounts	**(normal bal.)**	**Decrease**
Asset	Debit	Credit
Liability	Credit	Debit
Common stock	Credit	Debit
Dividends	Debit	Credit
Revenue	Credit	Debit
Expense	Debit	Credit

Point: Technology does not provide the judgment required to analyze most business transactions. Analysis requires the expertise of skilled and ethical professionals.

EXHIBIT 2.13

Ledger for FastForward (in T-Account Form)

Assets				=	Liabilities			+	Equity		

Assets

Cash   101

(1)	30,000	(2)	2,500
(5)	4,200	(3)	26,000
(9)	1,900	(6)	1,000
(12)	3,000	(7)	700
		(10)	900
		(11)	200
		(13)	2,400
		(14)	120
		(15)	230
		(16)	700
Balance	4,350		

Accounts Receivable   106

(8)	1,900	(9)	1,900
Balance	0		

Supplies   126

(2)	2,500		
(4)	7,100		
(14)	120		
Balance	9,720		

Prepaid Insurance   128

(13)	2,400		

Equipment   167

(3)	26,000		

Liabilities

Accounts Payable   201

(10)	900	(4)	7,100
		Balance	6,200

Unearned Consulting Revenue   236

		(12)	3,000

Equity

Common Stock   307

		(1)	30,000

Dividends   319

(11)	200		

Consulting Revenue   403

		(5)	4,200
		(8)	1,600
		Balance	5,800

Rental Revenue   406

		(8)	300

Salaries Expense   622

(7)	700		
(16)	700		
Balance	1,400		

Rent Expense   640

(6)	1,000		

Utilities Expense   690

(15)	230		

Accounts in this white area reflect those reported on the income statement.

$42,470	=	$9,200	+	$33,270

Quick Check

Answers—p. 75

8. What types of transactions increase equity? What types decrease equity?

9. Why are accounting systems called *double entry*?

10. For each transaction, double-entry accounting requires which of the following: (*a*) Debits to asset accounts must create credits to liability or equity accounts, (*b*) a debit to a liability account must create a credit to an asset account, or (*c*) total debits must equal total credits.

11. An owner invests $15,000 cash along with equipment having a market value of $23,000 in a company in exchange for common stock. Prepare the necessary journal entry.

12. Explain what a compound journal entry is.

13. Why are posting reference numbers entered in the journal when entries are posted to ledger accounts?

Trial Balance

Double-entry accounting ensures that the sum of debit account balances equals the sum of credit account balances. A trial balance is used to confirm this. A **trial balance** is a list of accounts and their balances at a point in time. Account balances are reported in their appropriate debit or credit columns of a trial balance. A trial balance can be used to confirm this and to follow up on any abnormal or unusual balances. Exhibit 2.14 shows the trial balance for FastForward after its 16 entries have been posted to the ledger. (This is an *unadjusted* trial balance—Chapter 3 explains the necessary adjustments.)

Video2.1

Accounting System: Exhibit 2-14

File Edit Maintain Tasks Analysis Options Reports Window Help

FASTFORWARD
Trial Balance
December 31, 2009

	Debit	Credit
Cash	$ 4,350	
Accounts receivable	0	
Supplies	9,720	
Prepaid insurance	2,400	
Equipment	26,000	
Accounts payable		$ 6,200
Unearned consulting revenue		3,000
Common stock		30,000
Dividends	200	
Consulting revenue		5,800
Rental revenue		300
Salaries expense	1,400	
Rent expense	1,000	
Utilities expense	230	
Totals	$ 45,300	$ 45,300

Sales   Purchases   General Ledger   Payroll   Inventory   Company   Analysis

EXHIBIT 2.14

Trial Balance (unadjusted)

Point: The ordering of accounts in a trial balance typically follows their identification number from the chart of accounts.

Preparing a Trial Balance

Preparing a trial balance involves three steps:

1. List each account title and its amount (from ledger) in the trial balance. If an account has a zero balance, list it with a zero in its normal balance column (or omit it entirely).
2. Compute the total of debit balances and the total of credit balances.
3. Verify (*prove*) total debit balances equal total credit balances.

The total of debit balances equals the total of credit balances for the trial balance in Exhibit 2.14. Equality of these two totals does not guarantee that no errors were made. For example, the column totals still will be equal when a debit or credit of a correct amount is made to a wrong account. Another error that does not cause unequal column totals is the entering of equal debits and credits of an incorrect amount.

P2 Prepare and explain the use of a trial balance.

Point: A trial balance is *not* a financial statement but a mechanism for checking equality of debits and credits in the ledger. Financial statements do not have debit and credit columns.

Searching for and Correcting Errors If the trial balance does not balance (when its columns are not equal), the error (or errors) must be found and corrected. An efficient

Example: If a credit to Unearned Revenue was incorrectly posted from the journal as a credit to the Revenue ledger account, would the ledger still balance? Would the financial statements be correct? *Answers:* The ledger would balance, but liabilities would be understated, equity would be overstated, and income would be overstated (all because of overstated revenues).

Point: The IRS requires companies to keep records that can be audited.

way to search for an error is to check the journalizing, posting, and trial balance preparation in *reverse order*. Step 1 is to verify that the trial balance columns are correctly added. If step 1 fails to find the error, step 2 is to verify that account balances are accurately entered from the ledger. Step 3 is to see whether a debit (or credit) balance is mistakenly listed in the trial balance as a credit (or debit). A clue to this error is when the difference between total debits and total credits equals twice the amount of the incorrect account balance. If the error is still undiscovered, Step 4 is to recompute each account balance in the ledger. Step 5 is to verify that each journal entry is properly posted. Step 6 is to verify that the original journal entry has equal debits and credits. At this point, the errors should be uncovered.[3]

If an error in a journal entry is discovered before the error is posted, it can be corrected in a manual system by drawing a line through the incorrect information. The correct information is written above it to create a record of change for the auditor. Many computerized systems allow the operator to replace the incorrect information directly.

If an error in a journal entry is not discovered until after it is posted, we do not strike through both erroneous entries in the journal and ledger. Instead, we correct this error by creating a *correcting entry* that removes the amount from the wrong account and records it to the correct account. As an example, suppose a $100 purchase of supplies is journalized with an incorrect debit to Equipment, and then this incorrect entry is posted to the ledger. The Supplies ledger account balance is understated by $100, and the Equipment ledger account balance is overstated by $100. The correcting entry is: debit Supplies and credit Equipment (both for $100).

Using a Trial Balance to Prepare Financial Statements

P3 Prepare financial statements from business transactions.

This section shows how to prepare *financial statements* from the trial balance in Exhibit 2.14 and from information on the December transactions of FastForward. These statements differ from those in Chapter 1 because of several additional transactions. These statements are also more precisely called *unadjusted statements* because we need to make some further accounting adjustments (described in Chapter 3).

EXHIBIT 2.15

Links between Financial Statements Across Time

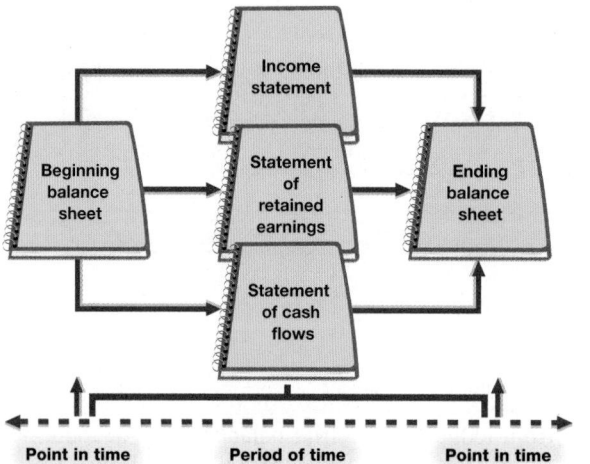

How financial statements are linked in time is illustrated in Exhibit 2.15. A balance sheet reports on an organization's financial position at a *point in time*. The income statement, statement of retained earnings, and statement of cash flows report on financial performance over a *period of time*. The three statements in the middle column of Exhibit 2.15 link balance sheets from the beginning to the end of a reporting period. They explain how financial position changes from one point to another.

---

[3] *Transposition* occurs when two digits are switched, or transposed, within a number. If transposition is the only error, it yields a difference between the two trial balance totals that is evenly divisible by 9. For example, assume that a $691 debit in an entry is incorrectly posted to the ledger as $619. Total credits in the trial balance are then larger than total debits by $72 ($691 − $619). The $72 error is *evenly* divisible by 9 (72/9 = 8). The first digit of the quotient (in our example it is 8) equals the difference between the digits of the two transposed numbers (the 9 and the 1). The number of digits in the quotient also tells the location of the transposition, starting from the right. The quotient in our example had only one digit (8), so it tells us the transposition is in the first digit. Consider another example where a transposition error involves posting $961 instead of the correct $691. The difference in these numbers is $270, and its quotient is 30 (270/9). The quotient has two digits, so it tells us to check the second digit from the right for a transposition of two numbers that have a difference of 3.

Preparers and users (including regulatory agencies) determine the length of the reporting period. A one-year, or annual, reporting period is common, as are semiannual, quarterly, and monthly periods. The one-year reporting period is known as the *accounting,* or *fiscal, year.* Businesses whose accounting year begins on January 1 and ends on December 31 are known as *calendar-year* companies. Many companies choose a fiscal year ending on a date other than December 31. **Best Buy** is a *noncalendar-year* company as reflected in the headings of its February 28 year-end financial statements in Appendix A near the end of the book.

Income Statement An income statement reports the revenues earned less the expenses incurred by a business over a period of time. FastForward's income statement for December is shown at the top of Exhibit 2.16. Information about revenues and expenses is conveniently taken from the trial balance in Exhibit 2.14. Net income of $3,470 is reported at the bottom of the statement. Owner investments and dividends are *not* part of income.

Statement of Retained Earnings The statement of retained earnings reports information about how retained earnings changes over the reporting period. FastForward's statement of retained earnings is the second report in Exhibit 2.16. It shows the $3,470 of

Point: A statement's heading lists the 3 W's: **W**ho—name of organization, **W**hat—name of statement, **W**hen—statement's point in time or period of time.

EXHIBIT 2.16

Financial Statements and Their Links

FASTFORWARD Income Statement For Month Ended December 31, 2009		
Revenues		
Consulting revenue ($4,200 + $1,600)	$ 5,800	
Rental revenue	300	
Total revenues		$ 6,100
Expenses		
Rent expense	1,000	
Salaries expense	1,400	
Utilities expense	230	
Total expenses		2,630
Net income		$ 3,470

Point: Arrow lines show how the statements are linked.

FASTFORWARD Statement of Retained Earnings For Month Ended December 31, 2009	
Retained earnings, December 1, 2009	$ 0
Plus: Net income	3,470
	3,470
Less: Cash dividends	200
Retained earnings, December 31, 2009	$ 3,270

FASTFORWARD Balance Sheet December 31, 2009			
Assets		**Liabilities**	
Cash	$ 4,350	Accounts payable	$ 6,200
Supplies	9,720	Unearned revenue	3,000
Prepaid insurance ..	2,400	Total liabilities	9,200
Equipment	26,000	**Equity**	
		Common stock	30,000
		Retained earnings	3,270
		Total equity	33,270
Total assets	$42,470	Total liabilities and equity .	$42,470

Point: To *foot* a column of numbers is to add them.

net income, the $200 dividend, and the $3,270 end-of-period balance. (The beginning balance in the statement of retained earnings is rarely zero. An exception is for the first period of operations. The beginning retained earnings balance in January 2010 is $3,270, which is December's ending balance.)

Balance Sheet　The balance sheet reports the financial position of a company at a point in time, usually at the end of a month, quarter, or year. FastForward's balance sheet is the third report in Exhibit 2.16. This statement refers to financial condition at the close of business on December 31. The left side of the balance sheet lists its assets: cash, supplies, prepaid insurance, and equipment. The upper right side of the balance sheet shows that it owes $6,200 to creditors and $3,000 in services to customers who paid in advance. The equity section shows an ending balance of $33,270. Note the link between the ending balance of the statement of retained earnings and the retained earnings balance. (Recall that this presentation of the balance sheet is called the *account form:* assets on the left and liabilities and equity on the right. Another presentation is the *report form:* assets on top, followed by liabilities and then equity. Either presentation is acceptable.)

Decision Maker

Entrepreneur　You open a wholesale business selling entertainment equipment to retail outlets. You find that most of your customers demand to buy on credit. How can you use the balance sheets of these customers to decide which ones to extend credit to? [Answer—p. 74]

off the mark.com　by Mark Parisi
offthemark.com

HE CONTINUED ACCOUNTING RIGHT THROUGH HIS COFFEE BREAK...THEN HIS LUNCH BREAK. CLEARLY, MYRON WAS "IN THE ZONE."

Presentation Issues　Dollar signs are not used in journals and ledgers. They do appear in financial statements and other reports such as trial balances. The usual practice is to put dollar signs beside only the first and last numbers in a column. **Best Buy**'s financial statements in Appendix A show this. When amounts are entered in a journal, ledger, or trial balance, commas are optional to indicate thousands, millions, and so forth. However, commas are always used in financial statements. Companies also commonly round amounts in reports to the nearest dollar, or even to a higher level. Best Buy is typical of many companies in that it rounds its financial statement amounts to the nearest million. This decision is based on the perceived impact of rounding for users' business decisions.

Quick Check
Answers—p. 75

14. Where are dollar signs typically entered in financial statements?
15. If a $4,000 debit to Equipment in a journal entry is incorrectly posted to the ledger as a $4,000 credit, and the ledger account has a resulting debit balance of $20,000, what is the effect of this error on the Trial Balance column totals?
16. Describe the link between the income statement and the statement of retained earnings.
17. Explain the link between the balance sheet and the statement of retained earnings.
18. Define and describe revenues and expenses.
19. Define and describe assets, liabilities, and equity.

Global View

Financial accounting according to U.S. GAAP is similar, but not identical, to IFRS. This section discusses differences in analyzing and recording transactions, and with the preparation of financial statements.

Analyzing and Recording Transactions

Both U.S. GAAP and IFRS include broad and similar guidance for financial accounting. As the FASB and IASB work toward a common conceptual framework over the next few years, even those differences will fade. Further, both U.S. GAAP and IFRS apply transaction analysis and recording as shown in this chapter—using the same debit and credit system and accrual accounting. Although some variations exist in revenue and expense recognition and other accounting principles, all of the transactions in this chapter are accounted for identically under these two systems.

Financial Statements

Both U.S. GAAP and IFRS prepare the same four basic financial statements. A few differences within each statement do exist and we will discuss those throughout the book. For example, both U.S. GAAP and IFRS require balance sheets to separate current items from noncurrent items. However, while U.S. GAAP balance sheets report current items first, IFRS balance sheets normally (but are not required to) present noncurrent items first, and equity before liabilities. To illustrate, a condensed version of **GOME**'s balance sheet follows (numbers using Renminbi in thousands).

GOME Balance Sheet (in RMB 000s) December 31, 2008			
Assets		**Equity and Liabilities**	
Noncurrent assets	9,012,393	Total equity	8,700,035
Current assets	18,482,711	Noncurrent liabilities	3,647,822
		Current liabilities	15,147,247
Total assets	27,495,104	Total equity and liabilities	27,495,104

Accounting Controls and Assurance

Accounting systems depend on control procedures that assure the proper principles were applied in processing accounting information. The passage of SOX legislation strengthened U.S. control procedures in recent years. However, global standards for control are diverse and so are enforcement activities. Consequently, while global accounting standards are converging, their application in different countries can yield different outcomes depending on the quality of their auditing standards and enforcement.

Decision Insight

SOX: Data Control Recording valid transactions, and not recording fraudulent transactions, enhances the quality of financial statements. The graph here shows the percentage of employees in information technology that report observing specific types of misconduct within the past year. [Source: KPMG 2009]

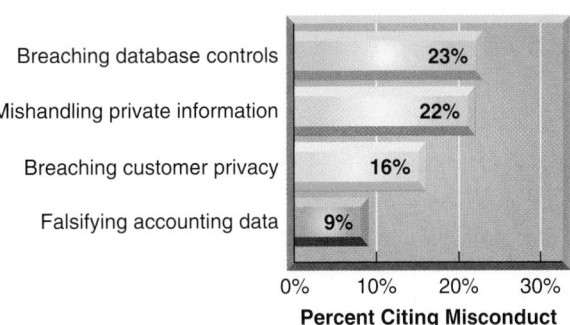

Debt Ratio	**Decision Analysis**

An important business objective is gathering information to help assess a company's risk of failing to pay its debts. Companies finance their assets with either liabilities or equity. A company that finances a relatively large portion of its assets with liabilities is said to have a high degree of *financial leverage*. Higher financial leverage involves greater risk because liabilities must be repaid and often require regular interest payments (equity financing does not). The risk that a company might not be able to meet such required payments is higher if it has more liabilities (is more highly leveraged). One way

A2 Compute the debt ratio and describe its use in analyzing financial condition.

to assess the risk associated with a company's use of liabilities is to compute the **debt ratio** as in Exhibit 2.17.

EXHIBIT 2.17

Debt Ratio

$$\text{Debt ratio} = \frac{\text{Total liabilities}}{\text{Total assets}}$$

Point: Compare the equity amount to the liability amount to assess the extent of owner versus nonowner financing.

To see how to apply the debt ratio, let's look at **Skechers**'s liabilities and assets. The company designs, markets and sells footwear for men, women and children under the Skechers brand. Exhibit 2.18 computes and reports its debt ratio at the end of each year from 2004 to 2008.

EXHIBIT 2.18

Computation and Analysis of Debt Ratio

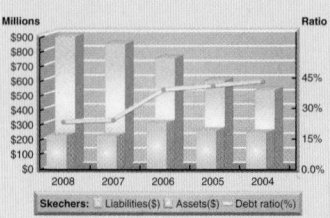

$ in millions	2008	2007	2006	2005	2004
Total liabilities	$204	$201	$288	$238	$224
Total assets	$876	$828	$737	$582	$519
Debt ratio	0.23	0.24	0.39	0.41	0.43
Industry debt ratio	0.50	0.46	0.48	0.47	0.48

Skechers's debt ratio ranges from a low of 0.23 to a high of 0.43—also, see graph in margin. Its ratio is lower, and has been declining, compared with the industry ratio. This analysis implies a low risk from its financial leverage. Is financial leverage good or bad for Skechers? To answer that question we need to compare the company's return on the borrowed money to the rate it is paying creditors. If the company's return is higher, it is successfully borrowing money to make more money. A company's success with making money from borrowed money can quickly turn unprofitable if its own return drops below the rate it is paying creditors.

 Decision Maker ▬▬▬▬▬

Investor   You consider buying stock in **Converse**. As part of your analysis, you compute its debt ratio for 2006, 2007, and 2008 as: 0.35, 0.74, and 0.94, respectively. Based on the debt ratio, is Converse a low-risk investment? Has the risk of buying Converse stock changed over this period? (The industry debt ratio averages 0.40.) [Answer—p. 74]

Demonstration Problem

(This problem extends the demonstration problem of Chapter 1.) After several months of planning, Jasmine Worthy started a haircutting business called Expressions. The following events occurred during its first month.

a. On August 1, Worthy invested $3,000 cash and $15,000 of equipment in Expressions in exchange for its common stock.

b. On August 2, Expressions paid $600 cash for furniture for the shop.

c. On August 3, Expressions paid $500 cash to rent space in a strip mall for August.

d. On August 4, it purchased $1,200 of equipment on credit for the shop (using a long-term note payable).

e. On August 5, Expressions opened for business. Cash received from haircutting services in the first week and a half of business (ended August 15) was $825.

f. On August 15, it provided $100 of haircutting services on account.

g. On August 17, it received a $100 check for services previously rendered on account.

h. On August 17, it paid $125 to an assistant for hours worked during the grand opening.

i. Cash received from services provided during the second half of August was $930.

j. On August 31, it paid a $400 installment toward principal on the note payable entered into on August 4.

k. On August 31, it paid $900 cash for dividends.

Required

1. Open the following ledger accounts in balance column format (account numbers are in parentheses): Cash (101); Accounts Receivable (102); Furniture (161); Store Equipment (165); Note Payable (240); Common Stock (307); Dividends (319); Haircutting Services Revenue (403); Wages Expense (623); and Rent Expense (640). Prepare general journal entries for the transactions.
2. Post the journal entries from (1) to the ledger accounts.
3. Prepare a trial balance as of August 31.
4. Prepare an income statement for August.
5. Prepare a statement of retained earnings for August.
6. Prepare a balance sheet as of August 31.
7. Determine the debt ratio as of August 31.

Extended Analysis

8. In the coming months, Expressions will experience a greater variety of business transactions. Identify which accounts are debited and which are credited for the following transactions. (*Hint:* We must use some accounts not opened in part 1.)
   a. Purchase supplies with cash.
   b. Pay cash for future insurance coverage.
   c. Receive cash for services to be provided in the future.
   d. Purchase supplies on account.

Planning the Solution

- Analyze each transaction and use the debit and credit rules to prepare a journal entry for each.
- Post each debit and each credit from journal entries to their ledger accounts and cross-reference each amount in the posting reference (PR) columns of the journal and ledger.
- Calculate each account balance and list the accounts with their balances on a trial balance.
- Verify that total debits in the trial balance equal total credits.
- To prepare the income statement, identify revenues and expenses. List those items on the statement, compute the difference, and label the result as *net income* or *net loss*.
- Use information in the ledger to prepare the statement of retained earnings.
- Use information in the ledger to prepare the balance sheet.
- Calculate the debt ratio by dividing total liabilities by total assets.
- Analyze the future transactions to identify the accounts affected and apply debit and credit rules.

Solution to Demonstration Problem

1. General journal entries:

GENERAL JOURNAL

Page 1

Date	Account Titles and Explanation	PR	Debit	Credit
Aug. 1	Cash	101	3,000	
	Store Equipment	165	15,000	
	Common Stock	307		18,000
	Owner's investment.			
2	Furniture	161	600	
	Cash	101		600
	Purchased furniture for cash.			
3	Rent Expense	640	500	
	Cash	101		500
	Paid rent for August.			
4	Store Equipment	165	1,200	
	Note Payable	240		1,200
	Purchased additional equipment on credit.			

[continued on next page]

[continued from previous page]

15	Cash	101	825	
	Haircutting Services Revenue	403		825
	Cash receipts from first half of August.			
15	Accounts Receivable	102	100	
	Haircutting Services Revenue	403		100
	To record revenue for services provided on account.			
17	Cash	101	100	
	Accounts Receivable	102		100
	To record cash received as payment on account.			
17	Wages Expense	623	125	
	Cash	101		125
	Paid wages to assistant.			
31	Cash	101	930	
	Haircutting Services Revenue	403		930
	Cash receipts from second half of August.			
31	Note Payable	240	400	
	Cash	101		400
	Paid an installment on the note payable.			
31	Dividends	319	900	
	Cash	101		900
	Paid cash dividend.			

2. Post journal entries from part 1 to the ledger accounts:

General Ledger

Cash — Account No. 101

Date	PR	Debit	Credit	Balance
Aug. 1	G1	3,000		3,000
2	G1		600	2,400
3	G1		500	1,900
15	G1	825		2,725
17	G1	100		2,825
17	G1		125	2,700
31	G1	930		3,630
31	G1		400	3,230
31	G1		900	2,330

Accounts Receivable — Account No. 102

Date	PR	Debit	Credit	Balance
Aug. 15	G1	100		100
17	G1		100	0

Furniture — Account No. 161

Date	PR	Debit	Credit	Balance
Aug. 2	G1	600		600

Store Equipment — Account No. 165

Date	PR	Debit	Credit	Balance
Aug. 1	G1	15,000		15,000
4	G1	1,200		16,200

Note Payable — Account No. 240

Date	PR	Debit	Credit	Balance
Aug. 4	G1		1,200	1,200
31	G1	400		800

Common Stock — Account No. 307

Date	PR	Debit	Credit	Balance
Aug. 1	G1		18,000	18,000

Dividends — Account No. 319

Date	PR	Debit	Credit	Balance
Aug. 31	G1	900		900

Haircutting Services Revenue — Account No. 403

Date	PR	Debit	Credit	Balance
Aug. 15	G1		825	825
15	G1		100	925
31	G1		930	1,855

Wages Expense — Account No. 623

Date	PR	Debit	Credit	Balance
Aug. 17	G1	125		125

Rent Expense — Account No. 640

Date	PR	Debit	Credit	Balance
Aug. 3	G1	500		500

3. Prepare a trial balance from the ledger:

EXPRESSIONS Trial Balance August 31		
	Debit	**Credit**
Cash	$ 2,330	
Accounts receivable	0	
Furniture	600	
Store equipment	16,200	
Note payable		$ 800
Common stock		18,000
Dividends	900	
Haircutting services revenue		1,855
Wages expense	125	
Rent expense	500	
Totals	$20,655	$20,655

4.

EXPRESSIONS Income Statement For Month Ended August 31		
Revenues		
Haircutting services revenue		$1,855
Operating expenses		
Rent expense	$500	
Wages expense	125	
Total operating expenses		625
Net income		$1,230

5.

EXPRESSIONS Statement of Retained Earnings For Month Ended August 31	
Retained earnings, August 1	$ 0
Plus: Net income	1,230
	1,230
Less: Cash dividends	900
Retained earnings, August 31	$ 330

6.

EXPRESSIONS Balance Sheet August 31			
Assets		**Liabilities**	
Cash	$ 2,330	Note payable	$ 800
Furniture	600	**Equity**	
Store equipment	16,200	Common stock	18,000
		Retained earnings	330
		Total equity	18,330
Total assets	$19,130	Total liabilities and equity	$19,130

7. Debt ratio $= \dfrac{\text{Total liabilities}}{\text{Total assets}} = \dfrac{\$800}{\$19,130} = \underline{\underline{\textbf{4.18\%}}}$

8a. Supplies *debited*   **8c.** Cash *debited*
       Cash *credited*   Unearned Services Revenue *credited*

8b. Prepaid Insurance *debited*   **8d.** Supplies *debited*
       Cash *credited*   Accounts Payable *credited*

Summary

C1 **Explain the steps in processing transactions.** The accounting process identifies business transactions and events, analyzes and records their effects, and summarizes and prepares information useful in making decisions. Transactions and events are the starting points in the accounting process. Source documents help in their analysis. The effects of transactions and events are recorded in journals. Posting along with a trial balance helps summarize and classify these effects.

C2 **Describe source documents and their purpose.** Source documents identify and describe transactions and events. Examples are sales tickets, checks, purchase orders, bills, and bank statements. Source documents provide objective and reliable evidence, making information more useful.

C3 **Describe an account and its use in recording transactions.** An account is a detailed record of increases and decreases in a specific asset, liability, equity, revenue, or expense. Information from accounts is analyzed, summarized, and presented in reports and financial statements for decision makers.

C4 **Describe a ledger and a chart of accounts.** The ledger (or general ledger) is a record containing all accounts used by a company and their balances. It is referred to as the *books*. The chart of accounts is a list of all accounts and usually includes an identification number assigned to each account.

C5 **Define *debits* and *credits* and explain double-entry accounting.** *Debit* refers to left, and *credit* refers to right. Debits increase assets, expenses, and dividends while credits decrease them. Credits increase liabilities, common stock, and revenues; debits decrease them. Double-entry accounting means each transaction affects at least two accounts and has at least one debit and one credit. The system for recording debits and credits follows from the accounting equation. The left side of an account is the normal balance for assets, dividends, and expenses, and the right side is the normal balance for liabilities, common stock, and revenues.

A1 **Analyze the impact of transactions on accounts and financial statements.** We analyze transactions using concepts of double-entry accounting. This analysis is performed by determining a transaction's effects on accounts. These effects are recorded in journals and posted to ledgers.

A2 **Compute the debt ratio and describe its use in analyzing financial condition.** A company's debt ratio is computed as total liabilities divided by total assets. It reveals how much of the assets are financed by creditor (nonowner) financing. The higher this ratio, the more risk a company faces because liabilities must be repaid at specific dates.

P1 **Record transactions in a journal and post entries to a ledger.** Transactions are recorded in a journal. Each entry in a journal is posted to the accounts in the ledger. This provides information that is used to produce financial statements. Balance column accounts are widely used and include columns for debits, credits, and the account balance.

P2 **Prepare and explain the use of a trial balance.** A trial balance is a list of accounts from the ledger showing their debit or credit balances in separate columns. The trial balance is a summary of the ledger's contents and is useful in preparing financial statements and in revealing recordkeeping errors.

P3 **Prepare financial statements from business transactions.** The balance sheet, the statement of retained earnings, the income statement, and the statement of cash flows use data from the trial balance (and other financial statements) for their preparation.

Guidance Answers to **Decision Maker** and **Decision Ethics**

Cashier The advantages to the process proposed by the assistant manager include improved customer service, fewer delays, and less work for you. However, you should have serious concerns about internal control and the potential for fraud. In particular, the assistant manager could steal cash and simply enter fewer sales to match the remaining cash. You should reject her suggestion without the manager's approval. Moreover, you should have an ethical concern about the assistant manager's suggestion to ignore store policy.

Entrepreneur We can use the accounting equation (Assets = Liabilities + Equity) to help us identify risky customers to whom we would likely not want to extend credit. A balance sheet provides amounts for each of these key components. The lower a customer's equity is relative to liabilities, the less likely you would extend credit. A low equity means the business has little value that does not already have creditor claims to it.

Investor The debt ratio suggests the stock of Converse is of higher risk than normal and that this risk is rising. The average industry ratio of 0.40 further supports this conclusion. The 2008 debt ratio for Converse is twice the industry norm. Also, a debt ratio approaching 1.0 indicates little to no equity.

Guidance Answers to **Quick Checks**

1. Examples of source documents are sales tickets, checks, purchase orders, charges to customers, bills from suppliers, employee earnings records, and bank statements.

2. Source documents serve many purposes, including record-keeping and internal control. Source documents, especially if obtained from outside the organization, provide objective and reliable evidence about transactions and their amounts.

3.

Assets	Liabilities	Equity
a,c,e	b,d	—

4. An account is a record in an accounting system that records and stores the increases and decreases in a specific asset, liability, equity, revenue, or expense. The ledger is a collection of all the accounts of a company.

5. A company's size and diversity affect the number of accounts in its accounting system. The types of accounts depend on information the company needs to both effectively operate and report its activities in financial statements.

6. No. Debit and credit both can mean increase or decrease. The particular meaning in a circumstance depends on the *type of account*. For example, a debit increases the balance of asset, dividends, and expense accounts, but it decreases the balance of liability, common stock, and revenue accounts.

7. A chart of accounts is a list of all of a company's accounts and their identification numbers.

8. Equity is increased by revenues and by owner investments. Equity is decreased by expenses and dividends.

9. The name *double entry* is used because all transactions affect at least two accounts. There must be at least one debit in one account and at least one credit in another account.

10. Answer is (*c*).

11.

Cash	15,000	
Equipment	23,000	
Common Stock		38,000

Investment by owner of cash and equipment.

12. A compound journal entry affects three or more accounts.

13. Posting reference numbers are entered in the journal when posting to the ledger as a cross-reference that allows the record-keeper or auditor to trace debits and credits from one record to another.

14. At a minimum, dollar signs are placed beside the first and last numbers in a column. It is also common to place dollar signs beside any amount that appears after a ruled line to indicate that an addition or subtraction has occurred.

15. The Equipment account balance is incorrectly reported at $20,000—it should be $28,000. The effect of this error understates the trial balance's Debit column total by $8,000. This results in an $8,000 difference between the column totals.

16. An income statement reports a company's revenues and expenses along with the resulting net income or loss. A statement of retained earnings reports changes in retained earnings, including that from net income or loss. Both statements report transactions occurring over a period of time.

17. The balance sheet describes a company's financial position (assets, liabilities, and equity) at a point in time. The retained earnings amount in the balance sheet is obtained from the statement of retained earnings.

18. Revenues are inflows of assets in exchange for products or services provided to customers as part of the main operations of a business. Expenses are outflows or the using up of assets that result from providing products or services to customers.

19. Assets are the resources a business owns or controls that carry expected future benefits. Liabilities are the obligations of a business, representing the claims of others against the assets of a business. Equity reflects the owner's claims on the assets of the business after deducting liabilities.

Key Terms

Account (p. 51)	**Debit** (p. 55)	**Journalizing** (p. 56)
Account balance (p. 55)	**Debt ratio** (p. 70)	**Ledger** (p. 51)
Balance column account (p. 58)	**Debtors** (p. 51)	**Posting** (p. 56)
Chart of accounts (p. 54)	**Dividends** (p. 53)	**Posting reference (PR) column** (p. 58)
Common stock (p. 53)	**Double-entry accounting** (p. 55)	**Source documents** (p. 50)
Compound journal entry (p. 61)	**General journal** (p. 57)	**T-account** (p. 55)
Credit (p. 55)	**General ledger** (p. 51)	**Trial balance** (p. 65)
Creditors (p. 52)	**Journal** (p. 56)	**Unearned revenue** (p. 53)

Multiple Choice Quiz   Answers on p. 91   mhhe.com/wildFA5e

Additional Quiz Questions are available at the book's Website.

1. Amalia Company received its utility bill for the current period of $700 and immediately paid it. Its journal entry to record this transaction includes a
  a. Credit to Utility Expense for $700.
  b. Debit to Utility Expense for $700.
  c. Debit to Accounts Payable for $700.
  d. Debit to Cash for $700.
  e. Credit to Common Stock for $700.

2. On May 1, Mattingly Lawn Service collected $2,500 cash from a customer in advance of five months of lawn service. Mattingly's journal entry to record this transaction includes a
  a. Credit to Unearned Lawn Service Fees for $2,500.
  b. Debit to Lawn Service Fees Earned for $2,500.
  c. Credit to Cash for $2,500.
  d. Debit to Unearned Lawn Service Fees for $2,500.
  e. Credit to Common Stock for $2,500.

3. Liang Shue contributed $250,000 cash and land worth $500,000 in exchange for common stock to open his new business, Shue Consulting. Which of the following journal entries does Shue Consulting make to record this transaction?

  a. Cash Assets 750,000
       Common Stock   750,000
  b. Common Stock 750,000
       Assets   750,000
  c. Cash 250,000
     Land 500,000
       Common Stock   750,000

  d. Common Stock 750,000
     Cash   250,000
     Land   500,000

4. A trial balance prepared at year-end shows total credits exceed total debits by $765. This discrepancy could have been caused by
  a. An error in the general journal where a $765 increase in Accounts Payable was recorded as a $765 decrease in Accounts Payable.
  b. The ledger balance for Accounts Payable of $7,650 being entered in the trial balance as $765.
  c. A general journal error where a $765 increase in Accounts Receivable was recorded as a $765 increase in Cash.
  d. The ledger balance of $850 in Accounts Receivable was entered in the trial balance as $85.
  e. An error in recording a $765 increase in Cash as a credit.

5. Bonaventure Company has total assets of $1,000,000, liabilities of $400,000, and equity of $600,000. What is its debt ratio (rounded to a whole percent)?
  a. 250%
  b. 167%
  c. 67%
  d. 150%
  e. 40%

Discussion Questions

1. Provide the names of two (*a*) asset accounts, (*b*) liability accounts, and (*c*) equity accounts.

2. What is the difference between a note payable and an account payable?

3. ♟ Discuss the steps in processing business transactions.

4. What kinds of transactions can be recorded in a general journal?

5. Are debits or credits typically listed first in general journal entries? Are the debits or the credits indented?

6. If assets are valuable resources and asset accounts have debit balances, why do expense accounts also have debit balances?

7. Should a transaction be recorded first in a journal or the ledger? Why?

8. ♟ Why does the recordkeeper prepare a trial balance?

9. If an incorrect amount is journalized and posted to the accounts, how should the error be corrected?

10. Identify the four financial statements of a business.

11. ♟ What information is reported in an income statement?

12. ♟ Why does the user of an income statement need to know the time period that it covers?

13. ♟ What information is reported in a balance sheet?

14. Define (*a*) *assets*, (*b*) *liabilities*, (*c*) *equity*, and (*d*) *net assets*.

15. Which financial statement is sometimes called the *statement of financial position*?

16. ♟ Review the **Best Buy** balance sheet in Appendix A. Identify three accounts on its balance sheet that carry debit balances and three accounts on its balance sheet that carry credit balances. **BEST BUY**

17. Review the **RadioShack** balance sheet in Appendix A. Identify an asset with the word *receivable* in its account title and a liability with the word *payable* in its account title.

18. Locate **Apple**'s income statement in Appendix A. What is the title of its revenue account?

19. Refer to **GOME**'s balance sheet in Appendix A. What does GOME title its current asset referring to merchandise available for sale?

♟ *Denotes Discussion Questions that involve decision making.*

connect™   Available with Connect Accounting

Identify the items from the following list that are likely to serve as source documents.

a. Trial balance   **d.** Income statement   **g.** Prepaid insurance
b. Telephone bill   **e.** Company revenue account   **h.** Bank statement
c. Sales ticket   **f.** Invoice from supplier   **i.** Balance sheet

QUICK STUDY

QS 2-1
Identifying source documents   C2

Identify the financial statement(s) where each of the following items appears. Use I for income statement, E for statement of retained earnings, and B for balance sheet.

a. Service fees earned   **d.** Accounts payable   **g.** Office supplies
b. Cash dividends   **e.** Cash   **h.** Prepaid rent
c. Office equipment   **f.** Utilities expenses **i.** Unearned fees

QS 2-2
Identifying financial
statement items

C3   P3

Identify the normal balance (debit or credit) for each of the following accounts.

a. Office supplies   **d.** Wages Expense   **g.** Wages Payable
b. Dividends   **e.** Cash   **h.** Building
c. Fees Earned   **f.** Prepaid Insurance **i.** Common Stock

QS 2-3
Identifying normal balance

C5

Indicate whether a debit or credit *decreases* the normal balance of each of the following accounts.

a. Repair Services Revenue   **e.** Common Stock   **i.** Dividends
b. Interest Payable   **f.** Prepaid Insurance **j.** Unearned Revenue
c. Accounts Receivable   **g.** Buildings   **k.** Accounts Payable
d. Salaries Expense   **h.** Interest Revenue   **l.** Office Supplies

QS 2-4
Linking debit or credit with
normal balance

C5

Identify whether a debit or credit yields the indicated change for each of the following accounts.

a. To increase Land   **f.** To decrease Prepaid Insurance
b. To decrease Cash   **g.** To increase Notes Payable
c. To increase Utilities Expense **h.** To decrease Accounts Receivable
d. To increase Fees Earned   **i.** To increase Common Stock
e. To decrease Unearned Revenue **j.** To increase Store Equipment

QS 2-5
Analyzing debit or credit
by account

C5   A1 ♟

Prepare journal entries for each of the following selected transactions.

a. On January 13, DeShawn Tyler opens a landscaping company called Elegant Lawns by investing $80,000 cash along with equipment having a $30,000 value in exchange for common stock.
b. On January 21, Elegant Lawns purchases office supplies on credit for $820.
c. On January 29, Elegant Lawns receives $8,700 cash for performing landscaping services.
d. On January 30, Elegant Lawns receives $4,000 cash in advance of providing landscaping services to a customer.

QS 2-6
Preparing journal entries

P1

A trial balance has total debits of $20,000 and total credits of $24,500. Which one of the following errors would create this imbalance? Explain.

a. A $2,250 credit to Consulting Fees Earned in a journal entry is incorrectly posted to the ledger as a $2,250 debit, leaving the Consulting Fees Earned account with a $6,300 credit balance.
b. A $4,500 debit to Salaries Expense in a journal entry is incorrectly posted to the ledger as a $4,500 credit, leaving the Salaries Expense account with a $750 debit balance.
c. A $2,250 debit to Rent Expense in a journal entry is incorrectly posted to the ledger as a $2,250 credit, leaving the Rent Expense account with a $3,000 debit balance.
d. A $2,250 debit posting to Accounts Receivable was posted mistakenly to Cash.
e. A $4,500 debit posting to Equipment was posted mistakenly to Supplies.
f. An entry debiting Cash and crediting Notes Payable for $4,500 was mistakenly not posted.

QS 2-7
Identifying a posting error

P2 ♟

Indicate the financial statement on which each of the following items appears. Use I for income statement, E for statement of retained earnings, and B for balance sheet.

a. Rental Revenue   **e.** Accounts Receivable **i.** Buildings
b. Insurance Expense   **f.** Salaries Expense   **j.** Interest Revenue
c. Services Revenue   **g.** Equipment   **k.** Dividends
d. Interest Payable   **h.** Prepaid Insurance   **l.** Office Supplies

QS 2-8
Classifying accounts in
financial statements

P3

QS 2-9
International accounting standards

C5

Answer each of the following questions related to international accounting standards.

a. What type of entry system is applied when accounting follows IFRS?

b. Identify the number and usual titles of the financial statements prepared under IFRS.

c. How do differences in accounting controls and enforcement impact accounting reports prepared across different countries?

Available with Connect Accounting CONNECT

EXERCISES

Exercise 2-1
Identifying type and normal balances of accounts

C3 C5

For each of the following (1) identify the type of account as an asset, liability, equity, revenue, or expense, (2) enter *debit* (*Dr.*) or *credit* (*Cr.*) to identify the kind of entry that would increase the account balance, and (3) identify the normal balance of the account.

a. Common Stock
b. Accounts Receivable
c. Dividends
d. Cash

e. Equipment
f. Fees Earned
g. Wages Expense
h. Unearned Revenue

i. Accounts Payable
j. Postage Expense
k. Prepaid Insurance
l. Land

Exercise 2-2
Analyzing account entries and balances

A1

Use the information in each of the following separate cases to calculate the unknown amount.

a. During October, Alcorn Company had $104,750 of cash receipts and $101,607 of cash disbursements. The October 31 Cash balance was $17,069. Determine how much cash the company had at the close of business on September 30.

b. On September 30, Mordish Co. had a $83,250 balance in Accounts Receivable. During October, the company collected $75,924 from its credit customers. The October 31 balance in Accounts Receivable was $85,830. Determine the amount of sales on account that occurred in October.

c. Strong Co. had $148,000 of accounts payable on September 30 and $137,492 on October 31. Total purchases on account during October were $271,876. Determine how much cash was paid on accounts payable during October.

Exercise 2-3
Analyzing effects of transactions on accounts

A1

Nology Co. bills a client $65,000 for services provided and agrees to accept the following three items in full payment: (1) $12,000 cash, (2) computer equipment worth $90,000, and (3) to assume responsibility for a $37,000 note payable related to the computer equipment. The entry Nology makes to record this transaction includes which one or more of the following?

a. $37,000 increase in a liability account
b. $12,000 increase in the Cash account
c. $12,000 increase in a revenue account

d. $65,000 increase in an asset account
e. $65,000 increase in a revenue account
f. $37,000 increase in an equity account

Exercise 2-4
Preparing general journal entries

A1 P1

Prepare general journal entries for the following transactions of a new company called Special Pics.

Aug. 1   Madison Harris, the owner, invested $14,250 cash and $61,275 of photography equipment in the company in exchange for its common stock.
      2   The company paid $3,300 cash for an insurance policy covering the next 24 months.
      5   The company purchased office supplies for $2,707 cash.
      20 The company received $3,250 cash in photography fees earned.
      31 The company paid $871 cash for August utilities.

Exercise 2-5
Preparing T-accounts (ledger) and a trial balance

C3 P2

Use the information in Exercise 2-4 to prepare an August 31 trial balance for Special Pics. Begin by opening these T-accounts: Cash; Office Supplies; Prepaid Insurance; Photography Equipment; Common Stock; Photography Fees Earned; and Utilities Expense. Then, post the general journal entries to these T-accounts (which will serve as the ledger), and prepare the trial balance.

Exercise 2-6
Recording effects of transactions in T-accounts

C5 A1

Record the transactions below for Amena Company by recording the debit and credit entries directly in the following T-accounts: Cash; Accounts Receivable; Office Supplies; Office Equipment; Accounts Payable; Common Stock; Dividends; Fees Earned; and Rent Expense. Use the letters beside each transaction to identify entries. Determine the ending balance of each T-account.

a. Sergey Amena, owner, invested $14,000 cash in the company in exchange for its common stock.

b. The company purchased office supplies for $406 cash.

c. The company purchased $7,742 of office equipment on credit.

d. The company received $1,652 cash as fees for services provided to a customer.

e. The company paid $7,742 cash to settle the payable for the office equipment purchased in transaction *c*.

f. The company billed a customer $2,968 as fees for services provided.

g. The company paid $510 cash for the monthly rent.

h. The company collected $1,246 cash as partial payment for the account receivable created in transaction *f*.

i. The company paid $1,200 cash for dividends.

Check Cash ending balance, $7,040

After recording the transactions of Exercise 2-6 in T-accounts and calculating the balance of each account, prepare a trial balance. Use May 31, 2011, as its report date.

Exercise 2-7
Preparing a trial balance   P2

Examine the following transactions and identify those that create expenses for Thomas Services. Prepare general journal entries to record those expense transactions and explain why the other transactions did not create expenses.

a. The company paid $12,200 cash for office supplies that were purchased more than 1 year ago.

b. The company paid $1,233 cash for the just completed two-week salary of the receptionist.

c. The company paid $39,200 cash for equipment purchased.

d. The company paid $870 cash for this month's utilities.

e. The company paid $4,500 cash for dividends.

Exercise 2-8
Analyzing and journalizing expense transactions

A1 P1

Examine the following transactions and identify those that create revenues for Thomas Services, a company owned by Brina Thomas. Prepare general journal entries to record those revenue transactions and explain why the other transactions did not create revenues.

a. Brina Thomas invests $39,350 cash in the company in exchange for its common stock.

b. The company provided $2,300 of services on credit.

c. The company provided services to a client and immediately received $875 cash.

d. The company received $10,200 cash from a client in payment for services to be provided next year.

e. The company received $3,500 cash from a client in partial payment of an account receivable.

f. The company borrowed $120,000 cash from the bank by signing a promissory note.

Exercise 2-9
Analyzing and journalizing revenue transactions

A1 P1

On October 1, Diondre Shabazz organized a new consulting firm called Tech Talk. On October 31, the company's records show the following accounts and amounts. Use this information to prepare an October income statement for the business.

Cash	$ 12,614	Dividends	$ 2,000
Accounts receivable	25,648	Consulting fees earned	25,620
Office supplies	4,903	Rent expense	6,859
Land	69,388	Salaries expense	12,405
Office equipment	27,147	Telephone expense	560
Accounts payable	12,070	Miscellaneous expenses	280
Common stock	124,114		

Exercise 2-10
Preparing an income statement

C4 P3

Check Net income, $5,516

Use the information in Exercise 2-10 to prepare an October statement of retained earnings for Tech Talk.

Exercise 2-11
Preparing a statement of retained earnings   P3

Check End. ret. earnings, $3,516

Use the information in Exercise 2-10 (if completed, you can also use your solution to Exercise 2-11) to prepare an October 31 balance sheet for Tech Talk.

Exercise 2-12
Preparing a balance sheet   P3

Exercise 2-13
Computing net income
A1 P3

A corporation had the following assets and liabilities at the beginning and end of a recent year.

	Assets	Liabilities
Beginning of the year	$131,000	$56,159
End of the year	180,000	72,900

Determine the net income earned or net loss incurred by the business during the year for each of the following *separate* cases:

a. Owner made no investments in the business and no dividends were paid during the year.

b. Owner made no investments in the business but dividends were $650 cash per month.

c. No dividends were paid during the year but the owner invested an additional $45,000 cash in exchange for common stock.

d. Dividends were $650 cash per month and the owner invested an additional $25,000 cash in exchange for common stock.

Exercise 2-14
Analyzing changes in a
company's equity
C5 P3

Compute the missing amount in each of the following separate companies *a* through *d*.

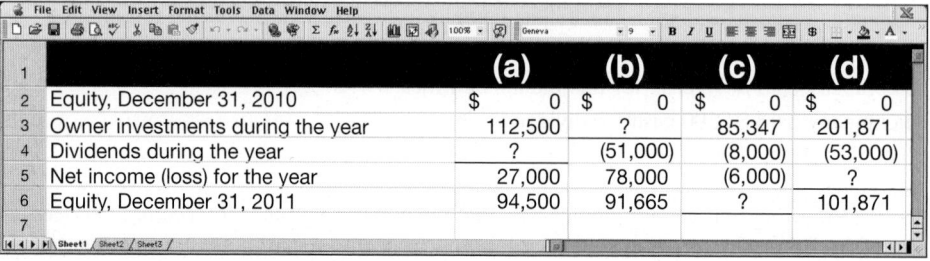

	(a)	(b)	(c)	(d)
2 Equity, December 31, 2010	$ 0	$ 0	$ 0	$ 0
3 Owner investments during the year	112,500	?	85,347	201,871
4 Dividends during the year	?	(51,000)	(8,000)	(53,000)
5 Net income (loss) for the year	27,000	78,000	(6,000)	?
6 Equity, December 31, 2011	94,500	91,665	?	101,871

Exercise 2-15
Interpreting and describing
transactions from T-accounts
C1 A1

Assume the following T-accounts reflect Belle Co.'s general ledger and that seven transactions *a* through *g* are posted to them. Provide a short description of each transaction. Include the amounts in your descriptions.

Cash			
(a)	12,000	(b)	4,800
(e)	9,000	(c)	2,000
		(f)	4,600
		(g)	820

Office Supplies	
(c)	2,000
(d)	300

Prepaid Insurance	
(b)	4,800

Equipment	
(a)	15,200
(d)	9,700

Automobiles	
(a)	24,000

Accounts Payable			
(f)	4,600	(d)	10,000

Common Stock			
		(a)	51,200

Delivery Services Revenue			
		(e)	9,000

Gas and Oil Expense	
(g)	820

Exercise 2-16
Preparing general
journal entries A1 P1

Use information from the T-accounts in Exercise 2-15 to prepare general journal entries for each of the seven transactions *a* through *g*.

Exercise 2-17
Identifying effects of
posting errors on the
trial balance A1 P2

Several posting errors are identified in the following table. In column (1), enter the amount of the difference between the two trial balance columns (debit and credit) due to the error. In column (2), identify the trial balance column (debit or credit) with the larger amount if they are not equal. In column (3), identify the account(s) affected by the error. In column (4), indicate the amount by which the account(s) in column (3) is under- or overstated. Item (a) is completed as an example.

Description of Posting Error	(1) Difference between Debit and Credit Columns	(2) Column with the Larger Total	(3) Identify Account(s) Incorrectly Stated	(4) Amount that Account(s) is Over- or Understated
a.	$1,870 debit to Rent Expense is posted as a $1,780 debit.	$90	Credit	Rent Expense	Rent Expense understated $90
b.	$3,560 credit to Cash is posted twice as two credits to Cash.				
c.	$7,120 debit to the Dividends account is debited to Common Stock.				
d.	$1,630 debit to Prepaid Insurance is posted as a debit to Insurance Expense.				
e.	$31,150 debit to Machinery is posted as a debit to Accounts Payable.				
f.	$4,460 credit to Services Revenue is posted as a $446 credit.				
g.	$820 debit to Store Supplies is not posted.				

You are told the column totals in a trial balance are not equal. After careful analysis, you discover only one error. Specifically, a correctly journalized credit purchase of a computer for $11,250 is posted from the journal to the ledger with a $11,250 debit to Office Equipment and another $11,250 debit to Accounts Payable. The Office Equipment account has a debit balance of $26,663 on the trial balance. Answer each of the following questions and compute the dollar amount of any misstatement.

Exercise 2-18
Analyzing a trial balance error

A1 P2

a. Is the debit column total of the trial balance overstated, understated, or correctly stated?

b. Is the credit column total of the trial balance overstated, understated, or correctly stated?

c. Is the Office Equipment account balance overstated, understated, or correctly stated in the trial balance?

d. Is the Accounts Payable account balance overstated, understated, or correctly stated in the trial balance?

e. If the debit column total of the trial balance is $236,250 before correcting the error, what is the total of the credit column before correction?

a. Calculate the debt ratio and the return on assets using the year-end information for each of the following six separate companies ($ thousands).

Exercise 2-19
Interpreting the debt ratio and return on assets

A2

Case	Assets	Liabilities	Average Assets	Net Income
Company 1	$ 147,000	$ 56,000	$ 200,000	$ 21,000
Company 2	104,500	51,500	70,000	12,000
Company 3	90,500	12,000	100,000	20,000
Company 4	92,000	31,000	40,000	7,500
Company 5	64,000	47,000	40,000	3,800
Company 6	32,500	26,500	50,000	660

b. Of the six companies, which business relies most heavily on creditor financing?

c. Of the six companies, which business relies most heavily on equity financing?

d. Which two companies indicate the greatest risk?

e. Which two companies earn the highest return on assets?

f. Which one company would investors likely prefer based on the risk–return relation?

Exercise 2-20
Preparing a balance sheet following IFRS

P3

BMW reports the following balance sheet accounts for the year ended December 31, 2008 (euro in millions.) Prepare the balance sheet for this company as of December 31, 2008, following the usual IFRS formats.

Current liabilities	€ 7,998	Noncurrent liabilities	€9,980
Current assets	16,673	Noncurrent assets	6,643
Total equity	5,338		

Available with Connect Accounting **connect**™

PROBLEM SET A

Problem 2-1A
Preparing and posting journal entries; preparing a trial balance

C4 C5 A1 P1 P2

Lancet Engineering completed the following transactions in the month of June.

a. Jenna Lancet, the owner, invested $195,000 cash, office equipment with a value of $8,200, and $80,000 of drafting equipment to launch the company in exchange for its common stock.

b. The company purchased land worth $52,000 for an office by paying $8,900 cash and signing a long-term note payable for $43,100.

c. The company purchased a portable building with $55,000 cash and moved it onto the land acquired in *b*.

d. The company paid $2,300 cash for the premium on an 18-month insurance policy.

e. The company completed and delivered a set of plans for a client and collected $6,600 cash.

f. The company purchased $24,000 of additional drafting equipment by paying $9,600 cash and signing a long-term note payable for $14,400.

g. The company completed $14,500 of engineering services for a client. This amount is to be received in 30 days.

h. The company purchased $1,100 of additional office equipment on credit.

i. The company completed engineering services for $23,000 on credit.

j. The company received a bill for rent of equipment that was used on a recently completed job. The $1,410 rent cost must be paid within 30 days.

k. The company collected $8,000 cash in partial payment from the client described in transaction *g*.

l. The company paid $2,500 cash for wages to a drafting assistant.

m. The company paid $1,100 cash to settle the account payable created in transaction *h*.

n. The company paid $970 cash for minor maintenance of its drafting equipment.

o. The company paid $10,450 cash for dividends.

p. The company paid $2,000 cash for wages to a drafting assistant.

q. The company paid $2,400 cash for advertisements in the local newspaper during June.

Required

1. Prepare general journal entries to record these transactions (use the account titles listed in part 2).

Check (2) Ending balances: Cash, $114,380; Accounts Receivable, $29,500; Accounts Payable, $1,410

2. Open the following ledger accounts—their account numbers are in parentheses (use the balance column format): Cash (101); Accounts Receivable (106); Prepaid Insurance (108); Office Equipment (163); Drafting Equipment (164); Building (170); Land (172); Accounts Payable (201); Notes Payable (250); Common Stock (307); Dividends (319); Engineering Fees Earned (402); Wages Expense (601); Equipment Rental Expense (602); Advertising Expense (603); and Repairs Expense (604). Post the journal entries from part 1 to the accounts and enter the balance after each posting—in the date column enter instead the reference to which transaction from (*a*) through (*q*).

(3) Trial balance totals, $386,210

3. Prepare a trial balance as of the end of June.

Problem 2-2A
Preparing and posting journal entries; preparing a trial balance

C4 C5 A1 P1 P2

mhhe.com/wildFA5e

Denzel Brooks opens a Web consulting business called Venture Consultants and completes the following transactions in March.

March 1 Brooks invested $180,000 cash along with $30,000 of office equipment in the company in exchange for its common stock.

2 The company prepaid $8,000 cash for six months' rent for an office. (*Hint:* Debit Prepaid Rent for $8,000.)

3 The company made credit purchases of office equipment for $3,300 and office supplies for $1,400. Payment is due within 10 days.

6 The company completed services for a client and immediately received $6,000 cash.

9 The company completed a $9,200 project for a client, who must pay within 30 days.

12 The company paid $4,700 cash to settle the account payable created on March 3.

19   The company paid $7,500 cash for the premium on a 12-month insurance policy.
22   The company received $4,300 cash as partial payment for the work completed on March 9.
25   The company completed work for another client for $3,590 on credit.
29   The company paid $4,900 cash for dividends.
30   The company purchased $1,700 of additional office supplies on credit.
31   The company paid $500 cash for this month's utility bill.

Required

1. Prepare general journal entries to record these transactions (use the account titles listed in part 2).

2. Open the following ledger accounts—their account numbers are in parentheses (use the balance column format): Cash (101); Accounts Receivable (106); Office Supplies (124); Prepaid Insurance (128); Prepaid Rent (131); Office Equipment (163); Accounts Payable (201); Common Stock (307); Dividends (319); Services Revenue (403); and Utilities Expense (690). Post the journal entries from part 1 to the ledger accounts and enter the balance after each posting.

3. Prepare a trial balance as of the end of March.

Check (2) Ending balances: Cash, $164,700; Accounts Receivable, $8,490; Accounts Payable, $1,700

(3) Total debits, $230,490

Jayden Lanelle opens a computer consulting business called Viva Consultants and completes the following transactions in its first month of operations.

Problem 2-3A
Preparing and posting journal entries; preparing a trial balance

C4 C5 A1 P1 P2

April 1   Lanelle invests $95,000 cash along with office equipment valued at $22,800 in the company in exchange for its common stock.
     2   The company prepaid $7,200 cash for twelve months' rent for office space. (*Hint:* Debit Prepaid Rent for $7,200.)
     3   The company made credit purchases for $11,400 in office equipment and $2,280 in office supplies. Payment is due within 10 days.
     6   The company completed services for a client and immediately received $2,000 cash.
     9   The company completed a $7,600 project for a client, who must pay within 30 days.
    13   The company paid $13,680 cash to settle the account payable created on April 3.
    19   The company paid $6,000 cash for the premium on a 12-month insurance policy. (*Hint:* Debit Prepaid Insurance for $6,000.)
    22   The company received $6,080 cash as partial payment for the work completed on April 9.
    25   The company completed work for another client for $2,640 on credit.
    28   The company paid $6,200 cash for dividends.
    29   The company purchased $760 of additional office supplies on credit.
    30   The company paid $700 cash for this month's utility bill.

Required

1. Prepare general journal entries to record these transactions (use account titles listed in part 2).

2. Open the following ledger accounts—their account numbers are in parentheses (use the balance column format): Cash (101); Accounts Receivable (106); Office Supplies (124); Prepaid Insurance (128); Prepaid Rent (131); Office Equipment (163); Accounts Payable (201); Common Stock (307); Dividends (319); Services Revenue (403); and Utilities Expense (690). Post journal entries from part 1 to the ledger accounts and enter the balance after each posting.

3. Prepare a trial balance as of April 30.

Check (2) Ending balances: Cash, $69,300; Accounts Receivable, $4,160; Accounts Payable, $760

(3) Total debits, $130,800

The accounting records of Faviana Shipping show the following assets and liabilities as of December 31, 2010, and 2011.

Problem 2-4A
Computing net income from equity analysis, preparing a balance sheet, and computing the debt ratio

C3 A1 A2 P3

*e**X**cel*
mhhe.com/wildFA5e

December 31	2010	2011
Cash	$ 47,867	$ 8,154
Accounts receivable	25,983	20,370
Office supplies	4,098	3,002
Office equipment	125,816	134,018
Trucks	49,236	58,236
Building	0	164,124
Land	0	40,956
Accounts payable	68,310	33,879
Note payable	0	85,080

Late in December 2011, the business purchased a small office building and land for $205,080. It paid $120,000 cash toward the purchase and an $85,080 note payable was signed for the balance. Ms. Faviana had to invest $34,000 cash in the business (in exchange for stock) to enable it to pay the $120,000 cash. The business also pays $2,400 cash per month for dividends.

Required

1. Prepare balance sheets for the business as of December 31, 2010, and 2011. (*Hint:* Report only total equity on the balance sheet and remember that total equity equals the difference between assets and liabilities.)

Check (2) Net income, $120,011

2. By comparing equity amounts from the balance sheets and using the additional information presented in this problem, prepare a calculation to show how much net income was earned by the business during 2011.

(3) Debt ratio, 27.7%

3. Compute the 2011 year-end debt ratio for the business.

Problem 2-5A

Analyzing account balances and reconstructing transactions

C1 C4 A1 P2

Yi Min started an engineering firm called Min Engineering. He began operations and completed seven transactions in May, which included his initial investment of $18,000 cash. After those seven transactions, the ledger included the following accounts with normal balances.

Cash	$44,132
Office supplies	1,090
Prepaid insurance	4,700
Office equipment	11,200
Accounts payable	11,200
Common stock	18,000
Dividends	4,328
Engineering fees earned	44,000
Rent expense	7,750

Required

Check (1) Trial balance totals, $73,200

1. Prepare a trial balance for this business as of the end of May.

Analysis Components

2. Analyze the accounts and their balances and prepare a list that describes each of the seven most likely transactions and their amounts.

(3) Cash paid, $17,868

3. Prepare a report of cash received and cash paid showing how the seven transactions in part 2 yield the $44,132 ending Cash balance.

Problem 2-6A

Recording transactions; posting to ledger; preparing a trial balance

C4 A1 P1 P2

Business transactions completed by Alanna Emitt during the month of September are as follows.

a. Emitt invested $82,000 cash along with office equipment valued at $22,000 in exchange for common stock of a new company named AE Consulting.

b. The company purchased land valued at $40,000 and a building valued at $165,000. The purchase is paid with $25,000 cash and a long-term note payable for $180,000.

c. The company purchased $1,700 of office supplies on credit.

d. Emitt invested her personal automobile in the company in exchange for more common stock. The automobile has a value of $16,800 and is to be used exclusively in the business.

e. The company purchased $5,900 of additional office equipment on credit.

f. The company paid $1,500 cash salary to an assistant.

g. The company provided services to a client and collected $7,600 cash.

h. The company paid $630 cash for this month's utilities.

i. The company paid $1,700 cash to settle the account payable created in transaction *c.*

j. The company purchased $20,200 of new office equipment by paying $20,200 cash.

k. The company completed $6,750 of services for a client, who must pay within 30 days.

l. The company paid $2,000 cash salary to an assistant.

m. The company received $4,000 cash in partial payment on the receivable created in transaction *k.*

n. The company paid $2,900 cash for dividends.

Required

1. Prepare general journal entries to record these transactions (use account titles listed in part 2).
2. Open the following ledger accounts—their account numbers are in parentheses (use the balance column format): Cash (101); Accounts Receivable (106); Office Supplies (108); Office Equipment (163); Automobiles (164); Building (170); Land (172); Accounts Payable (201); Notes Payable (250); Common Stock (307); Dividends (319); Fees Earned (402); Salaries Expense (601); and Utilities Expense (602). Post the journal entries from part 1 to the ledger accounts and enter the balance after each posting—in the date column enter instead the reference to which transaction from (*a*) through (*n*).
3. Prepare a trial balance as of the end of September.

Check (2) Ending balances: Cash, $39,670; Office Equipment, $48,100

(3) Trial balance totals, $321,050

At the beginning of April, Vanessa Wende launched a custom computer solutions company called Softworks. The company had the following transactions during April.

a. Vanessa Wende invested $155,000 cash, office equipment with a value of $5,100, and $78,000 of computer equipment in the company in exchange for its common stock.

b. The company purchased land worth $55,000 for an office by paying $8,700 cash and signing a long-term note payable for $46,300.

c. The company purchased a portable building with $59,000 cash and moved it onto the land acquired in *b*.

d. The company paid $3,500 cash for the premium on a two-year insurance policy.

e. The company provided services to a client and immediately collected $7,000 cash.

f. The company purchased $26,000 of additional computer equipment by paying $11,800 cash and signing a long-term note payable for $14,200.

g. The company completed $16,500 of services for a client. This amount is to be received within 30 days.

h. The company purchased $1,800 of additional office equipment on credit.

i. The company completed client services for $28,000 on credit.

j. The company received a bill for rent of a computer testing device that was used on a recently completed job. The $1,685 rent cost must be paid within 30 days.

k. The company collected $10,000 cash in partial payment from the client described in transaction *i*.

l. The company paid $1,300 cash for wages to an assistant.

m. The company paid $1,800 cash to settle the payable created in transaction *h*.

n. The company paid $985 cash for minor maintenance of the company's computer equipment.

o. The company paid $10,230 cash for dividends.

p. The company paid $1,300 cash for wages to an assistant.

q. The company paid $4,300 cash for advertisements in the local newspaper during April.

PROBLEM SET B

Problem 2-1B
Preparing and posting journal entries; preparing a trial balance

C4 C5 A1 P1 P2

Required

1. Prepare general journal entries to record these transactions (use account titles listed in part 2).
2. Open the following ledger accounts—their account numbers are in parentheses (use the balance column format): Cash (101); Accounts Receivable (106); Prepaid Insurance (108); Office Equipment (163); Computer Equipment (164); Building (170); Land (172); Accounts Payable (201); Notes Payable (250); Common Stock (307); Dividends (319); Fees Earned (402); Wages Expense (601); Computer Rental Expense (602); Advertising Expense (603); and Repairs Expense (604). Post the journal entries from part 1 to the accounts and enter the balance after each posting—in the date column enter instead the reference to which transaction from (*a*) through (*q*).
3. Prepare a trial balance as of the end of April.

Check (2) Ending balances: Cash, $69,085; Accounts Receivable, $34,500; Accounts Payable, $1,685

(3) Trial balance totals, $351,785

Kylan Management Services opens for business and completes these transactions in November.

Nov. 1 Rollie Kylan, the owner, invested $190,000 cash along with $29,000 of office equipment in the company in exchange for its common stock.
2 The company prepaid $10,000 cash for six months' rent for an office. (*Hint:* Debit Prepaid Rent for $10,000.)
4 The company made credit purchases of office equipment for $4,300 and of office supplies for $2,100. Payment is due within 10 days.
8 The company completed work for a client and immediately received $7,000 cash.
12 The company completed a $9,200 project for a client, who must pay within 30 days.

Problem 2-2B
Preparing and posting journal entries; preparing a trial balance

C4 C5 A1 P1 P2

13   The company paid $6,400 cash to settle the payable created on November 4.
19   The company paid $4,100 cash for the premium on a 24-month insurance policy.
22   The company received $3,700 cash as partial payment for the work completed on November 12.
24   The company completed work for another client for $4,010 on credit.
28   The company paid $6,300 cash for dividends.
29   The company purchased $1,200 of additional office supplies on credit.
30   The company paid $1,100 cash for this month's utility bill.

Required

1. Prepare general journal entries to record these transactions (use account titles listed in part 2).

Check (2) Ending balances: Cash, $172,800; Accounts Receivable, $9,510; Accounts Payable, $1,200

2. Open the following ledger accounts—their account numbers are in parentheses (use the balance column format): Cash (101); Accounts Receivable (106); Office Supplies (124); Prepaid Insurance (128); Prepaid Rent (131); Office Equipment (163); Accounts Payable (201); Common Stock (307); Dividends (319); Services Revenue (403); and Utilities Expense (690). Post the journal entries from part 1 to the ledger accounts and enter the balance after each posting.

(3) Total debits, $240,410

3. Prepare a trial balance as of the end of November.

Problem 2-3B
Preparing and posting journal entries; preparing a trial balance

C4 C5 A1 P1 P2

Hassan Management Services opens for business and completes these transactions in September.

Sept. 1   Jamal Hassan, the owner, invests $130,000 cash along with office equipment valued at $31,200 in the company in exchange for its common stock.
        2   The company prepaid $7,200 cash for twelve months' rent for office space. (*Hint:* Debit Prepaid Rent for $7,200.)
        4   The company made credit purchases for $15,600 in office equipment and $3,120 in office supplies. Payment is due within 10 days.
        8   The company completed work for a client and immediately received $2,000 cash.
       12   The company completed a $10,400 project for a client, who must pay within 30 days.
       13   The company paid $18,720 cash to settle the payable created on September 4.
       19   The company paid $6,000 cash for the premium on an 18-month insurance policy. (*Hint:* Debit Prepaid Insurance for $6,000.)
       22   The company received $8,320 cash as partial payment for the work completed on September 12.
       24   The company completed work for another client for $2,640 on credit.
       28   The company paid $6,200 cash for dividends.
       29   The company purchased $1,040 of additional office supplies on credit.
       30   The company paid $700 cash for this month's utility bill.

Required

1. Prepare general journal entries to record these transactions (use account titles listed in part 2).

Check (2) Ending balances: Cash, $101,500; Accounts Receivable, $4,720; Accounts Payable, $1,040

2. Open the following ledger accounts—their account numbers are in parentheses (use the balance column format): Cash (101); Accounts Receivable (106); Office Supplies (124); Prepaid Insurance (128); Prepaid Rent (131); Office Equipment (163); Accounts Payable (201); Common Stock (307); Dividends (319); Service Fees Earned (401); and Utilities Expense (690). Post journal entries from part 1 to the ledger accounts and enter the balance after each posting.

(3) Total debits, $177,280

3. Prepare a trial balance as of the end of September.

Problem 2-4B
Computing net income from equity analysis, preparing a balance sheet, and computing the debt ratio

C3 A1 A2 P3

The accounting records of Trinity Co. show the following assets and liabilities as of December 31, 2010, and 2011.

December 31	2010	2011
Cash	$ 54,773	$ 10,629
Accounts receivable	29,731	23,309
Office supplies	4,689	3,435
Office equipment	$143,968	153,353
Machinery	56,339	65,339
Building	0	187,802
Land	0	46,864
Accounts payable	78,165	38,767
Note payable	0	114,666

Late in December 2011, the business purchased a small office building and land for $234,666. It paid $120,000 cash toward the purchase and a $114,666 note payable was signed for the balance. Ms. Trinity, the owner, had to invest an additional $35,000 cash (in exchange for stock) to enable it to pay the $120,000 cash toward the purchase. The business also pays $4,000 cash per month in dividends.

Required

1. Prepare balance sheets for the business as of December 31, 2010, and 2011. (*Hint:* Report only to- tal equity on the balance sheet and remember that total equity equals the difference between assets and liabilities.)

2. By comparing equity amounts from the balance sheets and using the additional information presented in the problem, prepare a calculation to show how much net income was earned by the business dur- ing 2011.

Check   (2) Net income, $138,963

3. Calculate the December 31, 2011, debt ratio for the business.

(3) Debt ratio, 31.3%

Roshaun Gould started a Web consulting firm called Gould Solutions. He began operations and completed seven transactions in April that resulted in the following accounts, which all have normal balances.

Problem 2-5B
Analyzing account balances and reconstructing transactions

C1 C4 A1 P2

Cash	$46,518
Office supplies	850
Prepaid rent	4,700
Office equipment	11,300
Accounts payable	11,300
Common stock	22,500
Dividends	4,172
Consulting fees earned	43,000
Operating expenses	9,260

Required

1. Prepare a trial balance for this business as of the end of April.

Check   (1) Trial balance total, $76,800

Analysis Component

2. Analyze the accounts and their balances and prepare a list that describes each of the seven most likely transactions and their amounts.

3. Prepare a report of cash received and cash paid showing how the seven transactions in part 2 yield the $46,518 ending Cash balance.

(3) Cash paid, $18,982

Witter Consulting completed the following transactions during June.

a. D. Witter, the owner, invested $82,000 cash along with office equipment valued at $23,000 in the new company in exchange for common stock.

b. The company purchased land valued at $50,000 and a building valued at $165,000. The purchase is paid with $30,000 cash and a long-term note payable for $185,000.

c. The company purchased $2,200 of office supplies on credit.

d. D. Witter invested his personal automobile in the business in exchange for more common stock. The automobile has a value of $16,800 and is to be used exclusively in the business.

e. The company purchased $5,100 of additional office equipment on credit.

f. The company paid $1,500 cash salary to an assistant.

g. The company provided services to a client and collected $8,000 cash.

h. The company paid $630 cash for this month's utilities.

i. The company paid $2,200 cash to settle the payable created in transaction *c*.

j. The company purchased $20,400 of new office equipment by paying $20,400 cash.

k. The company completed $6,500 of services for a client, who must pay within 30 days.

l. The company paid $2,000 cash salary to an assistant.

m. The company received $4,000 cash in partial payment on the receivable created in transaction *k*.

n. The company paid $2,700 cash for dividends.

Problem 2-6B
Recording transactions; posting to ledger; preparing a trial balance

C4 A1 P1 P2

Required

1. Prepare general journal entries to record these transactions (use account titles listed in part 2).

2. Open the following ledger accounts—their account numbers are in parentheses (use the balance column format): Cash (101); Accounts Receivable (106); Office Supplies (108); Office Equipment (163); Automobiles (164); Building (170); Land (172); Accounts Payable (201); Notes Payable (250); Common Stock (307); Dividends (319); Fees Earned (402); Salaries Expense (601); and Utilities Expense (602). Post the journal entries from part 1 to the ledger accounts and enter the balance after each posting—in the date column enter instead the reference to which transaction from (a) through (n).

3. Prepare a trial balance as of the end of June.

SERIAL PROBLEM

Success Systems

A1 P1 P2

(This serial problem started in Chapter 1 and continues through most of the chapters. If the Chapter 1 segment was not completed, the problem can begin at this point. It is helpful, but not necessary, to use the Working Papers that accompany this book.)

SP 2   On October 1, 2009, Adriana Lopez launched a computer services company called Success Systems, which provides consulting services, computer system installations, and custom program development. Lopez adopts the calendar year for reporting purposes and expects to prepare the company's first set of financial statements on December 31, 2009. The company's initial chart of accounts follows.

Account	No.	Account	No.
Cash	101	Common Stock	307
Accounts Receivable	106	Dividends	319
Computer Supplies	126	Computer Services Revenue	403
Prepaid Insurance	128	Wages Expense	623
Prepaid Rent	131	Advertising Expense	655
Office Equipment	163	Mileage Expense	676
Computer Equipment	167	Miscellaneous Expenses	677
Accounts Payable	201	Repairs Expense—Computer	684

Required

1. Prepare journal entries to record each of the following transactions for Success Systems.

Oct. 1 Lopez invested $55,000 cash, a $20,000 computer system, and $8,000 of office equipment in the company in exchange for its common stock.

2 The company paid $3,300 cash for four months' rent. (*Hint:* Debit Prepaid Rent for $3,300.)

3 The company purchased $1,420 of computer supplies on credit from Harris Office Products.

5 The company paid $2,220 cash for one year's premium on a property and liability insurance policy. (*Hint:* Debit Prepaid Insurance for $2,220.)

6 The company billed Easy Leasing $4,800 for services performed in installing a new Web server.

8 The company paid $1,420 cash for the computer supplies purchased from Harris Office Products on October 3.

10 The company hired Lyn Addie as a part-time assistant for $125 per day, as needed.

12 The company billed Easy Leasing another $1,400 for services performed.

15 The company received $4,800 cash from Easy Leasing as partial payment on its account.

17 The company paid $805 cash to repair computer equipment that was damaged when moving it.

20 The company paid $1,940 cash for an advertisement in the local newspaper.

22 The company received $1,400 cash from Easy Leasing on its account.

28 The company billed IFM Company $5,208 for services performed.

31 The company paid $875 cash for Lyn Addie's wages for seven days' work.

31 The company paid $3,600 cash for dividends.

Nov. 1   The company reimbursed Lopez in cash for business automobile mileage allowance (Lopez logged 1,000 miles at $0.32 per mile).

2   The company received $4,633 cash from Liu Corporation for computer services performed.

5   The company purchased computer supplies for $1,125 cash from Harris Office Products.

8   The company billed Gomez Co. $5,668 for services performed.

13 The company received notification from Alex's Engineering Co. that Success Systems' bid of $3,950 for an upcoming project is accepted.

18 The company received $2,208 cash from IFM Company as partial payment of the October 28 bill.

22 The company donated $250 cash to the United Way in the company's name.

24 The company completed work for Alex's Engineering Co. and sent it a bill for $3,950.

25 The company sent another bill to IFM Company for the past-due amount of $3,000.

28 The company reimbursed Lopez in cash for business automobile mileage (1,200 miles at $0.32 per mile).

30 The company paid $1,750 cash for Lyn Addie's wages for 14 days' work.

30 The company paid $2,000 cash for dividends.

2. Open ledger accounts (in balance column format) and post the journal entries from part 1 to them.

3. Prepare a trial balance as of the end of November.

Check (2) Cash, Nov. 30 bal., $48,052

(3) Trial bal. totals, $108,659

BEYOND THE NUMBERS

BTN 2-1   Refer to **Best Buy**'s financial statements in Appendix A for the following questions.

Required

1. What amount of total liabilities does it report for each of the fiscal years ended March 1, 2008, and February 28, 2009?

2. What amount of total assets does it report for each of the fiscal years ended March 1, 2008, and February 28, 2009?

3. Compute its debt ratio for each of the fiscal years ended March 1, 2008, and February 28, 2009.

4. In which fiscal year did it employ more financial leverage (March 1, 2008, or February 28, 2009)? Explain.

Fast Forward

5. Access its financial statements (10-K report) for a fiscal year ending after February 28, 2009, from its Website (**BestBuy.com**) or the SEC's EDGAR database (**www.SEC.gov**). Recompute its debt ratio for any subsequent year's data and compare it with the debt ratio for 2008 and 2009.

REPORTING IN ACTION

A1 A2

BTN 2-2   Key comparative figures for **Best Buy** and **RadioShack** follow.

($ millions)	Best Buy		RadioShack	
	Current Year	Prior Year	Current Year	Prior Year
Total liabilities	$11,183	$ 8,274	$1,466.2	$1,219.9
Total assets	15,826	12,758	2,283.5	1,989.6

COMPARATIVE ANALYSIS

A1 A2

1. What is the debt ratio for Best Buy in the current year and for the prior year?

2. What is the debt ratio for RadioShack in the current year and for the prior year?

3. Which of the two companies has the higher degree of financial leverage? What does this imply?

ETHICS CHALLENGE

C1 C2

BTN 2-3 Review the *Decision Ethics* case from the first part of this chapter involving the cashier. The guidance answer suggests that you should not comply with the assistant manager's request.

Required

Propose and evaluate two other courses of action you might consider, and explain why.

COMMUNICATING IN PRACTICE

C1 C3 A1 P3

BTN 2-4 Mora Stanley is an aspiring entrepreneur and your friend. She is having difficulty understanding the purposes of financial statements and how they fit together across time.

Required

Write a one-page memorandum to Stanley explaining the purposes of the four financial statements and how they are linked across time.

TAKING IT TO THE NET

A1

BTN 2-5 Access EDGAR online (www.SEC.gov) and locate the 2008 year 10-K report of **Amazon.com** (ticker AMZN) filed on January 1, 2009. Review its financial statements reported for years ended 2008, 2007, and 2006 to answer the following questions.

Required

1. What are the amounts of its net income or net loss reported for each of these three years?
2. Does Amazon's operating activities provide cash or use cash for each of these three years?
3. If Amazon has a 2008 net income of more than $600 million and 2008 operating cash flows of more than $1,500 million, how is it possible that its cash balance at December 31, 2008, increases by less than $250 million relative to its balance at December 31, 2007?

TEAMWORK IN ACTION

C1 C3 C5 A1

BTN 2-6 The expanded accounting equation consists of assets, liabilities, common stock, dividends, revenues, and expenses. It can be used to reveal insights into changes in a company's financial position.

Required

1. Form *learning teams* of six (or more) members. Each team member must select one of the six components and each team must have at least one expert on each component: (*a*) assets, (*b*) liabilities, (*c*) common stock, (*d*) dividends, (*e*) revenues, and (*f*) expenses.
2. Form *expert teams* of individuals who selected the same component in part 1. Expert teams are to draft a report that each expert will present to his or her learning team addressing the following:
   a. Identify for its component the (i) increase and decrease side of the account and (ii) normal balance side of the account.
   b. Describe a transaction, with amounts, that increases its component.
   c. Using the transaction and amounts in (*b*), verify the equality of the accounting equation and then explain any effects on the income statement and statement of cash flows.
   d. Describe a transaction, with amounts, that decreases its component.
   e. Using the transaction and amounts in (*d*), verify the equality of the accounting equation and then explain any effects on the income statement and statement of cash flows.
3. Each expert should return to his/her learning team. In rotation, each member presents his/her expert team's report to the learning team. Team discussion is encouraged.

ENTREPRENEURIAL DECISION

A1 A2 P3

BTN 2-7 Angel Fender is a young entrepreneur who operates Fender Music Services, offering singing lessons and instruction on musical instruments. Fender wishes to expand but needs a $30,000 loan. The bank requests Fender to prepare a balance sheet and key financial ratios. Fender has not kept formal records but is able to provide the following accounts and their amounts as of December 31, 2011.

Cash	$ 3,600	Accounts Receivable	$ 9,600	Prepaid Insurance	$ 1,500
Prepaid Rent	9,400	Store Supplies	6,600	Equipment	50,000
Accounts Payable	2,200	Unearned Lesson Fees	15,600	Total Equity*	62,900
Annual net income	40,000				

* The total equity amount reflects all owner investments, dividends, revenues, and expenses as of December 31, 2011.

Required

1. Prepare a balance sheet as of December 31, 2011, for Fender Music Services. (Report only the total equity amount on the balance sheet.)
2. Compute Fender's debt ratio and its return on assets (the latter ratio is defined in Chapter 1). Assume average assets equal its ending balance.
3. Do you believe the prospects of a $30,000 bank loan are good? Why or why not?

BTN 2-8 Assume Sara Blakely of **SPANX** plans on expanding her business to accommodate more product lines. She is considering financing her expansion in one of two ways: (1) contributing more of her own funds to the business or (2) borrowing the funds from a bank.

A1 A2 P3

Required

Identify the issues that Blakely should consider when trying to decide on the method for financing her expansion.

BTN 2-9 Obtain a recent copy of the most prominent newspaper distributed in your area. Research the classified section and prepare a report answering the following questions (attach relevant classified clippings to your report). Alternatively, you may want to search the Web for the required information. One suitable Website is **CareerOneStop** (www.CareerOneStop.org). For documentation, you should print copies of Websites accessed.

HITTING THE ROAD

C1

1. Identify the number of listings for accounting positions and the various accounting job titles.
2. Identify the number of listings for other job titles, with examples, that require or prefer accounting knowledge/experience but are not specifically accounting positions.
3. Specify the salary range for the accounting and accounting-related positions if provided.
4. Indicate the job that appeals to you, the reason for its appeal, and its requirements.

BTN 2-10 GOME (www.GOME.com.hk) is the leading chain retailer of consumer electronic products and household appliances in China, and it competes to some extent with **Best Buy** and **RadioShack**. Key financial ratios for the current fiscal year follow.

GLOBAL DECISION

A2

Key Figure	GOME	Best Buy	RadioShack
Return on assets	3.7%	7.0%	9.0%
Debt ratio	68.4%	70.7%	64.2%

Required

1. Which company is most profitable according to its return on assets?
2. Which company is most risky according to the debt ratio?
3. Which company deserves increased investment based on a joint analysis of return on assets and the debt ratio? Explain.

ANSWERS TO MULTIPLE CHOICE QUIZ

1. b; debit Utility Expense for $700, and credit Cash for $700.
2. a; debit Cash for $2,500, and credit Unearned Lawn Service Fees for $2,500.
3. c; debit Cash for $250,000, debit Land for $500,000, and credit Common Stock for $750,000.

4. d
5. e; Debt ratio = $400,000/$1,000,000 = 40%

3

Adjusting Accounts and Preparing Financial Statements

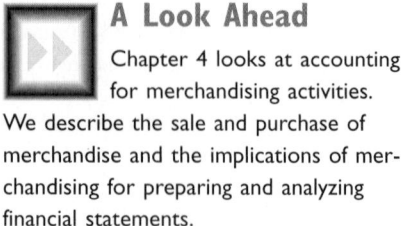

"Get a good accountant"—Jason Kapalka (from left: John Vechey, Brian Feite, Jason Kapalka)

A Look Back

Chapter 2 explained the analysis and recording of transactions. We showed how to apply and interpret company accounts, T-accounts, double-entry accounting, ledgers, postings, and trial balances.

A Look at This Chapter

This chapter explains the timing of reports and the need to adjust accounts. Adjusting accounts is important for recognizing revenues and expenses in the proper period. We describe how to prepare financial statements from an adjusted trial balance, and how the closing process works.

A Look Ahead

Chapter 4 looks at accounting for merchandising activities. We describe the sale and purchase of merchandise and the implications of merchandising for preparing and analyzing financial statements.

High Score Biz

SEATTLE—Jason Kapalka met John Vechey and Brian Feite, both 19 at the time, after the two had created an online game. "We hit it off really well," explains Jason. "We were all a little unhappy with our jobs. We thought, 'Hey, we could start our own company.'" Their start-up company, **PopCap Games (PopCap.com),** is a creator and provider of downloadable games. Jason recalls that their friends considered them crazy.

Undaunted, the three scraped together the little cash they had. Jason explains that they worked out of their respective apartments to save money. "We survived," admits Jason, "because we didn't have many expenses." The young trio quickly developed a system to account for everything, including cash, revenues, receivables, and payables. They also had to learn about the deferral and accrual of revenues and expenses. Setting up a good accounting system is an important part of success, explains Jason. "Don't wait until . . . everything is a big mess."

Most of PopCap's sales are paid for in advance of game delivery. This means few uncollectible accounts. The team also defers payment of their expenses to the time permitted—which is good management. "We're trying to keep a very simple business model," insists Jason. The team continues to fine-tune their accounting system as they remain focused on revenues, income, assets, and liabilities. "No matter what you do," argues Jason, "there's always something that you haven't done." This includes reaping benefits from their accounting system.

Financial statement preparation and analysis is a process that the three continue to work on. Although they insist on timely and accurate accounting reports, Jason says "it really helped us to keep things simple." To help make it simple, they took time to understand accounting adjustments and their effects. It is part of the larger picture. "You're not going to get breaks unless you're working hard." And, working hard at accounting is something they take seriously.

Today, PopCap is a success story. "Now we can afford mac and cheese, and the occasional bottle of water," laughs Jason. "Life is good!"

[Sources: *PopCap Website,* January 2010; *Entrepreneur,* February 2008; *Wired,* March 2008; *2o2p Magazine,* September 2006; *Washington Post,* March 2008]

CAP

Conceptual

C1 Explain the importance of periodic reporting and the time period assumption. *(p. 94)*

C2 Explain accrual accounting and how it improves financial statements. *(p. 95)*

C3 Identify steps in the accounting cycle. *(p. 112)*

C4 Explain and prepare a classified balance sheet. *(p. 113)*

Analytical

A1 Explain how accounting adjustments link to financial statements. *(p. 105)*

A2 Compute profit margin and describe its use in analyzing company performance. *(p. 116)*

A3 Compute the current ratio and describe what it reveals about a company's financial condition. *(p. 117)*

Procedural

P1 Prepare and explain adjusting entries. *(p. 96)*

P2 Explain and prepare an adjusted trial balance. *(p. 106)*

P3 Prepare financial statements from an adjusted trial balance. *(p. 106)*

P4 Describe and prepare closing entries. *(p. 108)*

P5 Explain and prepare a post-closing trial balance. *(p. 110)*

P6 *Appendix 3A*—Explain the alternatives in accounting for prepaids. *(p. 122)*

P7 *Appendix 3B*—Prepare a work sheet and explain its usefulness. *(p. 124)*

P8 *Appendix 3C*—Prepare reversing entries and explain their purpose. *(p. 126)*

Chapters 1 and 2 described how transactions and events are analyzed, journalized, and posted. This chapter describes important adjustments that are often necessary to properly reflect revenues when earned and expenses when incurred. This chapter also describes financial statement preparation. It

explains the closing process that readies revenue, expense, and dividend accounts for the next reporting period and updates retained earnings. It also explains how accounts are classified on a balance sheet to increase their usefulness to decision makers.

Adjusting Accounts and Preparing Financial Statements

Timing and Reporting
- Accounting period
- Accrual versus cash
- Recognition of revenues and expenses

Adjusting Accounts
- Prepaid expenses
- Unearned revenues
- Accrued expenses
- Accrued revenues
- Adjusted trial balance

Preparing Financial Statements
- Income statement
- Statement of retained earnings
- Balance sheet

Closing Process
- Temporary and permanent accounts
- Closing entries
- Post-closing trial balance
- Accounting cycle summary

Classified Balance Sheet
- Classification structure
- Classification categories

Timing and Reporting

This section describes the importance of reporting accounting information at regular intervals and its impact for recording revenues and expenses.

The Accounting Period

C1 Explain the importance of periodic reporting and the time period assumption.

"Best Buy announces income of . . ."

Video3.1

The value of information is often linked to its timeliness. Useful information must reach decision makers frequently and promptly. To provide timely information, accounting systems prepare reports at regular intervals. This results in an accounting process impacted by the time period (or periodicity) assumption. The **time period assumption** presumes that an organization's activities can be divided into specific time periods such as a month, a three-month quarter, a six-month interval, or a year. Exhibit 3.1 shows various **accounting,** or *reporting,* **periods.** Most organizations use a year as their primary accounting period. Reports covering a one-year period are known as **annual financial statements.** Many organizations also prepare **interim financial statements** covering one, three, or six months of activity.

EXHIBIT 3.1

Accounting Periods

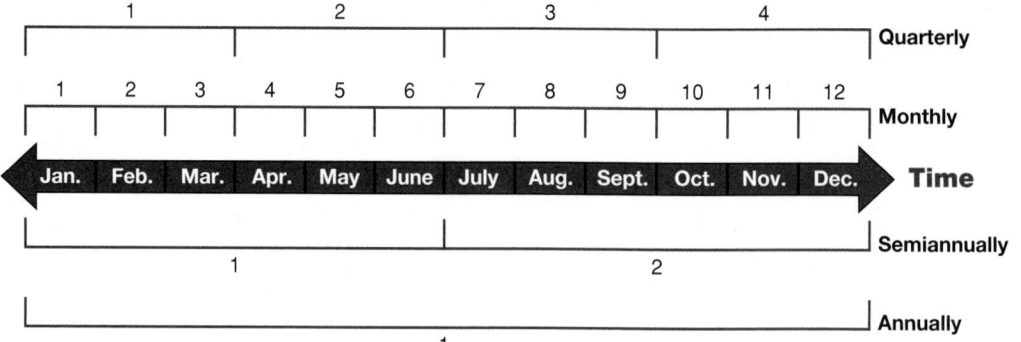

The annual reporting period is not always a calendar year ending on December 31. An organization can adopt a **fiscal year** consisting of any 12 consecutive months. It is also acceptable to adopt an annual reporting period of 52 weeks. For example, **Gap**'s fiscal year consistently ends the final week of January or the first week of February each year.

Companies with little seasonal variation in sales often choose the calendar year as their fiscal year. For example, the financial statements of **Marvel Enterprises** (the company that controls characters such as Spider-Man, Fantastic Four, and Shang-Chi) reflect a fiscal year that ends on December 31. Companies experiencing seasonal variations in sales often choose a **natural business year** end, which is when sales activities are at their lowest level for the year. The natural business year for retailers such as **Wal-Mart**, **Target**, and **Macy's** usually ends around January 31, after the holiday season.

Accrual Basis versus Cash Basis

After external transactions and events are recorded, several accounts still need adjustments before their balances appear in financial statements. This need arises because internal transactions and events remain unrecorded. **Accrual basis accounting** uses the adjusting process to recognize revenues when earned and expenses when incurred (matched with revenues).

C2 Explain accrual accounting and how it improves financial statements.

Cash basis accounting recognizes revenues when cash is received and records expenses when cash is paid. This means that cash basis net income for a period is the difference between cash receipts and cash payments. Cash basis accounting is not consistent with generally accepted accounting principles (neither U.S. GAAP nor IFRS).

It is commonly held that accrual accounting better reflects business performance than information about cash receipts and payments. Accrual accounting also increases the *comparability* of financial statements from one period to another. Yet cash basis accounting is useful for several business decisions—which is the reason companies must report a statement of cash flows.

To see the difference between these two accounting systems, let's consider FastForward's Prepaid Insurance account. FastForward paid $2,400 for 24 months of insurance coverage beginning on December 1, 2009. Accrual accounting requires that $100 of insurance expense be reported on December 2009's income statement. Another $1,200 of expense is reported in year 2010, and the remaining $1,100 is reported as expense in the first 11 months of 2011. Exhibit 3.2 illustrates this allocation of insurance cost across these three years. Any unexpired premium is reported as a Prepaid Insurance asset on the accrual basis balance sheet.

EXHIBIT 3.2

Accrual Accounting for Allocating Prepaid Insurance to Expense

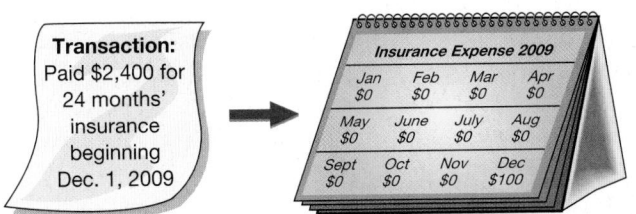

Alternatively, a cash basis income statement for December 2009 reports insurance expense of $2,400, as shown in Exhibit 3.3. The cash basis income statements for years 2010 and 2011 report no insurance expense. The cash basis balance sheet never reports an insurance asset because it is immediately expensed. This shows that cash basis income for 2009–2011 fails to match the cost of insurance with the insurance benefits received for those years and months.

EXHIBIT 3.3

Cash Accounting for Allocating Prepaid Insurance to Expense

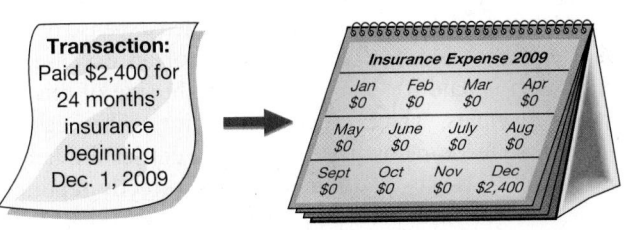
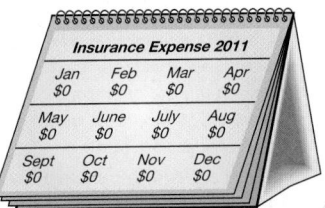

Recognizing Revenues and Expenses

We use the time period assumption to divide a company's activities into specific time periods, but not all activities are complete when financial statements are prepared. Thus, adjustments often are required to get correct account balances.

We rely on two principles in the adjusting process: revenue recognition and expense recognition (the latter is often referred to as *matching*). Chapter 1 explained that the *revenue recognition principle* requires that revenue be recorded when earned, not before and not after. Most companies earn revenue when they provide services and products to customers. A major goal of the adjusting process is to have revenue recognized (reported) in the time period when it is earned. The *expense recognition* (or *matching*) *principle* aims to record expenses in the same accounting period as the revenues that are earned as a result of those expenses. This matching of expenses with the revenue benefits is a major part of the adjusting process.

Matching expenses with revenues often requires us to predict certain events. When we use financial statements, we must understand that they require estimates and therefore include measures that are not precise. **Walt Disney**'s annual report explains that its production costs from movies, such as *Pirates of the Caribbean,* are matched to revenues based on a ratio of current revenues from the movie divided by its predicted total revenues.

Decision Insight

Improper Adjustments   Revenue recognition and expense matching are key to recording accounting adjustments. Good adjustments require good management judgment. Failure in judgment led to improper adjustments at **Fannie Mae, AOL Time Warner, WorldCom,** and **Xerox.**

Quick Check   Answers—p. 129

1. Describe a company's annual reporting period.
2. Why do companies prepare interim financial statements?
3. What two accounting principles most directly drive the adjusting process?
4. Is cash basis accounting consistent with the matching principle? Why or why not?
5. If your company pays a $4,800 premium on April 1, 2011, for two years' insurance coverage, how much insurance expense is reported in 2012 using cash basis accounting?

Adjusting Accounts

Adjusting accounts is a 3-step process:

> **Step 1:** Determine what the current account balance *equals.*
> **Step 2:** Determine what the current account balance *should equal.*
> **Step 3:** Record an adjusting entry to get from step *1* to step *2*.

Framework for Adjustments

Adjustments are necessary for transactions and events that extend over more than one period. It is helpful to group adjustments by the timing of cash receipt or cash payment in relation to the recognition of the related revenues or expenses. Exhibit 3.4 identifies four types of adjustments.

The left side of this exhibit shows prepaid expenses (including depreciation) and unearned revenues, which reflect transactions when cash is paid or received *before* a related expense or revenue is recognized. They are also called *deferrals* because the recognition of an expense (or revenue) is *deferred* until after the related cash is paid (or received). The right side of this exhibit shows accrued expenses and accrued revenues, which reflect transactions when cash is paid or received *after* a related expense or revenue is recognized. Adjusting entries are necessary for each of these so that revenues, expenses, assets, and liabilities are correctly reported.

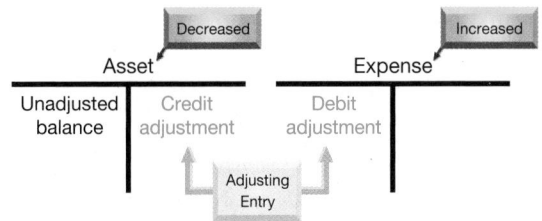

EXHIBIT 3.4

Types of Adjustments

*Includes depreciation.

Specifically, an **adjusting entry** is made at the end of an accounting period to reflect a transaction or event that is not yet recorded. Each adjusting entry affects one or more income statement accounts *and* one or more balance sheet accounts (but never the Cash account).

Prepaid (Deferred) Expenses

Prepaid expenses refer to items *paid for* in advance of receiving their benefits. Prepaid expenses are assets. When these assets are used, their costs become expenses. Adjusting entries for prepaids increase expenses and decrease assets as shown in the T-accounts of Exhibit 3.5. Such adjustments reflect transactions and events that use up prepaid expenses (including passage of time). To illustrate the accounting for prepaid expenses, we look at prepaid insurance, supplies, and depreciation.

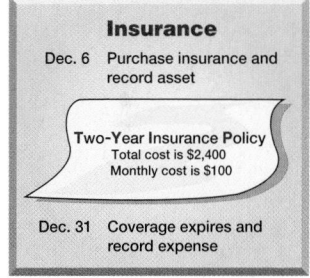

EXHIBIT 3.5

Adjusting for Prepaid Expenses

Prepaid Insurance   We use our 3-step process for this and all accounting adjustments.

Step 1:   We determine the current balance of FastForward's prepaid insurance as equal to its $2,400 payment for 24 months of insurance benefits beginning on December 1, 2009.

Step 2:   With the passage of time, the benefits of the insurance gradually expire and a portion of the Prepaid Insurance asset becomes expense. For instance, one month's insurance coverage expires by December 31, 2009. This expense is $100, or 1/24 of $2,400, which leaves $2,300.

Step 3:   The adjusting entry to record this expense and reduce the asset, along with T-account postings, follows:

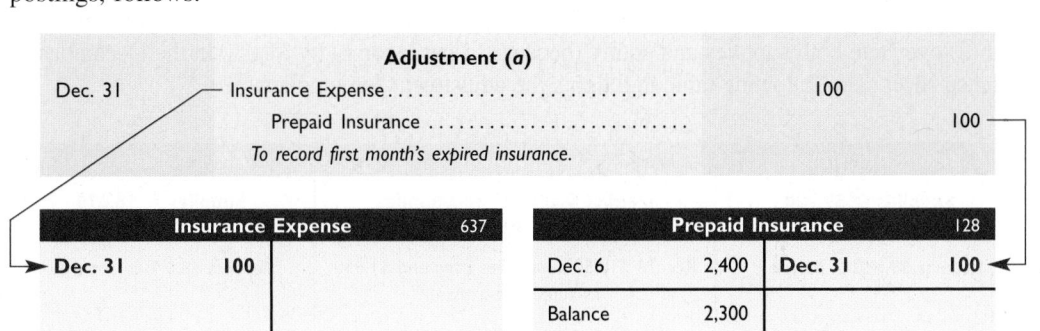

Assets = Liabilities + Equity
−100   −100

Explanation   After adjusting and posting, the $100 balance in Insurance Expense and the $2,300 balance in Prepaid Insurance are ready for reporting in financial statements. *Not* making the adjustment on or before December 31 would (1) understate expenses by $100 and overstate net income by $100 for the December income statement and (2) overstate both prepaid insurance (assets) and equity (because of net income) by $100 in the December 31 balance sheet. (Exhibit 3.2 showed that 2010's adjustments must transfer a total of $1,200 from Prepaid

Point: Many companies record adjusting entries only at the end of each year because of the time and cost necessary.

Insurance to Insurance Expense, and 2011's adjustments must transfer the remaining $1,100 to Insurance Expense.) The following table highlights the December 31, 2009, adjustment for prepaid insurance.

Before Adjustment	Adjustment	After Adjustment
Prepaid Insurance = $2,400	**Deduct $100 from Prepaid Insurance** **Add $100 to Insurance Expense**	**Prepaid Insurance = $2,300**
Reports $2,400 policy for 24-months' coverage.	Record current month's $100 insurance expense and $100 reduction in prepaid amount.	Reports $2,300 in coverage for remaining 23 months.

Supplies   Supplies are a prepaid expense requiring adjustment.

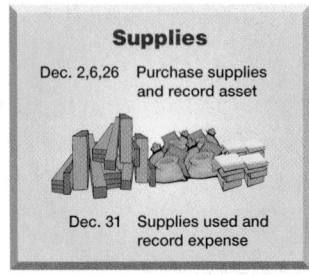

Supplies

Dec. 2,6,26   Purchase supplies and record asset

Dec. 31   Supplies used and record expense

Step 1:   FastForward purchased $9,720 of supplies in December and some of them were used during this month. When financial statements are prepared at December 31, the cost of supplies used during December must be recognized.

Step 2:   When FastForward computes (takes physical count of) its remaining unused supplies at December 31, it finds $8,670 of supplies remaining of the $9,720 total supplies. The $1,050 difference between these two amounts is December's supplies expense.

Step 3:   The adjusting entry to record this expense and reduce the Supplies asset account, along with T-account postings, follows:

$$\text{Assets} = \text{Liabilities} + \text{Equity}$$
$$-1,050 \qquad\qquad\qquad -1,050$$

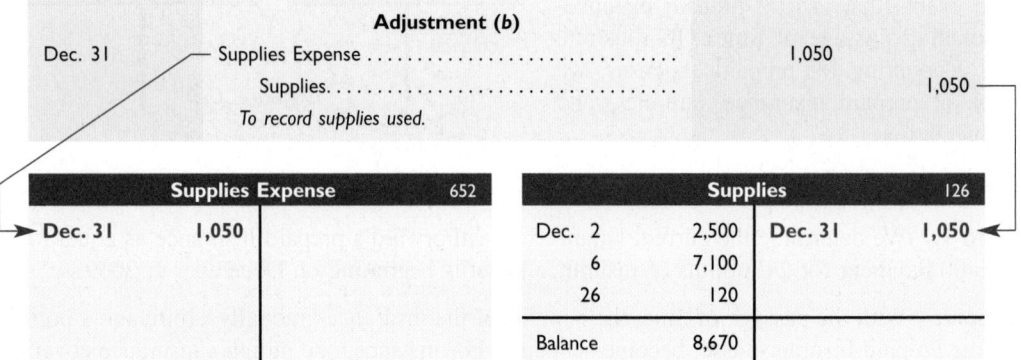

Adjustment (b)

Dec. 31	Supplies Expense	1,050	
	Supplies...................................		1,050
	To record supplies used.		

Supplies Expense		652
Dec. 31	1,050	

Supplies				126
Dec. 2	2,500	Dec. 31	1,050
6	7,100		
26	120		
Balance	8,670		

Explanation   The balance of the Supplies account is $8,670 after posting—equaling the cost of the remaining supplies. *Not* making the adjustment on or before December 31 would (1) understate expenses by $1,050 and overstate net income by $1,050 for the December income statement and (2) overstate both supplies and equity (because of net income) by $1,050 in the December 31 balance sheet. The following table highlights the adjustment for supplies.

Before Adjustment	Adjustment	After Adjustment
Supplies = $9,720	**Deduct $1,050 from Supplies** **Add $1,050 to Supplies Expense**	**Supplies = $8,670**
Reports $9,720 in supplies.	Record $1,050 in supplies used and $1,050 as supplies expense.	Reports $8,670 in supplies.

Other Prepaid Expenses   Other prepaid expenses, such as Prepaid Rent, are accounted for exactly as Insurance and Supplies are. We should note that some prepaid expenses are both paid for and fully used up within a single accounting period. One example is when a company pays monthly rent on the first day of each month. This payment creates a prepaid expense on the first day of each month that fully expires by the end of the month. In these special cases, we can record the cash paid with a debit to an expense account instead of an asset account. This practice is described more completely later in the chapter.

Point: We assume that prepaid and unearned items are recorded in balance sheet accounts. An alternative is to record them in income statement accounts; Appendix 3A discusses this alternative. The adjusted financial statements are identical.

Decision Maker

Investor A small publishing company signs a well-known athlete to write a book. The company pays the athlete $500,000 to sign plus future book royalties. A note to the company's financial statements says that "prepaid expenses include $500,000 in author signing fees to be matched against future expected sales." Is this accounting for the signing bonus acceptable? How does it affect your analysis? [Answer—p. 128]

Depreciation A special category of prepaid expenses is **plant assets,** which refers to long-term tangible assets used to produce and sell products and services. Plant assets are expected to provide benefits for more than one period. Examples of plant assets are buildings, machines, vehicles, and fixtures. All plant assets, with a general exception for land, eventually wear out or decline in usefulness. The costs of these assets are deferred but are gradually reported as expenses in the income statement over the assets' useful lives (benefit periods). **Depreciation** is the process of allocating the costs of these assets over their expected useful lives. Depreciation expense is recorded with an adjusting entry similar to that for other prepaid expenses.

Point: Plant assets are also called *Plant & Equipment,* or *Property, Plant & Equipment.*

Point: Depreciation does not necessarily measure decline in market value.

Point: An asset's expected value at the end of its useful life is called *salvage value.*

Step 1: Recall that FastForward purchased equipment for $26,000 in early December to use in earning revenue. This equipment's cost must be depreciated.

Step 2: The equipment is expected to have a useful life (benefit period) of four years and to be worth about $8,000 at the end of four years. This means the *net* cost of this equipment over its useful life is $18,000 ($26,000 − $8,000). We can use any of several methods to allocate this $18,000 net cost to expense. FastForward uses a method called **straight-line depreciation,** which allocates equal amounts of the asset's net cost to depreciation during its useful life. Dividing the $18,000 net cost by the 48 months in the asset's useful life gives a monthly cost of $375 ($18,000/48).

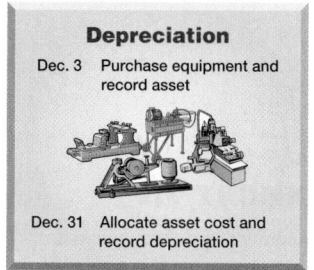

Step 3: The adjusting entry to record monthly depreciation expense, along with T-account postings, follows:

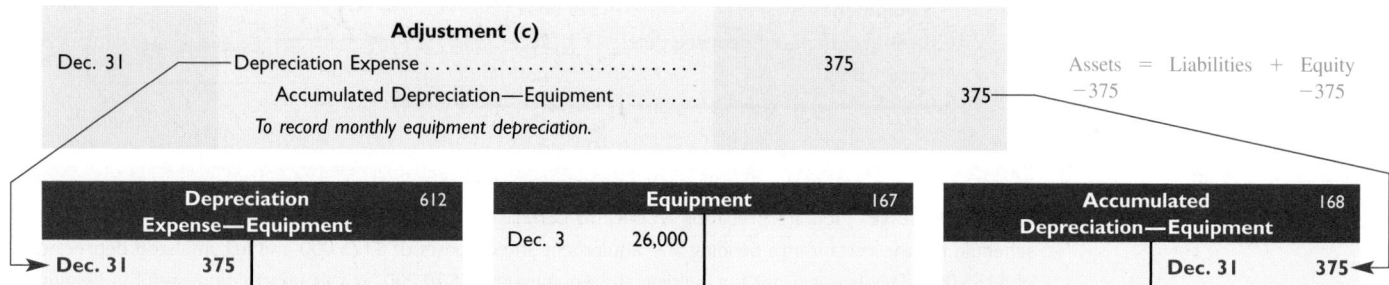

Explanation After posting the adjustment, the Equipment account ($26,000) less its Accumulated Depreciation ($375) account equals the $25,625 net cost (made up of $17,625 for the 47 remaining months in the benefit period plus the $8,000 value at the end of that time). The $375 balance in the Depreciation Expense account is reported in the December income statement. *Not* making the adjustment at December 31 would (1) understate expenses by $375 and overstate net income by $375 for the December income statement and (2) overstate both assets and equity (because of income) by $375 in the December 31 balance sheet. The following table highlights the adjustment for depreciation.

Before Adjustment	Adjustment	After Adjustment
Equipment, net = $26,000	Deduct $375 from Equipment, net Add $375 to Depreciation Expense	Equipment, net = $25,625
Reports $26,000 in equipment.	Record $375 in depreciation and $375 as accumulated depreciation, which is deducted from equipment.	Reports $25,625 in equipment, net of accumulated depreciation.

Accumulated depreciation is kept in a separate contra account. A **contra account** is an account linked with another account, it has an opposite normal balance, and it is reported as a subtraction from that other account's balance. For instance, FastForward's contra account of Accumulated Depreciation—Equipment is subtracted from the Equipment account in the balance sheet (see Exhibit 3.7). This contra account allows balance sheet readers to know both the full costs of assets and the total depreciation.

Point: The cost principle requires an asset to be initially recorded at acquisition cost. Depreciation causes the asset's book value (cost less accumulated depreciation) to decline over time.

Point: The net cost of equipment is also called the *depreciable basis*.

The title of the contra account, *Accumulated Depreciation,* reveals that this account includes total depreciation expense for all prior periods for which the asset was used. To illustrate, the Equipment and the Accumulated Depreciation accounts appear as in Exhibit 3.6 on February 28, 2010, after three months of adjusting entries. The $1,125 balance in the accumulated depreciation account can be subtracted from its related $26,000 asset cost. The difference ($24,875) between these two balances is the cost of the asset that has not yet been depreciated. This difference is called the **book value,** or the *net amount,* which equals the asset's costs less its accumulated depreciation.

EXHIBIT 3.6

Accounts after Three Months of Depreciation Adjustments

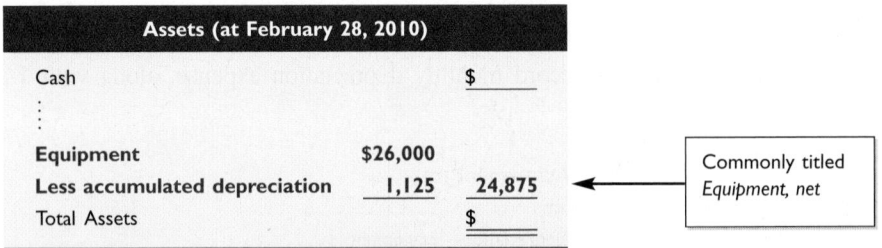

Equipment		167
Dec. 3	26,000	

Accumulated Depreciation—Equipment		168
	Dec. 31	375
	Jan. 31	375
	Feb. 28	375
	Balance	1,125

These account balances are reported in the assets section of the February 28 balance sheet in Exhibit 3.7.

EXHIBIT 3.7

Equipment and Accumulated Depreciation on February 28 Balance Sheet

Assets (at February 28, 2010)		
Cash		$ ___
⋮		
Equipment	$26,000	
Less accumulated depreciation	1,125	24,875
Total Assets		$ ___

← Commonly titled *Equipment, net*

 Decision Maker

Entrepreneur You are preparing an offer to purchase a family-run restaurant. The depreciation schedule for the restaurant's building and equipment shows costs of $175,000 and accumulated depreciation of $155,000. This leaves a net for building and equipment of $20,000. Is this information useful in helping you decide on a purchase offer? [Answer—p. 128]

Unearned (Deferred) Revenues

The term **unearned revenues** refers to cash received in advance of providing products and services. Unearned revenues, also called *deferred revenues,* are liabilities. When cash

EXHIBIT 3.8

Adjusting for Unearned Revenues

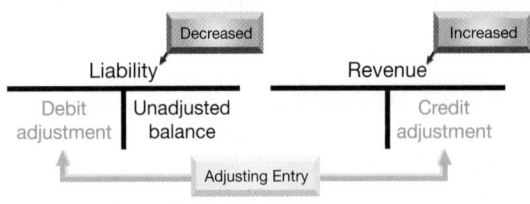

is accepted, an obligation to provide products or services is accepted. As products or services are provided, the unearned revenues become *earned* revenues. Adjusting entries for unearned revenues involve increasing revenues and decreasing unearned revenues, as shown in Exhibit 3.8.

Point: To *defer* is to postpone. We postpone reporting amounts received as revenues until they are earned.

An example of unearned revenues is from **The New York Times Company**, which reports unexpired (unearned) subscriptions of $81 million: "Proceeds from . . . subscriptions are deferred at the time of sale and are recognized in earnings on a pro rata basis over the terms of the subscriptions." Unearned revenues are nearly 10% of the current liabilities for the Times. Another example comes from the **Boston Celtics**. When the Celtics receive cash from advance ticket sales and broadcast fees, they record it in an unearned revenue account called *Deferred Game Revenues.* The Celtics recognize this unearned revenue with adjusting entries on a game-by-game basis. Since the NBA regular season begins in October and ends in April, revenue recognition is mainly limited to this period. For a recent season, the Celtics' quarterly revenues were $0 million for July–September; $34 million for October–December; $48 million for January–March; and $17 million for April–June.

Returning to FastForward, it has unearned revenues. It agreed on December 26 to provide consulting services to a client for a fixed fee of $3,000 for 60 days.

Step 1:   On December 26, the client paid the 60-day fee in advance, covering the period December 27 to February 24. The entry to record the cash received in advance is

Dec. 26	Cash	3,000	
	Unearned Consulting Revenue		3,000
	Received advance payment for services over the next 60 days.		

Assets = Liabilities + Equity
+3,000   +3,000

This advance payment increases cash and creates an obligation to do consulting work over the next 60 days.

Step 2:   As time passes, FastForward earns this payment through consulting. By December 31, it has provided five days' service and earned 5/60 of the $3,000 unearned revenue. This amounts to $250 ($3,000 × 5/60). The *revenue recognition principle* implies that $250 of unearned revenue must be reported as revenue on the December income statement.

Step 3:   The adjusting entry to reduce the liability account and recognize earned revenue, along with T-account postings, follows:

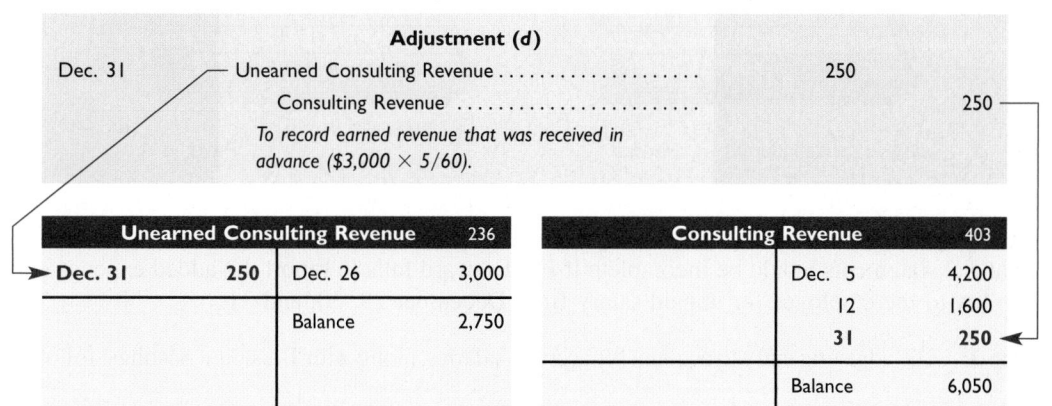

Assets = Liabilities + Equity
−250   +250

Explanation   The adjusting entry transfers $250 from unearned revenue (a liability account) to a revenue account. *Not* making the adjustment (1) understates revenue and net income by $250 in the December income statement and (2) overstates unearned revenue and understates equity by $250 on the December 31 balance sheet. The following highlights the adjustment for unearned revenue.

Before Adjustment	Adjustment	After Adjustment
Unearned Consulting Revenue = $3,000	**Deduct $250 from Unearned Consulting Revenue** **Add $250 to Consulting Revenue**	**Unearned Consulting Revenue = $2,750**
Reports $3,000 in unearned revenue for consulting services promised for 60 days.	Record 5 days of earned consulting revenue, which is 5/60 of unearned amount.	Reports $2,750 in unearned revenue for consulting services owed over next 55 days.

Accounting for unearned revenues is crucial to many companies. For example, the **National Retail Federation** reports that gift card sales, which are unearned revenues for sellers, exceed $20 billion annually. Gift cards are now the top selling holiday gift.

Accrued Expenses

Accrued expenses refer to costs that are incurred in a period but are both unpaid and unrecorded. Accrued expenses must be reported on the income statement of the period when incurred. Adjusting entries for recording accrued expenses involve increasing expenses and increasing liabilities as shown in Exhibit 3.9. This adjustment recognizes expenses incurred in a period but not yet paid. Common examples of accrued expenses are salaries, interest, rent, and taxes. We use salaries and interest to show how to adjust accounts for accrued expenses.

EXHIBIT 3.9

Adjusting for Accrued Expenses

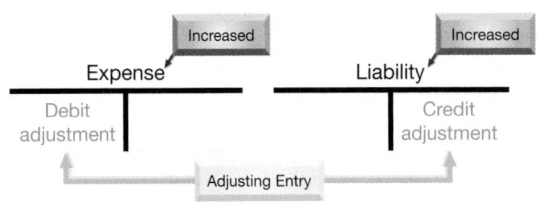

Accrued Salaries Expense   FastForward's employee earns $70 per day, or $350 for a five-day workweek beginning on Monday and ending on Friday.

Step 1:   Its employee is paid every two weeks on Friday. On December 12 and 26, the wages are paid, recorded in the journal, and posted to the ledger.

Step 2:   The calendar in Exhibit 3.10 shows three working days after the December 26 payday (29, 30, and 31). This means the employee has earned three days' salary by the close of

EXHIBIT 3.10

Salary Accrual and Paydays

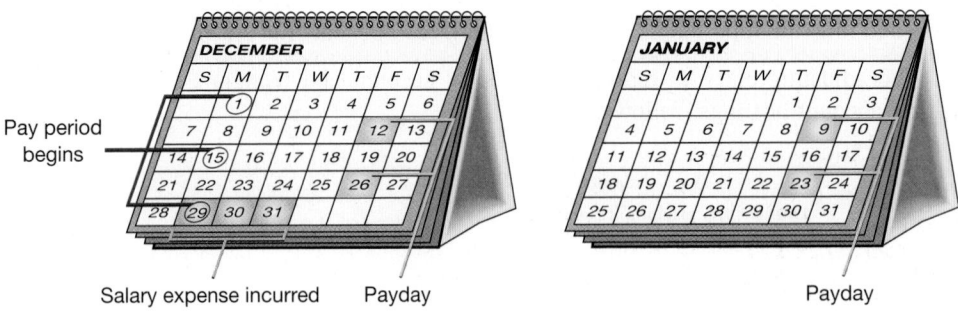

business on Wednesday, December 31, yet this salary cost has not been paid or recorded. The financial statements would be incomplete if FastForward fails to report the added expense and liability to the employee for unpaid salary from December 29, 30, and 31.

Step 3:   The adjusting entry to account for accrued salaries, along with T-account postings, follows:

Assets = Liabilities + Equity
         +210   −210

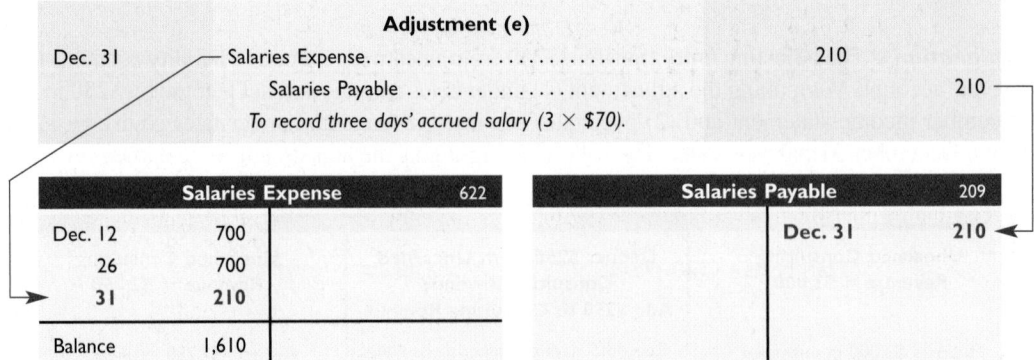

Explanation   Salaries expense of $1,610 is reported on the December income statement and $210 of salaries payable (liability) is reported in the balance sheet. *Not* making the adjustment (1) understates salaries expense and overstates net income by $210 in the December income statement and (2) understates salaries payable (liabilities) and overstates equity by $210 on the December 31 balance sheet. The following highlights the adjustment for salaries incurred.

Before Adjustment	Adjustment	After Adjustment
Salaries Payable = $0	Add $210 to Salaries Payable Add $210 to Salaries Expense	Salaries Payable = $210
Reports $0 from employee salaries incurred but not yet paid in cash.	Record 3 days' salaries owed to employee, but not yet paid, at $70 per day.	Reports $210 salaries payable to employee but not yet paid.

Accrued Interest Expense Companies commonly have accrued interest expense on notes payable and other long-term liabilities at the end of a period. Interest expense is incurred with the passage of time. Unless interest is paid on the last day of an accounting period, we need to adjust for interest expense incurred but not yet paid. This means we must accrue interest cost from the most recent payment date up to the end of the period. The formula for computing accrued interest is:

Principal amount owed × Annual interest rate × Fraction of year since last payment date.

To illustrate, if a company has a $6,000 loan from a bank at 6% annual interest, then 30 days' accrued interest expense is $30—computed as $6,000 × 0.06 × 30/360. The adjusting entry would be to debit Interest Expense for $30 and credit Interest Payable for $30.

Point: Interest computations assume a 360-day year; known as the *bankers' rule.*

Future Payment of Accrued Expenses Adjusting entries for accrued expenses foretell cash transactions in future periods. Specifically, accrued expenses at the end of one accounting period result in *cash payment* in a *future period*(s). To illustrate, recall that FastForward recorded accrued salaries of $210. On January 9, the first payday of the next period, the following entry settles the accrued liability (salaries payable) and records salaries expense for seven days of work in January:

Jan. 9	Salaries Payable (3 days at $70 per day)	210	
	Salaries Expense (7 days at $70 per day).	490	
	Cash		700
	Paid two weeks' salary including three days accrued in December.		

Assets = Liabilities + Equity
−700   −210   −490

The $210 debit reflects the payment of the liability for the three days' salary accrued on December 31. The $490 debit records the salary for January's first seven working days (including the New Year's Day holiday) as an expense of the new accounting period. The $700 credit records the total amount of cash paid to the employee.

Accrued Revenues

The term **accrued revenues** refers to revenues earned in a period that are both unrecorded and not yet received in cash (or other assets). An example is a technician who bills customers only when the job is done. If one-third of a job is complete by the end of a period, then the technician must record one-third of the expected billing as revenue in that period—even though there is no billing or collection. The adjusting entries for accrued revenues increase assets and increase revenues as shown in Exhibit 3.11. Accrued revenues commonly arise from services, products, interest, and rent. We use service fees and interest to show how to adjust for accrued revenues.

Point: Accrued revenues are also called *accrued assets.*

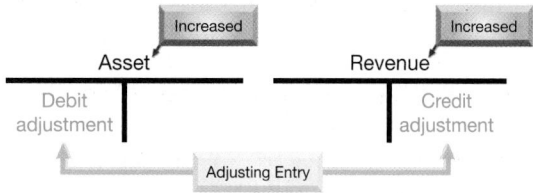

EXHIBIT 3.11

Adjusting for Accrued Revenues

Accrued Services Revenue Accrued revenues are not recorded until adjusting entries are made at the end of the accounting period. These accrued revenues are earned but unrecorded because either the buyer has not yet paid for them or the seller has not yet billed the buyer. FastForward provides an example.

Step 1: In the second week of December, it agreed to provide 30 days of consulting services to a local fitness club for a fixed fee of $2,700. The terms of the initial agreement call for FastForward to provide services from December 12, 2009, through January 10, 2010, or 30 days

Accrued Revenues

Dec. 31 Record revenue and receivable for services provided but unbilled

Pay me next month

Jan. 10 Receive cash and reduce receivable

Assets = Liabilities + Equity
+1,800 +1,800

of service. The club agrees to pay FastForward $2,700 on January 10, 2010, when the service period is complete.

Step 2: At December 31, 2009, 20 days of services have already been provided. Since the contracted services have not yet been entirely provided, FastForward has neither billed the club nor recorded the services already provided. Still, FastForward has earned two-thirds of the 30-day fee, or $1,800 ($2,700 × 20/30). The *revenue recognition principle* implies that it must report the $1,800 on the December income statement. The balance sheet also must report that the club owes FastForward $1,800.

Step 3: The year-end adjusting entry to account for accrued services revenue is

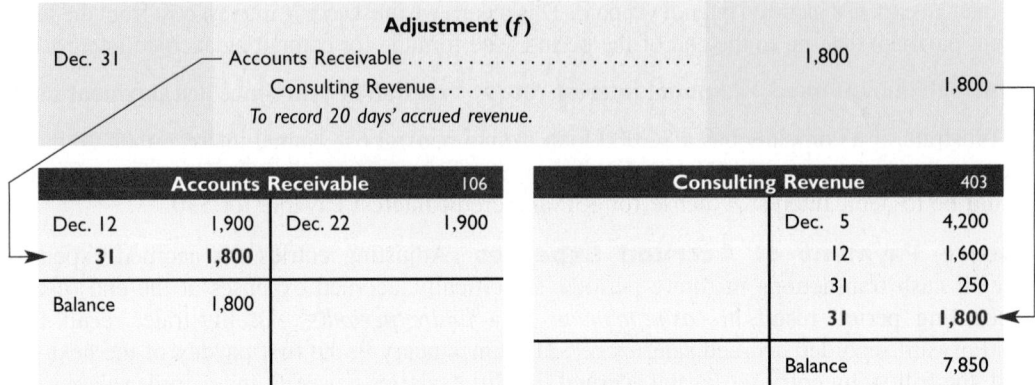

Adjustment (f)		
Dec. 31	Accounts Receivable	1,800
	Consulting Revenue	1,800
	To record 20 days' accrued revenue.	

Accounts Receivable			106
Dec. 12	1,900	Dec. 22	1,900
31	1,800		
Balance	1,800		

Consulting Revenue		403
	Dec. 5	4,200
	12	1,600
	31	250
	31	1,800
	Balance	7,850

Example: What is the adjusting entry if the 30-day consulting period began on December 22? *Answer:* One-third of the fee is earned:
Accounts Receivable ... 900
   Consulting Revenue ... 900

Explanation Accounts receivable are reported on the balance sheet at $1,800, and the $7,850 total of consulting revenue is reported on the income statement. *Not* making the adjustment would understate (1) both consulting revenue and net income by $1,800 in the December income statement and (2) both accounts receivable (assets) and equity by $1,800 on the December 31 balance sheet. The following table highlights the adjustment for accrued revenue.

Before Adjustment	Adjustment	After Adjustment
Accounts Receivable = $0	**Add $1,800 to Accounts Receivable** **Add $1,800 to Consulting Revenue**	**Accounts Receivable = $1,800**
Reports $0 from revenue earned but not yet received in cash.	Record 20 days of earned consulting revenue, which is 20/30 of total contract amount.	Reports $1,800 in accounts receivable from consulting services provided.

Accrued Interest Revenue In addition to the accrued interest expense we described earlier, interest can yield an accrued revenue when a debtor owes money (or other assets) to a company. If a company is holding notes or accounts receivable that produce interest revenue, we must adjust the accounts to record any earned and yet uncollected interest revenue. The adjusting entry is similar to the one for accruing services revenue. Specifically, we debit Interest Receivable (asset) and credit Interest Revenue.

Future Receipt of Accrued Revenues Accrued revenues at the end of one accounting period result in *cash receipts* in a *future* period(s). To illustrate, recall that FastForward made an adjusting entry for $1,800 to record 20 days' accrued revenue earned from its consulting contract. When FastForward receives $2,700 cash on January 10 for the entire contract amount, it makes the following entry to remove the accrued asset (accounts receivable) and recognize the revenue earned in January. The $2,700 debit reflects the cash received. The $1,800 credit reflects the removal of the receivable, and the $900 credit records the revenue earned in January.

Assets = Liabilities + Equity
+2,700 +900
−1,800

Jan. 10	Cash...	2,700	
	Accounts Receivable (20 days at $90 per day)		1,800
	Consulting Revenue (10 days at $90 per day)		900
	Received cash for the accrued asset and recorded *earned consulting revenue for January.*		

Decision Maker ▬▬▬▬▬▬▬▬▬▬▬▬▬▬▬▬▬▬▬

Loan Officer The owner of an electronics store applies for a business loan. The store's financial statements reveal large increases in current-year revenues and income. Analysis shows that these increases are due to a promotion that let consumers buy now and pay nothing until January 1 of next year. The store recorded these sales as accrued revenue. Does your analysis raise any concerns? [Answer—p. 128]

Links to Financial Statements

The process of adjusting accounts is intended to bring an asset or liability account balance to its correct amount. It also updates a related expense or revenue account. These adjustments are necessary for transactions and events that extend over more than one period. (Adjusting entries are posted like any other entry.)

Exhibit 3.12 summarizes the four types of transactions requiring adjustment. Understanding this exhibit is important to understanding the adjusting process and its importance to financial statements. Remember that each adjusting entry affects one or more income statement accounts *and* one or more balance sheet accounts (but never cash).

A1 Explain how accounting adjustments link to financial statements.

	BEFORE Adjusting		
Category	**Balance Sheet**	**Income Statement**	**Adjusting Entry**
Prepaid expenses†	Asset overstated	Expense understated	**Dr. Expense**
	Equity overstated		**Cr. Asset***
Unearned revenues†	Liability overstated	Revenue understated	Dr. Liability
	Equity understated		Cr. Revenue
Accrued expenses	Liability understated	Expense understated	**Dr. Expense**
	Equity overstated		**Cr. Liability**
Accrued revenues	Asset understated	Revenue understated	Dr. Asset
	Equity understated		Cr. Revenue

EXHIBIT 3.12

Summary of Adjustments and Financial Statement Links

* For depreciation, the credit is to Accumulated Depreciation (contra asset).

† Exhibit assumes that prepaid expenses are initially recorded as assets and that unearned revenues are initially recorded as liabilities.

Information about some adjustments is not always available until several days or even weeks after the period-end. This means that some adjusting and closing entries are recorded later than, but dated as of, the last day of the period. One example is a company that receives a utility bill on January 10 for costs incurred for the month of December. When it receives the bill, the company records the expense and the payable as of December 31. Other examples include long-distance phone usage and costs of many Web billings. The December income statement reflects these additional expenses incurred, and the December 31 balance sheet includes these payables, although the amounts were not actually known on December 31.

Decision Ethics ▬▬▬▬▬▬▬▬▬▬▬▬▬▬▬▬▬▬▬

Financial Officer At year-end, the president instructs you, the financial officer, not to record accrued expenses until next year because they will not be paid until then. The president also directs you to record in current-year sales a recent purchase order from a customer that requires merchandise to be delivered two weeks after the year-end. Your company would report a net income instead of a net loss if you carry out these instructions. What do you do? [Answer—p. 128]

Adjusted Trial Balance

P2   Explain and prepare an adjusted trial balance.

An **unadjusted trial balance** is a list of accounts and balances prepared *before* adjustments are recorded. An **adjusted trial balance** is a list of accounts and balances prepared *after* adjusting entries have been recorded and posted to the ledger.

Exhibit 3.13 shows both the unadjusted and the adjusted trial balances for FastForward at December 31, 2009. The order of accounts in the trial balance is usually set up to match the order in the chart of accounts. Several new accounts arise from the adjusting entries.

EXHIBIT 3.13

Unadjusted and Adjusted Trial Balances

File Edit View Insert Format Tools Data Window Help

FASTFORWARD
Trial Balances
December 31, 2009

Acct. No.	Account Title	Unadjusted Trial Balance Dr.	Cr.	Adjustments Dr.	Cr.	Adjusted Trial Balance Dr.	Cr.
101	Cash	$ 4,350				$ 4,350	
106	Accounts receivable	0		(f) $1,800		1,800	
126	Supplies	9,720			(b) $1,050	8,670	
128	Prepaid insurance	2,400			(a) 100	2,300	
167	Equipment	26,000				26,000	
168	Accumulated depreciation—Equip.		$ 0		(c) 375		$ 375
201	Accounts payable		6,200				6,200
209	Salaries payable		0		(e) 210		210
236	Unearned consulting revenue		3,000	(d) 250			2,750
307	Common stock		30,000				30,000
318	Retained earnings		0				0
319	Dividends	200				200	
403	Consulting revenue		5,800		(d) 250		7,850
					(f) 1,800		
406	Rental revenue		300				300
612	Depreciation expense—Equip.	0		(c) 375		375	
622	Salaries expense	1,400		(e) 210		1,610	
637	Insurance expense	0		(a) 100		100	
640	Rent expense	1,000				1,000	
652	Supplies expense	0		(b) 1,050		1,050	
690	Utilities expense	230				230	
	Totals	$45,300	$45,300	$3,785	$3,785	$47,685	$47,685

Sheet1   Sheet2   Sheet3

Each adjustment (see middle columns) is identified by a letter in parentheses that links it to an adjusting entry explained earlier. Each amount in the Adjusted Trial Balance columns is computed by taking that account's amount from the Unadjusted Trial Balance columns and adding or subtracting any adjustment(s). To illustrate, Supplies has a $9,720 Dr. balance in the unadjusted columns. Subtracting the $1,050 Cr. amount shown in the adjustments columns yields an adjusted $8,670 Dr. balance for Supplies. An account can have more than one adjustment, such as for Consulting Revenue. Also, some accounts might not require adjustment for this period, such as Accounts Payable.

Preparing Financial Statements

P3   Prepare financial statements from an adjusted trial balance.

We can prepare financial statements directly from information in the *adjusted* trial balance. An adjusted trial balance (see the right-most two columns in Exhibit 3.13) includes all accounts and balances appearing in financial statements, and is easier to work from than the entire ledger when preparing financial statements.

Exhibit 3.14 shows how revenue and expense balances are transferred from the adjusted trial balance to the income statement (red lines). Amounts for net income, retained earnings, and dividends are then used to prepare the statement of retained earnings (black lines). Asset, liability, and common stock balances on the adjusted trial balance are then transferred to the

Point: Each trial balance amount is used in only *one* financial statement and, when financial statements are completed, each account will have been used once.

EXHIBIT 3.14

Preparing Financial Statements (Adjusted Trial Balance from Exhibit 3.13)

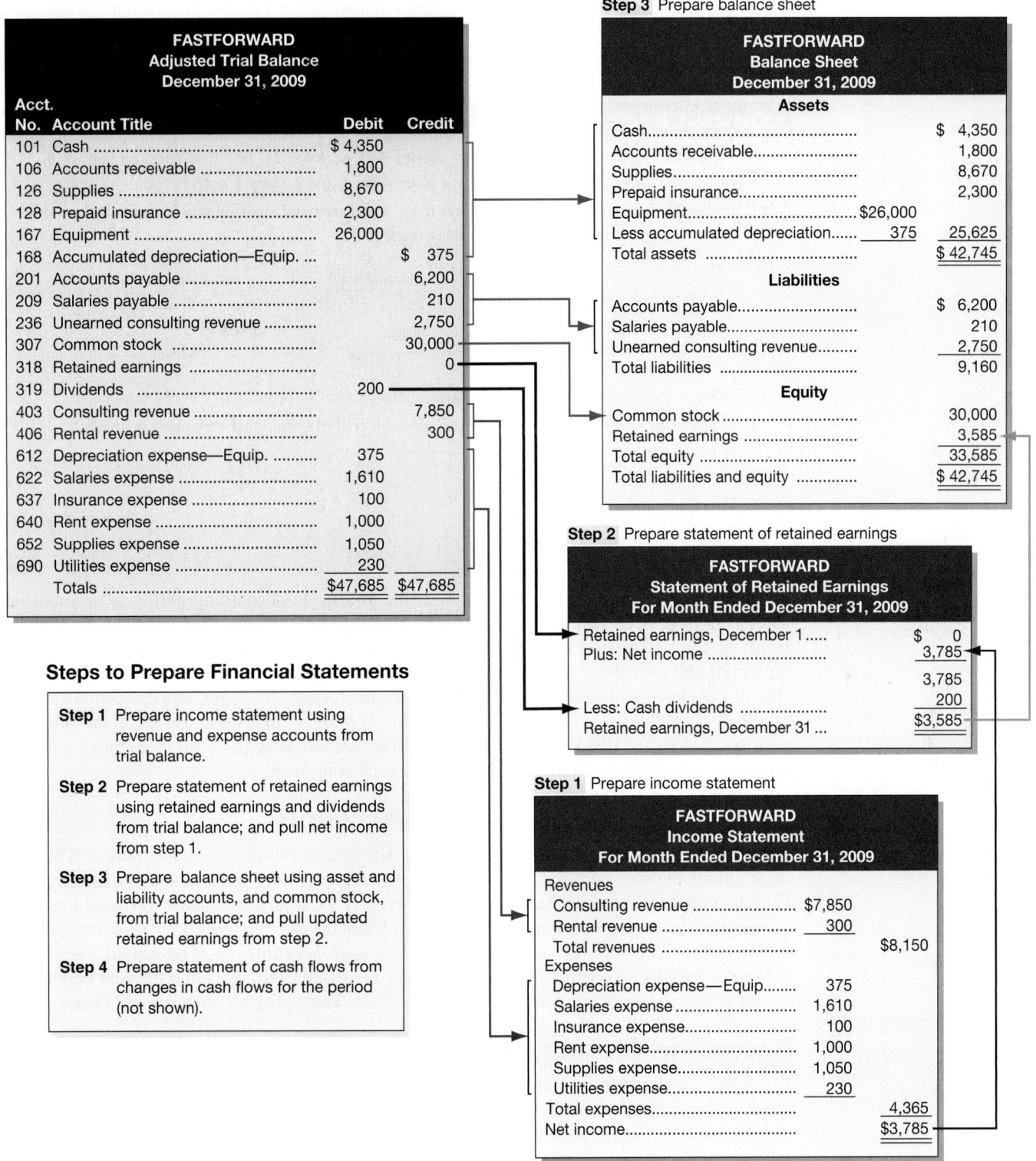

Steps to Prepare Financial Statements

Step 1 Prepare income statement using revenue and expense accounts from trial balance.

Step 2 Prepare statement of retained earnings using retained earnings and dividends from trial balance; and pull net income from step 1.

Step 3 Prepare balance sheet using asset and liability accounts, and common stock, from trial balance; and pull updated retained earnings from step 2.

Step 4 Prepare statement of cash flows from changes in cash flows for the period (not shown).

Point: Sarbanes-Oxley Act requires that financial statements filed with the SEC be certified by the CEO and CFO, including a declaration that the statements fairly present the issuer's operations and financial condition. Violators can receive fines and/or prison terms.

balance sheet (blue lines). The ending retained earnings is determined on the statement of retained earnings and transferred to the balance sheet (green line).

We prepare financial statements in the following order: income statement, statement of retained earnings, and balance sheet. This order makes sense because the balance sheet uses information from the statement of retained earnings, which in turn uses information from the income statement. The statement of cash flows is usually the final statement prepared.

Quick Check
Answers—p. 129

10. Music-Mart records $1,000 of accrued salaries on December 31. Five days later, on January 5 (the next payday), salaries of $7,000 are paid. What is the January 5 entry?

11. Jordan Air has the following information in its unadjusted and adjusted trial balances. What are the adjusting entries that Jordan Air likely recorded?

	Unadjusted		Adjusted	
	Debit	Credit	Debit	Credit
Prepaid insurance	$6,200		$5,900	
Salaries payable		$ 0		$1,400

12. What accounts are taken from the adjusted trial balance to prepare an income statement?

13. In preparing financial statements from an adjusted trial balance, what statement is usually prepared second?

Closing Process

P4 Describe and prepare closing entries.

Video3.1

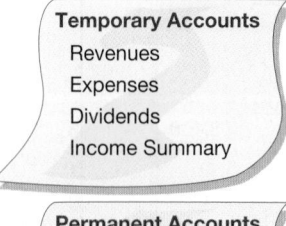

Temporary Accounts
Revenues
Expenses
Dividends
Income Summary

Permanent Accounts
Assets
Liabilities
Common Stock
Retained Earnings

The **closing process** is an important step at the end of an accounting period *after* financial statements have been completed. It prepares accounts for recording the transactions and the events of the *next* period. In the closing process we must (1) identify accounts for closing, (2) record and post the closing entries, and (3) prepare a post-closing trial balance. The purpose of the closing process is twofold. First, it resets revenue, expense, and dividends account balances to zero at the end of each period. This is done so that these accounts can properly measure income and dividends for the next period. Second, it helps in summarizing a period's revenues and expenses. This section explains the closing process.

Temporary and Permanent Accounts

Temporary (or *nominal*) **accounts** accumulate data related to one accounting period. They include all income statement accounts, the dividends account, and the Income Summary account. They are temporary because the accounts are opened at the beginning of a period, used to record transactions and events for that period, and then closed at the end of the period. *The closing process applies only to temporary accounts.* **Permanent** (or *real*) **accounts** report on activities related to one or more future accounting periods. They carry their ending balances into the next period and consist of balance sheet accounts. These asset, liability, and equity accounts are not closed.

Recording Closing Entries

To record and post **closing entries** is to transfer the end-of-period balances in revenue, expense, and dividends accounts to retained earnings. Closing entries are necessary at the end of each period after financial statements are prepared because

■ Revenue, expense, and dividends accounts must begin each period with zero balances.

■ Retained earnings must reflect prior periods' revenues, expenses, and dividends.

An income statement aims to report revenues and expenses for a *specific accounting period*. The statement of retained earnings reports similar information, including dividends. Since revenue, expense, and dividends accounts must accumulate information separately for each period, they must start each period with zero balances. To close these accounts, we transfer their balances first to an account called *Income Summary*. **Income Summary** is a temporary account (only used for the closing process) that contains a credit for the sum of all revenues (and gains) and a debit for the sum of all expenses (and losses). Its balance equals net income or net loss and it is transferred to retained earnings. Next, the dividends account balance is transferred to retained earnings. After these closing entries are posted, the revenue, expense, dividends, and Income Summary accounts have zero balances. These accounts are then said to be *closed* or *cleared*.

Point: To understand the closing process, focus on its *outcomes—updating* the retained earnings account balance to its proper ending balance, and getting *temporary accounts* to show *zero balances* for purposes of accumulating data for the next period.

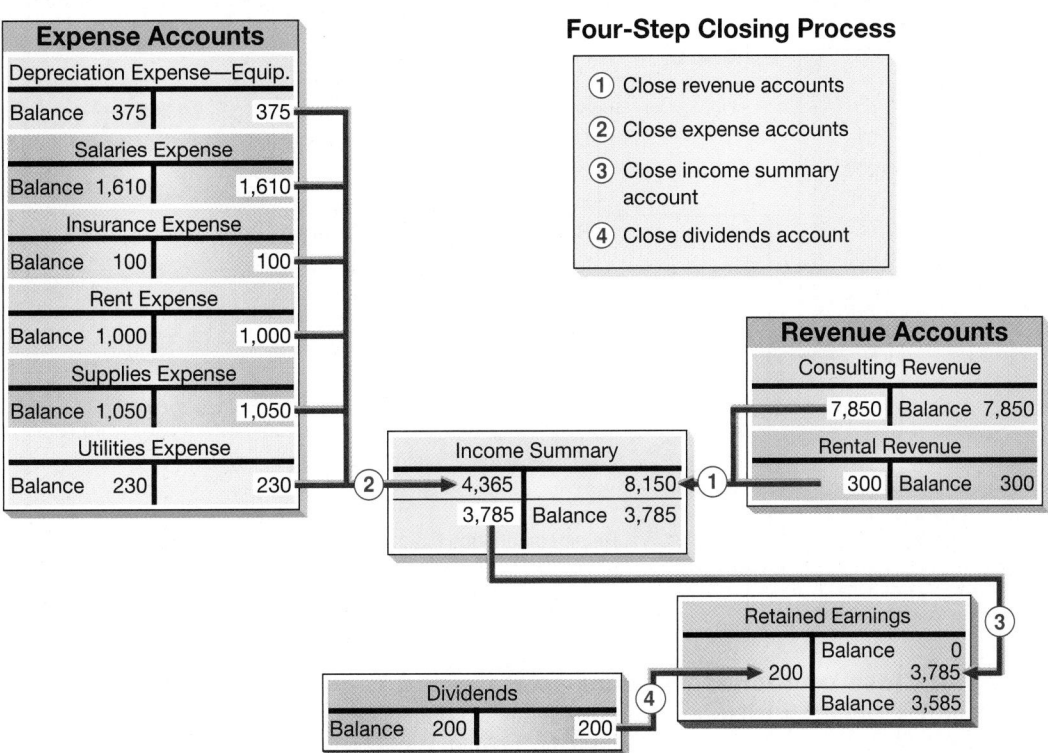

Four-Step Closing Process

1. Close revenue accounts
2. Close expense accounts
3. Close income summary account
4. Close dividends account

EXHIBIT 3.15

Four-Step Closing Process

Point: Retained Earnings is the only *permanent account* in Exhibit 3.15.

Exhibit 3.15 uses the adjusted account balances of FastForward (from the left side of Exhibit 3.14) to show the four steps necessary to close its temporary accounts. We explain each step.

Step 1: Close Credit Balances in Revenue Accounts to Income Summary The first closing entry transfers credit balances in revenue (and gain) accounts to the Income Summary account. We bring accounts with credit balances to zero by debiting them. For FastForward, this journal entry is step 1 in Exhibit 3.16. This entry closes revenue accounts and leaves them with zero balances. The accounts are now ready to record revenues when they occur in the next period. The $8,150 credit entry to Income Summary equals total revenues for the period.

Step 2: Close Debit Balances in Expense Accounts to Income Summary The second closing entry transfers debit balances in expense (and loss) accounts to the Income Summary account. We bring expense accounts' debit balances to zero by crediting them. With a balance of zero, these accounts are ready to accumulate a record of expenses for the next period. This second closing entry for FastForward is step 2 in Exhibit 3.16. Exhibit 3.15 shows that posting this entry gives each expense account a zero balance.

Point: It is possible to close revenue and expense accounts directly to retained earnings. Computerized accounting systems do this.

Step 3: Close Income Summary to Retained Earnings After steps 1 and 2, the balance of Income Summary is equal to December's net income of $3,785 ($8,150 credit less $4,365 debit). The third closing entry transfers the balance of the Income Summary account to retained earnings. This entry closes the Income Summary account–see step 3 in Exhibit 3.16. The Income Summary account has a zero balance after posting this entry. It continues to have a zero balance until the closing process again occurs at the end of the next period. (If a net loss occurred because expenses exceeded revenues, the third entry is reversed: debit Retained Earnings and credit Income Summary.)

EXHIBIT 3.16

Preparing Closing Entries

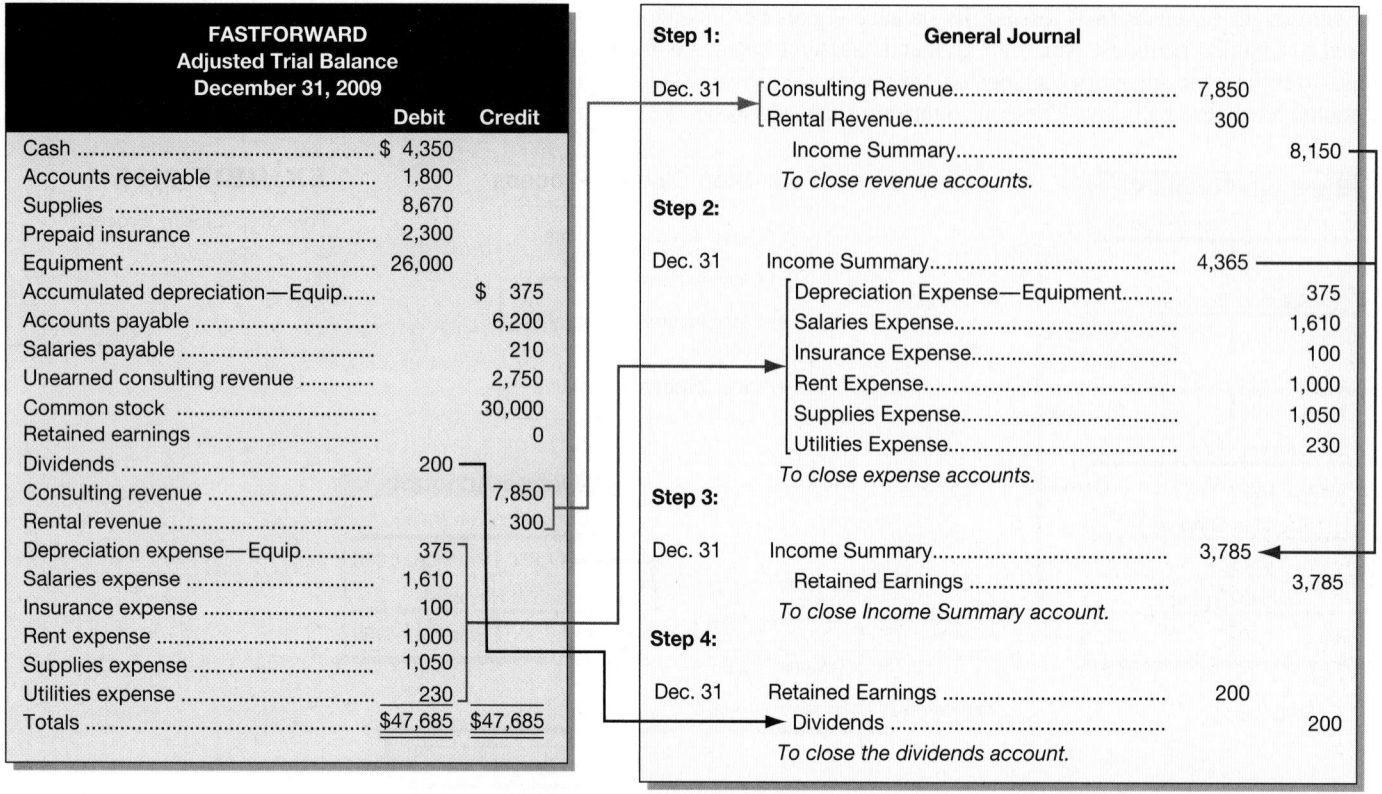

Step 4: Close Dividends Account to Retained Earnings

The fourth closing entry transfers any debit balance in the dividends account to retained earnings—see step 4 in Exhibit 3.16. This entry gives the dividends account a zero balance, and the account is now ready to accumulate next period's dividends. This entry also reduces the retained earnings balance to the $3,585 amount reported on the balance sheet.

We could also have selected the accounts and amounts needing to be closed by identifying individual revenue, expense, and dividends accounts in the ledger. (Information for closing entries is also in the financial statement columns of a work sheet—see Appendix 3B.)

Post-Closing Trial Balance

P5 Explain and prepare a post-closing trial balance.

Exhibit 3.17 shows the entire ledger of FastForward as of December 31 after adjusting and closing entries are posted. The temporary accounts (revenues, expenses, and dividends) have ending balances equal to zero.

A **post-closing trial balance** is a list of permanent accounts and their balances from the ledger after all closing entries have been journalized and posted. It lists the balances for all accounts not closed. These accounts comprise a company's assets, liabilities, and equity, which are identical to those in the balance sheet. The aim of a post-closing trial balance is to verify that (1) total debits equal total credits for permanent accounts and (2) all temporary accounts have zero balances. FastForward's post-closing trial balance is shown in Exhibit 3.18. The post-closing trial balance usually is the last step in the accounting process.

Quick Check   Answers—p. 129

14. What are the major steps in preparing closing entries?

15. Why are revenue and expense accounts called *temporary*? Identify and list the types of temporary accounts.

16. What accounts are listed on the post-closing trial balance?

EXHIBIT 3.17

General Ledger after the Closing Process for FastForward

Asset Accounts

Cash — Acct. No. 101

Date	Explan.	PR	Debit	Credit	Balance
2009					
Dec. 1	(1)	G1	30,000		30,000
2	(2)	G1		2,500	27,500
3	(3)	G1		26,000	1,500
5	(5)	G1	4,200		5,700
6	(13)	G1		2,400	3,300
12	(6)	G1		1,000	2,300
12	(7)	G1		700	1,600
22	(9)	G1	1,900		3,500
24	(10)	G1		900	2,600
24	(11)	G1		200	2,400
26	(12)	G1	3,000		5,400
26	(14)	G1		120	5,280
26	(15)	G1		230	5,050
26	(16)	G1		700	**4,350**

Accounts Receivable — Acct. No. 106

Date	Explan.	PR	Debit	Credit	Balance
2009					
Dec. 12	(8)	G1	1,900		1,900
22	(9)	G1		1,900	0
31	Adj.(f)	G1	1,800		**1,800**

Supplies — Acct. No. 126

Date	Explan.	PR	Debit	Credit	Balance
2009					
Dec. 2	(2)	G1	2,500		2,500
6	(4)	G1	7,100		9,600
26	(14)	G1	120		9,720
31	Adj.(b)	G1		1,050	**8,670**

Prepaid Insurance — Acct. No. 128

Date	Explan.	PR	Debit	Credit	Balance
2009					
Dec. 6	(13)	G1	2,400		2,400
31	Adj.(a)	G1		100	**2,300**

Equipment — Acct. No. 167

Date	Explan.	PR	Debit	Credit	Balance
2009					
Dec. 3	(3)	G1	26,000		**26,000**

Accumulated Depreciation—Equipment — Acct. No. 168

Date	Explan.	PR	Debit	Credit	Balance
2009					
Dec. 31	Adj.(c)	G1		375	**375**

Liability and Equity Accounts

Accounts Payable — Acct. No. 201

Date	Explan.	PR	Debit	Credit	Balance
2009					
Dec. 6	(4)	G1		7,100	7,100
24	(10)	G1	900		**6,200**

Salaries Payable — Acct. No. 209

Date	Explan.	PR	Debit	Credit	Balance
2009					
Dec. 31	Adj.(e)	G1		210	**210**

Unearned Consulting Revenue — Acct. No. 236

Date	Explan.	PR	Debit	Credit	Balance
2009					
Dec. 26	(12)	G1		3,000	3,000
31	Adj.(d)	G1	250		**2,750**

Common Stock — Acct. No. 307

Date	Explan.	PR	Debit	Credit	Balance
2009					
Dec. 1	(1)	G1		30,000	**30,000**

Retained Earnings — Acct. No. 318

Date	Explan.	PR	Debit	Credit	Balance
2009					
Dec. 31	Clos.(3)	G1		3,785	3,785
31	Clos.(4)	G1	200		3,585

Dividends — Acct. No. 319

Date	Explan.	PR	Debit	Credit	Balance
2009					
Dec. 24	(11)	G1	200		200
31	Clos.(4)	G1		200	0

Revenue and Expense Accounts (including Income Summary)

Consulting Revenue — Acct. No. 403

Date	Explan.	PR	Debit	Credit	Balance
2009					
Dec. 5	(5)	G1		4,200	4,200
12	(8)	G1		1,600	5,800
31	Adj.(d)	G1		250	6,050
31	Adj.(f)	G1		1,800	7,850
31	Clos.(1)	G1	7,850		0

Rental Revenue — Acct. No. 406

Date	Explan.	PR	Debit	Credit	Balance
2009					
Dec. 12	(8)	G1		300	300
31	Clos.(1)	G1	300		0

Depreciation Expense—Equipment — Acct. No. 612

Date	Explan.	PR	Debit	Credit	Balance
2009					
Dec. 31	Adj.(c)	G1	375		375
31	Clos.(2)	G1		375	0

Salaries Expense — Acct. No. 622

Date	Explan.	PR	Debit	Credit	Balance
2009					
Dec. 12	(7)	G1	700		700
26	(16)	G1	700		1,400
31	Adj.(e)	G1	210		1,610
31	Clos.(2)	G1		1,610	0

Insurance Expense — Acct. No. 637

Date	Explan.	PR	Debit	Credit	Balance
2009					
Dec. 31	Adj.(a)	G1	100		100
31	Clos.(2)	G1		100	0

Rent Expense — Acct. No. 640

Date	Explan.	PR	Debit	Credit	Balance
2009					
Dec. 12	(6)	G1	1,000		1,000
31	Clos.(2)	G1		1,000	0

Supplies Expense — Acct. No. 652

Date	Explan.	PR	Debit	Credit	Balance
2009					
Dec. 31	Adj.(b)	G1	1,050		1,050
31	Clos.(2)	G1		1,050	0

Utilities Expense — Acct. No. 690

Date	Explan.	PR	Debit	Credit	Balance
2009					
Dec. 26	(15)	G1	230		230
31	Clos.(2)	G1		230	0

Income Summary — Acct. No. 901

Date	Explan.	PR	Debit	Credit	Balance
2009					
Dec. 31	Clos.(1)	G1		8,150	8,150
31	Clos.(2)	G1	4,365		3,785
31	Clos.(3)	G1	3,785		0

EXHIBIT 3.18

Post-Closing Trial Balance

FASTFORWARD Post-Closing Trial Balance December 31, 2009	Debit	Credit
Cash	$ 4,350	
Accounts receivable	1,800	
Supplies	8,670	
Prepaid insurance	2,300	
Equipment	26,000	
Accumulated depreciation—Equipment		$ 375
Accounts payable		6,200
Salaries payable		210
Unearned consulting revenue		2,750
Common stock		30,000
Retained earnings		3,585
Totals	$43,120	$43,120

Accounting Cycle Summary

C3 Identify steps in the accounting cycle.

The term **accounting cycle** refers to the steps in preparing financial statements. It is called a *cycle* because the steps are repeated each reporting period. Exhibit 3.19 shows the 10 steps in the cycle, beginning with analyzing transactions and ending with a post-closing trial balance or reversing entries. Steps 1 through 3 usually occur regularly as a company enters into transactions. Steps 4 through 9 are done at the end of a period. *Reversing entries* in step 10 are optional and are explained in Appendix 3C, which is available on the book's Website.

EXHIBIT 3.19

Steps in the Accounting Cycle*

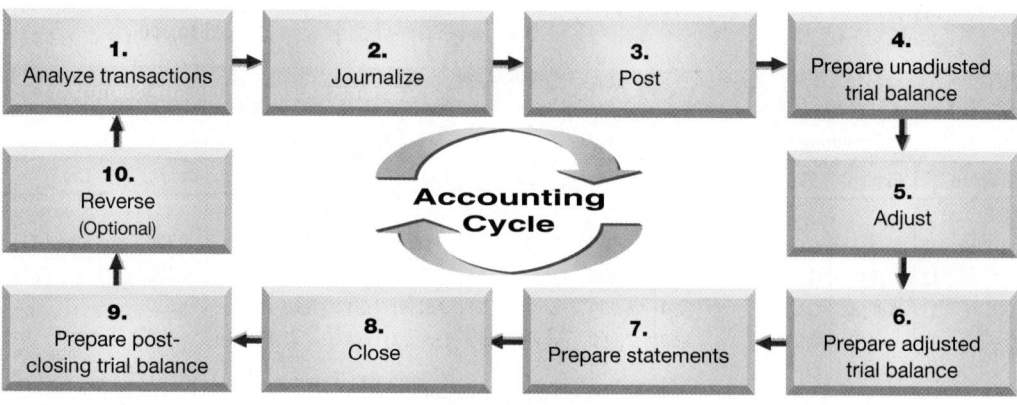

Explanations

1. Analyze transactions	Analyze transactions to prepare for journalizing.
2. Journalize	Record accounts, including debits and credits, in a journal.
3. Post	Transfer debits and credits from the journal to the ledger.
4. Prepare unadjusted trial balance	Summarize unadjusted ledger accounts and amounts.
5. Adjust	Record adjustments to bring account balances up to date; journalize and post adjustments.
6. Prepare adjusted trial balance	Summarize adjusted ledger accounts and amounts.
7. Prepare statements	Use adjusted trial balance to prepare financial statements.
8. Close	Journalize and post entries to close temporary accounts.
9. Prepare post-closing trial balance	Test clerical accuracy of the closing procedures.
10. Reverse (optional)	Reverse certain adjustments in the next period—optional step.

* Steps 4, 6, and 9 can be done on a work sheet. A work sheet is useful in *planning* adjustments, but adjustments (step 5) must always be journalized and posted. Steps 3, 4, 6, and 9 are automatic with a computerized system.

Classified Balance Sheet

Our discussion to this point has been limited to unclassified financial statements. This section describes a classified balance sheet. The next chapter describes a classified income statement. An **unclassified balance sheet** is one whose items are broadly grouped into assets, liabilities, and equity. One example is FastForward's balance sheet in Exhibit 3.14. A **classified balance sheet** organizes assets and liabilities into important subgroups that provide more information to decision makers.

C4 Explain and prepare a classified balance sheet.

Classification Structure

A classified balance sheet has no required layout, but it usually contains the categories in Exhibit 3.20. One of the more important classifications is the separation between current and noncurrent items for both assets and liabilities. Current items are those expected to come due (either collected or owed) within one year or the company's operating cycle, whichever is longer. The **operating cycle** is the time span from when *cash is used* to acquire goods and services until *cash is received* from the sale of goods and services. "Operating" refers to company operations and "cycle" refers to the circular flow of cash used for company inputs and then cash received from its outputs. The length of a company's operating cycle depends on its activities. For a service company, the operating cycle is the time span between (1) paying employees who perform the services and (2) receiving cash from customers. For a merchandiser selling products, the operating cycle is the time span between (1) paying suppliers for merchandise and (2) receiving cash from customers.

Video3.1

Assets	Liabilities and Equity
Current assets	Current liabilities
Noncurrent assets	Noncurrent liabilities
Long-term investments	Equity
Plant assets	
Intangible assets	

EXHIBIT 3.20

Typical Categories in a Classified Balance Sheet

Most operating cycles are less than one year. This means most companies use a one-year period in deciding which assets and liabilities are current. A few companies have an operating cycle longer than one year. For instance, producers of certain beverages (wine) and products (ginseng) that require aging for several years have operating cycles longer than one year. A balance sheet lists current assets before noncurrent assets and current liabilities before noncurrent liabilities. This consistency in presentation allows users to quickly identify current assets that are most easily converted to cash and current liabilities that are shortly coming due. Items in current assets and current liabilities are listed in the order of how quickly they will be converted to, or paid in, cash.

Classification Categories

This section describes the most common categories in a classified balance sheet. The balance sheet for Snowboarding Components in Exhibit 3.21 shows the typical categories. Its assets are classified as either current or noncurrent. Its noncurrent assets include three main categories: long-term investments, plant assets, and intangible assets. Its liabilities are classified as either current or long term. Not all companies use the same categories of assets and liabilities for their balance sheets. **K2 Inc.'s** balance sheet lists only three asset classes: current assets; property, plant and equipment; and other assets.

Current Assets **Current assets** are cash and other resources that are expected to be sold, collected, or used within one year or the company's operating cycle, whichever is longer. Examples are cash, short-term investments, accounts receivable, short-term notes receivable, goods for sale (called *merchandise* or *inventory*), and prepaid expenses. The individual prepaid expenses of a company are usually small in amount compared to many other assets and are often combined and shown as a single item. The prepaid expenses in Exhibit 3.21 likely include

Point: Current is also called *short term*, and noncurrent is also called *long term*.

EXHIBIT 3.21

Example of a Classified
Balance Sheet

SNOWBOARDING COMPONENTS Balance Sheet January 31, 2011		
Assets		
Current assets		
Cash	$ 6,500	
Short-term investments	2,100	
Accounts receivable	4,400	
Merchandise inventory	27,500	
Prepaid expenses	2,400	
Total current assets		$ 42,900
Long-term investments		
Notes receivable	1,500	
Investments in stocks and bonds	18,000	
Land held for future expansion	48,000	
Total long-term investments		67,500
Plant assets		
Equipment and buildings	203,200	
Less accumulated depreciation	53,000	
Equipment and buildings, net		150,200
Land		73,200
Total plant assets		223,400
Intangible assets		10,000
Total assets		$343,800
Liabilities		
Current liabilities		
Accounts payable	$15,300	
Wages payable	3,200	
Notes payable	3,000	
Current portion of long-term liabilities	7,500	
Total current liabilities		$ 29,000
Long-term liabilities (net of current portion)		150,000
Total liabilities		179,000
Equity		
Common stock		50,000
Retained earnings		114,800
Total equity		164,800
Total liabilities and equity		$343,800

items such as prepaid insurance, prepaid rent, office supplies, and store supplies. Prepaid expenses are usually listed last because they will not be converted to cash (instead, they are used).

Global: In the U.K. and many
countries influenced by U.K. reporting,
noncurrent assets are listed first and
current assets are listed second.

Long-Term Investments   A second major balance sheet classification is **long-term** (or *noncurrent*) **investments.** Notes receivable and investments in stocks and bonds are long-term assets when they are expected to be held for more than the longer of one year or the operating cycle. Land held for future expansion is a long-term investment because it is *not* used in operations.

Point: Plant assets are also called
fixed assets; property, plant and
equipment; or long-lived assets.

Plant Assets   Plant assets are tangible assets that are both *long lived* and *used to produce* or *sell products and services.* Examples are equipment, machinery, buildings, and land that are used to produce or sell products and services. The order listing for plant assets is usually from most liquid to least liquid such as equipment and machinery to buildings and land.

Intangible Assets   **Intangible assets** are long-term resources that benefit business operations, usually lack physical form, and have uncertain benefits. Examples are patents, trademarks, copyrights, franchises, and goodwill. Their value comes from the privileges or rights granted to or held by the owner. **K2, Inc.**, reports intangible assets of **$228 million**, which is nearly 20 percent of its total assets. Its intangibles include trademarks, patents, and licensing agreements.

Current Liabilities   **Current liabilities** are obligations due to be paid or settled within one year or the operating cycle, whichever is longer. They are usually settled by paying out current assets such as cash. Current liabilities often include accounts payable, notes payable, wages payable, taxes payable, interest payable, and unearned revenues. Also, any portion of a long-term liability due to be paid within one year or the operating cycle, whichever is longer, is a current liability. Unearned revenues are current liabilities when they will be settled by delivering products or services within one year or the operating cycle, whichever is longer. Current liabilities are reported in the order of those to be settled first.

Point: Many financial ratios are distorted if accounts are not classified correctly.

Long-Term Liabilities   **Long-term liabilities** are obligations *not* due within one year or the operating cycle, whichever is longer. Notes payable, mortgages payable, bonds payable, and lease obligations are common long-term liabilities. If a company has both short- and long-term items in each of these categories, they are commonly separated into two accounts in the ledger.

Point: Only assets and liabilities are classified as current or noncurrent.

Equity   Equity is the owner's claim on assets. The equity section for a corporation is divided into two main subsections, common stock (or contributed capital) and retained earnings.

Quick Check
Answers—p. 129

17. Identify the following assets as classified as (1) current assets, (2) plant assets, or (3) intangible assets: (*a*) land used in operations, (*b*) office supplies, (*c*) receivables from customers due in 10 months, (*d*) insurance protection for the next nine months, (*e*) trucks used to provide services to customers, (*f*) trademarks.
18. Cite two examples of assets classified as investments on the balance sheet.
19. Explain the operating cycle for a service company.

Global View

We explained that accounting under U.S. GAAP is similar, but not identical, to that under IFRS. This section discusses differences in adjusting accounts, preparing financial statements, and reporting assets and liabilities on a balance sheet.

Adjusting Accounts and the Closing Process

Both U.S. GAAP and IFRS include broad and similar guidance for adjusting accounts. Although some variations exist in revenue and expense recognition and other principles, all of the adjustments in this chapter are accounted for identically under the two systems. The closing process also is identical under U.S. GAAP and IFRS. In later chapters we describe how certain assets and liabilities can result in different adjusted amounts using fair value measurements.

Preparing Financial Statements

Both U.S. GAAP and IFRS prepare the same four basic financial statements following the same process discussed in this chapter. Some differences within each statement do exist and we will discuss those throughout the book. Chapter 2 explained how both U.S. GAAP and IFRS require current items to be separated from noncurrent items on the balance sheet (yielding a classified balance sheet). U.S. GAAP balance sheets report current items first. Assets are listed from most liquid to least liquid, where liquid refers to the ease of converting an asset to cash. Liabilities are listed from nearest to maturity to furthest from maturity, maturity refers to the nearness of paying off the liability. IFRS balance sheets normally present noncurrent items first (and equity before liabilities), but this is not a requirement. Other differences with financial statements exist, which we identify in later chapters. GOME provides the following example of IFRS reporting for its assets, liabilities, and equity within the balance sheet:

GOME Balance Sheet (in RMB 000s) December 31, 2008			
Assets		**Equity and Liabilities**	
Noncurrent assets		Total equity	8,700,035
Goodwill and other intangibles	3,497,253		
Property, plant and equipment	3,719,829	Noncurrent liabilities	
Other noncurrent assets	1,795,311	Deferred tax liabilities	78,269
Total noncurrent assets	9,012,393	Convertible bonds	3,569,553
Current assets		Total noncurrent liabilities	3,647,822
Investments, deposits and loans	3,630,399	Current liabilities	
Inventories	5,473,497	Interest-bearing bank loans	170,000
Other current assets	6,327,746	Trade and bills payables	12,917,958
Cash and cash equivalents	3,051,069	Tax payable and other current liabilities ...	2,059,289
Total current assets	18,482,711	Total current liabilities	15,147,247
Total assets	27,495,104	Total equity and liabilities	27,495,104

Reporting Assets and Liabilities

The definition of an asset is similar under U.S. GAAP and IFRS and involves three basic criteria: (1) the company owns or controls the right to use the item, (2) the right arises from a past transaction or event, and (3) the item can be reliably measured. Both systems define the initial asset value as historical cost for nearly all assets. After acquisition, one of two asset measurement systems is applied: historical cost or fair value (fair value includes replacement cost, realizable value, and present value). Generally, U.S. GAAP defines fair value as the amount to be received in an orderly sale. IFRS defines fair value as *exchange value*—either replacement cost or selling price. We describe these differences, and the assets to which they apply, in later chapters.

The definition of a liability is similar under U.S. GAAP and IFRS and involves three basic criteria: (1) the item is a *present* obligation requiring a probable future resource outlay, (2) the obligation arises from a past transaction or event, and (3) the obligation can be reliably measured. As with assets, both systems apply one of two measurement systems to specific liabilities: historical cost or fair value. Later chapters discuss specific differences.

IFRS

Adjusting with IFRS   Revenue and expense recognition are key to recording accounting adjustments. IFRS tends to be more *principles-based relative* to U.S. GAAP, which is viewed as more *rules-based*. A principles-based system depends heavily on control procedures to reduce the potential for fraud or misconduct. Failure in judgment led to improper accounting adjustments at **Fannie Mae, Xerox, WorldCom,** and others. A KPMG 2009 survey of accounting and finance employees found that 13% of them had witnessed falsification or manipulation of accounting data within the past year. Internal controls and governance processes are directed at curtailing such behavior.

Decision Analysis | Profit Margin and Current Ratio

A2   Compute profit margin and describe its use in analyzing company performance.

EXHIBIT 3.22

Profit Margin

Profit Margin

A useful measure of a company's operating results is the ratio of its net income to net sales. This ratio is called **profit margin,** or *return on sales,* and is computed as in Exhibit 3.22.

$$\text{Profit margin} = \frac{\text{Net income}}{\text{Net sales}}$$

This ratio is interpreted as reflecting the percent of profit in each dollar of sales. To illustrate how we compute and use profit margin, let's look at the results of **Limited Brands, Inc.,** in Exhibit 3.23 for its fiscal years 2006 through 2009.

$ in millions	2009	2008	2007	2006
Net income	$ 220	$ 718	$ 676	$ 683
Net sales	$9,043	$10,134	$10,671	$9,699
Profit margin	2.4%	7.1%	6.3%	7.0%
Industry profit margin	0.3%	1.1%	1.6%	1.5%

EXHIBIT 3.23

Limited Brands' Profit Margin

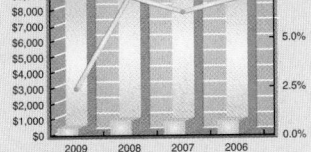

The Limited's average profit margin is 5.7% during this period. This favorably compares to the average industry profit margin of 1.1%. However, Limited's profit margin has declined in the most recent year—from 7.0% in 2006 to 2.4% for the recent recessionary period (see margin graph). Future success depends on Limited maintaining its market share and increasing its profit margin.

Current Ratio

An important use of financial statements is to help assess a company's ability to pay its debts in the near future. Such analysis affects decisions by suppliers when allowing a company to buy on credit. It also affects decisions by creditors when lending money to a company, including loan terms such as interest rate, due date, and collateral requirements. It can also affect a manager's decisions about using cash to pay debts when they come due. The **current ratio** is one measure of a company's ability to pay its short-term obligations. It is defined in Exhibit 3.24 as current assets divided by current liabilities.

A3 Compute the current ratio and describe what it reveals about a company's financial condition.

$$\text{Current ratio} = \frac{\text{Current assets}}{\text{Current liabilities}}$$

EXHIBIT 3.24

Current Ratio

Using financial information from **Limited Brands, Inc.**, we compute its current ratio for the recent four-year period. The results are in Exhibit 3.25.

$ in millions	2009	2008	2007	2006
Current assets	$2,867	$2,919	$2,771	$2,784
Current liabilities	$1,255	$1,374	$1,709	$1,575
Current ratio	2.3%	2.1%	1.6	1.8
Industry current ratio	2.0%	2.1%	2.3	2.4

EXHIBIT 3.25

Limited Brands' Current Ratio

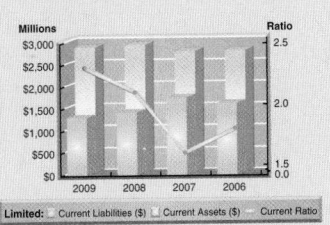

Limited Brands' current ratio averaged 2.0 for its fiscal years 2006 through 2009. The current ratio for each of these years suggests that the company's short-term obligations can be covered with its short-term assets. However, if its ratio would approach 1.0, Limited would expect to face challenges in covering liabilities. If the ratio were *less* than 1.0, current liabilities would exceed current assets, and the company's ability to pay short-term obligations could be in doubt.

Decision Maker

Analyst You are analyzing the financial condition of a company to assess its ability to meet upcoming loan payments. You compute its current ratio as 1.2. You also find that a major portion of accounts receivable is due from one client who has not made any payments in the past 12 months. Removing this receivable from current assets lowers the current ratio to 0.7. What do you conclude? [Answer—p. 129]

Demonstration Problem 1

The following information relates to Fanning's Electronics on December 31, 2011. The company, which uses the calendar year as its annual reporting period, initially records prepaid and unearned items in balance sheet accounts (assets and liabilities, respectively).

a. The company's weekly payroll is $8,750, paid each Friday for a five-day workweek. Assume December 31, 2011, falls on a Monday, but the employees will not be paid their wages until Friday, January 4, 2012.

b. Eighteen months earlier, on July 1, 2010, the company purchased equipment that cost $20,000. Its useful life is predicted to be five years, at which time the equipment is expected to be worthless (zero salvage value).

c. On October 1, 2011, the company agreed to work on a new housing development. The company is paid $120,000 on October 1 in advance of future installation of similar alarm systems in 24 new homes. That amount was credited to the Unearned Services Revenue account. Between October 1 and December 31, work on 20 homes was completed.

d. On September 1, 2011, the company purchased a 12-month insurance policy for $1,800. The transaction was recorded with an $1,800 debit to Prepaid Insurance.

e. On December 29, 2011, the company completed a $7,000 service that has not been billed and not recorded as of December 31, 2011.

Required

1. Prepare any necessary adjusting entries on December 31, 2011, in relation to transactions and events *a* through *e*. Assume that adjusting entries are made only at the end of the calendar year.

2. Prepare T-accounts for the accounts affected by adjusting entries, and post the adjusting entries. Determine the adjusted balances for the Unearned Revenue and the Prepaid Insurance accounts.

3. Complete the following table and determine the amounts and effects of your adjusting entries on the year 2011 income statement and the December 31, 2011, balance sheet. Use up (down) arrows to indicate an increase (decrease) in the Effect columns.

Entry	Amount in the Entry	Effect on Net Income	Effect on Total Assets	Effect on Total Liabilities	Effect on Total Equity

Planning the Solution

- Analyze each situation to determine which accounts need to be updated with an adjustment.
- Calculate the amount of each adjustment and prepare the necessary journal entries.
- Show the amount of each adjustment in the designated accounts, determine the adjusted balance, and identify the balance sheet classification of the account.
- Determine each entry's effect on net income for the year and on total assets, total liabilities, and total equity at the end of the year.

Solution to Demonstration Problem 1

1. Adjusting journal entries.

(a) Dec. 31	Wages Expense	1,750	
	Wages Payable		1,750
	To accrue wages for the last day of the year ($8,750 × 1/5).		
(b) Dec. 31	Depreciation Expense—Equipment	4,000	
	Accumulated Depreciation—Equipment		4,000
	To record depreciation expense for the year ($20,000/5 years = $4,000 per year).		
(c) Dec. 31	Unearned Services Revenue	100,000	
	Services Revenue...........................		100,000
	To recognize services revenue earned ($120,000 × 20/24).		
(d) Dec. 31	Insurance Expense.............................	600	
	Prepaid Insurance		600
	To adjust for expired portion of insurance ($1,800 × 4/12).		
(e) Dec. 31	Accounts Receivable	7,000	
	Services Revenue...........................		7,000
	To record services revenue earned.		

2. T-accounts for adjusting journal entries *a* through *e*.

Wages Expense	
(a) 1,750	

Wages Payable	
	(a) 1,750

Depreciation Expense—Equipment	
(b) 4,000	

Accumulated Depreciation—Equipment	
	(b) 4,000

Unearned Revenue	
	Unadj. Bal. 120,000
(c) 100,000	
	Adj. Bal. 20,000

Services Revenue	
	(c) 100,000
	(e) 7,000
	Adj. Bal. 107,000

Insurance Expense	
(d) 600	

Prepaid Insurance	
Unadj. Bal. 1,800	
	(d) 600
Adj. Bal. 1,200	

Accounts Receivable	
(e) 7,000	

3. Financial statement effects of adjusting journal entries.

Entry	Amount in the Entry	Effect on Net Income	Effect on Total Assets	Effect on Total Liabilities	Effect on Total Equity
a	$ 1,750	$ 1,750 ↓	No effect	$ 1,750 ↑	$ 1,750 ↓
b	4,000	4,000 ↓	$4,000 ↓	No effect	4,000 ↓
c	100,000	100,000 ↑	No effect	$100,000 ↓	100,000 ↑
d	600	600 ↓	$ 600 ↓	No effect	600 ↓
e	7,000	7,000 ↑	$7,000 ↑	No effect	7,000 ↑

Demonstration Problem 2

Use the following adjusted trial balance to answer questions 1 through 4.

CHOI COMPANY
Adjusted Trial Balance
December 31

	Debit	Credit
Cash	$ 3,050	
Accounts receivable	400	
Prepaid insurance	830	
Supplies	80	
Equipment	217,200	

[continued on next page]

[continued from previous page]

Accumulated depreciation—Equipment		$ 29,100
Wages payable		880
Interest payable		3,600
Unearned rent		460
Long-term notes payable		150,000
Common stock		10,000
Retained earnings		30,340
Dividends	21,000	
Rent earned		57,500
Wages expense	25,000	
Utilities expense	1,900	
Insurance expense	3,200	
Supplies expense	250	
Depreciation expense—Equipment	5,970	
Interest expense	3,000	
Totals	$281,880	$281,880

1. Prepare the annual income statement from the adjusted trial balance of Choi Company.

Answer:

CHOI COMPANY
Income Statement
For Year Ended December 31

Revenues		
Rent earned		$57,500
Expenses		
Wages expense	$25,000	
Utilities expense	1,900	
Insurance expense	3,200	
Supplies expense	250	
Depreciation expense—Equipment	5,970	
Interest expense	3,000	
Total expenses		39,320
Net income		$18,180

2. Prepare a statement of retained earnings from the adjusted trial balance of Choi Company.

Answer:

CHOI COMPANY
Statement of Retained Earnings
For Year Ended December 31

Retained earnings, December 31 (prior year)	$30,340
Plus: Net income	18,180
	48,520
Less: Cash dividends	21,000
Retained earnings, December 31 (current year)	$27,520

3. Prepare a classified balance sheet from the adjusted trial balance of Choi Company.

Answer:

CHOI COMPANY
Balance Sheet
December 31

Assets

Current assets		
Cash		$ 3,050
Accounts receivable		400
Prepaid insurance		830
Supplies		80
Total current assets		4,360
Plant assets		
Equipment	$217,200	
Less accumulated depreciation	29,100	
Total plant assets, net		188,100
Total assets		$192,460

Liabilities

Current liabilities		
Wages payable		$ 880
Interest payable		3,600
Unearned rent		460
Total current liabilities		4,940
Long-term liabilities		
Long-term notes payable		150,000
Total liabilities		154,940

Equity

Common stock		10,000
Retained earnings		27,520
Total equity		37,520
Total liabilities and equity		$192,460

4. Prepare the closing entries for Choi Company.

Dec. 31	Rent Earned.....................................	57,500	
	Income Summary.............................		57,500
	To close revenue accounts.		
Dec. 31	Income Summary.................................	39,320	
	Wages Expense		25,000
	Utilities Expense		1,900
	Insurance Expense...........................		3,200
	Supplies Expense		250
	Depreciation Expense—Equip.................		5,970
	Interest Expense		3,000
	To close expense accounts.		
Dec. 31	Income Summary.................................	18,180	
	Retained Earnings		18,180
	To close Income Summary account.		
Dec. 31	Retained Earnings................................	21,000	
	Dividends..................................		21,000
	To close the Dividends account.		

APPENDIX

3A Alternative Accounting for Prepayments

This appendix explains an alternative in accounting for prepaid expenses and unearned revenues.

Recording the Prepayment of Expenses in Expense Accounts

P6 Explain the alternatives in accounting for prepaids.

An alternative method is to record *all* prepaid expenses with debits to expense accounts. If any prepaids remain unused or unexpired at the end of an accounting period, then adjusting entries must transfer the cost of the unused portions from expense accounts to prepaid expense (asset) accounts. This alternative method is acceptable. The financial statements are identical under either method, but the adjusting entries are different. To illustrate the differences between these two methods, let's look at FastForward's cash payment of December 6 for 24 months of insurance coverage beginning on December 1. FastForward recorded that payment with a debit to an asset account, but it could have recorded a debit to an expense account. These alternatives are shown in Exhibit 3A.1.

EXHIBIT 3A.1

Alternative Initial Entries for Prepaid Expenses

		Payment Recorded as Asset	Payment Recorded as Expense
Dec. 6	Prepaid Insurance	2,400	
	Cash	2,400	
Dec. 6	Insurance Expense		2,400
	Cash		2,400

At the end of its accounting period on December 31, insurance protection for one month has expired. This means $100 ($2,400/24) of insurance coverage expired and is an expense for December. The adjusting entry depends on how the original payment was recorded. This is shown in Exhibit 3A.2.

EXHIBIT 3A.2

Adjusting Entry for Prepaid Expenses for the Two Alternatives

		Payment Recorded as Asset	Payment Recorded as Expense
Dec. 31	Insurance Expense	100	
	Prepaid Insurance	100	
Dec. 31	Prepaid Insurance		2,300
	Insurance Expense		2,300

When these entries are posted to the accounts in the ledger, we can see that these two methods give identical results. The December 31 adjusted account balances in Exhibit 3A.3 show Prepaid Insurance of $2,300 and Insurance Expense of $100 for both methods.

EXHIBIT 3A.3

Account Balances under Two Alternatives for Recording Prepaid Expenses

Payment Recorded as Asset			
Prepaid Insurance			128
Dec. 6	2,400	Dec. 31	100
Balance	2,300		

Insurance Expense			637
Dec. 31	100		

Payment Recorded as Expense			
Prepaid Insurance			128
Dec. 31	2,300		

Insurance Expense			637
Dec. 6	2,400	Dec. 31	2,300
Balance	100		

Recording the Prepayment of Revenues in Revenue Accounts

As with prepaid expenses, an alternative method is to record *all* unearned revenues with credits to revenue accounts. If any revenues are unearned at the end of an accounting period, then adjusting entries must transfer the unearned portions from revenue accounts to unearned revenue (liability) accounts. This alternative method is acceptable. The adjusting entries are different for these two alternatives, but the financial statements are identical. To illustrate the accounting differences between these two methods, let's look at FastForward's December 26 receipt of $3,000 for consulting services covering the period December 27 to February 24. FastForward recorded this transaction with a credit to a liability account. The alternative is to record it with a credit to a revenue account, as shown in Exhibit 3A.4.

		Receipt Recorded as Liability	Receipt Recorded as Revenue
Dec. 26	Cash	3,000	
	Unearned Consulting Revenue	3,000	
Dec. 26	Cash		3,000
	Consulting Revenue		3,000

EXHIBIT 3A.4

Alternative Initial Entries for Unearned Revenues

By the end of its accounting period on December 31, FastForward has earned $250 of this revenue. This means $250 of the liability has been satisfied. Depending on how the initial receipt is recorded, the adjusting entry is as shown in Exhibit 3A.5.

		Receipt Recorded as Liability	Receipt Recorded as Revenue
Dec. 31	Unearned Consulting Revenue	250	
	Consulting Revenue	250	
Dec. 31	Consulting Revenue		2,750
	Unearned Consulting Revenue		2,750

EXHIBIT 3A.5

Adjusting Entry for Unearned Revenues for the Two Alternatives

After adjusting entries are posted, the two alternatives give identical results. The December 31 adjusted account balances in Exhibit 3A.6 show unearned consulting revenue of $2,750 and consulting revenue of $250 for both methods.

Receipt Recorded as Liability			
Unearned Consulting Revenue			236
Dec. 31	250	Dec. 26	3,000
		Balance	**2,750**

Consulting Revenue			403
		Dec. 31	**250**

Receipt Recorded as Revenue			
Unearned Consulting Revenue			236
		Dec. 31	**2,750**

Consulting Revenue			403
Dec. 31	2,750	Dec. 26	3,000
		Balance	**250**

EXHIBIT 3A.6

Account Balances under Two Alternatives for Recording Unearned Revenues

APPENDIX

Work Sheet as a Tool

3B

Information preparers use various analyses and internal documents when organizing information for internal and external decision makers. Internal documents are often called **working papers.** One widely used working paper is the **work sheet,** which is a useful tool for preparers in working with accounting information. It is usually not available to external decision makers.

P7　Prepare a work sheet and explain its usefulness.

Benefits of a Work Sheet

A work sheet is *not* a required report, yet using a manual or electronic work sheet has several potential benefits. Specifically, a work sheet:

- ■ Aids the preparation of financial statements.
- ■ Reduces the possibility of errors when working with many accounts and adjustments.
- ■ Links accounts and adjustments to their impacts in financial statements.
- ■ Assists in planning and organizing an audit of financial statements—as it can be used to reflect any adjustments necessary.
- ■ Helps in preparing interim (monthly and quarterly) financial statements when the journalizing and posting of adjusting entries are postponed until the year-end.
- ■ Shows the effects of proposed or "what if" transactions.

Use of a Work Sheet

Point: Since a work sheet is *not* a required report or an accounting record, its format is flexible and can be modified by its user to fit his/her preferences.

When a work sheet is used to prepare financial statements, it is constructed at the end of a period before the adjusting process. The complete work sheet includes a list of the accounts, their balances and adjustments, and their sorting into financial statement columns. It provides two columns each for the unadjusted trial balance, the adjustments, the adjusted trial balance, the income statement, and the balance sheet. To describe and interpret the work sheet, we use the information from FastForward. Preparing the work sheet has five important steps. Each step, 1 through 5, is color-coded and explained with reference to Exhibit 3B.1.

① Step 1. Enter Unadjusted Trial Balance

The first step in preparing a work sheet is to list the title of every account and its account number that is expected to appear on its financial statements. This includes all accounts in the ledger plus any new ones from adjusting entries. Most adjusting entries—including expenses from salaries, supplies, depreciation, and insurance—are predictable and recurring. The unadjusted balance for each account is then entered in the appropriate Debit or Credit column of the unadjusted trial balance columns. The totals of these two columns must be equal. Exhibit 3B.1 shows FastForward's work sheet after completing this first step. Sometimes blank lines are left on the work sheet based on past experience to indicate where lines will be needed for adjustments to certain accounts. Exhibit 3B.1 shows Consulting Revenue as one example. An alternative is to squeeze adjustments on one line or to combine the effects of two or more adjustments in one amount. In the unusual case when an account is not predicted, we can add a new line for such an account following the *Totals* line.

② Step 2. Enter Adjustments

The second step in preparing a work sheet is to enter adjustments in the Adjustments columns. The adjustments shown are the same ones shown in Exhibit 3.13. An identifying letter links the debit and credit of each adjusting entry. This is called *keying* the adjustments. After preparing a work sheet, adjusting entries must still be entered in the journal and posted to the ledger. The Adjustments columns provide the information for those entries.

③ Step 3. Prepare Adjusted Trial Balance

Point: To avoid omitting the transfer of an account balance, start with the first line (cash) and continue in account order.

The adjusted trial balance is prepared by combining the adjustments with the unadjusted balances for each account. As an example, the Prepaid Insurance account has a $2,400 debit balance in the Unadjusted Trial Balance columns. This $2,400 debit is combined with the $100 credit in the Adjustments columns to give Prepaid Insurance a $2,300 debit in the Adjusted Trial Balance columns. The totals of the Adjusted Trial Balance columns confirm the equality of debits and credits.

④ Step 4. Sort Adjusted Trial Balance Amounts to Financial Statements

This step involves sorting account balances from the adjusted trial balance to their proper financial statement columns. Expenses go to the Income Statement Debit column and revenues to the Income Statement Credit column. Assets and Dividends go to the Balance Sheet Debit column. Liabilities, Retained Earnings, and Common Stock go to the Balance Sheet Credit column.

⑤ Step 5. Total Statement Columns, Compute Income or Loss, and Balance Columns

Each financial statement column (from Step 4) is totaled. The difference between the totals of the Income Statement columns is net income or net loss. This occurs because revenues are entered in the Credit

EXHIBIT 3B.1

Work Sheet

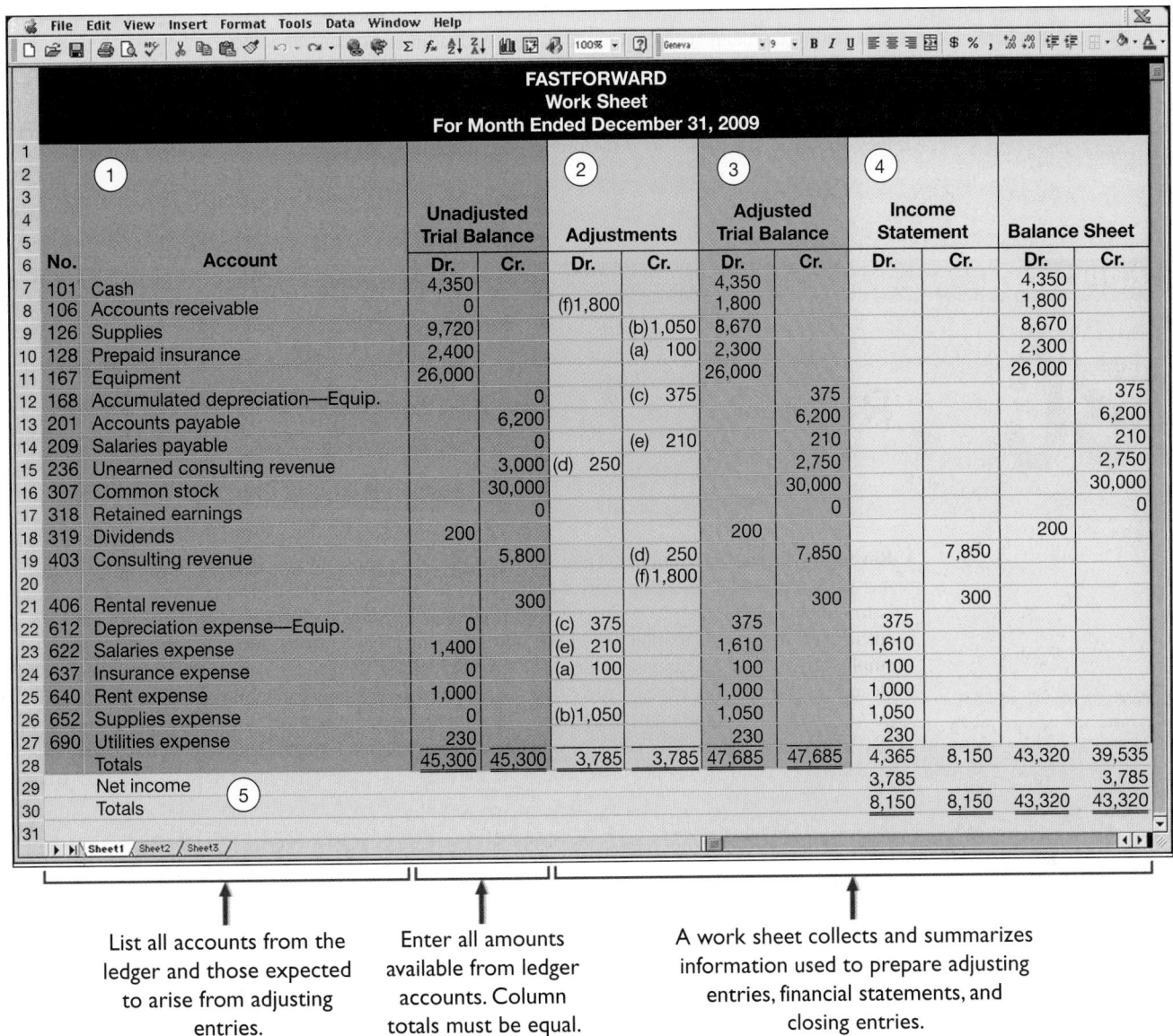

FASTFORWARD
Work Sheet
For Month Ended December 31, 2009

No.	Account	Unadjusted Trial Balance Dr.	Cr.	Adjustments Dr.	Cr.	Adjusted Trial Balance Dr.	Cr.	Income Statement Dr.	Cr.	Balance Sheet Dr.	Cr.
101	Cash	4,350				4,350				4,350	
106	Accounts receivable	0		(f)1,800		1,800				1,800	
126	Supplies	9,720			(b)1,050	8,670				8,670	
128	Prepaid insurance	2,400			(a) 100	2,300				2,300	
167	Equipment	26,000				26,000				26,000	
168	Accumulated depreciation—Equip.		0		(c) 375		375				375
201	Accounts payable		6,200				6,200				6,200
209	Salaries payable		0		(e) 210		210				210
236	Unearned consulting revenue		3,000	(d) 250			2,750				2,750
307	Common stock		30,000				30,000				30,000
318	Retained earnings		0				0				0
319	Dividends	200				200				200	
403	Consulting revenue		5,800		(d) 250		7,850		7,850		
					(f)1,800						
406	Rental revenue		300				300		300		
612	Depreciation expense—Equip.	0		(c) 375		375		375			
622	Salaries expense	1,400		(e) 210		1,610		1,610			
637	Insurance expense	0		(a) 100		100		100			
640	Rent expense	1,000				1,000		1,000			
652	Supplies expense	0		(b)1,050		1,050		1,050			
690	Utilities expense	230				230		230			
	Totals	45,300	45,300	3,785	3,785	47,685	47,685	4,365	8,150	43,320	39,535
	Net income							3,785			3,785
	Totals							8,150	8,150	43,320	43,320

Sheet1 / Sheet2 / Sheet3

List all accounts from the ledger and those expected to arise from adjusting entries.

Enter all amounts available from ledger accounts. Column totals must be equal.

A work sheet collects and summarizes information used to prepare adjusting entries, financial statements, and closing entries.

column and expenses in the Debit column. If the Credit total exceeds the Debit total, there is net income. If the Debit total exceeds the Credit total, there is a net loss. For FastForward, the Credit total exceeds the Debit total, giving a $3,785 net income.

The net income from the Income Statement columns is then entered in the Balance Sheet Credit column. Adding net income to the last Credit column implies that it is to be added to retained earnings. If a loss occurs, it is added to the Debit column. This implies that it is to be subtracted from retained earnings. The ending balance of retained earnings does not appear in the last two columns as a single amount, but it is computed in the statement of retained earnings using these account balances. When net income or net loss is added to the proper Balance Sheet column, the totals of the last two columns must balance. If they do not, one or more errors have been made. The error can either be mathematical or involve sorting one or more amounts to incorrect columns.

Work Sheet Applications and Analysis

A work sheet does not substitute for financial statements. It is a tool we can use at the end of an accounting period to help organize data and prepare financial statements. FastForward's financial statements are shown in Exhibit 3.14. Its income statement amounts are taken from the Income Statement columns of the work sheet. Similarly, amounts for its balance sheet and its statement of retained earnings are taken from the Balance Sheet columns of the work sheet.

Work sheets are also useful in analyzing the effects of proposed, or what-if, transactions. This is done by entering financial statement amounts in the Unadjusted (what-if) columns. Proposed transactions are then entered in the Adjustments columns. We then compute "adjusted" amounts from these proposed transactions. The extended amounts in the financial statement columns show the effects of these proposed transactions. These financial statement columns yield **pro forma financial statements** because they show the statements *as if* the proposed transactions occurred.

3C   Reversing Entries

Reversing entries are optional. They are recorded in response to accrued assets and accrued liabilities that were created by adjusting entries at the end of a reporting period. The purpose of reversing entries is to simplify a company's recordkeeping. Exhibit 3C.1 shows an example of FastForward's reversing entries. The top of the exhibit shows the adjusting entry FastForward recorded on December 31 for its employee's earned but unpaid salary. The entry recorded three days' salary of $210, which increased December's total salary expense to $1,610. The entry also recognized a liability of $210. The expense is reported on December's income statement. The expense account is then closed. The ledger on January 1, 2010, shows a $210 liability and a zero balance in the Salaries Expense account. At this point, the choice is made between using or not using reversing entries.

Point: As a general rule, adjusting entries that create new asset or liability accounts are likely candidates for reversing.

Accounting *without* Reversing Entries

The path down the left side of Exhibit 3C.1 is described in the chapter. To summarize here, when the next payday occurs on January 9, we record payment with a compound entry that debits both the expense and liability accounts and credits Cash. Posting that entry creates a $490 balance in the expense account and reduces the liability account balance to zero because the debt has been settled. The disadvantage of this approach is the slightly more complex entry required on January 9. Paying the accrued liability means that this entry differs from the routine entries made on all other paydays. To construct the proper entry on January 9, we must recall the effect of the December 31 adjusting entry. Reversing entries overcome this disadvantage.

Accounting *with* Reversing Entries

P8   Prepare reversing entries and explain their purpose.

The right side of Exhibit 3C.1 shows how a reversing entry on January 1 overcomes the disadvantage of the January 9 entry when not using reversing entries. A reversing entry is the exact opposite of an adjusting entry. For FastForward, the Salaries Payable liability account is debited for $210, meaning that this account now has a zero balance after the entry is posted. The Salaries Payable account temporarily understates the liability, but this is not a problem since financial statements are not prepared before the liability is settled on January 9. The credit to the Salaries Expense account is unusual because it gives the account an *abnormal credit balance*. We highlight an abnormal balance by circling it. Because of the reversing entry, the January 9 entry to record payment is straightforward. This entry debits the Salaries Expense account and credits Cash for the full $700 paid. It is the same as all other entries made to record 10 days' salary for the employee. Notice that after the payment entry is posted, the Salaries Expense account has a $490 balance that reflects seven days' salary of $70 per day (see the lower right side of Exhibit 3C.1). The zero balance in the Salaries Payable account is now correct. The lower section of Exhibit 3C.1 shows that the expense and liability accounts have exactly the same balances whether reversing entries are used or not. This means that both approaches yield identical results.

Accrue salaries expense on December 31, 2009

Salaries Expense 210
    Salaries Payable 210

Salaries Expense

Date	Expl.	Debit	Credit	Balance
2009				
Dec. 12	(7)	700		700
26	(16)	700		1,400
31	(e)	210		1,610

Salaries Payable

Date	Expl.	Debit	Credit	Balance
2009				
Dec. 31	(e)		210	210

EXHIBIT 3C.1

Reversing Entries for an
Accrued Expense

— OR —

No reversing entry recorded on
January 1, 2010

NO ENTRY

Salaries Expense

Date	Expl.	Debit	Credit	Balance
2010				

Salaries Payable

Date	Expl.	Debit	Credit	Balance
2009				
Dec. 31	(e)		210	210
2010				

Reversing entry recorded on
January 1, 2010

Salaries Payable 210
    Salaries Expense 210

Salaries Expense*

Date	Expl.	Debit	Credit	Balance
2010				
Jan. 1			210	(210)

Salaries Payable

Date	Expl.	Debit	Credit	Balance
2009				
Dec. 31	(e)		210	210
2010				
Jan. 1		210		0

Pay the accrued and current salaries on January 9, the first payday in 2010

Salaries Expense 490
Salaries Payable 210
    Cash 700

Salaries Expense

Date	Expl.	Debit	Credit	Balance
2010				
Jan. 9		490		490

Salaries Payable

Date	Expl.	Debit	Credit	Balance
2009				
Dec. 31	(e)		210	210
2010				
Jan. 9		210		0

Salaries Expense 700
    Cash 700

Salaries Expense*

Date	Expl.	Debit	Credit	Balance
2010				
Jan. 1			210	(210)
Jan. 9		700		490

Salaries Payable

Date	Expl.	Debit	Credit	Balance
2009				
Dec. 31	(e)		210	210
2010				
Jan. 1		210		0

Under both approaches, the expense and liability accounts have
identical balances after the cash payment on January 9.

Salaries Expense $490
Salaries Payable .... $ 0

*Circled numbers in the Balance column indicate abnormal balances.

Summary

C1 **Explain the importance of periodic reporting and the time period assumption.** The value of information is often linked to its timeliness. To provide timely information, accounting systems prepare periodic reports at regular intervals. The time period assumption presumes that an organization's activities can be divided into specific time periods for periodic reporting.

C2 **Explain accrual accounting and how it improves financial statements.** Accrual accounting recognizes revenue when earned and expenses when incurred—not necessarily when cash inflows and outflows occur. This information is valuable in assessing a company's financial position and performance.

C3 Identify steps in the accounting cycle. The accounting cycle consists of 10 steps: (1) analyze transactions, (2) journalize, (3) post, (4) prepare an unadjusted trial balance, (5) adjust accounts, (6) prepare an adjusted trial balance, (7) prepare statements, (8) close, (9) prepare a post-closing trial balance, and (10) prepare (optional) reversing entries.

C4 Explain and prepare a classified balance sheet. Classified balance sheets report assets and liabilities in two categories: current and noncurrent. Noncurrent assets often include long-term investments, plant assets, and intangible assets. A corporation separates equity into common stock and retained earnings.

A1 Explain how accounting adjustments link to financial statements. Accounting adjustments bring an asset or liability account balance to its correct amount. They also update related expense or revenue accounts. Every adjusting entry affects one or more income statement accounts *and* one or more balance sheet accounts. An adjusting entry never affects cash.

A2 Compute profit margin and describe its use in analyzing company performance. *Profit margin* is defined as the reporting period's net income divided by its net sales. Profit margin reflects on a company's earnings activities by showing how much income is in each dollar of sales.

A3 Compute the current ratio and describe what it reveals about a company's financial condition. A company's current ratio is defined as current assets divided by current liabilities. We use it to evaluate a company's ability to pay its current liabilities out of current assets.

P1 Prepare and explain adjusting entries. *Prepaid expenses* refer to items paid for in advance of receiving their benefits. Prepaid expenses are assets. Adjusting entries for prepaids involve increasing (debiting) expenses and decreasing (crediting) assets. *Unearned* (or *prepaid*) *revenues* refer to cash received in advance of providing products and services. Unearned revenues are liabilities. Adjusting entries for unearned revenues involve increasing (crediting) revenues and decreasing (debiting) unearned revenues. *Accrued expenses* refer to costs incurred in a period that are both unpaid and unrecorded. Adjusting entries for recording accrued expenses involve increasing (debiting) expenses and increasing (crediting) liabilities. *Accrued revenues* refer to revenues earned in a period that are both unrecorded and not yet received in cash. Adjusting entries for recording accrued revenues involve increasing (debiting) assets and increasing (crediting) revenues.

P2 Explain and prepare an adjusted trial balance. An adjusted trial balance is a list of accounts and balances prepared after recording and posting adjusting entries. Financial statements are often prepared from the adjusted trial balance.

P3 Prepare financial statements from an adjusted trial balance. Revenue and expense balances are reported on the income statement. Asset, liability, and equity balances are reported on the balance sheet. We usually prepare statements in the following order: income statement, statement of retained earnings, balance sheet, and statement of cash flows.

P4 Describe and prepare closing entries. Closing entries involve four steps: (1) close credit balances in revenue (and gain) accounts to Income Summary, (2) close debit balances in expense (and loss) accounts to Income Summary, (3) close Income Summary to Retained Earnings, and (4) close Dividends account to Retained Earnings.

P5 Explain and prepare a post-closing trial balance. A post-closing trial balance is a list of permanent accounts and their balances after all closing entries have been journalized and posted. Its purpose is to verify that (1) total debits equal total credits for permanent accounts and (2) all temporary accounts have zero balances.

P6^A Explain the alternatives in accounting for prepaids. Charging all prepaid expenses to expense accounts when they are purchased is acceptable. When this is done, adjusting entries must transfer any unexpired amounts from expense accounts to asset accounts. Crediting all unearned revenues to revenue accounts when cash is received is also acceptable. In this case, the adjusting entries must transfer any unearned amounts from revenue accounts to unearned revenue accounts.

P7^B Prepare a work sheet and explain its usefulness. A work sheet can be a useful tool in preparing and analyzing financial statements. It is helpful at the end of a period in preparing adjusting entries, an adjusted trial balance, and financial statements. A work sheet usually contains five pairs of columns: Unadjusted Trial Balance, Adjustments, Adjusted Trial Balance, Income Statement, and Balance Sheet.

P8^C Prepare reversing entries and explain their purpose. Reversing entries are an optional step. They are applied to accrued expenses and revenues. The purpose of reversing entries is to simplify subsequent journal entries. Financial statements are unaffected by the choice to use or not use reversing entries.

Guidance Answers to **Decision Maker** and **Decision Ethics**

Investor Prepaid expenses are items paid for in advance of receiving their benefits. They are assets and are expensed as they are used up. The publishing company's treatment of the signing bonus is acceptable provided future book sales can at least match the $500,000 expense. As an investor, you are concerned about the risk of future book sales. The riskier the likelihood of future book sales is, the more likely your analysis is to treat the $500,000, or a portion of it, as an expense, not a prepaid expense (asset).

Entrepreneur Depreciation is a process of cost allocation, not asset valuation. Knowing the depreciation schedule is not especially useful in your estimation of what the building and equipment are

currently worth. Your own assessment of the age, quality, and usefulness of the building and equipment is more important.

Loan Officer Your concern in lending to this store arises from analysis of current-year sales. While increased revenues and income are fine, your concern is with collectibility of these promotional sales. If the owner sold products to customers with poor records of paying bills, then collectibility of these sales is low. Your analysis must assess this possibility and recognize any expected losses.

Financial Officer Omitting accrued expenses and recognizing revenue early can mislead financial statement users. One action is to request a second meeting with the president so you can explain that accruing expenses when incurred and recognizing revenue when earned are required practices. If the president persists, you might discuss the situation with legal counsel and any auditors involved. Your ethical action might cost you this job, but the potential pitfalls for falsification of statements, reputation loss, personal integrity, and other costs are too great.

Analyst   A current ratio of 1.2 suggests that current assets are sufficient to cover current liabilities, but it implies a minimal buffer in case of errors in measuring current assets or current liabilities. Removing the tardy receivable reduces the current ratio to 0.7. Your assessment is that the company will have some difficulty meeting its loan payments.

Guidance Answers to **Quick Checks**

1. An annual reporting (or accounting) period covers one year and refers to the preparation of annual financial statements. The annual reporting period is not always a calendar year that ends on December 31. An organization can adopt a fiscal year consisting of any consecutive 12 months or 52 weeks.

2. Interim financial statements (covering less than one year) are prepared to provide timely information to decision makers.

3. The revenue recognition principle and the matching principle lead most directly to the adjusting process.

4. No. Cash basis accounting is not consistent with the matching principle because it reports expenses when paid, not in the period when revenue is earned as a result of those expenses.

5. No expense is reported in 2012. Under cash basis accounting, the entire $4,800 is reported as an expense in April 2011 when the premium is paid.

6. If the accrued revenues adjustment of $200 is not made, then both revenues and net income are understated by $200 on the current year's income statement, and both assets and equity are understated by $200 on the balance sheet.

7. A contra account is an account that is subtracted from the balance of a related account. Use of a contra account provides more information than simply reporting a net amount.

8. An accrued expense is a cost incurred in a period that is both unpaid and unrecorded prior to adjusting entries. One example is salaries earned but not yet paid at period-end.

9. An unearned revenue arises when a firm receives cash (or other assets) from a customer before providing the services or products to the customer. A magazine subscription paid in advance is one example; season ticket sales is another.

10. Salaries Payable 1,000
    Salaries Expense 6,000
         Cash 7,000
    Paid salary including accrual from December.

11. The probable adjusting entries of Jordan Air are:
    Insurance Expense 300
         Prepaid Insurance 300
    To record insurance expired.
    Salaries Expense 1,400
         Salaries Payable 1,400
    To record accrued salaries.

12. Revenue accounts and expense accounts.

13. Statement of retained earnings.

14. The major steps in preparing closing entries are to close (1) credit balances in revenue accounts to Income Summary, (2) debit balances in expense accounts to Income Summary, (3) Income Summary to Retained Earnings, and (4) any Dividends account to Retained Earnings.

15. Revenue (and gain) and expense (and loss) accounts are called *temporary* because they are opened and closed each period. The Income Summary and Dividends accounts are also temporary.

16. Permanent accounts make up the post-closing trial balance. These accounts are asset, liability, and equity accounts.

17. Current assets: (*b*), (*c*), (*d*). Plant assets: (*a*), (*e*). Item (*f*) is an intangible asset.

18. Investment in common stock, investment in bonds, and land held for future expansion.

19. For a service company, the operating cycle is the usual time between (1) paying employees who do the services and (2) receiving cash from customers for services provided.

Key Terms

Accounting cycle (p. 112)
Accounting period (p. 94)
Accrual basis accounting (p. 95)
Accrued expenses (p. 102)
Accrued revenues (p. 103)
Adjusted trial balance (p. 106)
Adjusting entry (p. 97)

Annual financial statements (p. 94)
Book value (p. 100)
Cash basis accounting (p. 95)
Classified balance sheet (p. 113)
Closing entries (p. 108)
Closing process (p. 108)
Contra account (p. 99)

Current assets (p. 113)
Current liabilities (p. 115)
Current ratio (p. 117)
Depreciation (p. 99)
Fiscal year (p. 95)
Income summary (p. 109)
Intangible assets (p. 114)

Interim financial statements (p. 94)	Plant assets (p. 99)	Temporary accounts (p. 108)
Long-term investments (p. 114)	Post-closing trial balance (p. 110)	Time period assumption (p. 94)
Long-term liabilities (p. 115)	Prepaid expenses (p. 97)	Unadjusted trial balance (p. 106)
Matching principle (p. 96)	Pro forma financial statements (p. 126)	Unclassified balance sheet (p. 113)
Natural business year (p. 95)	Profit margin (p. 116)	Unearned revenues (p. 100)
Operating cycle (p. 113)	Reversing entries (p. 126)	Working papers (p. 123)
Permanent accounts (p. 108)	Straight-line depreciation method (p. 99)	Work sheet (p. 123)

Multiple Choice Quiz   Answers on p. 153   mhhe.com/wildFA5e

Additional Quiz Questions are available at the book's Website.

1. A company forgot to record accrued and unpaid employee wages of $350,000 at period-end. This oversight would
  a. Understate net income by $350,000.
  b. Overstate net income by $350,000.
  c. Have no effect on net income.
  d. Overstate assets by $350,000.
  e. Understate assets by $350,000.

2. Prior to recording adjusting entries, the Supplies account has a $450 debit balance. A physical count of supplies shows $125 of unused supplies still available. The required adjusting entry is
  a. Debit Supplies $125; Credit Supplies Expense $125.
  b. Debit Supplies $325; Credit Supplies Expense $325.
  c. Debit Supplies Expense $325; Credit Supplies $325.
  d. Debit Supplies Expense $325; Credit Supplies $125.
  e. Debit Supplies Expense $125; Credit Supplies $125.

3. On May 1, 2011, a two-year insurance policy was purchased for $24,000 with coverage to begin immediately. What is the amount of insurance expense that appears on the company's income statement for the year ended December 31, 2011?
  a. $4,000
  b. $8,000
  c. $12,000
  d. $20,000
  e. $24,000

4. On November 1, 2011, Stockton Co. receives $3,600 cash from Hans Co. for consulting services to be provided evenly over the period November 1, 2011, to April 30, 2012—at which time Stockton credited $3,600 to Unearned Consulting Fees. The adjusting entry on December 31, 2011 (Stockton's year-end) would include a
  a. Debit to Unearned Consulting Fees for $1,200.
  b. Debit to Unearned Consulting Fees for $2,400.
  c. Credit to Consulting Fees Earned for $2,400.
  d. Debit to Consulting Fees Earned for $1,200.
  e. Credit to Cash for $3,600.

5. If a company had $15,000 in net income for the year, and its sales were $300,000 for the same year, what is its profit margin?
  a. 20%
  b. 2,000%
  c. $285,000
  d. $315,000
  e. 5%

Superscript letter ^{A} $^{(B,\,C)}$ denotes assignments based on Appendix 3A (3B, 3C).

Discussion Questions

1. What is the difference between the cash basis and the accrual basis of accounting?

2. ♟ Why is the accrual basis of accounting generally preferred over the cash basis?

3. What type of business is most likely to select a fiscal year that corresponds to its natural business year instead of the calendar year?

4. What is a prepaid expense and where is it reported in the financial statements?

5. ♟ What type of assets require adjusting entries to record depreciation?

6. ♟ What contra account is used when recording and reporting the effects of depreciation? Why is it used?

7. What is unearned revenue and where is it reported in financial statements?

8. What is an accrued revenue? Give an example.

9.^{A} If a company initially records prepaid expenses with debits to expense accounts, what type of account is debited in the adjusting entries for those prepaid expenses?

10. ♟ Review the balance sheet of **Best Buy** in Appendix A. Identify one asset account that requires adjustment before annual financial statements can be prepared. What would be the effect on the income statement if this asset account were not adjusted?

11. ♟ Review the balance sheet of **GOME** in Appendix A. Identify the amount for property, plant, and equipment. What adjusting entry is necessary (no numbers required) for this account when preparing financial statements?

12. ♟ Refer to **Apple**'s balance sheet in Appendix A. If it made an adjustment for unpaid wages at year-end, where would the accrued wages be reported on its balance sheet?

13. What accounts are affected by closing entries? What accounts are not affected?

14. ♟ What two purposes are accomplished by recording closing entries?

15. What are the steps in recording closing entries?

16. What is the purpose of the Income Summary account?

17. ♟ Explain whether an error has occurred if a post-closing trial balance includes a Depreciation Expense account.

18.ᴮWhat tasks are aided by a work sheet?

19.ᴮWhy are the debit and credit entries in the Adjustments columns of the work sheet identified with letters?

20. What is a company's operating cycle?

21. What classes of assets and liabilities are shown on a typical classified balance sheet?

22. How is unearned revenue classified on the balance sheet?

23. What are the characteristics of plant assets?

24. ♟ Refer to the balance sheet for **Best Buy** in Appendix A. What six main noncurrent asset categories are used on its classified balance sheet?

25. Refer to **GOME**'s balance sheet in Appendix A. Identify and list its 10 current assets.

26. ♟ Refer to **RadioShack**'s balance sheet in Appendix A. Identify the four accounts listed as current liabilities.

27. ♟ Refer to **Apple**'s financial statements in Appendix A. What journal entry was likely recorded as of September 27, 2008, to close its Income Summary account?

28.ᶜHow do reversing entries simplify recordkeeping?

29.ᶜIf a company recorded accrued salaries expense of $500 at the end of its fiscal year, what reversing entry could be made? When would it be made?

♟ **Denotes Discussion Questions that involve decision making.**

---

connect™ Available with Connect Accounting

In its first year of operations, Case Co. earned $60,000 in revenues and received $52,000 cash from these customers. The company incurred expenses of $37,500 but had not paid $6,000 of them at year-end. Case also prepaid $3,250 cash for expenses that would be incurred the next year.

a. Compute the first year's net income under the cash basis of accounting.

b. Compute the first year's net income under the accrual basis of accounting.

QUICK STUDY

QS 3-1
Computing accrual and cash income

C1   C2 ♟

Classify the following adjusting entries as involving prepaid expenses (PE), unearned revenues (UR), accrued expenses (AE), or accrued revenues (AR).

a. _____ To record wages expense incurred but not yet paid (nor recorded).

b. _____ To record expiration of prepaid insurance.

c. _____ To record revenue earned that was previously received as cash in advance.

d. _____ To record depreciation expense for the period.

e. _____ To record revenue earned but not yet billed (nor recorded).

QS 3-2
Identifying accounting adjustments

P1

Adjusting entries affect at least one balance sheet account and at least one income statement account. For the following entries, identify the account to be debited and the account to be credited. Indicate which of the accounts is the income statement account and which is the balance sheet account.

a. Entry to record revenue earned that was previously received as cash in advance.

b. Entry to record wage expenses incurred but not yet paid (nor recorded).

c. Entry to record revenue earned but not yet billed (nor recorded).

d. Entry to record expiration of prepaid insurance.

e. Entry to record depreciation expense for the period.

QS 3-3
Recording and analyzing adjusting entries

A1

---

a. On July 1, 2011, Rendex Company paid $3,000 for six months of insurance coverage. No adjustments have been made to the Prepaid Insurance account, and it is now December 31, 2011. Prepare the adjusting entry to reflect expiration of the insurance as of December 31, 2011.

b. Indus Company has a Supplies account balance of $900 on January 1, 2011. During 2011, it purchased $4,000 of supplies. As of December 31, 2011, a supplies inventory shows $750 of supplies available. Prepare the adjusting journal entry to correctly report the balance of the Supplies account and the Supplies Expense account as of December 31, 2011.

QS 3-4
Adjusting prepaid expenses

P1

QS 3-5
Adjusting for depreciation
P1

a. Andrews Company purchases $45,000 of equipment on January 1, 2011. The equipment is expected to last five years and be worth $3,000 at the end of that time. Prepare the entry to record one year's depreciation expense of $8,400 for the equipment as of December 31, 2011.

b. Fortel Company purchases $40,000 of land on January 1, 2011. The land is expected to last indefinitely. What depreciation adjustment, if any, should be made with respect to the Land account as of December 31, 2011?

QS 3-6
Accruing salaries
A1   P1

Lakia Rowell employs one college student every summer in her coffee shop. The student works the five weekdays and is paid on the following Monday. (For example, a student who works Monday through Friday, June 1 through June 5, is paid for that work on Monday, June 8.) Rowell adjusts her books monthly, if needed, to show salaries earned but unpaid at month-end. The student works the last week of July—Friday is August 1. If the student earns $100 per day, what adjusting entry must Rowell make on July 31 to correctly record accrued salaries expense for July?

QS 3-7
Adjusting for unearned revenues
A1   P1

a. Fortune Co. receives $30,000 cash in advance for four months of legal services on October 1, 2011, and records it by debiting Cash and crediting Unearned Revenue, both for $30,000. It is now December 31, 2011, and Fortune has provided legal services as planned. What adjusting entry should Fortune make to account for the work performed from October 1 through December 31, 2011?

b. Warner Co. started a new publication called *Contest News*. Its subscribers pay $24 to receive 12 issues. With every new subscriber, Warner debits Cash and credits Unearned Subscription Revenue for the amounts received. Warner has 100 new subscribers as of June 1, 2011. It sends *Contest News* to each of these subscribers every month from June through December. Assuming no changes in subscribers, prepare the journal entry that Warner must make as of December 31, 2011, to adjust the Subscription Revenue account and the Unearned Subscription Revenue account.

QS 3-8
Preparing adjusting entries
P1

During the year, Sonoma Co. recorded prepayments of expenses in asset accounts, and cash receipts of unearned revenues in liability accounts. At the end of its annual accounting period, the company must make three adjusting entries: (1) accrue salaries expense, (2) adjust the Unearned Services Revenue account to recognize earned revenue, and (3) record services revenue earned for which cash will be received the following period. For each of these adjusting entries (1), (2), and (3), indicate the account from *a* through *i* to be debited and the account to be credited.

a. Unearned Services Revenue   **d.** Prepaid Salaries   **g.** Salaries Payable

b. Accounts Receivable   **e.** Salaries Expense   **h.** Dividends

c. Accounts Payable   **f.** Services Revenue   **i.** Cash

QS 3-9
Interpreting adjusting entries
C2   P2

The following information is taken from Booker Company's unadjusted and adjusted trial balances.

	Unadjusted		Adjusted	
	Debit	**Credit**	**Debit**	**Credit**
Prepaid insurance	$4,100		$3,700	
Interest payable		$ 0		$800

Given this information, which of the following is likely included among its adjusting entries?

a. A $400 debit to Insurance Expense and an $800 debit to Interest Expense.

b. A $400 debit to Insurance Expense and an $800 debit to Interest Payable.

c. A $400 credit to Prepaid Insurance and an $800 debit to Interest Payable.

QS 3-10
Determining effects of closing entries
P4

Irvine Company began the current period with a $35,000 credit balance in the Retained Earnings account. At the end of the period, the company's adjusted account balances include the following temporary accounts with normal balances.

Service fees earned	$42,000	Interest revenue	$8,000
Salaries expense	31,000	Dividends	9,200
Depreciation expense	11,000	Utilities expense	5,000

After closing the revenue and expense accounts, what will be the balance of the Income Summary account? After all closing entries are journalized and posted, what will be the balance of the Retained Earnings account?

In making adjusting entries at the end of its accounting period, Chao Consulting failed to record $1,600 of insurance coverage that had expired. This $1,600 cost had been initially debited to the Prepaid Insurance account. The company also failed to record accrued salaries expense of $1,000. As a result of these two oversights, the financial statements for the reporting period will [choose one] (1) understate assets by $1,600; (2) understate expenses by $2,600; (3) understate net income by $1,000; or (4) overstate liabilities by $1,000.

QS 3-11
Determining effects of adjusting entries

P1   A1

List the following steps of the accounting cycle in their proper order.

a. Posting the journal entries.

b. Journalizing and posting adjusting entries.

c. Preparing the adjusted trial balance.

d. Journalizing and posting closing entries.

e. Analyzing transactions and events.

f. Preparing the financial statements.

g. Preparing the unadjusted trial balance.

h. Journalizing transactions and events.

i. Preparing the post-closing trial balance.

QS 3-12
Identifying the accounting cycle

C3

The following are common categories on a classified balance sheet:

A. Current assets

B. Long-term investments

C. Plant assets

D. Intangible assets

E. Current liabilities

F. Long-term liabilities

For each of the following items, select the letter that identifies the balance sheet category where the item typically would appear.

_____ **1.** Accounts payable

_____ **2.** Store equipment

_____ **3.** Wages payable

_____ **4.** Cash

_____ **5.** Land not currently used in operations

_____ **6.** Notes payable (due in three years)

_____ **7.** Accounts receivable

_____ **8.** Trademarks

QS 3-13
Classifying balance sheet items

C4

The ledger of Turner Company includes the following accounts with normal balances: Retained Earnings $24,000; Dividends $1,200; Services Revenue $40,000; Wages Expense $15,000; and Rent Expense $6,000. Prepare the necessary closing entries from the available information at December 31.

QS 3-14
Prepare closing entries from the ledger   P4

Identify the accounts listed in QS 3-14 that would be included in a post-closing trial balance.

QS 3-15
Identify post-closing accounts   P5

Miller Company reported net income of $78,750 and net sales of $630,000 for the current year. Compute Miller's profit margin and interpret the result. Assume that Miller's competitors achieve an average profit margin of 15%.

QS 3-16
Analyzing profit margin

A2

Compute Darrah Company's current ratio using the following information.

Accounts receivable	$18,000	Unearned services revenue	$ 3,000
Accounts payable	11,000	Long-term notes payable	21,000
Buildings	45,000	Office supplies	2,860
Cash	7,000	Prepaid insurance	3,500

QS 3-17
Identifying current accounts and computing the current ratio

C4   A3

Bevin Consulting initially records prepaid and unearned items in income statement accounts. Given Bevin Consulting's accounting practices, which of the following applies to the preparation of adjusting entries at the end of its first accounting period?

a. Unpaid salaries are recorded with a debit to Prepaid Salaries and a credit to Salaries Expense.

b. The cost of unused office supplies is recorded with a debit to Supplies Expense and a credit to Office Supplies.

c. Unearned fees (on which cash was received in advance earlier in the period) are recorded with a debit to Consulting Fees Earned and a credit to Unearned Consulting Fees.

d. Earned but unbilled (and unrecorded) consulting fees are recorded with a debit to Unearned Consulting Fees and a credit to Consulting Fees Earned.

QS 3-18^A
Preparing adjusting entries

P1   P6

QS 3-19[B]
Applying a work sheet
P7

In preparing a work sheet, indicate the financial statement Debit column to which a normal balance in the following accounts should be extended. Use I for the Income Statement Debit column and B for the Balance Sheet Debit column.

_____ **a.** Depreciation expense—Equipment   _____ **d.** Equipment

_____ **b.** Accounts receivable   _____ **e.** Dividends

_____ **c.** Insurance expense   _____ **f.** Prepaid rent

QS 3-20[B]
Preparing a partial work sheet
P7 ♟

The ledger of Edgardo Company includes the following unadjusted normal balances: Prepaid Rent $4,000, Services Revenue $65,000, and Wages Expense $30,000. Adjusting entries are required for (a) prepaid rent expired $800; (b) accrued services revenue $950; and (c) accrued wages expense $750. Enter these unadjusted balances and the necessary adjustments on a work sheet and complete the work sheet for these accounts. (*Hint:* Include the following accounts: Accounts Receivable, Wages Payable, and Rent Expense.)

QS 3-21[C]
Reversing entries
P8

On December 31, 2010, Yates Co. prepared an adjusting entry for $24,000 of earned but unrecorded management fees. On January 16, 2011, Yates received $37,500 cash in management fees, which included the accrued fees earned in 2010. Assuming the company uses reversing entries, prepare the January 1, 2011, reversing entry and the January 16, 2011, cash receipt entry.

QS 3-22
International accounting standards
C3 C4

Answer each of the following questions related to international accounting standards.

a. Explain how the closing process is different between accounting under IFRS versus U.S. GAAP.

b. Do financial statements prepared under IFRS normally present assets from least liquid to most liquid or vice-versa?

c. Do financial statements prepared under IFRS normally present liabilities from furthest from maturity to nearest to maturity or vice-versa?

Available with Connect Accounting **connect**

EXERCISES

Exercise 3-1
Preparing adjusting entries
P1

For each of the following separate cases, prepare adjusting entries required of financial statements for the year ended (date of) December 31, 2011. (Assume that prepaid expenses are initially recorded in asset accounts and that fees collected in advance of work are initially recorded as liabilities.)

a. One-third of the work related to $15,000 cash received in advance this period is performed.

b. Wages of $7,500 are earned by workers this period but not paid as of December 31, 2011.

c. Depreciation on the company's equipment for 2011 is $17,251.

d. The Supplies account had a $240 debit balance on December 31, 2010. During 2011, $6,102 of supplies are purchased. A physical count of supplies at December 31, 2011, shows $660 of supplies available.

Check (e) Dr. Insurance Expense, $2,700; (f) Cr. Interest Revenue, $1,400

e. The Prepaid Insurance account had a $4,000 balance on December 31, 2010. An analysis of insurance policies shows that $1,300 of unexpired insurance benefits remain at December 31, 2011.

f. The company has earned (but not recorded) $1,400 of interest from investments in CDs for the year ended December 31, 2011. The interest revenue will be received on January 10, 2012.

g. The company has a bank loan and has incurred (but not recorded) interest expense of $2,000 for the year ended December 31, 2011. The company must pay the interest on January 2, 2012.

Exercise 3-2
Preparing adjusting entries
P1

Prepare adjusting journal entries for the year ended (date of) December 31, 2011, for each of these separate situations. Assume that prepaid expenses are initially recorded in asset accounts, and that fees collected in advance of work are initially recorded as liabilities.

a. Depreciation on the company's equipment for 2011 is computed to be $16,000.

b. The Prepaid Insurance account had a $6,000 debit balance at December 31, 2011, before adjusting for the costs of any expired coverage. An analysis of the company's insurance policies showed that $640 of unexpired insurance coverage remains.

Check (c) Dr. Supplies Expense, $3,422; (e) Dr. Insurance Expense, $6,160

c. The Supplies account had a $325 debit balance on December 31, 2010; and $3,480 of supplies were purchased during 2011. The December 31, 2011, physical count showed $383 of supplies available.

d. One-fifth of the work related to $15,000 of cash received in advance this period was performed.

e. The Prepaid Insurance account had a $6,800 debit balance at December 31, 2011, before adjusting for the costs of any expired coverage. An analysis of insurance policies showed that $6,160 of coverage had expired.

f. Wage expenses of $2,700 have been incurred but are not paid as of December 31, 2011.

The following three separate situations require adjusting journal entries to prepare financial statements as of April 30. For each situation, present both the April 30 adjusting entry and the subsequent entry during May to record the payment of the accrued expenses.

a. On April 1, the company retained an attorney at a flat monthly fee of $4,500. Each monthly fee amount is payable on the 12th of the following month.

b. A $760,000 note payable requires $5,700 of interest to be paid at the end of each 30 days. The interest was last paid on April 20 and the next payment is due on May 20. As of April 30, $1,900 of interest expense has accrued.

c. Total weekly salaries expense for all employees is $12,000. This amount is paid at the end of the day on Friday of each five-day workweek. April 30 falls on Tuesday of this year, which means that the employees had worked two days since the last payday. The next payday is May 3.

Exercise 3-3
Adjusting and paying accrued expenses

A1 P1

Check (b) May 20 Dr. Interest Expense, $3,800

Arton Management has five part-time employees, each of whom earns $165 per day. They are normally paid on Fridays for work completed Monday through Friday of the same week. They were paid in full on Friday, December 28, 2011. The next week, the five employees worked only four days because New Year's Day was an unpaid holiday. Show (a) the adjusting entry that would be recorded on Monday, December 31, 2011, and (b) the journal entry that would be made to record payment of the employees' wages on Friday, January 4, 2012.

Exercise 3-4
Adjusting and paying accrued wages

C1 P1

Check (b) Cr. Cash $3,300

On November 1, 2010, a company paid a $15,300 premium on a 36-month insurance policy for coverage beginning on that date. Refer to that policy and fill in the blanks in the following table.

Balance Sheet Prepaid Insurance Asset Using			Insurance Expense Using		
	Accrual Basis	**Cash Basis**		**Accrual Basis**	**Cash Basis**
Dec. 31, 2010	$_____	$_____	2010	$_____	$_____
Dec. 31, 2011	_____	_____	2011	_____	_____
Dec. 31, 2012	_____	_____	2012	_____	_____
Dec. 31, 2013	_____	_____	2013	_____	_____
			Total	$_____	$_____

Exercise 3-5
Determining assets and expenses for accrual and cash accounting

C2

Check 2012 insurance expense: Accrual, $5,100; Cash, $0. Dec. 31, 2012, asset: Accrual, $4,250; Cash, $0.

The following adjusted trial balance contains the accounts and balances of Ferrara Company as of December 31, 2011, the end of its fiscal year. (1) Prepare the December 31, 2011, closing entries for Ferrara Company. (2) Prepare the December 31, 2011, post-closing trial balance for Ferrara Company.

No.	Account Title	Debit	Credit
101	Cash	$18,000	
126	Supplies	13,900	
128	Prepaid insurance	2,000	
167	Equipment	23,000	
168	Accumulated depreciation—Equipment		$ 6,500
307	Common stock		18,168
318	Retained earnings		30,000
319	Dividends	6,000	
404	Services revenue		37,200
612	Depreciation expense—Equipment	2,000	
622	Salaries expense	21,687	
637	Insurance expense	1,562	
640	Rent expense	2,492	
652	Supplies expense	1,227	
	Totals	$91,868	$91,868

Exercise 3-6
Preparing closing entries and a post-closing trial balance

P4 P5

Check (2) Retained Earnings (ending), $32,232; Total debits, $56,900

Exercise 3-7

Preparing an income statement
and statement of retained
earnings

C3

Use the following adjusted trial balance of Resource Trucking Company to prepare the (1) income statement, and (2) statement of retained earnings, for the year ended December 31, 2011.

Account Title	Debit	Credit
Cash	$ 5,800	
Accounts receivable	17,500	
Office supplies	3,000	
Trucks	156,000	
Accumulated depreciation—Trucks		$ 32,136
Land	85,000	
Accounts payable		9,800
Interest payable		4,000
Long-term notes payable		53,000
Common stock		86,901
Retained earnings		75,000
Dividends	20,000	
Trucking fees earned		121,000
Depreciation expense—Trucks	20,727	
Salaries expense	56,749	
Office supplies expense	6,655	
Repairs expense—Trucks	10,406	
Totals	$381,837	$381,837

Check   Net income $26,463

Exercise 3-8

Preparing a classified
balance sheet

C4

Check   Total Assets $235,164

Use the information in the adjusted trial balance reported in Exercise 3-7 to prepare Resource Trucking
Company's classified balance sheet as of December 31, 2011.

Exercise 3-9

Computing and interpreting
profit margin

A2

Use the information from Exercise 3-7 to calculate Resource Trucking Company's profit margin. Interpret
the profit margin for this company (assume the industry average is 15%).

Exercise 3-10

Computing the current ratio

A3

Use the information in the adjusted trial balance reported in Exercise 3-7 to compute the current ratio
as of the balance sheet date (round the ratio to one decimal). Interpret the current ratio for this company
(assume that the industry average for the current ratio is 1.5).

Exercise 3-11

Computing and interpreting
profit margin

A2

Use the following information to compute profit margin for each separate company *a* through *e*.

	Net Income	*Net Sales*		*Net Income*	*Net Sales*
a.	$ 6,039	$ 52,970	**d.**	$67,140	$1,721,520
b.	100,890	471,430	**e.**	84,780	513,800
c.	106,880	301,920			

Which of the five companies is the most profitable according to the profit margin ratio? Interpret that
company's profit margin ratio.

Compute the current ratio in each of the following separate cases (round the ratio to two decimals). Identify the company case with the strongest liquidity position. (These cases represent competing companies in the same industry.)

	Current Assets	Current Liabilities
Case 1	$ 76,000	$26,666
Case 2	101,080	64,351
Case 3	42,863	41,104
Case 4	82,308	69,156
Case 5	58,444	84,638

Exercise 3-12
Computing and analyzing the current ratio

A3

Colgate Company experienced the following events and transactions during July:

July 1 Received $2,800 cash in advance of performing work for Vivian Solana.
       6 Received $8,100 cash in advance of performing work for Iris Haru.
     12 Completed the job for Solana.
     18 Received $7,300 cash in advance of performing work for Amina Jordan.
     27 Completed the job for Haru.
     31 None of the work for Jordan has been performed.

a. Prepare journal entries (including any adjusting entries as of the end of the month) to record these events using the procedure of initially crediting the Unearned Fees account when payment is received from a customer in advance of performing services.

b. Prepare journal entries (including any adjusting entries as of the end of the month) to record these events using the procedure of initially crediting the Fees Earned account when payment is received from a customer in advance of performing services.

c. Under each method, determine the amount of earned fees reported on the income statement for July and the amount of unearned fees reported on the balance sheet as of July 31.

Exercise 3-13^A

Exercise 3-13ᴬ
Recording and reporting revenues received in advance

P6

Check (c) Fees Earned—using entries from part b, $10,900

Lowes Construction began operations on December 1. In setting up its accounting procedures, the company decided to debit expense accounts when it prepays its expenses and to credit revenue accounts when customers pay for services in advance. Prepare journal entries for items *a* through *d* and the adjusting entries as of its December 31 period-end for items *e* through *g*.

a. Supplies are purchased on December 1 for $2,000 cash.

b. The company prepaid its insurance premiums for $1,540 cash on December 2.

c. On December 15, the company receives an advance payment of $13,000 cash from a customer for remodeling work.

d. On December 28, the company receives $3,700 cash from another customer for remodeling work to be performed in January.

e. A physical count on December 31 indicates that Lowes has $1,840 of supplies available.

f. An analysis of the insurance policies in effect on December 31 shows that $340 of insurance coverage had expired.

g. As of December 31, the company had performed $5,570 of the services that the customer had paid for on December 15.

Exercise 3-14ᴬ
Adjusting for prepaids recorded as expenses and unearned revenues recorded as revenues

P6

Check (f) Cr. Insurance Expense, $1,200; (g) Dr. Remodeling Fees Earned, $7,430

The following unadjusted trial balance contains the accounts and balances of Santaga Delivery Company as of December 31, 2011.

1. Use the following information about the company's adjustments to complete a 10-column work sheet for Santaga.

   a. Unrecorded depreciation on the trucks at the end of the year is $16,000.

   b. The total amount of accrued interest expense at year-end is $8,000.

   c. The cost of unused office supplies still available at the year-end is $500.

Exercise 3-15ᴮ
Preparing a work sheet and recording closing entries

P4 P7

2. Prepare the year-end closing entries for Santaga, and determine the retained earnings to be reported on its year-end balance sheet.

Account Title	Debit	Credit
Cash	$ 15,000	
Accounts receivable	33,000	
Office supplies	4,000	
Trucks	340,000	
Accumulated depreciation—Trucks		$ 112,000
Land	150,000	
Accounts payable		23,550
Interest payable		6,000
Long-term notes payable		104,000
Common stock		100,000
Retained earnings		172,770
Dividends	38,000	
Delivery fees earned		274,350
Depreciation expense—Trucks	48,000	
Salaries expense	128,670	
Office supplies expense	14,000	
Interest expense	6,000	
Repairs expense—Trucks	16,000	
Totals	$792,670	$792,670

Check   Adj. trial balance totals, $810,670; Net income, $40,180

Exercise 3-16ᶜ

Preparing reversing entries

P8

The following two events occurred for Tankwell Co. on October 31, 2011, the end of its fiscal year:

a. Tankwell rents a building from its owner for $3,300 per month. By a prearrangement, the company delayed paying October's rent until November 5. On this date, the company paid the rent for both October and November.

b. Tankwell rents space in a building it owns to a tenant for $1,050 per month. By prearrangement, the tenant delayed paying the October rent until November 8. On this date, the tenant paid the rent for both October and November.

Required

1. Prepare adjusting entries that Tankwell must record for these events as of October 31.

2. Assuming Tankwell does *not* use reversing entries, prepare journal entries to record Tankwell's payment of rent on November 5 and the collection of rent on November 8 from Tankwell's tenant.

3. Assuming that Tankwell uses reversing entries, prepare reversing entries on November 1 and the journal entries to record Tankwell's payment of rent on November 5 and the collection of rent on November 8 from Tankwell's tenant.

Exercise 3-17ᶜ

Preparing reversing entries

P8

Scholl Company records prepaid assets and unearned revenues in balance sheet accounts. The following information was used to prepare adjusting entries for Scholl Company as of August 31, the end of the company's fiscal year.

a. The company has earned $4,500 in unrecorded service fees.

b. The expired portion of prepaid insurance is $3,750.

c. The company has earned $2,100 of its Unearned Service Fees account balance.

d. Depreciation expense for office equipment is $2,600.

e. Employees have earned but have not been paid salaries of $2,700.

Prepare any necessary reversing entries for the accounting adjustments *a* through *e* assuming that this company uses reversing entries in its accounting system.

adidas AG reports the following balance sheet accounts for the year ended December 31, 2008 (euros in thousands.) Prepare the balance sheet for this company as of December 31, 2008, following usual IFRS practices.

Exercise 3-18
Preparing a balance sheet following IFRS

C4 P3

Tangible and other assets	€3,440,472	Intangible assets	€ 57,569
Total equity	1,920,043	Total current liabilities	235,240
Receivables and investments	1,322,550	Inventories........................	21,428
Total noncurrent liabilities	2,813,993	Total liabilities	3,049,233
Cash and cash equivalents	1,593	Prepaid expenses	125,664
Common stock	193,516	Retained earnings and reserves	1,720,198
Total current assets	1,471,235	Total noncurrent assets	3,498,041

connect Available with Connect Accounting

Hormel Co. follows the practice of recording prepaid expenses and unearned revenues in balance sheet accounts. Hormel's annual accounting period ends on December 31, 2011. The following information concerns the adjusting entries to be recorded as of that date.

a. The Office Supplies account started the year with a $2,900 balance. During 2011, the company purchased supplies for $11,977, which was added to the Office Supplies account. The inventory of supplies available at December 31, 2011, totaled $2,552.

b. An analysis of the company's insurance policies provided the following facts:

Policy	Date of Purchase	Months of Coverage	Cost
A	April 1, 2010	24	$11,640
B	April 1, 2011	36	10,440
C	August 1, 2011	12	9,240

The total premium for each policy was paid in full (for all months) at the purchase date, and the Prepaid Insurance account was debited for the full cost. (Year-end adjusting entries for Prepaid Insurance were properly recorded in all prior years.)

c. The company has 15 employees, who earn a total of $1,830 in salaries each working day. They are paid each Monday for their work in the five-day workweek ending on the previous Friday. Assume that December 31, 2011, is a Tuesday, and all 15 employees worked the first two days of that week. Because New Year's Day is a paid holiday, they will be paid salaries for five full days on Monday, January 6, 2012.

d. The company purchased a building on January 1, 2011. It cost $800,000 and is expected to have a $45,000 salvage value at the end of its predicted 40-year life. Annual depreciation is $18,875.

e. Since the company is not large enough to occupy the entire building it owns, it rented space to a tenant at $3,000 per month, starting on November 1, 2011. The rent was paid on time on November 1, and the amount received was credited to the Rent Earned account. However, the tenant has not paid the December rent. The company has worked out an agreement with the tenant, who has promised to pay both December and January rent in full on January 15. The tenant has agreed not to fall behind again.

f. On November 1, the company rented space to another tenant for $2,718 per month. The tenant paid five months' rent in advance on that date. The payment was recorded with a credit to the Unearned Rent account.

Required

1. Use the information to prepare adjusting entries as of December 31, 2011.

2. Prepare journal entries to record the first subsequent cash transaction in 2012 for parts *c* and *e*.

PROBLEM SET A

Problem 3-1A
Preparing adjusting and subsequent journal entries

C1 A1 P1

Check   (1*b*) Dr. Insurance Expense, $12,280 (1*d*) Dr. Depreciation Expense, $18,875

Wells Teaching Institute (WTI), a school owned by Tracey Wells, provides training to individuals who pay tuition directly to the school. WTI also offers training to groups in off-site locations. Its unadjusted trial balance as of December 31, 2011, follows. WTI initially records prepaid expenses and unearned revenues in balance sheet accounts. Descriptions of items *a* through *h* that require adjusting entries on December 31, 2011, follow.

Problem 3-2A
Preparing adjusting entries, adjusted trial balance, and financial statements

A1 P1 P2 P3

Additional Information Items

a. An analysis of the school's insurance policies shows that $3,000 of coverage has expired.

b. An inventory count shows that teaching supplies costing $2,000 are available at year-end 2011.

c. Annual depreciation on the equipment is $10,000.

d. Annual depreciation on the professional library is $5,000.

e. On November 1, the school agreed to do a special six-month course (starting immediately) for a client. The contract calls for a monthly fee of $2,500, and the client paid the first five months' fees in advance. When the cash was received, the Unearned Training Fees account was credited. The fee for the sixth month will be recorded when it is earned and collected in 2012.

f. On October 15, the school agreed to teach a four-month class (beginning immediately) for an individual for $1,600 tuition per month payable at the end of the class. The services are being provided as agreed, and no payment has yet been received.

g. The school's two employees are paid weekly. As of the end of the year, two days' salaries have accrued at the rate of $120 per day for each employee.

h. The balance in the Prepaid Rent account represents rent for December.

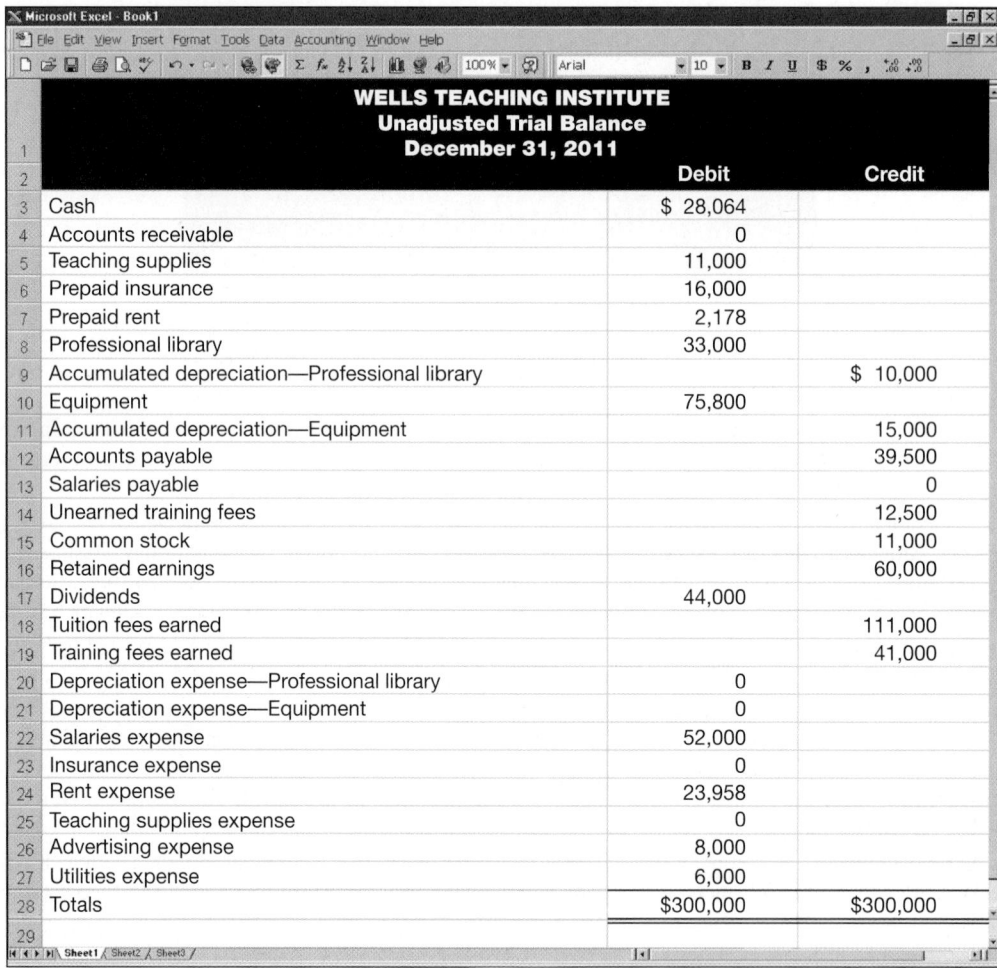

	WELLS TEACHING INSTITUTE Unadjusted Trial Balance December 31, 2011		
		Debit	Credit
3	Cash	$ 28,064	
4	Accounts receivable	0	
5	Teaching supplies	11,000	
6	Prepaid insurance	16,000	
7	Prepaid rent	2,178	
8	Professional library	33,000	
9	Accumulated depreciation—Professional library		$ 10,000
10	Equipment	75,800	
11	Accumulated depreciation—Equipment		15,000
12	Accounts payable		39,500
13	Salaries payable		0
14	Unearned training fees		12,500
15	Common stock		11,000
16	Retained earnings		60,000
17	Dividends	44,000	
18	Tuition fees earned		111,000
19	Training fees earned		41,000
20	Depreciation expense—Professional library	0	
21	Depreciation expense—Equipment	0	
22	Salaries expense	52,000	
23	Insurance expense	0	
24	Rent expense	23,958	
25	Teaching supplies expense	0	
26	Advertising expense	8,000	
27	Utilities expense	6,000	
28	Totals	$300,000	$300,000

Required

1. For accounts listed in the unadjusted trial balance, prepare T-accounts (representing the ledger) and enter the unadjusted balances.

2. Prepare the necessary adjusting journal entries for items *a* through *h* and post them to the T-accounts. Assume that adjusting entries are made only at year-end.

3. Update balances in the T-accounts for the adjusting entries and prepare an adjusted trial balance.

4. Prepare Wells Teaching Institute's income statement and statement of retained earnings for the year 2011 and prepare its balance sheet as of December 31, 2011.

The adjusted trial balance of Maytagg Repairs on December 31, 2011, follows.

Problem 3-3A
Preparing trial balances, closing
entries, and financial statements
C4 P4 P5

No.	MAYTAGG REPAIRS Adjusted Trial Balance December 31, 2011 Account Title	Debit	Credit
101	Cash	$ 13,000	
124	Office supplies	2,000	
128	Prepaid insurance	2,150	
167	Equipment	53,000	
168	Accumulated depreciation—Equipment		$ 8,000
201	Accounts payable		19,000
210	Wages payable		700
307	Common stock		13,200
318	Retained earnings		21,600
319	Dividends	16,500	
401	Repair fees earned		91,150
612	Depreciation expense—Equipment	7,000	
623	Wages expense	38,000	
637	Insurance expense	1,600	
640	Rent expense	11,400	
650	Office supplies expense	5,600	
690	Utilities expense	3,400	
	Totals	$153,650	$153,650

Required

1. Prepare an income statement and a statement of retained earnings for the year 2011, and a classified balance sheet as of December 31, 2011.

2. Enter the adjusted trial balance in the first two columns of a six-column table. Use columns three and four for closing entry information and the last two columns for a post-closing trial balance—see the headings below. Insert an Income Summary account as the last row in the trial balance.

Check (1) Ending Retained Earnings, $29,250

(2) P-C trial balance totals, $70,150

No.	Account Title	Adjusted Trial Balance Dr.	Cr.	Closing Entries Information Dr.	Cr.	Post-Closing Trial Balance Dr.	Cr.

3. Enter closing entry information in the six-column table and prepare journal entries for them.

Analysis Component

4. Assume for this part only that:

   a. None of the $1,600 insurance expense had expired during the year. Instead, assume it is a prepayment of the next period's insurance protection.

   b. There are no earned and unpaid wages at the end of the year. (*Hint:* Reverse the $700 wages payable accrual.)

   Describe the financial statement changes that would result from these two assumptions.

On April 1, 2011, Jiro Nozomi created a new travel agency, Adventure Travel. The following transactions occurred during the company's first month.

Problem 3-4A
Applying the accounting cycle
C3 P4 P5

mhhe.com/wildFA5e

April 1 Nozomi invested $32,000 cash and computer equipment worth $26,000 in the company in exchange for its common stock.

    2 The company rented furnished office space by paying $1,300 cash for the first month's (April) rent.

    3 The company purchased $2,500 of office supplies for cash.

10   The company paid $2,502 cash for the premium on a 12-month insurance policy. Coverage begins on April 11.

14   The company paid $2,300 cash for two weeks' salaries earned by employees.

24   The company collected $16,000 cash on commissions from airlines on tickets obtained for customers.

28   The company paid $2,400 cash for two weeks' salaries earned by employees.

29   The company paid $750 cash for minor repairs to the company's computer.

30   The company paid $550 cash for this month's telephone bill.

30   The company paid $1,200 cash for dividends.

The company's chart of accounts follows:

101	Cash	405	Commissions Earned
106	Accounts Receivable	612	Depreciation Expense—Computer Equip.
124	Office Supplies	622	Salaries Expense
128	Prepaid Insurance	637	Insurance Expense
167	Computer Equipment	640	Rent Expense
168	Accumulated Depreciation—Computer Equip.	650	Office Supplies Expense
209	Salaries Payable	684	Repairs Expense
307	Common Stock	688	Telephone Expense
318	Retained Earnings	901	Income Summary
319	Dividends		

Required

1. Use the balance column format to set up a ledger account for each account listed in its chart of accounts.

2. Prepare journal entries to record the April transactions and post them to the ledger accounts. The company records prepaid and unearned items in balance sheet accounts.

Check (3) Unadj. trial balance totals, $74,000

3. Prepare an unadjusted trial balance as of April 30.

(4a) Dr. Insurance Expense, $139

4. Use the following information to journalize and post adjusting entries for the month.
   a. Two-thirds of one month's insurance coverage has expired.
   b. At the end of the month, $700 of office supplies are still available.
   c. This month's depreciation on the computer equipment is $500.
   d. Employees earned $720 of unpaid and unrecorded salaries as of month-end.
   e. The company earned $3,050 of commissions that are not yet billed at month-end.

(5) Net income, $8,591; Retained Earnings (ending), $7,391; Total assets, $66,111

5. Prepare the income statement and the statement of retained earnings for the month of April and the balance sheet as of April 30, 2011.

6. Prepare journal entries to close the temporary accounts and post these entries to the ledger.

(7) P-C trial balance totals, $66,611

7. Prepare a post-closing trial balance.

Problem 3-5A

Determining balance sheet classifications

C4

In the blank space beside each numbered balance sheet item, enter the letter of its balance sheet classification. If the item should not appear on the balance sheet, enter a Z in the blank.

A. Current assets   **D.** Intangible assets   **F.** Long-term liabilities

B. Long-term investments   **E.** Current liabilities   **G.** Equity

C. Plant assets

_____ **1.** Prepaid rent   _____ **11.** Buildings

_____ **2.** Accounts payable   _____ **12.** Depreciation expense—Building

_____ **3.** Repairs expense   _____ **13.** Notes payable (due in 20 years)

_____ **4.** Long-term investment in stock   _____ **14.** Unearned services revenue

_____ **5.** Taxes payable   _____ **15.** Cash

_____ **6.** Office equipment   _____ **16.** Prepaid insurance

_____ **7.** Automobiles   _____ **17.** Interest receivable

_____ **8.** Accumulated depreciation—Trucks   _____ **18.** Office supplies

_____ **9.** Current portion of long-term   _____ **19.** Land (used in operations)
         note payable
                                          _____ **20.** Store supplies
_____ **10.** Common stock

Riso Co. had the following transactions in the last two months of its year ended December 31.

Nov. 1 Paid $2,000 cash for future newspaper advertising.
      1 Paid $2,466 cash for 12 months of insurance through October 31 of the next year.
     30 Received $4,200 cash for future services to be provided to a customer.
Dec. 1 Paid $2,400 cash for a consultant's services to be received over the next three months.
     15 Received $7,250 cash for future services to be provided to a customer.
     31 Of the advertising paid for on November 1, $1,300 worth is not yet used.
     31 A portion of the insurance paid for on November 1 has expired. No adjustment was made in November to Prepaid Insurance.
     31 Services worth $1,600 are not yet provided to the customer who paid on November 30.
     31 One-third of the consulting services paid for on December 1 have been received.
     31 The company has performed $4,350 of services that the customer paid for on December 15.

Problem 3-6Aᴬ
Recording prepaid expenses
and unearned revenues

P1 P6

Required

1. Prepare entries for these transactions under the method that records prepaid expenses as assets and records unearned revenues as liabilities. Also prepare adjusting entries at the end of the year.

2. Prepare entries for these transactions under the method that records prepaid expenses as expenses and records unearned revenues as revenues. Also prepare adjusting entries at the end of the year.

Analysis Component

3. Explain why the alternative sets of entries in requirements 1 and 2 do not result in different financial statement amounts.

The following unadjusted trial balance is for Ace Construction Co. as of the end of its 2011 fiscal year.

Problem 3-7Aᴮ
Preparing a work sheet, adjusting and closing entries, and financial statements

C4 P4 P7

File Edit View Insert Format Tools Data Window Help

ACE CONSTRUCTION CO.
Unadjusted Trial Balance
June 30, 2011

No.	Account Title	Debit	Credit
101	Cash	$ 19,500	
126	Supplies	9,500	
128	Prepaid insurance	5,000	
167	Equipment	152,160	
168	Accumulated depreciation—Equipment		$ 27,000
201	Accounts payable		5,800
203	Interest payable		0
208	Rent payable		0
210	Wages payable		0
213	Property taxes payable		0
251	Long-term notes payable		30,000
307	Common stock		46,000
318	Retained earnings		40,760
319	Dividends	32,000	
401	Construction fees earned		143,000
612	Depreciation expense—Equipment	0	
623	Wages expense	48,000	
633	Interest expense	3,300	
637	Insurance expense	0	
640	Rent expense	13,000	
652	Supplies expense	0	
683	Property taxes expense	4,500	
684	Repairs expense	2,600	
690	Utilities expense	3,000	
	Totals	$292,560	$292,560

Required

1. Prepare a 10-column work sheet for fiscal year 2011, starting with the unadjusted trial balance and including adjustments based on these additional facts:

   a. The supplies available at the end of fiscal year 2011 had a cost of $3,420.

   b. The cost of expired insurance for the fiscal year is $3,150.

    c. Annual depreciation on equipment is $9,000.

    d. The June utilities expense of $580 is not included in the unadjusted trial balance because the bill arrived after the trial balance was prepared. The $580 amount owed needs to be recorded.

    e. The company's employees have earned $1,200 of accrued wages at fiscal year-end.

    f. The rent expense incurred and not yet paid or recorded at fiscal year-end is $200.

    g. Additional property taxes of $1,000 have been assessed for this fiscal year but have not been paid or recorded in the accounts.

    h. The long-term note payable bears interest at 12% per year. The unadjusted Interest Expense account equals the amount paid for the first 11 months of the 2011 fiscal year. The $300 accrued interest for June has not yet been paid or recorded. (The company is required to make a $6,000 payment toward the note payable during the 2012 fiscal year.)

Check (3) Total assets, $140,930; Current liabilities, $15,080; Net income, $47,090

2. Use information on the accounting adjustments and the resulting balances entered into the work sheet in part *1* to journalize the adjusting and closing entries.

3. Prepare the income statement and the statement of retained earnings for the year ended June 30 and the classified balance sheet as of June 30, 2011.

Analysis Component

4. Analyze the following separate errors and describe how each would affect the 10-column work sheet. Explain whether the error is likely to be discovered in completing the work sheet and, if not, the effect of the error on the financial statements.

    a. Assume that the adjustment for supplies used consisted of a credit to Supplies for $3,420 and a debit for $3,420 to Supplies Expense.

    b. When the adjusted trial balance in the work sheet is completed, assume that the $19,500 Cash balance is incorrectly entered in the Credit column.

PROBLEM SET B

Problem 3-1B
Preparing adjusting and subsequent journal entries

C1 A1 P1

Wu-Tang Co. follows the practice of recording prepaid expenses and unearned revenues in balance sheet accounts. Wu-Tang's annual accounting period ends on October 31, 2011. The following information concerns the adjusting entries that need to be recorded as of that date.

a. The Office Supplies account started the fiscal year with a $3,950 balance. During the fiscal year, the company purchased supplies for $16,313, which was added to the Office Supplies account. The supplies available at October 31, 2011, totaled $3,476.

b. An analysis of the company's insurance policies revealed the following facts:

Policy	Date of Purchase	Months of Coverage	Cost
A	April 1, 2010	24 months	$10,824
B	April 1, 2011	36 months	9,540
C	August 1, 2011	12 months	8,424

The total premium for each policy was paid in full (for all months) at the purchase date, and the Prepaid Insurance account was debited for the full cost. (Year-end adjusting entries for Prepaid Insurance were properly recorded in all prior fiscal years.)

c. The company has 15 employees, who earn a total of $2,610 for each workday. They are paid each Monday for their work in the five-day workweek ending on the previous Friday. Assume that October 31, 2011, is a Tuesday, and all 15 employees worked the first two days of that week. They will be paid salaries for five full days on Monday, November 6, 2011.

d. The company purchased a building on November 1, 2010, that cost $695,000 and is expected to have a $41,000 salvage value at the end of its predicted 30-year life. Annual depreciation is $21,800.

e. Since the company does not occupy the entire building it owns, it rented space to a tenant at $3,200 per month, starting on September 1, 2011. The rent was paid on time on September 1, and the amount received was credited to the Rent Earned account. However, the October rent has not been paid. The company has worked out an agreement with the tenant, who has promised to pay both October and November rent in full on November 15. The tenant has agreed not to fall behind again.

f. On September 1, the company rented space to another tenant for $2,899 per month. The tenant paid five months' rent in advance on that date. The payment was recorded with a credit to the Unearned Rent account.

Required

1. Use the information to prepare adjusting entries as of October 31, 2011.
2. Prepare journal entries to record the first subsequent cash transaction in November 2011 for parts *c* and *e*.

Check (1*b*) Dr. Insurance Expense, $9,373; (1*d*) Dr. Depreciation Expense, $21,800.

Following is the unadjusted trial balance for Augustus Institute as of December 31, 2011, which initially records prepaid expenses and unearned revenues in balance sheet accounts. The Institute provides one-on-one training to individuals who pay tuition directly to the business and offers extension training to groups in off-site locations. Shown after the trial balance are items *a* through *h* that require adjusting entries as of December 31, 2011.

Problem 3-2B
Preparing adjusting entries, adjusted trial balance, and financial statements

A1 P1 P2 P3

	Debit	Credit
AUGUSTUS INSTITUTE		
Unadjusted Trial Balance		
December 31, 2011		
Cash	$ 27,000	
Accounts receivable	0	
Teaching supplies	10,000	
Prepaid insurance	16,000	
Prepaid rent	2,073	
Professional library	31,000	
Accumulated depreciation—Professional library		$ 9,000
Equipment	72,719	
Accumulated depreciation—Equipment		17,000
Accounts payable		35,600
Salaries payable		0
Unearned training fees		13,000
Common stock		10,000
Retained earnings		56,000
Dividends	41,000	
Tuition fees earned		106,000
Training fees earned		39,000
Depreciation expense—Professional library	0	
Depreciation expense—Equipment	0	
Salaries expense	50,000	
Insurance expense	0	
Rent expense	22,808	
Teaching supplies expense	0	
Advertising expense	7,000	
Utilities expense	6,000	
Totals	$285,600	$285,600

Additional Information Items

a. An analysis of the Institute's insurance policies shows that $3,000 of coverage has expired.

b. An inventory count shows that teaching supplies costing $3,000 are available at year-end 2011.

c. Annual depreciation on the equipment is $17,000.

d. Annual depreciation on the professional library is $6,000.

e. On November 1, the Institute agreed to do a special six-month course (starting immediately) for a client. The contract calls for a $2,600 monthly fee, and the client paid the first five months' fees in advance. When the cash was received, the Unearned Training Fees account was credited. The last one month's fees will be recorded when earned and collected in 2012.

f. On October 15, the Institute agreed to teach a four-month class (beginning immediately) to an individual for $3,900 tuition per month payable at the end of the class. The class started on October 15, but no payment has yet been received.

g. The Institute's only employee is paid weekly. As of the end of the year, two days' wages have accrued at the rate of $170 per day.

h. The balance in the Prepaid Rent account represents rent for December.

Required

1. For accounts listed in the unadjusted trial balance, prepare T-accounts (representing the ledger) and enter the unadjusted balances.

2. Prepare the necessary adjusting journal entries for items *a* through *h*, and post them to the T-accounts. Assume that adjusting entries are made only at year-end.

3. Update balances in the T-accounts for the adjusting entries and prepare an adjusted trial balance.

4. Prepare Augustus Institute's income statement and statement of retained earnings for the year 2011, and prepare its balance sheet as of December 31, 2011.

Problem 3-3B

Preparing trial balances, closing entries, and financial statements

C4 P4 P5

Goldsmith Company's adjusted trial balance on December 31, 2011, follows.

GOLDSMITH COMPANY
Adjusted Trial Balance
December 31, 2011

No.	Account Title	Debit	Credit
101	Cash	$ 10,300	
125	Store supplies	1,400	
128	Prepaid insurance	2,200	
167	Equipment	52,000	
168	Accumulated depreciation—Equipment		$ 9,000
201	Accounts payable		17,000
210	Wages payable		1,300
307	Common stock		13,200
318	Retained earnings		20,200
319	Dividends	16,500	
401	Repair fees earned		91,500
612	Depreciation expense—Equipment	8,500	
623	Wages expense	41,500	
637	Insurance expense	1,000	
640	Rent expense.............................	11,400	
651	Store supplies expense	4,400	
690	Utilities expense	3,000	
	Totals	$152,200	$152,200

Required

1. Prepare an income statement and a statement of retained earnings for the year 2011, and a classified balance sheet as of December 31, 2011.

2. Enter the adjusted trial balance in the first two columns of a six-column table. Use the middle two columns for closing entry information and the last two columns for a post-closing trial balance—see the headings below. Insert an Income Summary account as the last row in the trial balance.

No.	Account Title	Adjusted Trial Balance		Closing Entries Information		Post-Closing Trial Balance	
		Dr.	Cr.	Dr.	Cr.	Dr.	Cr.

3. Enter closing entry information in the six-column table and prepare journal entries for them.

Analysis Component

4. Assume for this part only that:

a. None of the $1,000 insurance expense had expired during the year. Instead, assume it is a prepayment of the next period's insurance protection.

b. There are no earned and unpaid wages at the end of the year. (*Hint:* Reverse the $1,300 wages payable accrual.)

Describe the financial statement changes that would result from these two assumptions.

On July 1, 2011, Lauren Plume created a new self-storage business, Safe Storage. The following transactions occurred during the company's first month.

Problem 3-4B
Applying the accounting cycle
C3 P4 P5

July 1   Plume invested $28,000 cash and buildings worth $20,000 in the company in exchange for its common stock.
2   The company rented equipment by paying $1,700 cash for the first month's (July) rent.
5   The company purchased $2,500 of office supplies for cash.
10   The company paid $3,000 cash for the premium on a 12-month insurance policy. Coverage begins on July 11.
14   The company paid an employee $1,700 cash for two weeks' salary earned.
24   The company collected $11,000 cash for storage fees from customers.
28   The company paid another $1,700 cash for two weeks' salary earned by an employee.
29   The company paid $700 cash for minor repairs to a leaking roof.
30   The company paid $600 cash for this month's telephone bill.
31   The company paid $900 cash for dividends.

The company's chart of accounts follows:

101	Cash	401	Storage Fees Earned
106	Accounts Receivable	606	Depreciation Expense—Buildings
124	Office Supplies	622	Salaries Expense
128	Prepaid Insurance	637	Insurance Expense
173	Buildings	640	Rent Expense
174	Accumulated Depreciation—Buildings	650	Office Supplies Expense
209	Salaries Payable	684	Repairs Expense
307	Common Stock	688	Telephone Expense
318	Retained Earnings	901	Income Summary
319	Dividends		

Required

1. Use the balance column format to set up a ledger account for each account listed in its chart of accounts.
2. Prepare journal entries to record the July transactions and post them to the ledger accounts. Record prepaid and unearned items in balance sheet accounts.
3. Prepare an unadjusted trial balance as of July 31.
4. Use the following information to journalize and post adjusting entries for the month.

a. Two-thirds of one month's insurance coverage has expired.
b. At the end of the month, $1,200 of office supplies are still available.
c. This month's depreciation on the buildings is $500.
d. An employee earned $120 of unpaid and unrecorded salary as of month-end.
e. The company earned $2,550 of storage fees that are not yet billed at month-end.

5. Prepare the income statement and the statement of retained earnings for the month of July and the balance sheet as of July 31, 2011.
6. Prepare journal entries to close the temporary accounts and post these entries to the ledger.
7. Prepare a post-closing trial balance.

Check (3) Unadj. trial balance totals, $59,000

(4a) Dr. Insurance Expense, $167

(5) Net income, $5,063; Retained Earnings (ending), $4,163; Total assets, $52,283

(7) P-C trial balance totals, $52,783

Problem 3-5B

Determining balance sheet classifications

C4

In the blank space beside each numbered balance sheet item, enter the letter of its balance sheet classification. If the item should not appear on the balance sheet, enter a Z in the blank.

A. Current assets
B. Long-term investments
C. Plant assets
D. Intangible assets

E. Current liabilities
F. Long-term liabilities
G. Equity

_____ **1.** Rent receivable
_____ **2.** Salaries payable
_____ **3.** Income taxes payable
_____ **4.** Prepaid insurance
_____ **5.** Office supplies
_____ **6.** Interest payable
_____ **7.** Rent revenue
_____ **8.** Notes receivable (due in 120 days)
_____ **9.** Land (used in operations)
_____ **10.** Depreciation expense—Trucks
_____ **11.** Commissions earned

_____ **12.** Interest receivable
_____ **13.** Long-term investment in stock
_____ **14.** Retained Earnings
_____ **15.** Machinery
_____ **16.** Notes payable (due in 15 years)
_____ **17.** Copyrights
_____ **18.** Current portion of long-term note payable
_____ **19.** Accumulated depreciation—Trucks
_____ **20.** Office equipment

Problem 3-6B^A

Recording prepaid expenses and unearned revenues

P1   P6

Jazz Co. had the following transactions in the last two months of its fiscal year ended May 31.

Apr. 1   Paid $2,600 cash to an accounting firm for future consulting services.
     1   Paid $2,484 cash for 12 months of insurance through March 31 of the next year.
     30 Received $4,600 cash for future services to be provided to a customer.
May 1   Paid $2,700 cash for future newspaper advertising.
     23 Received $7,450 cash for future services to be provided to a customer.
     31 Of the consulting services paid for on April 1, $1,700 worth has been received.
     31 A portion of the insurance paid for on April 1 has expired. No adjustment was made in April to Prepaid Insurance.
     31 Services worth $1,400 are not yet provided to the customer who paid on April 30.
     31 One-third of the advertising paid for on May 1 has not yet been provided.
     31 The company has performed $3,000 of services that the customer paid for on May 23.

Required

1. Prepare entries for these transactions under the method that records prepaid expenses and unearned revenues in balance sheet accounts. Also prepare adjusting entries at the end of the year.

2. Prepare entries for these transactions under the method that records prepaid expenses and unearned revenues in income statement accounts. Also prepare adjusting entries at the end of the year.

Analysis Component

3. Explain why the alternative sets of entries in parts 1 and 2 do not result in different financial statement amounts.

Problem 3-7B^B

Preparing a work sheet, adjusting and closing entries, and financial statements

C4   P4   P7

The following unadjusted trial balance is for Braun Demolition Company as of the end of its April 30, 2011, fiscal year.

File Edit View Insert Format Tools Data Window Help

BRAUN DEMOLITION COMPANY
Unadjusted Trial Balance
April 30, 2011

No.	Account Title	Debit	Credit
101	Cash	$ 17,000	
126	Supplies	9,500	
128	Prepaid insurance	6,500	
167	Equipment	140,460	
168	Accumulated depreciation—Equipment		$ 22,000
201	Accounts payable		6,000
203	Interest payable		0
208	Rent payable		0
210	Wages payable		0
213	Property taxes payable		0
251	Long-term notes payable		25,000
307	Common stock		44,000
318	Retained earnings		37,610
319	Dividends	25,500	
401	Demolition fees earned		140,000
612	Depreciation expense—Equipment	0	
623	Wages expense	48,000	
633	Interest expense	2,750	
637	Insurance expense	0	
640	Rent expense	15,400	
652	Supplies expense	0	
683	Property taxes expense	4,400	
684	Repairs expense	2,100	
690	Utilities expense	3,000	
	Totals	$274,610	$274,610

Sheet1 / Sheet2 / Sheet3

Required

1. Prepare a 10-column work sheet for fiscal year 2011, starting with the unadjusted trial balance and including adjustments based on these additional facts:

   a. The supplies available at the end of fiscal year 2011 had a cost of $3,420.

   b. The cost of expired insurance for the fiscal year is $4,095.

   c. Annual depreciation on equipment is $11,000.

   d. The April utilities expense of $580 is not included in the unadjusted trial balance because the bill arrived after the trial balance was prepared. The $580 amount owed needs to be recorded.

   e. The company's employees have earned $1,500 of accrued wages at fiscal year-end.

   f. The rent expense incurred and not yet paid or recorded at fiscal year-end is $1,400.

   g. Additional property taxes of $500 have been assessed for this fiscal year but have not been paid or recorded in the accounts.

   h. The long-term note payable bears interest at 12% per year. The unadjusted Interest Expense account equals the amount paid for the first 11 months of the 2011 fiscal year. The $250 accrued interest for April has not yet been paid or recorded. (The company is required to make a $5,000 payment toward the note payable during the 2012 fiscal year.)

2. Use information on the accounting adjustments and the resulting balances entered into the work sheet in part *1* to journalize the adjusting and closing entries.

3. Prepare the income statement and the statement of retained earnings for the year ended April 30, and the classified balance sheet as of April 30, 2011.

Check (3) Total assets, $130,285; Current liabilities, $15,230; Net income, $38,945

Analysis Component

4. Analyze the following separate errors and describe how each would affect the 10-column work sheet. Explain whether the error is likely to be discovered in completing the work sheet and, if not, the effect of the error on the financial statements.

   a. Assume the adjustment for expiration of the insurance coverage consisted of a credit to Prepaid Insurance for $2,405 and a debit for $2,405 to Insurance Expense.

   b. When the adjusted trial balance in the work sheet is completed, assume that the $2,100 Repairs Expense account balance is extended to the Debit column of the balance sheet columns.

SERIAL PROBLEM

Success Systems

This serial problem began in Chapter 1 and continues through most of the book. If previous chapter segments were not completed, the serial problem can still begin at this point. It is helpful, but not necessary, to use the Working Papers that accompany the book.

SP 3   After the success of the company's first two months, Adriana Lopez continues to operate Success Systems. (Transactions for the first two months are described in the serial problem of Chapter 2.) The unadjusted trial balance (along with some new accounts) at November 30 follows.

No.	Account Title	Debit	Credit
101	Cash	$ 48,052	
106	Accounts receivable	12,618	
126	Computer supplies	2,545	
128	Prepaid insurance	2,220	
131	Prepaid rent	3,300	
163	Office equipment	8,000	
164	Accumulated depreciation—Office equipment		$ 0
167	Computer equipment	20,000	
168	Accumulated depreciation—Computer equipment		0
201	Accounts payable		0
210	Wages payable		0
236	Unearned computer services revenue		0
307	Common stock		83,000
318	Retained earnings		0
319	Dividends	5,600	
403	Computer services revenue		25,659
612	Depreciation expense—Office equipment	0	
613	Depreciation expense—Computer equipment	0	
623	Wages expense	2,625	
637	Insurance expense	0	
640	Rent expense	0	
652	Computer supplies expense	0	
655	Advertising expense	1,940	
676	Mileage expense	704	
677	Miscellaneous expenses	250	
684	Repairs expense—Computer	805	
901	Income summary		0
	Totals	$108,659	$108,659

Success Systems had the following transactions and events in December 2009.

Dec. 2 Paid $1,025 cash to Hillside Mall for Success Systems' share of mall advertising costs.
      3 Paid $500 cash for minor repairs to the company's computer.
      4 Received $3,950 cash from Alex's Engineering Co. for the receivable from November.
     10 Paid cash to Lyn Addie for six days of work at the rate of $125 per day.
     14 Notified by Alex's Engineering Co. that Success's bid of $7,000 on a proposed project has been accepted. Alex's paid a $1,500 cash advance to Success Systems.
     15 Purchased $1,100 of computer supplies on credit from Harris Office Products.
     16 Sent a reminder to Gomez Co. to pay the fee for services recorded on November 8.
     20 Completed a project for Liu Corporation and received $5,625 cash.
  22–26 Took the week off for the holidays.
     28 Received $3,000 cash as partial payment from Gomez Co. on its receivable.
     29 Reimbursed Lopez's business automobile mileage (600 miles at $0.32 per mile).
     31 Paid $1,500 cash for dividends.

The following additional facts are collected for use in making adjusting entries prior to preparing financial statements for the company's first three months.

a. The December 31 inventory count of computer supplies shows $580 still available.

b. Three months have expired since the 12-month insurance premium was paid in advance.

c. As of December 31, Lyn Addie has not been paid for four days of work at $125 per day.

d. The company's computer is expected to have a four-year life with no salvage value.

e. The office equipment is expected to have a five-year life with no salvage value.

f. Three of the four months' prepaid rent has expired.

Required

1. Prepare journal entries to record each of the December transactions and events for Success Systems. Post those entries to the accounts in the ledger.

2. Prepare adjusting entries to reflect *a* through *f*. Post those entries to the accounts in the ledger.

3. Prepare an adjusted trial balance as of December 31, 2009.

4. Prepare an income statement and a statement of retained earnings for the three months ended December 31, 2009. Prepare a balance sheet as of December 31, 2009.

5. Record and post the necessary closing entries for Success Systems.

6. Prepare a post-closing trial balance as of December 31, 2009.

Check (3) Adjusted trial balance totals, $119,034

(4) Total assets, $93,248

(6) Post-closing trial balance totals, $94,898

BEYOND THE NUMBERS

BTN 3-1 Refer to **Best Buy**'s financial statements in Appendix A to answer the following.

1. Identify and write down the revenue recognition principle as explained in the chapter.

2. Research Best Buy's footnotes to discover how it applies the revenue recognition principle and when it recognizes revenue. Report what you discover.

3. What is Best Buy's profit margin for fiscal years ended March 1, 2008, and February 28, 2009.

4. For the fiscal year ended February 28, 2009, what amount is credited to Income Summary to summarize its revenues earned?

5. For the fiscal year ended February 28, 2009, what amount is debited to Income Summary to summarize its expenses incurred?

6. For the fiscal year ended February 28, 2009, what is the balance of its Income Summary account before it is closed?

Fast Forward

7. Access Best Buy's annual report (10-K) for fiscal years ending after February 28, 2009, at its Website (**BestBuy.com**) or the SEC's EDGAR database (**www.SEC.gov**). Compare and assess the February 28, 2009, fiscal year profit margin to any subsequent year's profit margin that you compute.

REPORTING IN ACTION

C1 C2 A1 A2 P4

BTN 3-2 Key figures for the recent two years of both **Best Buy** and **RadioShack** follow.

($ millions)	Best Buy		RadioShack	
	Current Year	Prior Year	Current Year	Prior Year
Net income	$ 1,003	$ 1,407	$ 192.4	$ 236.8
Net sales	45,015	40,023	4,224.5	4,251.7
Current assets	8,192	7,342	1,792.0	1,566.8
Current liabilities	8,435	6,769	637.2	748.0

COMPARATIVE ANALYSIS

A2 A3

Required

1. Compute profit margins for (*a*) Best Buy and (*b*) RadioShack for the two years of data shown.

2. Which company is more successful on the basis of profit margin? Explain.

3. Compute the current ratio for both years and both companies.

4. Which company has the better ability to pay short-term obligations according to the current ratio?

5. Analyze and comment on each company's current ratios for the past two years.

6. How do Best Buy's and RadioShack's current ratios compare to their industry average ratio of 1.3?

ETHICS CHALLENGE

C3

BTN 3-3   On January 20, 2011, Tamira Nelson, the accountant for Picton Enterprises, is feeling pressure to complete the annual financial statements. The company president has said he needs up-to-date financial statements to share with the bank on January 21 at a dinner meeting that has been called to discuss Picton's obtaining loan financing for a special building project. Tamira knows that she will not be able to gather all the needed information in the next 24 hours to prepare the entire set of adjusting entries that must be posted before the financial statements accurately portray the company's performance and financial position for the fiscal period ended December 31, 2010. Tamira ultimately decides to estimate several expense accruals at the last minute. When deciding on estimates for the expenses, she uses low estimates because she does not want to make the financial statements look worse than they are. Tamira finishes the financial statements before the deadline and gives them to the president without mentioning that several accounts use estimated balances.

Required

1. Identify several courses of action that Tamira could have taken instead of the one she took.

2. If you were in Tamira's situation, what would you have done? Briefly justify your response.

COMMUNICATING IN PRACTICE

P4

BTN 3-4   Assume that one of your classmates states that a company's accounting books should be ongoing and therefore not closed until that business is terminated. Write a one-half page memo to this classmate explaining the concept of the closing process by drawing analogies between (1) a scoreboard for an athletic event and the revenue and expense accounts of a business or (2) a sports team's record book and the equity (net asset) account. (*Hint:* Consider what would happen if the scoreboard were not cleared before the start of a new game.)

TAKING IT TO THE NET

C1   A2

BTN 3-5   Access the **Gap**'s Website (<u>GapInc.com</u>) to answer the following requirements.

Required

1. What are Gap's main brands?

2. Access Gap's 2009 fiscal year annual report (10-K) either at the company's Website or at <u>www.sec.gov</u>. What is Gap's fiscal year-end?

3. What is Gap's net sales for the period ended January 31, 2009?

4. What is Gap's net income for the period ended January 31, 2009?

5. Compute Gap's profit margin for the year ended January 31, 2009.

6. Do you believe Gap's decision to use a year-end of late January or early February relates to its natural business year? Explain.

A3

BTN 3-6   Access **Motley Fool**'s discussion of the current ratio at <u>Fool.com/School/Valuation/CurrentAndQuickRatio.htm</u>. (If the page changed, search that site for the *current ratio*.)

Required

1. What level for the current ratio is generally regarded as sufficient to meet near-term operating needs?

2. Once you have calculated the current ratio for a company, what should you compare it against?

3. What are the implications for a company that has a current ratio that is too high?

TEAMWORK IN ACTION

A1   P1

BTN 3-7   Four types of adjustments are described in the chapter for: (1) prepaid expenses, (2) unearned revenues, (3) accrued expenses, and (4) accrued revenues.

Required

1. Form *learning teams* of four (or more) members. Each team member must select one of the four adjustments as an area of expertise (each team must have at least one expert in each area).

2. Form *expert teams* from the individuals who have selected the same area of expertise. Expert teams are to discuss and write a report that each expert will present to his or her learning team addressing the following:

   a. Description of the adjustment and why it's necessary.

   b. Example of a transaction or event, with dates and amounts, that requires adjustment.

   c. Adjusting entry(ies) for the example in requirement *b*.

   d. Status of the affected account(s) before and after the adjustment in requirement *c*.

   e. Effects on financial statements of not making the adjustment.

3. Each expert should return to his or her learning team. In rotation, each member should present his or her expert team's report to the learning team. Team discussion is encouraged.

BTN 3-8 Review the opening feature of this chapter dealing with **PopCap Games.**

Required

1. Assume that PopCap sells a $300 gift certificate to a customer, collecting the $300 cash in advance. Prepare the journal entry for the (*a*) collection of the cash for delivery of the gift certificate to the customer and (*b*) revenue from the subsequent delivery of games when the gift certificate is used.

2. How can keeping no inventories help to improve PopCap's profit margin?

3. PopCap understands that many companies carry inventories, and the owners are thinking of carrying an inventory of games on CDs. The owners desire your advice on the pros and cons of carrying such inventory. Provide at least one reason for and one reason against carrying inventories.

ENTREPRENEURIAL DECISION

A3 C4 P4

BTN 3-9 Select a company that you can visit in person or interview on the telephone. Call ahead to the company to arrange a time when you can interview an employee (preferably an accountant) who helps prepare the annual financial statements. Inquire about the following aspects of its *accounting cycle:*

1. Does the company prepare interim financial statements? What reporting period(s) is used?

2. Does the company use the cash or accrual basis of accounting?

3. Does the company use a work sheet in preparing financial statements? Why or why not?

4. Does the company use a spreadsheet program? If so, which software program is used?

5. How long does it take after the end of its reporting period to complete annual statements?

HITTING THE ROAD

C3

BTN 3-10 GOME (www.GOME.com.hk) is the leading chain retailer of consumer electronic products and household appliances in China.

Required

1. Locate the notes to its December 31, 2008, financial statements at the company's Website, and read note *3 Revenue Recognition,* first paragraph only. When is revenue recognized by GOME?

2. Refer to GOME's financials in Appendix A. What is GOME's profit margin for the year ended December 31, 2008?

3. Refer to GOME's financials in Appendix A. Compute GOME's current ratio for both the current year and the prior year. (GOME's balance sheet is in a slightly different format than the U.S. GAAP examples in the chapter: current assets follow noncurrent assets, and current liabilities follow noncurrent liabilities.)

GLOBAL DECISION

A2 C1 C2

ANSWERS TO MULTIPLE CHOICE QUIZ

1. b; the forgotten adjusting entry is: *dr.* Wages Expense, *cr.* Wages Payable.

2. c; Supplies used = $450 − $125 = $325

3. b; Insurance expense = $24,000 × (8/24) = $8,000; adjusting entry is: *dr.* Insurance Expense for $8,000, *cr.* Prepaid Insurance for $8,000.

4. a; Consulting fees earned = $3,600 × (2/6) = $1,200; adjusting entry is: *dr.* Unearned Consulting Fee for $1,200, *cr.* Consulting Fees Earned for $1,200.

5. e; Profit margin = $15,000/$300,000 = 5%

Reporting and Analyzing Merchandising Operations

"We are changing history. And, . . . we are all going to make a whole lot of money!" —Selena Cuffe

A Look Back

Chapter 3 focused on the final steps of the accounting process. We explained the importance of proper revenue and expense recognition and described the adjusting and closing processes. We also prepared financial statements.

A Look at This Chapter

This chapter emphasizes merchandising activities. We explain how reporting merchandising activities differs from reporting service activities. We also analyze and record merchandise purchases and sales transactions, and explain the adjustments and closing process for merchandisers.

A Look Ahead

Chapter 5 extends our analysis of merchandising activities and focuses on the valuation of inventory. Topics include the items in inventory, costs assigned, costing methods used, and inventory estimation techniques.

Out of Africa

LOS ANGELES—Selena Cuffe was in Johannesburg as part of a student exchange program when she discovered wine at the Soweto Wine Festival. "They have wine here?" asked a puzzled Selena. That festival unleashed Selena's passion to pursue the merchandising of wine. But not just any wine—she would import and distribute wine produced by indigenous African vintners. She and her husband, Khary, launched **Heritage Link Brands (HeritageLinkBrands.com).** Our mission, says Selena, is "to showcase the very best wines from Africa and the African Diaspora."

But the start-up was a struggle. "Our business is a family business so whatever decisions we make have to be made with the best interest of my family and those we work with," explains Selena. She describes how the business required a merchandising accounting system that needed to account for purchases and sales transactions and to effectively track the levels of the various wines. Inventory was especially important to account for and monitor. Khary explains, "It is very easy to underestimate expenses."

To succeed, Selena and Khary needed to make smart business decisions. They set up an accounting system to capture and communicate costs and sales information. Tracking merchandising activities was necessary to set prices and to manage discounts, allowances, and returns of both sales and purchases. A perpetual inventory system enabled them to stock the right kind and amount of merchandise and to avoid the costs of out-of-stock and excess inventory. Khary stressed that they monitored current assets and current liabilities (working capital). "Understand working capital," insists Khary. "If you don't understand working capital, stop right here and open an accounting book."

Mastering accounting for merchandising is a means to an end for Selena and Khary. "My training is really about how to run a successful business," says Selena. "How to get the most profit you can out of something." Still, Selena recognizes that her merchandising business is much more. "What we're able to do and how we're able to make an impact with this business only matters in as much as the people here and on the continent are able to be successful and thrive."

[Sources: *Heritage Link Brands Website,* January 2010; *TIME,* September 2007; *Black Enterprise,* May 2009; *Inc,* March 2009]

CAP

Conceptual

C1 Describe merchandising activities and identify income components for a merchandising company. *(p. 156)*

C2 Identify and explain the inventory asset of a merchandising company. *(p. 157)*

C3 Describe both perpetual and periodic inventory systems. *(p. 157)*

C4 Analyze and interpret cost flows and operating activities of a merchandising company. *(p. 166)*

Analytical

A1 Compute the acid-test ratio and explain its use to assess liquidity. *(p. 172)*

A2 Compute the gross margin ratio and explain its use to assess profitability. *(p. 172)*

Procedural

P1 Analyze and record transactions for merchandise purchases using a perpetual system. *(p. 158)*

P2 Analyze and record transactions for merchandise sales using a perpetual system. *(p. 163)*

P3 Prepare adjustments and close accounts for a merchandising company. *(p. 166)*

P4 Define and prepare multiple-step and single-step income statements. *(p. 168)*

P5 *Appendix 4A*—Record and compare merchandising transactions using both periodic and perpetual inventory systems. *(p. 177)*

LP4

Buyers of merchandise expect many products, discount prices, inventory on demand, and high quality. This chapter introduces the accounting practices used by companies engaged in merchandising. We show how financial statements reflect merchandising activities and explain the new financial statement items created by merchandising activities. We also analyze and record merchandise purchases and sales, and explain the adjustments and the closing process for these companies.

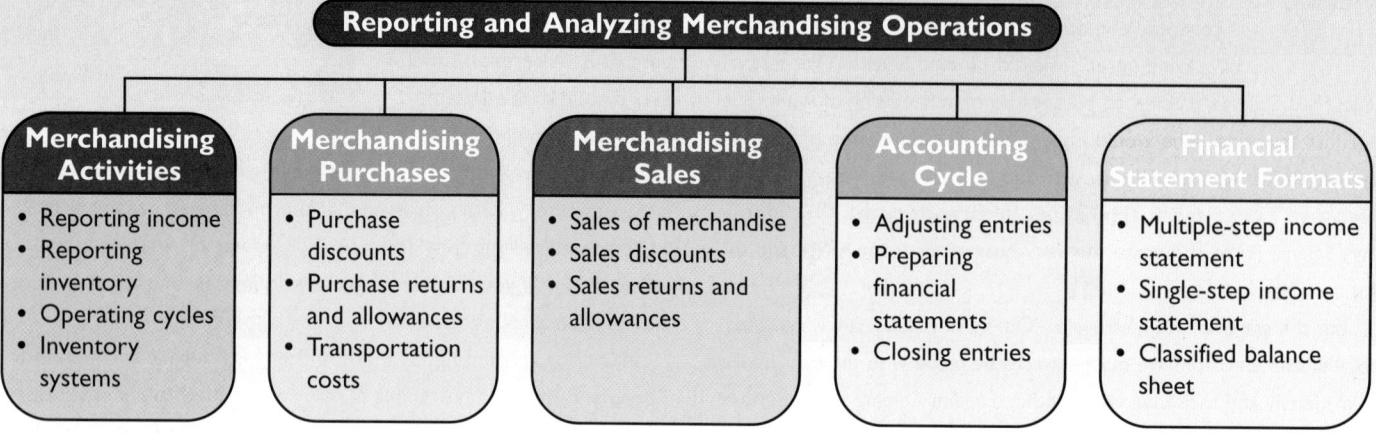

Reporting and Analyzing Merchandising Operations

Merchandising Activities	Merchandising Purchases	Merchandising Sales	Accounting Cycle	Financial Statement Formats
• Reporting income • Reporting inventory • Operating cycles • Inventory systems	• Purchase discounts • Purchase returns and allowances • Transportation costs	• Sales of merchandise • Sales discounts • Sales returns and allowances	• Adjusting entries • Preparing financial statements • Closing entries	• Multiple-step income statement • Single-step income statement • Classified balance sheet

Merchandising Activities

C1 Describe merchandising activities and identify income components for a merchandising company.

Video4.1

Previous chapters emphasized the accounting and reporting activities of service companies. A merchandising company's activities differ from those of a service company. **Merchandise** consists of products, also called *goods,* that a company acquires to resell to customers. A **merchandiser** earns net income by buying and selling merchandise. Merchandisers are often identified as either wholesalers or retailers. A **wholesaler** is an *intermediary* that buys products from manufacturers or other wholesalers and sells them to retailers or other wholesalers. A **retailer** is an intermediary that buys products from manufacturers or wholesalers and sells them to consumers. Many retailers sell both products and services.

Reporting Income for a Merchandiser

Net income for a merchandiser equals revenues from selling merchandise minus both the cost of merchandise sold to customers and the cost of other expenses for the period, see Exhibit 4.1.

EXHIBIT 4.1

Computing Income for a Merchandising Company versus a Service Company

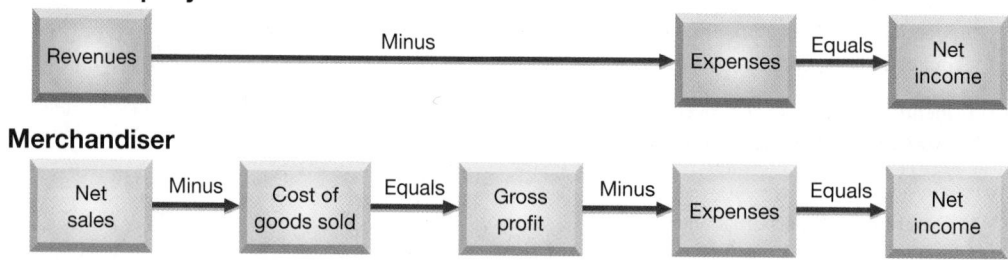

The usual accounting term for revenues from selling merchandise is *sales,* and the term used for the expense of buying and preparing the merchandise is **cost of goods sold.** (Some service companies use the term *sales* instead of revenues; and cost of goods sold is also called *cost of sales.*)

The income statement for Z-Mart in Exhibit 4.2 illustrates these key components of a merchandiser's net income. The first two lines show that products are acquired at a cost of $230,400 and sold for $314,700. The third line shows an $84,300 **gross profit,** also called

Point: Fleming, SuperValu, and SYSCO are wholesalers. Gap, Oakley, Target, and Wal-Mart are retailers.

Z-MART Income Statement For Year Ended December 31, 2009	
Net sales	$314,700
Cost of goods sold	230,400
Gross profit	84,300
Expenses	71,400
Net income	$ 12,900

EXHIBIT 4.2

Merchandiser's Income Statement

gross margin, which equals net sales less cost of goods sold. Additional expenses of $71,400 are reported, which leaves $12,900 in net income.

Point: Analysis of gross profit is important to effective business decisions, and is described later in the chapter.

Reporting Inventory for a Merchandiser

A merchandiser's balance sheet includes a current asset called *merchandise inventory,* an item not on a service company's balance sheet. **Merchandise inventory,** or simply *inventory,* refers to products that a company owns and intends to sell. The cost of this asset includes the cost incurred to buy the goods, ship them to the store, and make them ready for sale.

C2 Identify and explain the inventory asset of a merchandising company.

Operating Cycle for a Merchandiser

A merchandising company's operating cycle begins by purchasing merchandise and ends by collecting cash from selling the merchandise. The length of an operating cycle differs across the types of businesses. Department stores often have operating cycles of two to five months. Operating cycles for grocery merchants usually range from two to eight weeks.

Exhibit 4.3 illustrates an operating cycle for a merchandiser with credit sales. The cycle moves from (*a*) cash purchases of merchandise to (*b*) inventory for sale to (*c*) credit sales to (*d*) accounts receivable to (*e*) cash. Companies try to keep their operating cycles short because assets tied up in inventory and receivables are not productive. Cash sales shorten operating cycles.

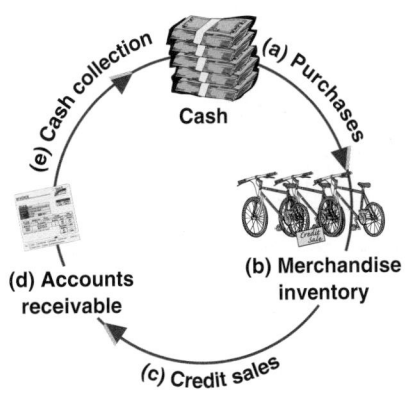

EXHIBIT 4.3

Merchandiser's Operating Cycle

Inventory Systems

Cost of goods sold is the cost of merchandise sold to customers during a period. It is often the largest single expense on a merchandiser's income statement. **Inventory** refers to products a company owns and expects to sell in its normal operations. Exhibit 4.4 shows that a company's merchandise available for sale consists of what it begins with (beginning

C3 Describe both perpetual and periodic inventory systems.

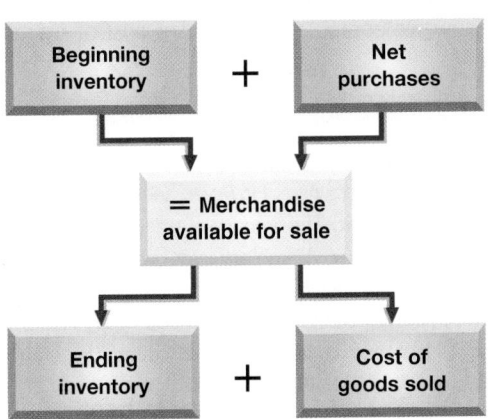

EXHIBIT 4.4

Merchandiser's Cost Flow for a Single Time Period

Point: Mathematically, Exhibit 4.4 says
BI + NP = MAS,
where BI is beginning inventory, NP is net purchases, and MAS is merchandise available for sale. Exhibit 4.4 also says
MAS = EI + COGS,
which can be rewritten as MAS − EI = COGS or MAS − COGS = EI, where EI is ending inventory and COGS is cost of goods sold.

inventory) and what it purchases (net purchases). The merchandise available is either sold (cost of goods sold) or kept for future sales (ending inventory).

Two alternative inventory accounting systems can be used to collect information about cost of goods sold and cost of inventory: *perpetual system* or *periodic system*. The **perpetual inventory system** continually updates accounting records for merchandising transactions—specifically, for those records of inventory available for sale and inventory sold. The **periodic inventory system** updates the accounting records for merchandise transactions only at the *end of a period*. Technological advances and competitive pressures have dramatically increased the use of the perpetual system. It gives managers immediate access to detailed information on sales and inventory levels, where they can strategically react to sales trends, cost changes, consumer tastes, and so forth, to increase gross profit. (Some companies use a *hybrid* system where the perpetual system is used for tracking units available and the periodic system is used to compute cost of sales.)

Point: Growth of superstores such as **Costco** and **Sam's** is fueled by efficient use of perpetual inventory.

Quick Check   Answers—p. 183

1. Describe a merchandiser's cost of goods sold.
2. What is gross profit for a merchandising company?
3. Explain why use of the perpetual inventory system has dramatically increased.

The following sections, consisting of the next 10 pages, on purchasing, selling, and adjusting merchandise use the perpetual system. Appendix 4A uses the periodic system (with the perpetual results on the side). An instructor can choose to cover either one or both inventory systems.

Accounting for Merchandise Purchases

P1 Analyze and record transactions for merchandise purchases using a perpetual system.

The cost of merchandise purchased for resale is recorded in the Merchandise Inventory asset account. To illustrate, Z-Mart records a $1,200 cash purchase of merchandise on November 2 as follows:

Assets = Liabilities + Equity
+1,200
−1,200

Nov. 2	Merchandise Inventory	1,200	
	Cash		1,200
	Purchased merchandise for cash.		

The invoice for this merchandise is shown in Exhibit 4.5. The buyer usually receives the original invoice, and the seller keeps a copy. This *source document* serves as the purchase invoice of Z-Mart (buyer) and the sales invoice for Trex (seller). The amount recorded for merchandise inventory includes its purchase cost, shipping fees, taxes, and any other costs necessary to make it ready for sale. This section explains how we compute the recorded cost of merchandise purchases.

Point: The Merchandise Inventory account reflects the cost of goods available for resale.

Decision Insight

Trade Discounts   When a manufacturer or wholesaler prepares a catalog of items it has for sale, it usually gives each item a **list price,** also called a *catalog price*. However, an item's intended *selling price* equals list price minus a given percent called a **trade discount.** The amount of trade discount usually depends on whether a buyer is a wholesaler, retailer, or final consumer. A wholesaler buying in large quantities is often granted a larger discount than a retailer buying in smaller quantities. A buyer records the net amount of list price minus trade discount. For example, in the November 2 purchase of merchandise by Z-Mart, the merchandise was listed in the seller's catalog at $2,000 and Z-Mart received a 40% trade discount. This meant that Z-Mart's purchase price was $1,200, computed as $2,000 − (40% × $2,000).

INVOICE

TREX

W9797 Cherry Rd.
Antigo, WI 54409

SOLD TO

Firm Name	Z-Mart
Attention of	Tom Novak, Purchasing Agent
Address	10 Michigan Street
City	Chicago
State	Illinois	Zip	60521

Invoice	
Date	Number
11/2/09	4657-2

P.O. Date	Salesperson	Terms	Freight	Ship
10/30/09	#141	2/10, n/30	FOB Destination	Via FedEx

Model No.	Description	Quantity	Price	Amount
CH015	Challenger X7	1	490	490
SD099	Speed Demon	1	710	710

See reverse for terms of sale and returns.

SubTotal	1,200
Shipping	—
Tax	—
Total	1,200

Key: ① Seller ② Invoice date ③ Purchaser ④ Order date ⑤ Credit terms
⑥ Freight terms ⑦ Goods ⑧ Total invoice amount

EXHIBIT 4.5

Invoice

Purchase Discounts

The purchase of goods on credit requires a clear statement of expected future payments and dates to avoid misunderstandings. **Credit terms** for a purchase include the amounts and timing of payments from a buyer to a seller. Credit terms usually reflect an industry's practices. To illustrate, when sellers require payment within 10 days after the end of the month of the invoice date, the invoice will show credit terms as "n/10 EOM," which stands for net 10 days after end of month (**EOM**). When sellers require payment within 30 days after the invoice date, the invoice shows credit terms of "n/30," which stands for *net 30 days.*

Exhibit 4.6 portrays credit terms. The amount of time allowed before full payment is due is called the **credit period.** Sellers can grant a **cash discount** to encourage buyers to pay earlier. A buyer views a cash discount as a **purchase discount.** A seller views a cash discount as a **sales discount.** Any cash discounts are described in the credit terms on the invoice. For example, credit terms of "2/10, n/60" mean that full payment is due within a 60-day credit period, but the buyer can deduct 2% of the invoice amount if payment is made within 10 days of the invoice date. This reduced payment applies only for the **discount period.**

Point: Since both the buyer and seller know the invoice date, this date is used in setting the discount and credit periods.

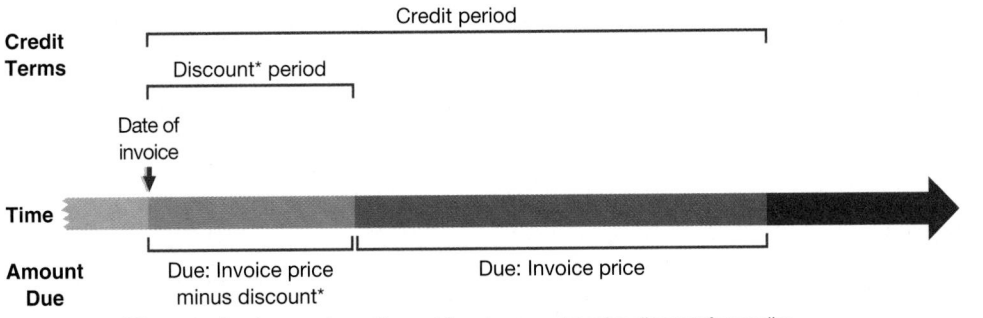

EXHIBIT 4.6

Credit Terms

Point: Appendix 4A repeats journal entries *a* through *f* using a periodic inventory system.

Assets = Liabilities + Equity
+1,200   +1,200

To illustrate how a buyer accounts for a purchase discount, assume that Z-Mart's $1,200 purchase of merchandise is on credit with terms of 2/10, n/30. Its entry is

(a) Nov. 2	Merchandise Inventory	1,200	
	Accounts Payable		1,200
	Purchased merchandise on credit, invoice dated Nov. 2, terms 2/10, n/30.		

If Z-Mart pays the amount due on (or before) November 12, the entry is

Assets = Liabilities + Equity
−24   −1,200
−1,176

(b) Nov. 12	Accounts Payable..............................	1,200	
	Merchandise Inventory		24
	Cash		1,176
	Paid for the $1,200 purchase of Nov. 2 less the discount of $24 (2% × $1,200).		

Point: These entries illustrate what is called the *gross method* of accounting for purchases with discount terms.

The Merchandise Inventory account after these entries reflects the net cost of merchandise purchased, and the Accounts Payable account shows a zero balance. Both ledger accounts, in T-account form, follow:

Merchandise Inventory					Accounts Payable				
Nov. 2	1,200	Nov. 12	24		Nov. 12	1,200	Nov. 2	1,200	
Balance	1,176						Balance	0	

A buyer's failure to pay within a discount period can be expensive. To illustrate, if Z-Mart does not pay within the 10-day 2% discount period, it can delay payment by 20 more days. This delay costs Z-Mart $24, computed as 2% × $1,200. Most buyers take advantage of a purchase discount because of the usually high interest rate implied from not taking it.[1] Also, good cash management means that no invoice is paid until the last day of the discount or credit period.

Decision Maker

Entrepreneur   You purchase a batch of products on terms of 3/10, n/90, but your company has limited cash and you must borrow funds at an 11% annual rate if you are to pay within the discount period. Do you take advantage of the purchase discount? [Answer—p. 182]

Purchase Returns and Allowances

Purchase returns refer to merchandise a buyer acquires but then returns to the seller. A *purchase allowance* is a reduction in the cost of defective or unacceptable merchandise that a buyer acquires. Buyers often keep defective but still marketable merchandise if the seller grants an acceptable allowance. When a buyer returns or takes an allowance on merchandise, the buyer issues a **debit memorandum** to inform the seller of a debit made to the seller's account in the buyer's records.

Point: The sender (maker) of a *debit memorandum* will debit the account of the memo's receiver. The memo's receiver will credit the sender's account.

---

[1] The *implied annual interest rate* formula is:

$$[365 \text{ days} \div (\text{Credit period} - \text{Discount period})] \times \text{Cash discount rate.}$$

For terms of 2/10, n/30, missing the 2% discount for an additional 20 days is equal to an annual interest rate of 36.5%, computed as [365 days/(30 days − 10 days)] × 2% discount rate. *Favorable purchase discounts* are those with implied annual interest rates that exceed the purchaser's annual rate for borrowing money.

Purchase Allowances To illustrate purchase allowances, assume that on November 15, Z-Mart (buyer) issues a $300 debit memorandum for an allowance from Trex for defective merchandise. Z-Mart's November 15 entry to update its Merchandise Inventory account to reflect the purchase allowance is

(c) Nov. 15	Accounts Payable................................	300	
	Merchandise Inventory		300
	Allowance for defective merchandise.		

Assets = Liabilities + Equity
−300   −300

The buyer's allowance for defective merchandise is usually offset against the buyer's current account payable balance to the seller. When cash is refunded, the Cash account is debited instead of Accounts Payable.

Purchase Returns Returns are recorded at the net costs charged to buyers. To illustrate the accounting for returns, suppose Z-Mart purchases $1,000 of merchandise on June 1 with terms 2/10, n/60. Two days later, Z-Mart returns $100 of goods before paying the invoice. When Z-Mart later pays on June 11, it takes the 2% discount only on the $900 remaining balance. When goods are returned, a buyer can take a purchase discount on only the remaining balance of the invoice. The resulting discount is $18 (2% × $900) and the cash payment is $882 ($900 − $18). The following entries reflect this illustration.

June 1	Merchandise Inventory	1,000	
	Accounts Payable...........................		1,000
	Purchased merchandise, invoice dated June 1,		
	terms 2/10, n/60.		
June 3	Accounts Payable...............................	100	
	Merchandise Inventory		100
	Returned merchandise to seller.		
June 11	Accounts Payable...............................	900	
	Merchandise Inventory		18
	Cash		882
	Paid for $900 merchandise ($1,000 − $100)		
	less $18 discount (2% × $900).		

Example: Assume Z-Mart pays $980 cash for $1,000 of merchandise purchased within its 2% discount period. Later, it returns $100 of the original $1,000 merchandise. The return entry is
Cash 98
   Merchandise Inventory   98

Decision Ethics

Credit Manager As a new credit manager, you are being trained by the outgoing manager. She explains that the system prepares checks for amounts net of favorable cash discounts, and the checks are dated the last day of the discount period. She also tells you that checks are not mailed until five days later, adding that "the company gets free use of cash for an extra five days, and our department looks better. When a supplier complains, we blame the computer system and the mailroom." Do you continue this payment policy? [Answer—p. 182]

Transportation Costs and Ownership Transfer

The buyer and seller must agree on who is responsible for paying any freight costs and who bears the risk of loss during transit for merchandising transactions. This is essentially the same as asking at what point ownership transfers from the seller to the buyer. The point of transfer is called the **FOB** (*free on board*) point, which determines who pays transportation costs (and often other incidental costs of transit such as insurance).

Exhibit 4.7 identifies two alternative points of transfer. (1) *FOB shipping point,* also called *FOB factory,* means the buyer accepts ownership when the goods depart the seller's place of business. The buyer is then responsible for paying shipping costs and bearing the risk of damage or loss when goods are in transit. The goods are part of the buyer's inventory when they are in transit since ownership has transferred to the buyer. **Cannondale,** a bike manufacturer,

EXHIBIT 4.7

Ownership Transfer and
Transportation Costs

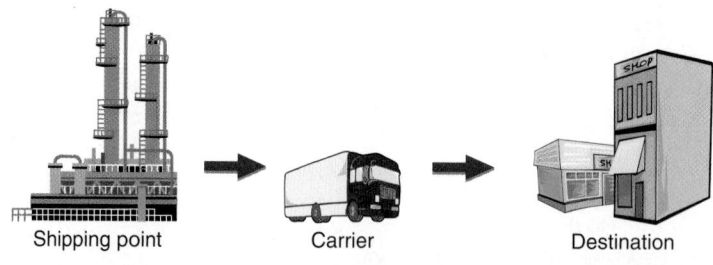

	Ownership Transfers when Goods Passed to	Transportation Costs Paid by
FOB shipping point	Carrier	Buyer
FOB destination	Buyer	Seller

Point: The party not responsible for shipping costs sometimes pays the carrier. In these cases, the party paying these costs either bills the party responsible or, more commonly, adjusts its account payable or account receivable with the other party. For example, a buyer paying a carrier when terms are FOB destination can decrease its account payable to the seller by the amount of shipping cost.

uses FOB shipping point. (2) *FOB destination* means ownership of goods transfers to the buyer when the goods arrive at the buyer's place of business. The seller is responsible for paying shipping charges and bears the risk of damage or loss in transit. The seller does not record revenue from this sale until the goods arrive at the destination because this transaction is not complete before that point.

Z-Mart's $1,200 purchase on November 2 is on terms of FOB destination. This means Z-Mart is not responsible for paying transportation costs. When a buyer is responsible for paying transportation costs, the payment is made to a carrier or directly to the seller depending on the agreement. The cost principle requires that any necessary transportation costs of a buyer (often called *transportation-in* or *freight-in*) be included as part of the cost of purchased merchandise. To illustrate, Z-Mart's entry to record a $75 freight charge from an independent carrier for merchandise purchased FOB shipping point is

Assets = Liabilities + Equity
+75
−75

(d) Nov. 24	Merchandise Inventory	75	
	Cash		75
	Paid freight costs on purchased merchandise.		

A seller records the costs of shipping goods to customers in a Delivery Expense account when the seller is responsible for these costs. Delivery Expense, also called *transportation-out* or *freight-out,* is reported as a selling expense in the seller's income statement.

In summary, purchases are recorded as debits to Merchandise Inventory. Any later purchase discounts, returns, and allowances are credited (decreases) to Merchandise Inventory. Transportation-in is debited (added) to Merchandise Inventory. Z-Mart's itemized costs of merchandise purchases for year 2009 are in Exhibit 4.8.

EXHIBIT 4.8

Itemized Costs of
Merchandise Purchases

Z-MART Itemized Costs of Merchandise Purchases For Year Ended December 31, 2009	
Invoice cost of merchandise purchases	$ 235,800
Less: Purchase discounts received	(4,200)
Purchase returns and allowances	(1,500)
Add: Costs of transportation-in	2,300
Total cost of merchandise purchases	**$232,400**

Point: Some companies have separate accounts for purchase discounts, returns and allowances, and transportation-in. These accounts are then transferred to Merchandise Inventory at period-end. This is a *hybrid system* of perpetual and periodic. That is, Merchandise Inventory is updated on a perpetual basis but only for purchases and cost of goods sold.

The accounting system described here does not provide separate records (accounts) for total purchases, total purchase discounts, total purchase returns and allowances, and total transportation-in. Yet nearly all companies collect this information in supplementary records because managers need this information to evaluate and control each of these cost elements. **Supplementary records,** also called *supplemental records,* refer to information outside the usual general ledger accounts.

Quick Check Answers—p. 183

4. How long are the credit and discount periods when credit terms are 2/10, n/60?

5. Identify which items are subtracted from the *list* amount and not recorded when computing purchase price: (*a*) freight-in; (*b*) trade discount; (*c*) purchase discount; (*d*) purchase return.

6. What does *FOB* mean? What does *FOB destination* mean?

Accounting for Merchandise Sales

Merchandising companies also must account for sales, sales discounts, sales returns and allowances, and cost of goods sold. A merchandising company such as Z-Mart reflects these items in its gross profit computation, as shown in Exhibit 4.9. This section explains how this information is derived from transactions.

EXHIBIT 4.9

Gross Profit Computation

Z-MART Computation of Gross Profit For Year Ended December 31, 2009		
Sales		$321,000
Less: Sales discounts	$4,300	
Sales returns and allowances	2,000	6,300
Net sales		314,700
Cost of goods sold		230,400
Gross profit		**$ 84,300**

Sales of Merchandise

Each sales transaction for a seller of merchandise involves two parts.

1. Revenue received in the form of an asset from the customer.
2. Recognition of the cost of merchandise sold to the customer.

P2 Analyze and record transactions for merchandise sales using a perpetual system.

Accounting for a sales transaction under the perpetual system requires recording information about both parts. This means that each sales transaction for merchandisers, whether for cash or on credit, requires *two entries:* one for revenue and one for cost. To illustrate, Z-Mart sold $2,400 of merchandise on credit on November 3. The revenue part of this transaction is recorded as

(e) Nov. 3	Accounts Receivable	2,400	
	Sales		2,400
	Sold merchandise on credit.		

Assets = Liabilities + Equity
+2,400   +2,400

This entry reflects an increase in Z-Mart's assets in the form of accounts receivable. It also shows the increase in revenue (Sales). If the sale is for cash, the debit is to Cash instead of Accounts Receivable.

The cost part of each sales transaction ensures that the Merchandise Inventory account under a perpetual inventory system reflects the updated cost of the merchandise available for sale. For example, the cost of the merchandise Z-Mart sold on November 3 is $1,600, and the entry to record the cost part of this sales transaction is

(e) Nov. 3	Cost of Goods Sold	1,600	
	Merchandise Inventory		1,600
	To record the cost of Nov. 3 sale.		

Assets = Liabilities + Equity
−1,600   −1,600

Sales Discounts

Sales discounts on credit sales can benefit a seller by decreasing the delay in receiving cash and reducing future collection efforts. At the time of a credit sale, a seller does not know whether a customer will pay within the discount period and take advantage of a discount. This means the seller usually does not record a sales discount until a customer actually pays within the discount period. To illustrate, Z-Mart completes a credit sale for $1,000 on November 12 with terms of 2/10, n/60. The entry to record the revenue part of this sale is

Assets = Liabilities + Equity
+1,000   +1,000

Nov. 12	Accounts Receivable	1,000	
	Sales		1,000
	Sold merchandise under terms of 2/10, n/60.		

This entry records the receivable and the revenue as if the customer will pay the full amount. The customer has two options, however. One option is to wait 60 days until January 11 and pay the full $1,000. In this case, Z-Mart records that payment as

Assets = Liabilities + Equity
+1,000
−1,000

Jan. 11	Cash	1,000	
	Accounts Receivable		1,000
	Received payment for Nov. 12 sale.		

The customer's second option is to pay $980 within a 10-day period ending November 22. If the customer pays on (or before) November 22, Z-Mart records the payment as

Assets = Liabilities + Equity
+980   −20
−1,000

Nov. 22	Cash	980	
	Sales Discounts	20	
	Accounts Receivable		1,000
	Received payment for Nov. 12 sale less discount.		

Sales Discounts is a contra revenue account, meaning the Sales Discounts account is deducted from the Sales account when computing a company's net sales (see Exhibit 4.9). Management monitors Sales Discounts to assess the effectiveness and cost of its discount policy.

Sales Returns and Allowances

Sales returns refer to merchandise that customers return to the seller after a sale. Many companies allow customers to return merchandise for a full refund. *Sales allowances* refer to reductions in the selling price of merchandise sold to customers. This can occur with damaged or defective merchandise that a customer is willing to purchase with a decrease in selling price. Sales returns and allowances usually involve dissatisfied customers and the possibility of lost future sales, and managers monitor information about returns and allowances.

Point: Published income statements rarely disclose sales discounts, returns and allowances.

Sales Returns   To illustrate, recall Z-Mart's sale of merchandise on November 3 for $2,400 that had cost $1,600. Assume that the customer returns part of the merchandise on November 6, and the returned items sell for $800 and cost $600. The revenue part of this transaction must reflect the decrease in sales from the customer's return of merchandise as follows:

(f) Nov. 6	Sales Returns and Allowances	800	
	Accounts Receivable		800
	Customer returns merchandise of Nov. 3 sale.		

Assets = Liabilities + Equity
−800   −800

If the merchandise returned to Z-Mart is not defective and can be resold to another customer, Z-Mart returns these goods to its inventory. The entry to restore the cost of such goods to the Merchandise Inventory account is

Nov. 6	Merchandise Inventory	600	
	Cost of Goods Sold		600
	Returned goods added to inventory.		

Assets = Liabilities + Equity
+600   +600

This entry changes if the goods returned are defective. In this case the returned inventory is recorded at its estimated value, not its cost. To illustrate, if the goods (costing $600) returned to Z-Mart are defective and estimated to be worth $150, the following entry is made: Dr. Merchandise Inventory for $150, Dr. Loss from Defective Merchandise for $450, and Cr. Cost of Goods Sold for $600.

Decision Insight

Return to Sender Book merchandisers such as **Barnes & Noble**, **Borders Books**, **Books-A-Million**, and **Waldenbooks** can return unsold books to publishers at purchase price. Publishers say returns of new hardcover books run between 35% and 50%.

Sales Allowances To illustrate sales allowances, assume that $800 of the merchandise Z-Mart sold on November 3 is defective but the buyer decides to keep it because Z-Mart offers a $100 price reduction. Z-Mart records this allowance as follows:

Nov. 6	Sales Returns and Allowances	100	
	Accounts Receivable		100
	To record sales allowance on Nov. 3 sale.		

Assets = Liabilities + Equity
−100   −100

The seller usually prepares a credit memorandum to confirm a buyer's return or allowance. A seller's **credit memorandum** informs a buyer of the seller's credit to the buyer's Account Receivable (on the seller's books).

Point: The sender (maker) of a credit memorandum will *credit* the account of the receiver. The receiver of a credit memorandum will *debit* the sender's account.

Quick Check

Answers—p. 183

7. Why are sales discounts and sales returns and allowances recorded in contra revenue accounts instead of directly in the Sales account?

8. Under what conditions are two entries necessary to record a sales return?

9. When merchandise is sold on credit and the seller notifies the buyer of a price allowance, does the seller create and send a credit memorandum or a debit memorandum?

Completing the Accounting Cycle

C4   Analyze and interpret cost flows and operating activities of a merchandising company.

Exhibit 4.10 shows the flow of merchandising costs during a period and where these costs are reported at period-end. Specifically, beginning inventory plus the net cost of purchases is the merchandise available for sale. As inventory is sold, its cost is recorded in cost of goods sold on the income statement; what remains is ending inventory on the balance sheet. A period's ending inventory is the next period's beginning inventory.

EXHIBIT 4.10

Merchandising Cost Flow in the Accounting Cycle

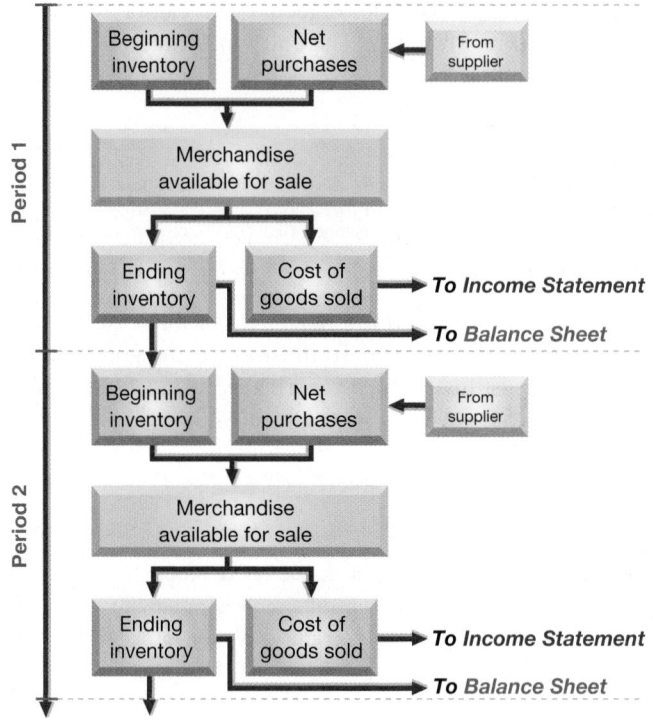

Adjusting Entries for Merchandisers

P3   Prepare adjustments and close accounts for a merchandising company.

Each of the steps in the accounting cycle described in the prior chapter for a service company applies to a merchandiser. This section and the next two further explain three steps of the accounting cycle for a merchandiser—adjustments, statement preparation, and closing.

Adjusting entries are generally the same for merchandising companies and service companies, including those for prepaid expenses (including depreciation), accrued expenses, unearned revenues, and accrued revenues. However, a merchandiser using a perpetual inventory system is usually required to make another adjustment to update the Merchandise Inventory account to reflect any loss of merchandise, including theft and deterioration. **Shrinkage** is the term used to refer to the loss of inventory and it is computed by comparing a physical count of inventory with recorded amounts. A physical count is usually performed at least once annually.

To illustrate, Z-Mart's Merchandise Inventory account at the end of year 2009 has a balance of $21,250, but a physical count reveals that only $21,000 of inventory exists. The adjusting entry to record this $250 shrinkage is

Point: About two-thirds of shoplifting losses are thefts by employees.

Assets = Liabilities + Equity
−250   −250

Dec. 31	Cost of Goods Sold	250	
	Merchandise Inventory		250
	To adjust for $250 shrinkage revealed by a physical count of inventory.		

Preparing Financial Statements

The financial statements of a merchandiser, and their preparation, are similar to those for a service company described in Chapters 2 and 3. The income statement mainly differs by the inclusion of *cost of goods sold* and *gross profit*. Also, net sales is affected by discounts, returns, and allowances, and some additional expenses are possible such as delivery expense and loss from defective merchandise. The balance sheet mainly differs by the inclusion of *merchandise inventory* as part of current assets. The statement of retained earnings is unchanged. A work sheet can be used to help prepare these statements, and one is illustrated in Appendix 4B for Z-Mart.

Point: Staples's costs of shipping merchandise to its stores is included in its costs of inventories as required by the cost principle.

Closing Entries for Merchandisers

Closing entries are similar for service companies and merchandising companies using a perpetual system. The difference is that we must close some new temporary accounts that arise from merchandising activities. Z-Mart has several temporary accounts unique to merchandisers: Sales (of goods), Sales Discounts, Sales Returns and Allowances, and Cost of Goods Sold. Their existence in the ledger means that the first two closing entries for a merchandiser are slightly different from the ones described in the prior chapter for a service company. These differences are set in **red boldface** in the closing entries of Exhibit 4.11.

Point: The Inventory account is not affected by the closing process under a perpetual system.

EXHIBIT 4.11

Closing Entries for a Merchandiser

Step 1: Close Credit Balances in Temporary Accounts to Income Summary.

Dec. 31	**Sales**	**321,000**	
	Income Summary		321,000
	To close credit balances in temporary accounts.		

Step 2: Close Debit Balances in Temporary Accounts to Income Summary.

Dec. 31	Income Summary	308,100	
	Sales Discounts		**4,300**
	Sales Returns and Allowances		**2,000**
	Cost of Goods Sold		**230,400**
	Depreciation Expense		3,700
	Salaries Expense		43,800
	Insurance Expense		600
	Rent Expense		9,000
	Supplies Expense		3,000
	Advertising Expense		11,300
	To close debit balances in temporary accounts.		

Step 3: Close Income Summary to Retained Earnings.

The third closing entry is identical for a merchandising company and a service company. The $12,900 amount is net income reported on the income statement.

Dec. 31	Income Summary	12,900	
	Retained Earnings		12,900
	To close the Income Summary account.		

Step 4: Close Dividends Account to Retained Earnings.

The fourth closing entry is identical for a merchandising company and a service company. It closes the Dividends account and adjusts the Retained Earnings account to the amount shown on the balance sheet.

Dec. 31	Retained Earnings	4,000	
	Dividends		4,000
	To close the Dividends account.		

Summary of Merchandising Entries

Exhibit 4.12 summarizes the key adjusting and closing entries of a merchandiser (using a perpetual inventory system) that are different from those of a service company described in prior chapters (the Demonstration Problem 2 illustrates these merchandising entries).

EXHIBIT 4.12

Summary of Merchandising Entries

Merchandising Transactions		Merchandising Entries	Dr.	Cr.
Purchases	Purchasing merchandise for resale.	Merchandise Inventory	#	
		Cash or Accounts Payable		#
	Paying freight costs on purchases; FOB shipping point.	Merchandise Inventory	#	
		Cash		#
	Paying within discount period.	Accounts Payable	#	
		Merchandise Inventory		#
		Cash		#
	Recording purchase returns or allowances.	Cash or Accounts Payable	#	
		Merchandise Inventory		#
Sales	Selling merchandise.	Cash or Accounts Receivable	#	
		Sales		#
		Cost of Goods Sold	#	
		Merchandise Inventory		#
	Receiving payment within discount period.	Cash	#	
		Sales Discounts	#	
		Accounts Receivable		#
	Granting sales returns or allowances.	Sales Returns and Allowances	#	
		Cash or Accounts Receivable		#
		Merchandise Inventory	#	
		Cost of Goods Sold		#
	Paying freight costs on sales; FOB destination.	Delivery Expense	#	
		Cash		#

Merchandising Events		Adjusting and Closing Entries		
Adjusting	Adjusting due to shrinkage (occurs when recorded amount larger than physical inventory).	Cost of Goods Sold	#	
		Merchandise Inventory		#
Closing	Closing temporary accounts with credit balances.	Sales	#	
		Income Summary		#
	Closing temporary accounts with debit balances.	Income Summary	#	
		Sales Returns and Allowances		#
		Sales Discounts		#
		Cost of Goods Sold		#
		Delivery Expense		#
		"Other Expenses"		#

Quick Check

Answers—p. 183

10. When a merchandiser uses a perpetual inventory system, why is it sometimes necessary to adjust the Merchandise Inventory balance with an adjusting entry?

11. What temporary accounts do you expect to find in a merchandising business but not in a service business?

12. Describe the closing entries normally made by a merchandising company.

Financial Statement Formats

Generally accepted accounting principles do not require companies to use any one presentation format for financial statements so we see many different formats in practice. This section describes two common income statement formats: multiple-step and single-step. The classified balance sheet of a merchandiser is also explained.

P4 Define and prepare multiple-step and single-step income statements.

Multiple-Step Income Statement

A **multiple-step income statement** format shows detailed computations of net sales and other costs and expenses, and reports subtotals for various classes of items. Exhibit 4.13 shows a

EXHIBIT 4.13

Multiple-Step Income Statement

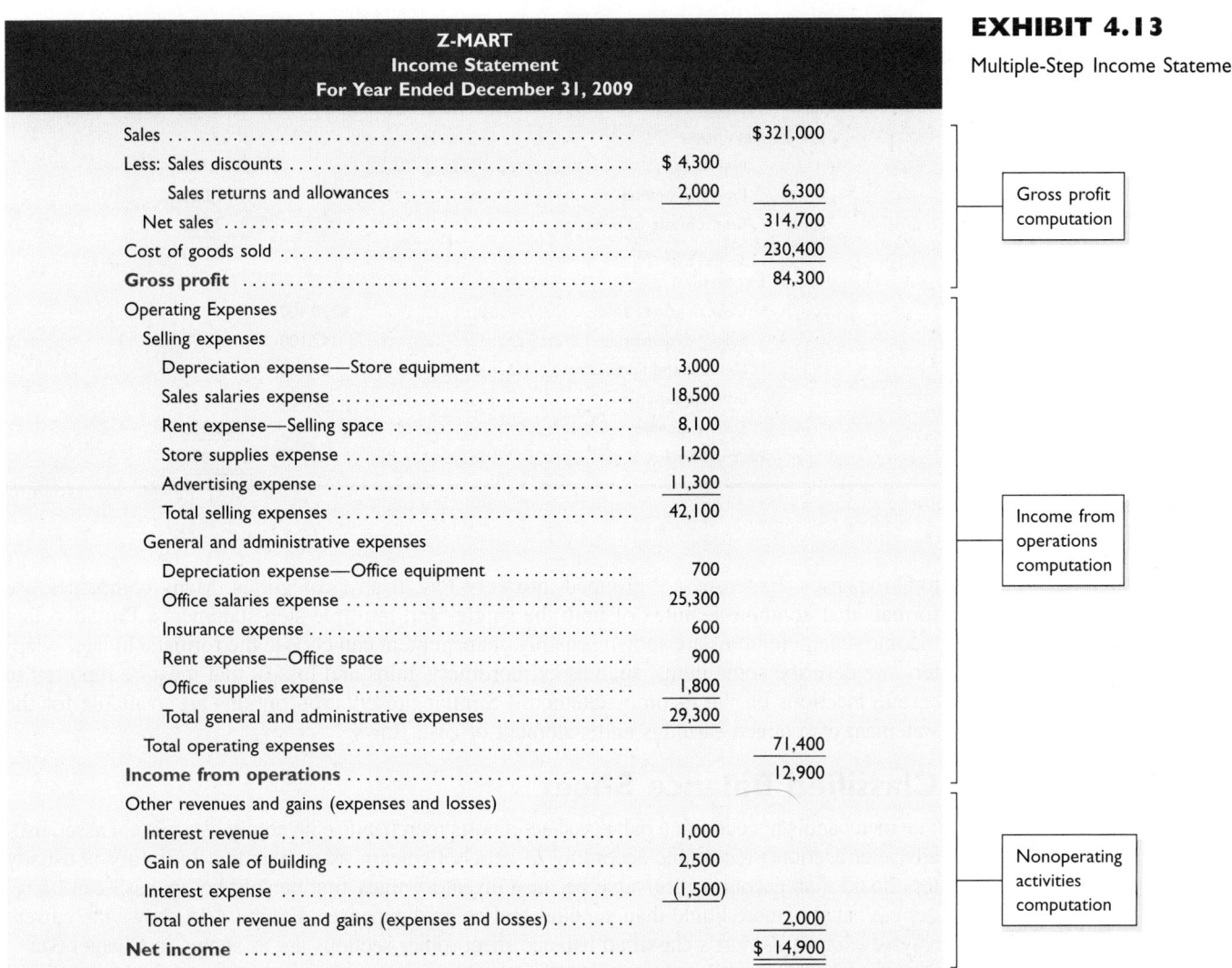

Z-MART Income Statement For Year Ended December 31, 2009			
Sales			$321,000
Less: Sales discounts		$ 4,300	
Sales returns and allowances		2,000	6,300
Net sales			314,700
Cost of goods sold			230,400
Gross profit			84,300
Operating Expenses			
Selling expenses			
Depreciation expense—Store equipment		3,000	
Sales salaries expense		18,500	
Rent expense—Selling space		8,100	
Store supplies expense		1,200	
Advertising expense		11,300	
Total selling expenses		42,100	
General and administrative expenses			
Depreciation expense—Office equipment		700	
Office salaries expense		25,300	
Insurance expense		600	
Rent expense—Office space		900	
Office supplies expense		1,800	
Total general and administrative expenses		29,300	
Total operating expenses			71,400
Income from operations			12,900
Other revenues and gains (expenses and losses)			
Interest revenue		1,000	
Gain on sale of building		2,500	
Interest expense		(1,500)	
Total other revenue and gains (expenses and losses)			2,000
Net income			$ 14,900

Gross profit computation

Income from operations computation

Nonoperating activities computation

multiple-step income statement for Z-Mart. The statement has three main parts: (1) *gross profit,* determined by net sales less cost of goods sold, (2) *income from operations,* determined by gross profit less operating expenses, and (3) *net income,* determined by income from operations adjusted for nonoperating items.

Operating expenses are classified into two sections. **Selling expenses** include the expenses of promoting sales by displaying and advertising merchandise, making sales, and delivering goods to customers. **General and administrative expenses** support a company's overall operations and include expenses related to accounting, human resource management, and financial management. Expenses are allocated between sections when they contribute to more than one. Z-Mart allocates rent expense of $9,000 from its store building between two sections: $8,100 to selling expense and $900 to general and administrative expense.

Nonoperating activities consist of other expenses, revenues, losses, and gains that are unrelated to a company's operations. *Other revenues and gains* commonly include interest revenue, dividend revenue, rent revenue, and gains from asset disposals. *Other expenses and losses* commonly include interest expense, losses from asset disposals, and casualty losses. When a company has no reportable nonoperating activities, its income from operations is simply labeled net income.

Point: Z-Mart did not have any nonoperating activities, however, Exhibit 4.13 includes some for illustrative purposes.

Single-Step Income Statement

A **single-step income statement** is another widely used format and is shown in Exhibit 4.14 for Z-Mart. It lists cost of goods sold as another expense and shows only one subtotal for

EXHIBIT 4.14

Single-Step Income Statement

Z-MART Income Statement For Year Ended December 31, 2009		
Revenues		
Net sales		$314,700
Interest revenue		1,000
Gain on sale of building		2,500
Total revenues		318,200
Expenses		
Cost of goods sold	$230,400	
Selling expenses	42,100	
General and administrative expenses	29,300	
Interest expense	1,500	
Total expenses		303,300
Net income		$ 14,900

Point: Many companies report interest expense and interest revenue in separate categories after operating income and before subtracting income tax expense. As one example, see **RadioShack**'s income statement in Appendix A.

total expenses. Expenses are grouped into very few, if any, categories. Many companies use formats that combine features of both the single- and multiple-step statements. Provided that income statement items are shown sensibly, management can choose the format. (In later chapters, we describe some items, such as extraordinary gains and losses, that must be reported in certain locations on the income statement.) Similar presentation options are available for the statement of retained earnings and statement of cash flows.

Classified Balance Sheet

The merchandiser's classified balance sheet reports merchandise inventory as a current asset, usually after accounts receivable according to an asset's nearness to liquidity. Inventory is usually less liquid than accounts receivable because inventory must first be sold before cash can be received; but it is more liquid than supplies and prepaid expenses. Exhibit 4.15 shows the current asset section of Z-Mart's classified balance sheet (other sections are as shown in Chapter 3).

EXHIBIT 4.15

Classified Balance Sheet (partial) of a Merchandiser

Z-MART Balance Sheet (partial) December 31, 2009	
Assets	
Cash	$ 8,200
Accounts receivable	11,200
Merchandise inventory	**21,000**
Office supplies	550
Store supplies	250
Prepaid insurance	300
Total current assets	$ 41,500

Decision Insight

Merchandising Shenanigans   Accurate invoices are important to both sellers and buyers. Merchandisers rely on invoices to make certain they receive all monies for products provided—no more, no less. To achieve this, controls are set up. Still, failures arise. A survey reports that 9% of employees in sales and marketing witnessed false or misleading invoices sent to customers. Another 14% observed employees violating contract terms with customers (KPMG 2009).

Global View

This section discusses similarities and differences between U.S. GAAP and IFRS in accounting and reporting for merchandise purchases and sales, and for the income statement.

Accounting for Merchandise Purchases and Sales

Both U.S. GAAP and IFRS include broad and similar guidance for the accounting of merchandise purchases and sales. Specifically, all of the transactions presented and illustrated in this chapter are accounted for identically under the two systems. The closing process for merchandisers also is identical for U.S. GAAP and IFRS. In the next chapter we describe how inventory valuation can, in some cases, be different for the two systems.

Income Statement Presentation

We explained that net income, profit, and earnings refer to the same (*bottom line*) item. However, IFRS tends to use the term *profit* more than any other term, whereas U.S. statements tend to use *net income* more than any other term. Both U.S. GAAP and IFRS income statements begin with the net sales or net revenues (*top line*) item. For merchandisers and manufacturers, this is followed by cost of goods sold. The presentation is similar for the remaining items with the following differences.

- ■ U.S. GAAP offers little guidance about the presentation or order of expenses. IFRS requires separate disclosures for financing costs (interest expense), income tax expense, and some other special items.
- ■ Both systems require separate disclosure of items when their size, nature, or frequency are important for proper interpretation.
- ■ IFRS permits expenses to be presented by their function or their nature. U.S. GAAP provides no direction but the SEC requires presentation by function.
- ■ Neither U.S. GAAP nor IFRS define *operating* income; this means classification of expenses into operating or nonoperating reflects considerable management discretion.
- ■ IFRS permits alternative measures of income on the income statement; U.S. GAAP prohibits disclosure of alternative income measures in financial statements.

GOME provides the following example of income statement reporting.

GOME Income Statement (in RMB 000s) For Year Ended December 31, 2008	
Revenue	45,889,257
Cost of sales	(41,381,223)
Gross profit	4,508,034
Other income and gain	3,266,244
Selling and distribution costs	(4,487,131)
Administrative expenses	(828,028)
Other expenses	(515,357)
Profit from operating activities	1,943,762
Finance costs	(212,118)
Finance income	441,017
Other loss and impairment	(638,812)
Profit before tax	1,533,849
Tax	(435,156)
Profit for the year	1,098,693

Balance Sheet Presentation

Chapters 2 and 3 explained how both U.S. GAAP and IFRS require current items to be separated from noncurrent items on the balance sheet (yielding a *classified balance sheet*). As discussed, U.S. GAAP balance sheets report current items first. Assets are listed from most liquid to least liquid, whereas liabilities are listed from nearest to maturity to furthest from maturity. IFRS balance sheets normally present noncurrent items first (and equity before liabilities), but this is *not* a requirement. **GOME** provides an example of IFRS reporting for the balance sheet in Appendix A.

Acid-Test Ratio

A1 Compute the acid-test ratio and explain its use to assess liquidity.

For many merchandisers, inventory makes up a large portion of current assets. Inventory must be sold and any resulting accounts receivable must be collected before cash is available. Chapter 3 explained that the current ratio, defined as current assets divided by current liabilities, is useful in assessing a company's ability to pay current liabilities. Because it is sometimes unreasonable to assume that inventories are a source of payment for current liabilities, we look to other measures.

One measure of a merchandiser's ability to pay its current liabilities (referred to as its *liquidity*) is the acid-test ratio. It differs from the current ratio by excluding less liquid current assets such as inventory and prepaid expenses that take longer to be converted to cash. The **acid-test ratio,** also called *quick ratio,* is defined as *quick assets* (cash, short-term investments, and current receivables) divided by current liabilities—see Exhibit 4.16.

EXHIBIT 4.16

Acid-Test (Quick) Ratio

$$\text{Acid-test ratio} = \frac{\text{Cash and cash equivalents} + \text{Short-term investments} + \text{Current receivables}}{\text{Current liabilities}}$$

Exhibit 4.17 shows both the acid-test and current ratios of retailer **JCPenney** for fiscal years 2007 through 2009—also see margin graph. JCPenney's acid-test ratio reveals a general increase from 2007 through 2009 that exceeds the industry average. Further, JCPenney's current ratio (never less than 1.90) suggests that its short-term obligations can be confidently covered with short-term assets.

EXHIBIT 4.17

JCPenney's Acid-Test and Current Ratios

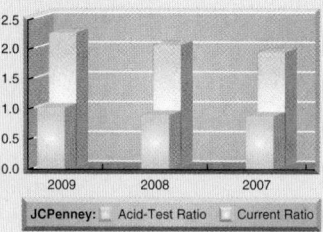

JCPenney: Acid-Test Ratio   Current Ratio

($ millions)	2009	2008	2007
Total quick assets	$2,704	$2,845	$2,901
Total current assets	$6,220	$6,751	$6,648
Total current liabilities	$2,794	$3,338	$3,492
Acid-test ratio	**0.97**	**0.85**	**0.83**
Current ratio	**2.23**	**2.02**	**1.90**
Industry acid-test ratio	0.63	0.62	0.58
Industry current ratio	2.31	2.39	2.43

An acid-test ratio less than 1.0 means that current liabilities exceed quick assets. A rule of thumb is that the acid-test ratio should have a value near, or higher than, 1.0 to conclude that a company is unlikely to face near-term liquidity problems. A value much less than 1.0 raises liquidity concerns unless a company can generate enough cash from inventory sales or if much of its liabilities are not due until late in the next period. Similarly, a value slightly larger than 1.0 can hide a liquidity problem if payables are due shortly and receivables are not collected until late in the next period. Analysis of JCPenney shows no need for concern regarding its liquidity even though its acid-test ratio is less than one. This is because retailers such as JCPenney pay many current liabilities from inventory sales. Further, in all years, JCPenney's acid-test ratios exceed the industry norm (and its inventory is fairly liquid).

Point: Successful use of a just-in-time inventory system can narrow the gap between the acid-test ratio and the current ratio.

Decision Maker

Supplier   A retailer requests to purchase supplies on credit from your company. You have no prior experience with this retailer. The retailer's current ratio is 2.1, its acid-test ratio is 0.5, and inventory makes up most of its current assets. Do you extend credit? [Answer—p. 183]

Gross Margin Ratio

A2 Compute the gross margin ratio and explain its use to assess profitability.

The cost of goods sold makes up much of a merchandiser's expenses. Without sufficient gross profit, a merchandiser will likely fail. Users often compute the gross margin ratio to help understand this relation. It differs from the profit margin ratio in that it excludes all costs except cost of goods sold. The **gross margin ratio** (also called *gross profit ratio*) is defined as *gross margin* (net sales minus cost of goods sold) divided by net sales—see Exhibit 4.18.

EXHIBIT 4.18

Gross Margin Ratio

$$\text{Gross margin ratio} = \frac{\text{Net sales} - \text{Cost of goods sold}}{\text{Net sales}}$$

Exhibit 4.19 shows the gross margin ratio of **JCPenney** for fiscal years 2007 through 2009. For JCPenney, each $1 of sales in 2009 yielded about 37.4¢ in gross margin to cover all other expenses and still produce a net income. This 37.4¢ margin is down from 39.3¢ in 2007. This decrease is an important (and negative) development. Success for merchandisers such as JCPenney depends on adequate gross margin. For example, the 1.9¢ decline in the gross margin ratio, computed as 39.3¢ − 37.4¢, means that JCPenney has $351 million less in gross margin! (This is computed as net sales of $18,486 million multiplied by the 1.9% decline in gross margin.). Management's discussion in its annual report blames this on "the slowdown in consumer spending" tied to the recessionary period.

Point: The power of a ratio is often its ability to identify areas for more detailed analysis.

($ millions)	2009	2008	2007
Gross margin	$ 6,915	$ 7,671	$ 7,825
Net sales	$18,486	$19,860	$19,903
Gross margin ratio	37.4%	38.6%	39.3%

EXHIBIT 4.19

JCPenney's Gross Margin Ratio

Decision Maker

Financial Officer Your company has a 36% gross margin ratio and a 17% net profit margin ratio. Industry averages are 44% for gross margin and 16% for net profit margin. Do these comparative results concern you? [Answer—p. 183]

Demonstration Problem 1

Use the following adjusted trial balance and additional information to complete the requirements.

KC ANTIQUES Adjusted Trial Balance December 31, 2009	Debit	Credit
Cash	$ 7,000	
Accounts receivable	13,000	
Merchandise inventory	60,000	
Store supplies	1,500	
Equipment	45,600	
Accumulated depreciation—Equipment		$ 16,600
Accounts payable		9,000
Salaries payable		2,000
Common stock		20,000
Retained earnings		59,000
Dividends	10,000	
Sales		343,250
Sales discounts	5,000	
Sales returns and allowances	6,000	
Cost of goods sold	159,900	
Depreciation expense—Store equipment	4,100	
Depreciation expense—Office equipment	1,600	
Sales salaries expense	30,000	
Office salaries expense	34,000	
Insurance expense	11,000	
Rent expense (70% is store, 30% is office)	24,000	
Store supplies expense	5,750	
Advertising expense	31,400	
Totals	$449,850	$449,850

KC Antiques' *supplementary records* for 2009 reveal the following itemized costs for merchandising activities:

Invoice cost of merchandise purchases	$150,000
Purchase discounts received	2,500
Purchase returns and allowances	2,700
Cost of transportation-in	5,000

Required

1. Use the supplementary records to compute the total cost of merchandise purchases for 2009.
2. Prepare a 2009 multiple-step income statement. (Inventory at December 31, 2008, is $70,100.)
3. Prepare a single-step income statement for 2009.
4. Prepare closing entries for KC Antiques at December 31, 2009.
5. Compute the acid-test ratio and the gross margin ratio. Explain the meaning of each ratio and interpret them for KC Antiques.

Planning the Solution

- Compute the total cost of merchandise purchases for 2009.
- To prepare the multiple-step statement, first compute net sales. Then, to compute cost of goods sold, add the net cost of merchandise purchases for the year to beginning inventory and subtract the cost of ending inventory. Subtract cost of goods sold from net sales to get gross profit. Then classify expenses as selling expenses or general and administrative expenses.
- To prepare the single-step income statement, begin with net sales. Then list and subtract the expenses.
- The first closing entry debits all temporary accounts with credit balances and opens the Income Summary account. The second closing entry credits all temporary accounts with debit balances. The third entry closes the Income Summary account to the retained earnings account, and the fourth entry closes the dividends account to the retained earnings account.
- Identify the quick assets on the adjusted trial balance. Compute the acid-test ratio by dividing quick assets by current liabilities. Compute the gross margin ratio by dividing gross profit by net sales.

Solution to Demonstration Problem 1

1.

Invoice cost of merchandise purchases	$150,000
Less: Purchases discounts received	2,500
Purchase returns and allowances	2,700
Add: Cost of transportation-in	5,000
Total cost of merchandise purchases	$149,800

2. Multiple-step income statement

KC ANTIQUES		
Income Statement		
For Year Ended December 31, 2009		
Sales		$343,250
Less: Sales discounts	$ 5,000	
Sales returns and allowances	6,000	11,000
Net sales		332,250
Cost of goods sold*		159,900
Gross profit		172,350
Expenses		
Selling expenses		
Depreciation expense—Store equipment	4,100	
Sales salaries expense	30,000	
Rent expense—Selling space	16,800	
Store supplies expense	5,750	
Advertising expense	31,400	
Total selling expenses	88,050	

[continued on next page]

[continued from previous page]

General and administrative expenses

Depreciation expense—Office equipment	1,600	
Office salaries expense	34,000	
Insurance expense	11,000	
Rent expense—Office space	7,200	
Total general and administrative expenses	53,800	
Total operating expenses		141,850
Net income		$ 30,500

* Cost of goods sold can also be directly computed (applying concepts from Exhibit 4.4):

Merchandise inventory, December 31, 2008	$ 70,100
Total cost of merchandise purchases (from part 1)	149,800
Goods available for sale	219,900
Merchandise inventory, December 31, 2009	60,000
Cost of goods sold	$159,900

3. Single-step income statement

KC ANTIQUES
Income Statement
For Year Ended December 31, 2009

Net sales		$332,250
Expenses		
Cost of goods sold	$159,900	
Selling expenses	88,050	
General and administrative expenses	53,800	
Total expenses		301,750
Net income		$ 30,500

4.

Dec. 31	Sales	343,250	
	Income Summary		343,250
	To close credit balances in temporary accounts.		
Dec. 31	Income Summary	312,750	
	Sales Discounts		5,000
	Sales Returns and Allowances		6,000
	Cost of Goods Sold		159,900
	Depreciation Expense—Store Equipment		4,100
	Depreciation Expense—Office Equipment		1,600
	Sales Salaries Expense		30,000
	Office Salaries Expense		34,000
	Insurance Expense		11,000
	Rent Expense		24,000
	Store Supplies Expense		5,750
	Advertising Expense		31,400
	To close debit balances in temporary accounts.		
Dec. 31	Income Summary	30,500	
	Retained Earnings		30,500
	To close the Income Summary account.		
Dec. 31	Retained Earnings	10,000	
	Dividends		10,000
	To close the Dividends account.		

5. Acid-test ratio = (Cash and equivalents + Short-term investments + Current receivables)/ Current liabilities

= (Cash + Accounts receivable/(Accounts payable + Salaries payable)

= ($7,000 + $13,000)/($9,000 + $2,000) = $20,000/$11,000 = 1.82

Gross margin ratio = Gross profit/Net sales = $172,350/$332,250 = 0.52 (or 52%)

KC Antiques has a healthy acid-test ratio of 1.82. This means it has more than $1.80 in liquid assets to satisfy each $1.00 in current liabilities. The gross margin of 0.52 shows that KC Antiques spends 48¢ ($1.00 − $0.52) of every dollar of net sales on the costs of acquiring the merchandise it sells. This leaves 52¢ of every dollar of net sales to cover other expenses incurred in the business and to provide a net profit.

Demonstration Problem 2

Prepare journal entries to record the following merchandising transactions for both the seller (BMX) and buyer (Sanuk).

May 4 BMX sold $1,500 of merchandise on account to Sanuk, terms FOB shipping point, n/45, invoice dated May 4. The cost of the merchandise was $900.

May 6 Sanuk paid transportation charges of $30 on the May 4 purchase from BMX.

May 8 BMX sold $1,000 of merchandise on account to Sanuk, terms FOB destination, n/30, invoice dated May 8. The cost of the merchandise was $700.

May 10 BMX paid transportation costs of $50 for delivery of merchandise sold to Sanuk on May 8.

May 16 BMX issued Sanuk a $200 credit memorandum for merchandise returned. The merchandise was purchased by Sanuk on account on May 8. The cost of the merchandise returned was $140.

May 18 BMX received payment from Sanuk for purchase of May 8.

May 21 BMX sold $2,400 of merchandise on account to Sanuk, terms FOB shipping point, 2/10, n/EOM. BMX prepaid transportation costs of $100, which were added to the invoice. The cost of the merchandise was $1,440.

May 31 BMX received payment from Sanuk for purchase of May 21, less discount (2% × $2,400).

Solution to Demonstration Problem 2

BMX (Seller)

Date	Account	Debit	Credit
May 4	Accounts Receivable—Sanuk	1,500	
	Sales		1,500
	Cost of Goods Sold	900	
	Merchandise Inventory		900
6	No entry.		
8	Accounts Receivable—Sanuk	1,000	
	Sales		1,000
	Cost of Goods Sold	700	
	Merchandise Inventory		700
10	Delivery Expense	50	
	Cash		50
16	Sales Returns & Allowances	200	
	Accounts Receivable—Sanuk		200
	Merchandise Inventory	140	
	Cost of Goods Sold		140
18	Cash	800	
	Accounts Receivable—Sanuk		800
21	Accounts Receivable—Sanuk	2,400	
	Sales		2,400
	Accounts Receivable—Sanuk	100	
	Cash		100
	Cost of Goods Sold	1,440	
	Merchandise Inventory		1,440
31	Cash	2,452	
	Sales Discounts	48	
	Accounts Receivable—Sanuk		2,500

Sanuk (Buyer)

Account	Debit	Credit
Merchandise Inventory	1,500	
Accounts Payable—BMX		1,500
Merchandise Inventory	30	
Cash		30
Merchandise Inventory	1,000	
Accounts Payable—BMX		1,000
No entry.		
Accounts Payable—BMX	200	
Merchandise Inventory		200
Accounts Payable—BMX	800	
Cash		800
Merchandise Inventory	2,500	
Accounts Payable—BMX		2,500
Accounts Payable—BMX	2,500	
Merchandise Inventory		48
Cash		2,452

Periodic Inventory System

4A

A **periodic inventory system** requires updating the inventory account only at the *end of a period* to reflect the quantity and cost of both the goods available and the goods sold. Thus, during the period, the Merchandise Inventory balance remains unchanged. It reflects the beginning inventory balance until it is updated at the end of the period. During the period the cost of merchandise is recorded in a temporary *Purchases* account. When a company sells merchandise, it records revenue **but not the cost of the goods sold.** At the end of the period when a company prepares financial statements, it takes a *physical count of inventory* by counting the quantities and costs of merchandise available. The cost of goods sold is then computed by subtracting the ending inventory amount from the cost of merchandise available for sale.

Recording Merchandise Transactions

Under a periodic system, purchases, purchase returns and allowances, purchase discounts, and transportation-in transactions are recorded in separate temporary accounts. At period-end, each of these temporary accounts is closed and the Merchandise Inventory account is updated. To illustrate, journal entries under the periodic inventory system are shown for the most common transactions (codes *a* through *f* link these transactions to those in the chapter, and we drop explanations for simplicity). For comparison, perpetual system journal entries are shown to the right of each periodic entry, where differences are in green font.

P5 Record and compare merchandising transactions using both periodic and perpetual inventory systems.

Purchases The periodic system uses a temporary *Purchases* account that accumulates the cost of all purchase transactions during each period. Z-Mart's November 2 entry to record the purchase of merchandise for $1,200 on credit with terms of 2/10, n/30 is

(a)

Periodic			Perpetual		
Purchases	1,200		Merchandise Inventory	1,200	
Accounts Payable		1,200	Accounts Payable		1,200

Purchase Discounts The periodic system uses a temporary *Purchase Discounts* account that accumulates discounts taken on purchase transactions during the period. If payment in (*a*) is delayed until after the discount period expires, the entry is to debit Accounts Payable and credit Cash for $1,200 each. However, if Z-Mart pays the supplier for the previous purchase in (*a*) within the discount period, the required payment is $1,176 ($1,200 × 98%) and is recorded as

(b)

Periodic			Perpetual		
Accounts Payable	1,200		Accounts Payable	1,200	
Purchase Discounts		24	Merchandise Inventory		24
Cash		1,176	Cash		1,176

Purchase Returns and Allowances Z-Mart returned merchandise purchased on November 2 because of defects. In the periodic system, the temporary *Purchase Returns and Allowances* account accumulates the cost of all returns and allowances during a period. The recorded cost (including discounts) of the defective merchandise is $300, and Z-Mart records the November 15 return with this entry:

(c)

Periodic			Perpetual		
Accounts Payable	300		Accounts Payable	300	
Purchase Returns and Allowances		300	Merchandise Inventory		300

Transportation-In Z-Mart paid a $75 freight charge to transport merchandise to its store. In the periodic system, this cost is charged to a temporary *Transportation-In* account.

(d)

Periodic			Perpetual		
Transportation-In	75		Merchandise Inventory	75	
Cash		75	Cash		75

Sales   Under the periodic system, the cost of goods sold is *not* recorded at the time of each sale. (We later show how to compute total cost of goods sold at the end of a period.) Z-Mart's November 3 entry to record sales of $2,400 in merchandise on credit (when its cost is $1,600) is:

(e)

Periodic			Perpetual		
Accounts Receivable	2,400		Accounts Receivable	2,400	
Sales		2,400	Sales		2,400
			Cost of Goods Sold	1,600	
			Merchandise Inventory		1,600

Sales Returns   A customer returned part of the merchandise from the transaction in (*e*), where the returned items sell for $800 and cost $600. (*Recall:* The periodic system records only the revenue effect, not the cost effect, for sales transactions.) Z-Mart restores the merchandise to inventory and records the November 6 return as

(f)

Periodic			Perpetual		
Sales Returns and			Sales Returns and		
Allowances	800		Allowances	800	
Accounts Receivable . . .		800	Accounts Receivable		800
			Merchandise Inventory	600	
			Cost of Goods Sold		600

Sales Discounts   To illustrate sales discounts, assume that the remaining $1,600 of receivables (computed as $2,400 from *e* less $800 for *f*) has credit terms of 3/10, n/90 and that customers all pay within the discount period. Z-Mart records this payment as

Periodic			Perpetual		
Cash	1,552		Cash	1,552	
Sales Discounts ($1,600 × .03)	48		Sales Discounts ($1,600 × .03) . .	48	
Accounts Receivable . . .		1,600	Accounts Receivable		1,600

Adjusting and Closing Entries

The periodic and perpetual inventory systems have slight differences in adjusting and closing entries. The period-end Merchandise Inventory balance (unadjusted) is $19,000 under the periodic system and $21,250 under the perpetual system. Since the periodic system does not update the Merchandise Inventory balance during the period, the $19,000 amount is the beginning inventory. However, the $21,250 balance under the perpetual system is the recorded ending inventory before adjusting for any inventory shrinkage.

A physical count of inventory taken at the end of the period reveals $21,000 of merchandise available. The adjusting and closing entries for the two systems are shown in Exhibit 4A.1. The periodic system records the ending inventory of $21,000 in the Merchandise Inventory account (which includes

EXHIBIT 4A.1

Comparison of Adjusting and Closing Entries—Periodic and Perpetual

PERIODIC			PERPETUAL		
Adjusting Entry—Shrinkage			**Adjusting Entry—Shrinkage**		
None			Cost of Goods Sold	250	
			Merchandise Inventory		250

[continued on next page]

[continued from previous page]

PERIODIC		
Closing Entries		
(1) Sales	321,000	
Merchandise Inventory	21,000	
Purchase Discounts	4,200	
Purchase Returns and Allowances	1,500	
Income Summary		347,700
(2) Income Summary	334,800	
Sales Discounts		4,300
Sales Returns and Allowances		2,000
Merchandise Inventory		19,000
Purchases		235,800
Transportation-In		2,300
Depreciation Expense		3,700
Salaries Expense		43,800
Insurance Expense		600
Rent Expense		9,000
Supplies Expense		3,000
Advertising Expense		11,300
(3) Income Summary	12,900	
Retained Earnings		12,900
(4) Retained Earnings	4,000	
Dividends		4,000

PERPETUAL		
Closing Entries		
(1) Sales	321,000	
Income Summary		321,000
(2) Income Summary	308,100	
Sales Discounts		4,300
Sales Returns and Allowances		2,000
Cost of Goods Sold		230,400
Depreciation Expense		3,700
Salaries Expense		43,800
Insurance Expense		600
Rent Expense		9,000
Supplies Expense		3,000
Advertising Expense		11,300
(3) Income Summary	12,900	
Retained Earnings		12,900
(4) Retained Earnings	4,000	
Dividends		4,000

shrinkage) in the first closing entry and removes the $19,000 beginning inventory balance from the account in the second closing entry.[2]

By updating Merchandise Inventory and closing Purchases, Purchase Discounts, Purchase Returns and Allowances, and Transportation-In, the periodic system transfers the cost of goods sold amount to Income Summary. Review the periodic side of Exhibit 4A.1 and notice that the boldface items affect Income Summary as follows.

Credit to Income Summary in the first closing entry includes amounts from:	
Merchandise inventory (ending)	$ 21,000
Purchase discounts	4,200
Purchase returns and allowances	1,500
Debit to Income Summary in the second closing entry includes amounts from:	
Merchandise inventory (beginning)	(19,000)
Purchases	(235,800)
Transportation-in	(2,300)
Net effect on Income Summary	**$(230,400)**

This $230,400 effect on Income Summary is the cost of goods sold amount. The periodic system transfers cost of goods sold to the Income Summary account but without using a Cost of Goods Sold account. Also, the periodic system does not separately measure shrinkage. Instead, it computes cost of goods

---

[2] This approach is called the *closing entry method*. An alternative approach, referred to as the *adjusting entry method*, would not make any entries to Merchandise Inventory in the closing entries of Exhibit 4A.1, but instead would make two adjusting entries. Using Z-Mart data, the two adjusting entries would be: (1) Dr. Income Summary and Cr. Merchandise Inventory for $19,000 each, and (2) Dr. Merchandise Inventory and Cr. Income Summary for $21,000 each. The first entry removes the beginning balance of Merchandise Inventory, and the second entry records the actual ending balance.

available for sale, subtracts the cost of ending inventory, and defines the difference as cost of goods sold, which includes shrinkage.

Preparing Financial Statements

The financial statements of a merchandiser using the periodic system are similar to those for a service company described in prior chapters. The income statement mainly differs by the inclusion of *cost of goods sold* and *gross profit*—of course, net sales is affected by discounts, returns, and allowances. The cost of goods sold section under the periodic system follows

Calculation of Cost of Goods Sold For Year Ended December 31, 2009	
Beginning inventory	$ 19,000
Cost of goods purchased	232,400
Cost of goods available for sale	251,400
Less ending inventory	21,000
Cost of goods sold	$230,400

The balance sheet mainly differs by the inclusion of *merchandise inventory* in current assets—see Exhibit 4.15. The statement of retained earnings is unchanged. A work sheet can be used to help prepare these statements. The only differences under the periodic system from the work sheet illustrated in Appendix 4B using the perpetual system are highlighted as follows in blue boldface font.

File Edit View Insert Format Tools Data Accounting Window Help

No.	Account	Unadjusted Trial Balance Dr.	Cr.	Adjustments Dr.	Cr.	Adjusted Trial Balance Dr.	Cr.	Income Statement Dr.	Cr.	Balance Sheet Dr.	Cr.
101	Cash	8,200				8,200				8,200	
106	Accounts receivable	11,200				11,200				11,200	
119	**Merchandise Inventory**	19,000				19,000		19,000	21,000	21,000	
126	Supplies	3,800			(b) 3,000	800				800	
128	Prepaid insurance	900			(a) 600	300				300	
167	Equipment	34,200				34,200				34,200	
168	Accumulated depr.—Equip.		3,700		(c) 3,700		7,400				7,400
201	Accounts payable		16,000				16,000				16,000
209	Salaries payable				(d) 800		800				800
307	Common stock		10,000				10,000				10,000
318	Retained earnings		32,600				32,600				32,600
319	Dividends	4,000				4,000				4,000	
413	Sales		321,000				321,000		321,000		
414	Sales returns and allowances	2,000				2,000		2,000			
415	Sales discounts	4,300				4,300		4,300			
505	**Purchases**	235,800				235,800		235,800			
506	**Purchases returns & allowance**		1,500				1,500		1,500		
507	**Purchases discounts**		4,200				4,200		4,200		
508	**Transportation-in**	2,300				2,300		2,300			
612	Depreciation expense—Equip.			(c) 3,700		3,700		3,700			
622	Salaries expense	43,000		(d) 800		43,800		43,800			
637	Insurance expense			(a) 600		600		600			
640	Rent expense	9,000				9,000		9,000			
652	Supplies expense			(b) 3,000		3,000		3,000			
655	Advertising expense	11,300				11,300		11,300			
	Totals	389,000	389,000	8,100	8,100	393,500	393,500	334,800	347,700	79,700	66,800
	Net income							12,900			12,900
	Totals							347,700	347,700	79,700	79,700

Sheet1 Sheet2 Sheet3

Quick Check

Answers—p. 183

13. What account is used in a perpetual inventory system but not in a periodic system?

14. Which of the following accounts are temporary accounts under a periodic system:
(a) Merchandise Inventory; (b) Purchases; (c) Transportation-In?

15. How is cost of goods sold computed under a periodic inventory system?

16. Do reported amounts of ending inventory and net income differ if the adjusting entry method of recording the change in inventory is used instead of the closing entry method?

APPENDIX

Work Sheet—Perpetual System

4B

Exhibit 4B.1 shows the work sheet for preparing financial statements of a merchandiser. It differs slightly from the work sheet layout in Chapter 3—the differences are in **red boldface**. Also, the adjustments in the work sheet reflect the following: (a) Expiration of $600 of prepaid insurance. (b) Use of $3,000 of supplies. (c) Depreciation of $3,700 for equipment. (d) Accrual of $800 of unpaid salaries. (e) Inventory shrinkage of $250. Once the adjusted amounts are extended into the financial statement columns, the information is used to develop financial statements.

EXHIBIT 4B.1

Work Sheet for Merchandiser (using a perpetual system)

No.	Account	Unadjusted Trial Balance Dr.	Cr.	Adjustments Dr.	Cr.	Adjusted Trial Balance Dr.	Cr.	Income Statement Dr.	Cr.	Balance Sheet Dr.	Cr.
101	Cash	8,200				8,200				8,200	
106	Accounts receivable	11,200				11,200				11,200	
119	**Merchandise Inventory**	21,250			(g) 250	21,000				21,000	
126	Supplies	3,800			(b) 3,000	800				800	
128	Prepaid insurance	900			(a) 600	300				300	
167	Equipment	34,200				34,200				34,200	
168	Accumulated depr.—Equip.		3,700		(c) 3,700		7,400				7,400
201	Accounts payable		16,000				16,000				16,000
209	Salaries payable				(d) 800		800				800
307	Common stock		10,000				10,000				10,000
318	Retained earnings		32,600				32,600				32,600
319	Dividends	4,000				4,000				4,000	
413	**Sales**		321,000				321,000		321,000		
414	**Sales returns and allowances**	2,000				2,000		2,000			
415	**Sales discounts**	4,300				4,300		4,300			
502	**Cost of goods sold**	230,150		(g) 250 (c) 3,700		230,400		230,400			
612	Depreciation expense—Equip.			(c) 3,700		3,700		3,700			
622	Salaries expense	43,000		(d) 800		43,800		43,800			
637	Insurance expense			(a) 600		600		600			
640	Rent expense	9,000				9,000		9,000			
652	Supplies expense			(b) 3,000		3,000		3,000			
655	Advertising expense	11,300				11,300		11,300			
	Totals	383,300	383,300	8,350	8,350	387,800	387,800	308,100	321,000	79,700	66,800
	Net income							12,900			12,900
	Totals							321,000	321,000	79,700	79,700

Summary

C1 **Describe merchandising activities and identify income components for a merchandising company.** Merchandisers buy products and resell them. Examples of merchandisers include Wal-Mart, Home Depot, The Limited, and Barnes & Noble. A merchandiser's costs on the income statement include an amount for cost of goods sold. Gross profit, or gross margin, equals sales minus cost of goods sold.

C2 **Identify and explain the inventory asset of a merchandising company.** The current asset section of a merchandising company's balance sheet includes *merchandise inventory,* which refers to the products a merchandiser sells and are available for sale at the balance sheet date.

C3 **Describe both perpetual and periodic inventory systems.** A perpetual inventory system continuously tracks the cost of goods available for sale and the cost of goods sold. A periodic system accumulates the cost of goods purchased during the period and does not compute the amount of inventory or the cost of goods sold until the end of a period.

C4 **Analyze and interpret cost flows and operating activities of a merchandising company.** Cost of merchandise purchases flows into Merchandise Inventory and from there to Cost of Goods Sold on the income statement. Any remaining inventory is reported as a current asset on the balance sheet.

A1 **Compute the acid-test ratio and explain its use to assess liquidity.** The acid-test ratio is computed as quick assets (cash, short-term investments, and current receivables) divided by current liabilities. It indicates a company's ability to pay its current liabilities with its existing quick assets. An acid-test ratio equal to or greater than 1.0 is often adequate.

A2 **Compute the gross margin ratio and explain its use to assess profitability.** The gross margin ratio is computed as gross margin (net sales minus cost of goods sold) divided by net sales. It indicates a company's profitability before considering other expenses.

P1 **Analyze and record transactions for merchandise purchases using a perpetual system.** For a perpetual inventory system, purchases of inventory (net of trade discounts) are added to the Merchandise Inventory account. Purchase discounts and purchase returns and allowances are subtracted from Merchandise Inventory, and transportation-in costs are added to Merchandise Inventory.

P2 **Analyze and record transactions for merchandise sales using a perpetual system.** A merchandiser records sales at list price less any trade discounts. The cost of items sold is transferred from Merchandise Inventory to Cost of Goods Sold. Refunds or credits given to customers for unsatisfactory merchandise are recorded in Sales Returns and Allowances, a contra account to Sales. If merchandise is returned and restored to inventory, the cost of this merchandise is removed from Cost of Goods Sold and transferred back to Merchandise Inventory. When cash discounts from the sales price are offered and customers pay within the discount period, the seller records Sales Discounts, a contra account to Sales.

P3 **Prepare adjustments and close accounts for a merchandising company.** With a perpetual system, it is often necessary to make an adjustment for inventory shrinkage. This is computed by comparing a physical count of inventory with the Merchandise Inventory balance. Shrinkage is normally charged to Cost of Goods Sold. Temporary accounts closed to Income Summary for a merchandiser include Sales, Sales Discounts, Sales Returns and Allowances, and Cost of Goods Sold.

P4 **Define and prepare multiple-step and single-step income statements.** Multiple-step income statements include greater detail for sales and expenses than do single-step income statements. They also show details of net sales and report expenses in categories reflecting different activities.

P5^A **Record and compare merchandising transactions using both periodic and perpetual inventory systems.** Transactions involving the sale and purchase of merchandise are recorded and analyzed under both the periodic and perpetual inventory systems. Adjusting and closing entries for both inventory systems are illustrated and explained.

Guidance Answers to **Decision Maker** and **Decision Ethics**

Entrepreneur For terms of 3/10, n/90, missing the 3% discount for an additional 80 days equals an implied annual interest rate of 13.69%, computed as (365 days ÷ 80 days) × 3%. Since you can borrow funds at 11% (assuming no other processing costs), it is better to borrow and pay within the discount period. You save 2.69% (13.69% − 11%) in interest costs by paying early.

Credit Manager Your decision is whether to comply with prior policy or to create a new policy and not abuse discounts offered by suppliers. Your first step should be to meet with your superior to find out if the late payment policy is the actual policy and, if so, its rationale. If it is the policy to pay late, you must apply your own sense of ethics. One point of view is that the late payment policy is unethical. A deliberate plan to make late payments means the company lies when it pretends to make payment within the discount period. Another view is that the late payment policy is acceptable. In some markets, attempts to take discounts through late payments are accepted as a continued phase of "price negotiation." Also, your company's suppliers can respond by billing your company for the discounts not accepted because of late payments. However, this is a dubious viewpoint, especially since the prior manager proposes that you dishonestly explain late payments as computer or mail problems and since some suppliers have complained.

Supplier A current ratio of 2.1 suggests sufficient current assets to cover current liabilities. An acid-test ratio of 0.5 suggests, however, that quick assets can cover only about one-half of current liabilities. This implies that the retailer depends on money from sales of inventory to pay current liabilities. If sales of inventory decline or profit margins decrease, the likelihood that this retailer will default on its payments increases. Your decision is probably not to extend credit. If you do extend credit, you are likely to closely monitor the retailer's financial condition. (It is better to hold unsold inventory than uncollectible receivables.)

Financial Officer Your company's net profit margin is about equal to the industry average and suggests typical industry performance. However, gross margin reveals that your company is paying far more in cost of goods sold or receiving far less in sales price than competitors. Your attention must be directed to finding the problem with cost of goods sold, sales, or both. One positive note is that your company's expenses make up 19% of sales (36% − 17%). This favorably compares with competitors' expenses that make up 28% of sales (44% − 16%).

Guidance Answers to **Quick Checks**

1. Cost of goods sold is the cost of merchandise purchased from a supplier that is sold to customers during a specific period.

2. Gross profit (or gross margin) is the difference between net sales and cost of goods sold.

3. Widespread use of computing and related technology has dramatically increased the use of the perpetual inventory system.

4. Under credit terms of 2/10, n/60, the credit period is 60 days and the discount period is 10 days.

5. (*b*) trade discount.

6. *FOB* means "free on board." It is used in identifying the point when ownership transfers from seller to buyer. *FOB destination* means that the seller transfers ownership of goods to the buyer when they arrive at the buyer's place of business. It also means that the seller is responsible for paying shipping charges and bears the risk of damage or loss during shipment.

7. Recording sales discounts and sales returns and allowances separately from sales gives useful information to managers for internal monitoring and decision making.

8. When a customer returns merchandise *and* the seller restores the merchandise to inventory, two entries are necessary. One entry records the decrease in revenue and credits the customer's account. The second entry debits inventory and reduces cost of goods sold.

9. Credit memorandum—seller credits accounts receivable from buyer.

10. Merchandise Inventory may need adjusting to reflect shrinkage.

11. Sales (of goods), Sales Discounts, Sales Returns and Allowances, and Cost of Goods Sold (and maybe Delivery Expense).

12. Four closing entries: (1) close credit balances in temporary accounts to Income Summary, (2) close debit balances in temporary accounts to Income Summary, (3) close Income Summary to Retained Earnings, and (4) close Dividends account to Retained Earnings.

13. Cost of Goods Sold.

14. (*b*) Purchases and (*c*) Transportation-In.

15. Under a periodic inventory system, the cost of goods sold is determined at the end of an accounting period by adding the net cost of goods purchased to the beginning inventory and subtracting the ending inventory.

16. Both methods report the same ending inventory and income.

 **Key Terms**

Acid-test ratio (p. 172)	**Gross margin** (p. 157)	**Purchase discount** (p. 159)
Cash discount (p. 159)	**Gross margin ratio** (p. 172)	**Retailer** (p. 156)
Cost of goods sold (p. 156)	**Gross profit** (p. 156)	**Sales discount** (p. 159)
Credit memorandum (p. 165)	**Inventory** (p. 157)	**Selling expenses** (p. 169)
Credit period (p. 159)	**List price** (p. 158)	**Shrinkage** (p. 166)
Credit terms (p. 159)	**Merchandise** (p. 156)	**Single-step income statement** (p. 169)
Debit memorandum (p. 160)	**Merchandise inventory** (p. 157)	**Supplementary records** (p. 162)
Discount period (p. 159)	**Merchandiser** (p. 156)	**Trade discount** (p. 158)
EOM (p. 159)	**Multiple-step income statement** (p. 168)	**Wholesaler** (p. 156)
FOB (p. 161)	**Periodic inventory system** (pp. 158, 177)	
General and administrative expenses (p. 169)	**Perpetual inventory system** (p. 158)	

Multiple Choice Quiz   Answers on p. 201   **mhhe.com/wildFA5e**

Additional Quiz Questions are available at the book's Website.

1. A company has $550,000 in net sales and $193,000 in gross profit. This means its cost of goods sold equals
   a. $743,000
   b. $550,000
   c. $357,000
   d. $193,000
   e. $(193,000)

2. A company purchased $4,500 of merchandise on May 1 with terms of 2/10, n/30. On May 6, it returned $250 of that merchandise. On May 8, it paid the balance owed for merchandise, taking any discount it is entitled to. The cash paid on May 8 is
   a. $4,500
   b. $4,250
   c. $4,160
   d. $4,165
   e. $4,410

3. A company has cash sales of $75,000, credit sales of $320,000, sales returns and allowances of $13,700, and sales discounts of $6,000. Its net sales equal
   a. $395,000
   b. $375,300

   c. $300,300
   d. $339,700
   e. $414,700

4. A company's quick assets are $37,500, its current assets are $80,000, and its current liabilities are $50,000. Its acid-test ratio equals
   a. 1.600
   b. 0.750
   c. 0.625
   d. 1.333
   e. 0.469

5. A company's net sales are $675,000, its costs of goods sold are $459,000, and its net income is $74,250. Its gross margin ratio equals
   a. 32%
   b. 68%
   c. 47%
   d. 11%
   e. 34%

Superscript letter ^{A} (^{B}) denotes assignments based on Appendix 4A (4B).

Discussion Questions

1. In comparing the accounts of a merchandising company with those of a service company, what additional accounts would the merchandising company likely use, assuming it employs a perpetual inventory system?

2. What items appear in financial statements of merchandising companies but not in the statements of service companies?

3. ♟ Explain how a business can earn a positive gross profit on its sales and still have a net loss.

4. ♟ Why do companies offer a cash discount?

5. How does a company that uses a perpetual inventory system determine the amount of inventory shrinkage?

6. Distinguish between cash discounts and trade discounts. Is the amount of a trade discount on purchased merchandise recorded in the accounts?

7. What is the difference between a sales discount and a purchase discount?

8. ♟ Why would a company's manager be concerned about the quantity of its purchase returns if its suppliers allow unlimited returns?

9. Does the sender (maker) of a debit memorandum record a debit or a credit in the recipient's account? What entry (debit or credit) does the recipient record?

10. What is the difference between the single-step and multiple-step income statement formats?

11. ♟ Refer to the balance sheet and income statement for **Best Buy** in Appendix A. What does the company title its inventory account? Does the company present a detailed calculation of its cost of goods sold?

12. Refer to **GOME**'s income statement in Appendix A. What title does it use for cost of goods sold?

13. Refer to the income statement for **RadioShack** in Appendix A. What does RadioShack title its cost of goods sold account?

14. Refer to the income statement of **Apple** in Appendix A. Does its income statement report a gross profit figure? If yes, what is the amount?

15. ♟ Buyers negotiate purchase contracts with suppliers. What type of shipping terms should a buyer attempt to negotiate to minimize freight-in costs?

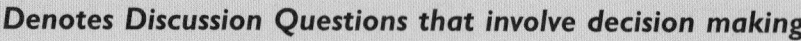

♟ Denotes Discussion Questions that involve decision making.

connect ™ Available with Connect Accounting

Prepare journal entries to record each of the following purchases transactions of a merchandising company. Show supporting calculations and assume a perpetual inventory system.

Mar. 5   Purchased 1,000 units of product at a cost of $12 per unit. Terms of the sale are 2/10, n/60; the invoice is dated March 5.
Mar. 7   Returned 50 defective units from the March 5 purchase and received full credit.
Mar. 15   Paid the amount due from the March 5 purchase, less the return on March 7.

QUICK STUDY

QS 4-1
Recording purchases—
perpetual system   P1

Prepare journal entries to record each of the following sales transactions of a merchandising company. Show supporting calculations and assume a perpetual inventory system.

Apr. 1   Sold merchandise for $5,000, granting the customer terms of 2/10, EOM; invoice dated April 1. The cost of the merchandise is $3,000.
Apr. 4   The customer in the April 1 sale returned merchandise and received credit for $1,000. The merchandise, which had cost $600, is returned to inventory.
Apr. 11   Received payment for the amount due from the April 1 sale less the return on April 4.

QS 4-2
Recording sales—
perpetual system
P2

Compute net sales, gross profit, and the gross margin ratio for each separate case *a* through *d*. Interpret the gross margin ratio for case *a*.

	a	b	c	d
Sales	$140,000	$378,000	$42,500	$593,000
Sales discounts	1,700	6,000	400	2,500
Sales returns and allowances	9,000	17,000	3,400	15,300
Cost of goods sold	82,493	222,230	28,676	451,532

QS 4-3
Computing and analyzing
gross margin
C1   A2

Crystal Company's ledger on July 31, its fiscal year-end, includes the following selected accounts that have normal balances (Crystal uses the perpetual inventory system).

Merchandise inventory	$ 42,000	Sales returns and allowances	$ 7,600
Common stock	50,000	Cost of goods sold	115,000
Retained earnings	74,900	Depreciation expense	12,000
Sales	275,300	Salaries expense	45,000
Sales discounts	5,200	Miscellaneous expenses	7,000

A physical count of its July 31 year-end inventory discloses that the cost of the merchandise inventory still available is $40,600. Prepare the entry to record any inventory shrinkage.

QS 4-4
Accounting for shrinkage—
perpetual system
P3

Refer to QS 4-4 and prepare journal entries to close the balances in temporary revenue and expense accounts. Remember to consider the entry for shrinkage that is made to solve QS 4-4.

QS 4-5
Closing entries   P3

Use the following information on current assets and current liabilities to compute and interpret the acid-test ratio. Explain what the acid-test ratio of a company measures.

Cash	$ 3,000	Prepaid expenses	$ 1,400
Accounts receivable	5,580	Accounts payable	11,500
Inventory	12,000	Other current liabilities	1,700

QS 4-6
Computing and interpreting
acid-test ratio
A1

Identify similarities and differences between the acid-test ratio and the current ratio. Compare and describe how the two ratios reflect a company's ability to meet its current obligations.

QS 4-7
Contrasting liquidity ratios   A1

QS 4-8^A
Contrasting periodic and perpetual systems   C3

Identify whether each description best applies to a periodic or a perpetual inventory system.
a. Requires an adjusting entry to record inventory shrinkage.
b. Markedly increased in frequency and popularity in business within the past decade.
c. Provides more timely information to managers.
d. Records cost of goods sold each time a sales transaction occurs.
e. Updates the inventory account only at period-end.

QS 4-9^A
Recording purchases—periodic system   P5

Refer to QS 4-1 and prepare journal entries to record each of the merchandising transactions assuming that the periodic inventory system is used.

QS 4-10^A
Recording purchases—periodic system   P5

Refer to QS 4-2 and prepare journal entries to record each of the merchandising transactions assuming that the periodic inventory system is used.

QS 4-11
IFRS income statement presentation   P4

Income statement information for **adidas Group**, a German footwear, apparel, and accessories manufacturer, for the year ended December 31, 2008, follows. The company applies IFRS, as adopted by the European Union, and reports its results in millions of Euros. Prepare its calendar year 2008 (1) multiple-step income statement and (2) single-step income statement.

Net income	€ 644
Financial income	37
Financial expenses	203
Operating profit	1,070
Cost of sales	5,543
Income taxes	260
Income before taxes	904
Gross profit	5,256
Royalty and commission income	89
Other operating income	103
Other operating expenses	4,378
Net sales	10,799

QS 4-12
International accounting standards

C1   C3

Answer each of the following questions related to international accounting standards.
a. Explain how the accounting for merchandise purchases and sales is different between accounting under IFRS versus U.S. GAAP.
b. Income statements prepared under IFRS usually report an item titled *finance costs*. What do finance costs refer to?
c. U.S. GAAP prohibits alternative measures of income reported on the income statement. Does IFRS permit such alternative measures on the income statement?

Available with Connect Accounting **connect**

EXERCISES

Prepare journal entries to record the following transactions for a retail store. Assume a perpetual inventory system.

Exercise 4-1
Recording entries for merchandise purchases   P1

Apr. 2   Purchased merchandise from Johns Company under the following terms: $5,900 price, invoice dated April 2, credit terms of 2/15, n/60, and FOB shipping point.
      3   Paid $330 for shipping charges on the April 2 purchase.
      4   Returned to Johns Company unacceptable merchandise that had an invoice price of $900.
     17   Sent a check to Johns Company for the April 2 purchase, net of the discount and the returned merchandise.
     18   Purchased merchandise from William Corp. under the following terms: $12,250 price, invoice dated April 18, credit terms of 2/10, n/30, and FOB destination.
     21   After negotiations, received from William a $3,250 allowance on the April 18 purchase.
     28   Sent check to William paying for the April 18 purchase, net of the discount and allowance.

Check   April 28, Cr. Cash $8,820

Fortuna Company purchased merchandise for resale from Lemar Company with an invoice price of $30,000 and credit terms of 2/10, n/60. The merchandise had cost Lemar $20,100. Fortuna paid within the discount period. Assume that both buyer and seller use a perpetual inventory system.

1. Prepare entries that the buyer should record for (*a*) the purchase and (*b*) the cash payment.

2. Prepare entries that the seller should record for (*a*) the sale and (*b*) the cash collection.

3. Assume that the buyer borrowed enough cash to pay the balance on the last day of the discount period at an annual interest rate of 8% and paid it back on the last day of the credit period. Compute how much the buyer saved by following this strategy. (Assume a 365-day year and round dollar amounts to the nearest cent.)

Exercise 4-2
Analyzing and recording merchandise transactions—both buyer and seller
P1 P2
Check   (3) $278 savings (rounded)

Enter the letter for each term in the blank space beside the definition that it most closely matches.

A. Cash discount   **E.** FOB shipping point   **H.** Purchase discount
B. Credit period   **F.** Gross profit   **I.** Sales discount
C. Discount period   **G.** Merchandise inventory   **J.** Trade discount
D. FOB destination

_____ **1.** Time period in which a cash discount is available.
_____ **2.** Reduction below list or catalog price that is negotiated in setting the price of goods.
_____ **3.** Reduction in a receivable or payable if it is paid within the discount period.
_____ **4.** Time period that can pass before a customer's payment is due.
_____ **5.** Difference between net sales and the cost of goods sold.
_____ **6.** Ownership of goods is transferred when the seller delivers goods to the carrier.
_____ **7.** Ownership of goods is transferred when delivered to the buyer's place of business.
_____ **8.** Goods a company owns and expects to sell to its customers.
_____ **9.** Purchaser's description of a cash discount received from a supplier of goods.
_____ **10.** Seller's description of a cash discount granted to buyers in return for early payment.

Exercise 4-3
Applying merchandising terms
C1

Mechanic Parts was organized on May 1, 2011, and made its first purchase of merchandise on May 3. The purchase was for 1,200 units at a price of $7 per unit. On May 5, Mechanic Parts sold 720 of the units for $11 per unit to Radica Co. Terms of the sale were 2/10, n/60. Prepare entries for Mechanic Parts to record the May 5 sale and each of the following separate transactions *a* through *c* using a perpetual inventory system.

a. On May 7, Radica returns 251 units because they did not fit the customer's needs. Mechanic Parts restores the units to its inventory.

b. On May 8, Radica discovers that 60 units are damaged but are still of some use and, therefore, keeps the units. Mechanic Parts sends Radica a credit memorandum for $180 to compensate for the damage.

c. On May 15, Radica discovers that 72 units are the wrong color. Radica keeps 43 of these units because Mechanic sends a $92 credit memorandum to compensate. However, Radica returns the remaining 29 units to Mechanic. Mechanic restores the 29 returned units to its inventory.

Exercise 4-4
Recording sales returns and allowances P2
Check (c) Dr. Sales Returns and Allowances $411

Refer to Exercise 4-4 and prepare the appropriate journal entries for Radica Co. to record the May 5 purchase and each of the three separate transactions *a* through *c*. Radica is a retailer that uses a perpetual inventory system and purchases these units for resale.

Exercise 4-5
Recording purchase returns and allowances   P1

On May 11, York Co. accepts delivery of $38,000 of merchandise it purchases for resale from Troy Corporation. With the merchandise is an invoice dated May 11, with terms of 3/10, n/90, FOB shipping point. The goods cost Troy $25,460. When the goods are delivered, York pays $520 to Express Shipping for delivery charges on the merchandise. On May 12, York returns $2,000 of goods to Troy, who receives them one day later and restores them to inventory. The returned goods had cost Troy $1,393. On May 20, York mails a check to Troy Corporation for the amount owed. Troy receives it the following day. (Both York and Troy use a perpetual inventory system.)

1. Prepare journal entries that York Co. records for these transactions.

2. Prepare journal entries that Troy Corporation records for these transactions.

Exercise 4-6
Analyzing and recording merchandise transactions—both buyer and seller
P1 P2
Check   (1) May 20, Cr. Cash $34,920

Exercise 4-7
Sales returns and allowances

C1   P2 ♟

Business decision makers desire information on sales returns and allowances. (1) Explain why a company's manager wants the accounting system to record customers' returns of unsatisfactory goods in the Sales Returns and Allowances account instead of the Sales account. (2) Explain whether this information would be useful for external decision makers.

Exercise 4-8
Computing revenues, expenses, and income

C1   C4

Using your accounting knowledge, fill in the blanks in the following separate income statements *a* through *e*. Identify any negative amount by putting it in parentheses.

	a	b	c	d	e
Sales	$82,800	$58,622	$50,094	$?	$32,540
Cost of goods sold					
Merchandise inventory (beginning)	7,866	3,507	10,519	9,902	3,351
Total cost of merchandise purchases	35,439	?	?	45,252	7,439
Merchandise inventory (ending)	?	(3,714)	(12,019)	(9,527)	?
Cost of goods sold	34,950	21,932	?	?	8,359
Gross profit	?	?	4,606	62,013	?
Expenses	9,000	10,650	14,923	32,600	6,100
Net income (loss)	$?	$26,040	$(10,317)	$29,413	$?

Exercise 4-9
Recording effects of merchandising activities

C4

The following supplementary records summarize Tandy Company's merchandising activities for year 2011. Set up T-accounts for Merchandise Inventory and Cost of Goods Sold. Then record the summarized activities in those T-accounts and compute account balances.

Cost of merchandise sold to customers in sales transactions	$296,000
Merchandise inventory, December 31, 2010	42,979
Invoice cost of merchandise purchases	303,459
Shrinkage determined on December 31, 2011	790
Cost of transportation-in	3,034
Cost of merchandise returned by customers and restored to inventory	2,700
Purchase discounts received	2,427
Purchase returns and allowances	3,900

Check   Year-End Merchandise
Inventory Dec. 31, $49,055

Exercise 4-10
Preparing adjusting and closing entries for a merchandiser

P3

The following list includes selected permanent accounts and all of the temporary accounts from the December 31, 2011, unadjusted trial balance of Yamiko Co., a business owned by Kumi Yamiko. Use these account balances along with the additional information to journalize (*a*) adjusting entries and (*b*) closing entries. Yamiko Co. uses a perpetual inventory system.

	Debit	Credit
Merchandise inventory	$ 30,200	
Prepaid selling expenses	4,000	
Dividends	1,600	
Sales		$543,600
Sales returns and allowances	20,656	
Sales discounts	5,783	
Cost of goods sold	267,451	
Sales salaries expense	59,796	
Utilities expense	17,395	
Selling expenses	46,749	
Administrative expenses	120,135	

Additional Information

Accrued sales salaries amount to $1,700. Prepaid selling expenses of $1,600 have expired. A physical count of year-end merchandise inventory shows $29,626 of goods still available.

A retail company recently completed a physical count of ending merchandise inventory to use in preparing adjusting entries. In determining the cost of the counted inventory, company employees failed to consider that $5,000 of incoming goods had been shipped by a supplier on December 31 under an FOB shipping point agreement. These goods had been recorded in Merchandise Inventory as a purchase, but they were not included in the physical count because they were in transit. Explain how this overlooked fact affects the company's financial statements and the following ratios: return on assets, debt ratio, current ratio, profit margin ratio, and acid-test ratio.

Exercise 4-11
Interpreting a physical count error as inventory shrinkage

A1 A2 P3

Compute the current ratio and acid-test ratio for each of the following separate cases. Which company case is in the best position to meet short-term obligations? Explain.

Exercise 4-12
Computing and analyzing acid-test and current ratios

A1

	Case X	Case Y	Case Z
Cash	$ 920	$ 1,046	$1,220
Short-term investments	0	0	500
Current receivables	0	1,126	890
Inventory	2,300	1,136	4,600
Prepaid expenses	1,200	679	900
Total current assets	$4,420	$3,987	$8,110
Current liabilities	$2,563	$1,281	$4,254

Journalize the following merchandising transactions for Chiller Systems assuming it uses a perpetual inventory system.

1. On November 1, Chiller Systems purchases merchandise for $2,800 on credit with terms of 2/5, n/30, FOB shipping point; invoice dated November 1.

2. On November 5, Chiller Systems pays cash for the November 1 purchase.

3. On November 7, Chiller Systems discovers and returns $100 of defective merchandise purchased on November 1 for a cash refund.

4. On November 10, Chiller Systems pays $140 cash for transportation costs with the November 1 purchase.

5. On November 13, Chiller Systems sells merchandise for $3,024 on credit. The cost of the merchandise is $1,512.

6. On November 16, the customer returns merchandise from the November 13 transaction. The returned items sell for $205 and cost $115.

Exercise 4-13
Preparing journal entries—perpetual system

P1 P2

Refer to Exercise 4-1 and prepare journal entries to record each of the merchandising transactions assuming that the periodic inventory system is used.

Exercise 4-14ᴬ
Recording purchases—periodic system   P5

Refer to Exercise 4-2 and prepare journal entries to record each of the merchandising transactions assuming that the periodic inventory system is used by both the buyer and the seller. (Skip the part 3 requirement.)

Exercise 4-15ᴬ
Recording purchases and sales—periodic system   P5

Exercise 4-16ᴬ

Buyer and seller transactions—periodic system   P5

Refer to Exercise 4-6 and prepare journal entries to record each of the merchandising transactions assuming that the periodic inventory system is used by both the buyer and the seller.

Exercise 4-17ᴬ

Recording purchases—periodic system   P5

Refer to Exercise 4-13 and prepare journal entries to record each of the merchandising transactions assuming that the periodic inventory system is used.

Exercise 4-18

Preparing an income statement following IFRS

P4

L'Oréal reports the following income statement accounts for the year ended December 31, 2008 (euros in millions). Prepare the income statement for this company for the year ended December 31, 2008, following usual IFRS practices.

Net profit	€ 1,950.9	Income tax expense	€ 680.7
Finance costs	174.2	Profit before tax expense	2,631.6
Net sales	17,541.8	Research and development expense	581.3
Gross profit	12,301.7	Selling, general and administrative expense	3,779.4
Other income	139.4	Advertising and promotion expense	5,274.6
Cost of sales	5,240.1		

Available with Connect Accounting **connect**

PROBLEM SET A

Problem 4-1A

Preparing journal entries for merchandising activities—perpetual system

P1 P2

Prepare journal entries to record the following merchandising transactions of Flora Company, which applies the perpetual inventory system. (*Hint:* It will help to identify each receivable and payable; for example, record the purchase on July 1 in Accounts Payable—Arch.)

July   1 Purchased merchandise from Arch Company for $6,400 under credit terms of 1/15, n/30, FOB shipping point, invoice dated July 1.

   2 Sold merchandise to Driver Co. for $900 under credit terms of 1/10, n/60, FOB shipping point, invoice dated July 2. The merchandise had cost $533.

   3 Paid $130 cash for freight charges on the purchase of July 1.

   8 Sold merchandise that had cost $1,700 for $2,100 cash.

   9 Purchased merchandise from Kew Co. for $2,200 under credit terms of 1/15, n/60, FOB destination, invoice dated July 9.

   11 Received a $200 credit memorandum from Kew Co. for the return of part of the merchandise purchased on July 9.

Check July 12, Dr. Cash $891

   July 16, Cr. Cash $6,336

   12 Received the balance due from Driver Co. for the invoice dated July 2, net of the discount.

   16 Paid the balance due to Arch Company within the discount period.

   19 Sold merchandise that cost $800 to Surtis Co. for $1,200 under credit terms of 1/15, n/60, FOB shipping point, invoice dated July 19.

   21 Issued a $200 credit memorandum to Surtis Co. for an allowance on goods sold on July 19.

July 24, Cr. Cash $1,980

July 30, Dr. Cash $990

   24 Paid Kew Co. the balance due after deducting the discount.

   30 Received the balance due from Surtis Co. for the invoice dated July 19, net of discount.

   31 Sold merchandise that cost $5,200 to Driver Co. for $6,900 under credit terms of 1/10, n/60, FOB shipping point, invoice dated July 31.

Problem 4-2A

Preparing journal entries for merchandising activities—perpetual system

P1 P2

Prepare journal entries to record the following merchandising transactions of Gore Company, which applies the perpetual inventory system. (*Hint:* It will help to identify each receivable and payable; for example, record the purchase on August 1 in Accounts Payable—Arotek.)

Aug.   1 Purchased merchandise from Arotek Company for $7,800 under credit terms of 1/10, n/30, FOB destination, invoice dated August 1.

   4 At Arotek's request, Gore paid $270 cash for freight charges on the August 1 purchase, reducing the amount owed to Arotek.

   5 Sold merchandise to Larton Corp. for $5,460 under credit terms of 2/10, n/60, FOB destination, invoice dated August 5. The merchandise had cost $3,898.

   8 Purchased merchandise from Frees Corporation for $7,100 under credit terms of 1/10, n/45, FOB shipping point, invoice dated August 8. The invoice showed that at Gore's request, Frees paid the $240 shipping charges and added that amount to the bill. (*Hint:* Discounts are not applied to freight and shipping charges.)

Check Aug. 9, Dr. Delivery
Expense, $120

9 Paid $120 cash for shipping charges related to the August 5 sale to Larton Corp.
10 Larton returned merchandise from the August 5 sale that had cost Gore $649 and been sold for $910. The merchandise was restored to inventory.
12 After negotiations with Frees Corporation concerning problems with the merchandise purchased on August 8, Gore received a credit memorandum from Frees granting a price reduction of $1,100.
15 Received balance due from Larton Corp. for the August 5 sale less the return on August 10.
18 Paid the amount due Frees Corporation for the August 8 purchase less the price reduction granted.

Aug. 18, Cr. Cash $6,180

19 Sold merchandise to Jones Co. for $4,680 under credit terms of 1/10, n/30, FOB shipping point, invoice dated August 19. The merchandise had cost $3,247.
22 Jones requested a price reduction on the August 19 sale because the merchandise did not meet specifications. Gore sent Jones a $780 credit memorandum to resolve the issue.
29 Received Jones's cash payment for the amount due from the August 19 sale.

Aug. 29, Dr. Cash $3,861

30 Paid Arotek Company the amount due from the August 1 purchase.

The following unadjusted trial balance is prepared at fiscal year-end for Helix Company.

Problem 4-3A
Preparing adjusting entries and income statements; and computing gross margin, acid-test, and current ratios

A1 A2 P3 P4

mhhe.com/wildFA5e

File Edit View Insert Format Tools Data Accounting Window Help

100% Arial 10 B I U $ %

HELIX COMPANY
Unadjusted Trial Balance
January 31, 2009

		Debit	Credit
2	Cash	$ 28,750	
3	Merchandise inventory	13,000	
4	Store supplies	5,500	
5	Prepaid insurance	2,400	
6	Store equipment	42,600	
7	Accumulated depreciation—Store equipment		$ 19,750
8	Accounts payable		14,000
9	Common stock		19,000
10	Retained earnings		20,000
11	Dividends	2,000	
12	Sales		115,800
13	Sales discounts	1,900	
14	Sales returns and allowances	2,300	
15	Cost of good sold	38,000	
16	Depreciation expense—Store equipment	0	
17	Salaries expense	27,400	
18	Insurance expense	0	
19	Rent expense	15,000	
20	Store supplies expense	0	
21	Advertising expense	9,700	
22	Totals	$188,550	$188,550

Sheet1 Sheet2 Sheet3

Rent expense and salaries expense are equally divided between selling activities and the general and administrative activities. Helix Company uses a perpetual inventory system.

Required

1. Prepare adjusting journal entries to reflect each of the following:
   a. Store supplies still available at fiscal year-end amount to $2,550.
   b. Expired insurance, an administrative expense, for the fiscal year is $1,450.
   c. Depreciation expense on store equipment, a selling expense, is $1,975 for the fiscal year.
   d. To estimate shrinkage, a physical count of ending merchandise inventory is taken. It shows $10,300 of inventory is still available at fiscal year-end.
2. Prepare a multiple-step income statement for fiscal year 2009.
3. Prepare a single-step income statement for fiscal year 2009.
4. Compute the current ratio, acid-test ratio, and gross margin ratio as of January 31, 2009.

Check (2) Gross profit, $70,900;
(3) Total expenses, $99,175; Net income, $12,425

Problem 4-4A

Computing merchandising amounts and formatting income statements

C4   P4

Rusio Company's adjusted trial balance on August 31, 2009, its fiscal year-end, follows.

	Debit	Credit
Merchandise inventory	$ 43,500	
Other (noninventory) assets	174,000	
Total liabilities		$ 50,242
Common stock		83,481
Retained earnings		58,555
Dividends	8,000	
Sales		297,540
Sales discounts	4,552	
Sales returns and allowances	19,637	
Cost of goods sold	114,571	
Sales salaries expense	40,762	
Rent expense—Selling space	13,984	
Store supplies expense	3,570	
Advertising expense	25,290	
Office salaries expense	37,192	
Rent expense—Office space	3,570	
Office supplies expense	1,190	
Totals	$489,818	$489,818

On August 31, 2008, merchandise inventory was $35,104. Supplementary records of merchandising activities for the year ended August 31, 2009, reveal the following itemized costs.

Invoice cost of merchandise purchases	$127,890
Purchase discounts received	2,685
Purchase returns and allowances	6.138
Costs of transportation-in	3,900

Required

1. Compute the company's net sales for the year.

Check   (2) $122,967;

2. Compute the company's total cost of merchandise purchased for the year.

(3) Gross profit, $158,780;
Net income, $33,222;

3. Prepare a multiple-step income statement that includes separate categories for selling expenses and for general and administrative expenses.

(4) Total expenses, $240,129

4. Prepare a single-step income statement that includes these expense categories: cost of goods sold, selling expenses, and general and administrative expenses.

Problem 4-5A

Preparing closing entries and interpreting information about discounts and returns

C4   P3

Use the data for Rusio Company in Problem 4-4A to complete the following requirements.

Required

1. Prepare closing entries as of August 31, 2009 (the perpetual inventory system is used).

Analysis Component

Check   (1) $33,222 Dr. to close
Income Summary
(3) Current-year rate, 6.6%

2. The company makes all purchases on credit, and its suppliers uniformly offer a 3% sales discount. Does it appear that the company's cash management system is accomplishing the goal of taking all available discounts? Explain.

3. In prior years, the company experienced a 4% returns and allowance rate on its sales, which means approximately 4% of its gross sales were eventually returned outright or caused the company to grant allowances to customers. How do this year's results compare to prior years' results?

Refer to the data and information in Problem 4-3A.

Required

Prepare and complete the entire 10-column work sheet for Helix Company. Follow the structure of Exhibit 4B.1 in Appendix 4B.

Problem 4-6A[B]
Preparing a work sheet for a merchandiser
P3

Prepare journal entries to record the following merchandising transactions of Yarvelle Company, which applies the perpetual inventory system. (*Hint:* It will help to identify each receivable and payable; for example, record the purchase on May 2 in Accounts Payable—Pearl.)

May 2	Purchased merchandise from Pearl Co. for $6,600 under credit terms of 3/15, n/30, FOB shipping point, invoice dated May 2.
4	Sold merchandise to Miller Co. for $1,000 under credit terms of 3/10, n/60, FOB shipping point, invoice dated May 4. The merchandise had cost $550.
5	Paid $120 cash for freight charges on the purchase of May 2.
9	Sold merchandise that had cost $1,900 for $2,300 cash.
10	Purchased merchandise from Verte Co. for $2,500 under credit terms of 3/15, n/60, FOB destination, invoice dated May 10.
12	Received a $500 credit memorandum from Verte Co. for the return of part of the merchandise purchased on May 10.
14	Received the balance due from Miller Co. for the invoice dated May 4, net of the discount.
17	Paid the balance due to Pearl Co. within the discount period.
20	Sold merchandise that cost $800 to Stephen Co. for $1,200 under credit terms of 3/15, n/60, FOB shipping point, invoice dated May 20.
22	Issued a $100 credit memorandum to Stephen Co. for an allowance on goods sold from May 20.
25	Paid Verte Co. the balance due after deducting the discount.
30	Received the balance due from Stephen Co. for the invoice dated May 20, net of discount and allowance.
31	Sold merchandise that cost $5,400 to Miller Co. for $7,100 under credit terms of 3/10, n/60, FOB shipping point, invoice dated May 31.

PROBLEM SET B

Problem 4-1B
Preparing journal entries for merchandising activities—perpetual system
P1 P2

Check May 14, Dr. Cash $970
May 17, Cr. Cash $6,402

May 30, Dr. Cash $1,067

Prepare journal entries to record the following merchandising transactions of Allou Company, which applies the perpetual inventory system. (*Hint:* It will help to identify each receivable and payable; for example, record the purchase on July 3 in Accounts Payable—Magar.)

July 3	Purchased merchandise from Magar Corp. for $4,100 under credit terms of 1/10, n/30, FOB destination, invoice dated July 3.
4	At Magar's request, Allou paid $500 cash for freight charges on the July 3 purchase, reducing the amount owed to Magar.
7	Sold merchandise to Konop Co. for $2,870 under credit terms of 2/10, n/60, FOB destination, invoice dated July 7. The merchandise had cost $2,049.
10	Purchased merchandise from Payak Corporation for $3,400 under credit terms of 1/10, n/45, FOB shipping point, invoice dated July 10. The invoice showed that at Allou's request, Payak paid the $240 shipping charges and added that amount to the bill. (*Hint:* Discounts are not applied to freight and shipping charges.)
11	Paid $120 cash for shipping charges related to the July 7 sale to Konop Co.
12	Konop returned merchandise from the July 7 sale that had cost Allou $341 and been sold for $470. The merchandise was restored to inventory.
14	After negotiations with Payak Corporation concerning problems with the merchandise purchased on July 10, Allou received a credit memorandum from Payak granting a price reduction of $500.
17	Received balance due from Konop Co. for the July 7 sale less the return on July 12.
20	Paid the amount due Payak Corporation for the July 10 purchase less the price reduction granted.
21	Sold merchandise to Vescio for $2,460 under credit terms of 1/10, n/30, FOB shipping point, invoice dated July 21. The merchandise had cost $1,707.
24	Vescio requested a price reduction on the July 21 sale because the merchandise did not meet specifications. Allou sent Vescio a credit memorandum for $360 to resolve the issue.
30	Received Vescio's cash payment for the amount due from the July 21 sale.
31	Paid Magar Corp. the amount due from the July 3 purchase.

Problem 4-2B
Preparing journal entries for merchandising activities—perpetual system
P1 P2

Check July 17, Dr. Cash $2,352
July 20, Cr. Cash $3,111

July 30, Dr. Cash $2,079

Problem 4-3B

Preparing adjusting entries and income statements; and computing gross margin, acid-test, and current ratios

A1 A2 P3 P4

The following unadjusted trial balance is prepared at fiscal year-end for Giaccio Products Company.

File Edit View Insert Format Tools Data Accounting Window Help		
GIACCIO PRODUCTS COMPANY **Unadjusted Trial Balance** **October 31, 2009**		
1	**Debit**	**Credit**
2 Cash	$ 30,150	
3 Merchandise inventory	13,000	
4 Store supplies	5,300	
5 Prepaid insurance	2,700	
6 Store equipment	42,900	
7 Accumulated depreciation—Store equipment		$ 19,900
8 Accounts payable		15,000
9 Common stock		18,000
10 Retained earnings		20,000
11 Dividends	2,050	
12 Sales		116,250
13 Sales discounts	1,950	
14 Sales returns and allowances	2,300	
15 Cost of goods sold	39,000	
16 Depreciation expense—Store equipment	0	
17 Salaries expense	26,000	
18 Insurance expense	0	
19 Rent expense	14,000	
20 Store supplies expense	0	
21 Advertising expense	9,800	
22 Totals	$ 189,150	$ 189,150
23		

Rent expense and salaries expense are equally divided between selling activities and the general and administrative activities. Giaccio Products Company uses a perpetual inventory system.

Required

1. Prepare adjusting journal entries to reflect each of the following.

   a. Store supplies still available at fiscal year-end amount to $1,650.

   b. Expired insurance, an administrative expense, for the fiscal year is $1,300.

   c. Depreciation expense on store equipment, a selling expense, is $1,990 for the fiscal year.

   d. To estimate shrinkage, a physical count of ending merchandise inventory is taken. It shows $11,600 of inventory is still available at fiscal year-end.

Check (2) Gross profit, $71,600;
(3) Total expenses, $97,140;
Net income, $14,860

2. Prepare a multiple-step income statement for fiscal year 2009.

3. Prepare a single-step income statement for fiscal year 2009.

4. Compute the current ratio, acid-test ratio, and gross margin ratio as of October 31, 2009.

Problem 4-4B

Computing merchandising amounts and formatting income statements

C1 C4 P4

Frisco Company's adjusted trial balance on March 31, 2009, its fiscal year-end, follows.

	Debit	Credit
Merchandise inventory	$ 34,500	
Other (noninventory) assets	138,000	
Total liabilities		$ 39,847
Common stock		68,670
Retained earnings		46,440
Dividends	8,000	

[continued on next page]

[continued from previous page]

Sales		235,980
Sales discounts	3,610	
Sales returns and allowances	15,574	
Cost of goods sold	91,673	
Sales salaries expense	32,329	
Rent expense—Selling space	11,091	
Store supplies expense	2,831	
Advertising expense	20,058	
Office salaries expense	29,497	
Rent expense—Office space	2,831	
Office supplies expense	943	
Totals	$390,937	$390,937

On March 31, 2008, merchandise inventory was $27,841. Supplementary records of merchandising activities for the year ended March 31, 2009, reveal the following itemized costs.

Invoice cost of merchandise purchases	$101,430
Purchase discounts received	2,130
Purchase returns and allowances	4,868
Costs of transportation-in	3,900

Required

1. Calculate the company's net sales for the year.
2. Calculate the company's total cost of merchandise purchased for the year.
3. Prepare a multiple-step income statement that includes separate categories for selling expenses and for general and administrative expenses.
4. Prepare a single-step income statement that includes these expense categories: cost of goods sold, selling expenses, and general and administrative expenses.

Check (2) $98,332;

(3) Gross profit, $125,123;
   Net income, $25,543;

(4) Total expenses, $191,253

Use the data for Frisco Company in Problem 4-4B to complete the following requirements.

Problem 4-5B
Preparing closing entries and interpreting information about discounts and returns

C4 P3

Required

1. Prepare closing entries as of March 31, 2009 (the perpetual inventory system is used).

Analysis Component

2. The company makes all purchases on credit, and its suppliers uniformly offer a 3% sales discount. Does it appear that the company's cash management system is accomplishing the goal of taking all available discounts? Explain.
3. In prior years, the company experienced a 5% returns and allowance rate on its sales, which means approximately 5% of its gross sales were eventually returned outright or caused the company to grant allowances to customers. How do this year's results compare to prior years' results?

Check (1) $25,543 Dr. to close
   Income Summary

(3) Current-year rate, 6.6%

Refer to the data and information in Problem 4-3B.

Problem 4-6B[B]
Preparing a work sheet for a merchandiser

Required

Prepare and complete the entire 10-column work sheet for Giaccio Products Company. Follow the structure of Exhibit 4B.1 in Appendix 4B.

P3

SERIAL PROBLEM

Success Systems

(This serial problem began in Chapter 1 and continues through most of the book. If previous chapter segments were not completed, the serial problem can begin at this point. It is helpful, but not necessary, to use the Working Papers that accompany the book.)

SP 4   Adriana Lopez created Success Systems on October 1, 2009. The company has been successful, and its list of customers has grown. To accommodate the growth, the accounting system is modified to set up separate accounts for each customer. The following chart of accounts includes the account number used for each account and any balance as of December 31, 2009. Lopez decided to add a fourth digit with a decimal point to the 106 account number that had been used for the single Accounts Receivable account. This change allows the company to continue using the existing chart of accounts.

No.	Account Title	Dr.	Cr.
101	Cash	$58,160	
106.1	Alex's Engineering Co.	0	
106.2	Wildcat Services	0	
106.3	Easy Leasing	0	
106.4	IFM Co.	3,000	
106.5	Liu Corp.	0	
106.6	Gomez Co.	2,668	
106.7	Delta Co.	0	
106.8	KC, Inc.	0	
106.9	Dream, Inc.	0	
119	Merchandise inventory	0	
126	Computer supplies	580	
128	Prepaid insurance	1,665	
131	Prepaid rent	825	
163	Office equipment	8,000	
164	Accumulated depreciation—Office equipment		400
167	Computer equipment	20,000	
168	Accumulated depreciation—Computer equipment		1,250
201	Accounts payable		1,100

No.	Account Title	Dr.	Cr.
210	Wages payable		500
236	Unearned computer services revenue		1,500
307	Common stock		83,000
318	Retained earnings		7,148
319	Dividends	0	
403	Computer services revenue		0
413	Sales		0
414	Sales returns and allowances	0	
415	Sales discounts	0	
502	Cost of goods sold	0	
612	Depreciation expense—Office equipment	0	
613	Depreciation expense—Computer equipment	0	
623	Wages expense	0	
637	Insurance expense	0	
640	Rent expense	0	
652	Computer supplies expense	0	
655	Advertising expense	0	
676	Mileage expense	0	
677	Miscellaneous expenses	0	
684	Repairs expense—Computer	0	

In response to requests from customers, Lopez will begin selling computer software. The company will extend credit terms of 1/10, n/30, FOB shipping point, to all customers who purchase this merchandise. However, no cash discount is available on consulting fees. Additional accounts (Nos. 119, 413, 414, 415, and 502) are added to its general ledger to accommodate the company's new merchandising activities. Also, Success Systems does not use reversing entries and, therefore, all revenue and expense accounts have zero beginning balances as of January 1, 2010. Its transactions for January through March follow:

Jan. 4   The company paid cash to Lyn Addie for five days' work at the rate of $125 per day. Four of the five days relate to wages payable that were accrued in the prior year.

5   Adriana Lopez invested an additional $25,000 cash in the company in exchange for more common stock.

7   The company purchased $5,800 of merchandise from Kansas Corp. with terms of 1/10, n/30, FOB shipping point, invoice dated January 7.

9   The company received $2,668 cash from Gomez Co. as full payment on its account.

11   The company completed a five-day project for Alex's Engineering Co. and billed it $5,500, which is the total price of $7,000 less the advance payment of $1,500.

13   The company sold merchandise with a retail value of $5,200 and a cost of $3,560 to Liu Corp., invoice dated January 13.

Check Jan. 11, Dr. Unearned
Computer Services Revenue $1,500

15 The company paid $600 cash for freight charges on the merchandise purchased on January 7.

16 The company received $4,000 cash from Delta Co. for computer services provided.

17 The company paid Kansas Corp. for the invoice dated January 7, net of the discount.

20 Liu Corp. returned $500 of defective merchandise from its invoice dated January 13. The returned merchandise, which had a $320 cost, is discarded. (The policy of Success Systems is to leave the cost of defective products in cost of goods sold.)

Check Jan. 20, No entry to Cost of Goods Sold

22 The company received the balance due from Liu Corp., net of both the discount and the credit for the returned merchandise.

24 The company returned defective merchandise to Kansas Corp. and accepted a credit against future purchases. The defective merchandise invoice cost, net of the discount, was $496.

26 The company purchased $9,000 of merchandise from Kansas Corp. with terms of 1/10, n/30, FOB destination, invoice dated January 26.

26 The company sold merchandise with a $4,640 cost for $5,800 on credit to KC, Inc., invoice dated January 26.

29 The company received a $496 credit memorandum from Kansas Corp. concerning the merchandise returned on January 24.

31 The company paid cash to Lyn Addie for 10 days' work at $125 per day.

Feb. 1 The company paid $2,475 cash to Hillside Mall for another three months' rent in advance.

3 The company paid Kansas Corp. for the balance due, net of the cash discount, less the $496 amount in the credit memorandum.

5 The company paid $600 cash to the local newspaper for an advertising insert in today's paper.

11 The company received the balance due from Alex's Engineering Co. for fees billed on January 11.

15 The company paid $4,800 cash for dividends.

23 The company sold merchandise with a $2,660 cost for $3,220 on credit to Delta Co., invoice dated February 23.

26 The company paid cash to Lyn Addie for eight days' work at $125 per day.

27 The company reimbursed Adriana Lopez for business automobile mileage (600 miles at $0.32 per mile).

Mar. 8 The company purchased $2,730 of computer supplies from Harris Office Products on credit, invoice dated March 8.

9 The company received the balance due from Delta Co. for merchandise sold on February 23.

11 The company paid $960 cash for minor repairs to the company's computer.

16 The company received $5,260 cash from Dream, Inc., for computing services provided.

19 The company paid the full amount due to Harris Office Products, consisting of amounts created on December 15 (of $1,100) and March 8.

24 The company billed Easy Leasing for $8,900 of computing services provided.

25 The company sold merchandise with a $2,002 cost for $2,800 on credit to Wildcat Services, invoice dated March 25.

30 The company sold merchandise with a $1,100 cost for $2,220 on credit to IFM Company, invoice dated March 30.

31 The company reimbursed Adriana Lopez for business automobile mileage (400 miles at $0.32 per mile).

The following additional facts are available for preparing adjustments on March 31 prior to financial statement preparation:

a. The March 31 amount of computer supplies still available totals $2,005.

b. Three more months have expired since the company purchased its annual insurance policy at a $2,220 cost for 12 months of coverage.

c. Lyn Addie has not been paid for seven days of work at the rate of $125 per day.

d. Three months have passed since any prepaid rent has been transferred to expense. The monthly rent expense is $825.

e. Depreciation on the computer equipment for January 1 through March 31 is $1,250.

f. Depreciation on the office equipment for January 1 through March 31 is $400.

g. The March 31 amount of merchandise inventory still available totals $704.

Required

1. Prepare journal entries to record each of the January through March transactions.

2. Post the journal entries in part 1 to the accounts in the company's general ledger. (*Note:* Begin with the ledger's post-closing adjusted balances as of December 31, 2009.)

Check (2) Ending balances: Cash, $77,845; Sales, $19,240;

(3) Unadj. totals, $161,198;
Adj. totals, $163,723;

(4) Net income, $18,686;

(5) Retained Earnings
(3/31/10), $21,034;

(6) Total assets, $129,909

3. Prepare a partial work sheet consisting of the first six columns (similar to the one shown in Exhibit 4B.1) that includes the unadjusted trial balance, the March 31 adjustments (*a*) through (*g*), and the adjusted trial balance. Do not prepare closing entries and do not journalize the adjustments or post them to the ledger.

4. Prepare an income statement (from the adjusted trial balance in part 3) for the three months ended March 31, 2010. Use a single-step format. List all expenses without differentiating between selling expenses and general and administrative expenses.

5. Prepare a statement of retained earnings (from the adjusted trial balance in part 3) for the three months ended March 31, 2010.

6. Prepare a classified balance sheet (from the adjusted trial balance) as of March 31, 2010.

BEYOND THE NUMBERS

REPORTING IN ACTION

C4 A1

BTN 4-1   Refer to **Best Buy**'s financial statements in Appendix A to answer the following.

Required

1. Assume that the amounts reported for inventories and cost of sales reflect items purchased in a form ready for resale. Compute the net cost of goods purchased for the fiscal year ended February 28, 2009.

2. Compute the current ratio and acid-test ratio as of February 28, 2009, and March 1, 2008. Interpret and comment on the ratio results. How does Best Buy compare to the industry average of 1.3 for the current ratio and 0.5 for the acid-test ratio?

Fast Forward

3. Access Best Buy's financial statements (form 10-K) for fiscal years ending after February 28, 2009, from its Website (**BestBuy.com**) or the SEC's EDGAR database (**www.SEC.gov**). Recompute and interpret the current ratio and acid-test ratio for these current fiscal years.

COMPARATIVE ANALYSIS

A2

BTN 4-2   Key comparative figures for both **Best Buy** and **RadioShack** follow.

($ millions)	Best Buy		RadioShack	
	Current Year	Prior Year	Current Year	Prior Year
Revenues (net sales)	$45,015	$40,023	$4,224.5	$4,251.7
Cost of sales	34,017	30,477	2,301.8	2,225.9

Required

1. Compute the dollar amount of gross margin and the gross margin ratio for the two years shown for each of these companies.

2. Which company earns more in gross margin for each dollar of net sales? How do they compare to the industry average of 26.5%?

3. Did the gross margin ratio improve or decline for these companies?

ETHICS CHALLENGE

C1 P2

BTN 4-3   Ashton Martin is a student who plans to attend approximately four professional events a year at her college. Each event necessitates a financial outlay of $100 to $200 for a new suit and accessories. After incurring a major hit to her savings for the first event, Ashton developed a different approach. She buys the suit on credit the week before the event, wears it to the event, and returns it the next week to the store for a full refund on her charge card.

Required

1. Comment on the ethics exhibited by Ashton and possible consequences of her actions.

2. How does the merchandising company account for the suits that Ashton returns?

BTN 4-4   You are the financial officer for Music Plus, a retailer that sells goods for home entertainment needs. The business owner, Jamie Madsen, recently reviewed the annual financial statements you prepared and sent you an e-mail stating that he thinks you overstated net income. He explains that although he has invested a great deal in security, he is sure shoplifting and other forms of inventory shrinkage have occurred, but he does not see any deduction for shrinkage on the income statement. The store uses a perpetual inventory system.

COMMUNICATING IN PRACTICE

C3 C4 P3

Required

Prepare a brief memorandum that responds to the owner's concerns.

BTN 4-5   Access the SEC's EDGAR database (www.SEC.gov) and obtain the March 23, 2009, filing of its fiscal 2009 10-K report (for year ended January 31, 2009) for **J. Crew Group, Inc.**

TAKING IT TO THE NET

A2 C1

Required

Prepare a table that reports the gross margin ratios for J. Crew using the revenues and cost of goods sold data from J. Crew's income statement for each of its most recent three years. Analyze and comment on the trend in its gross margin ratio.

BTN 4-6   Best Brands' general ledger and supplementary records at the end of its current period reveal the following.

TEAMWORK IN ACTION

C1 C4

Sales	$600,000	Merchandise inventory (beginning of period)	$ 98,000
Sales returns	20,000	Invoice cost of merchandise purchases	360,000
Sales discounts	13,000	Purchase discounts received	9,000
Cost of transportation-in	22,000	Purchase returns and allowances	11,000
Operating expenses	50,000	Merchandise inventory (end of period)	84,000

Required

1. *Each* member of the team is to assume responsibility for computing *one* of the following items. You are not to duplicate your teammates' work. Get any necessary amounts to compute your item from the appropriate teammate. Each member is to explain his or her computation to the team in preparation for reporting to the class.

   a. Net sales   **d.** Gross profit

   b. Total cost of merchandise purchases   **e.** Net income

   c. Cost of goods sold

2. Check your net income with the instructor. If correct, proceed to step 3.

3. Assume that a physical inventory count finds that actual ending inventory is $76,000. Discuss how this affects previously computed amounts in step 1.

Point: In teams of four, assign the same student *a* and *e*. Rotate teams for reporting on a different computation and the analysis in step 3.

BTN 4-7   Refer to the opening feature about **Heritage Link Brands**. Assume that Selena and Khary Cuffe reports current annual sales at approximately $10 million and disclose the following income statement.

Heritage Link Brands Income Statement For Year Ended January 31, 2010	
Net sales	$10,000,000
Cost of sales	6,100,000
Expenses (other than cost of sales)	2,000,000
Net income	$ 1,900,000

Selena and Khary Cuffe sell to various individuals and retailers, ranging from small shops to large chains. Assume that they currently offer credit terms of 1/15, n/60, and ship FOB destination. To improve their cash flow, they are considering changing credit terms to 3/10, n/30. In addition, they propose to change shipping terms to FOB shipping point. They expect that the increase in discount rate will increase net sales by 9%, but the gross margin ratio (and ratio of cost of sales divided by net sales) is expected to remain unchanged. They also expect that delivery expenses will be zero under this proposal; thus, expenses other than cost of sales are expected to increase only 6%.

Required

1. Prepare a forecasted income statement for the year ended January 31, 2011, based on the proposal.
2. Based on the forecasted income statement alone (from your part 1 solution), do you recommend that Selena and Khary implement the new sales policies? Explain.
3. What else should Selena and Khary consider before deciding whether or not to implement the new policies? Explain.

 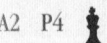
BTN 4-8   Arrange an interview (in person or by phone) with the manager of a retail shop in a mall or in the downtown area of your community. Explain to the manager that you are a student studying merchandising activities and the accounting for sales returns and sales allowances. Ask the manager what the store policy is regarding returns. Also find out if sales allowances are ever negotiated with customers. Inquire whether management perceives that customers are abusing return policies and what actions management takes to counter potential abuses. Be prepared to discuss your findings in class.

BTN 4-9   GOME (www.GOME.com.hk), **Best Buy**, and **RadioShack** are competitors in the global marketplace. Key comparative figures for each company follow.

	Net Sales	Cost of Sales
GOME*	45,889,257	41,381,223
Best Buy†	$ 45,015	$ 34,017
RadioShack†	$ 4,224.5	$ 2,301.8

* RMB thousands for GOME.

† $ millions for Best Buy and RadioShack.

Required

1. Rank the four companies (highest to lowest) based on the gross margin ratio.
2. Which of the companies uses a multiple-step income statement format? (These companies' income statements are in Appendix A.)
3. Which company's income statement is more readily usable by potential investors? Provide a brief justification for your choice.

ANSWERS TO MULTIPLE CHOICE QUIZ

1. c; Gross profit = $550,000 − $193,000 = $\underline{\$357,000}$

2. d; ($4,500 − $250) × (100% − 2%) = $\underline{\$4,165}$

3. b; Net sales = $75,000 + $320,000 − $13,700 − $6,000 = $\underline{\$375,300}$

4. b; Acid-test ratio = $37,500/$50,000 = $\underline{0.750}$

5. a; Gross margin ratio = ($675,000 − $459,000)/$675,000 = $\underline{32\%}$

5

Reporting and Analyzing Inventories

"Believe in yourself, your product and services" —Jacquelyn Tran

A Look Back

Chapter 4 focused on merchandising activities and how they are reported. We analyzed and recorded purchases and sales and explained accounting adjustments and closing for merchandisers.

A Look at This Chapter

This chapter emphasizes accounting for inventory. We describe methods for assigning costs to inventory and we explain the items and costs making up merchandise inventory. We also discuss methods of estimating and measuring inventory.

A Look Ahead

Chapter 6 focuses on internal controls and accounting for cash and cash equivalents. We explain good internal control procedures and their importance for accounting and analysis.

Scent of Success

HUNTINGTON BEACH, CA—As U.S. immigrants, Jacquelyn Tran and her family had no money and did not speak English. "They [her family] took the risk," explains Jacquelyn, in the hope of opportunity. A few years passed and Jacquelyn caught a glimpse of her future. "I saw an opportunity to take . . . the retail perfume business to the next level." She launched **Beauty Encounter (BeautyEncounter.com)** to provide perfume and beauty products to consumers.

The entrepreneurial road was rough at times. Jacquelyn struggled with inventory and sales, and had to deal with discounts, returns, and allowances. A major challenge was maintaining appropriate inventories while controlling costs. "I made plenty of mistakes," admits Jacquelyn. "I just had to throw myself in there and learn."

Learn she did. Applying modern inventory management, and trial and error, Jacquelyn learned to fill orders, collect money, and stock the right inventory. "We have something for everyone," explains Jacquelyn, and her perpetual inventory system accounts for inventory sales and purchases in real time. "It's really important for customers to be able to find products . . . [and for me] to give them what they want."

But business success requires more than good products and perpetual inventory management, insists Jacquelyn. "[It] requires a lot of patience, energy and faith." We focus on customer satisfaction, says Jacquelyn. As a result, "we have very loyal customers."

Although Jacquelyn continues to measure, monitor, and manage inventories and costs, her success and growth are pushing her to a more managerial role. "We are moving into a larger warehouse, allowing us to expand our selection," explains Jacquelyn. Her inventory procedures contribute to her success and allow her customers to know which products are hot. "I never imagined I would be where I am today," says Jacquelyn. "It is really cool."

[Sources: *Beauty Encounter Website*, January 2010; *USA Today*, April 2008; *CNN Money*, June 2005; *Inc.com*, July 2007; *Entrepreneur*, December 2007; *MyWomanOwnedBusiness.com*, August 2007]

CAP

Conceptual

C1 Identify the items making up merchandise inventory. *(p. 204)*

C2 Identify the costs of merchandise inventory. *(p. 205)*

Analytical

A1 Analyze the effects of inventory methods for both financial and tax reporting. *(p. 212)*

A2 Analyze the effects of inventory errors on current and future financial statements. *(p. 215)*

A3 Assess inventory management using both inventory turnover and days' sales in inventory. *(p. 217)*

LP5

Procedural

P1 Compute inventory in a perpetual system using the methods of specific identification, FIFO, LIFO, and weighted average. *(p. 206)*

P2 Compute the lower of cost or market amount of inventory. *(p. 213)*

P3 *Appendix 5A*—Compute inventory in a periodic system using the methods of specific identification, FIFO, LIFO, and weighted average. *(p. 223)*

P4 *Appendix 5B*—Apply both the retail inventory and gross profit methods to estimate inventory. *(p. 228)*

Merchandisers' activities include the purchasing and reselling of merchandise. We explained accounting for merchandisers in Chapter 4, including that for purchases and sales. In this chapter, we extend the study and analysis of inventory by explaining the methods used to assign costs to merchandise inventory *and* to cost of goods sold. Retailers, wholesalers, and other merchandising companies that purchase products for resale use the principles and methods described here. Understanding inventory accounting helps in the analysis and interpretation of financial statements, and in helping people run their businesses.

Reporting and Analyzing Inventories

Inventory Basics
- Determining inventory items
- Determining inventory costs
- Internal control of inventory
- Taking a physical count

Inventory Costing under a Perpetual System
- Cost flow assumptions
- Specific identification
- First-in, first-out
- Last-in, first-out
- Weighted average
- Financial statement effects

Inventory Valuation and Errors
- Inventory valuation at lower of cost or market
- Financial statement effects of inventory errors

Inventory Basics

This section identifies the items and costs making up merchandise inventory. It also describes the importance of internal controls in taking a physical count of inventory.

Determining Inventory Items

C1 Identify the items making up merchandise inventory.

Merchandise inventory includes all goods that a company owns and holds for sale. This rule holds regardless of where the goods are located when inventory is counted. Certain inventory items require special attention, including goods in transit, goods on consignment, and goods that are damaged or obsolete.

Goods in Transit Does a purchaser's inventory include goods in transit from a supplier? The answer is that if ownership has passed to the purchaser, the goods are included in the purchaser's inventory. We determine this by reviewing the shipping terms: *FOB destination* or *FOB shipping point*. If the purchaser is responsible for paying freight, ownership passes when goods are loaded on the transport vehicle. If the seller is responsible for paying freight, ownership passes when goods arrive at their destination.

Goods on Consignment Goods on consignment are goods shipped by the owner, called the **consignor**, to another party, the **consignee**. A consignee sells goods for the owner. The consignor continues to own the consigned goods and reports them in its inventory. **Upper Deck**, for instance, pays sports celebrities such as Tiger Woods to sign memorabilia, which are offered to shopping networks on consignment. Upper Deck, the consignor, must report these items in its inventory until sold.

Goods Damaged or Obsolete Damaged and obsolete (and deteriorated) goods are not counted in inventory if they cannot be sold. If these goods can be sold at a reduced price, they are included in inventory at a conservative estimate of their **net realizable value.** Net realizable value is sales price minus the cost of making the sale. The period when damage or obsolescence (or deterioration) occurs is the period when the loss in value is reported.

A wireless portable device with a two-way radio allows clerks to quickly record inventory by scanning bar codes and to instantly send and receive inventory data. It gives managers access to up-to-date information on inventory and its location.

Determining Inventory Costs

Merchandise inventory includes costs of expenditures necessary, directly or indirectly, to bring an item to a salable condition and location. This means that the cost of an inventory item includes its invoice cost minus any discount, and plus any incidental costs necessary to put it in a place and condition for sale. Incidental costs can include import duties, freight, storage, insurance, and costs incurred in an aging process (for example, aging wine or cheese).

> **C2** Identify the costs of merchandise inventory.

Accounting principles prescribe that incidental costs be added to inventory. Also, the *matching (expense recognition) principle* states that inventory costs should be recorded against revenue in the period when inventory is sold. However, some companies use the *materiality constraint (cost-to-benefit constraint)* to avoid assigning some incidental costs of acquiring merchandise to inventory. Instead, they expense them when incurred. These companies argue either that those incidental costs are immaterial or that the effort in assigning them outweighs the benefit.

Internal Controls and Taking a Physical Count

The Inventory account under a perpetual system is updated for each purchase and sale, but events can cause the Inventory account balance to differ from the actual inventory available. Such events include theft, loss, damage, and errors. Thus, nearly all companies take a *physical count of inventory* at least once each year—informally called *taking an inventory.* This often occurs at the end of a fiscal year or when inventory amounts are low. This physical count is used to adjust the Inventory account balance to the actual inventory available.

A company applies internal controls when taking a physical count of inventory that usually include the following:

- *Prenumbered inventory tickets* are prepared and distributed to the *counters*—each ticket must be accounted for.
- Counters of inventory are assigned and do not include those responsible for inventory.
- Counters confirm the validity of inventory, including its existence, amount, and quality.
- A second count is taken by a different counter.
- A manager confirms that all inventories are ticketed once, and only once.

> **Point:** The Inventory account is a controlling account for the inventory subsidiary ledger. This *subsidiary ledger* contains a separate record (units and costs) for each separate product, and it can be in electronic or paper form. Subsidiary records assist managers in planning and monitoring inventory.

Quick Check   Answers—p. 231

1. What accounting principle most guides the allocation of cost of goods available for sale between ending inventory and cost of goods sold?

2. If **Skechers** sells goods to **Target** with terms FOB shipping point, which company reports these goods in its inventory while they are in transit?

3. An art gallery purchases a painting for $11,400 on terms FOB shipping point. Additional costs in obtaining and offering the artwork for sale include $130 for transportation-in, $150 for import duties, $100 for insurance during shipment, $180 for advertising, $400 for framing, and $800 for office salaries. For computing inventory, what cost is assigned to the painting?

Inventory Costing under a Perpetual System

Accounting for inventory affects both the balance sheet and the income statement. A major goal in accounting for inventory is to properly match costs with sales. We use the *matching principle* to decide how much of the cost of the goods available for sale is deducted from sales and how much is carried forward as inventory and matched against future sales.

Video5.1

Management decisions in accounting for inventory involve the following

■ Items included in inventory and their costs.

■ Costing method (specific identification, FIFO, LIFO, or weighted average).

■ Inventory system (perpetual or periodic).

■ Use of market values or other estimates.

The first point was explained on the prior two pages. The second and third points will be addressed now. The fourth point is the focus at the end of this chapter. Decisions on these points affect the reported amounts for inventory, cost of goods sold, gross profit, income, current assets, and other accounts.

One of the most important issues in accounting for inventory is determining the per unit costs assigned to inventory items. When all units are purchased at the same unit cost, this process is simple. When identical items are purchased at different costs, however, a question arises as to which amounts to record in cost of goods sold and which amounts remain in inventory.

Four methods are commonly used to assign costs to inventory and to cost of goods sold: (1) specific identification; (2) first-in, first-out; (3) last-in, first-out; and (4) weighted average. Exhibit 5.1 shows the frequency in the use of these methods.

EXHIBIT 5.1

Frequency in Use of
Inventory Methods

Other* 4%

FIFO 46%

Weighted
Average 20%

LIFO 30%

*Includes specific identification.

Each method assumes a particular pattern for how costs flow through inventory. Each of these four methods is acceptable whether or not the actual physical flow of goods follows the cost flow assumption. Physical flow of goods depends on the type of product and the way it is stored. (Perishable goods such as fresh fruit demand that a business attempt to sell them in a first-in, first-out physical flow. Other products such as crude oil and minerals such as coal, gold, decorative stone can be sold in a last-in, first-out physical flow.) **Physical flow and cost flow need not be the same.**

Inventory Cost Flow Assumptions

This section introduces inventory cost flow assumptions. For this purpose, assume that three identical units are purchased separately at the following three dates and costs: May 1 at $45, May 3 at $65, and May 6 at $70. One unit is then sold on May 7 for $100. Exhibit 5.2 gives a visual layout of the flow of costs to either the gross profit section of the income statement or the inventory reported on the balance sheet for FIFO, LIFO, and weighted average.

(1) *FIFO assumes costs flow in the order incurred.* The unit purchased on May 1 for $45 is the earliest cost incurred—it is sent to cost of goods sold on the income statement first. The remaining two units ($65 and $70) are reported in inventory on the balance sheet.

(2) *LIFO assumes costs flow in the reverse order incurred.* The unit purchased on May 6 for $70 is the most recent cost incurred—it is sent to cost of goods sold on the income statement. The remaining two units ($45 and $65) are reported in inventory on the balance sheet.

(3) *Weighted average assumes costs flow at an average of the costs available.* The units available at the May 7 sale average $60 in cost, computed as ($45 + $65 + $70)/3. One unit's $60 average cost is sent to cost of goods sold on the income statement. The remaining two units' average costs are reported in inventory at $120 on the balance sheet.

Cost flow assumptions can markedly impact gross profit and inventory numbers. Exhibit 5.2 shows that gross profit as a percent of net sales ranges from 30% to 55% due to nothing else but the cost flow assumption.

P1 Compute inventory in a perpetual system using the methods of specific identification, FIFO, LIFO, and weighted average.

Point: It is helpful to recall the cost flow of inventory from Exhibit 4.4.

Beginning inventory	+	Net purchases

= Merchandise available for sale

| Ending inventory | + | Cost of goods sold |

The following sections on inventory costing use the perpetual system. Appendix 5A uses the periodic system. An instructor can choose to cover either one or both systems. If the perpetual system is skipped, then read Appendix 5A and return to the section (7 pages ahead) titled "Valuing Inventory at LCM and . . ."

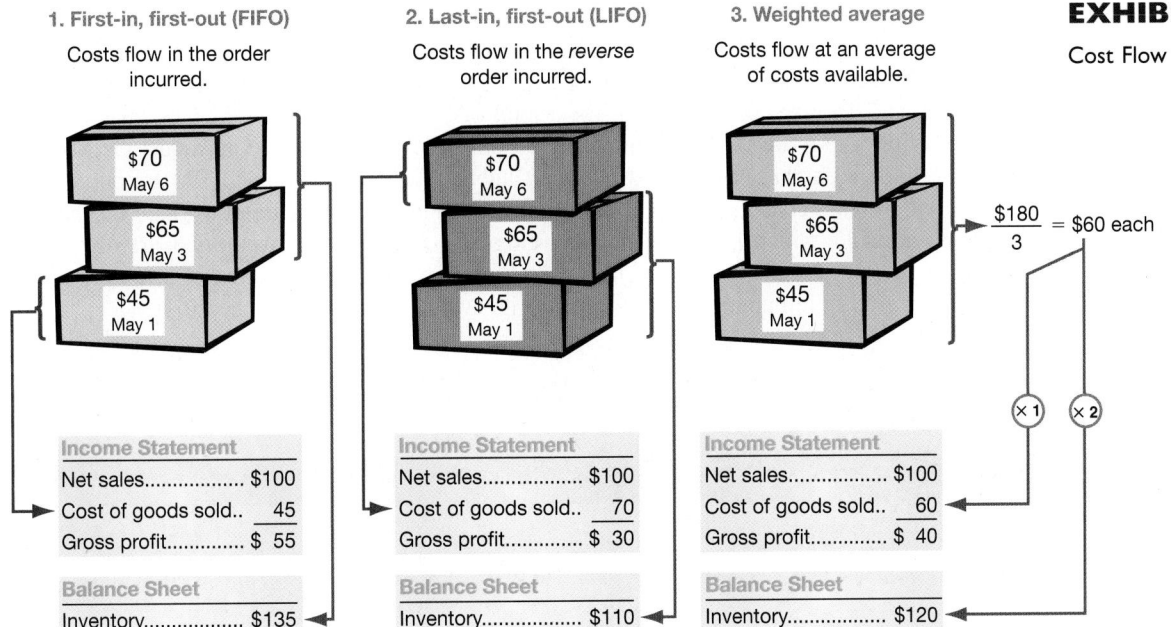

EXHIBIT 5.2

Cost Flow Assumptions

Inventory Costing Illustration

This section provides a comprehensive illustration of inventory costing methods. We use information from Trekking, a sporting goods store. Among its many products, Trekking carries one type of mountain bike whose sales are directed at resorts that provide inexpensive mountain bikes for complimentary guest use. Its customers usually purchase in amounts of 10 or more bikes. We use Trekking's data from August. Its mountain bike (unit) inventory at the beginning of August and its purchases and sales during August are shown in Exhibit 5.3. It ends August with 12 bikes remaining in inventory.

EXHIBIT 5.3

Purchases and Sales of Goods

Date	Activity	Units Acquired at Cost	Units Sold at Retail	Unit Inventory
Aug. 1	Beginning inventory	10 units @ $ 91 = $ 910		10 units
Aug. 3	Purchases	15 units @ $106 = $ 1,590		25 units
Aug. 14	Sales		20 units @ $130	5 units
Aug. 17	Purchases	20 units @ $115 = $ 2,300		25 units
Aug. 28	Purchases	10 units @ $119 = $ 1,190		35 units
Aug. 31	Sales		23 units @ $150	12 units
	Totals	55 units $5,990	43 units	

Trekking uses the perpetual inventory system, which means that its merchandise inventory account is continually updated to reflect purchases and sales. **(Appendix 5A describes the assignment of costs to inventory using a periodic system.)** Regardless of what inventory method or system is used, cost of goods available for sale must be allocated between cost of goods sold and ending inventory.

Point: The perpetual inventory system is now the most dominant system for U.S. businesses.

Point: Cost of goods sold plus ending inventory equals cost of goods available for sale.

Specific Identification

When each item in inventory can be identified with a specific purchase and invoice, we can use **specific identification** (also called *specific invoice inventory pricing*) to assign costs. We also need sales records that identify exactly which items were sold and when. Trekking's internal documents reveal the following specific unit sales:

August 14   Sold 8 bikes costing $91 each and 12 bikes costing $106 each
August 31   Sold 2 bikes costing $91 each, 3 bikes costing $106 each, 15 bikes costing $115 each, and 3 bikes costing $119 each

Applying specific identification, and using the information above and from Exhibit 5.3, we prepare Exhibit 5.4. This exhibit starts with 10 bikes at $91 each in beginning inventory. On August 3, 15 more bikes are purchased at $106 each for $1,590. Inventory available now consists of 10 bikes at $91 each and 15 bikes at $106 each, for a total of $2,500. On August 14 (see sales above), 20 bikes costing $2,000 are sold—leaving 5 bikes costing $500 in inventory. On August 17, 20 bikes costing $2,300 are purchased, and on August 28, another 10 bikes costing $1,190 are purchased, for a total of 35 bikes costing $3,990 in inventory. On August 31 (see sales above), 23 bikes costing $2,582 are sold, which leaves 12 bikes costing $1,408 in ending inventory. Carefully study this exhibit and the boxed explanations to see the flow of costs both in and out of inventory. Each unit, whether sold or remaining in inventory, has its own specific cost attached to it.

EXHIBIT 5.4

Specific Identification Computations

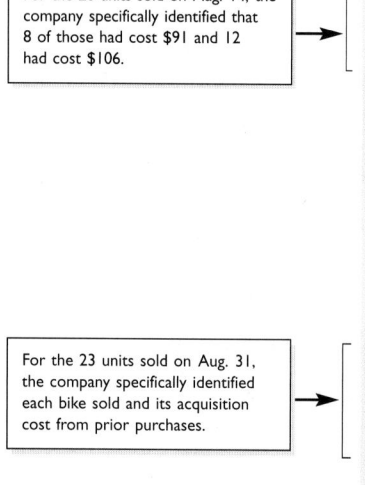

For the 20 units sold on Aug. 14, the company specifically identified that 8 of those had cost $91 and 12 had cost $106.

For the 23 units sold on Aug. 31, the company specifically identified each bike sold and its acquisition cost from prior purchases.

	"goods in"	"goods out"	"what's left"
Date	**Goods Purchased**	**Cost of Goods Sold**	**Inventory Balance**
Aug. 1	Beginning balance		10 @ $ 91 = $ 910
Aug. 3	15 @ $106 = $1,590		10 @ $ 91 } 15 @ $106 } = $2,500
Aug. 14		8 @ $ 91 = $ 728 } 12 @ $106 = $1,272 } = $2,000*	2 @ $ 91 } 3 @ $106 } = $ 500
Aug. 17	20 @ $115 = $2,300		2 @ $ 91 } 3 @ $106 } 20 @ $115 } = $2,800
Aug. 28	10 @ $119 = $1,190		2 @ $ 91 } 3 @ $106 } 20 @ $115 } 10 @ $119 } = $3,990
Aug. 31		2 @ $ 91 = $ 182 } 3 @ $106 = $ 318 } 15 @ $115 = $1,725 } 3 @ $119 = $ 357 } = $2,582*	5 @ $115 } 7 @ $119 } = $1,408
		$4,582	

* Identification of items sold (and their costs) is obtained from internal documents that track each unit from its purchase to its sale.

When using specific identification, Trekking's cost of goods sold reported on the income statement totals **$4,582**, the sum of $2,000 and $2,582 from the third column of Exhibit 5.4. Trekking's ending inventory reported on the balance sheet is **$1,408**, which is the final inventory balance from the fourth column of Exhibit 5.4.

The purchases and sales entries for Exhibit 5.4 follow (the colored boldface numbers are those impacted by the cost flow assumption).

Purchases		
Aug. 3	Merchandise Inventory	1,590	
	Accounts Payable		1,590
17	Merchandise Inventory	2,300	
	Accounts Payable		2,300
28	Merchandise Inventory	1,190	
	Accounts Payable		1,190

Sales		
Aug. 14	Accounts Receivable	2,600	
	Sales		2,600
14	Cost of Goods Sold	**2,000**	
	Merchandise Inventory		**2,000**
31	Accounts Receivable	3,450	
	Sales		3,450
31	Cost of Goods Sold	**2,582**	
	Merchandise Inventory		**2,582**

First-In, First-Out

The **first-in, first-out (FIFO)** method of assigning costs to both inventory and cost of goods sold assumes that inventory items are sold in the order acquired. When sales occur, the costs of the earliest units acquired are charged to cost of goods sold. This leaves the costs from the most recent purchases in ending inventory. Use of FIFO for computing the cost of inventory and cost of goods sold is shown in Exhibit 5.5.

Point: The "Goods Purchased" column is identical for all methods. Data are taken from Exhibit 5.3.

This exhibit starts with beginning inventory of 10 bikes at $91 each. On August 3, 15 more bikes costing $106 each are bought for $1,590. Inventory now consists of 10 bikes at $91 each and 15 bikes at $106 each, for a total of $2,500. On August 14, 20 bikes are sold—applying FIFO, the first 10 sold cost $91 each and the next 10 sold cost $106 each, for a total cost of $1,970. This leaves 5 bikes costing $106 each, or $530, in inventory. On August 17, 20 bikes costing $2,300 are purchased, and on August 28, another 10 bikes costing $1,190 are purchased, for a total of 35 bikes costing $4,020 in inventory. On August 31, 23 bikes are sold—applying FIFO, the first 5 bikes sold cost $530 and the next 18 sold cost $2,070, which leaves 12 bikes costing $1,420 in ending inventory.

EXHIBIT 5.5

FIFO Computations—Perpetual System

Date	Goods Purchased	Cost of Goods Sold	Inventory Balance
Aug. 1	Beginning balance		10 @ $91 = $ 910
Aug. 3	15 @ $106 = $1,590		10 @ $91 ⎱ = $2,500 15 @ $106 ⎰
Aug. 14		10 @ $91 = $ 910 ⎱ = $1,970 10 @ $106 = $1,060 ⎰	5 @ $106 = $ 530
Aug. 17	20 @ $115 = $2,300		5 @ $106 ⎱ = $2,830 20 @ $115 ⎰
Aug. 28	10 @ $119 = $1,190		5 @ $106 ⎱ 20 @ $115 ⎰ = $4,020 10 @ $119 ⎰
Aug. 31		5 @ $106 = $ 530 ⎱ = $2,600 18 @ $115 = $2,070 ⎰ **$4,570**	2 @ $115 ⎱ = **$1,420** 10 @ $119 ⎰

For the 20 units sold on Aug. 14, the first 10 sold are assigned the earliest cost of $91 (from beg. bal.). The next 10 sold are assigned the next earliest cost of $106.

For the 23 units sold on Aug. 31, the first 5 sold are assigned the earliest available cost of $106 (from Aug. 3 purchase). The next 18 sold are assigned the next earliest cost of $115 (from Aug. 17 purchase).

Trekking's FIFO cost of goods sold reported on its income statement (reflecting the 43 units sold) is **$4,570** ($1,970 + $2,600), and its ending inventory reported on the balance sheet (reflecting the 12 units unsold) is **$1,420**.

The purchases and sales entries for Exhibit 5.5 follow (the colored boldface numbers are those affected by the cost flow assumption).

Point: Under FIFO, a unit sold is assigned the earliest (oldest) cost from inventory. This leaves the most recent costs in ending inventory.

Purchases

Aug. 3	Merchandise Inventory	1,590	
	Accounts Payable		1,590
17	Merchandise Inventory	2,300	
	Accounts Payable		2,300
28	Merchandise Inventory	1,190	
	Accounts Payable		1,190

Sales

Aug. 14	Accounts Receivable	2,600	
	Sales		2,600
14	Cost of Goods Sold	**1,970**	
	Merchandise Inventory		**1,970**
31	Accounts Receivable	3,450	
	Sales		3,450
31	Cost of Goods Sold	**2,600**	
	Merchandise Inventory		**2,600**

Last-In, First-Out

The **last-in, first-out (LIFO)** method of assigning costs assumes that the most recent purchases are sold first. These more recent costs are charged to the goods sold, and the costs of the earliest purchases are assigned to inventory. As with other methods, LIFO is acceptable even when the physical flow of goods does not follow a last-in, first-out pattern. One appeal of LIFO is that by assigning costs from the most recent purchases to cost of goods sold, LIFO comes closest to matching current costs of goods sold with revenues (compared to FIFO or weighted average).

Exhibit 5.6 shows the LIFO computations. It starts with beginning inventory of 10 bikes at $91 each. On August 3, 15 more bikes costing $106 each are bought for $1,590. Inventory now consists of 10 bikes at $91 each and 15 bikes at $106 each, for a total of $2,500. On August 14, 20 bikes are sold—applying LIFO, the first 15 sold are from the most recent purchase costing $106 each, and the next 5 sold are from the next most recent purchase costing $91 each, for a total cost of $2,045. This leaves 5 bikes costing $91 each, or $455, in inventory. On August 17, 20 bikes costing $2,300 are purchased, and on August 28, another 10 bikes costing $1,190 are purchased, for a total of 35 bikes costing $3,945 in inventory. On August 31, 23 bikes are sold—applying LIFO, the first 10 bikes sold are from the most recent purchase costing $1,190, and the next 13 sold are from the next most recent purchase costing $1,495, which leaves 12 bikes costing $1,260 in ending inventory.

EXHIBIT 5.6

LIFO Computations—
Perpetual System

For the 20 units sold on Aug. 14, the first 15 sold are assigned the most recent cost of $106. The next 5 sold are assigned the next most recent cost of $91.

For the 23 units sold on Aug. 31, the first 10 sold are assigned the most recent cost of $119. The next 13 sold are assigned the next most recent cost of $115.

Date	Goods Purchased	Cost of Goods Sold	Inventory Balance
Aug. 1	Beginning balance		10 @ $ 91 = $ 910
Aug. 3	15 @ $106 = $1,590		10 @ $ 91 ⎫ = $ 2,500 15 @ $106 ⎭
Aug. 14		15 @ $106 = $1,590 ⎫ = $2,045 5 @ $ 91 = $ 455 ⎭	5 @ $ 91 = $ 455
Aug. 17	20 @ $115 = $2,300		5 @ $ 91 ⎫ = $ 2,755 20 @ $115 ⎭
Aug. 28	10 @ $119 = $1,190		5 @ $ 91 ⎫ 20 @ $115 ⎬ = $ 3,945 10 @ $119 ⎭
Aug. 31		10 @ $119 = $1,190 ⎫ = $2,685 13 @ $115 = $1,495 ⎭	5 @ $ 91 ⎫ = $1,260 7 @ $115 ⎭
		$4,730	

Trekking's LIFO cost of goods sold reported on the income statement is **$4,730** ($2,045 + $2,685), and its ending inventory reported on the balance sheet is **$1,260**.

The purchases and sales entries for Exhibit 5.6 follow (the colored boldface numbers are those affected by the cost flow assumption).

Purchases		
Aug. 3 Merchandise Inventory.........	1,590	
Accounts Payable		1,590
17 Merchandise Inventory.........	2,300	
Accounts Payable		2,300
28 Merchandise Inventory.........	1,190	
Accounts Payable		1,190

Sales		
Aug. 14 Accounts Receivable..........	2,600	
Sales....................		2,600
14 Cost of Goods Sold..........	**2,045**	
Merchandise Inventory		**2,045**
31 Accounts Receivable..........	3,450	
Sales....................		3,450
31 Cost of Goods Sold..........	**2,685**	
Merchandise Inventory		**2,685**

Weighted Average

The **weighted average** (also called **average cost**) method of assigning cost requires that we use the weighted average cost per unit of inventory at the time of each sale. Weighted average cost per unit at the time of each sale equals the cost of goods available for sale divided by the units available. The results using weighted average (WA) for Trekking are shown in Exhibit 5.7.

EXHIBIT 5.7

Weighted Average
Computations—Perpetual System

Date	Goods Purchased	Cost of Goods Sold	Inventory Balance
Aug. 1	Beginning balance		10 @ $ 91 = $ 910
Aug. 3	15 @ $106 = $1,590		10 @ $ 91 } = $2,500 (or $100 per unit)[a] 15 @ $106 }
Aug. 14		20 @ $100 = $2,000	5 @ $100 = $ 500 (or $100 per unit)[b]
Aug. 17	20 @ $115 = $2,300		5 @ $100 } = $2,800 (or $112 per unit)[c] 20 @ $115 }
Aug. 28	10 @ $119 = $1,190		5 @ $100 } 20 @ $115 } = $3,990 (or $114 per unit)[d] 10 @ $119 }
Aug. 31		23 @ $114 = $2,622 $4,622	12 @ $114 = $1,368 (or $114 per unit)[e]

For the 20 units sold on Aug. 14, the cost assigned is the $100 *average cost* per unit from the inventory balance column at the time of sale.

For the 23 units sold on Aug. 31, the cost assigned is the $114 *average cost* per unit from the inventory balance column at the time of sale.

[a] $100 per unit = ($2,500 inventory balance ÷ 25 units in inventory).
[b] $100 per unit = ($500 inventory balance ÷ 5 units in inventory).
[c] $112 per unit = ($2,800 inventory balance ÷ 25 units in inventory).
[d] $114 per unit = ($3,990 inventory balance ÷ 35 units in inventory).
[e] $114 per unit = ($1,368 inventory balance ÷ 12 units in inventory).

This exhibit starts with beginning inventory of 10 bikes at $91 each. On August 3, 15 more bikes costing $106 each are bought for $1,590. Inventory now consists of 10 bikes at $91 each and 15 bikes at $106 each, for a total of $2,500. The average cost per bike for that inventory is $100, computed as $2,500/(10 bikes + 15 bikes). On August 14, 20 bikes are sold—applying WA, the 20 sold are assigned the $100 average cost, for a total cost of $2,000. This leaves 5 bikes with an average cost of $100 each, or $500, in inventory. On August 17, 20 bikes costing $2,300 are purchased, and on August 28, another 10 bikes costing $1,190 are purchased, for a total of 35 bikes costing $3,990 in inventory at August 28. The average cost per bike for the August 28 inventory is $114, computed as $3,990/(5 bikes + 20 bikes + 10 bikes). On August 31, 23 bikes are sold—applying WA, the 23 sold are assigned the $114 average cost, for a total cost of $2,622. This leaves 12 bikes costing $1,368 in ending inventory.

Trekking's cost of goods sold reported on the income statement (reflecting the 43 units sold) is **$4,622** ($2,000 + $2,622), and its ending inventory reported on the balance sheet (reflecting the 12 units unsold) is **$1,368**.

The purchases and sales entries for Exhibit 5.7 follow (the colored boldface numbers are those affected by the cost flow assumption).

Point: Under weighted average, a unit sold is assigned the average cost of all items currently available for sale at the date of each sale.

	Purchases				Sales		
Aug. 3	Merchandise Inventory	1,590		Aug. 14	Accounts Receivable	2,600	
	Accounts Payable		1,590		Sales		2,600
17	Merchandise Inventory	2,300		14	Cost of Goods Sold	**2,000**	
	Accounts Payable		2,300		Merchandise Inventory		**2,000**
28	Merchandise Inventory	1,190		31	Accounts Receivable	3,450	
	Accounts Payable		1,190		Sales		3,450
				31	Cost of Goods Sold	**2,622**	
					Merchandise Inventory		**2,622**

Advances in technology have greatly reduced the cost of a perpetual inventory system. Many companies are now asking whether they can afford *not* to have a perpetual inventory system because timely access to inventory information is a competitive advantage and it can help reduce the level of inventory, which reduces costs.

Decision Insight

SOX: Inventory Control   SOX demands that companies safeguard inventory and properly report it. Safeguards include restricted access, use of authorized requisitions, security measures, and controlled environments to prevent damage. Proper accounting includes matching inventory received with purchase order terms and quality requirements, preventing misstatements, and controlling access to inventory records. A study reports that 23% of employees in purchasing and procurement observed inappropriate kickbacks or gifts from suppliers (KPMG 2009). Another 23% of employees in production witnessed fabrication of product quality results.

Financial Statement Effects of Costing Methods

A1 Analyze the effects of inventory methods for both financial and tax reporting.

When purchase prices do not change, each inventory costing method assigns the same cost amounts to inventory and to cost of goods sold. When purchase prices are different, however, the methods nearly always assign different cost amounts. We show these differences in Exhibit 5.8 using Trekking's data.

EXHIBIT 5.8

Financial Statement Effects of Inventory Costing Methods

TREKKING COMPANY For Month Ended August 31				
	Specific Identification	FIFO	LIFO	Weighted Average
Income Statement				
Sales	$6,050	$6,050	$6,050	$6,050
Cost of goods sold	4,582	4,570	4,730	4,622
Gross profit	1,468	1,480	1,320	1,428
Expenses	450	450	450	450
Income before taxes	1,018	1,030	870	978
Income tax expense (30%)	305	309	261	293
Net income	$ 713	$ 721	$ 609	$ 685
Balance Sheet				
Inventory	$1,408	$1,420	$1,260	$1,368

This exhibit reveals two important results. First, when purchase costs *regularly rise,* as in Trekking's case, the following occurs:

- FIFO assigns the lowest amount to cost of goods sold—yielding the highest gross profit and net income.
- LIFO assigns the highest amount to cost of goods sold—yielding the lowest gross profit and net income, which also yields a temporary tax advantage by postponing payment of some income tax.
- Weighted average yields results between FIFO and LIFO.
- Specific identification always yields results that depend on which units are sold.

Point: FIFO is preferred when costs are rising *and* managers have incentives to report higher income for reasons such as bonus plans, job security, and reputation.

Point: LIFO inventory is often less than the inventory's replacement cost because LIFO inventory is valued using the oldest inventory purchase costs.

Second, when costs *regularly decline,* the reverse occurs for FIFO and LIFO. Namely, FIFO gives the highest cost of goods sold—yielding the lowest gross profit and income. However, LIFO then gives the lowest cost of goods sold—yielding the highest gross profit and income.

All four inventory costing methods are acceptable. However, a company must disclose the inventory method it uses in its financial statements or notes. Each method offers certain advantages as follows:

- FIFO assigns an amount to inventory on the balance sheet that approximates its current cost; it also mimics the actual flow of goods for most businesses.
- LIFO assigns an amount to cost of goods sold on the income statement that approximates its current cost; it also better matches current costs with revenues in computing gross profit.
- Weighted average tends to smooth out erratic changes in costs.
- Specific identification exactly matches the costs of items with the revenues they generate.

Tax Effects of Costing Methods   Trekking's segment income statement in Exhibit 5.8 includes income tax expense (at a rate of 30%) because it was formed as a corporation. Since inventory costs affect net income, they have potential tax effects. Trekking gains a temporary tax advantage by using LIFO. Many companies use LIFO for this reason.

Companies can and often do use different costing methods for financial reporting and tax reporting. *The only exception is when LIFO is used for tax reporting; in this case, the IRS requires that it also be used in financial statements*—called the LIFO conformity rule.

Decision Maker

Financial Planner   One of your clients asks if the inventory account of a company using FIFO needs any "adjustments" for analysis purposes in light of recent inflation. What is your advice? Does your advice depend on changes in the costs of these inventories? [Answer—p. 230]

Consistency in Using Costing Methods

The **consistency concept** prescribes that a company use the same accounting methods period after period so that financial statements are comparable across periods—the only exception is when a change from one method to another will improve its financial reporting. The *full-disclosure principle* prescribes that the notes to the statements report this type of change, its justification, and its effect on income.

The consistency concept does *not* require a company to use one method exclusively. For example, it can use different methods to value different categories of inventory.

Decision Ethics

Inventory Manager   Your compensation as inventory manager includes a bonus plan based on gross profit. Your superior asks your opinion on changing the inventory costing method from FIFO to LIFO. Since costs are expected to continue to rise, your superior predicts that LIFO would match higher current costs against sales, thereby lowering taxable income (and gross profit). What do you recommend? [Answer—p. 230]

Quick Check   Answers—p. 231

4. Describe one advantage for each of the inventory costing methods: specific identification, FIFO, LIFO, and weighted average.
5. When costs are rising, which method reports higher net income—LIFO or FIFO?
6. When costs are rising, what effect does LIFO have on a balance sheet compared to FIFO?
7. A company takes a physical count of inventory at the end of 2009 and finds that ending inventory is understated by $10,000. Would this error cause cost of goods sold to be overstated or understated in 2009? In year 2010? If so, by how much?

Valuing Inventory at LCM and the Effects of Inventory Errors

This section examines the role of market costs in determining inventory on the balance sheet and also the financial statement effects of inventory errors.

Lower of Cost or Market

We explained how to assign costs to ending inventory and cost of goods sold using one of four costing methods (FIFO, LIFO, weighted average, or specific identification). However, *accounting principles require that inventory be reported at the market value (cost) of replacing inventory when market value is lower than cost.* Merchandise inventory is then said to be reported on the balance sheet at the **lower of cost or market (LCM).**

 P2 Compute the lower of cost or market amount of inventory.

Computing the Lower of Cost or Market   *Market* in the term *LCM* is defined as the current replacement cost of purchasing the same inventory items in the usual manner.

Video5.1

A decline in replacement cost reflects a loss of value in inventory. When the recorded cost of inventory is higher than the replacement cost, a loss is recognized. When the recorded cost is lower, no adjustment is made.

LCM is applied in one of three ways: (1) to each individual item separately, (2) to major categories of items, or (3) to the whole of inventory. The less similar the items that make up inventory, the more likely companies are to apply LCM to individual items or categories. To illustrate, we apply LCM to the ending inventory of a motorsports retailer in Exhibit 5.9.

EXHIBIT 5.9

Lower of Cost or Market Computations

Items: $140,000 is the lower of $160,000 or $140,000

Categories: $200,000 is the lower of $210,000 or $200,000

Whole: $287,000 is the lower of $295,000 or $287,000

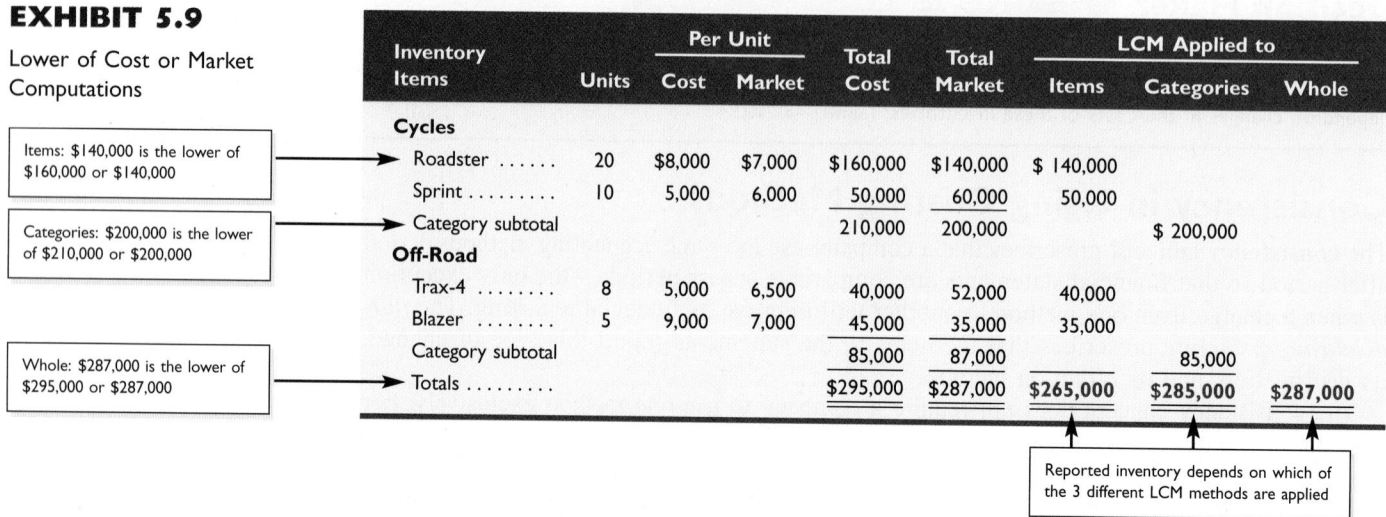

Inventory Items	Units	Per Unit Cost	Per Unit Market	Total Cost	Total Market	LCM Applied to Items	LCM Applied to Categories	LCM Applied to Whole
Cycles								
Roadster	20	$8,000	$7,000	$160,000	$140,000	$ 140,000		
Sprint	10	5,000	6,000	50,000	60,000	50,000		
Category subtotal				210,000	200,000		$ 200,000	
Off-Road								
Trax-4	8	5,000	6,500	40,000	52,000	40,000		
Blazer	5	9,000	7,000	45,000	35,000	35,000		
Category subtotal				85,000	87,000		85,000	
Totals				$295,000	$287,000	$265,000	$285,000	$287,000

Reported inventory depends on which of the 3 different LCM methods are applied

LCM to Whole   When LCM is applied to the *whole* inventory, it is determined from *one* comparison. We compare the $295,000 total from the Total Cost column with the $287,000 total from the Total Market column and select the lower amount. This yields a $287,000 reported inventory on the balance sheet.

LCM to Categories   When LCM is applied to the major *categories* of inventory, it is computed from two comparisons, where the number of comparisons equals the number of categories. First, for cycles, $200,000 is the lower of the $210,000 cost and the $200,000 market. Second, for off-road, $85,000 is the lower of the $85,000 cost and the $87,000 market. This yields a $285,000 reported inventory, computed from $200,000 for category one plus $85,000 for category two.

LCM to Items   When LCM is applied to individual *items* of inventory, the number of comparisons equals the number of items. For Roadster, $140,000 is the lower of the $160,000 cost and the $140,000 market. For Sprint, $50,000 is the lower of the $50,000 cost and the $60,000 market. For Trax-4, $40,000 is the lower of the $40,000 cost and the $52,000 market. For Blazer, $35,000 is the lower of the $45,000 cost and the $35,000 market. This yields a $265,000 reported inventory, computed from $140,000 for Roadster plus $50,000 for Sprint plus $40,000 for Trax-4 plus $35,000 for Blazer.

Point: Advances in technology encourage the individual-item approach for LCM.

Any one of these three applications of LCM is acceptable. The retailer **Best Buy** applies LCM and reports that its "merchandise inventories are recorded at the lower of average cost or market."

Recording the Lower of Cost or Market   Inventory must be adjusted downward when market is less than cost. To illustrate, if LCM is applied to the individual items of inventory in Exhibit 5.9, the Merchandise Inventory account must be adjusted from the $295,000 recorded cost down to the $265,000 market amount as follows.

Cost of Goods Sold	30,000	
Merchandise Inventory		30,000
To adjust inventory cost to market.		

Accounting rules require that inventory be adjusted to market when market is less than cost, but inventory normally cannot be written up to market when market exceeds cost. If recording inventory down to market is acceptable, why are companies not allowed to record inventory up to market? One view is that a gain from a market increase should not be realized until a sales transaction verifies the gain. However, this problem also applies when market is less than cost. A second and primary reason is the **conservatism constraint,** which prescribes the use of the less optimistic amount when more than one estimate of the amount to be received or paid exists and these estimates are about equally likely.

Financial Statement Effects of Inventory Errors

Companies must take care in both taking a physical count of inventory and in assigning a cost to it. An inventory error causes misstatements in cost of goods sold, gross profit, net income, current assets, and equity. It also causes misstatements in the next period's statements because ending inventory of one period is the beginning inventory of the next. As we consider the financial statement effects in this section, it is helpful if we recall the following *inventory relation.*

A2 Analyze the effects of inventory errors on current and future financial statements.

Beginning inventory $+$ Net purchases $-$ Ending inventory $=$ Cost of goods sold

Income Statement Effects Exhibit 5.10 shows the effects of inventory errors on key amounts in the current and next periods' income statements. Let's look at row 1 and year 1. We see that understating ending inventory overstates cost of goods sold. This can be seen from the above inventory relation where we subtract a smaller ending inventory amount in computing cost of goods sold. Then, a higher cost of goods sold yields a lower income.

To understand year 2 of row 1, remember that an understated ending inventory for year 1 becomes an understated beginning inventory for year 2. Using the above inventory relation, we see that if beginning inventory is understated, then cost of goods sold is understated (because we are starting with a smaller amount). A lower cost of goods sold yields a higher income.

Turning to overstatements, let's look at row 2 and year 1. If ending inventory is overstated, we use the inventory relation to see that cost of goods sold is understated. A lower cost of goods sold yields a higher income.

For year 2 of row 2, we again recall that an overstated ending inventory for year 1 becomes an overstated beginning inventory for year 2. If beginning inventory is overstated, we use the inventory relation to see that cost of goods sold is overstated. A higher cost of goods sold yields a lower income.

EXHIBIT 5.10

Effects of Inventory Errors on the Income Statement

	Year 1		Year 2	
Ending Inventory	**Cost of Goods Sold**	**Net Income**	**Cost of Goods Sold**	**Net Income**
Understated	Overstated	Understated	Understated	Overstated
Overstated*	Understated	Overstated	Overstated	Understated

* This error is less likely under a perpetual system because it implies more inventory than is recorded (or less shrinkage than expected). Management will normally follow up and discover and correct this error before it impacts any accounts.

To illustrate, consider an inventory error for a company with $100,000 in sales for each of the years 2008, 2009, and 2010. If this company maintains a steady $20,000 inventory level during this period and makes $60,000 in purchases in each of these years, its cost of goods sold is $60,000 and its gross profit is $40,000 each year.

Ending Inventory Understated—Year 1 Assume that this company errs in computing its 2008 ending inventory and reports $16,000 instead of the correct amount of $20,000. The effects of this error are shown in Exhibit 5.11. The $4,000 understatement of 2008 ending inventory causes a $4,000 overstatement in 2008 cost of goods sold and a $4,000 understatement in both gross profit and net income for 2008. We see that these effects match the effects predicted in Exhibit 5.10.

Ending Inventory Understated—Year 2   The 2008 understated ending inventory becomes the 2009 understated *beginning* inventory. We see in Exhibit 5.11 that this error causes an understatement in 2009 cost of goods sold and a $4,000 overstatement in both gross profit and net income for 2009.

Ending Inventory Understated—Year 3   Exhibit 5.11 shows that the 2008 ending inventory error only affects that period and the next. It does not affect 2010 results nor any period thereafter. An inventory error is said to be *self-correcting* because it always yields an offsetting error in the next period. This does not reduce the severity of inventory errors. Managers, lenders, owners, and others make important decisions from analysis of income and costs.

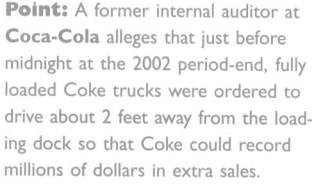

Point: A former internal auditor at **Coca-Cola** alleges that just before midnight at the 2002 period-end, fully loaded Coke trucks were ordered to drive about 2 feet away from the loading dock so that Coke could record millions of dollars in extra sales.

EXHIBIT 5.11

Effects of Inventory Errors on Three Periods' Income Statements

Correct income is $30,000 for each year

	Income Statements		
	2008	**2009**	**2010**
Sales	$100,000	$100,000	$100,000
Cost of goods sold			
Beginning inventory	$20,000	→ $16,000*	→ $20,000
Cost of goods purchased	60,000	60,000	60,000
Goods available for sale	80,000	76,000	80,000
Ending inventory	16,000*	20,000	20,000
Cost of goods sold	64,000†	56,000†	60,000
Gross profit	36,000	44,000	40,000
Expenses	10,000	10,000	10,000
Net income	$ 26,000	$ 34,000	$ 30,000

* Correct amount is $20,000.   † Correct amount is $60,000.

Example: If 2008 ending inventory in Exhibit 5.11 is overstated by $3,000 (not understated by $4,000), what is the effect on cost of goods sold, gross profit, assets, and equity? *Answer:* Cost of goods sold is understated by $3,000 in 2008 and overstated by $3,000 in 2009. Gross profit and net income are overstated in 2008 and understated in 2009. Assets and equity are overstated in 2008.

We can also do an analysis of beginning inventory errors. The income statement effects are the opposite of those for ending inventory.

Balance Sheet Effects   Balance sheet effects of an inventory error can be seen by considering the accounting equation: Assets = Liabilities + Equity. For example, understating ending inventory understates both current and total assets. An understatement in ending inventory also yields an understatement in equity because of the understatement in net income. Exhibit 5.12 shows the effects of inventory errors on the current period's balance sheet amounts. Errors in *beginning* inventory do not yield misstatements in the end-of-period balance sheet, but they do affect that current period's income statement.

EXHIBIT 5.12

Effects of Inventory Errors on Current Period's Balance Sheet

Ending Inventory	Assets	Equity
Understated	Understated	Understated
Overstated	Overstated	Overstated

Quick Check

Answers—p. 231

8. Use LCM applied separately to the following individual items to compute ending inventory.

Product	Units	Unit Recorded Cost	Unit Market Cost
A	20	$ 6	$ 5
B	40	9	8
C	10	12	15

Global View

This section discusses differences between U.S. GAAP and IFRS in the items and costs making up merchandise inventory, in the methods to assign costs to inventory, and in the methods to estimate inventory values.

Items and Costs Making Up Inventory

Both U.S. GAAP and IFRS include broad and similar guidance for the items and costs making up merchandise inventory. Specifically, under both accounting systems, merchandise inventory includes all items that a company owns and holds for sale. Further, merchandise inventory includes costs of expenditures necessary, directly or indirectly, to bring those items to a salable condition and location.

Assigning Costs to Inventory

Both U.S. GAAP and IFRS allow companies to use specific identification in assigning costs to inventory. Further, both systems allow companies to apply a *cost flow assumption*. The usual cost flow assumptions are: FIFO, Weighted Average, and LIFO. However, IFRS does not (currently) allow use of LIFO. As the convergence project progresses, this prohibition may or may not persist.

Estimating Inventory Costs

The value of inventory can change while it awaits sale to customers. That value can decrease or increase.

Decreases in Inventory Value Both U.S. GAAP and IFRS require companies to write down (reduce the cost recorded for) inventory when its value falls below the cost presently recorded. This is referred to as the *lower of cost or market* method explained in this chapter. U.S. GAAP prohibits any later increase in the recorded value of that inventory even if that decline in value is reversed through value increases in later periods. However, IFRS allows reversals of those write downs up to the original acquisition cost. For example, if **Best Buy** wrote down its 2010 inventory from $995 million to $950 million, it could not reverse this in future periods even if its value increased to more than $995 million. However, if Best Buy applied IFRS, it could reverse that previous loss. (Another difference is that value refers to *replacement cost* under U.S. GAAP, but *net realizable value* under IFRS.)

Increases in Inventory Value Neither U.S. GAAP nor IFRS allow inventory to be adjusted upward beyond the original cost. (One exception is that IFRS requires agricultural assets such as animals, forests, and plants to be measured at fair value less point-of-sale costs.)

GOME provides the following description of its inventory valuation procedures:

> Inventories comprise merchandise purchased for resale . . . and are stated at the lower of cost and net realisable value. Cost is determined on the first-in, first-out basis. The net realisable value is determined based on the estimated selling prices less any estimated costs to be incurred to disposal.

Inventory Turnover and Days' Sales in Inventory | Decision Analysis

Inventory Turnover

Earlier chapters described two important ratios useful in evaluating a company's short-term liquidity: current ratio and acid-test ratio. A merchandiser's ability to pay its short-term obligations also depends on how quickly it sells its merchandise inventory. **Inventory turnover,** also called *merchandise inventory turnover,* is one ratio used to assess this and is defined in Exhibit 5.13.

A3   Assess inventory management using both inventory turnover and days' sales in inventory.

$$\text{Inventory turnover} = \frac{\text{Cost of goods sold}}{\text{Average inventory}}$$

EXHIBIT 5.13

Inventory Turnover

This ratio reveals how many *times* a company turns over (sells) its inventory during a period. If a company's inventory greatly varies within a year, average inventory amounts can be computed from interim periods such as quarters or months.

Users apply inventory turnover to help analyze short-term liquidity and to assess whether management is doing a good job controlling the amount of inventory available. A low ratio compared to that of competitors suggests inefficient use of assets. The company may be holding more inventory than it needs to support its sales volume. Similarly, a very high ratio compared to that of competitors suggests inventory might be too low. This can cause lost sales if customers must back-order merchandise. Inventory turnover has no simple rule except to say *a high ratio is preferable provided inventory is adequate to meet demand.*

Days' Sales in Inventory

To better interpret inventory turnover, many users measure the adequacy of inventory to meet sales demand. **Days' sales in inventory,** also called *days' stock on hand,* is a ratio that reveals how much inventory is available in terms of the number of days' sales. It can be interpreted as the number of days one can sell from inventory if no new items are purchased. This ratio is often viewed as a measure of the buffer against out-of-stock inventory and is useful in evaluating liquidity of inventory. It is defined in Exhibit 5.14.

EXHIBIT 5.14

Days' Sales in Inventory

$$\text{Days' sales in inventory} = \frac{\text{Ending inventory}}{\text{Cost of goods sold}} \times 365$$

Days' sales in inventory focuses on ending inventory and it estimates how many days it will take to convert inventory at the end of a period into accounts receivable or cash. Days' sales in inventory focuses on *ending* inventory whereas inventory turnover focuses on *average* inventory.

Decision Insight

Dell-ocity   From its roots in a college dorm room, **Dell** now sells over 50 million dollars' worth of computers each day from its Website. The speed of Web technology has allowed Dell to slash inventories. Dell's inventory turnover is 88 and its days' sales in inventory is 5 days. Michael Dell asserts, "Speed is everything in this business."

Analysis of Inventory Management

Inventory management is a major emphasis for merchandisers. They must both plan and control inventory purchases and sales. **Toys "R" Us** is one of those merchandisers. Its inventory in fiscal year 2009 was $1,781 million. This inventory constituted 59% of its current assets and 21% of its total assets. We apply the analysis tools in this section to Toys "R" Us, as shown in Exhibit 5.15—also see margin graph.

EXHIBIT 5.15

Inventory Turnover and Days' Sales in Inventory for Toys "R" Us

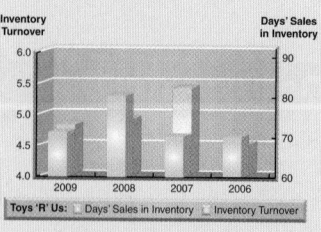

($ millions)	2009	2008	2007	2006
Cost of goods sold	$8,976	$8,987	$8,638	$7,652
Ending inventory	$1,781	$1,998	$1,690	$1,488
Inventory turnover	4.8 times	4.9 times	5.4 times	4.5 times
Industry inventory turnover	3.2 times	3.4 times	3.0 times	2.8 times
Days' sales in inventory	72 days	81 days	71 days	71 days
Industry days' sales in inventory	124 days	135 days	129 days	135 days

Its 2009 inventory turnover of 4.8 times means that Toys "R" Us turns over its inventory 4.8 times per year, or once every 76 days (365 days ÷ 4.8). We prefer inventory turnover to be high provided inventory is not out of stock and the company is not losing customers. The second metric, the 2009 days' sales in inventory of 72 days, reveals that it is carrying 72 days of sales in inventory. This inventory buffer seems more than adequate. Toys "R" Us would benefit from further management efforts to increase inventory turnover and reduce inventory levels.

Decision Maker

Entrepreneur Analysis of your retail store yields an inventory turnover of 5.0 and a days' sales in inventory of 73 days. The industry norm for inventory turnover is 4.4 and for days' sales in inventory is 74 days. What is your assessment of inventory management? [Answer—p. 230]

Frank and Ernest used with the permission of the Thaves and the Cartoonist Group. All rights reserved.

Demonstration Problem

Craig Company uses a perpetual inventory system for its one product. Its beginning inventory, purchases, and sales during calendar year 2009 follow.

Date	Activity	Units Acquired at Cost	Units Sold at Retail	Unit Inventory
Jan. 1	Beg. Inventory ..	400 units @ $14 = $ 5,600		400 units
Jan. 15	Sale		200 units @ $30	200 units
March 10	Purchase	200 units @ $15 = $ 3,000		400 units
April 1	Sale		200 units @ $30	200 units
May 9	Purchase	300 units @ $16 = $ 4,800		500 units
Sept. 22	Purchase	250 units @ $20 = $ 5,000		750 units
Nov. 1	Sale		300 units @ $35	450 units
Nov. 28	Purchase	100 units @ $21 = $ 2,100		550 units
	Totals	1,250 units $20,500	700 units	

Additional tracking data for specific identification: (1) January 15 sale—200 units @ $14, (2) April 1 sale—200 units @ $15, and (3) November 1 sale—200 units @ $14 and 100 units @ $20.

Required

1. Calculate the cost of goods available for sale.
2. Apply the four different methods of inventory costing (FIFO, LIFO, weighted average, and specific identification) to calculate ending inventory and cost of goods sold under each method.
3. Compute gross profit earned by the company for each of the four costing methods in part 2. Also, report the inventory amount reported on the balance sheet for each of the four methods.
4. In preparing financial statements for year 2009, the financial officer was instructed to use FIFO but failed to do so and instead computed cost of goods sold according to LIFO. Determine the impact on year 2009's income from the error. Also determine the effect of this error on year 2010's income. Assume no income taxes.
5. Management wants a report that shows how changing from FIFO to another method would change net income. Prepare a table showing (1) the cost of goods sold amount under each of the four methods, (2) the amount by which each cost of goods sold total is different from the FIFO cost of goods sold, and (3) the effect on net income if another method is used instead of FIFO.

Planning the Solution

- Compute cost of goods available for sale by multiplying the units of beginning inventory and each purchase by their unit costs to determine the total cost of goods available for sale.
- Prepare a perpetual FIFO table starting with beginning inventory and showing how inventory changes after each purchase and after each sale (see Exhibit 5.5).
- Prepare a perpetual LIFO table starting with beginning inventory and showing how inventory changes after each purchase and after each sale (see Exhibit 5.6).
- Make a table of purchases and sales recalculating the average cost of inventory prior to each sale to arrive at the weighted average cost of ending inventory. Total the average costs associated with each sale to determine cost of goods sold (see Exhibit 5.7).
- Prepare a table showing the computation of cost of goods sold and ending inventory using the specific identification method (see Exhibit 5.4).
- Compare the year-end 2009 inventory amounts under FIFO and LIFO to determine the misstatement of year 2009 income that results from using LIFO. The errors for year 2009 and 2010 are equal in amount but opposite in effect.
- Create a table showing cost of goods sold under each method and how net income would differ from FIFO net income if an alternate method is adopted.

Solution to Demonstration Problem

1. Cost of goods available for sale (this amount is the same for all methods).

Date		Units	Unit Cost	Cost
Jan. 1	Beg. Inventory	400	$14	$ 5,600
March 10	Purchase	200	15	3,000
May 9	Purchase	300	16	4,800
Sept. 22	Purchase	250	20	5,000
Nov. 28	Purchase	100	21	2,100
Total goods available for sale		1,250		$20,500

2a. FIFO perpetual method.

Date	Goods Purchased	Cost of Goods Sold	Inventory Balance
Jan. 1	Beginning balance		400 @ $14 = $ 5,600
Jan. 15		200 @ $14 = $2,800	200 @ $14 = $ 2,800
Mar. 10	200 @ $15 = $3,000		200 @ $14 200 @ $15 } = $ 5,800
April 1		200 @ $14 = $2,800	200 @ $15 = $ 3,000
May 9	300 @ $16 = $4,800		200 @ $15 300 @ $16 } = $ 7,800
Sept. 22	250 @ $20 = $5,000		200 @ $15 300 @ $16 250 @ $20 } = $12,800
Nov. 1		200 @ $15 = $3,000 100 @ $16 = $1,600	200 @ $16 250 @ $20 } = $ 8,200
Nov. 28	100 @ $21 = $2,100		200 @ $16 250 @ $20 100 @ $21 } = $10,300
Total cost of goods sold		**$10,200**	

Note to students: **In a classroom situation,** once we compute cost of goods available for sale, we can compute the amount for either cost of goods sold or ending inventory—it is a matter of preference. **In practice,** the costs of items sold are identified as sales are made and immediately transferred from the inventory account to the cost of goods sold account. The previous solution showing the line-by-line approach illustrates actual application in practice. The following alternate solutions illustrate that, once the concepts are understood, other solution approaches are available. Although this is only shown for FIFO, it could be shown for all methods.

Alternate Methods to Compute FIFO Perpetual Numbers

[FIFO Alternate No. 1: Computing cost of goods sold first]

Cost of goods available for sale (from part 1)			$ 20,500
Cost of goods sold			
Jan. 15	Sold (200 @ $14)	$2,800	
April 1	Sold (200 @ $14)	2,800	
Nov. 1	Sold (200 @ $15 and 100 @ $16)	4,600	10,200
Ending inventory			$10,300

[FIFO Alternate No. 2: Computing ending inventory first]

Cost of goods available for sale (from part 1)			$ 20,500
Ending inventory*			
Nov. 28	Purchase (100 @ $21)	$2,100	
Sept. 22	Purchase (250 @ $20)	5,000	
May 9	Purchase (200 @ $16)	3,200	
Ending inventory			10,300
Cost of goods sold			$10,200

* Since FIFO assumes that the earlier costs are the first to flow out, we determine ending inventory by assigning the most recent costs to the remaining items.

2b. LIFO perpetual method.

Date	Goods Purchased	Cost of Goods Sold	Inventory Balance
Jan. 1	Beginning balance		400 @ $14 = $ 5,600
Jan. 15		200 @ $14 = $2,800	200 @ $14 = $ 2,800
Mar. 10	200 @ $15 = $3,000		200 @ $14 ⎱ 200 @ $15 ⎰ = $ 5,800
April 1		200 @ $15 = $3,000	200 @ $14 = $ 2,800
May 9	300 @ $16 = $4,800		200 @ $14 ⎱ 300 @ $16 ⎰ = $ 7,600
Sept. 22	250 @ $20 = $5,000		200 @ $14 ⎱ 300 @ $16 ⎬ = $12,600 250 @ $20 ⎰
Nov. 1		250 @ $20 = $5,000 50 @ $16 = $ 800	200 @ $14 ⎱ 250 @ $16 ⎰ = $ 6,800
Nov. 28	100 @ $21 = $2,100		200 @ $14 ⎱ 250 @ $16 ⎬ = $ 8,900 100 @ $21 ⎰
	Total cost of goods sold	$11,600	

2c. Weighted average perpetual method.

Date	Goods Purchased	Cost of Goods Sold	Inventory Balance
Jan. 1	Beginning balance		400 @ $14 = $ 5,600
Jan. 15		200 @ $14 = $2,800	200 @ $14 = $ 2,800
Mar. 10	200 @ $15 = $3,000		200 @ $14 200 @ $15 } = $ 5,800 (avg. cost is $14.5)
April 1		200 @ $14.5 = $2,900	200 @ $14.5 = $ 2,900
May 9	300 @ $16 = $4,800		200 @ $14.5 300 @ $16 } = $ 7,700 (avg. cost is $15.4)
Sept. 22	250 @ $20 = $5,000		200 @ $14.5 300 @ $16 } = $ 12,700 250 @ $20 (avg. cost is $16.93)
Nov. 1		300 @ $16.93 = $5,079	450 @ $16.93 = $ 7,618.5
Nov. 28	100 @ $21 = $2,100		450 @ $16.93 100 @ $21 } = **$9,718.5**
Total cost of goods sold*		**$10,779**	

* The cost of goods sold ($10,779) plus ending inventory ($9,718.5) is $2.5 less than the cost of goods available for sale ($20,500) due to rounding.

2d. Specific identification method.

Date	Goods Purchased	Cost of Goods Sold	Inventory Balance
Jan. 1	Beginning balance		400 @ $14 = $ 5,600
Jan. 15		200 @ $14 = $2,800	200 @ $14 = $ 2,800
Mar. 10	200 @ $15 = $3,000		200 @ $14 200 @ $15 } = $ 5,800
April 1		200 @ $15 = $3,000	200 @ $14 = $ 2,800
May 9	300 @ $16 = $4,800		200 @ $14 300 @ $16 } = $ 7,600
Sept. 22	250 @ $20 = $5,000		200 @ $14 300 @ $16 } = $12,600 250 @ $20
Nov. 1		200 @ $14 = $2,800 100 @ $20 = $2,000	300 @ $16 150 @ $20 } = $ 7,800
Nov. 28	100 @ $21 = $2,100		300 @ $16 150 @ $20 } = **$ 9,900** 100 @ $21
Total cost of goods sold		**$10,600**	

3.

	FIFO	LIFO	Weighted Average	Specific Identification
Income Statement				
Sales*	$ 22,500	$22,500	$ 22,500	$22,500
Cost of goods sold	10,200	11,600	10,779	10,600
Gross profit	$ 12,300	$10,900	$ 11,721	$11,900
Balance Sheet				
Inventory	$10,300	$ 8,900	$9,718.5	$ 9,900

* Sales = (200 units × $30) + (200 units × $30) + (300 units × $35) = $22,500

4. Mistakenly using LIFO when FIFO should have been used overstates cost of goods sold in year 2009 by $1,400, which is the difference between the FIFO and LIFO amounts of ending inventory. It understates income in 2009 by $1,400. In year 2010, income is overstated by $1,400 because of the understatement in beginning inventory.

5. Analysis of the effects of alternative inventory methods.

	Cost of Goods Sold	Difference from FIFO Cost of Goods Sold	Effect on Net Income if Adopted Instead of FIFO
FIFO	$10,200	—	—
LIFO	11,600	+$1,400	$1,400 lower
Weighted average	10,779	+ 579	579 lower
Specific identification	10,600	+ 400	400 lower

Inventory Costing Under a Periodic System

5A

The basic aim of the periodic system and the perpetual system is the same: to assign costs to inventory and cost of goods sold. The same four methods are used to assign costs under both systems: specific identification; first-in, first-out; last-in, first-out; and weighted average. We use information from Trekking to show how to assign costs using these four methods with a periodic system. Data for sales and purchases are in Exhibit 5A.1. Also, recall that we explained the accounting entries under a periodic system in Appendix 4A.

 **P3** Compute inventory in a periodic system using the methods of specific identification, FIFO, LIFO, and weighted average.

EXHIBIT 5A.1

Purchases and Sales of Goods

Date	Activity	Units Acquired at Cost	Units Sold at Retail	Unit Inventory
Aug. 1	Beginning inventory	10 units @ $ 91 = $ 910		10 units
Aug. 3	Purchases	15 units @ $106 = $ 1,590		25 units
Aug. 14	Sales		20 units @ $130	5 units
Aug. 17	Purchases	20 units @ $115 = $ 2,300		25 units
Aug. 28	Purchases	10 units @ $119 = $ 1,190		35 units
Aug. 31	Sales		23 units @ $150	12 units
	Totals	55 units $5,990	43 units	

Specific Identification

We use the above sales and purchases information and the specific identification method to assign costs to ending inventory and units sold. Trekking's internal data reveal the following specific unit sales:

August 14   Sold 8 bikes costing $91 each and 12 bikes costing $106 each
August 31   Sold 2 bikes costing $91 each, 3 bikes costing $106 each, 15 bikes costing $115 each, and 3 bikes costing $119 each

Applying specific identification and using the information above, we prepare Exhibit 5A.2. This exhibit starts with 10 bikes at $91 each in beginning inventory. On August 3, 15 more bikes are purchased at $106 each for $1,590. Inventory available now consists of 10 bikes at $91 each and 15 bikes at $106 each, for a total of $2,500. On August 14 (see specific sales data above), 20 bikes costing $2,000 are sold—leaving 5 bikes costing $500 in inventory. On August 17, 20 bikes costing $2,300 are purchased, and on August 28, another 10 bikes costing $1,190 are purchased, for a total of 35 bikes costing $3,990 in inventory. On August 31 (see specific sales above), 23 bikes costing $2,582 are sold, which leaves 12 bikes costing $1,408 in ending inventory. Carefully study Exhibit 5A.2 to see the flow of costs both in and out of inventory. Each unit, whether sold or remaining in inventory, has its own specific cost attached to it.

EXHIBIT 5A.2

Specific Identification Computations

For the 20 units sold on Aug. 14, the company specifically identified that 8 of those had cost $91 and 12 had cost $106.

For the 23 units sold on Aug. 31, the company specifically identified each bike sold and its acquisition cost from prior purchases.

Date	Goods Purchased	Cost of Goods Sold	Inventory Balance
Aug. 1	Beginning balance		10 @ $ 91 = $ 910
Aug. 3	15 @ $106 = $1,590		10 @ $ 91 } 15 @ $106 } = $2,500
Aug. 14		8 @ $ 91 = $ 728 } 12 @ $106 = $1,272 } = $2,000*	2 @ $ 91 } 3 @ $106 } = $ 500
Aug. 17	20 @ $115 = $2,300		2 @ $ 91 } 3 @ $106 } 20 @ $115 } = $2,800
Aug. 28	10 @ $119 = $1,190		2 @ $ 91 } 3 @ $106 } 20 @ $115 } 10 @ $119 } = $3,990
Aug. 31		2 @ $ 91 = $ 182 } 3 @ $106 = $ 318 } 15 @ $115 = $1,725 } 3 @ $119 = $ 357 } = $2,582*	5 @ $115 } 7 @ $119 } = $1,408
		$4,582	

* Identification of items sold (and their costs) is obtained from internal documents that track each unit from its purchase to its sale.

Point: The assignment of costs to the goods sold and to inventory using specific identification is the same for both the perpetual and periodic systems.

When using specific identification, Trekking's cost of goods sold reported on the income statement totals **$4,582**, the sum of $2,000 and $2,582 from the third column of Exhibit 5A.2. Trekking's ending inventory reported on the balance sheet is **$1,408**, which is the final inventory balance from the fourth column. The purchases and sales entries for Exhibit 5A.2 follow (the colored boldface numbers are those affected by the cost flow assumption).

Purchases

Aug. 3	Purchases	1,590	
	Accounts Payable		1,590
17	Purchases	2,300	
	Accounts Payable		2,300
28	Purchases	1,190	
	Accounts Payable		1,190

Sales

Aug. 14	Accounts Receivable	2,600	
	Sales...................		2,600
31	Accounts Receivable	3,450	
	Sales...................		3,450

Adjusting Entry

31	Merchandise Inventory	1,408	
	Income Summary		498
	Merchandise Inventory....		910

First-In, First-Out

The first-in, first-out (FIFO) method of assigning costs to inventory assumes that inventory items are sold in the order acquired. When sales occur, the costs of the earliest units acquired are charged to cost of goods sold. This leaves the costs from the most recent purchases in ending inventory. Use of FIFO for computing the cost of inventory and cost of goods sold is shown in Exhibit 5A.3.

This exhibit starts with computing $5,990 in total units available for sale—this is given to us at the start of this appendix. Applying FIFO, we know that the 12 units in ending inventory will be reported at the cost of the most recent 12 purchases. Reviewing purchases in reverse order, we assign costs to the 12 bikes in ending inventory as follows: $119 cost to 10 bikes and $115 cost to 2 bikes. This yields 12 bikes costing $1,420 in ending inventory. We then subtract this $1,420 in ending inventory from $5,990 in cost of goods available to get $4,570 in cost of goods sold.

Total cost of 55 units available for sale (from Exhibit 5A.1)		$5,990
Less ending inventory priced using FIFO		
10 units from August 28 purchase at $119 each	$1,190	
2 units from August 17 purchase at $115 each	230	
Ending inventory		1,420
Cost of goods sold		$4,570

EXHIBIT 5A.3

FIFO Computations— Periodic System

> Exhibit 5A.1 shows that the 12 units in ending inventory consist of 10 units from the latest purchase on Aug. 28 and 2 units from the next latest purchase on Aug. 17.

Trekking's ending inventory reported on the balance sheet is **$1,420**, and its cost of goods sold reported on the income statement is **$4,570**. These amounts are the same as those computed using the perpetual system. This always occurs because the most recent purchases are in ending inventory under both systems. The purchases and sales entries for Exhibit 5A.3 follow (the colored boldface numbers are those affected by the cost flow assumption).

Point: The assignment of costs to the goods sold and to inventory using FIFO is the same for both the perpetual and periodic systems.

Purchases			
Aug. 3	Purchases.	1,590	
	Accounts Payable		1,590
17	Purchases.	2,300	
	Accounts Payable		2,300
28	Purchases.	1,190	
	Accounts Payable		1,190

Sales			
Aug. 14	Accounts Receivable	2,600	
	Sales		2,600
31	Accounts Receivable	3,450	
	Sales		3,450
	Adjusting Entry		
31	Merchandise Inventory.	**1,420**	
	Income Summary		510
	Merchandise Inventory		910

Last-In, First-Out

The last-in, first-out (LIFO) method of assigning costs assumes that the most recent purchases are sold first. These more recent costs are charged to the goods sold, and the costs of the earliest purchases are assigned to inventory. LIFO results in costs of the most recent purchases being assigned to cost of goods sold, which means that LIFO comes close to matching current costs of goods sold with revenues. Use of LIFO for computing cost of inventory and cost of goods sold is shown in Exhibit 5A.4.

This exhibit starts with computing $5,990 in total units available for sale—this is given to us at the start of this appendix. Applying LIFO, we know that the 12 units in ending inventory will be reported at the cost of the earliest 12 purchases. Reviewing the earliest purchases in order, we assign costs to the 12 bikes in ending inventory as follows: $91 cost to 10 bikes and $106 cost to 2 bikes. This yields 12 bikes costing $1,122 in ending inventory. We then subtract this $1,122 in ending inventory from $5,990 in cost of goods available to get $4,868 in cost of goods sold.

Total cost of 55 units available for sale (from Exhibit 5A.1)		$5,990
Less ending inventory priced using LIFO		
10 units in beginning inventory at $91 each	$910	
2 units from August 3 purchase at $106 each	212	
Ending inventory		1,122
Cost of goods sold		$4,868

EXHIBIT 5A.4

LIFO Computations— Periodic System

> Exhibit 5A.1 shows that the 12 units in ending inventory consist of 10 units from the earliest purchase (beg. inv.) and 2 units from the next earliest purchase on Aug. 3.

Trekking's ending inventory reported on the balance sheet is **$1,122**, and its cost of goods sold reported on the income statement is **$4,868**. When LIFO is used with the periodic system, cost of goods sold is assigned costs from the most recent purchases for the period. With a perpetual system, cost of goods sold is assigned costs from the most recent purchases at the point of *each sale*. The purchases and sales entries for Exhibit 5A.4 follow (the colored boldface numbers are those affected by the cost flow assumption).

Purchases			**Sales**		
Aug. 3 Purchases	1,590		Aug. 14 Accounts Receivable	2,600	
Accounts Payable		1,590	Sales		2,600
17 Purchases	2,300		31 Accounts Receivable	3,450	
Accounts Payable		2,300	Sales		3,450
28 Purchases	1,190		**Adjusting Entry**		
Accounts Payable		1,190	31 Merchandise Inventory	1,122	
			Income Summary		212
			Merchandise Inventory		910

Weighted Average

The **weighted average, WA,** (also called **average cost**) method of assigning cost requires that we use the average cost per unit of inventory at the end of the period. Weighted average cost per unit equals the cost of goods available for sale divided by the units available. The weighted average method of assigning cost involves three important steps. The first two steps are shown in Exhibit 5A.5. First, multiply the per unit cost for beginning inventory and each particular purchase by the corresponding number of units (from Exhibit 5A.1). Second, add these amounts and divide by the total number of units available for sale to find the weighted average cost per unit.

EXHIBIT 5A.5

Weighted Average Cost per Unit

Example: In Exhibit 5A.5, if 5 more units had been purchased at $120 each, what would be the weighted average cost per unit?
Answer: $109.83 ($6,590/60)

Step 1:	10 units @ $ 91 = $ 910	
	15 units @ $106 = 1,590	
	20 units @ $115 = 2,300	
	10 units @ $119 = 1,190	
	55 $5,990	
Step 2:	$5,990/55 units = $108.91 weighted average cost per unit	

The third step is to use the weighted average cost per unit to assign costs to inventory and to the units sold as shown in Exhibit 5A.6.

EXHIBIT 5A.6

Weighted Average Computations—Periodic

Step 3:	Total cost of 55 units available for sale (from Exhibit 5A.1)	$ 5,990
	Less **ending inventory** priced on a weighted average cost basis: 12 units at $108.91 each (from Exhibit 5A.5)	1,307
	Cost of goods sold	$4,683

Point: Weighted average usually yields different results for the perpetual and the periodic systems because under a perpetual system it recomputes the per unit cost prior to each sale, whereas under a periodic system, the per unit cost is computed only at the end of a period.

Trekking's ending inventory reported on the balance sheet is **$1,307**, and its cost of goods sold reported on the income statement is **$4,683** when using the weighted average (periodic) method. The purchases and sales entries for Exhibit 5A.6 follow (the colored boldface numbers are those affected by the cost flow assumption).

Purchases			**Sales**		
Aug. 3 Purchases	1,590		Aug. 14 Accounts Receivable	2,600	
Accounts Payable		1,590	Sales		2,600
17 Purchases	2,300		31 Accounts Receivable	3,450	
Accounts Payable		2,300	Sales		3,450
28 Purchases	1,190		**Adjusting Entry**		
Accounts Payable		1,190	31 Merchandise Inventory	1,307	
			Income Summary		397
			Merchandise Inventory		910

Financial Statement Effects

When purchase prices do not change, each inventory costing method assigns the same cost amounts to inventory and to cost of goods sold. When purchase prices are different, however, the methods nearly always assign different cost amounts. We show these differences in Exhibit 5A.7 using Trekking's data.

Point: LIFO inventory is often less than the inventory's replacement cost because LIFO inventory is valued using the oldest inventory purchase costs.

EXHIBIT 5A.7

Financial Statement Effects of Inventory Costing Methods

TREKKING COMPANY For Month Ended August 31				
	Specific Identification	FIFO	LIFO	Weighted Average
Income Statement				
Sales	$ 6,050	$ 6,050	$ 6,050	$ 6,050
Cost of goods sold	4,582	4,570	4,868	4,683
Gross profit	1,468	1,480	1,182	1,367
Expenses	450	450	450	450
Income before taxes	1,018	1,030	732	917
Income tax expense (30%)	305	309	220	275
Net income	$ 713	$ 721	$ 512	$ 642
Balance Sheet				
Inventory	$1,408	$1,420	$1,122	$1,307

This exhibit reveals two important results. First, when purchase costs *regularly rise,* as in Trekking's case, observe the following:

■ FIFO assigns the lowest amount to cost of goods sold—yielding the highest gross profit and net income.

■ LIFO assigns the highest amount to cost of goods sold—yielding the lowest gross profit and net income, which also yields a temporary tax advantage by postponing payment of some income tax.

■ Weighted average yields results between FIFO and LIFO.

■ Specific identification always yields results that depend on which units are sold.

Second, when costs *regularly decline,* the reverse occurs for FIFO and LIFO. FIFO gives the highest cost of goods sold—yielding the lowest gross profit and income. And, LIFO gives the lowest cost of goods sold—yielding the highest gross profit and income.

All four inventory costing methods are acceptable in practice. A company must disclose the inventory method it uses. Each method offers certain advantages as follows:

■ FIFO assigns an amount to inventory on the balance sheet that approximates its current cost; it also mimics the actual flow of goods for most businesses.

■ LIFO assigns an amount to cost of goods sold on the income statement that approximates its current cost; it also better matches current costs with revenues in computing gross profit.

■ Weighted average tends to smooth out erratic changes in costs.

■ Specific identification exactly matches the costs of items with the revenues they generate.

Quick Check
Answers—p. 231

9. A company reports the following beginning inventory and purchases, and it ends the period with 30 units in inventory.

Beginning Inventory	100 units at $10 cost per unit
Purchase 1	40 units at $12 cost per unit
Purchase 2	20 units at $14 cost per unit

a. Compute ending inventory using the FIFO periodic system.

b. Compute cost of goods sold using the LIFO periodic system.

5B   Inventory Estimation Methods

P4   Apply both the retail inventory and gross profit methods to estimate inventory.

Inventory sometimes requires estimation for two reasons. First, companies often require **interim statements** (financial statements prepared for periods of less than one year), but they only annually take a physical count of inventory. Second, companies may require an inventory estimate if some casualty such as fire or flood makes taking a physical count impossible. Estimates are usually only required for companies that use the periodic system. Companies using a perpetual system would presumably have updated inventory data.

This appendix describes two methods to estimate inventory.

Retail Inventory Method

Point: When a retailer takes a physical inventory, it can restate the retail value of inventory to a cost basis by applying the cost-to-retail ratio. It can also estimate the amount of shrinkage by comparing the inventory computed with the amount from a physical inventory.

To avoid the time-consuming and expensive process of taking a physical inventory each month or quarter, some companies use the **retail inventory method** to estimate cost of goods sold and ending inventory. Some companies even use the retail inventory method to prepare the annual statements. **Home Depot**, for instance, says in its annual report: "Inventories are stated at the lower of cost (first-in, first-out) or market, as determined by the retail inventory method." A company may also estimate inventory for audit purposes or when inventory is damaged or destroyed.

The retail inventory method uses a three-step process to estimate ending inventory. We need to know the amount of inventory a company had at the beginning of the period in both *cost* and *retail* amounts. We already explained how to compute the cost of inventory. The *retail amount of inventory* refers to its dollar amount measured using selling prices of inventory items. We also need to know the net amount of goods purchased (minus returns, allowances, and discounts) in the period, both at cost and at retail. The amount of net sales at retail is also needed. The process is shown in Exhibit 5B.1.

The reasoning behind the retail inventory method is that if we can get a good estimate of the cost-to-retail ratio, we can multiply ending inventory at retail by this ratio to estimate ending inventory at cost. We show in Exhibit 5B.2 how these steps are applied to estimate

EXHIBIT 5B.1

Retail Inventory Method of Inventory Estimation

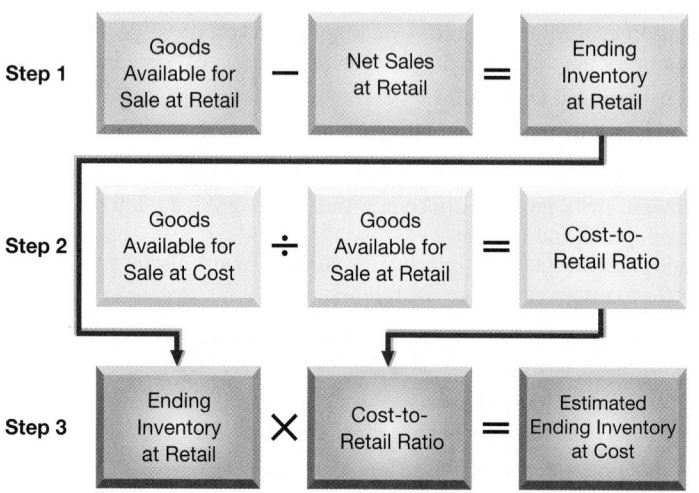

EXHIBIT 5B.2

Estimated Inventory Using the Retail Inventory Method

		At Cost	At Retail
Goods available for sale			
Beginning inventory		$ 20,500	$ 34,500
Cost of goods purchased		39,500	65,500
Step 1: { Goods available for sale		60,000	100,000
Deduct net sales at retail			70,000
Ending inventory at retail			$ 30,000
Step 2:	Cost-to-retail ratio: ($60,000 ÷ $100,000) = 60%		
Step 3:	Estimated ending inventory at cost ($30,000 × 60%)	$18,000	

ending inventory for a typical company. First, we find that $100,000 of goods (at retail selling prices) was available for sale. We see that $70,000 of these goods were sold, leaving $30,000 (retail value) of merchandise in ending inventory. Second, the cost of these goods is 60% of the $100,000 retail value. Third, since cost for these goods is 60% of retail, the estimated cost of ending inventory is $18,000.

Example: What is the cost of ending inventory in Exhibit 5B.2 if the cost of beginning inventory is $22,500 and its retail value is $34,500? *Answer:* $30,000 × 62% = $18,600

Gross Profit Method

The **gross profit method** estimates the cost of ending inventory by applying the gross profit ratio to net sales (at retail). This type of estimate often is needed when inventory is destroyed, lost, or stolen. These cases require an inventory estimate so that a company can file a claim with its insurer. Users also apply this method to see whether inventory amounts from a physical count are reasonable. This method uses the historical relation between cost of goods sold and net sales to estimate the proportion of cost of goods sold making up current sales. This cost of goods sold estimate is then subtracted from cost of goods available for sale to estimate the ending inventory at cost. These two steps are shown in Exhibit 5B.3.

To illustrate, assume that a company's inventory is destroyed by fire in March 2009. When the fire occurs, the company's accounts show the following balances for January through March: sales, $31,500; sales returns, $1,500; inventory (January 1, 2009), $12,000; and cost of goods purchased, $20,500. If this company's gross profit ratio is 30%, then 30% of each net sales dollar is gross profit and 70% is cost of goods sold. We show in Exhibit 5B.4 how this 70% is used to estimate lost inventory of $11,500. To understand this exhibit, think of subtracting cost of goods sold from the goods available for sale to get ending inventory.

EXHIBIT 5B.3

Gross Profit Method of Inventory Estimation

EXHIBIT 5B.4

Estimated Inventory Using the Gross Profit Method

Point: A fire or other catastrophe can result in an insurance claim for lost inventory or income. Backup and off-site storage of data help ensure coverage for such losses.

Point: Reliability of the gross profit method depends on a good estimate of the gross profit ratio.

Goods available for sale		
Inventory, January 1, 2009		$12,000
Cost of goods purchased		20,500
Goods available for sale (at cost)		32,500
Net sales at retail ($31,500 − $1,500)		$30,000
Step 1: Estimated cost of goods sold ($30,000 × 70%)		(21,000) ← × 0.70
Step 2: Estimated March inventory at cost		$11,500

Quick Check
Answer—p. 231

10. Using the retail method and the following data, estimate the cost of ending inventory.

	Cost	Retail
Beginning inventory	$324,000	$530,000
Cost of goods purchased	195,000	335,000
Net sales		320,000

Summary

C1 **Identify the items making up merchandise inventory.**
Merchandise inventory refers to goods owned by a company and held for resale. Three special cases merit our attention. Goods in transit are reported in inventory of the company that holds ownership rights. Goods on consignment are reported in the consignor's inventory. Goods damaged or obsolete are reported in inventory at their net realizable value.

C2 **Identify the costs of merchandise inventory.** Costs of merchandise inventory include expenditures necessary to bring an item to a salable condition and location. This includes its invoice cost minus any discount plus any added or incidental costs necessary to put it in a place and condition for sale.

A1   **Analyze the effects of inventory methods for both financial and tax reporting.** When purchase costs are rising or falling, the inventory costing methods are likely to assign different costs to inventory. Specific identification exactly matches costs and revenues. Weighted average smooths out cost changes. FIFO assigns an amount to inventory closely approximating current replacement cost. LIFO assigns the most recent costs incurred to cost of goods sold and likely better matches current costs with revenues.

A2   **Analyze the effects of inventory errors on current and future financial statements.** An error in the amount of ending inventory affects assets (inventory), net income (cost of goods sold), and equity for that period. Since ending inventory is next period's beginning inventory, an error in ending inventory affects next period's cost of goods sold and net income. Inventory errors in one period are offset in the next period.

A3   **Assess inventory management using both inventory turnover and days' sales in inventory.** We prefer a high inventory turnover, provided that goods are not out of stock and customers are not turned away. We use days' sales in inventory to assess the likelihood of goods being out of stock. We prefer a small number of days' sales in inventory if we can serve customer needs and provide a buffer for uncertainties.

P1   **Compute inventory in a perpetual system using the methods of specific identification, FIFO, LIFO, and weighted average.** Costs are assigned to the cost of goods sold account *each time* a sale occurs in a perpetual system. Specific identification assigns a cost to each item sold by referring to its actual cost (for example, its net invoice cost). Weighted average assigns a cost to items sold by dividing the current balance in the inventory account by the total items available for sale to determine cost per unit. We then multiply the number of units sold by this cost per unit to get the cost of each sale. FIFO assigns cost to items sold assuming that the earliest units purchased are the first units sold. LIFO assigns cost to items sold assuming that the most recent units purchased are the first units sold.

P2   **Compute the lower of cost or market amount of inventory.** Inventory is reported at market cost when market is *lower* than recorded cost, called the *lower of cost or market (LCM) inventory*. Market is typically measured as replacement cost. Lower of cost or market can be applied separately to each item, to major categories of items, or to the entire inventory.

P3[A]   **Compute inventory in a periodic system using the methods of specific identification, FIFO, LIFO, and weighted average.** Periodic inventory systems allocate the cost of goods available for sale between cost of goods sold and ending inventory *at the end of a period.* Specific identification and FIFO give identical results whether the periodic or perpetual system is used. LIFO assigns costs to cost of goods sold assuming the last units purchased for the period are the first units sold. The weighted average cost per unit is computed by dividing the total cost of beginning inventory and net purchases for the period by the total number of units available. Then, it multiplies cost per unit by the number of units sold to give cost of goods sold.

P4[B]   **Apply both the retail inventory and gross profit methods to estimate inventory.** The retail inventory method involves three steps: (1) goods available at retail minus net sales at retail equals ending inventory at retail, (2) goods available at cost divided by goods available at retail equals the cost-to-retail ratio, and (3) ending inventory at retail multiplied by the cost-to-retail ratio equals estimated ending inventory at cost. The gross profit method involves two steps: (1) net sales at retail multiplied by 1 minus the gross profit ratio equals estimated cost of goods sold, and (2) goods available at cost minus estimated cost of goods sold equals estimated ending inventory at cost.

Guidance Answers to **Decision Maker** and **Decision Ethics**

Financial Planner   The FIFO method implies that the oldest costs are the first ones assigned to cost of goods sold. This leaves the most recent costs in ending inventory. You report this to your client and note that in most cases, the ending inventory of a company using FIFO is reported at or near its replacement cost. This means that your client need not in most cases adjust the reported value of inventory. Your answer changes only if there are major increases in replacement cost compared to the cost of recent purchases reported in inventory. When major increases in costs occur, your client might wish to adjust inventory (for internal reports) for the difference between the reported cost of inventory and its replacement cost. (*Note:* Decreases in costs of purchases are recognized under the lower of cost or market adjustment.)

Inventory Manager   It seems your company can save (or at least postpone) taxes by switching to LIFO, but the switch is likely to reduce bonus money that you think you have earned and deserve. Since the U.S. tax code requires companies that use LIFO for tax reporting also to use it for financial reporting, your options are further constrained. Your best decision is to tell your superior about the tax savings with LIFO. You also should discuss your bonus plan and how this is likely to hurt you unfairly. You might propose to compute inventory under the LIFO method for reporting purposes but use the FIFO method for your bonus calculations. Another solution is to revise the bonus plan to reflect the company's use of the LIFO method.

Entrepreneur   Your inventory turnover is markedly higher than the norm, whereas days' sales in inventory approximates the norm. Since your turnover is already 14% better than average, you are probably best served by directing attention to days' sales in inventory. You should see whether you can reduce the level of inventory while maintaining service to customers. Given your higher turnover, you should be able to hold less inventory.

Guidance Answers to **Quick Checks**

1. The matching principle.

2. Target reports these goods in its inventory.

3. Total cost assigned to the painting is $12,180, computed as $11,400 + $130 + $150 + $100 + $400.

4. Specific identification exactly matches costs and revenues. Weighted average tends to smooth out cost changes. FIFO assigns an amount to inventory that closely approximates current replacement cost. LIFO assigns the most recent costs incurred to cost of goods sold and likely better matches current costs with revenues.

5. FIFO—it gives a lower cost of goods sold, a higher gross profit, and a higher net income when costs are rising.

6. When costs are rising, LIFO gives a lower inventory figure on the balance sheet as compared to FIFO. FIFO's inventory amount approximates current replacement costs.

7. Cost of goods sold would be overstated by $10,000 in 2009 and understated by $10,000 in year 2010.

8. The reported LCM inventory amount (using items) is $540, computed as $[(20 \times \$5) + (40 \times \$8) + (10 \times \$12)]$.

9.^{A}a. FIFO periodic inventory $= (20 \times \$14) + (10 \times \$12)$
$= \$400$

b. LIFO periodic cost of goods sold
$= (20 \times \$14) + (40 \times \$12) + (70 \times \$10)$
$= \$1,460$

10.^{B} Estimated ending inventory (at cost) is $327,000. It is computed as follows:

Step 1: $(\$530,000 + \$335,000) - \$320,000 = \$545,000$

Step 2: $\dfrac{\$324,000 + \$195,000}{\$530,000 + \$335,000} = 60\%$

Step 3: $\$545,000 \times 60\% = \underline{\underline{\$327,000}}$

Key Terms

Average cost (pp. 210, 226)	**First-in, first-out (FIFO)** (p. 209)	**Net realizable value** (p. 204)
Conservatism constraint (p. 215)	**Gross profit method** (p. 229)	**Retail inventory method** (p. 228)
Consignee (p. 204)	**Interim statements** (p. 228)	**Specific identification** (p. 207)
Consignor (p. 204)	**Inventory turnover** (p. 217)	**Weighted average** (pp. 210, 226)
Consistency concept (p. 213)	**Last-in, first-out (LIFO)** (p. 209)	
Days' sales in inventory (p. 218)	**Lower of cost or market (LCM)** (p. 213)	

Multiple Choice Quiz   Answers on p. 247   mhhe.com/wildFA5e

Additional Quiz Questions are available at the book's Website.

Use the following information from Marvel Company for the month of July to answer questions 1 through 4.

July 1	Beginning inventory	75 units @ $25 each
July 3	Purchase	348 units @ $27 each
July 8	Sale	300 units
July 15	Purchase	257 units @ $28 each
July 23	Sale	275 units

1. Assume that Marvel uses a perpetual FIFO inventory system. What is the dollar value of its ending inventory?
a. $2,940   **d.** $2,852
b. $2,685   **e.** $2,705
c. $2,625

2. Assume that Marvel uses a perpetual LIFO inventory system. What is the dollar value of its ending inventory?
a. $2,940   **d.** $2,852
b. $2,685   **e.** $2,705
c. $2,625

3. Assume that Marvel uses a perpetual specific identification inventory system. Its ending inventory consists of 20 units from beginning inventory, 40 units from the July 3 purchase, and 45 units from the July 15 purchase. What is the dollar value of its ending inventory?
a. $2,940   **d.** $2,852
b. $2,685   **e.** $2,840
c. $2,625

4.^{A} Assume that Marvel uses a *periodic* FIFO inventory system. What is the dollar value of its ending inventory?
a. $2,940   **d.** $2,852
b. $2,685   **e.** $2,705
c. $2,625

5. A company has cost of goods sold of $85,000 and ending inventory of $18,000. Its days' sales in inventory equals:
a. 49.32 days   **d.** 77.29 days
b. 0.21 days   **e.** 1,723.61 days
c. 4.72 days

Superscript letter ^A (^B) *denotes assignments based on Appendix 5A (5B).*

Discussion Questions

1. Describe how costs flow from inventory to cost of goods sold for the following methods: (*a*) FIFO and (*b*) LIFO.

2. Where is the amount of merchandise inventory disclosed in the financial statements?

3. Why are incidental costs sometimes ignored in inventory costing? Under what accounting constraint is this permitted?

4. ♟ If costs are declining, will the LIFO or FIFO method of inventory valuation yield the lower cost of goods sold? Why?

5. What does the full-disclosure principle prescribe if a company changes from one acceptable accounting method to another?

6. Can a company change its inventory method each accounting period? Explain.

7. ♟ Does the accounting concept of consistency preclude any changes from one accounting method to another?

8. ♟ If inventory errors are said to correct themselves, why are accounting users concerned when such errors are made?

9. Explain the following statement: "Inventory errors correct themselves."

10. What is the meaning of *market* as it is used in determining the lower of cost or market for inventory?

11. ♟ What guidance does the accounting constraint of conservatism offer?

12. What factors contribute to (or cause) inventory shrinkage?

13.^AWhat accounts are used in a periodic inventory system but not in a perpetual inventory system?

14. Refer to **Best Buy**'s financial statements in Appendix A. On February 28, 2009, what percent of current assets are represented by inventory?

15. Refer to **RadioShack**'s financial statements in Appendix A and compute its cost of goods available for sale for the year ended December 31, 2008.

16. Refer to **GOME**'s financial statements in Appendix A. Compute its cost of goods available for sale for the year ended December 31, 2008.

17. Refer to **Apple**'s financial statements in Appendix A. What percent of its current assets are inventory as of September 27, 2008, and as of September 29, 2007?

18.^BWhen preparing interim financial statements, what two methods can companies utilize to estimate cost of goods sold and ending inventory?

♟ *Denotes Discussion Questions that involve decision making.*

Available with Connect Accounting **connect**

QUICK STUDY

QS 5-1
Inventory costing with FIFO perpetual

P1

A company reports the following beginning inventory and purchases for the month of January. On January 26, the company sells 360 units. What is the cost of the 155 units that remain in ending inventory at January 31, assuming costs are assigned based on a perpetual inventory system and use of FIFO? (Round per unit costs to three decimals, but inventory balances to the dollar.)

	Units	Unit Cost
Beginning inventory on January 1	320	$6.00
Purchase on January 9	85	6.40
Purchase on January 25	110	6.60

QS 5-2
Inventory costing with LIFO perpetual   P1

Refer to the information in QS 5-1 and assume the perpetual inventory system is used. Determine the costs assigned to ending inventory when costs are assigned based on LIFO. (Round per unit costs to three decimals, but inventory balances to the dollar.)

QS 5-3
Inventory costing with weighted average perpetual   P1

Check $960

Refer to the information in QS 5-1 and assume the perpetual inventory system is used. Determine the costs assigned to ending inventory when costs are assigned based on weighted average. (Round per unit costs to three decimals, but inventory balances to the dollar.)

QS 5-4
Computing goods available for sale

P1

Rosen Company reports beginning inventory of 10 units at $28 each. Every week for four weeks it purchases an additional 10 units at respective costs of $30, $31, $32, and $34 per unit for weeks 1 through 4. Calculate the cost of goods available for sale and the units available for sale for this four-week period. Assume that no sales occur during those four weeks.

Mercedes Brown starts a merchandising business on December 1 and enters into three inventory purchases:

December 7	10 units @ $ 9 cost
December 14	20 units @ $10 cost
December 21	15 units @ $12 cost

Brown sells 18 units for $35 each on December 15. Seven of the sold units are from the December 7 purchase and eleven are from the December 14 purchase. Brown uses a perpetual inventory system. Determine the costs assigned to the December 31 ending inventory based on FIFO. (Round per unit costs to three decimals, but inventory balances to the dollar.)

QS 5-5
Assigning costs with FIFO perpetual

P1

Refer to the information in QS 5-5 and assume the perpetual inventory system is used. Determine the costs assigned to ending inventory when costs are assigned based on LIFO. (Round per unit costs to three decimals, but inventory balances to the dollar.)

QS 5-6
Inventory costing with LIFO perpetual

P1

Refer to the information in QS 5-5 and assume the perpetual inventory system is used. Determine the costs assigned to ending inventory when costs are assigned based on weighted average. (Round per unit costs to three decimals, but inventory balances to the dollar.)

QS 5-7
Inventory costing with weighted average perpetual   P1

Check $296

Refer to the information in QS 5-5 and assume the perpetual inventory system is used. Determine the costs assigned to ending inventory when costs are assigned based on specific identification. (Round per unit costs to three decimals, but inventory balances to the dollar.)

QS 5-8
Inventory costing with specific identification perpetual

P1

Identify the inventory costing method best described by each of the following separate statements. Assume a period of increasing costs.

1. Results in a balance sheet inventory amount approximating replacement cost.
2. The preferred method when each unit of product has unique features that markedly affect cost.
3. Matches recent costs against net sales.
4. Yields a balance sheet inventory amount often markedly less than its replacement cost.
5. Provides a tax advantage (deferral) to a corporation when costs are rising.

QS 5-9
Contrasting inventory costing methods

A1

Homestead Crafts, a distributor of handmade gifts, operates out of owner Emma Flynn's house. At the end of the current period, Emma reports she has 800 units (products) in her basement, 10 of which were damaged by water and cannot be sold. She also has another 400 units in her van, ready to deliver per a customer order, terms FOB destination, and another 100 units out on consignment to a friend who owns a retail store. How many units should Emma include in her company's period-end inventory?

QS 5-10
Inventory ownership

C1

---

1. Jabar Company has shipped $600 of goods to Chi Co., and Chi Co. has arranged to sell the goods for Jabar. Identify the consignor and the consignee. Which company should include any unsold goods as part of its inventory?
2. At year-end, Liu Co. had shipped $750 of merchandise FOB destination to Kwon Co. Which company should include the $750 of merchandise in transit as part of its year-end inventory?

QS 5-11
Inventory ownership

C1

Rivers Associates, antique dealers, purchased the contents of an estate for $75,000. Terms of the purchase were FOB shipping point, and the cost of transporting the goods to Rivers Associates' warehouse was $1,800. Rivers Associates insured the shipment at a cost of $300. Prior to putting the goods up for sale, they cleaned and refurbished them at a cost of $1,750. Determine the cost of the inventory acquired from the estate.

QS 5-12
Inventory costs

C2

QS 5-13
Inventory costs
C2

A car dealer acquires a used car for $17,500, terms FOB shipping point. Additional costs in obtaining and offering the car for sale include $300 for transportation-in, $1,000 for import duties, $250 for insurance during shipment, $400 for advertising, and $3,000 for sales staff salaries. For computing inventory, what cost is assigned to the used car?

QS 5-14
Applying LCM to inventories
P2

Paoli Trading Co. has the following products in its ending inventory. Compute lower of cost or market for inventory (*a*) as a whole and (*b*) applied separately to each product.

Product	Quantity	Cost per Unit	Market per Unit
Mountain bikes	20	$650	$500
Skateboards	22	400	450
Gliders	40	850	790

QS 5-15
Inventory errors
A2

In taking a physical inventory at the end of year 2009, Peña Company erroneously forgot to count certain units. Explain how this error affects the following: (*a*) 2009 cost of goods sold, (*b*) 2009 gross profit, (*c*) 2009 net income, (*d*) 2010 net income, (*e*) the combined two-year income, and (*f*) income for years after 2010.

QS 5-16
Analyzing inventory
A3

Civic Company begins the year with $75,075 of goods in inventory. At year-end, the amount in inventory has increased to $89,925. Cost of goods sold for the year is $602,250. Compute Civic's inventory turnover and days' sales in inventory. Assume that there are 365 days in the year.

QS 5-17[A]
Assigning costs with FIFO
periodic   P3

Refer to the information in QS 5-1 and assume the periodic inventory system is used. Determine the costs assigned to the ending inventory when costs are assigned based on FIFO. (Round per unit costs to three decimals, but inventory balances to the dollar.)

QS 5-18[A]
Inventory costing with LIFO
periodic   P3

Refer to the information in QS 5-1 and assume the periodic inventory system is used. Determine the costs assigned to ending inventory when costs are assigned based on LIFO. (Round per unit costs to three decimals, but inventory balances to the dollar.)

QS 5-19[A]
Inventory costing with weighted average periodic   P3

Refer to the information in QS 5-1 and assume the periodic inventory system is used. Determine the costs assigned to ending inventory when costs are assigned based on weighted average. (Round per unit costs to three decimals, but inventory balances to the dollar.)

QS 5-20[A]
Inventory costing with FIFO
periodic   P3

Refer to the information in QS 5-5 and assume the periodic inventory system is used. Determine the costs assigned to the December 31 ending inventory when costs are assigned based on FIFO. (Round per unit costs to three decimals, but inventory balances to the dollar.)

QS 5-21[A]
Inventory costing with LIFO
periodic   P3

Refer to the information in QS 5-5 and assume the periodic inventory system is used. Determine the costs assigned to ending inventory when costs are assigned based on LIFO. (Round per unit costs to three decimals, but inventory balances to the dollar.)

QS 5-22[A]
Inventory costing with weighted average periodic   P3

Refer to the information in QS 5-5 and assume the periodic inventory system is used. Determine the costs assigned to ending inventory when costs are assigned based on weighted average. (Round per unit costs to three decimals, but inventory balances to the dollar.)

QS 5-23[A]
Inventory costing with specific identification periodic   P3

Refer to the information in QS 5-5 and assume the periodic inventory system is used. Determine the costs assigned to ending inventory when costs are assigned based on specific identification. (Round per unit costs to three decimals, but inventory balances to the dollar.)

Kaysee Store's inventory is destroyed by a fire on September 5, 2011. The following data for year 2011 are available from the accounting records. Estimate the cost of the inventory destroyed.

Jan. 1 inventory..........................	$230,000
Jan. 1 through Sept. 5 purchases (net)	$492,000
Jan. 1 through Sept. 5 sales (net)	$850,000
Year 2011 estimated gross profit rate	37%

QS 5-24ᴮ
Estimating inventories—gross profit method

P4

Answer each of the following questions related to international accounting standards.

a. Explain how the accounting for items and costs making up merchandise inventory is different between IFRS and U.S. GAAP.

b. Can companies reporting under IFRS apply a cost flow assumption in assigning costs to inventory? If yes, identify at least two acceptable cost flow assumptions.

c. Both IFRS and U.S. GAAP apply the lower of cost or market method for reporting inventory values. If inventory is written down from applying the lower of cost or market method, explain in general terms how IFRS and U.S. GAAP differ in accounting for any subsequent period reversal of that reported decline in inventory value.

QS 5-25
International accounting standards

C1   C2   P2

connect™ Available with Connect Accounting

Liberty Company reported the following January purchases and sales data for its only product.

EXERCISES

Exercise 5-1
Inventory costing methods—perpetual

P1

Date		Activities	Units Acquired at Cost	Units Sold at Retail
Jan.	1	Beginning inventory	140 units @ $7.00 = $ 980	
Jan.	10	Sales		90 units @ $15
Jan.	20	Purchase	220 units @ $6.00 = 1,320	
Jan.	25	Sales		145 units @ $15
Jan.	30	Purchase	100 units @ $5.00 = 500	
		Totals	460 units $2,800	235 units

Liberty uses a perpetual inventory system. Ending inventory consists of 225 units, 100 from the January 30 purchase, 80 from the January 20 purchase, and 45 from beginning inventory. Determine the cost assigned to ending inventory and to cost of goods sold using (*a*) specific identification, (*b*) weighted average, (*c*) FIFO, and (*d*) LIFO. (Round per unit costs to three decimals, but inventory balances to the dollar.)

Check   Ending inventory: LIFO, $1,300; WA, $1,273

Use the data in Exercise 5-1 to prepare comparative income statements for the month of January for Liberty Company similar to those shown in Exhibit 5.8 for the four inventory methods. Assume expenses are $1,250, and that the applicable income tax rate is 30%.

1. Which method yields the highest net income?

2. Does net income using weighted average fall between that using FIFO and LIFO?

3. If costs were rising instead of falling, which method would yield the highest net income?

Exercise 5-2
Income effects of inventory methods

A1

Harper Co. reported the following current-year purchases and sales data for its only product.

Exercise 5-3
Inventory costing methods (perpetual)—FIFO and LIFO

P1

Date		Activities	Units Acquired at Cost	Units Sold at Retail
Jan.	1	Beginning inventory	126 units @ $8 = $ 1,008	
Jan.	10	Sales		113 units @ $40
Mar.	14	Purchase	315 units @ $13 = 4,095	
Mar.	15	Sales		180 units @ $40
July	30	Purchase	250 units @ $18 = 4,500	
Oct.	5	Sales		378 units @ $40
Oct.	26	Purchase	50 units @ $23 = 1,150	
		Totals	741 units $10,753	671 units

Check Ending inventory: LIFO, $1,345

Harper uses a perpetual inventory system. Determine the costs assigned to ending inventory and to cost of goods sold using (a) FIFO and (b) LIFO. Compute the gross margin for each method.

Exercise 5-4
Specific identification
P1

Refer to the data in Exercise 5-3. Assume that ending inventory is made up of 5 units from the March 14 purchase, 15 units from the July 30 purchase, and all the units of the October 26 purchase. Using the specific identification method, calculate (a) the cost of goods sold and (b) the gross profit.

Exercise 5-5
Lower of cost or market
P2

Maya Company's ending inventory includes the following items. Compute the lower of cost or market for ending inventory (a) as a whole and (b) applied separately to each product.

		Per Unit	
Product	Units	Cost	Market
Helmets	19	$45	$49
Bats	12	73	67
Shoes	33	90	86
Uniforms	37	31	31

Check (b) $5,644

Exercise 5-6
Analysis of inventory errors
A2

Abco Company had $1,100,000 of sales in each of three consecutive years 2008–2010, and it purchased merchandise costing $700,000 in each of those years. It also maintained a $280,000 physical inventory from the beginning to the end of that three-year period. In accounting for inventory, it made an error at the end of year 2008 that caused its year-end 2008 inventory to appear on its statements as $262,000 rather than the correct $280,000.

Check 2008 reported gross profit, $382,000

1. Determine the correct amount of the company's gross profit in each of the years 2008–2010.

2. Prepare comparative income statements as in Exhibit 5.11 to show the effect of this error on the company's cost of goods sold and gross profit for each of the years 2008–2010.

Exercise 5-7
Inventory turnover and days' sales in inventory
A3

Use the following information for Palmer Co. to compute inventory turnover for 2011 and 2010, and its days' sales in inventory at December 31, 2011 and 2010. (Round answers to one decimal.) Comment on Palmer's efficiency in using its assets to increase sales from 2010 to 2011.

	2011	2010	2009
Cost of goods sold	$667,134	$442,104	$405,600
Ending inventory	92,232	87,840	97,600

Exercise 5-8
Comparing LIFO numbers to FIFO numbers; ratio analysis
A1 A3

Cook Company uses LIFO for inventory costing and reports the following financial data. It also recomputed inventory and cost of goods sold using FIFO for comparison purposes.

	2011	2010
LIFO inventory	$110	$177
LIFO cost of goods sold	760	828
FIFO inventory	270	457
FIFO cost of goods sold	680	645
Current assets (using LIFO)	250	200
Current liabilities	225	180

Check (1) FIFO: Current ratio, 1.8; Inventory turnover, 1.9 times

1. Compute its current ratio, inventory turnover, and days' sales in inventory for 2011 using (a) LIFO numbers and (b) FIFO numbers. (Round answers to one decimal.)

2. Comment on and interpret the results of part 1.

Exercise 5-9^A
Inventory costing—
periodic system   P3

Refer to Exercise 5-1 and assume the periodic inventory system is used. Determine the costs assigned to ending inventory and to cost of goods sold using (a) specific identification, (b) weighted average, (c) FIFO, and (d) LIFO. (Round per unit costs to three decimals, but inventory balances to the dollar.)

Refer to Exercise 5-3 and assume the periodic inventory system is used. Determine the costs assigned to ending inventory and to cost of goods sold using (*a*) FIFO, and (*b*) LIFO. Compute the gross margin for each method.

Exercise 5-10[A]

Inventory costing—periodic system P3

Martinez Co. reported the following current-year data for its only product. The company uses a periodic inventory system, and its ending inventory consists of 405 units—135 from each of the last three purchases. Determine the cost assigned to ending inventory and to cost of goods sold using (*a*) specific identification, (*b*) weighted average, (*c*) FIFO, and (*d*) LIFO. (Round per unit costs to three decimals, but inventory balances to the dollar.) Which method yields the highest net income?

Exercise 5-11[A]

Alternative cost flow assumptions—periodic

P3

Jan. 1	Beginning inventory	270 units @ $1.90 = $ 513
Mar. 7	Purchase	540 units @ $2.05 = 1,107
July 28	Purchase	1,350 units @ $2.30 = 3,105
Oct. 3	Purchase	1,230 units @ $2.60 = 3,198
Dec. 19	Purchase	390 units @ $2.70 = 1,053
	Totals	3,780 units $8,976

Check Inventory; LIFO, $790; FIFO, $1,092

Genesis Gifts reported the following current-year data for its only product. The company uses a periodic inventory system, and its ending inventory consists of 360 units—120 from each of the last three purchases. Determine the cost assigned to ending inventory and to cost of goods sold using (*a*) specific identification, (*b*) weighted average, (*c*) FIFO, and (*d*) LIFO. (Round per unit costs to three decimals, but inventory balances to the dollar.) Which method yields the lowest net income?

Exercise 5-12[A]

Alternative cost flow assumptions—periodic

P3

Jan. 1	Beginning inventory	290 units @ $2.80 = $ 812
Mar. 7	Purchase	610 units @ $2.70 = 1,647
July 28	Purchase	810 units @ $2.40 = 1,944
Oct. 3	Purchase	1,110 units @ $2.20 = 2,442
Dec. 19	Purchase	260 units @ $1.90 = 494
	Totals	3,080 units $7,339

Check Inventory: LIFO, $1,001; FIFO, $714

In 2011, Dakota Company had net sales (at retail) of $219,800. The following additional information is available from its records at the end of 2011. Use the retail inventory method to estimate Dakota's 2011 ending inventory at cost.

Exercise 5-13[B]

Estimating ending inventory—retail method

P4

	At Cost	At Retail
Beginning inventory	$ 57,100	$108,200
Cost of goods purchased	97,740	168,300

Check End. Inventory, $31,752

On January 1, Java Shop had $360,000 of inventory at cost. In the first quarter of the year, it purchased $1,267,200 of merchandise, returned $11,450, and paid freight charges of $18,100 on purchased merchandise, terms FOB shipping point. The company's gross profit averages 34%, and the store had $1,594,800 of net sales (at retail) in the first quarter of the year. Use the gross profit method to estimate its cost of inventory at the end of the first quarter.

Exercise 5-14[B]

Estimating ending inventory—gross profit method

P4

Samsung Electronics reports the following regarding its accounting for inventories.

Exercise 5-15

Accounting for inventory following IFRS

P2

Inventories are stated at the lower of cost or net realizable value. Cost is determined using the average cost method, except for materials-in-transit which are stated at actual cost as determined using the specific identification method. Losses on valuation of inventories and losses on inventory obsolescence are recorded as part of cost of sales. As of December 31, 2008, losses on valuation of inventories amounted to ₩651,296 million (₩ is Korean won).

1. What cost flow assumption(s) does Samsung apply in assigning costs to its inventories?

2. What has Samsung recorded for 2008 as a write down on valuation of its inventories?

3. If at year-end 2009 there was an increase in the value of its inventories such that there was a reversal of ₩900 million for the 2008 write down, how would Samsung account for this under IFRS? Would Samsung's accounting be different for this reversal if it reported under U.S. GAAP? Explain.

Available with Connect Accounting **connect**™

PROBLEM SET A

Problem 5-1A
Alternative cost flows—perpetual

P1

Ammons Company uses a perpetual inventory system. It entered into the following purchases and sales transactions for January.

Date	Activities	Units Acquired at Cost	Units Sold at Retail
Jan. 1	Beginning inventory	5 units @ $500/unit	
Jan. 5	Purchase	20 units @ $550/unit	
Jan. 9	Sales		21 units @ $850/unit
Jan. 18	Purchase	6 units @ $600/unit	
Jan. 25	Purchase	10 units @ $620/unit	
Jan. 29	Sales		8 units @ $950/unit
	Totals	41 units	29 units

Required

1. Compute cost of goods available for sale and the number of units available for sale.

2. Compute the number of units in ending inventory.

Check (3) Ending Inventory: FIFO, $7,400; LIFO, $6,840, WA, $7,176

3. Compute the cost assigned to ending inventory using (a) FIFO, (b) LIFO, (c) weighted average, and (d) specific identification. (Round per unit costs to three decimals, but inventory balances to the dollar.) For specific identification, the January 9 sale consisted of 4 units from beginning inventory and 17 units from the January 5 purchase; the January 29 sale consisted of 2 units from the January 18 purchase and 6 units from the January 25 purchase.

(4) LIFO gross profit, $8,990

4. Compute gross profit earned by the company for each of the four costing methods in part 3.

Problem 5-2A
Alternative cost flows—perpetual

P1 ♟

Marlow Company uses a perpetual inventory system. It entered into the following calendar-year 2011 purchases and sales transactions.

Date	Activities	Units Acquired at Cost	Units Sold at Retail
Jan. 1	Beginning inventory	770 units @ $50/unit	
Feb. 10	Purchase	420 units @ $41/unit	
Mar. 13	Purchase	260 units @ $25/unit	
Mar. 15	Sales		770 units @ $75/unit
Aug. 21	Purchase	180 units @ $49/unit	
Sept. 5	Purchase	585 units @ $42/unit	
Sept. 10	Sales		650 units @ $75/unit
	Totals	2,215 units	1,420 units

Required

1. Compute cost of goods available for sale and the number of units available for sale.

2. Compute the number of units in ending inventory.

Check (3) Ending inventory: FIFO, $34,140; LIFO, $39,635; WA, $34,424;

3. Compute the cost assigned to ending inventory using (a) FIFO, (b) LIFO, (c) specific identification—ending inventory consists of 95 units from beginning inventory, 175 from the February 10 purchase, 70 from the March 13 purchase, and 455 from the September 5 purchase, and (d) weighted average. (Round per unit costs to three decimals, but inventory balances to the dollar.)

(4) LIFO gross profit, $50,525

4. Compute gross profit earned by the company for each of the four costing methods in part 3.

Analysis Component

5. If the company's manager earns a bonus based on a percent of gross profit, which method of inventory costing will the manager likely prefer?

A physical inventory of SoundLand Company taken at December 31 reveals the following.

Problem 5-3A
Lower of cost or market
P2

File Edit View Insert Format Tools Data Accounting Window Help			
	Per Unit		
Item	**Units**	**Cost**	**Market**
Audio equipment			
Receivers	343	$ 88	$ 96
CD players	255	109	98
MP3 players	323	84	93
Speakers	198	50	39
Video equipment			
Handheld LCDs	481	148	123
VCRs	288	91	82
Camcorders	206	308	320
Car audio equipment			
Satellite radios	179	68	82
CD/MP3 radios	164	95	103

Sheet1 / Sheet2 / Sheet3 /

Required

Calculate the lower of cost or market for the inventory (*a*) as a whole, (*b*) by major category, and (*c*) applied separately to each item.

Check (*b*) $271,462; (*c*) $264,007

Nikita Company's financial statements show the following. The company recently discovered that in making physical counts of inventory, it had made the following errors: Inventory on December 31, 2008, is understated by $56,000, and inventory on December 31, 2009, is overstated by $25,000.

Problem 5-4A
Analysis of inventory errors
A2

mhhe.com/wildFA5e

For Year Ended December 31	2008	2009	2010
(a) Cost of goods sold	$ 623,000	$ 955,000	$ 780,000
(b) Net income	230,000	275,000	250,000
(c) Total current assets	1,247,000	1,360,000	1,230,000
(d) Total equity	1,387,000	1,580,000	1,245,000

Required

1. For each key financial statement figure—(*a*), (*b*), (*c*), and (*d*) above—prepare a table similar to the following to show the adjustments necessary to correct the reported amounts.

Figure: _____	2008	2009	2010
Reported amount			
Adjustments for: 12/31/2008 error			
12/31/2009 error			
Corrected amount			

Check (1) Corrected net income: 2008, $286,000; 2009, $194,000; 2010, $275,000

Analysis Component

2. What is the error in total net income for the combined three-year period resulting from the inventory errors? Explain.

3. Explain why the understatement of inventory by $56,000 at the end of 2008 results in an understatement of equity by the same amount in that year.

Problem 5-5A^A
Alternative cost flows—periodic

P3

Austin Company began year 2011 with 33,000 units of product in its January 1 inventory costing $17 each. It made successive purchases of its product in year 2011 as follows. The company uses a periodic inventory system. On December 31, 2011, a physical count reveals that 40,000 units of its product remain in inventory.

Mar. 7	38,000 units @ $19 each
May 25	34,000 units @ $22 each
Aug. 1	26,000 units @ $26 each
Nov. 10	22,000 units @ $30 each

Required

Check (2) Cost of goods sold: FIFO, $2,239,000; LIFO, $2,673,000; WA, $2,486,720

1. Compute the number and total cost of the units available for sale in year 2011.

2. Compute the amounts assigned to the 2011 ending inventory and the cost of goods sold using (*a*) FIFO, (*b*) LIFO, and (*c*) weighted average. (Round per unit costs to three decimals, but inventory balances to the dollar.)

Problem 5-6A^A
Income comparisons and cost flows—periodic

A1 P3

Bay Corp. sold 6,500 units of its product at $50 per unit in year 2011 and incurred operating expenses of $5 per unit in selling the units. It began the year with 900 units in inventory and made successive purchases of its product as follows.

Jan. 1	Beginning inventory	900 units @ $21 per unit
Feb. 20	Purchase	1,950 units @ $22 per unit
May 16	Purchase	1,050 units @ $25 per unit
Oct. 3	Purchase	700 units @ $26 per unit
Dec. 11	Purchase	2,750 units @ $27 per unit
	Total	7,350 units

Required

Check (1) Net income: FIFO, $80,970; LIFO, $77,910; WA, $79,724

1. Prepare comparative income statements similar to Exhibit 5.8 for the three inventory costing methods of FIFO, LIFO, and weighted average. (Round per unit costs to three decimals, but inventory balances to the dollar.) Include a detailed cost of goods sold section as part of each statement. The company uses a periodic inventory system, and its income tax rate is 40%.

2. How would the financial results from using the three alternative inventory costing methods change if Bay had been experiencing declining costs in its purchases of inventory?

3. What advantages and disadvantages are offered by using (*a*) LIFO and (*b*) FIFO? Assume the continuing trend of increasing costs.

Problem 5-7A^B
Retail inventory method

P4

mhhe.com/wildFA5e

The records of Ultra Company provide the following information for the year ended December 31.

	At Cost	At Retail
January 1 beginning inventory	$ 476,600	$ 927,950
Cost of goods purchased	3,481,060	6,401,050
Sales		5,565,800
Sales returns		49,800

Required

Check (1) Inventory, $979,020 cost; (2) Inventory shortage at cost, $55,134

1. Use the retail inventory method to estimate the company's year-end inventory at cost.

2. A year-end physical inventory at retail prices yields a total inventory of $1,710,900. Prepare a calculation showing the company's loss from shrinkage at cost and at retail.

Problem 5-8A^B
Gross profit method

P4

Optek Company wants to prepare interim financial statements for the first quarter. The company wishes to avoid making a physical count of inventory. Optek's gross profit rate averages 39%. The following information for the first quarter is available from its records.

January 1 beginning inventory	$ 312,580
Cost of goods purchased	944,040
Sales	1,391,160
Sales returns	8,760

Required

Use the gross profit method to estimate the company's first-quarter ending inventory.

Check Estimated ending inventory, $413,356

Sheila Company uses a perpetual inventory system. It entered into the following purchases and sales transactions for May.

PROBLEM SET B

Problem 5-1B
Alternative cost flows—perpetual
P1

Date	Activities	Units Acquired at Cost	Units Sold at Retail
May 1	Beginning inventory	150 units @ $300/unit	
May 6	Purchase	350 units @ $350/unit	
May 9	Sales		180 units @ $1,200/unit
May 17	Purchase	80 units @ $450/unit	
May 25	Purchase	100 units @ $458/unit	
May 30	Sales		300 units @ $1,400/unit
	Total	680 units	480 units

Required

1. Compute cost of goods available for sale and the number of units available for sale.
2. Compute the number of units in ending inventory.
3. Compute the cost assigned to ending inventory using (*a*) FIFO, (*b*) LIFO, (*c*) weighted average, and (*d*) specific identification. (Round per unit costs to three decimals, but inventory balances to the dollar.) For specific identification, the May 9 sale consisted of 80 units from beginning inventory and 100 units from the May 6 purchase; the May 30 sale consisted of 200 units from the May 6 purchase and 100 units from the May 25 purchase.
4. Compute gross profit earned by the company for each of the four costing methods in part 3.

Check (3) Ending inventory: FIFO, $88,800; LIFO, $62,500; WA, $75,600;

(4) LIFO gross profit, $449,200

Hawaii Pacific Company uses a perpetual inventory system. It entered into the following calendar-year 2011 purchases and sales transactions.

Problem 5-2B
Alternative cost flows—perpetual
P1

Date	Activities	Units Acquired at Cost	Units Sold at Retail
Jan. 1	Beginning inventory	520 units @ $45/unit	
Jan. 10	Purchase	350 units @ $50/unit	
Feb. 13	Purchase	200 units @ $51/unit	
Feb. 15	Sales		620 units @ $75/unit
July 21	Purchase	260 units @ $52/unit	
Aug. 5	Purchase	595 units @ $53/unit	
Aug. 10	Sales		660 units @ $75/unit
	Total	1,925 units	1,280 units

Required

1. Compute cost of goods available for sale and the number of units available for sale.
2. Compute the number of units in ending inventory.
3. Compute the cost assigned to ending inventory using (*a*) FIFO, (*b*) LIFO, (*c*) specific identification— ending inventory consists of 105 units from beginning inventory, 140 units from the January 10 purchase, 105 units from the February 13 purchase, 50 units from the July 21 purchase, and 245 units from the August 5 purchase, and (*d*) weighted average. (Round per unit costs to three decimals, but inventory balances to the dollar.)
4. Compute gross profit earned by the company for each of the four costing methods in part 3.

Check (3) Ending inventory: FIFO, $34,135; LIFO, $30,390; WA, $32,890;

(4) LIFO gross profit, $30,235

Analysis Component

5. If the company's manager earns a bonus based on a percent of gross profit, which method of inventory costing will the manager likely prefer?

Problem 5-3B
Lower of cost or market

P2

A physical inventory of Office Mart taken at December 31 reveals the following.

File Edit View Insert Format Tools Data Accounting Window Help			
Item	**Units**	**Per Unit Cost**	**Market**
Office furniture			
Desks	376	$231	$239
Credenzas	280	198	207
Chairs	725	36	33
Bookshelves	218	103	99
Filing cabinets			
Two-drawer	136	85	82
Four-drawer	317	129	126
Lateral	92	114	118
Office equipment			
Fax machines	352	55	65
Copiers	430	405	396
Telephones	515	63	61

Required

Check (b) $477,375; (c) $470,440

Compute the lower of cost or market for the inventory (a) as a whole, (b) by major category, and (c) applied separately to each item.

Problem 5-4B
Analysis of inventory errors

A2

Watson Company's financial statements show the following. The company recently discovered that in making physical counts of inventory, it had made the following errors: Inventory on December 31, 2008, is overstated by $64,000, and inventory on December 31, 2009, is understated by $35,000.

For Year Ended December 31	2008	2009	2010
(a) Cost of goods sold	$ 615,000	$ 957,000	$ 786,000
(b) Net income	225,000	285,000	244,000
(c) Total current assets	1,251,000	1,360,000	1,265,000
(d) Total equity	1,387,000	1,520,000	1,250,000

Required

1. For each key financial statement figure—(a), (b), (c), and (d) above—prepare a table similar to the following to show the adjustments necessary to correct the reported amounts.

Figure: _____	2008	2009	2010
Reported amount			
Adjustments for: 12/31/2008 error			
12/31/2009 error			
Corrected amount			

Check (1) Corrected net income:
2008, $161,000; 2009, $384,000;
2010, $209,000

Analysis Component

2. What is the error in total net income for the combined three-year period resulting from the inventory errors? Explain.

3. Explain why the overstatement of inventory by $64,000 at the end of 2008 results in an overstatement of equity by the same amount in that year.

Problem 5-5B[A]
Alternative cost flows—periodic

P3

Solaris Co. began year 2011 with 39,000 units of product in its January 1 inventory costing $21 each. It made successive purchases of its product in year 2011 as follows. The company uses a periodic inventory system. On December 31, 2011, a physical count reveals that 40,000 units of its product remain in inventory.

Jan. 4	34,000 units @ $20 each
May 18	32,000 units @ $19 each
July 9	18,000 units @ $16 each
Nov. 21	36,000 units @ $14 each

Required

1. Compute the number and total cost of the units available for sale in year 2011.

2. Compute the amounts assigned to the 2011 ending inventory and the cost of goods sold using (*a*) FIFO, (*b*) LIFO, and (*c*) weighted average. (Round per unit costs to three decimals, but inventory balances to the dollar.)

Check   (2) Cost of goods sold: FIFO, $2,331,000; LIFO, $2,060,000; WA, $2,169,680

Shasta Company sold 6,850 units of its product at $63 per unit in year 2011 and incurred operating expenses of $5 per unit in selling the units. It began the year with 1,100 units in inventory and made successive purchases of its product as follows.

Problem 5-6B[A]

Income comparisons and cost flows—periodic

A1   P3

Jan. 1	Beginning inventory	1,100 units @ $23 per unit
April 2	Purchase	2,100 units @ $24 per unit
June 14	Purchase	1,250 units @ $25 per unit
Aug. 29	Purchase	1,200 units @ $27 per unit
Nov. 18	Purchase	2,250 units @ $29 per unit
	Total	7,900 units

Required

1. Prepare comparative income statements similar to Exhibit 5.8 for the three inventory costing methods of FIFO, LIFO, and weighted average. (Round per unit costs to three decimals, but inventory balances to the dollar.) Include a detailed cost of goods sold section as part of each statement. The company uses a periodic inventory system, and its income tax rate is 30%.

2. How would the financial results from using the three alternative inventory costing methods change if the company had been experiencing decreasing prices in its purchases of inventory?

3. What advantages and disadvantages are offered by using (*a*) LIFO and (*b*) FIFO? Assume the continuing trend of increasing costs.

Check   (1) Net income: LIFO, $151,795; FIFO, $156,205; WA, $153,926

The records of Mercury Co. provide the following information for the year ended December 31.

Problem 5-7B[B]

Retail inventory method

P4

	At Cost	At Retail
January 1 beginning inventory	$ 468,010	$ 934,950
Cost of goods purchased	3,383,110	6,471,050
Sales		5,573,800
Sales returns		48,800

Required

1. Use the retail inventory method to estimate the company's year-end inventory.

2. A year-end physical inventory at retail prices yields a total inventory of $1,701,900. Prepare a calculation showing the company's loss from shrinkage at cost and at retail.

Check   (1) Inventory, $978,120 cost; (2) Inventory shortage at cost, $93,132

Tacita Equipment Co. wants to prepare interim financial statements for the first quarter. The company wishes to avoid making a physical count of inventory. Tacita's gross profit rate averages 40%. The following information for the first quarter is available from its records.

Problem 5-8B[B]

Gross profit method

P4

January 1 beginning inventory	$ 301,580
Cost of goods purchased	941,040
Sales	1,401,160
Sales returns	9,100

Required

Use the gross profit method to estimate the company's first quarter ending inventory.

Check   Estim. ending inventory, $407,384

(This serial problem began in Chapter 1 and continues through most of the book. If previous chapter segments were not completed, the serial problem can begin at this point.)

SERIAL PROBLEM

Success Systems

SP 5

Part A

Adriana Lopez of Success Systems is evaluating her inventory to determine whether it must be adjusted based on lower of cost or market rules. Lopez has three different types of software in her inventory and the following information is available for each.

Inventory Items	Units	Per Unit Cost	Per Unit Market
Office productivity	3	$ 76	$ 74
Desktop publishing	2	103	100
Accounting	3	90	96

Required

1. Compute the lower of cost or market for ending inventory assuming Lopez applies the lower of cost or market rule to inventory as a whole. Must Lopez adjust the reported inventory value? Explain.

2. Assume that Lopez had instead applied the lower of cost or market rule to each product in inventory. Under this assumption, must Lopez adjust the reported inventory value? Explain.

Part B

Selected accounts and balances for the three months ended March 31, 2010, for Success Systems follows.

January 1 beginning inventory	$ 0
Cost of goods sold	14,052
March 31 ending inventory	704

Required

1. Compute inventory turnover and days' sales in inventory for the three months ended March 31, 2010.

2. Assess the company's performance if competitors average 10 times for inventory turnover and 29 days for days' sales in inventory.

BEYOND THE NUMBERS

REPORTING IN ACTION

C2 A3

BTN 5-1   Refer to **Best Buy**'s financial statements in Appendix A to answer the following.

Required

1. What amount of inventories did Best Buy report as a current asset on February 28, 2009? On March 1, 2008?

2. Inventories represent what percent of total assets on February 28, 2009? On March 1, 2008?

3. Comment on the relative size of Best Buy's inventories compared to its other types of assets.

4. What accounting method did Best Buy use to compute inventory amounts on its balance sheet?

5. Compute inventory turnover for fiscal year ended February 28, 2009, and days' sales in inventory as of February 28, 2009.

Fast Forward

6. Access Best Buy's financial statements for fiscal years ended after February 28, 2009, from its Website (**BestBuy.com**) or the SEC's EDGAR database (**www.SEC.gov**). Answer questions 1 through 5 using the current Best Buy information and compare results to those prior years.

COMPARATIVE ANALYSIS

A3

BTN 5-2   Comparative figures for **Best Buy** and **RadioShack** follow.

($ millions)	Best Buy Current Year	Best Buy One Year Prior	Best Buy Two Years Prior	RadioShack Current Year	RadioShack One Year Prior	RadioShack Two Years Prior
Inventory	$ 4,753	$ 4,708	$ 4,028	$ 636.3	$ 705.4	$ 752.1
Cost of sales	34,017	30,477	27,165	2,301.8	2,225.9	2,648.1

Required

1. Compute inventory turnover for each company for the most recent two years shown.
2. Compute days' sales in inventory for each company for the three years shown.
3. Comment on and interpret your findings from parts 1 and 2. Assume an industry average for inventory turnover of 6.3.

BTN 5-3   Golf Depot is a retail sports store carrying golf apparel and equipment. The store is at the end of its second year of operation and is struggling. A major problem is that its cost of inventory has continually increased in the past two years. In the first year of operations, the store assigned inventory costs using LIFO. A loan agreement the store has with its bank, its prime source of financing, requires the store to maintain a certain profit margin and current ratio. The store's owner is currently looking over Golf Depot's preliminary financial statements for its second year. The numbers are not favorable. The only way the store can meet the required financial ratios agreed on with the bank is to change from LIFO to FIFO. The store originally decided on LIFO because of its tax advantages. The owner recalculates ending inventory using FIFO and submits those numbers and statements to the loan officer at the bank for the required bank review. The owner thankfully reflects on the available latitude in choosing the inventory costing method.

ETHICS CHALLENGE

A1

Required

1. How does Golf Depot's use of FIFO improve its net profit margin and current ratio?
2. Is the action by Golf Depot's owner ethical? Explain.

BTN 5-4   You are a financial adviser with a client in the wholesale produce business that just completed its first year of operations. Due to weather conditions, the cost of acquiring produce to resell has escalated during the later part of this period. Your client, Javonte Cruz, mentions that because her business sells perishable goods, she has striven to maintain a FIFO flow of goods. Although sales are good, the increasing cost of inventory has put the business in a tight cash position. Cruz has expressed concern regarding the ability of the business to meet income tax obligations.

COMMUNICATING IN PRACTICE

A1

Required

Prepare a memorandum that identifies, explains, and justifies the inventory method you recommend your client, Ms. Cruz, adopt.

BTN 5-5   Access the 2006 annual 10-K report for **Oakley, Inc.** (Ticker OO), filed on March 9, 2007, from the EDGAR filings at www.SEC.gov.

TAKING IT TO THE NET

A3

Required

1. What product does Oakley sell that is especially popular with college students?
2. What inventory method does Oakley use? (*Hint:* See the notes to its financial statements.)
3. Compute Oakley's gross margin and gross margin ratio for the 2006 calendar year. Comment on your computations—assume an industry average of 35% for the gross margin ratio.
4. Compute Oakley's inventory turnover and days' sales in inventory for the year ended December 31, 2006. Comment on your computations—assume an industry average of 3.9 for inventory turnover.

BTN 5-6   Each team member has the responsibility to become an expert on an inventory method. This expertise will be used to facilitate teammates' understanding of the concepts relevant to that method.

1. Each learning team member should select an area for expertise by choosing one of the following inventory methods: specific identification, LIFO, FIFO, or weighted average.
2. Form expert teams made up of students who have selected the same area of expertise. The instructor will identify where each expert team will meet.
3. Using the following data, each expert team must collaborate to develop a presentation that illustrates the relevant concepts and procedures for its inventory method. Each team member must write the presentation in a format that can be shown to the learning team.

TEAMWORK IN ACTION

A1 P1

Point: Step 1 allows four choices or areas for expertise. Larger teams will have some duplication of choice, but the specific identification method should not be duplicated.

Data

The company uses a perpetual inventory system. It had the following beginning inventory and current year purchases of its product.

Jan. 1	Beginning inventory	50 units @ $100 =	$ 5,000
Jan. 14	Purchase	150 units @ $120 =	18,000
Apr. 30	Purchase	200 units @ $150 =	30,000
Sept. 26	Purchase	300 units @ $200 =	60,000

The company transacted sales on the following dates at a $350 per unit sales price.

Jan. 10	30 units	(specific cost: 30 @ $100)
Feb. 15	100 units	(specific cost: 100 @ $120)
Oct. 5	350 units	(specific cost: 100 @ $150 and 250 @ $200)

Concepts and Procedures to Illustrate in Expert Presentation

   a. Identify and compute the costs to assign to the units sold. (Round per unit costs to three decimals.)

   b. Identify and compute the costs to assign to the units in ending inventory. (Round inventory balances to the dollar.)

   c. How likely is it that this inventory costing method will reflect the actual physical flow of goods? How relevant is that factor in determining whether this is an acceptable method to use?

   d. What is the impact of this method versus others in determining net income and income taxes?

   e. How closely does the ending inventory amount reflect replacement cost?

4. Re-form learning teams. In rotation, each expert is to present to the team the presentation developed in part 3. Experts are to encourage and respond to questions.

ENTREPRENEURIAL DECISION

A3

BTN 5-7   Review the chapter's opening feature highlighting Jacquelyn Tran and her company, **Beauty Encounter**. Assume that Beauty Encounter consistently maintains an inventory level of $300,000, meaning that its average and ending inventory levels are the same. Also assume its annual cost of sales is $1,200,000. To cut costs, Jacquelyn proposes to slash inventory to a constant level of $150,000 with no impact on cost of sales. She plans to work with suppliers to get quicker deliveries and to order smaller quantities more often.

Required

1. Compute the company's inventory turnover and its days' sales in inventory under (*a*) current conditions and (*b*) proposed conditions.

2. Evaluate and comment on the merits of Jacquelyn's proposal given your analysis for part 1. Identify any concerns you might have about the proposal.

HITTING THE ROAD

C1 C2

BTN 5-8   Visit four retail stores with another classmate. In each store, identify whether the store uses a bar-coding system to help manage its inventory. Try to find at least one store that does not use bar-coding. If a store does not use bar-coding, ask the store's manager or clerk whether he or she knows which type of inventory method the store employs. Create a table that shows columns for the name of store visited, type of merchandise sold, use or nonuse of bar-coding, and the inventory method used if bar-coding is not employed. You might also inquire as to what the store's inventory turnover is and how often physical inventory is taken.

GLOBAL DECISION

A3

BTN 5-9   Key figures (RMB 000s) for **GOME** (www.GOME.com.hk), which is the leading chain retailer of consumer electronic products and household appliances in China, follow.

RMB 000s	Current Year	One Year Prior	Two Years Prior
Inventory	5,473,497	5,383,039	4,882,754
Cost of sales	41,381,223	38,383,276	22,369,445

Required

1. Use these data and those from BTN 5-2 to compute (*a*) inventory turnover and (*b*) days' sales in inventory for the most recent two years shown for **GOME, Best Buy** and **RadioShack.**

2. Comment on and interpret your findings from part 1.

ANSWERS TO MULTIPLE CHOICE QUIZ

1. a; FIFO perpetual

Date	Goods Purchased	Cost of Goods Sold	Inventory Balance
July 1			75 units @ $25 = $ 1,875
July 3	348 units @ $27 = $9,396		75 units @ $25 } 348 units @ $27 } = $ 11,271
July 8		75 units @ $25 } 225 units @ $27 } = $ 7,950	123 units @ $27 = $ 3,321
July 15	257 units @ $28 = $7,196		123 units @ $27 } 257 units @ $28 } = $ 10,517
July 23		123 units @ $27 } 152 units @ $28 } = $ 7,577	105 units @ $28 = $ 2,940
		$15,527	

2. b; LIFO perpetual

Date	Goods Purchased	Cost of Goods Sold	Inventory Balance
July 1			75 units @ $25 = $ 1,875
July 3	348 units @ $27 = $9,396		75 units @ $25 } 348 units @ $27 } = $ 11,271
July 8		300 units @ $27 = $ 8,100	75 units @ $25 } 48 units @ $27 } = $ 3,171
July 15	257 units @ $28 = $7,196		75 units @ $25 } 48 units @ $27 } 257 units @ $28 } = $ 10,367
July 23		257 units @ $28 } 18 units @ $27 } = $ 7,682	75 units @ $25 } 30 units @ $27 } = $ 2,685
		$15,782	

3. e; Specific identification perpetual—Ending inventory computation.

20 units @ $25	$ 500
40 units @ $27	1,080
45 units @ $28	1,260
105 units	$2,840

4. a; FIFO periodic—Ending inventory computation.

105 units @ $28 each = $2,940; The FIFO periodic inventory computation is identical to the FIFO perpetual inventory computation (see question 1).

5. d; Days' sales in inventory = (Ending inventory/Cost of goods sold × 365)
= ($18,000/$85,000) × 365 = 77.29 days

Reporting and Analyzing Cash and Internal Controls

"It's a creative outlet for me . . . it doesn't feel like work"   —Dylan Lauren

A Look Back

Chapters 4 and 5 focused on merchandising activities and accounting for inventory. We explained the inventory system, accounting for inventory transactions, and methods for assigning costs to inventory.

A Look at This Chapter

This chapter extends our study of accounting to internal control and the analysis of cash. We describe procedures that are good for internal control. We also explain the control of and the accounting for cash, including control features of banking activities.

A Look Ahead

Chapter 7 focuses on receivables. We explain how to account and report on receivables and their related accounts. This includes estimating uncollectible receivables and computing interest earned.

Candyland Biz

NEW YORK—A 10-foot chocolate bunny greets you as you enter the store—that should be warning enough! This elite designer candy store, christened **Dylan's Candy Bar (DylansCandyBar.com),** is the brainchild of co-founder Dylan Lauren. Explains Dylan, "I got a business plan together and set out to make candy my livelihood."

This sweet-lovers heaven offers more than 5,000 different choices of sweets from all over the world. It has become a hip hangout for locals and tourists—and it has made candy cool. Says Dylan, "Park Avenue women come in, and the first thing they ask for is Gummi bears. They love that it's very childhood, nostalgic."

Although marketing is an important part of its success, Dylan's management of internal controls and cash is equally impressive. Several control procedures monitor its business activities and safeguard its assets. An example is the biometric time and attendance control system using fingerprint characteristics. Says Dylan, "There's no fooling the system! It is going to help us remotely manage our employees while eliminating human error and dishonesty. [It] is a cost-effective and

important business management tool." Similar controls are applied throughout the store. Dylan explains that such controls raise productivity and cut expenses.

The store's cash management practices are equally impressive, including controls over cash receipts, disbursements, and petty cash. The use of bank reconciliations further helps with the store's control and management of cash. Dylan explains that she takes advantage of available banking services to enhance controls over cash.

Internal controls are crucial when on a busy day its stores bring in thousands of customers, and their cash. They have already expanded to three stores in New York, and one each in Houston and Orlando. Through it all, Dylan says it is "totally fun."

[Sources: *Dylan's Candy Bar Website*, January 2010; *Entrepreneur*, June 2005; *NYC Official City Guide*, July 2009; *The New York Times*, June & March 2009; *Dolce Vita Magazine*, June 2009; *Luxury Insider*, March 2009.]

CAP

Conceptual

C1 Define internal control and identify its purpose and principles. *(p. 250)*

C2 Define cash and cash equivalents and explain how to report them. *(p. 255)*

C3 Identify control features of banking activities. *(p. 262)*

Analytical

A1 Compute the days' sales uncollected ratio and use it to assess liquidity. *(p. 270)*

Procedural

P1 Apply internal control to cash receipts and disbursements. *(p. 256)*

P2 Explain and record petty cash fund transactions. *(p. 260)*

P3 Prepare a bank reconciliation. *(p. 265)*

P4 *Appendix 6A*—Describe the use of documentation and verification to control cash disbursements. *(p. 273)*

P5 *Appendix 6B*—Apply the net method to control purchase discounts. *(p. 276)*

LP6

We all are aware of theft and fraud. They affect us in several ways: We lock doors, chain bikes, review sales receipts, and acquire alarm systems. A company also takes actions to safeguard, control, and manage what it owns. Experience tells us that small companies are most vulnerable, usually due to weak internal controls. It is management's responsibility to set up policies and procedures to safeguard a company's assets, especially cash. To do so, management *and* employees must understand and apply principles of internal control. This chapter describes these principles and how to apply them. It focuses special attention on cash because it is easily transferable and is often at high risk of loss.

Reporting and Analyzing Cash and Internal Controls

Internal Control

- Purpose of controls
- Principles of controls
- Technology and controls
- Limitations of controls

Control of Cash

- Cash, cash equivalents, and liquidity
- Control of receipts
- Control of disbursements

Banking Activities as Controls

- Basic bank services
- Bank statement
- Bank reconciliation

Internal Control

This section describes internal control and its fundamental principles. We also discuss the impact of technology on internal control and the limitations of control procedures.

Purpose of Internal Control

C1 Define internal control and identify its purpose and principles.

Managers (or owners) of small businesses often control the entire operation. These managers usually purchase all assets, hire and manage employees, negotiate all contracts, and sign all checks. They know from personal contact and observation whether the business is actually receiving the assets and services paid for. Most companies, however, cannot maintain this close personal supervision. They must delegate responsibilities and rely on formal procedures rather than personal contact in controlling business activities.

Internal Control System   Managers use an internal control system to monitor and control business activities. An **internal control system** consists of the policies and procedures managers use to

- ■ Protect assets.
- ■ Ensure reliable accounting.
- ■ Promote efficient operations.
- ■ Urge adherence to company policies.

Video6.1

A properly designed internal control system is a key part of systems design, analysis, and performance. Managers place a high priority on internal control systems because they can prevent avoidable losses, help managers plan operations, and monitor company and employee performance. Internal controls do not provide guarantees, but they lower the company's risk of loss.

Sarbanes-Oxley Act (SOX)   The **Sarbanes-Oxley Act (SOX)** requires the managers and auditors of companies whose stock is traded on an exchange (called *public companies*) to document and certify the system of internal controls. Following are some of the specific requirements:

- ■ Auditors must evaluate internal controls and issue an internal control report.
- ■ Auditors of a client are restricted as to what consulting services they can provide that client.

- The person leading an audit can serve no more than seven years without a two-year break.
- Auditors' work is overseen by the *Public Company Accounting Oversight Board* (PCAOB).
- Harsh penalties exist for violators—sentences up to 25 years in prison with severe fines.

SOX has markedly impacted companies, and the costs of its implementation are high. Importantly, *Section 404* of SOX requires that managers document and assess the effectiveness of all internal control processes that can impact financial reporting. The benefits include greater confidence in accounting systems and their related reports. However, the public continues to debate the costs versus the benefits of SOX as nearly all business activities of these companies are impacted by SOX. Section 404 of SOX requires that managers document and assess their internal controls *and* that auditors provide an opinion on managers' documentation and assessment. Costs of complying with Section 404 for companies is reported to average $4 million (source: Financial Executives Institute).

Principles of Internal Control

Internal control policies and procedures vary from company to company according to such factors as the nature of the business and its size. Certain fundamental internal control principles apply to all companies. The **principles of internal control** are to

1. Establish responsibilities.
2. Maintain adequate records.
3. Insure assets and bond key employees.
4. Separate recordkeeping from custody of assets.
5. Divide responsibility for related transactions.
6. Apply technological controls.
7. Perform regular and independent reviews.

This section explains these seven principles and describes how internal control procedures minimize the risk of fraud and theft. These procedures also increase the reliability and accuracy of accounting records. A framework for how these seven principles improve the quality of financial reporting is provided by the ***Committee of Sponsoring Organizations (COSO),*** see **www.COSO.org.** Specifically, these principles link to five aspects of internal control: control activities, control environment, risk assessment, monitoring, and communication.

Point: Sarbanes-Oxley Act (SOX) requires that each annual report contain an *internal control report*, which must: (1) state managers' responsibility for establishing and maintaining adequate internal controls for financial reporting; and (2) assess the effectiveness of those controls.

Establish Responsibilities Proper internal control means that responsibility for a task is clearly established and assigned to one person. When a problem occurs in a company where responsibility is not identified, determining who is at fault is difficult. For instance, if two sales-clerks share the same cash register and there is a cash shortage, neither clerk can be held accountable. To prevent this problem, one clerk might be given responsibility for handling all cash sales. Alternately, a company can use a register with separate cash drawers for each clerk. Most of us have waited at a retail counter during a shift change while employees swap cash drawers.

Point: Many companies have a mandatory vacation policy for employees who handle cash. When another employee must cover for the one on vacation, it is more difficult to hide cash frauds.

Maintain Adequate Records Good recordkeeping is part of an internal control system. It helps protect assets and ensures that employees use prescribed procedures. Reliable records are also a source of information that managers use to monitor company activities. When detailed records of equipment are kept, for instance, items are unlikely to be lost or stolen without detection. Similarly, transactions are less likely to be entered in wrong accounts if a chart of accounts is set up and carefully used. Many preprinted forms and internal documents are also designed for use in a good internal control system. When sales slips are properly designed, for instance, sales personnel can record needed information efficiently with less chance of errors or delays to customers. When sales slips are prenumbered and controlled, each one issued is the responsibility of one salesperson, preventing the salesperson from pocketing cash by making a sale and destroying the sales slip. Computerized point-of-sale systems achieve the same control results.

Point: The Association of Certified Fraud Examiners (**cfenet.com**) estimates that employee fraud costs small companies more than $100,000 per incident.

Insure Assets and Bond Key Employees   Good internal control means that assets are adequately insured against casualty and that employees handling large amounts of cash and easily transferable assets are bonded. An employee is *bonded* when a company purchases an insurance policy, or a bond, against losses from theft by that employee. Bonding reduces the risk of loss. It also discourages theft because bonded employees know an independent bonding company will be involved when theft is uncovered and is unlikely to be sympathetic with an employee involved in theft.

Decision Insight

Tag Control   A novel technique exists for marking physical assets. It involves embedding a less than one-inch-square tag of fibers that creates a unique optical signature recordable by scanners. Manufacturers hope to embed tags in everything from compact discs and credit cards to designer clothes for purposes of internal control and efficiency.

Separate Recordkeeping from Custody of Assets   A person who controls or has access to an asset must not keep that asset's accounting records. This principle reduces the risk of theft or waste of an asset because the person with control over it knows that another person keeps its records. Also, a recordkeeper who does not have access to the asset has no reason to falsify records. This means that to steal an asset and hide the theft from the records, two or more people must *collude*—or agree in secret to commit the fraud.

Divide Responsibility for Related Transactions   Good internal control divides responsibility for a transaction or a series of related transactions between two or more individuals or departments. This is to ensure that the work of one individual acts as a check on the other. This principle, often called *separation of duties,* is not a call for duplication of work. Each employee or department should perform unduplicated effort. Examples of transactions with divided responsibility are placing purchase orders, receiving merchandise, and paying vendors. These tasks should not be given to one individual or department. Assigning responsibility for two or more of these tasks to one party increases mistakes and perhaps fraud. Having an independent person, for example, check incoming goods for quality and quantity encourages more care and attention to detail than having the person who placed the order do the checking. Added protection can result from identifying a third person to approve payment of the invoice. A company can even designate a fourth person with authority to write checks as another protective measure.

Point: There's a new security device—a person's ECG (electrocardiogram) reading—that is as unique as a fingerprint and a lot harder to lose or steal than a PIN. ECGs can be read through fingertip touches. An ECG also shows that a living person is actually there, whereas fingerprint and facial recognition software can be fooled.

Apply Technological Controls   Cash registers, check protectors, time clocks, and personal identification scanners are examples of devices that can improve internal control. Technology often improves the effectiveness of controls. A cash register with a locked-in tape or electronic file makes a record of each cash sale. A check protector perforates the amount of a check into its face and makes it difficult to alter the amount. A time clock registers the exact time an employee both arrives at and departs from the job. Mechanical change and currency counters quickly and accurately count amounts, and personal scanners limit access to only authorized individuals. Each of these and other technological controls are an effective part of many internal control systems.

Decision Insight

About Face   Face-recognition software snaps a digital picture of the face and converts key facial features—say, the distance between the eyes—into a series of numerical values. These can be stored on an ID or ATM card as a simple bar code to prohibit unauthorized access.

Perform Regular and Independent Reviews   Changes in personnel, stress of time pressures, and technological advances present opportunities for shortcuts and lapses. To counter

1. Principles of internal control suggest that (choose one): (*a*) Responsibility for a series of related transactions (such as placing orders, receiving and paying for merchandise) should be assigned to one employee; (*b*) Responsibility for individual tasks should be shared by more than one employee so that one serves as a check on the other; or (*c*) Employees who handle considerable cash and easily transferable assets should be bonded.

2. What are some impacts of computing technology on internal control?

Control of Cash

Cash is a necessary asset of every company. Most companies also own *cash equivalents* (defined below), which are assets similar to cash. Cash and cash equivalents are the most liquid of all assets and are easily hidden and moved. An effective system of internal controls protects these assets and it should meet three basic guidelines:

1. Handling cash is separate from recordkeeping of cash.
2. Cash receipts are promptly deposited in a bank.
3. Cash disbursements are made by check.

Video6.1

The first guideline applies separation of duties to minimize errors and fraud. When duties are separated, two or more people must collude to steal cash and conceal this action in the accounting records. The second guideline uses immediate (say, daily) deposits of all cash receipts to produce a timely independent record of the cash received. It also reduces the likelihood of cash theft (or loss) and the risk that an employee could personally use the money before depositing it. The third guideline uses payments by check to develop an independent bank record of cash disbursements. This guideline also reduces the risk of cash theft (or loss).

   This section begins with definitions of cash and cash equivalents. Discussion then focuses on controls and accounting for both cash receipts and disbursements. The exact procedures used to achieve control over cash vary across companies. They depend on factors such as company size, number of employees, volume of cash transactions, and sources of cash.

Cash, Cash Equivalents, and Liquidity

Good accounting systems help in managing the amount of cash and controlling who has access to it. Cash is the usual means of payment when paying for assets, services, or liabilities. **Liquidity** refers to a company's ability to pay for its near-term obligations. Cash and similar assets are called **liquid assets** because they can be readily used to settle such obligations. A company needs liquid assets to effectively operate.

   Cash includes currency and coins along with the amounts on deposit in bank accounts, checking accounts (called *demand deposits*), and many savings accounts (called *time deposits*). Cash also includes items that are acceptable for deposit in these accounts such as customer checks, cashier checks, certified checks, and money orders. **Cash equivalents** are short-term, highly liquid investment assets meeting two criteria: (1) readily convertible to a known cash amount and (2) sufficiently close to their due date so that their market value is not sensitive to interest rate changes. Only investments purchased within three months of their due date usually satisfy these criteria. Examples of cash equivalents are short-term investments in assets such as U.S. Treasury bills and money market funds. To increase their return, many companies invest idle cash in cash equivalents. Most companies combine cash equivalents with cash as a single item on the balance sheet.

C2   Define cash and cash equivalents and explain how to report them.

Point: The most liquid assets are usually reported first on a balance sheet; the least liquid assets are reported last.

Point: Google reports cash and cash equivalents of $3,544 million in its balance sheet. This amount makes up nearly 20% of its total assets.

Cash Management

When companies fail, one of the most common causes is their inability to manage cash. Companies must plan both cash receipts and cash payments. The goals of cash management are twofold:

1. Plan cash receipts to meet cash payments when due.
2. Keep a minimum level of cash necessary to operate.

The *treasurer* of the company is responsible for cash management. Effective cash management involves applying the following cash management principles.

- **Encourage collection of receivables.** The more quickly customers and others pay the company, the more quickly that company can use the money. Some companies have cash-only sales policies. Others might offer discounts for payments received early.

- **Delay payment of liabilities.** The more delayed a company is in paying others, the more time it has to use the money. Some companies regularly wait until the last possible day required to pay their bills—although, a company must take care not to hurt its credit standing.

- **Keep only necessary levels of assets.** The less money tied up in idle assets, the more money to invest in productive assets. Some companies maintain *just-in-time* inventory; meaning they plan inventory to be available at the same time orders are filled. Others might lease out excess warehouse space or rent equipment instead of buying it.

- **Plan expenditures.** Money should be spent only when it is available. Companies must look at seasonal and business cycles to plan expenditures.

- **Invest excess cash.** Excess cash earns no return and should be invested. Excess cash from seasonal cycles can be placed in a bank account or other short-term investment for income. Excess cash beyond what's needed for regular business should be invested in productive assets like factories and inventories.

Decision Insight

Days' Cash Expense Coverage The ratio of *cash (and cash equivalents) to average daily cash expenses* indicates the number of days a company can operate without additional cash inflows. It reflects on company liquidity and on the potential of excess cash.

Control of Cash Receipts

P1 Apply internal control to cash receipts and disbursements.

Internal control of cash receipts ensures that cash received is properly recorded and deposited. Cash receipts can arise from transactions such as cash sales, collections of customer accounts, receipts of interest earned, bank loans, sales of assets, and owner investments. This section explains internal control over two important types of cash receipts: over-the-counter and by mail.

Over-the-Counter Cash Receipts For purposes of internal control, over-the-counter cash receipts from sales should be recorded on a cash register at the time of each sale. To help ensure that correct amounts are entered, each register should be located so customers can read the amounts entered. Clerks also should be required to enter each sale before wrapping merchandise and to give the customer a receipt for each sale. The design of each cash register should provide a permanent, locked-in record of each transaction. In many systems, the register is directly linked with computing and accounting services. Less advanced registers simply print a record of each transaction on a paper tape or electronic file locked inside the register.

Proper internal control prescribes that custody over cash should be separate from its recordkeeping. For over-the-counter cash receipts, this separation begins with the cash sale. The clerk who has access to cash in the register should not have access to its locked-in record. At the end of the clerk's work period, the clerk should count the cash in the register, record the amount, and turn over the cash and a record of its amount to the company cashier. The cashier, like the clerk, has access to the cash but should not have access to accounting records (or the register tape or file). A third employee, often a supervisor, compares the record of total register transactions (or the register tape or file) with the cash receipts reported by the cashier. This record is the basis for a journal entry recording over-the-counter cash receipts. The third employee has access to the records for cash but not to the actual cash. The clerk and the cashier have access to cash but not to the accounting records. None of them can make a mistake or divert cash without the difference being revealed—see the following diagram.

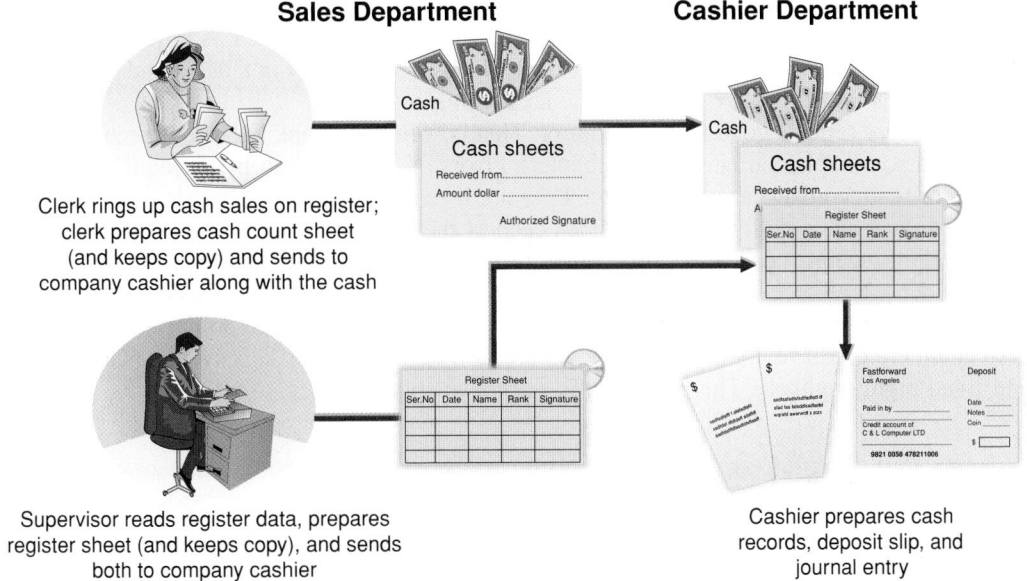

Cash over and short.   Sometimes errors in making change are discovered from differences between the cash in a cash register and the record of the amount of cash receipts. Although a clerk is careful, one or more customers can be given too much or too little change. This means that at the end of a work period, the cash in a cash register might not equal the record of cash receipts. This difference is reported in the **Cash Over and Short** account, also called *Cash Short and Over,* which is an income statement account recording the income effects of cash overages and cash shortages. To illustrate, if a cash register's record shows $550 but the count of cash in the register is $555, the entry to record cash sales and its overage is

Cash	555	
Cash Over and Short		5
Sales		550
To record cash sales and a cash overage.		

Assets = Liabilities + Equity
+555   + 5
                  +550

On the other hand, if a cash register's record shows $625 but the count of cash in the register is $621, the entry to record cash sales and its shortage is

Cash	621	
Cash Over and Short	4	
Sales		625
To record cash sales and a cash shortage.		

Assets = Liabilities + Equity
+621   − 4
                  +625

Since customers are more likely to dispute being shortchanged than being given too much change, the Cash Over and Short account usually has a debit balance at the end of an accounting period. A debit balance reflects an expense. It is reported on the income statement as part of general and administrative expenses. (Since the amount is usually small, it is often combined with other small expenses and reported as part of *miscellaneous expenses;* or as part of *miscellaneous revenues* if it has a credit balance.)

Cash Receipts by Mail   Control of cash receipts that arrive through the mail starts with the person who opens the mail. Preferably, two people are assigned the task of, and are present for, opening the mail. In this case, theft of cash receipts by mail requires collusion between these two employees. Specifically, the person(s) opening the mail enters a list (in triplicate) of money received. This list should contain a record of each sender's name, the amount, and an explanation of why the money is sent. The first copy is sent with the money to the cashier. A second copy is sent to the recordkeeper in the accounting area. A third copy is kept by the clerk(s) who opened the mail. The cashier deposits the money in a bank, and the recordkeeper records the amounts received in the accounting records.

This process reflects good internal control. That is, when the bank balance is reconciled by another person (explained later in the chapter), errors or acts of fraud by the mail clerks, the cashier, or the recordkeeper are revealed. They are revealed because the bank's record of cash deposited must agree with the records from each of the three. Moreover, if the mail clerks do not report all receipts correctly, customers will question their account balances. If the cashier does not deposit all receipts, the bank balance does not agree with the recordkeeper's cash balance. The recordkeeper and the person who reconciles the bank balance do not have access to cash and therefore have no opportunity to divert cash to themselves. This system makes errors and fraud highly unlikely. The exception is employee collusion.

Decision Insight

Perpetual Accounting   Wal-Mart uses a network of information links with its point-of-sale cash registers to coordinate sales, purchases, and distribution. Its supercenters, for instance, ring up 15,000 separate sales on heavy days. By using cash register information, the company can fix pricing mistakes quickly and capitalize on sales trends.

Control of Cash Disbursements

Control of cash disbursements is especially important as most large thefts occur from payment of fictitious invoices. One key to controlling cash disbursements is to require all expenditures to be made by check. The only exception is small payments made from petty cash. Another key is to deny access to the accounting records to anyone other than the owner who has the authority to sign checks. A small business owner often signs checks and knows from personal contact that the items being paid for are actually received. This arrangement is impossible in large businesses. Instead, internal control procedures must be substituted for personal contact. Such procedures are designed to assure the check signer that the obligations recorded are properly incurred and should be paid. This section describes these and other internal control procedures, including the voucher system and petty cash system. A method for management of cash disbursements for purchases is described in Appendix 6B.

Decision Insight

Cash Budget   Projected cash receipts and cash disbursements are often summarized in a *cash budget*. Provided that sufficient cash exists for effective operations, companies wish to minimize the cash they hold because of its risk of theft and its low return versus other investment opportunities.

Voucher System of Control   A **voucher system** is a set of procedures and approvals designed to control cash disbursements and the acceptance of obligations. The voucher system of control establishes procedures for

■ Verifying, approving, and recording obligations for eventual cash disbursement.
■ Issuing checks for payment of verified, approved, and recorded obligations.

A reliable voucher system follows standard procedures for every transaction. This applies even when multiple purchases are made from the same supplier.

A voucher system's control over cash disbursements begins when a company incurs an obligation that will result in payment of cash. A key factor in this system is that only approved departments and individuals are authorized to incur such obligations. The system often limits the type of obligations that a department or individual can incur. In a large retail store, for instance, only a purchasing department should be authorized to incur obligations for merchandise inventory. Another key factor is that procedures for purchasing, receiving, and paying for merchandise are divided among several departments (or individuals). These departments include the one requesting the purchase, the purchasing department, the receiving department, and the accounting department. To coordinate and control responsibilities of these departments, a company uses several different business documents. Exhibit 6.1 shows how documents are accumulated in a **voucher,** which is an internal document (or file) used to accumulate information to control cash disbursements and to ensure that a transaction is properly recorded. This specific example begins with a *purchase requisition* and concludes with a *check* drawn against cash. Appendix 6A describes the documentation and verification necessary for a voucher system of control. It also describes the internal control objective served by each document.

Point: MCI, formerly <u>WorldCom</u>, paid a whopping $500 million in SEC fines for accounting fraud. Among the charges were that it inflated earnings by as much as $10 billion. Its CEO, Bernard Ebbers, was sentenced to 25 years.

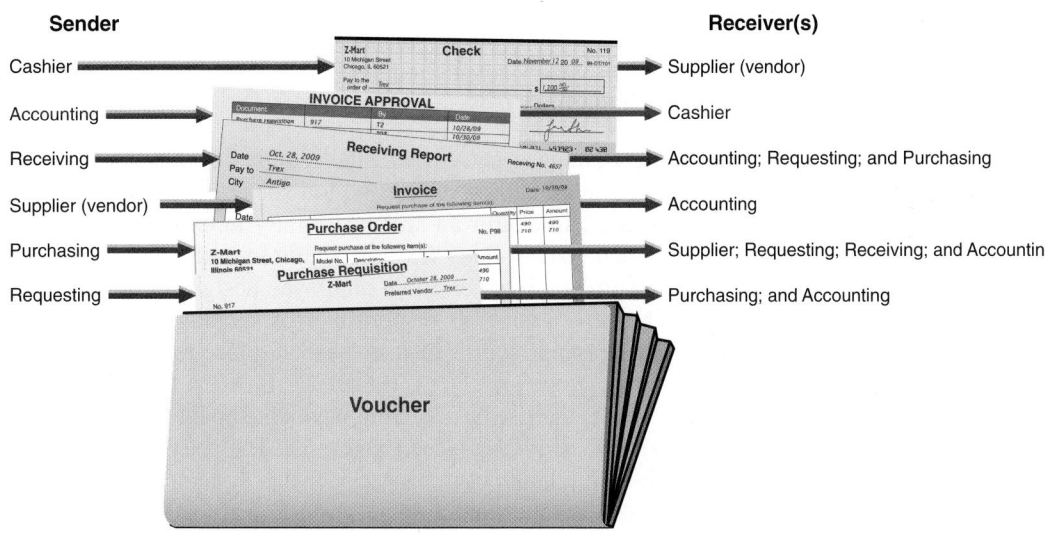

EXHIBIT 6.1

Document Flow in a Voucher System

A voucher system should be applied not only to purchases of inventory but to all expenditures. To illustrate, when a company receives a monthly telephone bill, it should review and verify the charges, prepare a voucher (file), and insert the bill. This transaction is then recorded with a journal entry. If the amount is currently due, a check is issued. If not, the voucher is filed for payment on its due date. If no voucher is prepared, verifying the invoice and its amount after several days or weeks can be difficult. Also, without records, a dishonest employee could collude with a dishonest supplier to get more than one payment for an obligation, payment for excessive amounts, or payment for goods and services not received. An effective voucher system helps prevent such frauds.

Point: A *voucher* is an internal document (or file).

Point: The basic purposes of paper and electronic documents are similar. However, the internal control system must change to reflect different risks, including confidential and competitive-sensitive information that is at greater risk in electronic systems.

Decision Insight

Cyber Setup The FTC is on the cutting edge of cybersleuthing. Opportunists in search of easy money are lured to <u>WeMarket4U.net/netops</u>. Take the bait and you get warned—and possibly targeted. The top 4 fraud complaints as compiled by the Internet Crime Complaint Center are shown to the right.

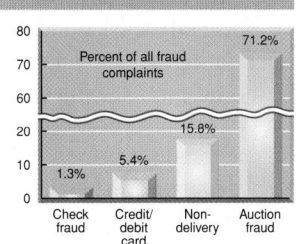

3. Why must a company hold liquid assets?

4. Why does a company hold cash equivalent assets in addition to cash?

5. Identify at least two assets that are classified as cash equivalents.

6. Good internal control procedures for cash include which of the following? (*a*) All cash disbursements, other than those for very small amounts, are made by check; (*b*) One employee counts cash received from sales and promptly deposits cash receipts; or (*c*) Cash receipts by mail are opened by one employee who is then responsible for recording and depositing them.

7. Should all companies require a voucher system? At what point in a company's growth would you recommend a voucher system?

P2   Explain and record petty cash fund transactions.

Petty Cash System of Control   A basic principle for controlling cash disbursements is that all payments must be made by check. An exception to this rule is made for *petty cash disbursements,* which are the small payments required for items such as postage, courier fees, minor repairs, and low-cost supplies. To avoid the time and cost of writing checks for small amounts, a company sets up a petty cash fund to make small payments. (**Petty cash** activities are part of an *imprest system,* which designates advance money to establish the fund, to withdraw from the fund, and to reimburse the fund.)

Operating a petty cash fund.   Establishing a petty cash fund requires estimating the total amount of small payments likely to be made during a short period such as a week or month. A check is then drawn by the company cashier for an amount slightly in excess of this estimate. This check is recorded with a debit to the Petty Cash account (an asset) and a credit to Cash. The check is cashed, and the currency is given to an employee designated as the *petty cashier* or *petty cash custodian.* The petty cashier is responsible for keeping this cash safe, making payments from the fund, and keeping records of it in a secure place referred to as the *petty cashbox.*

Point: A petty cash fund is used only for business expenses.

When each cash disbursement is made, the person receiving payment should sign a prenumbered *petty cash receipt,* also called *petty cash ticket*—see Exhibit 6.2. The petty cash receipt is then placed in the petty cashbox with the remaining money. Under this system, the sum of all receipts plus the remaining cash equals the total fund amount. A $100 petty cash fund, for instance, contains any combination of cash and petty cash receipts that totals $100 (examples are $80 cash plus $20 in receipts, or $10 cash plus $90 in receipts). Each disbursement reduces cash and increases the amount of receipts in the petty cashbox.

EXHIBIT 6.2

Petty Cash Receipt

Point: Petty cash receipts with either no signature or a forged signature usually indicate misuse of petty cash. Companies respond with surprise petty cash counts for verification.

The petty cash fund should be reimbursed when it is nearing zero and at the end of an accounting period when financial statements are prepared. For this purpose, the petty cashier sorts the paid receipts by the type of expense or account and then totals the receipts. The petty cashier presents all paid receipts to the company cashier, who stamps all receipts *paid* so they cannot be reused, files them for recordkeeping, and gives the petty cashier a check for their sum. When this check is cashed and the money placed in the cashbox, the total money in the cashbox is restored to its original amount. The fund is now ready for a new cycle of petty cash payments.

Illustrating a petty cash fund.   To illustrate, assume Z-Mart establishes a petty cash fund on November 1 and designates one of its office employees as the petty cashier. A $75 check is drawn, cashed, and the proceeds given to the petty cashier. The entry to record the setup of this petty cash fund is

Nov. 1	Petty Cash	75	
	Cash		75
	To establish a petty cash fund.		

Assets = Liabilities + Equity
+75
−75

After the petty cash fund is established, the Petty Cash account is not debited or credited again unless the amount of the fund is changed. (A fund should be increased if it requires reimbursement too frequently. On the other hand, if the fund is too large, some of its money should be redeposited in the Cash account.)

Next, assume that Z-Mart's petty cashier makes several November payments from petty cash. Each person who received payment is required to sign a receipt. On November 27, after making a $26.50 cash payment for tile cleaning, only $3.70 cash remains in the fund. The petty cashier then summarizes and totals the petty cash receipts as shown in Exhibit 6.3.

Point: Reducing or eliminating a petty cash fund requires a credit to Petty Cash.

Point: Although *individual* petty cash disbursements are not evidenced by a check, the initial petty cash fund is evidenced by a check, and later petty cash expenditures are evidenced by a check to replenish them *in total.*

EXHIBIT 6.3

Petty Cash Payments Report

Z-MART		
Petty Cash Payments Report		
Miscellaneous Expenses		
Nov. 2 Cleaning of LCD panels	$20.00	
Nov. 27 Tile cleaning	26.50	$ 46.50
Merchandise Inventory (transportation-in)		
Nov. 5 Transport of merchandise purchased	6.75	
Nov. 20 Transport of merchandise purchased	8.30	15.05
Delivery Expense		
Nov. 18 Customer's package delivered		5.00
Office Supplies Expense		
Nov. 15 Purchase of office supplies immediately used		4.75
Total		**$71.30**

Point: This report can also include receipt number and names of those who approved and received cash payment (see Demo Problem 2).

The petty cash payments report and all receipts are given to the company cashier in exchange for a $71.30 check to reimburse the fund. The petty cashier cashes the check and puts the $71.30 cash in the petty cashbox. The company records this reimbursement as follows.

Nov. 27	Miscellaneous Expenses	46.50	
	Merchandise Inventory	15.05	
	Delivery Expense	5.00	
	Office Supplies Expense	4.75	
	Cash		71.30
	To reimburse petty cash.		

Assets = Liabilities + Equity
−71.30   −46.50
                              −15.05
                              − 5.00
                              − 4.75

A petty cash fund is usually reimbursed at the end of an accounting period so that expenses are recorded in the proper period, even if the fund is not low on money. If the fund is not reimbursed at the end of a period, the financial statements would show both an overstated cash asset and understated expenses (or assets) that were paid out of petty cash. Some companies do not reimburse the petty cash fund at the end of each period under the notion that this amount is immaterial to users of financial statements.

Point: To avoid errors in recording petty cash reimbursement, follow these steps: (1) prepare payments report, (2) compute cash needed by subtracting cash remaining from total fund amount, (3) record entry, and (4) check "Dr. = Cr." in entry. Any difference is Cash Over and Short.

Increasing or decreasing a petty cash fund.   A decision to increase or decrease a petty cash fund is often made when reimbursing it. To illustrate, assume Z-Mart decides to *increase* its petty cash fund from $75 to $100 on November 27 when it reimburses the fund. The entries required are to (1) reimburse the fund as usual (see the preceding November 27 entry), and (2) increase the fund amount as follows.

Event	Petty Cash	Cash	Expenses
Set up fund	Dr.	Cr.	—
Reimburse fund ..	—	Cr.	Dr.
Increase fund	Dr.	Cr.	—
Decrease fund ...	Cr.	Dr.	—

Nov. 27	Petty Cash	25	
	Cash		25
	To increase the petty cash fund amount.		

Alternatively, if Z-Mart *decreases* the petty cash fund from $75 to $55 on November 27, the entry is to (1) credit Petty Cash for $20 (decreasing the fund from $75 to $55) and (2) debit Cash for $20 (reflecting the $20 transfer from Petty Cash to Cash).

$200 Petty Cash Fund

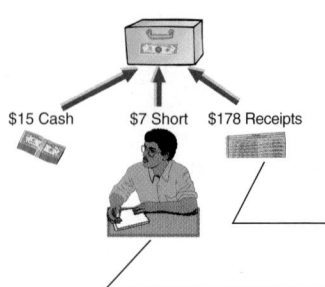

$15 Cash $7 Short $178 Receipts

Cash over and short.   Sometimes a petty cashier fails to get a receipt for payment or overpays for the amount due. When this occurs and the fund is later reimbursed, the petty cash payments report plus the cash remaining will not total to the fund balance. This mistake causes the fund to be *short*. This shortage is recorded as an expense in the reimbursing entry with a debit to the Cash Over and Short account. (An overage in the petty cash fund is recorded with a credit to Cash Over and Short in the reimbursing entry.) To illustrate, prepare the June 1 entry to reimburse a $200 petty cash fund when its payments report shows $178 in miscellaneous expenses and $15 cash remains.

June 1	Miscellaneous Expenses..........................	178	
	Cash Over and Short........................	7	
	Cash		185
	To reimburse petty cash.		

Decision Insight

Warning Signs   There are clues to internal control violations. Warning signs from accounting include: (1) an increase in customer refunds—could be fake, (2) missing documents—could be used for fraud, (3) differences between bank deposits and cash receipts—could be cash embezzled, and (4) delayed recording—could reflect fraudulent records. Warning signs from employees include: (1) lifestyle change—could be embezzlement, (2) too close with suppliers—could signal fraudulent transactions, and (3) failure to leave job, even for vacations—could conceal fraudulent activities.

Quick Check   Answers—p. 278

   8. Why are some cash payments made from a petty cash fund, and not by check?

   9. Why should a petty cash fund be reimbursed at the end of an accounting period?

   10. Identify at least two results of reimbursing a petty cash fund.

Banking Activities as Controls

Banks (and other financial institutions) provide many services, including helping companies control cash. Banks safeguard cash, provide detailed and independent records of cash transactions, and are a source of cash financing. This section describes these services and the documents provided by banking activities that increase managers' control over cash.

Basic Bank Services

C3 Identify control features of banking activities.

This section explains basic bank services—such as the bank account, the bank deposit, and checking—that contribute to the control of cash.

Bank Account, Deposit, and Check   A *bank account* is a record set up by a bank for a customer. It permits a customer to deposit money for safekeeping and helps control withdrawals. To limit access to a bank account, all persons authorized to write checks on the account must sign a **signature card,** which bank employees use to verify signatures on checks. Many companies have more than one bank account to serve different needs and to handle special transactions such as payroll.

Each bank deposit is supported by a **deposit ticket,** which lists items such as currency, coins, and checks deposited along with their corresponding dollar amounts. The bank gives the customer a copy of the deposit ticket or a deposit receipt as proof of the deposit. Exhibit 6.4 shows one type of deposit ticket.

Point: Online banking services include the ability to stop payment on a check, move money between accounts, get up-to-date balances, and identify cleared checks and deposits.

EXHIBIT 6.4

Deposit Ticket

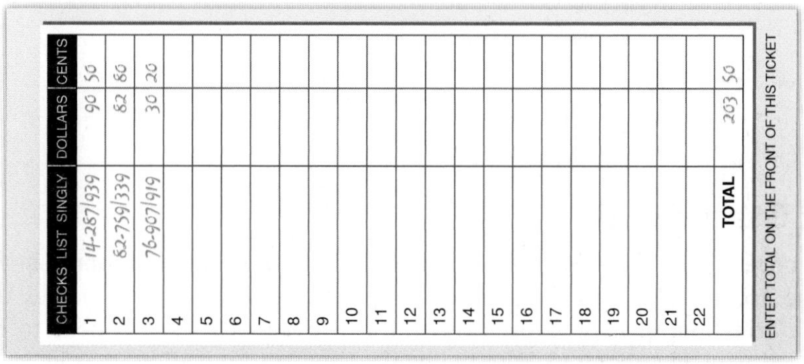

To withdraw money from an account, the depositor can use a **check,** which is a document signed by the depositor instructing the bank to pay a specified amount of money to a designated recipient. A check involves three parties: a *maker* who signs the check, a *payee* who is the recipient, and a *bank* (or *payer*) on which the check is drawn. The bank provides a depositor the checks that are serially numbered and imprinted with the name and address of both the depositor and bank. Both checks and deposit tickets are imprinted with identification codes in magnetic ink for computer processing. Exhibit 6.5 shows one type of check. It is accompanied with an optional *remittance advice* explaining the payment. When a remittance advice is unavailable, the *memo* line is often used for a brief explanation.

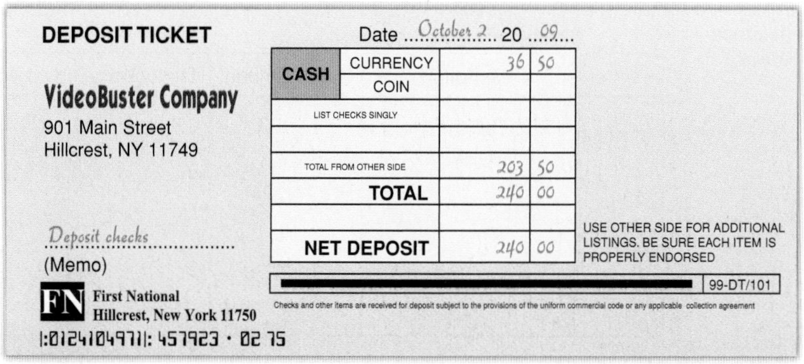

Electronic Funds Transfer   **Electronic funds transfer (EFT)** is the electronic transfer of cash from one party to another. No paper documents are necessary. Banks simply transfer cash from one account to another with a journal entry. Companies are increasingly using EFT because of its convenience and low cost. For instance, it can cost up to 50 cents to process a check through the banking system, whereas EFT cost is near zero. We now commonly see items such as payroll, rent, utilities, insurance, and interest payments being handled by EFT. The bank statement lists cash withdrawals by EFT with the checks and other deductions. Cash receipts by EFT are listed with deposits and other additions. A bank statement is sometimes a depositor's only notice of an EFT. *Automated teller machines*

EXHIBIT 6.5

Check with Remittance Advice

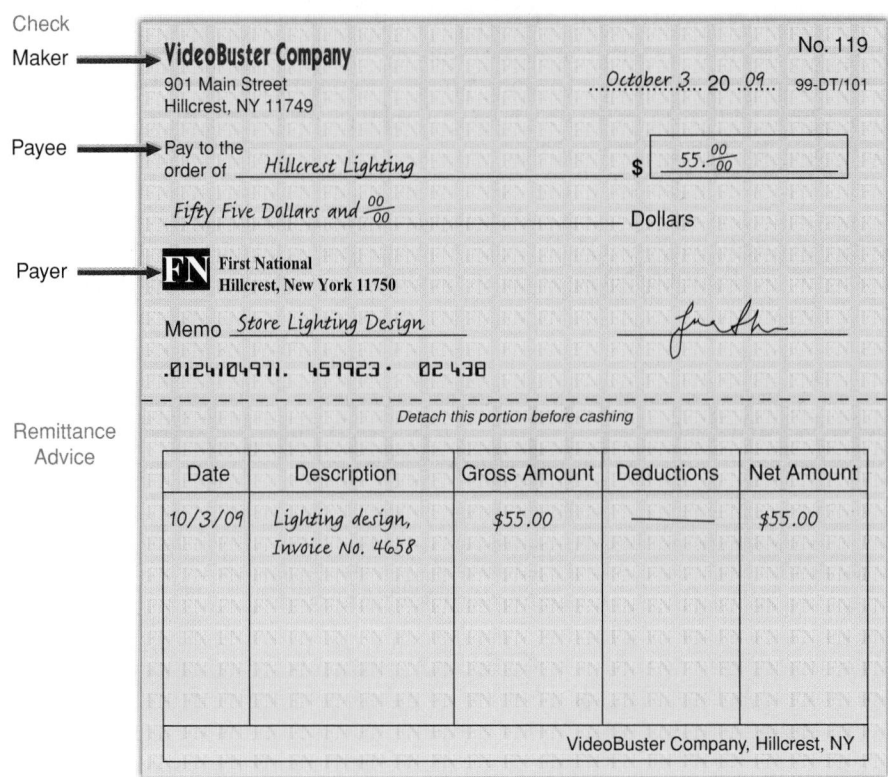

(ATMs) are one form of EFT, which allows bank customers to deposit, withdraw, and transfer cash.

Bank Statement

Usually once a month, the bank sends each depositor a **bank statement** showing the activity in the account. Although a monthly statement is common, companies often regularly access information on its banking transactions. (Companies can choose to record any accounting adjustments required from the bank statement immediately or later, say, at the end of each day, week, month, or when reconciling a bank statement.) Different banks use different formats for their bank statements, but all of them include the following items of information:

1. Beginning-of-period balance of the depositor's account.
2. Checks and other debits decreasing the account during the period.
3. Deposits and other credits increasing the account during the period.
4. End-of-period balance of the depositor's account.

This information reflects the bank's records. Exhibit 6.6 shows one type of bank statement. Identify each of these four items in that statement. Part Ⓐ of Exhibit 6.6 summarizes changes in the account. Part Ⓑ lists paid checks along with other debits. Part Ⓒ lists deposits and credits to the account, and part Ⓓ shows the daily account balances.

In reading a bank statement note that a depositor's account is a liability on the bank's records. This is so because the money belongs to the depositor, not the bank. When a depositor increases the account balance, the bank records it with a *credit* to that liability account. This means that debit memos from the bank produce *credits* on the depositor's books, and credit memos from the bank produce *debits* on the depositor's books.

Enclosed with a bank statement is a list of the depositor's canceled checks (or the actual canceled checks) along with any debit or credit memoranda affecting the account. Increasingly,

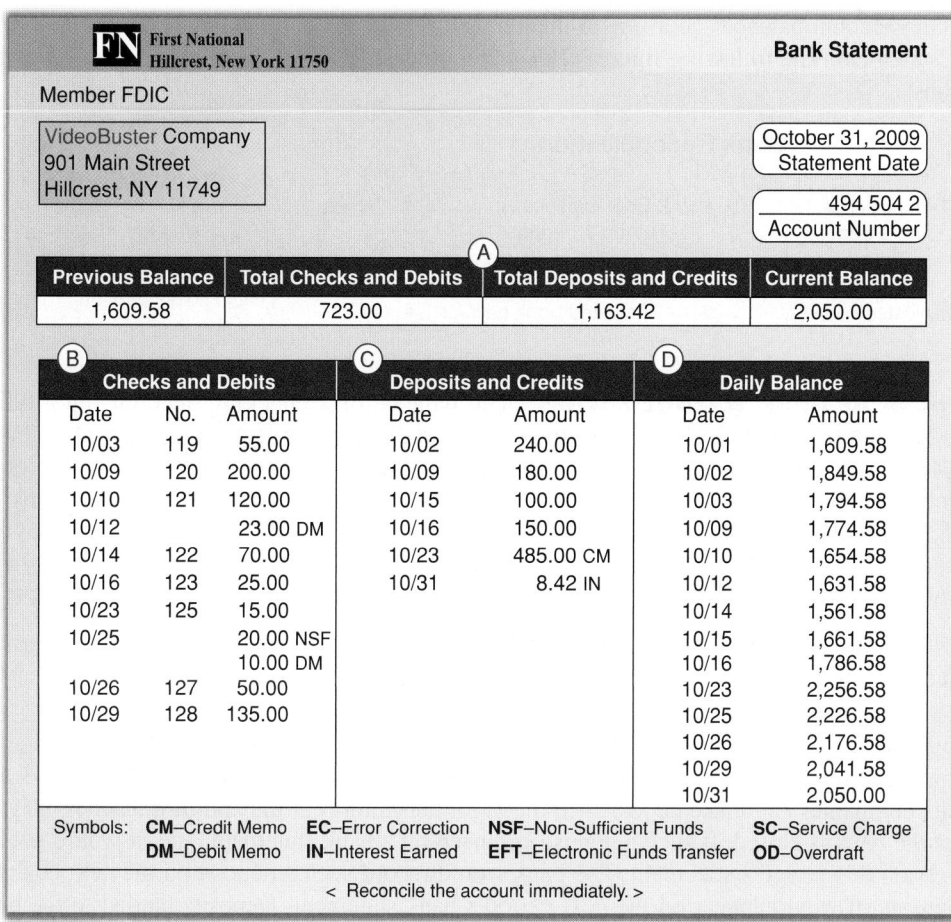

EXHIBIT 6.6

Bank Statement

Point: Many banks separately report other debits and credits apart from checks and deposits.

banks are showing canceled checks electronically via online access to accounts. **Canceled checks** are checks the bank has paid and deducted from the customer's account during the period. Other deductions that can appear on a bank statement include (1) service charges and fees assessed by the bank, (2) checks deposited that are uncollectible, (3) corrections of previous errors, (4) withdrawals through automated teller machines (ATMs), and (5) periodic payments arranged in advance by a depositor. (Most company checking accounts do not allow ATM withdrawals because of the company's desire to make all disbursements by check.) Except for service charges, the bank notifies the depositor of each deduction with a debit memorandum when the bank reduces the balance. A copy of each debit memorandum is usually sent with the statement (again, this information is often available earlier via online access and notifications).

Global: If cash is in more than one currency, a company usually translates these amounts into U.S. dollars using the exchange rate as of the balance sheet date. Also, a company must disclose any restrictions on cash accounts located outside the U.S.

   Transactions that increase the depositor's account include amounts the bank collects on behalf of the depositor and the corrections of previous errors. Credit memoranda notify the depositor of all increases when they are recorded. A copy of each credit memorandum is often sent with the bank statement. Banks that pay interest on checking accounts often compute the amount of interest earned on the average cash balance and credit it to the depositor's account each period. In Exhibit 6.6, the bank credits $8.42 of interest to the account.

Bank Reconciliation

When a company deposits all cash receipts and makes all cash payments (except petty cash) by check, it can use the bank statement for proving the accuracy of its cash records. This is done using a **bank reconciliation,** which is a report explaining any differences between the

P3 Prepare a bank reconciliation.

checking account balance according to the depositor's records and the balance reported on the bank statement. The following figure reflects this process, which we describe in the following sections.

Bank Reconciliation

Bank Balance		
Bank Statement		
• Checks & debits	#	
• Deposits & credits....	#	

Bank balance..............	#	Book balance..............	#
Add & deduct:		Add & deduct:	
• Timing differences	#	• Timing differences	#
• Any errors	#	• Any errors	#
Adjusted bank bal.......	#	Adjusted book bal.......	#

Book Balance		
Cash Account		
• Cash receipts	#	
• Cash disbursements		#

Purpose of Bank Reconciliation The balance of a checking account reported on the bank statement rarely equals the balance in the depositor's accounting records. This is usually due to information that one party has that the other does not. We must therefore prove the accuracy of both the depositor's records and those of the bank. This means we must *reconcile* the two balances and explain or account for any differences in them. Among the factors causing the bank statement balance to differ from the depositor's book balance are these:

■ **Outstanding checks. Outstanding checks** are checks written (or drawn) by the depositor, deducted on the depositor's records, and sent to the payees but not yet received by the bank for payment at the bank statement date.

■ **Deposits in transit** (also called **outstanding deposits**). **Deposits in transit** are deposits made and recorded by the depositor but not yet recorded on the bank statement. For example, companies can make deposits (in the night depository) at the end of a business day after the bank is closed. If such a deposit occurred on a bank statement date, it would not appear on this period's statement. The bank would record such a deposit on the next business day, and it would appear on the next period's bank statement. Deposits mailed to the bank near the end of a period also can be in transit and unrecorded when the statement is prepared.

■ **Deductions for uncollectible items and for services.** A company sometimes deposits another party's check that is uncollectible (usually meaning the balance in that party's account is not large enough to cover the check). This check is called a *non-sufficient funds (NSF)* check. The bank would have initially credited the depositor's account for the amount of the check. When the bank learns the check is uncollectible, it debits (reduces) the depositor's account for the amount of that check. The bank may also charge the depositor a fee for processing an uncollectible check and notify the depositor of the deduction by sending a debit memorandum. The depositor should record each deduction when a debit memorandum is received, but an entry is sometimes not made until the bank reconciliation is prepared. Other possible bank charges to a depositor's account that are first reported on a bank statement include printing new checks and service fees.

■ **Additions for collections and for interest.** Banks sometimes act as collection agents for their depositors by collecting notes and other items. Banks can also receive electronic funds transfers to the depositor's account. When a bank collects an item, it is added to the depositor's account, less any service fee. The bank also sends a credit memorandum to notify the depositor of the transaction. When the memorandum is received, the depositor should record it; yet it sometimes remains unrecorded until the bank reconciliation is prepared. The bank statement also includes a credit for any interest earned.

■ **Errors.** Both banks and depositors can make errors. Bank errors might not be discovered until the depositor prepares the bank reconciliation. Also, depositor errors are sometimes discovered when the bank balance is reconciled. Error testing includes: (a) comparing deposits on the bank statement with deposits in the accounting records and (b) comparing canceled checks on the bank statement with checks recorded in the accounting records.

Forms of Check Fraud (CkFraud.org)

• Forged signatures—legitimate blank checks with fake payer signature

• Forged endorsements—stolen check that is endorsed and cashed by someone other than the payee

• Counterfeit checks—fraudulent checks with fake payer signature

• Altered checks—legitimate check altered (such as changed payee or amount) to benefit perpetrator

• Check kiting—deposit check from one bank account (without sufficient funds) into a second bank account

---

Point: Small businesses with few employees often allow recordkeepers to both write checks and keep the general ledger. If this is done, it is essential that the owner do the bank reconciliation.

Point: The person preparing the bank reconciliation should not be responsible for processing cash receipts, managing checks, or maintaining cash records.

Illustration of a Bank Reconciliation   We follow nine steps in preparing the bank reconciliation. It is helpful to refer to the bank reconciliation in Exhibit 6.7 when studying steps ① through ⑨.

EXHIBIT 6.7

Bank Reconciliation

	VIDEOBUSTER Bank Reconciliation October 31, 2009					
①	Bank statement balance		$ 2,050.00	⑤ Book balance		$ 1,404.58
②	Add			⑥ Add		
	Deposit of Oct. 31 in transit . . .		145.00	Collect $500 note less $15 fee . . .	$485.00	
			2,195.00	Interest earned	8.42	493.42
③	Deduct					1,898.00
	Outstanding checks			⑦ Deduct		
	No. 124	$150.00		Check printing charge	23.00	
	No. 126	200.00	350.00	NSF check plus service fee	30.00	53.00
④	**Adjusted bank balance**		**$1,845.00**	⑧ **Adjusted book balance**		**$1,845.00**
			↑ ⑨ Balances are equal (reconciled)			↑

① Identify the bank statement balance of the cash account (*balance per bank*). VideoBuster's bank balance is $2,050.

② Identify and list any unrecorded deposits and any bank errors understating the bank balance. Add them to the bank balance. VideoBuster's $145 deposit placed in the bank's night depository on October 31 is not recorded on its bank statement.

③ Identify and list any outstanding checks and any bank errors overstating the bank balance. Deduct them from the bank balance. VideoBuster's comparison of canceled checks with its books shows two checks outstanding: No. 124 for $150 and No. 126 for $200.

④ Compute the *adjusted bank balance,* also called the *corrected* or *reconciled balance.*

⑤ Identify the company's book balance of the cash account (*balance per book*). VideoBuster's book balance is $1,404.58.

⑥ Identify and list any unrecorded credit memoranda from the bank, any interest earned, and errors understating the book balance. Add them to the book balance. VideoBuster's bank statement includes a credit memorandum showing the bank collected a note receivable for the company on October 23. The note's proceeds of $500 (minus a $15 collection fee) are credited to the company's account. VideoBuster's bank statement also shows a credit of $8.42 for interest earned on the average cash balance. There was no prior notification of this item, and it is not yet recorded.

⑦ Identify and list any unrecorded debit memoranda from the bank, any service charges, and errors overstating the book balance. Deduct them from the book balance. Debits on VideoBuster's bank statement that are not yet recorded include (a) a $23 charge for check printing and (b) an NSF check for $20 plus a related $10 processing fee. (The NSF check is dated October 16 and was included in the book balance.)

⑧ Compute the *adjusted book balance,* also called *corrected* or *reconciled balance.*

⑨ Verify that the two adjusted balances from steps 4 and 8 are equal. If so, they are reconciled. If not, check for accuracy and missing data to achieve reconciliation.

Point: Outstanding checks are identified by comparing canceled checks on the bank statement with checks recorded. This includes identifying any outstanding checks listed on the *previous* period's bank reconciliation that are not included in the canceled checks on this period's bank statement.

Point: Adjusting entries can be combined into one compound entry.

Adjusting Entries from a Bank Reconciliation   A bank reconciliation often identifies unrecorded items that need recording by the company. In VideoBuster's reconciliation, the adjusted balance of $1,845 is the correct balance as of October 31. But the company's accounting records show a $1,404.58 balance. We must prepare journal entries to adjust the book balance to the correct balance. It is important to remember that only the items reconciling the *book balance* require adjustment. A review of Exhibit 6.7 indicates that four entries are required for VideoBuster.

Collection of note.   The first entry is to record the proceeds of its note receivable collected by the bank less the expense of having the bank perform that service.

Assets = Liabilities + Equity
+485   −15
−500

Oct. 31	Cash	485	
	Collection Expense	15	
	Notes Receivable........................		500
	To record the collection fee and proceeds		
	for a note collected by the bank.		

Interest earned.   The second entry records interest credited to its account by the bank.

Assets = Liabilities + Equity
+8.42   +8.42

Oct. 31	Cash	8.42	
	Interest Revenue		8.42
	To record interest earned on the cash		
	balance in the checking account.		

Check printing.   The third entry records expenses for the check printing charge.

Assets = Liabilities + Equity
−23   −23

Oct. 31	Miscellaneous Expenses..........................	23	
	Cash		23
	Check printing charge.		

NSF check.   The fourth entry records the NSF check that is returned as uncollectible. The $20 check was originally received from T. Woods in payment of his account and then deposited. The bank charged $10 for handling the NSF check and deducted $30 total from VideoBuster's account. This means the entry must reverse the effects of the original entry made when the check was received and must record (add) the $10 bank fee.

Point: The company will try to collect the entire NSF amount of $30.

Oct. 31	Accounts Receivable—T. Woods	30	
	Cash		30
	To charge Woods' account for $20 NSF check		
	and $10 bank fee.		

Assets = Liabilities + Equity
+30
−30

Point: The Demo Problem I shows an adjusting entry for an error correction.

After these four entries are recorded, the book balance of cash is adjusted to the correct amount of $1,845 (computed as $1,404.58 + $485 + $8.42 − $23 − $30). The Cash T-account to the side shows the same computation, where entries are keyed to the numerical codes in Exhibit 6.7.

Cash			
Unadj. bal.	1,404.58		
⑥	485.00	⑦	23.00
⑥	8.42	⑦	30.00
Adj. bal.	1,845.00		

Decision Insight

Fraud   A survey reports that 74% of employees had 'personally seen' or had 'firsthand knowledge of' fraud or misconduct in their company within the past year. These employees also identified factors that would drive employees and managers to engage in misconduct. They cited pressures to meet targets, lack of standards, and other root causes—see graphic (KPMG 2009).

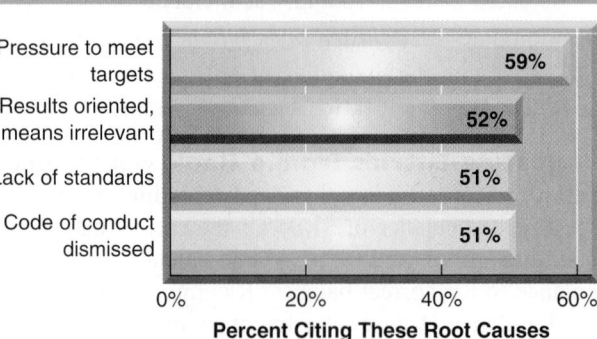

Quick Check

Answers—pp. 278–279

11. What is a bank statement?

12. What is the meaning of the phrase *to reconcile a bank balance?*

13. Why do we reconcile the bank statement balance of cash and the depositor's book balance of cash?

14. List at least two items affecting the bank balance side of a bank reconciliation and indicate whether the items are added or subtracted.

15. List at least three items affecting the book balance side of a bank reconciliation and indicate whether the items are added or subtracted.

Global View

This section discusses similarities and differences between U.S. GAAP and IFRS regarding internal controls and in the accounting and reporting of cash.

Internal Control Purposes, Principles, and Procedures

Both U.S. GAAP and IFRS aim for high-quality financial reporting. That aim translates into enhanced internal controls worldwide. Specifically, the purposes and principles of internal control systems are fundamentally the same across the globe. However, culture and other realities suggest different emphases on the mix of control procedures, and some sensitivity to different customs and environments when establishing that mix. Nevertheless, the discussion in this chapter applies internationally. **GOME** provides the following description of its control activities.

> Management had implemented a system of internal controls to provide reasonable assurance that the Group's assets are safeguarded, proper accounting records are maintained, appropriate legislation and regulations are complied with, reliable financial information is provided for management and publication purposes, and investment and business risks affecting the Group are identified and managed.

Control of Cash

Accounting definitions for cash are similar for U.S. GAAP and IFRS. **GOME** provides the following definition for cash.

> For the purpose of the balance sheets, cash and cash equivalents comprise cash on hand and at banks, including term deposits, which are not restricted as to use.

The need for control of cash is universal and applies globally. This means that companies worldwide desire to apply cash management procedures as explained in this chapter and aim to control both cash receipts and disbursements. Accordingly, systems that employ tools such as cash monitoring mechanisms, verification of documents, and petty cash processes are applied worldwide. The basic techniques explained in this chapter are part of those control procedures.

Banking Activities as Controls

There is a global demand for banking services, bank statements, and bank reconciliations. To the extent feasible, companies utilize banking services as part of their effective control procedures. Further, bank statements are similarly used along with bank reconciliations to control and monitor cash.

IFRS

Internal controls are crucial to companies that convert from U.S. GAAP to IFRS. Major risks include misstatement of financial information and fraud. Other risks are ineffective communication of the impact of this change for investors, creditors and others, and management's inability to certify the effectiveness of controls over financial reporting.

Decision Analysis | Days' Sales Uncollected

A1 Compute the days' sales uncollected ratio and use it to assess liquidity.

An important part of cash management is monitoring the receipt of cash from receivables. If customers and others who owe money to a company are delayed in payment, then that company can find it difficult to pay its obligations when they are due. A company's customers are crucial partners in its cash management. Many companies attract customers by selling to them on credit. This means that cash receipts from customers are delayed until accounts receivable are collected.

One measure of how quickly a company can convert its accounts receivable into cash is the **days' sales uncollected,** also called *days' sales in receivables*. This measure is computed by dividing the current balance of receivables by net credit sales over the year just completed and then multiplying by 365 (number of days in a year). Since net credit sales usually are not reported to external users, the net sales (or revenues) figure is commonly used in the computation as in Exhibit 6.8.

EXHIBIT 6.8

Days' Sales Uncollected

$$\text{Days' sales uncollected} = \frac{\text{Accounts receivable}}{\text{Net sales}} \times 365$$

We use days' sales uncollected to estimate how much time is likely to pass before the current amount of accounts receivable is received in cash. For evaluation purposes, we need to compare this estimate to that for other companies in the same industry. We also make comparisons between current and prior periods.

To illustrate, we select data from the annual reports of two toy manufacturers, **Hasbro** and **Mattel**. Their days' sales uncollected figures are shown in Exhibit 6.9.

EXHIBIT 6.9

Analysis Using Days' Sales Uncollected

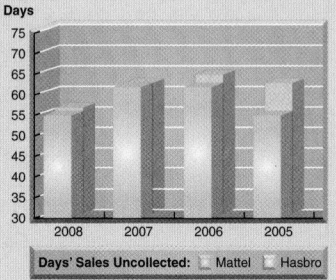

Days' Sales Uncollected: Mattel Hasbro

Company	Figure ($ millions)	2008	2007	2006	2005
Hasbro	Accounts receivable	$612	$655	$556	$523
	Net sales	$4,022	$3,838	$3,151	$3,088
	Days' sales uncollected	56 days	62 days	64 days	62 days
Mattel	Accounts receivable	$874	$991	$944	$761
	Net sales	$5,918	$5,970	$5,650	$5,179
	Days' sales uncollected	54 days	61 days	61 days	54 days

Days' sales uncollected for Hasbro in 2008 is computed as ($612/$4,022) × 365 days = 56 days. This means that it will take about 56 days to collect cash from ending accounts receivable. This number reflects one or more of the following factors: a company's ability to collect receivables, customer financial health, customer payment strategies, and discount terms. To further assess days' sales uncollected for Hasbro, we compare it to three prior years and to those of Mattel. We see that Hasbro's days' sales uncollected has generally improved over the past 4 years—from 62 days down to 56 days. In comparison, Mattel fluctuated on days' sales uncollected for each of those years—from 54 days, to 61 days for two years, and then back down to 54 days. Yet, for all years, Mattel is superior to Hasbro on this measure of cash management. The less time that money is tied up in receivables often translates into increased profitability.

 Decision Maker

Sales Representative   The sales staff is told to take action to help reduce days' sales uncollected for cash management purposes. What can you, a salesperson, do to reduce days' sales uncollected? [Answer—p. 278]

Demonstration Problem 1

Prepare a bank reconciliation for Jamboree Enterprises for the month ended November 30, 2009. The following information is available to reconcile Jamboree Enterprises' book balance of cash with its bank statement balance as of November 30, 2009:

a. After all posting is complete on November 30, the company's book balance of Cash has a $16,380 debit balance, but its bank statement shows a $38,520 balance.

b. Checks No. 2024 for $4,810 and No. 2026 for $5,000 are outstanding.

c. In comparing the canceled checks on the bank statement with the entries in the accounting records, it is found that Check No. 2025 in payment of rent is correctly drawn for $1,000 but is erroneously entered in the accounting records as $880.

d. The November 30 deposit of $17,150 was placed in the night depository after banking hours on that date, and this amount does not appear on the bank statement.

e. In reviewing the bank statement, a check written by Jumbo Enterprises in the amount of $160 was erroneously drawn against Jamboree's account.

f. A credit memorandum enclosed with the bank statement indicates that the bank collected a $30,000 note and $900 of related interest on Jamboree's behalf. This transaction was not recorded by Jamboree prior to receiving the statement.

g. A debit memorandum for $1,100 lists a $1,100 NSF check received from a customer, Marilyn Welch. Jamboree had not recorded the return of this check before receiving the statement.

h. Bank service charges for November total $40. These charges were not recorded by Jamboree before receiving the statement.

Planning the Solution

- Set up a bank reconciliation with a bank side and a book side (as in Exhibit 6.7). Leave room to both add and deduct items. Each column will result in a reconciled, equal balance.
- Examine each item *a* through *h* to determine whether it affects the book or the bank balance and whether it should be added or deducted from the bank or book balance.
- After all items are analyzed, complete the reconciliation and arrive at a reconciled balance between the bank side and the book side.
- For each reconciling item on the book side, prepare an adjusting entry. Additions to the book side require an adjusting entry that debits Cash. Deductions on the book side require an adjusting entry that credits Cash.

Solution to Demonstration Problem 1

JAMBOREE ENTERPRISES
Bank Reconciliation
November 30, 2009

Bank statement balance		$ 38,520	Book balance		$ 16,380
Add			Add		
Deposit of Nov. 30	$17,150		Collection of note	$30,000	
Bank error (Jumbo)	160	17,310	Interest earned	900	30,900
		55,830			47,280
Deduct			Deduct		
Outstanding checks			NSF check (M. Welch) ...	1,100	
No. 2024	4,810		Recording error (# 2025) .	120	
No. 2026	5,000	9,810	Service charge	40	1,260
Adjusted bank balance ...		**$46,020**	**Adjusted book balance ..**		**$46,020**

Required Adjusting Entries for Jamboree

Nov. 30	Cash	30,900	
	Notes Receivable		30,000
	Interest Earned		900
	To record collection of note with interest.		
Nov. 30	Accounts Receivable—M. Welch	1,100	
	Cash		1,100
	To reinstate account due from an NSF check.		
Nov. 30	Rent Expense	120	
	Cash		120
	To correct recording error on check no. 2025.		

[continued on next page]

[continued from previous page]

Nov. 30	Bank Service Charges	40	
	Cash		40
	To record bank service charges.		

Demonstration Problem 2

Bacardi Company established a $150 petty cash fund with Dean Martin as the petty cashier. When the fund balance reached $19 cash, Martin prepared a petty cash payment report, which follows.

Petty Cash Payments Report

Receipt No.	Account Charged		Approved by	Received by
12	Delivery Expense	$ 29	Martin	A. Smirnoff
13	Merchandise Inventory	18	Martin	J. Daniels
15	(Omitted)	32	Martin	C. Carlsberg
16	Miscellaneous Expense	41	(Omitted)	J. Walker
	Total	$120		

Required

1. Identify four internal control weaknesses from the payment report.

2. Prepare general journal entries to record:

    a. Establishment of the petty cash fund.

    b. Reimbursement of the fund. (Assume for this part only that petty cash receipt no. 15 was issued for miscellaneous expenses.)

3. What is the Petty Cash account balance immediately before reimbursement? Immediately after reimbursement?

Solution to Demonstration Problem 2

1. Four internal control weaknesses are

    a. Petty cash ticket no. 14 is missing. Its omission raises questions about the petty cashier's management of the fund.

    b. The $19 cash balance means that $131 has been withdrawn ($150 − $19 = $131). However, the total amount of the petty cash receipts is only $120 ($29 + $18 + $32 + $41). The fund is $11 short of cash ($131 − $120 = $11). Was petty cash receipt no. 14 issued for $11? Management should investigate.

    c. The petty cashier (Martin) did not sign petty cash receipt no. 16. This omission could have been an oversight on his part or he might not have authorized the payment. Management should investigate.

    d. Petty cash receipt no. 15 does not indicate which account to charge. This omission could have been an oversight on the petty cashier's part. Management could check with C. Carlsberg and the petty cashier (Martin) about the transaction. Without further information, debit Miscellaneous Expense.

2. Petty cash general journal entries.

    a. Entry to establish the petty cash fund.   **b.** Entry to reimburse the fund.

Petty Cash	150	
Cash		150

Delivery Expense	29	
Merchandise Inventory	18	
Miscellaneous Expense ($41 + $32)	73	
Cash Over and Short	11	
Cash		131

3. The Petty Cash account balance *always* equals its fund balance, in this case $150. This account balance does not change unless the fund is increased or decreased.

Documentation and Verification

6A.1

This appendix describes the important business documents of a voucher system of control.

Purchase Requisition   Department managers are usually not allowed to place orders directly with suppliers for control purposes. Instead, a department manager must inform the purchasing department of its needs by preparing and signing a **purchase requisition**, which lists the merchandise needed and requests that it be purchased—see Exhibit 6A.1. Two copies of the purchase requisition are sent to the purchasing department, which then sends one copy to the accounting department. When the accounting department receives a purchase requisition, it creates and maintains a voucher for this transaction. The requesting department keeps the third copy.

P4 Describe the use of documentation and verification to control cash disbursements.

EXHIBIT 6A.1

Purchase Requisition

Z-Mart

PURCHASE REQUISITION   No. 917

From _Sporting Goods Department_   Date _October 28, 2009_
To _Purchasing Department_   Preferred Vendor _Trex_

Request purchase of the following item(s):

MODEL NO.	DESCRIPTION	QUANTITY
CH 015	Challenger X7	1
SD 099	SpeedDemon	1

Reason for Request _Replenish inventory_
Approval for Request _T.Z._

For Purchasing Department use only: Order Date _10/30/09_   P.O. No. _P98_

Purchase Order   A **purchase order** is a document the purchasing department uses to place an order with a **vendor** (seller or supplier). A purchase order authorizes a vendor to ship ordered merchandise at the stated price and terms—see Exhibit 6A.2. When the purchasing department receives a purchase requisition, it prepares at least five copies of a purchase order. The copies are distributed as follows: *copy 1* to the vendor as a purchase request and as authority to ship merchandise; *copy 2,* along with a copy of the purchase requisition, to the accounting department, where it is entered in the voucher and used in approving payment of the invoice; *copy 3* to the requesting department to inform its manager that action is being taken; *copy 4* to the receiving department without order quantity so it can compare with goods received and provide independent count of goods received; and *copy 5* retained on file by the purchasing department.

Invoice   An **invoice** is an itemized statement of goods prepared by the vendor listing the customer's name, items sold, sales prices, and terms of sale. An invoice is also a bill sent to the buyer from the supplier. From the vendor's point of view, it is a *sales invoice*. The buyer, or **vendee**, treats it as a *purchase invoice*. When receiving a purchase order, the vendor ships the ordered merchandise to the buyer and includes or mails a copy of the invoice covering the shipment to the buyer. The invoice is sent to the buyer's accounting department where it is placed in the voucher. (Refer back to Exhibit 4.5, which shows Z-Mart's purchase invoice.)

Point: It is important to note that a voucher system is designed to uniquely meet the needs of a specific business. Thus, you should read this appendix as one example of a common voucher system design, but *not* the only design.

EXHIBIT 6A.2

Purchase Order

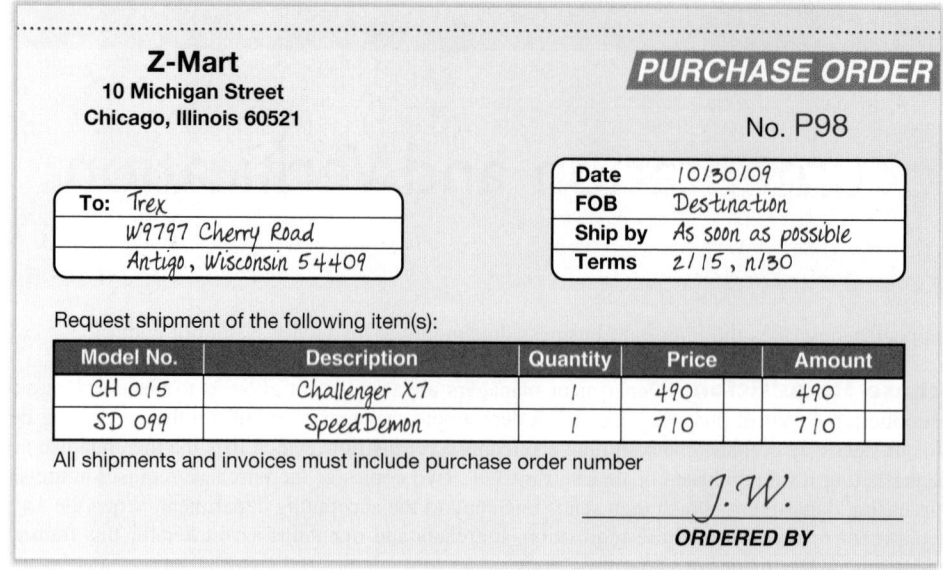

Receiving Report   Many companies maintain a separate department to receive all merchandise and purchased assets. When each shipment arrives, this receiving department counts the goods and checks them for damage and agreement with the purchase order. It then prepares four or more copies of a **receiving report,** which is used within the company to notify the appropriate persons that ordered goods have been received and to describe the quantities and condition of the goods. One copy is sent to accounting and placed in the voucher. Copies are also sent to the requesting department and the purchasing department to notify them that the goods have arrived. The receiving department retains a copy in its files.

Invoice Approval   When a receiving report arrives, the accounting department should have copies of the following documents in the voucher: purchase requisition, purchase order, and invoice. With the information in these documents, the accounting department can record the purchase and approve its payment. In approving an invoice for payment, it checks and compares information across all documents. To facilitate this checking and to ensure that no step is omitted, it often uses an **invoice approval,** also called *check authorization*—see Exhibit 6A.3. An invoice approval is a checklist of steps necessary for approving an invoice for recording and payment. It is a separate document either filed in the voucher or preprinted (or stamped) on the voucher.

EXHIBIT 6A.3

Invoice Approval

INVOICE APPROVAL				
DOCUMENT			**BY**	**DATE**
Purchase requisition		917	TZ	10/28/09
Purchase order		P98	JW	10/30/09
Receiving report		R85	SK	11/03/09
Invoice:		4657		11/12/09
Price			JK	11/12/09
Calculations			JK	11/12/09
Terms			JK	11/12/09
Approved for payment			BC	

As each step in the checklist is approved, the person initials the invoice approval and records the current date. Final approval implies the following steps have occurred:

1. **Requisition check:** Items on invoice are requested per purchase requisition.
2. **Purchase order check:** Items on invoice are ordered per purchase order.
3. **Receiving report check:** Items on invoice are received, per receiving report.
4. **Invoice check: Price:** Invoice prices are as agreed with the vendor.
           Calculations: Invoice has no mathematical errors.
           Terms: Terms are as agreed with the vendor.

Point: Recording a purchase is initiated by an invoice approval, not an invoice. An invoice approval verifies that the amount is consistent with that requested, ordered, and received. This controls and verifies purchases and related liabilities.

Voucher   Once an invoice has been checked and approved, the voucher is complete. A complete voucher is a record summarizing a transaction. Once the voucher certifies a transaction, it authorizes recording an obligation. A voucher also contains approval for paying the obligation on an appropriate date. The physical form of a voucher varies across companies. Many are designed so that the invoice and other related source documents are placed inside the voucher, which can be a folder.

Completion of a voucher usually requires a person to enter certain information on both the inside and outside of the voucher. Typical information required on the inside of a voucher is shown in Exhibit 6A.4, and that for the outside is shown in Exhibit 6A.5. This information is taken from the invoice and the supporting documents filed in the voucher. A complete voucher is sent to an authorized individual (often called an *auditor*). This person performs a final review, approves the accounts and amounts for debiting (called the *accounting distribution*), and authorizes recording of the voucher.

EXHIBIT 6A.4

Inside of a Voucher

Z-Mart
Chicago, Illinois

Voucher No. 4657

Date __Oct. 28, 2009__
Pay to __Trex__
City __Antigo__ _____ State __Wisconsin__

For the following: (attach all invoices and supporting documents)

DATE OF INVOICE	TERMS	INVOICE NUMBER AND OTHER DETAILS	TERMS
Nov. 2, 2009	2/15, n/30	Invoice No. 4657	1,200
		Less discount	24
		Net amount payable	1,176

Payment approved

N. O. Neal
Auditor

After a voucher is approved and recorded (in a journal called a **voucher register**), it is filed by its due date. A check is then sent on the payment date from the cashier, the voucher is marked "paid," and the voucher is sent to the accounting department and recorded (in a journal called the **check register**). The person issuing checks relies on the approved voucher and its signed supporting documents as proof that an obligation has been incurred and must be paid. The purchase requisition and purchase order confirm the purchase was authorized. The receiving report shows that items have been received, and the invoice approval form verifies that the invoice has been checked for errors. There is little chance for error and even less chance for fraud without collusion unless all the documents and signatures are forged.

EXHIBIT 6A.5

Outside of a Voucher

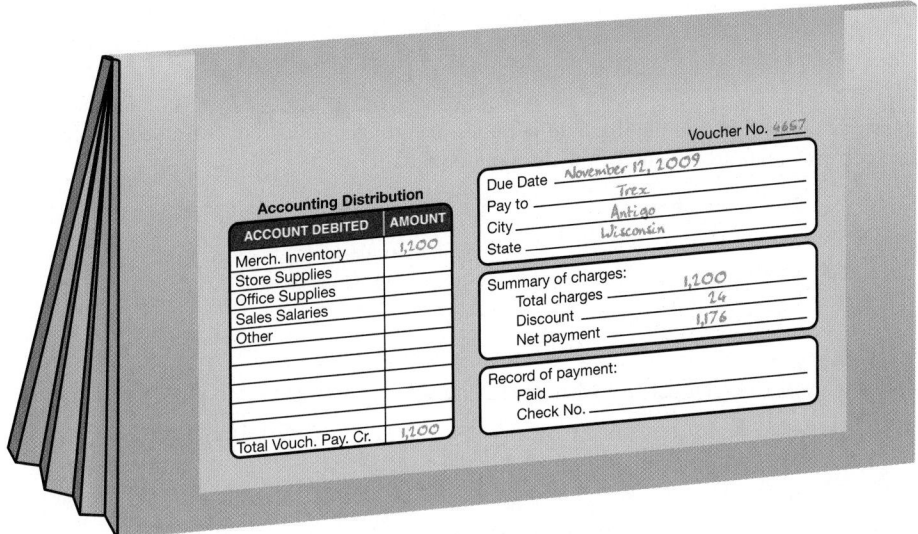

Voucher No. 4657

Accounting Distribution

ACCOUNT DEBITED	AMOUNT
Merch. Inventory	1,200
Store Supplies	
Office Supplies	
Sales Salaries	
Other	
Total Vouch. Pay. Cr.	1,200

Due Date __November 12, 2009__
Pay to __Trex__
City __Antigo__
State __Wisconsin__

Summary of charges:
Total charges ____ 1,200
Discount ____ 24
Net payment ____ 1,176

Record of payment:
Paid _____
Check No. _____

APPENDIX

6B

Control of Purchase Discounts

P5   Apply the net method to control purchase discounts.

This appendix explains how a company can better control its cash *disbursements* to take advantage of favorable purchases discounts. Chapter 4 described the entries to record the receipt and payment of an invoice for a merchandise purchase with and without discount terms. Those entries were prepared under what is called the **gross method** of recording purchases, which initially records the invoice at its *gross* amount ignoring any cash discount.

The **net method** is another means of recording purchases, which initially records the invoice at its *net* amount of any cash discount. The net method gives management an advantage in controlling and monitoring cash payments involving purchase discounts.

To explain, when invoices are recorded at *gross* amounts, the amount of any discounts taken is deducted from the balance of the Merchandise Inventory account when cash payment is made. This means that the amount of any discounts lost is not reported in any account or on the income statement. Lost discounts recorded in this way are unlikely to come to the attention of management. When purchases are recorded at *net* amounts, a **Discounts Lost** expense account is recorded and brought to management's attention. Management can then seek to identify the reason for discounts lost such as oversight, carelessness, or unfavorable terms. (Chapter 4 explains how managers assess whether a discount is favorable or not.)

Perpetual Inventory System   To illustrate, assume that a company purchases merchandise on November 2 at a $1,200 invoice price with terms of 2/10, n/30. Its November 2 entries under the gross and net methods are

Gross Method			**Net Method**		
Merchandise Inventory	1,200		Merchandise Inventory	1,176	
Accounts Payable		1,200	Accounts Payable		1,176

If the invoice is paid on November 12 within the discount period, it records the following

Gross Method			**Net Method**		
Accounts Payable	1,200		Accounts Payable	1,176	
Merchandise Inventory		24	Cash		1,176
Cash		1,176			

If the invoice is *not* paid within the discount period, it records the following November 12 entry (which is the date corresponding to the end of the discount period)

Gross Method			**Net Method**		
No entry			**Discounts Lost**	24	
			Accounts Payable		24

Then, when the invoice is later paid on December 2, outside the discount period, it records the following

Gross Method			**Net Method**		
Accounts Payable	1,200		Accounts Payable	1,200	
Cash		1,200	Cash		1,200

(The discount lost can be recorded when the cash payment is made with a single entry. However, in this case, when financial statements are prepared after a discount is lost and before the cash payment is made, an adjusting entry is required to recognize any unrecorded discount lost in the period when incurred.)

Periodic Inventory System The preceding entries assume a perpetual inventory system. If a company is using a *periodic system,* its November 2 entries under the gross and net methods are

Gross Method—Periodic			Net Method—Periodic		
Purchases	1,200		Purchases	1,176	
Accounts Payable		1,200	Accounts Payable		1,176

If the invoice is paid on November 12 within the discount period, it records the following

Gross Method—Periodic			Net Method—Periodic		
Accounts Payable	1,200		Accounts Payable	1,176	
Purchases Discounts		24	Cash		1,176
Cash		1,176			

If the invoice is *not* paid within the discount period, it records the following November 12 entry

Gross Method—Periodic			Net Method—Periodic		
No entry			Discounts Lost	24	
			Accounts Payable		24

Then, when the invoice is later paid on December 2, outside the discount period, it records the following

Gross Method—Periodic			Net Method—Periodic		
Accounts Payable	1,200		Accounts Payable	1,200	
Cash		1,200	Cash		1,200

Summary

C1 Define internal control and identify its purpose and principles. An internal control system consists of the policies and procedures managers use to protect assets, ensure reliable accounting, promote efficient operations, and urge adherence to company policies. It can prevent avoidable losses and help managers both plan operations and monitor company and human performance. Principles of good internal control include establishing responsibilities, maintaining adequate records, insuring assets and bonding employees, separating recordkeeping from custody of assets, dividing responsibilities for related transactions, applying technological controls, and performing regular independent reviews.

C2 Define cash and cash equivalents and explain how to report them. Cash includes currency, coins, and amounts on (or acceptable for) deposit in checking and savings accounts. Cash equivalents are short-term, highly liquid investment assets readily convertible to a known cash amount and sufficiently close to their maturity date so that market value is not sensitive to interest rate changes. Cash and cash equivalents are liquid assets because they are readily converted into other assets or can be used to pay for goods, services, or liabilities.

C3 Identify control features of banking activities. Banks offer several services that promote the control and safeguarding of cash. A bank account is a record set up by a bank permitting a customer to deposit money for safekeeping and to draw checks on it. A bank deposit is money contributed to the account with a deposit ticket as proof. A check is a document signed by the depositor instructing the bank to pay a specified amount of money to a designated recipient.

A1 Compute the days' sales uncollected ratio and use it to assess liquidity. Many companies attract customers by selling to them on credit. This means that cash receipts from customers are delayed until accounts receivable are collected. Users want to know how quickly a company can convert its accounts receivable into cash. The days' sales uncollected ratio, one measure reflecting company liquidity, is computed by dividing the ending balance of receivables by annual net sales, and then multiplying by 365.

P1 **Apply internal control to cash receipts and disbursements.** Internal control of cash receipts ensures that all cash received is properly recorded and deposited. Attention focuses on two important types of cash receipts: over-the-counter and by mail. Good internal control for over-the-counter cash receipts includes use of a cash register, customer review, use of receipts, a permanent transaction record, and separation of the custody of cash from its recordkeeping. Good internal control for cash receipts by mail includes at least two people assigned to open mail and a listing of each sender's name, amount, and explanation.

P2 **Explain and record petty cash fund transactions.** Petty cash disbursements are payments of small amounts for items such as postage, courier fees, minor repairs, and supplies. A company usually sets up one or more petty cash funds. A petty fund cashier is responsible for safekeeping the cash, making payments from this fund, and keeping receipts and records. A Petty Cash account is debited only when the fund is established or increased in amount. When the fund is replenished, petty cash disbursements are recorded with debits to expense (or asset) accounts and a credit to cash.

P3 **Prepare a bank reconciliation.** A bank reconciliation proves the accuracy of the depositor's and the bank's records. The bank statement balance is adjusted for items such as outstanding checks and unrecorded deposits made on or before the bank statement date but not reflected on the statement. The book balance is adjusted for items such as service charges, bank collections for the depositor, and interest earned on the account.

P4^A **Describe the use of documentation and verification to control cash disbursements.** A voucher system is a set of procedures and approvals designed to control cash disbursements and acceptance of obligations. The voucher system of control relies on several important documents, including the voucher and its supporting files. A key factor in this system is that only approved departments and individuals are authorized to incur certain obligations.

P5^B **Apply the net method to control purchase discounts.** The net method aids management in monitoring and controlling purchase discounts. When invoices are recorded at gross amounts, the amount of discounts taken is deducted from the balance of the Inventory account. This means that the amount of any discounts lost is not reported in any account and is unlikely to come to the attention of management. When purchases are recorded at net amounts, a Discounts Lost account is brought to management's attention as an operating expense. Management can then seek to identify the reason for discounts lost, such as oversight, carelessness, or unfavorable terms.

Guidance Answers to **Decision Maker** and **Decision Ethics**

Entrepreneur A forced vacation policy is part of a good system of internal controls. When employees are forced to take vacations, their ability to hide any fraudulent behavior decreases because others must perform the vacationers' duties. A replacement employee potentially can uncover fraudulent behavior or falsified records. A forced vacation policy is especially important for employees in sensitive positions of handling money or in control of easily transferable assets.

Sales Representative A salesperson can take several steps to reduce days' sales uncollected. These include (1) decreasing the ratio of sales on account to total sales by encouraging more cash sales, (2) identifying customers most delayed in their payments and encouraging earlier payments or cash sales, and (3) applying stricter credit policies to eliminate credit sales to customers that never pay.

Guidance Answers to **Quick Checks**

1. (c)

2. Technology reduces processing errors. It also allows more extensive testing of records, limits the amount of hard evidence, and highlights the importance of separation of duties.

3. A company holds liquid assets so that it can purchase other assets, buy services, and pay obligations.

4. It owns cash equivalents because they yield a return greater than what cash earns (and are readily exchanged for cash).

5. Examples of cash equivalents are 90-day (or less) U.S. Treasury bills, money market funds, and commercial paper (notes).

6. (a)

7. A voucher system is used when an owner/manager can no longer control purchasing procedures through personal supervision and direct participation.

8. If all cash payments are made by check, numerous checks for small amounts must be written. Since this practice is expensive and time-consuming, a petty cash fund is often established for making small (immaterial) cash payments.

9. If the petty cash fund is not reimbursed at the end of an accounting period, the transactions involving petty cash are not yet recorded and the petty cash asset is overstated.

10. First, petty cash transactions are recorded when the petty cash fund is reimbursed. Second, reimbursement provides cash to allow the fund to continue being used. Third, reimbursement identifies any cash shortage or overage in the fund.

11. A bank statement is a report prepared by the bank describing the activities in a depositor's account.

12. To reconcile a bank balance means to explain the difference between the cash balance in the depositor's accounting records and the cash balance on the bank statement.

13. The purpose of the bank reconciliation is to determine whether the bank or the depositor has made any errors and whether the bank has entered any transactions affecting the account that the depositor has not recorded.

14. Unrecorded deposits—added
Outstanding checks—subtracted

15. Interest earned—added   Debit memos—subtracted
Credit memos—added   NSF checks—subtracted
                            Bank service charges—subtracted

Key Terms

Bank reconciliation (p. 265)	Deposits in transit (p. 266)	Principles of internal control (p. 251)
Bank statement (p. 264)	Discounts lost (p. 276)	Purchase order (p. 273)
Canceled checks (p. 265)	Electronic funds transfer (EFT) (p. 263)	Purchase requisition (p. 273)
Cash (p. 255)	Gross method (p. 276)	Receiving report (p. 274)
Cash equivalents (p. 255)	Internal control system (p. 250)	Sarbanes-Oxley Act (p. 250)
Cash over and short (p. 257)	Invoice (p. 273)	Section 404 (of SOX) (p. 251)
Check (p. 263)	Invoice approval (p. 274)	Signature card (p. 263)
Check register (p. 275)	Liquid assets (p. 255)	Vendee (p. 273)
Committee of Sponsoring Organizations (COSO) (p. 251)	Liquidity (p. 255)	Vendor (p. 273)
	Net method (p. 276)	Voucher (p. 259)
Days' sales uncollected (p. 270)	Outstanding checks (p. 266)	Voucher register (p. 275)
Deposit ticket (p. 263)	Petty cash (p. 260)	Voucher system (p. 258)

Multiple Choice Quiz   Answers on p. 293   mhhe.com/wildFA5e

Additional Quiz Questions are available at the book's Website.

1. A company needs to replenish its $500 petty cash fund. Its petty cash box has $75 cash and petty cash receipts of $420. The journal entry to replenish the fund includes
   a. A debit to Cash for $75.
   b. A credit to Cash for $75.
   c. A credit to Petty Cash for $420.
   d. A credit to Cash Over and Short for $5.
   e. A debit to Cash Over and Short for $5.

2. The following information is available for Hapley Company:
   • The November 30 bank statement shows a $1,895 balance.
   • The general ledger shows a $1,742 balance at November 30.
   • A $795 deposit placed in the bank's night depository on November 30 does not appear on the November 30 bank statement.
   • Outstanding checks amount to $638 at November 30.
   • A customer's $335 note was collected by the bank in November. A collection fee of $15 was deducted by the bank and the difference deposited in Hapley's account.
   • A bank service charge of $10 is deducted by the bank and appears on the November 30 bank statement.

   How will the customer's note appear on Hapley's November 30 bank reconciliation?
   a. $320 appears as an addition to the book balance of cash.
   b. $320 appears as a deduction from the book balance of cash.
   c. $320 appears as an addition to the bank balance of cash.
   d. $320 appears as a deduction from the bank balance of cash.

   e. $335 appears as an addition to the bank balance of cash.

3. Using the information from question 2, what is the reconciled balance on Hapley's November 30 bank reconciliation?
   a. $2,052
   b. $1,895
   c. $1,742
   d. $2,201
   e. $1,184

4. A company had net sales of $84,000 and accounts receivable of $6,720. Its days' sales uncollected is
   a. 3.2 days
   b. 18.4 days
   c. 230.0 days
   d. 29.2 days
   e. 12.5 days

5. [B] A company records its purchases using the net method. On August 1, it purchases merchandise on account for $6,000 with terms of 2/10, n/30. The August 1 journal entry to record this transaction includes a
   a. Debit to Merchandise Inventory for $6,000.
   b. Debit to Merchandise Inventory for $5,880.
   c. Debit to Merchandise Inventory for $120.
   d. Debit to Accounts Payable for $5,880.
   e. Credit to Accounts Payable for $6,000.

Superscript letter ^{A} (^{B}) denotes assignments based on Appendix 6A (6B).

Discussion Questions

1. List the seven broad principles of internal control.

2. ♟ Internal control procedures are important in every business, but at what stage in the development of a business do they become especially critical?

3. ♟ Why should responsibility for related transactions be divided among different departments or individuals?

4. ♟ Why should the person who keeps the records of an asset not be the person responsible for its custody?

5. ♟ When a store purchases merchandise, why are individual departments not allowed to directly deal with suppliers?

6. What are the limitations of internal controls?

7. Which of the following assets is most liquid? Which is least liquid? Inventory, building, accounts receivable, or cash.

8. What is a petty cash receipt? Who should sign it?

9. Why should cash receipts be deposited on the day of receipt?

10. **Best Buy**'s statement of cash flows in Appendix A describes changes in cash and cash equivalents for **BEST BUY** the year ended February 28, 2009. What total amount is provided (used) by investing activities? What amount is provided (used) by financing activities?

11. Refer to **RadioShack**'s financial statements in Appendix A. Identify RadioShack's net income for the year ended December 31, 2008. Is its net income equal to the increase in cash and cash equivalents for the year? Explain the difference between net income and the increase in cash and cash equivalents.

12. ♟ Refer to **GOME**'s balance sheet in Appendix A. How does its cash compare with its other current assets (both in amount and percent) as of December 31, 2008? Compare and assess the cash amount at December 31, 2008, with its amount at December 31, 2007.

13. ♟ **Apple**'s balance sheet in Appendix A reports that cash and equivalents increased during the fiscal year ended September 27, 2008. Identify the cash generated (or used) by operating activities, by investing activities, and by financing activities.

♟ *Denotes Discussion Questions that involve decision making.*

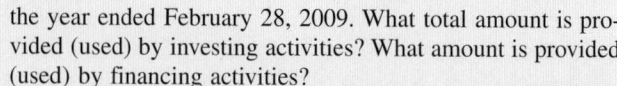
Available with Connect Accounting **connect**

QUICK STUDY

QS 6-1
Internal control objectives

C1 ♟

An internal control system consists of all policies and procedures used to protect assets, ensure reliable accounting, promote efficient operations, and urge adherence to company policies.

1. What is the main objective of internal control procedures? How is that objective achieved?

2. Why should recordkeeping for assets be separated from custody over those assets?

3. Why should the responsibility for a transaction be divided between two or more individuals or departments?

QS 6-2
Cash and equivalents

C2

Good accounting systems help in managing cash and controlling who has access to it.

1. What items are included in the category of cash?

2. What items are included in the category of cash equivalents?

3. What does the term *liquidity* refer to?

QS 6-3
Cash, liquidity, and return

C1   C2

Good accounting systems help with the management and control of cash and cash equivalents.

1. Define and contrast the terms *liquid asset* and *cash equivalent*.

2. Why would companies invest their idle cash in cash equivalents?

3. Identify five principles of effective cash management.

QS 6-4
Internal control for cash

P1 ♟

A good system of internal control for cash provides adequate procedures for protecting both cash receipts and cash disbursements.

1. What are three basic guidelines that help achieve this protection?

2. Identify two control systems or procedures for cash disbursements.

QS 6-5
Petty cash accounting

P2

1. The petty cash fund of the Kaley Agency is established at $75. At the end of the current period, the fund contained $8.18 and had the following receipts: film rentals, $26.50, refreshments for meetings, $32.17 (both expenditures to be classified as Entertainment Expense); postage, $5.15; and printing, $3. Prepare journal entries to record (*a*) establishment of the fund and (*b*) reimbursement of the fund at the end of the current period.

2. Identify the two events that cause a Petty Cash account to be credited in a journal entry.

1. For each of the following items, indicate whether its amount (i) affects the bank or book side of a bank reconciliation and (ii) represents an addition or a subtraction in a bank reconciliation.

   a. Unrecorded deposits   **d.** Debit memos   **g.** NSF checks

   b. Interest on cash balance   **e.** Outstanding checks

   c. Bank service charges   **f.** Credit memos

2. Which of the items in part 1 require an adjusting journal entry?

QS 6-6
Bank reconciliation
P3

Madison Company deposits all cash receipts on the day when they are received and it makes all cash payments by check. At the close of business on July 31, 2011, its Cash account shows a $2,025 debit balance. Madison's July 31 bank statement shows $1,800 on deposit in the bank. Prepare a bank reconciliation for Madison Company using the following information.

a. The July 31 bank statement included a $30 debit memorandum for bank services; Madison has not yet recorded the cost of these services.

b. In reviewing the bank statement, a $90 check written by Madsen Company was mistakenly drawn against Madison's account.

c. July 31 cash receipts of $210 were placed in the bank's night depository after banking hours and were not recorded on the July 31 bank statement.

d. Outstanding checks as of July 31 total $100.

e. The bank statement included a $5 credit for interest earned on the cash in the bank.

QS 6-7
Bank reconciliation
P3

The following annual account balances are taken from Mizuno Sports at December 31.

	2011	2010
Accounts receivable	$ 93,700	$ 90,450
Net sales	1,357,600	1,259,680

What is the change in the number of days' sales uncollected between years 2010 and 2011? According to this analysis, is the company's collection of receivables improving? Explain.

QS 6-8
Days' sales uncollected
A1

Management uses a voucher system to help control and monitor cash disbursements. Identify and describe at least four key documents that are part of a voucher system of control.

QS 6-9ᴬ
Documents in a voucher system
P4

An important part of cash management is knowing when, and if, to take purchase discounts.

a. Which accounting method uses a Discounts Lost account?

b. What is the advantage of this method for management?

QS 6-10ᴮ
Purchase discounts
P5

Answer each of the following related to international accounting standards.

a. Explain how the purposes and principles of internal controls are different between accounting systems reporting under IFRS versus U.S. GAAP.

b. Cash presents special internal control challenges. How do internal controls for cash differ for accounting systems reporting under IFRS versus U.S. GAAP? How do the procedures applied differ across those two accounting systems?

QS 6-11
International accounting and internal controls
C1 P1

---

connect Available with Connect Accounting

Pacific Company is a rapidly growing start-up business. Its recordkeeper, who was hired one year ago, left town after the company's manager discovered that a large sum of money had disappeared over the past six months. An audit disclosed that the recordkeeper had written and signed several checks made payable to her fiancé and then recorded the checks as salaries expense. The fiancé, who cashed the checks but never worked for the company, left town with the recordkeeper. As a result, the company incurred an uninsured loss of $184,000. Evaluate Pacific's internal control system and indicate which principles of internal control appear to have been ignored.

EXERCISES

Exercise 6-1
Analyzing internal control
C1

Some of Chapman Company's cash receipts from customers are received by the company with the regular mail. Chapman's recordkeeper opens these letters and deposits the cash received each day. (*a*) Identify any internal control problem(s) in this arrangement. (*b*) What changes to its internal control system do you recommend?

Exercise 6-2
Control of cash receipts by mail
P1

Exercise 6-3
Internal control recommendations
C1 ♟

What internal control procedures would you recommend in each of the following situations?

1. A concession company has one employee who sells sunscreen, T-shirts, and sunglasses at the beach. Each day, the employee is given enough sunscreen, shirts and sunglasses to last through the day and enough cash to make change. The money is kept in a box at the stand.

2. An antique store has one employee who is given cash and sent to garage sales each weekend. The employee pays cash for any merchandise acquired that the antique store resells.

Exercise 6-4
Petty cash fund accounting
P2

Check (2) Cr. Cash $210

Fresno Co. establishes a $350 petty cash fund on January 1. On January 8, the fund shows $140 in cash along with receipts for the following expenditures: postage, $67; transportation-in, $35; delivery expenses, $52; and miscellaneous expenses, $56. Fresno uses the perpetual system in accounting for merchandise inventory. Prepare journal entries to (1) establish the fund on January 1, (2) reimburse it on January 8, and (3) both reimburse the fund and increase it to $550 on January 8, assuming no entry in part 2. (*Hint*: Make two separate entries for part 3.)

Exercise 6-5
Petty cash fund with a shortage
P2

Check (2) Cr. Cash $216 and (3) Cr. Cash $50

Reichard Company establishes a $250 petty cash fund on September 9. On September 30, the fund shows $34 in cash along with receipts for the following expenditures: transportation-in, $47; postage expenses, $62; and miscellaneous expenses, $103. The petty cashier could not account for a $4 shortage in the fund. Reichard uses the perpetual system in accounting for merchandise inventory. Prepare (1) the September 9 entry to establish the fund, (2) the September 30 entry to reimburse the fund, and (3) an October 1 entry to increase the fund to $300.

Exercise 6-6
Bank reconciliation and adjusting entries
P3

Prepare a table with the following headings for a monthly bank reconciliation dated September 30.

Bank Balance		Book Balance			Not Shown on the Reconciliation
Add	Deduct	Add	Deduct	Adjust	

For each item 1 through 12, place an *x* in the appropriate column to indicate whether the item should be added to or deducted from the book or bank balance, or whether it should not appear on the reconciliation. If the book balance is to be adjusted, place a *Dr.* or *Cr.* in the Adjust column to indicate whether the Cash balance should be debited or credited. At the left side of your table, number the items to correspond to the following list.

1. NSF check from customer is returned on September 25 but not yet recorded by this company.
2. Interest earned on the September cash balance in the bank.
3. Deposit made on September 5 and processed by the bank on September 6.
4. Checks written by another depositor but charged against this company's account.
5. Bank service charge for September.
6. Checks outstanding on August 31 that cleared the bank in September.
7. Check written against the company's account and cleared by the bank; erroneously not recorded by the company's recordkeeper.
8. Principal and interest on a note receivable to this company is collected by the bank but not yet recorded by the company.
9. Checks written and mailed to payees on October 2.
10. Checks written by the company and mailed to payees on September 30.
11. Night deposit made on September 30 after the bank closed.
12. Special bank charge for collection of note in part 8 on this company's behalf.

Exercise 6-7
Voucher system
P1

The voucher system of control is designed to control cash disbursements and the acceptance of obligations.
1. The voucher system of control establishes procedures for what two processes?
2. What types of expenditures should be overseen by a voucher system of control?
3. When is the voucher initially prepared? Explain.

Austin Clinic deposits all cash receipts on the day when they are received and it makes all cash payments by check. At the close of business on June 30, 2011, its Cash account shows an $15,671 debit balance. Austin Clinic's June 30 bank statement shows $15,382 on deposit in the bank. Prepare a bank reconciliation for Austin Clinic using the following information:

a. Outstanding checks as of June 30 total $2,700.

b. The June 30 bank statement included a $65 debit memorandum for bank services.

c. Check No. 919, listed with the canceled checks, was correctly drawn for $489 in payment of a utility bill on June 15. Austin Clinic mistakenly recorded it with a debit to Utilities Expense and a credit to Cash in the amount of $498.

d. The June 30 cash receipts of $2,933 were placed in the bank's night depository after banking hours and were not recorded on the June 30 bank statement.

Exercise 6-8
Bank reconciliation
P3

Check   Reconciled bal., $15,615

Prepare the adjusting journal entries that Austin Clinic must record as a result of preparing the bank reconciliation in Exercise 6-8.

Exercise 6-9
Adjusting entries from
bank reconciliation   P3

Walsh Company deposits all cash receipts on the day when they are received and it makes all cash payments by check. At the close of business on May 31, 2011, its Cash account shows a $7,750 debit balance. Walsh's May 31 bank statement shows $6,900 on deposit in the bank. Prepare a bank reconciliation for Walsh Company using the following information.

a. May 31 cash receipts of $1,100 were placed in the bank's night depository after banking hours and were not recorded on the May 31 bank statement.

b. Outstanding checks as of May 31 total $800.

c. The May 31 bank statement included a $50 debit memorandum for bank services; Walsh has not yet recorded the cost of these services.

d. In reviewing the bank statement, a $200 check written by Wald Company was mistakenly drawn against Walsh's account.   *Bank Error*

e. A debit memorandum for $300 refers to a $300 NSF check from a customer; Walsh has not yet recorded this NSF check.

Exercise 6-10
Bank reconciliation
P3

Check   Reconciled bal., $7,400

Todd Co. reported annual net sales for 2010 and 2011 of $664,000 and $746,000, respectively. Its year-end balances of accounts receivable follow: December 31, 2010, $65,000; and December 31, 2011, $93,000. (*a*) Calculate its days' sales uncollected at the end of each year. (*b*) Evaluate and comment on any changes in the amount of liquid assets tied up in receivables.

Exercise 6-11
Liquid assets and
accounts receivable

A1

Match each document in a voucher system in column one with its description in column two.

Document

1. Purchase requisition

2. Purchase order

3. Invoice

4. Receiving report

5. Invoice approval

6. Voucher

Description

A. An itemized statement of goods prepared by the vendor listing the customer's name, items sold, sales prices, and terms of sale.

B. An internal file used to store documents and information to control cash disbursements and to ensure that a transaction is properly authorized and recorded.

C. A document used to place an order with a vendor that authorizes the vendor to ship ordered merchandise at the stated price and terms.

D. A checklist of steps necessary for the approval of an invoice for recording and payment; also known as a check authorization.

E. A document used by department managers to inform the purchasing department to place an order with a vendor.

F. A document used to notify the appropriate persons that ordered goods have arrived, including a description of the quantities and condition of goods.

Exercise 6-12ᴬ
Documents in a voucher system

P4

Exercise 6-13[B]
Record invoices at
gross or net amounts

P5

World Imports uses the perpetual system in accounting for merchandise inventory and had the following transactions during the month of October. Prepare entries to record these transactions assuming that World Imports records invoices (*a*) at gross amounts and (*b*) at net amounts.

Oct.　2　Purchased merchandise at a $5,600 price, invoice dated October 2, terms 1/10, n/30.
　　　10　Received a $900 credit memorandum (at full invoice price) for the return of merchandise that it purchased on October 2.
　　　17　Purchased merchandise at a $5,950 price, invoice dated October 16, terms 2/10, n/30.
　　　26　Paid for the merchandise purchased on October 17, less the discount.
　　　31　Paid for the merchandise purchased on October 2. Payment was delayed because the invoice was mistakenly filed for payment today. This error caused the discount to be lost.

Available with Connect Accounting **connect**

PROBLEM SET A

For each of these five separate cases, identify the principle(s) of internal control that is violated. Recommend what the business should do to ensure adherence to principles of internal control.

Problem 6-1A
Analyzing internal control

C1

1. Chi Han records all incoming customer cash receipts for his employer and posts the customer payments to their respective accounts.

2. At Tico Company, Jenn and Kirsten alternate lunch hours. Jenn is the petty cash custodian, but if someone needs petty cash when she is at lunch, Kirsten fills in as custodian.

3. Nori Nozumi posts all patient charges and payments at the Hopeville Medical Clinic. Each night Nori backs up the computerized accounting system to a tape and stores the tape in a locked file at her desk.

4. Sanjay Shales prides himself on hiring quality workers who require little supervision. As office manager, Sanjay gives his employees full discretion over their tasks and for years has seen no reason to perform independent reviews of their work.

5. Cala Farah's manager has told her to reduce costs. Cala decides to raise the deductible on the plant's property insurance from $5,000 to $10,000. This cuts the property insurance premium in half. In a related move, she decides that bonding the plant's employees is a waste of money since the company has not experienced any losses due to employee theft. Cala saves the entire amount of the bonding insurance premium by dropping the bonding insurance.

Problem 6-2A
Establish, reimburse, and increase
petty cash

P2

Beard Gallery had the following petty cash transactions in February of the current year.

Feb.　2　Wrote a $300 check, cashed it, and gave the proceeds and the petty cashbox to Reggie Gore, the petty cashier.
　　　5　Purchased bond paper for the copier for $14.55 that is immediately used.
　　　9　Paid $32.50 COD shipping charges on merchandise purchased for resale, terms FOB shipping point. Beard uses the perpetual system to account for merchandise inventory.
　　　12　Paid $7.85 postage to express mail a contract to a client.
　　　14　Reimbursed Jonny Carr, the manager, $66 for business mileage on her car.
　　　20　Purchased stationery for $67.67 that is immediately used.
　　　23　Paid a courier $23 to deliver merchandise sold to a customer, terms FOB destination.
　　　25　Paid $10.30 COD shipping charges on merchandise purchased for resale, terms FOB shipping point.
　　　27　Paid $55 for postage expenses.
　　　28　The fund had $20.82 remaining in the petty cash box. Sorted the petty cash receipts by accounts affected and exchanged them for a check to reimburse the fund for expenditures.
　　　28　The petty cash fund amount is increased by $100 to a total of $400.

Required

1. Prepare the journal entry to establish the petty cash fund.

2. Prepare a petty cash payments report for February with these categories: delivery expense, mileage expense, postage expense, merchandise inventory (for transportation-in), and office supplies expense. Sort the payments into the appropriate categories and total the expenditures in each category.

Check　(3a) Cr. Cash $279.18

3. Prepare the journal entries for part 2 to both (*a*) reimburse and (*b*) increase the fund amount.

Dylan Co. set up a petty cash fund for payments of small amounts. The following transactions involving the petty cash fund occurred in May (the last month of the company's fiscal year).

Problem 6-3A
Establish, reimburse, and adjust petty cash
P2

May 1   Prepared a company check for $350 to establish the petty cash fund.
     15   Prepared a company check to replenish the fund for the following expenditures made since May 1.
          a.   Paid $109.20 for janitorial services.
          b.   Paid $89.15 for miscellaneous expenses.
          c.   Paid postage expenses of $60.90.
          d.   Paid $80.01 to *The County Gazette* (the local newspaper) for an advertisement.
          e.   Counted $16.84 remaining in the petty cash box.
     16   Prepared a company check for $200 to increase the fund to $550.
     31   The petty cashier reports that $390.27 cash remains in the fund. A company check is drawn to replenish the fund for the following expenditures made since May 15.
          f.   Paid postage expenses of $59.10.
          g.   Reimbursed the office manager for business mileage, $47.05.
          h.   Paid $48.58 to deliver merchandise to a customer, terms FOB destination.
     31   The company decides that the May 16 increase in the fund was too large. It reduces the fund by $50, leaving a total of $500.

Required

1. Prepare journal entries to establish the fund on May 1, to replenish it on May 15 and on May 31, and to reflect any increase or decrease in the fund balance on May 16 and May 31.

Check (1) Cr. to Cash: May 15, $333.16; May 16, $200

Analysis Component

2. Explain how the company's financial statements are affected if the petty cash fund is not replenished and no entry is made on May 31.

The following information is available to reconcile Hamilton Company's book balance of cash with its bank statement cash balance as of July 31, 2011.

Problem 6-4A
Prepare a bank reconciliation and record adjustments
P3

mhhe.com/wildFA5e

a. On July 31, the company's Cash account has a $25,862 debit balance, but its July bank statement shows a $28,575 cash balance.

b. Check No. 3031 for $1,670 and Check No. 3040 for $827 were outstanding on the June 30 bank reconciliation. Check No. 3040 is listed with the July canceled checks, but Check No. 3031 is not. Also, Check No. 3065 for $611 and Check No. 3069 for $2,438, both written in July, are not among the canceled checks on the July 31 statement.

c. In comparing the canceled checks on the bank statement with the entries in the accounting records, it is found that Check No. 3056 for July rent was correctly written and drawn for $1,250 but was erroneously entered in the accounting records as $1,240.

d. A credit memorandum enclosed with the July bank statement indicates the bank collected $6,000 cash on a noninterest-bearing note for Hamilton, deducted a $30 collection fee, and credited the remainder to its account. Hamilton had not recorded this event before receiving the statement.

e. A debit memorandum for $805 lists a $795 NSF check plus a $10 NSF charge. The check had been received from a customer, Evan Shaw. Hamilton has not yet recorded this check as NSF.

f. Enclosed with the July statement is a $9 debit memorandum for bank services. It has not yet been recorded because no previous notification had been received.

g. Hamilton's July 31 daily cash receipts of $7,152 were placed in the bank's night depository on that date, but do not appear on the July 31 bank statement.

Required

1. Prepare the bank reconciliation for this company as of July 31, 2011.
2. Prepare the journal entries necessary to bring the company's book balance of cash into conformity with the reconciled cash balance as of July 31, 2011.

Check (1) Reconciled balance, $31,008; (2) Cr. Note Receivable $6,000

Analysis Component

3. Assume that the July 31, 2011, bank reconciliation for this company is prepared and some items are treated incorrectly. For each of the following errors, explain the effect of the error on (i) the adjusted bank statement cash balance and (ii) the adjusted cash account book balance.
   a. The company's unadjusted cash account balance of $25,862 is listed on the reconciliation as $25,682.
   b. The bank's collection of the $6,000 note less the $30 collection fee is added to the bank statement cash balance on the reconciliation.

Problem 6-5A

Prepare a bank reconciliation and record adjustments

P3

mhhe.com/wildFA5e

Madison Company most recently reconciled its bank statement and book balances of cash on August 31 and it reported two checks outstanding, No. 5888 for $1,089 and No. 5893 for $542. The following information is available for its September 30, 2011, reconciliation.

From the September 30 Bank Statement

PREVIOUS BALANCE	TOTAL CHECKS AND DEBITS	TOTAL DEPOSITS AND CREDITS	CURRENT BALANCE
18,500	9,799	11,463	20,164

CHECKS AND DEBITS			DEPOSITS AND CREDITS		DAILY BALANCE	
Date	No.	Amount	Date	Amount	Date	Amount
09/03	5888	1,089	09/05	1,145	08/31	18,500
09/04	5902	711	09/12	2,282	09/03	17,411
09/07	5901	1,805	09/21	4,072	09/04	16,700
09/17		631 NSF	09/25	2,323	09/05	17,845
09/20	5905	986	09/30	23 IN	09/07	16,040
09/22	5903	402	09/30	1,618 CM	09/12	18,322
09/22	5904	2,073			09/17	17,691
09/28	5907	213			09/20	16,705
09/29	5909	1,889			09/21	20,777
					09/22	18,302
					09/25	20,625
					09/28	20,412
					09/29	18,523
					09/30	20,164

From Madison Company's Accounting Records

Cash Receipts Deposited			
Date			Cash Debit
Sept.	5		1,145
	12		2,282
	21		4,072
	25		2,323
	30		1,753
			11,575

Cash Disbursements		
Check No.		Cash Credit
5901		1,805
5902		711
5903		402
5904		2,037
5905		986
5906		1,003
5907		213
5908		378
5909		1,889
		9,424

Cash						Acct. No. 101
Date		Explanation	PR	Debit	Credit	Balance
Aug.	31	Balance				16,869
Sept.	30	Total receipts	R12	11,575		28,444
	30	Total disbursements	D23		9,424	19,020

Additional Information

Check No. 5904 is correctly drawn for $2,073 to pay for computer equipment; however, the recordkeeper misread the amount and entered it in the accounting records with a debit to Computer Equipment and a credit to Cash of $2,037. The NSF check shown in the statement was originally received from a customer, S. Nilson, in payment of her account. Its return has not yet been recorded by the company. The credit memorandum is from the collection of a $1,640 note for Madison Company by the bank. The bank deducted a $22 collection fee. The collection and fee are not yet recorded.

Required

1. Prepare the September 30, 2011, bank reconciliation for this company.

2. Prepare the journal entries to adjust the book balance of cash to the reconciled balance.

Check (1) Reconciled balance, $19,994 (2) Cr. Note Receivable $1,640

Analysis Component

3. The bank statement reveals that some of the prenumbered checks in the sequence are missing. Describe three situations that could explain this.

For each of these five separate cases, identify the principle(s) of internal control that is violated. Recommend what the business should do to ensure adherence to principles of internal control.

1. Latisha Tally is the company's computer specialist and oversees its computerized payroll system. Her boss recently asked her to put password protection on all office computers. Latisha has put a password in place that allows only the boss access to the file where pay rates are changed and personnel are added or deleted from the payroll.

2. Marker Theater has a computerized order-taking system for its tickets. The system is active all week and backed up every Friday night.

3. Sutton Company has two employees handling acquisitions of inventory. One employee places purchase orders and pays vendors. The second employee receives the merchandise.

4. The owner of Super Pharmacy uses a check protector to perforate checks, making it difficult for anyone to alter the amount of the check. The check protector is on the owner's desk in an office that contains company checks and is normally unlocked.

5. Lavina Company is a small business that has separated the duties of cash receipts and cash disbursements. The employee responsible for cash disbursements reconciles the bank account monthly.

PROBLEM SET B

Problem 6-1B
Analyzing internal control

C1

Music City Center had the following petty cash transactions in March of the current year.

March	5	Wrote a $300 check, cashed it, and gave the proceeds and the petty cashbox to Abby Rode, the petty cashier.
	6	Paid $16.75 COD shipping charges on merchandise purchased for resale, terms FOB shipping point. Music City uses the perpetual system to account for merchandise inventory.
	11	Paid $44.50 delivery charges on merchandise sold to a customer, terms FOB destination.
	12	Purchased file folders for $7.95 that are immediately used.
	14	Reimbursed Alys Mingle, the manager, $68 for office supplies purchased and used.
	18	Purchased printer paper for $20 that is immediately used.
	27	Paid $11.60 COD shipping charges on merchandise purchased for resale, terms FOB shipping point.
	28	Paid postage expenses of $60.
	30	Reimbursed Mingle $56.80 for business car mileage.
	31	Cash of $16.81 remained in the fund. Sorted the petty cash receipts by accounts affected and exchanged them for a check to reimburse the fund for expenditures.
	31	The petty cash fund amount is increased by $50 to a total of $350.

Problem 6-2B
Establish, reimburse, and increase petty cash

P2

Required

1. Prepare the journal entry to establish the petty cash fund.

2. Prepare a petty cash payments report for March with these categories: delivery expense, mileage expense, postage expense, merchandise inventory (for transportation-in), and office supplies expense. Sort the payments into the appropriate categories and total the expenses in each category.

3. Prepare the journal entries for part 2 to both (*a*) reimburse and (*b*) increase the fund amount.

Check (2) Total expenses $285.60

(3a) Cr. Cash $283.19

Problem 6-3B

Establishing, reimbursing, and adjusting petty cash

P2

Lansing Co. establishes a petty cash fund for payments of small amounts. The following transactions involving the petty cash fund occurred in January (the last month of the company's fiscal year).

Jan. 3   A company check for $150 is written and made payable to the petty cashier to establish the petty cash fund.

14   A company check is written to replenish the fund for the following expenditures made since January 3.

   a.   Purchased office supplies for $17.52 that are immediately used up.

   b.   Paid $20.50 COD shipping charges on merchandise purchased for resale, terms FOB shipping point. Lansing uses the perpetual system to account for inventory.

   c.   Paid $55.30 to All-Tech for minor repairs to a computer.

   d.   Paid $19.63 for items classified as miscellaneous expenses.

   e.   Counted $35.05 remaining in the petty cash box.

15   Prepared a company check for $50 to increase the fund to $200.

31   The petty cashier reports that $29.57 remains in the fund. A company check is written to replenish the fund for the following expenditures made since January 14.

   f.   Paid $52 to *The Smart Shopper* for an advertisement in January's newsletter.

   g.   Paid $55.61 for postage expenses.

   h.   Paid $65 to FedEx for delivery of merchandise, terms FOB destination.

31   The company decides that the January 15 increase in the fund was too little. It increases the fund by another $50, leaving a total of $250.

Required

Check   (1) Cr. to Cash: Jan. 14, $114.95; Jan. 15, $50

1. Prepare journal entries to establish the fund on January 3, to replenish it on January 14 and January 31, and to reflect any increase or decrease in the fund balance on January 15 and 31.

Analysis Component

2. Explain how the company's financial statements are affected if the petty cash fund is not replenished and no entry is made on January 31.

Problem 6-4B

Prepare a bank reconciliation and record adjustments

P3

The following information is available to reconcile Gardenia Co.'s book balance of cash with its bank statement cash balance as of December 31, 2011.

a. The December 31 cash balance according to the accounting records is $13,599, and the bank statement cash balance for that date is $26,379.

b. Check No. 1273 for $1,800 and Check No. 1282 for $892, both written and entered in the accounting records in December, are not among the canceled checks. Two checks, No. 1231 for $676 and No. 1242 for $2,568, were outstanding on the most recent November 30 reconciliation. Check No. 1231 is listed with the December canceled checks, but Check No. 1242 is not.

c. When the December checks are compared with entries in the accounting records, it is found that Check No. 1267 had been correctly drawn for $1,230 to pay for office supplies but was erroneously entered in the accounting records as $1,320.

d. Two debit memoranda are enclosed with the statement and are unrecorded at the time of the reconciliation. One debit memorandum is for $805 and dealt with an NSF check for $795 received from a customer, Millard Industries, in payment of its account. The bank assessed a $10 fee for processing it. The second debit memorandum is a $99 charge for check printing. Gardenia did not record these transactions before receiving the statement.

e. A credit memorandum indicates that the bank collected $19,000 cash on a note receivable for the company, deducted a $14 collection fee, and credited the balance to the company's Cash account. Gardenia did not record this transaction before receiving the statement.

f. Gardenia's December 31 daily cash receipts of $10,652 were placed in the bank's night depository on that date, but do not appear on the December 31 bank statement.

Required

Check   (1) Reconciled balance, $31,771; (2) Cr. Note Receivable $19,000

1. Prepare the bank reconciliation for this company as of December 31, 2011.

2. Prepare the journal entries necessary to bring the company's book balance of cash into conformity with the reconciled cash balance as of December 31, 2011.

Analysis Component

3. Explain the nature of the communications conveyed by a bank when the bank sends the depositor (*a*) a debit memorandum and (*b*) a credit memorandum.

Tamzen Systems most recently reconciled its bank balance on April 30 and reported two checks outstanding at that time, No. 1771 for $1,037 and No. 1780 for $516. The following information is available for its May 31, 2011, reconciliation.

Problem 6-5B
Prepare a bank reconciliation and record adjustments

P3

From the May 31 Bank Statement

PREVIOUS BALANCE	TOTAL CHECKS AND DEBITS	TOTAL DEPOSITS AND CREDITS	CURRENT BALANCE
18,500	8,041	11,611	22,070

CHECKS AND DEBITS			DEPOSITS AND CREDITS		DAILY BALANCE	
Date	No.	Amount	Date	Amount	Date	Amount
05/01	1771	1,037	05/04	1,109	04/30	18,500
05/02	1783	782	05/14	2,280	05/01	17,463
05/04	1782	1,801	05/22	4,304	05/02	16,681
05/11	1784	424	05/25	1,520 CM	05/04	15,989
05/18		688 NSF	05/26	2,398	05/11	15,565
05/25	1787	993			05/14	17,845
05/26	1785	2,056			05/18	17,157
05/29	1788	238			05/22	21,461
05/31		22 SC			05/25	21,988
					05/26	23,330
					05/29	22,092
					05/31	22,070

From Tamzen Systems' Accounting Records

Cash Receipts Deposited			
Date			Cash Debit
May	4		1,109
	14		2,280
	22		4,304
	26		2,398
	31		1,716
			11,807

Cash Disbursements		
Check No.		Cash Credit
1782		1,801
1783		782
1784		424
1785		2,056
1786		935
1787		993
1788		228
1789		371
		7,590

Cash						Acct. No. 101
Date		Explanation	PR	Debit	Credit	Balance
Apr.	30	Balance				16,947
May	31	Total receipts	R2	11,807		28,754
	31	Total disbursements	D23		7,590	21,164

Additional Information

Check No. 1788 is correctly drawn for $238 to pay for May utilities; however, the recordkeeper misread the amount and entered it in the accounting records with a debit to Utilities Expense and a credit to Cash for $228. The bank paid and deducted the correct amount. The NSF check shown in the statement was originally received from a customer, W. Sox, in payment of her account. The company has not yet recorded its return. The credit memorandum is from a $1,540 note that the bank collected for the company. The bank deducted a $20 collection fee and deposited the remainder in the company's account. The collection and fee have not yet been recorded.

Required

1. Prepare the May 31, 2011, bank reconciliation for Tamzen Systems.

2. Prepare the journal entries to adjust the book balance of cash to the reconciled balance.

Analysis Component

3. The bank statement reveals that some of the prenumbered checks in the sequence are missing. Describe three possible situations to explain this.

SERIAL PROBLEM

Success Systems

P3

(This serial problem began in Chapter 1 and continues through most of the book. If previous chapter segments were not completed, the serial problem can begin at this point. It is helpful, but not necessary, to use the Working Papers that accompany the book.)

SP 6   Adriana Lopez receives the March bank statement for Success Systems on April 11, 2010. The March 31 bank statement shows an ending cash balance of $77,354. A comparison of the bank statement with the general ledger Cash account, No. 101, reveals the following.

a. Lopez notices that the bank erroneously cleared a $500 check against her account in March that she did not issue. The check documentation included with the bank statement shows that this check was actually issued by a company named Sierra Systems.

b. On March 25, the bank issued a $50 debit memorandum for the safety deposit box that Success Systems agreed to rent from the bank beginning March 25.

c. On March 26, the bank issued a $102 debit memorandum for printed checks that Success Systems ordered from the bank.

d. On March 31, the bank issued a credit memorandum for $33 interest earned on Success Systems' checking account for the month of March.

e. Lopez notices that the check she issued for $128 on March 31, 2010, has not yet cleared the bank.

f. Lopez verifies that all deposits made in March do appear on the March bank statement.

g. The general ledger Cash account, No. 101, shows an ending cash balance per books of $77,845 as of March 31 (prior to any reconciliation).

Required

1. Prepare a bank reconciliation for Success Systems for the month ended March 31, 2010.

2. Prepare any necessary adjusting entries. Use Miscellaneous Expenses, No. 677, for any bank charges. Use Interest Revenue, No. 404, for any interest earned on the checking account for the month of March.

BEYOND THE NUMBERS

REPORTING IN ACTION

C2 A1

BTN 6-1   Refer to Best Buy's financial statements in Appendix A to answer the following.

1. For both fiscal year-ends February 28, 2009, and March 1, 2008, identify the total amount of cash and cash equivalents. Determine the percent this amount represents of total current assets, total current liabilities, total shareholders' equity, and total assets for both years. Comment on any trends.

2. For fiscal years ended February 28, 2009, and March 1, 2008, use the information in the statement of cash flows to determine the percent change between the beginning and ending year amounts of cash and cash equivalents.

3. Compute the days' sales uncollected as of February 28, 2009, and March 1, 2008. Has the collection of receivables improved? Are accounts receivable an important asset for Best Buy? Explain.

Fast Forward

4. Access Best Buy's financial statements for fiscal years ending after February 28, 2009, from its Website (**BestBuy.com**) or the SEC's EDGAR database (**www.SEC.gov**). Recompute its days' sales uncollected for fiscal years ending after February 28, 2009. Compare this to the days' sales uncollected for 2009 and 2008.

BTN 6-2 Key comparative figures for **Best Buy** and **RadioShack** follow.

($ millions)	Best Buy		RadioShack	
	Current Year	Prior Year	Current Year	Prior Year
Accounts receivable	$ 1,868	$ 549	$ 241.9	$ 256.0
Net sales	45,015	40,023	4,224.5	4,251.7

Required

Compute days' sales uncollected for these companies for each of the two years shown. Comment on any trends for the companies. Which company has the largest percent change in days' sales uncollected?

BTN 6-3 Harriet Knox, Ralph Patton, and Marcia Diamond work for a family physician, Dr. Gwen Conrad, who is in private practice. Dr. Conrad is knowledgeable about office management practices and has segregated the cash receipt duties as follows. Knox opens the mail and prepares a triplicate list of money received. She sends one copy of the list to Patton, the cashier, who deposits the receipts daily in the bank. Diamond, the recordkeeper, receives a copy of the list and posts payments to patients' accounts. About once a month the office clerks have an expensive lunch they pay for as follows. First, Patton endorses a patient's check in Dr. Conrad's name and cashes it at the bank. Knox then destroys the remittance advice accompanying the check. Finally, Diamond posts payment to the customer's account as a miscellaneous credit. The three justify their actions by their relatively low pay and knowledge that Dr. Conrad will likely never miss the money.

Required

1. Who is the best person in Dr. Conrad's office to reconcile the bank statement?
2. Would a bank reconciliation uncover this office fraud?
3. What are some procedures to detect this type of fraud?
4. Suggest additional internal controls that Dr. Conrad could implement.

BTN 6-4[B] Assume you are a business consultant. The owner of a company sends you an e-mail expressing concern that the company is not taking advantage of its discounts offered by vendors. The company currently uses the gross method of recording purchases. The owner is considering a review of all invoices and payments from the previous period. Due to the volume of purchases, however, the owner recognizes this is time-consuming and costly. The owner seeks your advice about monitoring purchase discounts in the future. Provide a response in memorandum form.

BTN 6-5 Visit the Association of Certified Fraud Examiners Website at **cfenet.com**. Find and open the file "2008 Report to the Nation." Read the two-page Executive Summary and fill in the following blanks. (The report is under its *Fraud Resources* tab or under its *About the ACFE* tab [under Press Room]; we can also use the *Search* tab.)

1. The median loss caused by occupational frauds was $_____.
2. Nearly _____ of fraud cases caused at least $1 million in losses.
3. Companies lose ___% of their annual revenues to fraud; this figure translates to $_____ billion in fraud losses.
4. The typical length of fraud schemes was _____ years from the time the fraud began until it was detected.
5. Companies that conducted surprise audits suffered a median loss of $_____, whereas those without surprise audits had a median loss of $_____.

6. The median loss suffered by companies with fewer than 100 employees was $_____ per scheme.

7. _____ and _____ were the most common small business fraud schemes.

8. ___% of respondents cited inadequate internal controls as the primary contributing factor in the frauds investigated.

9. Only ___% of the perpetrators had convictions prior to committing their frauds.

TEAMWORK IN ACTION

C1

BTN 6-6   Organize the class into teams. Each team must prepare a list of 10 internal controls a consumer could observe in a typical retail department store. When called upon, the team's spokesperson must be prepared to share controls identified by the team that have not been shared by another team's spokesperson.

ENTREPRENEURIAL DECISION

C1   P1

BTN 6-7   Review the opening feature of this chapter that highlights Dylan Lauren and Jeff Rubin and their company **Dylan's Candy Bar**.

Required

1. List the seven principles of internal control and explain how Dylan and Jeff could implement each of them in their retail stores.

2. Do you believe that they will need to add additional controls as their business expands? Explain.

HITTING THE ROAD

C1

BTN 6-8   Visit an area of your college that serves the student community with either products or services. Some examples are food services, libraries, and book stores. Identify and describe between four and eight internal controls being implemented.

GLOBAL DECISION

C2   A1

BTN 6-9   The following information is from **GOME** (www.GOME.com.hk), which is the leading chain retailer of consumer electronic products and household appliances in China.

RMB 000s	Current Year	Prior Year
Cash	3,051,069	6,269,996
Accounts receivable	45,092	97,719
Current assets	18,482,711	22,337,559
Total assets	27,495,104	29,837,493
Current liabilities	15,147,247	16,180,091
Shareholders' equity	8,700,035	10,392,668
Net sales	45,889,257	42,478,523

Required

1. For each year, compute the percentage that cash represents of current assets, total assets, current liabilities, and shareholders' equity. Comment on any trends in these percentages.

2. Determine the percentage change between the current and prior year cash balances.

3. Compute the days' sales uncollected at the end of both the current year and the prior year. Has the collection of receivables improved? Explain.

ANSWERS TO MULTIPLE CHOICE QUIZ

1. e; The entry follows.

Debits to expenses (or assets)	420
Cash Over and Short	5
Cash	425

2. a; recognizes cash collection of note by bank.

3. a; the bank reconciliation follows.

4. d; ($6,720/$84,000) × 365 = 29.2 days

5. b; The entry follows.

Merchandise Inventory*	5,880	
Accounts Payable		5,880

*$6,000 × 98%

Bank Reconciliation November 30			
Balance per bank statement	$1,895	Balance per books	$1,742
Add: Deposit in transit	795	Add: Note collected less fee	320
Deduct: Outstanding checks	(638)	Deduct: Service charge	(10)
Reconciled balance	$2,052	Reconciled balance	$2,052

7

Reporting and Analyzing Receivables

"Create what the industry is missing . . . it is worth the hardships" —Kevin Plank (center)

A Look Back

Chapter 6 focused on internal control and reporting for cash. We described internal control procedures and the accounting for and management of cash.

A Look at This Chapter

This chapter emphasizes receivables. We explain that they are liquid assets and describe how companies account for and report them. We also discuss the importance of estimating uncollectibles.

A Look Ahead

Chapter 8 focuses on plant assets, natural resources, and intangible assets. We explain how to account for, report, and analyze these long-term assets.

No Sweat!

BALTIMORE, MD—"There was a void in apparel and I decided to fill it," says Kevin Plank, the founder of **Under Armour (UnderArmour.com),** a manufacturer of athletic apparel using a polyester fabric that wicks perspiration away. He invested his life savings of $20,000 and began by working out of his grandma's basement.

As sales grew, Kevin partnered with a factory in Ohio and hit it off with the factory manager, Sal Fasciana. Sal spent many evenings and weekends teaching Kevin about accounting and costs. "I said, 'OK, kid. This is the way it's going to be done,'" recalls Sal. Attention to details carried over to where Kevin learned to monitor receivables. Decisions on credit sales and policies for extending credit can make or break a start-up.

Kevin applied well what Sal taught him. He ensured that credit sales were extended to customers in good credit standing. Kevin knows his customers, including who pays and when. Says Kevin, we understand our customers—inside and out—including cash payment patterns that allow us to estimate uncollectibles and minimize bad debts. His company's financial report says, "We make ongoing estimates relating to the collectibility of our accounts receivable and maintain a reserve for estimated losses resulting from the inability of our customers to make required payments."

A commitment to quality customers is propelling Under Armour's sales and shattering Kevin's most optimistic goals. "It's about educating consumers . . . investing in the product." Kevin has also issued notes receivable to select employees. Both accounts and notes receivables receive his attention. His financial report discloses that the company "reviews the allowance for doubtful accounts monthly."

"When I first started . . . I was a young punk who thought he knew everything," explains Kevin. Now, he explains, my accounting reports must show profits for long-term success. "Most people out there are saying we're going to trip up at some point," says Kevin. "Our job is to prove them wrong." He might also prove Thomas Edison right: genius is 99 percent perspiration and 1 percent inspiration; and Kevin is after the 99 percent.

[Sources: *Under Armour Website,* January 2010; *Under Armour 10-K Report,* Filed February 2009; *Entrepreneur,* November 2003; *FastCompany,* 2005 and 2002; *USA Today,* December 2004; *Inc.com,* 2003 and 2004; *All Headline News,* August 2005; *Entrepreneur's Journey,* November 2007]

CAP

Conceptual

C1 Describe accounts receivable and how they occur and are recorded. *(p. 296)*

C2 Describe a note receivable and the computation of its maturity date and interest. *(p. 306)*

C3 Explain how receivables can be converted to cash before maturity. *(p. 310)*

Analytical

A1 Compute accounts receivable turnover and use it to help assess financial condition. *(p. 312)*

Procedural

P1 Apply the direct write-off and allowance methods to account for accounts receivable. *(p. 300)*

P2 Estimate uncollectibles using methods based on sales and accounts receivable. *(p. 303)*

P3 Record the receipt of a note receivable. *(p. 308)*

P4 Record the honoring and dishonoring of a note and adjustments for interest. *(p. 308)*

LP7

This chapter focuses on accounts receivable and short-term notes receivable. We describe each of these assets, their uses, and how they are accounted for and reported in financial statements. This knowledge helps us use accounting information to make better business decisions. It can also help in predicting future company performance and financial condition as well as in managing one's own business.

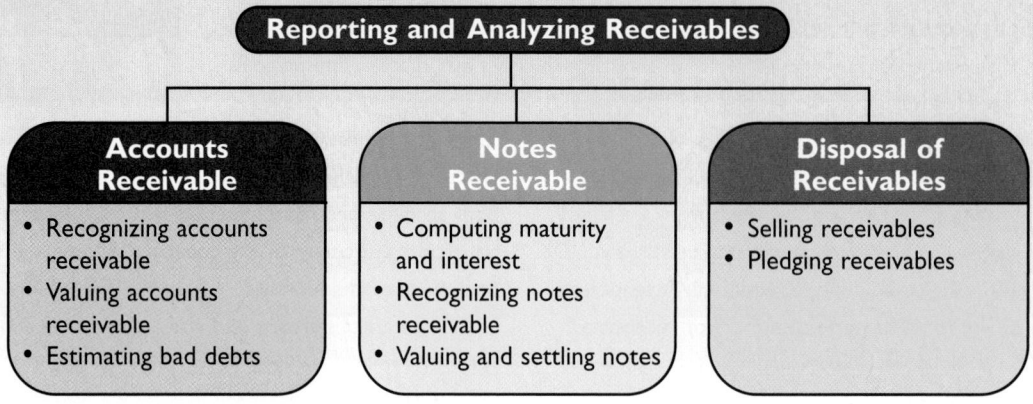

Reporting and Analyzing Receivables

Accounts Receivable
- Recognizing accounts receivable
- Valuing accounts receivable
- Estimating bad debts

Notes Receivable
- Computing maturity and interest
- Recognizing notes receivable
- Valuing and settling notes

Disposal of Receivables
- Selling receivables
- Pledging receivables

Accounts Receivable

Video7.1

A *receivable* is an amount due from another party. The two most common receivables are accounts receivable and notes receivable. Other receivables include interest receivable, rent receivable, tax refund receivable, and receivables from employees. **Accounts receivable** are amounts due from customers for credit sales. This section begins by describing how accounts receivable occur. It includes receivables that occur when customers use credit cards issued by third parties and when a company gives credit directly to customers. When a company does extend credit directly to customers, it (1) maintains a separate account receivable for each customer and (2) accounts for bad debts from credit sales.

Recognizing Accounts Receivable

C1 Describe accounts receivable and how they occur and are recorded.

Accounts receivable occur from credit sales to customers. The amount of credit sales has increased in recent years, reflecting several factors including an efficient financial system. Retailers such as **Limited Brands** and **Best Buy** hold millions of dollars in accounts receivable. Similar amounts are held by wholesalers such as **SUPERVALU** and **SYSCO**. Exhibit 7.1 shows recent dollar amounts of accounts receivable and their percent of total assets for four well-known companies.

Sales on Credit Credit sales are recorded by increasing (debiting) Accounts Receivable. A company must also maintain a separate account for each customer that tracks how much that

EXHIBIT 7.1

Accounts Receivable for Selected Companies

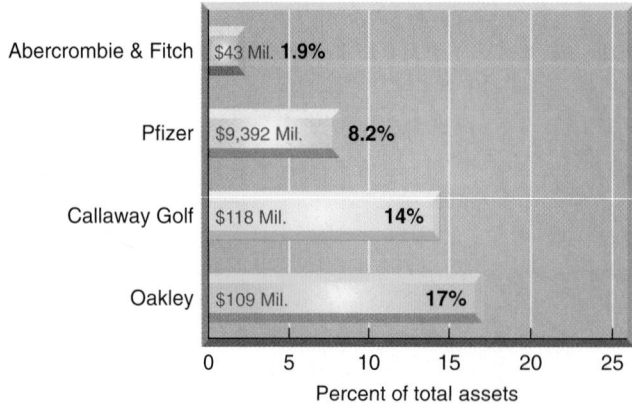

customer purchases, has already paid, and still owes. This information provides the basis for sending bills to customers and for other business analyses. To maintain this information, companies that extend credit directly to their customers keep a separate account receivable for each one of them. The general ledger continues to have a single Accounts Receivable account along with the other financial statement accounts, but a supplementary record is created to maintain a separate account for each customer. This supplementary record is called the *accounts receivable ledger.*

Exhibit 7.2 shows the relation between the Accounts Receivable account in the general ledger and its individual customer accounts in the accounts receivable ledger for TechCom, a small electronics wholesaler. This exhibit reports a $3,000 ending balance of TechCom's accounts receivable for June 30. TechCom's transactions are mainly in cash, but it has two major credit customers: CompStore and RDA Electronics. Its *schedule of accounts receivable* shows that the $3,000 balance of the Accounts Receivable account in the general ledger equals the total of its two customers' balances in the accounts receivable ledger.

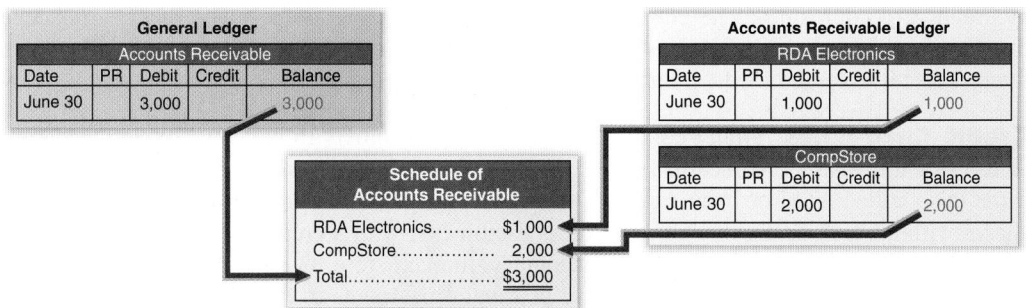

EXHIBIT 7.2

General Ledger and the Accounts Receivable Ledger (before July 1 transactions)

To see how accounts receivable from credit sales are recognized in the accounting records, we look at two transactions on July 1 between TechCom and its credit customers—see Exhibit 7.3. The first is a credit sale of $950 to CompStore. A credit sale is posted with both a debit to the Accounts Receivable account in the general ledger and a debit to the customer account in the accounts receivable ledger. The second transaction is a collection of $720 from RDA Electronics from a prior credit sale. Cash receipts from a credit customer are posted with a credit to the Accounts Receivable account in the general ledger and flows through to credit the customer account in the accounts receivable ledger. (Posting debits or credits to Accounts Receivable in two separate ledgers does not violate the requirement that debits equal credits. The equality of debits and credits is maintained in the general ledger. The accounts receivable ledger is a *supplementary* record providing information on each customer.)

EXHIBIT 7.3

Accounts Receivable Transactions

July 1	Accounts Receivable—CompStore	950	
	Sales		950
	*To record credit sales**		
July 1	Cash	720	
	Accounts Receivable—RDA Electronics		720
	To record collection of credit sales.		

Assets = Liabilities + Equity
+ 950   +950

Assets = Liabilities + Equity
+720
−720

* We omit the entry to Dr. Cost of Sales and Cr. Merchandise Inventory to focus on sales and receivables.

Exhibit 7.4 shows the general ledger and the accounts receivable ledger after recording the two July 1 transactions. The general ledger shows the effects of the sale, the collection, and the resulting balance of $3,230. These events are also reflected in the individual customer accounts: RDA Electronics has an ending balance of $280, and CompStore's ending balance is $2,950. The $3,230 sum of the individual accounts equals the debit balance of the Accounts Receivable account in the general ledger.

EXHIBIT 7.4

General Ledger and
the Accounts Receivable Ledger
(after July 1 transactions)

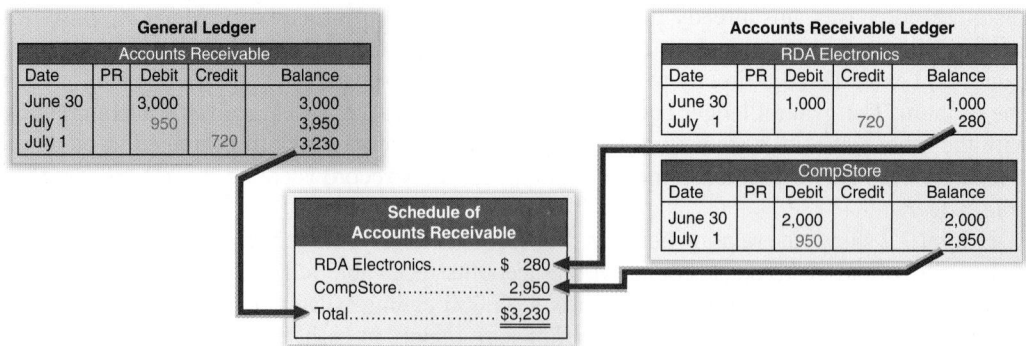

Like TechCom, many large retailers such as **Sears** and **JCPenney** sell on credit. Many also maintain their own credit cards to grant credit to approved customers and to earn interest on any balance not paid within a specified period of time. This allows them to avoid the fee charged by credit card companies. The entries in this case are the same as those for TechCom except for the possibility of added interest revenue. If a customer owes interest on a bill, we debit Interest Receivable and credit Interest Revenue for that amount.

Credit Card Sales   Many companies allow their customers to pay for products and services using third-party credit cards such as **Visa**, **MasterCard**, or **American Express**, and debit cards (also called ATM or bank cards). This practice gives customers the ability to make purchases without cash or checks. Once credit is established with a credit card company or bank, the customer does not have to open an account with each store. Customers using these cards can make single monthly payments instead of several payments to different creditors and can defer their payments.

Many sellers allow customers to use third-party credit cards and debit cards instead of granting credit directly for several reasons. First, the seller does not have to evaluate each customer's credit standing or make decisions about who gets credit and how much. Second, the seller avoids the risk of extending credit to customers who cannot or do not pay. This risk is transferred to the card company. Third, the seller typically receives cash from the card company sooner than had it granted credit directly to customers. Fourth, a variety of credit options for customers offers a potential increase in sales volume. **Sears** historically offered credit only to customers using a Sears card but later changed its policy to permit customers to charge purchases to third-party credit card companies in a desire to increase sales. It reported: "SearsCharge increased its share of Sears retail sales even as the company expanded the payment options available to its customers with the acceptance . . . of Visa, MasterCard, and American Express in addition to the [Sears] Card."

There are guidelines in how companies account for credit card and debit card sales. Some credit cards, but mostly debit cards, credit a seller's Cash account immediately upon deposit. In this case the seller deposits a copy of each card sales receipt in its bank account just as it deposits a customer's check. Some other cards require the seller to remit a copy (often electronically) of each receipt to the card company. Until payment is received, the seller has an account receivable from the card company. In both cases, the seller pays a fee for services provided by the card company, often ranging from 1% to 5% of card sales. This charge is deducted from the credit to the seller's account or the cash payment to the seller.

Decision Insight

Debit Card vs. Credit Card   A buyer's debit card purchase reduces the buyer's cash account balance at the card company, which is often a bank. Since the buyer's cash account balance is a liability (with a credit balance) for the card company to the buyer, the card company would debit that account for a buyer's purchase—hence, the term *debit card*. A credit card reflects authorization by the card company of a line of credit for the buyer with preset interest rates and payment terms—hence, the term *credit card*. Most card companies waive interest charges if the buyer pays its balance each month.

The procedures used in accounting for credit card sales depend on whether cash is received immediately on deposit or cash receipt is delayed until the credit card company makes the payment. To illustrate, if TechCom has $100 of credit card sales with a 4% fee, and its $96 cash is received immediately on deposit, the entry is

July 15	Cash	96	
	Credit Card Expense	4	
	Sales		100
	*To record credit card sales less a 4% credit card expense.**		

Assets = Liabilities + Equity
+96   +100
                              −4

* We omit the entry to Dr. Cost of Sales and Cr. Merchandise Inventory to focus on credit card expense.

However, if instead TechCom must remit electronically the credit card sales receipts to the credit card company and wait for the $96 cash payment, the entry on the date of sale is

July 15	**Accounts Receivable—Credit Card Co.**	96	
	Credit Card Expense	4	
	Sales		100
	*To record credit card sales less 4% credit card expense.**		

Assets = Liabilities + Equity
+96   +100
                              −4

* We omit the entry to Dr. Cost of Sales and Cr. Merchandise Inventory to focus on credit card expense.

When cash is later received from the credit card company, usually through electronic funds transfer, the entry is

July 20	Cash	96	
	Accounts Receivable—Credit Card Co.		96
	To record cash receipt.		

Assets = Liabilities + Equity
+96
−96

Some firms report credit card expense in the income statement as a type of discount deducted from sales to get net sales. Other companies classify it as a selling expense or even as an administrative expense. Arguments can be made for each approach.

Installment Sales and Receivables Many companies allow their credit customers to make periodic payments over several months. For example, **Ford Motor Company** reports more than $70 billion in installment receivables. The seller refers to such assets as *installment accounts receivable,* which are amounts owed by customers from credit sales for which payment is required in periodic amounts over an extended time period. Source documents for installment accounts receivable include sales slips or invoices describing the sales transactions. The customer is usually charged interest. Although installment accounts receivable can have credit periods of more than one year, they are classified as current assets if the seller regularly offers customers such terms.

Decision Maker

Entrepreneur As a small retailer, you are considering allowing customers to buy merchandise using credit cards. Until now, your store accepted only cash and checks. What analysis do you use to make this decision? [Answer—p. 315]

Quick Check

Answers—p. 316

1. In recording credit card sales, when do you debit Accounts Receivable and when do you debit Cash?

2. A company accumulates sales receipts and remits them to the credit card company for payment. When are the credit card expenses recorded? When are these expenses incurred?

Valuing Accounts Receivable—Direct Write-Off Method

P1	Apply the direct write-off and allowance methods to account for accounts receivable.

When a company directly grants credit to its customers, it expects that some customers will not pay what they promised. The accounts of these customers are *uncollectible accounts,* commonly called **bad debts.** The total amount of uncollectible accounts is an expense of selling on credit. Why do companies sell on credit if they expect some accounts to be uncollectible? The answer is that companies believe that granting credit will increase total sales and net income enough to offset bad debts. Companies use two methods to account for uncollectible accounts: (1) direct write-off method and (2) allowance method. We describe both.

Point: Managers realize that some portion of credit sales will be uncollectible, but which credit sales are uncollectible is unknown.

Recording and Writing Off Bad Debts   The **direct write-off method** of accounting for bad debts records the loss from an uncollectible account receivable when it is determined to be uncollectible. No attempt is made to predict bad debts expense. To illustrate, if TechCom determines on January 23 that it cannot collect $520 owed to it by its customer J. Kent, it recognizes the loss using the direct write-off method as follows:

Assets = Liabilities + Equity
−520   −520

Jan. 23	Bad Debts Expense.............................	520	
	Accounts Receivable—J. Kent................		520
	To write off an uncollectible account.		

The debit in this entry charges the uncollectible amount directly to the current period's Bad Debts Expense account. The credit removes its balance from the Accounts Receivable account in the general ledger (and its subsidiary ledger).

Point: If a customer fails to pay within the credit period, most companies send out repeated billings and make other efforts to collect.

Recovering a Bad Debt   Although uncommon, sometimes an account written off is later collected. This can be due to factors such as continual collection efforts or a customer's good fortune. If the account of J. Kent that was written off directly to Bad Debts Expense is later collected in full, the following two entries record this recovery.

Assets = Liabilities + Equity
+520   +520

Assets = Liabilities + Equity
+520
−520

Mar. 11	Accounts Receivable—J. Kent....................	520	
	Bad Debts Expense.........................		520
	To reinstate account previously written off.		
Mar. 11	Cash..	520	
	Accounts Receivable—J. Kent................		520
	To record full payment of account.		

Assessing the Direct Write-Off Method   Examples of companies that use the direct write-off method include **Rand Medical Billing, Gateway Distributors, Microwave Satellite Technologies, Frebon International, Interscope Technologies, On Line Payroll Services**, and **Sub Surface Waste Management**. The following disclosure by **Pharma-Bio Serv** is typical of the justification for this method: Bad debts are accounted for using the direct write-off method whereby an expense is recognized only when a specific account is determined to be uncollectible. The effect of using this method approximates that of the allowance method. Companies must weigh at least two accounting concepts when considering the use of the direct write-off method: the (1) matching principle and (2) materiality constraint.

Matching principle applied to bad debts.   The **matching (expense recognition) principle** requires expenses to be reported in the same accounting period as the sales they helped produce. This means that if extending credit to customers helped produce sales, the bad debts expense linked to those sales is matched and reported in the same period. The direct write-off method usually does *not* best match sales and expenses because bad debts expense is not recorded until an account becomes uncollectible, which often occurs in a period after that of the credit sale. To match bad debts expense with the sales it produces therefore requires a company to estimate future uncollectibles.

Point: **Oakley** reports $15 million of bad debts expense matched against $762 million of sales in a recent year.

Materiality constraint applied to bad debts. The **materiality constraint** states that an amount can be ignored if its effect on the financial statements is unimportant to users' business decisions. The materiality constraint permits the use of the direct write-off method when bad debts expenses are very small in relation to a company's other financial statement items such as sales and net income.

Valuing Accounts Receivable—Allowance Method

The **allowance method** of accounting for bad debts matches the *estimated* loss from uncollectible accounts receivable against the sales they helped produce. We must use estimated losses because when sales occur, management does not know which customers will not pay their bills. This means that at the end of each period, the allowance method requires an estimate of the total bad debts expected to result from that period's sales. This method has two advantages over the direct write-off method: (1) it records estimated bad debts expense in the period when the related sales are recorded and (2) it reports accounts receivable on the balance sheet at the estimated amount of cash to be collected.

Point: Under direct write-off, expense is recorded each time an account is written off. Under the allowance method, expense is recorded with an adjusting entry equal to the total estimated uncollectibles for that period's sales.

Recording Bad Debts Expense The allowance method estimates bad debts expense at the end of each accounting period and records it with an adjusting entry. TechCom, for instance, had credit sales of $300,000 during its first year of operations. At the end of the first year, $20,000 of credit sales remained uncollected. Based on the experience of similar businesses, TechCom estimated that $1,500 of its accounts receivable would be uncollectible. This estimated expense is recorded with the following adjusting entry.

Dec. 31	Bad Debts Expense	1,500	
	Allowance for Doubtful Accounts		1,500
	To record estimated bad debts.		

Assets = Liabilities + Equity
−1,500   −1,500

The estimated Bad Debts Expense of $1,500 is reported on the income statement (as either a selling expense or an administrative expense) and offsets the $300,000 credit sales it helped produce. The **Allowance for Doubtful Accounts** is a contra asset account. A contra account is used instead of reducing accounts receivable directly because at the time of the adjusting entry, the company does not know which customers will not pay. After the bad debts adjusting entry is posted, TechCom's account balances (in T-account form) for Accounts Receivable and its Allowance for Doubtful Accounts are as shown in Exhibit 7.5.

Point: Credit approval is usually not assigned to the selling dept. because its goal is to increase sales, and it may approve customers at the cost of increased bad debts. Instead, approval is assigned to a separate credit-granting or administrative dept.

Accounts Receivable				Allowance for Doubtful Accounts		
Dec. 31	20,000				Dec. 31	1,500

EXHIBIT 7.5

General Ledger Entries after Bad Debts Adjusting Entry

The Allowance for Doubtful Accounts credit balance of $1,500 has the effect of reducing accounts receivable to its estimated realizable value. **Realizable value** refers to the expected proceeds from converting an asset into cash. Although credit customers owe $20,000 to TechCom, only $18,500 is expected to be realized in cash collections from these customers. In the balance sheet, the Allowance for Doubtful Accounts is subtracted from Accounts Receivable and is often reported as shown in Exhibit 7.6.

Point: Bad Debts Expense is also called *Uncollectible Accounts Expense.* The Allowance for Doubtful Accounts is also called *Allowance for Uncollectible Accounts.*

Current assets		
Accounts receivable	$20,000	
Less allowance for doubtful accounts	1,500	$18,500

EXHIBIT 7.6

Balance Sheet Presentation of the Allowance for Doubtful Accounts

Sometimes the Allowance for Doubtful Accounts is not reported separately. This alternative presentation is shown in Exhibit 7.7 (also see Appendix A).

EXHIBIT 7.7

Alternative Presentation of the Allowance for Doubtful Accounts

Current assets	
Accounts receivable (net of $1,500 doubtful accounts)	$18,500

Writing Off a Bad Debt   When specific accounts are identified as uncollectible, they are written off against the Allowance for Doubtful Accounts. To illustrate, TechCom decides that J. Kent's $520 account is uncollectible and makes the following entry to write it off.

Assets = Liabilities + Equity
+520
−520

Jan. 23	Allowance for Doubtful Accounts	520	
	Accounts Receivable—J. Kent		520
	To write off an uncollectible account.		

Point: The Bad Debts Expense account is not debited in the write-off entry because it was recorded in the period when sales occurred.

Posting this write-off entry to the Accounts Receivable account removes the amount of the bad debt from the general ledger (it is also posted to the accounts receivable subsidiary ledger). The general ledger accounts now appear as in Exhibit 7.8 (assuming no other transactions affecting these accounts).

EXHIBIT 7.8

General Ledger Entries after Write-Off

Accounts Receivable				Allowance for Doubtful Accounts			
Dec. 31	20,000					Dec. 31	1,500
		Jan. 23	520	Jan. 23	520		

Point: In posting a write-off, the ledger's Explanation column indicates the reason for this credit so it is not misinterpreted as payment in full.

The write-off does *not* affect the realizable value of accounts receivable as shown in Exhibit 7.9. Neither total assets nor net income is affected by the write-off of a specific account. Instead, both assets and net income are affected in the period when bad debts expense is predicted and recorded with an adjusting entry.

EXHIBIT 7.9

Realizable Value before and after Write-Off of a Bad Debt

	Before Write-Off	After Write-Off
Accounts receivable	$ 20,000	$ 19,480
Less allowance for doubtful accounts	1,500	980
Estimated realizable accounts receivable	**$18,500**	**$18,500**

Recovering a Bad Debt   When a customer fails to pay and the account is written off as uncollectible, his or her credit standing is jeopardized. To help restore credit standing, a customer sometimes volunteers to pay all or part of the amount owed. A company makes two entries when collecting an account previously written off by the allowance method. The first is to reverse the write-off and reinstate the customer's account. The second entry records the collection of the reinstated account. To illustrate, if on March 11 Kent pays in full his account previously written off, the entries are

Assets = Liabilities + Equity
+520
−520

Assets = Liabilities + Equity
+520
−520

Mar. 11	Accounts Receivable—J. Kent	520	
	Allowance for Doubtful Accounts		520
	To reinstate account previously written off.		
Mar. 11	Cash	520	
	Accounts Receivable—J. Kent		520
	To record full payment of account.		

In this illustration, Kent paid the entire amount previously written off, but sometimes a customer pays only a portion of the amount owed. A question then arises as to whether the entire balance of the account or just the amount paid is returned to accounts receivable. This is a matter of judgment. If we believe this customer will later pay in full, we return the entire amount owed to accounts receivable, but if we expect no further collection, we return only the amount paid.

Example: If TechCom used a collection agency and paid a 35% commission on $520 collected from Kent, how is this recorded? *Answer:*

Cash 338
Collection Expense 182
   Accts. Recble.—J. Kent ...   520

Decision Insight

PayPal PayPal is legally just a money transfer agent, but it is increasingly challenging big credit card brands—see chart. PayPal is successful because: (1) online credit card processing fees often exceed $0.15 per dollar, but PayPal's fees are under $0.10 per dollar. (2) PayPal's merchant fraud losses are under 0.2% of revenues, which compares to 1.8% for online merchants using credit cards.

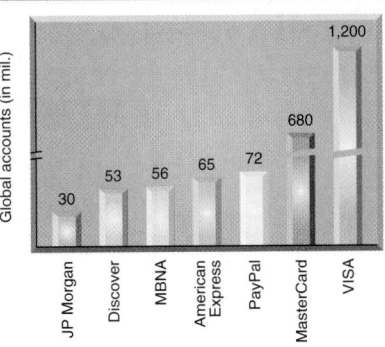

Estimating Bad Debts—Percent of Sales Method

The allowance method requires an estimate of bad debts expense to prepare an adjusting entry at the end of each accounting period. There are two common methods. One is based on the income statement relation between bad debts expense and sales. The second is based on the balance sheet relation between accounts receivable and the allowance for doubtful accounts.

The *percent of sales method,* also referred to as the *income statement method,* is based on the idea that a given percent of a company's credit sales for the period are uncollectible. To illustrate, assume that Musicland has credit sales of $400,000 in year 2009. Based on past experience, Musicland estimates 0.6% of credit sales to be uncollectible. This implies that Musicland expects $2,400 of bad debts expense from its sales (computed as $400,000 \times 0.006$). The adjusting entry to record this estimated expense is

P2 Estimate uncollectibles using methods based on sales and accounts receivable.

Point: Focus is on *credit* sales because cash sales do not produce bad debts. If cash sales are a small or stable percent of credit sales, total sales can be used.

Dec. 31	Bad Debts Expense	2,400	
	Allowance for Doubtful Accounts		2,400
	To record estimated bad debts.		

Assets = Liabilities + Equity
−2,400   −2,400

The allowance account ending balance on the balance sheet for this method would rarely equal the bad debts expense on the income statement. This is so because unless a company is in its first period of operations, its allowance account has a zero balance only if the prior amounts written off as uncollectible *exactly* equal the prior estimated bad debts expenses. (When computing bad debts expense as a percent of sales, managers monitor and adjust the percent so it is not too high or too low.)

Point: When using the *percent of sales method* for estimating uncollectibles, the estimate of bad debts is the number used in the adjusting entry.

Estimating Bad Debts—Percent of Receivables Method

The *accounts receivable methods,* also referred to as *balance sheet methods,* use balance sheet relations to estimate bad debts—mainly the relation between accounts receivable and the allowance amount. The goal of the bad debts adjusting entry for these methods is to make the Allowance for Doubtful Accounts balance equal to the portion of accounts receivable that is estimated to be uncollectible. The estimated balance for the allowance account is obtained in one of two ways: (1) computing the percent uncollectible from the total accounts receivable or (2) aging accounts receivable.

The *percent of accounts receivable method* assumes that a given percent of a company's receivables is uncollectible. This percent is based on past experience and is impacted by current conditions such as economic trends and customer difficulties. The total dollar amount of all receivables is multiplied by this percent to get the estimated dollar amount of uncollectible accounts—reported in the balance sheet as the Allowance for Doubtful Accounts.

To illustrate, assume that Musicland has $50,000 of accounts receivable on December 31, 2009. Experience suggests 5% of its receivables are uncollectible. This means that *after* the adjusting entry is posted, we want the Allowance for Doubtful Accounts to show a $2,500 credit balance (5% of $50,000). We are also told that its beginning balance is $2,200, which is 5% of the $44,000 accounts receivable on December 31, 2008—see Exhibit 7.10.

Point: When using an accounts receivable method for estimating uncollectibles, the allowance account balance is adjusted to equal the estimate of uncollectibles.

EXHIBIT 7.10

Allowance for Doubtful Accounts after Bad Debts Adjusting Entry

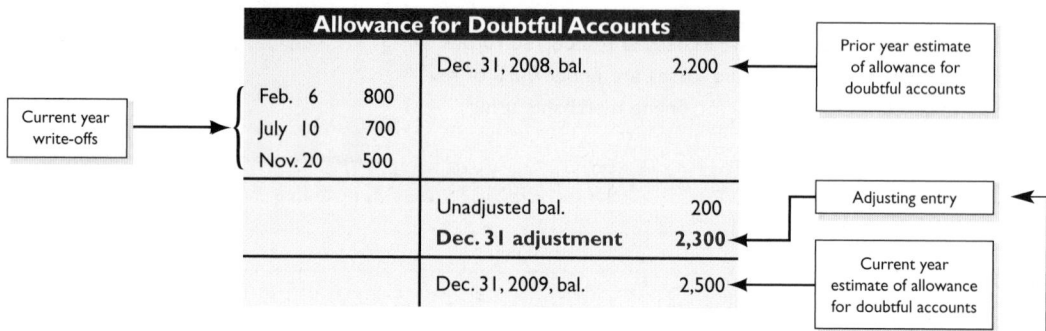

During 2009, accounts of customers are written off on February 6, July 10, and November 20. Thus, the account has a $200 credit balance *before* the December 31, 2009, adjustment. The adjusting entry to give the allowance account the estimated $2,500 balance is

Assets = Liabilities + Equity
−2,300   −2,300

Dec. 31	Bad Debts Expense	2,300	
	Allowance for Doubtful Accounts		2,300
	To record estimated bad debts.		

Decision Insight

Aging Pains Experience shows that the longer a receivable is past due, the lower is the likelihood of its collection. An *aging schedule* uses this knowledge to estimate bad debts. The chart here is from a survey that reported estimates of bad debts for receivables grouped by how long they were past their due dates. Each company sets its own estimates based on its customers and its experiences with those customers' payment patterns.

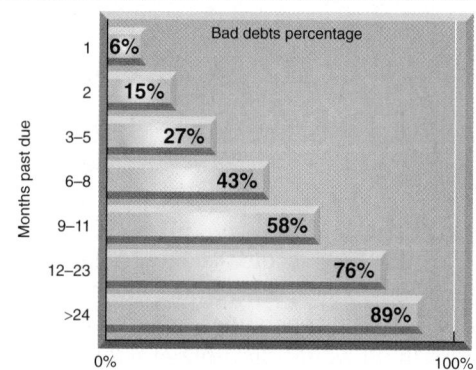

Estimating Bad Debts—Aging of Receivables Method

The **aging of accounts receivable** method uses both past and current receivables information to estimate the allowance amount. Specifically, each receivable is classified by how long it is past its due date. Then estimates of uncollectible amounts are made assuming that the longer an amount is past due, the more likely it is to be uncollectible. Classifications are often based on 30-day periods. After the amounts are classified (or aged), experience is used to estimate the percent of each uncollectible class. These percents are applied to the amounts in each class and then totaled to get the estimated balance of the Allowance for Doubtful Accounts. This computation is performed by setting up a schedule such as Exhibit 7.11.

EXHIBIT 7.11

Aging of Accounts Receivable

| | | | 1 to 30 | 31 to 60 | 61 to 90 | Over |
| **MUSICLAND** Schedule of Accounts Receivable by Age December 31, 2009 | | Not Yet | Days | Days | Days | 90 Days |
Customer	Totals	Due	Past Due	Past Due	Past Due	Past Due
Carlie Abbott..............	$ 450	$ 450				
Jamie Allen.................	710			$ 710		
Chavez Andres............	500	300	$ 200			
Balicia Company..........	740				$ 100	$ 640
Zamora Services.........	1,000	810	190			
Total receivables.......	$50,000	$37,000	$6,500	$3,700	$1,900	$ 900
Percent uncollectible.....		× 2%	× 5%	× 10%	× 25%	× 40%
Estimated uncollectible..	$ 2,270	$ 740	$ 325	$ 370	$ 475	$ 360

- Each receivable is grouped by how long it is past its due date
- Each age group is multiplied by its estimated bad debts percent
- Estimated bad debts for each group are totaled

Exhibit 7.11 lists each customer's individual balances assigned to one of five classes based on its days past due. The amounts in each class are totaled and multiplied by the estimated percent of uncollectible accounts for each class. The percents used are regularly reviewed to reflect changes in the company and economy.

To explain, Musicland has $3,700 in accounts receivable that are 31 to 60 days past due. Its management estimates 10% of the amounts in this age class are uncollectible, or a total of $370 (computed as $3,700 × 10%). Similar analysis is done for each of the other four classes. The final total of $2,270 ($740 + $325 +370 + $475 + $360) shown in the first column is the estimated balance for the Allowance for Doubtful Accounts. Exhibit 7.12 shows that since the allowance

EXHIBIT 7.12

Computation of the Required Adjustment for the Accounts Receivable Method

Unadjusted balance	$ 200 credit
Estimated balance	2,270 credit
Required adjustment	**$2,070 credit**

account has an unadjusted credit balance of $200, the required adjustment to the Allowance for Doubtful Accounts is $2,070. This yields the following end-of-period adjusting entry.

Dec. 31	Bad Debts Expense	2,070	
	Allowance for Doubtful Accounts		2,070
	To record estimated bad debts.		

Assets = Liabilities + Equity
−2,070   −2,070

Alternatively, if the allowance account had an unadjusted *debit* balance of $500 (instead of the $200 credit balance), its required adjustment would be computed as follows.

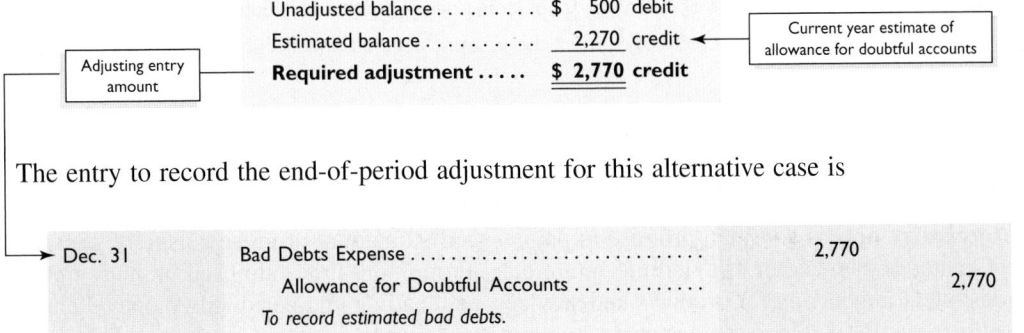

Unadjusted balance	$ 500 debit
Estimated balance	2,270 credit
Required adjustment	**$ 2,770 credit**

Adjusting entry amount

Current year estimate of allowance for doubtful accounts

The entry to record the end-of-period adjustment for this alternative case is

Dec. 31	Bad Debts Expense	2,770	
	Allowance for Doubtful Accounts		2,770
	To record estimated bad debts.		

Assets = Liabilities + Equity
−2,770   −2,770

The aging of accounts receivable method is an examination of specific accounts and is usually the most reliable of the estimation methods.

EXHIBIT 7.13

Methods to Estimate Bad Debts

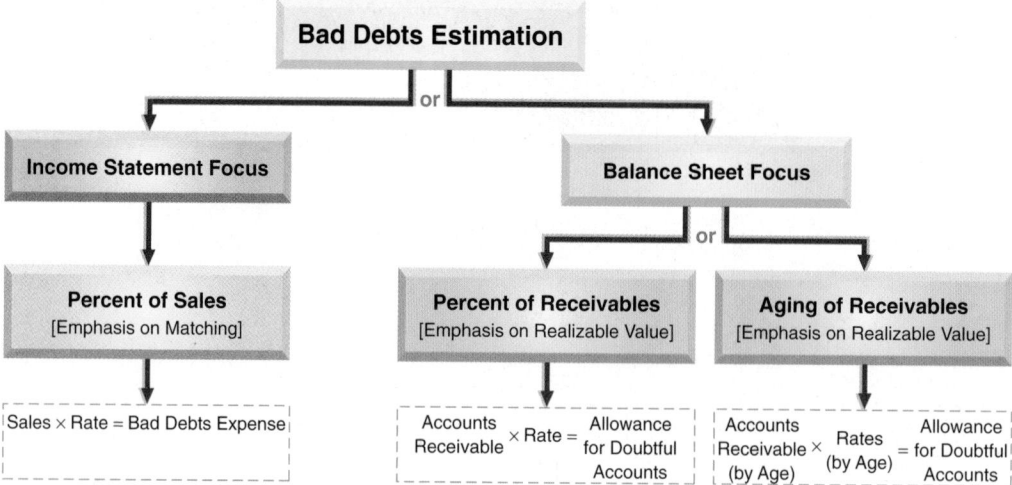

Estimating Bad Debts—Summary of Methods   Exhibit 7.13 summarizes the principles guiding all three estimation methods and their focus of analysis. Percent of sales, with its income statement focus, does a good job at matching bad debts expense with sales. The accounts receivable methods, with their balance sheet focus, do a better job at reporting accounts receivable at realizable value.

 Decision Maker

Labor Union Chief   One week prior to labor contract negotiations, financial statements are released showing no income growth. A 10% growth was predicted. Your analysis finds that the company increased its allowance for uncollectibles from 1.5% to 4.5% of receivables. Without this change, income would show a 9% growth. Does this analysis impact negotiations? [Answer—p. 316]

Quick Check

Answers—p. 316

3. Why must bad debts expense be estimated if such an estimate is possible?

4. What term describes the balance sheet valuation of Accounts Receivable less the Allowance for Doubtful Accounts?

5. Why is estimated bad debts expense credited to a contra account (Allowance for Doubtful Accounts) rather than to the Accounts Receivable account?

6. SnoBoard Company's year-end balance in its Allowance for Doubtful Accounts is a credit of $440. By aging accounts receivable, it estimates that $6,142 is uncollectible. Prepare SnoBoard's year-end adjusting entry for bad debts.

7. Record entries for these transactions assuming the allowance method is used:

Jan.   10   The $300 account of customer Cool Jam is determined uncollectible.

April 12   Cool Jam unexpectedly pays in full the account deemed uncollectible on Jan. 10.

Notes Receivable

 C2   Describe a note receivable and the computation of its maturity date and interest.

A **promissory note** is a written promise to pay a specified amount of money, usually with interest, either on demand or at a definite future date. Promissory notes are used in many transactions, including paying for products and services, and lending and borrowing money. Sellers sometimes ask for a note to replace an account receivable when a customer requests additional time to pay a past-due account. For legal reasons, sellers generally prefer to receive notes when the credit period is long and when the receivable is for a large amount. If a lawsuit is needed to collect from a customer, a note is the buyer's written acknowledgment of the debt, its amount, and its terms.

Exhibit 7.14 shows a simple promissory note dated July 10, 2009. For this note, Julia Browne promises to pay TechCom or to its order (according to TechCom's instructions) a specified amount of money ($1,000), called the **principal of a note,** at a definite future date (October 8, 2009). As the one who signed the note and promised to pay it at maturity, Browne is the **maker of the note.** As the person to whom the note is payable, TechCom is the **payee of the note.** To Browne, the note is a liability called a *note payable.* To TechCom, the same note is an asset called a *note receivable.* This note bears interest at 12%, as written on the note. **Interest** is the charge for using the money until its due date. To a borrower, interest is an expense. To a lender, it is revenue.

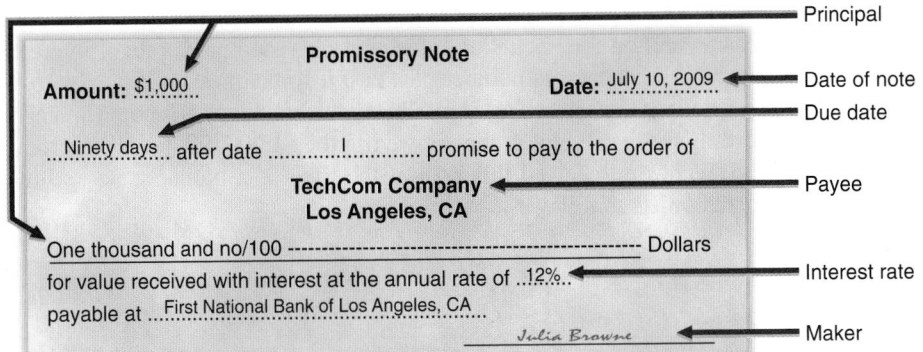

EXHIBIT 7.14

Promissory Note

Computing Maturity and Interest

This section describes key computations for notes including the determination of maturity date, period covered, and interest computation.

Video7.1

Maturity Date and Period   The **maturity date of a note** is the day the note (principal and interest) must be repaid. The *period* of a note is the time from the note's (contract) date to its maturity date. Many notes mature in less than a full year, and the period they cover is often expressed in days. When the time of a note is expressed in days, its maturity date is the specified number of days after the note's date. As an example, a five-day note dated June 15 matures and is due on June 20. A 90-day note dated July 10 matures on October 8. This October 8 due date is computed as shown in Exhibit 7.15. The period of a note is sometimes expressed in months or years. When months are used, the note matures and is payable in the month of its maturity on the *same day of the month* as its original date. A nine-month note dated July 10, for instance, is payable on April 10. The same analysis applies when years are used.

Days in July	31	
Minus the date of the note	10	
Days remaining in July	21	July 11–31
Add days in August	31	Aug. 1–31
Add days in September	30	Sept. 1–30
Days to equal 90 days, or **maturity date of October 8**	8	Oct. 1–8
Period of the note in days	90	

EXHIBIT 7.15

Maturity Date Computation

Interest Computation   *Interest* is the cost of borrowing money for the borrower or, alternatively, the profit from lending money for the lender. Unless otherwise stated, the rate of interest on a note is the rate charged for the use of the principal for one year. The formula for computing interest on a note is shown in Exhibit 7.16.

$$\frac{\text{Principal}}{\text{of the note}} \times \frac{\text{Annual}}{\text{interest rate}} \times \frac{\text{Time expressed}}{\text{in years}} = \text{Interest}$$

EXHIBIT 7.16

Computation of Interest Formula

To simplify interest computations, a year is commonly treated as having 360 days (called the *banker's rule* in the business world and widely used in commercial transactions). **We treat a year as having 360 days for interest computations in the examples and assignments.** Using the promissory note in Exhibit 7.14 where we have a 90-day, 12%, $1,000 note, the total interest is computed as follows.

$$\$1,000 \times 12\% \times \frac{90}{360} = \$1,000 \times 0.12 \times 0.25 = \$30$$

Recognizing Notes Receivable

P3   Record the receipt of a note receivable.

Notes receivable are usually recorded in a single Notes Receivable account to simplify record-keeping. The original notes are kept on file, including information on the maker, rate of interest, and due date. (When a company holds a large number of notes, it sometimes sets up a controlling account and a subsidiary ledger for notes. This is similar to the handling of accounts receivable.) To illustrate the recording for the receipt of a note, we use the $1,000, 90-day, 12% promissory note in Exhibit 7.14. TechCom received this note at the time of a product sale to Julia Browne. This transaction is recorded as follows.

Assets = Liabilities + Equity
+1,000   +1,000

July 10*	Notes Receivable..............................	1,000	
	Sales		1,000
	Sold goods in exchange for a 90-day, 12% note.		

* We omit the entry to Dr. Cost of Sales and Cr. Merchandise Inventory to focus on sales and receivables.

When a seller accepts a note from an overdue customer as a way to grant a time extension on a past-due account receivable, it will often collect part of the past-due balance in cash. This partial payment forces a concession from the customer, reduces the customer's debt (and the seller's risk), and produces a note for a smaller amount. To illustrate, assume that TechCom agreed to accept $232 in cash along with a $600, 60-day, 15% note from Jo Cook to settle her $832 past-due account. TechCom made the following entry to record receipt of this cash and note.

Point: Notes receivable often are a major part of a company's assets. Likewise, notes payable often are a large part of a company's liabilities.

Assets = Liabilities + Equity
+232
+600
−832

Oct. 5	Cash...	232	
	Notes Receivable..............................	600	
	Accounts Receivable—J. Cook		832
	Received cash and note to settle account.		

Valuing and Settling Notes

P4   Record the honoring and dishonoring of a note and adjustments for interest.

Recording an Honored Note The principal and interest of a note are due on its maturity date. The maker of the note usually *honors* the note and pays it in full. To illustrate, when J. Cook pays the note above on its due date, TechCom records it as follows.

Assets = Liabilities + Equity
+615   +15
−600

Dec. 4	Cash...	615	
	Notes Receivable		600
	Interest Revenue		15
	Collect note with interest of $600 × 15% × 60/360.		

Interest Revenue, also called *Interest Earned,* is reported on the income statement.

Recording a Dishonored Note When a note's maker is unable or refuses to pay at maturity, the note is *dishonored.* The act of dishonoring a note does not relieve the maker of the obligation to pay. The payee should use every legitimate means to collect. How do companies report this event? The balance of the Notes Receivable account should include only those notes that have not matured. Thus, when a note is dishonored, we remove the amount of this note from the Notes Receivable account and charge it back to an account receivable from its maker. To illustrate, TechCom holds an $800, 12%, 60-day note of Greg Hart. At maturity, Hart dishonors the note. TechCom records this dishonoring of the note as follows.

Point: When posting a dishonored note to a customer's account, an explanation is included so as not to misinterpret the debit as a sale on account.

Oct. 14	Accounts Receivable—G. Hart	816	
	Interest Revenue		16
	Notes Receivable		800
	To charge account of G. Hart for a dishonored note and interest of $800 × 12% × 60/360.		

Assets = Liabilities + Equity
+816   +16
−800

Charging a dishonored note back to the account of its maker serves two purposes. First, it removes the amount of the note from the Notes Receivable account and records the dishonored note in the maker's account. Second, and more important, if the maker of the dishonored note applies for credit in the future, his or her account will reveal all past dealings, including the dishonored note. Restoring the account also reminds the company to continue collection efforts from Hart for both principal and interest. The entry records the full amount, including interest, to ensure that it is included in collection efforts.

Point: Reporting the details of notes is consistent with the **full disclosure principle,** which requires financial statements (including footnotes) to report all relevant information.

Recording End-of-Period Interest Adjustment   When notes receivable are outstanding at the end of a period, any accrued interest earned is computed and recorded. To illustrate, on December 16, TechCom accepts a $3,000, 60-day, 12% note from a customer in granting an extension on a past-due account. When TechCom's accounting period ends on December 31, $15 of interest has accrued on this note ($3,000 × 12% × 15/360). The following adjusting entry records this revenue.

Dec. 31	Interest Receivable	15	
	Interest Revenue		15
	To record accrued interest earned.		

Assets = Liabilities + Equity
+15   +15

Interest Revenue appears on the income statement, and Interest Receivable appears on the balance sheet as a current asset. When the December 16 note is collected on February 14, TechCom's entry to record the cash receipt is

Feb. 14	Cash	3,060	
	Interest Revenue		45
	Interest Receivable		15
	Notes Receivable		3,000
	Received payment of note and its interest.		

Assets = Liabilities + Equity
+3,060   +45
−15
−3,000

Total interest earned on the 60-day note is $60. The $15 credit to Interest Receivable on February 14 reflects the collection of the interest accrued from the December 31 adjusting entry. The $45 interest earned reflects TechCom's revenue from holding the note from January 1 to February 14 of the current period.

Quick Check   Answers—p. 316

8. Irwin purchases $7,000 of merchandise from Stamford on December 16, 2009. Stamford accepts Irwin's $7,000, 90-day, 12% note as payment. Stamford's accounting period ends on December 31, and it does not make reversing entries. Prepare entries for Stamford on December 16, 2009, and December 31, 2009.

9. Using the information in Quick Check 8, prepare Stamford's March 16, 2010, entry if Irwin dishonors the note.

Disposing of Receivables

Companies can convert receivables to cash before they are due. Reasons for this include the need for cash or the desire not to be involved in collection activities. Converting receivables is usually done either by (1) selling them or (2) using them as security for a loan. A recent survey shows that about 20% of companies obtain cash from either selling receivables or pledging them as security. In some industries such as textiles, apparel and furniture, this is common practice.

Selling Receivables

C3 Explain how receivables can be converted to cash before maturity.

Global: Firms in export sales increasingly sell their receivables to factors.

A company can sell all or a portion of its receivables to a finance company or bank. The buyer, called a *factor,* charges the seller a *factoring fee* and then the buyer takes ownership of the receivables and receives cash when they come due. By incurring a factoring fee, the seller receives cash earlier and can pass the risk of bad debts to the factor. The seller can also choose to avoid costs of billing and accounting for the receivables. To illustrate, if TechCom sells $20,000 of its accounts receivable and is charged a 4% factoring fee, it records this sale as follows.

Assets = Liabilities + Equity
+19,200 −800
−20,000

Aug. 15	Cash	19,200	
	Factoring Fee Expense	800	
	Accounts Receivable		20,000
	Sold accounts receivable for cash, less 4% fee.		

The accounting for sales of notes receivable is similar to that for accounts receivable. The detailed entries are covered in advanced courses.

Pledging Receivables

A company can raise cash by borrowing money and *pledging* its receivables as security for the loan. Pledging receivables does not transfer the risk of bad debts to the lender because the borrower retains ownership of the receivables. If the borrower defaults on the loan, the lender has a right to be paid from the cash receipts of the receivable when collected. To illustrate, when TechCom borrows $35,000 and pledges its receivables as security, it records this transaction as follows.

Assets = Liabilities + Equity
+35,000 +35,000

Aug. 20	Cash	35,000	
	Notes Payable		35,000
	Borrowed money with a note secured by pledging receivables.		

Since pledged receivables are committed as security for a specific loan, the borrower's financial statements disclose the pledging of them. TechCom, for instance, includes the following note with its statements: Accounts receivable of $40,000 are pledged as security for a $35,000 note payable.

Decision Insight

What's the Proper Allowance? How can we assess whether a company has properly estimated its allowance for uncollectibles? One way is to compute the ratio of the allowance account to the gross accounts receivable. When this ratio is analyzed over several consecutive periods, trends often emerge that reflect on the adequacy of the allowance amount.

Global View

This section discusses similarities and differences between U.S. GAAP and IFRS regarding the recognition, measurement, and disposition of receivables.

Recognition of Receivables

Both U.S. GAAP and IFRS have similar asset criteria that apply to recognition of receivables. Further, receivables that arise from revenue-generating activities are subject to broadly similar criteria for U.S. GAAP and IFRS. Specifically, both refer to the realization principle and an earnings process. The realization principle under U.S. GAAP implies an *arm's-length transaction* occurs, whereas under IFRS this notion is applied in terms of reliable measurement and likelihood of economic benefits. Regarding U.S. GAAP's reference to an earnings process, IFRS instead refers to risk transfer and ownership reward. However, while these criteria are broadly similar, differences do exist, and they arise mainly from industry-specific guidance under U.S. GAAP, which is very limited under IFRS. For its recognition of receivables, **GOME** applies the following guidance:

> Revenue is recognised when it is probable that the economic benefits will flow to the Group and when the revenue can be measured reliably.

Valuation of Receivables

Both U.S. GAAP and IFRS require that receivables be reported net of estimated uncollectibles. Further, both systems require that the expense for estimated uncollectibles be recorded in the same period when any revenues from those receivables are recorded. This means that in the case of accounts receivable, both U.S. GAAP and IFRS require the allowance method for uncollectibles (unless uncollectibles are immaterial). The allowance method using percent of sales, percent of receivables, or aging was explained in this chapter. **GOME** prepares an aging of receivables analysis, which is reported in its annual report (per its Note 25). Interestingly, GOME estimates zero uncollectibles, which it justifies as follows:

> Receivables that were past due . . . [are from] customers which have long business relationships with the Group. The directors are of the opinion that no provision for impairment is necessary at this stage because there has not been a significant change in credit quality of the individual debtors and the balances are considered fully recoverable.

Disposition of Receivables

Both U.S. GAAP and IFRS apply broadly similar rules in recording dispositions of receivables. Those rules are discussed in this chapter. We should be aware of an important difference in terminology. Companies reporting under U.S. GAAP disclose Bad Debts Expense, which is also referred to as Provision for Bad Debts or the Provision for Uncollectible Accounts. For U.S. GAAP, *provision* here refers to expense. However, under IFRS, the term *provision* usually refers to a liability whose amount or timing (or both) is uncertain. **GOME** provides the following approach for its provision:

> In relation to trade and other receivables, a provision for impairment is made when there is objective evidence (such as the probability of insolvency or significant financial difficulties of the debtor and significant changes in the technological, market, economic or legal environment that have an adverse effect on the debtor) that the Group will not be able to collect all of the amounts due under the original terms of an invoice. The carrying amount of the receivables is reduced through the use of an allowance account. Impaired debts are derecognised when they are assessed as uncollectible.

Decision Analysis | Accounts Receivable Turnover

A1   Compute accounts receivable turnover and use it to help assess financial condition.

For a company selling on credit, we want to assess both the quality and liquidity of its accounts receivable. *Quality* of receivables refers to the likelihood of collection without loss. Experience shows that the longer receivables are outstanding beyond their due date, the lower the likelihood of collection. *Liquidity* of receivables refers to the speed of collection. **Accounts receivable turnover** is a measure of both the quality and liquidity of accounts receivable. It indicates how often, on average, receivables are received and collected during the period. The formula for this ratio is shown in Exhibit 7.17.

EXHIBIT 7.17

Accounts Receivable Turnover

Video7.1

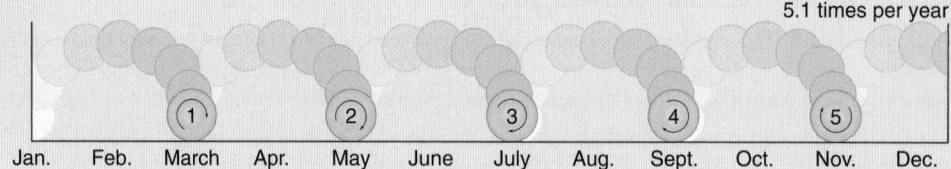

$$\text{Accounts receivable turnover} = \frac{\text{Net sales}}{\text{Average accounts receivable, net}}$$

We prefer to use net *credit* sales in the numerator because cash sales do not create receivables. However, since financial statements rarely report net credit sales, our analysis uses net sales. The denominator is the *average* accounts receivable balance, computed as (Beginning balance + Ending balance) ÷ 2. TechCom has an accounts receivable turnover of 5.1. This indicates its average accounts receivable balance is converted into cash 5.1 times during the period. Exhibit 7.18 shows graphically this turnover activity for TechCom.

EXHIBIT 7.18

Rate of Accounts Receivable Turnover for TechCom

5.1 times per year

① ② ③ ④ ⑤

Jan.   Feb.   March   Apr.   May   June   July   Aug.   Sept.   Oct.   Nov.   Dec.

Point: Credit risk ratio is computed by dividing the Allowance for Doubtful Accounts by Accounts Receivable. The higher this ratio, the higher is credit risk.

Accounts receivable turnover also reflects how well management is doing in granting credit to customers in a desire to increase sales. A high turnover in comparison with competitors suggests that management should consider using more liberal credit terms to increase sales. A low turnover suggests management should consider stricter credit terms and more aggressive collection efforts to avoid having its resources tied up in accounts receivable.

To illustrate, we take fiscal year data from two competitors: **Dell** and **Apple**. Exhibit 7.19 shows accounts receivable turnover for both companies.

EXHIBIT 7.19

Analysis Using Accounts Receivable Turnover

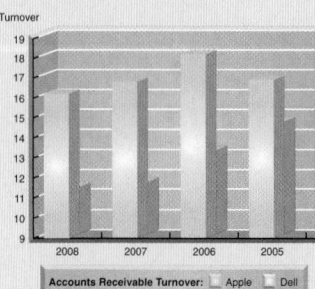

Company	Figure ($ millions)	2008	2007	2006	2005
Dell	Net sales	$61,101	$61,133	$57,420	$55,788
	Average accounts receivable, net	$ 5,346	$ 5,292	$ 4,352	$ 3,826
	Accounts receivable turnover	11.4	11.6	13.2	14.6
Apple	Net sales	$32,479	$24,006	$19,315	$13,931
	Average accounts receivable, net	$ 2,030	$ 1,445	$ 1,074	$ 835
	Accounts receivable turnover	16.0	16.6	18.0	16.7

Dell's 2008 turnover is 11.4, computed as $61,101/$5,346 ($ millions). This means that Dell's average accounts receivable balance was converted into cash 11.4 times in 2008. Its turnover declined in 2008, as it has for each of the past 3 years. Apple's turnover exceeds that for Dell in each of the past 4 years. Is either company's turnover too high? Since sales are stable or markedly growing over this time period, each company's turnover rate does not appear to be too high. Instead, both Dell and

Apple seem to be doing well in managing receivables. This is especially true given the recessionary period of 2008 and 2009. Turnover for competitors is generally in the range of 7 to 12 for this same period.[1]

Decision Maker

Family Physician Your medical practice is barely profitable, so you hire a health care analyst. The analyst highlights several points including the following: *"Accounts receivable turnover is too low. Tighter credit policies are recommended along with discontinuing service to those most delayed in payments."* How do you interpret these recommendations? What actions do you take? [Answer—p. 316]

Demonstration Problem

Clayco Company completes the following selected transactions during year 2009.

July 14 Writes off a $750 account receivable arising from a sale to Briggs Company that dates to 10 months ago. (Clayco Company uses the allowance method.)

    30 Clayco Company receives a $1,000, 90-day, 10% note in exchange for merchandise sold to Sumrell Company (the merchandise cost $600).

Aug. 15 Receives $2,000 cash plus a $10,000 note from JT Co. in exchange for merchandise that sells for $12,000 (its cost is $8,000). The note is dated August 15, bears 12% interest, and matures in 120 days.

Nov. 1 Completed a $200 credit card sale with a 4% fee (the cost of sales is $150). The cash is received immediately from the credit card company.

     3 Sumrell Company refuses to pay the note that was due to Clayco Company on October 28. Prepare the journal entry to charge the dishonored note plus accrued interest to Sumrell Company's accounts receivable.

     5 Completed a $500 credit card sale with a 5% fee (the cost of sales is $300). The payment from the credit card company is received on Nov. 9.

    15 Received the full amount of $750 from Briggs Company that was previously written off on July 14. Record the bad debts recovery.

Dec. 13 Received payment of principal plus interest from JT for the August 15 note.

Required

1. Prepare journal entries to record these transactions on Clayco Company's books.

2. Prepare an adjusting journal entry as of December 31, 2009, assuming the following:

   a. Bad debts are estimated to be $20,400 by aging accounts receivable. The unadjusted balance of the Allowance for Doubtful Accounts is $1,000 debit.

   b. Alternatively, assume that bad debts are estimated using the percent of sales method. The Allowance for Doubtful Accounts had a $1,000 debit balance before adjustment, and the company estimates bad debts to be 1% of its credit sales of $2,000,000.

Planning the Solution

- Examine each transaction to determine the accounts affected, and then record the entries.
- For the year-end adjustment, record the bad debts expense for the two approaches.

---

[1] As an estimate of *average days' sales uncollected*, we compute how many days (*on average*) it takes to collect receivables as follows: 365 days ÷ accounts receivable turnover. An increase in this *average collection period* can signal a decline in customers' financial condition.

Solution to Demonstration Problem

1.

July 14	Allowance for Doubtful Accounts	750	
	Accounts Receivable—Briggs Co.		750
	Wrote off an uncollectible account.		
July 30	Notes Receivable—Sumrell Co.	1,000	
	Sales		1,000
	Sold merchandise for a 90-day, 10% note.		
July 30	Cost of Goods Sold	600	
	Merchandise Inventory		600
	To record the cost of July 30 sale.		
Aug. 15	Cash	2,000	
	Notes Receivable—JT Co.	10,000	
	Sales		12,000
	Sold merchandise to customer for $2,000 cash and $10,000 note.		
Aug. 15	Cost of Goods Sold	8,000	
	Merchandise Inventory		8,000
	To record the cost of Aug. 15 sale.		
Nov. 1	Cash	192	
	Credit Card Expense	8	
	Sales		200
	To record credit card sale less a 4% credit card expense.		
Nov. 1	Cost of Goods Sold	150	
	Merchandise Inventory		150
	To record the cost of Nov. 1 sale.		
Nov. 3	Accounts Receivable—Sumrell Co.	1,025	
	Interest Revenue		25
	Notes Receivable—Sumrell Co...............		1,000
	To charge account of Sumrell Company for a $1,000 dishonored note and interest of $1,000 × 10% × 90/360.		
Nov. 5	Accounts Receivable—Credit Card Co.	475	
	Credit Card Expense..........................	25	
	Sales		500
	To record credit card sale less a 5% credit card expense.		
Nov. 5	Cost of Goods Sold	300	
	Merchandise Inventory		300
	To record the cost of Nov. 5 sale.		
Nov. 9	Cash.......................................	475	
	Accounts Receivable—Credit Card Co.		475
	To record cash receipt from Nov. 5 sale.		
Nov. 15	Accounts Receivable—Briggs Co.	750	
	Allowance for Doubtful Accounts		750
	To reinstate the account of Briggs Company previously written off.		
Nov. 15	Cash.......................................	750	
	Accounts Receivable—Briggs Co.		750
	Cash received in full payment of account.		
Dec. 13	Cash.......................................	10,400	
	Interest Revenue		400
	Note Receivable—JT Co.		10,000
	Collect note with interest of $10,000 × 12% × 120/360.		

2a. Aging of accounts receivable method.

Dec. 31	Bad Debts Expense.............................	21,400	
	Allowance for Doubtful Accounts.............		21,400
	To adjust allowance account from a $1,000 debit balance to a $20,400 credit balance.		

2b. Percent of sales method.*

Dec. 31	Bad Debts Expense.............................	20,000	
	Allowance for Doubtful Accounts.............		20,000
	To provide for bad debts as 1% × $2,000,000 in credit sales.		

---

* For the income statement approach, which requires estimating bad debts as a percent of sales or credit sales, the Allowance account balance is *not* considered when making the adjusting entry.

Summary

C1 **Describe accounts receivable and how they occur and are recorded.** Accounts receivable are amounts due from customers for credit sales. A subsidiary ledger lists amounts owed by each customer. Credit sales arise from at least two sources: (1) sales on credit and (2) credit card sales. *Sales on credit* refers to a company's granting credit directly to customers. Credit card sales involve customers' use of third-party credit cards.

C2 **Describe a note receivable and the computation of its maturity date and interest.** A note receivable is a written promise to pay a specified amount of money at a definite future date. The maturity date is the day the note (principal and interest) must be repaid. Interest rates are normally stated in annual terms. The amount of interest on the note is computed by expressing time as a fraction of one year and multiplying the note's principal by this fraction and the annual interest rate.

C3 **Explain how receivables can be converted to cash before maturity.** Receivables can be converted to cash before maturity in three ways. First, a company can sell accounts receivable to a factor, who charges a factoring fee. Second, a company can borrow money by signing a note payable that is secured by pledging the accounts receivable. Third, notes receivable can be discounted at (sold to) a financial institution.

A1 **Compute accounts receivable turnover and use it to help assess financial condition.** Accounts receivable turnover is a measure of both the quality and liquidity of accounts receivable. The accounts receivable turnover measure indicates how often, on average, receivables are received and collected during the period. Accounts receivable turnover is computed as net sales divided by average accounts receivable.

P1 **Apply the direct write-off and allowance methods to account for accounts receivable.** The direct write-off method charges Bad Debts Expense when accounts are written off as uncollectible. This method is acceptable only when the amount of bad debts expense is immaterial. Under the allowance method, bad debts expense is recorded with an adjustment at the end of each accounting period that debits the Bad Debts Expense account and credits the Allowance for Doubtful Accounts. The uncollectible accounts are later written off with a debit to the Allowance for Doubtful Accounts.

P2 **Estimate uncollectibles using methods based on sales and accounts receivable.** Uncollectibles are estimated by focusing on either (1) the income statement relation between bad debts expense and credit sales or (2) the balance sheet relation between accounts receivable and the allowance for doubtful accounts. The first approach emphasizes the matching principle using the income statement. The second approach emphasizes realizable value of accounts receivable using the balance sheet.

P3 **Record the receipt of a note receivable.** A note received is recorded at its principal amount by debiting the Notes Receivable account. The credit amount is to the asset, product, or service provided in return for the note.

P4 **Record the honoring and dishonoring of a note and adjustments for interest.** When a note is honored, the payee debits the money received and credits both Notes Receivable and Interest Revenue. Dishonored notes are credited to Notes Receivable and debited to Accounts Receivable (to the account of the maker in an attempt to collect), and Interest Revenue is recorded for interest earned for the time the note is held.

Guidance Answers to **Decision Maker** and **Decision Ethics**

Entrepreneur Analysis of credit card sales should weigh the benefits against the costs. The primary benefit is the potential to increase sales by attracting customers who prefer the convenience of credit cards. The primary cost is the fee charged by the credit card company for providing this service. Analysis should therefore estimate the expected increase in dollar sales from allowing credit card sales and then subtract (1) the normal costs and expenses and (2) the credit card fees associated with this expected increase in dollar sales. If your analysis shows an increase in profit from allowing credit card sales, your store should probably accept them.

Labor Union Chief Yes, this information is likely to impact your negotiations. The obvious question is why the company markedly increased this allowance. The large increase in this allowance means a substantial increase in bad debts expense *and* a decrease in earnings. This change (coming immediately prior to labor contract discussions) also raises concerns since it reduces the union's bargaining power for increased compensation. You want to ask management for supporting documentation justifying this increase. You also want data for two or three prior years and similar data from competitors. These data should give you some

sense of whether the change in the allowance for uncollectibles is justified.

Family Physician The recommendations are twofold. First, the analyst suggests more stringent screening of patients' credit standing. Second, the analyst suggests dropping patients who are most overdue in payments. You are likely bothered by both suggestions. They are probably financially wise recommendations, but you are troubled by eliminating services to those less able to pay. One alternative is to follow the recommendations while implementing a care program directed at patients less able to pay for services. This allows you to continue services to patients less able to pay and lets you discontinue services to patients able but unwilling to pay.

Guidance Answers to **Quick Checks**

1. If cash is immediately received when credit card sales receipts are deposited, the company debits Cash at the time of sale. If the company does not receive payment until after it submits receipts to the credit card company, it debits Accounts Receivable at the time of sale. (Cash is later debited when payment is received from the credit card company.)

2. Credit card expenses are usually *recorded* and *incurred* at the time of their related sales, not when cash is received from the credit card company.

3. If possible, bad debts expense must be matched with the sales that gave rise to the accounts receivable. This requires that companies estimate future bad debts at the end of each period before they learn which accounts are uncollectible.

4. Realizable value (also called *net realizable value*).

5. The estimated amount of bad debts expense cannot be credited to the Accounts Receivable account because the specific customer accounts that will prove uncollectible cannot yet be identified and removed from the accounts receivable subsidiary ledger. Moreover, if only the Accounts Receivable account is credited, its balance would not equal the sum of its subsidiary account balances.

6.

Dec. 31	Bad Debts Expense......................	5,702	
	Allowance for Doubtful Accounts......		5,702

7.

Jan. 10	Allowance for Doubtful Accounts..........	300	
	Accounts Receivable—Cool Jam.......		300
Apr. 12	Accounts Receivable—Cool Jam...........	300	
	Allowance for Doubtful Accounts......		300
Apr. 12	Cash	300	
	Accounts Receivable—Cool Jam.......		300

8.

Dec. 16	Note Receivable—Irwin.................	7,000	
	Sales...............................		7,000
Dec. 31	Interest Receivable......................	35	
	Interest Revenue.....................		35
	($7,000 × 12% × 15/360)		

9.

Mar. 16	Accounts Receivable—Irwin	7,210	
	Interest Revenue.....................		175
	Interest Receivable...................		35
	Notes Receivable—Irwin.............		7,000

Key Terms

Accounts receivable (p. 296)	**Direct write-off method** (p. 300)	**Payee of the note** (p. 307)
Accounts receivable turnover (p. 312)	**Interest** (p. 307)	**Principal of a note** (p. 307)
Aging of accounts receivable (p. 304)	**Maker of the note** (p. 307)	**Promissory note** (or **note**) (p. 306)
Allowance for doubtful accounts (p. 301)	**Matching principle** (p. 300)	**Realizable value** (p. 301)
Allowance method (p. 301)	**Materiality constraint** (p. 301)	
Bad debts (p. 300)	**Maturity date of a note** (p. 307)	

Multiple Choice Quiz   Answers on p. 329   mhhe.com/wildFA5e

Additional Quiz Questions are available at the book's Website.

1. A company's Accounts Receivable balance at its December 31 year-end is $125,650, and its Allowance for Doubtful Accounts has a credit balance of $328 before year-end adjustment. Its net sales are $572,300. It estimates that 4% of outstanding accounts receivable are uncollectible. What amount of Bad Debts Expense is recorded at December 31?
a. $5,354
b. $328
c. $5,026
d. $4,698
e. $34,338

2. A company's Accounts Receivable balance at its December 31 year-end is $489,300, and its Allowance for Doubtful Accounts has a debit balance of $554 before year-end adjustment. Its net sales are $1,300,000. It estimates that 6% of outstanding accounts receivable are uncollectible. What amount of Bad Debts Expense is recorded at December 31?
a. $29,912
b. $28,804
c. $78,000
d. $29,358
e. $554

3. Total interest to be earned on a $7,500, 5%, 90-day note is
a. $93.75
b. $375.00
c. $1,125.00
d. $31.25
e. $125.00

4. A company receives a $9,000, 8%, 60-day note. The maturity value of the note is
a. $120
b. $9,000
c. $9,120
d. $720
e. $9,720

5. A company has net sales of $489,600 and average accounts receivable of $40,800. What is its accounts receivable turnover?
a. 0.08
b. 30.41
c. 1,341.00
d. 12.00
e. 111.78

Discussion Questions

1. ♟ How do sellers benefit from allowing their customers to use credit cards?

2. ♟ Why does the direct write-off method of accounting for bad debts usually fail to match revenues and expenses?

3. Explain the accounting constraint of materiality.

4. Explain why writing off a bad debt against the Allowance for Doubtful Accounts does not reduce the estimated realizable value of a company's accounts receivable.

5. ♟ Why does the Bad Debts Expense account usually not have the same adjusted balance as the Allowance for Doubtful Accounts?

6. Why might a business prefer a note receivable to an account receivable?

7. ♟ Refer to the financial statements of **Best Buy** in Appendix A. In its presentation of accounts receivable,

Best Buy does not mention uncollectible accounts, nor does it list its receivables as "net." Why do you believe that Best Buy does not include information about uncollectible accounts?

8. ♟ Refer to the balance sheet of **RadioShack** in Appendix A. Does it use the direct write-off method or allowance method in accounting for its Accounts and Note Receivable? What is the realizable value of its receivable's balance as of December 31, 2008?

9. Refer to the financial statements of **Apple** in Appendix A. What are Apple's gross accounts receivable at September 27, 2008? What percentage of its accounts receivable does Apple believe to be uncollectible at this date?

♟ *Denotes Discussion Questions that involve decision making.*

---

connect Available with Connect Accounting

Prepare journal entries for the following credit card sales transactions (the company uses the perpetual inventory system).

1. Sold $16,000 of merchandise, that cost $7,000, on MasterCard credit cards. The net cash receipts from sales are immediately deposited in the seller's bank account. MasterCard charges a 4% fee.

2. Sold $18,000 of merchandise, that cost $7,800, on an assortment of credit cards. Net cash receipts are received 5 days later, and a 3% fee is charged.

QUICK STUDY

QS 7-1
Credit card sales
C1

QS 7-2
Allowance method for bad debts
P1

Kordas Corp. uses the allowance method to account for uncollectibles. On October 31, it wrote off a $750 account of a customer, D. Elwick. On December 9, it receives a $400 payment from Elwick.

1. Prepare the journal entry or entries for October 31.

2. Prepare the journal entry or entries for December 9; assume no additional money is expected from Elwick.

QS 7-3
Percent of accounts receivable method
P1

Darius Company's year-end unadjusted trial balance shows accounts receivable of $95,000, allowance for doubtful accounts of $550 (credit), and sales of $350,000. Uncollectibles are estimated to be 1.5% of accounts receivable.

1. Prepare the December 31 year-end adjusting entry for uncollectibles.

2. What amount would have been used in the year-end adjusting entry if the allowance account had a year-end unadjusted debit balance of $150?

QS 7-4
Percent of sales method   P2

Assume the same facts as in QS 7-3, except that Darius estimates uncollectibles as 0.5% of sales. Prepare the December 31 year-end adjusting entry for uncollectibles.

QS 7-5
Note receivable
P3   P4

On August 2, 2011, Passat Co. receives a $9,000, 90-day, 6% note from customer Dee Kissick as payment on her $9,000 account. Prepare Passat's journal entries for August 2 and for the note's maturity date assuming the note is honored by Kissick.

QS 7-6
Note receivable
C2   P4

Marlin Company's December 31 year-end unadjusted trial balance shows a $24,000 balance in Notes Receivable. This balance is from one 6% note dated December 1, with a period of 45 days. Prepare any necessary journal entries for December 31 and for the note's maturity date assuming it is honored.

QS 7-7
Accounts receivable turnover
A1

The following data are taken from the comparative balance sheets of Despina Company. Compute and interpret its accounts receivable turnover for year 2011 (competitors average a turnover of 7.5).

	2011	2010
Accounts receivable, net	$138,500	$153,400
Net sales	910,600	854,200

QS 7-8
International accounting standards

C1

Answer each of the following related to international accounting standards.

a. Explain (in general terms) how the accounting for recognition of receivables is different between IFRS and U.S. GAAP.

b. Explain (in general terms) how the accounting for valuation of receivables is different between IFRS and U.S. GAAP.

Available with Connect Accounting **connect**

EXERCISES

Exercise 7-1
Accounting for credit card sales
C1

Hue Company uses the perpetual inventory system and allows customers to use two credit cards in charging purchases. With the Omni Bank Card, Hue receives an immediate credit to its account when it deposits sales receipts. Omni assesses a 4% service charge for credit card sales. The second credit card that Hue accepts is the Continental Card. Hue sends its accumulated receipts to Continental on a weekly basis and is paid by Continental about a week later. Continental assesses a 2.5% charge on sales for using its card. Prepare journal entries to record the following selected credit card transactions of Hue Company.

Apr. 8 Sold merchandise for $5,600 (that had cost $4,138) and accepted the customer's Omni Bank Card. The Omni receipts are immediately deposited in Hue's bank account.

12 Sold merchandise for $6,000 (that had cost $4,400) and accepted the customer's Continental Card. Transferred $6,000 of credit card receipts to Continental, requesting payment.

20 Received Continental's check for the April 12 billing, less the service charge.

Beachum Company recorded the following selected transactions during November 2011.

Nov. 5	Accounts Receivable—Ski Shop....................	5,817	
	Sales		5,817
10	Accounts Receivable—Welcome Enterprises	1,774	
	Sales		1,774
13	Accounts Receivable—Kit Ronin...................	1,040	
	Sales		1,040
21	Sales Returns and Allowances	268	
	Accounts Receivable—Kit Ronin..............		268
30	Accounts Receivable—Ski Shop..................	3,698	
	Sales		3,698

Exercise 7-2
Accounts receivable subsidiary ledger; schedule of accounts receivable

C1

1. Open a general ledger having T-accounts for Accounts Receivable, Sales, and Sales Returns and Allowances. Also open an accounts receivable subsidiary ledger having a T-account for each customer. Post these entries to both the general ledger and the accounts receivable ledger.
2. Prepare a schedule of accounts receivable (see Exhibit 7.4) and compare its total with the balance of the Accounts Receivable controlling account as of November 30.

Check Accounts Receivable ending balance, $12,061

At year-end (December 31), Terner Company estimates its bad debts as 0.6% of its annual credit sales of $858,000. Terner records its Bad Debts Expense for that estimate. On the following February 1, Terner decides that the $429 account of D. Fidel is uncollectible and writes it off as a bad debt. On June 5, Fidel unexpectedly pays the amount previously written off. Prepare the journal entries of Terner to record these transactions and events of December 31, February 1, and June 5.

Exercise 7-3
Percent of sales method; write-off

P1 P2

At each calendar year-end, Rivka Supply Co. uses the percent of accounts receivable method to estimate bad debts. On December 31, 2011, it has outstanding accounts receivable of $139,500, and it estimates that 2% will be uncollectible. Prepare the adjusting entry to record bad debts expense for year 2011 under the assumption that the Allowance for Doubtful Accounts has (*a*) a $2,371 credit balance before the adjustment and (*b*) a $487 debit balance before the adjustment.

Exercise 7-4
Percent of accounts receivable method

P1 P2

Paloma Company estimates uncollectible accounts using the allowance method at December 31. It prepared the following aging of receivables analysis.

Exercise 7-5
Aging of receivables method

P1 P2

		Days Past Due				
	Total	0	1 to 30	31 to 60	61 to 90	Over 90
Accounts receivable	$95,000	$66,000	$15,000	$6,000	$3,000	$5,000
Percent uncollectible		1%	2%	4%	7%	12%

a. Estimate the balance of the Allowance for Doubtful Accounts using the aging of accounts receivable method.
b. Prepare the adjusting entry to record Bad Debts Expense using the estimate from part *a*. Assume the unadjusted balance in the Allowance for Doubtful Accounts is a $300 debit.
c. Prepare the adjusting entry to record Bad Debts Expense using the estimate from part *a*. Assume the unadjusted balance in the Allowance for Doubtful Accounts is a $200 credit.

Refer to the information in Exercise 7-5 to complete the following requirements.
a. Estimate the balance of the Allowance for Doubtful Accounts assuming the company uses 2% of total accounts receivable to estimate uncollectibles, instead of the aging of receivables method.
b. Prepare the adjusting entry to record Bad Debts Expense using the estimate from part *a*. Assume the unadjusted balance in the Allowance for Doubtful Accounts is a $300 debit.
c. Prepare the adjusting entry to record Bad Debts Expense using the estimate from part *a*. Assume the unadjusted balance in the Allowance for Doubtful Accounts is a $200 credit.

Exercise 7-6
Percent of receivables method

P1 P2

Exercise 7-7

Writing off receivables

P1 P2

Refer to the information in Exercise 7-5 to complete the following requirements.

a. On February 1 of the next period, the company determined that $950 in customer accounts is uncollectible; specifically, $200 for Laguna Co. and $750 for Malibu Co. Prepare the journal entry to write off those accounts.

b. On June 5 of that next period, the company unexpectedly received a $200 payment on a customer account, Laguna Company, that had previously been written off in part *a*. Prepare the entries necessary to reinstate the account and to record the cash received.

Exercise 7-8

Estimating bad debts

P1 P2

At December 31, Bowie Company reports the following results for its calendar-year.

Cash sales	$400,000
Credit sales	300,000

Its year-end unadjusted trial balance includes the following items.

Accounts receivable	$65,000 debit
Allowance for doubtful accounts	1,000 debit

Check Dr. Bad Debts Expense:
(*a*) $6,000

(*c*) $6,200

a. Prepare the adjusting entry to record Bad Debts Expense assuming uncollectibles are estimated to be 2% of credit sales.

b. Prepare the adjusting entry to record Bad Debts Expense assuming uncollectibles are estimated to be 1% of total sales.

c. Prepare the adjusting entry to record Bad Debts Expense assuming uncollectibles are estimated to be 8% of year-end accounts receivable.

Exercise 7-9

Selling and pledging accounts receivable

C3

On June 30, Twain Co. has $145,600 of accounts receivable. Prepare journal entries to record the following selected July transactions. Also prepare any footnotes to the July 31 financial statements that result from these transactions. (The company uses the perpetual inventory system.)

July	4	Sold $7,160 of merchandise (that had cost $4,582) to customers on credit.
	9	Sold $20,300 of accounts receivable to Main Bank. Main charges a 5% factoring fee.
	17	Received $3,938 cash from customers in payment on their accounts.
	27	Borrowed $11,000 cash from Main Bank, pledging $14,700 of accounts receivable as security for the loan.

Exercise 7-10

Honoring a note

P4

Prepare journal entries to record these selected transactions for Alvarez Company.

Nov.	1	Accepted a $15,000, 180-day, 7% note dated November 1 from Carlos Cruz in granting a time extension on his past-due account receivable.
Dec.	31	Adjusted the year-end accounts for the accrued interest earned on the Cruz note.
Apr.	30	Cruz honors his note when presented for payment; February has 28 days for the current year.

Exercise 7-11

Dishonoring a note

P4

Prepare journal entries to record the following selected transactions of Calio Company.

Mar.	21	Accepted a $17,200, 180-day, 7% note dated March 21 from James Penn in granting a time extension on his past-due account receivable.
Sept.	17	Penn dishonors his note when it is presented for payment.
Dec.	31	After exhausting all legal means of collection, Calio Company writes off Penn's account against the Allowance for Doubtful Accounts.

Exercise 7-12

Notes receivable transactions and entries

C2 P3 P4

Check Dec. 31, Cr. Interest Revenue $63

Feb. 11, Dr. Cash $14,210

Prepare journal entries for the following selected transactions of Hirona Company.

2010

Dec.	13	Accepted a $14,000, 60-day, 9% note dated December 13 in granting Allie Sumera a time extension on her past-due account receivable.
	31	Prepared an adjusting entry to record the accrued interest on the Sumera note.

2011

Feb.	11	Received Sumera's payment for principal and interest on the note dated December 13.
Mar.	3	Accepted a $10,000, 9%, 90-day note dated March 3 in granting a time extension on the past-due account receivable of Kudak Company.

17   Accepted a $9,000, 30-day, 8% note dated March 17 in granting Rod Burgess a time exten-
     sion on his past-due account receivable.
Apr. 16   Burgess dishonors his note when presented for payment.
May 1   Wrote off the Burgess account against the Allowance for Doubtful Accounts.
June 1   Received the Kudak payment for principal and interest on the note dated March 3.

June 1, Dr. Cash $10,225

The following information is from the annual financial statements of Lucilla Company. Compute its accounts receivable turnover for 2010 and 2011. Compare the two years' results and give a possible explanation for any change (competitors average a turnover of 7).

Exercise 7-13
Accounts receivable turnover

A1

	2011	2010	2009
Net sales	$262,000	$193,000	$245,000
Accounts receivable, net (year-end)	42,700	40,500	37,200

Hitachi, Ltd., reports total revenues of ¥10,000,369 million (in yen) for its fiscal year ending March 31,
2009, and its March 31, 2009, unadjusted trial balance reports a debit balance for trade receivables (gross)
of ¥2,179,764 million.

a. Prepare the adjusting entry to record its Bad Debts Expense assuming uncollectibles are estimated to
be 0.4% of total revenues and its unadjusted trial balance reports a credit balance of ¥10,000 million.

b. Prepare the adjusting entry to record Bad Debts Expense assuming uncollectibles are estimated to be
2.1% of year-end accounts receivable (gross) and its unadjusted trial balance reports a credit balance
of ¥10,000 million.

Exercise 7-14
Accounting for bad debts
following IFRS

P2

---

connect Available with Connect Accounting

Bantay Co. allows select customers to make purchases on credit. Its other customers can use either of two
credit cards: Zisa or Access. Zisa deducts a 3.5% service charge for sales on its credit card and credits
the bank account of Bantay immediately when credit card receipts are deposited. Bantay deposits the Zisa
credit card receipts each business day. When customers use Access credit cards, Bantay accumulates the
receipts for several days before submitting them to Access for payment. Access deducts a 2.5% service
charge and usually pays within one week of being billed. Bantay completes the following transactions in
June. (The terms of all credit sales are 2/15, n/30, and all sales are recorded at the gross price.)

June 4   Sold $700 of merchandise (that had cost $220) on credit to Alfredia Bullaro.
     5   Sold $8,400 of merchandise (that had cost $4,300) to customers who used their Zisa cards.
     6   Sold $6,000 of merchandise (that had cost $3,680) to customers who used their Access cards.
     8   Sold $4,480 of merchandise (that had cost $2,600) to customers who used their Access cards.
     10   Submitted Access card receipts accumulated since June 6 to the credit card company for payment.
     13   Wrote off the account of Trenton Wanek against the Allowance for Doubtful Accounts. The
           $467 balance in Wanek's account stemmed from a credit sale in October of last year.
     17   Received the amount due from Access.
     18   Received Bullaro's check in full payment for the purchase of June 4.

PROBLEM SET A

Problem 7-1A
Sales on account and
credit card sales

C1

Check June 17, Dr. Cash $10,218

Required

Prepare journal entries to record the preceding transactions and events. (The company uses the perpetual inventory system. Round amounts to the nearest dollar.)

Ming Company began operations on January 1, 2010. During its first two years, the company completed
a number of transactions involving sales on credit, accounts receivable collections, and bad debts. These
transactions are summarized as follows.

2010

a. Sold $1,347,700 of merchandise (that had cost $982,500) on credit, terms n/30.

b. Wrote off $20,676 of uncollectible accounts receivable.

c. Received $671,100 cash in payment of accounts receivable.

d. In adjusting the accounts on December 31, the company estimated that 1.3% of accounts receivable
will be uncollectible.

Problem 7-2A
Accounts receivable transactions
and bad debts adjustments

C1 P1 P2

Check (d) Dr. Bad Debts Expense
$29,203

2011

e. Sold $1,517,800 of merchandise (that had cost $1,302,200) on credit, terms n/30.

f. Wrote off $32,624 of uncollectible accounts receivable.

g. Received $1,118,100 cash in payment of accounts receivable.

(h) Dr. Bad Debts Expense
$37,396

h. In adjusting the accounts on December 31, the company estimated that 1.3% of accounts receivable will be uncollectible.

Required

Prepare journal entries to record Ming's 2010 and 2011 summarized transactions and its year-end adjustments to record bad debts expense. (The company uses the perpetual inventory system. Round amounts to the nearest dollar.)

Problem 7-3A
Estimating and reporting bad debts

P1   P2

At December 31, 2011, Vizarro Company reports the following results for its calendar-year.

Cash sales	$2,184,700
Credit sales	3,720,000

In addition, its unadjusted trial balance includes the following items.

Accounts receivable	$1,127,500 debit
Allowance for doubtful accounts	29,030 debit

Required

1. Prepare the adjusting entry for Vizarro Co. to recognize bad debts under each of the following independent assumptions.

   a. Bad debts are estimated to be 1.5% of credit sales.

Check Bad Debts Expense:
(1*a*) $55,800, (1*c*) $62,855

   b. Bad debts are estimated to be 1% of total sales.

   c. An aging analysis estimates that 3% of year-end accounts receivable are uncollectible.

2. Show how Accounts Receivable and the Allowance for Doubtful Accounts appear on its December 31, 2011, balance sheet given the facts in part 1*a*.

3. Show how Accounts Receivable and the Allowance for Doubtful Accounts appear on its December 31, 2011, balance sheet given the facts in part 1*c*.

Problem 7-4A
Aging accounts receivable and accounting for bad debts

P1   P2

Ghosh Company has credit sales of $2.8 million for year 2011. On December 31, 2011, the company's Allowance for Doubtful Accounts has an unadjusted credit balance of $22,800. Ghosh prepares a schedule of its December 31, 2011, accounts receivable by age. On the basis of past experience, it estimates the percent of receivables in each age category that will become uncollectible. This information is summarized here.

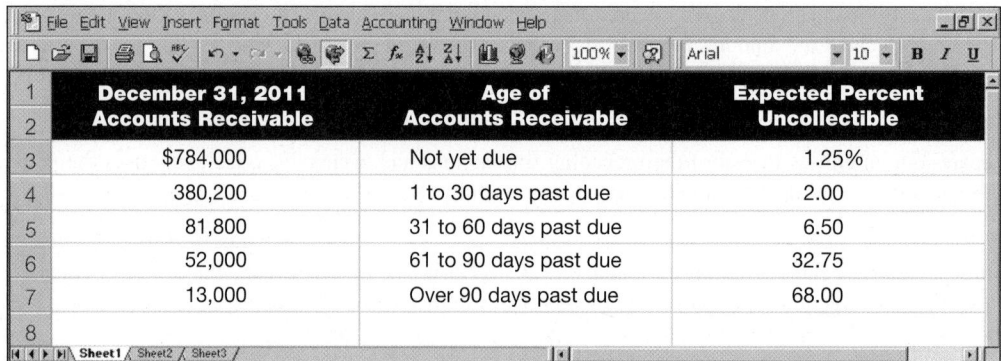

December 31, 2011 Accounts Receivable	Age of Accounts Receivable	Expected Percent Uncollectible
$784,000	Not yet due	1.25%
380,200	1 to 30 days past due	2.00
81,800	31 to 60 days past due	6.50
52,000	61 to 90 days past due	32.75
13,000	Over 90 days past due	68.00

Required

1. Estimate the required balance of the Allowance for Doubtful Accounts at December 31, 2011, using the aging of accounts receivable method.

Check (2) Dr. Bad Debts Expense
$25,791

2. Prepare the adjusting entry to record bad debts expense at December 31, 2011.

Analysis Component

3. On June 30, 2012, Ghosh Company concludes that a customer's $4,750 receivable (created in 2011) is uncollectible and that the account should be written off. What effect will this action have on Ghosh's 2012 net income? Explain.

The following selected transactions are from Chantay Company.

2010

Dec. 16   Accepted a $14,400, 60-day, 8% note dated this day in granting Adam Bakko a time extension on his past-due account receivable.

31   Made an adjusting entry to record the accrued interest on the Bakko note.

2011

Feb. 14   Received Bakko's payment of principal and interest on the note dated December 16.

Mar. 2   Accepted an $8,000, 9%, 90-day note dated this day in granting a time extension on the past-due account receivable from Mayday Co.

17   Accepted a $2,200, 30-day, 6% note dated this day in granting Carrie Kadin a time extension on her past-due account receivable.

Apr. 16   Kadin dishonored her note when presented for payment.

June 2   Mayday Co. refuses to pay the note that was due to Chantay Co. on May 31. Prepare the journal entry to charge the dishonored note plus accrued interest to Mayday Co.'s accounts receivable.

July 17   Received payment from Mayday Co. for the maturity value of its dishonored note plus interest for 46 days beyond maturity at 9%.

Aug. 7   Accepted an $8,400, 90-day, 12% note dated this day in granting a time extension on the past-due account receivable of Trenton Co.

Sept. 3   Accepted a $3,335, 60-day, 9% note dated this day in granting Collin Marin a time extension on his past-due account receivable.

Nov. 2   Received payment of principal plus interest from Marin for the September 3 note.

Nov. 5   Received payment of principal plus interest from Trenton for the August 7 note.

Dec. 1   Wrote off the Carrie Kadin account against Allowance for Doubtful Accounts.

Required

1. Prepare journal entries to record these transactions and events. (Round amounts to the nearest dollar.)

Analysis Component

2. What reporting is necessary when a business pledges receivables as security for a loan and the loan is still outstanding at the end of the period? Explain the reason for this requirement and the accounting principle being satisfied.

Problem 7-5A
Analyzing and journalizing notes receivable transactions

C2 C3 P3 P4

Check Feb. 14, Cr. Interest Revenue $144

June 2, Cr. Interest Revenue $180

Nov. 2, Cr. Interest Revenue $50

Marbus Co. allows select customers to make purchases on credit. Its other customers can use either of two credit cards: Commerce Bank or Aztec. Commerce Bank deducts a 2% service charge for sales on its credit card and immediately credits the bank account of Marbus when credit card receipts are deposited. Marbus deposits the Commerce Bank credit card receipts each business day. When customers use the Aztec card, Marbus accumulates the receipts for several days and then submits them to Aztec for payment. Aztec deducts a 1% service charge and usually pays within one week of being billed. Marbus completed the following transactions in August (terms of all credit sales are 2/15, n/30; and all sales are recorded at the gross price).

Aug. 4   Sold $600 of merchandise (that had cost $470) on credit to Kirby Carpen.

10   Sold $6,100 of merchandise (that had cost $5,100) to customers who used their Commerce Bank credit cards.

11   Sold $7,200 of merchandise (that had cost $6,150) to customers who used their Aztec cards.

14   Received Carpen's check in full payment for the purchase of August 4.

15   Sold $4,900 of merchandise (that had cost $3,500) to customers who used their Aztec cards.

18   Submitted Aztec card receipts accumulated since August 11 to the credit card company for payment.

PROBLEM SET B

Problem 7-1B
Sales on account and credit card sales

C1

22   Wrote off the account of Rayvac Co. against the Allowance for Doubtful Accounts. The $568 balance in Rayvac's account stemmed from a credit sale in November of last year.

Check   Aug. 25, Dr. Cash $11,979

25   Received the amount due from Aztec.

Required

Prepare journal entries to record the preceding transactions and events. (The company uses the perpetual inventory system. Round amounts to the nearest dollar.)

Problem 7-2B
Accounts receivable transactions and bad debts adjustments

C1   P1   P2

Freeman Co. began operations on January 1, 2010, and completed several transactions during 2010 and 2011 that involved sales on credit, accounts receivable collections, and bad debts. These transactions are summarized as follows.

2010

a. Sold $1,346,800 of merchandise (that had cost $980,300) on credit, terms n/30.

b. Received $666,300 cash in payment of accounts receivable.

c. Wrote off $21,000 of uncollectible accounts receivable.

Check   (d) Dr. Bad Debts Expense $28,914

d. In adjusting the accounts on December 31, the company estimated that 1.2% of accounts receivable will be uncollectible.

2011

e. Sold $1,562,400 of merchandise (that had cost $1,339,300) on credit, terms n/30.

f. Received $1,168,400 cash in payment of accounts receivable.

g. Wrote off $30,400 of uncollectible accounts receivable.

(h) Dr. Bad Debts Expense $34,763

h. In adjusting the accounts on December 31, the company estimated that 1.2% of accounts receivable will be uncollectible.

Required

Prepare journal entries to record Freeman's 2010 and 2011 summarized transactions and its year-end adjusting entry to record bad debts expense. (The company uses the perpetual inventory system. Round amounts to the nearest dollar.)

Problem 7-3B
Estimating and reporting bad debts

P1   P2

At December 31, 2011, Tobie Company reports the following results for the year.

Cash sales	$1,600,000
Credit sales	2,926,000

In addition, its unadjusted trial balance includes the following items.

Accounts receivable	$886,000 debit
Allowance for doubtful accounts	2,300 credit

Required

1. Prepare the adjusting entry for Tobie Co. to recognize bad debts under each of the following independent assumptions.

   a. Bad debts are estimated to be 1.2% of credit sales.

Check   Bad debts expense:
(1b) $31,682, (1c) $42,000

   b. Bad debts are estimated to be 0.7% of total sales.

   c. An aging analysis estimates that 5% of year-end accounts receivable are uncollectible.

2. Show how Accounts Receivable and the Allowance for Doubtful Accounts appear on its December 31, 2011, balance sheet given the facts in part 1a.

3. Show how Accounts Receivable and the Allowance for Doubtful Accounts appear on its December 31, 2011, balance sheet given the facts in part 1c.

Margrett Company has credit sales of $2.2 million for year 2011. At December 31, 2011, the company's Allowance for Doubtful Accounts has an unadjusted debit balance of $2,800. Margrett prepares a schedule of its December 31, 2011, accounts receivable by age. On the basis of past experience, it estimates the percent of receivables in each age category that will become uncollectible. This information is summarized here.

Problem 7-4B

Aging accounts receivable and accounting for bad debts

P1   P2

December 31, 2011 Accounts Receivable	Age of Accounts Receivable	Expected Percent Uncollectible
$616,000	Not yet due	0.90%
298,000	1 to 30 days past due	1.65
64,000	31 to 60 days past due	6.15
41,000	61 to 90 days past due	31.00
9,200	Over 90 days past due	64.00

Required

1. Compute the required balance of the Allowance for Doubtful Accounts at December 31, 2011, using the aging of accounts receivable method.

2. Prepare the adjusting entry to record bad debts expense at December 31, 2011.

Check (2) Dr. Bad Debts Expense $35,795

Analysis Component

3. On July 31, 2012, Margrett concludes that a customer's $3,455 receivable (created in 2011) is uncollectible and that the account should be written off. What effect will this action have on Margrett's 2012 net income? Explain.

The following selected transactions are from Castella Company.

Problem 7-5B

Analyzing and journalizing notes receivable transactions

C2   C3   P3   P4

2010

Nov. 1   Accepted a $13,560, 90-day, 10% note dated this day in granting Eric Merklin a time extension on his past-due account receivable.

Dec. 31 Made an adjusting entry to record the accrued interest on the Merklin note.

2011

Jan. 30 Received Merklin's payment for principal and interest on the note dated November 1.

Mar. 1   Accepted a $6,000, 8%, 30-day note dated this day in granting a time extension on the past-due account receivable from Zada Co.

Mar. 2   Accepted a $4,080, 60-day, 5% note dated this day in granting Shane Patru a time extension on his past-due account receivable.

   31 The Zada Co. dishonored its note when presented for payment.

May 1   Received payment of principal plus interest from S. Patru for the March 2 note.

June 15 Accepted a $9,000, 60-day, 11% note dated this day in granting a time extension on the past-due account receivable of Mary Braff.

   21 Accepted a $3,160, 90-day, 10% note dated this day in granting Harris Guam a time extension on his past-due account receivable.

Aug. 14 Received payment of principal plus interest from M. Braff for the note of June 15.

Sept. 19 Received payment of principal plus interest from H. Guam for the June 21 note.

Nov. 30 Wrote off Zada Co.'s account against Allowance for Doubtful Accounts.

Check Jan. 30, Cr. Interest Revenue $113

May 1, Cr. Interest Revenue $34

Sept. 19, Cr. Interest Revenue $79

Required

1. Prepare journal entries to record these transactions and events. (Round amounts to the nearest dollar.)

Analysis Component

2. What reporting is necessary when a business pledges receivables as security for a loan and the loan is still outstanding at the end of the period? Explain the reason for this requirement and the accounting principle being satisfied.

SERIAL PROBLEM

Success Systems

(This serial problem began in Chapter 1 and continues through most of the book. If previous chapter segments were not completed, the serial problem can begin at this point. It is helpful, but not necessary, to use the Working Papers that accompany the book.)

SP 7   Adriana Lopez, owner of Success Systems, realizes that she needs to begin accounting for bad debts expense. Assume that Success Systems has total revenues of $43,853 during the first three months of 2010, and that the Accounts Receivable balance on March 31, 2010, is $22,720.

Required

1. Prepare the adjusting entry needed for Success Systems to recognize bad debts expense on March 31, 2010, under each of the following independent assumptions (assume a zero unadjusted balance in the Allowance for Doubtful Accounts at March 31).

    a. Bad debts are estimated to be 1% of total revenues. (Round amounts to the nearest dollar.)

    b. Bad debts are estimated to be 2% of accounts receivable. (Round amounts to the nearest dollar.)

Check   (2) Bad Debts Expense, $51

2. Assume that Success Systems' Accounts Receivable balance at June 30, 2010, is $20,250 and that one account of $100 has been written off against the Allowance for Doubtful Accounts since March 31, 2010. If Lopez uses the method prescribed in Part 1*b*, what adjusting journal entry must be made to recognize bad debts expense on June 30, 2010?

3. Should Lopez consider adopting the direct write-off method of accounting for bad debts expense rather than one of the allowance methods considered in part 1? Explain.

BEYOND THE NUMBERS

REPORTING IN ACTION

A1

BTN 7-1   Refer to **Best Buy**'s financial statements in Appendix A to answer the following.

1. What is the amount of Best Buy's accounts receivable as of February 28, 2009?
2. Compute Best Buy's accounts receivable turnover as of February 28, 2009.
3. How long does it take, *on average,* for Best Buy to collect receivables? Why is this period so short? Do you believe that customers actually pay the amounts due within this short period? Explain.
4. Best Buy's most liquid assets include (*a*) cash and cash equivalents, (*b*) short-term investments, and (*c*) receivables. Compute the percentage that these liquid assets make up of current liabilities as of February 28, 2009. Do the same computations for March 1, 2008. Comment on the company's ability to satisfy its current liabilities as of its 2009 fiscal year-end compared to its 2008 fiscal year-end.
5. What criteria did Best Buy use to classify items as cash equivalents?

Fast Forward

6. Access Best Buy's financial statements for fiscal years after February 28, 2009, at its Website (**www.BestBuy.com**) or the SEC's EDGAR database (**www.sec.gov**). Recompute parts 2 and 4 and comment on any changes since February 28, 2009.

COMPARATIVE ANALYSIS

A1   P2

BTN 7-2   Comparative figures for **Best Buy** and **RadioShack** follow.

($ millions)	Best Buy			RadioShack		
	Current Year	One Year Prior	Two Years Prior	Current Year	One Year Prior	Two Years Prior
Accounts receivable, net	$ 1,868	$ 549	$ 548	$ 241.9	$ 256.0	$ 247.9
Net sales	45,015	40,023	35,934	4,224.5	4,251.7	4,777.5

Required

1. Compute the accounts receivable turnover for Best Buy and RadioShack for each of the two most recent years using the data shown.

2. Using results from part 1, compute how many days it takes each company, *on average,* to collect receivables. Why are these periods so short? Do you believe that receivables are actually collected this quickly? Explain.

3. Which company is more efficient in collecting its accounts receivable? Explain.

Hint: Average collection period equals 365 divided by the accounts receivable turnover.

BTN 7-3   Astin Blair is the manager of a medium-size company. A few years ago, Blair persuaded the owner to base a part of his compensation on the net income the company earns each year. Each December he estimates year-end financial figures in anticipation of the bonus he will receive. If the bonus is not as high as he would like, he offers several recommendations to the accountant for year-end adjustments. One of his favorite recommendations is for the controller to reduce the estimate of doubtful accounts.

ETHICS CHALLENGE

P1   P2   ♟

Required

1. What effect does lowering the estimate for doubtful accounts have on the income statement and balance sheet?

2. Do you believe Blair's recommendation to adjust the allowance for doubtful accounts is within his right as manager, or do you believe this action is an ethics violation? Justify your response.

3. What type of internal control(s) might be useful for this company in overseeing the manager's recommendations for accounting changes?

BTN 7-4   As the accountant for Pure-Air Distributing, you attend a sales managers' meeting devoted to a discussion of credit policies. At the meeting, you report that bad debts expense is estimated to be $59,000 and accounts receivable at year-end amount to $1,750,000 less a $43,000 allowance for doubtful accounts. Sid Omar, a sales manager, expresses confusion over why bad debts expense and the allowance for doubtful accounts are different amounts. Write a one-page memorandum to him explaining why a difference in bad debts expense and the allowance for doubtful accounts is not unusual. The company estimates bad debts expense as 2% of sales.

COMMUNICATING IN PRACTICE

P1   P2   ♟

BTN 7-5   Access eBay's, February 20, 2009, filing of its 10-K report for the year ended December 31, 2008, at www.sec.gov.

TAKING IT TO THE NET

C1

Required

1. What is the amount of eBay's net accounts receivable at December 31, 2008, and at December 31, 2007?

2. "Financial Statement Schedule II" to its financial statements lists eBay's allowance for doubtful accounts (including authorized credits). For the two years ended December 31, 2008 and 2007, compute its allowance for doubtful accounts (including authorized credits) as a percent of gross accounts receivable.

3. Do you believe that these percentages are reasonable based on what you know about eBay? Explain.

BTN 7-6   Each member of a team is to participate in estimating uncollectibles using the aging schedule and percents shown in Problem 7-4A. The division of labor is up to the team. Your goal is to accurately complete this task as soon as possible. After estimating uncollectibles, check your estimate with the instructor. If the estimate is correct, the team then should prepare the adjusting entry and the presentation of accounts receivable (net) for the December 31, 2011, balance sheet.

TEAMWORK IN ACTION

P2

ENTREPRENEURIAL DECISION

C1

BTN 7-7 Kevin Plank of **Under Armour** is introduced in the chapter's opening feature. Kevin currently sells his products through multiple outlets. Assume that he is considering two new selling options.

Plan A. Under Armour would begin selling products online directly to customers. Online customers would use their credit cards. It currently has the capability of selling through its Website with no additional investment in hardware or software. Credit sales are expected to increase by $250,000 per year. Costs associated with this plan are: cost of these sales will be $135,500, credit card fees will be 4.75% of sales, and additional recordkeeping and shipping costs will be 6% of sales. These online sales will reduce the sales to stores by $35,000 because some customers will now purchase items online. Sales to stores have a 25% gross margin percentage.

Plan B. Under Armour would expand its market to more stores. It would make additional credit sales of $500,000 to those stores. Costs associated with those sales are: cost of sales will be $375,000, additional recordkeeping and shipping will be 4% of sales, and uncollectible accounts will be 6.2% of sales.

Required

Check (1b) Net income, $74,000

1. Compute the additional annual net income or loss expected under (a) Plan A and (b) Plan B.

2. Should Under Armour pursue either plan? Discuss both the financial and nonfinancial factors relevant to this decision.

HITTING THE ROAD

C1

BTN 7-8 Many commercials include comments similar to the following: "We accept **VISA**" or "We do not accept **American Express.**" Conduct your own research by contacting at least five companies via interviews, phone calls, or the Internet to determine the reason(s) companies discriminate in their use of credit cards. Collect information on the fees charged by the different cards for the companies contacted. (The instructor can assign this as a team activity.)

GLOBAL DECISION

C1 P1

BTN 7-9 Key information from **GOME (www.GOME.com.hk)**, which is the leading chain retailer of consumer electronic products and household appliances in China, follows.

RMB 000s	Current Year	Prior Year
Accounts receivable, net*	45,092	97,719
Sales	45,889,257	42,478,523

*GOME refers to it as "Trade and bills receivables."

1. Compute the accounts receivable turnover for the current year.

2. How long does it take on average for GOME to collect receivables?

3. Refer to BTN 7-2. How does GOME compare to Best Buy and RadioShack in terms of its accounts receivable turnover and its collection period?

4. GOME reports an aging analysis of its receivables, based on invoice dates, as follows (in RMB 000s) as of December 31, 2008. Compute the percent of receivables in each category.

RMB 000s	Total Receivables
Within 3 months	41,787
3 to 6 months	1,615
6 months to 1 year	1,043
Over 1 year	647

5. GOME reports more than 7% of its receivables are "over 3 months past due." However, it provides no allowance as its "directors are of the opinion that no provision for impairment is necessary . . . because there has not been a significant change in credit quality of the individual debtors." Does this finding impact your assessment of GOME?

ANSWERS TO MULTIPLE CHOICE QUIZ

1. d; Desired balance in Allowance for Doubtful Accounts = $ 5,026 cr.
($125,650 × 0.04)

Current balance in Allowance for Doubtful Accounts = (328) cr.

Bad Debts Expense to be recorded = $ 4,698

2. a; Desired balance in Allowance for Doubtful Accounts = $29,358 cr.
($489,300 × 0.06)

Current balance in Allowance for Doubtful Accounts = 554 dr.

Bad Debts Expense to be recorded = $29,912

3. a; $7,500 × 0.05 × 90/360 = $93.75

4. c; Principal amount $9,000

Interest accrued . . . . 120 ($9,000 × 0.08 × 60/360)

Maturity value $9,120

5. d; $489,600/$40,800 = 12

8

Reporting and Analyzing Long-Term Assets

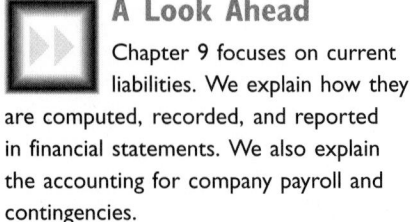

"The best way to predict the future is to create it" —Jeremy Black (from left: E. Nichols, R. Black, T. Baumgardner, J. Black)

A Look Back

Chapters 6 and 7 focused on short-term assets: cash, cash equivalents, and receivables. We explained why they are known as liquid assets and described how companies account and report for them.

A Look at This Chapter

This chapter introduces us to long-term assets. We explain how to account for a long-term asset's cost, the allocation of an asset's cost to periods benefiting from it, the recording of additional costs after an asset is purchased, and the disposal of an asset.

A Look Ahead

Chapter 9 focuses on current liabilities. We explain how they are computed, recorded, and reported in financial statements. We also explain the accounting for company payroll and contingencies.

Fruitful Assets

SAN CLEMENTE, CA—Surfing is the common bond for Ryan Black, Ed Nichols, and Jeremy Black. It also was the driving force for an excursion to ride the waves of Brazil. But what they encountered would change their lives forever.

The three surfers discovered beachgoers eating a purple berry called *acai* (ah-sigh-ee). "We too fell in love with it," says Ed. "We didn't want to leave Brazil without it." Adds Jeremy, "When people start eating acai, they want it . . . every day."

The three decided to become business missionaries and introduce acai to the masses. They launched **Sambazon (Sambazon.com),** short for Sustainable Management of the Brazilian Amazon, to manufacture and distribute acai. Scraping up just enough money, they started operations. Says Jeremy, "Financing our equipment, machinery, and other assets was a struggle as our operating cycle is long. We must pay cash to Brazilian acai growers, then pay for processing and shipping, and finally package and distribute acai products to buyers."

The power of the wave was with them. Sambazon now employs 120 workers, churns out numerous acai products, and generates nearly $20 million in annual sales. A continuing challenge is maintaining the right kind and amount of plant assets to meet demand and be profitable. Explains Jeremy, Sambazon's success depends on monitoring and controlling plant asset costs, which range from bottling and packaging equipment to delivery vehicles, plant facilities, and land.

Sambazon must account for, manage, and recover all costs of long-term assets. "We built Sambazon on a triple bottom line business model . . . economic, environmental, and social," says Ryan. "[And, we] recognize some things that are not just on our balance sheet."

Their success in asset management permits them to pursue other passions. "We've been given this incredible opportunity to make a lot of positive change with this berry," declares Jeremy. "It's not just a job . . . it's a mission!"

[Sources: *Sambazon Website,* January 2010; *The Wall Street Journal,* March 2007; *San Clemente Times,* March 2006; *CU Business Portfolio,* Spring 2007; *Entrepreneur,* November 2007]

Learning Objectives

CAP

Conceptual

C1 Describe plant assets and issues in accounting for them. *(p. 332)*

C2 Explain depreciation and the factors affecting its computation. *(p. 335)*

C3 Explain depreciation for partial years and changes in estimates. *(p. 340)*

Analytical

A1 Compare and analyze alternative depreciation methods. *(p. 339)*

A2 Compute total asset turnover and apply it to analyze a company's use of assets. *(p. 352)*

Procedural

P1 Apply the cost principle to compute the cost of plant assets. *(p. 333)*

P2 Compute and record depreciation using the straight-line, units-of-production, and declining-balance methods. *(p. 336)*

P3 Distinguish between revenue and capital expenditures, and account for them. *(p. 342)*

P4 Account for asset disposal through discarding or selling an asset. *(p. 344)*

P5 Account for natural resource assets and their depletion. *(p. 346)*

P6 Account for intangible assets. *(p. 348)*

P7 *Appendix 8A*—Account for asset exchanges. *(p. 355)*

This chapter focuses on long-term assets, which can be grouped into plant assets, natural resource assets, and intangible assets. Plant assets make up a large part of assets on most balance sheets, and they yield depreciation, often one of the largest expenses on income statements. The acquisition or building of a plant asset is often referred to as a *capital expenditure*. Capital expenditures are important events because they impact both the short- and long-term success of a company. Natural resource assets and intangible assets have similar impacts. This chapter describes the purchase and use of these assets. We also explain what distinguishes these assets from other types of assets, how to determine their cost, how to allocate their costs to periods benefiting from their use, and how to dispose of them.

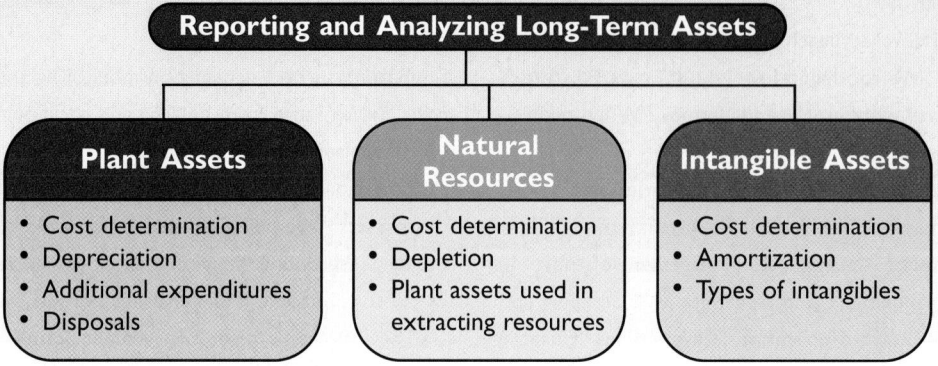

Reporting and Analyzing Long-Term Assets

Plant Assets
- Cost determination
- Depreciation
- Additional expenditures
- Disposals

Natural Resources
- Cost determination
- Depletion
- Plant assets used in extracting resources

Intangible Assets
- Cost determination
- Amortization
- Types of intangibles

Section 1—Plant Assets

Plant assets are tangible assets used in a company's operations that have a useful life of more than one accounting period. Plant assets are also called *plant and equipment; property, plant, and equipment;* or *fixed assets.* For many companies, plant assets make up the single largest class of assets they own. Exhibit 8.1 shows plant assets as a percent of total assets for several companies. Not only do they make up a large percent of many companies' assets but their dollar values are large.

EXHIBIT 8.1

Plant Assets of Selected Companies

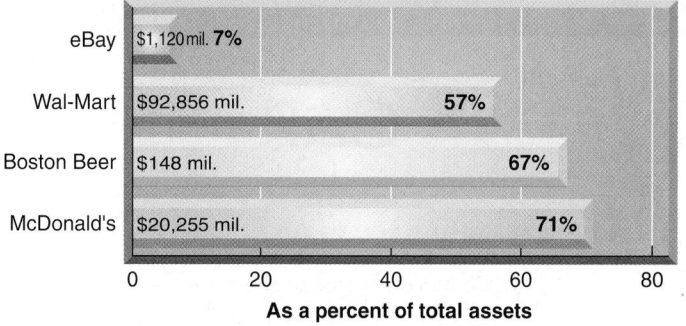

eBay | $1,120 mil. **7%**
Wal-Mart | $92,856 mil. | **57%**
Boston Beer | $148 mil. | **67%**
McDonald's | $20,255 mil. | **71%**

0   20   40   60   80
As a percent of total assets

McDonald's plant assets, for instance, are reported at more than $20 billion, and **Wal-Mart** reports plant assets of more than $92 billion.

Plant assets are set apart from other assets by two important features. First, *plant assets are used in operations.* This makes them different from, for instance, inventory that is held for sale and not used in operations. The distinctive feature here is use, not type of asset. A company that purchases a computer to resell it, reports it on the balance sheet as inventory. If the same company purchases this computer to use in operations, however, it is a plant asset. Another example is land held for future expansion, which is reported as a long-term investment. However, if this land holds a factory used in operations, the land is part of plant assets. Another example is equipment held for use in the event of a breakdown or for peak periods of production, which is reported in plant assets. If this same equipment is removed from use and held for sale, however, it is not reported in plant assets.

The second important feature is that *plant assets have useful lives extending over more than one accounting period.* This makes plant assets different from current assets such as supplies that are normally consumed in a short time period after they are placed in use.

The accounting for plant assets reflects these two features. Since plant assets are used in operations, we try to match their costs against the revenues they generate. Also, since their useful lives extend over more than one period, our matching of costs and revenues must extend over several periods. Specifically, we value plant assets (balance sheet effect) and then, for many of them, we allocate their costs to periods benefiting from their use (income statement effect). An important exception is land; land cost is not allocated to expense when we expect it to have an indefinite life.

Point: It can help to view plant assets as prepaid expenses that benefit several future accounting periods.

Exhibit 8.2 shows four main issues in accounting for plant assets: (1) computing the costs of plant assets, (2) allocating the costs of most plant assets (less any salvage amounts) against revenues for the periods they benefit, (3) accounting for expenditures such as repairs and improvements to plant assets, and (4) recording the disposal of plant assets. The following sections discuss these issues.

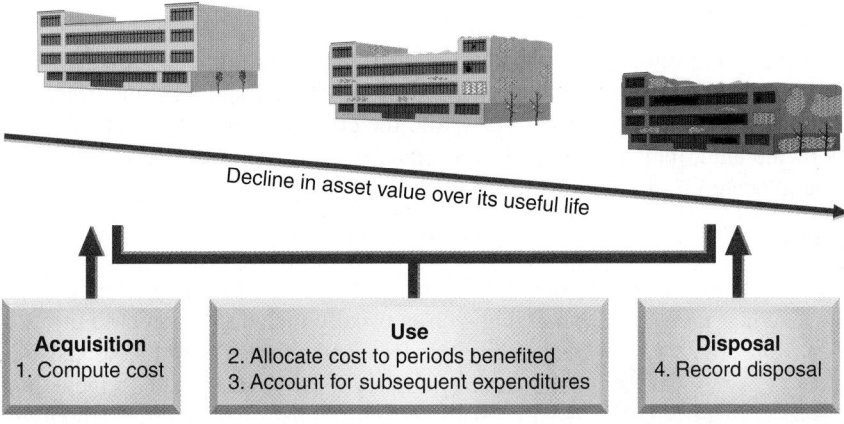

EXHIBIT 8.2

Issues in Accounting for Plant Assets

Decline in asset value over its useful life

Acquisition
1. Compute cost

Use
2. Allocate cost to periods benefited
3. Account for subsequent expenditures

Disposal
4. Record disposal

Cost Determination

Plant assets are recorded at cost when acquired. This is consistent with the *cost principle.* **Cost** includes all normal and reasonable expenditures necessary to get the asset in place and ready for its intended use. The cost of a factory machine, for instance, includes its invoice cost less any cash discount for early payment, plus any necessary freight, unpacking, assembling, installing, and testing costs. Examples are the costs of building a base or foundation for a machine, providing electrical hook-ups, and testing the asset before using it in operations.

Video8.1

To be recorded as part of the cost of a plant asset, an expenditure must be normal, reasonable, and necessary in preparing it for its intended use. If an asset is damaged during unpacking, the repairs are not added to its cost. Instead, they are charged to an expense account. Nor is a paid traffic fine for moving heavy machinery on city streets without a proper permit part of the machinery's cost; but payment for a proper permit is included in the cost of machinery. Charges are sometimes incurred to modify or customize a new plant asset. These charges are added to the asset's cost. We explain in this section how to determine the cost of plant assets for each of its four major classes.

Land

When land is purchased for a building site, its cost includes the total amount paid for the land, including any real estate commissions, title insurance fees, legal fees, and any accrued property taxes paid by the purchaser. Payments for surveying, clearing, grading, and draining also are included in the cost of land. Other costs include government assessments, whether incurred at the time of

P1   Apply the cost principle to compute the cost of plant assets.

purchase or later, for items such as public roadways, sewers, and sidewalks. These assessments are included because they permanently add to the land's value. Land purchased as a building site sometimes includes structures that must be removed. In such cases, the total purchase price is charged to the Land account as is the cost of removing the structures, less any amounts recovered through sale of salvaged materials. To illustrate, assume that **Starbucks** paid $167,000 cash to acquire land for a retail store.

EXHIBIT 8.3

Computing Cost of Land

Cash price of land	$ 167,000
Net cost of garage removal	13,000
Closing costs	10,000
Cost of land	**$190,000**

This land had an old service garage that was removed at a net cost of $13,000 ($15,000 in costs less $2,000 proceeds from salvaged materials). Additional closing costs total $10,000, consisting of brokerage fees ($8,000), legal fees ($1,500), and title costs ($500). The cost of this land to Starbucks is $190,000 and is computed as shown in Exhibit 8.3.

Land Improvements

Land has an indefinite (unlimited) life and is not usually used up over time. **Land improvements** such as parking lot surfaces, driveways, fences, shrubs, and lighting systems, however, have limited useful lives and are used up. While the costs of these improvements increase the usefulness of the land, they are charged to a separate Land Improvement account so that their costs can be allocated to the periods they benefit.

Buildings

A Building account is charged for the costs of purchasing or constructing a building that is used in operations. When purchased, a building's costs usually include its purchase price, brokerage

fees, taxes, title fees, and attorney fees. Its costs also include all expenditures to ready it for its intended use, including any necessary repairs or renovations such as wiring, lighting, flooring, and wall coverings. When a company constructs a building or any plant asset for its own use, its costs include materials and labor plus a reasonable amount of indirect overhead cost. Overhead includes the costs of items such as heat, lighting, power, and depreciation on machinery used to construct the asset. Costs of construction also include design fees, building permits, and insurance during construction. However, costs such as insurance to cover the asset *after* it is placed in use are operating expenses.

Machinery and Equipment

The costs of machinery and equipment consist of all costs normal and necessary to purchase them and prepare them for their intended use. These include the purchase price, taxes, transportation charges, insurance while in transit, and the installing, assembling, and testing of the machinery and equipment.

Lump-Sum Purchase

Example: If appraised values in Exhibit 8.4 are land, $24,000; land improvements, $12,000; and building, $84,000, what cost is assigned to the building? *Answer:*
(1) $24,000 + $12,000 + $84,000 = $120,000 (total appraisal)
(2) $84,000/$120,000 = 70% (building's percent of total)
(3) 70% × $90,000 = $63,000 (building's apportioned cost)

Plant assets sometimes are purchased as a group in a single transaction for a lump-sum price. This transaction is called a *lump-sum purchase,* or *group, bulk,* or *basket purchase.* When this occurs, we allocate the cost of the purchase among the different types of assets acquired based on their *relative market values,* which can be estimated by appraisal or by using the tax-assessed valuations of the assets. To illustrate, assume **Oakley** paid $90,000 cash to acquire a group of items consisting of land appraised at $30,000, land improvements appraised at $10,000, and a building appraised at $60,000. The $90,000 cost is allocated on the basis of these appraised values as shown in Exhibit 8.4.

EXHIBIT 8.4

Computing Costs in a Lump-Sum Purchase

	Appraised Value	Percent of Total	Apportioned Cost
Land	$ 30,000	30% ($30,000/$100,000)	**$27,000** ($90,000 × 30%)
Land improvements	10,000	10 ($10,000/$100,000)	**9,000** ($90,000 × 10%)
Building	60,000	60 ($60,000/$100,000)	**54,000** ($90,000 × 60%)
Totals	$100,000	100%	$ 90,000

Depreciation

Depreciation is the process of allocating the cost of a plant asset to expense in the accounting periods benefiting from its use. Depreciation does not measure the decline in the asset's market value each period, nor does it measure the asset's physical deterioration. Since depreciation reflects the cost of using a plant asset, depreciation charges are only recorded when the asset is actually in service. This section describes the factors we must consider in computing depreciation, the depreciation methods used, revisions in depreciation, and depreciation for partial periods.

Video8.1

Factors in Computing Depreciation

Factors that determine depreciation are (1) cost, (2) salvage value, and (3) useful life.

Cost   The **cost** of a plant asset consists of all necessary and reasonable expenditures to acquire it and to prepare it for its intended use.

Salvage Value   The total amount of depreciation to be charged off over an asset's benefit period equals the asset's cost minus its salvage value. **Salvage value,** also called *residual value* or *scrap value,* is an estimate of the asset's value at the end of its benefit period. This is the amount the owner expects to receive from disposing of the asset at the end of its benefit period. If the asset is expected to be traded in on a new asset, its salvage value is the expected trade-in value.

Useful Life   The **useful life** of a plant asset is the length of time it is productively used in a company's operations. Useful life, also called *service life,* might not be as long as the asset's total productive life. For example, the productive life of a computer can be eight years or more. Some companies, however, trade in old computers for new ones every two years. In this case, these computers have a two-year useful life, meaning the cost of these computers (less their expected trade-in values) is charged to depreciation expense over a two-year period.

Several variables often make the useful life of a plant asset difficult to predict. A major variable is the wear and tear from use in operations. Two other variables, inadequacy and obsolescence, also require consideration. **Inadequacy** refers to the insufficient capacity of a company's plant assets to meet its growing productive demands. **Obsolescence** refers to a plant asset that is no longer useful in producing goods or services with a competitive advantage because of new inventions and improvements. Both inadequacy and obsolescence are difficult to predict because of demand changes, new inventions, and improvements. A company usually disposes of an inadequate or obsolete asset before it wears out.

A company is often able to better predict a new asset's useful life when it has past experience with a similar asset. When it has no such experience, a company relies on the experience of others or on engineering studies and judgment. In note 1 of its annual report, **Tootsie Roll,** a snack food manufacturer, reports the following useful lives:

Buildings	20–35 years
Machinery and Equipment	5–20 years

C2   Explain depreciation and the factors affecting its computation.

Point: If we expect additional costs in preparing a plant asset for disposal, the salvage value equals the expected amount from disposal less any disposal costs.

Point: Useful life and salvage value are estimates. Estimates require judgment based on all available information.

Depreciation Methods

Depreciation methods are used to allocate a plant asset's cost over the accounting periods in its useful life. The most frequently used method of depreciation is the straight-line method. Another common depreciation method is the units-of-production method. We explain both of these methods in this section. This section also describes accelerated depreciation methods, with a focus on the declining-balance method.

The computations in this section use information about a machine that inspects athletic shoes before packaging. Manufacturers such as **Converse, Reebok, adidas,** and **Fila** use this machine. Data for this machine are in Exhibit 8.5.

EXHIBIT 8.5

Data for Athletic Shoe-Inspecting Machine

Cost	$10,000
Salvage value	1,000
Depreciable cost	$ 9,000
Useful life	
Accounting periods	5 years
Units inspected	36,000 shoes

P2 Compute and record depreciation using the straight-line, units-of-production, and declining-balance methods.

Straight-Line Method   **Straight-line depreciation** charges the same amount of expense to each period of the asset's useful life. A two-step process is used. We first compute the *depreciable cost* of the asset; also called the *cost to be depreciated*. It is computed by subtracting the asset's salvage value from its total cost. Second, depreciable cost is divided by the number of accounting periods in the asset's useful life. The formula for straight-line depreciation, along with its computation for the inspection machine described above, is shown in Exhibit 8.6.

EXHIBIT 8.6

Straight-Line Depreciation Formula and Example

$$\frac{\text{Cost} - \text{Salvage value}}{\text{Useful life in periods}} = \frac{\$10,000 - \$1,000}{5 \text{ years}} = \$1,800 \text{ per year}$$

If this machine is purchased on December 31, 2008, and used throughout its predicted useful life of five years, the straight-line method allocates an equal amount of depreciation to each of the years 2009 through 2013. We make the following adjusting entry at the end of each of the five years to record straight-line depreciation of this machine.

Assets = Liabilities + Equity
−1,800   −1,800

Dec. 31	Depreciation Expense	1,800	
	Accumulated Depreciation—Machinery		1,800
	To record annual depreciation.		

Example: If salvage value of the machine is $2,500, what is the annual depreciation? *Answer:* ($10,000 − $2,500)/5 years = $1,500

The $1,800 Depreciation Expense is reported on the income statement among operating expenses. The $1,800 Accumulated Depreciation is a contra asset account to the Machinery account in the balance sheet. The graph on the left in Exhibit 8.7 shows the $1,800 per year expenses reported in each of the five years. The graph on the right shows the amounts reported on each of the six December 31 balance sheets.

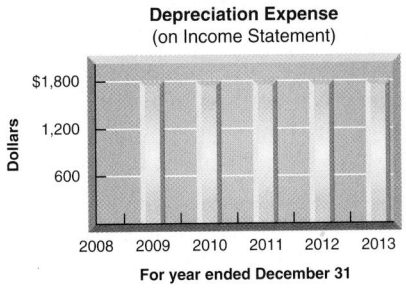

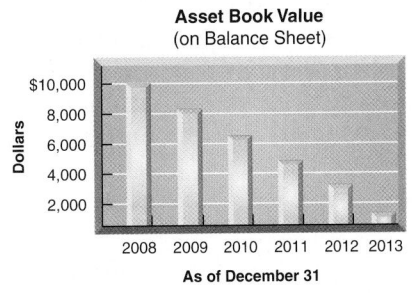

EXHIBIT 8.7

Financial Statement Effects of Straight-Line Depreciation

The net balance sheet amount is the **asset book value,** or simply *book value,* and is computed as the asset's total cost less its accumulated depreciation. For example, at the end of year 2 (December 31, 2010), its book value is $6,400 and is reported in the balance sheet as follows:

Machinery $10,000
Less accumulated depreciation 3,600 $6,400

The book value of this machine declines by $1,800 each year due to depreciation. From the graphs in Exhibit 8.7 we can see why this method is called straight line.

We also can compute the *straight-line depreciation rate,* defined as 100% divided by the number of periods in the asset's useful life. For the inspection machine, this rate is 20% (100% ÷ 5 years, or 1/5 per period). We use this rate, along with other information, to compute the machine's *straight-line depreciation schedule* shown in Exhibit 8.8. Note three points in this exhibit. First, depreciation expense is the same each period. Second, accumulated depreciation is the sum of current and prior periods' depreciation expense. Third, book value declines each period until it equals salvage value at the end of the machine's useful life.

Point: Depreciation requires estimates for salvage value and useful life. Ethics are relevant when managers might be tempted to choose estimates to achieve desired results on financial statements.

Annual Period	Depreciation for the Period			End of Period	
	Depreciable Cost*	Depreciation Rate	Depreciation Expense	Accumulated Depreciation	Book Value†
2008	—	—	—	—	$10,000
2009	$9,000	20%	$1,800	$1,800	8,200
2010	9,000	20	1,800	3,600	6,400
2011	9,000	20	1,800	5,400	4,600
2012	9,000	20	1,800	7,200	2,800
2013	9,000	20	1,800	9,000	1,000

EXHIBIT 8.8

Straight-Line Depreciation Schedule

* $10,000 − $1,000.   † Book value is total cost minus accumulated depreciation.

Units-of-Production Method   The straight-line method charges an equal share of an asset's cost to each period. If plant assets are used up in about equal amounts each accounting period, this method produces a reasonable matching of expenses with revenues. However, the use of some plant assets varies greatly from one period to the next. A builder, for instance, might use a piece of construction equipment for a month and then not use it again for several months. When equipment use varies from period to period, the units-of-production depreciation method can better match expenses with revenues. **Units-of-production depreciation** charges a varying amount to expense for each period of an asset's useful life depending on its usage.

A two-step process is used to compute units-of-production depreciation. We first compute *depreciation per unit* by subtracting the asset's salvage value from its total cost and then dividing by the total number of units expected to be produced during its useful life. Units of production can be expressed in product or other units such as hours used or miles driven. The second step is to compute depreciation expense for the period by multiplying the units produced in the period by the depreciation per unit. The formula for units-of-production depreciation, along with its computation for the machine described in Exhibit 8.5, is shown in Exhibit 8.9. (7,000 shoes are inspected and sold in its first year.)

EXHIBIT 8.9

Units-of-Production
Depreciation Formula
and Example

Step 1

$$\text{Depreciation per unit} = \frac{\text{Cost} - \text{Salvage value}}{\text{Total units of production}} = \frac{\$10,000 - \$1,000}{36,000 \text{ shoes}} = \$0.25 \text{ per shoe}$$

Step 2

$$\text{Depreciation expense} = \text{Depreciation per unit} \times \text{Units produced in period}$$
$$\$0.25 \text{ per shoe} \times 7,000 \text{ shoes} = \$1,750$$

Using data on the number of shoes inspected by the machine, we can compute the *units-of-production depreciation schedule* shown in Exhibit 8.10. For example, depreciation for the first year is $1,750 (7,000 shoes at $0.25 per shoe). Depreciation for the second year is $2,000 (8,000 shoes at $0.25 per shoe). Other years are similarly computed. Exhibit 8.10 shows that (1) depreciation expense depends on unit output, (2) accumulated depreciation is the sum of current and prior periods' depreciation expense, and (3) book value declines each period until it equals salvage value at the end of the asset's useful life. **Boise Cascade** is one of many companies using the units-of-production depreciation method. It reports that most of its "paper and wood products manufacturing facilities determine depreciation by a units-of-production method." **Kimberly-Clark** also reports that much of its "depreciable property is depreciated on the . . . units-of-production method."

Example: Refer to Exhibit 8.10. If the number of shoes inspected in 2013 is 5,500, what is depreciation for 2013? *Answer:* $1,250 (never depreciate below salvage value)

EXHIBIT 8.10

Units-of-Production
Depreciation Schedule

Annual Period	Depreciation for the Period			End of Period	
	Number of Units	Depreciation per Unit	Depreciation Expense	Accumulated Depreciation	Book Value
2008	—	—	—	—	$10,000
2009	7,000	$0.25	$1,750	$1,750	8,250
2010	8,000	0.25	2,000	3,750	6,250
2011	9,000	0.25	2,250	6,000	4,000
2012	7,000	0.25	1,750	7,750	2,250
2013	5,000	0.25	1,250	9,000	1,000

Declining-Balance Method   An **accelerated depreciation method** yields larger depreciation expenses in the early years of an asset's life and less depreciation in later years. The most common accelerated method is the **declining-balance method** of depreciation, which uses a depreciation rate that is a multiple of the straight-line rate and applies it to the asset's beginning-of-period book value. The amount of depreciation declines each period because book value declines each period.

A common depreciation rate for the declining-balance method is double the straight-line rate. This is called the *double-declining-balance (DDB)* method. This method is applied in three steps: (1) compute the asset's straight-line depreciation rate, (2) double the straight-line rate, and (3) compute depreciation expense by multiplying this rate by the asset's beginning-of-period book value. To illustrate, let's return to the machine in Exhibit 8.5 and apply the double-declining-balance method to compute depreciation expense. Exhibit 8.11 shows the first-year depreciation computation for the machine. The three-step process is to (1) divide

Point: In the DDB method, *double* refers to the rate and *declining balance* refers to book value. The rate is applied to beginning book value each period.

100% by five years to determine the straight-line rate of 20%, or 1/5, per year, (2) double this 20% rate to get the declining-balance rate of 40%, or 2/5, per year, and (3) compute depreciation expense as 40%, or 2/5, multiplied by the beginning-of-period book value.

EXHIBIT 8.11

Double-Declining-Balance Depreciation Formula*

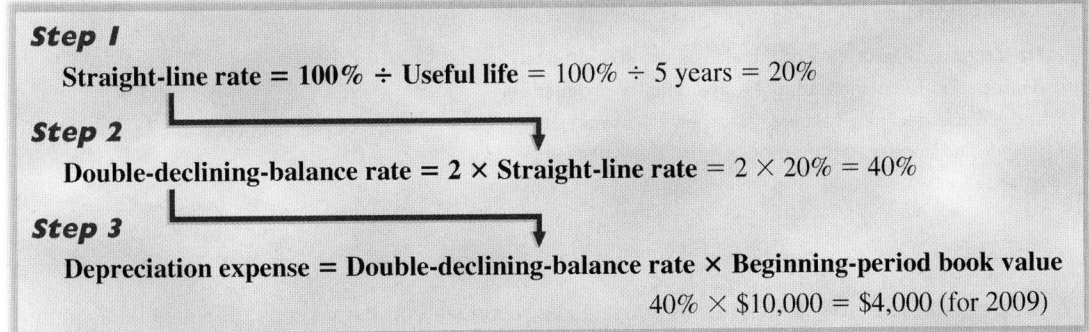

Step 1

   Straight-line rate = 100% ÷ Useful life = 100% ÷ 5 years = 20%

Step 2

   Double-declining-balance rate = 2 × Straight-line rate = 2 × 20% = 40%

Step 3

   Depreciation expense = Double-declining-balance rate × Beginning-period book value

                                40% × $10,000 = $4,000 (for 2009)

* To simplify: DDB depreciation = (2 × Beginning-period book value)/Useful life.

The *double-declining-balance depreciation schedule* is shown in Exhibit 8.12. The schedule follows the formula except for year 2013, when depreciation expense is $296. This $296 is not equal to 40% × $1,296, or $518.40. If we had used the $518.40 for depreciation expense in 2013, ending book value would equal $777.60, which is less than the $1,000 salvage value. Instead, the $296 is computed by subtracting the $1,000 salvage value from the $1,296 book value at the beginning of the fifth year (the year when DDB depreciation cuts into salvage value).

Example: What is DDB depreciation expense in year 2012 if the salvage value is $2,000? *Answer:* $2,160 − $2,000 = $160

EXHIBIT 8.12

Double-Declining-Balance Depreciation Schedule

Annual Period	Depreciation for the Period			End of Period	
	Beginning of Period Book Value	Depreciation Rate	Depreciation Expense	Accumulated Depreciation	Book Value
2008	—	—	—	—	$10,000
2009	$10,000	40%	$4,000	$4,000	6,000
2010	6,000	40	2,400	6,400	3,600
2011	3,600	40	1,440	7,840	2,160
2012	2,160	40	864	8,704	1,296
2013	1,296	40	296*	9,000	**1,000**

* Year 2013 depreciation is $1,296 − $1,000 = $296 (never depreciate book value below salvage value).

Comparing Depreciation Methods   Exhibit 8.13 shows depreciation expense for each year of the machine's useful life under each of the three depreciation methods. While depreciation expense per period differs for different methods, total depreciation expense of $9,000 is the same over the machine's useful life.

A1 Compare and analyze alternative depreciation methods.

EXHIBIT 8.13

Depreciation Expense for the Different Methods

Period	Straight-Line	Units-of-Production	Double-Declining-Balance
2009	$1,800	$1,750	$4,000
2010	1,800	2,000	2,400
2011	1,800	2,250	1,440
2012	1,800	1,750	864
2013	1,800	1,250	296
Totals	$9,000	$9,000	$9,000

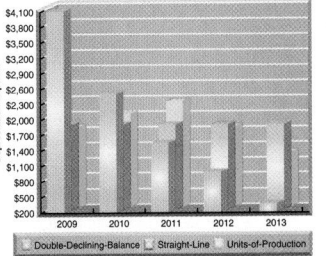

Each method starts with a total cost of $10,000 and ends with a salvage value of $1,000. The difference is the pattern in depreciation expense over the useful life. The book value of the asset when using straight-line is always greater than the book value from using double-declining-balance, except at the beginning and end of the asset's useful life, when it is the same.

Point: Depreciation is higher and income lower in the short run when using accelerated versus straight-line methods.

Also, the straight-line method yields a steady pattern of depreciation expense while the units-of-production depreciation depends on the number of units produced. Each of these methods is acceptable because it allocates cost in a systematic and rational manner.

Decision Insight

In Vogue   About 85% of companies use straight-line depreciation for plant assets, 4% use units-of-production, and 4% use declining-balance. Another 7% use an unspecified accelerated method—most likely declining-balance.

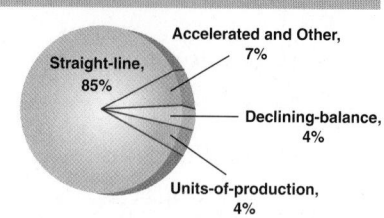

Accelerated and Other, 7%

Straight-line, 85%

Declining-balance, 4%

Units-of-production, 4%

Point: Understanding depreciation for financial accounting will help in learning MACRS for tax accounting. Rules for MACRS are available from **www.IRS.gov.**

Depreciation for Tax Reporting   The records a company keeps for financial accounting purposes are usually separate from the records it keeps for tax accounting purposes. This is so because financial accounting aims to report useful information on financial performance and position, whereas tax accounting reflects government objectives in raising revenues. Differences between these two accounting systems are normal and expected. Depreciation is a common example of how the records differ. For example, many companies use accelerated depreciation in computing taxable income. Reporting higher depreciation expense in the early years of an asset's life reduces the company's taxable income in those years and increases it in later years, when the depreciation expense is lower. The company's goal here is to *postpone* its tax payments.

The U.S. federal income tax law has rules for depreciating assets. These rules include the **Modified Accelerated Cost Recovery System (MACRS),** which allows straight-line depreciation for some assets, but it requires accelerated depreciation for most kinds of assets. MACRS separates depreciable assets into different classes and defines the depreciable life and rate for each class. MACRS is *not* acceptable for financial reporting because it often allocates costs over an arbitrary period that is less than the asset's useful life and it fails to estimate salvage value. Details of MACRS are covered in tax accounting courses.

Partial-Year Depreciation

C3   Explain depreciation for partial years and changes in estimates.

Plant assets are purchased and disposed of at various times. When an asset is purchased (or disposed of) at a time other than the beginning or end of an accounting period, depreciation is recorded for part of a year. This is done so that the year of purchase or the year of disposal is charged with its share of the asset's depreciation.

To illustrate, assume that the machine in Exhibit 8.5 is purchased and placed in service on October 8, 2008, and the annual accounting period ends on December 31. Since this machine is purchased and used for nearly three months in 2008, the calendar-year income statement should report depreciation expense on the machine for that part of the year. Normally, depreciation assumes that the asset is purchased on the first day of the month nearest the actual date of purchase. In this case, since the purchase occurred on October 8, we assume an October 1 purchase date. This means that three months' depreciation is recorded in 2008. Using straight-line depreciation, we compute three months' depreciation of $450 as follows.

$$\frac{\$10,000 - \$1,000}{5 \text{ years}} \times \frac{3}{12} = \$450$$

Example: If the machine's salvage value is zero and purchase occurs on Oct. 8, 2008, how much depreciation is recorded at Dec. 31, 2008? *Answer:* $10,000/5 × 3/12 = $500

A similar computation is necessary when an asset disposal occurs during a period. To illustrate, assume that the machine is sold on June 24, 2013. Depreciation is recorded for the period January 1 through June 24 when it is disposed of. This partial year's depreciation, computed to the nearest whole month, is

$$\frac{\$10,000 - \$1,000}{5 \text{ years}} \times \frac{6}{12} = \$900$$

Change in Estimates for Depreciation

Depreciation is based on estimates of salvage value and useful life. During the useful life of an asset, new information may indicate that these estimates are inaccurate. If our estimate of an asset's useful life and/or salvage value changes, what should we do? The answer is to use the new estimate to compute depreciation for current and future periods. This means that we revise the depreciation expense computation by spreading the cost yet to be depreciated over the remaining useful life. This approach is used for all depreciation methods.

Point: Remaining depreciable cost equals book value less revised salvage value at the point of revision.

Let's return to the machine described in Exhibit 8.8 using straight-line depreciation. At the beginning of this asset's third year, its book value is $6,400, computed as $10,000 minus $3,600. Assume that at the beginning of its third year, the estimated number of years remaining in its useful life changes from three to four years *and* its estimate of salvage value changes from $1,000 to $400. Straight-line depreciation for each of the four remaining years is computed as shown in Exhibit 8.14.

Point: Income is overstated (and depreciation understated) when useful life is too high; when useful life is too low, the opposite results.

$$\frac{\text{Book value} - \text{Revised salvage value}}{\text{Revised remaining useful life}} = \frac{\$6,400 - \$400}{4 \text{ years}} = \$1,500 \text{ per year}$$

EXHIBIT 8.14

Computing Revised Straight-Line Depreciation

Thus, $1,500 of depreciation expense is recorded for the machine at the end of the third through sixth years—each year of its remaining useful life. Since this asset was depreciated at $1,800 per year for the first two years, it is tempting to conclude that depreciation expense was overstated in the first two years. However, these expenses reflected the best information available at that time. We do not go back and restate prior years' financial statements for this type of new information. Instead, we adjust the current and future periods' statements to reflect this new information. Revising an estimate of the useful life or salvage value of a plant asset is referred to as a **change in an accounting estimate** and is reflected in current and future financial statements, not in prior statements.

Example: If at the beginning of its second year the machine's remaining useful life changes from four to three years and salvage value from $1,000 to $400, how much straight-line depreciation is recorded in remaining years? *Answer:* Revised depreciation = ($8,200 − $400)/3 = $2,600.

Reporting Depreciation

Both the cost and accumulated depreciation of plant assets are reported on the balance sheet or in its notes. **Dale Jarrett Racing Adventure**, for instance, reports the following.

Office furniture and equipment	$ 45,386
Shop and track equipment	123,378
Race vehicles and other	775,363
Property and equipment, gross	944,127
Less accumulated depreciation	715,435
Property and equipment, net	$228,692

Many companies also show plant assets on one line with the net amount of cost less accumulated depreciation. When this is done, the amount of accumulated depreciation is disclosed in a note. **RadioShack** reports only the net amount of its property and equipment in its balance sheet in Appendix A. To satisfy the full-disclosure principle, RadioShack describes its depreciation methods in its Note 2 and the amounts comprising plant assets in its Note 3—see its 10-K at SEC.gov.

Point: A company usually keeps records for each asset showing its cost and depreciation to date. The combined records for individual assets are a type of *plant asset subsidiary ledger.*

Reporting both the cost and accumulated depreciation of plant assets helps users compare the assets of different companies. For example, a company holding assets costing $50,000 and accumulated depreciation of $40,000 is likely in a situation different from a company with new assets costing $10,000. While the net undepreciated cost of $10,000 is the same in both cases, the first company may have more productive capacity available but likely is facing the need to replace older assets. These insights are not provided if the two balance sheets report only the $10,000 book values.

Users must remember that plant assets are reported on a balance sheet at their undepreciated costs (book value), not at fair (market) values. This emphasis on costs rather than fair values is based on the *going-concern assumption* described in Chapter 1. This assumption states that, unless there is evidence to the contrary, we assume that a company continues in business. This implies that plant assets are held and used long enough to recover their cost through the sale of products and services. Since plant assets are not for sale, their fair values are not reported. An exception is when there is a *permanent decline* in the fair value of an asset relative to its book value; called an asset **impairment.** In this case the company writes the asset down to this fair value (details for the two-step process for assessing and computing the impairment loss are in advanced courses).

Accumulated Depreciation is a contra asset account with a normal credit balance. It does *not* reflect funds accumulated to buy new assets when the assets currently owned are replaced. If a company has funds available to buy assets, the funds are shown on the balance sheet among liquid assets such as Cash or Investments.

Example: Assume equipment carries a book value of $800 ($900 cost less $100 accumulated depreciation) and a fair (market) value of $750, *and* this $50 decline in value meets the 2-step impairment test. The entry to record this impairment is:

Impairment Loss $50
   Accum Depr-Equip. $50

Decision Ethics

Controller You are the controller for a struggling company. Its operations require regular investments in equipment, and depreciation is its largest expense. Its competitors frequently replace equipment—often depreciated over three years. The company president instructs you to revise useful lives of equipment from three to six years and to use a six-year life on all new equipment. What actions do you take? [Answer—p. 358]

Quick Check
Answers—p. 358

4. On January 1, 2009, a company pays $77,000 to purchase office furniture with a zero salvage value. The furniture's useful life is somewhere between 7 and 10 years. What is the year 2009 straight-line depreciation on the furniture using (*a*) a 7-year useful life and (*b*) a 10-year useful life?

5. What does the term *depreciation* mean in accounting?

6. A company purchases a machine for $96,000 on January 1, 2009. Its useful life is five years or 100,000 units of product, and its salvage value is $8,000. During 2009, 10,000 units of product are produced. Compute the book value of this machine on December 31, 2009, assuming (*a*) straight-line depreciation and (*b*) units-of-production depreciation.

7. In early January 2009, a company acquires equipment for $3,800. The company estimates this equipment to have a useful life of three years and a salvage value of $200. Early in 2011, the company changes its estimates to a total four-year useful life and zero salvage value. Using the straight-line method, what is depreciation for the year ended 2011?

Additional Expenditures

P3 Distinguish between revenue and capital expenditures, and account for them.

After a company acquires a plant asset and puts it into service, it often makes additional expenditures for that asset's operation, maintenance, repair, and improvement. In recording these expenditures, it must decide whether to capitalize or expense them (to capitalize an expenditure is to debit the asset account). The issue is whether these expenditures are reported as current period expenses or added to the plant asset's cost and depreciated over its remaining useful life.

Revenue expenditures, also called *income statement expenditures,* are additional costs of plant assets that do not materially increase the asset's life or productive capabilities. They are recorded as expenses and deducted from revenues in the current period's income statement. Examples of revenue expenditures are cleaning, repainting, adjustments, and lubricants. **Capital expenditures,** also called *balance sheet expenditures,* are additional costs of plant assets that provide benefits extending beyond the current period. They are debited to asset accounts and reported on the balance sheet. Capital expenditures increase or improve the type or amount of service an asset provides. Examples are roofing replacement, plant expansion, and major overhauls of machinery and equipment.

Financial Statement Effect		
	Accounting	Expense Timing
Revenue expenditure	Income stmt. account debited	Expensed currently
Capital expenditure	Balance sheet account debited	Expensed in future

Financial statements are affected for several years by the accounting choice of recording costs as either revenue expenditures or capital expenditures. This decision is based on whether the expenditures are identified as ordinary repairs or as betterments and extraordinary repairs.

Ordinary Repairs

Ordinary repairs are expenditures to keep an asset in normal, good operating condition. They are necessary if an asset is to perform to expectations over its useful life. Ordinary repairs do not extend an asset's useful life beyond its original estimate or increase its productivity beyond original expectations. Examples are normal costs of cleaning, lubricating, adjusting, and replacing small parts of a machine. Ordinary repairs are treated as *revenue expenditures*. This means their costs are reported as expenses on the current period income statement. Following this rule, **Brunswick** reports that "maintenance and repair costs are expensed as incurred." If Brunswick's current year repair costs are $9,500, it makes the following entry.

Point: Many companies apply the *materiality constraint* to treat *low-cost plant assets* (say, less than $500) as revenue expenditures.

Dec. 31	Repairs Expense..............................	9,500	
	Cash		9,500
	To record ordinary repairs of equipment.		

Assets = Liabilities + Equity
−9,500   −9,500

Betterments and Extraordinary Repairs

Accounting for betterments and extraordinary repairs is similar—both are treated as *capital expenditures*.

Video8.1

Betterments (Improvements)   **Betterments,** also called *improvements,* are expenditures that make a plant asset more efficient or productive. A betterment often involves adding a component to an asset or replacing one of its old components with a better one, and does not always increase an asset's useful life. An example is replacing manual controls on a machine with automatic controls. One special type of betterment is an *addition,* such as adding a new wing or dock to a warehouse. Since a betterment benefits future periods, it is debited to the asset account as a capital expenditure. The new book value (less salvage value) is then depreciated over the asset's remaining useful life. To illustrate, suppose a company pays $8,000 for a machine with an eight-year useful life and no salvage value. After three years and $3,000 of depreciation, it adds an automated control system to the machine at a cost of $1,800. This results in reduced labor costs in future periods. The cost of the betterment is added to the Machinery account with this entry.

Example: Assume a firm owns a Web server. Identify each cost as a revenue or capital expenditure: (1) purchase price, (2) necessary wiring, (3) platform for operation, (4) circuits to increase capacity, (5) cleaning after each month of use, (6) repair of a faulty switch, and (7) replaced a worn fan. *Answer:* Capital expenditures: 1, 2, 3, 4; Revenue expenditures: 5, 6, 7.

Jan. 2	Machinery....................................	1,800	
	Cash		1,800
	To record installation of automated system.		

Assets = Liabilities + Equity
+1,800
−1,800

After the betterment is recorded, the remaining cost to be depreciated is $6,800, computed as $8,000 − $3,000 + $1,800. Depreciation expense for the remaining five years is $1,360 per year, computed as $6,800/5 years.

Point: Both extraordinary repairs and betterments require revising future depreciation.

Extraordinary Repairs (Replacements)   **Extraordinary repairs** are expenditures extending the asset's useful life beyond its original estimate. Extraordinary repairs are *capital expenditures* because they benefit future periods. Their costs are debited to the asset account (or to accumulated depreciation). For example, **America West Airlines** reports: "cost of major scheduled airframe, engine and certain component overhauls are capitalized (and expensed) . . . over the periods benefited."

Decision Maker ▬▬▬▬▬▬▬▬▬▬▬▬▬▬▬▬▬▬▬▬▬▬▬▬▬▬▬

Entrepreneur Your start-up Internet services company needs cash, and you are preparing financial statements to apply for a short-term loan. A friend suggests that you treat as many expenses as possible as capital expenditures. What are the impacts on financial statements of this suggestion? What do you think is the aim of this suggestion? [Answer—p. 358]

Disposals of Plant Assets

Plant assets are disposed of for several reasons. Some are discarded because they wear out or become obsolete. Others are sold because of changing business plans. Regardless of the reason, disposals of plant assets occur in one of three basic ways: discarding, sale, or exchange. The general steps in accounting for a disposal of plant assets is described in Exhibit 8.15.

EXHIBIT 8.15

Accounting for Disposals of Plant Assets

1. Record depreciation up to the date of disposal—this also updates Accumulated Depreciation.
2. Record the removal of the disposed asset's account balances—including its Accumulated Depreciation.
3. Record any cash (and/or other assets) received or paid in the disposal.
4. Record any gain or loss—computed by comparing the disposed asset's book value with the market value of any assets received.*

* An exception to step 4 is the case of an exchange that lacks *commercial substance*—See Appendix 8A.

Discarding Plant Assets

P4 Account for asset disposal through discarding or selling an asset.

A plant asset is *discarded* when it is no longer useful to the company and it has no market value. To illustrate, assume that a machine costing $9,000 with accumulated depreciation of $9,000 is discarded. When accumulated depreciation equals the asset's cost, it is said to be *fully depreciated* (zero book value). The entry to record the discarding of this asset is

Assets = Liabilities + Equity
+9,000
−9,000

June 5	Accumulated Depreciation—Machinery	9,000	
	Machinery.		9,000
	To discard fully depreciated machinery.		

This entry reflects all four steps of Exhibit 8.15. Step 1 is unnecessary since the machine is fully depreciated. Step 2 is reflected in the debit to Accumulated Depreciation and credit to Machinery. Since no other asset is involved, step 3 is irrelevant. Finally, since book value is zero and no other asset is involved, no gain or loss is recorded in step 4.

How do we account for discarding an asset that is not fully depreciated or one whose depreciation is not up-to-date? To answer this, consider equipment costing $8,000 with accumulated depreciation of $6,000 on December 31 of the prior fiscal year-end. This equipment is being depreciated using the straight-line method over eight years with zero salvage. On July 1 of the current year it is discarded. Step 1 is to bring depreciation up-to-date.

Point: Recording depreciation expense up-to-date gives an up-to-date book value for determining gain or loss.

Assets = Liabilities + Equity
−500   −500

July 1	Depreciation Expense	500	
	Accumulated Depreciation—Equipment		500
	To record 6 months' depreciation ($1,000 × 6/12).		

Steps 2 through 4 of Exhibit 8.15 are reflected in the second (and final) entry.

Assets = Liabilities + Equity
+6,500   −1,500
−8,000

July 1	Accumulated Depreciation—Equipment	6,500	
	Loss on Disposal of Equipment	1,500	
	Equipment		8,000
	To discard equipment with a $1,500 book value.		

This loss is computed by comparing the equipment's $1,500 book value ($8,000 − $6,000 − $500) with the zero net cash proceeds. The loss is reported in the Other Expenses and Losses section of the income statement. Discarding an asset can sometimes require a cash payment that would increase the loss.

Point: Gain or loss is determined by comparing "value given" (book value) to "value received."

Selling Plant Assets

Companies often sell plant assets when they restructure or downsize operations. To illustrate the accounting for selling plant assets, we consider BTO's March 31 sale of equipment that cost $16,000 and has accumulated depreciation of $12,000 at December 31 of the prior calendar year-end. Annual depreciation on this equipment is $4,000 computed using straight-line depreciation. Step 1 of this sale is to record depreciation expense and update accumulated depreciation to March 31 of the current year.

March 31	Depreciation Expense	1,000	
	Accumulated Depreciation—Equipment		1,000
	To record 3 months' depreciation ($4,000 × 3/12).		

Assets = Liabilities + Equity
−1,000   −1,000

Steps 2 through 4 of Exhibit 8.15 can be reflected in one final entry that depends on the amount received from the asset's sale. We consider three different possibilities.

Sale at Book Value   If BTO receives $3,000 cash, an amount equal to the equipment's book value as of March 31 (book value = $16,000 − $12,000 − $1,000), no gain or loss occurs on disposal. The entry is

March 31	Cash	3,000	
	Accumulated Depreciation—Equipment	13,000	
	Equipment		16,000
	To record sale of equipment for no gain or loss.		

Assets = Liabilities + Equity
+3,000
+13,000
−16,000

Sale above Book Value   If BTO receives $7,000, an amount that is $4,000 above the equipment's $3,000 book value as of March 31, a gain on disposal occurs. The entry is

March 31	Cash	7,000	
	Accumulated Depreciation—Equipment	13,000	
	Gain on Disposal of Equipment		4,000
	Equipment		16,000
	To record sale of equipment for a $4,000 gain.		

Assets = Liabilities + Equity
+7,000   +4,000
+13,000
−16,000

Sale below Book Value   If BTO receives $2,500, an amount that is $500 below the equipment's $3,000 book value as of March 31, a loss on disposal occurs. The entry is

March 31	Cash	2,500	
	Loss on Disposal of Equipment	500	
	Accumulated Depreciation—Equipment	13,000	
	Equipment		16,000
	To record sale of equipment for a $500 loss.		

Assets = Liabilities + Equity
+2,500   −500
+13,000
−16,000

IFRS

Unlike U.S. GAAP, IFRS requires an annual review of useful life and salvage value estimates. IFRS also permits revaluation of plant assets to market value if market value is reliably determined.

Quick Check

Answers—p. 358

8. Early in the fifth year of a machine's six-year useful life, it is overhauled, and its useful life is extended to nine years. This machine originally cost $108,000 and the overhaul cost is $12,000. Prepare the entry to record the overhaul cost.

9. Explain the difference between revenue expenditures and capital expenditures and how both are recorded.

10. What is a betterment? How is a betterment recorded?

11. A company acquires equipment on January 10, 2009, at a cost of $42,000. Straight-line depreciation is used with a five-year life and $7,000 salvage value. On June 27, 2010, the company sells this equipment for $32,000. Prepare the entry(ies) for June 27, 2010.

Section 2—Natural Resources

P5 Account for natural resource assets and their depletion.

Natural resources are assets that are physically consumed when used. Examples are standing timber, mineral deposits, and oil and gas fields. Since they are consumed when used, they are often called *wasting assets*. These assets represent soon-to-be inventories of raw materials that will be converted into one or more products by cutting, mining, or pumping. Until that conversion takes place, they are noncurrent assets and are shown in a balance sheet using titles such as timberlands, mineral deposits, or oil reserves. Natural resources are reported under either plant assets or its own separate category. **Alcoa**, for instance, reports its natural resources under the balance sheet title *Properties, plants and equipment*. In a note to its financial statements, Alcoa reports a separate amount for *Land and land rights, including mines*. **Weyerhaeuser**, on the other hand, reports its timber holdings in a separate balance sheet category titled *Timber and timberlands*.

Cost Determination and Depletion

Natural resources are recorded at cost, which includes all expenditures necessary to acquire the resource and prepare it for its intended use. **Depletion** is the process of allocating the cost of a natural resource to the period when it is consumed. Natural resources are reported on the balance sheet at cost less *accumulated depletion*. The depletion expense per period is usually based on units extracted from cutting, mining, or pumping. This is similar to units-of-production depreciation. **Exxon Mobil** uses this approach to amortize the costs of discovering and operating its oil wells.

To illustrate depletion of natural resources, let's consider a mineral deposit with an estimated 250,000 tons of available ore. It is purchased for $500,000, and we expect zero salvage value. The depletion charge per ton of ore mined is $2, computed as $500,000 ÷ 250,000 tons. If 85,000 tons are mined and sold in the first year, the depletion charge for that year is $170,000. These computations are detailed in Exhibit 8.16.

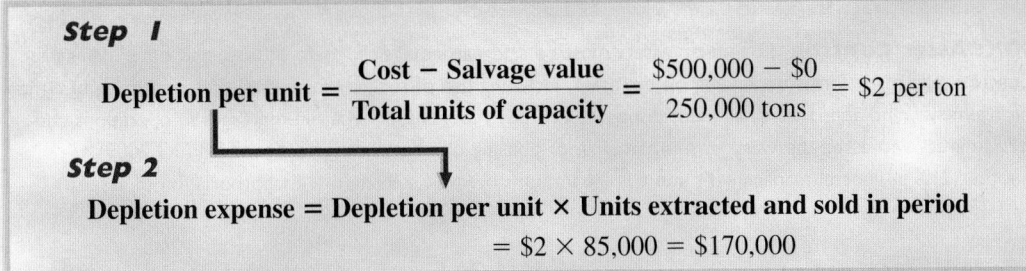

EXHIBIT 8.16

Depletion Formula and Example

Step 1

$$\text{Depletion per unit} = \frac{\text{Cost} - \text{Salvage value}}{\text{Total units of capacity}} = \frac{\$500,000 - \$0}{250,000 \text{ tons}} = \$2 \text{ per ton}$$

Step 2

Depletion expense = Depletion per unit × Units extracted and sold in period

$$= \$2 \times 85,000 = \$170,000$$

Depletion expense for the first year is recorded as follows.

Dec. 31	Depletion Expense—Mineral Deposit	170,000	
	Accumulated Depletion—Mineral Deposit		170,000
	To record depletion of the mineral deposit.		

Assets = Liabilities + Equity
−170,000   −170,000

The period-end balance sheet reports the mineral deposit as shown in Exhibit 8.17.

Mineral deposit	$500,000	
Less accumulated depletion	**170,000**	$330,000

EXHIBIT 8.17

Balance Sheet Presentation of Natural Resources

Since all 85,000 tons of the mined ore are sold during the year, the entire $170,000 of deple-tion is reported on the income statement. If some of the ore remains unsold at year-end, how-ever, the depletion related to the unsold ore is carried forward on the balance sheet and re-ported as Ore Inventory, a current asset. To illustrate, and continuing with our example, assume that 40,000 tons are mined in the second year, but only 34,000 tons are sold. We record deple-tion of $68,000 (34,000 tons × $2 depletion per unit) and the remaining Ore Inventory of $12,000 (6,000 tons × $2 depletion per unit) as follows.

Dec. 31	Depletion Expense—Mineral Deposit	68,000	
	Ore Inventory	12,000	
	Accumulated Depletion—Mineral Deposit		80,000
	To record depletion and inventory of mineral deposit.		

Assets = Liabilities + Equity
−80,000   −68,000
+12,000

Plant Assets Used in Extracting

The conversion of natural resources by mining, cutting, or pumping usually requires machin-ery, equipment, and buildings. When the usefulness of these plant assets is directly related to the depletion of a natural resource, their costs are depreciated using the units-of-production method in proportion to the depletion of the natural resource. For example, if a machine is per-manently installed in a mine and 10% of the ore is mined and sold in the period, then 10% of the machine's cost (less any salvage value) is allocated to depreciation expense. The same pro-cedure is used when a machine is abandoned once resources have been extracted. If, however, a machine will be moved to and used at another site when extraction is complete, the machine is depreciated over its own useful life.

Video8.1

Decision Insight ▮▮▮▮▮▮▮▮▮▮▮▮▮

SOX: Asset Control   Long-term assets must be safeguarded against theft, misuse, and other damages. Controls take many forms depending on the asset, including use of security tags, the legal monitoring of rights infringements, and approvals of all asset disposals. A study reports that 44% of employees in operations and service areas witnessed the wasting, mismanaging, or abusing of assets in the past year (KPMG 2009). Another 21% in general management and administration observed stealing or misappropriation of assets.

Section 3—Intangible Assets

P6   Account for intangible assets.

Intangible assets are nonphysical assets (used in operations) that confer on their owners long-term rights, privileges, or competitive advantages. Examples are patents, copyrights, licenses, leaseholds, franchises, goodwill, and trademarks. Lack of physical substance does not necessarily imply an intangible asset. Notes and accounts receivable, for instance, lack physical substance, but they are not intangibles. This section identifies the more common types of intangible assets and explains the accounting for them.

Cost Determination and Amortization

An intangible asset is recorded at cost when purchased. Intangibles are then separated into those with limited lives or indefinite lives. If an intangible has a **limited life,** its cost is systematically allocated to expense over its estimated useful life through the process of **amortization.** If an intangible asset has an **indefinite life**—meaning that no legal, regulatory, contractual, competitive, economic, or other factors limit its useful life—it should not be amortized. (If an intangible with an indefinite life is later judged to have a limited life, it is amortized over that limited life.) Amortization of intangible assets is similar to depreciation of plant assets and the depletion of natural resources in that it is a process of cost allocation. However, only the straight-line method is used for amortizing intangibles *unless* the company can show that another method is preferred. The effects of amortization are recorded in a contra account (Accumulated Amortization). The gross acquisition cost of intangible assets is disclosed in the balance sheet along with their accumulated amortization (these disclosures are new). The eventual disposal of an intangible asset involves removing its book value, recording any other asset(s) received or given up, and recognizing any gain or loss for the difference.

Point: The cost to acquire a Website address is an intangible asset.

Point: Goodwill is not amortized; instead, it is annually tested for impairment.

Many intangibles have limited lives due to laws, contracts, or other asset characteristics. Examples are patents, copyrights, and leaseholds. Other intangibles such as goodwill, trademarks, and trade names have lives that cannot be easily determined. The cost of intangible assets is amortized over the periods expected to benefit by their use, but in no case can this period be longer than the asset's legal existence. The values of some intangible assets such as goodwill continue indefinitely into the future and are not amortized. (An intangible asset that is not amortized is tested annually for **impairment**—if necessary, an impairment loss is recorded. Details for this test are in advanced courses.)

Intangible assets are often shown in a separate section of the balance sheet immediately after plant assets. **Callaway Golf**, for instance, follows this approach in reporting nearly $150 million of intangible assets in its balance sheet. Companies usually disclose their amortization periods for intangibles. The remainder of our discussion focuses on accounting for specific types of intangible assets.

Types of Intangibles

Patents   The federal government grants patents to encourage the invention of new technology, mechanical devices, and production processes. A **patent** is an exclusive right granted to its owner to manufacture and sell a patented item or to use a process for 20 years. When patent rights are purchased, the cost to acquire the rights is debited to an account called Patents. If the owner engages in lawsuits to successfully defend a patent, the cost of lawsuits is debited to the Patents account. However, the costs of research and development leading to a new patent are expensed when incurred.

A patent's cost is amortized over its estimated useful life (not to exceed 20 years). If we purchase a patent costing $25,000 with a useful life of 10 years, we make the following adjusting entry at the end of each of the 10 years to amortize one-tenth of its cost.

Dec. 31	Amortization Expense—Patents	2,500	
	Accumulated Amortization—Patents		2,500
	To amortize patent costs over its useful life.		

Assets = Liabilities + Equity
−2,500   −2,500

The $2,500 debit to Amortization Expense appears on the income statement as a cost of the product or service provided under protection of the patent. The Accumulated Amortization—Patents account is a contra asset account to Patents.

Decision Insight

Mention "drug war" and most people think of illegal drug trade. But another drug war is under way: Brand-name drugmakers are fighting to stop generic copies of their products from hitting the market once patents expire. Delaying a generic rival can yield millions in extra sales.

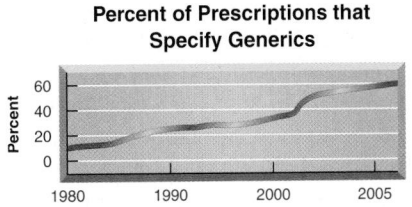

Percent of Prescriptions that Specify Generics

Copyrights   A **copyright** gives its owner the exclusive right to publish and sell a musical, literary, or artistic work during the life of the creator plus 70 years, although the useful life of most copyrights is much shorter. The costs of a copyright are amortized over its useful life. The only identifiable cost of many copyrights is the fee paid to the Copyright Office of the federal government or international agency granting the copyright. If this fee is immaterial, it is charged directly to an expense account, but if the identifiable costs of a copyright are material, they are capitalized (recorded in an asset account) and periodically amortized by debiting an account called Amortization Expense—Copyrights.

Franchises and Licenses   **Franchises** and **licenses** are rights that a company or government grants an entity to deliver a product or service under specified conditions. Many organizations grant franchise and license rights—**McDonald's**, **Pizza Hut**, and **Major League Baseball** are just a few examples. The costs of franchises and licenses are debited to a Franchises and Licenses asset account and are amortized over the lives of the agreements. If an agreement is for an indefinite or perpetual period, those costs are not amortized.

Trademarks and Trade Names   Companies often adopt unique symbols or select unique names and brands in marketing their products. A **trademark** or **trade (brand) name** is a symbol, name, phrase, or jingle identified with a company, product, or service. Examples are Nike swoosh, Marlboro Man, Big Mac, Coca-Cola, and Corvette. Ownership and exclusive right to use a trademark or trade name is often established by showing that one company used it before another. Ownership is best established by registering a trademark or trade name with the government's Patent Office. The cost of developing, maintaining, or enhancing the value of a trademark or trade name (such as advertising) is charged to expense when incurred. If a trademark or trade name is purchased, however, its cost is debited to an asset account and then amortized over its expected life. If the company plans to renew indefinitely its right to the trademark or trade name, the cost is not amortized.

Point: McDonald's "golden arches" is one of the world's most valuable trademarks, yet this asset is not shown on McDonald's balance sheet.

Goodwill   **Goodwill** has a specific meaning in accounting. Goodwill is the amount by which a company's value exceeds the value of its individual assets and liabilities. This usually implies that the company as a whole has certain valuable attributes not measured among its individual assets and liabilities. These can include superior management, skilled workforce, good supplier or customer relations, quality products or services, good location, or other competitive advantages.

Point: Amortization of goodwill is different for financial accounting and tax accounting. The IRS requires the amortization of goodwill over 15 years.

Example: Assume goodwill carries a book value of $500 and has an implied fair value of $475, *and* this $25 decline in value meets the 2-step impairment test. The entry to record this impairment is:

Impairment Loss $25
    Goodwill $25

To keep accounting information from being too subjective, goodwill is not recorded unless an entire company or business segment is purchased. Purchased goodwill is measured by taking the purchase price of the company and subtracting the market value of its individual net assets (excluding goodwill). For instance, **Yahoo!** paid nearly $3.0 billion to acquire **GeoCities**; about $2.8 of the $3.0 billion was for goodwill and other intangibles.

Goodwill is measured as the excess of the cost of an acquired entity over the value of the acquired net assets. Goodwill is recorded as an asset, and it is *not* amortized. Instead, goodwill is annually tested for impairment. If the book value of goodwill does not exceed its fair (market) value, goodwill is not impaired. However, if the book value of goodwill does exceed its fair value, an impairment loss is recorded equal to that excess. (Details of this test are in advanced courses.)

Leaseholds   Property is rented under a contract called a **lease.** The property's owner, called the **lessor,** grants the lease. The one who secures the right to possess and use the property is called the **lessee. A leasehold** refers to the rights the lessor grants to the lessee under the terms of the lease. A leasehold is an intangible asset for the lessee.

Certain leases require no advance payment from the lessee but require monthly rent payments. In this case, we do not set up a Leasehold account. Instead, the monthly payments are debited to a Rent Expense account. If a long-term lease requires the lessee to pay the final period's rent in advance when the lease is signed, the lessee records this advance payment with a debit to the Leasehold account. Since the advance payment is not used until the final period, the Leasehold account balance remains intact until that final period when its balance is transferred to Rent Expense. (Some long-term leases give the lessee essentially the same rights as a purchaser. This results in a tangible asset and a liability reported by the lessee. Chapter 10 describes these so-called *capital leases*.)

Point: A leasehold account implies existence of future benefits that the lessee controls because of a prepayment. It also meets the definition of an asset.

A long-term lease can increase in value when current rental rates for similar property rise while the required payments under the lease remain constant. This increase in value of a lease is not reported on the lessee's balance sheet. However, if the property is subleased and the new tenant makes a cash payment to the original lessee for the rights under the old lease, the new tenant debits this payment to a Leasehold account, which is amortized to Rent Expense over the remaining life of the lease.

Leasehold Improvements   A lessee sometimes pays for alterations or improvements to the leased property such as partitions, painting, and storefronts. These alterations and improvements are called **leasehold improvements,** and the lessee debits these costs to a Leasehold Improvements account. Since leasehold improvements become part of the property and revert to the lessor at the end of the lease, the lessee amortizes these costs over the life of the lease or the life of the improvements, whichever is shorter. The amortization entry debits Amortization Expense—Leasehold Improvements and credits Accumulated Amortization— Leasehold Improvements.

Other Intangibles   There are other types of intangible assets such as *software, noncompete covenants, customer lists,* and so forth. Our accounting for them is the same. First, we record the intangible asset's costs. Second, we determine whether the asset has a limited or indefinite life. If limited, we allocate its costs over that period. If indefinite, its costs are not amortized.

Quick Check   Answers—p. 358

12. Give an example of a natural resource and of an intangible asset.

13. A company pays $650,000 for an ore deposit. The deposit is estimated to have 325,000 tons of ore that will be mined over the next 10 years. During the first year, it mined, processed, and sold 91,000 tons. What is that year's depletion expense?

14. On January 6, 2011, a company pays $120,000 for a patent with a remaining 17-year legal life to produce a toy expected to be marketable for three years. Prepare entries to record its acquisition and the December 31, 2011, amortization entry.

Global View

This section discusses similarities and differences between U.S. GAAP and IFRS in accounting and reporting for plant assets and intangible assets.

Accounting for Plant Assets

Issues involving cost determination, depreciation, additional expenditures, and disposals of plant assets are subject to broadly similar guidance for both U.S. GAAP and IFRS. Although differences exist, the similarities vastly outweigh the differences. **GOME** describes its accounting for plant assets as follows:

> The cost of an item of property, plant and equipment comprises its purchase price and any directly attributable costs of bringing the asset to its working condition and location for its intended use. Expenditure incurred after items of property, plant and equipment have been put into operation, such as repairs and maintenance, is normally charged to the income statement in the period in which it is incurred. In situations where it can be clearly demonstrated that the expenditure has resulted in an increase in the future economic benefits expected to be obtained from the use of an item of property, plant and equipment, and where the cost of the item can be measured reliably, the expenditure is capitalised as an additional cost of that asset or as a replacement.

There is one area where notable differences exist, and that is in accounting for changes in the value of plant assets (between the time they are acquired and disposed of). Namely, how does IFRS and U.S. GAAP treat decreases and increases in the value of plant assets subsequent to acquisition?

Decreases in the Value of Plant Assets   When the value of plant assets declines after acquisition, but before disposition, both U.S. GAAP and IFRS require companies to record those decreases as *impairment losses*. While the *test for impairment* uses a different base between U.S. GAAP and IFRS, a more fundamental difference is that U.S. GAAP revalues impaired plant assets to *fair value* whereas IFRS revalues them to a *recoverable amount* (defined as fair value less costs to sell). **GOME** describes its accounting for decreases in the value of plant assets as follows:

> Where an indication of impairment exists . . . the asset's recoverable amount is estimated. An impairment loss is recognised only if the carrying amount of an asset exceeds its recoverable amount. An impairment loss is charged to the income statement in the period in which it arises. . . . An assessment is made at each reporting date as to whether there is any indication that previously recognised impairment losses may no longer exist or may have decreased.

Increases in the Value of Plant Assets   U.S. GAAP prohibits companies to record increases in the value of plant assets. However, IFRS permits upward *asset revaluations*. Namely, under IFRS, if an impairment was previously recorded, a company would reverse that impairment to the extent necessary and record that increase in income. If the increase is beyond the original cost, that increase is recorded in comprehensive income.

Accounting for Intangible Assets

For intangible assets, accounting for cost determination, depreciation, additional expenditures, and disposals of intangible assets is subject to broadly similar guidance for U.S. GAAP and IFRS. Although differences exist, the similarities vastly outweigh the differences. Again, and consistent with the accounting for plant assets, U.S. GAAP and IFRS handle decreases and increases in the value of intangible assets differently. However, IFRS requirements for recording increases in the value of intangible assets are so restrictive that such increases are rare. **GOME** describes its accounting for intangible assets as follows:

> The useful lives of intangible assets are assessed to be either finite or indefinite. Intangible assets with finite lives are amortised over the useful economic life and assessed for impairment whenever there is an indication that the intangible asset may be impaired. The amortisation period and the amortisation method for an intangible asset with a finite useful life are reviewed at least at each balance sheet date.

Decision Analysis — Total Asset Turnover

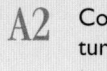

Compute total asset turnover and apply it to analyze a company's use of assets.

A company's assets are important in determining its ability to generate sales and earn income. Managers devote much attention to deciding what assets a company acquires, how much it invests in assets, and how to use assets most efficiently and effectively. One important measure of a company's ability to use its assets is **total asset turnover,** defined in Exhibit 8.18.

EXHIBIT 8.18

Total Asset Turnover

$$\text{Total asset turnover} = \frac{\text{Net sales}}{\text{Average total assets}}$$

The numerator reflects the net amounts earned from the sale of products and services. The denominator reflects the average total resources devoted to operating the company and generating sales.

To illustrate, let's look at total asset turnover in Exhibit 8.19 for two competing companies: **Molson Coors** and **Boston Beer.**

EXHIBIT 8.19

Analysis Using Total Asset Turnover

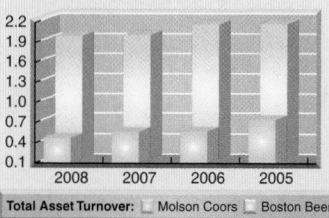

Total Asset Turnover: Molson Coors   Boston Beer

Company	Figure ($ millions)	2008	2007	2006	2005
Molson Coors	Net sales	$ 4,774.3	$ 6,190.6	$ 5,845.0	$ 5,506.9
	Average total assets	$11,934.1	$12,527.5	$11,701.4	$ 8,228.4
	Total asset turnover	0.40	0.49	0.50	0.67
Boston Beer	Net sales	$ 398.400	$ 341.647	$ 285.431	$238.304
	Average total assets	$ 208.856	$ 176.215	$ 136.765	$113.258
	Total asset turnover	1.91	1.94	2.09	2.10

Point: An estimate of **plant asset useful life** equals the plant asset cost divided by depreciation expense.

Point: The **plant asset age** is estimated by dividing accumulated depreciation by depreciation expense. Older plant assets can signal needed asset replacements; it may also signal less efficient assets.

To show how we use total asset turnover, let's look at Molson Coors. We express Molson Coors's use of assets in generating net sales by saying "it turned its assets over 0.40 times during 2008." This means that each $1.00 of assets produced $0.40 of net sales. Is a total asset turnover of 0.40 good or bad? It is safe to say that all companies desire a high total asset turnover. Like many ratio analyses, however, a company's total asset turnover must be interpreted in comparison with that of prior years and of its competitors. Interpreting the total asset turnover also requires an understanding of the company's operations. Some operations are capital intensive, meaning that a relatively large amount is invested in assets to generate sales. This suggests a relatively lower total asset turnover. Other companies' operations are labor intensive, meaning that they generate sales more by the efforts of people than the use of assets. In that case, we expect a higher total asset turnover. Companies with low total asset turnover require higher profit margins (examples are hotels and real estate); companies with high total asset turnover can succeed with lower profit margins; examples are food stores and toy merchandisers. Molson Coors's turnover recently declined, and is now much lower than that for Boston Beer and many other competitors. Total asset turnover for Molson Coors's competitors, available in industry publications such as Dun & Bradstreet, is generally in the range of 0.7 to 1.0 over this same period. Overall, Molson Coors must improve relative to its competitors on total asset turnover.

Decision Maker

Environmentalist A paper manufacturer claims it cannot afford more environmental controls. It points to its low total asset turnover of 1.9 and argues that it cannot compete with companies whose total asset turnover is much higher. Examples cited are food stores (5.5) and auto dealers (3.8). How do you respond? [Answer—p. 358]

Demonstration Problem

On July 14, 2009, Tulsa Company pays $600,000 to acquire a fully equipped factory. The purchase involves the following assets and information.

Asset	Appraised Value	Salvage Value	Useful Life	Depreciation Method
Land	$160,000			Not depreciated
Land improvements	80,000	$ 0	10 years	Straight-line
Building	320,000	100,000	10 years	Double-declining-balance
Machinery	240,000	20,000	10,000 units	Units-of-production*
Total	$800,000			

* The machinery is used to produce 700 units in 2009 and 1,800 units in 2010.

Required

1. Allocate the total $600,000 purchase cost among the separate assets.
2. Compute the 2009 (six months) and 2010 depreciation expense for each asset, and compute the company's total depreciation expense for both years.
3. On the last day of calendar year 2011, Tulsa discarded machinery that had been on its books for five years. The machinery's original cost was $12,000 (estimated life of five years) and its salvage value was $2,000. No depreciation had been recorded for the fifth year when the disposal occurred. Journalize the fifth year of depreciation (straight-line method) and the asset's disposal.
4. At the beginning of year 2011, Tulsa purchased a patent for $100,000 cash. The company estimated the patent's useful life to be 10 years. Journalize the patent acquisition and its amortization for the year 2011.
5. Late in the year 2011, Tulsa acquired an ore deposit for $600,000 cash. It added roads and built mine shafts for an additional cost of $80,000. Salvage value of the mine is estimated to be $20,000. The company estimated 330,000 tons of available ore. In year 2011, Tulsa mined and sold 10,000 tons of ore. Journalize the mine's acquisition and its first year's depletion.
6. AOn the first day of 2011, Tulsa exchanged the machinery that was acquired on July 14, 2009, along with $5,000 cash for machinery with a $210,000 market value. Journalize the exchange of these assets assuming the exchange lacked commercial substance. (Refer to background information in parts 1 and 2.)

Planning the Solution

- Complete a three-column table showing the following amounts for each asset: appraised value, percent of total value, and apportioned cost.
- Using allocated costs, compute depreciation for 2009 (only one-half year) and 2010 (full year) for each asset. Summarize those computations in a table showing total depreciation for each year.
- Remember that depreciation must be recorded up-to-date before discarding an asset. Calculate and record depreciation expense for the fifth year using the straight-line method. Since salvage value is not received at the end of a discarded asset's life, the amount of any salvage value becomes a loss on disposal. Record the loss on the disposal as well as the removal of the discarded asset and its related accumulated depreciation.
- Record the patent (an intangible asset) at its purchase price. Use straight-line amortization over its useful life to calculate amortization expense.
- Record the ore deposit (a natural resource asset) at its cost, including any added costs to ready the mine for use. Calculate depletion per ton using the depletion formula. Multiply the depletion per ton by the amount of tons mined and sold to calculate depletion expense for the year.
- Remember that gains and losses on asset exchanges that lack commercial substance are not recognized. Make a journal entry to add the acquired machinery to the books and to remove the old machinery, along with its accumulated depreciation, and to record the cash given in the exchange.

Solution to Demonstration Problem

1. Allocation of the total cost of $600,000 among the separate assets.

Asset	Appraised Value	Percent of Total Value	Apportioned Cost
Land	$160,000	20%	**$120,000** ($600,000 × 20%)
Land improvements	80,000	10	**60,000** ($600,000 × 10%)
Building	320,000	40	**240,000** ($600,000 × 40%)
Machinery	240,000	30	**180,000** ($600,000 × 30%)
Total	$800,000	100%	$ 600,000

2. Depreciation for each asset. (Land is not depreciated.)

Land Improvements

Cost	$ 60,000
Salvage value	0
Depreciable cost	$ 60,000
Useful life	10 years
Annual depreciation expense ($60,000/10 years)	$ 6,000
2009 depreciation ($6,000 × 6/12)	**$ 3,000**
2010 depreciation	**$ 6,000**

Building

Straight-line rate = 100%/10 years = 10%
Double-declining-balance rate = 10% × 2 = 20%

2009 depreciation ($240,000 × 20% × 6/12)	**$ 24,000**
2010 depreciation [($240,000 − $24,000) × 20%]	**$ 43,200**

Machinery

Cost	$ 180,000
Salvage value	20,000
Depreciable cost	$ 160,000
Total expected units of production	10,000 units
Depreciation per unit ($160,000/10,000 units)	$ 16
2009 depreciation ($16 × 700 units)	**$ 11,200**
2010 depreciation ($16 × 1,800 units)	**$ 28,800**

Total depreciation expense for each year:

	2009	2010
Land improvements	$ 3,000	$ 6,000
Building	24,000	43,200
Machinery	11,200	28,800
Total	$38,200	$78,000

3. Record the depreciation up to date on the discarded asset.

Depreciation Expense—Machinery	2,000	
Accumulated Depreciation—Machinery		2,000
To record depreciation on date of disposal: ($12,000 − $2,000)/5		

Record the removal of the discarded asset and its loss on disposal.

Accumulated Depreciation—Machinery	10,000	
Loss on Disposal of Machinery	2,000	
Machinery		12,000
To record the discarding of machinery with a $2,000 book value.		

4.

Patent	100,000	
Cash		100,000
To record patent acquisition.		

Amortization Expense—Patent	10,000	
Accumulated Amortization—Patent		10,000
To record amortization expense: $100,000/10 years = $10,000.		

5.

Ore Deposit	680,000	
Cash		680,000
To record ore deposit acquisition and its related costs.		

Depletion Expense—Ore Deposit	20,000	
Accumulated Depletion—Ore Deposit		20,000
To record depletion expense: ($680,000 − $20,000)/330,000 tons =		
$2 per ton. 10,000 tons mined and sold × $2 = $20,000 depletion.		

6. Record the asset exchange: The book value on the exchange date is $180,000 (cost) − $40,000 (accumulated depreciation). The book value of the machinery given up in the exchange ($140,000) plus the $5,000 cash paid is less than the $210,000 value of the machine acquired. The entry to record this exchange of assets that lacks commercial substance does not recognize the $65,000 "gain."

Machinery (new)	145,000*	
Accumulated Depreciation—Machinery (old)	40,000	
Machinery (old)		180,000
Cash		5,000
To record asset exchange that lacks commercial substance.		

* Market value of the acquired asset of $210,000 minus $65,000 "gain."

APPENDIX

Exchanging Plant Assets

8A

Many plant assets such as machinery, automobiles, and office equipment are disposed of by exchanging them for newer assets. In a typical exchange of plant assets, a *trade-in allowance* is received on the old asset and the balance is paid in cash. Accounting for the exchange of assets depends on whether the transaction has *commercial substance* (per *SFAS 153;* commercial substance implies that it alters the company's future cash flows). If an asset exchange has commercial substance, a gain or loss is recorded based on the difference between the book value of the asset(s) given up and the market value of the asset(s) received. If an asset exchange lacks commercial substance, no gain or loss is recorded, and the asset(s) received is recorded based on the book value of the asset(s) given up. An exchange has commercial substance if the company's future cash flows change as a result of the transaction. This section describes the accounting for the exchange of assets.

P7A Account for asset exchanges.

Exchange with Commercial Substance: A Loss   A company acquires $42,000 in new equipment. In exchange, the company pays $33,000 cash and trades in old equipment. The old equipment originally cost $36,000 and has accumulated depreciation of $20,000, which implies a $16,000 book value at the time of exchange. We are told this exchange has commercial substance and that the old equipment has a trade-in allowance of $9,000. This exchange yields a loss as computed in the middle (Loss) columns of Exhibit 8A.1; loss computed as Asset received − Assets given = $42,000 − $49,000 = $(7,000). We can also compute the loss as: Trade-in allowance − Book value of asset given = $9,000 − $16,000 = $(7,000).

EXHIBIT 8A.1

Computing Gain or Loss on Asset Exchange with Commercial Substance

Asset Exchange Has Commercial Substance		Loss		Gain
Market value of asset received		$ 42,000		$ 52,000
Book value of assets given:				
Equipment ($36,000 − $20,000)	$16,000		$16,000	
Cash	33,000	49,000	33,000	49,000
Gain (loss) on exchange		$(7,000)		$ 3,000

The entry to record this asset exchange is

Assets = Liabilities + Equity
+42,000   −7,000
+20,000
−36,000
−33,000

Jan. 3	Equipment (new)................................	42,000	
	Loss on Exchange of Assets	7,000	
	Accumulated Depreciation—Equipment (old)	20,000	
	Equipment (old).............................		36,000
	Cash		33,000
	To record exchange (with commercial substance) of old equipment and cash for new equipment.		

Point: Parenthetical notes to "new" and "old" equipment are for illustration only. Both the debit and credit are to the same Equipment account.

Exchange with Commercial Substance: A Gain   Let's assume the same facts as in the preceding asset exchange *except* that the new equipment received has a market value of $52,000 instead of $42,000. We are told this exchange has commercial substance and that the old equipment has a trade-in allowance of $19,000. This exchange yields a gain as computed in the right-most (Gain) columns of Exhibit 8A.1; gain computed as Asset received − Assets given = $52,000 − $49,000 = $3,000. We can also compute the gain as: Trade-in allowance − Book value of asset given = $19,000 − $16,000 = $3,000. The entry to record this asset exchange is

Assets = Liabilities + Equity
+52,000   +3,000
+20,000
−36,000
−33,000

Jan. 3	Equipment (new)................................	52,000	
	Accumulated Depreciation—Equipment (old)	20,000	
	Equipment (old).............................		36,000
	Cash		33,000
	Gain on Exchange of Assets..................		3,000
	To record exchange (with commercial substance) of old equipment and cash for new equipment.		

Exchanges without Commercial Substance   Let's assume the same facts as in the preceding asset exchange involving new equipment received with a market value of $52,000, but let's instead assume the transaction *lacks commercial substance*. The entry to record this asset exchange is

Assets = Liabilities + Equity
+49,000
+20,000
−36,000
−33,000

Jan. 3	Equipment (new)................................	49,000	
	Accumulated Depreciation—Equipment (old)	20,000	
	Equipment (old).............................		36,000
	Cash		33,000
	To record exchange (without commercial substance) of old equipment and cash for new equipment.		

Point: No gain or loss is recorded for exchanges *without* commercial substance.

The $3,000 gain recorded when the transaction has commercial substance is *not* recognized in this entry because of the rule prohibiting recording a gain or loss on asset exchanges without commercial substance. The $49,000 recorded for the new equipment equals its cash price ($52,000) less the unrecognized gain ($3,000) on the exchange. The $49,000 cost recorded is called the *cost basis* of the new machine. This cost basis is the amount we use to compute depreciation and its book value. The cost basis of the new asset also can be computed by summing the book values of the assets given up as shown in Exhibit 8A.2. The same analysis and approach is taken for a loss on an asset exchange without commercial substance.

EXHIBIT 8A.2

Cost Basis of New Asset when Gain Not Recorded on Asset Exchange without Commercial Substance

Cost of old equipment	$ 36,000
Less accumulated depreciation	20,000
Book value of old equipment	16,000
Cash paid in the exchange	33,000
Cost recorded for new equipment	**$49,000**

Quick Check

Answer—p. 358

15. A company trades an old Web server for a new one. The cost of the old server is $30,000, and its accumulated depreciation at the time of the trade is $23,400. The new server has a cash price of $45,000. Prepare entries to record the trade under two different assumptions where the company receives a trade-in allowance of (*a*) $3,000 and the exchange has commercial substance, and (*b*) $7,000 and the exchange lacks commercial substance.

Summary

C1   Describe plant assets and issues in accounting for them.
Plant assets are tangible assets used in the operations of a company and have a useful life of more than one accounting period. Plant assets are set apart from other tangible assets by two important features: use in operations and useful lives longer than one period. The four main accounting issues with plant assets are (1) computing their costs, (2) allocating their costs to the periods they benefit, (3) accounting for subsequent expenditures, and (4) recording their disposal.

C2   Explain depreciation and the factors affecting its computation. *Depreciation* is the process of allocating to expense the cost of a plant asset over the accounting periods that benefit from its use. Depreciation does not measure the decline in a plant asset's market value or its physical deterioration. Three factors determine depreciation: cost, salvage value, and useful life. Salvage value is an estimate of the asset's value at the end of its benefit period. Useful (service) life is the length of time an asset is productively used.

C3   Explain depreciation for partial years and changes in estimates. Partial-year depreciation is often required because assets are bought and sold throughout the year. Depreciation is revised when changes in estimates such as salvage value and useful life occur. If the useful life of a plant asset changes, for instance, the remaining cost to be depreciated is spread over the remaining (revised) useful life of the asset.

A1   Compare and analyze alternative depreciation methods.
The amount of depreciation expense per period is usually different for different methods, yet total depreciation expense over an asset's life is the same for all methods. Each method starts with the same total cost and ends with the same salvage value. The difference is in the pattern of depreciation expense over the asset's life. Common methods are straight-line, double-declining-balance, and units-of-production.

A2   Compute total asset turnover and apply it to analyze a company's use of assets. Total asset turnover measures a company's ability to use its assets to generate sales. It is defined as net sales divided by average total assets. While all companies desire a high total asset turnover, it must be interpreted in comparison with that for prior years and its competitors.

P1   Apply the cost principle to compute the cost of plant assets. Plant assets are recorded at cost when purchased. Cost includes all normal and reasonable expenditures necessary to get the asset in place and ready for its intended use. The cost of a lump-sum purchase is allocated among its individual assets.

P2   Compute and record depreciation using the straight-line, units-of-production, and declining-balance methods. The straight-line method divides cost less salvage value by the asset's useful life to determine depreciation expense per period. The units-of-production method divides cost less salvage value by the estimated number of units the asset will produce over its life to determine depreciation per unit. The declining-balance method multiplies the asset's beginning-of-period book value by a factor that is often double the straight-line rate.

P3   Distinguish between revenue and capital expenditures, and account for them. Revenue expenditures expire in the current period and are debited to expense accounts and matched with current revenues. Ordinary repairs are an example of revenue expenditures. Capital expenditures benefit future periods and are debited to asset accounts. Examples of capital expenditures are extraordinary repairs and betterments.

P4   Account for asset disposal through discarding or selling an asset. When a plant asset is discarded or sold, its cost and accumulated depreciation are removed from the accounts. Any cash proceeds from discarding or selling an asset are recorded and compared to the asset's book value to determine gain or loss.

P5   Account for natural resource assets and their depletion.
The cost of a natural resource is recorded in a noncurrent asset account. Depletion of a natural resource is recorded by allocating its cost to depletion expense using the units-of-production method. Depletion is credited to an Accumulated Depletion account.

P6   Account for intangible assets. An intangible asset is recorded at the cost incurred to purchase it. The cost of an intangible asset with a definite useful life is allocated to expense using the straight-line method, and is called *amortization*. Goodwill and intangible assets with an indefinite useful life are not amortized—they are annually tested for impairment. Intangible assets include patents, copyrights, leaseholds, goodwill, and trademarks.

P7A   Account for asset exchanges. For an asset exchange with commercial substance, a gain or loss is recorded based on the difference between the book value of the asset given up and the market value of the asset received. For an asset exchange without commercial substance, no gain or loss is recorded, and the asset received is recorded based on book value of the asset given up.

Guidance Answers to **Decision Maker** and **Decision Ethics**

Controller The president's instructions may reflect an honest and reasonable prediction of the future. Since the company is struggling financially, the president may have concluded that the normal pattern of replacing assets every three years cannot continue. Perhaps the strategy is to avoid costs of frequent replacements and stretch use of equipment a few years longer until financial conditions improve. However, if you believe the president's decision is unprincipled, you might confront the president with your opinion that it is unethical to change the estimate to increase income. Another possibility is to wait and see whether the auditor will prohibit this change in estimate. In either case, you should insist that the statements be based on reasonable estimates.

Entrepreneur Treating an expense as a capital expenditure means that reported expenses will be lower and income higher in the short run. This is so because a capital expenditure is not expensed immedi-

ately but is spread over the asset's useful life. Treating an expense as a capital expenditure also means that asset and equity totals are reported at larger amounts in the short run. This continues until the asset is fully depreciated. Your friend is probably trying to help, but the suggestion is misguided. Only an expenditure benefiting future periods is a capital expenditure.

Environmentalist The paper manufacturer's comparison of its total asset turnover with food stores and auto dealers is misdirected. These other industries' turnovers are higher because their profit margins are lower (about 2%). Profit margins for the paper industry are usually 3% to 3.5%. You need to collect data from competitors in the paper industry to show that a 1.9 total asset turnover is about the norm for this industry. You might also want to collect data on this company's revenues and expenses, along with compensation data for its high-ranking officers and employees.

Guidance Answers to **Quick Checks**

1. **a.** Supplies—current assets
   b. Office equipment—plant assets
   c. Inventory—current assets
   d. Land for future expansion—long-term investments
   e. Trucks used in operations—plant assets

2. **a.** Land   **b.** Land Improvements

3. $700,000 + $49,000 − $21,000 + $3,500
   + $3,000 + $2,500 = $737,000

4. **a.** Straight-line with 7-year life: ($77,000/7) = $11,000
   b. Straight-line with 10-year life: ($77,000/10) = $7,700

5. Depreciation is a process of allocating the cost of plant assets to the accounting periods that benefit from the assets' use.

6. **a.** Book value using straight-line depreciation:
   $96,000 − [($96,000 − $8,000)/5] = $78,400
   b. Book value using units of production:
   $96,000 − [($96,000 − $8,000) × (10,000/100,000)]
   = $87,200

7. ($3,800 − $200)/3 = $1,200 (original depreciation per year)
   $1,200 × 2 = $2,400 (accumulated depreciation)
   ($3,800 − $2,400)/2 = $700 (revised depreciation)

8.

Machinery	12,000	
Cash		12,000

9. A revenue expenditure benefits only the current period and should be charged to expense in the current period. A capital expenditure yields benefits that extend beyond the end of the current period and should be charged to an asset.

10. A betterment involves modifying an existing plant asset to make it more efficient, usually by replacing part of the asset with an improved or superior part. The cost of a betterment is debited to the asset account.

11.

Depreciation Expense	3,500	
Accumulated Depreciation		3,500
Cash	32,000	
Accumulated Depreciation	10,500	
Gain on Sale of Equipment		500
Equipment		42,000

12. Examples of natural resources are timberlands, mineral deposits, and oil reserves. Examples of intangible assets are patents, copyrights, leaseholds, leasehold improvements, goodwill, trademarks, and licenses.

13. ($650,000/325,000 tons) × 91,000 tons = $182,000

14.

Jan. 6	Patents	120,000	
	Cash		120,000
Dec. 31	Amortization Expense	40,000*	
	Accumulated Amortization—Patents		40,000

* $120,000/3 years = $40,000.

15.

(a)	Equipment (new)	45,000	
	Loss on Exchange of Assets	3,600	
	Accumulated Depreciation—Equipment (old)	23,400	
	Equipment (old)		30,000
	Cash ($45,000 − $3,000)		42,000
(b)	Equipment (new)*	44,600	
	Accumulated Depreciation—Equipment (old)	23,400	
	Equipment (old)		30,000
	Cash ($45,000 − $7,000)		38,000

* Includes $400 unrecognized gain.

Key Terms

Accelerated depreciation method (p. 338)	Impairment (pp. 342, 348)	Natural resources (p. 346)
Amortization (p. 348)	Inadequacy (p. 335)	Obsolescence (p. 335)
Asset book value (p. 337)	Indefinite life (p. 348)	Ordinary repairs (p. 343)
Betterments (p. 343)	Intangible assets (p. 348)	Patent (p. 348)
Capital expenditures (p. 342)	Land improvements (p. 334)	Plant assets (p. 332)
Change in an accounting estimate (p. 341)	Lease (p. 350)	Revenue expenditures (p. 342)
Copyright (p. 349)	Leasehold (p. 350)	Salvage value (p. 335)
Cost (pp. 333, 335)	Leasehold improvements (p. 350)	Straight-line depreciation (p. 336)
Declining-balance method (p. 338)	Lessee (p. 350)	Total asset turnover (p. 352)
Depletion (p. 346)	Lessor (p. 350)	Trademark or trade (brand) name (p. 349)
Depreciation (p. 335)	Licenses (p. 349)	
Extraordinary repairs (p. 343)	Limited life (p. 349)	Units-of-production depreciation (p. 337)
Franchises (p. 349)	Modified Accelerated Cost Recovery System (MACRS) (p. 340)	Useful life (p. 335)
Goodwill (p. 349)		

Multiple Choice Quiz   Answers on p. 373   mhhe.com/wildFA5e

Additional Quiz Questions are available at the book's Website.

1. A company paid $326,000 for property that included land, land improvements, and a building. The land was appraised at $175,000, the land improvements were appraised at $70,000, and the building was appraised at $105,000. What is the allocation of property costs to the three assets purchased?
  a. Land, $150,000; Land Improvements, $60,000; Building, $90,000
  b. Land, $163,000; Land Improvements, $65,200; Building, $97,800
  c. Land, $150,000; Land Improvements, $61,600; Building, $92,400
  d. Land, $159,000; Land Improvements, $65,200; Building, $95,400
  e. Land, $175,000; Land Improvements, $70,000; Building, $105,000

2. A company purchased a truck for $35,000 on January 1, 2009. The truck is estimated to have a useful life of four years and an estimated salvage value of $1,000. Assuming that the company uses straight-line depreciation, what is depreciation expense on the truck for the year ended December 31, 2010?
  a. $8,750
  b. $17,500
  c. $8,500
  d. $17,000
  e. $25,500

3. A company purchased machinery for $10,800,000 on January 1, 2009. The machinery has a useful life of 10 years

and an estimated salvage value of $800,000. What is depreciation expense on the machinery for the year ended December 31, 2010, assuming that the double-declining-balance method is used?
  a. $2,160,000
  b. $3,888,000
  c. $1,728,000
  d. $2,000,000
  e. $1,600,000

4. A company sold a machine that originally cost $250,000 for $120,000 when accumulated depreciation on the machine was $100,000. The gain or loss recorded on the sale of this machine is
  a. $0 gain or loss.
  b. $120,000 gain.
  c. $30,000 loss.
  d. $30,000 gain.
  e. $150,000 loss.

5. A company had average total assets of $500,000, gross sales of $575,000, and net sales of $550,000. The company's total asset turnover is
  a. 1.15
  b. 1.10
  c. 0.91
  d. 0.87
  e. 1.05

Superscript letter ᴬ *denotes assignments based on Appendix 8A.*

Discussion Questions

1. ♟ What characteristics of a plant asset make it different from other assets?
2. What is the general rule for cost inclusion for plant assets?
3. What is different between land and land improvements?
4. Why is the cost of a lump-sum purchase allocated to the individual assets acquired?
5. ♟ Does the balance in the Accumulated Depreciation—Machinery account represent funds to replace the machinery when it wears out? If not, what does it represent?
6. Why is the Modified Accelerated Cost Recovery System not generally accepted for financial accounting purposes?
7. ♟ What accounting concept justifies charging low-cost plant asset purchases immediately to an expense account?
8. What is the difference between ordinary repairs and extraordinary repairs? How should each be recorded?
9. ♟ Identify events that might lead to disposal of a plant asset.
10. What is the process of allocating the cost of natural resources to expense as they are used?
11. Is the declining-balance method an acceptable way to compute depletion of natural resources? Explain.
12. What are the characteristics of an intangible asset?

13. What general procedures are applied in accounting for the acquisition and potential cost allocation of intangible assets?
14. ♟ When do we know that a company has goodwill? When can goodwill appear in a company's balance sheet?
15. ♟ Assume that a company buys another business and pays for its goodwill. If the company plans to incur costs each year to maintain the value of the goodwill, must it also amortize this goodwill?
16. ♟ How is total asset turnover computed? Why would a financial statement user be interested in total asset turnover?
17. Refer to **Best Buy**'s balance sheet in Appendix A. What plant and equipment assets does Best Buy list on its balance sheet? What is the book value of its total plant and equipment assets at February 28, 2009?
18. **RadioShack** lists its plant assets as "Property, plant and equipment, net." What does "net" mean in this title?
19. ♟ Refer to **GOME**'s balance sheet in Appendix A. What does it title its plant assets? What is the book value of its plant assets at December 31, 2008?
20. Refer to the September 27, 2008, balance sheet of **Apple** in Appendix A. What long-term assets discussed in this chapter are reported by the company?

♟ **Denotes Discussion Questions that involve decision making.**

Available with Connect Accounting **connect**

QUICK STUDY

QS 8-1
Cost of plant assets
P1 ♟

Marlin Bowling installs automatic scorekeeping equipment with an invoice cost of $350,000. The electrical work required for the installation costs $10,000. Additional costs are $4,000 for delivery and $21,000 for sales tax. During the installation, a component of the equipment is carelessly left on a lane and hit by the automatic lane-cleaning machine. The cost of repairing the component is $4,200. What is the total recorded cost of the automatic scorekeeping equipment?

QS 8-2
Defining assets
C1 ♟

Identify the main difference between (1) plant assets and current assets, (2) plant assets and inventory, and (3) plant assets and long-term investments.

QS 8-3
Straight-line depreciation
P2

On January 2, 2011, the Deadra Band acquires sound equipment for concert performances at a cost of $32,500. The band estimates it will use this equipment for four years, during which time it anticipates performing about 200 concerts. It estimates that after four years it can sell the equipment for $2,500. During year 2011, the band performs 47 concerts. Compute the year 2011 depreciation using the straight-line method.

QS 8-4
Units-of-production depreciation
P2

Refer to the information in QS 8-3. Compute the year 2011 depreciation using the units-of-production method.

QS 8-5
Computing revised depreciation
C3

Refer to the facts in QS 8-3. Assume that Deadra Band uses straight-line depreciation but realizes at the start of the second year that due to concert bookings beyond expectations, this equipment will last only a total of three years. The salvage value remains unchanged. Compute the revised depreciation for both the second and third years.

A fleet of refrigerated delivery trucks is acquired on January 5, 2011, at a cost of $1,200,000 with an estimated useful life of eight years and an estimated salvage value of $100,000. Compute the depreciation expense for the first three years using the double-declining-balance method.

QS 8-6
Double-declining-balance method
P2

---

1. Classify the following as either a revenue or a capital expenditure.
  a. Paid $40,000 cash to replace a compressor on a refrigeration system that extends its useful life by four years.
  b. Paid $200 cash per truck for the cost of their annual tune-ups.
  c. Paid $175 for the monthly cost of replacement filters on an air-conditioning system.
  d. Completed an addition to an office building for $225,000 cash.
2. Prepare the journal entries to record transactions *a* and *d* of part 1.

QS 8-7
Revenue and capital expenditures
P3 ♟

Tresler Co. owns equipment that cost $92,500, with accumulated depreciation of $54,000. Tresler sells the equipment for cash. Record the sale of the equipment assuming Tresler sells the equipment for (1) $42,000 cash, (2) $38,500 cash, and (3) $31,000 cash.

QS 8-8
Disposal of assets
P4

Crandon Company acquires an ore mine at a cost of $6,300,000. It incurs additional costs of $500,000 to access the mine, which is estimated to hold 1,000,000 tons of ore. The estimated value of the land after the ore is removed is $900,000.
1. Prepare the entry(ies) to record the cost of the ore mine.
2. Prepare the year-end adjusting entry if 125,000 tons of ore are mined and sold the first year.

QS 8-9
Natural resources and depletion
P5

Which of the following assets are reported on the balance sheet as intangible assets? Which are reported as natural resources? (*a*) Oil well, (*b*) Trademark, (*c*) Leasehold, (*d*) Gold mine, (*e*) Building, (*f*) Copyright, (*g*) Franchise, (*h*) Timberland.

QS 8-10
Classify assets
P5 P6 ♟

On January 4 of this year, Brasen Boutique incurs a $275,000 cost to modernize its store. Improvements include new floors, ceilings, wiring, and wall coverings. These improvements are estimated to yield benefits for 10 years. Brasen leases its store and has eight years remaining on the lease. Prepare the entry to record (1) the cost of modernization and (2) amortization at the end of this current year.

QS 8-11
Intangible assets and amortization
P6

Camden Company reports the following ($ 000s): net sales of $14,880 for 2011 and $13,990 for 2010; end-of-year total assets of $15,869 for 2011 and $17,819 for 2010. Compute its total asset turnover for 2011, and assess its level if competitors average a total asset turnover of 2.0 times.

QS 8-12
Computing total asset turnover
A2 ♟

Gamma Co. owns a machine that costs $84,800 with accumulated depreciation of $36,800. Gamma exchanges the machine for a newer model that has a market value of $104,000. (1) Record the exchange assuming Gamma paid $60,000 cash and the exchange has commercial substance. (2) Record the exchange assuming Gamma pays $44,000 cash and the exchange lacks commercial substance.

QS 8-13^A
Asset exchange
P7

QS 8-13A
Asset exchange
P7

Answer each of the following related to international accounting standards.
a. Explain how the accounting for plant assets involving cost determination, depreciation, additional expenditures, and disposals is broadly different between IFRS and U.S. GAAP. Identify one notable difference between IFRS and U.S. GAAP in accounting for plant assets.
b. Describe how IFRS and U.S. GAAP treat increases in the value of plant assets subsequent to their acquisition (but before their disposition).

QS 8-14
International accounting standards
C1 C2

---

connect Available with Connect Accounting

Kruz Co. purchases a machine for $10,400, terms 1/10, n/60, FOB shipping point. The seller prepaid the $235 freight charges, adding the amount to the invoice and bringing its total to $10,635. The machine requires special steel mounting and power connections costing $719. Another $339 is paid to assemble the machine and get it into operation. In moving the machine to its steel mounting, $250 in damages occurred. Materials costing $40 are used in adjusting the machine to produce a satisfactory product. The adjustments are normal for this machine and are not the result of the damages. Compute the cost recorded for this machine. (Kruz pays for this machine within the cash discount period.)

EXERCISES

Exercise 8-1
Cost of plant assets
P1

Exercise 8-2
Recording costs of assets
C1 P1

Fisk Manufacturing purchases a large lot on which an old building is located as part of its plans to build a new plant. The negotiated purchase price is $209,000 for the lot plus $104,000 for the old building. The company pays $40,400 to tear down the old building and $59,722 to fill and level the lot. It also pays a total of $1,663,150 in construction costs—this amount consists of $1,564,400 for the new building and $98,750 for lighting and paving a parking area next to the building. Prepare a single journal entry to record these costs incurred by Fisk, all of which are paid in cash.

Exercise 8-3
Lump-sum purchase
of plant assets   C1

Dillon Company pays $404,000 for real estate plus $21,500 in closing costs. The real estate consists of land appraised at $217,140; land improvements appraised at $83,160; and a building appraised at $161,700. Allocate the total cost among the three purchased assets and prepare the journal entry to record the purchase.

Exercise 8-4
Straight-line depreciation
P2

In early January 2009, Sanchez Builders purchases equipment for $102,000 to use in operating activities for the next five years. It estimates the equipment's salvage value at $21,000. Prepare a table showing depreciation and book value for each of the five years assuming straight-line depreciation.

Exercise 8-5
Double-declining-balance
P2

Refer to the information in Exercise 8-4. Prepare a table showing depreciation and book value for each of the five years assuming double-declining-balance depreciation.

Exercise 8-6
Straight-line depreciation
P2

Sarita Company installs a computerized manufacturing machine in its factory at the beginning of the year at a cost of $67,000. The machine's useful life is estimated at 10 years, or 420,000 units of product, with a $4,000 salvage value. During its second year, the machine produces 29,900 units of product. Determine the machine's second-year depreciation under the straight-line method.

Exercise 8-7
Units-of-production
P2

Refer to the information in Exercise 8-6. Determine the machine's second-year depreciation using the units-of-production method.

Exercise 8-8
Double-declining-balance
P2

Refer to the information in Exercise 8-6. Determine the machine's second-year depreciation using the double-declining-balance method.

Exercise 8-9
Straight-line; partial year
depreciation   C3

On April 1, 2010, Bricen Backhoe Co. purchases a trencher for $253,000. The machine is expected to last five years and have a salvage value of $25,300. Compute depreciation expense for year 2011 assuming the company uses the straight-line method.

Exercise 8-10
Double-declining-balance;
partial year depreciation   C3

Refer to the information in Exercise 8-9. Compute depreciation expense for year 2011 assuming the company uses the double-declining-balance method.

Exercise 8-11
Revising depreciation
C3

Check   (2) $4,200

Siness Fitness Club uses straight-line depreciation for a machine costing $26,400, with an estimated four-year life and a $2,900 salvage value. At the beginning of the third year, Siness determines that the machine has three more years of remaining useful life, after which it will have an estimated $2,050 salvage value. Compute (1) the machine's book value at the end of its second year and (2) the amount of depreciation for each of the final three years given the revised estimates.

Exercise 8-12
Straight-line depreciation and
income effects

A1

Echo Enterprises pays $274,900 for equipment that will last five years and have a $41,000 salvage value. By using the equipment in its operations for five years, the company expects to earn $86,800 annually, after deducting all expenses except depreciation. Prepare a table showing income before depreciation, depreciation expense, and net (pretax) income for each year and for the total five-year period, assuming straight-line depreciation.

Refer to the information in Exercise 8-12. Prepare a table showing income before depreciation, depreciation expense, and net (pretax) income for each year and for the total five-year period, assuming double-declining-balance depreciation is used.

Exercise 8-13
Double-declining-balance
A1

Check Year 3 NI, $47,214

Horizon Company owns a building that appears on its prior year-end balance sheet at its original $620,000 cost less $496,000 accumulated depreciation. The building is depreciated on a straight-line basis assuming a 20-year life and no salvage value. During the first week in January of the current calendar year, major structural repairs are completed on the building at a $74,000 cost. The repairs extend its useful life for 7 years beyond the 20 years originally estimated.

1. Determine the building's age (plant asset age) as of the prior year-end balance sheet date.
2. Prepare the entry to record the cost of the structural repairs that are paid in cash.
3. Determine the book value of the building immediately after the repairs are recorded.
4. Prepare the entry to record the current calendar year's depreciation.

Exercise 8-14
Extraordinary repairs;
plant asset age
P3

Check (3) $198,000

Bera Company pays $264,900 for equipment expected to last four years and have a $30,000 salvage value. Prepare journal entries to record the following costs related to the equipment.

1. During the second year of the equipment's life, $29,500 cash is paid for a new component expected to increase the equipment's productivity by 10% a year.
2. During the third year, $7,375 cash is paid for normal repairs necessary to keep the equipment in good working order.
3. During the fourth year, $22,450 is paid for repairs expected to increase the useful life of the equipment from four to five years.

Exercise 8-15
Ordinary repairs, extraordinary
repairs and betterments
P3

Sydney Company owns a milling machine that cost $250,000 and has accumulated depreciation of $182,000. Prepare the entry to record the disposal of the milling machine on January 3 under each of the following independent situations.

1. The machine needed extensive repairs, and it was not worth repairing. Sydney disposed of the machine, receiving nothing in return.
2. Sydney sold the machine for $35,000 cash.
3. Sydney sold the machine for $68,000 cash.
4. Sydney sold the machine for $80,000 cash.

Exercise 8-16
Disposal of assets
P4

Rayya Co. purchases and installs a machine on January 1, 2009, at a total cost of $94,000. Straight-line depreciation is taken each year for four years assuming an eight-year life and no salvage value. The machine is disposed of on July 1, 2013, during its fifth year of service. Prepare entries to record the partial year's depreciation on July 1, 2013, and to record the disposal under the following separate assumptions: (1) the machine is sold for $43,593 cash and (2) Rayya receives an insurance settlement of $39,480 resulting from the total destruction of the machine in a fire.

Exercise 8-17
Partial year depreciation; disposal
of plant asset
P4

On April 2, 2011, Mitzu Mining Co. pays $3,920,000 for an ore deposit containing 1,400,000 tons. The company installs machinery in the mine costing $210,000, with an estimated seven-year life and no salvage value. The machinery will be abandoned when the ore is completely mined. Mitzu began mining on May 1, 2011, and mined and sold 178,200 tons of ore during the remaining eight months of 2011. Prepare the December 31, 2011, entries to record both the ore deposit depletion and the mining machinery depreciation. Mining machinery depreciation should be in proportion to the mine's depletion.

Exercise 8-18
Depletion of natural resources
P2 P5

Galvano Gallery purchases the copyright on an oil painting for $432,000 on January 1, 2011. The copyright legally protects its owner for 19 more years. However, the company plans to market and sell prints of the original for only 15 years. Prepare entries to record the purchase of the copyright on January 1, 2011, and its annual amortization on December 31, 2011.

Exercise 8-19
Amortization of intangible assets
P6

Exercise 8-20
Goodwill

P6

On January 1, 2011, Jeffrey Company purchased Perrow Company at a price of $2,500,000. The fair market value of the net assets purchased equals $1,800,000.

1. What is the amount of goodwill that Jeffrey records at the purchase date?

2. Explain how Jeffrey would determine the amount of goodwill amortization for the year ended December 31, 2011?

3. Jeffrey Company believes that its employees provide superior customer services, and through their efforts, Jeffrey Company believes it has created $900,000 of goodwill. How would Jeffrey Company record this goodwill?

Exercise 8-21
Cash flows related to assets

C1

Refer to the statement of cash flows for **RadioShack** in Appendix A for the year ended December 31, 2008, to answer the following.

1. What amount of cash is used to purchase property, plant, and equipment?

2. How much depreciation and amortization are recorded?

3. What total amount of net cash is used in investing activities?

Exercise 8-22
Evaluating efficient use of assets

A2

Teridan Co. reports net sales of $4,796,000 for 2010 and $8,758,000 for 2011. End-of-year balances for total assets are: 2009, $1,578,000; 2010, $1,824,000; and 2011, $1,946,000. (*a*) Compute Teridan's total asset turnover for 2010 and 2011. (*b*) Comment on Teridan's efficiency in using its assets if its competitors average a total asset turnover of 3.0.

Exercise 8-23^A

Exercise 8-23^A
Exchanging assets

P7

Corin Construction trades in an old tractor for a new tractor, receiving a $24,500 trade-in allowance and paying the remaining $71,750 in cash. The old tractor had cost $83,000, and straight-line accumulated depreciation of $45,000 had been recorded to date under the assumption that it would last eight years and have an $11,000 salvage value. Answer the following questions assuming the exchange has commercial substance.

1. What is the book value of the old tractor at the time of exchange?

Check (2) $13,500

2. What is the loss on this asset exchange?

3. What amount should be recorded (debited) in the asset account for the new tractor?

Exercise 8-24^A
Recording plant asset disposals

P4 P7

Check (2) Dr. Machinery (new), $68,120

On January 2, 2011, Bering Co. disposes of a machine costing $52,400 with accumulated depreciation of $28,227. Prepare the entries to record the disposal under each of the following separate assumptions.

1. Machine is sold for $20,274 cash.

2. Machine is traded in on a newer machine having a $68,900 cash price. A $24,953 trade-in allowance is received, and the balance is paid in cash. Assume the asset exchange lacks commercial substance.

3. Machine is traded in on a newer machine having a $68,900 cash price. An $18,714 trade-in allowance is received, and the balance is paid in cash. Assume the asset exchange has commercial substance.

Exercise 8-25
Accounting for plant assets under IFRS

P2 P3 P4

Volkswagen Group reports the following information for property, plant and equipment as of December 31, 2008, along with additions, disposals, depreciation, and impairments for the year ended December 31, 2008 (euros in millions):

Property, plant and equipment, net	€23,121
Additions to property, plant and equipment	6,651
Disposals of property, plant and equipment	2,322
Depreciation on property, plant and equipment	4,625
Impairments to property, plant and equipment	184

1. Prepare Volkswagen's journal entry to record its depreciation for 2008.

2. Prepare Volkswagen's journal entry to record its additions for 2008 assuming they are paid in cash and are treated as "betterments (improvements)" to the assets.

3. Prepare Volkswagen's journal entry to record its €2,322 in disposals for 2008 assuming it receives €700 cash in return and the accumulated depreciation on the disposed assets totals €1,322.

4. Volkswagen reports €184 of impairments. Do these impairments increase or decrease the property, plant and equipment account? And, by what amount?

Available with Connect Accounting

Teness Construction negotiates a lump-sum purchase of several assets from a company that is going out of business. The purchase is completed on January 1, 2011, at a total cash price of $900,000 for a building, land, land improvements, and four vehicles. The estimated market values of the assets are building, $514,250; land, $271,150; land improvements, $65,450; and four vehicles, $84,150. The company's fiscal year ends on December 31.

Required

1. Prepare a table to allocate the lump-sum purchase price to the separate assets purchased. Prepare the journal entry to record the purchase.
2. Compute the depreciation expense for year 2011 on the building using the straight-line method, assuming a 15-year life and a $30,000 salvage value.
3. Compute the depreciation expense for year 2011 on the land improvements assuming a five-year life and double-declining-balance depreciation.

Analysis Component

4. Defend or refute this statement: Accelerated depreciation results in payment of less taxes over the asset's life.

PROBLEM SET A

Problem 8-1A
Plant asset costs;
depreciation methods

C1 C2 A1 P1 P2

mhhe.com/wildFA5e

Check (2) $31,000
(3) $25,200

In January 2011, Solaris Co. pays $2,650,000 for a tract of land with two buildings on it. It plans to demolish Building 1 and build a new store in its place. Building 2 will be a company office; it is appraised at $692,530, with a useful life of 20 years and an $85,000 salvage value. A lighted parking lot near Building 1 has improvements (Land Improvements 1) valued at $451,650 that are expected to last another 12 years with no salvage value. Without the buildings and improvements, the tract of land is valued at $1,866,820. Solaris also incurs the following additional costs:

Cost to demolish Building 1	$ 342,400
Cost of additional land grading	193,400
Cost to construct new building (Building 3), having a useful life of 25 years and a $400,000 salvage value	2,282,000
Cost of new land improvements (Land Improvements 2) near Building 2 having a 20-year useful life and no salvage value	168,000

Required

1. Prepare a table with the following column headings: Land, Building 2, Building 3, Land Improvements 1, and Land Improvements 2. Allocate the costs incurred by Solaris to the appropriate columns and total each column.
2. Prepare a single journal entry to record all the incurred costs assuming they are paid in cash on January 1, 2011.
3. Using the straight-line method, prepare the December 31 adjusting entries to record depreciation for the 12 months of 2011 when these assets were in use.

Problem 8-2A
Asset cost allocation;
straight-line depreciation

C1 C2 P1 P2

mhhe.com/wildFA5e

Check (1) Land costs, $2,178,800;
Building 2 costs, $609,500

(3) Depr. Exp.—Land Improv.
1 and 2, $33,125 and $8,400

Maxil Contractors completed the following transactions and events involving the purchase and operation of equipment in its business.

2010

Jan. 1 Paid $293,660 cash plus $11,740 in sales tax and $1,500 in transportation (FOB shipping point) for a new loader. The loader is estimated to have a four-year life and a $36,000 salvage value. Loader costs are recorded in the Equipment account.

Jan. 3 Paid $5,100 to enclose the cab and install air conditioning in the loader to enable operations under harsher conditions. This increased the estimated salvage value of the loader by another $1,000.

Dec. 31 Recorded annual straight-line depreciation on the loader.

2011

Jan. 1 Paid $4,500 to overhaul the loader's engine, which increased the loader's estimated useful life by two years.

Feb. 17 Paid $1,125 to repair the loader after the operator backs it into a tree.

Dec. 31 Recorded annual straight-line depreciation on the loader.

Problem 8-3A
Computing and revising
depreciation; revenue and
capital expenditures

C3 P1 P3

Check Dec. 31, 2010, Dr. Depr.
Expense—Equip., $68,750

Check Dec. 31, 2011, Dr. Depr.
Expense—Equip., $42,150

Required

Prepare journal entries to record these transactions and events.

Problem 8-4A
Computing and revising depreciation; selling plant assets

C3 P2 P4

Dakota Company completed the following transactions and events involving its delivery trucks.

2010

Jan. 1 Paid $25,015 cash plus $1,485 in sales tax for a new delivery truck estimated to have a five-year life and a $2,000 salvage value. Delivery truck costs are recorded in the Trucks account.
Dec. 31 Recorded annual straight-line depreciation on the truck.

2011

Check Dec. 31, 2011, Dr. Depr. Expense—Trucks, $6,300

Dec. 31 Due to new information obtained earlier in the year, the truck's estimated useful life was changed from five to four years, and the estimated salvage value was increased to $2,700. Recorded annual straight-line depreciation on the truck.

2012

Dec. 31, 2012, Dr. Loss on Disposal of Trucks, $3,400

Dec. 31 Recorded annual straight-line depreciation on the truck.
Dec. 31 Sold the truck for $5,600 cash.

Required

Prepare journal entries to record these transactions and events.

Problem 8-5A
Depreciation methods

A1 P2

A machine costing $320,000 with a four-year life and an estimated $33,000 salvage value is installed in Luther Company's factory on January 1. The factory manager estimates the machine will produce 512,500 units of product during its life. It actually produces the following units: year 1, 127,500; year 2, 129,000; year 3, 128,500; and year 4, 127,900. The total number of units produced by the end of year 4 exceeds the original estimate—this difference was not predicted. (The machine must not be depreciated below its estimated salvage value.)

Required

Prepare a table with the following column headings and compute depreciation for each year (and total depreciation of all years combined) for the machine under each depreciation method.

Check Year 4: Units-of-Production Depreciation, $71,400; DDB Depreciation, $7,000

Year	Straight-Line	Units-of-Production	Double-Declining-Balance

---

Problem 8-6A
Disposal of plant assets

P1 P2 P4

Platero Co. purchases a used machine for $198,750 cash on January 2 and readies it for use the next day at an $11,000 cost. On January 3, it is installed on a required operating platform costing $3,410, and it is further readied for operations. The company predicts the machine will be used for six years and have a $16,960 salvage value. Depreciation is to be charged on a straight-line basis. On December 31, at the end of its fifth year in operations, it is disposed of.

Required

1. Prepare journal entries to record the machine's purchase and the costs to ready and install it. Cash is paid for all costs incurred.

Check (2b) Depr. Exp., $32,700

2. Prepare journal entries to record depreciation of the machine at December 31 of (a) its first year in operations and (b) the year of its disposal.

3. Prepare journal entries to record the machine's disposal under each of the following separate assumptions: (a) it is sold for $21,000 cash; (b) it is sold for $73,500 cash; and (c) it is destroyed in a fire and the insurance company pays $31,500 cash to settle the loss claim.

(3c) Dr. Loss from Fire, $18,160

Problem 8-7A
Natural resources

P5

On July 23 of the current year, Serena Mining Co. pays $4,612,500 for land estimated to contain 5,125,000 tons of recoverable ore. It installs machinery costing $512,500 that has a 10-year life and no salvage value and is capable of mining the ore deposit in eight years. The machinery is paid for on July 25, seven days before mining operations begin. The company removes and sells 490,000 tons of ore during its first five months of operations ending on December 31. Depreciation of the machinery is in proportion to the mine's depletion as the machinery will be abandoned after the ore is mined.

Required

Prepare entries to record (*a*) the purchase of the land, (*b*) the cost and installation of machinery, (*c*) the first five months' depletion assuming the land has a net salvage value of zero after the ore is mined, and (*d*) the first five months' depreciation on machinery.

Check (*c*) Depletion, $441,000
(*d*) Depreciation, $49,000

Analysis Component

Describe both the similarities and differences in amortization, depletion, and depreciation.

On July 1, 2006, Harper Company signed a contract to lease space in a building for 15 years. The lease contract calls for annual (prepaid) rental payments of $80,000 on each July 1 throughout the life of the lease and for the lessee to pay for all additions and improvements to the leased property. On June 25, 2011, Harper decides to sublease the space to Bosio & Associates for the remaining 10 years of the lease—Bosio pays $260,000 to Harper for the right to sublease and it agrees to assume the obligation to pay the $80,000 annual rent to the building owner beginning July 1, 2011. After taking possession of the leased space, Bosio pays for improving the office portion of the leased space at a $160,000 cost. The improvements are paid for by Bosio on July 5, 2011, and are estimated to have a useful life equal to the 16 years remaining in the life of the building.

Problem 8-8A
Intangible assets

P6

Required

1. Prepare entries for Bosio to record (*a*) its payment to Harper for the right to sublease the building space, (*b*) its payment of the 2011 annual rent to the building owner, and (*c*) its payment for the office improvements.

2. Prepare Bosio's year-end adjusting entries required at December 31, 2011, to (*a*) amortize the $260,000 cost of the sublease, (*b*) amortize the office improvements, and (*c*) record rent expense.

Check Dr. Rent Expense for:
(*2a*) $13,000, (*2c*) $40,000

Clinton Company negotiates a lump-sum purchase of several assets from a contractor who is relocating. The purchase is completed on January 1, 2011, at a total cash price of $930,000 for a building, land, land improvements, and four trucks. The estimated market values of the assets are building, $469,200; land, $303,600; land improvements, $36,800; and four trucks, $110,400. The company's fiscal year ends on December 31.

PROBLEM SET B

Problem 8-1B
Plant asset costs;
depreciation methods

C1 C2 A1 P1 P2

Required

1. Prepare a table to allocate the lump-sum purchase price to the separate assets purchased. Prepare the journal entry to record the purchase.

2. Compute the depreciation expense for year 2011 on the building using the straight-line method, assuming a 15-year life and a $30,000 salvage value.

3. Compute the depreciation expense for year 2011 on the land improvements assuming a 5-year life and double-declining-balance depreciation.

Check (2) $29,620

(3) $14,880

Analysis Component

4. Defend or refute this statement: Accelerated depreciation results in payment of more taxes over the asset's life.

In January 2011, Boulware Co. pays $2,750,000 for a tract of land with two buildings. It plans to demolish Building A and build a new shop in its place. Building B will be a company office; it is appraised at $687,700, with a useful life of 20 years and an $85,000 salvage value. A lighted parking lot near Building B has improvements (Land Improvements B) valued at $478,400 that are expected to last another 10 years with no salvage value. Without the buildings and improvements, the tract of land is valued at $1,823,900. Boulware also incurs the following additional costs.

Problem 8-2B
Asset cost allocation;
straight-line depreciation

C1 C2 P1 P2

Cost to demolish Building A	$ 345,400
Cost of additional land grading	185,400
Cost to construct new building (Building C), having a useful life of 25 years and a $400,000 salvage value	2,282,000
Cost of new land improvements (Land Improvements C) near Building C, having a 20-year useful life and no salvage value	173,000

Required

1. Prepare a table with the following column headings: Land, Building B, Building C, Land Improvements B, and Land Improvements C. Allocate the costs incurred by Boulware to the appropriate columns and total each column.

2. Prepare a single journal entry to record all incurred costs assuming they are paid in cash on January 1, 2011.

3. Using the straight-line method, prepare the December 31 adjusting entries to record depreciation for the 12 months of 2011 when these assets were in use.

Problem 8-3B
Computing and revising depreciation; revenue and capital expenditures

C3 P1 P3

Zander Delivery Service completed the following transactions and events involving the purchase and operation of equipment for its business.

2010

Jan. 1 Paid $58,000 cash plus $4,000 in sales tax for a new delivery van that was estimated to have a four-year life and a $3,000 salvage value. Van costs are recorded in the Equipment account.

Jan. 3 Paid $2,900 to install sorting racks in the van for more accurate and quicker delivery of packages. This increases the estimated salvage value of the van by another $200.

Dec. 31 Recorded annual straight-line depreciation on the van.

2011

Jan. 1 Paid $4,300 to overhaul the van's engine, which increased the van's estimated useful life by two years.

May 10 Paid $1,075 to repair the van after the driver backed it into a loading dock.

Dec. 31 Record annual straight-line depreciation on the van. (Round to the nearest dollar.)

Required

Prepare journal entries to record these transactions and events.

Problem 8-4B
Computing and revising depreciation; selling plant assets

C3 P2 P4

Walsh Instruments completed the following transactions and events involving its machinery.

2010

Jan. 1 Paid $20,515 cash plus $1,485 in sales tax for a new machine. The machine is estimated to have a five-year life and a $2,000 salvage value.

Dec. 31 Recorded annual straight-line depreciation on the machinery.

2011

Dec. 31 Due to new information obtained earlier in the year, the machine's estimated useful life was changed from five to four years, and the estimated salvage value was increased to $2,550. Recorded annual straight-line depreciation on the machinery.

2012

Dec. 31 Recorded annual straight-line depreciation on the machinery.
Dec. 31 Sold the machine for $5,600 cash.

Required

Prepare journal entries to record these transactions and events.

Problem 8-5B
Depreciation methods

A1 P2

On January 2, Gillette Co. purchases and installs a new machine costing $360,000 with a five-year life and an estimated $33,000 salvage value. Management estimates the machine will produce 2,180,000 units of product during its life. Actual production of units is as follows: year 1, 425,000; year 2, 452,000; year 3, 445,000; year 4, 438,000; and year 5, 441,000. The total number of units produced by the end of year 5 exceeds the original estimate—this difference was not predicted. (The machine must not be depreciated below its estimated salvage value.)

Required

Prepare a table with the following column headings and compute depreciation for each year (and total depreciation of all years combined) for the machine under each depreciation method.

Year	Straight-Line	Units-of-Production	Double-Declining-Balance

Check   DDB Depreciation, Year 3, $51,840; U-of-P Depreciation, Year 4, $65,700

On January 1, Ammons purchases a used machine for $238,500 and readies it for use the next day at a cost of $11,000. On January 4, it is mounted on a required operating platform costing $3,600, and it is further readied for operations. Management estimates the machine will be used for six years and have a $22,100 salvage value. Depreciation is to be charged on a straight-line basis. On December 31, at the end of its fifth year of use, the machine is disposed of.

Problem 8-6B
Disposal of plant assets

P1   P2   P4

Required

1. Prepare journal entries to record the machine's purchase and the costs to ready and install it. Cash is paid for all costs incurred.
2. Prepare journal entries to record depreciation of the machine at December 31 of (*a*) its first year in operations and, (*b*) the year of its disposal.
3. Prepare journal entries to record the machine's disposal under each of the following separate assumptions: (*a*) it is sold for $20,500 cash; (*b*) it is sold for $71,750 cash; and (*c*) it is destroyed in a fire and the insurance company pays $31,000 cash to settle the loss claim.

Check   (2*b*) Depr. Exp., $38,500

(3*c*) Dr. Loss from Fire, $29,600

On February 19 of the current year, Javier Co. pays $6,000,000 for land estimated to contain 4 million tons of recoverable ore. It installs machinery costing $480,000 that has a 16-year life and no salvage value and is capable of mining the ore deposit in 12 years. The machinery is paid for on March 21, seven days before mining operations begin. The company removes and sells 380,000 tons of ore during its first nine months of operations ending on December 31. Depreciation of the machinery is in proportion to the mine's depletion as the machinery will be abandoned after the ore is mined.

Problem 8-7B
Natural resources

P5

Required

Prepare entries to record (*a*) the purchase of the land, (*b*) the cost and installation of machinery, (*c*) the first nine months' depletion assuming the land has a net salvage value of zero after the ore is mined, and (*d*) the first nine months' depreciation on machinery.

Check   (*c*) Depletion, $570,000; (*d*) Depreciation, $45,600

Analysis Component

Describe both the similarities and differences in amortization, depletion, and depreciation.

On January 1, 2004, Palos Co. entered into a 12-year lease on a building. The lease contract requires (1) annual (prepaid) rental payments of $90,000 each January 1 throughout the life of the lease and (2) for the lessee to pay for all additions and improvements to the leased property. On January 1, 2011, Palos decides to sublease the space to Callahan Co. for the remaining five years of the lease—Callahan pays $200,000 to Palos for the right to sublease and agrees to assume the obligation to pay the $90,000 annual rent to the building owner beginning January 1, 2011. After taking possession of the leased space, Callahan pays for improving the office portion of the leased space at a $150,000 cost. The improvements are paid for by Callahan on January 3, 2011, and are estimated to have a useful life equal to the 13 years remaining in the life of the building.

Problem 8-8B
Intangible assets

P6

Required

1. Prepare entries for Callahan to record (*a*) its payment to Palos for the right to sublease the building space, (*b*) its payment of the 2011 annual rent to the building owner, and (*c*) its payment for the office improvements.
2. Prepare Callahan's year-end adjusting entries required on December 31, 2011, to (*a*) amortize the $200,000 cost of the sublease, (*b*) amortize the office improvements, and (*c*) record rent expense.

Check   Dr. Rent Expense: (2*a*) $40,000, (2*c*) $90,000

SERIAL PROBLEM

Success Systems

(This serial problem began in Chapter 1 and continues through most of the book. If previous chapter segments were not completed, the serial problem can begin at this point. It is helpful, but not necessary, to use the Working Papers that accompany the book.)

SP 8   Selected ledger account balances for Success Systems follow.

	For Three Months Ended December 31, 2009	For Three Months Ended March 31, 2010
Office equipment	$ 8,000	$ 8,000
Accumulated depreciation—		
Office equipment	400	800
Computer equipment	20,000	20,000
Accumulated depreciation—		
Computer equipment	1,250	2,500
Total revenue	31,284	43,853
Total assets	93,248	129,909

Required

1. Assume that Success Systems does not acquire additional office equipment or computer equipment in 2010. Compute the amounts for the year ended December 31, 2010, for Depreciation Expense—Office Equipment and for Depreciation Expense—Computer Equipment (assume use of the straight-line method).

2. Given the assumptions in part 1, what is the book value of both the office equipment and the computer equipment as of December 31, 2010?

Check   (3) Three-month (annual) turnover = 0.39 (1.56 annual)

3. Compute the 3-month total asset turnover for Success Systems as of March 31, 2010. Use total revenue for the numerator and average the December 31, 2009, total assets and the March 31, 2010, total assets for the denominator. Interpret its total asset turnover if competitors average 2.5 for annual periods.

BEYOND THE NUMBERS

REPORTING IN ACTION

A1   A2

BTN 8-1   Refer to the financial statements of **Best Buy** in Appendix A to answer the following.

1. What percent of the original cost of Best Buy's property and equipment remains to be depreciated as of February 28, 2009, and at March 1, 2008? Assume these assets have no salvage value.

2. Over what length(s) of time is Best Buy depreciating its major categories of property and equipment?

3. What is the change in total property and equipment (before accumulated depreciation) for the year ended February 28, 2009? What is the amount of cash provided (used) by investing activities for property and equipment for the year ended February 28, 2009? What is one possible explanation for the difference between these two amounts?

4. Compute its total asset turnover for the year ended February 28, 2009, and the year ended March 1, 2008. Assume total assets at March 3, 2007, are $13,570 ($ millions).

Fast Forward

5. Access Best Buy's financial statements for fiscal years ending after February 28, 2009, at its Website (**BestBuy.com**) or the SEC's EDGAR database (**www.SEC.gov**). Recompute Best Buy's total asset turnover for the additional years' data you collect. Comment on any differences relative to the turnover computed in part 4.

COMPARATIVE ANALYSIS

A2

BTN 8-2   Comparative figures for **Best Buy** and **RadioShack** follow.

($ millions)	Best Buy			RadioShack		
	Current Year	One Year Prior	Two Years Prior	Current Year	One Year Prior	Two Years Prior
Total assets	$15,826	$12,758	$13,570	$2,283.5	$1,989.6	$2,070.0
Net sales	45,015	40,023	35,934	4,224.5	4,251.7	4,777.5

Required

1. Compute total asset turnover for the most recent two years for Best Buy and RadioShack using the data shown.
2. Which company is more efficient in generating net sales given the total assets it employs? Assume an industry average of 2.6.

BTN 8-3   Carmel Choi owns a small business and manages its accounting. Her company just finished a year in which a large amount of borrowed funds was invested in a new building addition as well as in equipment and fixture additions. Choi's banker requires her to submit semiannual financial statements so he can monitor the financial health of her business. He has warned her that if profit margins erode, he might raise the interest rate on the borrowed funds to reflect the increased loan risk from the bank's point of view. Choi knows profit margin is likely to decline this year. As she prepares year-end adjusting entries, she decides to apply the following depreciation rule: All asset additions are considered to be in use on the first day of the following month. (The previous rule assumed assets are in use on the first day of the month nearest to the purchase date.)

ETHICS CHALLENGE

C1 C2

Required

1. Identify decisions that managers like Choi must make in applying depreciation methods.
2. Is Choi's rule an ethical violation, or is it a legitimate decision in computing depreciation?
3. How will Choi's new depreciation rule affect the profit margin of her business?

BTN 8-4   Teams are to select an industry, and each team member is to select a different company in that industry. Each team member is to acquire the financial statements (form 10-K) of the company selected—see the company's Website or the SEC's EDGAR database (www.SEC.gov). Use the financial statements to compute total asset turnover. Communicate with teammates via a meeting, e-mail, or telephone to discuss the meaning of this ratio, how different companies compare to each other, and the industry norm. The team must prepare a one-page report that describes the ratios for each company and identifies the conclusions reached during the team's discussion.

COMMUNICATING IN PRACTICE

A2

BTN 8-5   Access the **Yahoo!** (ticker: YHOO) 10-K report for the year ended December 31, 2008, filed on February 27, 2009, at www.SEC.gov.

TAKING IT TO THE NET

C1 P6

Required

1. What amount of goodwill is reported on Yahoo!'s balance sheet? What percentage of total assets does its goodwill represent? Is goodwill a major asset for Yahoo! Explain.
2. Locate Note 5 to its financial statements. Identify the change in goodwill from December 31, 2007, to December 31, 2008. Comment on the change in goodwill over this period.
3. Locate Note 6 to its financial statements. What are the three categories of intangible assets that Yahoo! reports at December 31, 2008? What proportion of total assets do the intangibles represent?
4. What does Yahoo! indicate is the life of "Trademark, trade name, and domain name" according to its Note 6? Comment on the difference between the estimated useful life and the legal life of Yahoo!'s trademark.

BTN 8-6   Each team member is to become an expert on one depreciation method to facilitate teammates' understanding of that method. Follow these procedures:

a. Each team member is to select an area for expertise from one of the following depreciation methods: straight-line, units-of-production, or double-declining-balance.
b. Expert teams are to be formed from those who have selected the same area of expertise. The instructor will identify the location where each expert team meets.

TEAMWORK IN ACTION

C2 A1 P2

c. Using the following data, expert teams are to collaborate and develop a presentation answering the requirements. Expert team members must write the presentation in a format they can show to their learning teams.

Data and Requirements On January 8, 2007, Whitewater Riders purchases a van to transport rafters back to the point of departure at the conclusion of the rafting adventures they operate. The cost of the van is $44,000. It has an estimated salvage value of $2,000 and is expected to be used for four years and driven 60,000 miles. The van is driven 12,000 miles in 2007, 18,000 miles in 2008, 21,000 in 2009, and 10,000 in 2010.

   1. Compute annual depreciation expense for each year of the van's estimated useful life.

   2. Explain when and how annual depreciation is recorded.

   3. Explain the impact on income of this depreciation method versus others over the van's life.

   4. Identify the van's book value for each year of its life and illustrate the reporting of this amount for any one year.

d. Re-form original learning teams. In rotation, experts are to present to their teams the results from part *c*. Experts are to encourage and respond to questions.

ENTREPRENEURIAL DECISION

A2

BTN 8-7   Review the chapter's opening feature involving **Sambazon**. Assume that the company currently has net sales of $8,000,000, and that it is planning an expansion that will increase net sales by $4,000,000. To accomplish this expansion, Sambazon must increase its average total assets from $2,500,000 to $3,000,000.

Required

1. Compute the company's total asset turnover under (*a*) current conditions and (*b*) proposed conditions.

2. Evaluate and comment on the merits of the proposal given your analysis in part 1. Identify any concerns you would express about the proposal.

HITTING THE ROAD

C1 P5 P6

BTN 8-8   Team up with one or more classmates for this activity. Identify companies in your community or area that must account for at least one of the following assets: natural resource; patent; lease; leasehold improvement; copyright; trademark; or goodwill. You might find a company having more than one type of asset. Once you identify a company with a specific asset, describe the accounting this company uses to allocate the cost of that asset to the periods benefited from its use.

GLOBAL DECISION

A2

BTN 8-9   GOME (www.GOME.com.hk), **Best Buy**, and **RadioShack** are all competitors in the global marketplace. Comparative figures for these companies' recent annual accounting periods follow.

(in millions, except turnover)	GOME (RMB millions)			Best Buy		RadioShack	
	Current Year	Prior Year	Two Years Prior	Current Year	Prior Year	Current Year	Prior Year
Total assets	27,495	29,837	21,176	$15,826	$12,758	$2,283.5	$1,989.6
Net sales	45,889	42,479	24,729	45,015	40,023	4,224.5	4,251.7
Total asset turnover	?	?	—	3.15	3.04	1.98	2.09

Required

1. Compute total asset turnover for the most recent two years for GOME using the data shown.

2. Which company is most efficient in generating net sales given the total assets it employs?

ANSWERS TO MULTIPLE CHOICE QUIZ

1. b;

	Appraisal Value	%	Total Cost	Allocated
Land	$175,000	50%	$326,000	$163,000
Land improvements	70,000	20	326,000	65,200
Building	105,000	30	326,000	97,800
Totals	$350,000			$326,000

2. c; ($35,000 − $1,000)/4 years = $8,500 per year.

3. c; 2009: $10,800,000 × (2 × 10%) = $2,160,000
     2010: ($10,800,000 − $2,160,000) × (2 × 10%) = $1,728,000

4. c;

Cost of machine	$250,000
Accumulated depreciation	100,000
Book value	150,000
Cash received	120,000
Loss on sale	$ 30,000

5. b; $550,000/$500,000 = 1.10

9

Reporting and Analyzing Current Liabilities

"Being a first-time entrepreneur . . . is like running full speed through the dark over unfamiliar terrain" —Aaron Kennedy

A Look Back

Chapter 8 focused on long-term assets including plant assets, natural resources, and intangibles. We showed how to account for and analyze those assets.

A Look at This Chapter

This chapter explains how to identify, compute, record, and report current liabilities in financial statements. We also analyze and interpret these liabilities, including those related to employee costs.

A Look Ahead

Chapter 10 focuses on long-term liabilities. We explain how to value, record, amortize, and report those liabilities in financial statements.

Using His Noodle

BOULDER, CO—Aaron Kennedy never planned to be an entrepreneur. An evening dinner at a noodle shop in New York's Greenwich Village changed all that. "All of a sudden this idea hit me," says Kennedy. "There are noodle dishes all over the world. I thought, 'What if they were all on one menu? Why not bring all of these influences together and make it affordable and fast.'"

Kennedy quickly developed his global noodle concept: "high-quality food made to order." He wanted his noodles "quick and convenient, very affordable, and served in a very appealing dining environment." This led to his launch of **Noodles & Company (Noodles.com)**. "We're not fast food—we're casual dining," explains Kennedy.

Kennedy devoted himself to financial success, including the important task of managing liabilities for payroll, supplies, employee benefits, vacations, training, and taxes. He insists that effective management of liabilities, especially payroll and employee benefits, is crucial to success. Kennedy stresses that monitoring and controlling liabilities are a must.

With grit and determination, Kennedy launched his first noodle shop in Denver, followed by a second in Madison, Wisconsin. "The first two restaurants nearly killed us—physically and fiscally," recalls Kennedy. Yet Noodles not only achieved the income to pay the liabilities but also produced revenue growth for expansion. Kennedy then took on additional financing, which he successfully predicted would "culminate in accelerating growth."

Kennedy admits he is both surprised and humbled by Noodles' success but realizes that simple concepts are often the best. "Noodles are staples," Kennedy says. Our task is to "bring the noodles to the people." By all accounts, Kennedy has applied his noodles well.

[Sources: *Noodles & Co. Website*, January 2010; *Pinoy Business*, November 2008; *Rocky Mountain News*, February 2002; *Augustana Magazine*, Fall 2002; *Inc. Magazine*, January and October 2007; *Food Business Review*, April 2008.]

CAP

Conceptual

C1 Describe current and long-term liabilities and their characteristics. *(p. 376)*

C2 Identify and describe known current liabilities. *(p. 378)*

C3 Explain how to account for contingent liabilities. *(p. 388)*

Analytical

A1 Compute the times interest earned ratio and use it to analyze liabilities. *(p. 390)*

Procedural

P1 Prepare entries to account for short-term notes payable. *(p. 379)*

P2 Compute and record *employee* payroll deductions and liabilities. *(p. 381)*

P3 Compute and record *employer* payroll expenses and liabilities. *(p. 383)*

P4 Account for estimated liabilities, including warranties and bonuses. *(p. 385)*

P5 *Appendix 9A*—Identify and describe the details of payroll reports, records, and procedures. *(p. 393)*

LP9

Previous chapters introduced liabilities such as accounts payable, notes payable, wages payable, and unearned revenues. This chapter further explains these liabilities and additional ones such as warranties, taxes, payroll, vacation pay, and bonuses. It also describes contingent liabilities and introduces long-term liabilities. The focus is on how to define, classify, measure, report, and analyze these liabilities so that this information is useful to business decision makers.

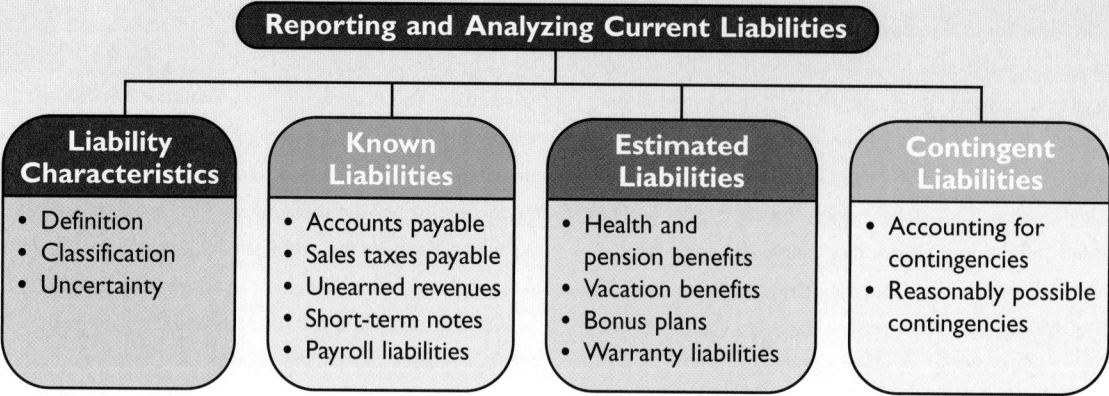

Reporting and Analyzing Current Liabilities

Liability Characteristics	Known Liabilities	Estimated Liabilities	Contingent Liabilities
• Definition • Classification • Uncertainty	• Accounts payable • Sales taxes payable • Unearned revenues • Short-term notes • Payroll liabilities	• Health and pension benefits • Vacation benefits • Bonus plans • Warranty liabilities	• Accounting for contingencies • Reasonably possible contingencies

Characteristics of Liabilities

This section discusses important characteristics of liabilities and how liabilities are classified and reported.

Defining Liabilities

C1 Describe current and long-term liabilities and their characteristics.

A *liability* is a probable future payment of assets or services that a company is presently obligated to make as a result of past transactions or events. This definition includes three crucial factors:

1. A past transaction or event.
2. A present obligation.
3. A future payment of assets or services.

These three important elements are portrayed visually in Exhibit 9.1. Liabilities reported in financial statements exhibit those characteristics. No liability is reported when one or more of those characteristics is absent. For example, most companies expect to pay wages to their employees in upcoming months and years, but these future payments are *not* liabilities because no past event such as employee work resulted in a present obligation. Instead, such liabilities arise when employees perform their work and earn the wages.

EXHIBIT 9.1

Characteristics of a Liability

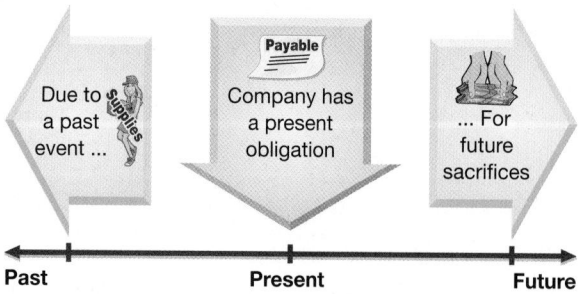

Past   Present   Future

Due to a past event ...   Company has a present obligation   ... For future sacrifices

Classifying Liabilities

Information about liabilities is more useful when the balance sheet identifies them as either current or long term. Decision makers need to know when obligations are due so they can plan for them and take appropriate action.

Video9.1

Current Liabilities **Current liabilities,** also called *short-term liabilities,* are obligations due within one year or the company's operating cycle, whichever is longer. They are expected to be paid using current assets or by creating other current liabilities. Common examples of current liabilities are accounts payable, short-term notes payable, wages payable, warranty liabilities, lease liabilities, taxes payable, and unearned revenues.

Point: Improper classification of liabilities can distort ratios used in financial statement analysis and business decisions.

Current liabilities differ across companies because they depend on the type of company operations. **Univision Communications,** for instance, included the following current liabilities related to its Spanish-language media operations ($000s):

Music copyright and artist royalties	$53,054
Program rights obligations	15,658

Harley-Davidson reports a much different set of current liabilities. It discloses current liabilities made up of items such as warranty, recall, and dealer incentive liabilities.

Long-Term Liabilities A company's obligations not expected to be paid within the longer of one year or the company's operating cycle are reported as **long-term liabilities.** They can include long-term notes payable, warranty liabilities, lease liabilities, and bonds payable. They are sometimes reported on the balance sheet in a single long-term liabilities total or in multiple categories. **Domino's Pizza,** for instance, reports long-term liabilities of $982 million. They are reported after current liabilities. A single liability also can be divided between the current and noncurrent sections if a company expects to make payments toward it in both the short and long term. Domino's reports ($ millions) long-term debt, $789.9; and current portion of long-term debt, $1.5. The second item is reported in current liabilities. We sometimes see liabilities that do not have a fixed due date but instead are payable on the creditor's demand. These are reported as current liabilities because of the possibility of payment in the near term. Exhibit 9.2 shows amounts of current liabilities and as a percent of total liabilities for selected companies.

Point: The current ratio is overstated if a company fails to classify any portion of long-term debt due next period as a current liability.

EXHIBIT 9.2

Current Liabilities of Selected Companies

Company	As a percent of total liabilities	Amount
Six Flags	10%	$291 mil.
AMF Bowling	25%	$69 mil.
K2 Inc	41%	$284 mil.
Apple	86%	$9,299 mil.

As a percent of total liabilities

Uncertainty in Liabilities

Accounting for liabilities involves addressing three important questions: Whom to pay? When to pay? How much to pay? Answers to these questions are often decided when a liability is incurred. For example, if a company has a $100 account payable to a specific individual, payable on March 15, the answers are clear. The company knows whom to pay, when to pay, and how much to pay. However, the answers to one or more of these questions are uncertain for some liabilities.

Uncertainty in Whom to Pay Liabilities can involve uncertainty in whom to pay. For instance, a company can create a liability with a known amount when issuing a note that is payable to its holder. In this case, a specific amount is payable to the note's holder at a specified date, but the company does not know who the holder is until that date. Despite this uncertainty, the company reports this liability on its balance sheet.

Point: An *accrued expense* is an unpaid expense, and is also called an *accrued liability.*

Uncertainty in When to Pay   A company can have an obligation of a known amount to a known creditor but not know when it must be paid. For example, a legal services firm can accept fees in advance from a client who plans to use the firm's services in the future. This means that the firm has a liability that it settles by providing services at an unknown future date. Although this uncertainty exists, the legal firm's balance sheet must report this liability. These types of obligations are reported as current liabilities because they are likely to be settled in the short term.

Uncertainty in How Much to Pay   A company can be aware of an obligation but not know how much will be required to settle it. For example, a company using electrical power is billed only after the meter has been read. This cost is incurred and the liability created before a bill is received. A liability to the power company is reported as an estimated amount if the balance sheet is prepared before a bill arrives.

IFRS

IFRS records a contingent liability when an obligation exists from a past event if there is a 'probable' outflow of resources *and* the amount can be estimated reliably. However, IFRS defines probable as 'more likely than not' while U.S. GAAP defines it as 'likely to occur.'

Quick Check   Answers—p. 401

1. What is a liability? Identify its crucial characteristics.
2. Is every expected future payment a liability?
3. If a liability is payable in 15 months, is it classified as current or long term?

Known Liabilities

Video9.1

Most liabilities arise from situations with little uncertainty. They are set by agreements, contracts, or laws and are measurable. These liabilities are **known liabilities,** also called *definitely determinable liabilities.* Known liabilities include accounts payable, notes payable, payroll, sales taxes, unearned revenues, and leases. We describe how to account for these known liabilities in this section.

Accounts Payable

C2 | Identify and describe known current liabilities.

Accounts payable, or trade accounts payable, are amounts owed to suppliers for products or services purchased on credit. Accounting for accounts payable is primarily explained and illustrated in our discussion of merchandising activities in Chapters 4 and 5.

Sales Taxes Payable

Nearly all states and many cities levy taxes on retail sales. Sales taxes are stated as a percent of selling prices. The seller collects sales taxes from customers when sales occur and remits these collections (often monthly) to the proper government agency. Since sellers currently owe these collections to the government, this amount is a current liability. **Home Depot,** for instance, reports sales taxes payable of $475 million in its recent annual report. To illustrate, if Home Depot sells materials on August 31 for $6,000 cash that are subject to a 5% sales tax, the revenue portion of this transaction is recorded as follows:

Assets = Liabilities + Equity
+6,300   +300   +6,000

Aug. 31	Cash	6,300	
	Sales		6,000
	Sales Taxes Payable ($6,000 × 0.05)		300
	To record cash sales and 5% sales tax.		

Sales Taxes Payable is debited and Cash credited when it remits these collections to the government. Sales Taxes Payable is not an expense. It arises because laws require sellers to collect this cash from customers for the government.[1]

Unearned Revenues

Unearned revenues (also called *deferred revenues, collections in advance,* and *prepayments*) are amounts received in advance from customers for future products or services. Advance ticket sales for sporting events or music concerts are examples. **Bon Jovi**, for instance, has "deferred revenues" from advance ticket sales. To illustrate, assume that Bon Jovi sells $5 million in tickets for eight concerts; the entry is

Point: To *defer* a revenue means to postpone recognition of a revenue collected in advance until it is earned. Sport teams must defer recognition of ticket sales until games are played.

June 30	Cash...	5,000,000	
	Unearned Ticket Revenue....................		5,000,000
	To record sale of concert tickets.		

Assets = Liabilities + Equity
+5,000,000   +5,000,000

When a concert is played, Bon Jovi would record revenue for the portion earned.

Oct. 31	Unearned Ticket Revenue	625,000	
	Ticket Revenue		625,000
	To record concert ticket revenues earned.		

Assets = Liabilities + Equity
            −625,000   +625,000

Unearned Ticket Revenue is an unearned revenue account and is reported as a current liability. Unearned revenues also arise with airline ticket sales, magazine subscriptions, construction projects, hotel reservations, and custom orders.

Decision Insight

Reward Programs Gift card sales now exceed $100 billion annually, and reward (also called loyalty) programs are growing. There are no exact rules for how retailers account for rewards. When **Best Buy** launched its "Reward Zone," shoppers earned $5 on each $125 spent and had 90 days to spend it. Retailers make assumptions about how many reward program dollars will be spent and how to report it. Best Buy sets up a liability and reduces revenue by the same amount. **Talbots** does not reduce revenue but instead increases selling expense. **Men's Wearhouse** records rewards in cost of goods sold, whereas **Neiman Marcus** subtracts them from revenue. The FASB is reviewing reward programs.

Short-Term Notes Payable

A **short-term note payable** is a written promise to pay a specified amount on a definite future date within one year or the company's operating cycle, whichever is longer. These promissory notes are negotiable (as are checks), meaning they can be transferred from party to party by endorsement. The written documentation provided by notes is helpful in resolving disputes and for pursuing legal actions involving these liabilities. Most notes payable bear interest to compensate for use of the money until payment is made. Short-term notes payable can arise from many transactions. A company that purchases merchandise on credit can sometimes extend the credit period by signing a note to replace an account payable. Such notes also can arise when money is borrowed from a bank. We describe both of these cases.

P1 Prepare entries to account for short-term notes payable.

Point: Required characteristics for negotiability of a note: (1) unconditional promise, (2) in writing, (3) specific amount, and (4) definite due date.

---

[1] Sales taxes can be computed from total sales receipts when sales taxes are not separately identified on the register. To illustrate, assume a 5% sales tax and $420 in total sales receipts (which includes sales taxes). Sales are computed as follows:

$$\text{Sales} = \text{Total sales receipts}/(1 + \text{Sales tax percentage}) = \$420/1.05 = \$400$$

Thus, the sales tax amount equals total sales receipts minus sales, or $420 − $400 = $20.

Note Given to Extend Credit Period   A company can replace an account payable with a note payable. A common example is a creditor that requires the substitution of an interest-bearing note for an overdue account payable that does not bear interest. A less common situation occurs when a debtor's weak financial condition motivates the creditor to accept a note, sometimes for a lesser amount, and to close the account to ensure that this customer makes no additional credit purchases.

To illustrate, let's assume that on August 23, Brady Company asks to extend its past-due $600 account payable to McGraw. After some negotiations, McGraw agrees to accept $100 cash and a 60-day, 12%, $500 note payable to replace the account payable. Brady records the transaction with this entry:

Assets = Liabilities + Equity
−100   −600
           +500

Aug. 23	Accounts Payable—McGraw......................	600	
	Cash		100
	Notes Payable—McGraw		500
	Gave $100 cash and a 60-day, 12% note for payment on account.		

Signing the note does not resolve Brady's debt. Instead, the form of debt is changed from an account payable to a note payable. McGraw prefers the note payable over the account payable because it earns interest and it is written documentation of the debt's existence, term, and amount. When the note comes due, Brady pays the note and interest by giving McGraw a check for $510. Brady records that payment with this entry:

Assets = Liabilities + Equity
−510   −500   −10

Oct. 22	Notes Payable—McGraw	500	
	Interest Expense	10	
	Cash		510
	Paid note with interest ($500 × 12% × 60/360).		

Interest expense is computed by multiplying the principal of the note ($500) by the annual interest rate (12%) for the fraction of the year the note is outstanding (60 days/360 days).

Note Given to Borrow from Bank   A bank nearly always requires a borrower to sign a promissory note when making a loan. When the note matures, the borrower repays the note with an amount larger than the amount borrowed. The difference between the amount borrowed and the amount repaid is *interest.* This section considers a type of note whose signer promises to pay *principal* (the amount borrowed) plus interest. In this case, the *face value* of the note equals principal. Face value is the value shown on the face (front) of the note. To illustrate, assume that a company needs $2,000 for a project and borrows this money from a bank at 12% annual interest. The loan is made on September 30, 2009, and is due in 60 days. Specifically, the borrowing company signs a note with a face value equal to the amount borrowed. The note includes a statement similar to this: *"I promise to pay $2,000 plus interest at 12% within 60 days after September 30."* This simple note is shown in Exhibit 9.3.

EXHIBIT 9.3

Note with Face Value Equal to Amount Borrowed

Promissory Note

$2,000   *Sept. 30, 2009*

Face Value   **Date**

Sixty days after date, _____*I*_____ promise to pay to the order of

National Bank
Boston, MA

Two thousand and no/100 ------------------------ **Dollars**

plus interest at the annual rate of _*12%*_ .

Janet Lee

The borrower records its receipt of cash and the new liability with this entry:

Sept. 30	Cash	2,000	
	Notes Payable		2,000
	Borrowed $2,000 cash with a 60-day, 12%, $2,000 note.		

Assets = Liabilities + Equity
+2,000   +2,000

When principal and interest are paid, the borrower records payment with this entry:

Nov. 29	Notes Payable	2,000	
	Interest Expense	40	
	Cash		2,040
	Paid note with interest ($2,000 × 12% × 60/360).		

Assets = Liabilities + Equity
−2,040   −2,000   −40

End-of-period interest adjustment.   When the end of an accounting period occurs between the signing of a note payable and its maturity date, the *matching principle* requires us to record the accrued but unpaid interest on the note. To illustrate, let's return to the note in Exhibit 9.3, but assume that the company borrows $2,000 cash on December 16, 2009, instead of September 30. This 60-day note matures on February 14, 2010, and the company's fiscal year ends on December 31. Thus, we need to record interest expense for the final 15 days in December. This means that one-fourth (15 days/60 days) of the $40 total interest is an expense of year 2009. The borrower records this expense with the following adjusting entry:

2009			
Dec. 31	Interest Expense	10	
	Interest Payable		10
	To record accrued interest on note ($2,000 × 12% × 15/360).		

Assets = Liabilities + Equity
              +10   −10

When this note matures on February 14, the borrower must recognize 45 days of interest expense for year 2010 and remove the balances of the two liability accounts:

Example: If this note is dated Dec. 1 instead of Dec. 16, how much expense is recorded on Dec. 31? *Answer:* $2,000 × 12% × 30/360 = $20

2010			
Feb. 14	Interest Expense*............................	30	
	Interest Payable	10	
	Notes Payable	2,000	
	Cash		2,040
	*Paid note with interest. *($2,000 × 12% × 45/360)*		

Assets = Liabilities + Equity
−2,040   −10   −30
                −2,000

Many franchisors such as **Geeks on Call**, **Techs in a Sec**, and **Nerds on Site**, use notes to help entrepreneurs acquire their own franchises, including using notes to pay for the franchise fee and any equipment. Payments on these notes are usually collected monthly and often are secured by the franchisees' assets.

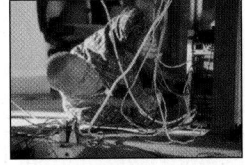

Payroll Liabilities

An employer incurs several expenses and liabilities from having employees. These expenses and liabilities are often large and arise from salaries and wages earned, from employee benefits, and from payroll taxes levied on the employer. **Anheuser-Busch**, for instance, reports payroll-related current liabilities of more than $374.3 million from "accrued salaries, wages and benefits." We discuss payroll liabilities and related accounts in this section. Appendix 9A describes details about payroll reports, records, and procedures.

P2 Compute and record *employee* payroll deductions and liabilities.

Employee Payroll Deductions   **Gross pay** is the total compensation an employee earns including wages, salaries, commissions, bonuses, and any compensation earned before deductions such as taxes. (*Wages* usually refer to payments to employees at an hourly rate. *Salaries* usually refer to payments to employees at a monthly or yearly rate.) **Net pay,** also called *take-home pay,* is gross pay less all deductions. **Payroll deductions,** commonly called *withholdings,* are amounts withheld from an employee's gross pay, either required or voluntary. Required deductions result from laws and include income taxes and Social Security taxes. Voluntary deductions, at an employee's option, include pension and health contributions, union dues, and charitable giving. Exhibit 9.4 shows the typical payroll deductions of an employee. The employer withholds payroll deductions from employees' pay and is obligated to transmit this money to the designated organization. The employer records payroll deductions as current liabilities until these amounts are transmitted. This section discusses the major payroll deductions.

EXHIBIT 9.4

Payroll Deductions

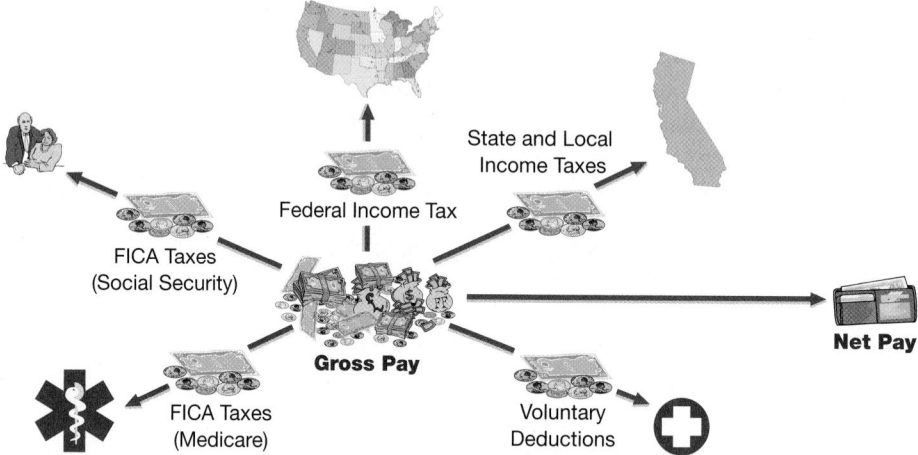

Employee FICA taxes.   The federal Social Security system provides retirement, disability, survivorship, and medical benefits to qualified workers. Laws *require* employers to withhold **Federal Insurance Contributions Act (FICA) taxes** from employees' pay to cover costs of the system. Employers usually separate FICA taxes into two groups: (1) retirement, disability, and survivorship and (2) medical. For the first group, the Social Security system provides monthly cash payments to qualified retired workers for the rest of their lives. These payments are often called *Social Security benefits.* Taxes related to this group are often called *Social Security taxes.* For the second group, the system provides monthly payments to deceased workers' surviving families and to disabled workers who qualify for assistance. These payments are commonly called *Medicare benefits;* like those in the first group, they are paid with *Medicare taxes* (part of FICA taxes).

Law requires employers to withhold FICA taxes from each employee's salary or wages on each payday. The taxes for Social Security and Medicare are computed separately. For example, for the year 2009, the amount withheld from each employee's pay for Social Security tax was 6.2% of the first $106,800 the employee earns in the calendar year, or a maximum of $6,621.60. The Medicare tax was 1.45% of *all* amounts the employee earns; there is no maximum limit to Medicare tax.

Employers must pay withheld taxes to the Internal Revenue Service (IRS) on specific filing dates during the year. Employers who fail to send the withheld taxes to the IRS on time can be assessed substantial penalties. Until all the taxes are sent to the IRS, they are included in employers' current liabilities. For any changes in rates or with the maximum earnings level, check the IRS Website at **www.IRS.gov** or the SSA Website at **www.SSA.gov**.

Employee income tax.   Most employers are required to withhold federal income tax from each employee's paycheck. The amount withheld is computed using tables published by the IRS. The amount depends on the employee's annual earnings rate and the number of *withholding allowances* the employee claims. Allowances reduce the amount of taxes one owes the government. The more allowances one claims, the less tax the employer will withhold. Employees can claim allowances for themselves and their dependents. They also can claim additional allowances if they expect major declines in their taxable income for medical expenses. (An employee who claims more allowances than appropriate is subject to a fine.) Most states and many local governments require employers to withhold income taxes from employees' pay and to remit them promptly to the proper government agency. Until they are paid, withholdings are reported as a current liability on the employer's balance sheet.

Point: IRS withholding tables are based on projecting weekly (or other period) pay into an annual figure.

Employee voluntary deductions.   Beyond Social Security, Medicare, and income taxes, employers often withhold other amounts from employees' earnings. These withholdings arise from employee requests, contracts, unions, or other agreements. They can include amounts for charitable giving, medical insurance premiums, pension contributions, and union dues. Until they are paid, such withholdings are reported as part of employers' current liabilities.

Recording employee payroll deductions.   Employers must accrue payroll expenses and liabilities at the end of each pay period. To illustrate, assume that an employee earns a salary of $2,000 per month. At the end of January, the employer's entry to accrue payroll expenses and liabilities for this employee is

Jan. 31	Salaries Expense................................	2,000	
	FICA—Social Security Taxes Payable (6.2%).....		124
	FICA—Medicare Taxes Payable (1.45%).........		29
	Employee Federal Income Taxes Payable*.......		213
	Employee Medical Insurance Payable*.........		85
	Employee Union Dues Payable*..............		25
	Salaries Payable		1,524
	To record accrued payroll for January.		

Assets = Liabilities + Equity
      +124   −2,000
      +29
      +213
      +85
      +25
      +1,524

* Amounts taken from employer's accounting records.

Salaries Expense (debit) shows that the employee earns a gross salary of $2,000. The first five payables (credits) show the liabilities the employer owes on behalf of this employee to cover FICA taxes, income taxes, medical insurance, and union dues. The Salaries Payable account (credit) records the $1,524 net pay the employee receives from the $2,000 gross pay earned. When the employee is paid, another entry (or a series of entries) is required to record the check written and distributed (or funds transferred). The entry to record cash payment to this employee is to debit Salaries Payable and credit Cash for $1,524.

Decision Insight

A company's delay or failure to pay withholding taxes to the government has severe consequences. For example, a 100% penalty can be levied, with interest, on the unpaid balance. The government can even close a company, take its assets, and pursue legal actions against those involved.

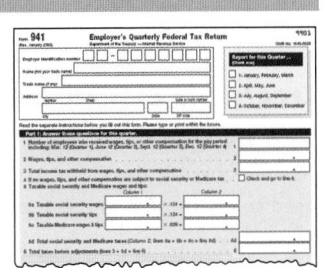

Employer Payroll Taxes   Employers must pay payroll taxes in addition to those required of employees. Employer taxes include FICA and unemployment taxes.

P3 Compute and record *employer* payroll expenses and liabilities.

Employer FICA tax.   Employers must pay FICA taxes *equal in amount to* the FICA taxes withheld from their employees. An employer's tax is credited to the same FICA Taxes Payable accounts used to record the Social Security and Medicare taxes withheld from employees. (A self-employed person must pay both the employee and employer FICA taxes.)

Federal and state unemployment taxes.   The federal government participates with states in a joint federal and state unemployment insurance program. Each state administers its program. These programs provide unemployment benefits to qualified workers. The federal government approves state programs and pays a portion of their administrative expenses.

Federal Unemployment Taxes (FUTA). Employers are subject to a federal unemployment tax on wages and salaries paid to their employees. For the year 2009, employers were required to pay FUTA taxes of as much as 6.2% of the first $7,000 earned by each employee. This federal tax can be reduced by a credit of up to 5.4% for taxes paid to a state program. As a result, the net federal unemployment tax is often only 0.8%.

State Unemployment Taxes (SUTA). All states support their unemployment insurance programs by placing a payroll tax on employers. (A few states require employees to make a contribution. In the book's assignments, we assume that this tax is only on the employer.) In most states, the base rate for SUTA taxes is 5.4% of the first $7,000 paid each employee. This base rate is adjusted according to an employer's merit rating. The state assigns a **merit rating** that reflects a company's stability or instability in employing workers. A good rating reflects stability in employment and means an employer can pay less than the 5.4% base rate. A low rating reflects high turnover or seasonal hirings and layoffs. To illustrate, an employer with 50 employees each of whom earns $7,000 or more per year saves $15,400 annually if it has a merit rating of 1.0% versus 5.4%. This is computed by comparing taxes of $18,900 at the 5.4% rate to only $3,500 at the 1.0% rate.

Recording employer payroll taxes.   Employer payroll taxes are an added expense beyond the wages and salaries earned by employees. These taxes are often recorded in an entry separate from the one recording payroll expenses and deductions. To illustrate, assume that the $2,000 recorded salaries expense from the previous example is earned by an employee whose earnings have not yet reached $5,000 for the year. This means the entire salaries expense for this period is subject to tax because year-to-date pay is under $7,000. Also assume that the federal unemployment tax rate is 0.8% and the state unemployment tax rate is 5.4%. Consequently, the FICA portion of the employer's tax is $153, computed by multiplying both the 6.2% and 1.45% by the $2,000 gross pay. Moreover, state unemployment (SUTA) taxes are $108 (5.4% of the $2,000 gross pay), and federal unemployment (FUTA) taxes are $16 (0.8% of $2,000). The entry to record the employer's payroll tax expense and related liabilities is

Example: If the employer's merit rating in this example reduces its SUTA rate to 2.9%, what is its SUTA liability?
Answer: SUTA payable = $2,000 × 2.9% = $58

Assets = Liabilities + Equity
+124   −277
+29
+108
+16

Jan. 31	Payroll Taxes Expense	277	
	FICA—Social Security Taxes Payable (6.2%)		124
	FICA—Medicare Taxes Payable (1.45%)		29
	State Unemployment Taxes Payable		108
	Federal Unemployment Taxes Payable		16
	To record employer payroll taxes.		

Decision Ethics

Web Designer   You take a summer job working for a family friend who runs a small IT service. On your first payday, the owner slaps you on the back, gives you full payment in cash, winks, and adds: "No need to pay those high taxes, eh." What action, if any, do you take? [Answer—p. 401]

Multi-Period Known Liabilities

Many known liabilities extend over multiple periods. These often include unearned revenues and notes payable. For example, if **Sports Illustrated** sells a four-year magazine subscription, it records amounts received for this subscription in an Unearned Subscription Revenues account. Amounts in this account are liabilities, but are they current or long term? They are *both.* The portion of the Unearned Subscription Revenues account that will be fulfilled in the next year is reported as a current liability. The remaining portion is reported as a long-term liability.

The same analysis applies to notes payable. For example, a borrower reports a three-year note payable as a long-term liability in the first two years it is outstanding. In the third year, the borrower reclassifies this note as a current liability since it is due within one year or the operating cycle, whichever is longer. The **current portion of long-term debt** refers to that part of long-term debt due within one year or the operating cycle, whichever is longer.

Long-term debt is reported under long-term liabilities, but the *current portion due* is reported under current liabilities. To illustrate, assume that a $7,500 debt is paid in installments of $1,500 per year for five years. The $1,500 due within the year is reported as a current liability. No journal entry is necessary for this reclassification. Instead, we simply classify the amounts for debt as either current or long term when the balance sheet is prepared.

    Some known liabilities are rarely reported in long-term liabilities. These include accounts payable, sales taxes, and wages and salaries.

Point: Alternatively, some accounting systems do make an entry to transfer the current amount due out of Long-Term Debt and into the Current Portion of Long-Term Debt.

Decision Insight

Liability Limits   Probably the greatest number of frauds involve payroll. Companies must safeguard payroll activities. Controls include proper approvals and processes for employee additions, deletions, and pay rate changes. A common fraud is a manager adding a fictitious employee to the payroll and then cashing the fictitious employee's check. A study reports that 28% of employees in operations and service areas witnessed violations of employee wage, overtime, or benefit rules in the past year (KPMG 2009). Another 21% observed falsifying of time and expense reports.

Quick Check   Answers—p. 401

4. Why does a creditor prefer a note payable to a past-due account payable?

5. A company pays its one employee $3,000 per month. This company's FUTA rate is 0.8% on the first $7,000 earned; its SUTA rate is 4.0% on the first $7,000; its Social Security tax rate is 6.2% of the first $106,800; and its Medicare tax rate is 1.45% of all amounts earned. The entry to record this company's March payroll includes what amount for total payroll taxes expense?

6. Identify whether the employer or employee or both incurs each of the following: (*a*) FICA taxes, (*b*) FUTA taxes, (*c*) SUTA taxes, and (*d*) withheld income taxes.

Estimated Liabilities

An **estimated liability** is a known obligation that is of an uncertain amount but that can be reasonably estimated. Common examples are employee benefits such as pensions, health care and vacation pay, and warranties offered by a seller. We discuss each of these in this section. Other examples of estimated liabilities include property taxes and certain contracts to provide future services.

P4 Account for estimated liabilities, including warranties and bonuses.

Health and Pension Benefits

Many companies provide **employee benefits** beyond salaries and wages. An employer often pays all or part of medical, dental, life, and disability insurance. Many employers also contribute to *pension plans,* which are agreements by employers to provide benefits (payments) to employees after retirement. Many companies also provide medical care and insurance benefits to their retirees. When payroll taxes and charges for employee benefits are totaled, payroll cost often exceeds employees' gross earnings by 25% or more.

    To illustrate, assume that an employer agrees to (1) pay an amount for medical insurance equal to $8,000 and (2) contribute an additional 10% of the employees' $120,000 gross salary to a retirement program. The entry to record these accrued benefits is

Dec. 31	Employee Benefits Expense......................	20,000	
	Employee Medical Insurance Payable...........		8,000
	Employee Retirement Program Payable.........		12,000
	To record costs of employee benefits.		

Assets = Liabilities + Equity
+8,000   −20,000
+12,000

Decision Insight

Postgame Spoils Baseball was the first pro sport to set up a pension, originally up to $100 per month depending on years played. Many former players now take home six-figure pensions. Cal Ripken Jr.'s pension when he reaches 62 is estimated at $160,000 per year (he played 21 seasons). The requirement is only 43 games for a full pension and just one game for full medical benefits.

Vacation Benefits

Many employers offer paid vacation benefits, also called *paid absences*. To illustrate, assume that salaried employees earn 2 weeks' vacation per year. This benefit increases employers' payroll expenses because employees are paid for 52 weeks but work for only 50 weeks. Total annual salary is the same, but the cost per week worked is greater than the amount paid per week. For example, if an employee is paid $20,800 for 52 weeks but works only 50 weeks, the total weekly expense to the employer is $416 ($20,800/50 weeks) instead of the $400 cash paid weekly to the employee ($20,800/52 weeks). The $16 difference between these two amounts is recorded weekly as follows:

Assets = Liabilities + Equity
+16   −16

Vacation Benefits Expense......................	16	
Vacation Benefits Payable		16
To record vacation benefits accrued.		

Vacation Benefits Expense is an operating expense, and Vacation Benefits Payable is a current liability. When the employee takes a vacation, the employer reduces (debits) the Vacation Benefits Payable and credits Cash (no additional expense is recorded).

Bonus Plans

Many companies offer bonuses to employees, and many of the bonuses depend on net income. To illustrate, assume that an employer offers a bonus to its employees equal to 5% of the company's annual net income (to be equally shared by all). The company's expected annual net income is $210,000. The year-end adjusting entry to record this benefit is

Assets = Liabilities + Equity
+10,000   −10,000

Dec. 31	Employee Bonus Expense*	10,000	
	Bonus Payable		10,000
	To record expected bonus costs.		

* Bonus Expense (B) equals 5% of net income, which equals $210,000 minus the bonus; this is computed as:

$$B = 0.05 (\$210,000 - B)$$
$$B = \$10,500 - 0.05B$$
$$1.05B = \$10,500$$
$$\mathbf{B = \$10,500/1.05 = \$10,000}$$

When the bonus is paid, Bonus Payable is debited and Cash is credited for $10,000.

Point: Kodak recently reported $60 million in warranty obligations.

Warranty Liabilities

A **warranty** is a seller's obligation to replace or correct a product (or service) that fails to perform as expected within a specified period. Most new cars, for instance, are sold with a warranty covering parts for a specified period of time. **Ford Motor Company** reported more than $15 billion in "dealer and customer allowances and claims" in its annual report. To comply with the *full disclosure* and *matching principles,* the seller reports the expected warranty expense in the period when revenue from the sale of the product or service is reported. The seller reports this warranty obligation as a liability, although the existence, amount, payee, and date of future sacrifices are uncertain. This is because such warranty costs are probable and the amount can be estimated using, for instance, past experience with warranties.

To illustrate, a dealer sells a used car for $16,000 on December 1, 2009, with a maximum one-year or 12,000-mile warranty covering parts. This dealer's experience shows that warranty expense averages about 4% of a car's selling price, or $640 in this case ($16,000 × 4%). The dealer records the estimated expense and liability related to this sale with this entry:

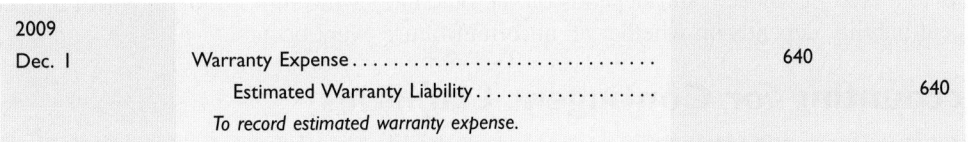

2009			
Dec. 1	Warranty Expense............................	640	
	Estimated Warranty Liability..................		640
	To record estimated warranty expense.		

Assets = Liabilities + Equity
         +640   −640

This entry alternatively could be made as part of end-of-period adjustments. Either way, the estimated warranty expense is reported on the 2009 income statement and the warranty liability on the 2009 balance sheet. To further extend this example, suppose the customer returns the car for warranty repairs on January 9, 2010. The dealer performs this work by replacing parts costing $200. The entry to record partial settlement of the estimated warranty liability is

Point: Recognition of warranty liabilities is necessary to comply with the matching and full disclosure principles.

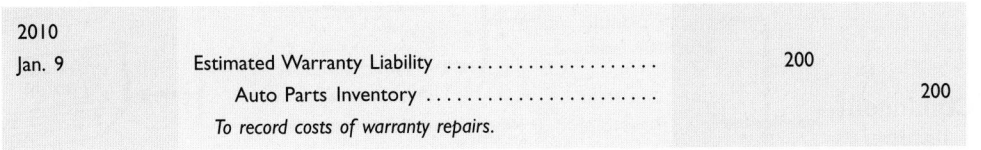

2010			
Jan. 9	Estimated Warranty Liability	200	
	Auto Parts Inventory		200
	To record costs of warranty repairs.		

Assets = Liabilities + Equity
−200   −200

This entry reduces the balance of the estimated warranty liability. Warranty expense was previously recorded in 2009, the year the car was sold with the warranty. Finally, what happens if total warranty expenses are more or less than the estimated 4%, or $640? The answer is that management should monitor actual warranty expenses to see whether the 4% rate is accurate. If experience reveals a large difference from the estimate, the rate for current and future sales should be changed. Differences are expected, but they should be small.

Point: Both U.S. GAAP and IFRS account for restructuring costs in a manner similar to accounting for warranties.

Decision Insight

Guaranteed Profits Best Buy's profits from sales of extended-warranty contracts with their electronics are reported in the table to the side [*BusinessWeek*, 2004].

Warranty contracts as a percentage of sales	4.0%
Warranty contracts as a percentage of operating profit	45
Profit margin on warranty contracts	60

Multi-Period Estimated Liabilities

Estimated liabilities can be both current and long term. For example, pension liabilities to employees are long term to workers who will not retire within the next period. For employees who are retired or will retire within the next period, a portion of pension liabilities is current. Other examples include employee health benefits and warranties. Specifically, many warranties are for 30 or 60 days in length. Estimated costs under these warranties are properly reported in current liabilities. Many other automobile warranties are for three years or 36,000 miles. A portion of these warranties is reported as long term.

Quick Check

Answers—p. 401

7. Estimated liabilities involve an obligation to pay which of these? (*a*) An uncertain but reasonably estimated amount owed on a known obligation or (*b*) A known amount to a specific entity on an uncertain due date.

8. A car is sold for $15,000 on June 1, 2009, with a one-year warranty on parts. Warranty expense is estimated at 1.5% of selling price at each calendar year-end. On March 1, 2010, the car is returned for warranty repairs costing $135. The amount recorded as warranty expense on March 1 is (*a*) $0; (*b*) $60; (*c*) $75; (*d*) $135; (*e*) $225.

Contingent Liabilities

C3	Explain how to account for contingent liabilities.

A **contingent liability** is a potential obligation that depends on a future event arising from a past transaction or event. An example is a pending lawsuit. Here, a past transaction or event leads to a lawsuit whose result depends on the outcome of the suit. Future payment of a contingent liability depends on whether an uncertain future event occurs.

Accounting for Contingent Liabilities

Accounting for contingent liabilities depends on the likelihood that a future event will occur and the ability to estimate the future amount owed if this event occurs. Three different possibilities are identified in the following chart: record liability, disclose in notes, or no disclosure.

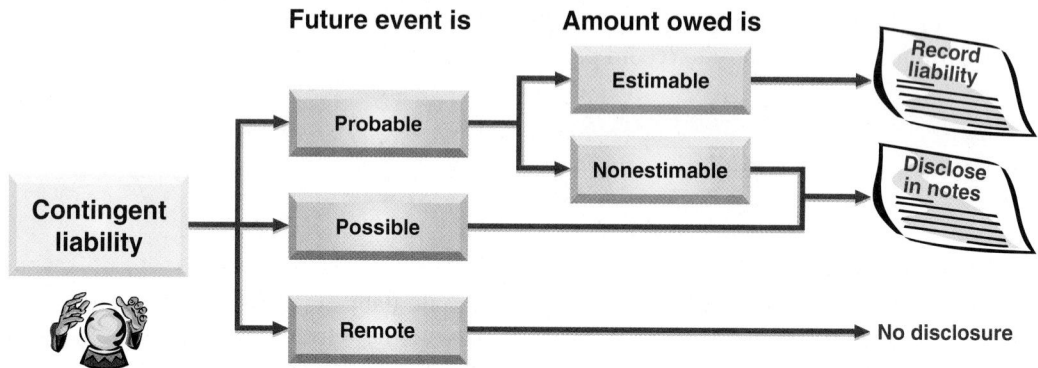

The conditions that determine each of these three possibilities follow:

1. The future event is *probable* (likely) and the amount owed can be *reasonably estimated*. We then record this amount as a liability. Examples are the estimated liabilities described earlier such as warranties, vacation pay, and income taxes.
2. The future event is *reasonably possible* (could occur). We disclose information about this type of contingent liability in notes to the financial statements.
3. The future event is *remote* (unlikely). We do not record or disclose information on remote contingent liabilities.

Point: A contingency is an *if*. Namely, if a future event occurs, then financial consequences are likely for the entity.

Reasonably Possible Contingent Liabilities

This section identifies and discusses contingent liabilities that commonly fall in the second category—when the future event is reasonably possible. Disclosing information about contingencies in this category is motivated by the *full-disclosure principle*, which requires information relevant to decision makers be reported and not ignored.

Point: A sale of a note receivable is often a contingent liability. It becomes a liability if the original signer of the note fails to pay it at maturity.

Potential Legal Claims   Many companies are sued or at risk of being sued. The accounting issue is whether the defendant should recognize a liability on its balance sheet or disclose a contingent liability in its notes while a lawsuit is outstanding and not yet settled. The answer is that a potential claim is recorded in the accounts *only* if payment for damages is probable and the amount can be reasonably estimated. If the potential claim cannot be reasonably estimated or is less than probable but reasonably possible, it is disclosed. **Ford Motor Company**, for example, includes the following note in its annual report: "Various legal actions, governmental investigations and proceedings and claims are pending . . . arising out of alleged defects in our products."

Debt Guarantees   Sometimes a company guarantees the payment of debt owed by a supplier, customer, or another company. The guarantor usually discloses the guarantee in its financial statement notes as a contingent liability. If it is probable that the debtor will default, the guarantor needs to record and report the guarantee in its financial statements as a liability. The **Boston Celtics** report a unique guarantee when it comes to coaches and players: "Certain of the contracts provide for guaranteed payments which must be paid even if the employee [player] is injured or terminated."

Other Contingencies   Other examples of contingencies include environmental damages, possible tax assessments, insurance losses, and government investigations. **Sunoco**, for instance, reports that "federal, state and local laws . . . result in liabilities and loss contingencies. Sunoco accrues . . . cleanup costs [that] are probable and reasonably estimable. Management believes it is reasonably possible (i.e., less than probable but greater than remote) that additional . . . losses will be incurred." Many of Sunoco's contingencies are revealed only in notes.

Point: Auditors and managers often have different views about whether a contingency is recorded, disclosed, or omitted.

Decision Insight

Pricing Priceless   What's it worth to see from one side of the Grand Canyon to the other? What's the cost when beaches are closed due to pollution? A method to measure environmental liabilities is *contingent valuation,* by which people answer such questions. Regulators use their answers to levy fines and assess punitive damages.

Uncertainties That Are Not Contingencies

All organizations face uncertainties from future events such as natural disasters and the development of new competing products or services. These uncertainties are not contingent liabilities because they are future events *not* arising from past transactions. Accordingly, they are not disclosed.

Quick Check   Answers—p. 401

9. A future payment is reported as a liability on the balance sheet if payment is contingent on a future event that (*a*) is reasonably possible but the payment cannot be reasonably estimated; (*b*) is probable and the payment can be reasonably estimated; or (*c*) is not probable but the payment is known.

10. Under what circumstances is a future payment reported in the notes to the financial statements as a contingent liability?

Global View

This section discusses similarities and differences between U.S. GAAP and IFRS in accounting and reporting for current liabilities.

Characteristics of Liabilities

The definitions and characteristics of current liabilities are broadly similar for both U.S. GAAP and IFRS. Although differences exist, the similarities vastly outweigh any differences. Remembering that "provision" is typically used under IFRS to refer to "liability" under U.S. GAAP, **GOME** describes its recognition of liabilities as follows:

> A provision is recognised when a present obligation (legal or constructive) has arisen as a result of a past event and it is probable that a future outflow of resources will be required to settle the obligation, provided that a reliable estimate can be made of the amount of the obligation.

Known (Determinable) Liabilities

When there is little uncertainty surrounding current liabilities, both U.S. GAAP and IFRS require companies to record them in a similar manner. This correspondence in accounting applies to accounts payable, sales taxes payable, unearned revenues, short-term notes, and payroll liabilities. Of course, tax regulatory systems of countries are different, which implies use of different rates and levels. Still, the basic approach is the same. **GOME**, which references a subset of these liabilities as *financial liabilities,* applies the following policy:

> Financial liabilities including trade and other payables . . . and interest-bearing loans and borrowings are initially stated at fair value less directly attributable transaction costs and are subsequently measured at amortised cost, using the effective interest method unless the effect of discounting would be immaterial, in which case they are stated at cost. The related interest expense is recognised within "finance costs" in the income statement.

Estimated Liabilities

When there is a known current obligation that involves an uncertain amount, but one that can be reasonably estimated, both U.S. GAAP and IFRS require similar treatment. This treatment extends to many obligations such as those arising from vacations, warranties, restructurings, pensions, and health care. Both accounting systems require that companies record estimated expenses related to these obligations when they can reasonably estimate the amounts. GOME reports wages, salaries and bonuses of RMB (000s) 1,212,757. It also reports pension contributions of RMB (000s) 249,985. The accounting for these is described as follows:

> Salaries, bonuses, paid annual leave, and the cost to the Group of non-monetary benefits are accrued in the year in which the associated services are rendered by employees of the Group.

Decision Analysis	Times Interest Earned Ratio

A1 Compute the times interest earned ratio and use it to analyze liabilities.

A company incurs interest expense on many of its current and long-term liabilities. Examples extend from its short-term notes and the current portion of long-term liabilities to its long-term notes and bonds. Interest expense is often viewed as a *fixed expense* because the amount of these liabilities is likely to remain in one form or another for a substantial period of time. This means that the amount of interest is unlikely to vary due to changes in sales or other operating activities. While fixed expenses can be advantageous when a company is growing, they create risk. This risk stems from the possibility that a company might be unable to pay fixed expenses if sales decline. To illustrate, consider Diego Co.'s results for 2009 and two possible outcomes for year 2010 in Exhibit 9.5.

EXHIBIT 9.5

Actual and Projected Results

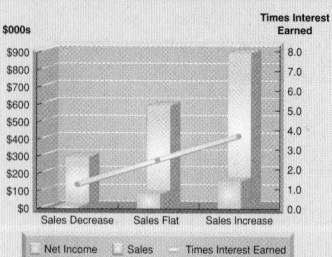

($ thousands)	2009	2010 Projections	
		Sales Increase	Sales Decrease
Sales	$600	$900	$300
Expenses (75% of sales)	450	675	225
Income before interest	150	225	75
Interest expense (fixed)	60	60	60
Net income	$ 90	$165	$ 15

Expenses excluding interest are at, and expected to remain at, 75% of sales. Expenses such as these that change with sales volume are called *variable expenses.* However, interest expense is at, and expected to remain at, $60,000 per year due to its fixed nature.

The middle numerical column of Exhibit 9.5 shows that Diego's income increases by 83% to $165,000 if sales increase by 50% to $900,000. In contrast, the far right column shows that income decreases by 83% if sales decline by 50%. These results reveal that the amount of fixed interest expense affects a company's risk of its ability to pay interest, which is numerically reflected in the **times interest earned** ratio in Exhibit 9.6.

EXHIBIT 9.6

Times Interest Earned

$$\text{Times interest earned} = \frac{\text{Income before interest expense and income taxes}}{\text{Interest expense}}$$

For 2009, Diego's times interest earned is computed as $150,000/$60,000, or 2.5 times. This ratio suggests that Diego faces low to moderate risk because its sales must decline sharply before it would be unable to cover its interest expenses. (Diego is an LLC and does not pay income taxes.)

Experience shows that when times interest earned falls below 1.5 to 2.0 and remains at that level or lower for several periods, the default rate on liabilities increases sharply. This reflects increased risk for companies and their creditors. We also must interpret the times interest earned ratio in light of information about the variability of a company's income before interest. If income is stable from year to year or if it is growing, the company can afford to take on added risk by borrowing. If its income greatly varies from year to year, fixed interest expense can increase the risk that it will not earn enough income to pay interest.

Decision Maker

Entrepreneur   You wish to invest in a franchise for either one of two national chains. Each franchise has an expected annual net income *after* interest and taxes of $100,000. Net income for the first franchise includes a regular fixed interest charge of $200,000. The fixed interest charge for the second franchise is $40,000. Which franchise is riskier to you if sales forecasts are not met? Does your decision change if the first franchise has more variability in its income stream? [Answer—p. 401]

Demonstration Problem

The following transactions and events took place at Kern Company during its recent calendar-year reporting period (Kern does not use reversing entries).

a. In September 2009, Kern sold $140,000 of merchandise covered by a 180-day warranty. Prior experience shows that costs of the warranty equal 5% of sales. Compute September's warranty expense and prepare the adjusting journal entry for the warranty liability as recorded at September 30. Also prepare the journal entry on October 8 to record a $300 cash expenditure to provide warranty service on an item sold in September.

b. On October 12, 2009, Kern arranged with a supplier to replace Kern's overdue $10,000 account payable by paying $2,500 cash and signing a note for the remainder. The note matures in 90 days and has a 12% interest rate. Prepare the entries recorded on October 12, December 31, and January 10, 2010, related to this transaction.

c. In late December, Kern learns it is facing a product liability suit filed by an unhappy customer. Kern's lawyer advises that although it will probably suffer a loss from the lawsuit, it is not possible to estimate the amount of damages at this time.

d. Sally Bline works for Kern. For the pay period ended November 30, her gross earnings are $3,000. Bline has $800 deducted for federal income taxes and $200 for state income taxes from each paycheck. Additionally, a $35 premium for her health care insurance and a $10 donation for the United Way are deducted. Bline pays FICA Social Security taxes at a rate of 6.2% and FICA Medicare taxes at a rate of 1.45%. She has not earned enough this year to be exempt from any FICA taxes. Journalize the accrual of salaries expense of Bline's wages by Kern.

e. On November 1, Kern borrows $5,000 cash from a bank in return for a 60-day, 12%, $5,000 note. Record the note's issuance on November 1 and its repayment with interest on December 31.

f.[B] Kern has estimated and recorded its quarterly income tax payments. In reviewing its year-end tax adjustments, it identifies an additional $5,000 of income tax expense that should be recorded. A portion of this additional expense, $1,000, is deferrable to future years. Record this year-end income taxes expense adjusting entry.

g. For this calendar-year, Kern's net income is $1,000,000, its interest expense is $275,000, and its income taxes expense is $225,000. Calculate Kern's times interest earned ratio.

Planning the Solution

- For *a*, compute the warranty expense for September and record it with an estimated liability. Record the October expenditure as a decrease in the liability.
- For *b*, eliminate the liability for the account payable and create the liability for the note payable. Compute interest expense for the 80 days that the note is outstanding in 2009 and record it as an additional liability. Record the payment of the note, being sure to include the interest for the 10 days in 2010.

- For *c,* decide whether the company's contingent liability needs to be disclosed or accrued (recorded) according to the two necessary criteria: probable loss and reasonably estimable.
- For *d,* set up payable accounts for all items in Bline's paycheck that require deductions. After deducting all necessary items, credit the remaining amount to Salaries Payable.
- For *e,* record the issuance of the note. Calculate 60 days' interest due using the 360-day convention in the interest formula.
- For *f,* determine how much of the income taxes expense is payable in the current year and how much needs to be deferred.
- For *g,* apply and compute times interest earned.

Solution to Demonstration Problem

a. Warranty expense = 5% × $140,000 = $7,000

Sept. 30	Warranty Expense................................	7,000	
	Estimated Warranty Liability...................		7,000
	To record warranty expense for the month.		
Oct. 8	Estimated Warranty Liability......................	300	
	Cash		300
	To record the cost of the warranty service.		

b. Interest expense for 2009 = 12% × $7,500 × 80/360 = $200

Interest expense for 2010 = 12% × $7,500 × 10/360 = $25

Oct. 12	Accounts Payable................................	10,000	
	Notes Payable		7,500
	Cash		2,500
	Paid $2,500 cash and gave a 90-day, 12% note to extend the due date on the account.		
Dec. 31	Interest Expense	200	
	Interest Payable		200
	To accrue interest on note payable.		
Jan. 10	Interest Expense	25	
	Interest Payable	200	
	Notes Payable	7,500	
	Cash		7,725
	Paid note with interest, including the accrued interest payable.		

c. Disclose the pending lawsuit in the financial statement notes. Although the loss is probable, no liability can be accrued since the loss cannot be reasonably estimated.

d.

Nov. 30	Salaries Expense.................................	3,000.00	
	FICA—Social Security Taxes Payable (6.2%)		186.00
	FICA—Medicare Taxes Payable (1.45%).........		43.50
	Employee Federal Income Taxes Payable........		800.00
	Employee State Income Taxes Payable..........		200.00
	Employee Medical Insurance Payable		35.00
	Employee United Way Payable		10.00
	Salaries Payable		1,725.50
	To record Bline's accrued payroll.		

e.

Nov. 1	Cash..	5,000	
	Notes Payable		5,000
	Borrowed cash with a 60-day, 12% note.		

When the note and interest are paid 60 days later, Kern Company records this entry:

Dec. 31	Notes Payable	5,000	
	Interest Expense	100	
	Cash		5,100
	Paid note with interest ($5,000 × 12% × 60/360).		

f.

Dec. 31	Income Taxes Expense..........................	5,000	
	Income Taxes Payable		4,000
	Deferred Income Tax Liability		1,000
	To record added income taxes expense and the deferred tax liability.		

g. Times interest earned $= \dfrac{\$1,000,000 + \$275,000 + \$225,000}{\$275,000} = \underline{\underline{5.45 \text{ times}}}$

APPENDIX

Payroll Reports, Records, and Procedures

9A

Understanding payroll procedures and keeping adequate payroll reports and records are essential to a company's success. This appendix focuses on payroll accounting and its reports, records, and procedures.

Payroll Reports

Most employees and employers are required to pay local, state, and federal payroll taxes. Payroll expenses involve liabilities to individual employees, to federal and state governments, and to other organizations such as insurance companies. Beyond paying these liabilities, employers are required to prepare and submit reports explaining how they computed these payments.

P5 Identify and describe the details of payroll reports, records, and procedures.

Reporting FICA Taxes and Income Taxes   The Federal Insurance Contributions Act (FICA) requires each employer to file an Internal Revenue Service (IRS) **Form 941,** the *Employer's Quarterly Federal Tax Return,* within one month after the end of each calendar quarter. A sample Form 941 is shown in Exhibit 9A.1 for Phoenix Sales & Service, a landscape design company. Accounting information and software are helpful in tracking payroll transactions and reporting the accumulated information on Form 941. Specifically, the employer reports total wages subject to income tax withholding on line 2 of Form 941. (For simplicity, this appendix uses *wages* to refer to both wages and salaries.) The income tax withheld is reported on line 3. The combined amount of employee and employer FICA (Social Security) taxes for Phoenix Sales & Service is reported on line 5a (taxable Social Security wages, $36,599 × 12.4% = $4,538.28$). The 12.4% is the sum of the Social Security tax withheld, computed as 6.2% tax withheld from the employee wages for the quarter plus the 6.2% tax levied on the employer. The combined amount of employee Medicare wages is reported on line 5c. The 2.9% is the sum of 1.45% withheld from employee wages for the quarter plus 1.45% tax levied on the employer. Total FICA taxes are reported on line 5d and are added to the total income taxes withheld of $3,056.47 to yield a total of $8,656.12. For this year, assume that income up to $106,800 is subject to Social Security tax. There is

Form 941

Employer's QUARTERLY Federal Tax Return

Department of the Treasury — Internal Revenue Service

(EIN)
Employer identification number 8 6 – 3 2 1 4 5 8 7

Name (not your trade name) Phoenix Sales & Service

Trade name (if any)

Address 1214 Mill Road
Number Street Suite or room number
Phoenix AZ 85621
City State ZIP code

Report for this Quarter ...
(Check one.)

☐ 1: January, February, March
☐ 2: April, May, June
☐ 3: July, August, September
☒ 4: October, November, December

Part 1: Answer these questions for this quarter.

1 Number of employees who received wages, tips, or other compensation for the pay period including: *Mar. 12* (Quarter 1), *June 12* (Quarter 2), *Sept. 12* (Quarter 3), *Dec. 12* (Quarter 4)	1	1
2 Wages, tips, and other compensation	2	36,599.00
3 Total income tax withheld from wages, tips, and other compensation	3	3,056.47
4 If no wages, tips, and other compensation are subject to social security or Medicare tax	☐ Check and go to line 6.	

5 Taxable social security and Medicare wages and tips:

	Column 1		Column 2
5a Taxable social security wages	36,599.00	× .124 =	4,538.28
5b Taxable social security tips		× .124 =	
5c Taxable Medicare wages & tips	36,599.00	× .029 =	1,061.37

5d Total social security and Medicare taxes (Column 2, lines 5a + 5b + 5c = line 5d)	5d	5,599.65
6 Total taxes before adjustments (lines 3 + 5d = line 6)	6	8,656.12

7 TAX ADJUSTMENTS (Read the instructions for line 7 before completing lines 7a through 7h.):

7a Current quarter's fractions of cents		
7b Current quarter's sick pay		
7c Current quarter's adjustments for tips and group-term life insurance		
7d Current year's income tax withholding (attach Form 941c)		
7e Prior quarters' social security and Medicare taxes (attach Form 941c)		
7f Special additions to federal income tax (attach Form 941c)		
7g Special additions to social security and Medicare (attach Form 941c)		
7h TOTAL ADJUSTMENTS (Combine all amounts: lines 7a through 7g.)	7h	0.00
8 Total taxes after adjustments (Combine lines 6 and 7h.)	8	8,656.12
9 Advance earned income credit (EIC) payments made to employees	9	.
10 Total taxes after adjustment for advance EIC (lines 8 – line 9 = line 10)	10	8,656.12
11 Total deposits for this quarter, including overpayment applied from a prior quarter	11	8,656.12
12 Balance due (If line 10 is more than line 11, write the difference here.) Make checks payable to *United States Treasury*.	12	0.00

13 Overpayment (If line 11 is more than line 10, write the difference here.) 0.00 Check one ☐ Apply to next return.
☐ Send a refund.

Part 2: Tell us about your deposit schedule and tax liability for this quarter.

If you are unsure about whether you are a monthly schedule depositor or a semiweekly schedule depositor, see *Pub. 15 (Circular E)*, section 11.

14 A Z Write the state abbreviation for the state where you made your deposits OR write "MU" if you made your deposits in *multiple* states.

15 Check one: ☐ Line 10 is less than $2,500. Go to Part 3.

☒ You were a monthly schedule depositor for the entire quarter. Fill out your tax liability for each month. Then go to Part 3.

Tax liability:	Month 1	3,079.11
	Month 2	2,049.77
	Month 3	3,527.24
	Total liability for quarter	8,656.12	Total must equal line 10.

☐ You were a semiweekly schedule depositor for any part of this quarter. Fill out Schedule B (Form 941): *Report of Tax Liability for Semiweekly Schedule Depositors*, and attach it to this form.

Part 3: Tell us about your business. If a question does NOT apply to your business, leave it blank.

16 If your business has closed or you stopped paying wages ☐ Check here, and
enter the final date you paid wages / /

17 If you are a seasonal employer and you do not have to file a return for every quarter of the year ☐ Check here.

Part 4: May we speak with your third-party designee?

Do you want to allow an employee, a paid tax preparer, or another person to discuss this return with the IRS? See the instructions for details.

☐ Yes. Designee's name

Phone (   )   –   Personal Identification Number (PIN) ☐☐☐☐☐

☒ No.

Part 5: Sign here. You MUST fill out both sides of this form and SIGN it.

Under penalties of perjury, I declare that I have examined this return, including accompanying schedules and statements, and to the best of my knowledge and belief, it is true, correct, and complete.

✗ Sign your name here

Print name and title

Date / / Phone (   )   –

no income limit on amounts subject to Medicare tax. Congress sets annual limits on the amount owed for Social Security tax.

Federal depository banks are authorized to accept deposits of amounts payable to the federal government. Deposit requirements depend on the amount of tax owed. For example, when the sum of FICA taxes plus the employee income taxes is less than $2,500 for a quarter, the taxes can be paid when Form 941 is filed. Companies with large payrolls are often required to pay monthly or even semiweekly.

Reporting FUTA Taxes and SUTA Taxes   An employer's federal unemployment taxes (FUTA) are reported on an annual basis by filing an *Annual Federal Unemployment Tax Return,* IRS **Form 940.** It must be mailed on or before January 31 following the end of each tax year. Ten more days are allowed if all required tax deposits are filed on a timely basis and the full amount of tax is paid on or before January 31. FUTA payments are made quarterly to a federal depository bank if the total amount due exceeds $500. If $500 or less is due, the taxes are remitted annually. Requirements for paying and reporting state unemployment taxes (SUTA) vary depending on the laws of each state. Most states require quarterly payments and reports.

Reporting Wages and Salaries   Employers are required to give each employee an annual report of his or her wages subject to FICA and federal income taxes along with the amounts of these taxes withheld. This report is called a *Wage and Tax Statement,* or **Form W-2.** It must be given to employees before January 31 following the year covered by the report. Exhibit 9A.2 shows Form W-2 for one of the employees at Phoenix Sales & Service. Copies of the W-2 Form must be sent to the Social Security Administration, where the amount of the employee's wages subject to FICA taxes and FICA taxes withheld are posted to each employee's Social Security account. These posted amounts become the basis for determining an employee's retirement and survivors' benefits. The Social Security Administration also transmits to the IRS the amount of each employee's wages subject to federal income taxes and the amount of taxes withheld.

Payroll Records

Employers must keep payroll records in addition to reporting and paying taxes. These records usually include a payroll register and an individual earnings report for each employee.

Payroll Register   A **payroll register** usually shows the pay period dates, hours worked, gross pay, deductions, and net pay of each employee for each pay period. Exhibit 9A.3 shows a payroll register for Phoenix Sales & Service. It is organized into nine columns:

Col. 1   Employee identification (ID); Employee name; Social Security number (SS No.); Reference (check number); and Date (date check issued)
Col. 2   Pay Type (regular and overtime)
Col. 3   Pay Hours (number of hours worked as regular and overtime)
Col. 4   Gross Pay (amount of gross pay)[2]
Col. 5   FIT (federal income taxes withheld); FUTA (federal unemployment taxes)
Col. 6   SIT (state income taxes withheld); SUTA (state unemployment taxes)
Col. 7   FICA-SS_EE (social security taxes withheld, employee); FICA-SS_ER (social security taxes, employer)
Col. 8   FICA-Med_EE (medicare tax withheld, employee); FICA-Med_ER (medicare tax, employer)
Col. 9   Net pay (Gross pay less amounts withheld from employees)

Net pay for each employee is computed as gross pay minus the items on the first line of columns 5–8. The employer's payroll tax for each employee is computed as the sum of items on the third line of columns 5–8. A payroll register includes all data necessary to record payroll. In some software programs the entries to record payroll are made in a special *payroll journal.*

---

[2] The Gross Pay column shows regular hours worked on the first line multiplied by the regular pay rate—this equals regular pay. Overtime hours multiplied by the overtime premium rate equals overtime premium pay reported on the second line. If employers are engaged in interstate commerce, federal law sets a minimum overtime rate of pay to employees. For this company, workers earn 150% of their regular rate for hours in excess of 40 per week.

EXHIBIT 9A.2

Form W-2

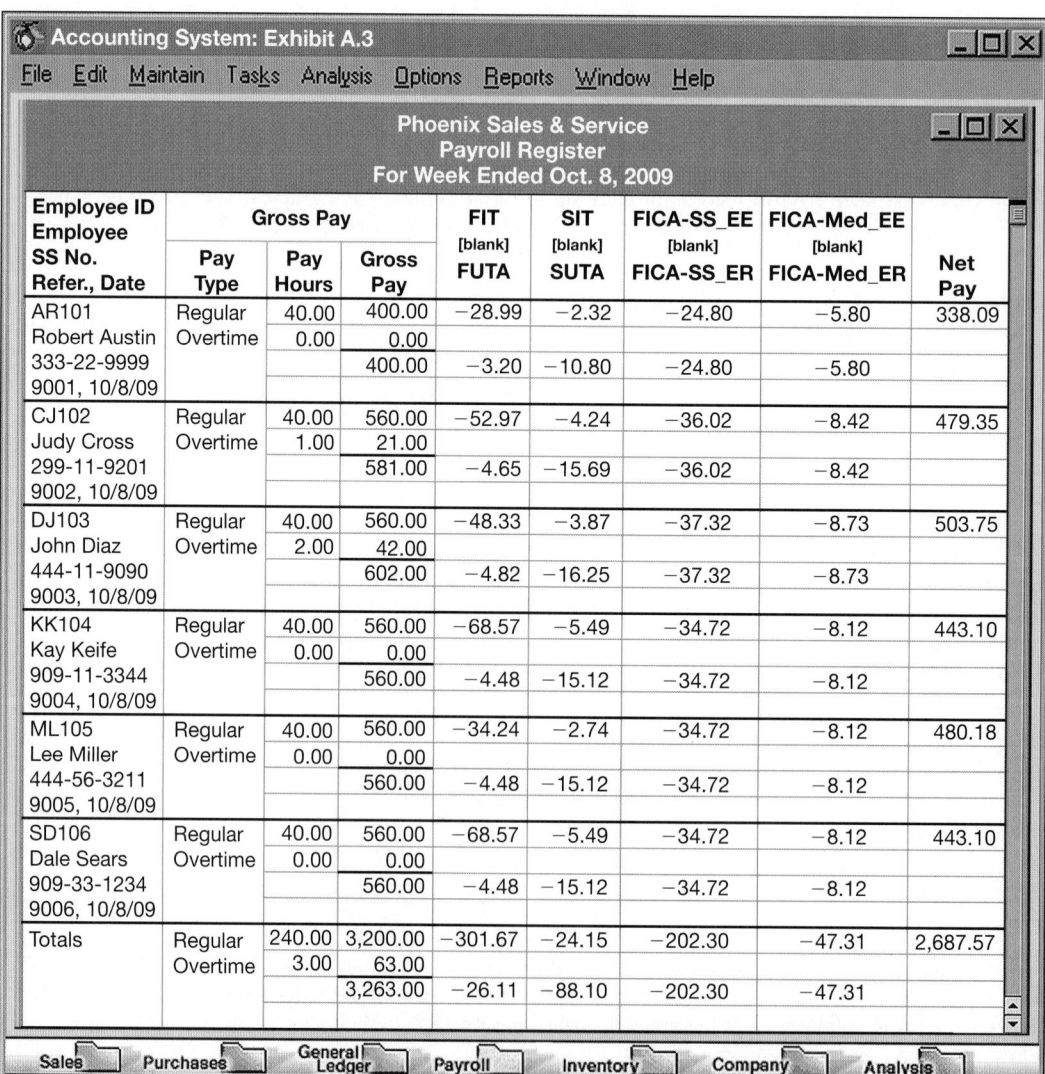

Form **W-2** Wage and Tax Statement				Department of Treasury—Internal Revenue Service

Copy 1–For State, City, or Local Tax Department

a Control number: AR101 — 22222 — OMB No. 1545-0006

b Employer identification number (EIN): 86-3214587

1 Wages, tips, other compensation: 4,910.00
2 Federal income tax withheld: 333.37

c Employer's name, address and ZIP code:
Phoenix Sales & Service
1214 Mill Road
Phoenix, AZ 85621

3 Social security wages: 4,910.00
4 Social security tax withheld: 304.42

5 Medicare wages and tips: 4,910.00
6 Medicare tax withheld: 71.20

7 Social security tips
8 Allocated tips

d Employee's social security number: 333-22-9999

9 Advance EIC payment
10 Dependent care benefits

e Employee's first name and initial: Robert J. — Last name: Austin

11 Nonqualified plans
12a Code

f Employee's address and ZIP code:
18 Roosevelt Blvd., Apt. C
Tempe, AZ 86322

13 Statutory employee / Retirement plan / Third-party sick pay
14 Other
12b Code
12c Code
12d Code

15 State: AZ — Employer's state ID number: 13-902319
16 State wages, tips, etc.: 4,910.00
17 State income tax: 26.68
18 Local wages, tips, etc.
19 Local income tax
20 Locality name

EXHIBIT 9A.3

Payroll Register

Accounting System: Exhibit A.3

File Edit Maintain Tasks Analysis Options Reports Window Help

Phoenix Sales & Service
Payroll Register
For Week Ended Oct. 8, 2009

Employee ID Employee SS No. Refer., Date	Pay Type	Pay Hours	Gross Pay	FIT [blank] FUTA	SIT [blank] SUTA	FICA-SS_EE [blank] FICA-SS_ER	FICA-Med_EE [blank] FICA-Med_ER	Net Pay
AR101 Robert Austin 333-22-9999 9001, 10/8/09	Regular	40.00	400.00	−28.99	−2.32	−24.80	−5.80	338.09
	Overtime	0.00	0.00					
			400.00	−3.20	−10.80	−24.80	−5.80	
CJ102 Judy Cross 299-11-9201 9002, 10/8/09	Regular	40.00	560.00	−52.97	−4.24	−36.02	−8.42	479.35
	Overtime	1.00	21.00					
			581.00	−4.65	−15.69	−36.02	−8.42	
DJ103 John Diaz 444-11-9090 9003, 10/8/09	Regular	40.00	560.00	−48.33	−3.87	−37.32	−8.73	503.75
	Overtime	2.00	42.00					
			602.00	−4.82	−16.25	−37.32	−8.73	
KK104 Kay Keife 909-11-3344 9004, 10/8/09	Regular	40.00	560.00	−68.57	−5.49	−34.72	−8.12	443.10
	Overtime	0.00	0.00					
			560.00	−4.48	−15.12	−34.72	−8.12	
ML105 Lee Miller 444-56-3211 9005, 10/8/09	Regular	40.00	560.00	−34.24	−2.74	−34.72	−8.12	480.18
	Overtime	0.00	0.00					
			560.00	−4.48	−15.12	−34.72	−8.12	
SD106 Dale Sears 909-33-1234 9006, 10/8/09	Regular	40.00	560.00	−68.57	−5.49	−34.72	−8.12	443.10
	Overtime	0.00	0.00					
			560.00	−4.48	−15.12	−34.72	−8.12	
Totals	Regular	240.00	3,200.00	−301.67	−24.15	−202.30	−47.31	2,687.57
	Overtime	3.00	63.00					
			3,263.00	−26.11	−88.10	−202.30	−47.31	

Sales   Purchases   General Ledger   Payroll   Inventory   Company   Analysis

Payroll Check   Payment of payroll is usually done by check or electronic funds transfer. Exhibit 9A.4 shows a *payroll check* for a Phoenix employee. This check is accompanied with a detachable *statement of earnings* (at top) showing gross pay, deductions, and net pay.

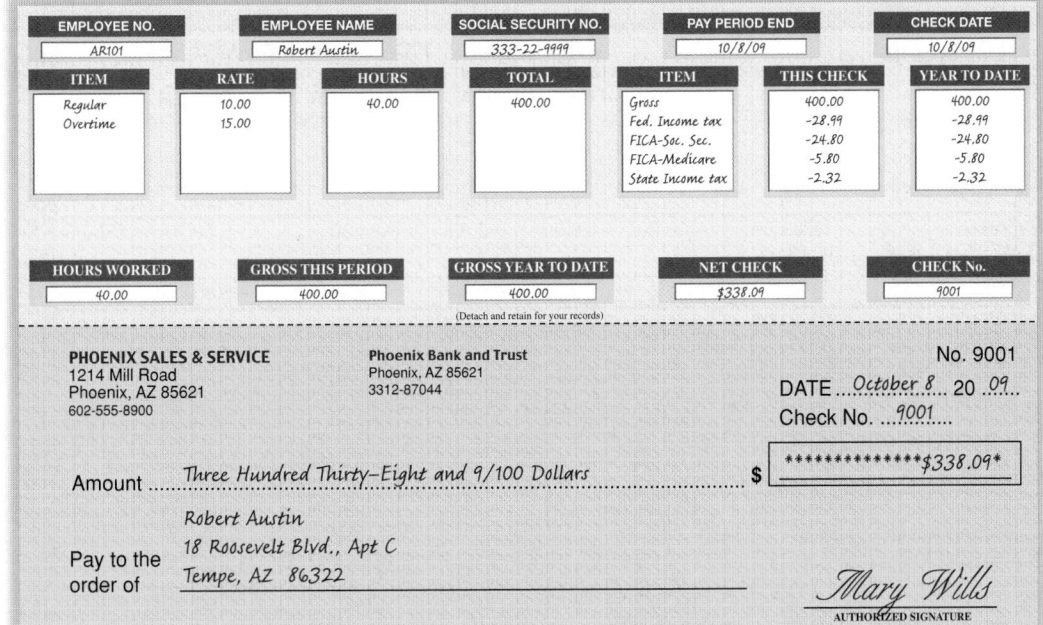

EXHIBIT 9A.4

Check and Statement of Earnings

Employee Earnings Report   An **employee earnings report** is a cumulative record of an employee's hours worked, gross earnings, deductions, and net pay. Payroll information on this report is taken from the payroll register. The employee earnings report for R. Austin at Phoenix Sales & Service is shown in Exhibit 9A.5. An employee earnings report accumulates information that can show when an employee's earnings reach the tax-exempt points for FICA, FUTA, and SUTA taxes. It also gives data an employer needs to prepare Form W-2.

Payroll Procedures

Employers must be able to compute federal income tax for payroll purposes. This section explains how we compute this tax and how to use a payroll bank account.

Computing Federal Income Taxes   To compute the amount of taxes withheld from each employee's wages, we need to determine both the employee's wages earned and the employee's number of *withholding allowances*. Each employee records the number of withholding allowances claimed on a withholding allowance certificate, **Form W-4,** filed with the employer. When the number of withholding allowances increases, the amount of income taxes withheld decreases.

Employers often use a **wage bracket withholding table** similar to the one shown in Exhibit 9A.6 to compute the federal income taxes withheld from each employee's gross pay. The table in Exhibit 9A.6 is for a single employee paid weekly. Tables are also provided for married employees and for biweekly, semimonthly, and monthly pay periods (most payroll software includes these tables). When using a wage bracket withholding table to compute federal income tax withheld from an employee's gross wages, we need to locate an employee's wage bracket within the first two columns. We then find the amount withheld by looking in the withholding allowance column for that employee.

Payroll Bank Account   Companies with few employees often pay them with checks drawn on the company's regular bank account. Companies with many employees often use a special **payroll bank account** to pay employees. When this account is used, a company either (1) draws one check for total payroll on the regular bank account and deposits it in the payroll bank account or (2) executes an *electronic funds transfer* to the payroll bank account. Individual payroll checks are then drawn on this payroll bank account. Since only one check for the total payroll is drawn on the regular bank account each payday, use of a special payroll bank account helps with internal control. It also helps in reconciling the

EXHIBIT 9A.5

Employee Earnings Report

```
Accounting System: Exhibit A.5                                    _ □ X
File  Edit  Maintain  Tasks  Analysis  Options  Reports  Window  Help
```

Phoenix Sales & Service
Employee Earnings Report
For Month Ended Dec. 31, 2009

Employee ID Employee SS No.	Date Reference	Gross Pay	FIT [blank] FUTA	SIT [blank] SUTA	FICA-SS_EE [blank] FICA-SS_ER	FICA-Med_EE [blank] FICA-Med_ER	Net Pay
Beginning Balance for Robert Austin		2,910.00	−188.42	−15.08	−180.42	−42.20	2,483.88
			−23.28	−78.57	−180.42	−42.20	
AR101 Robert Austin 333-22-9999	12/03/09 9049	400.00	−28.99	−2.32	−24.80	−5.80	338.09
			−3.20	−10.80	−24.80	−5.80	
AR101 Robert Austin 333-22-9999	12/10/09 9055	400.00	−28.99	−2.32	−24.80	−5.80	338.09
			−3.20	−10.80	−24.80	−5.80	
AR101 Robert Austin 333-22-9999	12/17/09 9061	400.00	−28.99	−2.32	−24.80	−5.80	338.09
			−3.20	−10.80	−24.80	−5.80	
AR101 Robert Austin 333-22-9999	12/24/09 9067	400.00	−28.99	−2.32	−24.80	−5.80	338.09
			−3.20	−10.80	−24.80	−5.80	
AR101 Robert Austin 333-22-9999	12/31/09 9073	400.00	−28.99	−2.32	−24.80	−5.80	338.09
			−3.20	−10.80	−24.80	−5.80	
Total 12/01/09 thru 12/31/09		2,000.00	−144.95	−11.60	−124.00	−29.00	1,690.45
			−16.00	−54.00	−124.00	−29.00	
Year-to-date Total for Robert Austin		4,910.00	−333.37	−26.68	−304.42	−71.20	4,174.33
			−39.28	−132.57	−304.42	−71.20	

```
Sales    Purchases    General     Payroll    Inventory    Company    Analysis
                       Ledger
```

EXHIBIT 9A.6

Wage Bracket Withholding Table

SINGLE Persons—WEEKLY Payroll Period

If the wages are—		And the number of withholding allowances claimed is—										
At least	But less than	0	1	2	3	4	5	6	7	8	9	10
		The amount of income tax to be withheld is—										
$600	$610	$76	$67	$58	$49	$39	$30	$21	$12	$6	$0	$0
610	620	79	69	59	50	41	32	22	13	7	1	0
620	630	81	70	61	52	42	33	24	15	8	2	0
630	640	84	72	62	53	44	35	25	16	9	3	0
640	650	86	73	64	55	45	36	27	18	10	4	0
650	660	89	75	65	56	47	38	28	19	11	5	0
660	670	91	76	67	58	48	39	30	21	12	6	0
670	680	94	78	68	59	50	41	31	22	13	7	1
680	690	96	81	70	61	51	42	33	24	14	8	2
690	700	99	83	71	62	53	44	34	25	16	9	3
700	710	101	86	73	64	54	45	35	27	17	10	4
710	720	104	88	74	65	56	47	37	28	19	11	5
720	730	106	91	76	67	57	48	39	30	20	12	6
730	740	109	93	78	68	59	50	40	31	22	13	7
740	750	111	96	80	70	60	51	42	33	23	14	8

regular bank account. When companies use a payroll bank account, they usually include check numbers in the payroll register. The payroll register in Exhibit 9A.3 shows check numbers in column 1. For instance, Check No. 9001 is issued to Robert Austin. With this information, the payroll register serves as a supplementary record of wages earned by and paid to employees.

Who Pays What Payroll Taxes and Benefits

We conclude this appendix with the following table identifying who pays which payroll taxes and which common employee benefits such as medical, disability, pension, charitable, and union costs. Who pays which employee benefits, and what portion, is subject to agreements between companies and their workers. Also, self-employed workers must pay both the employer and employee FICA taxes for Social Security and Medicare.

Employer Payroll Taxes and Costs	Employee Payroll Deductions
• FICA—Social Security Taxes	• FICA—Social Security taxes
• FICA—Medicare Taxes	• FICA—Medicare taxes
• FUTA (Federal Unemployment Taxes)	• Federal Income taxes
• SUTA (State Unemployment Taxes)	• State and local income taxes
• Share of medical coverage, if any	• Share of medical coverage, if any
• Share of pension coverage, if any	• Share of pension coverage, if any
• Share of other benefits, if any	• Share of other benefits, if any

Quick Check   Answers—p. 401

11. What three items determine the amount deducted from an employee's wages for federal income taxes?

12. What amount of income tax is withheld from the salary of an employee who is single with three withholding allowances and earnings of $675 in a week? (*Hint:* Use the wage bracket withholding table in Exhibit 9A.6.)

13. Which of the following steps are executed when a company draws one check for total payroll and deposits it in a special payroll bank account? (*a*) Write a check to the payroll bank account for the total payroll and record it with a debit to Salaries Payable and a credit to Cash. (*b*) Deposit a check (or transfer funds) for the total payroll in the payroll bank account. (*c*) Issue individual payroll checks drawn on the payroll bank account. (*d*) All of the above.

APPENDIX

Corporate Income Taxes

9B

This appendix explains current liabilities involving income taxes for corporations.

Income Tax Liabilities   Corporations are subject to income taxes and must estimate their income tax liability when preparing financial statements. Since income tax expense is created by earning income, a liability is incurred when income is earned. This tax must be paid quarterly under federal regulations. To illustrate, consider a corporation that prepares monthly financial statements. Based on its income in January 2009, this corporation estimates that it owes income taxes of $12,100. The following adjusting entry records this estimate:

Jan. 31	Income Taxes Expense	12,100	
	Income Taxes Payable		12,100
	To accrue January income taxes.		

Assets = Liabilities + Equity
+12,100   −12,100

The tax liability is recorded each month until the first quarterly payment is made. If the company's estimated taxes for this first quarter total $30,000, the entry to record its payment is

Assets = Liabilities + Equity
−30,000   −30,000

Apr. 10	Income Taxes Payable	30,000	
	Cash		30,000
	Paid estimated quarterly income taxes based on first quarter income.		

This process of accruing and then paying estimated income taxes continues through the year. When annual financial statements are prepared at year-end, the corporation knows its actual total income and the actual amount of income taxes it must pay. This information allows it to properly record income taxes expense for the fourth quarter so that the total of the four quarters' expense amounts equals the actual taxes paid to the government.

Deferred Income Tax Liabilities An income tax liability for corporations can arise when the amount of income before taxes that the corporation reports on its income statement is not the same as the amount of income reported on its income tax return. This difference occurs because income tax laws and GAAP measure income differently. (Differences between tax laws and GAAP arise because Congress uses tax laws to generate receipts, stimulate the economy, and influence behavior, whereas GAAP are intended to provide financial information useful for business decisions. Also, tax accounting often follows the cash basis, whereas GAAP follows the accrual basis.)

Some differences between tax laws and GAAP are temporary. *Temporary differences* arise when the tax return and the income statement report a revenue or expense in different years. As an example, companies are often able to deduct higher amounts of depreciation in the early years of an asset's life and smaller amounts in later years for tax reporting in comparison to GAAP. This means that in the early years, depreciation for tax reporting is often more than depreciation on the income statement. In later years, depreciation for tax reporting is often less than depreciation on the income statement. When temporary differences exist between taxable income on the tax return and the income before taxes on the income statement, corporations compute income taxes expense based on the income reported on the income statement. The result is that income taxes expense reported in the income statement is often different from the amount of income taxes payable to the government. This difference is the **deferred income tax liability.**

To illustrate, assume that in recording its usual quarterly income tax payments, a corporation computes $25,000 of income taxes expense. It also determines that only $21,000 is currently due and $4,000 is deferred to future years (a timing difference). The entry to record this end-of-period adjustment is

Assets = Liabilities + Equity
              +21,000   −25,000
              +4,000

Dec. 31	Income Taxes Expense	25,000	
	Income Taxes Payable		21,000
	Deferred Income Tax Liability		4,000
	To record tax expense and deferred tax liability.		

The credit to Income Taxes Payable reflects the amount currently due to be paid. The credit to Deferred Income Tax Liability reflects tax payments deferred until future years when the temporary difference reverses.

Temporary differences also can cause a company to pay income taxes *before* they are reported on the income statement as expense. If so, the company reports a *Deferred Income Tax Asset* on its balance sheet.

Summary

C1 Describe current and long-term liabilities and their characteristics. Liabilities are probable future payments of assets or services that past transactions or events obligate an entity to make. Current liabilities are due within one year or the operating cycle, whichever is longer. All other liabilities are long term.

C2 Identify and describe known current liabilities. Known (determinable) current liabilities are set by agreements or laws and are measurable with little uncertainty. They include accounts payable, sales taxes payable, unearned revenues, notes payable, payroll liabilities, and the current portion of long-term debt.

C3 Explain how to account for contingent liabilities. If an uncertain future payment depends on a probable future event and the amount can be reasonably estimated, the payment is recorded as a liability. The uncertain future payment is reported as a contingent liability (in the notes) if (*a*) the future event is reasonably possible but not probable or (*b*) the event is probable but the payment amount cannot be reasonably estimated.

A1 Compute the times interest earned ratio and use it to analyze liabilities. Times interest earned is computed by dividing a company's net income before interest expense and income taxes by the amount of interest expense. The times interest earned ratio reflects a company's ability to pay interest obligations.

P1 Prepare entries to account for short-term notes payable. Short-term notes payable are current liabilities; most bear interest. When a short-term note's face value equals the amount borrowed, it identifies a rate of interest to be paid at maturity.

P2   **Compute and record *employee* payroll deductions and liabilities.** Employee payroll deductions include FICA taxes, income taxes, and voluntary deductions such as for pensions and charities. They make up the difference between gross and net pay.

P3   **Compute and record *employer* payroll expenses and liabilities.** An employer's payroll expenses include employees' gross earnings, any employee benefits, and the payroll taxes levied on the employer. Payroll liabilities include employees' net pay amounts, withholdings from employee wages, any employer-promised benefits, and the employer's payroll taxes.

P4   **Account for estimated liabilities, including warranties and bonuses.** Liabilities for health and pension benefits, warranties, and bonuses are recorded with estimated amounts. These items are recognized as expenses when incurred and matched with revenues generated.

P5[A]   **Identify and describe the details of payroll reports, records, and procedures.** Employers report FICA taxes and federal income tax withholdings using Form 941. FUTA taxes are reported on Form 940. Earnings and deductions are reported to each employee and the federal government on Form W-2. An employer's payroll records often include a payroll register for each pay period, payroll checks and statements of earnings, and individual employee earnings reports.

Guidance Answers to **Decision Maker** and **Decision Ethics**

Web Designer   You need to be concerned about being an accomplice to unlawful payroll activities. Not paying federal and state taxes on wages earned is illegal and unethical. Such payments also will not provide the employee with Social Security and some Medicare credits. The best course of action is to request payment by check. If this fails to change the owner's payment practices, you must consider quitting this job.

Entrepreneur   Risk is partly reflected by the times interest earned ratio. This ratio for the first franchise is 1.5 [($100,000 + $200,000)/$200,000], whereas the ratio for the second franchise is 3.5 [($100,000 + $40,000)/$40,000]. This analysis shows that the first franchise is more at risk of incurring a loss if its sales decline. The second question asks about variability of income. If income greatly varies, this increases the risk an owner will not earn sufficient income to cover interest. Since the first franchise has the greater variability, it is a riskier investment.

Guidance Answers to **Quick Checks**

1. A liability involves a probable future payment of assets or services that an entity is presently obligated to make as a result of past transactions or events.

2. No, an expected future payment is not a liability unless an existing obligation was created by a past event or transaction.

3. In most cases, a liability due in 15 months is classified as long term. It is classified as a current liability if the company's operating cycle is 15 months or longer.

4. A creditor prefers a note payable instead of a past-due account payable so as to (*a*) charge interest and/or (*b*) have evidence of the debt and its terms for potential litigation or disputes.

5. $1,000* × (.008) + $1,000* × (.04) + $3,000 × (.062) + $3,000 × (.0145) = $277.50

---

* $1,000 of the $3,000 March pay is subject to FUTA and SUTA—the entire $6,000 pay from January and February was subject to them.

6. (*a*) FICA taxes are incurred by both employee and employer.
   (*b*) FUTA taxes are incurred by the employer.
   (*c*) SUTA taxes are incurred by the employer.
   (*d*) Withheld income taxes are incurred by the employee.

7. (*a*)

8. (*a*) Warranty expense was previously estimated and recorded.

9. (*b*)

10. A future payment is reported in the notes as a contingent liability if (*a*) the uncertain future event is probable but the amount of payment cannot be reasonably estimated or (*b*) the uncertain future event is not probable but has a reasonable possibility of occurring.

11. An employee's marital status, gross earnings and number of withholding allowances determine the deduction for federal income taxes.

12. $59

13. (*d*)

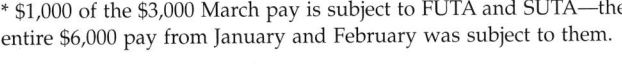

Key Terms

Contingent liability (p. 388)	Employee earnings report (p. 397)	Federal Unemployment Taxes (FUTA) (p. 384)
Current liabilities (p. 377)	Estimated liability (p. 385)	Form 940 (p. 395)
Current portion of long-term debt (p. 384)	Federal depository bank (p. 395)	Form 941 (p. 393)
Deferred income tax liability (p. 400)	Federal Insurance Contributions Act (FICA) Taxes (p. 382)	Form W-2 (p. 395)
Employee benefits (p. 385)		Form W-4 (p. 397)

Gross pay (p. 382)
Known liabilities (p. 378)
Long-term liabilities (p. 377)
Merit rating (p. 384)
Net pay (p. 382)

Payroll bank account (p. 397)
Payroll deductions (p. 382)
Payroll register (p. 395)
Short-term note
payable (p. 379)

State Unemployment Taxes
(SUTA) (p. 384)
Times interest earned (p. 390)
Wage bracket withholding table (p. 397)
Warranty (p. 386)

Multiple Choice Quiz   Answers on p. 417   mhhe.com/wildFA5e

Additional Quiz Questions are available at the book's Website.

1. On December 1, a company signed a $6,000, 90-day, 5% note payable, with principal plus interest due on March 1 of the following year. What amount of interest expense should be accrued at December 31 on the note?
   a. $300
   b. $25
   c. $100
   d. $75
   e. $0

2. An employee earned $50,000 during the year. FICA tax for social security is 6.2% and FICA tax for Medicare is 1.45%. The employer's share of FICA taxes is
   a. Zero, since the employee's pay exceeds the FICA limit.
   b. Zero, since FICA is not an employer tax.
   c. $3,100
   d. $725
   e. $3,825

3. Assume the FUTA tax rate is 0.8% and the SUTA tax rate is 5.4%. Both taxes are applied to the first $7,000 of an employee's pay. What is the total unemployment tax an employer must pay on an employee's annual wages of $40,000?
   a. $2,480
   b. $434
   c. $56
   d. $378
   e. Zero; the employee's wages exceed the $7,000 maximum.

4. A company sells big screen televisions for $3,000 each. Each television has a two-year warranty that covers the replacement of defective parts. It is estimated that 1% of all televisions sold will be returned under warranty at an average cost of $250 each. During July, the company sold 10,000 big screen televisions, and 80 were serviced under the warranty during July at a total cost of $18,000. The credit balance in the Estimated Warranty Liability account at July 1 was $26,000. What is the company's warranty expense for the month of July?
   a. $51,000
   b. $1,000
   c. $25,000
   d. $33,000
   e. $18,000

5. Employees earn vacation pay at the rate of 1 day per month. During October, 150 employees qualify for one vacation day each. Their average daily wage is $175 per day. What is the amount of vacation benefit expense for October?
   a. $26,250
   b. $175
   c. $2,100
   d. $63,875
   e. $150

Superscript letter ^{A} (^{B}) denotes assignments based on Appendix 9A (9B).

Discussion Questions

1. What are the three important questions concerning the uncertainty of liabilities?
2. What is the difference between a current and a long-term liability?
3. What is an estimated liability?
4. If $988 is the total of a sale that includes its sales tax of 4%, what is the selling price of the item only?
5. What is the combined amount (in percent) of the employee and employer Social Security tax rate?
6. What is the current Medicare tax rate? This rate is applied to what maximum level of salary and wages?

7. What determines the amount deducted from an employee's wages for federal income taxes?
8. Which payroll taxes are the employee's responsibility and which are the employer's responsibility?
9. What is an employer's unemployment merit rating? How are these ratings assigned to employers?
10. Why are warranty liabilities usually recognized on the balance sheet as liabilities even when they are uncertain?
11. Suppose that a company has a facility located where disastrous weather conditions often occur. Should it report a probable loss from a future disaster as a liability on its balance sheet? Explain.

12.ᴬ What is a wage bracket withholding table?

13.ᴬ What amount of income tax is withheld from the salary of an employee who is single with two withholding allowances and earning $725 per week? What if the employee earned $625 and has no withholding allowances? (Use Exhibit 9A.6.)

14. ♟ Refer to **Best Buy**'s balance sheet in Appendix A. What payroll-related liability does Best Buy report at February 28, 2009?

15. Refer to **RadioShack**'s balance sheet in Appendix A. What is the amount of RadioShack's accounts payable as of December 31, 2008?

16. ♟ Refer to **Apple**'s balance sheet in Appendix A. List Apple's current liabilities as of September 27, 2008.

17. ♟ Refer to **GOME**'s balance sheet in Appendix A. What current liabilities related to income taxes are on its balance sheet? Explain the meaning of each income tax account identified.

♟ *Denotes Discussion Questions that involve decision making.*

---

connect Available with Connect Accounting

Which of the following items are normally classified as a current liability for a company that has a 15-month operating cycle?

1. Note payable due in 18 months.

2. Note payable maturing in 2 years.

3. Portion of long-term note due in 15 months.

4. Salaries payable.

5. FICA taxes payable.

6. Note payable due in 11 months.

QUICK STUDY

QS 9-1
Classifying liabilities   C1 ♟

Tickets, Inc., receives $7,500,000 cash in advance ticket sales for a five-date tour of Bruce Springsteen. Record the advance ticket sales on October 31. Record the revenue earned for the first concert date of November 5, assuming it represents one-fifth of the advance ticket sales.

QS 9-2
Unearned revenue   C2

Wheeling Computing sells merchandise for $12,000 cash on September 30 (cost of merchandise is $7,800). The sales tax law requires Wheeling to collect 6% sales tax on every dollar of merchandise sold. Record the entry for the $12,000 sale and its applicable sales tax. Also record the entry that shows the remittance of the 6% tax on this sale to the state government on October 15.

QS 9-3
Accounting for sales taxes
C2

On November 7, 2011, Stockmann Company borrows $80,000 cash by signing a 90-day, 8% note payable with a face value of $80,000. (1) Compute the accrued interest payable on December 31, 2011, (2) prepare the journal entry to record the accrued interest expense at December 31, 2011, and (3) prepare the journal entry to record payment of the note at maturity.

QS 9-4
Interest-bearing note transactions
P1

DeNise Co. has five employees, each of whom earns $3,000 per month and has been employed since January 1. FICA Social Security taxes are 6.2% of the first $106,800 paid to each employee, and FICA Medicare taxes are 1.45% of gross pay. FUTA taxes are 0.8% and SUTA taxes are 5.4% of the first $7,000 paid to each employee. Prepare the March 31 journal entry to record the March payroll taxes expense.

QS 9-5
Record employer payroll taxes
P2 P3

Chavez Co.'s salaried employees earn four weeks vacation per year. It pays $156,000 in total employee salaries for 52 weeks but its employees work only 48 weeks. This means Chavez's total weekly expense is $3,250 ($156,000/48 weeks) instead of the $3,000 cash paid weekly to the employees ($156,000/52 weeks). Record Chavez's weekly vacation benefits expense.

QS 9-6
Accounting for vacations
P4

Erik Company offers an annual bonus to employees if the company meets certain net income goals. Prepare the journal entry to record a $15,000 bonus owed to its workers (to be shared equally) at calendar year-end.

QS 9-7
Accounting for bonuses   P4

On September 11, 2010, Lawn Outfitters sells a mower for $750 with a one-year warranty that covers parts. Warranty expense is estimated at 3% of sales. On July 24, 2011, the mower is brought in for repairs covered under the warranty requiring $55 in materials taken from the Repair Parts Inventory. Prepare the July 24, 2011, entry to record the warranty repairs.

QS 9-8
Recording warranty repairs
P4

The following legal claims exist for VanBeek Co. Identify the accounting treatment for each claim as either (*a*) a liability that is recorded or (*b*) an item described in notes to its financial statements.

1. VanBeek (defendant) estimates that a pending lawsuit could result in damages of $250,000; it is reasonably possible that the plaintiff will win the case.

2. VanBeek faces a probable loss on a pending lawsuit; the amount is not reasonably estimable.

3. VanBeek estimates damages in a case at $1,500,000 with a high probability of losing the case.

QS 9-9
Accounting for contingent liabilities

C3 ♟

QS 9-10
Times interest earned

A1

Compute the times interest earned for Zelma Company, which reports income before interest expense and income taxes of $1,044,000, and interest expense of $145,000. Interpret its times interest earned (assume that its competitors average a times interest earned of 4.0).

QS 9-11^B
Record deferred income tax liability P4

Eastwood Corporation has made and recorded its quarterly income tax payments. After a final review of taxes for the year, the company identifies an additional $40,000 of income tax expense that should be recorded. A portion of this additional expense, $6,000, is deferred for payment in future years. Record Eastwood's year-end adjusting entry for income tax expense.

QS 9-12
International accounting standards

C1 C2

Answer each of the following related to international accounting standards.

a. In general, how similar or different are the definitions and characteristics of current liabilities between IFRS and U.S. GAAP?

b. Companies reporting under IFRS often reference a set of current liabilities with the title *financial liabilities*. Identify two current liabilities that would be classified under financial liabilities per IFRS. (*Hint:* GOME provides examples in this chapter.)

Available with Connect Accounting **connect**

EXERCISES

Exercise 9-1
Classifying liabilities

C1

The following items appear on the balance sheet of a company with a two-month operating cycle. Identify the proper classification of each item as follows: C if it is a current liability, L if it is a long-term liability, or N if it is not a liability.

_____ **1.** Notes payable (due in 120 days).
_____ **2.** Notes payable (due in 6 to 12 months).
_____ **3.** Notes payable (due in 13 to 24 months).
_____ **4.** Accounts receivable.
_____ **5.** FUTA taxes payable.

_____ **6.** Notes payable (mature in five years).
_____ **7.** Current portion of long-term debt.
_____ **8.** Sales taxes payable.
_____ **9.** Wages payable.
_____ **10.** Salaries payable.

Exercise 9-2
Adjusting entries for liabilities

C2 C3 P4

Prepare any necessary adjusting entries at December 31, 2011, for Madison Company's year-end financial statements for each of the following separate transactions and events.

1. During December, Madison Company sold 4,100 units of a product that carries a 60-day warranty. December sales for this product total $164,000. The company expects 6% of the units to need warranty repairs, and it estimates the average repair cost per unit will be $14.

2. A disgruntled employee is suing Madison Company. Legal advisers believe that the company will probably need to pay damages, but the amount cannot be reasonably estimated.

3. Employees earn vacation pay at a rate of one day per month. During December, 28 employees qualify for one vacation day each. Their average daily wage is $105 per employee.

4. Madison Company guarantees the $13,000 debt of a supplier. The supplier will probably not default on the debt.

5. Madison Company records an adjusting entry for $520,000 of previously unrecorded cash sales (costing $260,000) and its sales taxes at a rate of 7%.

6. The company earned $104,000 of $260,000 previously received in advance for services.

Exercise 9-3
Computing and recording bonuses C2

Check (1) $50,000

For the year ended December 31, 2009, Kava Company has implemented an employee bonus program equal to 4% of Kava's net income, which employees will share equally. Kava's net income (prebonus) is expected to be $1,300,000, and bonus expense is deducted in computing net income.

1. Compute the amount of the bonus payable to the employees at year-end (use the method described in the chapter and round to the nearest dollar).

2. Prepare the journal entry at December 31, 2009, to record the bonus due the employees.

3. Prepare the journal entry at January 19, 2010, to record payment of the bonus to employees.

Exercise 9-4
Accounting for note payable

P1
Check (2b) Interest expense, $6,165

Motora Systems borrows $137,000 cash on May 15, 2009, by signing a 180-day, 9% note.

1. On what date does this note mature?

2. Suppose the face value of the note equals $137,000, the principal of the loan. Prepare the journal entries to record (*a*) issuance of the note and (*b*) payment of the note at maturity.

Keshena Co. borrows $240,000 cash on November 1, 2009, by signing a 180-day, 10% note with a face value of $240,000.

1. On what date does this note mature? (Assume February of 2010 has 28 days.)

2. How much interest expense results from this note in 2009? (Assume a 360-day year.)

3. How much interest expense results from this note in 2010? (Assume a 360-day year.)

4. Prepare journal entries to record (*a*) issuance of the note, (*b*) accrual of interest at the end of 2009, and (*c*) payment of the note at maturity.

Exercise 9-5
Interest-bearing notes payable with year-end adjustments
P1

Check (2) $4,000
(3) $8,000

RNG Co. has one employee, and the company is subject to the following taxes.

Tax	Rate	Applied To
FICA—Social Security	6.20%	First $106,800
FICA—Medicare	1.45	All gross pay
FUTA	0.80	First $7,000
SUTA	2.90	First $7,000

Compute RNG's amounts for each of these four taxes as applied to the employee's gross earnings for September under each of three separate situations (*a*), (*b*), and (*c*).

	Gross Pay through August	Gross Pay for September
a.	$ 5,900	$2,100
b.	17,700	2,500
c.	100,500	7,400

Exercise 9-6
Computing payroll taxes
P2 P3

Check (*a*) FUTA, $8.80; SUTA, $31.90

Using the data in situation *a* of Exercise 9-6, prepare the employer's September 30 journal entries to record (1) salary expense and its related payroll liabilities for this employee and (2) the employer's payroll taxes expense and its related liabilities. The employee's federal income taxes withheld by the employer are $250 for this pay period.

Exercise 9-7
Payroll-related journal entries
P2 P3

Lee Co. sold a copier costing $6,500 with a two-year parts warranty to a customer on August 16, 2009, for $9,400 cash. Lee uses the perpetual inventory system. On November 22, 2010, the copier requires on-site repairs that are completed the same day. The repairs cost $125 for materials taken from the Repair Parts Inventory. These are the only repairs required in 2010 for this copier. Based on experience, Lee expects to incur warranty costs equal to 3% of dollar sales. It records warranty expense with an adjusting entry at the end of each year.

1. How much warranty expense does the company report in 2009 for this copier?

2. How much is the estimated warranty liability for this copier as of December 31, 2009?

3. How much warranty expense does the company report in 2010 for this copier?

4. How much is the estimated warranty liability for this copier as of December 31, 2010?

5. Prepare journal entries to record (*a*) the copier's sale; (*b*) the adjustment on December 31, 2009, to recognize the warranty expense; and (*c*) the repairs that occur in November 2010.

Exercise 9-8
Warranty expense and liability computations and entries
P4

Check (1) $282

(4) $157

Use the following information from separate companies *a* through *f* to compute times interest earned. Which company indicates the strongest ability to pay interest expense as it comes due?

	Net Income (Loss)	Interest Expense	Income Taxes
a.	$122,000	$36,600	$ 30,500
b.	116,600	11,660	41,976
c.	125,100	7,506	60,048
d.	103,700	31,110	43,554
e.	79,300	9,516	30,134
f.	(34,160)	74,469	0

Exercise 9-9
Computing and interpreting times interest earned
A1

Check (b) 14.60

Exercise 9-10^A
Net pay and tax computations
P5

The payroll records of Simplex Software show the following information about Ken LeShon, an employee, for the weekly pay period ending September 30, 2009. LeShon is single and claims one allowance. Compute his Social Security tax (6.2%), Medicare tax (1.45%), federal income tax withholding, state income tax (0.5%), and net pay for the current pay period. The state income tax is 0.5 percent on the first $9,000 earned. (Use the withholding table in Exhibit 9A.6, and round tax amounts to the nearest cent.)

Total (gross) earnings for current pay period	$ 735
Cumulative earnings of previous pay periods	9,500

Check   Net pay, $585.77

Exercise 9-11^A
Gross and net pay computation
P5

Tad Newbern, an unmarried employee, works 47 hours in the week ended January 12. His pay rate is $12 per hour, and his wages are subject to no deductions other than FICA—Social Security, FICA—Medicare, and federal income taxes. He claims two withholding allowances. Compute his regular pay, overtime pay (overtime premium is 50% of the regular rate for hours in excess of 40 per week), and gross pay. Then compute his FICA tax deduction (use 6.2% for the Social Security portion and 1.45% for the Medicare portion), income tax deduction (use the wage bracket withholding table of Exhibit 9A.6), total deductions, and net pay. (Round tax amounts to the nearest cent.)

Check   Net pay, $501.64

Exercise 9-12^B
Accounting for income taxes
P4

Florita Corporation prepares financial statements for each month-end. As part of its accounting process, estimated income taxes are accrued each month for 34% of the current month's net income. The income taxes are paid in the first month of each quarter for the amount accrued for the prior quarter. The following information is available for the fourth quarter of year 2009. When tax computations are completed on January 20, 2010, Florita determines that the quarter's Income Taxes Payable account balance should be $46,693 on December 31, 2009 (its unadjusted balance is $42,364).

October 2009 net income	$45,200
November 2009 net income	29,400
December 2009 net income	50,000

Check   (1) $4,329

1. Determine the amount of the accounting adjustment (dated as of December 31, 2009) to produce the proper ending balance in the Income Taxes Payable account.
2. Prepare journal entries to record (*a*) the December 31, 2009, adjustment to the Income Taxes Payable account and (*b*) the January 20, 2010, payment of the fourth-quarter taxes.

Exercise 9-13
Accounting for current liabilities under IFRS
P4

Volvo Group reports the following information for its product warranty costs as of December 31, 2008, along with provisions and utilizations of warranty liabilities for the year ended December 31, 2008 (SEK in millions).

Product warranty costs

Estimated costs for product warranties are charged to cost of sales when the products are sold. Estimated warranty costs include contractual warranty and goodwill warranty. Warranty provisions are estimated with consideration of historical claims statistics, the warranty period, the average time-lag between faults occurring and claims to the company, and anticipated changes in quality indexes. Differences between actual warranty claims and the estimated claims generally affect the recognized expense and provisions in future periods. At December 31, 2008, warranty cost provisions amounted to 10,354.

Product warranty liabilities, December 31, 2007	SEK 9,373
Additional provisions to product warranty liabilities	6,201
Utilizations and reductions of product warranty liabilities	(5,220)
Product warranty liabilities, December 31, 2008	10,354

1. Prepare Volvo's journal entry to record its estimated warranty liabilities (provisions) for 2008.
2. Prepare Volvo's journal entry to record its costs (utilizations) related to its warranty program for 2008. Assume those costs involve replacements taken out of Inventory, with no cash involved.
3. How much warranty expense does Volvo report for 2008?

connect™ Available with Connect Accounting

Montag Co. entered into the following transactions involving short-term liabilities in 2010 and 2011.

PROBLEM SET A

Problem 9-1A
Short-term notes payable
transactions and entries

P1

eXcel
mhhe.com/wildFA5e

2010

Apr. 20   Purchased $48,250 of merchandise on credit from Locust, terms are 1/10, n/30. Montag uses the perpetual inventory system.

May 19   Replaced the April 20 account payable to Locust with a 120-day, $39,000 note bearing 9% annual interest along with paying $9,250 in cash.

July 8   Borrowed $120,000 cash from National Bank by signing a 120-day, 8.5% interest-bearing note with a face value of $120,000.

___?___   Paid the amount due on the note to Locust at the maturity date.

___?___   Paid the amount due on the note to National Bank at the maturity date.

Nov. 28   Borrowed $60,000 cash from Fargo Bank by signing a 60-day, 8% interest-bearing note with a face value of $60,000.

Dec. 31   Recorded an adjusting entry for accrued interest on the note to Fargo Bank.

2011

___?___   Paid the amount due on the note to Fargo Bank at the maturity date.

Required

1. Determine the maturity date for each of the three notes described.

2. Determine the interest due at maturity for each of the three notes. (Assume a 360-day year.)

3. Determine the interest expense to be recorded in the adjusting entry at the end of 2010.

4. Determine the interest expense to be recorded in 2011.

5. Prepare journal entries for all the preceding transactions and events for years 2010 and 2011.

Check (2) Locust, $1,170
(3) $440
(4) $360

On October 29, 2010, Bram Co. began operations by purchasing razors for resale. Bram uses the perpetual inventory method. The razors have a 90-day warranty that requires the company to replace any nonworking razor. When a razor is returned, the company discards it and mails a new one from Merchandise Inventory to the customer. The company's cost per new razor is $16 and its retail selling price is $60 in both 2010 and 2011. The manufacturer has advised the company to expect warranty costs to equal 7% of dollar sales. The following transactions and events occurred.

Problem 9-2A
Warranty expense and
liability estimation

P4

2010

Nov. 11   Sold 75 razors for $4,500 cash.
     30   Recognized warranty expense related to November sales with an adjusting entry.
Dec. 9   Replaced 15 razors that were returned under the warranty.
     16   Sold 210 razors for $12,600 cash.
     29   Replaced 30 razors that were returned under the warranty.
     31   Recognized warranty expense related to December sales with an adjusting entry.

2011

Jan. 5   Sold 130 razors for $7,800 cash.
     17   Replaced 35 razors that were returned under the warranty.
     31   Recognized warranty expense related to January sales with an adjusting entry.

Required

1. Prepare journal entries to record these transactions and adjustments for 2010 and 2011.

2. How much warranty expense is reported for November 2010 and for December 2010?

3. How much warranty expense is reported for January 2011?

4. What is the balance of the Estimated Warranty Liability account as of December 31, 2010?

5. What is the balance of the Estimated Warranty Liability account as of January 31, 2011?

Check (3) $546
(4) $477 Cr.
(5) $463 Cr.

Problem 9-3A
Computing and analyzing times interest earned

A1

Shown here are condensed income statements for two different companies (both are organized as LLCs and pay no income taxes).

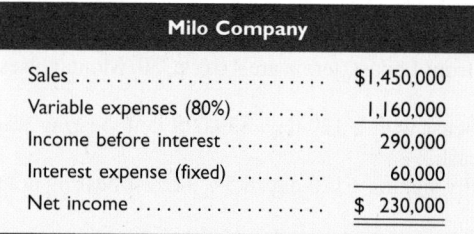

Milo Company	
Sales	$1,450,000
Variable expenses (80%)	1,160,000
Income before interest	290,000
Interest expense (fixed)	60,000
Net income	$ 230,000

Warner Company	
Sales	$1,450,000
Variable expenses (60%)	870,000
Income before interest	580,000
Interest expense (fixed)	350,000
Net income	$ 230,000

Required

1. Compute times interest earned for Milo Company.
2. Compute times interest earned for Warner Company.
3. What happens to each company's net income if sales increase by 40%?
4. What happens to each company's net income if sales increase by 50%?
5. What happens to each company's net income if sales increase by 80%?
6. What happens to each company's net income if sales decrease by 20%?
7. What happens to each company's net income if sales decrease by 30%?
8. What happens to each company's net income if sales decrease by 40%?

Check   (4) Milo net income, $375,000 (63% increase)

(6) Warner net income, $114,000 (50% decrease)

Analysis Component

9. Comment on the results from parts 3 through 8 in relation to the fixed-cost strategies of the two companies and the ratio values you computed in parts 1 and 2.

Problem 9-4A
Payroll expenses, withholdings, and taxes

P2   P3

mhhe.com/wildFA5e

Pardee Co. pays its employees each week. Its employees' gross pay is subject to these taxes.

Tax	Rate	Applied To
FICA—Social Security	6.20%	First $106,800
FICA—Medicare	1.45	All gross pay
FUTA	0.80	First $7,000
SUTA	2.15	First $7,000

The company is preparing its payroll calculations for the week ended August 25. Payroll records show the following information for the company's four employees.

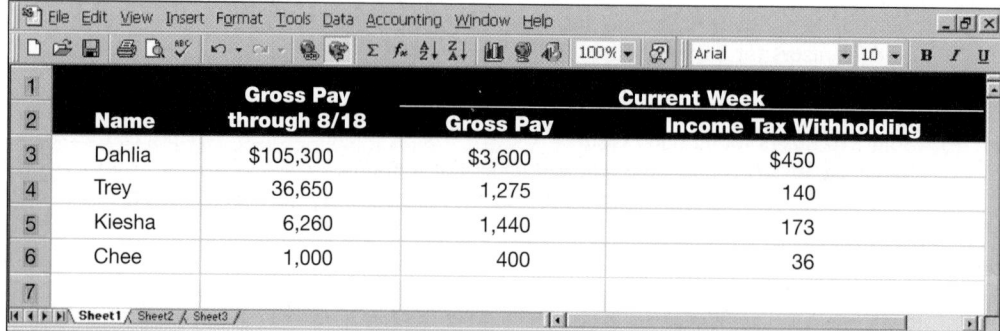

Name	Gross Pay through 8/18	Current Week	
		Gross Pay	Income Tax Withholding
Dahlia	$105,300	$3,600	$450
Trey	36,650	1,275	140
Kiesha	6,260	1,440	173
Chee	1,000	400	36

In addition to gross pay, the company must pay one-half of the $22 per employee weekly health insurance; each employee pays the remaining one-half. The company also contributes an extra 8% of each employee's gross pay (at no cost to employees) to a pension fund.

Required

Compute the following for the week ended August 25 (round amounts to the nearest cent):

1. Each employee's FICA withholdings for Social Security.
2. Each employee's FICA withholdings for Medicare.

Check   (3) $286.13

3. Employer's FICA taxes for Social Security.

4. Employer's FICA taxes for Medicare.

(4) $97.37
(5) $9.12

5. Employer's FUTA taxes.

6. Employer's SUTA taxes.

7. Each employee's net (take-home) pay.

(7) Total net pay, $5,488.50

8. Employer's total payroll-related expense for each employee.

On January 8, the end of the first weekly pay period of the year, Regal Company's payroll register showed that its employees earned $27,760 of office salaries and $70,240 of sales salaries. Withholdings from the employees' salaries include FICA Social Security taxes at the rate of 6.2%, FICA Medicare taxes at the rate of 1.45%, $13,360 of federal income taxes, $1,350 of medical insurance deductions, and $840 of union dues. No employee earned more than $7,000 in this first period.

Problem 9-5A
Entries for payroll transactions
P2   P3

Required

1. Calculate FICA Social Security taxes payable and FICA Medicare taxes payable. Prepare the journal entry to record Regal Company's January 8 (employee) payroll expenses and liabilities.

2. Prepare the journal entry to record Regal's (employer) payroll taxes resulting from the January 8 payroll. Regal's merit rating reduces its state unemployment tax rate to 5% of the first $7,000 paid each employee. The federal unemployment tax rate is 0.8%.

Check   (1) Cr. Salaries Payable,
$74,953.00

(2) Dr. Payroll Taxes
Expense, $13,181.00

Franco Company has 20 employees, each of whom earns $3,000 per month and is paid on the last day of each month. All 20 have been employed continuously at this amount since January 1. Franco uses a payroll bank account and special payroll checks to pay its employees. On March 1, the following accounts and balances exist in its general ledger:

Problem 9-6A^A
Entries for payroll transactions
P2   P3   P5

a. FICA—Social Security Taxes Payable, $7,440; FICA—Medicare Taxes Payable, $1,740. (The balances of these accounts represent total liabilities for *both* the employer's and employees' FICA taxes for the February payroll only.)

b. Employees' Federal Income Taxes Payable, $5,250 (liability for February only).

c. Federal Unemployment Taxes Payable, $960 (liability for January and February together).

d. State Unemployment Taxes Payable, $4,800 (liability for January and February together).

During March and April, the company had the following payroll transactions.

Mar. 15   Issued check payable to Swift Bank, a federal depository bank authorized to accept employers' payments of FICA taxes and employee income tax withholdings. The $14,430 check is in payment of the February FICA and employee income taxes.

31   Recorded the March payroll and transferred funds from the regular bank account to the payroll bank account. Issued checks payable to each employee in payment of the March payroll. The payroll register shows the following summary totals for the March pay period.

Check   March 31: Cr. Salaries
Payable, $50,160

Salaries and Wages		Gross Pay	FICA Taxes*	Federal Income Taxes	Net Pay
Office Salaries	Shop Wages				
$24,000	$36,000	$60,000	$3,720	$5,250	$50,160
			$ 870		

* FICA taxes are Social Security and Medicare, respectively.

31   Recorded the employer's payroll taxes resulting from the March payroll. The company has a merit rating that reduces its state unemployment tax rate to 4.0% of the first $7,000 paid each employee. The federal rate is 0.8%.

March 31: Dr. Payroll Taxes
Expenses, $5,550

Apr. 15   Issued check to Swift Bank in payment of the March FICA and employee income taxes.

15   Issued check to the State Tax Commission for the January, February, and March state unemployment taxes. Mailed the check and the first quarter tax return to the Commission.

April 15: Cr. Cash, $14,430
(Swift Bank)

30   Issued check payable to Swift Bank in payment of the employer's FUTA taxes for the first quarter of the year.

30   Mailed Form 941 to the IRS, reporting the FICA taxes and the employees' federal income tax withholdings for the first quarter.

Required

Prepare journal entries to record the transactions and events for both March and April.

PROBLEM SET B

Nix Co. entered into the following transactions involving short-term liabilities in 2010 and 2011.

Problem 9-1B

Short-term notes payable
transactions and entries

P1

2010

Apr. 22   Purchased $6,000 of merchandise on credit from Wolf Products, terms are 1/10, n/30. Nix uses the perpetual inventory system.

May 23   Replaced the April 22 account payable to Wolf Products with a 60-day, $5,400 note bearing 8% annual interest along with paying $600 in cash.

July 15   Borrowed $8,500 cash from Autumn Bank by signing a 90-day, 8% interest-bearing note with a face value of $8,500.

____?____   Paid the amount due on the note to Wolf Products at maturity.

____?____   Paid the amount due on the note to Autumn Bank at maturity.

Dec. 6   Borrowed $9,600 cash from City Bank by signing a 90-day, 6% interest-bearing note with a face value of $9,600.

      31   Recorded an adjusting entry for accrued interest on the note to City Bank.

2011

____?____   Paid the amount due on the note to City Bank at maturity. (February of 2011 has 28 days.)

Required

1. Determine the maturity date for each of the three notes described.

2. Determine the interest due at maturity for each of the three notes. (Assume a 360-day year.)

3. Determine the interest expense to be recorded in the adjusting entry at the end of 2010.

4. Determine the interest expense to be recorded in 2011.

5. Prepare journal entries for all the preceding transactions and events for years 2010 and 2011.

Check   (2) Wolf, $72
               (3) $40
               (4) $104

Problem 9-2B

Warranty expense and
liability estimation

P4

On November 10, 2009, Lorna Co. began operations by purchasing coffee grinders for resale. Lorna uses the perpetual inventory method. The grinders have a 90-day warranty that requires the company to re-place any nonworking grinder. When a grinder is returned, the company discards it and mails a new one from Merchandise Inventory to the customer. The company's cost per new grinder is $15 and its retail selling price is $85 in both 2009 and 2010. The manufacturer has advised the company to expect warranty costs to equal 8% of dollar sales. The following transactions and events occurred.

2009

Nov. 16   Sold 50 grinders for $4,250 cash.
      30   Recognized warranty expense related to November sales with an adjusting entry.
Dec. 12   Replaced 11 grinders that were returned under the warranty.
      18   Sold 160 grinders for $13,600 cash.
      28   Replaced 22 grinders that were returned under the warranty.
      31   Recognized warranty expense related to December sales with an adjusting entry.

2010

Jan. 7   Sold 95 grinders for $8,075 cash.
      21   Replaced 45 grinders that were returned under the warranty.
      31   Recognized warranty expense related to January sales with an adjusting entry.

Required

1. Prepare journal entries to record these transactions and adjustments for 2009 and 2010.

2. How much warranty expense is reported for November 2009 and for December 2009?

3. How much warranty expense is reported for January 2010?

4. What is the balance of the Estimated Warranty Liability account as of December 31, 2009?

5. What is the balance of the Estimated Warranty Liability account as of January 31, 2010?

Check   (3) $646
               (4) $933 Cr.
               (5) $904 Cr.

Shown here are condensed income statements for two different companies (both are organized as LLCs and pay no income taxes).

Problem 9-3B
Computing and analyzing times interest earned

A1

Ellis Company	
Sales	$250,000
Variable expenses (50%)	125,000
Income before interest	125,000
Interest expense (fixed)	75,000
Net income	$ 50,000

Seidel Company	
Sales	$250,000
Variable expenses (75%)	187,500
Income before interest	62,500
Interest expense (fixed)	12,500
Net income	$ 50,000

Required

1. Compute times interest earned for Ellis Company.
2. Compute times interest earned for Seidel Company.
3. What happens to each company's net income if sales increase by 40%?
4. What happens to each company's net income if sales increase by 50%?
5. What happens to each company's net income if sales increase by 80%?
6. What happens to each company's net income if sales decrease by 20%?
7. What happens to each company's net income if sales decrease by 30%?
8. What happens to each company's net income if sales decrease by 40%?

Check   (3) Ellis net income, $100,000
(100% increase)

(6) Seidel net income,
$37,500 (25% decrease)

Analysis Component

9. Comment on the results from parts 3 through 8 in relation to the fixed-cost strategies of the two companies and the ratio values you computed in parts 1 and 2.

Fishing Guides Co. pays its employees each week. Employees' gross pay is subject to these taxes.

Problem 9-4B
Payroll expenses, withholdings, and taxes

P2 P3

Tax	Rate	Applied To
FICA—Social Security	6.20%	First $106,800
FICA—Medicare	1.45	All gross pay
FUTA	0.80	First $7,000
SUTA	1.75	First $7,000

The company is preparing its payroll calculations for the week ended September 30. Payroll records show the following information for the company's four employees.

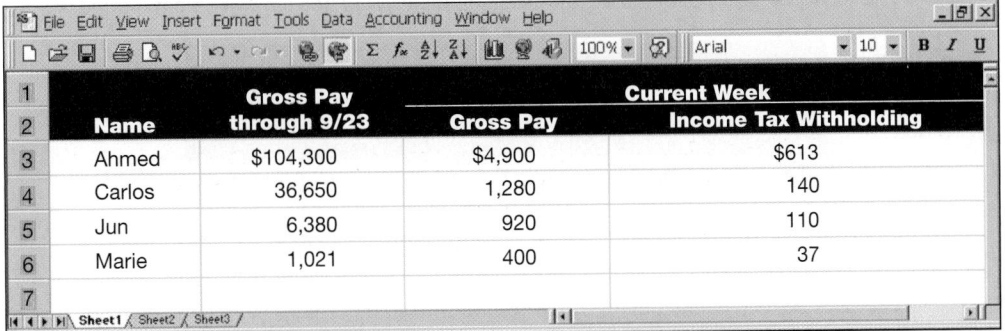

Name	Gross Pay through 9/23	Current Week	
		Gross Pay	Income Tax Withholding
Ahmed	$104,300	$4,900	$613
Carlos	36,650	1,280	140
Jun	6,380	920	110
Marie	1,021	400	37

In addition to gross pay, the company must pay one-half of the $20 per employee weekly health insurance; each employee pays the remaining one-half. The company also contributes an extra 8% of each employee's gross pay (at no cost to employees) to a pension fund.

Required

Compute the following for the week ended September 30 (round amounts to the nearest cent):

1. Each employee's FICA withholdings for Social Security.
2. Each employee's FICA withholdings for Medicare.
3. Employer's FICA taxes for Social Security.
4. Employer's FICA taxes for Medicare.
5. Employer's FUTA taxes.

Check   (3) $316.20
(4) $108.75
(5) $8.16

(7) Total net pay, $6,135.05

6. Employer's SUTA taxes.

7. Each employee's net (take-home) pay.

8. Employer's total payroll-related expense for each employee.

Problem 9-5B
Entries for payroll transactions

P2 P3

Ravello Company's first weekly pay period of the year ends on January 8. On that date, the column totals in Ravello's payroll register indicate its sales employees earned $20,160, its office employees earned $70,840, and its delivery employees earned $3,000. The employees are to have withheld from their wages FICA Social Security taxes at the rate of 6.2%, FICA Medicare taxes at the rate of 1.45%, $12,760 of federal income taxes, $1,350 of medical insurance deductions, and $820 of union dues. No employee earned more than $7,000 in the first pay period.

Required

Check (1) Cr. Salaries Payable, $71,879.00

(2) Dr. Payroll Taxes Expense, $9,823.00

1. Calculate FICA Social Security taxes payable and FICA Medicare taxes payable. Prepare the journal entry to record Ravello Company's January 8 (employee) payroll expenses and liabilities.

2. Prepare the journal entry to record Ravello's (employer) payroll taxes resulting from the January 8 payroll. Ravello's merit rating reduces its state unemployment tax rate to 2% of the first $7,000 paid each employee. The federal unemployment tax rate is 0.8%.

Problem 9-6B^A
Entries for payroll transactions

P2 P3 P5

JLS Company has 12 employees, each of whom earns $3,000 per month and is paid on the last day of each month. All 12 have been employed continuously at this amount since January 1. JLS uses a payroll bank account and special payroll checks to pay its employees. On March 1, the following accounts and balances exist in its general ledger:

a. FICA—Social Security Taxes Payable, $4,464; FICA—Medicare Taxes Payable, $1,044. (The balances of these accounts represent total liabilities for *both* the employer's and employees' FICA taxes for the February payroll only.)

b. Employees' Federal Income Taxes Payable, $4,050 (liability for February only).

c. Federal Unemployment Taxes Payable, $576 (liability for January and February together).

d. State Unemployment Taxes Payable, $3,600 (liability for January and February together).

During March and April, the company had the following payroll transactions.

March 15 Issued check payable to Security Bank, a federal depository bank authorized to accept employers' payments of FICA taxes and employee income tax withholdings. The $9,558 check is in payment of the February FICA and employee income taxes.

Check Mar. 31: Cr. Salaries Payable, $29,196

31 Recorded the March payroll and transferred funds from the regular bank account to the payroll bank account. Issued checks payable to each employee in payment of the March payroll. The payroll register shows the following summary totals for the March pay period.

Salaries and Wages				Federal	
Office Salaries	Shop Wages	Gross Pay	FICA Taxes*	Income Taxes	Net Pay
$21,000	$15,000	$36,000	$2,232	$4,050	$29,196
			$ 522		

* FICA taxes are Social Security and Medicare, respectively.

Check March 31: Dr. Payroll Taxes Expenses, $3,450

31 Recorded the employer's payroll taxes resulting from the March payroll. The company has a merit rating that reduces its state unemployment tax rate to 5.0% of the first $7,000 paid each employee. The federal rate is 0.8%.

April 15: Cr. Cash $9,558 (Security Bank)

April 15 Issued check payable to Security Bank in payment of the March FICA and employee income taxes.

15 Issued check to the State Tax Commission for the January, February, and March state unemployment taxes. Mailed the check and the second quarter tax return to the State Tax Commission.

30 Issued check payable to Security Bank in payment of the employer's FUTA taxes for the first quarter of the year.

30 Mailed Form 941 to the IRS, reporting the FICA taxes and the employees' federal income tax withholdings for the first quarter.

Required

Prepare journal entries to record the transactions and events for both March and April.

SERIAL PROBLEM

Success Systems

(This serial problem began in Chapter 1 and continues through most of the book. If previous chapter segments were not completed, the serial problem can begin at this point. It is helpful, but not necessary, to use the Working Papers that accompany the book.)

SP 9   Review the February 26 and March 25 transactions for Success Systems (SP 4) from Chapter 4.

Required

1. Assume that Lyn Addie is an unmarried employee. Her $1,000 of wages are subject to no deductions other than FICA Social Security taxes, FICA Medicare taxes, and federal income taxes. Her federal income taxes for this pay period total $159. Compute her net pay for the eight days' work paid on February 26. (Round amounts to the nearest cent.)

2. Record the journal entry to reflect the payroll payment to Lyn Addie as computed in part 1.

3. Record the journal entry to reflect the (employer) payroll tax expenses for the February 26 payroll payment. Assume Lyn Addie has not met earnings limits for FUTA and SUTA—the FUTA rate is 0.8% and the SUTA rate is 4% for Success Systems. (Round amounts to the nearest cent.)

4. Record the entry(ies) for the merchandise sold on March 25 if a 4% sales tax rate applies.

COMPREHENSIVE PROBLEM

Bug-Off Exterminators
(Review of Chapters 1–9)

CP 9   Bug-Off Exterminators provides pest control services and sells extermination products manufactured by other companies. The following six-column table contains the company's unadjusted trial balance as of December 31, 2009.

BUG-OFF EXTERMINATORS December 31, 2009	Unadjusted Trial Balance		Adjustments		Adjusted Trial Balance	
Cash	$ 17,000					
Accounts receivable	4,000					
Allowance for doubtful accounts		$ 828				
Merchandise inventory	11,700					
Trucks	32,000					
Accum. depreciation—Trucks		0				
Equipment	45,000					
Accum. depreciation—Equipment		12,200				
Accounts payable		5,000				
Estimated warranty liability		1,400				
Unearned services revenue		0				
Interest payable		0				
Long-term notes payable		15,000				
Common stock		10,000				
Retained earnings		49,700				
Dividends	10,000					
Extermination services revenue		60,000				
Interest revenue		872				
Sales (of merchandise)		71,026				
Cost of goods sold	46,300					
Depreciation expense—Trucks	0					
Depreciation expense—Equipment	0					
Wages expense	35,000					
Interest expense	0					
Rent expense	9,000					
Bad debts expense	0					
Miscellaneous expense	1,226					
Repairs expense	8,000					
Utilities expense	6,800					
Warranty expense	0					
Totals	$226,026	$226,026				

The following information in *a* through *h* applies to the company at the end of the current year.

a. The bank reconciliation as of December 31, 2009, includes the following facts.

Cash balance per bank	$15,100
Cash balance per books	17,000
Outstanding checks	1,800
Deposit in transit	2,450
Interest earned (on bank account)	52
Bank service charges (miscellaneous expense)	15

Reported on the bank statement is a canceled check that the company failed to record. (Information from the bank reconciliation allows you to determine the amount of this check, which is a payment on an account payable.)

b. An examination of customers' accounts shows that accounts totaling $679 should be written off as uncollectible. Using an aging of receivables, the company determines that the ending balance of the Allowance for Doubtful Accounts should be $700.

c. A truck is purchased and placed in service on January 1, 2009. Its cost is being depreciated with the straight-line method using the following facts and estimates.

Original cost	$32,000
Expected salvage value	8,000
Useful life (years)	4

d. Two items of equipment (a sprayer and an injector) were purchased and put into service in early January 2007. They are being depreciated with the straight-line method using these facts and estimates.

	Sprayer	Injector
Original cost	$27,000	$18,000
Expected salvage value	3,000	2,500
Useful life (years)	8	5

e. On August 1, 2009, the company is paid $3,840 cash in advance to provide monthly service for an apartment complex for one year. The company began providing the services in August. When the cash was received, the full amount was credited to the Extermination Services Revenue account.

f. The company offers a warranty for the services it sells. The expected cost of providing warranty service is 2.5% of the extermination services revenue of $57,760 for 2009. No warranty expense has been recorded for 2009. All costs of servicing warranties in 2009 were properly debited to the Estimated Warranty Liability account.

g. The $15,000 long-term note is an 8%, five-year, interest-bearing note with interest payable annually on December 31. The note was signed with First National Bank on December 31, 2009.

h. The ending inventory of merchandise is counted and determined to have a cost of $11,700. Bug-Off uses a perpetual inventory system.

Required

1. Use the preceding information to determine amounts for the following items.

Check (1*a*) Cash bal. $15,750
(1*b*) $551 credit

   a. Correct (reconciled) ending balance of Cash, and the amount of the omitted check.

   b. Adjustment needed to obtain the correct ending balance of the Allowance for Doubtful Accounts.

   c. Depreciation expense for the truck used during year 2009.

   d. Depreciation expense for the two items of equipment used during year 2009.

   e. The adjusted 2009 ending balances of the Extermination Services Revenue and Unearned Services Revenue accounts.

(1*f*) Estim. warranty liability,
$2,844 Cr.

   f. The adjusted 2009 ending balances of the accounts for Warranty Expense and Estimated Warranty Liability.

   g. The adjusted 2009 ending balances of the accounts for Interest Expense and Interest Payable. (Round amounts to nearest whole dollar.)

2. Use the results of part 1 to complete the six-column table by first entering the appropriate adjustments for items *a* through *g* and then completing the adjusted trial balance columns. (*Hint:* Item *b* requires two adjustments.)

3. Prepare journal entries to record the adjustments entered on the six-column table. Assume Bug-Off's adjusted balance for Merchandise Inventory matches the year-end physical count.

4. Prepare a single-step income statement, a statement of retained earnings (cash dividends declared during 2009 were $10,000), and a classified balance sheet.

(2) Adjusted trial balance totals, $238,207

(4) Net income, $9,274; Total assets, $82,771

BEYOND THE NUMBERS

BTN 9-1   Refer to the financial statements of **Best Buy** in Appendix A to answer the following.

1. Compute times interest earned for the fiscal years ended 2009, 2008, and 2007. Comment on Best Buy's ability to cover its interest expense for this period. Assume an industry average of 18.1.

2. Best Buy's current liabilities include "Unredeemed gift card liabilities." Explain how this liability is created and how Best Buy satisfies this liability.

3. Does Best Buy have any commitments or contingencies? Briefly explain them.

REPORTING IN ACTION

A1   P4

Fast Forward

4. Access Best Buy's financial statements for fiscal years ending after February 28, 2009, at its Website (BestBuy.com) or the SEC's EDGAR database (www.SEC.gov). Compute its times interest earned for years ending after February 28, 2009, and compare your results to those in part 1.

BTN 9-2   Key figures for **Best Buy** and **RadioShack** follow.

COMPARATIVE ANALYSIS

A1

	Best Buy			RadioShack		
($ millions)	Current Year	One Year Prior	Two Years Prior	Current Year	One Year Prior	Two Years Prior
Net income	$1,003	$1,407	$1,377	$192.4	$236.8	$73.4
Income taxes	674	815	752	111.9	129.8	38.0
Interest expense	94	62	31	29.9	38.8	44.3

Required

1. Compute times interest earned for the three years' data shown for each company.

2. Comment on which company appears stronger in its ability to pay interest obligations if income should decline. Assume an industry average of 18.1.

BTN 9-3   Connor Bly is a sales manager for an automobile dealership. He earns a bonus each year based on revenue from the number of autos sold in the year less related warranty expenses. Actual warranty expenses have varied over the prior 10 years from a low of 3% of an automobile's selling price to a high of 10%. In the past, Bly has tended to estimate warranty expenses on the high end to be conservative. He must work with the dealership's accountant at year-end to arrive at the warranty expense accrual for cars sold each year.

1. Does the warranty accrual decision create any ethical dilemma for Bly?

2. Since warranty expenses vary, what percent do you think Bly should choose for the current year? Justify your response.

ETHICS CHALLENGE

P4

BTN 9-4   Dustin Clemens is the accounting and finance manager for a manufacturer. At year-end, he must determine how to account for the company's contingencies. His manager, Madeline Pretti, objects to Clemens's proposal to recognize an expense and a liability for warranty service on units of a new product introduced in the fourth quarter. Pretti comments, "There's no way we can estimate this warranty

COMMUNICATING IN PRACTICE

C3

cost. We don't owe anyone anything until a product fails and it is returned. Let's report an expense if and when we do any warranty work."

Required

Prepare a one-page memorandum for Clemens to send to Pretti defending his proposal.

TAKING IT TO THE NET

C1 A1

BTN 9-5   Access the February 25, 2009, filing of the December 31, 2008, annual 10-K report of **McDonald's Corporation** (Ticker: MCD), which is available from **www.SEC.gov**.

Required

1. Identify the current liabilities on McDonald's balance sheet as of December 31, 2008.
2. What portion (in percent) of McDonald's long-term debt matures within the next 12 months?
3. Use the consolidated statement of income for the year ended December 31, 2008, to compute McDonald's times interest earned ratio. Comment on the result. Assume an industry average of 7.9.

TEAMWORK IN ACTION

C2 P1

BTN 9-6   Assume that your team is in business and you must borrow $6,000 cash for short-term needs. You have been shopping banks for a loan, and you have the following two options.

A. Sign a $6,000, 90-day, 10% interest-bearing note dated June 1.
B. Sign a $6,000, 120-day, 8% interest-bearing note dated June 1.

Required

1. Discuss these two options and determine the best choice. Ensure that all teammates concur with the decision and understand the rationale.
2. Each member of the team is to prepare *one* of the following journal entries.
    a. Option A—at date of issuance.
    b. Option B—at date of issuance.
    c. Option A—at maturity date.
    d. Option B—at maturity date.
3. In rotation, each member is to explain the entry he or she prepared in part 2 to the team. Ensure that all team members concur with and understand the entries.
4. Assume that the funds are borrowed on December 1 (instead of June 1) and your business operates on a calendar-year reporting period. Each member of the team is to prepare *one* of the following entries.
    a. Option A—the year-end adjustment.
    b. Option B—the year-end adjustment.
    c. Option A—at maturity date.
    d. Option B—at maturity date.
5. In rotation, each member is to explain the entry he or she prepared in part 4 to the team. Ensure that all team members concur with and understand the entries.

ENTREPRENEURIAL DECISION

A1

BTN 9-7   Review the chapter's opening feature about Aaron Kennedy and his start-up company, **Noodles & Company**. Assume that Aaron is considering expanding his business to open an outlet in Hawaii. Assume the current income statement is as follows.

NOODLES & COMPANY Income Statement For Year Ended December 31, 2011	
Sales	$1,000,000
Cost of goods sold (30%)	300,000
Gross profit	700,000
Operating expenses (25%)	250,000
Net income	$ 450,000

Noodles & Company currently has no interest-bearing debt. If Noodles & Company expands to open a Hawaiian location, it will require a $300,000 loan. Noodles & Company has found a bank that will loan it the money on a 7% note payable. The company believes that, at least for the first few years, sales at its Hawaiian location will be $250,000, and that all expenses (including cost of goods sold) will follow the same patterns as the current locations.

Required

1. Prepare an income statement (separately for current outlets, Hawaii, and total) for Noodles & Company assuming that he borrows the funds and expands to Hawaii. Annual revenues at the current locations are expected to remain at $1,000,000.

2. Compute Noodles & Company's times interest earned under the expansion assumptions in part 1.

3. Assume sales at the Hawaii location are $400,000. Prepare an income statement (separately for current outlets, Hawaii, and total) for Noodles & Company and compute times interest earned.

4. Assume sales at the Hawaii location are $100,000. Prepare an income statement (separately for current outlets, Hawaii, and total) for Noodles & Company and compute times interest earned.

5. Comment on your results from parts 1 through 4.

HITTING THE ROAD

P2

BTN 9-8 Check your phone book or the Social Security Administration Website (www.SSA.gov) to locate the Social Security office near you. Visit the office to request a personal earnings and estimate form. Fill out the form and mail according to the instructions. You will receive a statement from the Social Security Administration regarding your earnings history and future Social Security benefits you can receive. (Formerly the request could be made online. The online service has been discontinued and is now under review by the Social Security Administration due to security concerns.) It is good to request an earnings and benefit statement every 5 to 10 years to make sure you have received credit for all wages earned and for which you and your employer have paid taxes into the system.

GLOBAL DECISION

A1

BTN 9-9 **GOME**, **Best Buy**, and **RadioShack** are all competitors in the global marketplace. Comparative figures for GOME (www.GOME.com.hk), along with selected figures from Best Buy and RadioShack, follow.

Key Figures	GOME (RMB millions) Current Year	GOME (RMB millions) Prior Year	Best Buy Current Year	Best Buy Prior Year	RadioShack Current Year	RadioShack Prior Year
Net income	1,048	1,127	—	—	—	—
Income taxes	435	360	—	—	—	—
Interest expense*	212	193	—	—	—	—
Times interest earned	?	?	18.8	36.8	11.2	10.4

* Titled finance costs for GOME.

Required

1. Compute the times interest earned ratio for the most recent two years for GOME using the data shown.

2. Which company of the three presented provides the best coverage of interest expense? Explain.

ANSWERS TO MULTIPLE CHOICE QUIZ

1. b; $6,000 × 0.05 × 30/360 = $25

2. e; $50,000 × (.062 + .0145) = $3,825

3. b; $7,000 × (.008 + .054) = $434

4. c; 10,000 television sets × .01 × $250 = $25,000

5. a; 150 employees × $175 per day × 1 vacation day earned = $26,250

10

Reporting and Analyzing Long-Term Liabilities

"Get a clear vision and stick to it" —Jason Osborn

A Look Back

Chapter 9 focused on how current liabilities are identified, computed, recorded, and reported. Attention was directed at notes, payroll, sales taxes, warranties, employee benefits, and contingencies.

A Look at This Chapter

This chapter describes the accounting for and analysis of bonds and notes. We explain their characteristics, payment patterns, interest computations, retirement, and reporting requirements. An appendix to this chapter introduces leases and pensions.

A Look Ahead

Chapter 11 focuses on corporate equity transactions, including stock issuances and dividends. We also explain how to report and analyze income, earnings per share, and retained earnings.

Granola Gurus

NEW YORK—Jason Osborn never planned to be an entrepreneur. "It was sort of an accident," explains Osborn. "I was looking for a healthy snack food as an alternative to cookies and brownies." Osborn starting cooking with granola and his concoctions caught on. After sharing it with his buddy, Jason Wright, the two decided to launch **Feed Granola Company (FeedGranola.com),** a provider of granola snacks made with organic multi-grains.

"We started peddling it . . . to a few different coffee shops and one natural health food store," recalls Osborn. "That created a small demand and we realized we had a viable product." Adds Wright, "I had no idea that I would have a granola company one day!" Their commitment to healthy food carries over to the financial side. The two especially focus on the important task of managing liabilities for payroll, supplies, employee benefits, training, and taxes. Both insist that effective management of liabilities, especially long-term financing from sources such as bonds and notes, is crucial to success. They stress that monitoring and controlling liabilities are a must.

To help control liabilities, Osborn describes how they began by trading their granola products for kitchen space to reduce their financing needs using bonds and notes. "We partnered with a meal delivery service and bartered to use their kitchen space," explains Osborn. "We'd bake our granola during the night when they weren't using it and we paid for the usage in granola. That's how we paid rent." Creative payment of liabilities and the financing of the business can mean success or failure.

The two continue to monitor liabilities and their payment patterns. "Trying to balance receivables versus payables is always a big challenge," explains Wright. "When you are a small, growing company, cash flow is always a problem." The two insist that accounting for and monitoring liabilities of long-term financing are key to a successful start-up. Their company now generates sufficient income to pay for liabilities of interest and principal on long-term debt and still produces revenue growth for expansion. "We want to expand our product line," says Osborn. "[Soon] we'll be available in almost every region of the country."

[Sources: *Feed Granola Website*, January 2010; *BusinessWeek*, September 2007; *Inc.com*, July and October 2007; *The Wall Street Journal*, May 2008]

CAP

Conceptual

C1 Explain the types and payment patterns of notes. (p. 430)

C2 *Appendix 10A*—Explain and compute the present value of an amount(s) to be paid at a future date(s). (p. 438)

C3 *Appendix 10C*—Describe the accrual of bond interest when bond payments do not align with accounting periods. (p. 443)

C4 *Appendix 10D*—Describe accounting for leases and pensions. (p. 445)

Analytical

A1 Compare bond financing with stock financing. (p. 420)

A2 Assess debt features and their implications. (p. 434)

A3 Compute the debt-to-equity ratio and explain its use. (p. 435)

LP10

Procedural

P1 Prepare entries to record bond issuance and bond interest expense. (p. 422)

P2 Compute and record amortization of bond discount. (p. 423)

P3 Compute and record amortization of bond premium. (p. 426)

P4 Record the retirement of bonds. (p. 429)

P5 Prepare entries to account for notes. (p. 432)

Individuals, companies, and governments issue bonds to finance their activities. In return for financing, bonds promise to repay the lender with interest. This chapter explains the basics of bonds and the accounting for their issuance and retirement. The chapter also describes long-term notes as another financ-

ing source. We explain how present value concepts impact both the accounting for and reporting of bonds and notes. Appendixes to this chapter discuss present value concepts applicable to liabilities, effective interest amortization, and the accounting for leases and pensions.

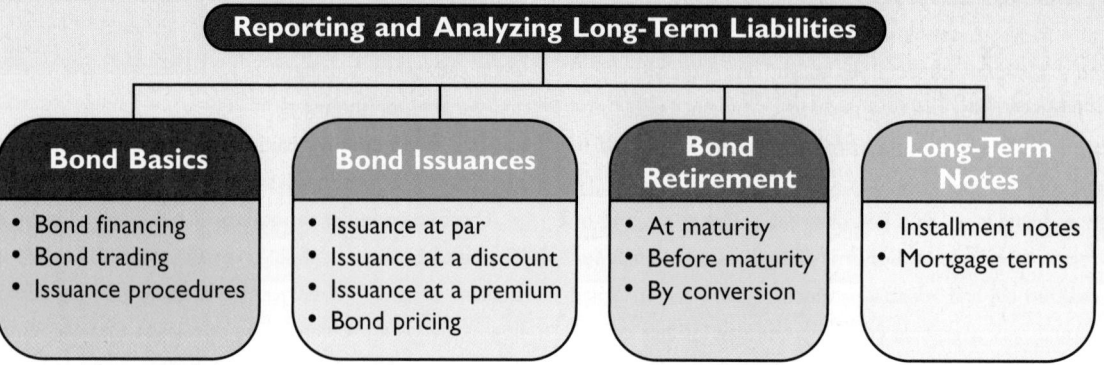

Reporting and Analyzing Long-Term Liabilities			
Bond Basics	**Bond Issuances**	**Bond Retirement**	**Long-Term Notes**
• Bond financing • Bond trading • Issuance procedures	• Issuance at par • Issuance at a discount • Issuance at a premium • Bond pricing	• At maturity • Before maturity • By conversion	• Installment notes • Mortgage terms

Basics of Bonds

Video 10.2

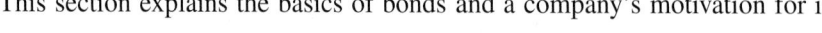

A1	Compare bond financing with stock financing.

This section explains the basics of bonds and a company's motivation for issuing them.

Bond Financing

Projects that demand large amounts of money often are funded from bond issuances. (Both for-profit and nonprofit companies, as well as governmental units, such as nations, states, cities, and school districts, issue bonds.) A **bond** is its issuer's written promise to pay an amount identified as the par value of the bond with interest. The **par value of a bond,** also called the *face amount* or *face value,* is paid at a specified future date known as the bond's *maturity date.* Most bonds also require the issuer to make semiannual interest payments. The amount of interest paid each period is determined by multiplying the par value of the bond by the bond's contract rate of interest. This section explains both advantages and disadvantages of bond financing.

Advantages of Bonds   There are three main advantages of bond financing:

1. *Bonds do not affect owner control.* Equity financing reflects ownership in a company, whereas bond financing does not. A person who contributes $1,000 of a company's $10,000 equity financing typically controls one-tenth of all owner decisions. A person who owns a $1,000, 11%, 20-year bond has no ownership right. This person, or bond-holder, is to receive from the bond issuer 11% interest, or $110, each year the bond is outstanding and $1,000 when it matures in 20 years.

2. *Interest on bonds is tax deductible.* Bond interest payments are tax deductible for the issuer, but equity payments (distributions) to owners are not. To illustrate, assume that a corporation with no bond financing earns $15,000 in income *before* paying taxes at a 40% tax rate, which amounts to $6,000 ($15,000 × 40%) in taxes. If a portion of its financing is in bonds, however, the resulting bond interest is deducted in computing taxable income. That is, if bond interest expense is $10,000, the taxes owed would be $2,000 ([$15,000 − $10,000] × 40%), which is less than the $6,000 owed with no bond financing.

3. *Bonds can increase return on equity.* A company that earns a higher return with borrowed funds than it pays in interest on those funds increases its return on equity. This process is called *financial leverage* or *trading on the equity.*

Point: Financial leverage reflects issuance of bonds, notes, or preferred stock.

To illustrate the third point, consider Magnum Co., which has $1 million in equity and is planning a $500,000 expansion to meet increasing demand for its product. Magnum predicts the

$500,000 expansion will yield $125,000 in additional income before paying any interest. It currently earns $100,000 per year and has no interest expense. Magnum is considering three plans. Plan A is to not expand. Plan B is to expand and raise $500,000 from equity financing. Plan C is to expand and issue $500,000 of bonds that pay 10% annual interest ($50,000). Exhibit 10.1 shows how these three plans affect Magnum's net income, equity, and return on equity (net income/equity). The owner(s) will earn a higher return on equity if expansion occurs. Moreover, the preferred expansion plan is to issue bonds. Projected net income under Plan C ($175,000) is smaller than under Plan B ($225,000), but the return on equity is larger because of less equity investment. Plan C has another advantage if income is taxable. This illustration reflects a general rule: *Return on equity increases when the expected rate of return from the new assets is higher than the rate of interest expense on the debt financing.*

Example: Compute return on equity for all three plans if Magnum currently earns $150,000 instead of $100,000. *Answer ($ 000s):*
Plan A = 15%   ($150/$1,000)
Plan B = 18.3%   ($275/$1,500)
Plan C = 22.5%   ($225/$1,000)

EXHIBIT 10.1

Financing with Bonds versus Equity

	Plan A Do Not Expand	Plan B Equity Financing	Plan C Bond Financing
Income before interest expense	$ 100,000	$ 225,000	$ 225,000
Interest expense	—	—	(50,000)
Net income	$ 100,000	$ 225,000	$ 175,000
Equity	$1,000,000	$1,500,000	$1,000,000
Return on equity	10.0%	15.0%	17.5%

Disadvantages of Bonds   The two main disadvantages of bond financing are:

1. *Bonds can decrease return on equity.* When a company earns a lower return with the borrowed funds than it pays in interest, it decreases its return on equity. This downside risk of financial leverage is more likely to arise when a company has periods of low income or net losses.

2. *Bonds require payment of both periodic interest and the par value at maturity.* Bond payments can be especially burdensome when income and cash flow are low. Equity financing, in contrast, does not require any payments because cash withdrawals (dividends) are paid at the discretion of the owner (or board).

Point: Debt financing is desirable when interest is tax deductible, when owner control is preferred, and when return on equity exceeds the debt's interest rate.

A company must weigh the risks and returns of the disadvantages and advantages of bond financing when deciding whether to issue bonds to finance operations.

Bond Trading

Bonds are securities that can be readily bought and sold. A large number of bonds trade on both the New York Exchange and the American Exchange. A bond *issue* consists of a number of bonds, usually in denominations of $1,000 or $5,000, and is sold to many different lenders. After bonds are issued, they often are bought and sold by investors, meaning that any particular bond probably has a number of owners before it matures. Since bonds are exchanged (bought and sold) in the market, they have a market value (price). For convenience, bond market values are expressed as a percent of their par (face) value. For example, a company's bonds might be trading at 103½, meaning they can be bought or sold for 103.5% of their par value. Bonds can also trade below par value. For instance, if a company's bonds are trading at 95, they can be bought or sold at 95% of their par value.

Decision Insight

Quotes   The **IBM** bond quote here is interpreted (left to right) as **Bonds,** issuer name; **Rate,** contract interest rate (7%); **Mat,** matures in year 2025 when

Bonds	Rate	Mat	Yld	Vol	Close	Chg
IBM	7	25	5.9	130	119¼	+1¼

principal is paid; **Yld,** yield rate (5.9%) of bond at current price; **Vol,** daily dollar worth ($130,000) of trades (in 1,000s); **Close,** closing price (119.25) for the day as percent of par value; **Chg,** change (+1.25) in closing price from prior day's close.

Bond-Issuing Procedures

State and federal laws govern bond issuances. Bond issuers also want to ensure that they do not violate any of their existing contractual agreements when issuing bonds. Authorization of bond issuances includes the number of bonds authorized, their par value, and the contract interest rate.

EXHIBIT 10.2

Bond Certificate

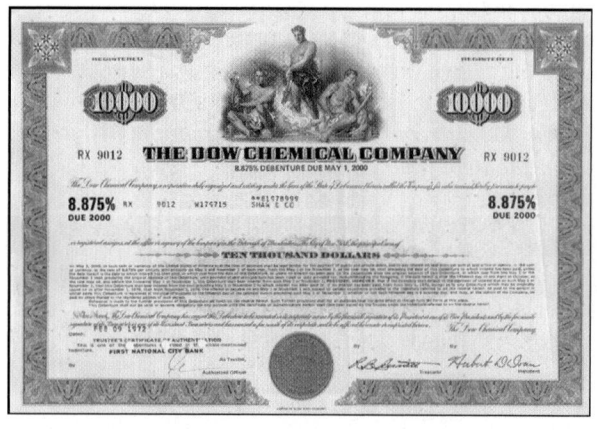

The legal document identifying the rights and obligations of both the bond-holders and the issuer is called the **bond indenture,** which is the legal contract between the issuer and the bond-holders. A bondholder may also receive a bond certificate as evidence of the company's debt. A **bond certificate,** such as that shown in Exhibit 10.2, includes specifics such as the issuer's name, the par value, the contract interest rate, and the maturity date. Many companies reduce costs by not issuing paper certificates to bondholders.[1]

Point: *Indenture* refers to a bond's legal contract; *debenture* refers to an unsecured bond.

Bond Issuances

Video10.2

This section explains accounting for bond issuances at par, below par (discount), and above par (premium). It also describes how to amortize a discount or premium and record bonds issued between interest payment dates.

Issuing Bonds at Par

P1 Prepare entries to record bond issuance and bond interest expense.

To illustrate an issuance of bonds at par value, suppose a company receives authorization to issue $800,000 of 9%, 20-year bonds dated January 1, 2009, that mature on December 31, 2028, and pay interest semiannually on each June 30 and December 31. After accepting the bond indenture on behalf of the bondholders, the trustee can sell all or a portion of the bonds to an underwriter. If all bonds are sold at par value, the issuer records the sale as:

Assets   = Liabilities + Equity
+800,000   +800,000

2009			
Jan. 1	Cash...	800,000	
	Bonds Payable		800,000
	Sold bonds at par.		

This entry reflects increases in the issuer's cash *and* long-term liabilities.

The issuer records the first semiannual interest payment as follows.

Assets = Liabilities + Equity
−36,000   −36,000

2009			
June 30	Bond Interest Expense	36,000	
	Cash....................................		36,000
	Paid semiannual interest (9% × $800,000 × ½ year).		

Point: The *spread* between the dealer's cost and what buyers pay can be huge. Dealers earn more than $25 billion in annual spread revenue.

Global: In the United Kingdom, government bonds are called *gilts*—short for gilt-edged investments.

---

[1] The issuing company normally sells its bonds to an investment firm called an *underwriter,* which resells them to the public. An issuing company can also sell bonds directly to investors. When an underwriter sells bonds to a large number of investors, a *trustee* represents and protects the bondholders' interests. The trustee monitors the issuer to ensure that it complies with the obligations in the bond indenture. Most trustees are large banks or trust companies. The trustee writes and accepts the terms of a bond indenture before it is issued. When bonds are offered to the public, called *floating an issue,* they must be registered with the Securities and Exchange Commission (SEC). SEC registration requires the issuer to file certain financial information. Most company bonds are issued in par value units of $1,000 or $5,000. *A baby bond* has a par value of less than $1,000, such as $100.

The issuer pays and records its semiannual interest obligation every six months until the bonds mature. When they mature, the issuer records its payment of principal as:

2028			
Dec. 31	Bonds Payable	800,000	
	Cash		800,000
	Paid bond principal at maturity.		

Assets   = Liabilities + Equity
−800,000   −800,000

Bond Discount or Premium

The bond issuer pays the interest rate specified in the indenture, the **contract rate,** also referred to as the *coupon rate, stated rate,* or *nominal rate.* The annual interest paid is determined by multiplying the bond par value by the contract rate. The contract rate is usually stated on an annual basis, even if interest is paid semiannually. For example, if a company issues a $1,000, 8% bond paying interest semiannually, it pays annual interest of $80 (8% × $1,000) in two semiannual payments of $40 each.

The contract rate sets the amount of interest the issuer pays in *cash,* which is not necessarily the *bond interest expense* actually incurred by the issuer. Bond interest expense depends on the bond's market value at issuance, which is determined by market expectations of the risk of lending to the issuer. The bond's **market rate** of interest is the rate that borrowers are willing to pay and lenders are willing to accept for a particular bond and its risk level. As the risk level increases, the rate increases to compensate purchasers for the bonds' increased risk. Also, the market rate is generally higher when the time period until the bond matures is longer due to the risk of adverse events occurring over a longer time period.

Many bond issuers try to set a contract rate of interest equal to the market rate they expect as of the bond issuance date. When the contract rate and market rate are equal, a bond sells at par value, but when they are not equal, a bond does not sell at par value. Instead, it is sold at a *premium* above par value or at a *discount* below par value. Exhibit 10.3 shows the relation between the contract rate, market rate, and a bond's issue price.

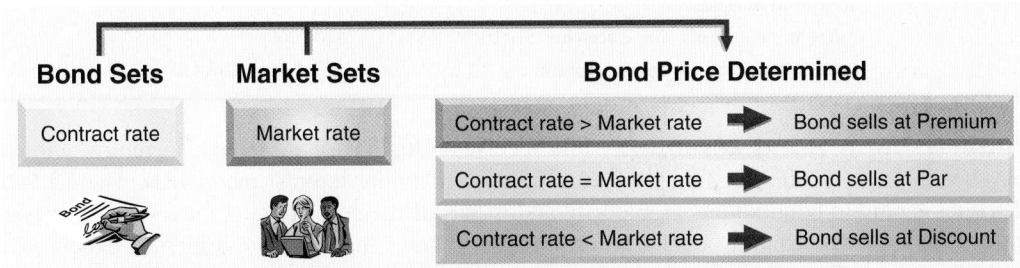

EXHIBIT 10.3

Relation between Bond Issue Price, Contract Rate, and Market Rate

Quick Check   Answers—p. 448

1. A company issues $10,000 of 9%, 5-year bonds dated January 1, 2011, that mature on December 31, 2015, and pay interest semiannually on each June 30 and December 31. Prepare the entry to record this bond issuance and the first semiannual interest payment.

2. How do you compute the amount of interest a bond issuer pays in cash each year?

3. When the contract rate is above the market rate, do bonds sell at a premium or a discount? Do purchasers pay more or less than the par value of the bonds?

Issuing Bonds at a Discount

A **discount on bonds payable** occurs when a company issues bonds with a contract rate less than the market rate. This means that the issue price is less than par value. To illustrate, assume that **Fila** announces an offer to issue bonds with a $100,000 par value, an 8% annual contract rate (paid semiannually), and a two-year life. Also assume that the market rate for Fila

P2 Compute and record amortization of bond discount.

bonds is 10%. These bonds then will sell at a discount since the contract rate is less than the market rate. The exact issue price for these bonds is stated as 96.454 (implying 96.454% of par value, or $96,454); we show how to compute this issue price later in the chapter. These bonds obligate the issuer to pay two separate types of future cash flows.

1. Par value of $100,000 cash at the end of the bonds' two-year life.
2. Cash interest payments of $4,000 (4% × $100,000) at the end of each semiannual period during the bonds' two-year life.

The exact pattern of cash flows for the Fila bonds is shown in Exhibit 10.4.

EXHIBIT 10.4

Cash Flows for Fila Bonds

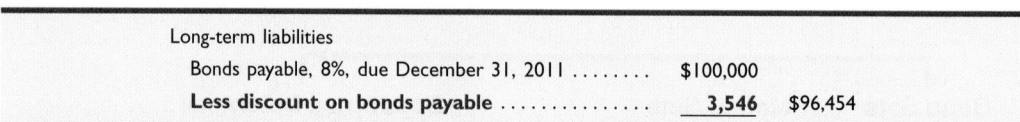

	$4,000	$4,000	$4,000	$100,000 $4,000
0	6 mo.	12 mo.	18 mo.	24 mo.

When Fila accepts $96,454 cash for its bonds on the issue date of December 31, 2009, it records the sale as follows.

Dec. 31	Cash	96,454	
	Discount on Bonds Payable	3,546	
	Bonds Payable		100,000
	Sold bonds at a discount on their issue date.		

These bonds are reported in the long-term liability section of the issuer's December 31, 2009, balance sheet as shown in Exhibit 10.5. A discount is deducted from the par value of bonds to yield the **carrying (book) value of bonds.** Discount on Bonds Payable is a contra liability account.

EXHIBIT 10.5

Balance Sheet Presentation of Bond Discount

Long-term liabilities		
Bonds payable, 8%, due December 31, 2011	$100,000	
Less discount on bonds payable	**3,546**	**$96,454**

Amortizing a Bond Discount   Fila receives $96,454 for its bonds; in return it must pay bondholders $100,000 after two years (plus semiannual interest payments). The $3,546 discount is paid to bondholders at maturity and is part of the cost of using the $96,454 for two years. The upper portion of panel A in Exhibit 10.6 shows that total bond interest expense of $19,546 is the difference between the total amount repaid to bondholders ($116,000) and the amount borrowed from bondholders ($96,454). Alternatively, we can compute total bond interest expense as the sum of the 4 interest payments and the bond discount. This alternative computation is shown in the lower portion of panel A.

The total $19,546 bond interest expense must be allocated across the 4 semiannual periods in the bonds' life, and the bonds' carrying value must be updated at each balance sheet date. This is accomplished using the straight-line method (or the effective interest method in Appendix 10B). Both methods systematically reduce the bond discount to zero over the two-year life. This process is called *amortizing a bond discount*.

Video 10.2

Straight-Line Method   The **straight-line bond amortization** method allocates an equal portion of the total bond interest expense to each interest period. To apply the straight-line method to Fila's bonds, we divide the total bond interest expense of $19,546 by 4 (the number of semiannual periods in the bonds' life). This gives a bond interest expense of $4,887 per period, which is $4,886.5 rounded to the nearest dollar per period (all computations, including those for assignments, are rounded to the nearest whole dollar). Alternatively, we can find this number by first dividing the $3,546 discount by 4, which yields the $887 amount of discount to be amortized each interest period. When the $887 is added to the $4,000 cash payment, the

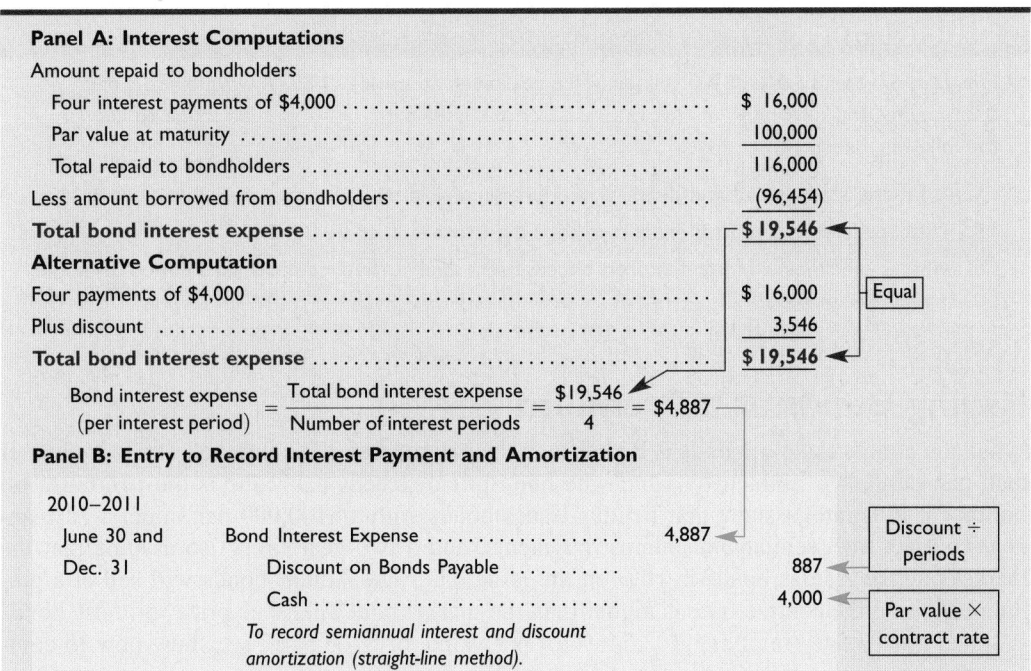

EXHIBIT 10.6

Interest Computation and Entry for Bonds Issued at a Discount

bond interest expense for each period is $4,887. Panel B of Exhibit 10.6 shows how the issuer records bond interest expense and updates the balance of the bond liability account at the end of *each* of the 4 semiannual interest periods (June 30, 2010, through December 31, 2011).

Exhibit 10.7 shows the pattern of decreases in the Discount on Bonds Payable account and the pattern of increases in the bonds' carrying value. The following points summarize the discount bonds' straight-line amortization.

1. At issuance, the $100,000 par value consists of the $96,454 cash received by the issuer plus the $3,546 discount.

2. During the bonds' life, the (unamortized) discount decreases each period by the $887 amortization ($3,546/4), and the carrying value (par value less unamortized discount) increases each period by $887.

Semiannual Period-End	Unamortized Discount*	Carrying Value†
(0) 12/31/2009	$3,546	$ 96,454
(1) 6/30/2010	2,659	97,341
(2) 12/31/2010	1,772	98,228
(3) 6/30/2011	885	99,115
(4) 12/31/2011	0‡	100,000

EXHIBIT 10.7

Straight-Line Amortization of Bond Discount

* Total bond discount (of $3,546) less accumulated periodic amortization ($887 per semiannual interest period).

† Bond par value (of $100,000) less unamortized discount.

‡ Adjusted for rounding.

> The two columns always sum to par value for a discount bond.

3. At maturity, the unamortized discount equals zero, and the carrying value equals the $100,000 par value that the issuer pays the holder.

We see that the issuer incurs a $4,887 bond interest expense each period but pays only $4,000 cash. The $887 unpaid portion of this expense is added to the bonds' carrying value. (The total $3,546 unamortized discount is "paid" when the bonds mature; $100,000 is paid at maturity but only $96,454 was received at issuance.)

Decision Insight

Ratings Game   Many bond buyers rely on rating services to assess bond risk. The best known are **Standard & Poor's, Moody's,** and **Fitch.** These services focus on the issuer's financial statements and other factors in setting ratings. Standard & Poor's ratings, from best quality to default, are AAA, AA, A, BBB, BB, B, CCC, CC, C, and D. Ratings can include a plus (+) or minus (−) to show relative standing within a category.

Quick Check   Answers—p. 448

Five-year, 6% bonds with a $100,000 par value are issued at a price of $91,893. Interest is paid semiannually, and the bonds' market rate is 8% on the issue date. Use this information to answer the following questions:

4. Are these bonds issued at a discount or a premium? Explain your answer.

5. What is the issuer's journal entry to record the issuance of these bonds?

6. What is the amount of bond interest expense recorded at the first semiannual period using the straight-line method?

Issuing Bonds at a Premium

P3   Compute and record amortization of bond premium.

When the contract rate of bonds is higher than the market rate, the bonds sell at a price higher than par value. The amount by which the bond price exceeds par value is the **premium on bonds.** To illustrate, assume that **Adidas** issues bonds with a $100,000 par value, a 12% annual contract rate, semiannual interest payments, and a two-year life. Also assume that the market rate for Adidas bonds is 10% on the issue date. The Adidas bonds will sell at a premium because the contract rate is higher than the market rate. The issue price for these bonds is stated as 103.546 (implying 103.546% of par value, or $103,546); we show how to compute this issue price later in the chapter. These bonds obligate the issuer to pay out two separate future cash flows.

1. Par value of $100,000 cash at the end of the bonds' two-year life.
2. Cash interest payments of $6,000 (6% × $100,000) at the end of each semiannual period during the bonds' two-year life.

The exact pattern of cash flows for the Adidas bonds is shown in Exhibit 10.8.

EXHIBIT 10.8

Cash Flows for Adidas Bonds

				$100,000
$6,000	$6,000	$6,000	$6,000	
0	6 mo.	12 mo.	18 mo.	24 mo.

When Adidas accepts $103,546 cash for its bonds on the issue date of December 31, 2009, it records this transaction as follows.

Assets = Liabilities + Equity
+103,546   +100,000
                +3,546

Dec. 31	Cash	103,546	
	Premium on Bonds Payable		3,546
	Bonds Payable		100,000
	Sold bonds at a premium on their issue date.		

These bonds are reported in the long-term liability section of the issuer's December 31, 2009, balance sheet as shown in Exhibit 10.9. A premium is added to par value to yield the carrying (book) value of bonds. Premium on Bonds Payable is an adjunct (also called *accretion*) liability account.

EXHIBIT 10.9

Balance Sheet Presentation of Bond Premium

Long-term liabilities		
Bonds payable, 12%, due December 31, 2011	$100,000	
Plus premium on bonds payable	**3,546**	$103,546

Amortizing a Bond Premium   Adidas receives $103,546 for its bonds; in return, it pays bondholders $100,000 after two years (plus semiannual interest payments). The $3,546 premium not repaid to issuer's bondholders at maturity goes to reduce the issuer's expense of using the $103,546 for two years. The upper portion of panel A of Exhibit 10.10 shows that total bond interest expense of $20,454 is the difference between the total amount repaid to bondholders ($124,000) and the amount borrowed from bondholders ($103,546). Alternatively, we can

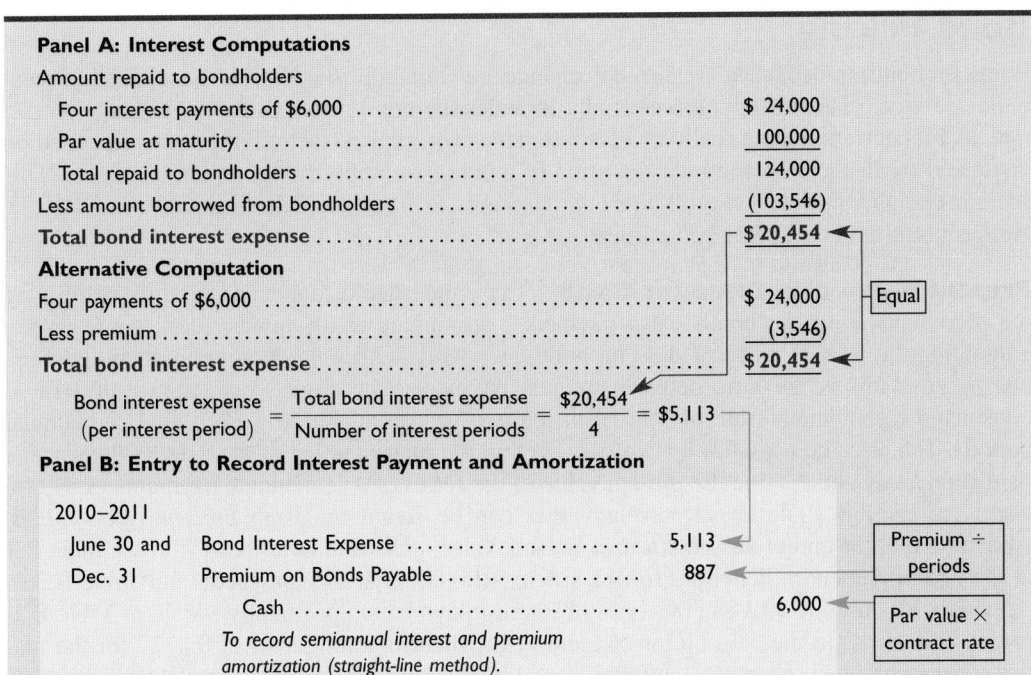

EXHIBIT 10.10

Interest Computation and Entry for Bonds Issued at a Premium

compute total bond interest expense as the sum of the 4 interest payments less the bond premium. The premium is subtracted because it will not be paid to bondholders when the bonds mature; see the lower portion of panel A. Total bond interest expense must be allocated over the 4 semi-annual periods using the straight-line method (or the effective interest method in Appendix 10B).

Straight-Line Method The straight-line method allocates an equal portion of total bond interest expense to each of the bonds' semiannual interest periods. To apply this method to Adidas bonds, we divide the two years' total bond interest expense of $20,454 by 4 (the number of semi-annual periods in the bonds' life). This gives a total bond interest expense of $5,113 per period, which is $5,113.5 rounded down so that the journal entry balances and for simplicity in presentation (alternatively, one could carry cents). Panel B of Exhibit 10.10 shows how the issuer records bond interest expense and updates the balance of the bond liability account for *each* semiannual period (June 30, 2010, through December 31, 2011).

Point: A premium decreases Bond Interest Expense; a discount increases it.

Exhibit 10.11 shows the pattern of decreases in the unamortized Premium on Bonds Payable account and in the bonds' carrying value. The following points summarize straight-line amortization of the premium bonds.

EXHIBIT 10.11

Straight-Line Amortization of Bond Premium

Semiannual Period-End	Unamortized Premium*	Carrying Value†
(0) 12/31/2009	$3,546	$103,546
(1) 6/30/2010	2,659	102,659
(2) 12/31/2010	1,772	101,772
(3) 6/30/2011	885	100,885
(4) 12/31/2011	0‡	100,000

* Total bond premium (of $3,546) less accumulated periodic amortization ($887 per semiannual interest period).

† Bond par value (of $100,000) plus unamortized premium.

‡ Adjusted for rounding.

During the bond life, carrying value is adjusted to par and the amortized premium to zero.

1. At issuance, the $100,000 par value plus the $3,546 premium equals the $103,546 cash received by the issuer.

2. During the bonds' life, the (unamortized) premium decreases each period by the $887 amortization ($3,546/4), and the carrying value decreases each period by the same $887.

3. At maturity, the unamortized premium equals zero, and the carrying value equals the $100,000 par value that the issuer pays the holder.

The next section describes bond pricing. An instructor can choose to cover bond pricing or not. Assignments requiring the next section are: Quick Study 10-4, Exercises 10-9 & 10-10, Problems 10-1A & 10-1B and 10-4A & 10-4B.

Bond Pricing

Prices for bonds traded on an organized exchange are often published in newspapers and through online services. This information normally includes the bond price (called *quote*), its contract rate, and its current market (called *yield*) rate. However, only a fraction of bonds are traded on organized exchanges. To compute the price of a bond, we apply present value concepts. This section explains how to use *present value concepts* to price the Fila discount bond and the Adidas premium bond described earlier.

Present Value of a Discount Bond   The issue price of bonds is found by computing the present value of the bonds' cash payments, discounted at the bonds' market rate. When computing the present value of the Fila bonds, we work with *semiannual* compounding periods because this is the time between interest payments; the annual market rate of 10% is considered a semiannual rate of 5%. Also, the two-year bond life is viewed as 4 semiannual periods. The price computation is twofold: (1) find the present value of the $100,000 par value paid at maturity and (2) find the present value of the series of 4 semiannual payments of $4,000 each; see Exhibit 10.4. These present values can be found by using *present value tables*. Appendix B at the end of this book shows present value tables and describes their use. Table B.1 at the end of Appendix B is used for the single $100,000 maturity payment, and Table B.3 in Appendix B is used for the $4,000 series of interest payments. Specifically, we go to Table B.1, row 4, and across to the 5% column to identify the present value factor of 0.8227 for the maturity payment. Next, we go to Table B.3, row 4, and across to the 5% column, where the present value factor is 3.5460 for the series of interest payments. We compute bond price by multiplying the cash flow payments by their corresponding present value factors and adding them together; see Exhibit 10.12.

EXHIBIT 10.12

Computing Issue Price for the Fila Discount Bonds

Cash Flow	Table	Present Value Factor	Amount	Present Value
$100,000 par (maturity) value	B.1	0.8227	× $100,000 =	$ 82,270
$4,000 interest payments	B.3	3.5460	× 4,000 =	14,184
Price of bond				$96,454

Present Value of a Premium Bond   We find the issue price of the Adidas bonds by using the market rate to compute the present value of the bonds' future cash flows. When computing the present value of these bonds, we again work with *semiannual* compounding periods because this is the time between interest payments. The annual 10% market rate is applied as a semiannual rate of 5%, and the two-year bond life is viewed as 4 semiannual periods. The computation is twofold: (1) find the present value of the $100,000 par value paid at maturity and (2) find the present value of the series of 4 payments of $6,000 each; see Exhibit 10.8. These present values can be found by using present value tables. First, go to Table B.1, row 4, and across to the 5% column where the present value factor is 0.8227 for the maturity payment. Second, go to Table B.3, row 4, and across to the 5% column, where the present value factor is 3.5460 for the series of interest payments. The bonds' price is computed by multiplying the cash flow payments by their corresponding present value factors and adding them together; see Exhibit 10.13.

EXHIBIT 10.13

Computing Issue Price for the Adidas Premium Bonds

Cash Flow	Table	Present Value Factor	Amount	Present Value
$100,000 par (maturity) value	B.1	0.8227	× $100,000 =	$ 82,270
$6,000 interest payments	B.3	3.5460	× 6,000 =	21,276
Price of bond				$103,546

Quick Check
Answers—p. 448

On December 31, 2010, a company issues 16%, 10-year bonds with a par value of $100,000. Interest is paid on June 30 and December 31. The bonds are sold to yield a 14% annual market rate at an issue price of $110,592. Use this information to answer questions 7 through 9:

7. Are these bonds issued at a discount or a premium? Explain your answer.

8. Using the straight-line method to allocate bond interest expense, the issuer records the second interest payment (on December 31, 2011) with a debit to Premium on Bonds Payable in the amount of (*a*) $7,470, (*b*) $530, (*c*) $8,000, or (*d*) $400.

9. How are these bonds reported in the long-term liability section of the issuer's balance sheet as of December 31, 2011?

Bond Retirement

This section describes the retirement of bonds (1) at maturity, (2) before maturity, and (3) by conversion to stock.

P4 Record the retirement of bonds.

Bond Retirement at Maturity

The carrying value of bonds at maturity always equals par value. For example, both Exhibits 10.7 (a discount) and 10.11 (a premium) show that the carrying value of bonds at the end of their lives equals par value ($100,000). The retirement of these bonds at maturity, assuming interest is already paid and entered, is recorded as follows:

2011			
Dec. 31	Bonds Payable	100,000	
	Cash		100,000
	To record retirement of bonds at maturity.		

Assets = Liabilities + Equity
−100,000   −100,000

Bond Retirement before Maturity

Issuers sometimes wish to retire some or all of their bonds prior to maturity. For instance, if interest rates decline greatly, an issuer may wish to replace high-interest-paying bonds with new low-interest bonds. Two common ways to retire bonds before maturity are to (1) exercise a call option or (2) purchase them on the open market. In the first instance, an issuer can reserve the right to retire bonds early by issuing callable bonds. The bond indenture can give the issuer an option to *call* the bonds before they mature by paying the par value plus a *call premium* to bondholders. In the second case, the issuer retires bonds by repurchasing them on the open market at their current price. Whether bonds are called or repurchased, the issuer is unlikely to pay a price that exactly equals their carrying value. When a difference exists between the bonds' carrying value and the amount paid, the issuer records a gain or loss equal to the difference.

To illustrate the accounting for retiring callable bonds, assume that a company issued callable bonds with a par value of $100,000. The call option requires the issuer to pay a call premium of $3,000 to bondholders in addition to the par value. Next, assume that after the June 30, 2009, interest payment, the bonds have a carrying value of $104,500. Then on July 1, 2009, the issuer calls these bonds and pays $103,000 to bondholders. The issuer recognizes a $1,500 gain from the difference between the bonds' carrying value of $104,500 and the retirement price of $103,000. The issuer records this bond retirement as:

Point: Bond retirement is also referred to as *bond redemption*.

Point: Gains and losses from retiring bonds were *previously* reported as extraordinary items. New standards require that they now be judged by the "unusual and infrequent" criteria for reporting purposes.

July 1	Bonds Payable	100,000	
	Premium on Bonds Payable.....................	4,500	
	Gain on Bond Retirement....................		1,500
	Cash		103,000
	To record retirement of bonds before maturity.		

Assets = Liabilities + Equity
−103,000   −100,000   +1,500
            −4,500

An issuer usually must call all bonds when it exercises a call option. However, to retire as many or as few bonds as it desires, an issuer can purchase them on the open market. If it retires less than the entire class of bonds, it recognizes a gain or loss for the difference between the carrying value of those bonds retired and the amount paid to acquire them.

Bond Retirement by Conversion

Convertible Bond

Holders of convertible bonds have the right to convert their bonds to stock. When conversion occurs, the bonds' carrying value is transferred to equity accounts and no gain or loss is recorded. (We further describe convertible bonds in the Decision Analysis section of this chapter.)

To illustrate, assume that on January 1 the $100,000 par value bonds of **Converse**, with a carrying value of $100,000, are converted to 15,000 shares of $2 par value common stock. The entry to record this conversion follows (the market prices of the bonds and stock are *not* relevant to this entry; the material in Chapter 11 is helpful in understanding this transaction):

Assets = Liabilities + Equity
−100,000   +30,000
          +70,000

Jan. 1	Bonds Payable	100,000	
	Common Stock		30,000
	Paid-In Capital in Excess of Par Value		70,000
	To record retirement of bonds by conversion.		

Decision Insight

Junk Bonds   Junk bonds are company bonds with low credit ratings due to a higher than average likelihood of default. On the upside, the high risk of junk bonds can yield high returns if the issuer survives and repays its debt.

Quick Check
Answer—p. 448

10. Six years ago, a company issued $500,000 of 6%, eight-year bonds at a price of 95. The current carrying value is $493,750. The company decides to retire 50% of these bonds by buying them on the open market at a price of 102½. What is the amount of gain or loss on retirement of these bonds?

Long-Term Notes Payable

Video10.1

Like bonds, notes are issued to obtain assets such as cash. Unlike bonds, notes are typically transacted with a *single* lender such as a bank. An issuer initially records a note at its selling price; that is, the note's face value minus any discount or plus any premium. Over the note's life, the amount of interest expense allocated to each period is computed by multiplying the market rate (at issuance of the note) by the beginning-of-period note balance. The note's carrying (book) value at any time equals its face value minus any unamortized discount or plus any unamortized premium; carrying value is also computed as the present value of all remaining payments, discounted using the market rate at issuance.

Installment Notes

C1 Explain the types and payment patterns of notes.

An **installment note** is an obligation requiring a series of payments to the lender. Installment notes are common for franchises and other businesses when lenders and borrowers agree to spread payments over several periods. To illustrate, assume that Foghog borrows $60,000 from a bank to purchase equipment. It signs an 8% installment note requiring six annual payments of principal plus interest and it records the note's issuance at January 1, 2009, as follows.

Assets = Liabilities + Equity
+60,000   +60,000

Jan. 1	Cash	60,000	
	Notes Payable		60,000
	Borrowed $60,000 by signing an 8%, six-year installment note.		

Payments on an installment note normally include the accrued interest expense plus a portion of the amount borrowed (the *principal*). This section describes an installment note with equal payments.

The equal total payments pattern consists of changing amounts of both interest and principal. To illustrate, assume that Foghog borrows $60,000 by signing a $60,000 note that requires six *equal payments* of $12,979 at the end of each year. (The present value of an annuity of six annual payments of $12,979, discounted at 8%, equals $60,000; we show this computation in footnote 2 on the next page.) The $12,979 includes both interest and principal, the amounts of which change with each payment. Exhibit 10.14 shows the pattern of equal total payments and its two parts, interest and principal. Column A shows the note's beginning balance. Column B shows accrued interest for each year at 8% of the beginning note balance. Column C shows the impact on the note's principal, which equals the difference between the total payment in column D and the interest expense in column B. Column E shows the note's year-end balance.

Years

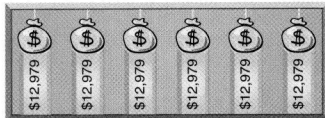

2009 2010 2011 2012 2013 2014

Point: Most consumer notes are installment notes that require equal total payments.

EXHIBIT 10.14

Installment Note: Equal Total Payments

Period Ending Date	(A) Beginning Balance	(B) Debit Interest Expense 8% × (A)	+	(C) Debit Notes Payable (D) − (B)	=	(D) Credit Cash (computed)	(E) Ending Balance (A) − (C)
(1) 12/31/2009	$60,000	$ 4,800		$ 8,179		$12,979	$51,821
(2) 12/31/2010	51,821	4,146		8,833		12,979	42,988
(3) 12/31/2011	42,988	3,439		9,540		12,979	33,448
(4) 12/31/2012	33,448	2,676		10,303		12,979	23,145
(5) 12/31/2013	23,145	1,852		11,127		12,979	12,018
(6) 12/31/2014	12,018	961		12,018		12,979	0
		$17,874		$60,000		$77,874	

Payments

☐ Interest   ☐ Principal

Decreasing Accrued Interest →

Increasing Principal Component →

Equal Total Payments →

End of Year	Interest	Principal
2009	$4,800	$8,179
2010	$4,146	$8,833
2011	$3,439	$9,540
2012	$2,676	$10,303
2013	$1,852	$11,127
2014	$961	$12,018

0   $2,500 $5,000 $7,500 $10,000 $12,500 $15,000

Cash Payment Pattern

Decision Insight

SOX: Hidden Debt   A study reports that 13% of employees in finance and accounting witnessed the falsifying or manipulating of accounting information in the past year (KPMG 2009). This is of special concern with long-term liabilities. For example, Enron violated GAAP to keep debt off its balance sheet. This concern extends to hidden environment liabilities. That same study reports 27% of employees in quality, safety, and environmental areas observed violations of environmental standards, which can yield massive liabilities.

Point: The Truth-in-Lending Act requires lenders to provide information about loan costs including finance charges and interest rate.

P5   Prepare entries to account for notes.

Assets = Liabilities + Equity
−12,979   −8,179   −4,800

Assets = Liabilities + Equity
−12,979   −8,833   −4,146

Although the six cash payments are equal, accrued interest decreases each year because the principal balance of the note declines. As the amount of interest decreases each year, the portion of each payment applied to principal increases. This pattern is graphed in the lower part of Exhibit 10.14. Foghog uses the amounts in Exhibit 10.14 to record its first two payments (for years 2009 and 2010) as follows:

2009		
Dec. 31	Interest Expense 4,800	
	Notes Payable 8,179	
	Cash	12,979
	To record first installment payment.	

2010		
Dec. 31	Interest Expense 4,146	
	Notes Payable 8,833	
	Cash	12,979
	To record second installment payment.	

Foghog records similar entries but with different amounts for each of the remaining four payments. After six years, the Notes Payable account balance is zero.[2]

Mortgage Notes and Bonds

A **mortgage** is a legal agreement that helps protect a lender if a borrower fails to make required payments on notes or bonds. A mortgage gives the lender a right to be paid from the cash proceeds of the sale of a borrower's assets identified in the mortgage. A legal document, called a *mortgage contract,* describes the mortgage terms.

Mortgage notes carry a mortgage contract pledging title to specific assets as security for the note. Mortgage notes are especially popular in the purchase of homes and the acquisition of plant assets. Less common *mortgage bonds* are backed by the issuer's assets. Accounting for mortgage notes and bonds is similar to that for unsecured notes and bonds, except that the mortgage agreement must be disclosed. For example, Musicland reports that its "**mortgage note payable is collateralized by land, buildings and certain fixtures.**"

Global: Countries vary in the preference given to debtholders vs. stockholders when a company is in financial distress. Some countries such as Germany, France, and Japan give preference to stockholders over debtholders.

♟ **Decision Maker** ▬▬▬▬▬▬▬▬▬▬▬▬▬▬▬▬▬▬▬▬▬▬▬▬▬▬▬▬▬▬

Entrepreneur   You are an electronics retailer planning a holiday sale on a custom stereo system that requires no payments for two years. At the end of two years, buyers must pay the full amount. The system's suggested retail price is $4,100, but you are willing to sell it today for $3,000 cash. What is your holiday sale price if payment will not occur for two years and the market interest rate is 10%? [Answer—p. 447]

▬▬

---

[2] Table B.3 in Appendix B is used to compute the dollar amount of the six payments that equal the initial note balance of $60,000 at 8% interest. We go to Table B.3, row 6, and across to the 8% column, where the present value factor is 4.6229. The dollar amount is then computed by solving this relation:

Table	**Present Value Factor**		**Dollar Amount**		**Present Value**
B.3	4.6229	×	?	=	$60,000

The dollar amount is computed by dividing $60,000 by 4.6229, yielding $12,979.

Example: Suppose the $60,000 installment loan has an 8% interest rate with eight equal annual payments. What is the annual payment? *Answer* (using Table B.3): $60,000/5.7466 = $10,441

Quick Check Answers—p. 448

11. Which of the following is true for an installment note requiring a series of equal total cash payments? (*a*) Payments consist of increasing interest and decreasing principal; (*b*) Payments consist of changing amounts of principal but constant interest; or (*c*) Payments consist of decreasing interest and increasing principal.

12. How is the interest portion of an installment note payment computed?

13. When a borrower records an interest payment on an installment note, how are the balance sheet and income statement affected?

Global View

This section discusses similarities and differences between U.S. GAAP and IFRS in accounting and reporting for long-term liabilities such as bonds and notes.

Accounting and Reporting for Bonds and Notes

The definitions and characteristics of bonds and notes are broadly similar for both U.S. GAAP and IFRS. Although slight differences exist, accounting for bonds and notes under U.S. GAAP and IFRS is similar. Specifically, the accounting for issuances (including recording discounts and premiums), market pricing, and retirement of both bonds and notes follows the procedures in this chapter. **GOME** describes its accounting for bonds, which follows the amortized cost approach explained in this chapter (and in Appendix 10B), as follows:

> The component of convertible bonds that exhibits characteristics of a liability is recognised as a liability in the balance sheet, net of transaction costs. On issuance of convertible bonds, the fair value of the liability component is determined using a market rate for an equivalent non-convertible bond; and this amount is carried as a long term liability on the amortised cost basis.

Both U.S. GAAP and IFRS allow companies to account for bonds and notes using fair value (different from the amortized value described in this chapter). This method is referred to as the **fair value option.** This method is similar to that applied in measuring and accounting for debt and equity securities. *Fair value* is the amount a company would receive if it settled a liability (or sold an asset) in an orderly transaction as of the balance sheet date. Companies can use several sources of inputs to determine fair value, and those inputs fall into three classes (ranked in order of preference):

Level 1: Observable quoted market prices in active markets for identical items.
Level 2: Observable inputs other than those in Level 1 such as prices from inactive markets or from similar, but not identical, items.
Level 3: Unobservable inputs reflecting a company's assumptions about value.

The exact procedures for marking these liabilities to fair value at each balance sheet date are in advanced courses.

Accounting and Reporting for Leases and Pensions

Both U.S. GAAP and IFRS require companies to distinguish between operating leases and capital leases; the latter is referred to as *finance leases* under IFRS. The accounting and reporting for leases are broadly similar for both U.S. GAAP and IFRS. The main difference is the criteria for identifying a lease as a capital lease are more general under IFRS. However, the basic approach applies. **GOME** describes its accounting for leases as follows:

> The Group has entered into commercial property leases for its retail business. The Group has determined that the lessor retains all the significant risks and rewards of relevant properties and so [GOME] accounts for them as operating leases.

For pensions, both U.S. GAAP and IFRS require companies to record costs of retirement benefits as employees work and earn them. The basic methods are similar in accounting and reporting for pensions. **GOME** reports the following regarding its pension obligations:

> Contributions to defined contribution retirement plans are recognised as an expense in the income statement as incurred. Pursuant to the relevant PRC laws and regulations, the employees of the Group's PRC subsidiaries are required to participate in a central pension scheme operated by the local municipal government. This subsidiary is required to contribute a certain percentage of the salaries of its employees to the central pension scheme. The only obligation of the subsidiary with respect to the central pension scheme is the ongoing required contributions. Contributions made to the retirement benefit scheme are charged to the income statement as they become payable in accordance with the rules of the central pension scheme.

Decision Analysis	**Debt Features and the Debt-to-Equity Ratio**

Collateral agreements can reduce the risk of loss for both bonds and notes. Unsecured bonds and notes are riskier because the issuer's obligation to pay interest and principal has the same priority as all other unsecured liabilities in the event of bankruptcy. If a company is unable to pay its debts in full, the unsecured creditors (including the holders of debentures) lose all or a portion of their balances. These types of legal agreements and other characteristics of long-term liabilities are crucial for effective business decisions. The first part of this section describes the different types of features sometimes included with bonds and notes. The second part explains and applies the debt-to-equity ratio.

A2 Assess debt features and their implications.

Features of Bonds and Notes

This section describes common features of debt securities.

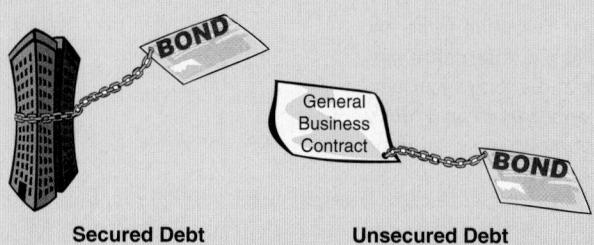

Secured Debt   **Unsecured Debt**

Secured or Unsecured   **Secured bonds** (and notes) have specific assets of the issuer pledged (or *mortgaged*) as collateral. This arrangement gives holders added protection against the issuer's default. If the issuer fails to pay interest or par value, the secured holders can demand that the collateral be sold and the proceeds used to pay the obligation. **Unsecured bonds** (and notes), also called *debentures,* are backed by the issuer's general credit standing. Unsecured debt is riskier than secured debt. *Subordinated debentures* are liabilities that are not repaid until the claims of the more senior, unsecured (and secured) liabilities are settled.

Term or Serial   **Term bonds** (and notes) are scheduled for maturity on one specified date. **Serial bonds** (and notes) mature at more than one date (often in series) and thus are usually repaid over a number of periods. For instance, $100,000 of serial bonds might mature at the rate of $10,000 each year from 6 to 15 years after they are issued. Many bonds are **sinking fund bonds,** which to reduce the holder's risk, require the issuer to create a *sinking fund* of assets set aside at specified amounts and dates to repay the bonds.

Registered or Bearer   Bonds issued in the names and addresses of their holders are **registered bonds.** The issuer makes bond payments by sending checks (or cash transfers) to registered holders. A registered holder must notify the issuer of any ownership change. Registered bonds offer the issuer the practical advantage of not having to actually issue bond certificates. Bonds payable to whoever holds them (the *bearer*) are called **bearer bonds** or *unregistered bonds*. Sales or exchanges might not be recorded, so the holder of a bearer bond is presumed to be its rightful owner. As a result, lost bearer bonds are difficult to replace. Many bearer bonds are also **coupon bonds.** This term reflects interest coupons that are attached to the bonds. When each coupon matures, the holder presents it to a bank or broker for collection. At maturity, the holder follows the same process and presents the bond certificate for collection. Issuers of coupon bonds cannot deduct the related interest expense for taxable income. This is to prevent abuse by taxpayers who own coupon bonds but fail to report interest income on their tax returns.

Convertible and/or Callable **Convertible bonds** (and notes) can be exchanged for a fixed number of shares of the issuing corporation's common stock. Convertible debt offers holders the potential to participate in future increases in stock price. Holders still receive periodic interest while the debt is held and the par value if they hold the debt to maturity. In most cases, the holders decide whether and when to convert debt to stock. **Callable bonds** (and notes) have an option exercisable by the issuer to retire them at a stated dollar amount before maturity.

Convertible Debt

Callable Debt

Decision Insight

Munis More than a million municipal bonds, or "munis," exist, and many are tax exempt. Munis are issued by state, city, town, and county governments to pay for public projects including schools, libraries, roads, bridges, and stadiums.

Debt-to-Equity Ratio

Beyond assessing different characteristics of debt as described above, we want to know the level of debt, especially in relation to total equity. Such knowledge helps us assess the risk of a company's financing structure. A company financed mainly with debt is more risky because liabilities must be repaid—usually with periodic interest—whereas equity financing does not. A measure to assess the risk of a company's financing structure is the **debt-to-equity ratio** (see Exhibit 10.15).

A3 Compute the debt-to-equity ratio and explain its use.

$$\text{Debt-to-equity} = \frac{\text{Total liabilities}}{\text{Total equity}}$$

EXHIBIT 10.15

Debt-to-Equity Ratio

The debt-to-equity ratio varies across companies and industries. Industries that are more variable tend to have lower ratios, while more stable industries are less risky and tend to have higher ratios. To apply the debt-to-equity ratio, let's look at this measure for **Cedar Fair** in Exhibit 10.16.

EXHIBIT 10.16

Cedar Fair's Debt-to-Equity Ratio

($ millions)	2008	2007	2006	2005
Total liabilities	$2,079.297	$2,133.576	$2,100.306	$590.560
Total equity	106.786	285.092	410.615	434.234
Debt-to-equity	19.5	7.5	5.1	1.4
Industry debt-to-equity	10.3	5.7	3.2	1.2

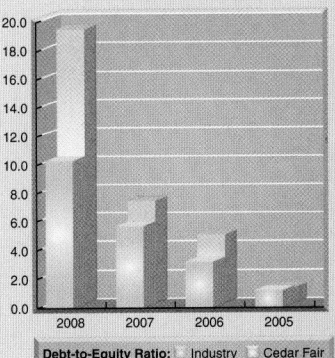

Cedar Fair's 2008 debt-to-equity ratio is 19.5, meaning that debtholders contributed $19.5 for each $1 contributed by equityholders. This implies a fairly risky financing structure for Cedar Fair. A similar concern is drawn from a comparison of Cedar Fair with its competitors, where the 2008 industry ratio is 10.3. Analysis across the years shows that Cedar Fair's financing structure has grown increasingly risky in recent years. Given its sluggish revenues and increasing operating expenses in recent years (see its annual report), Cedar Fair is increasingly at risk of financial distress.

Decision Maker

Bond Investor You plan to purchase debenture bonds from one of two companies in the same industry that are similar in size and performance. The first company has $350,000 in total liabilities, and $1,750,000 in equity. The second company has $1,200,000 in total liabilities, and $1,000,000 in equity. Which company's debenture bonds are less risky based on the debt-to-equity ratio? [Answer—p. 447]

Demonstration Problem

Water Sports Company (WSC) patented and successfully test-marketed a new product. To expand its ability to produce and market the new product, WSC needs to raise $800,000 of financing. On January 1, 2009, the company obtained the money in two ways:

a. WSC signed a $400,000, 10% installment note to be repaid with five equal annual installments to be made on December 31 of 2009 through 2013.

b. WSC issued five-year bonds with a par value of $400,000. The bonds have a 12% annual contract rate and pay interest on June 30 and December 31. The bonds' annual market rate is 10% as of January 1, 2009.

Required

1. For the installment note, (a) compute the size of each annual payment, (b) prepare an amortization table such as Exhibit 10.14, and (c) prepare the journal entry for the first payment.

2. For the bonds, (a) compute their issue price; (b) prepare the January 1, 2009, journal entry to record their issuance; (c) prepare an amortization table using the straight-line method; (d) prepare the June 30, 2009, journal entry to record the first interest payment; and (e) prepare a journal entry to record retiring the bonds at a $416,000 call price on January 1, 2011.

3.**B**Redo parts 2(c), 2(d), and 2(e) assuming the bonds are amortized using the effective interest method.

Planning the Solution

- For the installment note, divide the borrowed amount by the annuity factor (from Table B.3) using the 10% rate and five payments to compute the amount of each payment. Prepare a table similar to Exhibit 10.14 and use the numbers in the table's first line for the journal entry.

- Compute the bonds' issue price by using the market rate to find the present value of their cash flows (use tables found in Appendix B). Then use this result to record the bonds' issuance. Next, prepare an amortization table like Exhibit 10.11 (and Exhibit 10B.2) and use it to get the numbers needed for the journal entry. Also use the table to find the carrying value as of the date of the bonds' retirement that you need for the journal entry.

Solution to Demonstration Problem

Part 1: Installment Note

a. Annual payment = Note balance/Annuity factor = $400,000/3.7908 = $105,519 (The annuity factor is for five payments and a rate of 10%.)

b. Amortization table follows.

Annual Period Ending	(a) Beginning Balance	(b) Debit Interest Expense	(c) Debit Notes Payable	(d) Credit Cash	(e) Ending Balance
(1) 12/31/2009	$400,000	$ 40,000	$ 65,519	$105,519	$334,481
(2) 12/31/2010	334,481	33,448	72,071	105,519	262,410
(3) 12/31/2011	262,410	26,241	79,278	105,519	183,132
(4) 12/31/2012	183,132	18,313	87,206	105,519	95,926
(5) 12/31/2013	95,926	9,593	95,926	105,519	0
		$127,595	$400,000	$527,595	

c. Journal entry for December 31, 2009, payment.

Dec. 31	Interest Expense	40,000	
	Notes Payable	65,519	
	Cash		105,519
	To record first installment payment.		

Part 2: Bonds (straight-line amortization)

a. Compute the bonds' issue price.

Cash Flow	Table	Present Value Factor*	Amount	Present Value
Par (maturity) value	B.1 in App. B (PV of 1)	0.6139	× 400,000	= $245,560
Interest payments	B.3 in App. B (PV of annuity)	7.7217	× 24,000	= 185,321
Price of bond				$430,881

* Present value factors are for 10 payments using a semiannual market rate of 5%.

b. Journal entry for January 1, 2009, issuance.

Jan. 1	Cash	430,881	
	Premium on Bonds Payable		30,881
	Bonds Payable		400,000
	Sold bonds at a premium.		

c. Straight-line amortization table for premium bonds.

Semiannual Period-End	Unamortized Premium	Carrying Value
(0) 1/1/2009	$30,881	$430,881
(1) 6/30/2009	27,793	427,793
(2) 12/31/2009	24,705	424,705
(3) 6/30/2010	21,617	421,617
(4) 12/31/2010	18,529	418,529
(5) 6/30/2011	15,441	415,441
(6) 12/31/2011	12,353	412,353
(7) 6/30/2012	9,265	409,265
(8) 12/31/2012	6,177	406,177
(9) 6/30/2013	3,089	403,089
(10) 12/31/2013	0*	400,000

* Adjusted for rounding.

d. Journal entry for June 30, 2009, bond payment.

June 30	Bond Interest Expense	20,912	
	Premium on Bonds Payable	3,088	
	Cash		24,000
	Paid semiannual interest on bonds.		

e. Journal entry for January 1, 2011, bond retirement.

Jan. 1	Bonds Payable	400,000	
	Premium on Bonds Payable	18,529	
	Cash		416,000
	Gain on Retirement of Bonds		2,529
	To record bond retirement (carrying value as of Dec. 31, 2010).		

Part 3: Bonds (effective interest amortization)[B]

c. Effective interest amortization table for premium bonds.

		(A) Cash Interest Paid 6% × $400,000	(B) Interest Expense 5% × Prior (E)	(C) Premium Amortization (A) − (B)	(D) Unamortized Premium Prior (D) − (C)	(E) Carrying Value $400,000 + (D)
	Semiannual Interest Period					
(0)	1/1/2009				$30,881	$430,881
(1)	6/30/2009	$ 24,000	$ 21,544	$ 2,456	28,425	428,425
(2)	12/31/2009	24,000	21,421	2,579	25,846	425,846
(3)	6/30/2010	24,000	21,292	2,708	23,138	423,138
(4)	12/31/2010	24,000	21,157	2,843	20,295	420,295
(5)	6/30/2011	24,000	21,015	2,985	17,310	417,310
(6)	12/31/2011	24,000	20,866	3,134	14,176	414,176
(7)	6/30/2012	24,000	20,709	3,291	10,885	410,885
(8)	12/31/2012	24,000	20,544	3,456	7,429	407,429
(9)	6/30/2013	24,000	20,371	3,629	3,800	403,800
(10)	12/31/2013	24,000	20,200*	3,800	0	400,000
		$240,000	$209,119	$30,881		

* Adjusted for rounding

d. Journal entry for June 30, 2009, bond payment.

June 30	Bond Interest Expense	21,544	
	Premium on Bonds Payable.	2,456	
	Cash		24,000
	Paid semiannual interest on bonds.		

e. Journal entry for January 1, 2011, bond retirement.

Jan. 1	Bonds Payable	400,000	
	Premium on Bonds Payable.	20,295	
	Cash		416,000
	Gain on Retirement of Bonds.		4,295
	To record bond retirement (carrying value as of December 31, 2010).		

APPENDIX

10A Present Values of Bonds and Notes

C2 Explain and compute the present value of an amount(s) to be paid at a future date(s).

This appendix explains how to apply present value techniques to measure a long-term liability when it is created and to assign interest expense to the periods until it is settled. Appendix B at the end of the book provides additional discussion of present value concepts.

Present Value Concepts

The basic present value concept is that cash paid (or received) in the future has less value now than the same amount of cash paid (or received) today. To illustrate, if we must pay $1 one year from now, its present value is less than $1. To see this, assume that we borrow $0.9259 today that must be paid back in one year with 8% interest. Our interest expense for this loan is computed as $0.9259 \times 8\%$, or $0.0741. When the $0.0741 interest is added to the $0.9259 borrowed, we get the $1 payment necessary to repay our loan with interest. This is formally com-

Amount borrowed	**$0.9259**
Interest for one year at 8%	0.0741
Amount owed after 1 year	$ 1.0000

EXHIBIT 10A.1

Components of a One-Year Loan

puted in Exhibit 10A.1. The $0.9259 borrowed is the present value of the $1 future payment. More generally, an amount borrowed equals the present value of the future payment. (This same interpretation applies to an investment. If $0.9259 is invested at 8%, it yields $0.0741 in revenue after one year. This amounts to $1, made up of principal and interest.)

To extend this example, assume that we owe $1 two years from now instead of one year, and the 8% interest is compounded annually. *Compounded* means that interest during the second period is based on the total of the amount borrowed plus the interest accrued from the first period. The second period's interest is then computed as 8% multiplied by the sum of the amount borrowed plus interest earned in the first period. Exhibit 10A.2 shows how we compute the present value of $1 to be paid in two years. This amount is $0.8573. The first year's interest of $0.0686 is added to the principal so that the second year's interest is based on $0.9259. Total interest for this two-year period is $0.1427, computed as $0.0686 plus $0.0741.

Point: Benjamin Franklin is said to have described compounding as "the money, money makes, makes more money."

Amount borrowed	**$0.8573**
Interest for first year ($0.8573 \times 8%)	0.0686
Amount owed after 1 year	0.9259
Interest for second year ($0.9259 \times 8%)	0.0741
Amount owed after 2 years	$ 1.0000

EXHIBIT 10A.2

Components of a Two-Year Loan

Present Value Tables

The present value of $1 that we must repay at some future date can be computed by using this formula: $1/(1 + i)^n$. The symbol i is the interest rate per period and n is the number of periods until the future payment must be made. Applying this formula to our two-year loan, we get $\$1/(1.08)^2$, or $0.8573. This

is the same value shown in Exhibit 10A.2. We can use this formula to find any present value. However, a simpler method is to use a *present value table,* which lists present values computed with this formula for various interest rates and time periods. Many people find it helpful in learning present value concepts to first work with the table and then move to using a calculator.

Exhibit 10A.3 shows a present value table for a future payment of 1 for up to 10 periods at three different interest rates. Present values in this table are rounded to four decimal places. This table is drawn from the larger and more complete Table B.1 in Appendix B at the end of the book. Notice that the first value in the 8% column is 0.9259, the value we computed earlier for the present value of a $1

	Rate		
Periods	**6%**	**8%**	**10%**
1	0.9434	**0.9259**	0.9091
2	0.8900	**0.8573**	0.8264
3	0.8396	0.7938	0.7513
4	0.7921	0.7350	0.6830
5	0.7473	0.6806	0.6209
6	0.7050	0.6302	0.5645
7	0.6651	0.5835	0.5132
8	0.6274	0.5403	0.4665
9	0.5919	0.5002	0.4241
10	0.5584	0.4632	0.3855

EXHIBIT 10A.3

Present Value of 1

loan for one year at 8% (see Exhibit 10A.1). Go to the second row in the same 8% column and find the present value of 1 discounted at 8% for two years, or 0.8573. This $0.8573 is the present value of our obligation to repay $1 after two periods at 8% interest (see Exhibit 10A.2).

Example: Use Exhibit 10A.3 to find the present value of $1 discounted for 2 years at 6%. *Answer:* $0.8900

Applying a Present Value Table

To illustrate how to measure a liability using a present value table, assume that a company plans to borrow cash and repay it as follows: $2,000 after one year, $3,000 after two years, and $5,000 after three years. How much does this company receive today if the interest rate on this loan is 10%? To answer, we need to compute the present value of the three future payments, discounted at 10%. This computation is shown in Exhibit 10A.4 using present values from Exhibit 10A.3. The company can borrow $8,054 today at 10% interest in exchange for its promise to make these three payments at the scheduled dates.

Periods	**Payments**	**Present Value of 1 at 10%**	**Present Value of Payments**
1	$2,000	0.9091	$ 1,818
2	3,000	0.8264	2,479
3	5,000	0.7513	3,757
Present value of all payments			**$8,054**

EXHIBIT 10A.4

Present Value of a Series of Unequal Payments

Present Value of an Annuity

The $8,054 present value for the loan in Exhibit 10A.4 equals the sum of the present values of the three payments. When payments are not equal, their combined present value is best computed by adding the individual present values as shown in Exhibit 10A.4. Sometimes payments follow an **annuity,** which is a series of *equal* payments at equal time intervals. The present value of an annuity is readily computed.

Periods	Payments	Present Value of 1 at 6%	Present Value of Payments
1	$5,000	0.9434	$ 4,717
2	5,000	0.8900	4,450
3	5,000	0.8396	4,198
4	5,000	0.7921	3,961
Present value of all payments		**3.4651**	**$17,326**

To illustrate, assume that a company must repay a 6% loan with a $5,000 payment at each year-end for the next four years. This loan amount equals the present value of the four payments discounted at 6%. Exhibit 10A.5 shows how to compute this loan's present value of $17,326 by multiplying each payment by its matching present value factor taken from Exhibit 10A.3.

However, the series of $5,000 payments is an annuity, so we can compute its present value with either of two shortcuts. First, the third column of Exhibit 10A.5 shows that the sum of the present values of 1 at 6% for periods 1 through 4 equals 3.4651. One shortcut is to multiply this total of 3.4651 by the $5,000 annual payment to get the combined present value of $17,326. It requires one multiplication instead of four.

Periods	Rate 6%	8%	10%
1	0.9434	0.9259	0.9091
2	1.8334	1.7833	1.7355
3	2.6730	2.5771	2.4869
4	3.4651	3.3121	3.1699
5	4.2124	3.9927	3.7908
6	4.9173	4.6229	4.3553
7	5.5824	5.2064	4.8684
8	6.2098	5.7466	5.3349
9	6.8017	6.2469	5.7590
10	7.3601	6.7101	6.1446

The second shortcut uses an *annuity table* such as the one shown in Exhibit 10A.6, which is drawn from the more complete Table B.3 in Appendix B. We go directly to the annuity table to get the present value factor for a specific number of payments and interest rate. We then multiply this factor by the amount of the payment to find the present value of the annuity. Specifically, find the row for four periods and go across to the 6% column, where the factor is 3.4651. This factor equals the present value of an annuity with four payments of 1, discounted at 6%. We then multiply 3.4651 by $5,000 to get the $17,326 present value of the annuity.

Compounding Periods Shorter than a Year

The present value examples all involved periods of one year. In many situations, however, interest is compounded over shorter periods. For example, the interest rate on bonds is usually stated as an annual rate but interest is often paid every six months (semiannually). This means that the present value of interest payments from such bonds must be computed using interest periods of six months.

Assume that a borrower wants to know the present value of a series of 10 *semiannual payments* of $4,000 made over five years at an *annual interest rate* of 12%. The interest rate is stated as an annual rate of 12%, but it is actually a rate of 6% per semiannual interest period. To compute the present value of this series of $4,000 payments, go to row 10 of Exhibit 10A.6 and across to the 6% column to find the factor 7.3601. The present value of this annuity is $29,440 (7.3601 × $4,000).

Appendix B further describes present value concepts and includes more complete present value tables and assignments.

Quick Check

Answers—p. 448

14. A company enters into an agreement to make four annual year-end payments of $1,000 each, starting one year from now. The annual interest rate is 8%. The present value of these four payments is (a) $2,923, (b) $2,940, or (c) $3,312.

15. Suppose a company has an option to pay either (a) $10,000 after one year or (b) $5,000 after six months and another $5,000 after one year. Which choice has the lower present value?

Effective Interest Amortization

10B

Effective Interest Amortization of a Discount Bond

The straight-line method yields changes in the bonds' carrying value while the amount for bond interest expense remains constant. This gives the impression of a changing interest rate when users divide a constant bond interest expense over a changing carrying value. As a result, accounting standards allow use of the straight-line method only when its results do not differ materially from those obtained using the effective interest method. The **effective interest method,** or simply *interest method,* allocates total bond interest expense over the bonds' life in a way that yields a constant rate of interest. This constant rate of interest is the market rate at the issue date. Thus, bond interest expense for a period equals the carrying value of the bond at the beginning of that period multiplied by the market rate when issued.

Point: The effective interest method computes bond interest expense using the market rate at issuance. This rate is applied to a changing carrying value.

Exhibit 10B.1 shows an effective interest amortization table for the Fila bonds (as described in Exhibit 10.4). The key difference between the effective interest and straight-line methods lies in computing bond interest expense. Instead of assigning an equal amount of bond interest expense to each period, the effective interest method assigns a bond interest expense amount that increases over the life of a discount bond. **Both methods allocate the *same* $19,546 of total bond interest expense to the bonds' life, but in different patterns.** Specifically, the amortization table in Exhibit 10B.1 shows that the balance of the discount (column D) is amortized until it reaches zero. Also, the bonds' carrying value (column E) changes each period until it equals par value at maturity. Compare columns D and E to the corresponding columns in Exhibit 10.7 to see the amortization patterns. Total bond interest expense is $19,546, consisting of $16,000 of semiannual cash payments and $3,546 of the original bond discount, the same for both methods.

EXHIBIT 10B.1

Effective Interest Amortization of Bond Discount

Bonds: $100,000 Par Value, Semiannual Interest Payments, Two-Year Life, 4% Semiannual Contract Rate, 5% Semiannual Market Rate

Semiannual Interest Period-End	(A) Cash Interest Paid	(B) Bond Interest Expense	(C) Discount Amortization	(D) Unamortized Discount	(E) Carrying Value
(0) 12/31/2009				$3,546	$ 96,454
(1) 6/30/2010	$4,000	$4,823	$ 823	2,723	97,277
(2) 12/31/2010	4,000	4,864	864	1,859	98,141
(3) 6/30/2011	4,000	4,907	907	952	99,048
(4) 12/31/2011	4,000	4,952	952	0	100,000
	$16,000	$19,546	$3,546		

Column (**A**) is par value ($100,000) multiplied by the semiannual contract rate (4%).

Column (**B**) is prior period's carrying value multiplied by the semiannual market rate (5%).

Column (**C**) is the difference between interest paid and bond interest expense, or [(B) − (A)].

Column (**D**) is the prior period's unamortized discount less the current period's discount amortization.

Column (**E**) is par value less unamortized discount, or [$100,000 − (D)].

Except for differences in amounts, journal entries recording the expense and updating the liability balance are the same under the effective interest method and the straight-line method. We can use the numbers in Exhibit 10B.1 to record each semiannual entry during the bonds' two-year life (June 30,

2010, through December 31, 2011). For instance, we record the interest payment at the end of the first semiannual period as:

Assets = Liabilities + Equity
−4,000   +823   −4,823

2010			
June 30	Bond Interest Expense	4,823	
	Discount on Bonds Payable		823
	Cash		4,000
	To record semiannual interest and discount amortization (effective interest method).		

Effective Interest Amortization of a Premium Bond

Exhibit 10B.2 shows the amortization table using the effective interest method for the Adidas bonds (as described in Exhibit 10.8). Column A lists the semiannual cash payments. Column B shows the amount of bond interest expense, computed as the 5% semiannual market rate at issuance multiplied by the beginning-of-period carrying value. The amount of cash paid in column A is larger than the bond interest expense because the cash payment is based on the higher 6% semiannual contract rate. The excess cash payment over the interest expense reduces the principal. These amounts are shown in column C. Column E shows the carrying value after deducting the amortized premium in column C from the prior period's carrying value. Column D shows the premium's reduction by periodic amortization. When the

EXHIBIT 10B.2

Effective Interest Amortization of Bond Premium

Bonds: $100,000 Par Value, Semiannual Interest Payments, Two-Year Life, 6% Semiannual Contract Rate, 5% Semiannual Market Rate

Semiannual Interest Period-End	(A) Cash Interest Paid	(B) Bond Interest Expense	(C) Premium Amortization	(D) Unamortized Premium	(E) Carrying Value
(0) 12/31/2009				$3,546	$103,546
(1) 6/30/2010	$6,000	$5,177	$ 823	2,723	102,723
(2) 12/31/2010	6,000	5,136	864	1,859	101,859
(3) 6/30/2011	6,000	5,093	907	952	100,952
(4) 12/31/2011	6,000	5,048	952	0	100,000
	$24,000	$20,454	$3,546		

Column (A) is par value ($100,000) multiplied by the semiannual contract rate (6%).
Column (B) is prior period's carrying value multiplied by the semiannual market rate (5%).
Column (C) is the difference between interest paid and bond interest expense, or [(A) − (B)].
Column (D) is the prior period's unamortized premium less the current period's premium amortization.
Column (E) is par value plus unamortized premium, or [$100,000 + (D)].

issuer makes the first semiannual interest payment, the effect of premium amortization on bond interest expense and bond liability is recorded as follows:

Assets = Liabilities + Equity
−6,000   −823   −5,177

2010			
June 30	Bond Interest Expense	5,177	
	Premium on Bonds Payable	823	
	Cash		6,000
	To record semiannual interest and premium amortization (effective interest method).		

Similar entries with different amounts are recorded at each payment date until the bond matures at the end of 2011. The effective interest method yields decreasing amounts of bond interest expense and increasing amounts of premium amortization over the bonds' life.

IFRS

Unlike U.S. GAAP, IFRS requires that interest expense be computed using the effective interest method with *no exemptions*.

Issuing Bonds between Interest Dates

10C

An issuer can sell bonds at a date other than an interest payment date. When this occurs, the buyers normally pay the issuer the purchase price plus any interest accrued since the prior interest payment date. This accrued interest is then repaid to these buyers on the next interest payment date. To illustrate, suppose **Avia** sells $100,000 of its 9% bonds at par on March 1, 2009, 60 days after the stated issue date. The interest on Avia bonds is payable semiannually on each June 30 and December 31. Since 60 days have passed, the issuer collects accrued interest from the buyers at the time of issuance. This amount is $1,500 ($100,000 × 9% × $^{60}/_{360}$ year). This case is reflected in Exhibit 10C.1.

C3 Describe the accrual of bond interest when bond payments do not align with accounting periods.

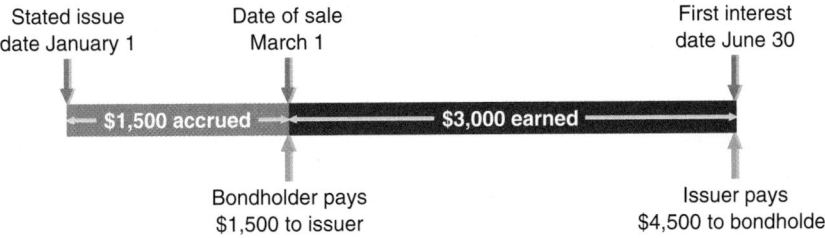

EXHIBIT 10C.1

Accruing Interest between Interest Payment Dates

Avia records the issuance of these bonds on March 1, 2009, as follows:

Mar. 1	Cash..	101,500	
	Interest Payable.............................		1,500
	Bonds Payable..............................		100,000
	Sold bonds at par with accrued interest.		

Assets = Liabilities + Equity
+101,500   +100,000
                 +1,500

Liabilities for interest payable and bonds payable are recorded in separate accounts. When the June 30, 2009, semiannual interest date arrives, Avia pays the full semiannual interest of $4,500 ($100,000 × 9% × ½ year) to the bondholders. This payment includes the four months' interest of $3,000 earned by the bondholders from March 1 to June 30 *plus* the repayment of the 60 days' accrued interest collected by Avia when the bonds were sold. Avia records this first semiannual interest payment as follows:

Example: How much interest is collected from a buyer of $50,000 of Avia bonds sold at par 150 days after the contract issue date? *Answer:* $1,875 (computed as $50,000 × 9% × $^{150}/_{360}$ year)

June 30	Interest Payable...............................	1,500	
	Bond Interest Expense........................	3,000	
	Cash.......................................		4,500
	Paid semiannual interest on the bonds.		

Assets = Liabilities + Equity
−4,500   −1,500   −3,000

The practice of collecting and then repaying accrued interest with the next interest payment is to simplify the issuer's administrative efforts. To explain, suppose an issuer sells bonds on 15 or 20 different dates between the stated issue date and the first interest payment date. If the issuer does not collect accrued interest from buyers, it needs to pay different amounts of cash to each of them according to the time that passed after purchasing the bonds. The issuer needs to keep detailed records of buyers and the dates they bought bonds. Issuers avoid this recordkeeping by having each buyer pay accrued interest at purchase. Issuers then pay the full semiannual interest to all buyers, regardless of when they bought bonds.

Accruing Bond Interest Expense

If a bond's interest period does not coincide with the issuer's accounting period, an adjusting entry is needed to recognize bond interest expense accrued since the most recent interest payment. To illustrate, assume that the stated issue date for Adidas bonds described in Exhibit 10.10 is September 1, 2009, instead of December 31, 2009, and that the bonds are sold on September 1, 2009. As a result, four months' interest (and premium amortization) accrue before the end of the 2009 calendar year. Interest for this period equals $3,409, or 4/6 of the first six months' interest of $5,113. Also, the premium amortization is $591, or 4/6 of the first six months' amortization of $887. The sum of the bond interest expense and the amortization is $4,000 ($3,409 + $591), which equals 4/6 of the $6,000 cash payment due on February 28, 2010. Adidas records these effects with an adjusting entry at December 31, 2009.

Point: Computation of accrued bond interest may use months instead of days for simplicity purposes. For example, the accrued interest computation for the Adidas bonds is based on months.

Assets = Liabilities + Equity
        −591   −3,409
        +4,000

Dec. 31	Bond Interest Expense	3,409	
	Premium on Bonds Payable	591	
	Interest Payable		4,000
	To record four months' accrued interest and premium amortization.		

Similar entries are made on each December 31 throughout the bonds' two-year life. When the $6,000 cash payment occurs on each February 28 interest payment date, Adidas must recognize bond interest expense and amortization for January and February. It must also eliminate the interest payable liability created by the December 31 adjusting entry. For example, Adidas records its payment on February 28, 2010, as:

Assets = Liabilities + Equity
−6,000   −4,000   −1,705
         −295

Feb. 28	Interest Payable	4,000	
	Bond Interest Expense ($5,113 × 2/6)	1,705	
	Premium on Bonds Payable ($887 × 2/6)	295*	
	Cash		6,000
	To record 2 months' interest and amortization, and eliminate accrued interest liability.		

*Adjusted for rounding.

The interest payments made each August 31 are recorded as usual because the entire six-month interest period is included within this company's calendar-year reporting period.

 Decision Maker ▬▬▬▬▬▬▬▬▬▬▬▬▬▬▬▬▬▬▬▬▬▬▬▬▬▬▬▬▬▬▬▬▬▬▬▬

Bond Rater You must assign a rating to a bond that reflects its risk to bondholders. Identify factors you consider in assessing bond risk. Indicate the likely levels (relative to the norm) for the factors you identify for a bond that sells at a discount. [Answer—p. 447]

Quick Check   Answer—p. 448

16. On May 1, a company sells 9% bonds with a $500,000 par value that pay semiannual interest on each January 1 and July 1. The bonds are sold at par plus interest accrued since January 1. The issuer records the first semiannual interest payment on July 1 with (a) a debit to Interest Payable for $15,000, (b) a debit to Bond Interest Expense for $22,500, or (c) a credit to Interest Payable for $7,500.

APPENDIX

Leases and Pensions

10D

This appendix briefly explains the accounting and analysis for both leases and pensions.

C4 Describe accounting for leases and pensions.

Lease Liabilities

A **lease** is a contractual agreement between a *lessor* (asset owner) and a *lessee* (asset renter or tenant) that grants the lessee the right to use the asset for a period of time in return for cash (rent) payments. Nearly one-fourth of all equipment purchases is financed with leases. The advantages of lease financing include the lack of an immediate large cash payment and the potential to deduct rental payments in computing taxable income. From an accounting perspective, leases can be classified as either operating or capital leases.

Operating Leases   **Operating leases** are short-term (or cancelable) leases in which the lessor retains the risks and rewards of ownership. Examples include most car and apartment rental agreements. The lessee records such lease payments as expenses; the lessor records them as revenue. The lessee does not report the leased item as an asset or a liability (it is the lessor's asset). To illustrate, if an employee of Amazon leases a car for $300 at an airport while on company business, Amazon (lessee) records this cost as:

Point: Home Depot reports that its rental expenses from operating leases total more than $900 million.

July 4	Rental Expense.	300	
	Cash		300
	To record lease rental payment.		

Assets = Liabilities + Equity
−300   −300

Capital Leases   **Capital leases** are long-term (or noncancelable) leases by which the lessor transfers substantially all risks and rewards of ownership to the lessee.[3] Examples include most leases of airplanes and department store buildings. The lessee records the leased item as its own asset along with a lease liability at the start of the lease term; the amount recorded equals the present value of all lease payments. To illustrate, assume that K2 Co. enters into a six-year lease of a building in which it will sell sporting equipment. The lease transfers all building ownership risks and rewards to K2 (the present value of its $12,979 annual lease payments is $60,000). K2 records this transaction as follows:

2009			
Jan. 1	Leased Asset—Building.	60,000	
	Lease Liability.		60,000
	To record leased asset and lease liability.		

Assets = Liabilities + Equity
+60,000   +60,000

K2 reports the leased asset as a plant asset and the lease liability as a long-term liability. The portion of the lease liability expected to be paid in the next year is reported as a current liability.[4] At each year-end,

---

[3] A *capital lease* meets any one or more of four criteria: (1) transfers title of leased asset to lessee, (2) contains a bargain purchase option, (3) has a lease term that is 75% or more of the leased asset's useful life, or (4) has a present value of lease payments that is 90% or more of the leased asset's market value.

[4] Most lessees try to keep leased assets and lease liabilities off their balance sheets by failing to meet any one of the four criteria of a capital lease. This is because a lease liability increases a company's total liabilities, making it more difficult to obtain additional financing. The acquisition of assets without reporting any related liabilities (or other asset outflows) on the balance sheet is called **off-balance-sheet financing.**

Assets = Liabilities + Equity
−10,000   −10,000

K2 records depreciation on the leased asset (assume straight-line depreciation, six-year lease term, and no salvage value) as follows:

Dec. 31	Depreciation Expense—Building	10,000	
	Accumulated Depreciation—Building.		10,000
	To record depreciation on leased asset.		

K2 also accrues interest on the lease liability at each year-end. Interest expense is computed by multiplying the remaining lease liability by the interest rate on the lease. Specifically, K2 records its annual interest expense as part of its annual lease payment ($12,979) as follows (for its first year):

Assets = Liabilities + Equity
−12,979   −8,179   −4,800

2009			
Dec. 31	Interest Expense	4,800	
	Lease Liability.	8,179	
	Cash		12,979
	*To record first annual lease payment.**		

* These numbers are computed from a *lease payment schedule*. For simplicity, we use the same numbers from Exhibit 10.14 for this lease payment schedule—with different headings as follows:

		Payments			
	(A)	(B) *Debit*	(C) *Debit*	(D) *Credit*	(E)
Period Ending Date	**Beginning Balance of Lease Liability**	**Interest on Lease + Liability 8% × (A)**	**Lease = Liability (D) − (B)**	**Cash Lease Payment**	**Ending Balance of Lease Liability (A) − (C)**
12/31/2009	$60,000	$ 4,800	$ 8,179	$12,979	$51,821
12/31/2010	51,821	4,146	8,833	12,979	42,988
12/31/2011	42,988	3,439	9,540	12,979	33,448
12/31/2012	33,448	2,676	10,303	12,979	23,145
12/31/2013	23,145	1,852	11,127	12,979	12,018
12/31/2014	12,018	961	12,018	12,979	0
		$17,874	$60,000	$77,874	

Pension Liabilities

A **pension plan** is a contractual agreement between an employer and its employees for the employer to provide benefits (payments) to employees after they retire. Most employers pay the full cost of the pension, but sometimes employees pay part of the cost. An employer records its payment into a pension plan with a debit to Pension Expense and a credit to Cash. A *plan administrator* receives payments from the employer, invests them in pension assets, and makes benefit payments to *pension recipients* (retired employees). Insurance and trust companies often serve as pension plan administrators.

Many pensions are known as *defined benefit plans* that define future benefits; the employer's contributions vary, depending on assumptions about future pension assets and liabilities. Several disclosures are necessary in this case. Specifically, a pension liability is reported when the accumulated benefit obligation is *more than* the plan assets, a so-called *underfunded plan*. The accumulated benefit obligation is the present value of promised future pension payments to retirees. *Plan assets* refer to the market value of assets the plan administrator holds. A pension asset is reported when the accumulated benefit obligation is *less than* the plan assets, a so-called *overfunded plan*. An employer reports pension expense when it receives the benefits from the employees' services, which is sometimes decades before it pays pension benefits to employees. (*Other Postretirement Benefits* refer to nonpension benefits such as health care and life insurance benefits. Similar to a pension, costs of these benefits are estimated and liabilities accrued when the employees earn them.)

Summary

C1 Explain the types and payment patterns of notes. Notes repaid over a period of time are called *installment notes* and usually follow one of two payment patterns: (1) decreasing payments of interest plus equal amounts of principal or (2) equal total payments. Mortgage notes also are common.

C2^A Explain and compute the present value of an amount(s) to be paid at a future date(s). The basic concept of present value is that an amount of cash to be paid or received in the future is worth less than the same amount of cash to be paid or received today. Another important present value concept is that interest is compounded, meaning interest is added to the balance and used to determine interest for succeeding periods. An annuity is a series of equal payments occurring at equal time intervals. An annuity's present value can be computed using the present value table for an annuity (or a calculator).

C3^C Describe the accrual of bond interest when bond payments do not align with accounting periods. Issuers and buyers of debt record the interest accrued when issue dates or accounting periods do not coincide with debt payment dates.

C4^D Describe accounting for leases and pensions. A lease is a rental agreement between the lessor and the lessee. When the lessor retains the risks and rewards of asset ownership (an *operating lease*), the lessee debits Rent Expense and credits Cash for its lease payments. When the lessor substantially transfers the risks and rewards of asset ownership to the lessee (a *capital lease*), the lessee capitalizes the leased asset and records a lease liability. Pension agreements can result in either pension assets or pension liabilities.

A1 Compare bond financing with stock financing. Bond financing is used to fund business activities. Advantages of bond financing versus stock include (1) no effect on owner control, (2) tax savings, and (3) increased earnings due to financial leverage. Disadvantages include (1) interest and principal payments and (2) amplification of poor performance.

A2 Assess debt features and their implications. Certain bonds are secured by the issuer's assets; other bonds, called *debentures,* are unsecured. Serial bonds mature at different points in time; term bonds mature at one time. Registered bonds have each bondholder's name recorded by the issuer; bearer bonds are payable to the holder. Convertible bonds are exchangeable for shares of the issuer's stock. Callable bonds can be retired by the issuer at a set price. Debt features alter the risk of loss for creditors.

A3 Compute the debt-to-equity ratio and explain its use. Both creditors and equity holders are concerned about the relation between the amount of liabilities and the amount of equity. A company's financing structure is at less risk when the debt-to-equity ratio is lower, as liabilities must be paid and usually with periodic interest.

P1 Prepare entries to record bond issuance and bond interest expense. When bonds are issued at par, Cash is debited and Bonds Payable is credited for the bonds' par value. At bond interest payment dates (usually semiannual), Bond Interest Expense is debited and Cash credited; the latter for an amount equal to the bond par value multiplied by the bond contract rate.

P2 Compute and record amortization of bond discount. Bonds are issued at a discount when the contract rate is less than the market rate, making the issue (selling) price less than par. When this occurs, the issuer records a credit to Bonds Payable (at par) and debits both Discount on Bonds Payable and Cash. The amount of bond interest expense assigned to each period is computed using either the straight-line or effective interest method.

P3 Compute and record amortization of bond premium. Bonds are issued at a premium when the contract rate is higher than the market rate, making the issue (selling) price greater than par. When this occurs, the issuer records a debit to Cash and credits both Premium on Bonds Payable and Bonds Payable (at par). The amount of bond interest expense assigned to each period is computed using either the straight-line or effective interest method. The Premium on Bonds Payable is allocated to reduce bond interest expense over the life of the bonds.

P4 Record the retirement of bonds. Bonds are retired at maturity with a debit to Bonds Payable and a credit to Cash at par value. The issuer can retire the bonds early by exercising a call option or purchasing them in the market. Bondholders can also retire bonds early by exercising a conversion feature on convertible bonds. The issuer recognizes a gain or loss for the difference between the amount paid and the bond carrying value.

P5 Prepare entries to account for notes. Interest is allocated to each period in a note's life by multiplying its beginning-period carrying value by its market rate at issuance. If a note is repaid with equal payments, the payment amount is computed by dividing the borrowed amount by the present value of an annuity factor (taken from a present value table) using the market rate and the number of payments.

Guidance Answers to **Decision Maker**

Entrepreneur This is a "present value" question. The market interest rate (10%) and present value ($3,000) are known, but the payment required two years later is unknown. This amount ($3,630) can be computed as $3,000 \times 1.10 \times 1.10$. Thus, the sale price is $3,630 when no payments are received for two years. The $3,630 received two years from today is equivalent to $3,000 cash today.

Bond Investor The debt-to-equity ratio for the first company is 0.2 ($350,000/$1,750,000) and for the second company is 1.2 ($1,200,000/$1,000,000), suggesting that the financing structure of

the second company is more risky than that of the first company. Consequently, as a buyer of unsecured debenture bonds, you prefer the first company (all else equal).

Bond Rater Bonds with longer repayment periods (life) have higher risk. Also, bonds issued by companies in financial difficulties or facing higher than normal uncertainties have higher risk. Moreover, companies with higher than normal debt and large fluctuations in earnings are considered of higher risk. Discount bonds are more risky on one or more of these factors.

Guidance Answers to **Quick Checks**

1.

2011			
Jan. 1	Cash	10,000	
	Bonds Payable		10,000
June 30	Bond Interest Expense	450	
	Cash		450

2. Multiply the bond's par value by its contract rate of interest.

3. Bonds sell at a premium when the contract rate exceeds the market rate and the purchasers pay more than their par value.

4. The bonds are issued at a discount, meaning that issue price is less than par value. A discount occurs because the bond contract rate (6%) is less than the market rate (8%).

5.

Cash......................................	91,893	
Discount on Bonds Payable	8,107	
Bonds Payable		100,000

6. $3,811 (Total bond interest expense of $38,107 divided by 10 periods; or the $3,000 semiannual cash payment plus the $8,107 discount divided by 10 periods.)

7. The bonds are issued at a premium, meaning issue price is higher than par value. A premium occurs because the bonds' contract rate (16%) is higher than the market rate (14%).

8. (*b*) For each semiannual period: $10,592/20 periods = $530 premium amortization.

9.

Bonds payable, 16%, due 12/31/2020	$100,000	
Plus premium on bonds payable	9,532*	$109,532

* Original premium balance of $10,592 less $530 and $530 amortized on 6/30/2011 and 12/31/2011, respectively.

10. $9,375 loss. Computed as the difference between the repurchase price of $256,250 [50% of ($500,000 × 102.5%)] and the carrying value of $246,875 (50% of $493,750).

11. (*c*)

12. The interest portion of an installment payment equals the period's beginning loan balance multiplied by the market interest rate at the time of the note's issuance.

13. On the balance sheet, the account balances of the related liability (note payable) and asset (cash) accounts are decreased. On the income statement, interest expense is recorded.

14. (*c*) Computed as 3.3121 × $1,000 = $3,312.

15. The option of paying $10,000 after one year has a lower present value. It postpones paying the first $5,000 by six months. More generally, the present value of a further delayed payment is always lower than a less delayed payment.

16. (*a*) Reflects payment of accrued interest recorded back on May 1; $500,000 × 9% × 4/12 = $15,000.

Key Terms

Annuity (p. 440)	Coupon bonds (p. 434)	Par value of a bond (p. 420)
Bearer bonds (p. 434)	Debt-to-equity ratio (p. 435)	Pension plan (p. 446)
Bond (p. 420)	Discount on bonds payable (p. 423)	Premium on bonds (p. 426)
Bond certificate (p. 422)	Effective interest method (p. 441)	Registered bonds (p. 434)
Bond indenture (p. 422)	Installment note (p. 430)	Secured bonds (p. 434)
Callable bonds (p. 435)	Lease (p. 445)	Serial bonds (p. 434)
Capital leases (p. 445)	Market rate (p. 423)	Sinking fund bonds (p. 434)
Carrying (book) value of bonds (p. 424)	Mortgage (p. 432)	Straight-line bond amortization (p. 424)
Contract rate (p. 423)	Off-balance-sheet financing (p. 445)	Term bonds (p. 434)
Convertible bonds (p. 435)	Operating leases (p. 445)	Unsecured bonds (p. 434)

Multiple Choice Quiz   Answers on p. 461   mhhe.com/wildFA5e

Additional Quiz Questions are available at the book's Website.

1. A bond traded at 97½ means that:
   a. The bond pays 97½% interest.
   b. The bond trades at $975 per $1,000 bond.
   c. The market rate of interest is below the contract rate of interest for the bond.
   d. The bonds can be retired at $975 each.
   e. The bond's interest rate is 2½%.

2. A bondholder that owns a $1,000, 6%, 15-year bond has:
   a. The right to receive $1,000 at maturity.
   b. Ownership rights in the bond issuing entity.
   c. The right to receive $60 per month until maturity.
   d. The right to receive $1,900 at maturity.
   e. The right to receive $600 per year until maturity.

3. A company issues 8%, 20-year bonds with a par value of $500,000. The current market rate for the bonds is 8%. The amount of interest owed to the bondholders for each semiannual interest payment is:

  a. $40,000.
  b. $0.
  c. $20,000.
  d. $800,000.
  e. $400,000.

4. A company issued 5-year, 5% bonds with a par value of $100,000. The company received $95,735 for the bonds. Using the straight-line method, the company's interest expense for the first semiannual interest period is:

  a. $2,926.50.
  b. $5,853.00.

  c. $2,500.00.
  d. $5,000.00.
  e. $9,573.50.

5. A company issued 8-year, 5% bonds with a par value of $350,000. The company received proceeds of $373,745. Interest is payable semiannually. The amount of premium amortized for the first semiannual interest period, assuming straight-line bond amortization, is:

  a. $2,698.
  b. $23,745.
  c. $8,750.
  d. $9,344.
  e. $1,484.

Superscript letter ^{B} ($^{C, D}$) denotes assignments based on Appendix 10B (10C, 10D).

Discussion Questions

1. What is the main difference between a bond and a share of stock?

2. What is the main difference between notes payable and bonds payable?

3. ♟ What is the advantage of issuing bonds instead of obtaining financing from the company's owners?

4. What are the duties of a trustee for bondholders?

5. What is a bond indenture? What provisions are usually included in it?

6. What are the *contract* rate and the *market* rate for bonds?

7. ♟ What factors affect the market rates for bonds?

8.^{B}♟ Does the straight-line or effective interest method produce an interest expense allocation that yields a constant rate of interest over a bond's life? Explain.

9.^{C}Why does a company that issues bonds between interest dates collect accrued interest from the bonds' purchasers?

10. ♟ If you know the par value of bonds, the contract rate, and the market rate, how do you compute the bonds' price?

11. What is the issue price of a $2,000 bond sold at 98¼? What is the issue price of a $6,000 bond sold at 101½?

12. Describe the debt-to-equity ratio and explain how creditors and owners would use this ratio to evaluate a company's risk.

13. ♟ What obligation does an entrepreneur (owner) have to investors that purchase bonds to finance the business?

14. Refer to **Best Buy**'s annual report in Appendix A. Is there any indication that Best Buy has issued bonds?

15. By what amount did **RadioShack**'s long-term debt increase or decrease in 2008?

16. Refer to the statement of cash flows for **GOME** in Appendix A. For the year ended December 31, 2008, what was the amount for repayment of bank loans?

17. Refer to the annual report for **Apple** in Appendix A. For the year ended September 27, 2008, what is its debt-to-equity ratio? What does this ratio tell us?

18.^{D}When can a lease create both an asset and a liability for the lessee?

19.^{D}Compare and contrast an operating lease with a capital lease.

20.^{D}Describe the two basic types of pension plans.

♟ **Denotes Discussion Questions that involve decision making.**

---

connect Available with Connect Accounting

Round dollar amounts to the nearest whole dollar.

Randell Company issues 7%, 10-year bonds with a par value of $150,000 and semiannual interest payments. On the issue date, the annual market rate for these bonds is 8%, which implies a selling price of 93¼. The straight-line method is used to allocate interest expense.

1. What are the issuer's cash proceeds from issuance of these bonds?

2. What total amount of bond interest expense will be recognized over the life of these bonds?

3. What is the amount of bond interest expense recorded on the first interest payment date?

QUICK STUDY

QS 10-1
Bond computations—
straight-line P1 P2

QS 10-2[B]

Bond computations—
effective interest

P1   P3

Elton Company issues 7%, 15-year bonds with a par value of $350,000 and semiannual interest payments. On the issue date, the annual market rate for these bonds is 6%, which implies a selling price of 109¾. The effective interest method is used to allocate interest expense.

   1. What are the issuer's cash proceeds from issuance of these bonds?

   2. What total amount of bond interest expense will be recognized over the life of these bonds?

   3. What amount of bond interest expense is recorded on the first interest payment date?

QS 10-3

Journalize bond issuance   P1

Prepare the journal entry for the issuance of the bonds in both QS 10-1 and QS 10-2. Assume that both bonds are issued for cash on January 1, 2011.

QS 10-4

Computing bond price   P2   P3

Using the bond details in both QS 10-1 and QS 10-2, confirm that the bonds' selling prices given in each problem are approximately correct. Use the present value tables B.1 and B.3 in Appendix B.

QS 10-5

Recording bond issuance and discount amortization

P1   P2

Boulware Company issues 8%, 5-year bonds, on December 31, 2010, with a par value of $100,000 and semiannual interest payments. Use the following straight-line bond amortization table and prepare journal entries to record (a) the issuance of bonds on December 31, 2010; (b) the first interest payment on June 30, 2011; and (c) the second interest payment on December 31, 2011.

Semiannual Period-End	Unamortized Discount	Carrying Value
(0) 12/31/2010	$7,723	$92,277
(1) 6/30/2011	6,951	93,049
(2) 12/31/2011	6,179	93,821

QS 10-6

Bond retirement by call option

P4

On July 1, 2011, Teller Company exercises a $4,000 call option (plus par value) on its outstanding bonds that have a carrying value of $208,000 and par value of $200,000. The company exercises the call option after the semiannual interest is paid on June 30, 2011. Record the entry to retire the bonds.

QS 10-7

Bond retirement by stock conversion   P4

On January 1, 2011, the $1,000,000 par value bonds of Staten Company with a carrying value of $1,000,000 are converted to 500,000 shares of $1.00 par value common stock. Record the entry for the conversion of the bonds.

QS 10-8

Computing payments for an installment note   C1

Jordyn Company borrows $600,000 cash from a bank and in return signs an installment note for five annual payments of equal amount, with the first payment due one year after the note is signed. Use Table B.3 in Appendix B to compute the amount of the annual payment for each of the following annual market rates: (a) 4%, (b) 6%, and (c) 8%.

QS 10-9

Bond features and terminology

A2

Enter the letter of the description A through H that best fits each term or phrase 1 through 8.

   A. Records and tracks the bondholders' names.

   B. Is unsecured; backed only by the issuer's credit standing.

   C. Has varying maturity dates for amounts owed.

   D. Identifies rights and responsibilities of the issuer and the bondholders.

   E. Can be exchanged for shares of the issuer's stock.

   F. Is unregistered; interest is paid to whoever possesses them.

   G. Maintains a separate asset account from which bondholders are paid at maturity.

   H. Pledges specific assets of the issuer as collateral.

1. _____ Convertible bond	**5.** _____ Registered bond
2. _____ Bond indenture	**6.** _____ Serial bond
3. _____ Sinking fund bond	**7.** _____ Secured bond
4. _____ Debenture	**8.** _____ Bearer bond

Compute the debt-to-equity ratio for each of the following companies. Which company appears to have a riskier financing structure? Explain.

QS 10-10
Debt-to-equity ratio

A2

	NLF Company	ABL Company
Total liabilities	$615,000	$ 480,000
Total equity	820,000	1,500,000

Knapp Company plans to issue 6% bonds on January 1, 2011, with a par value of $2,000,000. The company sells $1,800,000 of the bonds on January 1, 2011. The remaining $200,000 sells at par on March 1, 2011. The bonds pay interest semiannually as of June 30 and December 31. Record the entry for the March 1 cash sale of bonds.

QS 10-11ᶜ
Issuing bonds between
interest dates   P1

Lu Villena, an employee of ETrain.com, leases a car at O'Hare airport for a three-day business trip. The rental cost is $400. Prepare the entry by ETrain.com to record Lu Villena's short-term car lease cost.

QS 10-12ᴰ
Recording operating leases   C4

Artel, Inc., signs a five-year lease for office equipment with Office Solutions. The present value of the lease payments is $13,500. Prepare the journal entry that Artel records at the inception of this capital lease.

QS 10-13ᴰ
Recording capital leases   C4

Vodafone Group Plc reports the following information among its bonds payable as of March 31, 2009 (pounds in millions).

QS 10-14
International liabilities disclosures

P1   P2

Financial Long-Term Liabilities Measured at Amortised Cost			
(£ millions)	Nominal (par) Value	Carrying Value	Fair Value
4.625% (US dollar 500 million) bond due July 2018	£350	£392	£315

a. What is the par value of the 4.625% bond issuance? What is its book (carrying) value?

b. Was the 4.625% bond sold at a discount or a premium? Explain.

Refer to the information in QS 10-14 for **Vodafone Group Plc**. The following price quotes (from Yahoo! Finance Bond Center) relate to its bonds payable as of late 2009. For example, the price quote indicates that the 4.625% bonds have a market price of 98.0 (98.0% of par value), resulting in a yield to maturity of 4.899%.

QS 10-15
International liabilities disclosures
and interpretations

P1   P2

Price	Contract Rate (coupon)	Maturity Date	Market Rate (YTM)
98.0	4.625%	15-Jul-2018	4.899%

a. Assuming that the 4.625% bonds were originally issued at par value, what does the market price reveal about interest rate changes since bond issuance? (Assume that Vodafone's credit rating has remained the same.)

b. Does the change in market rates since the issuance of these bonds affect the amount of interest expense reported on Vodafone's income statement? Explain.

c. How much cash would Vodafone need to pay to repurchase the 4.625% bonds at the quoted market price of 98.0? (Assume no interest is owed when the bonds are repurchased.)

d. Assuming that the 4.625% bonds remain outstanding until maturity, at what market price will the bonds sell on the due date in 2018?

connect Available with Connect Accounting

Round dollar amounts to the nearest whole dollar. Assume no reversing entries are used.

EXERCISES

On January 1, 2011, Bartel Enterprises issues bonds that have a $3,650,000 par value, mature in 20 years, and pay 10% interest semiannually on June 30 and December 31. The bonds are sold at par.

Exercise 10-1
Recording bond issuance and
interest

P1

1. How much interest will Bartel pay (in cash) to the bondholders every six months?

2. Prepare journal entries to record (*a*) the issuance of bonds on January 1, 2011; (*b*) the first interest payment on June 30, 2011; and (*c*) the second interest payment on December 31, 2011.

3. Prepare the journal entry for issuance assuming the bonds are issued at (*a*) 98 and (*b*) 105.

Exercise 10-2
Straight-line amortization of bond discount
P2

Sears issues bonds with a par value of $175,000 on January 1, 2009. The bonds' annual contract rate is 4%, and interest is paid semiannually on June 30 and December 31. The bonds mature in three years. The annual market rate at the date of issuance is 6%, and the bonds are sold for $165,523.

1. What is the amount of the discount on these bonds at issuance?

2. How much total bond interest expense will be recognized over the life of these bonds?

3. Prepare an amortization table like the one in Exhibit 10.7 for these bonds; use the straight-line method to amortize the discount.

Exercise 10-3ᴮ
Effective interest amortization of bond discount
P2

Ritter issues bonds dated January 1, 2009, with a par value of $300,000. The bonds' annual contract rate is 9%, and interest is paid semiannually on June 30 and December 31. The bonds mature in three years. The annual market rate at the date of issuance is 12%, and the bonds are sold for $277,872.

1. What is the amount of the discount on these bonds at issuance?

2. How much total bond interest expense will be recognized over the life of these bonds?

3. Prepare an amortization table like the one in Exhibit 10B.1 for these bonds; use the effective interest method to amortize the discount.

Exercise 10-4
Straight-line amortization of bond premium   P3

Dell Co. issues bonds dated January 1, 2009, with a par value of $450,000. The bonds' annual contract rate is 9%, and interest is paid semiannually on June 30 and December 31. The bonds mature in three years. The annual market rate at the date of issuance is 8%, and the bonds are sold for $461,795.

1. What is the amount of the premium on these bonds at issuance?

2. How much total bond interest expense will be recognized over the life of these bonds?

3. Prepare an amortization table like the one in Exhibit 10.11 for these bonds; use the straight-line method to amortize the premium.

Exercise 10-5ᴮ
Effective interest amortization of bond premium   P3

Refer to the bond details in Exercise 10-4 and prepare an amortization table like the one in Exhibit 10B.2 for these bonds using the effective interest method to amortize the premium.

Exercise 10-6
Recording bond issuance and premium amortization
P1   P3

Anna Company issues 8%, 5-year bonds, on December 31, 2010, with a par value of $100,000 and semiannual interest payments. Use the following straight-line bond amortization table and prepare journal entries to record (a) the issuance of bonds on December 31, 2010; (b) the first interest payment on June 30, 2011; and (c) the second interest payment on December 31, 2011.

Semiannual Period-End	Unamortized Premium	Carrying Value
(0) 12/31/2010	$7,720	$107,720
(1) 6/30/2011	6,948	106,948
(2) 12/31/2011	6,176	106,176

Exercise 10-7
Recording bond issuance and discount amortization
P1   P2

St. Charles Company issues 10%, 4-year bonds, on December 31, 2009, with a par value of $100,000 and semiannual interest payments. Use the following straight-line bond amortization table and prepare journal entries to record (a) the issuance of bonds on December 31, 2009; (b) the first interest payment on June 30, 2010; and (c) the second interest payment on December 31, 2010.

Semiannual Period-End	Unamortized Discount	Carrying Value
(0) 12/31/2009	$8,000	$92,000
(1) 6/30/2010	7,000	93,000
(2) 12/31/2010	6,000	94,000

Exercise 10-8
Recording bond issuance and discount amortization   P1   P2

Zander Company issues 6%, 2-year bonds, on December 31, 2009, with a par value of $100,000 and semiannual interest payments. Use the following straight-line bond amortization table and prepare journal entries to record (a) the issuance of bonds on December 31, 2009; (b) the first through fourth interest payments on each June 30 and December 31; and (c) the maturity of the bond on December 31, 2011.

Semiannual Period-End	Unamortized Discount	Carrying Value
(0) 12/31/2009	$4,000	$ 96,000
(1) 6/30/2010	3,000	97,000
(2) 12/31/2010	2,000	98,000
(3) 6/30/2011	1,000	99,000
(4) 12/31/2011	0	100,000

Target Company issues bonds with a par value of $950,000 on their stated issue date. The bonds mature in 15 years and pay 10% annual interest in semiannual payments. On the issue date, the annual market rate for the bonds is 12%.

1. What is the amount of each semiannual interest payment for these bonds?
2. How many semiannual interest payments will be made on these bonds over their life?
3. Use the interest rates given to determine whether the bonds are issued at par, at a discount, or at a premium.
4. Compute the price of the bonds as of their issue date.
5. Prepare the journal entry to record the bonds' issuance.

Exercise 10-9
Computing bond interest and price; recording bond issuance

P2

Check   (4) $819,223

Boston Company issues bonds with a par value of $160,000 on their stated issue date. The bonds mature in six years and pay 8% annual interest in semiannual payments. On the issue date, the annual market rate for the bonds is 6%.

1. What is the amount of each semiannual interest payment for these bonds?
2. How many semiannual interest payments will be made on these bonds over their life?
3. Use the interest rates given to determine whether the bonds are issued at par, at a discount, or at a premium.
4. Compute the price of the bonds as of their issue date.
5. Prepare the journal entry to record the bonds' issuance.

Exercise 10-10
Computing bond interest and price; recording bond issuance

P3

Check   (4) $175,930

On January 1, 2009, Seldon issues $450,000 of 10%, 15-year bonds at a price of 93¼. Six years later, on January 1, 2015, Seldon retires 20% of these bonds by buying them on the open market at 109¾. All interest is accounted for and paid through December 31, 2014, the day before the purchase. The straight-line method is used to amortize any bond discount.

1. How much does the company receive when it issues the bonds on January 1, 2009?
2. What is the amount of the discount on the bonds at January 1, 2009?
3. How much amortization of the discount is recorded on the bonds for the entire period from January 1, 2009, through December 31, 2014?
4. What is the carrying (book) value of the bonds as of the close of business on December 31, 2014? What is the carrying value of the 20% soon-to-be-retired bonds on this same date?
5. How much did the company pay on January 1, 2015, to purchase the bonds that it retired?
6. What is the amount of the recorded gain or loss from retiring the bonds?
7. Prepare the journal entry to record the bond retirement at January 1, 2015.

Exercise 10-11
Bond computations, straight-line amortization, and bond retirement

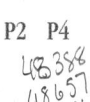

P2 P4

Check   (6) $12,420 loss

On May 1, 2011, Bradley Enterprises issues bonds dated January 1, 2011, that have a $1,950,000 par value, mature in 20 years, and pay 8% interest semiannually on June 30 and December 31. The bonds are sold at par plus four months' accrued interest.

1. How much accrued interest do the bond purchasers pay Bradley on May 1, 2011?
2. Prepare Bradley's journal entries to record (a) the issuance of bonds on May 1, 2011; (b) the first interest payment on June 30, 2011; and (c) the second interest payment on December 31, 2011.

Exercise 10-12ᶜ
Recording bond issuance with accrued interest

C4 P1

Check   (1) $52,000

Stockton Co. issues four-year bonds with a $50,000 par value on June 1, 2009, at a price of $47,850. The annual contract rate is 8%, and interest is paid semiannually on November 30 and May 31.

1. Prepare an amortization table like the one in Exhibit 10.7 for these bonds. Use the straight-line method of interest amortization.
2. Prepare journal entries to record the first two interest payments and to accrue interest as of December 31, 2009.

Exercise 10-13
Straight-line amortization and accrued bond interest expense

P1 P2

Exercise 10-14

Installment note with equal total payments C1 P5

Check (1) $25,381

On January 1, 2009, American Eagle borrows $90,000 cash by signing a four-year, 5% installment note. The note requires four equal total payments of accrued interest and principal on December 31 of each year from 2009 through 2012.

1. Compute the amount of each of the four equal total payments.

2. Prepare an amortization table for this installment note like the one in Exhibit 10.14.

Exercise 10-15

Installment note entries P5

Use the information in Exercise 10-14 to prepare the journal entries for American Eagle to record the loan on January 1, 2009, and the four payments from December 31, 2009, through December 31, 2012.

Exercise 10-16

Applying debt-to-equity ratio

A3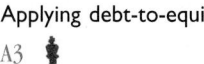

Motin Company is considering a project that will require a $250,000 loan. It presently has total liabilities of $110,000, and total assets of $310,000.

1. Compute Motin's (a) present debt-to-equity ratio and (b) the debt-to-equity ratio assuming it borrows $250,000 to fund the project.

2. Evaluate and discuss the level of risk involved if Motin borrows the funds to pursue the project.

Exercise 10-17[D]

Identifying capital and operating leases

C4

Indicate whether the company in each separate case 1 through 3 has entered into an operating lease or a capital lease.

1. The lessor retains title to the asset, and the lease term is three years on an asset that has a five-year useful life.

2. The title is transferred to the lessee, the lessee can purchase the asset for $1 at the end of the lease, and the lease term is five years. The leased asset has an expected useful life of six years.

3. The present value of the lease payments is 95% of the leased asset's market value, and the lease term is 70% of the leased asset's useful life.

Exercise 10-18[D]

Accounting for capital lease

C4

Hartel (lessee) signs a five-year capital lease for office equipment with a $21,000 annual lease payment. The present value of the five annual lease payments is $88,460, based on a 6% interest rate.

1. Prepare the journal entry Hartel will record at inception of the lease.

2. If the leased asset has a 5-year useful life with no salvage value, prepare the journal entry Hartel will record each year to recognize depreciation expense related to the leased asset.

Exercise 10-19[D]

Analyzing lease options

C2 C3 C4

General Motors advertised three alternatives for a 25-month lease on a new Blazer: (1) zero dollars down and a lease payment of $2,522 per month for 25 months, (2) $5,000 down and $2,240 per month for 25 months, or (3) $55,000 down and no payments for 25 months. Use the present value Table B.3 in Appendix B to determine which is the best alternative (assume you have enough cash to accept any alternative and the annual interest rate is 12% compounded monthly).

Exercise 10-20

Accounting for long-term liabilities under IFRS

P1 P2 P3

Heineken N.V. reports the following information for its Loans and Borrowings as of December 31, 2008, including proceeds and repayments for the year ended December 31, 2008 (euros in millions).

Loans and borrowings (noncurrent liabilities)	
Loans and borrowings, December 31, 2008	€ 9,084
Proceeds (cash) from issuances of loans and borrowings	6,361
Repayments (in cash) of loans and borrowings	(2,532)

1. Prepare Heineken's journal entry to record its cash proceeds from issuances of its loans and borrowings for 2008. Assume that the par value of these issuances is €6,000.

2. Prepare Heineken's journal entry to record its cash repayments of its loans and borrowings for 2008. Assume that the par value of these issuances is €2,400, and the premium on them is €32.

3. Compute the discount or premium on its loans and borrowings as of December 31, 2008, assuming that the par value of these liabilities is €9,000.

4. Given the facts in part 3 and viewing the entirety of loans and borrowings as one issuance, was the contract rate on these loans and borrowings higher or lower than the market rate at the time of issuance? Explain. (Assume that Heineken's credit rating has remained the same.)

connect Available with Connect Accounting

Round dollar amounts to the nearest whole dollar. Assume no reversing entries are used.

Harvard Research issues bonds dated January 1, 2011, that pay interest semiannually on June 30 and December 31. The bonds have a $45,000 par value, an annual contract rate of 6%, and mature in 6 years.

Required

For each of the following three separate situations, (*a*) determine the bonds' issue price on January 1, 2011, and (*b*) prepare the journal entry to record their issuance.

1. Market rate at the date of issuance is 4%.
2. Market rate at the date of issuance is 6%.
3. Market rate at the date of issuance is 8%.

Problem 10-1A
Computing bond price and recording issuance

P1   P2   P3

Check (1) Premium, $4,760

(3) Discount, $4,223

Braeburn issues $3,500,000 of 8%, 15-year bonds dated January 1, 2009, that pay interest semiannually on June 30 and December 31. The bonds are issued at a price of $3,024,000.

Required

1. Prepare the January 1, 2009, journal entry to record the bonds' issuance.
2. For each semiannual period, compute (*a*) the cash payment, (*b*) the straight-line discount amortization, and (*c*) the bond interest expense.
3. Determine the total bond interest expense to be recognized over the bonds' life.
4. Prepare the first two years of an amortization table like Exhibit 10.7 using the straight-line method.
5. Prepare the journal entries to record the first two interest payments.
6. Assume that the bonds are issued at a price of $4,284,000. Repeat parts 1 through 5.

Problem 10-2A
Straight-line amortization of bond discount and bond premium

P1   P2   P3   **eXcel**
mhhe.com/wildFA5e

Check (3) $4,676,000

(4) 12/31/2010 carrying value, $3,087,468

Jules issues 4.5%, five-year bonds dated January 1, 2009, with a $230,000 par value. The bonds pay interest on June 30 and December 31 and are issued at a price of $235,160. The annual market rate is 4% on the issue date.

Required

1. Calculate the total bond interest expense over the bonds' life.
2. Prepare a straight-line amortization table like Exhibit 10.11 for the bonds' life.
3. Prepare the journal entries to record the first two interest payments.

Problem 10-3A
Straight-line amortization of bond premium

P1   P3   **eXcel**
mhhe.com/wildFA5e

Check (2) 6/30/2009 carrying value, $234,644

Refer to the bond details in Problem 10-3A.

Required

1. Compute the total bond interest expense over the bonds' life.
2. Prepare an effective interest amortization table like the one in Exhibit 10B.2 for the bonds' life.
3. Prepare the journal entries to record the first two interest payments.
4. Use the market rate at issuance to compute the present value of the remaining cash flows for these bonds as of December 31, 2011. Compare your answer with the amount shown on the amortization table as the balance for that date (from part 2) and explain your findings.

Problem 10-4A[B]
Effective interest amortization of bond premium; computing bond price   P1   P3

Check (2) 6/30/2011 carrying value, $232,704

(4) $232,179

Legacy issues $345,000 of 5%, four-year bonds dated January 1, 2009, that pay interest semiannually on June 30 and December 31. They are issued at $332,888 and their market rate is 6% at the issue date.

Required

1. Prepare the January 1, 2009, journal entry to record the bonds' issuance.
2. Determine the total bond interest expense to be recognized over the bonds' life.
3. Prepare a straight-line amortization table like the one in Exhibit 10.7 for the bonds' first two years.
4. Prepare the journal entries to record the first two interest payments.

Analysis Component

5. Assume the market rate on January 1, 2009, is 4% instead of 6%. Without providing numbers, describe how this change affects the amounts reported on Legacy's financial statements.

Problem 10-5A
Straight-line amortization of bond discount

P1   P2

Check (2) $81,112

(3) 12/31/2010 carrying value, $338,944

Problem 10-6A[B]
Effective interest amortization of
bond discount   P1   P2

Check (2) $81,112

(3) 12/31/2010 carrying
value, $338,586

eXcel
mhhe.com/wildFA5e

Refer to the bond details in Problem 10-5A.

Required

1. Prepare the January 1, 2009, journal entry to record the bonds' issuance.

2. Determine the total bond interest expense to be recognized over the bonds' life.

3. Prepare an effective interest amortization table like the one in Exhibit 10B.1 for the bonds' first two years.

4. Prepare the journal entries to record the first two interest payments.

Problem 10-7A[B]
Effective interest amortization of
bond premium; retiring bonds

P1   P3   P4

Check (3) 6/30/2010 carrying
value, $187,494

(5) $7,256 gain

eXcel
mhhe.com/wildFA5e

Shopko issues $185,000 of 12%, three-year bonds dated January 1, 2009, that pay interest semiannually on June 30 and December 31. They are issued at $189,620. Their market rate is 11% at the issue date.

Required

1. Prepare the January 1, 2009, journal entry to record the bonds' issuance.

2. Determine the total bond interest expense to be recognized over the bonds' life.

3. Prepare an effective interest amortization table like Exhibit 10B.2 for the bonds' first two years.

4. Prepare the journal entries to record the first two interest payments.

5. Prepare the journal entry to record the bonds' retirement on January 1, 2011, at 97.

Analysis Component

6. Assume that the market rate on January 1, 2009, is 13% instead of 11%. Without presenting numbers, describe how this change affects amounts reported on Shopko's financial statements.

Problem 10-8A
Installment notes

C1   P5

Check (2) 10/31/2013 ending
balance, $159,556

On November 1, 2009, Norwood borrows $700,000 cash from a bank by signing a five-year installment note bearing 7% interest. The note requires equal total payments each year on October 31.

Required

1. Compute the total amount of each installment payment.

2. Complete an amortization table for this installment note similar to the one in Exhibit 10.14.

3. Prepare the journal entries in which Norwood (*a*) records accrued interest as of December 31, 2009 (the end of its annual reporting period), and (*b*) the first annual payment on the note.

Problem 10-9A
Applying the debt-to-equity ratio

A3

At the end of the current year, the following information is available for both the Pulaski Company and the Scott Company.

	Pulaski Company	Scott Company
Total assets	$1,800,000	$900,000
Total liabilities	723,600	478,800
Total equity	1,080,000	420,000

Required

1. Compute the debt-to-equity ratio for both companies.

2. Comment on your results and discuss the riskiness of each company's financing structure.

Problem 10-10A[D]
Capital lease accounting

C4

Check (1) $55,898

(3) Year 3 ending balance,
$24,966

Thomas Company signs a five-year capital lease with Universal Company for office equipment. The annual lease payment is $14,000, and the interest rate is 8%.

Required

1. Compute the present value of Thomas' five-year lease payments.

2. Prepare the journal entry to record Thomas' capital lease at its inception.

3. Complete a lease payment schedule for the five years of the lease with the following headings. Assume that the beginning balance of the lease liability (present value of lease payments) is $55,898. (*Hint:* To find the amount allocated to interest in year 1, multiply the interest rate by the beginning-of-year lease liability. The amount of the annual lease payment not allocated to interest is allocated to principal. Reduce the lease liability by the amount allocated to principal to update the lease liability at each year-end.)

Period Ending Date	Beginning Balance of Lease Liability	Interest on Lease Liability	Reduction of Lease Liability	Cash Lease Payment	Ending Balance of Lease Liability

4. Use straight-line depreciation and prepare the journal entry to depreciate the leased asset at the end of year 1. Assume zero salvage value and a five-year life for the office equipment.

Round dollar amounts to the nearest whole dollar. Assume no reversing entries are used.

PROBLEM SET B

Fortune Systems issues bonds dated January 1, 2011, that pay interest semiannually on June 30 and December 31. The bonds have a $35,000 par value, an annual contract rate of 4%, and mature in four years.

Required

For each of the following three separate situations, (*a*) determine the bonds' issue price on January 1, 2011, and (*b*) prepare the journal entry to record their issuance.

1. Market rate at the date of issuance is 2%.

2. Market rate at the date of issuance is 4%.

3. Market rate at the date of issuance is 6%.

Problem 10-1B
Computing bond price and recording issuance

P1 P2 P3

Check (1) Premium, $2,679

(3) Discount, $2,457

Long Beach issues $4,500,000 of 8%, 15-year bonds dated January 1, 2009, that pay interest semiannually on June 30 and December 31. The bonds are issued at a price of $3,888,000.

Required

1. Prepare the January 1, 2009, journal entry to record the bonds' issuance.

2. For each semiannual period, compute (*a*) the cash payment, (*b*) the straight-line discount amortization, and (*c*) the bond interest expense.

3. Determine the total bond interest expense to be recognized over the bonds' life.

4. Prepare the first two years of an amortization table like Exhibit 10.7 using the straight-line method.

5. Prepare the journal entries to record the first two interest payments.

6. Assume that the bonds are issued at a price of $5,508,000. Repeat parts 1 through 5.

Problem 10-2B
Straight-line amortization of bond discount and bond premium

P1 P2 P3

Check (3) $6,012,000

(4) 6/30/2010 carrying value, $3,949,200

San Mateo Company issues 7%, five-year bonds dated January 1, 2009, with a $220,000 par value. The bonds pay interest on June 30 and December 31 and are issued at a price of $229,385. Their annual market rate is 6% on the issue date.

Required

1. Calculate the total bond interest expense over the bonds' life.

2. Prepare a straight-line amortization table like Exhibit 10.11 for the bonds' life.

3. Prepare the journal entries to record the first two interest payments.

Problem 10-3B
Straight-line amortization of bond premium

P1 P3

Check (2) 12/31/2011 carrying value, $223,751

Refer to the bond details in Problem 10-3B.

Required

1. Compute the total bond interest expense over the bonds' life.

2. Prepare an effective interest amortization table like the one in Exhibit 10B.2 for the bonds' life.

3. Prepare the journal entries to record the first two interest payments.

4. Use the market rate at issuance to compute the present value of the remaining cash flows for these bonds as of December 31, 2011. Compare your answer with the amount shown on the amortization table as the balance for that date (from part 2) and explain your findings.

Problem 10-4B[B]
Effective interest amortization of bond premium; computing bond price P1 P3

Check (2) 6/30/2011 carrying value, $225,041

(4) $224,092

Problem 10-5B
Straight-line amortization of bond discount

P1   P2

Check   (2) $250,737

(3) 6/30/2010 carrying value, $259,437

Kelly issues $315,000 of 4%, 15-year bonds dated January 1, 2009, that pay interest semiannually on June 30 and December 31. They are issued at $253,263, and their market rate is 6% at the issue date.

Required

1. Prepare the January 1, 2009, journal entry to record the bonds' issuance.
2. Determine the total bond interest expense to be recognized over the life of the bonds.
3. Prepare a straight-line amortization table like the one in Exhibit 10.7 for the bonds' first two years.
4. Prepare the journal entries to record the first two interest payments.

Problem 10-6B[B]
Effective interest amortization of bond discount

P1   P2

Check   (2) $250,737;

(3) 6/30/2010 carrying value, $257,275

Refer to the bond details in Problem 10-5B.

Required

1. Prepare the January 1, 2009, journal entry to record the bonds' issuance.
2. Determine the total bond interest expense to be recognized over the bonds' life.
3. Prepare an effective interest amortization table like the one in Exhibit 10B.1 for the bonds' first two years.
4. Prepare the journal entries to record the first two interest payments.

Problem 10-7B[B]
Effective interest amortization of bond premium; retiring bonds

P1   P3   P4

Check   (3) 6/30/2010 carrying value, $177,380

(5) $7,126 loss

Kendall issues $175,000 of 11%, three-year bonds dated January 1, 2009, that pay interest semiannually on June 30 and December 31. They are issued at $179,439, and their market rate is 10% at the issue date.

Required

1. Prepare the January 1, 2009, journal entry to record the bonds' issuance.
2. Determine the total bond interest expense to be recognized over the bonds' life.
3. Prepare an effective interest amortization table like the one in Exhibit 10B.2 for the bonds' first two years.
4. Prepare the journal entries to record the first two interest payments.
5. Prepare the journal entry to record the bonds' retirement on January 1, 2011, at 105.

Analysis Component

6. Assume that the market rate on January 1, 2009, is 12% instead of 10%. Without presenting numbers, describe how this change affects amounts reported on Kendall's financial statements.

Problem 10-8B
Installment notes

C1   P5

Check   (2) 9/30/2011 ending balance, $71,223

On October 1, 2009, Miami Enterprises borrows $200,000 cash from a bank by signing a three-year installment note bearing 7% interest. The note requires equal total payments each year on September 30.

Required

1. Compute the total amount of each installment payment.
2. Complete an amortization table for this installment note similar to the one in Exhibit 10.14.
3. Prepare the journal entries to record (a) accrued interest as of December 31, 2009 (the end of its annual reporting period) and (b) the first annual payment on the note.

Problem 10-9B
Applying the debt-to-equity ratio

A3

At the end of the current year, the following information is available for both Caesar Company and Delta Company.

	Caesar Company	Delta Company
Total assets	$360,000	$1,500,000
Total liabilities	162,360	1,125,000
Total equity	198,000	375,000

Required

1. Compute the debt-to-equity ratio for both companies.
2. Comment on your results and discuss what they imply about the relative riskiness of these companies.

Allan Company signs a five-year capital lease with Vortal Company for office equipment. The annual lease payment is $13,000, and the interest rate is 8%.

Problem 10-10B^D
Capital lease accounting

C4

Required

1. Compute the present value of Allan's lease payments.

Check   (1) $51,905

2. Prepare the journal entry to record Allan's capital lease at its inception.

3. Complete a lease payment schedule for the five years of the lease with the following headings. Assume that the beginning balance of the lease liability (present value of lease payments) is $51,905. (*Hint:* To find the amount allocated to interest in year 1, multiply the interest rate by the beginning-of-year lease liability. The amount of the annual lease payment not allocated to interest is allocated to principal. Reduce the lease liability by the amount allocated to principal to update the lease liability at each year-end.)

(3) Year 3 ending balance,
$23,182

Period Ending Date	Beginning Balance of Lease Liability	Interest on Lease Liability	Reduction of Lease Liability	Cash Lease Payment	Ending Balance of Lease Liability

4. Use straight-line depreciation and prepare the journal entry to depreciate the leased asset at the end of year 1. Assume zero salvage value and a five-year life for the office equipment.

(This serial problem began in Chapter 1 and continues through most of the book. If previous chapter segments were not completed, the serial problem can begin at this point. It is helpful, but not necessary, to use the Working Papers that accompany the book.)

SERIAL PROBLEM

Success Systems

SP 10   Adriana Lopez has consulted with her local banker and is considering financing an expansion of her business by obtaining a long-term bank loan. Selected account balances at March 31, 2010, for Success Systems follow.

Total assets $129,909	Total liabilities $875	Total equity $129,034

Required

1. The bank has offered a long-term secured note to Success Systems. The bank's loan procedures require that a client's debt-to-equity ratio not exceed 0.8. As of March 31, 2010, what is the maximum amount that Success Systems could borrow from this bank (rounded to nearest dollar)?

Check   (1) $102,352

2. If Success Systems borrows the maximum amount allowed from the bank, what percentage of assets would be financed (*a*) by debt, and (*b*) by equity?

3. What are some factors Lopez should consider before borrowing the funds?

BEYOND THE NUMBERS

BTN 10-1   Refer to **Best Buy**'s financial statements in Appendix A to answer the following.

REPORTING IN ACTION

A1   A2

1. Identify the items that make up Best Buy's long-term debt at February 28, 2009. (Hint: See its note 6.)

2. How much annual cash interest must be paid on its convertible debentures assuming a 2.25% interest rate?

3. How much cash did it generate from issuance of debt for the year-ended February 28, 2009? How much cash did it use for repayments of debt for that same year?

Fast Forward

4. Access Best Buy's financial statements for the years ending after February 28, 2009, from its Website (**BestBuy.com**) or the SEC's EDGAR database (**www.SEC.gov**). Has it issued additional long-term debt since the year-end February 28, 2009? If yes, identify the amount(s).

COMPARATIVE ANALYSIS

A3

BTN 10-2   Key figures for **Best Buy** and **RadioShack** follow.

($ millions)	Best Buy Current Year	Best Buy Prior Year	RadioShack Current Year	RadioShack Prior Year
Total Assets	$15,826	$12,758	$2,283.5	$1,989.6
Total Liabilities	11,183	8,274	1,466.2	1,219.9
Total Equity	4,643	4,484	817.3	769.7

Required

1. Compute the debt-to-equity ratio for Best Buy and RadioShack for both the current year and the prior year.
2. Use the ratio you computed in part 1 to determine which company's financing structure is less risky. Assume an industry average of 1.07 for debt-to-equity.

ETHICS CHALLENGE

C4 A1

BTN 10-3   Brevard County needs a new county government building that would cost $24 million. The politicians feel that voters will not approve a municipal bond issue to fund the building since it would increase taxes. They opt to have a state bank issue $24 million of tax-exempt securities to pay for the building construction. The county then will make yearly lease payments (of principal and interest) to repay the obligation. Unlike conventional municipal bonds, the lease payments are not binding obligations on the county and, therefore, require no voter approval.

Required

1. Do you think the actions of the politicians and the bankers in this situation are ethical?
2. How do the tax-exempt securities used to pay for the building compare in risk to a conventional municipal bond issued by Brevard County?

COMMUNICATING IN PRACTICE

P3

BTN 10-4   Your business associate mentions that she is considering investing in corporate bonds currently selling at a premium. She says that since the bonds are selling at a premium, they are highly valued and her investment will yield more than the going rate of return for the risk involved. Reply with a memorandum to confirm or correct your associate's interpretation of premium bonds.

TAKING IT TO THE NET

A2

BTN 10-5   Access the April 2, 2009, filing of the 10-K report of **Home Depot** for the year ended February 1, 2009, from www.SEC.gov (Ticker: HD). Refer to Home Depot's balance sheet, including its Note 4 (on debt).

Required

1. Identify Home Depot's long-term liabilities and the amounts for those liabilities from Home Depot's balance sheet at February 1, 2009.
2. Review Home Depot's Note 6. Among its list of long-term debt is $1,000 million of "5.20% Senior Notes; due March 1, 2011; interest payable semi-annually on March 1 and September 1." How much cash interest must Home Depot pay each March 1 and September 1 on this specific debt?

TEAMWORK IN ACTION

P2 P3

BTN 10-6[B]   Break into teams and complete the following requirements related to effective interest amortization for a premium bond.

1. Each team member is to independently prepare a blank table with proper headings for amortization of a bond premium. When all have finished, compare tables and ensure all are in agreement.

Parts 2 and 3 require use of these facts: On January 1, 2008, BC issues $100,000, 9%, five-year bonds at 104.1. The market rate at issuance is 8%. BC pays interest semiannually on June 30 and December 31.

2. In rotation, *each* team member must explain how to complete *one* line of the bond amortization table, including all computations for his or her line. (Round amounts to the nearest dollar.) All members are to fill in their tables during this process. You need not finish the table; stop after all members have explained a line.
3. In rotation, *each* team member is to identify a separate column of the table and indicate what the final number in that column will be and explain the reasoning.

4. Reach a team consensus as to what the total bond interest expense on this bond issue will be if the bond is not retired before maturity.

5. As a team, prepare a list of similarities and differences between the amortization table just prepared and the amortization table if the bond had been issued at a discount.

BTN 10-7   Jason Osborn and Jason Wright are the founders of **Feed Granola Company**. Assume that their company currently has $250,000 in equity; and they are considering a $100,000 expansion to meet increased demand. The $100,000 expansion would yield $16,000 in additional annual income before interest expense. Assume that the business currently earns $40,000 annual income before interest expense of $10,000, yielding a return on equity of 12% ($30,000/$250,000). To fund the expansion, they are considering the issuance of a 10-year, $100,000 note with annual interest payments (the principal due at the end of 10 years).

ENTREPRENEURIAL DECISION

A1

Required

1. Using return on equity as the decision criterion, show computations to support or reject the expansion if interest on the $100,000 note is (a) 10%, (b) 15%, (c) 16%, (d) 17%, and (e) 20%.

2. What general rule do the results in part 1 illustrate?

BTN 10-8   Visit your city or county library. Ask the librarian to help you locate the recent financial records of your city or county government. Examine those records.

HITTING THE ROAD

A1

Required

1. Determine the amount of long-term bonds and notes currently outstanding.

2. Read the supporting information to your municipality's financial statements and record:

    a. Market interest rate(s) when the bonds and/or notes were issued.

    b. Date(s) when the bonds and/or notes will mature.

    c. Any rating(s) on the bonds and/or notes received from **Moody's, Standard & Poor's**, or another rating agency.

BTN 10-9   GOME (www.GOME.com.hk), **Best Buy**, and **RadioShack** are competitors in the global marketplace. Selected results from these companies follow.

GLOBAL DECISION

A3

Key Figures	GOME (RMB millions) Current Year	GOME (RMB millions) Prior Year	Best Buy ($ millions) Current Year	Best Buy ($ millions) Prior Year	RadioShack ($ millions) Current Year	RadioShack ($ millions) Prior Year
Total assets	27,495.104	29,837.493	$15,826	$12,758	$2,283.5	$1,989.6
Total liabilities	18,795.069	19,444.825	11,183	8,274	1,466.2	1,219.9
Total equity	8,700.035	10,392.668	4,643	4,484	817.3	769.7
Debt-to-equity ratio	?	?	2.41	1.85	1.79	1.58

Required

1. Compute GOME's debt-to-equity ratio for the current year and the prior year.

2. Use the data provided and the ratios you computed in part 1 to determine which company's financing structure is least risky.

ANSWERS TO MULTIPLE CHOICE QUIZ

1. b

2. a

3. c; $500,000 × 0.08 × ½ year = $20,000

4. a; Cash interest paid = $100,000 × 5% × ½ year = $2,500

Discount amortization = ($100,000 − $95,735)/10 periods = $426.50

Interest expense = $2,500.00 + $426.50 = $2,926.50

5. e; ($373,745 − $350,000)/16 periods = $1,484

11

Reporting and Analyzing Equity

"We weren't planning on starting a company" —Ali Perry (from left: B. Taylor, A. Perry, B. Myers)

A Look Back

Chapter 10 focused on long-term liabilities. We explained how to value, record, amortize, and report these liabilities in financial statements.

A Look at This Chapter

This chapter emphasizes details of the corporate form of organization. The accounting concepts and procedures for equity transactions are explained. We also describe how to report and analyze income, earnings per share, and retained earnings.

A Look Ahead

Chapter 12 focuses on reporting and analyzing a company's cash flows. Special emphasis is directed at the statement of cash flows—reported under the indirect method.

Breathing New Life

SANTA BARBARA, CA—"My grandma has COPD [chronic obstructive pulmonary disease] and she got put on oxygen," explains Ali Perry. "Her quality of life got destroyed because she couldn't go anywhere, she couldn't do anything. Everything was limited by how much she had in her bottles of compressed oxygen." Ali dreamed to help her grandma. COPD is a disease where the airways of the lungs narrow, which limits the flow of air and causes shortness of breath.

To make her dream a reality, Ali enlisted the aid of two college classmates, Byron Myers and Brenton Taylor. The three of them designed a portable oxygen system, wrote a business plan, and set off to secure financing. Their company, named **Inogen**, which is a combination of the words innovation and oxygen **(Inogen.net),** has already sold more than 10,000 units to date. "We worked really hard at the technology," explains Ali. "We saw the value of the company was in creating technology that was thought impossible in the marketplace."

The three founders insist that none of this would have been possible without equity financing. To make it happen, says Ali, they prepared analyses of corporate formation, equity issuances, stock types, retained earnings, and dividend yields to raise a whopping $4 million

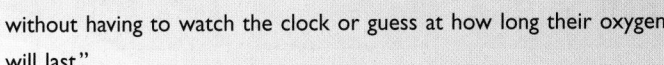

from a venture capital firm. Still, explains Ali, the focus is on helping folks, including her grandma. Adds Byron, "Oxygen users can now take off on a moment's notice, without having to watch the clock or guess at how long their oxygen will last."

The success of their corporate structure and their equity financing "brings both opportunities and challenges," explains Byron. "New patients do not know anything about oxygen therapy. All they know is that their life has changed and they now need to have a supply of oxygen with them whenever and wherever." Inogen answers that call. Their joint focus on corporate accounting and on people continues to reap rewards as they recently secured another $22 million in equity financing. As Byron put it: "[Inogen] makes old ways of thinking and operating inadequate." And it shows accounting for equity as a tool to aid those in need.

[Sources: *Inogen Website*, January 2010; *HME Business*, January 2006; *Daily Nexus*, January 2004; *Goleta Valley Voice*, December 2003; *Inc.com*, July 2007]

CAP

Conceptual

C1 Identify characteristics of corporations and their organization. *(p. 464)*

C2 Describe the components of stockholders' equity. *(p. 467)*

C3 Explain characteristics of common and preferred stock. *(p. 475)*

C4 Explain the items reported in retained earnings. *(p. 481)*

Analytical

A1 Compute earnings per share and describe its use. *(p. 483)*

A2 Compute price-earnings ratio and describe its use in analysis. *(p. 484)*

A3 Compute dividend yield and explain its use in analysis. *(p. 484)*

A4 Compute book value and explain its use in analysis. *(p. 485)*

Procedural

P1 Record the issuance of corporate stock. *(p. 468)*

P2 Record transactions involving cash dividends. *(p. 471)*

P3 Account for stock dividends and stock splits. *(p. 472)*

P4 Distribute dividends between common stock and preferred stock. *(p. 475)*

P5 Record purchases and sales of treasury stock and the retirement of stock. *(p. 478)*

LP11

This chapter focuses on equity transactions. The first part of the chapter describes the basics of the corporate form of organization and explains the accounting for common and preferred stock. We then focus on several special financing transactions, including cash and stock dividends, stock splits, and treasury stock. The final section considers accounting for retained earnings, including prior period adjustments, retained earnings restrictions, and reporting guidelines.

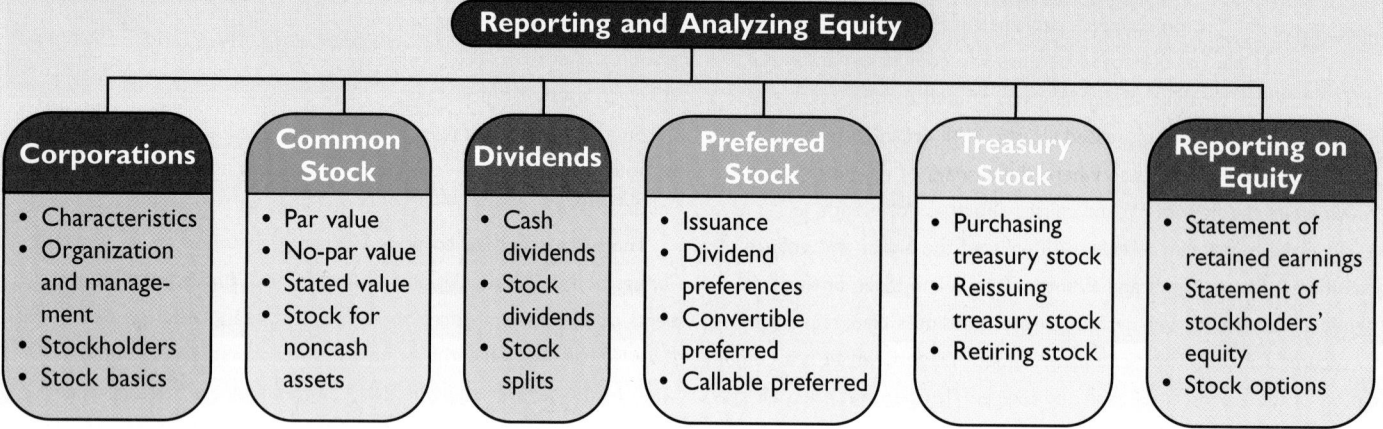

Reporting and Analyzing Equity

Corporations	Common Stock	Dividends	Preferred Stock	Treasury Stock	Reporting on Equity
• Characteristics • Organization and management • Stockholders • Stock basics	• Par value • No-par value • Stated value • Stock for noncash assets	• Cash dividends • Stock dividends • Stock splits	• Issuance • Dividend preferences • Convertible preferred • Callable preferred	• Purchasing treasury stock • Reissuing treasury stock • Retiring stock	• Statement of retained earnings • Statement of stockholders' equity • Stock options

Corporate Form of Organization

Video11.1

A **corporation** is an entity created by law that is separate from its owners. It has most of the rights and privileges granted to individuals. Owners of corporations are called *stockholders* or *shareholders*. Corporations can be separated into two types. A *privately held* (or *closely held*) corporation does not offer its stock for public sale and usually has few stockholders. A *publicly held* corporation offers its stock for public sale and can have thousands of stockholders. *Public sale* usually refers to issuance and trading on an organized stock market.

Characteristics of Corporations

C1 Identify characteristics of corporations and their organization.

Corporations represent an important type of organization. Their unique characteristics offer advantages and disadvantages.

Advantages of Corporate Characteristics

- **Separate legal entity:** A corporation conducts its affairs with the same rights, duties, and responsibilities of a person. It takes actions through its agents, who are its officers and managers.
- **Limited liability of stockholders:** Stockholders are liable for neither corporate acts nor corporate debt.
- **Transferable ownership rights:** The transfer of shares from one stockholder to another usually has no effect on the corporation or its operations except when this causes a change in the directors who control or manage the corporation.
- **Continuous life:** A corporation's life continues indefinitely because it is not tied to the physical lives of its owners.
- **Lack of mutual agency for stockholders:** A corporation acts through its agents, who are its officers and managers. Stockholders, who are not its officers and managers, do not have the power to bind the corporation to contracts—referred to as *lack of mutual agency*.
- **Ease of capital accumulation:** Buying stock is attractive to investors because (1) stockholders are not liable for the corporation's acts and debts, (2) stocks usually are transferred easily, (3) the life of the corporation is unlimited, and (4) stockholders are not corporate agents. These advantages enable corporations to accumulate large amounts of capital from the combined investments of many stockholders.

Point: The *business entity assumption* requires a corporation to be accounted for separately from its owners (shareholders).

Global: U.S., U.K., and Canadian corporations finance much of their operations with stock issuances, but companies in countries such as France, Germany, and Japan finance mainly with note and bond issuances.

Disadvantages of Corporate Characteristics

■ **Government regulation:** A corporation must meet requirements of a state's incorporation laws, which subject the corporation to state regulation and control. Proprietorships and partnerships avoid many of these regulations and governmental reports.

■ **Corporate taxation:** Corporations are subject to the same property and payroll taxes as proprietorships and partnerships plus *additional* taxes. The most burdensome of these are federal and state income taxes that together can take 40% or more of corporate pretax income. Moreover, corporate income is usually taxed a second time as part of stockholders' personal income when they receive cash distributed as dividends. This is called *double taxation*. (The usual dividend tax is 15%; however, it is less than 15% for lower income taxpayers, and in some cases zero.)

Point: Proprietorships and partnerships are not subject to income taxes. Their income is taxed as the personal income of their owners.

Point: Double taxation is less severe when a corporation's owner-manager collects a salary that is taxed only once as part of his or her personal income.

Decision Insight

Stock Financing Marc Andreessen cofounded **Netscape** at age 22, only four months after earning his degree. One year later, he and friends issued Netscape shares to the public. The stock soared, making Andreessen a multimillionaire.

Corporate Organization and Management

This section describes the incorporation, costs, and management of corporate organizations.

Point: A corporation is not required to have an office in its state of incorporation.

Incorporation A corporation is created by obtaining a charter from a state government. A charter application usually must be signed by the prospective stockholders called *incorporators* or *promoters* and then filed with the proper state official. When the application process is complete and fees paid, the charter is issued and the corporation is formed. Investors then purchase the corporation's stock, meet as stockholders, and elect a board of directors. Directors oversee a corporation's affairs.

Organization Expenses **Organization expenses** (also called *organization costs*) are the costs to organize a corporation; they include legal fees, promoters' fees, and amounts paid to obtain a charter. The corporation records (debits) these costs to an expense account called *Organization Expenses*. Organization costs are expensed as incurred because it is difficult to determine the amount and timing of their future benefits.

Management of a Corporation The ultimate control of a corporation rests with stockholders who control a corporation by electing its *board of directors,* or simply, *directors.* Each stockholder usually has one vote for each share of stock owned. This control relation is shown in Exhibit 11.1. Directors are responsible for and have final authority for managing corporate activities. A board can act only as a collective body and usually limits its actions to setting general policy.

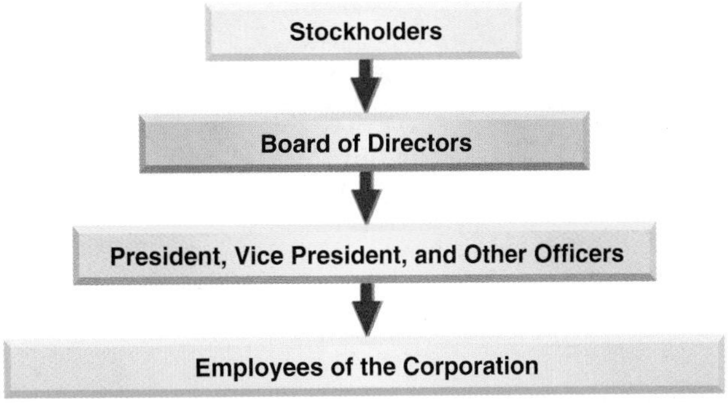

A corporation usually holds a stockholder meeting at least once a year to elect directors and transact business as its bylaws require. A group of stockholders owning or controlling votes of more than a 50% share of a corporation's stock can elect the board and control the corporation. Stockholders who do not attend stockholders' meetings must have an opportunity to delegate their voting rights to an agent by signing a **proxy,** a document that gives a designated agent the right to vote the stock.

Day-to-day direction of corporate business is delegated to executive officers appointed by the board. A corporation's chief executive officer (CEO) is often its president. Several vice

EXHIBIT 11.1

Corporate Structure

Point: *Bylaws* are guidelines that govern the behavior of individuals employed by and managing the corporation.

presidents, who report to the president, are commonly assigned specific areas of management responsibility such as finance, production, and marketing. One person often has the dual role of chairperson of the board of directors and CEO. In this case, the president is usually designated the chief operating officer (COO).

Decision Insight

Seed Money   Sources for start-up money include (1) "angel" investors such as family, friends, or anyone who believes in a company, (2) employees, investors, and even suppliers who can be paid with stock, and (3) venture capitalists (investors) who have a record of entrepreneurial success. See the National Venture Capital Association (**NVCA.org**) for information.

Stockholders of Corporations

This section explains stockholder rights, stock purchases and sales, and the role of registrar and transfer agents.

Rights of Stockholders   When investors buy stock, they acquire all *specific* rights the corporation's charter grants to stockholders. They also acquire *general* rights granted stockholders by the laws of the state in which the company is incorporated. When a corporation has only one class of stock, it is identified as **common stock.** State laws vary, but common stockholders usually have the general right to

1. Vote at stockholders' meetings.
2. Sell or otherwise dispose of their stock.
3. Purchase their proportional share of any common stock later issued by the corporation. This **preemptive right** protects stockholders' proportionate interest in the corporation. For example, a stockholder who owns 25% of a corporation's common stock has the first opportunity to buy 25% of any new common stock issued.
4. Receive the same dividend, if any, on each common share of the corporation.
5. Share in any assets remaining after creditors and preferred stockholders are paid when, and if, the corporation is liquidated. Each common share receives the same amount.

Stockholders also have the right to receive timely financial reports.

Stock Certificates and Transfer   Investors who buy a corporation's stock, sometimes receive a *stock certificate* as proof of share ownership. Many corporations issue only one certificate for each block of stock purchased. A certificate can be for any number of shares. Exhibit 11.2 shows a stock certificate of the **Green Bay Packers**. A certificate shows the company name, stockholder name, number of shares, and other crucial information. Issuance of certificates is becoming less common. Instead, many stockholders maintain accounts with the corporation or their stockbrokers and never receive actual certificates.

EXHIBIT 11.2

Stock Certificate

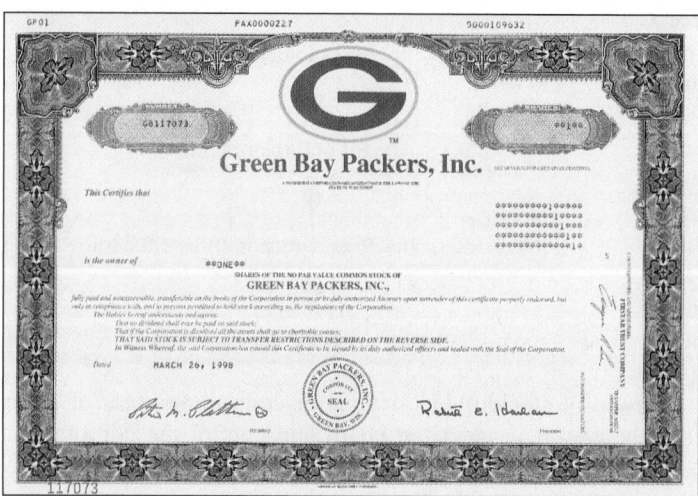

Registrar and Transfer Agents   If a corporation's stock is traded on a major stock exchange, the corporation must have a registrar and a transfer agent. A *registrar* keeps stockholder records and prepares official lists of stockholders for stockholder meetings and dividend payments. A *transfer agent* assists with purchases and sales of shares by receiving and issuing certificates as necessary. Registrars and transfer agents are usually large banks or trust companies with computer facilities and staff to do this work.

Decision Insight

Pricing Stock   A prospectus accompanies a stock's initial public offering (IPO), giving financial information about the company issuing the stock. A prospectus should help answer these questions to price an IPO: (1) Is the underwriter reliable? (2) Is there growth in revenues, profits, and cash flows? (3) What is management's view of operations? (4) Are current owners selling? (5) What are the risks?

Basics of Capital Stock

Capital stock is a general term that refers to any shares issued to obtain capital (owner financing). This section introduces terminology and accounting for capital stock.

C2   Describe the components of stockholders' equity.

Authorized Stock   **Authorized stock** is the number of shares that a corporation's charter allows it to sell. The number of authorized shares usually exceeds the number of shares issued (and outstanding), often by a large amount. (*Outstanding stock* refers to issued stock held by stockholders.) No formal journal entry is required for stock authorization. A corporation must apply to the state for a change in its charter if it wishes to issue more shares than previously authorized. A corporation discloses the number of shares authorized in the equity section of its balance sheet or notes. **Best Buy**'s balance sheet in Appendix A reports 1 billion shares authorized as of the start of its 2010 fiscal year.

Subcategories of Authorized Stock

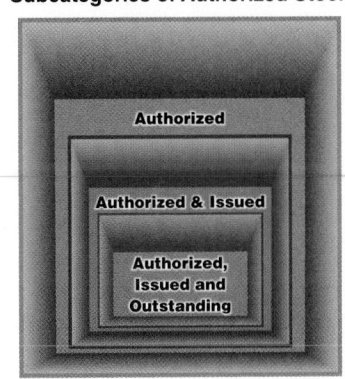

Selling (Issuing) Stock   A corporation can sell stock directly or indirectly. To *sell directly,* it advertises its stock issuance to potential buyers. This type of issuance is most common with privately held corporations. To *sell indirectly,* a corporation pays a brokerage house (investment banker) to issue its stock. Some brokerage houses *underwrite* an indirect issuance of stock; that is, they buy the stock from the corporation and take all gains or losses from its resale.

Market Value of Stock   **Market value per share** is the price at which a stock is bought and sold. Expected future earnings, dividends, growth, and other company and economic factors influence market value. Traded stocks' market values are available daily in newspapers such as *The Wall Street Journal* and online. The current market value of previously issued shares (for example, the price of stock in trades between investors) does not impact the issuing corporation's stockholders' equity.

Classes of Stock   When all authorized shares have the same rights and characteristics, the stock is called *common stock.* A corporation is sometimes authorized to issue more than one class of stock, including preferred stock and different classes of common stock. **American Greetings**, for instance, has two types of common stock: Class A stock has 1 vote per share and Class B stock has 10 votes per share.

Par Value Stock   **Par value stock** is stock that is assigned a **par value,** which is an amount assigned per share by the corporation in its charter. For example, Best Buy's common stock has a par value of $0.10. Other commonly assigned par values are $10, $5, $1 and $0.01. There is no restriction on the assigned par value. In many states, the par value of a stock establishes **minimum legal capital,** which refers to the least amount that the buyers of stock must contribute to the corporation or be subject to paying at a future date. For example, if a corporation issues 1,000 shares of $10 par value stock, the corporation's minimum legal capital in these states would be $10,000. Minimum legal capital is intended to protect a corporation's creditors. Since creditors cannot demand payment from stockholders' personal assets, their claims are limited to the corporation's assets and any minimum legal capital. At liquidation, creditor claims are paid before any amounts are distributed to stockholders.

Point: Managers are motivated to set a low par value when minimum legal capital or state issuance taxes are based on par value.

Point: Minimum legal capital was intended to protect creditors by requiring a minimum level of net assets.

No-Par Value Stock   **No-par value stock,** or simply *no-par stock,* is stock *not* assigned a value per share by the corporate charter. Its advantage is that it can be issued at any price without the possibility of a minimum legal capital deficiency.

Point: Par, no-par, and stated value do *not* set the stock's market value.

EXHIBIT 11.3

Equity Composition

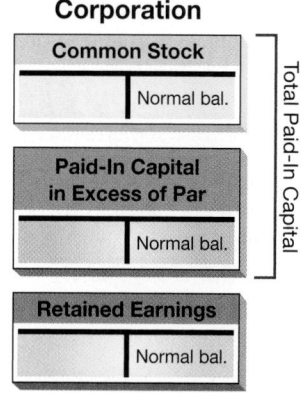

Point: Paid-in capital comes from stock-related transactions, whereas retained earnings comes from operations.

Corporation

Stated Value Stock   **Stated value stock** is no-par stock to which the directors assign a "stated" value per share. Stated value per share becomes the minimum legal capital per share in this case.

Stockholders' Equity   A corporation's equity is known as **stockholders' equity,** also called *shareholders' equity* or *corporate capital*. Stockholders' equity consists of (1) paid-in (or contributed) capital and (2) retained earnings; see Exhibit 11.3. **Paid-in capital** is the total amount of cash and other assets the corporation receives from its stockholders in exchange for its stock. **Retained earnings** is the cumulative net income (and loss) not distributed as dividends to its stockholders.

Decision Insight

Stock Quote   The **Best Buy** stock quote is interpreted as (left to right): **Hi,** highest price in past 52 weeks; **Lo,** lowest price in past 52 weeks; **Sym,** company exchange symbol; **Div,** dividends paid per share in past year; **Yld %,** dividend divided by closing price; **PE,** stock price per share divided by earnings per share; **Vol mil.,** number (in millions) of shares traded; **Hi,** highest price for the day; **Lo,** lowest price for the day; **Close,** closing price for the day; **Net Chg,** change in closing price from prior day.

52 Weeks						Yld		Vol				Net
Hi	Lo	Sym	Div	%	PE	mil.	Hi	Lo	Close	Chg
54.15	41.85	BBY	0.13	0.98	19	7.2	53.14	52.36	52.91	+0.20

Quick Check

Answers—p. 490

1. Which of the following is *not* a characteristic of the corporate form of business? (*a*) Ease of capital accumulation, (*b*) Stockholder responsibility for corporate debts, (*c*) Ease in transferability of ownership rights, or (*d*) Double taxation.

2. Why is a corporation's income said to be taxed twice?

3. What is a proxy?

Common Stock

P1 Record the issuance of corporate stock.

Video 11.2

Accounting for the issuance of common stock affects only paid-in (contributed) capital accounts; no retained earnings accounts are affected.

Issuing Par Value Stock

Par value stock can be issued at par, at a premium (above par), or at a discount (below par). In each case, stock can be exchanged for either cash or noncash assets.

Issuing Par Value Stock at Par   When common stock is issued at par value, we record amounts for both the asset(s) received and the par value stock issued. To illustrate, the entry to record Dillon Snowboards' issuance of 30,000 shares of $10 par value stock for $300,000 cash on June 5, 2009, follows.

Assets   = Liabilities +   Equity
+300,000   +300,000

June 5	Cash..	300,000	
	Common Stock, $10 Par Value...............		300,000
	Issued 30,000 shares of $10 par value		
	common stock at par.		

Exhibit 11.4 shows the stockholders' equity of Dillon Snowboards at year-end 2009 (its first year of operations) after income of $65,000 and no dividend payments.

EXHIBIT 11.4

Stockholders' Equity for Stock Issued at Par

Stockholders' Equity

Common Stock—$10 par value; 50,000 shares authorized; 30,000 shares issued and outstanding	$300,000
Retained earnings	65,000
Total stockholders' equity	$365,000

Issuing Par Value Stock at a Premium   A **premium on stock** occurs when a corporation sells its stock for more than par (or stated) value. To illustrate, if Dillon Snowboards issues its $10 par value common stock at $12 per share, its stock is sold at a $2 per share premium. The premium, known as **paid-in capital in excess of par value,** is reported as part of equity; it is not revenue and is not listed on the income statement. The entry to record Dillon Snowboards' issuance of 30,000 shares of $10 par value stock for $12 per share on June 5, 2009, follows

Point: A *premium* is the amount by which issue price exceeds par (or stated) value. It is recorded in the "Paid-In Capital in Excess of Par Value, Common Stock" account; also called "Additional Paid-In Capital, Common Stock."

June 5	Cash	360,000	
	Common Stock, $10 Par Value		300,000
	Paid-In Capital in Excess of Par Value, Common Stock		60,000
	Sold and issued 30,000 shares of $10 par value common stock at $12 per share.		

Assets	= Liabilities +	Equity
+360,000		+300,000
		+60,000

The Paid-In Capital in Excess of Par Value account is added to the par value of the stock in the equity section of the balance sheet as shown in Exhibit 11.5.

Point: The *Paid-In Capital* terminology is interchangeable with *Contributed Capital.*

EXHIBIT 11.5

Stockholders' Equity for Stock Issued at a Premium

Stockholders' Equity

Common Stock—$10 par value; 50,000 shares authorized; 30,000 shares issued and outstanding	$300,000
Paid-in capital in excess of par value, common stock	60,000
Retained earnings	65,000
Total stockholders' equity	$425,000

Issuing Par Value Stock at a Discount   A **discount on stock** occurs when a corporation sells its stock for less than par (or stated) value. Most states prohibit the issuance of stock at a discount. In states that allow stock to be issued at a discount, its buyers usually become contingently liable to creditors for the discount. If stock is issued at a discount, the amount by which issue price is less than par is debited to a *Discount on Common Stock* account, a contra to the common stock account, and its balance is subtracted from the par value of stock in the equity section of the balance sheet. This discount is not an expense and does not appear on the income statement.

Point: Retained earnings can be negative, reflecting accumulated losses. Amazon.com had an accumulated deficit of $1.8 billion at the start of 2007.

Issuing No-Par Value Stock

When no-par stock is issued and is not assigned a stated value, the amount the corporation receives becomes legal capital and is recorded as Common Stock. This means that the entire proceeds are credited to a no-par stock account. To illustrate, a corporation records its October 20 issuance of 1,000 shares of no-par stock for $40 cash per share as follows.

Oct. 20	Cash	40,000	
	Common Stock, No-Par Value		40,000
	Issued 1,000 shares of no-par value common stock at $40 per share.		

Assets	= Liabilities +	Equity
+40,000		+40,000

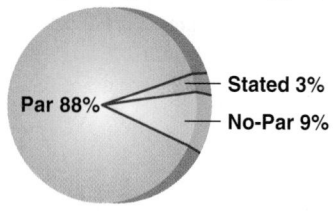
Issuing Stated Value Stock

When no-par stock is issued and assigned a stated value, its stated value becomes legal capital and is credited to a stated value stock account. Assuming that stated value stock is issued at an amount in excess of stated value (the usual case), the excess is credited to Paid-In Capital in Excess of Stated Value, Common Stock, which is reported in the stockholders' equity section. To illustrate, a corporation that issues 1,000 shares of no-par common stock having a stated value of $40 per share in return for $50 cash per share records this as follows.

Assets = Liabilities + Equity
+50,000   +40,000
                         +10,000

Oct. 20	Cash	50,000	
	Common Stock, $40 Stated Value		40,000
	Paid-In Capital in Excess of Stated Value, Common Stock		10,000
	Issued 1,000 shares of $40 per share stated value stock at $50 per share.		

Issuing Stock for Noncash Assets

Point: Stock issued for noncash assets should be recorded at the market value of either the stock or the noncash asset, whichever is more clearly determinable.

A corporation can receive assets other than cash in exchange for its stock. (It can also assume liabilities on the assets received such as a mortgage on property received.) The corporation records the assets received at their market values as of the date of the transaction. The stock given in exchange is recorded at its par (or stated) value with any excess recorded in the Paid-In Capital in Excess of Par (or Stated) Value account. (If no-par stock is issued, the stock is recorded at the assets' market value.) To illustrate, the entry to record receipt of land valued at $105,000 in return for issuance of 4,000 shares of $20 par value common stock on June 10 is

Assets = Liabilities + Equity
+105,000   +80,000
                         +25,000

June 10	Land	105,000	
	Common Stock, $20 Par Value...............		80,000
	Paid-In Capital in Excess of Par Value, Common Stock		25,000
	Exchanged 4,000 shares of $20 par value common stock for land.		

Point: Any type of stock can be issued for noncash assets.

A corporation sometimes gives shares of its stock to promoters in exchange for their services in organizing the corporation, which the corporation records as **Organization Expenses.** The entry to record receipt of services valued at $12,000 in organizing the corporation in return for 600 shares of $15 par value common stock on June 5 is

Assets = Liabilities + Equity
                        −12,000
                        +9,000
                        +3,000

June 5	Organization Expenses	12,000	
	Common Stock, $15 Par Value...............		9,000
	Paid-In Capital in Excess of Par Value, Common Stock		3,000
	Gave promoters 600 shares of $15 par value common stock in exchange for their services.		

Quick Check

Answers—p. 490

4. A company issues 7,000 shares of its $10 par value common stock in exchange for equipment valued at $105,000. The entry to record this transaction includes a credit to (*a*) Paid-In Capital in Excess of Par Value, Common Stock, for $35,000. (*b*) Retained Earnings for $35,000. (*c*) Common Stock, $10 Par Value, for $105,000.

5. What is a premium on stock issuance?

6. Who is intended to be protected by minimum legal capital?

Dividends

This section describes both cash and stock dividend transactions.

P2 Record transactions involving cash dividends.

Video11.2

Cash Dividends

The decision to pay cash dividends rests with the board of directors and involves more than evaluating the amounts of retained earnings and cash. The directors, for instance, may decide to keep the cash to invest in the corporation's growth, to meet emergencies, to take advantage of unexpected opportunities, or to pay off debt. Alternatively, many corporations pay cash dividends to their stockholders at regular dates. These cash flows provide a return to investors and almost always affect the stock's market value.

Accounting for Cash Dividends Dividend payment involves three important dates: declaration, record, and payment. **Date of declaration** is the date the directors vote to declare and pay a dividend. This creates a legal liability of the corporation to its stockholders. **Date of record** is the future date specified by the directors for identifying those stockholders listed in the corporation's records to receive dividends. The date of record usually follows the date of declaration by at least two weeks. Persons who own stock on the date of record receive dividends. **Date of payment** is the date when the corporation makes payment; it follows the date of record by enough time to allow the corporation to arrange checks, money transfers, or other means to pay dividends.

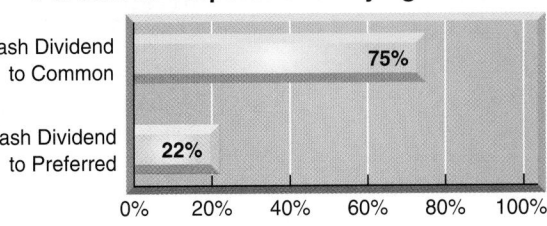

Percent of Corporations Paying Dividends

To illustrate, the entry to record a January 9 declaration of a $1 per share cash dividend by the directors of Z-Tech, Inc., with 5,000 outstanding shares is

Date of Declaration

Jan. 9	Retained Earnings.............................	5,000	
	Common Dividend Payable..................		5,000
	Declared $1 per common share cash dividend.[1]		

Assets = Liabilities + Equity
              +5,000   −5,000

Common Dividend Payable is a current liability. The date of record for the Z-Tech dividend is January 22. *No formal journal entry is needed on the date of record.* The February 1 date of payment requires an entry to record both the settlement of the liability and the reduction of the cash balance, as follows:

Date of Payment

Feb. 1	Common Dividend Payable.....................	5,000	
	Cash.......................................		5,000
	Paid $1 per common share cash dividend.		

Assets = Liabilities + Equity
−5,000   −5,000

Deficits and Cash Dividends A corporation with a debit (abnormal) balance for retained earnings is said to have a **retained earnings deficit,** which arises when a company incurs cumulative losses and/or pays more dividends than total earnings from current and prior years. A deficit is reported as a deduction on the balance sheet, as shown in Exhibit 11.6. Most states prohibit a corporation with a deficit from paying a cash dividend to its stockholders. This legal restriction is designed to protect creditors by preventing distribution of assets to stockholders when the company may be in financial difficulty.

Point: It is often said a dividend is a distribution of retained earnings, but it is more precise to describe a dividend as a distribution of assets to satisfy stockholder claims.

Point: The Retained Earnings Deficit account is also called *Accumulated Deficit.*

---

[1] An alternative entry is to debit Dividends instead of Retained Earnings. The balance in Dividends is then closed to Retained Earnings at the end of the reporting period. The effect is the same: Retained Earnings is decreased and a Dividend Payable is increased. For simplicity, all assignments in this chapter use the Retained Earnings account to record dividend declarations.

EXHIBIT 11.6

Stockholders' Equity
with a Deficit

Common stock—$10 par value, 5,000 shares authorized, issued, and outstanding	$50,000
Retained earnings deficit	(6,000)
Total stockholders' equity	$44,000

Some state laws allow cash dividends to be paid by returning a portion of the capital contributed by stockholders. This type of dividend is called a **liquidating cash dividend,** or simply *liquidating dividend,* because it returns a part of the original investment back to the stockholders. This requires a debit entry to one of the contributed capital accounts instead of Retained Earnings at the declaration date.

Point: Amazon.com has never declared a cash dividend.

Decision Insight

Accounting Quality The quality of information is at least as important as the quantity of information. A study reports that 13% of employees in the regulatory and government affairs areas witnessed inappropriate information provided to analysts or investors in the past year (KPMG 2009). Another 12% observed false or misleading information provided to regulators like the SEC. Legendary investor Warren Buffett says three ingredients are necessary for success: intelligence, initiative, and integrity. He cautions that without integrity, the other two will destroy you.

Quick Check

Answers—p. 491

7. What type of an account is the Common Dividend Payable account?

8. What three crucial dates are involved in the process of paying a cash dividend?

9. When does a dividend become a company's legal obligation?

Stock Dividends

P3 Account for stock dividends and stock splits.

A **stock dividend,** declared by a corporation's directors, is a distribution of additional shares of the corporation's own stock to its stockholders without the receipt of any payment in return. Stock dividends and cash dividends are different. A stock dividend does not reduce assets and equity but instead transfers a portion of equity from retained earnings to contributed capital.

Reasons for Stock Dividends Stock dividends exist for at least two reasons. First, directors are said to use stock dividends to keep the market price of the stock affordable. For example, if a corporation continues to earn income but does not issue cash dividends, the price of its common stock likely increases. The price of such a stock may become so high that it discourages some investors from buying the stock (especially in lots of 100 and 1,000). When a corporation has a stock dividend, it increases the number of outstanding shares and lowers the per share stock price. Another reason for a stock dividend is to provide evidence of management's confidence that the company is doing well and will continue to do well.

Accounting for Stock Dividends A stock dividend affects the components of equity by transferring part of retained earnings to contributed capital accounts, sometimes described as *capitalizing* retained earnings. Accounting for a stock dividend depends on whether it is a small or large stock dividend. A **small stock dividend** is a distribution of 25% or less of previously outstanding shares. It is recorded by capitalizing retained earnings for an amount equal to the market value of the shares to be distributed. A **large stock dividend** is a distribution of more than 25% of previously outstanding shares. A large stock dividend is recorded by capitalizing retained earnings for the minimum amount required by state law governing the corporation. Most states require capitalizing retained earnings equal to the par or stated value of the stock.

To illustrate stock dividends, we use the equity section of Quest's balance sheet shown in Exhibit 11.7 just *before* its declaration of a stock dividend on December 31.

Stockholders' Equity (before dividend)	
Common stock—$10 par value, 15,000 shares authorized, 10,000 shares issued and outstanding	$100,000
Paid-in capital in excess of par value, common stock	8,000
Retained earnings	35,000
Total stockholders' equity	$143,000

EXHIBIT 11.7

Stockholders' Equity *before* Declaring a Stock Dividend

Recording a small stock dividend.   Assume that Quest's directors declare a 10% stock dividend on December 31. This stock dividend of 1,000 shares, computed as 10% of its 10,000 issued and outstanding shares, is to be distributed on January 20 to the stockholders of record on January 15. Since the market price of Quest's stock on December 31 is $15 per share, this small stock dividend declaration is recorded as follows:

Point: Small stock dividends are recorded at market value.

Date of Declaration

Dec. 31	Retained Earnings.	15,000	
	Common Stock Dividend Distributable		10,000
	Paid-In Capital in Excess of Par Value, Common Stock		5,000
	Declared a 1,000-share (10%) stock dividend.		

Assets = Liabilities + Equity
$$-15,000$$
$$+10,000$$
$$+5,000$$

The $10,000 credit in the declaration entry equals the par value of the shares and is recorded in *Common Stock Dividend Distributable,* an equity account. Its balance exists only until the shares are issued. The $5,000 credit equals the amount by which market value exceeds par value. This amount increases the Paid-In Capital in Excess of Par Value account in anticipation of the issuance of shares. In general, the balance sheet changes in three ways when a stock dividend is declared. First, the amount of equity attributed to common stock increases; for Quest, from $100,000 to $110,000 for 1,000 additional declared shares. Second, paid-in capital in excess of par increases by the excess of market value over par value for the declared shares. Third, retained earnings decreases, reflecting the transfer of amounts to both common stock and paid-in capital in excess of par. The stockholders' equity of Quest is shown in Exhibit 11.8 *after* its 10% stock dividend is declared on December 31—the items impacted are in bold.

Point: The term *Distributable* (not *Payable*) is used for stock dividends. A stock dividend is never a liability because it never reduces assets.

Point: The credit to Paid-In Capital in Excess of Par Value is recorded when the stock dividend is declared. This account is not affected when stock is later distributed.

Stockholders' Equity (after dividend)	
Common stock—$10 par value, 15,000 shares authorized, 10,000 shares issued and outstanding	$100,000
Common stock dividend distributable—1,000 shares	**10,000**
Paid-in capital in excess of par value, common stock	**13,000**
Retained earnings	**20,000**
Total stockholders' equity	$143,000

EXHIBIT 11.8

Stockholders' Equity *after* Declaring a Stock Dividend

No entry is made on the date of record for a stock dividend. On January 20, the date of payment, Quest distributes the new shares to stockholders and records this entry:

Date of Payment

Jan. 20	Common Stock Dividend Distributable	10,000	
	Common Stock, $10 Par Value.		10,000
	To record issuance of common stock dividend.		

Assets = Liabilities + Equity
$$-10,000$$
$$+10,000$$

The combined effect of these stock dividend entries is to transfer (or capitalize) $15,000 of retained earnings to paid-in capital accounts. The amount of capitalized retained earnings equals the market value of the 1,000 issued shares ($15 × 1,000 shares). A stock dividend has no effect on the ownership percent of individual stockholders.

Recording a large stock dividend. A corporation capitalizes retained earnings equal to the minimum amount required by state law for a large stock dividend. For most states, this amount is the par or stated value of the newly issued shares. To illustrate, suppose Quest's board declares a stock dividend of 30% instead of 10% on December 31. Since this dividend is more than 25%, it is treated as a large stock dividend. Thus, the par value of the 3,000 dividend shares is capitalized at the date of declaration with this entry:

Date of Declaration

Dec. 31	Retained Earnings..............................	30,000	
	Common Stock Dividend Distributable.........		30,000
	Declared a 3,000-share (30%) stock dividend.		

This transaction decreases retained earnings and increases contributed capital by $30,000. On the date of payment the company debits Common Stock Dividend Distributable and credits Common Stock for $30,000. The effects from a large stock dividend on balance sheet accounts are similar to those for a small stock dividend except for the absence of any effect on paid-in capital in excess of par.

Before 5:1 Split: 1 share, $50 par

Stock Splits

A **stock split** is the distribution of additional shares to stockholders according to their percent ownership. When a stock split occurs, the corporation "calls in" its outstanding shares and issues more than one new share in exchange for each old share. Splits can be done in any ratio, including 2-for-1, 3-for-1, or higher. Stock splits reduce the par or stated value per share. The reasons for stock splits are similar to those for stock dividends.

After 5:1 Split: 5 shares, $10 par

To illustrate, CompTec has 100,000 outstanding shares of $20 par value common stock with a current market value of $88 per share. A 2-for-1 stock split cuts par value in half as it replaces 100,000 shares of $20 par value stock with 200,000 shares of $10 par value stock. Market value is reduced from $88 per share to about $44 per share. The split does not affect any equity amounts reported on the balance sheet or any individual stockholder's percent ownership. Both the Paid-In Capital and Retained Earnings accounts are unchanged by a split, and *no journal entry is made*. The only effect on the accounts is a change in the stock account description. CompTec's 2-for-1 split on its $20 par value stock means that after the split, it changes its stock account title to Common Stock, $10 Par Value. This stock's description on the balance sheet also changes to reflect the additional authorized, issued, and outstanding shares and the new par value.

The difference between stock splits and large stock dividends is often blurred. Many companies report stock splits in their financial statements without calling in the original shares by simply changing their par value. This type of "split" is really a large stock dividend and results in additional shares issued to stockholders by capitalizing retained earnings or transferring other paid-in capital to Common Stock. This approach avoids administrative costs of splitting the stock. **Harley-Davidson** recently declared a 2-for-1 stock split executed in the form of a 100% stock dividend.

♟ **Decision Maker** ▬▬▬▬▬▬▬▬▬

Entrepreneur A company you cofounded and own stock in announces a 50% stock dividend. Has the value of your stock investment increased, decreased, or remained the same? Would it make a difference if it was a 3-for-2 stock split executed in the form of a dividend? [Answer—p. 490]

10. How does a stock dividend impact assets and retained earnings?

11. What distinguishes a large stock dividend from a small stock dividend?

12. What amount of retained earnings is capitalized for a small stock dividend?

Preferred Stock

A corporation can issue two basic kinds of stock, common and preferred. **Preferred stock** has special rights that give it priority (or senior status) over common stock in one or more areas. Special rights typically include a preference for receiving dividends and for the distribution of assets if the corporation is liquidated. Preferred stock carries all rights of common stock unless the corporate charter nullifies them. Most preferred stock, for instance, does not confer the right to vote. Exhibit 11.9 shows that preferred stock is issued by about one-fourth of large corporations. All corporations issue common stock.

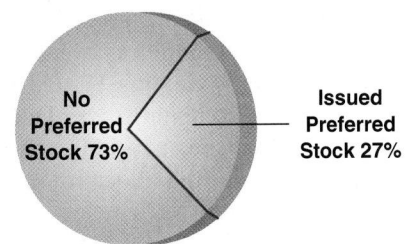

EXHIBIT 11.9

Corporations and Preferred Stock

Issuance of Preferred Stock

Preferred stock usually has a par value. Like common stock, it can be sold at a price different from par. Preferred stock is recorded in its own separate capital accounts. To illustrate, if Dillon Snowboards issues 50 shares of $100 par value preferred stock for $6,000 cash on July 1, 2009, the entry is

C3 Explain characteristics of common and preferred stock.

July 1	Cash..	6,000	
	Preferred Stock, $100 Par Value..............		5,000
	Paid-In Capital in Excess of Par Value,		
	Preferred Stock..........................		1,000
	Issued preferred stock for cash.		

Assets = Liabilities + Equity
+6,000   +5,000
                          +1,000

The equity section of the year-end balance sheet for Dillon Snowboards, including preferred stock, is shown in Exhibit 11.10. (This exhibit assumes that common stock was issued at par.) Issuing no-par preferred stock is similar to issuing no-par common stock. Also, the entries for issuing preferred stock for noncash assets are similar to those for common stock.

EXHIBIT 11.10

Stockholders' Equity with Common and Preferred Stock

Stockholders' Equity	
Common stock—$10 par value; 50,000 shares authorized;	
30,000 shares issued and outstanding	$300,000
Preferred stock—$100 par value; 1,000 shares authorized;	
50 shares issued and outstanding	5,000
Paid-in capital in excess of par value, preferred stock	1,000
Retained earnings	65,000
Total stockholders' equity	$371,000

Dividend Preference of Preferred Stock

Preferred stock usually carries a preference for dividends, meaning that preferred stockholders are allocated their dividends before any dividends are allocated to common stockholders. The dividends allocated to preferred stockholders are usually expressed as a dollar amount per

P4 Distribute dividends between common stock and preferred stock.

share or a percent applied to par value. A preference for dividends does *not* ensure dividends. If the directors do not declare a dividend, neither the preferred nor the common stockholders receive one.

Video11.2

Cumulative or Noncumulative Dividend   Most preferred stocks carry a cumulative dividend right. **Cumulative preferred stock** has a right to be paid both the current and all prior periods' unpaid dividends before any dividend is paid to common stockholders. When preferred stock is cumulative and the directors either do not declare a dividend to preferred stockholders or declare one that does not cover the total amount of cumulative dividend, the unpaid dividend amount is called **dividend in arrears.** Accumulation of dividends in arrears on cumulative preferred stock does not guarantee they will be paid. **Noncumulative preferred stock** confers no right to prior periods' unpaid dividends if they were not declared in those prior periods.

To illustrate the difference between cumulative and noncumulative preferred stock, assume that a corporation's outstanding stock includes (1) 1,000 shares of $100 par, 9% preferred stock—yielding $9,000 per year in potential dividends, and (2) 4,000 shares of $50 par value common stock. During 2008, the first year of operations, the directors declare cash dividends of $5,000. In year 2009, they declare cash dividends of $42,000. See Exhibit 11.11 for the allocation of dividends for these two years. Allocation of year 2009 dividends depends on whether the preferred stock is noncumulative or cumulative. With noncumulative preferred, the preferred stockholders never receive the $4,000 skipped in 2008. If the preferred stock is cumulative, the $4,000 in arrears is paid in 2009 before any other dividends are paid.

EXHIBIT 11.11

Allocation of Dividends (noncumulative vs. cumulative preferred stock)

	Preferred	Common
Preferred Stock Is Noncumulative		
Year 2008	$ 5,000	$ 0
Year 2009		
Step 1: Current year's preferred dividend	$ 9,000	
Step 2: Remainder to common		$33,000
Preferred Stock Is Cumulative		
Year 2008	$ 5,000	$ 0
Year 2009		
Step 1: Dividend in arrears	$ 4,000	
Step 2: Current year's preferred dividend	9,000	
Step 3: Remainder to common		$29,000
Totals for year 2009	$13,000	$29,000

A liability for a dividend does not exist until the directors declare a dividend. If a preferred dividend date passes and the corporation's board fails to declare the dividend on its cumulative preferred stock, the dividend in arrears is not a liability. The *full-disclosure principle* requires a corporation to report (usually in a note) the amount of preferred dividends in arrears as of the balance sheet date.

Participating or Nonparticipating Dividend   **Nonparticipating preferred stock** has a feature that limits dividends to a maximum amount each year. This maximum is often stated as a percent of the stock's par value or as a specific dollar amount per share. Once preferred stockholders receive this amount, the common stockholders receive any and all additional dividends. **Participating preferred stock** has a feature allowing preferred stockholders to share with common stockholders in any dividends paid in excess of the percent or dollar amount stated on the preferred stock. This participation feature does not apply until common stockholders receive dividends equal to the preferred stock's dividend percent. Many corporations are authorized to issue participating preferred stock but rarely do, and most managers never expect to issue it.[2]

Convertible Preferred Stock

Preferred stock is more attractive to investors if it carries a right to exchange preferred shares for a fixed number of common shares. **Convertible preferred stock** gives holders the option to exchange their preferred shares for common shares at a specified rate. When a company prospers and its common stock increases in value, convertible preferred stockholders can share in this success by converting their preferred stock into more valuable common stock.

Callable Preferred Stock

Callable preferred stock gives the issuing corporation the right to purchase (retire) this stock from its holders at specified future prices and dates. The amount paid to call and retire a preferred share is its **call price,** or *redemption value,* and is set when the stock is issued. The call price normally includes the stock's par value plus a premium giving holders additional return on their investment. When the issuing corporation calls and retires a preferred stock, the terms of the agreement often require it to pay the call price *and* any dividends in arrears.

Point: The issuing corporation has the right, or option, to retire its callable preferred stock.

IFRS

Like U.S. GAAP, IFRS requires that preferred stock be classified as debt or equity based on analysis of the stock's contractual terms. However, IFRS uses different criteria for such classification.

Reasons for Issuing Preferred Stock

Corporations issue preferred stock for several reasons. One is to raise capital without sacrificing control. For example, suppose a company's organizers have $100,000 cash to invest and organize a corporation that needs $200,000 of capital to start. If they sell $200,000 worth of common stock (with $100,000 to the organizers), they would have only 50% control and would need to negotiate extensively with other stockholders in making policy. However, if they issue $100,000 worth of common stock to themselves and sell outsiders $100,000 of 8%, cumulative preferred stock with no voting rights, they retain control.

A second reason to issue preferred stock is to boost the return earned by common stockholders. To illustrate, suppose a corporation's organizers expect to earn an annual after-tax income of $24,000 on an investment of $200,000. If they sell and issue $200,000 worth of common stock, the $24,000 income produces a 12% return on the $200,000 of common stockholders' equity. However, if they issue $100,000 of 8% preferred stock to outsiders and $100,000 of common stock to themselves, their own return increases to 16% per year, as shown in Exhibit 11.12.

---

[2] Participating preferred stock is usually authorized as a defense against a possible corporate *takeover* by an "unfriendly" investor (or a group of investors) who intends to buy enough voting common stock to gain control. Taking a term from spy novels, the financial world refers to this type of plan as a *poison pill* that a company swallows if enemy investors threaten its capture. A poison pill usually works as follows: A corporation's common stockholders on a given date are granted the right to purchase a large amount of participating preferred stock at a very low price. This right to purchase preferred shares is *not* transferable. If an unfriendly investor buys a large block of common shares (whose right to purchase participating preferred shares does *not* transfer to this buyer), the board can issue preferred shares at a low price to the remaining common shareholders who retained the right to purchase. Future dividends are then divided between the newly issued participating preferred shares and the common shares. This usually transfers value from common shares to preferred shares, causing the unfriendly investor's common stock to lose much of its value and reduces the potential benefit of a hostile takeover.

EXHIBIT 11.12

Return to Common Stockholders
When Preferred Stock Is Issued

Net (after-tax) income	$24,000
Less preferred dividends at 8%	(8,000)
Balance to common stockholders	$16,000
Return to common stockholders ($16,000/$100,000)	16%

Point: Financial leverage also occurs when debt is issued and the interest rate paid on it is less than the rate earned from using the assets the creditors lend the company.

Common stockholders earn 16% instead of 12% because assets contributed by preferred stockholders are invested to earn $12,000 while the preferred dividend is only $8,000. Use of preferred stock to increase return to common stockholders is an example of **financial leverage** (also called *trading on the equity*). As a general rule, when the dividend rate on preferred stock is less than the rate the corporation earns on its assets, the effect of issuing preferred stock is to increase (or *lever*) the rate earned by common stockholders.

Other reasons for issuing preferred stock include its appeal to some investors who believe that the corporation's common stock is too risky or that the expected return on common stock is too low.

 Decision Maker

Concert Organizer Assume that you alter your business strategy from organizing concerts targeted at under 1,000 people to those targeted at between 5,000 to 20,000 people. You also incorporate because of increased risk of lawsuits and a desire to issue stock for financing. It is important that you control the company for decisions on whom to schedule. What types of stock do you offer? [Answer—p. 490]

Quick Check

Answers—p. 491

13. In what ways does preferred stock often have priority over common stock?

14. Increasing the return to common stockholders by issuing preferred stock is an example of
    (*a*) Financial leverage. (*b*) Cumulative earnings. (*c*) Dividend in arrears.

15. A corporation has issued and outstanding (i) 9,000 shares of $50 par value, 10% cumulative, nonparticipating preferred stock and (ii) 27,000 shares of $10 par value common stock. No dividends have been declared for the two prior years. During the current year, the corporation declares $288,000 in dividends. The amount paid to common shareholders is (*a*) $243,000. (*b*) $153,000. (*c*) $135,000.

Treasury Stock

P5 Record purchases and sales of treasury stock and the retirement of stock.

Corporations acquire shares of their own stock for several reasons: (1) to use their shares to acquire another corporation, (2) to purchase shares to avoid a hostile takeover of the company, (3) to reissue them to employees as compensation, and (4) to maintain a strong market for their stock or to show management confidence in the current price.

A corporation's reacquired shares are called **treasury stock,** which is similar to unissued stock in several ways: (1) neither treasury stock nor unissued stock is an asset, (2) neither receives cash dividends or stock dividends, and (3) neither allows the exercise of voting rights. However, treasury stock does differ from unissued stock in one major way: The corporation can resell treasury stock at less than par without having the buyers incur a liability, provided it was originally issued at par value or higher. Treasury stock purchases also require management to exercise ethical sensitivity because funds are being paid to specific stockholders instead of all stockholders. Managers must be sure the purchase is in the best interest of all stockholders. These concerns cause companies to fully disclose treasury stock transactions.

Corporations and Treasury Stock

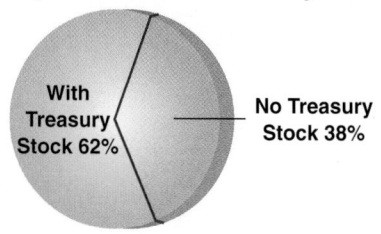

With Treasury Stock 62%

No Treasury Stock 38%

Purchasing Treasury Stock

Purchasing treasury stock reduces the corporation's assets and equity by equal amounts. (We describe the *cost method* of accounting for treasury stock, which is the most widely used method. The *par value* method is another method explained in advanced courses.) To illustrate, Exhibit 11.13 shows Cyber Corporation's account balances *before* any treasury stock purchase (Cyber has no liabilities).

Assets		Stockholders' Equity	
Cash	$ 30,000	Common stock—$10 par; 10,000 shares	
Other assets	95,000	authorized, issued, and outstanding	$100,000
		Retained earnings	25,000
Total assets	$125,000	Total stockholders' equity	$125,000

EXHIBIT 11.13

Account Balances *before* Purchasing Treasury Stock

Cyber then purchases 1,000 of its own shares for $11,500 on May 1, which is recorded as follows.

May 1	Treasury Stock, Common........................	11,500	
	Cash.....................................		11,500
	Purchased 1,000 treasury shares at $11.50 per share.		

Assets = Liabilities + Equity
−11,500   −11,500

This entry reduces equity through the debit to the Treasury Stock account, which is a contra equity account. Exhibit 11.14 shows account balances *after* this transaction.

Assets		Stockholders' Equity	
Cash	$ 18,500	Common stock—$10 par; 10,000 shares	
Other assets	95,000	authorized and issued; 1,000 shares in treasury	$100,000
		Retained earnings, $11,500 restricted by	
		treasury stock purchase	25,000
		Less cost of treasury stock	**(11,500)**
Total assets	$113,500	Total stockholders' equity	$113,500

EXHIBIT 11.14

Account Balances *after* Purchasing Treasury Stock

The treasury stock purchase reduces Cyber's cash, total assets, and total equity by $11,500 but does not reduce the balance of either the Common Stock or the Retained Earnings account. The equity reduction is reported by deducting the cost of treasury stock in the equity section. Also, two disclosures are evident. First, the stock description reveals that 1,000 issued shares are in treasury, leaving only 9,000 shares still outstanding. Second, the description for retained earnings reveals that it is partly restricted.

Point: The Treasury Stock account is *not* an asset. Treasury stock does not carry voting or dividend rights.

Point: A treasury stock purchase is also called a *stock buyback*.

Reissuing Treasury Stock

Treasury stock can be reissued by selling it at cost, above cost, or below cost.

Selling Treasury Stock at Cost   If treasury stock is reissued at cost, the entry is the reverse of the one made to record the purchase. For instance, if on May 21 Cyber reissues 100 of the treasury shares purchased on May 1 at the same $11.50 per share cost, the entry is

May 21	Cash...	1,150	
	Treasury Stock, Common...................		1,150
	Received $11.50 per share for 100 treasury		
	shares costing $11.50 per share.		

Assets = Liabilities + Equity
+1,150   +1,150

Point: Treasury stock does not represent ownership. A company cannot own a part of itself.

Selling Treasury Stock *above* Cost   If treasury stock is sold for more than cost, the amount received in excess of cost is credited to the Paid-In Capital, Treasury Stock account. This account is reported as a separate item in the stockholders' equity section. No gain is ever reported from the sale of treasury stock. To illustrate, if Cyber receives $12 cash per share for 400 treasury shares costing $11.50 per share on June 3, the entry is

Assets = Liabilities + Equity
+4,800   +4,600
                       +200

June 3	Cash	4,800	
	Treasury Stock, Common.....................		4,600
	Paid-In Capital, Treasury Stock............		**200**
	Received $12 per share for 400 treasury shares costing $11.50 per share.		

Point: The phrase *treasury stock* is believed to arise from the fact that reacquired stock is held in a corporation's treasury.

Selling Treasury Stock *below* Cost   When treasury stock is sold below cost, the entry to record the sale depends on whether the Paid-In Capital, Treasury Stock account has a credit balance. If it has a zero balance, the excess of cost over the sales price is debited to Retained Earnings. If the Paid-In Capital, Treasury Stock account has a credit balance, it is debited for the excess of the cost over the selling price but not to exceed the balance in this account. When the credit balance in this paid-in capital account is eliminated, any remaining difference between the cost and selling price is debited to Retained Earnings. To illustrate, if Cyber sells its remaining 500 shares of treasury stock at $10 per share on July 10, equity is reduced by $750 (500 shares × $1.50 per share excess of cost over selling price), as shown in this entry:

Point: The Paid-In Capital, Treasury Stock account can have a zero or credit balance but never a debit balance.

Assets = Liabilities + Equity
+5,000   −200
                      −550
                      +5,750

July 10	Cash	5,000	
	Paid-In Capital, Treasury Stock................	**200**	
	Retained Earnings	**550**	
	Treasury Stock, Common.....................		5,750
	Received $10 per share for 500 treasury shares costing $11.50 per share.		

This entry eliminates the $200 credit balance in the paid-in capital account created on June 3 and then reduces the Retained Earnings balance by the remaining $550 excess of cost over selling price. A company never reports a loss (or gain) from the sale of treasury stock.

Retiring Stock

A corporation can purchase its own stock and retire it. Retiring stock reduces the number of issued shares. Retired stock is the same as authorized and unissued shares. Purchases and retirements of stock are permissible under state law only if they do not jeopardize the interests of creditors and stockholders. When stock is purchased for retirement, we remove all capital amounts related to the retired shares. If the purchase price exceeds the net amount removed, this excess is debited to Retained Earnings. If the net amount removed from all capital accounts exceeds the purchase price, this excess is credited to the Paid-In Capital from Retirement of Stock account. A company's assets and equity are always reduced by the amount paid for the retiring stock.

Point: Recording stock retirement results in canceling the equity from the original issuance of the shares.

<table>
<tr><td colspan="2">**Quick Check**</td><td align="right">Answers—p. 491</td></tr>
</table>

16. Purchase of treasury stock (*a*) has no effect on assets; (*b*) reduces total assets and total equity by equal amounts; or (*c*) is recorded with a debit to Retained Earnings.

17. Southern Co. purchases shares of Northern Corp. Should either company classify these shares as treasury stock?

18. How does treasury stock affect the authorized, issued, and outstanding shares?

19. When a company purchases treasury stock, (*a*) retained earnings are restricted by the amount paid; (*b*) Retained Earnings is credited; or (*c*) it is retired.

Reporting of Equity

Statement of Retained Earnings

Retained earnings generally consist of a company's cumulative net income less any net losses and dividends declared since its inception. Retained earnings are part of stockholders' claims on the company's net assets, but this does *not* imply that a certain amount of cash or other assets is available to pay stockholders. For example, **RadioShack** has $2,153.2 million in retained earnings, but only $814.8 million in cash. This section describes events and transactions affecting retained earnings and how retained earnings are reported.

Restrictions and Appropriations   The term **restricted retained earnings** refers to both statutory and contractual restrictions. A common *statutory* (or *legal*) *restriction* is to limit treasury stock purchases to the amount of retained earnings. The balance sheet in Exhibit 11.14 provides an example. A common *contractual restriction* involves loan agreements that restrict paying dividends beyond a specified amount or percent of retained earnings. Restrictions are usually described in the notes. The term **appropriated retained earnings** refers to a voluntary transfer of amounts from the Retained Earnings account to the Appropriated Retained Earnings account to inform users of special activities that require funds.

Prior Period Adjustments   **Prior period adjustments** are corrections of material errors in prior period financial statements. These errors include arithmetic mistakes, unacceptable accounting, and missed facts. Prior period adjustments are reported in the *statement of retained earnings* (or the statement of stockholders' equity), net of any income tax effects. Prior period adjustments result in changing the beginning balance of retained earnings for events occurring prior to the earliest period reported in the current set of financial statements. To illustrate, assume that ComUS makes an error in a 2007 journal entry for the purchase of land by incorrectly debiting an expense account. When this is discovered in 2009, the statement of retained earnings includes a prior period adjustment, as shown in Exhibit 11.15. This exhibit also shows the usual format of the statement of retained earnings.

C4 Explain the items reported in retained earnings.

Video11.1

Point: If a year 2007 error is discovered in 2008, the company records the adjustment in 2008. But if the financial statements include 2007 and 2008 figures, the statements report the correct amounts for 2007, and a note describes the correction.

ComUS Statement of Retained Earnings For Year Ended December 31, 2009	
Retained earnings, Dec. 31, 2008, as previously reported	$4,745,000
Prior period adjustment	
Cost of land incorrectly expensed (net of $63,000 income taxes)	147,000
Retained earnings, Dec. 31, 2008, as adjusted	4,892,000
Plus net income	1,224,300
Less cash dividends declared	(301,800)
Retained earnings, Dec. 31, 2009	$5,814,500

EXHIBIT 11.15

Statement of Retained Earnings with a Prior Period Adjustment

Many items reported in financial statements are based on estimates. Future events are certain to reveal that some of these estimates were inaccurate even when based on the best data available at the time. These inaccuracies are *not* considered errors and are *not* reported as prior period adjustments. Instead, they are identified as **changes in accounting estimates** and are accounted for in current and future periods. To illustrate, we know that depreciation is based on estimated useful lives and salvage values. As time passes and new information becomes available, managers may need to change these estimates and the resulting depreciation expense for current and future periods.

Point: Accounting for changes in estimates is sometimes criticized as two wrongs to make a right. Consider a change in an asset's life. Depreciation neither before nor after the change is the amount computed if the revised estimate were originally selected. Regulators chose this approach to avoid restating prior period numbers.

Closing Process   The closing process was explained earlier in the book as: (1) Close credit balances in revenue accounts to Income Summary, (2) Close debit balances in expense accounts to Income Summary, and (3) Close Income Summary to Retained Earnings. If dividends are recorded in a Dividends account, and not as an immediate reduction to Retained Earnings (as shown in this chapter), a fourth step is necessary to close the Dividends account to Retained Earnings.

Statement of Stockholders' Equity

Instead of a separate statement of retained earnings, companies commonly report a statement of stockholders' equity that includes changes in retained earnings. A **statement of stockholders' equity** lists the beginning and ending balances of key equity accounts and describes the changes that occur during the period. The companies in Appendix A report such a statement. The usual format is to provide a column for each component of equity and use the rows to describe events occurring in the period. Exhibit 11.16 shows a condensed statement for **Apple**.

EXHIBIT 11.16

Statement of Stockholders' Equity

APPLE Statement of Stockholders' Equity					
($ millions, shares in thousands)	Common Stock Shares	Common Stock Amount	Retained Earnings	Other	Total Equity
Balance, Sept. 29, 2007	872,329	$5,368	$9,101	$63	$14,532
Net income	—	—	4,834	—	4,834
Issuance of Common Stock	15,997	481	(101)	—	380
Other	—	1,328	11	(55)	1,284
Cash Dividends ($0.00 per share)	—	—	—	—	—
Balance, Sept. 27, 2008	888,326	$7,177	$13,845	$ 8	$21,030

Reporting Stock Options

The majority of corporations whose shares are publicly traded issue **stock options,** which are rights to purchase common stock at a fixed price over a specified period. As the stock's price rises, the option's value increases. **Starbucks** and **Home Depot** offer stock options to both full- and part-time employees. Stock options are said to motivate managers and employees to (1) focus on company performance, (2) take a long-run perspective, and (3) remain with the company. A stock option is like having an investment with no risk ("a carrot with no stick").

To illustrate, Quantum grants each of its employees the option to purchase 100 shares of its $1 par value common stock at its current market price of $50 per share anytime within the next 10 years. If the stock price rises to $70 per share, an employee can exercise the option at a gain of $20 per share (acquire a $70 stock at the $50 option price). With 100 shares, a single employee would have a total gain of $2,000, computed as $20 × 100 shares. Companies report the cost of stock options in the income statement. Measurement of this cost is explained in advanced courses.

Video11.1

Global View

This section discusses similarities and differences between U.S. GAAP and IFRS in accounting and reporting for equity.

Accounting and Reporting for Common Stock

The accounting for and reporting of common stock under U.S. GAAP and IFRS are similar. Specifically, procedures for issuing common stock at par, at a premium, at a discount, and for noncash assets are similar across the two systems. However, we must be aware of legal and cultural differences across the world that can impact the rights and responsibilities of common shareholders. **GOME**'s terminology is a bit different as it uses the phrase "ordinary shares" in reference to what U.S. GAAP would title "common shares" (see Appendix A). It also discloses that it has authorized 200,000 million shares, but has only issued (and outstanding) shares of roughly 13,000 million.

Accounting and Reporting for Dividends

Accounting for and reporting of dividends under U.S. GAAP and IFRS are consistent. This applies to cash dividends, stock dividends, and stock splits. For **GOME**, a "dividend . . . amounting to a total of approximately RMB 344,486,000, was paid to the shareholders of the Company during the year." GOME, like many other companies, applies a regular dividend policy which follows:

> The Directors anticipate that the dividend payout ratio will be maintained at approximately 30% of the Group's distributable profit. Actual payout ratio . . . will be determined at the Directors' full discretion after taking into account . . . availability of investment and acquisition opportunities.

Accounting and Reporting for Preferred Stock

Accounting and reporting for preferred stock are similar for U.S. GAAP and IFRS, but there are some important differences. First, preferred stock that is redeemable at the option of the preferred stockholders is reported *between* liabilities and equity in U.S. GAAP balance sheets. However, that same stock is reported as a liability in IFRS balance sheets. Second, the issue price of convertible preferred stock (and bonds) is recorded entirely under preferred stock (or bonds) *and none to the conversion feature* under U.S. GAAP. However, IFRS requires that a portion of the issue price be allocated to the conversion feature when it exists. GOME has no preferred stock.

Accounting and Reporting for Treasury Stock

Both U.S. GAAP and IFRS apply the principle that companies do not record gains or losses on transactions involving their own stock. This applies to purchases, reissuances, and retirements of treasury stock. Consequently, the accounting for treasury stock explained in this chapter is consistent with that under IFRS. However, IFRS in this area is less detailed than that of U.S. GAAP. **GOME**'s policy regarding treasury stock follows:

> Own equity instruments which are reacquired are deducted from equity. No gain or loss is recognized in the income statement on the purchase, sale, issue or cancellation of the Group's own equity instruments.

Earnings per Share, Price-Earnings Ratio, Dividend Yield, and Book Value per Share	Decision Analysis

Earnings per Share

The income statement reports **earnings per share,** also called *EPS* or *net income per share,* which is the amount of income earned per each share of a company's outstanding common stock. The **basic earnings per share** formula is shown in Exhibit 11.17. When a company has no preferred stock, then preferred dividends are zero. The weighted-average common shares outstanding is measured over the income reporting period; its computation is explained in advanced courses.

A1 Compute earnings per share and describe its use.

$$\text{Basic earnings per share} = \frac{\text{Net income} - \text{Preferred dividends}}{\text{Weighted-average common shares outstanding}}$$

EXHIBIT 11.17

Basic Earnings per Share

To illustrate, assume that Quantum Co. earns $40,000 net income in 2009 and declares dividends of $7,500 on its noncumulative preferred stock. (If preferred stock is *non*cumulative, the income available [numerator] is the current period net income less any preferred dividends *declared* in that same period. If preferred stock is cumulative, the income available [numerator] is the current period net income less the preferred dividends whether declared or not.) Quantum has 5,000 weighted-average common shares outstanding during 2009. Its basic EPS[3] is

$$\text{Basic earnings per share} = \frac{\$40,000 - \$7,500}{5,000 \text{ shares}} = \$6.50$$

Price-Earnings Ratio

A2 Compute price-earnings ratio and describe its use in analysis.

A stock's market value is determined by its *expected* future cash flows. A comparison of a company's EPS and its market value per share reveals information about market expectations. This comparison is traditionally made using a **price-earnings (or PE) ratio,** expressed also as *price earnings, price to earnings,* or *PE.* Some analysts interpret this ratio as what price the market is willing to pay for a company's current earnings stream. Price-earnings ratios can differ across companies that have similar earnings because of either higher or lower expectations of future earnings. The price-earnings ratio is defined in Exhibit 11.18.

Point: The average PE ratio of stocks in the 1950–2010 period is about 14.

EXHIBIT 11.18

Price-Earnings Ratio

$$\text{Price-earnings ratio} = \frac{\textbf{Market value (price) per share}}{\textbf{Earnings per share}}$$

This ratio is often computed using EPS from the most recent period (for Amazon, its PE is 52; for Altria, its PE is 13). However, many users compute this ratio using *expected* EPS for the next period.

Some analysts view stocks with high PE ratios (higher than 20 to 25) as more likely to be overpriced and stocks with low PE ratios (less than 5 to 8) as more likely to be underpriced. These investors prefer to sell or avoid buying stocks with high PE ratios and to buy or hold stocks with low PE ratios. However, investment decision making is rarely so simple as to rely on a single ratio. For instance, a stock with a high PE ratio can prove to be a good investment if its earnings continue to increase beyond current expectations. Similarly, a stock with a low PE ratio can prove to be a poor investment if its earnings decline below expectations.

Point: Average PE ratios for U.S. stocks increased over the past two decades. Some analysts interpret this as a signal the market is overpriced. But higher ratios can at least partly reflect accounting changes that have reduced reported earnings.

 Decision Maker ▬▬▬▬▬▬▬▬▬▬▬▬▬▬▬▬▬

Money Manager You plan to invest in one of two companies identified as having identical future prospects. One has a PE of 19 and the other a PE of 25. Which do you invest in? Does it matter if your *estimate* of PE for these two companies is 29 as opposed to 22? [Answer—p. 490]

Dividend Yield

A3 Compute dividend yield and explain its use in analysis.

Investors buy shares of a company's stock in anticipation of receiving a return from either or both cash dividends and stock price increases. Stocks that pay large dividends on a regular basis, called *income stocks,* are attractive to investors who want recurring cash flows from their investments. In contrast, some stocks pay little or no dividends but are still attractive to investors because of their expected stock price increases. The stocks of companies that distribute little or no cash but use their cash to finance expansion are called *growth stocks.* One way to help identify whether a stock is an income stock or a growth stock is to analyze its dividend yield. **Dividend yield,** defined in Exhibit 11.19, shows the annual amount of cash dividends distributed to common shares relative to their market value.

EXHIBIT 11.19

Dividend Yield

$$\text{Dividend yield} = \frac{\textbf{Annual cash dividends per share}}{\textbf{Market value per share}}$$

---

[3] A corporation can be classified as having either a simple or complex capital structure. The term **simple capital structure** refers to a company with only common stock and nonconvertible preferred stock outstanding. The term **complex capital structure** refers to companies with dilutive securities. **Dilutive securities** include options, rights to purchase common stock, and any bonds or preferred stock that are convertible into common stock. A company with a complex capital structure must often report two EPS figures: basic and diluted. **Diluted earnings per share** is computed by adding all dilutive securities to the denominator of the basic EPS computation. It reflects the decrease in basic EPS *assuming* that all dilutive securities are converted into common shares.

Dividend yield can be computed for current and prior periods using actual dividends and stock prices and for future periods using expected values. Exhibit 11.20 shows recent dividend and stock price data for **Amazon** and **Altria Group** to compute dividend yield.

Company	Cash Dividends per Share	Market Value per Share	Dividend Yield
Amazon	$0.00	$80	0.0%
Altria Group	1.68	20	8.4

EXHIBIT 11.20

Dividend and Stock Price Information

Point: The *payout ratio* equals cash dividends declared on common stock divided by net income. A low payout ratio suggests that a company is retaining earnings for future growth.

Dividend yield is zero for Amazon, implying it is a growth stock. An investor in Amazon would look for increases in stock prices (and eventual cash from the sale of stock). Altria has a dividend yield of 8.4%, implying it is an income stock for which dividends are important in assessing its value.

Book Value per Share

Case 1: Common Stock (Only) Outstanding. **Book value per common share,** defined in Exhibit 11.21, reflects the amount of equity applicable to *common* shares on a per share basis. To illustrate, we use Dillon Snowboards' data from Exhibit 11.4. Dillon has 30,000 outstanding common shares, and the stockholders' equity applicable to common shares is $365,000. Dillon's book value per common share is $12.17, computed as $365,000 divided by 30,000 shares.

A4   Compute book value and explain its use in analysis.

$$\text{Book value per common share} = \frac{\text{Stockholders' equity applicable to common shares}}{\text{Number of common shares outstanding}}$$

EXHIBIT 11.21

Book Value per Common Share

Case 2: Common and Preferred Stock Outstanding. To compute book value when both common and preferred shares are outstanding, we allocate total equity between the two types of shares. The **book value per preferred share** is computed first; its computation is shown in Exhibit 11.22.

Point: Book value per share is also referred to as *stockholders' claim to assets on a per share basis.*

$$\text{Book value per preferred share} = \frac{\text{Stockholders' equity applicable to preferred shares}}{\text{Number of preferred shares outstanding}}$$

EXHIBIT 11.22

Book Value per Preferred Share

The equity applicable to preferred shares equals the preferred share's call price (or par value if the preferred is not callable) plus any cumulative dividends in arrears. The remaining equity is the portion applicable to common shares. To illustrate, consider LTD's equity in Exhibit 11.23. Its preferred stock is callable at $108 per share, and two years of cumulative preferred dividends are in arrears.

Stockholders' Equity

Preferred stock—$100 par value, 7% cumulative, 2,000 shares authorized, 1,000 shares issued and outstanding	$100,000
Common stock—$25 par value, 12,000 shares authorized, 10,000 shares issued and outstanding	250,000
Paid-in capital in excess of par value, common stock	15,000
Retained earnings	82,000
Total stockholders' equity	$447,000

EXHIBIT 11.23

Stockholders' Equity with Preferred and Common Stock

The book value computations are in Exhibit 11.24. Equity is first allocated to preferred shares before the book value of common shares is computed.

EXHIBIT 11.24

Computing Book Value per
Preferred and Common Share

Total stockholders' equity		$447,000
Less equity applicable to preferred shares		
Call price (1,000 shares × $108)	$108,000	
Dividends in arrears ($100,000 × 7% × 2 years)	14,000	(122,000)
Equity applicable to common shares		$325,000
Book value per preferred share ($122,000/1,000 shares)		**$ 122.00**
Book value per common share ($325,000/10,000 shares)		**$ 32.50**

Book value per share reflects the value per share if a company is liquidated at balance sheet amounts. Book value is also the starting point in many stock valuation models, merger negotiations, price setting for public utilities, and loan contracts. The main limitation in using book value is the potential difference between recorded value and market value for assets and liabilities. Investors often adjust their analysis for estimates of these differences.

♟ Decision Maker

Investor   You are considering investing in **BMX**, whose book value per common share is $4 and price per common share on the stock exchange is $7. From this information, are BMX's net assets priced higher or lower than its recorded values? [Answer—p. 490]

Demonstration Problem 1

Barton Corporation began operations on January 1, 2008. The following transactions relating to stockholders' equity occurred in the first two years of the company's operations.

2008

Jan. 1   Authorized the issuance of 2 million shares of $5 par value common stock and 100,000 shares of $100 par value, 10% cumulative, preferred stock.

Jan. 2   Issued 200,000 shares of common stock for $12 cash per share.

Jan. 3   Issued 100,000 shares of common stock in exchange for a building valued at $820,000 and merchandise inventory valued at $380,000.

Jan. 4   Paid $10,000 cash to the company's founders for organization activities.

Jan. 5   Issued 12,000 shares of preferred stock for $110 cash per share.

2009

June 4   Issued 100,000 shares of common stock for $15 cash per share.

Required

1. Prepare journal entries to record these transactions.

2. Prepare the stockholders' equity section of the balance sheet as of December 31, 2008, and December 31, 2009, based on these transactions.

3. Prepare a table showing dividend allocations and dividends per share for 2008 and 2009 assuming Barton declares the following cash dividends: 2008, $50,000, and 2009, $300,000.

4. Prepare the January 2, 2008, journal entry for Barton's issuance of 200,000 shares of common stock for $12 cash per share assuming

   a. Common stock is no-par stock without a stated value.

   b. Common stock is no-par stock with a stated value of $10 per share.

Planning the Solution

- Record journal entries for the transactions for 2008 and 2009.
- Determine the balances for the 2008 and 2009 equity accounts for the balance sheet.
- Prepare the contributed capital portion of the 2008 and 2009 balance sheets.
- Prepare a table similar to Exhibit 11.11 showing dividend allocations for 2008 and 2009.
- Record the issuance of common stock under both specifications of no-par stock.

Solution to Demonstration Problem 1

1. Journal entries.

2008			
Jan. 2	Cash	2,400,000	
	Common Stock, $5 Par Value.		1,000,000
	Paid-In Capital in Excess of Par Value, Common Stock		1,400,000
	Issued 200,000 shares of common stock.		
Jan. 3	Building.	820,000	
	Merchandise Inventory	380,000	
	Common Stock, $5 Par Value.		500,000
	Paid-In Capital in Excess of Par Value, Common Stock		700,000
	Issued 100,000 shares of common stock.		
Jan. 4	Organization Expenses	10,000	
	Cash		10,000
	Paid founders for organization costs.		
Jan. 5	Cash	1,320,000	
	Preferred Stock, $100 Par Value.		1,200,000
	Paid-In Capital in Excess of Par Value, Preferred Stock		120,000
	Issued 12,000 shares of preferred stock.		
2009			
June 4	Cash	1,500,000	
	Common Stock, $5 Par Value.		500,000
	Paid-In Capital in Excess of Par Value, Common Stock		1,000,000
	Issued 100,000 shares of common stock.		

2. Balance sheet presentations (at December 31 year-end).

	2009	2008
Stockholders' Equity		
Preferred stock—$100 par value, 10% cumulative, 100,000 shares authorized, 12,000 shares issued and outstanding	$1,200,000	$1,200,000
Paid-in capital in excess of par value, preferred stock	120,000	120,000
Total paid-in capital by preferred stockholders	1,320,000	1,320,000
Common stock—$5 par value, 2,000,000 shares authorized, 300,000 shares issued and outstanding in 2008, and 400,000 shares issued and outstanding in 2009	2,000,000	1,500,000
Paid-in capital in excess of par value, common stock	3,100,000	2,100,000
Total paid-in capital by common stockholders	5,100,000	3,600,000
Total paid-in capital	$6,420,000	$4,920,000

3. Dividend allocation table.

	Common	Preferred
2008 ($50,000)		
Preferred—current year (12,000 shares × $10 = $120,000)	$ 0	$ 50,000
Common—remainder (300,000 shares outstanding)	0	0
Total for the year	$ 0	$ 50,000
2009 ($300,000)		
Preferred—dividend in arrears from 2008 ($120,000 − $50,000)	$ 0	$ 70,000
Preferred—current year	0	120,000
Common—remainder (400,000 shares outstanding)	110,000	0
Total for the year	$110,000	$190,000
Dividends per share		
2008	$ 0.00	$ 4.17
2009	$ 0.28	$ 15.83

4. Journal entries.

a. For 2008 (no-par stock without a stated value):

Jan. 2	Cash	2,400,000	
	Common Stock, No-Par Value		2,400,000
	Issued 200,000 shares of no-par common		
	stock at $12 per share.		

b. For 2008 (no-par stock with a stated value):

Jan. 2	Cash	2,400,000	
	Common Stock, $10 Stated Value		2,000,000
	Paid-In Capital in Excess of		
	Stated Value, Common Stock		400,000
	Issued 200,000 shares of $10 stated value		
	common stock at $12 per share.		

Demonstration Problem 2

Precision Company began year 2008 with the following balances in its stockholders' equity accounts.

Common stock—$10 par, 500,000 shares authorized, 200,000 shares issued and outstanding	$2,000,000
Paid-in capital in excess of par, common stock	1,000,000
Retained earnings	5,000,000
Total	$8,000,000

All outstanding common stock was issued for $15 per share when the company was created. Prepare journal entries to account for the following transactions during year 2008.

Jan.	10	The board declared a $0.10 cash dividend per share to shareholders of record Jan. 28.
Feb.	15	Paid the cash dividend declared on January 10.
Mar.	31	Declared a 20% stock dividend. The market value of the stock is $18 per share.
May	1	Distributed the stock dividend declared on March 31.
July	1	Purchased 30,000 shares of treasury stock at $20 per share.
Sept.	1	Sold 20,000 treasury shares at $26 cash per share.
Dec.	1	Sold the remaining 10,000 shares of treasury stock at $7 cash per share.

Planning the Solution

- Calculate the total cash dividend to record by multiplying the cash dividend declared by the number of shares as of the date of record.
- Decide whether the stock dividend is a small or large dividend. Then analyze each event to determine the accounts affected and the appropriate amounts to be recorded.

Solution to Demonstration Problem 2

Jan. 10	Retained Earnings.............................	20,000	
	Common Dividend Payable		20,000
	Declared a $0.10 per share cash dividend.		
Feb. 15	Common Dividend Payable......................	20,000	
	Cash.......................................		20,000
	Paid $0.10 per share cash dividend.		
Mar. 31	Retained Earnings.............................	720,000	
	Common Stock Dividend Distributable.........		400,000
	Paid-In Capital in Excess of		
	Par Value, Common Stock		320,000
	Declared a small stock dividend of 20% or		
	40,000 shares; market value is $18 per share.		
May 1	Common Stock Dividend Distributable	400,000	
	Common Stock		400,000
	Distributed 40,000 shares of common stock.		
July 1	Treasury Stock, Common......................	600,000	
	Cash.......................................		600,000
	Purchased 30,000 common shares at $20 per share.		
Sept. 1	Cash.......................................	520,000	
	Treasury Stock, Common....................		400,000
	Paid-In Capital, Treasury Stock...............		120,000
	Sold 20,000 treasury shares at $26 per share.		
Dec. 1	Cash.......................................	70,000	
	Paid-In Capital, Treasury Stock..................	120,000	
	Retained Earnings............................	10,000	
	Treasury Stock, Common...................		200,000
	Sold 10,000 treasury shares at $7 per share.		

Summary

C1 Identify characteristics of corporations and their organization. Corporations are legal entities whose stockholders are not liable for its debts. Stock is easily transferred, and the life of a corporation does not end with the incapacity of a stock holder. A corporation acts through its agents, who are its officers and managers. Corporations are regulated and subject to income taxes.

C2 Describe the components of stockholders' equity. Authorized stock is the stock that a corporation's charter authorizes it to sell. Issued stock is the portion of authorized shares sold. Par value stock is a value per share assigned by the charter. No-par value stock is stock *not* assigned a value per share by the charter. Stated value stock is no-par stock to which the directors assign a value per share. Stockholders' equity is made up of (1) paid-in capital and (2) retained earnings. Paid-in capital consists of funds raised by stock issuances. Retained earnings consists of cumulative net income (losses) not distributed.

C3 Explain characteristics of common and preferred stock. Preferred stock has a priority (or senior status) relative to common stock in one or more areas, usually (1) dividends and (2) assets in case of liquidation. Preferred stock usually does not carry voting rights and can be convertible or callable. Convertibility permits the holder to convert preferred to common. Callability permits the issuer to buy back preferred stock under specified conditions.

C4 Explain the items reported in retained earnings. Many companies face statutory and contractual restrictions on retained earnings. Corporations can voluntarily appropriate retained earnings to inform others about their disposition. Prior period adjustments are corrections of errors in prior financial statements.

A1 Compute earnings per share and describe its use. A company with a simple capital structure computes basic EPS by dividing net income less any preferred dividends by the weighted-average number of outstanding common shares. A company with a complex capital structure must usually report both basic and diluted EPS.

A2 **Compute price-earnings ratio and describe its use in analysis.** A common stock's price-earnings (PE) ratio is computed by dividing the stock's market value (price) per share by its EPS. A stock's PE is based on expectations that can prove to be better or worse than eventual performance.

A3 **Compute dividend yield and explain its use in analysis.** Dividend yield is the ratio of a stock's annual cash dividends per share to its market value (price) per share. Dividend yield can be compared with the yield of other companies to determine whether the stock is expected to be an income or growth stock.

A4 **Compute book value and explain its use in analysis.** Book value per common share is equity applicable to common shares divided by the number of outstanding common shares. Book value per preferred share is equity applicable to preferred shares divided by the number of outstanding preferred shares.

P1 **Record the issuance of corporate stock.** When stock is issued, its par or stated value is credited to the stock account and any excess is credited to a separate contributed capital account. If a stock has neither par nor stated value, the entire proceeds are credited to the stock account. Stockholders must contribute assets equal to minimum legal capital or be potentially liable for the deficiency.

P2 **Record transactions involving cash dividends.** Cash dividends involve three events. On the date of declaration, the directors bind the company to pay the dividend. A dividend declaration reduces retained earnings and creates a current liability. On the date of record, recipients of the dividend are identified. On the date

of payment, cash is paid to stockholders and the current liability is removed.

P3 **Account for stock dividends and stock splits.** Neither a stock dividend nor a stock split alters the value of the company. However, the value of each share is less due to the distribution of additional shares. The distribution of additional shares is according to individual stockholders' ownership percent. Small stock dividends (≤25%) are recorded by capitalizing retained earnings equal to the market value of distributed shares. Large stock dividends (>25%) are recorded by capitalizing retained earnings equal to the par or stated value of distributed shares. Stock splits do not yield journal entries but do yield changes in the description of stock.

P4 **Distribute dividends between common stock and preferred stock.** Preferred stockholders usually hold the right to dividend distributions before common stockholders. When preferred stock is cumulative and in arrears, the amount in arrears must be distributed to preferred before any dividends are distributed to common.

P5 **Record purchases and sales of treasury stock and the retirement of stock.** When a corporation purchases its own previously issued stock, it debits the cost of these shares to Treasury Stock. Treasury stock is subtracted from equity in the balance sheet. If treasury stock is reissued, any proceeds in excess of cost are credited to Paid-In Capital, Treasury Stock. If the proceeds are less than cost, they are debited to Paid-In Capital, Treasury Stock to the extent a credit balance exists. Any remaining amount is debited to Retained Earnings. When stock is retired, all accounts related to the stock are removed.

Guidance Answers to **Decision Maker** and **Decision Ethics**

Entrepreneur The 50% stock dividend provides you no direct income. A stock dividend often reveals management's optimistic expectations about the future and can improve a stock's marketability by making it affordable to more investors. Accordingly, a stock dividend usually reveals "good news" and because of this, it likely increases (slightly) the market value for your stock. The same conclusions apply to the 3-for-2 stock split.

Concert Organizer You have two basic options: (1) different classes of common stock or (2) common and preferred stock. Your objective is to issue to yourself stock that has all or a majority of the voting power. The other class of stock would carry limited or no voting rights. In this way, you maintain control and are able to raise the necessary funds.

Money Manager Since one company requires a payment of $19 for each $1 of earnings, and the other requires $25, you would pre-

fer the stock with the PE of 19; it is a better deal given identical prospects. You should make sure these companies' earnings computations are roughly the same, for example, no extraordinary items, unusual events, and so forth. Also, your PE estimates for these companies do matter. If you are willing to pay $29 for each $1 of earnings for these companies, you obviously expect both to exceed current market expectations.

Investor Book value reflects recorded values. BMX's book value is $4 per common share. Stock price reflects the market's expectation of net asset value (both tangible and intangible items). BMX's market value is $7 per common share. Comparing these figures suggests BMX's market value of net assets is higher than its recorded values (by an amount of $7 versus $4 per share).

Guidance Answers to **Quick Checks**

1. (b)

2. A corporation pays taxes on its income, and its stockholders normally pay personal income taxes (at the 15% rate or lower) on any cash dividends received from the corporation.

3. A proxy is a legal document used to transfer a stockholder's right to vote to another person.

4. (a)

5. A stock premium is an amount in excess of par (or stated) value paid by purchasers of newly issued stock.

6. Minimum legal capital intends to protect creditors of a corporation by obligating stockholders to some minimum level of equity financing and by constraining a corporation from excessive payments to stockholders.

7. Common Dividend Payable is a current liability account.

8. The date of declaration, date of record, and date of payment.

9. A dividend is a legal liability at the date of declaration, on which date it is recorded as a liability.

10. A stock dividend does not transfer assets to stockholders, but it does require an amount of retained earnings to be transferred to a contributed capital account(s).

11. A small stock dividend is 25% or less of the previous outstanding shares. A large stock dividend is more than 25%.

12. Retained earnings equal to the distributable shares' market value should be capitalized for a small stock dividend.

13. Typically, preferred stock has a preference in receipt of dividends and in distribution of assets.

14. (*a*)

15. (*b*)

Total cash dividend	$288,000
To preferred shareholders	135,000*
Remainder to common shareholders	$153,000

* 9,000 × $50 × 10% × 3 years = $135,000.

16. (*b*)

17. No. The shares are an investment for Southern Co. and are issued and outstanding shares for Northern Corp.

18. Treasury stock does not affect the number of authorized or issued shares, but it reduces the outstanding shares.

19. (*a*)

Key Terms

Appropriated retained earnings (p. 481)	**Discount on stock** (p. 469)	**Preemptive right** (p. 466)
Authorized stock (p. 467)	**Dividend in arrears** (p. 476)	**Preferred stock** (p. 475)
Basic earnings per share (p. 483)	**Dividend yield** (p. 484)	**Premium on stock** (p. 469)
Book value per common share (p. 485)	**Earnings per share (EPS)** (p. 483)	**Price-earnings (PE) ratio** (p. 484)
Book value per preferred share (p. 485)	**Financial leverage** (p. 478)	**Prior period adjustments** (p. 481)
Call price (p. 477)	**Large stock dividend** (p. 472)	**Proxy** (p. 465)
Callable preferred stock (p. 477)	**Liquidating cash dividend** (p. 472)	**Restricted retained earnings** (p. 481)
Capital stock (p. 467)	**Market value per share** (p. 467)	**Retained earnings** (p. 468)
Changes in accounting estimates (p. 481)	**Minimum legal capital** (p. 467)	**Retained earnings deficit** (p. 471)
Common stock (p. 466)	**Noncumulative preferred stock** (p. 476)	**Reverse stock split** (p. 474)
Complex capital structure (p. 484)	**Nonparticipating preferred stock** (p. 476)	**Simple capital structure** (p. 484)
Convertible preferred stock (p. 477)	**No-par value stock** (p. 467)	**Small stock dividend** (p. 472)
Corporation (p. 464)	**Organization expenses** (pp. 465, 470)	**Stated value stock** (p. 468)
Cumulative preferred stock (p. 476)	**Paid-in capital** (p. 468)	**Statement of stockholders' equity** (p. 482)
Date of declaration (p. 471)	**Paid-in capital in excess of par value** (p. 469)	**Stock dividend** (p. 472)
Date of payment (p. 471)		**Stock options** (p. 482)
Date of record (p. 471)	**Par value** (p. 467)	**Stock split** (p. 474)
Diluted earnings per share (p. 484)	**Par value stock** (p. 467)	**Stockholders' equity** (p. 468)
Dilutive securities (p. 484)	**Participating preferred stock** (p. 476)	**Treasury stock** (p. 478)

Multiple Choice Quiz   Answers on p. 507   mhhe.com/wildFA5e

Additional Quiz Questions are available at the book's Website.

1. A corporation issues 6,000 shares of $5 par value common stock for $8 cash per share. The entry to record this transaction includes:

  a. A debit to Paid-In Capital in Excess of Par Value for $18,000.

  b. A credit to Common Stock for $48,000.

  c. A credit to Paid-In Capital in Excess of Par Value for $30,000.

  d. A credit to Cash for $48,000.

  e. A credit to Common Stock for $30,000.

2. A company reports net income of $75,000. Its weighted-average common shares outstanding is 19,000. It has no other stock outstanding. Its earnings per share is:

  a. $4.69

  b. $3.95

  c. $3.75

  d. $2.08

  e. $4.41

3. A company has 5,000 shares of $100 par preferred stock and 50,000 shares of $10 par common stock outstanding. Its total stockholders' equity is $2,000,000. Its book value per common share is:

     a. $100.00
     b. $ 10.00
     c. $ 40.00
     d. $ 30.00
     e. $ 36.36

4. A company paid cash dividends of $0.81 per share. Its earnings per share is $6.95 and its market price per share is $45.00. Its dividend yield is:

     a. 1.8%
     b. 11.7%

     c. 15.4%
     d. 55.6%
     e. 8.6%

5. A company's shares have a market value of $85 per share. Its net income is $3,500,000, and its weighted-average common shares outstanding is 700,000. Its price-earnings ratio is:

     a. 5.9
     b. 425.0
     c. 17.0
     d. 10.4
     e. 41.2

Discussion Questions

1. What are organization expenses? Provide examples.

2. How are organization expenses reported?

3. ♟ Who is responsible for directing a corporation's affairs?

4. What is the preemptive right of common stockholders?

5. List the general rights of common stockholders.

6. What is the difference between authorized shares and outstanding shares?

7. ♟ Why would an investor find convertible preferred stock attractive?

8. What is the difference between the market value per share and the par value per share?

9. What is the difference between the par value and the call price of a share of preferred stock?

10. Identify and explain the importance of the three dates relevant to corporate dividends.

11. Why is the term *liquidating dividend* used to describe cash dividends debited against paid-in capital accounts?

12. ♟ How does declaring a stock dividend affect the corporation's assets, liabilities, and total equity? What are the effects of the eventual distribution of that stock?

13. ♟ What is the difference between a stock dividend and a stock split?

14. ♟ Courts have ruled that a stock dividend is not taxable income to stockholders. What justifies this decision?

15. How does the purchase of treasury stock affect the purchaser's assets and total equity?

16. ♟ Why do laws place limits on treasury stock purchases?

17. How are EPS results computed for a corporation with a simple capital structure?

18. What is a stock option?

19. How is book value per share computed for a corporation with no preferred stock? What is the main limitation of using book value per share to value a corporation?

20. ♟ Refer to the balance sheet for **Best Buy** in Appendix A. What is the par value per share of its common stock? Suggest a rationale for the amount of par value it assigned.

21. Refer to **RadioShack**'s balance sheet in Appendix A. How many shares of common stock are authorized? How many shares of common stock are issued?

22. Review the balance sheet for **GOME** in Appendix A. What is its total "Issued capital" at year-end 2008?

23. ♟ Refer to the financial statements for **Apple** in Appendix A. What are its cash proceeds from issuance of common stock *and* its cash repurchases of common stock for the year ended September 27, 2008? Explain.

♟ *Denotes Discussion Questions that involve decision making.*

Available with Connect Accounting **connect**™

QUICK STUDY

QS 11-1
Characteristics of corporations

C1

Of the following statements, which are true for the corporate form of organization?

     1. Capital is more easily accumulated than with most other forms of organization.

     2. Corporate income that is distributed to shareholders is usually taxed twice.

     3. Owners have unlimited liability for corporate debts.

     4. Ownership rights cannot be easily transferred.

     5. Owners are not agents of the corporation.

     6. It is a separate legal entity.

     7. It has a limited life.

Prepare the journal entry to record Miltone Company's issuance of 50,000 shares of $1 par value common stock assuming the shares sell for:

a. $1 cash per share.

b. $3 cash per share.

QS 11-2
Issuance of common stock
P1

Prepare the journal entry to record Katrick Company's issuance of 75,000 shares of its common stock assuming the shares have a:

a. $5 par value and sell for $12 cash per share.

b. $5 stated value and sell for $12 cash per share.

QS 11-3
Issuance of par and stated value common stock
P1

Prepare the journal entry to record Gaylord Company's issuance of 52,000 shares of no-par value common stock assuming the shares:

a. Sell for $30 cash per share.

b. Are exchanged for land valued at $1,560,000.

QS 11-4
Issuance of no-par common stock
P1

Prepare the issuer's journal entry for each separate transaction. (*a*) On March 1, Atlantic Co. issues 37,500 shares of $5 par value common stock for $300,000 cash. (*b*) On April 1, BP Co. issues no-par value common stock for $90,000 cash. (*c*) On April 6, MPG issues 3,500 shares of $10 par value common stock for $20,000 of inventory, $130,000 of machinery, and acceptance of a $75,000 note payable.

QS 11-5
Issuance of common stock
P1

a. Prepare the journal entry to record Tamar Company's issuance of 6,000 shares of $100 par value 6% cumulative preferred stock for $102 cash per share.

b. Assuming the facts in part 1, if Tamar declares a year-end cash dividend, what is the amount of dividend paid to preferred shareholders? (Assume no dividends in arrears.)

QS 11-6
Issuance of preferred stock
C3

Prepare journal entries to record the following transactions for Forrest Corporation.

May 15   Declared a $32,000 cash dividend payable to common stockholders.

June 30   Paid the dividend declared on May 15.

QS 11-7
Accounting for cash dividends
P2

The stockholders' equity section of Atari Company's balance sheet as of April 1 follows. On April 2, Atari declares and distributes a 10% stock dividend. The stock's per share market value on April 2 is $18 (prior to the dividend). Prepare the stockholders' equity section immediately after the stock dividend.

QS 11-8
Accounting for small stock dividend
C2 P3

Common stock—$5 par value, 375,000 shares authorized, 200,000 shares issued and outstanding	$1,000,000
Paid-in capital in excess of par value, common stock	600,000
Retained earnings	833,000
Total stockholders' equity	$2,433,000

Stockholders' equity of Marwick Company consists of 10,000 shares of $20 par value, 8% cumulative preferred stock and 400,000 shares of $1 par value common stock. Both classes of stock have been outstanding since the company's inception. Marwick did not declare any dividends in the prior year, but it now declares and pays a $92,000 cash dividend at the current year-end. Determine the amount distributed to each class of stockholders for this two-year-old company.

QS 11-9
Dividend allocation between classes of shareholders
P4

On May 3, Winmac Corporation purchased 3,000 shares of its own stock for $45,000 cash. On November 4, Winmac reissued 850 shares of this treasury stock for $14,450. Prepare the May 3 and November 4 journal entries to record Winmac's purchase and reissuance of treasury stock.

QS 11-10
Purchase and sale of treasury stock   P5

QS 11-11

Accounting for changes in estimates; error adjustments

C4

Answer the following questions related to a company's activities for the current year:

1. A review of the notes payable files discovers that three years ago the company reported the entire amount of a payment (principal and interest) on an installment note payable as interest expense. This mistake had a material effect on the amount of income in that year. How should the correction be reported in the current year financial statements?

2. After using an expected useful life of seven years and no salvage value to depreciate its office equipment over the preceding three years, the company decided early this year that the equipment will last only two more years. How should the effects of this decision be reported in the current year financial statements?

QS 11-12

Basic earnings per share   A1

Campbell Company reports net income of $840,000 for the year. It has no preferred stock, and its weighted-average common shares outstanding is 300,000 shares. Compute its basic earnings per share.

QS 11-13

Basic earnings per share   A1

Epic Company earned net income of $950,000 this year. The number of common shares outstanding during the entire year was 400,000, and preferred shareholders received a $40,000 cash dividend. Compute Epic Company's basic earnings per share.

QS 11-14

Price-earnings ratio   A2

Compute Tripp Company's price-earnings ratio if its common stock has a market value of $31.50 per share and its EPS is $3.75. Would an analyst likely consider this stock potentially over- or underpriced? Explain.

QS 11-15

Dividend yield

A3

Payne Company expects to pay a $1.62 per share cash dividend this year on its common stock. The current market value of Payne stock is $22.50 per share. Compute the expected dividend yield on the Payne stock. Would you classify the Payne stock as a growth or an income stock? Explain.

QS 11-16

Book value per common share

A4

The stockholders' equity section of Klaus Company's balance sheet follows. The preferred stock's call price is $25. Determine the book value per share of the common stock.

Preferred stock—5% cumulative, $10 par value, 20,000 shares authorized, issued and outstanding	$ 200,000
Common stock—$5 par value, 200,000 shares authorized, 150,000 shares issued and outstanding	750,000
Retained earnings	889,500
Total stockholders' equity	$1,839,500

QS 11-17

International equity disclosures

P1

Air France-KLM reports the following equity information for its fiscal year ended March 31, 2009 (euros in millions). Prepare its journal entry, using its account titles, to record the issuance of capital stock assuming that its entire par value stock was issued on March 31, 2009, for cash.

March 31	2009
Issued capital	€2,552
Additional paid-in capital	765

Available with Connect Accounting **connect**

EXERCISES

Describe how each of the following characteristics of organizations applies to corporations.

Exercise 11-1

Characteristics of corporations

C1

1. Owner authority and control	5. Duration of life
2. Ease of formation	6. Owner liability
3. Transferability of ownership	7. Legal status
4. Ability to raise large capital amounts	8. Tax status of income

Rodriguez Corporation issues 12,000 shares of its common stock for $182,700 cash on February 20. Prepare journal entries to record this event under each of the following separate situations.

1. The stock has neither par nor stated value.

2. The stock has a $12 par value.

3. The stock has a $6 stated value.

Exercise 11-2
Accounting for par, stated, and no-par stock issuances
P1

Prepare journal entries to record the following four separate issuances of stock.

1. A corporation issued 2,500 shares of no-par common stock to its promoters in exchange for their efforts, estimated to be worth $43,500. The stock has no stated value.

2. A corporation issued 2,500 shares of no-par common stock to its promoters in exchange for their efforts, estimated to be worth $43,500. The stock has a $2 per share stated value.

3. A corporation issued 5,000 shares of $30 par value common stock for $180,000 cash.

4. A corporation issued 1,250 shares of $100 par value preferred stock for $168,500 cash.

Exercise 11-3
Recording stock issuances
P1

Soku Company issues 12,000 shares of $9 par value common stock in exchange for land and a building. The land is valued at $75,000 and the building at $120,000. Prepare the journal entry to record issuance of the stock in exchange for the land and building.

Exercise 11-4
Stock issuance for noncash assets
P1

Match each description 1 through 6 with the characteristic of preferred stock that it best describes by writing the letter of that characteristic in the blank next to each description.

A. Convertible   **B.** Cumulative   **C.** Noncumulative

D. Nonparticipating   **E.** Participating   **F.** Callable

_____ **1.** Holders of the stock are entitled to receive current and all past dividends before common stockholders receive any dividends.

_____ **2.** The issuing corporation can retire the stock by paying a prespecified price.

_____ **3.** Holders of the stock can receive dividends exceeding the stated rate under certain conditions.

_____ **4.** Holders of the stock are not entitled to receive dividends in excess of the stated rate.

_____ **5.** Holders of this stock can exchange it for shares of common stock.

_____ **6.** Holders of the stock lose any dividends that are not declared in the current year.

Exercise 11-5
Identifying characteristics of preferred stock
C2 C3

On June 30, 2011, Samson Corporation's common stock is priced at $30.50 per share before any stock dividend or split, and the stockholders' equity section of its balance sheet appears as follows.

Exercise 11-6
Stock dividends and splits
P3

Common stock—$8 par value, 80,000 shares authorized, 32,000 shares issued and outstanding	$256,000
Paid-in capital in excess of par value, common stock	100,000
Retained earnings	356,000
Total stockholders' equity	$712,000

1. Assume that the company declares and immediately distributes a 100% stock dividend. This event is recorded by capitalizing retained earnings equal to the stock's par value. Answer these questions about stockholders' equity as it exists *after* issuing the new shares.

   a. What is the retained earnings balance?

   b. What is the amount of total stockholders' equity?

   c. How many shares are outstanding?

2. Assume that the company implements a 2-for-1 stock split instead of the stock dividend in part 1. Answer these questions about stockholders' equity as it exists *after* issuing the new shares.

   a. What is the retained earnings balance?

   b. What is the amount of total stockholders' equity?

   c. How many shares are outstanding?

3. Explain the difference, if any, to a stockholder from receiving new shares distributed under a large stock dividend versus a stock split.

Check (1b) $712,000

(2a) $356,000

Exercise 11-7
Stock dividends and per share book values

P3 ♟

The stockholders' equity of Tyron Company at the beginning of the day on February 5 follows.

Common stock—$25 par value, 150,000 shares authorized, 64,000 shares issued and outstanding	$1,600,000
Paid-in capital in excess of par value, common stock	525,000
Retained earnings	671,800
Total stockholders' equity	$2,796,800

On February 5, the directors declare a 15% stock dividend distributable on February 28 to the February 15 stockholders of record. The stock's market value is $50 per share on February 5 before the stock dividend. The stock's market value is $43.60 per share on February 28.

1. Prepare entries to record both the dividend declaration and its distribution.

Check (2) Book value per share: before, $43.70; after, $38.00

2. One stockholder owned 900 shares on February 5 before the dividend. Compute the book value per share and total book value of this stockholder's shares immediately before *and* after the stock dividend of February 5.

3. Compute the total market value of the investor's shares in part 2 as of February 5 and February 28.

Exercise 11-8
Dividends on common and noncumulative preferred stock

P4

Norton's outstanding stock consists of (*a*) 13,000 shares of noncumulative 8% preferred stock with a $10 par value and (*b*) 32,500 shares of common stock with a $1 par value. During its first four years of operation, the corporation declared and paid the following total cash dividends.

2009	$ 8,000
2010	24,000
2011	120,000
2012	197,000

Check 4-Year total paid to preferred, $39,200

Determine the amount of dividends paid each year to each of the two classes of stockholders. Also compute the total dividends paid to each class for the four years combined.

Exercise 11-9
Dividends on common and cumulative preferred stock P4

Use the data in Exercise 11-8 to determine the amount of dividends paid each year to each of the two classes of stockholders assuming that the preferred stock is cumulative. Also determine the total dividends paid to each class for the four years combined.

Exercise 11-10
Recording and reporting treasury stock transactions

P5 ♟

On October 10, the stockholders' equity of Syntax Systems appears as follows.

Common stock—$10 par value, 72,000 shares authorized, issued, and outstanding	$ 720,000
Paid-in capital in excess of par value, common stock	216,000
Retained earnings	864,000
Total stockholders' equity	$1,800,000

1. Prepare journal entries to record the following transactions for Syntax Systems.

    a. Purchased 5,000 shares of its own common stock at $22 per share on October 11.

    b. Sold 1,000 treasury shares on November 1 for $28 cash per share.

Check (1c) Dr. Retained Earnings, $14,000

    c. Sold all remaining treasury shares on November 25 for $17 cash per share.

2. Explain how the company's equity section changes after the October 11 treasury stock purchase, and prepare the revised equity section of its balance sheet at that date.

Exercise 11-11
Preparing a statement of retained earnings

C4

The following information is available for Arturo Company for the year ended December 31, 2011.

a. Balance of retained earnings, December 31, 2010, prior to discovery of error, $1,375,000.

b. Cash dividends declared and paid during 2011, $43,000.

c. It neglected to record 2009 depreciation expense of $55,500, which is net of $4,500 in income taxes.

d. The company earned $126,000 in 2011 net income.

Prepare a 2011 statement of retained earnings for Arturo Company.

Grossmont Company reports $1,375,500 of net income for 2011 and declares $192,500 of cash dividends on its preferred stock for 2011. At the end of 2011, the company had 350,000 weighted-average shares of common stock.

1. What amount of net income is available to common stockholders for 2011?

2. What is the company's basic EPS for 2011?

Exercise 11-12
Earnings per share

A1

Check (2) $3.38

Franklin Company reports $1,875,000 of net income for 2011 and declares $262,500 of cash dividends on its preferred stock for 2011. At the end of 2011, the company had 250,000 weighted-average shares of common stock.

1. What amount of net income is available to common stockholders for 2011?

2. What is the company's basic EPS for 2011?

Exercise 11-13
Earnings per share

A1

Check (2) $6.45

Compute the price-earnings ratio for each of these four separate companies. Which stock might an analyst likely investigate as being potentially undervalued by the market? Explain.

Exercise 11-14
Price-earnings ratio computation and interpretation

A2

Company	Earnings per Share	Market Value per Share
1	$12.00	$145.20
2	11.00	116.60
3	7.80	74.10
4	43.20	60.48

Compute the dividend yield for each of these four separate companies. Which company's stock would probably *not* be classified as an income stock? Explain.

Exercise 11-15
Dividend yield computation and interpretation

A3

Company	Annual Cash Dividend per Share	Market Value per Share
1	$14.00	$229.51
2	11.00	110.00
3	5.52	60.00
4	1.90	118.75

The equity section of Westchester Corporation's balance sheet shows the following.

Exercise 11-16
Book value per share

A4

Preferred stock—6% cumulative, $30 par value, $35 call price, 10,000 shares issued and outstanding	$300,000
Common stock—$10 par value, 35,000 shares issued and outstanding	350,000
Retained earnings	267,500
Total stockholders' equity	$917,500

Determine the book value per share of the preferred and common stock under two separate situations.

1. No preferred dividends are in arrears.

2. Three years of preferred dividends are in arrears.

Check (1) Book value of common, $16.21

Unilever Group reports the following equity information for the years ended December 31, 2007 and 2008 (euros in millions).

Exercise 11-17
Accounting for equity under IFRS

C2 P1

December 31	2008	2007
Share capital	€ 484	€ 484
Share premium	121	153
Other reserves	(6,469)	(3,412)
Retained profit	15,812	15,162
Shareholders' equity	€ 9,948	€12,387

1. For each of the three account titles *share capital, share premium,* and *retained profit,* match it with the usual account title applied under U.S. GAAP from the following options:

   a. Paid-in capital in excess of par value, common stock

   b. Retained earnings

   c. Common stock, par value

2. Prepare Unilever's journal entry, using its account titles, to record the issuance of capital stock assuming that its entire par value stock was issued on December 31, 2007, for cash.

3. What were Unilever's 2008 dividends assuming that only dividends and income impacted retained profit for 2008 and that its 2008 income totaled €2,692?

Available with Connect Accounting **connect**™

PROBLEM SET A

Keshena Co. is incorporated at the beginning of this year and engages in a number of transactions. The following journal entries impacted its stockholders' equity during its first year of operations.

Problem 11-1A

Stockholders' equity transactions and analysis

C2　C3　P1 ♟

a.	Cash......................................	320,000	
	Common Stock, $25 Par Value...............		250,000
	Paid-In Capital in Excess of		
	Par Value, Common Stock		70,000
b.	Organization Expenses	160,000	
	Common Stock, $25 Par Value...............		125,000
	Paid-In Capital in Excess of		
	Par Value, Common Stock		35,000
c.	Cash......................................	45,500	
	Accounts Receivable	16,000	
	Building....................................	82,000	
	Notes Payable		59,500
	Common Stock, $25 Par Value...............		50,000
	Paid-In Capital in Excess of		
	Par Value, Common Stock		34,000
d.	Cash......................................	123,000	
	Common Stock, $25 Par Value...............		75,000
	Paid-In Capital in Excess of		
	Par Value, Common Stock		48,000

Required

1. Explain the transaction(s) underlying each journal entry (*a*) through (*d*).

Check (2) 20,000 shares

(3) $500,000

(4) $687,000

2. How many shares of common stock are outstanding at year-end?

3. What is the amount of minimum legal capital (based on par value) at year-end?

4. What is the total paid-in capital at year-end?

5. What is the book value per share of the common stock at year-end if total paid-in capital plus retained earnings equals $785,000?

Problem 11-2A

Cash dividends, treasury stock, and statement of retained earnings

C2　C4　P2　P5

Rocklin Corporation reports the following components of stockholders' equity on December 31, 2011.

Common stock—$25 par value, 100,000 shares authorized,	
45,000 shares issued and outstanding	$1,125,000
Paid-in capital in excess of par value, common stock	60,000
Retained earnings	460,000
Total stockholders' equity	$1,645,000

In year 2012, the following transactions affected its stockholders' equity accounts.

Jan. 1   Purchased 4,500 shares of its own stock at $25 cash per share.
Jan. 5   Directors declared a $3 per share cash dividend payable on Feb. 28 to the Feb. 5 stockholders of record.
Feb. 28   Paid the dividend declared on January 5.
July 6   Sold 1,688 of its treasury shares at $29 cash per share.
Aug. 22   Sold 2,812 of its treasury shares at $22 cash per share.
Sept. 5   Directors declared a $3 per share cash dividend payable on October 28 to the September 25 stockholders of record.
Oct. 28   Paid the dividend declared on September 5.
Dec. 31   Closed the $388,000 credit balance (from net income) in the Income Summary account to Retained Earnings.

Required

1. Prepare journal entries to record each of these transactions for 2012.
2. Prepare a statement of retained earnings for the year ended December 31, 2012.
3. Prepare the stockholders' equity section of the company's balance sheet as of December 31, 2012.

Check (2) Retained earnings, Dec. 31, 2012, $589,816.

At September 30, the end of Chan Company's third quarter, the following stockholders' equity accounts are reported.

Problem 11-3A
Equity analysis—journal entries and account balances

P2 P3

Common stock, $10 par value	$420,000
Paid-in capital in excess of par value, common stock	100,000
Retained earnings	400,000

In the fourth quarter, the following entries related to its equity are recorded.

Date	Account	Debit	Credit
Oct. 2	Retained Earnings	63,000	
	Common Dividend Payable		63,000
Oct. 25	Common Dividend Payable	63,000	
	Cash		63,000
Oct. 31	Retained Earnings	92,400	
	Common Stock Dividend Distributable		42,000
	Paid-In Capital in Excess of Par Value, Common Stock		50,400
Nov. 5	Common Stock Dividend Distributable	42,000	
	Common Stock, $10 Par Value		42,000
Dec. 1	Memo—Change the title of the common stock account to reflect the new par value of $5.		
Dec. 31	Income Summary	230,000	
	Retained Earnings		230,000

Required

1. Explain the transaction(s) underlying each journal entry.
2. Complete the following table showing the equity account balances at each indicated date (include the balances from September 30).

	Oct. 2	Oct. 25	Oct. 31	Nov. 5	Dec. 1	Dec. 31
Common stock	$____	$____	$____	$____	$____	$____
Common stock dividend distributable	____	____	____	____	____	____
Paid-in capital in excess of par, common stock	____	____	____	____	____	____
Retained earnings	____	____	____	____	____	____
Total equity	$____	$____	$____	$____	$____	$____

Check Total equity: Oct. 2, $857,000; Dec. 31, $1,087,000

Problem 11-4A

Analysis of changes in stockholders' equity accounts

C4   P2   P3   P5

The equity sections from Sierra Group's 2009 and 2010 year-end balance sheets follow.

Stockholders' Equity (December 31, 2009)

Common stock—$6 par value, 100,000 shares authorized, 45,000 shares issued and outstanding	$270,000
Paid-in capital in excess of par value, common stock	230,000
Retained earnings	340,000
Total stockholders' equity	$840,000

Stockholders' Equity (December 31, 2010)

Common stock—$6 par value, 100,000 shares authorized, 53,200 shares issued, 4,000 shares in treasury	$319,200
Paid-in capital in excess of par value, common stock	262,800
Retained earnings ($60,000 restricted by treasury stock)	400,000
	982,000
Less cost of treasury stock	(60,000)
Total stockholders' equity	$922,000

The following transactions and events affected its equity during year 2010.

Jan.   5   Declared a $0.50 per share cash dividend, date of record January 10.
Mar. 20   Purchased treasury stock for cash.
Apr.   5   Declared a $0.50 per share cash dividend, date of record April 10.
July   5   Declared a $0.50 per share cash dividend, date of record July 10.
July 31   Declared a 20% stock dividend when the stock's market value is $10 per share.
Aug. 14   Issued the stock dividend that was declared on July 31.
Oct.   5   Declared a $0.50 per share cash dividend, date of record October 10.

Required

1. How many common shares are outstanding on each cash dividend date?
2. What is the total dollar amount for each of the four cash dividends?
3. What is the amount of the capitalization of retained earnings for the stock dividend?
4. What is the per share cost of the treasury stock purchased?
5. How much net income did the company earn during year 2010?

Check   (3) $82,000
           (4) $15
           (5) $230,100

Problem 11-5A

Computation of book values and dividend allocations

C3   A4   P4

Folsom Corporation's common stock is currently selling on a stock exchange at $183 per share, and its current balance sheet shows the following stockholders' equity section.

Preferred stock—5% cumulative, $___ par value, 1,000 shares authorized, issued, and outstanding	$ 85,000
Common stock—$___ par value, 4,000 shares authorized, issued, and outstanding	200,000
Retained earnings	350,000
Total stockholders' equity	$635,000

Required

1. What is the current market value (price) of this corporation's common stock?
2. What are the par values of the corporation's preferred stock and its common stock?
3. If no dividends are in arrears, what are the book values per share of the preferred stock and the common stock?
4. If two years' preferred dividends are in arrears, what are the book values per share of the preferred stock and the common stock?
5. If two years' preferred dividends are in arrears and the preferred stock is callable at $95 per share, what are the book values per share of the preferred stock and the common stock?

Check   (4) Book value of common, $135.38
           (5) Book value of common, $132.88

6. If two years' preferred dividends are in arrears and the board of directors declares cash dividends of $24,750, what total amount will be paid to the preferred and to the common shareholders? What is the amount of dividends per share for the common stock?

(6) Dividends per common share, $3.00

Analysis Component

7. What are some factors that can contribute to a difference between the book value of common stock and its market value (price)?

Mayport Company is incorporated at the beginning of this year and engages in a number of transactions. The following journal entries impacted its stockholders' equity during its first year of operations.

PROBLEM SET B

Problem 11-1B
Stockholders' equity transactions and analysis

C2 C3 P1

a.	Cash	60,000	
	Common Stock, $1 Par Value................		1,500
	Paid-In Capital in Excess of		
	Par Value, Common Stock		58,500
b.	Organization Expenses	20,000	
	Common Stock, $1 Par Value................		500
	Paid-In Capital in Excess of		
	Par Value, Common Stock		19,500
c.	Cash	6,650	
	Accounts Receivable	4,000	
	Building...................................	18,500	
	Notes Payable		9,150
	Common Stock, $1 Par Value................		400
	Paid-In Capital in Excess of		
	Par Value, Common Stock		19,600
d.	Cash	30,000	
	Common Stock, $1 Par Value................		600
	Paid-In Capital in Excess of		
	Par Value, Common Stock		29,400

Required

1. Explain the transaction(s) underlying each journal entry (*a*) through (*d*).
2. How many shares of common stock are outstanding at year-end?
3. What is the amount of minimum legal capital (based on par value) at year-end?
4. What is the total paid-in capital at year-end?
5. What is the book value per share of the common stock at year-end if total paid-in capital plus retained earnings equals $141,500?

Check (2) 3,000 shares

(3) $3,000

(4) $130,000

San Marco Corp. reports the following components of stockholders' equity on December 31, 2011.

Problem 11-2B
Cash dividends, treasury stock, and statement of retained earnings

C2 C4 P2 P5

Common stock—$1 par value, 160,000 shares authorized, 100,000 shares issued and outstanding	$ 100,000
Paid-in capital in excess of par value, common stock	700,000
Retained earnings	1,080,000
Total stockholders' equity	$1,880,000

It completed the following transactions related to stockholders' equity in year 2012.

Jan. 10   Purchased 20,000 shares of its own stock at $12 cash per share.
Mar. 2   Directors declared a $1.50 per share cash dividend payable on March 31 to the March 15 stockholders of record.

Mar. 31 Paid the dividend declared on March 2.

Nov. 11 Sold 12,000 of its treasury shares at $13 cash per share.

Nov. 25 Sold 8,000 of its treasury shares at $9.50 cash per share.

Dec. 1 Directors declared a $2.50 per share cash dividend payable on January 2 to the December 10 stockholders of record.

Dec. 31 Closed the $536,000 credit balance (from net income) in the Income Summary account to Retained Earnings.

Required

1. Prepare journal entries to record each of these transactions for 2012.

Check (2) Retained earnings, Dec. 31, 2012, $1,238,000

2. Prepare a statement of retained earnings for the year ended December 31, 2012.

3. Prepare the stockholders' equity section of the company's balance sheet as of December 31, 2012.

Problem 11-3B

Equity analysis—journal entries and account balances

P2 P3

At December 31, the end of Santee Communication's third quarter, the following stockholders' equity accounts are reported.

Common stock, $10 par value	$480,000
Paid-in capital in excess of par value, common stock	192,000
Retained earnings	800,000

In the fourth quarter, the following entries related to its equity are recorded.

Jan. 17	Retained Earnings...............................	48,000	
	Common Dividend Payable		48,000
Feb. 5	Common Dividend Payable......................	48,000	
	Cash.......................................		48,000
Feb. 28	Retained Earnings...............................	126,000	
	Common Stock Dividend Distributable.........		60,000
	Paid-In Capital in Excess of Par Value, Common Stock		66,000
Mar. 14	Common Stock Dividend Distributable	60,000	
	Common Stock, $10 Par Value		60,000
Mar. 25	Memo—Change the title of the common stock account to reflect the new par value of $5.		
Mar. 31	Income Summary	360,000	
	Retained Earnings		360,000

Required

1. Explain the transaction(s) underlying each journal entry.

2. Complete the following table showing the equity account balances at each indicated date (include the balances from December 31).

	Jan. 17	Feb. 5	Feb. 28	Mar. 14	Mar. 25	Mar. 31
Common stock	$____	$____	$____	$____	$____	$____
Common stock dividend distributable	____	____	____	____	____	____
Paid-in capital in excess of par, common stock	____	____	____	____	____	____
Retained earnings	____	____	____	____	____	____
Total equity	$____	$____	$____	$____	$____	$____

Check Total equity: Jan. 17, $1,424,000; Mar. 31, $1,784,000

The equity sections from Kiwa Corporation's 2009 and 2010 balance sheets follow.

Problem 11-4B
Analysis of changes in stockholders' equity accounts
C4 P2 P3 P5

Stockholders' Equity (December 31, 2009)	
Common stock—$20 par value, 15,000 shares authorized, 8,500 shares issued and outstanding	$170,000
Paid-in capital in excess of par value, common stock	30,000
Retained earnings	135,000
Total stockholders' equity	$335,000

Stockholders' Equity (December 31, 2010)	
Common stock—$20 par value, 15,000 shares authorized, 9,500 shares issued, 500 shares in treasury	$190,000
Paid-in capital in excess of par value, common stock	52,000
Retained earnings ($20,000 restricted by treasury stock)	147,600
	389,600
Less cost of treasury stock	(20,000)
Total stockholders' equity	$369,600

The following transactions and events affected its equity during year 2010.

Feb. 15 Declared a $0.40 per share cash dividend, date of record five days later.
Mar. 2 Purchased treasury stock for cash.
May 15 Declared a $0.40 per share cash dividend, date of record five days later.
Aug. 15 Declared a $0.40 per share cash dividend, date of record five days later.
Oct. 4 Declared a 12.5% stock dividend when the stock's market value is $42 per share.
Oct. 20 Issued the stock dividend that was declared on October 4.
Nov. 15 Declared a $0.40 per share cash dividend, date of record five days later.

Required

1. How many common shares are outstanding on each cash dividend date?
2. What is the total dollar amount for each of the four cash dividends?
3. What is the amount of the capitalization of retained earnings for the stock dividend?
4. What is the per share cost of the treasury stock purchased?
5. How much net income did the company earn during year 2010?

Check (3) $42,000
(4) $40
(5) $68,000

Hansen Company's common stock is currently selling on a stock exchange at $90 per share, and its current balance sheet shows the following stockholders' equity section.

Problem 11-5B
Computation of book values and dividend allocations
C3 A4 P4

Preferred stock—8% cumulative, $___ par value, 1,500 shares authorized, issued, and outstanding	$ 187,500
Common stock—$___ par value, 18,000 shares authorized, issued, and outstanding	450,000
Retained earnings	562,500
Total stockholders' equity	$1,200,000

Required

1. What is the current market value (price) of this corporation's common stock?
2. What are the par values of the corporation's preferred stock and its common stock?
3. If no dividends are in arrears, what are the book values per share of the preferred stock and the common stock?
4. If two years' preferred dividends are in arrears, what are the book values per share of the preferred stock and the common stock?

Check (4) Book value of common, $54.58

(5) Book value of common, $53.33

(6) Dividends per common share, $0.28

5. If two years' preferred dividends are in arrears and the preferred stock is callable at $140 per share, what are the book values per share of the preferred stock and the common stock?

6. If two years' preferred dividends are in arrears and the board of directors declares cash dividends of $50,000, what total amount will be paid to the preferred and to the common shareholders? What is the amount of dividends per share for the common stock?

Analysis Component

7. Discuss why the book value of common stock is not always a good estimate of its market value.

SERIAL PROBLEM

Success Systems

(This serial problem began in Chapter 1 and continues through most of the book. If previous chapter segments were not completed, the serial problem can begin at this point. It is helpful, but not necessary, to use the Working Papers that accompany the book.)

SP 11   Adriana Lopez created Success Systems on October 1, 2009. The company has been successful, and Adriana plans to expand her business. She believes that an additional $86,000 is needed and is investigating three funding sources.

a. Adriana's sister Cicely is willing to invest $86,000 in the business as a common shareholder. Since Adriana currently has about $129,000 invested in the business, Cicely's investment will mean that Adriana will maintain about 60% ownership, and Cicely will have 40% ownership of Success Systems.

b. Adriana's uncle Marcello is willing to invest $86,000 in the business as a preferred shareholder. Marcello would purchase 860 shares of $100 par value, 7% preferred stock.

c. Adriana's banker is willing to lend her $86,000 on a 7%, 10-year note payable. Adriana would make monthly payments of $1,000 per month for 10 years.

Required

1. Prepare the journal entry to reflect the initial $86,000 investment under each of the options (a), (b), and (c).

2. Evaluate the three proposals for expansion, providing the pros and cons of each option.

3. Which option do you recommend Adriana adopt? Explain.

BEYOND THE NUMBERS

REPORTING IN ACTION

C2   C3   A1   A4

BTN 11-1   Refer to **Best Buy**'s financial statements in Appendix A to answer the following.

1. How many shares of common stock are issued and outstanding at February 28, 2009, and March 1, 2008? How do these numbers compare with the basic weighted-average common shares outstanding at February 28, 2009, and March 1, 2008?

2. What is the book value of its entire common stock at February 28, 2009?

3. What is the total amount of cash dividends paid to common stockholders for the years ended February 28, 2009, and March 1, 2008?

4. Identify and compare basic EPS amounts across fiscal years 2009, 2008, and 2007. Identify and comment on any notable changes.

5. How much does Best Buy hold in treasury stock, if any, as of February 28, 2009? March 1, 2008?

Fast Forward

6. Access Best Buy's financial statements for fiscal years ending after February 28, 2009, from its Website (**BestBuy.com**) or the SEC's database (**www.SEC.gov**). Has the number of common shares outstanding increased since February 28, 2009? Has Best Buy increased the total amount of cash dividends paid compared to the total amount for fiscal year 2009?

BTN 11-2 Key comparative figures for **Best Buy** and **RadioShack** follow.

Key Figures	Best Buy	RadioShack
Net income (in millions)	$1,003	$ 192.4
Cash dividends declared per common share	$ 0.54	$ 0.25
Common shares outstanding (in millions)	414	125.1
Weighted-average common shares outstanding (in mil.)	413	129.0
Market value (price) per share	$28.82	$11.94
Equity applicable to common shares (in millions)	$4,643	$817.3

Required

1. Compute the book value per common share for each company using these data.
2. Compute the basic EPS for each company using these data.
3. Compute the dividend yield for each company using these data. Does the dividend yield of either company characterize it as an income or growth stock? Explain.
4. Compute, compare, and interpret the price-earnings ratio for each company using these data.

BTN 11-3 Brianna Moore is an accountant for New World Pharmaceuticals. Her duties include tracking research and development spending in the new product development division. Over the course of the past six months, Brianna notices that a great deal of funds have been spent on a particular project for a new drug. She hears "through the grapevine" that the company is about to patent the drug and expects it to be a major advance in antibiotics. Brianna believes that this new drug will greatly improve company performance and will cause the company's stock to increase in value. Brianna decides to purchase shares of New World in order to benefit from this expected increase.

Required

What are Brianna's ethical responsibilities, if any, with respect to the information she has learned through her duties as an accountant for New World Pharmaceuticals? What are the implications to her planned purchase of New World shares?

BTN 11-4 Teams are to select an industry, and each team member is to select a different company in that industry. Each team member then is to acquire the selected company's financial statements (or Form 10-K) from the SEC site (www.SEC.gov). Use these data to identify basic EPS. Use the financial press (or finance.yahoo.com) to determine the market price of this stock, and then compute the price-earnings ratio. Communicate with teammates via a meeting, e-mail, or telephone to discuss the meaning of this ratio, how companies compare, and the industry norm. The team must prepare a single memorandum reporting the ratio for each company and identifying the team conclusions or consensus of opinion. The memorandum is to be duplicated and distributed to the instructor and teammates.

BTN 11-5 Access the February 25, 2009, filing of the December 31, 2008, calendar-year 10-K report of **McDonald's**, (ticker MCD) from www.SEC.gov.

Required

1. Review McDonald's balance sheet and identify how many classes of stock it has issued.
2. What are the par values, number of authorized shares, and issued shares of the classes of stock you identified in part 1?
3. Review its statement of cash flows and identify what total amount of cash it paid in 2008 to purchase treasury stock.
4. What amount did McDonald's pay out in common stock cash dividends for 2008?

TEAMWORK IN ACTION

P5

BTN 11-6   This activity requires teamwork to reinforce understanding of accounting for treasury stock.

1. Write a brief team statement (*a*) generalizing what happens to a corporation's financial position when it engages in a stock "buyback" and (*b*) identifying reasons that a corporation would engage in this activity.

2. Assume that an entity acquires 100 shares of its $100 par value common stock at a cost of $134 cash per share. Discuss the entry to record this acquisition. Next, assign *each* team member to prepare *one* of the following entries (assume each entry applies to all shares):

   a. Reissue treasury shares at cost.

   b. Reissue treasury shares at $150 per share.

   c. Reissue treasury shares at $120 per share; assume the paid-in capital account from treasury shares has a $1,500 balance.

   d. Reissue treasury shares at $120 per share; assume the paid-in capital account from treasury shares has a $1,000 balance.

   e. Reissue treasury shares at $120 per share; assume the paid-in capital account from treasury shares has a zero balance.

3. In sequence, each member is to present his/her entry to the team and explain the *similarities* and *differences* between that entry and the previous entry.

Hint: Instructor should be sure each team accurately completes part 1 before proceeding.

ENTREPRENEURIAL DECISION

C2   C3   P2

BTN 11-7   Assume that Ali Perry, Byron Myers, and Brenton Taylor of **Inogen** decide to launch a new retail chain to market their portable oxygen systems. This chain, named O-to-Go, requires $500,000 of start-up capital. The three contribute $375,000 of personal assets in return for 15,000 shares of common stock, but they need to raise another $125,000 in cash. There are two alternative plans for raising the additional cash. Plan A is to sell 3,750 shares of common stock to one or more investors for $125,000 cash. Plan B is to sell 1,250 shares of cumulative preferred stock to one or more investors for $125,000 cash (this preferred stock would have a $100 par value, an annual 8% dividend rate, and be issued at par).

1. If the new business is expected to earn $72,000 of after-tax net income in the first year, what rate of return on beginning equity will the three (as a group) earn under each alternative? Which plan will provide the higher expected return to them?

2. If the new business is expected to earn $16,800 of after-tax net income in the first year, what rate of return on beginning equity will the three (as a group) earn under each alternative? Which plan will provide the higher expected return to them?

3. Analyze and interpret the differences between the results for parts 1 and 2.

HITTING THE ROAD

A1   A2   A3

BTN 11-8   Review 30 to 60 minutes of financial news programming on television. Take notes on companies that are catching analysts' attention. You might hear reference to over- and undervaluation of firms and to reports about PE ratios, dividend yields, and earnings per share. Be prepared to give a brief description to the class of your observations.

GLOBAL DECISION

A1   C4

BTN 11-9   Assume the following financial information for **GOME** (www.GOME.com.hk), which is the leading chain retailer of consumer electronic products and household appliances in China (in RMB).

Net income (in millions)	1,098.693
Cash dividends declared per share	0.027
Number of shares outstanding (in millions)*	13,398.695
Equity applicable to shares (in millions)	8,700.035

* Assume that for GOME the year-end number of shares outstanding approximates the weighted-average shares outstanding.

Required

1. Compute book value per share for GOME.

2. Compute earnings per share (EPS) for GOME.

3. Compare GOME's dividends per share with its EPS. Is GOME paying out a large or small amount of its income as dividends? Explain.

ANSWERS TO MULTIPLE CHOICE QUIZ

1. e; Entry to record this stock issuance is:

Cash (6,000 × $8)	48,000	
Common Stock (6,000 × $5)		30,000
Paid-In Capital in Excess of Par Value, Common Stock		18,000

2. b; $75,000/19,000 shares = $3.95 per share

3. d; Preferred stock = 5,000 × $100 = $500,000
Book value per share = ($2,000,000 − $500,000)/50,000 shares = $30 per common share

4. a; $0.81/$45.00 = 1.8%

5. c; Earnings per share = $3,500,000/700,000 shares = $5 per share
PE ratio = $85/$5 = 17.0

12

Reporting and Analyzing Cash Flows

"If you put enough energy into your dream, you can make anything happen" —Jim Bonaminio

A Look Back

Chapter 11 focused on corporate transactions such as stock issuances and dividends. We also explained how to report and analyze equity accounts.

A Look at This Chapter

This chapter focuses on reporting and analyzing cash inflows and cash outflows. We emphasize how to prepare and interpret the statement of cash flows.

A Look Ahead

Chapter 13 focuses on tools to help us analyze financial statements. We also describe comparative analysis and the application of ratios for financial analysis.

Wizard of Odd

FAIRFIELD, OH—Jim Bonaminio built his roadside produce stand while living in an abandoned gas station. "I would get up and leave at 4 in the morning to buy everything fresh [and] my wife opened the market at 8 a.m.," recalls Jim. "By 10 o'clock at night, we'd be sitting on the bed balancing the register receipts . . . we worked seven days a week." The fruit of those early efforts is **Jungle Jim's International Market (JungleJims.com).**

Jungle Jim's is no Wal-Mart wannabe, but it is arguably America's wackiest supermarket. Instead of trying to beat the big chains at the price-squeezing game, Jim's is a funhouse maze of a store. A seven-foot Elvis lion sings "Jailhouse Rock," an antique fire engine rests atop cases of hot sauce, and Robin Hood greets customers with English food set within a 30-foot-tall Sherwood Forest. This is just a sampling.

"If you don't go out on a limb, then you're just like everybody else," insists Jim. "The stuff I've collected—all sorts of weird stuff—gets reused." Despite the wackiness, Jim is first and foremost a businessman. He learned firsthand about the importance of monitoring cash inflows and cash outflows. In the early days, recalls Jim, it was all about sales and profits. Then, inventory and asset growth yielded

negative cash flows, and Jim was in a pinch. That's when he realized that tracking cash flows was important, explains Jim.

Jim eventually learned how to monitor and control cash flows for each of his operating, investing, and financing activities. Today, says Jim, "I hire professional people to [help me monitor cash] . . . and to look for ways to make money." Yet Jim explains that he always reviews the statement of cash flows and the individual cash inflows and outflows. That review helps him focus on those products that are bringing in the most cash and those that are cash drains. He also uses cash flows to guide payment of invoices and asset purchases.

Yet cash management has not curtailed Jim's fun-loving approach to business. "I'm trying to create something that has never been done," laughs Jim. "I just want to see if I can do it and have fun."

[Sources: *Jungle Jim's Website,* March 2010; *BusinessWeek,* April 2005; *Country Living,* November 2004; *Miamian,* Summer 2004; *Plain Dealer,* November 2004; *Supermarket News,* September 2006; *Cintas,* August 2007]

CAP

Conceptual

C1 Explain the purpose and importance of cash flow information. (p. 510)

C2 Distinguish between operating, investing, and financing activities. (p. 511)

C3 Identify and disclose noncash investing and financing activities. (p. 513)

C4 Describe the format of the statement of cash flows. (p. 513)

Analytical

A1 Analyze the statement of cash flows. (p. 528)

A2 Compute and apply the cash flow on total assets ratio. (p. 529)

Procedural

P1 Prepare a statement of cash flows. (p. 514)

P2 Compute cash flows from operating activities using the indirect method. (p. 517)

P3 Determine cash flows from both investing and financing activities. (p. 523)

P4 *Appendix 12A*—Illustrate use of a spreadsheet to prepare a statement of cash flows. (p. 532)

P5 *Appendix 12B*—Compute cash flows from operating activities using the direct method. (p. 535)

A company cannot achieve or maintain profits without carefully managing cash. Managers and other users of information pay attention to a company's cash position and the events and transactions affecting cash. This chapter explains how we prepare, analyze, and interpret a statement of cash flows. It also discusses the importance of cash flow information for predicting future performance and making managerial decisions. More generally, effectively using the statement of cash flows is crucial for managing and analyzing the operating, investing, and financing activities of businesses.

Reporting and Analyzing Cash Flows

Basics of Cash Flow Reporting	Cash Flows from Operating	Cash Flows from Investing	Cash Flows from Financing
• Purpose • Importance • Measurement • Classification • Noncash activities • Format and preparation	• Indirect and direct methods of reporting • Application of indirect method of reporting • Summary of indirect method adjustments	• Three-stage process of analysis • Analysis of noncurrent assets • Analysis of other assets	• Three-stage process of analysis • Analysis of noncurrent liabilities • Analysis of equity

Basics of Cash Flow Reporting

This section describes the basics of cash flow reporting, including its purpose, measurement, classification, format, and preparation.

Purpose of the Statement of Cash Flows

C1 Explain the purpose and importance of cash flow information.

The purpose of the **statement of cash flows** is to report cash receipts (inflows) and cash payments (outflows) during a period. This includes separately identifying the cash flows related to operating, investing, and financing activities. The statement of cash flows does more than simply report changes in cash. It is the detailed disclosure of individual cash flows that makes this statement useful to users. Information in this statement helps users answer questions such as these:

■ How does a company obtain its cash?

■ Where does a company spend its cash?

■ What explains the change in the cash balance?

Point: Internal users rely on the statement of cash flows to make investing and financing decisions. External users rely on this statement to assess the amount and timing of a company's cash flows.

The statement of cash flows addresses important questions such as these by summarizing, classifying, and reporting a company's cash inflows and cash outflows for each period.

Importance of Cash Flows

Information about cash flows can influence decision makers in important ways. For instance, we look more favorably at a company that is financing its expenditures with cash from operations than one that does it by selling its assets. Information about cash flows helps users decide whether a company has enough cash to pay its existing debts as they mature. It is also relied upon to evaluate a company's ability to meet unexpected obligations and pursue unexpected opportunities. External information users especially want to assess a company's ability to take advantage of new business opportunities. Internal users such as managers use cash flow information to plan day-to-day operating activities and make long-term investment decisions.

Macy's striking turnaround is an example of how analysis and management of cash flows can lead to improved financial stability. Several years ago Macy's obtained temporary protection from bankruptcy, at which time it desperately needed to improve its cash flows. It did so by engaging in aggressive cost-cutting measures. As a result, Macy's annual cash flow rose to $210 million, up from a negative cash flow of $38.9 million in the prior year. Macy's eventually met its financial obligations and then successfully merged with **Federated Department Stores**.

The case of **W. T. Grant Co.** is a classic example of the importance of cash flow information in predicting a company's future performance and financial strength. Grant reported net income of more than $40 million per year for three consecutive years. At that same time, it was experiencing an alarming decrease in cash provided by operations. For instance, net cash outflow was more than $90 million by the end of that three-year period. Grant soon went bankrupt. Users who relied solely on Grant's income numbers were unpleasantly surprised. This reminds us that cash flows as well as income statement and balance sheet information are crucial in making business decisions.

Decision Insight

Cash Savvy   "A lender must have a complete understanding of a borrower's cash flows to assess both the borrowing needs and repayment sources. This requires information about the major types of cash inflows and outflows. I have seen many companies, whose financial statements indicate good profitability, experience severe financial problems because the owners or managers lacked a good understanding of cash flows."—Mary E. Garza, **Bank of America**.

Measurement of Cash Flows

Cash flows are defined to include both *cash* and *cash equivalents*. The statement of cash flows explains the difference between the beginning and ending balances of cash and cash equivalents. We continue to use the phrases *cash flows* and the *statement of cash flows,* but we must remember that both phrases refer to cash and cash equivalents. Recall that a cash equivalent must satisfy two criteria: (1) be readily convertible to a known amount of cash and (2) be sufficiently close to its maturity so its market value is unaffected by interest rate changes. In most cases, a debt security must be within three months of its maturity to satisfy these criteria. Companies must disclose and follow a clear policy for determining cash and cash equivalents and apply it consistently from period to period. **American Express**, for example, defines its cash equivalents as "time deposits and other highly liquid investments with original maturities of 90 days or less."

Classification of Cash Flows

Since cash and cash equivalents are combined, the statement of cash flows does not report transactions between cash and cash equivalents such as cash paid to purchase cash equivalents and cash received from selling cash equivalents. However, all other cash receipts and cash payments are classified and reported on the statement as operating, investing, or financing activities. Individual cash receipts and payments for each of these three categories are labeled to identify their originating transactions or events. A net cash inflow (source) occurs when the receipts in a category exceed the payments. A net cash outflow (use) occurs when the payments in a category exceed the receipts.

C2	Distinguish between operating, investing, and financing activities.

Operating Activities   **Operating activities** include those transactions and events that determine net income. Examples are the production and purchase of merchandise, the sale of goods and services to customers, and the expenditures to administer the business. Not all items in income, such as unusual gains and losses, are operating activities (we discuss these exceptions later in the chapter). Exhibit 12.1 lists the more common cash inflows and outflows from operating activities. (Although cash receipts and cash payments from buying and selling trading

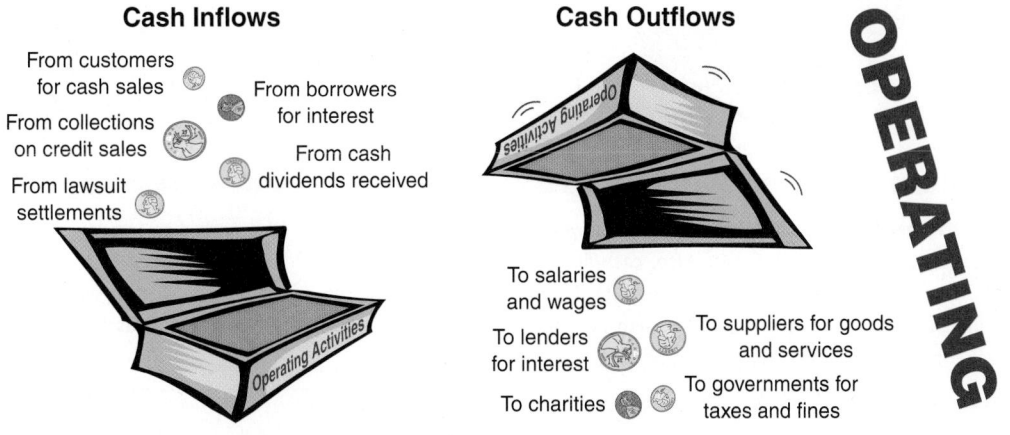

EXHIBIT 12.1

Cash Flows from Operating Activities

securities are often reported under operating activities, new standards require that these receipts and payments be classified based on the nature and purpose of those securities.)

Investing Activities   **Investing activities** generally include those transactions and events that affect long-term assets, namely, the purchase and sale of long-term assets. They also include the (1) purchase and sale of short-term investments in the securities of other entities, other than cash equivalents and trading securities and (2) lending and collecting money for notes receivable. Exhibit 12.2 lists examples of cash flows from investing activities. Proceeds from collecting the principal amounts of notes deserve special mention. If the note results from sales to customers, its cash receipts are classed as operating activities whether short term or long term. If the note results from a loan to another party apart from sales, however, the cash receipts from collecting the note principal are classed as an investing activity. The FASB requires the collection of interest on loans be reported as an operating activity.

Point: The FASB requires that *cash dividends received* and *cash interest received* be reported as operating activities.

EXHIBIT 12.2

Cash Flows from
Investing Activities

Cash Inflows

From selling investments in securities

From collecting principal on loans

From selling long-term productive assets

From selling (discounting) of notes

Investing Activities

Cash Outflows

INVESTING

To make loans to others

To purchase long-term productive assets

To purchase investments in securities

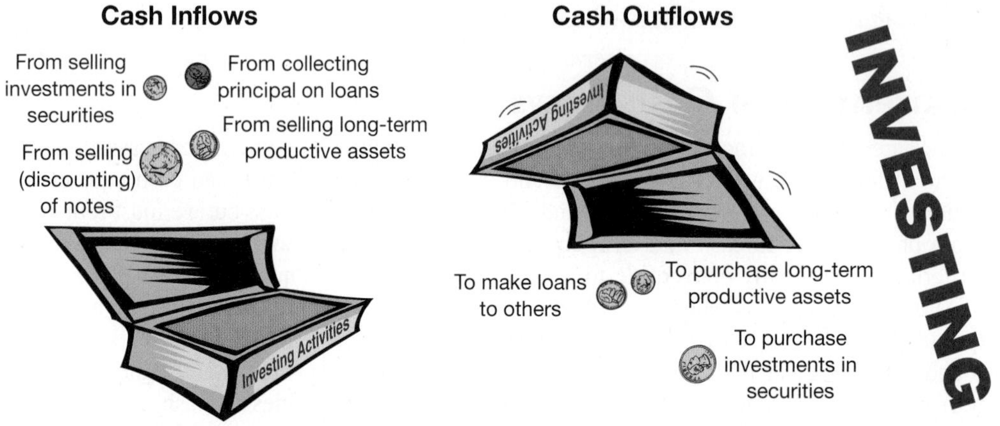

Financing Activities   **Financing activities** include those transactions and events that affect long-term liabilities and equity. Examples are (1) obtaining cash from issuing debt and repaying the amounts borrowed and (2) receiving cash from or distributing cash to owners. These activities involve transactions with a company's owners and creditors. They also often involve borrowing and repaying principal amounts relating to both short- and long-term debt. GAAP requires that payments of interest expense be classified as operating activities. Also, cash payments to settle credit purchases of merchandise, whether on account or by note, are operating activities. Exhibit 12.3 lists examples of cash flows from financing activities.

EXHIBIT 12.3

Cash Flows from
Financing Activities

Cash Inflows

From contributions by owners

From issuing its own equity stock

From issuing notes and bonds

From issuing short- and long-term debt

Financing Activities

Cash Outflows

FINANCING

To repay cash loans

To pay dividends to shareholders

To pay withdrawals by owners

To purchase treasury stock

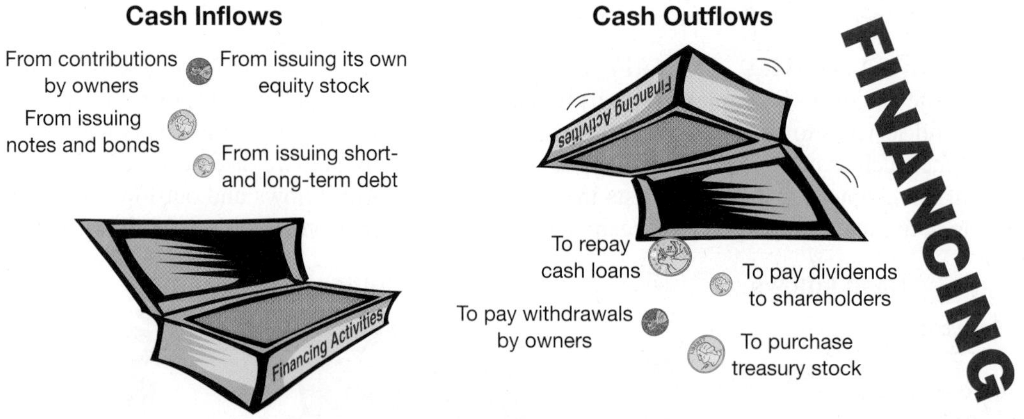

Point: Interest payments on a loan are classified as operating activities, but payments of loan principal are financing activities.

Decision Insight

Cash Monitoring   Cash flows can be delayed or accelerated at the end of a period to improve or reduce current period cash flows. Also, cash flows can be misclassified. Cash outflows reported under operations are interpreted as expense payments. However, cash outflows reported under investing activities are interpreted as a positive sign of growth potential. Thus, managers face incentives to misclassify cash flows. For these reasons, cash flow reporting warrants our scrutiny.

Noncash Investing and Financing

When important investing and financing activities do not affect cash receipts or payments, they are still disclosed at the bottom of the statement of cash flows or in a note to the statement because of their importance and the *full-disclosure principle*. One example of such a transaction is the purchase of long-term assets using a long-term note payable (loan). This transaction involves both investing and financing activities but does not affect any cash inflow or outflow and is not reported in any of the three sections of the statement of cash flows. This disclosure rule also extends to transactions with partial cash receipts or payments.

To illustrate, assume that Goorin purchases land for $12,000 by paying $5,000 cash and trading in used equipment worth $7,000. The investing section of the statement of cash flows reports only the $5,000 cash outflow for the land purchase. The $12,000 investing transaction is only partially described in the body of the statement of cash flows, yet this information is potentially important to users because it changes the makeup of assets. Goorin could either describe the transaction in a footnote or include information at the bottom of its statement that lists the $12,000 land purchase along with the cash financing of $5,000 and a $7,000 trade-in of equipment. As another example, Borg Co. acquired $900,000 of assets in exchange for $200,000 cash and a $700,000 long-term note, which should be reported as follows:

Fair value of assets acquired	$900,000
Less cash paid	200,000
Liabilities incurred or assumed	$700,000

Exhibit 12.4 lists transactions commonly disclosed as noncash investing and financing activities.

- Retirement of debt by issuing equity stock.
- Conversion of preferred stock to common stock.
- Lease of assets in a capital lease transaction.
- Purchase of long-term assets by issuing a note or bond.
- Exchange of noncash assets for other noncash assets.
- Purchase of noncash assets by issuing equity or debt.

Format of the Statement of Cash Flows

Accounting standards require companies to include a statement of cash flows in a complete set of financial statements. This statement must report information about a company's cash receipts and cash payments during the period. Exhibit 12.5 shows the usual format. A company must report cash flows from three activities: operating, investing, and financing. The statement explains how transactions and events impact the prior period-end cash (and cash equivalents) balance to produce its current period-end balance.

C3 Identify and disclose noncash investing and financing activities.

Point: A stock dividend transaction involving a transfer from retained earnings to common stock or a credit to contributed capital is *not* considered a noncash investing and financing activity because the company receives no consideration for shares issued.

EXHIBIT 12.4

Examples of Noncash Investing and Financing Activities

C4 Describe the format of the statement of cash flows.

EXHIBIT 12.5

Format of the Statement of Cash Flows

COMPANY NAME		
Statement of Cash Flows		
For *period* Ended *date*		
Cash flows from operating activities		
[List of individual inflows and outflows]		
Net cash provided (used) by operating activities	$ #	
Cash flows from investing activities		
[List of individual inflows and outflows]		
Net cash provided (used) by investing activities	#	
Cash flows from financing activities		
[List of individual inflows and outflows]		
Net cash provided (used) by financing activities	#	
Net increase (decrease) in cash	$ #	
Cash (and equivalents) balance at prior period-end	#	
Cash (and equivalents) balance at current period-end	$ #	

Separate schedule or note disclosure of any "noncash investing and financing transactions" is required.

Decision Maker ▬▬▬▬▬▬▬▬▬▬▬▬▬▬▬▬▬▬▬▬▬▬▬▬▬▬▬▬▬▬▬▬▬

Entrepreneur   You are considering purchasing a start-up business that recently reported a $110,000 annual net loss and a $225,000 annual net cash inflow. How are these results possible? [Answer—p. 541]

---

1. Does a statement of cash flows report the cash payments to purchase cash equivalents? Does it report the cash receipts from selling cash equivalents?

2. Identify the three categories of cash flows reported separately on the statement of cash flows.

3. Identify the cash activity category for each transaction: (*a*) purchase equipment for cash, (*b*) cash payment of wages, (*c*) sale of common stock for cash, (*d*) receipt of cash dividends from stock investment, (*e*) cash collection from customers, (*f*) notes issued for cash.

Preparing the Statement of Cash Flows

P1 Prepare a statement of cash flows.

Preparing a statement of cash flows involves five steps: (1) compute the net increase or decrease in cash; (2) compute and report net cash provided or used by operating activities (using either the direct or indirect method; both are explained); (3) compute and report net cash provided or used by investing activities; (4) compute and report net cash provided or used by financing activities; and (5) compute the net cash flow by combining net cash provided or used by operating, investing, and financing activities and then *prove it* by adding it to the beginning cash balance to show that it equals the ending cash balance.

Step 1: Compute net increase or decrease in cash

Step 2: Compute net cash from operating activities

Step 3: Compute net cash from investing activities

Step 4: Compute net cash from financing activities

Step 5: Prove and report beginning and ending cash balances

Computing the net increase or net decrease in cash is a simple but crucial computation. It equals the current period's cash balance minus the prior period's cash balance. This is the *bottom-line* figure for the statement of cash flows and is a check on accuracy. The information we need to prepare a statement of cash flows comes from various sources including comparative balance sheets at the beginning and end of the period, and an income statement for the period. There are two alternative approaches to preparing the statement: (1) analyzing the Cash account and (2) analyzing noncash accounts.

Analyzing the Cash Account   A company's cash receipts and cash payments are recorded in the Cash account in its general ledger. The Cash account is therefore a natural place to look for information about cash flows from operating, investing, and financing activities. To illustrate, review the summarized Cash T-account of Genesis, Inc., in Exhibit 12.6. Individual cash transactions are summarized in this Cash account according to the major types of cash receipts and cash payments. For instance, only the total of cash receipts from all customers is listed. Individual cash transactions underlying these totals can number in the thousands. Accounting software is available to provide summarized cash accounts.

Preparing a statement of cash flows from Exhibit 12.6 requires determining whether an individual cash inflow or outflow is an operating, investing, or financing activity, and then listing each

EXHIBIT 12.6

Summarized Cash Account

Accounting System:			
File Edit Maintain Tasks Analysis Options Reports Window Help			

Cash			
Balance, Dec. 31, 2008	12,000		
Receipts from customers	570,000	Payments for merchandise	319,000
Receipts from asset sales	12,000	Payments for wages and operating expenses	218,000
Receipts from stock issuance ..	15,000	Payments for interest	8,000
		Payments for taxes	5,000
		Payments for assets	10,000
		Payments for notes retirement	18,000
		Payments for dividends	14,000
Balance, Dec. 31, 2009	17,000		

Sales   Purchases   General Ledger   Payroll   Inventory   Company   Analysis

by activity. This yields the statement shown in Exhibit 12.7. However, preparing the statement of cash flows from an analysis of the summarized Cash account has two limitations. First, most companies have many individual cash receipts and payments, making it difficult to review them all. Accounting software minimizes this burden, but it is still a task requiring professional judgment for many transactions. Second, the Cash account does not usually carry an adequate description of each cash transaction, making assignment of all cash transactions according to activity difficult.

Point: View the change in cash as a *target* number that we will fully explain and prove in the statement of cash flows.

EXHIBIT 12.7

Statement of Cash Flows— Direct Method

Affects Net Income

Long term - Loan - buy/sell Assets - Invest fixed assets

Long term Liabilities or Equity - Pay back debt - borrow - Issue Stock - Pay Dividends - Issue Bonds

GENESIS Statement of Cash Flows For Year Ended December 31, 2009		
Cash flows from operating activities		
Cash received from customers	$570,000	
Cash paid for merchandise	(319,000)	
Cash paid for wages and other operating expenses	(218,000)	
Cash paid for interest	(8,000)	
Cash paid for taxes	(5,000)	
Net cash provided by operating activities		$20,000
Cash flows from investing activities		
Cash received from sale of plant assets	12,000	
Cash paid for purchase of plant assets	(10,000)	
Net cash provided by investing activities		2,000
Cash flows from financing activities		
Cash received from issuing stock	15,000	
Cash paid to retire notes	(18,000)	
Cash paid for dividends	(14,000)	
Net cash used in financing activities		(17,000)
Net increase in cash		$ 5,000
Cash balance at prior year-end		12,000
Cash balance at current year-end		$17,000

Analyzing Noncash Accounts A second approach to preparing the statement of cash flows is analyzing noncash accounts. This approach uses the fact that when a company records cash inflows and outflows with debits and credits to the Cash account (see Exhibit 12.6), it also records credits and debits in noncash accounts (reflecting double-entry accounting). Many of these noncash accounts are balance sheet accounts, for instance, from the sale of land for cash. Others are revenue and expense accounts that are closed to equity. For instance, the sale of services for cash yields a credit to Services Revenue that is closed to Retained Earnings for a corporation. In sum, *all cash transactions eventually affect noncash balance sheet accounts.* Thus, we can determine cash inflows and outflows by analyzing changes in noncash balance sheet accounts.

Exhibit 12.8 uses the accounting equation to show the relation between the Cash account and the noncash balance sheet accounts. This exhibit starts with the accounting equation at the top. It is then expanded in line (2) to separate cash from noncash asset accounts. Line (3) moves noncash asset accounts to the right-hand side of the equality where they are subtracted. This shows that cash equals the sum of the liability and equity accounts *minus* the noncash asset accounts. Line (4) points

EXHIBIT 12.8

Relation between Cash and
Noncash Accounts

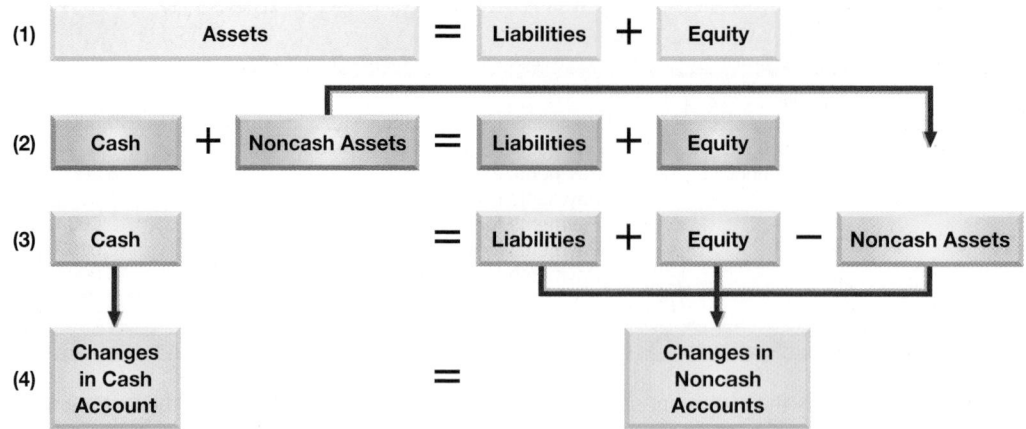

out that *changes* on one side of the accounting equation equal *changes* on the other side. It shows that we can explain changes in cash by analyzing changes in the noncash accounts consisting of liability accounts, equity accounts, and noncash asset accounts. By analyzing noncash balance sheet accounts and any related income statement accounts, we can prepare a statement of cash flows.

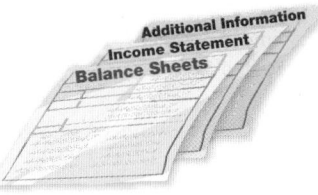

Information to Prepare the Statement   Information to prepare the statement of cash flows usually comes from three sources: (1) comparative balance sheets, (2) current income statement, and (3) additional information. Comparative balance sheets are used to compute changes in noncash accounts from the beginning to the end of the period. The current income statement is used to help compute cash flows from operating activities. Additional information often includes details on transactions and events that help explain both the cash flows and noncash investing and financing activities.

Decision Insight

e-Cash   Every credit transaction on the Net leaves a trail that a hacker or a marketer can pick up. Enter e-cash—or digital money. The encryption of e-cash protects your money from snoops and thieves and cannot be traced, even by the issuing bank.

Cash Flows from Operating

Indirect and Direct Methods of Reporting

Cash flows provided (used) by operating activities are reported in one of two ways: the *direct method* or the *indirect method.* **These two different methods apply only to the operating activities section.**

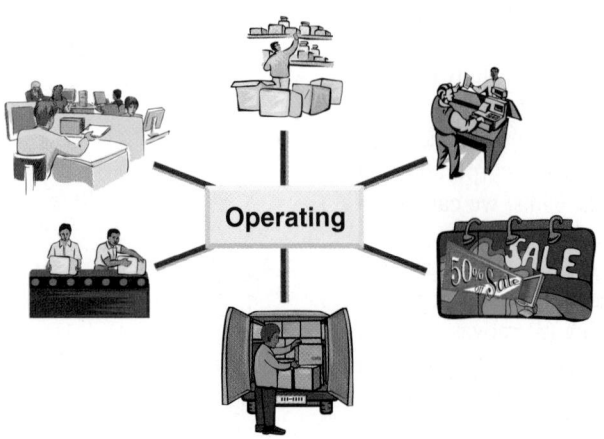

The **direct method** separately lists each major item of operating cash receipts (such as cash received from customers) and each major item of operating cash payments (such as cash paid for merchandise). The cash payments are subtracted from cash receipts to determine the net cash provided (used) by operating activities. The operating activities section of Exhibit 12.7 reflects the direct method of reporting operating cash flows.

The **indirect method** reports net income and then adjusts it for items necessary to obtain net cash provided or used by operating activities. It does *not* report individual items of cash inflows and cash outflows from operating activities. Instead, the indirect method reports the necessary adjustments to reconcile net income to net cash provided or used by operating activities. The operating activities section for Genesis prepared under the indirect method is shown in Exhibit 12.9.

Cash flows from operating activities		
Net income		$ 38,000
Adjustments to reconcile net income to net cash provided by operating activities		
Increase in accounts receivable	(20,000)	
Increase in merchandise inventory	(14,000)	
Increase in prepaid expenses	(2,000)	
Decrease in accounts payable	(5,000)	
Decrease in interest payable	(1,000)	
Increase in income taxes payable	10,000	
Depreciation expense	24,000	
Loss on sale of plant assets	6,000	
Gain on retirement of notes	(16,000)	
Net cash provided by operating activities		**$20,000**

EXHIBIT 12.9

Operating Activities Section—
Indirect Method

The net cash amount provided by operating activities is *identical* under both the direct and indirect methods. This equality always exists. The difference in these methods is with the computation and presentation of this amount. The FASB recommends the direct method, but because it is not required and the indirect method is arguably easier to compute, nearly all companies report operating cash flows using the indirect method.

To illustrate, we prepare the operating activities section of the statement of cash flows for Genesis. Exhibit 12.10 shows the December 31, 2008 and 2009, balance sheets of Genesis along with its 2009 income statement. We use this information to prepare a statement of cash flows that explains the $5,000 increase in cash for 2009 as reflected in its balance sheets. This $5,000 is computed as Cash of $17,000 at the end of 2009 minus Cash of $12,000 at the end of 2008. Genesis discloses additional information on its 2009 transactions:

a. The accounts payable balances result from merchandise inventory purchases.

b. Purchased $70,000 in plant assets by paying $10,000 cash and issuing $60,000 of notes payable.

c. Sold plant assets with an original cost of $30,000 and accumulated depreciation of $12,000 for $12,000 cash, yielding a $6,000 loss.

d. Received $15,000 cash from issuing 3,000 shares of common stock.

e. Paid $18,000 cash to retire notes with a $34,000 book value, yielding a $16,000 gain.

f. Declared and paid cash dividends of $14,000.

> The next section describes the indirect method. Appendix 12B describes the direct method. An instructor can choose to cover either one or both methods. Neither section depends on the other.

Point: To better understand the direct and indirect methods of reporting operating cash flows, identify similarities and differences between Exhibits 12.7 and 12.11.

Video12.1

Application of the Indirect Method of Reporting

Net income is computed using accrual accounting, which recognizes revenues when earned and expenses when incurred. Revenues and expenses do not necessarily reflect the receipt and payment of cash. The indirect method of computing and reporting net cash flows from operating activities involves adjusting the net income figure to obtain the net cash provided or used by operating activities. This includes subtracting noncash increases (credits) from net income and adding noncash charges (debits) back to net income.

To illustrate, the indirect method begins with Genesis's net income of $38,000 and adjusts it to obtain net cash provided by operating activities of $20,000. Exhibit 12.11 shows the results of the indirect method of reporting operating cash flows, which adjusts net income for three types of adjustments. There are adjustments ① to reflect changes in noncash current assets and current liabilities related to operating activities, ② to income statement items involving operating activities that do not affect cash inflows or outflows, and ③ to eliminate gains and losses resulting from investing and financing activities (not part of operating activities). This section describes each of these adjustments.

P2 Compute cash flows from operating activities using the indirect method.

Point: *Noncash credits* refer to *revenue* amounts reported on the income statement that are *not collected in cash* this period. *Noncash charges* refer to *expense* amounts reported on the income statement that are *not paid* this period.

EXHIBIT 12.10

Financial Statements

GENESIS Income Statement For Year Ended December 31, 2009		
Sales		$590,000
Cost of goods sold	$300,000	
Wages and other operating expenses ..	216,000	
Interest expense	7,000	
Depreciation expense	24,000	(547,000)
		43,000
Other gains (losses)		
Gain on retirement of notes	16,000	
Loss on sale of plant assets	(6,000)	10,000
Income before taxes		53,000
Income taxes expense		(15,000)
Net income		$ 38,000

GENESIS Balance Sheets December 31, 2009 and 2008		
	2009	**2008**
Assets		
Current assets		
Cash	$ 17,000	$ 12,000
Accounts receivable	60,000	40,000
Merchandise inventory	84,000	70,000
Prepaid expenses	6,000	4,000
Total current assets	167,000	126,000
Long-term assets		
Plant assets	250,000	210,000
Accumulated depreciation	(60,000)	(48,000)
Total assets	$357,000	$288,000
Liabilities		
Current liabilities		
Accounts payable	$ 35,000	$ 40,000
Interest payable	3,000	4,000
Income taxes payable	22,000	12,000
Total current liabilities	60,000	56,000
Long-term notes payable	90,000	64,000
Total liabilities	150,000	120,000
Equity		
Common stock, $5 par	95,000	80,000
Retained earnings	112,000	88,000
Total equity	207,000	168,000
Total liabilities and equity	$357,000	$288,000

① **Adjustments for Changes in Current Assets and Current Liabilities**   This section describes adjustments for changes in noncash current assets and current liabilities.

Adjustments for changes in noncash current assets.   Changes in noncash current assets normally result from operating activities. Examples are sales affecting accounts receivable and building usage affecting prepaid rent. Decreases in noncash current assets yield the following adjustment:

Decreases in noncash current assets are added to net income.

To see the logic for this adjustment, consider that a decrease in a noncash current asset such as accounts receivable suggests more available cash at the end of the period compared to the beginning. This is so because a decrease in accounts receivable implies higher cash receipts than reflected in sales. We add these higher cash receipts (from decreases in noncash current assets) to net income when computing cash flow from operations.

In contrast, an increase in noncash current assets such as accounts receivable implies less cash receipts than reflected in sales. As another example, an increase in prepaid rent indicates that more cash is paid for rent than is deducted as rent expense. Increases in noncash current assets yield the following adjustment:

Increases in noncash current assets are subtracted from net income.

To illustrate, these adjustments are applied to the noncash current assets in Exhibit 12.10.

Accounts receivable. Accounts Receivable *increase* $20,000, from a beginning balance of $40,000 to an ending balance of $60,000. This increase implies that Genesis collects less cash

than is reported in sales. That is, some of these sales were in the form of accounts recei
and that amount increased during the period. To see this it is helpful to use *account an*
This usually involves setting up a T-account and reconstructing its major entries to c
cash receipts or payments. The following reconstructed Accounts Receivable T-accoun
that cash receipts are less than sales:

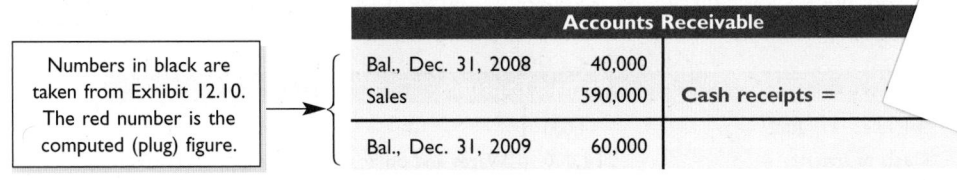

Accounts Receivable			
Bal., Dec. 31, 2008	40,000		
Sales	590,000	Cash receipts =	
Bal., Dec. 31, 2009	60,000		

Numbers in black are taken from Exhibit 12.10. The red number is the computed (plug) figure.

We see that sales are $20,000 greater than cash receipts. This $20,000—as reflected in the
$20,000 increase in Accounts Receivable—is subtracted from net income when computing cash
provided by operating activities (see Exhibit 12.11).

Merchandise inventory. Merchandise Inventory *increases* by $14,000, from a $70,000 beginning balance to an $84,000 ending balance. This increase implies that Genesis had greater
cash purchases than cost of goods sold. This larger amount of cash purchases is in the form of
inventory, as reflected in the following account analysis:

Merchandise Inventory			
Bal., Dec. 31, 2008	70,000		
Purchases =	314,000	Cost of goods sold	300,000
Bal., Dec. 31, 2009	84,000		

EXHIBIT 12.11

Statement of Cash Flows—
Indirect Method

GENESIS		
Statement of Cash Flows		
For Year Ended December 31, 2009		
Cash flows from operating activities		
Net income	$ 38,000	
Adjustments to reconcile net income to net cash provided by operating activities		
① ⎰ Increase in accounts receivable	(20,000)	
Increase in merchandise inventory	(14,000)	
Increase in prepaid expenses	(2,000)	
Decrease in accounts payable	(5,000)	
Decrease in interest payable	(1,000)	
⎱ Increase in income taxes payable	10,000	
② { Depreciation expense	24,000	
③ ⎰ Loss on sale of plant assets	6,000	
⎱ Gain on retirement of notes	(16,000)	
Net cash provided by operating activities		$20,000
Cash flows from investing activities		
Cash received from sale of plant assets	12,000	
Cash paid for purchase of plant assets	(10,000)	
Net cash provided by investing activities		2,000
Cash flows from financing activities		
Cash received from issuing stock	15,000	
Cash paid to retire notes	(18,000)	
Cash paid for dividends	(14,000)	
Net cash used in financing activities		(17,000)
Net increase in cash		$ 5,000
Cash balance at prior year-end		12,000
Cash balance at current year-end		$17,000

Handwritten annotations:

~ Paid Long term debt Interest

~ Paid Principle on Long term debt

Net Income
+ Assets = Sub
− = Add

Liabilities
+ = Add
− = Sub

Depreciation = Add

Gain = Sub
Loss = Add

+/− Adjustments

Point: Refer to Exhibit 12.10 and
identify the $5,000 change in cash.
This change is what the statement of
cash flows explains; it serves as a check.

The amount by which purchases exceed cost of goods sold—as reflected in the $14,000 increase in inventory—is subtracted from net income when computing cash provided by operating activities (see Exhibit 12.11).

Prepaid expenses. Prepaid Expenses *increase* $2,000, from a $4,000 beginning balance to a $6,000 ending balance, implying that Genesis's cash payments exceed its recorded prepaid expenses. These higher cash payments increase the amount of Prepaid Expenses, as reflected in its reconstructed T-account:

Prepaid Expenses			
Bal., Dec. 31, 2008	4,000		
Cash payments =	218,000	Wages and other operating exp.	216,000
Bal., Dec. 31, 2009	6,000		

The amount by which cash payments exceed the recorded operating expenses—as reflected in the $2,000 increase in Prepaid Expenses—is subtracted from net income when computing cash provided by operating activities (see Exhibit 12.11).

Adjustments for changes in current liabilities.   Changes in current liabilities normally result from operating activities. An example is a purchase that affects accounts payable. Increases in current liabilities yield the following adjustment to net income when computing operating cash flows:

Increases in current liabilities are added to net income.

To see the logic for this adjustment, consider that an increase in the Accounts Payable account suggests that cash payments are less than the related (cost of goods sold) expense. As another example, an increase in wages payable implies that cash paid for wages is less than the recorded wages expense. Since the recorded expense is greater than the cash paid, we add the increase in wages payable to net income to compute net cash flow from operations.

Conversely, when current liabilities decrease, the following adjustment is required:

Decreases in current liabilities are subtracted from net income.

To illustrate, these adjustments are applied to the current liabilities in Exhibit 12.10.

Accounts payable. Accounts Payable *decrease* $5,000, from a beginning balance of $40,000 to an ending balance of $35,000. This decrease implies that cash payments to suppliers exceed purchases by $5,000 for the period, which is reflected in the reconstructed Accounts Payable T-account:

Accounts Payable			
		Bal., Dec. 31, 2008	40,000
Cash payments =	319,000	Purchases	314,000
		Bal., Dec. 31, 2009	35,000

The amount by which cash payments exceed purchases—as reflected in the $5,000 decrease in Accounts Payable—is subtracted from net income when computing cash provided by operating activities (see Exhibit 12.11).

Interest payable. Interest Payable *decreases* $1,000, from a $4,000 beginning balance to a $3,000 ending balance. This decrease indicates that cash paid for interest exceeds interest expense by $1,000, which is reflected in the Interest Payable T-account:

Interest Payable			
		Bal., Dec. 31, 2008	4,000
Cash paid for interest =	8,000	Interest expense	7,000
		Bal., Dec. 31, 2009	3,000

The amount by which cash paid exceeds recorded expense—as reflected in the $1,000 decrease in Interest Payable—is subtracted from net income (see Exhibit 12.11).

Income taxes payable. Income Taxes Payable *increase* $10,000, from a $12,000 beginning balance to a $22,000 ending balance. This increase implies that reported income taxes exceed the cash paid for taxes, which is reflected in the Income Taxes Payable T-account:

Income Taxes Payable			
		Bal., Dec. 31, 2008	12,000
Cash paid for taxes =	5,000	Income taxes expense	15,000
		Bal., Dec. 31, 2009	22,000

The amount by which cash paid falls short of the reported taxes expense—as reflected in the $10,000 increase in Income Taxes Payable—is added to net income when computing cash provided by operating activities (see Exhibit 12.11).

Summary Adjustments for Changes in Current Assets and Current Liabilities		
Account	**Increases**	**Decreases**
Noncash current assets	Deduct from NI	Add to NI
Current liabilities	Add to NI	Deduct from NI

② **Adjustments for Operating Items Not Providing or Using Cash**   The income statement usually includes some expenses that do not reflect cash outflows in the period. Examples are depreciation, amortization, depletion, and bad debts expense. The indirect method for reporting operating cash flows requires that

Expenses with no cash outflows are added back to net income.

To see the logic of this adjustment, recall that items such as depreciation, amortization, depletion, and bad debts originate from debits to expense accounts and credits to noncash accounts. These entries have *no* cash effect, and we add them back to net income when computing net cash flows from operations. Adding them back cancels their deductions.

Similarly, when net income includes revenues that do not reflect cash inflows in the period, the indirect method for reporting operating cash flows requires that

Revenues with no cash inflows are subtracted from net income.

We apply these adjustments to the Genesis operating items that do not provide or use cash.

Depreciation.   Depreciation expense is the only Genesis operating item that has no effect on cash flows in the period. We must add back the $24,000 depreciation expense to net income when computing cash provided by operating activities. (We later explain that any cash outflow to acquire a plant asset is reported as an investing activity.)

③ **Adjustments for Nonoperating Items**   Net income often includes losses that are not part of operating activities but are part of either investing or financing activities. Examples are a loss from the sale of a plant asset and a loss from retirement of notes payable. The indirect method for reporting operating cash flows requires that

Nonoperating losses are added back to net income.

To see the logic, consider that items such as a plant asset sale and a notes retirement are normally recorded by recognizing the cash, removing all plant asset or notes accounts, and recognizing any loss or gain. The cash received or paid is not part of operating activities but is part of either investing or financing activities. *No* operating cash flow effect occurs. However, because the nonoperating loss is a deduction in computing net income, we need to add it back to net income when computing cash flow from operations. Adding it back cancels the deduction.

Point: An income statement reports revenues, gains, expenses, and losses on an accrual basis. The statement of cash flows reports cash received and cash paid for operating, financing, and investing activities.

Similarly, when net income includes gains not part of operating activities, the indirect method for reporting operating cash flows requires that

Nonoperating gains are subtracted from net income.

To illustrate these adjustments, we consider the nonoperating items of Genesis.

Loss on sale of plant assets.   Genesis reports a $6,000 loss on sale of plant assets as part of net income. This loss is a proper deduction in computing income, but it is *not part of operating activities*. Instead, a sale of plant assets is part of investing activities. Thus, the $6,000 nonoperating loss is added back to net income (see Exhibit 12.11). Adding it back cancels the loss. We later explain how to report the cash inflow from the asset sale in investing activities.

Gain on retirement of debt.   A $16,000 gain on retirement of debt is properly included in net income, but it is *not part of operating activities*. This means the $16,000 nonoperating gain must be subtracted from net income to obtain net cash provided by operating activities (see Exhibit 12.11). Subtracting it cancels the recorded gain. We later describe how to report the cash outflow to retire debt.

Summary of Adjustments for Indirect Method

Exhibit 12.12 summarizes the most common adjustments to net income when computing net cash provided or used by operating activities under the indirect method.

EXHIBIT 12.12

Summary of Selected
Adjustments for Indirect Method

Net Income

+Decrease in noncash current asset

−Increase in noncash current asset   ① Adjustments for changes in current
                                              assets and current liabilities
+Increase in current liability*

−Decrease in current liability*

+Depreciation, depletion, and amortization   ② Adjustments for operating items
                                                not providing or using cash

+Losses from disposal of long-term assets
 and retirement of debt   ③ Adjustments for nonoperating items

−Gains from disposal of long-term assets
 and retirement of debt

Net cash provided (used) by operating activities

* Excludes current portion of long-term debt and any (nonsales-related) short-term notes payable—both are financing activities.

The computations in determining cash provided or used by operating activities are different for the indirect and direct methods, but the result is identical. Both methods yield the same $20,000 figure for cash from operating activities for Genesis; see Exhibits 12.7 and 12.11.

Decision Insight

Cash or Income   The difference between net income and operating cash flows can be large and sometimes reflects on the quality of earnings. This bar chart shows net income and operating cash flows of three companies. Operating cash flows can be either higher or lower than net income.

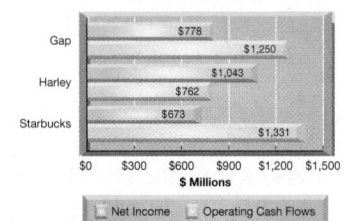

Quick Check

Answers—p. 541

4. Determine net cash provided or used by operating activities using the following data: net income, $74,900; decrease in accounts receivable, $4,600; increase in inventory, $11,700; decrease in accounts payable, $1,000; loss on sale of equipment, $3,400; payment of cash dividends, $21,500.

5. Why are expenses such as depreciation and amortization added to net income when cash flow from operating activities is computed by the indirect method?

6. A company reports net income of $15,000 that includes a $3,000 gain on the sale of plant assets. Why is this gain subtracted from net income in computing cash flow from operating activities using the indirect method?

Cash Flows from Investing

The third major step in preparing the statement of cash flows is to compute and report cash flows from investing activities. We normally do this by identifying changes in (1) all noncurrent asset accounts and (2) the current accounts for both notes receivable and investments in securities (excluding trading securities). We then analyze changes in these accounts to determine their effect, if any, on cash and report the cash flow effects in the investing activities section of the statement of cash flows. **Reporting of investing activities is identical under the direct method and indirect method.**

Three-Stage Process of Analysis

Information to compute cash flows from investing activities is usually taken from beginning and ending balance sheets and the income statement. We use a three-stage process to determine cash provided or used by investing activities: (1) identify changes in investing-related accounts, (2) explain these changes using reconstruction analysis, and (3) report their cash flow effects.

Video12.1

Analysis of Noncurrent Assets

Information about the Genesis transactions provided earlier reveals that the company both purchased and sold plant assets during the period. Both transactions are investing activities and are analyzed for their cash flow effects in this section.

Plant Asset Transactions   The first stage in analyzing the Plant Assets account and its related Accumulated Depreciation is to identify any changes in these accounts from comparative balance sheets in Exhibit 12.10. This analysis reveals a $40,000 increase in plant assets from $210,000 to $250,000 and a $12,000 increase in accumulated depreciation from $48,000 to $60,000.

The second stage is to explain these changes. Items *b* and *c* of the additional information for Genesis (page 517) are relevant in this case. Recall that the Plant Assets account is affected by both asset purchases and sales, while its Accumulated Depreciation account is normally increased from depreciation and decreased from the removal of accumulated depreciation in asset sales. To explain changes in these accounts and to identify their cash flow effects, we prepare *reconstructed entries* from prior transactions; *they are not the actual entries by the preparer.*

To illustrate, item *b* reports that Genesis purchased plant assets of $70,000 by issuing $60,000 in notes payable to the seller and paying $10,000 in cash. The reconstructed entry for analysis of item *b* follows:

Point: Investing activities include (1) purchasing and selling long-term assets, (2) lending and collecting on notes receivable, and (3) purchasing and selling short-term investments other than cash equivalents and trading securities.

Point: Financing and investing info is available in ledger accounts to help explain changes in comparative balance sheets. Post references lead to relevant entries and explanations.

Reconstruction	Plant Assets	70,000	
	Notes Payable		60,000
	Cash		**10,000**

This entry reveals a $10,000 cash outflow for plant assets and a $60,000 noncash investing and financing transaction involving notes exchanged for plant assets.

Next, item *c* reports that Genesis sold plant assets costing $30,000 (with $12,000 of accumulated depreciation) for $12,000 cash, resulting in a $6,000 loss. The reconstructed entry for analysis of item *c* follows:

Reconstruction	**Cash**	**12,000**	
	Accumulated Depreciation	12,000	
	Loss on Sale of Plant Assets	6,000	
	Plant Assets		30,000

This entry reveals a $12,000 cash inflow from assets sold. The $6,000 loss is computed by comparing the asset book value to the cash received and does not reflect any cash inflow or outflow. We also reconstruct the entry for Depreciation Expense using information from the income statement.

Reconstruction	Depreciation Expense	24,000	
	Accumulated Depreciation		24,000

This entry shows that Depreciation Expense results in no cash flow effect. These three reconstructed entries are reflected in the following plant asset and related T-accounts.

Plant Assets					Accumulated Depreciation—Plant Assets			
Bal., Dec. 31, 2008	210,000						Bal., Dec. 31, 2008	48,000
Purchase	70,000	Sale	30,000		Sale	12,000	Depr. expense	24,000
Bal., Dec. 31, 2009	250,000						Bal., Dec. 31, 2009	60,000

Example: If a plant asset costing $40,000 with $37,000 of accumulated depreciation is sold at a $1,000 loss, what is the cash flow? What is the cash flow if this asset is sold at a gain of $3,000? *Answers:* +$2,000; +$6,000.

This reconstruction analysis is complete in that the change in plant assets from $210,000 to $250,000 is fully explained by the $70,000 purchase and the $30,000 sale. Also, the change in accumulated depreciation from $48,000 to $60,000 is fully explained by depreciation expense of $24,000 and the removal of $12,000 in accumulated depreciation from an asset sale. (Preparers of the statement of cash flows have the entire ledger and additional information at their disposal, but for brevity reasons only the information needed for reconstructing accounts is given.)

The third stage looks at the reconstructed entries for identification of cash flows. The two identified cash flow effects are reported in the investing section of the statement as follows (also see Exhibit 12.7 or 12.11):

Cash flows from investing activities	
Cash received from sale of plant assets	$12,000
Cash paid for purchase of plant assets	(10,000)

The $60,000 portion of the purchase described in item *b* and financed by issuing notes is a noncash investing and financing activity. It is reported in a note or in a separate schedule to the statement as follows:

Noncash investing and financing activity	
Purchased plant assets with issuance of notes	$60,000

Analysis of Other Assets

Many other asset transactions (including those involving current notes receivable and investments in certain securities) are considered investing activities and can affect a company's cash flows. Since Genesis did not enter into other investing activities impacting assets, we do not need to extend our analysis to these other assets. If such transactions did exist, we would analyze them using the same three-stage process illustrated for plant assets.

Quick Check	Answer—p. 541

7. Equipment costing $80,000 with accumulated depreciation of $30,000 is sold at a loss of $10,000. What is the cash receipt from this sale? In what section of the statement of cash flows is this transaction reported?

Cash Flows from Financing

The fourth major step in preparing the statement of cash flows is to compute and report cash flows from financing activities. We normally do this by identifying changes in all noncurrent liability accounts (including the current portion of any notes and bonds) and the equity accounts. These accounts include long-term debt, notes payable, bonds payable, common stock, and retained earnings. Changes in these accounts are then analyzed using available information to determine their effect, if any, on cash. Results are reported in the financing activities section of the statement. **Reporting of financing activities is identical under the direct method and indirect method.**

Video12.1

Three-Stage Process of Analysis

We again use a three-stage process to determine cash provided or used by financing activities: (1) identify changes in financing-related accounts, (2) explain these changes using reconstruction analysis, and (3) report their cash flow effects.

Analysis of Noncurrent Liabilities

Information about Genesis provided earlier reveals two transactions involving noncurrent liabilities. We analyzed one of those, the $60,000 issuance of notes payable to purchase plant assets. This transaction is reported as a significant noncash investing and financing activity in a footnote or a separate schedule to the statement of cash flows. The other remaining transaction involving noncurrent liabilities is the cash retirement of notes payable.

Point: Financing activities generally refer to changes in the noncurrent liability and the equity accounts. Examples are (1) receiving cash from issuing debt or repaying amounts borrowed and (2) receiving cash from or distributing cash to owners.

Notes Payable Transactions The first stage in analysis of notes is to review the comparative balance sheets from Exhibit 12.10. This analysis reveals an increase in notes payable from $64,000 to $90,000.

The second stage explains this change. Item *e* of the additional information for Genesis (page 517) reports that notes with a carrying value of $34,000 are retired for $18,000 cash, resulting in a $16,000 gain. The reconstructed entry for analysis of item *e* follows:

Reconstruction	Notes Payable	34,000	
	Gain on retirement of debt		16,000
	Cash		**18,000**

This entry reveals an $18,000 cash outflow for retirement of notes and a $16,000 gain from comparing the notes payable carrying value to the cash received. This gain does not reflect any cash inflow or outflow. Also, item *b* of the additional information reports that Genesis purchased plant assets costing $70,000 by issuing $60,000 in notes payable to the seller and paying $10,000 in cash. We reconstructed this entry when analyzing investing activities: It showed a $60,000 increase to notes payable that is reported as a noncash investing and financing transaction. The Notes Payable account reflects (and is fully explained by) these reconstructed entries as follows:

Notes Payable			
		Bal., Dec. 31, 2008	64,000
Retired notes	**34,000**	**Issued notes**	**60,000**
		Bal., Dec. 31, 2009	90,000

The third stage is to report the cash flow effect of the notes retirement in the financing section of the statement as follows (also see Exhibit 12.7 or 12.11):

Cash flows from financing activities	
Cash paid to retire notes	$(18,000)

Analysis of Equity

The Genesis information reveals two transactions involving equity accounts. The first is the issuance of common stock for cash. The second is the declaration and payment of cash dividends. We analyze both.

Common Stock Transactions The first stage in analyzing common stock is to review the comparative balance sheets from Exhibit 12.10, which reveals an increase in common stock from $80,000 to $95,000.

The second stage explains this change. Item *d* of the additional information (page 517) reports that 3,000 shares of common stock are issued at par for $5 per share. The reconstructed entry for analysis of item *d* follows:

Reconstruction	Cash	15,000	
	Common Stock		15,000

This entry reveals a $15,000 cash inflow from stock issuance and is reflected in (and explains) the Common Stock account as follows:

Common Stock		
	Bal., Dec. 31, 2008	80,000
	Issued stock	**15,000**
	Bal., Dec. 31, 2009	95,000

The third stage discloses the cash flow effect from stock issuance in the financing section of the statement as follows (also see Exhibit 12.7 or 12.11):

Cash flows from financing activities	
Cash received from issuing stock	$15,000

Retained Earnings Transactions The first stage in analyzing the Retained Earnings account is to review the comparative balance sheets from Exhibit 12.10. This reveals an increase in retained earnings from $88,000 to $112,000.

The second stage explains this change. Item *f* of the additional information (page 517) reports that cash dividends of $14,000 are paid. The reconstructed entry follows:

Reconstruction	Retained Earnings.	14,000	
	Cash		14,000

This entry reveals a $14,000 cash outflow for cash dividends. Also see that the Retained Earnings account is impacted by net income of $38,000. (Net income was analyzed under the operating section of the statement of cash flows.) The reconstructed Retained Earnings account follows:

Retained Earnings			
		Bal., Dec. 31, 2008	88,000
Cash dividend	**14,000**	**Net income**	**38,000**
		Bal., Dec. 31, 2009	112,000

Point: Financing activities not affecting cash flow include *declaration* of a cash dividend, *declaration* of a stock dividend, payment of a stock dividend, and a stock split.

The third stage reports the cash flow effect from the cash dividend in the financing section of the statement as follows (also see Exhibit 12.7 or 12.11):

Cash flows from financing activities	
Cash paid for dividends	$(14,000)

We now have identified and explained all of the Genesis cash inflows and cash outflows and one noncash investing and financing transaction. Specifically, our analysis has reconciled changes in all noncash balance sheet accounts.

Global: There are no requirements to separate domestic and international cash flows, leading some users to ask "Where in the world is cash flow?"

Proving Cash Balances

The fifth and final step in preparing the statement is to report the beginning and ending cash balances and prove that the *net change in cash* is explained by operating, investing, and financing cash flows. This step is shown here for Genesis.

Net cash provided by operating activities	$20,000
Net cash provided by investing activities	2,000
Net cash used in financing activities	(17,000)
Net increase in cash	**$ 5,000**
Cash balance at 2008 year-end	12,000
Cash balance at 2009 year-end	$17,000

The preceding table shows that the $5,000 net increase in cash, from $12,000 at the beginning of the period to $17,000 at the end, is reconciled by net cash flows from operating ($20,000 inflow), investing ($2,000 inflow), and financing ($17,000 outflow) activities. This is formally reported at the bottom of the statement of cash flows as shown in both Exhibits 12.7 and 12.11.

Decision Maker

Reporter   Management is in labor contract negotiations and grants you an interview. It highlights a recent $600,000 net loss that involves a $930,000 extraordinary loss and a total net cash outflow of $550,000 (which includes net cash outflows of $850,000 for investing activities and $350,000 for financing activities). What is your assessment of this company? [Answer—p. 541]

Global View

The statement of cash flows, which explains changes in cash (including cash equivalents) from period to period, is required under both U.S. GAAP and IFRS. This section discusses similarities and differences between U.S. GAAP and IFRS in reporting that statement.

Reporting of Cash Flows from Operating

Both U.S. GAAP and IFRS permit the reporting of cash flows from operating activities using either the direct or indirect method. Further, the basic requirements underlying the application of both methods are fairly consistent across these two accounting systems. Appendix A shows that **GOME** reports its cash flows from operating activities using the indirect method, and in a manner similar to that explained in this chapter. Further, the definition of cash and cash equivalents is similar for U.S. GAAP and IFRS; GOME's definition follows:

> Cash and cash equivalents comprise cash on hand and demand deposits, and short term highly liquid investments that are readily convertible into known amounts of cash, are subject to an insignificant risk of changes in value, and have a short maturity of generally within three months when acquired, less bank overdrafts which are repayable on demand.

There are, however, some differences between U.S. GAAP and IFRS in reporting operating cash flows. We mention two of the more notable. First, U.S. GAAP requires cash inflows from interest revenue and dividend revenue be classified as operating, whereas IFRS permits classification under operating or investing provided that this classification is consistently applied across periods. GOME reports its cash from interest received under operating, consistent with U.S. GAAP (no mention is made of any dividends received). Second, U.S. GAAP requires cash outflows for interest expense be classified as operating, whereas IFRS again permits classification under operating or financing provided that it is consistently applied across periods. (Some believe that interest payments, like dividends payments, are better classified as financing because they represent payments to financiers.) GOME reports cash outflows for interest under financing, which is inconsistent with U.S. GAAP but acceptable under IFRS.

Reporting of Cash Flows from Investing and Financing

U.S. GAAP and IFRS are broadly similar in computing and classifying cash flows from investing and financing activities. A quick review of these two sections for GOME's statement of cash flows shows a structure similar to that explained in this chapter. One notable exception is that U.S. GAAP requires cash outflows for income tax be classified as operating, whereas IFRS permits the splitting of those cash flows among operating, investing, and financing depending on the sources of that tax. GOME reports its cash outflows for income tax under operating, which is similar to U.S. GAAP.

| **Decision Analysis** | **Cash Flow Analysis** |

Analyzing Cash Sources and Uses

A1   Analyze the statement of cash flows.

Most managers stress the importance of understanding and predicting cash flows for business decisions. Creditors evaluate a company's ability to generate cash before deciding whether to lend money. Investors also assess cash inflows and outflows before buying and selling stock. Information in the statement of cash flows helps address these and other questions such as (1) How much cash is generated from or used in operations? (2) What expenditures are made with cash from operations? (3) What is the source of cash for debt payments? (4) What is the source of cash for distributions to owners? (5) How is the increase in investing activities financed? (6) What is the source of cash for new plant assets? (7) Why is cash flow from operations different from income? (8) How is cash from financing used?

To effectively answer these questions, it is important to separately analyze investing, financing, and operating activities. To illustrate, consider data from three different companies in Exhibit 12.13. These companies operate in the same industry and have been in business for several years.

EXHIBIT 12.13

Cash Flows of Competing Companies

($ thousands)	BMX	ATV	Trex
Cash provided (used) by operating activities	$90,000	$40,000	$(24,000)
Cash provided (used) by investing activities			
Proceeds from sale of plant assets			26,000
Purchase of plant assets	(48,000)	(25,000)	
Cash provided (used) by financing activities			
Proceeds from issuance of debt			13,000
Repayment of debt	(27,000)		
Net increase (decrease) in cash	$15,000	$15,000	$ 15,000

Each company generates an identical $15,000 net increase in cash, but its sources and uses of cash flows are very different. BMX's operating activities provide net cash flows of $90,000, allowing it to purchase plant assets of $48,000 and repay $27,000 of its debt. ATV's operating activities provide $40,000 of cash flows, limiting its purchase of plant assets to $25,000. Trex's $15,000 net cash increase is due to selling plant assets and incurring additional debt. Its operating activities yield a net cash outflow of $24,000. Overall, analysis of these cash flows reveals that BMX is more capable of generating future cash flows than is ATV or Trex.

Free Cash Flows Many investors use cash flows to value company stock. However, cash-based valuation models often yield different stock values due to differences in measurement of cash flows. Most models require cash flows that are "free" for distribution to shareholders. These *free cash flows* are defined as cash flows available to shareholders after operating asset reinvestments and debt payments. Knowledge of the statement of cash flows is key to proper computation of free cash flows. A company's growth and financial flexibility depend on adequate free cash flows.

Cash Flow on Total Assets

Cash flow information has limitations, but it can help measure a company's ability to meet its obligations, pay dividends, expand operations, and obtain financing. Users often compute and analyze a cash-based ratio similar to return on total assets except that its numerator is net cash flows from operating activities. The **cash flow on total assets** ratio is in Exhibit 12.14.

A2 Compute and apply the cash flow on total assets ratio.

EXHIBIT 12.14

Cash Flow on Total Assets

$$\text{Cash flow on total assets} = \frac{\text{Cash flow from operations}}{\text{Average total assets}}$$

This ratio reflects actual cash flows and is not affected by accounting income recognition and measurement. It can help business decision makers estimate the amount and timing of cash flows when planning and analyzing operating activities.

To illustrate, the 2009 cash flow on total assets ratio for **Nike** is 13.5%—see Exhibit 12.15. Is a 13.5% ratio good or bad? To answer this question, we compare this ratio with the ratios of prior years (we could also compare its ratio with those of its competitors and the market). Nike's cash flow on total assets ratio for several prior years is in the second column of Exhibit 12.15. Results show that its 13.5% return is the lowest return over the past several years. This is probably reflective of the recent recessionary period.

EXHIBIT 12.15

Nike's Cash Flow on Total Assets

Year	Cash Flow on Total Assets	Return on Total Assets
2009	13.5%	11.6%
2008	16.7	16.3
2007	18.3	14.5
2006	17.9	14.9
2005	18.8	14.5

As an indicator of *earnings quality,* some analysts compare the cash flow on total assets ratio to the return on total assets ratio. Nike's return on total assets is provided in the third column of Exhibit 12.15. Nike's cash flow on total assets ratio exceeds its return on total assets in each of the five years, leading some analysts to infer that Nike's earnings quality is high for that period because more earnings are realized in the form of cash.

Cash Flow Ratios Analysts use various other cash-based ratios, including the following two:

(1) $$\text{Cash coverage of growth} = \frac{\text{Operating cash flow}}{\text{Cash outflow for plant assets}}$$

where a low ratio (less than 1) implies cash inadequacy to meet asset growth, whereas a high ratio implies cash adequacy for asset growth.

(2) $$\text{Operating cash flow to sales} = \frac{\text{Operating cash flow}}{\text{Net sales}}$$

when this ratio substantially and consistently differs from the operating income to net sales ratio, the risk of accounting improprieties increases.

Point: The following ratio helps assess whether operating cash flow is adequate to meet long-term obligations: **Cash coverage of debt** = Cash flow from operations ÷ Noncurrent liabilities. A low ratio suggests a higher risk of insolvency; a high ratio suggests a greater ability to meet long-term obligations.

Demonstration Problem

Umlauf's comparative balance sheets, income statement, and additional information follow.

UMLAUF COMPANY
Balance Sheets
December 31, 2009 and 2008

	2009	2008
Assets		
Cash	$ 43,050	$ 23,925
Accounts receivable	34,125	39,825
Merchandise inventory	156,000	146,475
Prepaid expenses	3,600	1,650
Equipment	135,825	146,700
Accum. depreciation—Equipment	(61,950)	(47,550)
Total assets	$310,650	$311,025
Liabilities and Equity		
Accounts payable	$ 28,800	$ 33,750
Income taxes payable	5,100	4,425
Dividends payable	0	4,500
Bonds payable	0	37,500
Common stock, $10 par	168,750	168,750
Retained earnings	108,000	62,100
Total liabilities and equity.............	$310,650	$311,025

UMLAUF COMPANY
Income Statement
For Year Ended December 31, 2009

Sales		$446,100
Cost of goods sold	$222,300	
Other operating expenses	120,300	
Depreciation expense	25,500	(368,100)
		78,000
Other gains (losses)		
Loss on sale of equipment	3,300	
Loss on retirement of bonds ..	825	(4,125)
Income before taxes		73,875
Income taxes expense		(13,725)
Net income		$ 60,150

Additional Information

a. Equipment costing $21,375 with accumulated depreciation of $11,100 is sold for cash.

b. Equipment purchases are for cash.

c. Accumulated Depreciation is affected by depreciation expense and the sale of equipment.

d. The balance of Retained Earnings is affected by dividend declarations and net income.

e. All sales are made on credit.

f. All merchandise inventory purchases are on credit.

g. Accounts Payable balances result from merchandise inventory purchases.

h. Prepaid expenses relate to "other operating expenses."

Required

1. Prepare a statement of cash flows using the indirect method for year 2009.

2.^B Prepare a statement of cash flows using the direct method for year 2009.

Planning the Solution

- Prepare two blank statements of cash flows with sections for operating, investing, and financing activities using the (1) indirect method format and (2) direct method format.

- Compute the cash paid for equipment and the cash received from the sale of equipment using the additional information provided along with the amount for depreciation expense and the change in the balances of equipment and accumulated depreciation. Use T-accounts to help chart the effects of the sale and purchase of equipment on the balances of the Equipment account and the Accumulated Depreciation account.

- Compute the effect of net income on the change in the Retained Earnings account balance. Assign the difference between the change in retained earnings and the amount of net income to dividends declared. Adjust the dividends declared amount for the change in the Dividends Payable balance.

- Compute cash received from customers, cash paid for merchandise, cash paid for other operating expenses, and cash paid for taxes as illustrated in the chapter.

- Enter the cash effects of reconstruction entries to the appropriate section(s) of the statement.

- Total each section of the statement, determine the total net change in cash, and add it to the beginning balance of cash to get the ending balance of cash.

Solution to Demonstration Problem

Supporting computations for cash receipts and cash payments.

(1)	*Cost of equipment sold	$ 21,375
	Accumulated depreciation of equipment sold	(11,100)
	Book value of equipment sold	10,275
	Loss on sale of equipment	(3,300)
	Cash received from sale of equipment	$ 6,975
	Cost of equipment sold	$ 21,375
	Less decrease in the equipment account balance	(10,875)
	Cash paid for new equipment	$ 10,500
(2)	Loss on retirement of bonds	$ 825
	Carrying value of bonds retired	37,500
	Cash paid to retire bonds	$ 38,325
(3)	Net income	$ 60,150
	Less increase in retained earnings	45,900
	Dividends declared	14,250
	Plus decrease in dividends payable	4,500
	Cash paid for dividends	$ 18,750
(4)[B]	Sales	$ 446,100
	Add decrease in accounts receivable	5,700
	Cash received from customers	$451,800
(5)[B]	Cost of goods sold	$ 222,300
	Plus increase in merchandise inventory	9,525
	Purchases	231,825
	Plus decrease in accounts payable	4,950
	Cash paid for merchandise	$236,775
(6)[B]	Other operating expenses	$ 120,300
	Plus increase in prepaid expenses	1,950
	Cash paid for other operating expenses	$122,250
(7)[B]	Income taxes expense	$ 13,725
	Less increase in income taxes payable	(675)
	Cash paid for income taxes	$ 13,050

* Supporting T-account analysis for part 1 follows:

Equipment			
Bal., Dec. 31, 2008	146,700		
Cash purchase	10,500	Sale	21,375
Bal., Dec. 31, 2009	135,825		

Accumulated Depreciation—Equipment			
		Bal., Dec. 31, 2008	47,550
Sale	11,100	Depr. expense	25,500
		Bal., Dec. 31, 2009	61,950

UMLAUF COMPANY
Statement of Cash Flows (Indirect Method)
For Year Ended December 31, 2009

Cash flows from operating activities	
Net income	$60,150
Adjustments to reconcile net income to net cash provided by operating activities	
Decrease in accounts receivable	5,700
Increase in merchandise inventory	(9,525)
Increase in prepaid expenses	(1,950)
Decrease in accounts payable	(4,950)
Increase in income taxes payable	675
Depreciation expense	25,500
Loss on sale of plant assets	3,300
Loss on retirement of bonds	825
Net cash provided by operating activities	$79,725

[continued on next page]

[continued from previous page]

Cash flows from investing activities		
Cash received from sale of equipment	6,975	
Cash paid for equipment	(10,500)	
Net cash used in investing activities		(3,525)
Cash flows from financing activities		
Cash paid to retire bonds payable	(38,325)	
Cash paid for dividends	(18,750)	
Net cash used in financing activities		(57,075)
Net increase in cash		$19,125
Cash balance at prior year-end		23,925
Cash balance at current year-end		$43,050

UMLAUF COMPANY
Statement of Cash Flows (Direct Method)
For Year Ended December 31, 2009

Cash flows from operating activities		
Cash received from customers	$451,800	
Cash paid for merchandise	(236,775)	
Cash paid for other operating expenses	(122,250)	
Cash paid for income taxes	(13,050)	
Net cash provided by operating activities		$79,725
Cash flows from investing activities		
Cash received from sale of equipment	6,975	
Cash paid for equipment	(10,500)	
Net cash used in investing activities		(3,525)
Cash flows from financing activities		
Cash paid to retire bonds payable	(38,325)	
Cash paid for dividends	(18,750)	
Net cash used in financing activities		(57,075)
Net increase in cash		$19,125
Cash balance at prior year-end		23,925
Cash balance at current year-end		$43,050

APPENDIX

12A Spreadsheet Preparation of the Statement of Cash Flows

This appendix explains how to use a spreadsheet to prepare the statement of cash flows under the indirect method.

Preparing the Indirect Method Spreadsheet

P4 Illustrate use of a spreadsheet to prepare a statement of cash flows.

Analyzing noncash accounts can be challenging when a company has a large number of accounts and many operating, investing, and financing transactions. A *spreadsheet,* also called *work sheet* or *working paper,* can help us organize the information needed to prepare a statement of cash flows. A spreadsheet also makes it easier to check the accuracy of our work. To illustrate, we return to the comparative balance sheets and income statement shown in Exhibit 12.10. We use the following identifying letters *a* through *g* to code changes in accounts, and letters *h* through *m* for additional information, to prepare the statement of cash flows:

a. Net income is $38,000.

b. Accounts receivable increase by $20,000.

c. Merchandise inventory increases by $14,000.

d. Prepaid expenses increase by $2,000.

e. Accounts payable decrease by $5,000.

f. Interest payable decreases by $1,000.

g. Income taxes payable increase by $10,000.

h. Depreciation expense is $24,000.

i. Plant assets costing $30,000 with accumulated depreciation of $12,000 are sold for $12,000 cash. This yields a loss on sale of assets of $6,000.

j. Notes with a book value of $34,000 are retired with a cash payment of $18,000, yielding a $16,000 gain on retirement.

k. Plant assets costing $70,000 are purchased with a cash payment of $10,000 and an issuance of notes payable for $60,000.

l. Issued 3,000 shares of common stock for $15,000 cash.

m. Paid cash dividends of $14,000.

Exhibit 12A.1 shows the indirect method spreadsheet for Genesis. We enter both beginning and ending balance sheet amounts on the spreadsheet. We also enter information in the Analysis of Changes columns (keyed to the additional information items *a* through *m*) to explain changes in the accounts and determine the cash flows for operating, investing, and financing activities. Information about noncash investing and financing activities is reported near the bottom.

Entering the Analysis of Changes on the Spreadsheet

The following sequence of procedures is used to complete the spreadsheet after the beginning and ending balances of the balance sheet accounts are entered:

① Enter net income as the first item in the Statement of Cash Flows section for computing operating cash inflow (debit) and as a credit to Retained Earnings.

② In the Statement of Cash Flows section, adjustments to net income are entered as debits if they increase cash flows and as credits if they decrease cash flows. Applying this same rule, adjust net income for the change in each noncash current asset and current liability account related to operating activities. For each adjustment to net income, the offsetting debit or credit must help reconcile the beginning and ending balances of a current asset or current liability account.

③ Enter adjustments to net income for income statement items not providing or using cash in the period. For each adjustment, the offsetting debit or credit must help reconcile a noncash balance sheet account.

④ Adjust net income to eliminate any gains or losses from investing and financing activities. Because the cash from a gain must be excluded from operating activities, the gain is entered as a credit in the operating activities section. Losses are entered as debits. For each adjustment, the related debit and/or credit must help reconcile balance sheet accounts and involve reconstructed entries to show the cash flow from investing or financing activities.

⑤ After reviewing any unreconciled balance sheet accounts and related information, enter the remaining reconciling entries for investing and financing activities. Examples are purchases of plant assets, issuances of long-term debt, stock issuances, and dividend payments. Some of these may require entries in the noncash investing and financing section of the spreadsheet (reconciled).

⑥ Check accuracy by totaling the Analysis of Changes columns and by determining that the change in each balance sheet account has been explained (reconciled).

We illustrate these steps in Exhibit 12A.1 for Genesis:

Point: Analysis of the changes on the spreadsheet are summarized as:

1. Cash flows from operating activities generally affect net income, current assets, and current liabilities.

2. Cash flows from investing activities generally affect noncurrent asset accounts.

3. Cash flows from financing activities generally affect noncurrent liability and equity accounts.

Step	Entries
①	(a)
②	(b) through (g)
③	(h)
④	(i) through (j)
⑤	(k) through (m)

EXHIBIT 12A.1

Spreadsheet for Preparing Statement of Cash Flows—Indirect Method

GENESIS
Spreadsheet for Statement of Cash Flows—Indirect Method
For Year Ended December 31, 2009

	Dec. 31, 2008		Analysis of Changes Debit		Credit	Dec. 31, 2009
Balance Sheet—Debits						
Cash	$ 12,000					$ 17,000
Accounts receivable	40,000	(b)	$ 20,000			60,000
Merchandise inventory	70,000	(c)	14,000			84,000
Prepaid expenses	4,000	(d)	2,000			6,000
Plant assets	210,000	(k1)	70,000	(i)	$ 30,000	250,000
	$336,000					$417,000
Balance Sheet—Credits						
Accumulated depreciation	$ 48,000	(i)	12,000	(h)	24,000	$ 60,000
Accounts payable	40,000	(e)	5,000			35,000
Interest payable	4,000	(f)	1,000			3,000
Income taxes payable	12,000			(g)	10,000	22,000
Notes payable	64,000	(j)	34,000	(k2)	60,000	90,000
Common stock, $5 par value	80,000			(l)	15,000	95,000
Retained earnings	88,000	(m)	14,000	(a)	38,000	112,000
	$336,000					$417,000
Statement of Cash Flows						
Operating activities						
Net income		(a)	38,000			
Increase in accounts receivable				(b)	20,000	
Increase in merchandise inventory				(c)	14,000	
Increase in prepaid expenses				(d)	2,000	
Decrease in accounts payable				(e)	5,000	
Decrease in interest payable				(f)	1,000	
Increase in income taxes payable		(g)	10,000			
Depreciation expense		(h)	24,000			
Loss on sale of plant assets		(i)	6,000			
Gain on retirement of notes				(j)	16,000	
Investing activities						
Receipts from sale of plant assets		(i)	12,000			
Payment for purchase of plant assets				(k1)	10,000	
Financing activities						
Payment to retire notes				(j)	18,000	
Receipts from issuing stock		(l)	15,000			
Payment of cash dividends				(m)	14,000	
Noncash Investing and Financing Activities						
Purchase of plant assets with notes		(k2)	60,000	(k1)	60,000	
			$337,000		$337,000	

Sheet1 Sheet2 Sheet3

Since adjustments *i, j,* and *k* are more challenging, we show them in the following debit and credit format. These entries are for purposes of our understanding; they are *not* the entries actually made in the journals. Changes in the Cash account are identified as sources or uses of cash.

i.	Loss from sale of plant assets	6,000	
	Accumulated depreciation..................................	12,000	
	Receipt from sale of plant assets **(source of cash)**	12,000	
	Plant assets		30,000
	To describe sale of plant assets.		

[continued on next page]

[continued from previous page]

j.	Notes payable	34,000	
	Payments to retire notes **(use of cash)**		18,000
	Gain on retirement of notes		16,000
	To describe retirement of notes.		
k1.	Plant assets	70,000	
	Payment to purchase plant assets **(use of cash)**		10,000
	Purchase of plant assets financed by notes		60,000
	To describe purchase of plant assets.		
k2.	Purchase of plant assets financed by notes	60,000	
	Notes payable		60,000
	To issue notes for purchase of assets.		

Direct Method of Reporting Operating Cash Flows

12B

We compute cash flows from operating activities under the direct method by adjusting accrual-based income statement items to the cash basis. The usual approach is to adjust income statement accounts related to operating activities for changes in their related balance sheet accounts as follows:

P5 Compute cash flows from operating activities using the direct method.

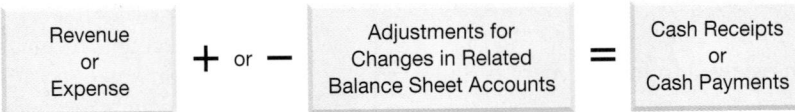

The framework for reporting cash receipts and cash payments for the operating section of the cash flow statement under the direct method is as in Exhibit 12B.1. We consider cash receipts first and then cash payments.

EXHIBIT 12B.1

Major Classes of Operating Cash Flows

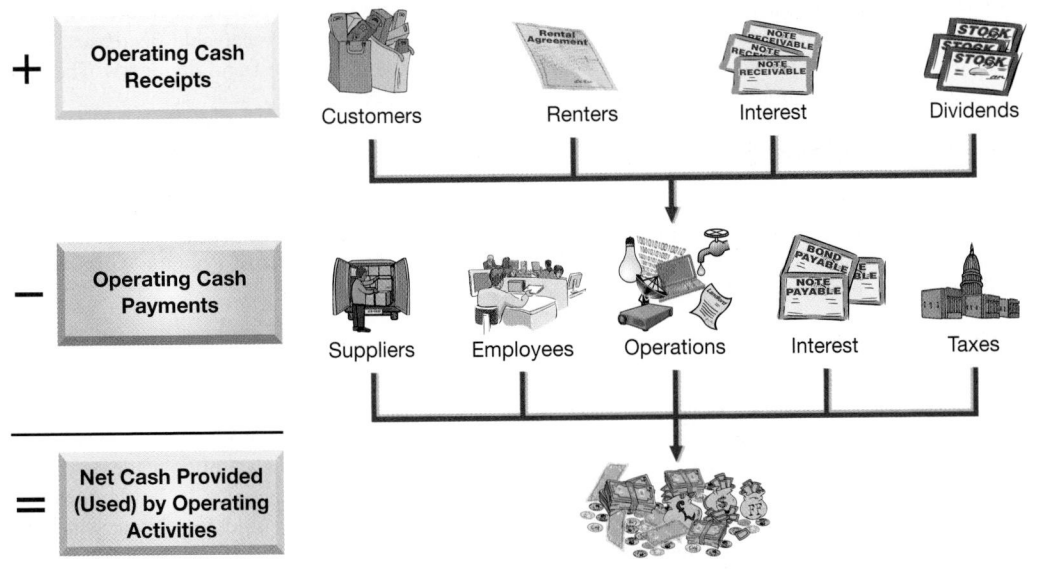

Operating Cash Receipts

A review of Exhibit 12.10 and the additional information reported by Genesis suggests only one potential cash receipt: sales to customers. This section, therefore, starts with sales to customers as reported on the income statement and then adjusts it as necessary to obtain cash received from customers to report on the statement of cash flows.

Cash Received from Customers   If all sales are for cash, the amount received from customers equals the sales reported on the income statement. When some or all sales are on account, however, we must adjust the amount of sales for the change in Accounts Receivable. It is often helpful to use *account analysis* to do this. This usually involves setting up a T-account and reconstructing its major entries, with emphasis on cash receipts and payments. To illustrate, we use a T-account that includes accounts receivable balances for Genesis on December 31, 2008 and 2009. The beginning balance is $40,000 and the ending balance is $60,000. Next, the income statement shows sales of $590,000, which we enter on the debit side of this account. We now can reconstruct the Accounts Receivable account to determine the amount of cash received from customers as follows:

Point: An accounts receivable increase implies cash received from customers is less than sales (the converse is also true).

Accounts Receivable			
Bal., Dec. 31, 2008	40,000		
Sales	590,000	Cash receipts =	570,000
Bal., Dec. 31, 2009	60,000		

Example: If the ending balance of accounts receivable is $20,000 (instead of $60,000), what is cash received from customers? *Answer:* $610,000

This T-account shows that the Accounts Receivable balance begins at $40,000 and increases to $630,000 from sales of $590,000, yet its ending balance is only $60,000. This implies that cash receipts from customers are $570,000, computed as $40,000 + $590,000 − [?] = $60,000. This computation can be rearranged to express cash received as equal to sales of $590,000 minus a $20,000 increase in accounts receivable. This computation is summarized as a general rule in Exhibit 12B.2. The statement of cash flows in Exhibit 12.7 reports the $570,000 cash received from customers as a cash inflow from operating activities.

EXHIBIT 12B.2

Formula to Compute Cash Received from Customers— Direct Method

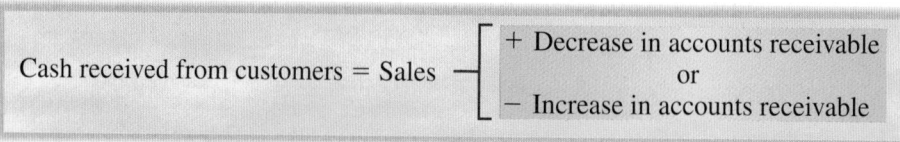

$$\text{Cash received from customers} = \text{Sales} \left\{ \begin{array}{c} + \text{ Decrease in accounts receivable} \\ \text{or} \\ - \text{ Increase in accounts receivable} \end{array} \right.$$

Other Cash Receipts   While Genesis's cash receipts are limited to collections from customers, we often see other types of cash receipts, most commonly cash receipts involving rent, interest, and dividends. We compute cash received from these items by subtracting an increase in their respective receivable or adding a decrease. For instance, if rent receivable increases in the period, cash received from renters is less than rent revenue reported on the income statement. If rent receivable decreases, cash received is more than reported rent revenue. The same logic applies to interest and dividends. The formulas for these computations are summarized later in this appendix.

Point: Net income is measured using accrual accounting. Cash flows from operations are measured using cash basis accounting.

Operating Cash Payments

A review of Exhibit 12.10 and the additional Genesis information shows four operating expenses: cost of goods sold; wages and other operating expenses; interest expense; and taxes expense. We analyze each expense to compute its cash amounts for the statement of cash flows. (We then examine depreciation and the other losses and gains.)

Cash Paid for Merchandise   We compute cash paid for merchandise by analyzing both cost of goods sold and merchandise inventory. If all merchandise purchases are for cash and the ending balance of Merchandise Inventory is unchanged from the beginning balance, the amount of cash paid for merchandise equals cost of goods sold—an uncommon situation. Instead, there normally is some change in the Merchandise Inventory balance. Also, some or all merchandise purchases are often made on credit, and this yields changes in the Accounts Payable balance. When the balances of both Merchandise Inventory and Accounts Payable change, we must adjust the cost of goods sold for changes in both accounts to compute cash paid for merchandise. This is a two-step adjustment.

First, we use the change in the account balance of Merchandise Inventory, along with the cost of goods sold amount, to compute cost of purchases for the period. An increase in merchandise inventory implies that we bought more than we sold, and we add this inventory increase to cost of goods sold to compute cost of purchases. A decrease in merchandise inventory implies that we bought less than we sold, and we subtract the inventory decrease from cost of goods sold to compute purchases. We illustrate the *first step* by reconstructing the Merchandise Inventory account of Genesis:

Merchandise Inventory			
Bal., Dec. 31, 2008	70,000		
Purchases =	314,000	Cost of goods sold	300,000
Bal., Dec. 31, 2009	84,000		

The beginning balance is $70,000, and the ending balance is $84,000. The income statement shows that cost of goods sold is $300,000, which we enter on the credit side of this account. With this information, we determine the amount for cost of purchases to be $314,000. This computation can be rearranged to express cost of purchases as equal to cost of goods sold of $300,000 plus the $14,000 increase in inventory.

The second step uses the change in the balance of Accounts Payable, and the amount of cost of purchases, to compute cash paid for merchandise. A decrease in accounts payable implies that we paid for more goods than we acquired this period, and we would then add the accounts payable decrease to cost of purchases to compute cash paid for merchandise. An increase in accounts payable implies that we paid for less than the amount of goods acquired, and we would subtract the accounts payable increase from purchases to compute cash paid for merchandise. The *second step* is applied to Genesis by reconstructing its Accounts Payable account:

Accounts Payable			
		Bal., Dec. 31, 2008	40,000
Cash payments =	319,000	Purchases	314,000
		Bal., Dec. 31, 2009	35,000

Its beginning balance of $40,000 plus purchases of $314,000 minus an ending balance of $35,000 yields cash paid of $319,000 (or $40,000 + $314,000 − [?] = $35,000). Alternatively, we can express cash paid for merchandise as equal to purchases of $314,000 plus the $5,000 decrease in accounts payable. The $319,000 cash paid for merchandise is reported on the statement of cash flows in Exhibit 12.7 as a cash outflow under operating activities.

We summarize this two-step adjustment to cost of goods sold to compute cash paid for merchandise inventory in Exhibit 12B.3.

Example: If the ending balances of Inventory and Accounts Payable are $60,000 and $50,000, respectively (instead of $84,000 and $35,000), what is cash paid for merchandise? *Answer:* $280,000

EXHIBIT 12B.3

Two Steps to Compute Cash Paid for Merchandise—Direct Method

Step 1

Purchases = Cost of goods sold ⎡ + Increase in merchandise inventory
                                  ⎢ or
                                  ⎣ − Decrease in merchandise inventory

Step 2

Cash paid for merchandise = Purchases ⎡ + Decrease in accounts payable
                                       ⎢ or
                                       ⎣ − Increase in accounts payable

Cash Paid for Wages and Operating Expenses (excluding depreciation)

The income statement of Genesis shows wages and other operating expenses of $216,000 (see Exhibit 12.10). To compute cash paid for wages and other operating expenses, we adjust this amount for any changes in their related balance sheet accounts. We begin by looking for any prepaid expenses and accrued liabilities related to wages and other operating expenses in the balance sheets of Genesis in

Exhibit 12.10. The balance sheets show prepaid expenses but no accrued liabilities. Thus, the adjustment is limited to the change in prepaid expenses. The amount of adjustment is computed by assuming that all cash paid for wages and other operating expenses is initially debited to Prepaid Expenses. This assumption allows us to reconstruct the Prepaid Expenses account:

Prepaid Expenses			
Bal., Dec. 31, 2008	4,000		
Cash payments =	218,000	Wages and other operating exp.	216,000
Bal., Dec. 31, 2009	6,000		

Point: A decrease in prepaid expenses implies that reported expenses include an amount(s) that did not require a cash outflow in the period.

Prepaid Expenses increase by $2,000 in the period, meaning that cash paid for wages and other operating expenses exceeds the reported expense by $2,000. Alternatively, we can express cash paid for wages and other operating expenses as equal to its reported expenses of $216,000 plus the $2,000 increase in prepaid expenses.[1]

Exhibit 12B.4 summarizes the adjustments to wages (including salaries) and other operating expenses. The Genesis balance sheet did not report accrued liabilities, but we include them in the formula to explain the adjustment to cash when they do exist. A decrease in accrued liabilities implies that we paid cash for more goods or services than received this period, so we add the decrease in accrued liabilities to the expense amount to obtain cash paid for these goods or services. An increase in accrued liabilities implies that we paid cash for less than what was acquired, so we subtract this increase in accrued liabilities from the expense amount to get cash paid.

EXHIBIT 12B.4

Formula to Compute Cash Paid for Wages and Operating Expenses—Direct Method

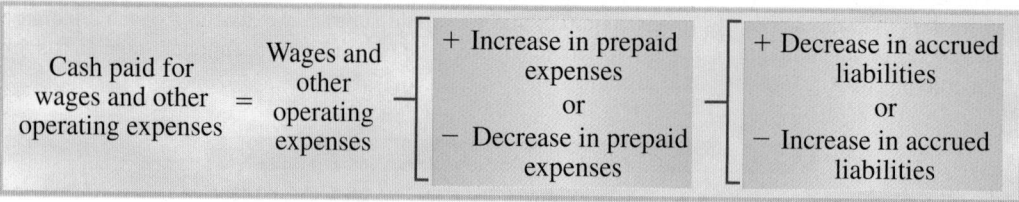

Cash Paid for Interest and Income Taxes Computing operating cash flows for interest and taxes is similar to that for operating expenses. Both require adjustments to their amounts reported on the income statement for changes in their related balance sheet accounts. We begin with the Genesis income statement showing interest expense of $7,000 and income taxes expense of $15,000. To compute the cash paid, we adjust interest expense for the change in interest payable and then the income taxes expense for the change in income taxes payable. These computations involve reconstructing both liability accounts:

Interest Payable			
		Bal., Dec. 31, 2008	4,000
Cash paid for interest =	8,000	Interest expense	7,000
		Bal., Dec. 31, 2009	3,000

Income Taxes Payable			
		Bal., Dec. 31, 2008	12,000
Cash paid for taxes =	5,000	Income taxes expense	15,000
		Bal., Dec. 31, 2009	22,000

These accounts reveal cash paid for interest of $8,000 and cash paid for income taxes of $5,000. The formulas to compute these amounts are in Exhibit 12B.5. Both of these cash payments are reported as operating cash outflows on the statement of cash flows in Exhibit 12.7.

---

[1] The assumption that all cash payments for wages and operating expenses are initially debited to Prepaid Expenses is not necessary for our analysis to hold. If cash payments are debited directly to the expense account, the total amount of cash paid for wages and other operating expenses still equals the $216,000 expense plus the $2,000 increase in Prepaid Expenses (which arise from end-of-period adjusting entries).

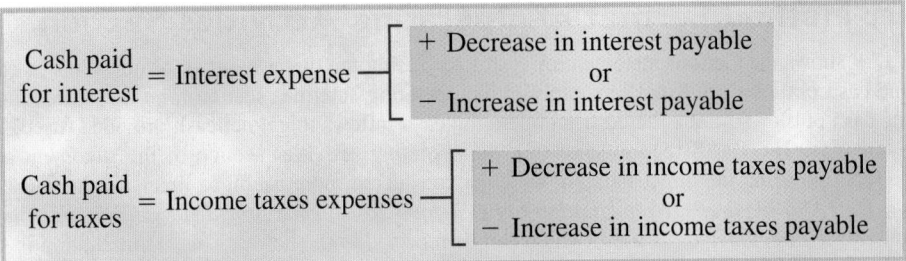

EXHIBIT 12B.5

Formulas to Compute Cash Paid for Both Interest and Taxes—Direct Method

Analysis of Additional Expenses, Gains, and Losses Genesis has three additional items reported on its income statement: depreciation, loss on sale of assets, and gain on retirement of debt. We must consider each for its potential cash effects.

Depreciation Expense Depreciation expense is $24,000. It is often called a *noncash expense* because depreciation has no cash flows. Depreciation expense is an allocation of an asset's depreciable cost. The cash outflow with a plant asset is reported as part of investing activities when it is paid for. Thus, depreciation expense is *never* reported on a statement of cash flows using the direct method, nor is depletion or amortization expense.

Loss on Sale of Assets Sales of assets frequently result in gains and losses reported as part of net income, but the amount of recorded gain or loss does *not* reflect any cash flows in these transactions. Asset sales result in cash inflow equal to the cash amount received, regardless of whether the asset was sold at a gain or a loss. This cash inflow is reported under investing activities. Thus, the loss or gain on a sale of assets is *never* reported on a statement of cash flows using the direct method.

Gain on Retirement of Debt Retirement of debt usually yields a gain or loss reported as part of net income, but that gain or loss does *not* reflect cash flow in this transaction. Debt retirement results in cash outflow equal to the cash paid to settle the debt, regardless of whether the debt is retired at a gain or loss. This cash outflow is reported under financing activities; the loss or gain from retirement of debt is *never* reported on a statement of cash flows using the direct method.

Point: The direct method is usually viewed as *user friendly* because less accounting knowledge is required to understand and use it.

Summary of Adjustments for Direct Method

Exhibit 12B.6 summarizes common adjustments for net income to yield net cash provided (used) by operating activities under the direct method.

EXHIBIT 12B.6

Summary of Selected Adjustments for Direct Method

Item	From Income Statement	Adjustments to Obtain Cash Flow Numbers		
Receipts				
From sales	Sales Revenue	+Decrease in Accounts Receivable −Increase in Accounts Receivable		
From rent	Rent Revenue	+Decrease in Rent Receivable −Increase in Rent Receivable		
From interest	Interest Revenue	+Decrease in Interest Receivable −Increase in Interest Receivable		
From dividends	Dividend Revenue	+Decrease in Dividends Receivable −Increase in Dividends Receivable		
Payments				
To suppliers	Cost of Goods Sold	+Increase in Inventory −Decrease in Inventory	+Decrease in Accounts Payable −Increase in Accounts Payable	
For operations	Operating Expense	+Increase in Prepaids −Decrease in Prepaids	+Decrease in Accrued Liabilities −Increase in Accrued Liabilities	
To employees	Wages (Salaries) Expense	+Decrease in Wages (Salaries) Payable −Increase in Wages (Salaries) Payable		
For interest	Interest Expense	+Decrease in Interest Payable −Increase in Interest Payable		
For taxes	Income Tax Expense	+Decrease in Income Tax Payable −Increase in Income Tax Payable		

Direct Method Format of Operating Activities Section

Point: Some preparers argue that it is easier to prepare a statement of cash flows using the indirect method. This likely explains its greater frequency in financial statements.

Exhibit 12.7 shows the Genesis statement of cash flows using the direct method. Major items of cash inflows and cash outflows are listed separately in the operating activities section. The format requires that operating cash outflows be subtracted from operating cash inflows to get net cash provided (used) by operating activities. The FASB recommends that the operating activities section of the statement of cash flows be reported using the direct method, which is considered more useful to financial statement users. *However, the FASB requires a reconciliation of net income to net cash provided (used) by operating activities when the direct method is used* (which can be reported in the notes). This reconciliation is similar to preparation of the operating activities section of the statement of cash flows using the indirect method.

IFRS

Like U.S. GAAP, IFRS allows cash flows from operating activities to be reported using either the indirect method or the direct method.

Quick Check

Answers—p. 541

8. Net sales in a period are $590,000, beginning accounts receivable are $120,000, and ending accounts receivable are $90,000. What cash amount is collected from customers in the period?

9. The Merchandise Inventory account balance decreases in the period from a beginning balance of $32,000 to an ending balance of $28,000. Cost of goods sold for the period is $168,000. If the Accounts Payable balance increases $2,400 in the period, what is the cash amount paid for merchandise inventory?

10. This period's wages and other operating expenses total $112,000. Beginning-of-period prepaid expenses totaled $1,200, and its ending balance is $4,200. There were no beginning-of-period accrued liabilities, but end-of-period wages payable equal $5,600. How much cash is paid for wages and other operating expenses?

Summary

C1 Explain the purpose and importance of cash flow information. The main purpose of the statement of cash flows is to report the major cash receipts and cash payments for a period. This includes identifying cash flows as relating to either operating, investing, or financing activities. Most business decisions involve evaluating activities that provide or use cash.

C2 Distinguish between operating, investing, and financing activities. Operating activities include transactions and events that determine net income. Investing activities include transactions and events that mainly affect long-term assets. Financing activities include transactions and events that mainly affect long-term liabilities and equity.

C3 Identify and disclose noncash investing and financing activities. Noncash investing and financing activities must be disclosed either in a note or a separate schedule to the statement of cash flows. Examples are the retirement of debt by issuing equity and the exchange of a note payable for plant assets.

C4 Describe the format of the statement of cash flows. The statement of cash flows separates cash receipts and cash payments into operating, investing, or financing activities.

A1 Analyze the statement of cash flows. To understand and predict cash flows, users stress identification of the sources and uses of cash flows by operating, investing, and financing activities. Emphasis is on operating cash flows since they derive from continuing operations.

A2 Compute and apply the cash flow on total assets ratio. The cash flow on total assets ratio is defined as operating cash flows divided by average total assets. Analysis of current and past values for this ratio can reflect a company's ability to yield regular and positive cash flows. It is also viewed as a measure of earnings quality.

P1 Prepare a statement of cash flows. Preparation of a statement of cash flows involves five steps: (1) Compute the net increase or decrease in cash; (2) compute net cash provided or used by operating activities (*using either the direct or indirect method*); (3) compute net cash provided or used by investing activities; (4) compute net cash provided or used by financing activities; and (5) report the beginning and ending cash balance and prove that it is explained by net cash flows. Noncash investing and financing activities are also disclosed.

P2 Compute cash flows from operating activities using the indirect method. The indirect method for reporting net cash provided or used by operating activities starts with net income and then adjusts it for three items: (1) changes in noncash current assets and current liabilities related to operating activities, (2) revenues and expenses not providing or using cash, and (3) gains and losses from investing and financing activities.

P3 Determine cash flows from both investing and financing activities. Cash flows from both investing and financing activities are determined by identifying the cash flow effects of transactions and events affecting each balance sheet account related to these activities. All cash flows from these activities are identified when we can explain changes in these accounts from the beginning to the end of the period.

P4[A] **Illustrate use of a spreadsheet to prepare a statement of cash flows.** A spreadsheet is a useful tool in preparing a statement of cash flows. Six key steps (see appendix) are applied when using the spreadsheet to prepare the statement.

P5[B] **Compute cash flows from operating activities using the direct method.** The direct method for reporting net cash provided or used by operating activities lists major operating cash inflows less cash outflows to yield net cash inflow or outflow from operations.

Guidance Answers to **Decision Maker**

Entrepreneur Several factors might explain an increase in net cash flows when a net loss is reported, including (1) early recognition of expenses relative to revenues generated (such as research and development), (2) cash advances on long-term sales contracts not yet recognized in income, (3) issuances of debt or equity for cash to finance expansion, (4) cash sale of assets, (5) delay of cash payments, and (6) cash prepayment on sales. Analysis needs to focus on the components of both the net loss and the net cash flows and their implications for future performance.

Reporter Your initial reaction based on the company's $600,000 loss with a $550,000 decrease in net cash flows is not positive. However, closer scrutiny reveals a more positive picture of this company's performance. Cash flow from operating activities is $650,000, computed as [?] − $850,000 − $350,000 = $(550,000). You also note that net income *before* the extraordinary loss is $330,000, computed as [?] − $930,000 = $(600,000).

Guidance Answers to **Quick Checks**

1. No to both. The statement of cash flows reports changes in the sum of cash plus cash equivalents. It does not report transfers between cash and cash equivalents.

2. The three categories of cash inflows and outflows are operating activities, investing activities, and financing activities.

3. **a.** Investing **c.** Financing **e.** Operating
   b. Operating **d.** Operating **f.** Financing

4. $74,900 + $4,600 − $11,700 − $1,000 + $3,400 = $70,200

5. Expenses such as depreciation and amortization do not require current cash outflows. Therefore, adding these expenses back to

net income eliminates these noncash items from the net income number, converting it to a cash basis.

6. A gain on the sale of plant assets is subtracted from net income because a sale of plant assets is not an operating activity; it is an investing activity for the amount of cash received from its sale. Also, such a gain yields no cash effects.

7. $80,000 − $30,000 − $10,000 = $40,000 cash receipt. The $40,000 cash receipt is reported as an investing activity.

8. $590,000 + ($120,000 − $90,000) = $620,000

9. $168,000 − ($32,000 − $28,000) − $2,400 = $161,600

10. $112,000 + ($4,200 − $1,200) − $5,600 = $109,400

Key Terms

Cash flow on total assets (p. 529)
Direct method (p. 516)
Financing activities (p. 512)

Indirect method (p. 516)
Investing activities (p. 512)

Operating activities (p. 511)
Statement of cash flows (p. 510)

Multiple Choice Quiz   Answers on p. 561   **mhhe.com/wildFA5e**

Additional Quiz Questions are available at the book's Website.

1. A company uses the indirect method to determine its cash flows from operating activities. Use the following information to determine its net cash provided or used by operating activities.

Net income	$15,200
Depreciation expense	10,000
Cash payment on note payable	8,000
Gain on sale of land	3,000
Increase in inventory	1,500
Increase in accounts payable	2,850

    a. $23,550 used by operating activities
    b. $23,550 provided by operating activities
    c. $15,550 provided by operating activities
    d. $42,400 provided by operating activities
    e. $20,850 provided by operating activities

2. A machine with a cost of $175,000 and accumulated depreciation of $94,000 is sold for $87,000 cash. The amount reported as a source of cash under cash flows from investing activities is:
    a. $81,000.
    b. $6,000.
    c. $87,000.
    d. Zero; this is a financing activity.
    e. Zero; this is an operating activity.

3. A company settles a long-term note payable plus interest by paying $68,000 cash toward the principal amount and $5,440 cash for interest. The amount reported as a use of cash under cash flows from financing activities is:
    a. Zero; this is an investing activity.
    b. Zero; this is an operating activity.
    c. $73,440.
    d. $68,000.
    e. $5,440.

4. The following information is available regarding a company's annual salaries and wages. What amount of cash is paid for salaries and wages?

Salaries and wages expense	$255,000
Salaries and wages payable, prior year-end	8,200
Salaries and wages payable, current year-end	10,900

    a. $252,300
    b. $257,700
    c. $255,000
    d. $274,100
    e. $235,900

5. The following information is available for a company. What amount of cash is paid for merchandise for the current year?

Cost of goods sold	$545,000
Merchandise inventory, prior year-end	105,000
Merchandise inventory, current year-end	112,000
Accounts payable, prior year-end	98,500
Accounts payable, current year-end	101,300

    a. $545,000
    b. $554,800
    c. $540,800
    d. $535,200
    e. $549,200

Superscript letter ^A(^B) denotes assignments based on Appendix 12A (12B).

Discussion Questions

1. What is the reporting purpose of the statement of cash flows? Identify at least two questions that this statement can answer.

2. Describe the direct method of reporting cash flows from operating activities.

3. When a statement of cash flows is prepared using the direct method, what are some of the operating cash flows?

4. Describe the indirect method of reporting cash flows from operating activities.

5. What are some investing activities reported on the statement of cash flows?

6. What are some financing activities reported on the statement of cash flows?

7. Where on the statement of cash flows is the payment of cash dividends reported?

8. Assume that a company purchases land for $100,000, paying $20,000 cash and borrowing the remainder with a long-term note payable. How should this transaction be reported on a statement of cash flows?

9. On June 3, a company borrows $50,000 cash by giving its bank a 160-day, interest-bearing note. On the statement of cash flows, where should this be reported?

10. If a company reports positive net income for the year, can it also show a net cash outflow from operating activities? Explain.

11. Is depreciation a source of cash flow?

12. Refer to **Best Buy**'s statement of cash flows in Appendix A. (*a*) Which method is used to compute its net cash provided by operating activities? (*b*) While its balance sheet shows an increase in receivables from fiscal years 2008 to 2009, why is this increase in receivables subtracted when computing net cash provided by operating activities for the year ended February 28, 2009?

13. Refer to **RadioShack**'s statement of cash flows in Appendix A. What are its cash flows from financing activities for the year ended December 31, 2008? List items and amounts.

14. Refer to **GOME**'s statement of cash flows in Appendix A. List its cash flows from operating activities, investing activities, and financing activities.

15. Refer to **Apple**'s statement of cash flows in Appendix A. What investing activities result in cash outflows for the year ended September 27, 2008? List items and amounts.

Denotes Discussion Questions that involve decision making.

connect™ Available with Connect Accounting

The statement of cash flows is one of the four primary financial statements.

1. Describe the content and layout of a statement of cash flows, including its three sections.
2. List at least three transactions classified as investing activities in a statement of cash flows.
3. List at least three transactions classified as financing activities in a statement of cash flows.
4. List at least three transactions classified as significant noncash financing and investing activities in the statement of cash flows.

QUICK STUDY

QS 12-1
Statement of cash flows

C1 C2 C3

Classify the following cash flows as operating, investing, or financing activities.

1. Sold long-term investments for cash.
2. Received cash payments from customers.
3. Paid cash for wages and salaries.
4. Purchased inventories for cash.
5. Paid cash dividends.
6. Issued common stock for cash.
7. Received cash interest on a note.
8. Paid cash interest on outstanding notes.
9. Received cash from sale of land at a loss.
10. Paid cash for property taxes on building.

QS 12-2
Transaction classification by activity

C2

Use the following information to determine this company's cash flows from operating activities using the indirect method.

QS 12-3
Computing cash from operations (indirect) P2

LOLLAND COMPANY
Selected Balance Sheet Information
December 31, 2011 and 2010

	2011	2010
Current assets		
Cash	$169,300	$ 53,600
Accounts receivable	50,000	64,000
Inventory	120,000	108,200
Current liabilities		
Accounts payable	60,800	51,400
Income taxes payable	4,100	4,400

LOLLAND COMPANY
Income Statement
For Year Ended December 31, 2011

Sales		$1,030,000
Cost of goods sold		663,200
Gross profit		366,800
Operating expenses		
Depreciation expense	$ 72,000	
Other expenses	243,000	315,000
Income before taxes		51,800
Income taxes expense		15,400
Net income		$ 36,400

The following selected information is from Manning Company's comparative balance sheets.

QS 12-4
Computing cash from asset sales
P3

At December 31	2011	2010
Furniture	$ 264,000	$ 369,000
Accumulated depreciation—Furniture	(174,400)	(221,400)

The income statement reports depreciation expense for the year of $36,000. Also, furniture costing $105,000 was sold for its book value. Compute the cash received from the sale of furniture.

The following selected information is from the Tanner Company's comparative balance sheets.

QS 12-5
Computing financing cash flows
P3

At December 31	2011	2010
Common stock, $10 par value	$ 210,000	$200,000
Paid-in capital in excess of par	1,134,000	684,000
Retained earnings	627,000	575,000

The company's net income for the year ended December 31, 2011, was $96,000.
1. Compute the cash received from the sale of its common stock during 2011.
2. Compute the cash paid for dividends during 2011.

QS 12-6

Computing cash from
operations (indirect)   P2

Use the following balance sheets and income statement to answer QS 12-6 through QS 12-11.

Use the indirect method to prepare the cash provided or used from operating activities section only of
the statement of cash flows for this company.

AMMONS, INC.
Comparative Balance Sheets
December 31, 2011

	2011	2010
Assets		
Cash	$189,600	$ 48,000
Accounts receivable, net	82,000	102,000
Inventory	171,600	191,600
Prepaid expenses	10,800	8,400
Furniture	218,000	238,000
Accum. depreciation—Furniture	(34,000)	(18,000)
Total assets	$638,000	$570,000
Liabilities and Equity		
Accounts payable	$ 30,000	$ 42,000
Wages payable	18,000	10,000
Income taxes payable	2,800	5,200
Notes payable (long-term)	58,000	138,000
Common stock, $5 par value	458,000	358,000
Retained earnings	71,200	16,800
Total liabilities and equity	$638,000	$570,000

AMMONS, INC.
Income Statement
For Year Ended December 31, 2011

Sales		$976,000
Cost of goods sold		628,000
Gross profit		348,000
Operating expenses		
Depreciation expense	$ 75,200	
Other expenses	178,200	253,400
Income before taxes		94,600
Income taxes expense		34,600
Net income		$ 60,000

QS 12-7

Computing cash
from asset sales   P3

Refer to the data in QS 12-6.

Furniture costing $110,000 is sold at its book value in 2011. Acquisitions of furniture total $90,000 cash,
on which no depreciation is necessary because it is acquired at year-end. What is the cash inflow related
to the sale of furniture?

QS 12-8

Computing financing
cash outflows   P3

Refer to the data in QS 12-6.

1. Assume that all common stock is issued for cash. What amount of cash dividends is paid during 2011?

2. Assume that no additional notes payable are issued in 2011. What cash amount is paid to reduce the
notes payable balance in 2011?

QS 12-9[B]

Computing cash received
from customers   P5

Refer to the data in QS 12-6.

1. How much cash is received from sales to customers for year 2011?

2. What is the net increase or decrease in cash for year 2011?

QS 12-10[B]

Computing operating
cash outflows   P5

Refer to the data in QS 12-6.

1. How much cash is paid to acquire merchandise inventory during year 2011?

2. How much cash is paid for operating expenses during year 2011?

QS 12-11[B]

Computing cash from
operations (direct)   P5

Refer to the data in QS 12-6.

Use the direct method to prepare the cash provided or used from operating activities section only of the
statement of cash flows for this company.

Financial data from three competitors in the same industry follow.

1. Which of the three competitors is in the strongest position as shown by its statement of cash flows?

2. Analyze and discuss the strength of Peña's cash flow on total assets ratio to that of Garcia.

QS 12-12
Analyses of sources
and uses of cash   A1   A2

($ thousands)	Peña	Garcia	Piniella
Cash provided (used) by operating activities	$ 140,000	$ 120,000	$ (48,000)
Cash provided (used) by investing activities			
Proceeds from sale of operating assets			52,000
Purchase of operating assets	(56,000)	(68,000)	
Cash provided (used) by financing activities			
Proceeds from issuance of debt			46,000
Repayment of debt	(12,000)		
Net increase (decrease) in cash	$ 72,000	$ 52,000	$ 50,000
Average total assets	$ 1,580,000	$ 1,250,000	$ 600,000

When a spreadsheet for a statement of cash flows is prepared, all changes in noncash balance sheet accounts are fully explained on the spreadsheet. Explain how these noncash balance sheet accounts are used to fully account for cash flows on a spreadsheet.

QS 12-13[A]
Noncash accounts
on a spreadsheet   P4

For each of the following separate cases, compute cash flows from operations. The list includes all balance sheet accounts related to operating activities.

QS 12-14
Computing cash flows from
operations (indirect)

P2

	Case A	Case B	Case C
Net income	$ 8,000	$200,000	$144,000
Depreciation expense	60,000	16,000	48,000
Accounts receivable increase (decrease)	80,000	40,000	(8,000)
Inventory increase (decrease)	(40,000)	(20,000)	21,000
Accounts payable increase (decrease)	48,000	(44,000)	28,000
Accrued liabilities increase (decrease)	(88,000)	24,000	(16,000)

Compute cash flows from investing activities using the following company information.

QS 12-15
Computing cash flows from
investing

P3

Sale of short-term investments	$12,000	Purchase of used equipment	$10,000
Cash collections from customers	32,000	Depreciation expense	4,000

Compute cash flows from financing activities using the following company information.

QS 12-16
Computing cash flows from
financing

P3

Additional short-term borrowings	$40,000	Cash dividends paid	$32,000
Purchase of short-term investments	10,000	Interest paid	16,000

Answer each of the following related to international accounting standards.

1. Which method, indirect or direct, is acceptable for reporting operating cash flows under IFRS?

2. For each of the following four cash flows, identify whether it is reported under the operating, investing or financing section (or some combination) within the indirect format of the statement of cash flows reported under IFRS and under U.S. GAAP.

QS 12-17
International cash flow
disclosures

C2   P2

Cash Flow Source	US GAAP Reporting	IFRS Reporting
a. Interest paid		
b. Dividends paid		
c. Interest received		
d. Dividends received		

Available with Connect Accounting **CONNECT**

EXERCISES

Exercise 12-1
Cash flow from
operations (indirect)

P2

Hehman Company reports net income of $530,000 for the year ended December 31, 2011. It also reports $95,400 depreciation expense and a $4,000 gain on the sale of machinery. Its comparative balance sheets reveal a $42,400 increase in accounts receivable, $21,730 increase in accounts payable, $11,660 decrease in prepaid expenses, and $16,430 decrease in wages payable.

Required

Prepare only the operating activities section of the statement of cash flows for 2011 using the *indirect method*.

Exercise 12-2
Cash flow classification
(indirect)   C2   C3   P2 ♟

The following transactions and events occurred during the year. Assuming that this company uses the *indirect method* to report cash provided by operating activities, indicate where each item would appear on its statement of cash flows by placing an *x* in the appropriate column.

	Statement of Cash Flows			Noncash Investing and Financing Activities	Not Reported on Statement or in Notes
	Operating Activities	Investing Activities	Financing Activities		
a. Paid cash to purchase inventory.	X				
b. Purchased land by issuing common stock.				X	
c. Accounts receivable decreased in the year.	X				
d. Sold equipment for cash, yielding a loss.		X			
e. Recorded depreciation expense.					
f. Income taxes payable increased in the year.					
g. Declared and paid a cash dividend.					
h. Accounts payable decreased in the year.					
i. Paid cash to settle notes payable					
j. Prepaid expenses increased in the year					

Exercise 12-3^B

Exercise 12-3[B]
Cash flow classification
(direct)   C2   C3   P5 ♟

The following transactions and events occurred during the year. Assuming that this company uses the *direct method* to report cash provided by operating activities, indicate where each item would appear on the statement of cash flows by placing an *x* in the appropriate column.

	Statement of Cash Flows			Noncash Investing and Financing Activities	Not Reported on Statement or in Notes
	Operating Activities	Investing Activities	Financing Activities		
a. Retired long-term notes payable by issuing common stock					
b. Recorded depreciation expense.					
c. Paid cash dividend that was declared in a prior period.					
d. Sold inventory for cash.					
e. Borrowed cash from bank by signing a 9-month note payable.					
f. Paid cash to purchase a patent.					
g. Accepted six-month note receivable in exchange for plant assets.					
h. Paid cash toward accounts payable.					
i. Collected cash from sales.					
j. Paid cash to acquire treasury stock.					

Zander Company's calendar-year 2011 income statement shows the following: Net Income, $395,000; Depreciation Expense, $48,980; Amortization Expense, $9,875; Gain on Sale of Plant Assets, $4,900. An examination of the company's current assets and current liabilities reveals the following changes (all from operating activities): Accounts Receivable decrease, $7,600; Merchandise Inventory decrease, $22,040; Prepaid Expenses increase, $2,000; Accounts Payable decrease, $5,000; Other Payables increase, $760. Use the *indirect method* to compute cash flow from operating activities.

Exercise
Cash flows from
activities (indirect)

P2

For each of the following three separate cases, use the information provided about the calendar-year 2010 operations of Kowa Company to compute the required cash flow information.

Exercise 12-5^B
Computation of cash
flows (direct)

P5

Case A: Compute cash received from customers:

Sales	$590,000
Accounts receivable, December 31, 2009	38,000
Accounts receivable, December 31, 2010	52,440

Case B: Compute cash paid for rent:

Rent expense	$117,400
Rent payable, December 31, 2009	6,700
Rent payable, December 31, 2010	5,561

Case C: Compute cash paid for merchandise:

Cost of goods sold	$651,000
Merchandise inventory, December 31, 2009	201,810
Accounts payable, December 31, 2009	84,760
Merchandise inventory, December 31, 2010	165,484
Accounts payable, December 31, 2010	105,102

Use the following income statement and information about changes in noncash current assets and current liabilities to prepare only the cash flows from operating activities section of the statement of cash flows using the *indirect* method.

Exercise 12-6
Cash flows from operating
activities (indirect)

P2

SEYMOUR COMPANY		
Income Statement		
For Year Ended December 31, 2011		
Sales		$2,175,000
Cost of goods sold		1,065,750
Gross profit		1,109,250
Operating expenses		
Salaries expense	$297,975	
Depreciation expense	52,200	
Rent expense	58,725	
Amortization expenses—Patents	6,525	
Utilities expense	23,925	439,350
		669,900
Gain on sale of equipment		8,700
Net income		$ 678,600

Changes in current asset and current liability accounts for the year that relate to operations follow.

Accounts receivable	$45,300 increase	Accounts payable	$10,075 decrease
Merchandise inventory	35,150 increase	Salaries payable	4,750 decrease

...er to the information about Seymour Company in Exercise 12-6.
... the *direct method* to prepare only the cash provided or used by operating activities section of the
...ement of cash flows for this company.

... the following information to determine this company's cash flows from investing activities.
...Equipment with a book value of $72,500 and an original cost of $158,000 was sold at a loss of $22,000.
...Paid $95,000 cash for a new truck.
...Sold land costing $315,000 for $400,000 cash, yielding a gain of $15,000.
d. Long-term investments in stock were sold for $94,700 cash, yielding a gain of $5,750.

Exercise 12-9
Cash flows from financing
activities

P3

Use the following information to determine this company's cash flows from financing activities.
a. Net income was $53,000.
b. Issued common stock for $75,000 cash.
c. Paid cash dividend of $13,000.
d. Paid $90,000 cash to settle a note payable at its $90,000 maturity value.
e. Paid $18,000 cash to acquire its treasury stock.
f. Purchased equipment for $67,000 cash.

Exercise 12-10
Preparation of statement of
cash flows (indirect)

C2 A2 P1 P2 P3

Use the following financial statements and additional information to (1) prepare a statement of cash flows
for the year ended June 30, 2011, using the *indirect method,* and (2) compute the company's cash flow
on total assets ratio for its fiscal year 2011.

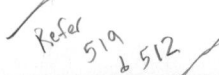
Refer 519 & 512

BOULWARE INC. Comparative Balance Sheets June 30, 2011 and 2010		
	2011	**2010**
Assets		
Cash	$ 84,663	$ 49,494
Accounts receivable, net	65,720	56,952
Inventory	62,620	106,107
Prepaid expenses	4,960	5,763
Equipment.........................	118,387	131,532
Accum. depreciation—Equipment	(26,350)	(10,848)
Total assets	$310,000	$339,000
Liabilities and Equity		
Accounts payable	$ 24,490	$ 35,256
Wages payable	6,510	17,628
Income taxes payable	2,170	4,068
Notes payable (long term)	31,953	76,953
Common stock, $5 par value	208,000	158,000
Retained earnings	36,877	47,095
Total liabilities and equity	$310,000	$339,000

BOULWARE INC. Income Statement For Year Ended June 30, 2011		
Sales		$976,600
Cost of goods sold		625,024
Gross profit		351,576
Operating expenses		
Depreciation expense	$ 88,753	
Other expenses	101,879	
Total operating expenses		190,632
		160,944
Other gains (losses)		
Gain on sale of equipment		3,125
Income before taxes		164,069
Income taxes expense		56,604
Net income		$107,465

Additional Information
a. A $45,000 note payable is retired at its carrying (book) value in exchange for cash.
b. The only changes affecting retained earnings are net income and cash dividends paid.
c. New equipment is acquired for $85,000 cash.

d. Received cash for the sale of equipment that had cost $98,145, yielding a $3,125 gain.

Net cash
used by operating

e. Prepaid Expenses and Wages Payable relate to Other Expenses on the income statement.

f. All purchases and sales of merchandise inventory are on credit.

204,833

Refer to the data in Exercise 12-10.

Using the *direct method,* prepare the statement of cash flows for the year ended June 30, 2011.

Exercise 12-11ᴮ

Preparation of statement of cash flows (direct)   C2 P1 P3 P5

Use the following information about the cash flows of Valencia Company to prepare a complete statement of cash flows (*direct method*) for the year ended December 31, 2011. Use a note disclosure for any noncash investing and financing activities.

Exercise 12-12ᴮ

Preparation of statement of cash flows (direct) and supporting note

C2 C3 C4 P1

Cash and cash equivalents balance, December 31, 2010	$ 43,000
Cash and cash equivalents balance, December 31, 2011	120,916
Cash received as interest	4,300
Cash paid for salaries	124,700
Bonds payable retired by issuing common stock (no gain or loss on retirement)	180,000
Cash paid to retire long-term notes payable	215,000
Cash received from sale of equipment	105,350
Cash received in exchange for six-month note payable	43,000
Land purchased by issuing long-term note payable	104,400
Cash paid for store equipment	40,850
Cash dividends paid	25,800
Cash paid for other expenses	68,800
Cash received from customers	834,200
Cash paid for merchandise	433,784

The following summarized Cash T-account reflects the total debits and total credits to the Cash account of Clarett Corporation for calendar year 2011.

(1) Use this information to prepare a complete statement of cash flows for year 2011. The cash provided or used by operating activities should be reported using the *direct method.*

(2) Refer to the statement of cash flows prepared for part 1 to answer the following questions *a* through *d*: (*a*) Which section—operating, investing, or financing—shows the largest cash (i) inflow and (ii) outflow? (*b*) What is the largest individual item among the investing cash outflows? (*c*) Are the cash proceeds larger from issuing notes or issuing stock? (*d*) Does the company have a net cash inflow or outflow from borrowing activities?

Exercise 12-13ᴮ

Preparation of statement of cash flows (direct) from Cash T-account

C2 A1 P1 P3 P5

```
Accounting System:                                                          _ □ ×
 File  Edit  Maintain  Tasks  Analysis  Options  Reports  Window  Help
┌──────────────────────────────────────── Cash ──────────────────────────── _ □ × ┐
│ Balance, Dec. 31, 2010 . . . . . . . . . . . . . . .   251,700                                   │
│ Receipts from customers . . . . . . . . . . . . . 7,074,800 │ Payments for merchandise . . . . . . . . . . . . . . . . .  2,934,822 │
│ Receipts from dividends . . . . . . . . . . . . . . .  876,180 │ Payments for wages . . . . . . . . . . . . . . . . . . . .  1,018,882 │
│ Receipts from land sale . . . . . . . . . . . . . . .  397,676 │ Payments for rent . . . . . . . . . . . . . . . . . . . . . .  586,964 │
│ Receipts from machinery sale . . . . . . .  606,826 │ Payments for interest . . . . . . . . . . . . . . . . . . .  398,693 │
│ Receipts from issuing stock . . . . . . . . . 2,846,224 │ Payments for taxes . . . . . . . . . . . . . . . . . . . . .  830,610 │
│ Receipts from borrowing . . . . . . . . . . . . 1,795,388 │ Payments for machinery . . . . . . . . . . . . . . . . .  3,130,900 │
│                                                    │ Payments for long-term investments . . . . . . .  2,295,200 │
│                                                    │ Payments for note payable . . . . . . . . . . . . . . .  905,787 │
│                                                    │ Payments for dividends . . . . . . . . . . . . . . . . . .  519,208 │
│                                                    │ Payments for treasury stock . . . . . . . . . . . . . .  398,693 │
│ Balance, Dec. 31, 2011 . . . . . . . . . . . . . $      ?                                                           │
└──────────────────────────────────────────────────────────────────────────┘
 Sales    Purchases    General    Payroll    Inventory    Company    Analysis
                        Ledger
```

Exercise 12-14
Reporting cash flows from operations (indirect)

C4 P2

Woodlock Company reports the following information for its recent calendar year.

Sales	$80,000	Accounts receivable increase	$ 5,000
Expenses		Inventory decrease	8,000
Cost of goods sold	50,000	Salaries payable increase	500
Salaries expense	12,000		
Depreciation expense	6,000		
Net income	$12,000		

Required

Prepare the operating activities section of the statement of cash flows for Woodlock Company using the indirect method.

Exercise 12-15
Reporting and interpreting cash flows from operations (indirect)

C4 P2

Portland Company disclosed the following information for its recent calendar year.

Revenues	$200,000	Accounts receivable decrease	$ 48,000
Expenses		Purchased a machine	20,000
Salaries expense	168,000	Salaries payable increase	36,000
Utilities expense	28,000	Other accrued liabilities decrease	16,000
Depreciation expense	29,200		
Other expenses	6,800		
Net loss	$ (32,000)		

Required

1. Prepare the operating activities section of the statement of cash flows using the indirect method.

2. What were the major reasons that this company was able to report a net loss but positive cash flow from operations?

3. Of the potential causes of differences between cash flow from operations and net income, which are the most important to investors?

Exercise 12-16
Statement of cash flows under IFRS (indirect)

P1 P2

Peugeot S.A. reports the following financial information for the year ended December 31, 2008 (euros in millions). Prepare its statement of cash flows under the indirect method.

Net loss	€ 500	Cash from sales of treasury stock and other	€ 812
Depreciation and amortization	3,679	Cash paid for dividends	361
Gains on disposals and other	(362)	Cash from disposal of plant assets and intangibles ...	88
Net increase in current assets	(417)	Cash paid for plant assets and intangibles	(3,331)
Net decrease in current liabilities ...	(2,338)	Cash and cash equivalents, December 31, 2007	5,937

Available with Connect Accounting **connect**

PROBLEM SET A

Problem 12-1A
Statement of cash flows (indirect method)

C2 C3 A1 P1 P2 P3

Georgia Company, a merchandiser, recently completed its calendar-year 2011 operations. For the year, (1) all sales are credit sales, (2) all credits to Accounts Receivable reflect cash receipts from customers, (3) all purchases of inventory are on credit, (4) all debits to Accounts Payable reflect cash payments for inventory, and (5) Other Expenses are paid in advance and are initially debited to Prepaid Expenses. The company's balance sheets and income statement follow.

(handwritten annotations) Know what goes in each Section – Statement of Cash Flows

GEORGIA COMPANY
Comparative Balance Sheets
December 31, 2011 and 2010

(handwritten) Skip cash at first

	2011	2010
Assets		
Cash	$ 49,800	$ 73,500
Accounts receivable	65,840	56,000
Merchandise inventory	277,000	252,000
Prepaid expenses	1,000	1,500
Equipment	158,500	107,500
Accum. depreciation—Equipment	(43,000)	(52,000)
Total assets	$509,140	$438,500
Liabilities and Equity		
Accounts payable	$ 42,965	$113,000
Short-term notes payable	10,000	7,000
Long-term notes payable	70,000	48,000
Common stock, $5 par value	162,750	151,000
Paid-in capital in excess		
of par, common stock	35,250	0
Retained earnings	188,175	119,500
Total liabilities and equity	$509,140	$438,500

(handwritten) LT Invest

GEORGIA COMPANY
Income Statement
For Year Ended December 31, 2011

Sales		$584,500
Cost of goods sold		281,000
Gross profit		303,500
Operating expenses		
Depreciation expense	$ 20,000	
Other expenses	132,800	152,800
Other gains (losses)		
Loss on sale of equipment		5,875
Income before taxes		144,825
Income taxes expense		24,250
Net income		$120,575

Additional Information on Year 2011 Transactions

a. The loss on the cash sale of equipment was $5,875 (details in *b*).

b. Sold equipment costing $46,500, with accumulated depreciation of $29,000, for $11,625 cash.

c. Purchased equipment costing $97,500 by paying $35,000 cash and signing a long-term note payable for the balance. *(handwritten)* Put at bottom under more infos

d. Borrowed $3,000 cash by signing a short-term note payable.

e. Paid $40,500 cash to reduce the long-term notes payable.

f. Issued 2,350 shares of common stock for $20 cash per share.

g. Declared and paid cash dividends of $51,900.

(handwritten) Put in operating section ~ Borrowed = Financing

Required

1. Prepare a complete statement of cash flows; report its operating activities using the *indirect method*. Disclose any noncash investing and financing activities in a note.

Check Cash from operating activities, $42,075

Analysis Component

2. Analyze and discuss the statement of cash flows prepared in part 1, giving special attention to the wisdom of the cash dividend payment.

Refer to the information reported about Georgia Company in Problem 12-1A.

Required

Prepare a complete statement of cash flows using a spreadsheet as in Exhibit 12A.1; report its operating activities using the indirect method. Identify the debits and credits in the Analysis of Changes columns with letters that correspond to the following list of transactions and events.

a. Net income was $120,575.

b. Accounts receivable increased.

c. Merchandise inventory increased.

d. Prepaid expenses decreased.

Problem 12-2A[A]
Cash flows spreadsheet
(indirect method)

P1 P2 P3 P4

e. Accounts payable decreased.

f. Depreciation expense was $20,000.

g. Sold equipment costing $46,500, with accumulated depreciation of $29,000, for $11,625 cash. This yielded a loss of $5,875.

h. Purchased equipment costing $97,500 by paying $35,000 cash and (i.) by signing a long-term note payable for the balance.

j. Borrowed $3,000 cash by signing a short-term note payable.

k. Paid $40,500 cash to reduce the long-term notes payable.

Check Analysis of Changes column totals, $594,850

l. Issued 2,350 shares of common stock for $20 cash per share.

m. Declared and paid cash dividends of $51,900.

Problem 12-3Aᴮ
Statement of cash flows (direct method)   C3 P1 P3 P5

Check Cash used in financing activities, $(42,400)

Refer to Georgia Company's financial statements and related information in Problem 12-1A.

Required

Prepare a complete statement of cash flows; report its operating activities according to the *direct method.* Disclose any noncash investing and financing activities in a note.

Problem 12-4A
Statement of cash flows (indirect method)   C3 P1 P2 P3

mhhe.com/wildFA5e

Memphis Corp., a merchandiser, recently completed its 2011 operations. For the year, (1) all sales are credit sales, (2) all credits to Accounts Receivable reflect cash receipts from customers, (3) all purchases of inventory are on credit, (4) all debits to Accounts Payable reflect cash payments for inventory, (5) Other Expenses are all cash expenses, and (6) any change in Income Taxes Payable reflects the accrual and cash payment of taxes. The company's balance sheets and income statement follow.

MEMPHIS CORPORATION
Comparative Balance Sheets
December 31, 2011 and 2010

	2011	2010
Assets		
Cash	$ 165,000	$137,000
Accounts receivable	82,000	74,000
Merchandise inventory	620,000	525,000
Equipment	345,000	240,000
Accum. depreciation—Equipment	(159,000)	(102,000)
Total assets	$1,053,000	$874,000
Liabilities and Equity		
Accounts payable	$ 160,000	$ 96,000
Income taxes payable	22,000	19,000
Common stock, $2 par value	588,000	560,000
Paid-in capital in excess of par value, common stock	201,000	159,000
Retained earnings	82,000	40,000
Total liabilities and equity	$1,053,000	$874,000

MEMPHIS CORPORATION
Income Statement
For Year Ended December 31, 2011

Sales		$1,794,000
Cost of goods sold		1,088,000
Gross profit		706,000
Operating expenses		
Depreciation expense	$ 57,000	
Other expenses	500,000	557,000
Income before taxes		149,000
Income taxes expense		22,000
Net income		$ 127,000

Additional Information on Year 2011 Transactions

a. Purchased equipment for $105,000 cash.

b. Issued 14,000 shares of common stock for $5 cash per share.

c. Declared and paid $85,000 in cash dividends.

Required

Prepare a complete statement of cash flows; report its cash inflows and cash outflows from operating activities according to the *indirect method*.

Check Cash from operating activities, $148,000

Refer to the information reported about Memphis Corporation in Problem 12-4A.

Required

Prepare a complete statement of cash flows using a spreadsheet as in Exhibit 12A.1; report operating activities under the indirect method. Identify the debits and credits in the Analysis of Changes columns with letters that correspond to the following list of transactions and events.

a. Net income was $127,000.

b. Accounts receivable increased.

c. Merchandise inventory increased.

d. Accounts payable increased.

e. Income taxes payable increased.

f. Depreciation expense was $57,000.

g. Purchased equipment for $105,000 cash.

h. Issued 14,000 shares at $5 cash per share.

i. Declared and paid $85,000 of cash dividends.

Problem 12-5A[A]

Cash flows spreadsheet (indirect method)

P1 P2 P3 P4

mhhe.com/wildFA5e

Check Analysis of Changes column totals, $614,000

Refer to Memphis Corporation's financial statements and related information in Problem 12-4A.

Required

Prepare a complete statement of cash flows; report its cash flows from operating activities according to the *direct method*.

Problem 12-6A[B]

Statement of cash flows (direct method) P1 P3 P5

mhhe.com/wildFA5e

Check Cash used in financing activities, $(15,000)

Rawling Company's 2011 income statement and selected balance sheet data at December 31, 2010 and 2011, follow ($ thousands).

Problem 12-7A

Computing cash flows from operations (indirect)

C4 P2

RAWLING COMPANY Selected Balance Sheet Accounts		
At Decmber 31	**2011**	**2010**
Accounts receivable	$280	$290
Inventory	99	77
Accounts payable	220	230
Salaries payable	44	35
Utilities payable	11	8
Prepaid insurance	13	14
Prepaid rent	11	9

RAWLING COMPANY Income Statement For Year Ended December 31, 2011	
Sales revenue	$48,600
Expenses	
Cost of goods sold	21,000
Depreciation expense	6,000
Salaries expense	9,000
Rent expense	4,500
Insurance expense	1,900
Interest expense	1,800
Utilities expense	1,400
Net income	$ 3,000

Required

Prepare the cash flows from operating activities section only of the company's 2011 statement of cash flows using the indirect method.

Check Cash from operating activities, $8,989

Problem 12-8A[B]
Computing cash flows from operations (direct)

C4 P5

Refer to the information in Problem 12-7A.

Required

Prepare the cash flows from operating activities section only of the company's 2011 statement of cash flows using the direct method.

PROBLEM SET B

Problem 12-1B
Statement of cash flows (indirect method)

C2 C3 A1 P1 P2 P3

Wilson Corporation, a merchandiser, recently completed its calendar-year 2011 operations. For the year, (1) all sales are credit sales, (2) all credits to Accounts Receivable reflect cash receipts from customers, (3) all purchases of inventory are on credit, (4) all debits to Accounts Payable reflect cash payments for inventory, and (5) Other Expenses are paid in advance and are initially debited to Prepaid Expenses. The company's balance sheets and income statement follow.

WILSON CORPORATION
Income Statement
For Year Ended December 31, 2011

Sales		$585,000
Cost of goods sold		285,000
Gross profit		300,000
Operating expenses		
Depreciation expense	$ 20,000	
Other expenses	134,000	
Total operating expenses		154,000
		146,000
Other gains (losses)		
Loss on sale of equipment		5,625
Income before taxes		140,375
Income taxes expense		24,250
Net income		$116,125

WILSON CORPORATION
Comparative Balance Sheets
December 31, 2011 and 2010

	2011	2010
Assets		
Cash	$ 49,400	$ 74,000
Accounts receivable	65,830	55,000
Merchandise inventory	277,000	252,000
Prepaid expenses	1,250	1,600
Equipment	158,500	107,500
Accum. depreciation—Equipment	(36,625)	(46,000)
Total assets	$515,355	$444,100
Liabilities and Equity		
Accounts payable	$ 55,380	$112,000
Short-term notes payable	9,000	7,000
Long-term notes payable	70,000	48,250
Common stock, $5 par	162,500	150,750
Paid-in capital in excess of par, common stock	35,250	0
Retained earnings	183,225	126,100
Total liabilities and equity	$515,355	$444,100

Additional Information on Year 2011 Transactions

a. The loss on the cash sale of equipment was $5,625 (details in *b*).

b. Sold equipment costing $46,500, with accumulated depreciation of $29,375, for $11,500 cash.

c. Purchased equipment costing $97,500 by paying $25,000 cash and signing a long-term note payable for the balance.

d. Borrowed $2,000 cash by signing a short-term note payable.

e. Paid $50,750 cash to reduce the long-term notes payable.

f. Issued 2,350 shares of common stock for $20 cash per share.

g. Declared and paid cash dividends of $59,000.

Required

Check Cash from operating activities, $49,650

1. Prepare a complete statement of cash flows; report its operating activities using the *indirect method*. Disclose any noncash investing and financing activities in a note.

Analysis Component

2. Analyze and discuss the statement of cash flows prepared in part 1, giving special attention to the wisdom of the cash dividend payment.

Refer to the information reported about Wilson Corporation in Problem 12-1B.

Problem 12-2B^A
Cash flows spreadsheet
(indirect method)

P1 P2 P3 P4

Required

Prepare a complete statement of cash flows using a spreadsheet as in Exhibit 12A.1; report its operating activities using the *indirect method*. Identify the debits and credits in the Analysis of Changes columns with letters that correspond to the following list of transactions and events.

  a. Net income was $116,125.

  b. Accounts receivable increased.

  c. Merchandise inventory increased.

  d. Prepaid expenses decreased.

  e. Accounts payable decreased.

  f. Depreciation expense was $20,000.

  g. Sold equipment costing $46,500, with accumulated depreciation of $29,375, for $11,500 cash. This yielded a loss of $5,625.

  h. Purchased equipment costing $97,500 by paying $25,000 cash and **(i.)** by signing a long-term note payable for the balance.

  j. Borrowed $2,000 cash by signing a short-term note payable.

  k. Paid $50,750 cash to reduce the long-term notes payable.

  l. Issued 2,350 shares of common stock for $20 cash per share.

  m. Declared and paid cash dividends of $59,000.

Check Analysis of Changes column totals, $604,175

Refer to Wilson Corporation's financial statements and related information in Problem 12-1B.

Problem 12-3B^B
Statement of cash flows (direct method)

C3 P1 P3 P5

Required

Prepare a complete statement of cash flows; report its operating activities according to the *direct method*. Disclose any noncash investing and financing activities in a note.

Check Cash used in financing activities, $(60,750)

Prius Company, a merchandiser, recently completed its 2011 operations. For the year, (1) all sales are credit sales, (2) all credits to Accounts Receivable reflect cash receipts from customers, (3) all purchases of inventory are on credit, (4) all debits to Accounts Payable reflect cash payments for inventory, (5) Other Expenses are cash expenses, and (6) any change in Income Taxes Payable reflects the accrual and cash payment of taxes. The company's balance sheets and income statement follow.

Problem 12-4B
Statement of cash flows (indirect method)

C3 P1 P2 P3

PRIUS COMPANY		
Comparative Balance Sheets		
December 31, 2011 and 2010		
	2011	**2010**
Assets		
Cash	$ 164,000	$ 131,000
Accounts receivable	82,000	70,000
Merchandise inventory	605,000	515,000
Equipment	350,000	276,000
Accum. depreciation—Equipment	(157,000)	(102,000)
Total assets	$1,044,000	$ 890,000
Liabilities and Equity		
Accounts payable	$ 173,000	$ 119,000
Income taxes payable	20,000	17,000
Common stock, $2 par value	580,000	560,000
Paid-in capital in excess		
of par, common stock	193,000	163,000
Retained earnings	78,000	31,000
Total liabilities and equity	$1,044,000	$ 890,000

PRIUS COMPANY		
Income Statement		
For Year Ended December 31, 2011		
Sales		$1,792,000
Cost of goods sold		1,087,000
Gross profit		705,000
Operating expenses		
Depreciation expense	$ 55,000	
Other expenses	494,000	549,000
Income before taxes		156,000
Income taxes expense		24,000
Net income		$ 132,000

Additional Information on Year 2011 Transactions

a. Purchased equipment for $74,000 cash.

b. Issued 10,000 shares of common stock for $5 cash per share.

c. Declared and paid $85,000 of cash dividends.

Required

Check Cash from operating
activities, $142,000

Prepare a complete statement of cash flows; report its cash inflows and cash outflows from operating activities according to the *indirect method*.

Problem 12-5B^A
Cash flows spreadsheet
(indirect method)

P1 P2 P3 P4

Refer to the information reported about Prius Company in Problem 12-4B.

Required

Prepare a complete statement of cash flows using a spreadsheet as in Exhibit 12A.1; report operating activities under the *indirect method*. Identify the debits and credits in the Analysis of Changes columns with letters that correspond to the following list of transactions and events.

a. Net income was $132,000.

b. Accounts receivable increased.

c. Merchandise inventory increased.

d. Accounts payable increased.

e. Income taxes payable increased.

f. Depreciation expense was $55,000.

g. Purchased equipment for $74,000 cash.

Check Analysis of Changes column
totals, $555,000

h. Issued 10,000 shares at $5 cash per share.

i. Declared and paid $85,000 of cash dividends.

Problem 12-6B^B
Statement of cash flows
(direct method)   P1 P3 P5

Check Cash used by financing
activities, $(35,000)

Refer to Prius Company's financial statements and related information in Problem 12-4B.

Required

Prepare a complete statement of cash flows; report its cash flows from operating activities according to the *direct method*.

Problem 12-7B
Computing cash flows from
operations (indirect)

C4 P2

Kodak Company's 2011 income statement and selected balance sheet data at December 31, 2010 and 2011, follow ($ thousands).

KODAK COMPANY
Income Statement
For Year Ended December 31, 2011

Sales revenue	$312,000
Expenses	
Cost of goods sold	144,000
Depreciation expense	64,000
Salaries expense	40,000
Rent expense	10,000
Insurance expense	5,200
Interest expense	4,800
Utilities expense	4,000
Net income	$ 40,000

KODAK COMPANY
Selected Balance Sheet Accounts

At December 31	2011	2010
Accounts receivable	$720	$600
Inventory	172	196
Accounts payable	480	520
Salaries payable	180	120
Utilities payable	40	0
Prepaid insurance	28	36
Prepaid rent	20	40

Required

Prepare the cash flows from operating activities section only of the company's 2011 statement of cash flows using the indirect method.

Check   Cash from operating activities, $103,992

Refer to the information in Problem 12-7B.

Problem 12-8B[B]
Computing cash flows from operations (direct)

C4   P5

Required

Prepare the cash flows from operating activities section only of the company's 2011 statement of cash flows using the direct method.

(This serial problem began in Chapter 1 and continues through most of the book. If previous chapter segments were not completed, the serial problem can begin at this point. It is helpful, but not necessary, to use the Working Papers that accompany the book.)

SERIAL PROBLEM

Success Systems

SP 12   Adriana Lopez, owner of Success Systems, decides to prepare a statement of cash flows for her business. (Although the serial problem allowed for various ownership changes in earlier chapters, we will prepare the statement of cash flows using the following financial data.)

SUCCESS SYSTEMS
Comparative Balance Sheets
December 31, 2009, and March 31, 2010

	2010	2009
Assets		
Cash	$ 77,845	$58,160
Accounts receivable	22,720	5,668
Merchandise inventory	704	0
Computer supplies	2,005	580
Prepaid insurance	1,110	1,665
Prepaid rent	825	825
Office equipment	8,000	8,000
Accumulated depreciation—Office equipment	(800)	(400)
Computer equipment	20,000	20,000
Accumulated depreciation— Computer equipment	(2,500)	(1,250)
Total assets	$129,909	$93,248
Liabilities and Equity		
Accounts payable	$ 0	$ 1,100
Wages payable	875	500
Unearned computer service revenue	0	1,500
Common stock	108,000	83,000
Retained earnings	21,034	7,148
Total liabilities and equity	$129,909	$93,248

SUCCESS SYSTEMS
Income Statement
For Three Months Ended March 31, 2010

Computer services revenue		$25,160
Net sales		18,693
Total revenue		43,853
Cost of goods sold	$14,052	
Depreciation expense— Office equipment	400	
Depreciation expense— Computer equipment	1,250	
Wages expense	3,250	
Insurance expense	555	
Rent expense	2,475	
Computer supplies expense	1,305	
Advertising expense	600	
Mileage expense	320	
Repairs expense—Computer	960	
Total expenses		25,167
Net income		$18,686

Required

Prepare a statement of cash flows for Success Systems using the *indirect method* for the three months ended March 31, 2010. Recall that the owner Adriana Lopez contributed $25,000 to the business in exchange for additional stock in the first quarter of 2010 and has received $4,800 in cash dividends.

Check   Cash flows used by operations: $(515)

BEYOND THE NUMBERS

**REPORTING IN
ACTION**

C4 A1

BTN 12-1   Refer to **Best Buy**'s financial statements in Appendix A to answer the following.

1. Is Best Buy's statement of cash flows prepared under the direct method or the indirect method? How do you know?
2. For each fiscal year 2009, 2008, and 2007, is the amount of cash provided by operating activities more or less than the cash paid for dividends?
3. What is the largest amount in reconciling the difference between net income and cash flow from operating activities in 2009? In 2008? In 2007?
4. Identify the largest cash inflow and outflow for investing *and* for financing activities in 2009 and in 2008.

Fast Forward

5. Obtain Best Buy's financial statements for a fiscal year ending after February 28, 2009, from either its Website (**BestBuy.com**) or the SEC's database (**WWW.SEC.gov**). Since February 28, 2009, what are Best Buy's largest cash outflows and cash inflows in the investing and in the financing sections of its statement of cash flows?

**COMPARATIVE
ANALYSIS**

A1 A2

BTN 12-2   Key figures for **Best Buy** and **RadioShack** follow.

($ millions)	Best Buy			RadioShack		
	Current Year	1 Year Prior	2 Years Prior	Current Year	1 Year Prior	2 Years Prior
Operating cash flows	$ 1,877	$ 2,025	$ 1,762	$ 274.6	$ 379.0	$ 314.8
Total assets	15,826	12,758	13,570	2,283.5	1,989.6	2,070.0

Required

1. Compute the recent two years' cash flow on total assets ratios for Best Buy and RadioShack.
2. What does the cash flow on total assets ratio measure?
3. Which company has the highest cash flow on total assets ratio for the periods shown?
4. Does the cash flow on total assets ratio reflect on the quality of earnings? Explain.

**ETHICS
CHALLENGE**

C1 C2 A1

BTN 12-3   Kaelyn Gish is preparing for a meeting with her banker. Her business is finishing its fourth year of operations. In the first year, it had negative cash flows from operations. In the second and third years, cash flows from operations were positive. However, inventory costs rose significantly in year 4, and cash flows from operations will probably be down 25%. Gish wants to secure a line of credit from her banker as a financing buffer. From experience, she knows the banker will scrutinize operating cash flows for years 1 through 4 and will want a projected number for year 5. Gish knows that a steady progression upward in operating cash flows for years 1 through 4 will help her case. She decides to use her discretion as owner and considers several business actions that will turn her operating cash flow in year 4 from a decrease to an increase.

Required

1. Identify two business actions Gish might take to improve cash flows from operations.
2. Comment on the ethics and possible consequences of Gish's decision to pursue these actions.

BTN 12-4 Your friend, Hanna Willard, recently completed the second year of her business and just received annual financial statements from her accountant. Willard finds the income statement and balance sheet informative but does not understand the statement of cash flows. She says the first section is especially confusing because it contains a lot of additions and subtractions that do not make sense to her. Willard adds, "The income statement tells me the business is more profitable than last year and that's most important. If I want to know how cash changes, I can look at comparative balance sheets."

COMMUNICATING IN PRACTICE

C1 C4

Required

Write a half-page memorandum to your friend explaining the purpose of the statement of cash flows. Speculate as to why the first section is so confusing and how it might be rectified.

BTN 12-5 Access the March 23, 2009, filing of the 10-K report (for fiscal year ending January 31, 2009) of **J. Crew Group, Inc.**, at <u>www.sec.gov</u>.

TAKING IT TO THE NET

A1

Required

1. Does J. Crew use the direct or indirect method to construct its consolidated statement of cash flows?
2. For the fiscal year ended January 31, 2009, what is the largest item in reconciling the net income to net cash provided by operating activities?
3. In the recent three years, has the company been more successful in generating operating cash flows or in generating net income? Identify the figures to support the answer.
4. In the year ended January 31, 2009, what was the largest cash outflow for investing activities *and* for financing activities?
5. What item(s) does J. Crew report as supplementary cash flow information?
6. Does J. Crew report any noncash financing activities for fiscal year 2009? Identify them, if any.

BTN 12-6 Team members are to coordinate and independently answer one question within each of the following three sections. Team members should then report to the team and confirm or correct teammates' answers.

TEAMWORK IN ACTION

C1 C4 A1 P2 P5

1. Answer *one* of the following questions about the statement of cash flows.
   a. What are this statement's reporting objectives?
   b. What two methods are used to prepare it? Identify similarities and differences between them.
   c. What steps are followed to prepare the statement?
   d. What types of analyses are often made from this statement's information?
2. Identify and explain the adjustment from net income to obtain cash flows from operating activities using the indirect method for *one* of the following items.
   a. Noncash operating revenues and expenses.
   b. Nonoperating gains and losses.
   c. Increases and decreases in noncash current assets.
   d. Increases and decreases in current liabilities.
3. [B]Identify and explain the formula for computing cash flows from operating activities using the direct method for *one* of the following items.
   a. Cash receipts from sales to customers.
   b. Cash paid for merchandise inventory.
   c. Cash paid for wages and operating expenses.
   d. Cash paid for interest and taxes.

Note: For teams of more than four, some pairing within teams is necessary. Use as an in-class activity or as an assignment. If used in class, specify a time limit on each part. Conclude with reports to the entire class, using team rotation. Each team can prepare responses on a transparency.

ENTREPRENEURIAL DECISION

C1   A1

BTN 12-7   Review the chapter's opener involving **Jungle Jim's International Market.**

Required

1. In a business such as Jungle Jim's, monitoring cash flow is always a priority. Even though Jungle Jim's now has thousands in annual sales and earns a positive net income, explain how cash flow can lag behind earnings.
2. Jungle Jim's is a closely held corporation. What are potential sources of financing for its future expansion?

C2   A1

BTN 12-8   Jenna and Matt Wilder are completing their second year operating Mountain High, a downhill ski area and resort. Mountain High reports a net loss of $(10,000) for its second year, which includes an $85,000 extraordinary loss from fire. This past year also involved major purchases of plant assets for renovation and expansion, yielding a year-end total asset amount of $800,000. Mountain High's net cash outflow for its second year is $(5,000); a summarized version of its statement of cash flows follows:

Net cash flow provided by operating activities	$295,000
Net cash flow used by investing activities	(310,000)
Net cash flow provided by financing activities	10,000

Required

Write a one-page memorandum to the Wilders evaluating Mountain High's current performance and assessing its future. Give special emphasis to cash flow data and their interpretation.

HITTING THE ROAD

C1

BTN 12-9   Visit **The Motley Fool**'s Website (**Fool.com**). Click on the sidebar link titled *Fool's School* (or *Fool.com/School*). Identify and select the link *How to Value Stocks.*

Required

1. Click on *Introduction to Valuation,* and then *Cash-Flow-Based Valuations.* How does the Fool's school define cash flow? What is the School's reasoning for this definition?
2. Per the school's instruction, why do analysts focus on earnings before interest and taxes (EBIT)?
3. Visit other links at this Website that interest you such as "How to Read a Balance Sheet," or find out what the "Fool's Ratio" is. Write a half-page report on what you find.

GLOBAL DECISION

C1   C2   C4

BTN 12-10   Key comparative information for **GOME** (**www.GOME.com.hk**), which is the leading chain retailer of consumer electronic products and household appliances in China, follows (in RMB).

(RMB millions)	Current Year	1 Year Prior	2 Years Prior
Operating cash flows	3,610,360	2,560,723	(116,931)
Total assets	27,495,104	29,837,493	21,176,229

Required

1. Compute the recent two years' cash flow on total assets ratio for GOME.
2. How does GOME's ratio compare to Best Buy's and RadioShack's ratios from BTN 12-2?

ANSWERS TO MULTIPLE CHOICE QUIZ

1. b;

Net income	$15,200
Depreciation expense	10,000
Gain on sale of land	(3,000)
Increase in inventory	(1,500)
Increase in accounts payable	2,850
Net cash provided by operations	$23,550

2. c; cash received from sale of machine is reported as an investing activity.

3. d; FASB requires cash interest paid to be reported under operating.

4. a; Cash paid for salaries and wages = $255,000 + $8,200 − $10,900 = $252,300

5. e; Increase in inventory = $112,000 − $105,000 = $7,000
Increase in accounts payable = $101,300 − $98,500 = $2,800
Cash paid for merchandise = $545,000 + $7,000 − $2,800 = $549,200

13

Analyzing and Interpreting Financial Statements

"What goes on at The Motley Fool . . . is similar to what goes on in a library"
—Tom Gardner (David Gardner on left)

◀◀ A Look Back

Chapter 12 focused on reporting and analyzing cash inflows and cash outflows. We explained how to prepare, analyze, and interpret the statement of cash flows.

◀▶ A Look at This Chapter

This chapter emphasizes the analysis and interpretation of financial statement information. We learn to apply horizontal, vertical, and ratio analyses to better understand company performance and financial condition.

Motley Fool

ALEXANDRIA, VA—In Shakespeare's Elizabethan comedy *As You Like It,* only the fool could speak truthfully to the King without getting his head lopped off. Inspired by Shakespeare's stage character, Tom and David Gardner vowed to become modern-day fools who tell it like it is. With under $10,000 in start-up money, the brothers launched **The Motley Fool (Fool.com).** And befitting of a Shakespearean play, the two say they are "dedicated to educating, amusing, and enriching individuals in search of the truth."

The Gardners do not fear the wrath of any King, real or fictional. They are intent on exposing the truth, as they see it, "that the financial world preys on ignorance and fear." As Tom explains, "There is such a great need in the general populace for financial information." Who can argue, given their brilliant success through practically every medium; including their Website, radio shows, newspaper columns, online store, investment newsletters, and global expansion.

Despite the brothers' best efforts, however, ordinary people still do not fully use information contained in financial statements. For instance, discussions keep appearing on The Motley Fool's online bulletin board that can be easily resolved using reliable and available accounting data. So, it would seem that the Fools must continue their work of "educating and enriching" individuals.

Resembling The Motley Fools' objectives, this chapter introduces horizontal and vertical analyses—tools used to reveal crucial trends and insights from financial information. It also expands on ratio analysis, which gives insight into a company's financial condition and performance. By arming ourselves with the information contained in this chapter and the investment advice of The Motley Fool, *we* can be sure not to play the fool in today's financial world.

[Sources: *Motley Fool Website,* March 2010; *Entrepreneur,* July 1997; *What to Do with Your Money Now,* June 2002; *USA Weekend,* July 2004; *Washington Post,* November 2007; *Money after 40,* April 2007]

Learning Objectives

CAP

Conceptual

C1 Explain the purpose of analysis. *(p. 564)*

C2 Identify the building blocks of analysis. *(p. 565)*

C3 Describe standards for comparisons in analysis. *(p. 566)*

C4 Identify the tools of analysis. *(p. 566)*

Analytical

A1 Summarize and report results of analysis. *(p. 585)*

A2 *Appendix 13A*—Explain the form and assess the content of a complete income statement. *(p. 588)*

LP13

Procedural

P1 Explain and apply methods of horizontal analysis. *(p. 566)*

P2 Describe and apply methods of vertical analysis. *(p. 571)*

P3 Define and apply ratio analysis. *(p. 575)*

This chapter shows how we use financial statements to evaluate a company's financial performance and condition. We explain financial statement analysis, its basic building blocks, the information available, standards for comparisons, and tools of analysis. Three major analysis tools are presented: horizontal analysis, vertical analysis, and ratio analysis. We apply each of these tools using **Best Buy**'s financial statements, and we introduce comparative analysis using **RadioShack** (and sometimes **GOME**). This chapter expands and organizes the ratio analyses introduced at the end of each chapter.

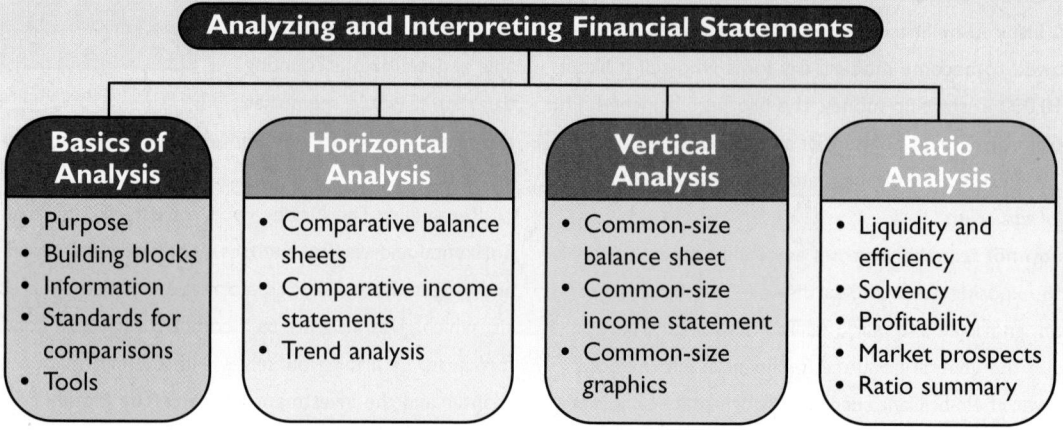

Analyzing and Interpreting Financial Statements

Basics of Analysis	Horizontal Analysis	Vertical Analysis	Ratio Analysis
• Purpose • Building blocks • Information • Standards for comparisons • Tools	• Comparative balance sheets • Comparative income statements • Trend analysis	• Common-size balance sheet • Common-size income statement • Common-size graphics	• Liquidity and efficiency • Solvency • Profitability • Market prospects • Ratio summary

Basics of Analysis

Video13.1

Financial statement analysis applies analytical tools to general-purpose financial statements and related data for making business decisions. It involves transforming accounting data into more useful information. Financial statement analysis reduces our reliance on hunches, guesses, and intuition as well as our uncertainty in decision making. It does not lessen the need for expert judgment; instead, it provides us an effective and systematic basis for making business decisions. This section describes the purpose of financial statement analysis, its information sources, the use of comparisons, and some issues in computations.

Purpose of Analysis

C1 Explain the purpose of analysis.

Internal users of accounting information are those involved in strategically managing and operating the company. They include managers, officers, internal auditors, consultants, budget directors, and market researchers. The purpose of financial statement analysis for these users is to provide strategic information to improve company efficiency and effectiveness in providing products and services.

External users of accounting information are *not* directly involved in running the company. They include shareholders, lenders, directors, customers, suppliers, regulators, lawyers, brokers, and the press. External users rely on financial statement analysis to make better and more informed decisions in pursuing their own goals.

Point: Financial statement analysis tools are also used for personal financial investment decisions.

Point: Financial statement analysis is a topic on the CPA, CMA, CIA, and CFA exams.

We can identify other uses of financial statement analysis. Shareholders and creditors assess company prospects to make investing and lending decisions. A board of directors analyzes financial statements in monitoring management's decisions. Employees and unions use financial statements in labor negotiations. Suppliers use financial statement information in establishing credit terms. Customers analyze financial statements in deciding whether to establish supply relationships. Public utilities set customer rates by analyzing financial statements. Auditors use financial statements in assessing the "fair presentation" of their clients' financial results. Analyst services such as **Dun & Bradstreet, Moody's,** and **Standard & Poor's** use financial statements in making buy-sell recommendations and in setting credit ratings. The common goal of these users is to evaluate company performance and financial condition. This includes evaluating (1) past and current performance, (2) current financial position, and (3) future performance and risk.

Building Blocks of Analysis

Financial statement analysis focuses on one or more elements of a company's financial condition or performance. Our analysis emphasizes four areas of inquiry—with varying degrees of importance. These four areas are described and illustrated in this chapter and are considered the *building blocks* of financial statement analysis:

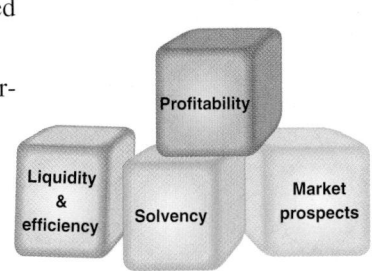

C2 Identify the building blocks of analysis.

- **Liquidity** and **efficiency**—ability to meet short-term obligations and to efficiently generate revenues.
- **Solvency**—ability to generate future revenues and meet long-term obligations.
- **Profitability**—ability to provide financial rewards sufficient to attract and retain financing.
- **Market prospects**—ability to generate positive market expectations.

Applying the building blocks of financial statement analysis involves determining (1) the objectives of analysis and (2) the relative emphasis among the building blocks. We distinguish among these four building blocks to emphasize the different aspects of a company's financial condition or performance, yet we must remember that these areas of analysis are interrelated. For instance, a company's operating performance is affected by the availability of financing and short-term liquidity conditions. Similarly, a company's credit standing is not limited to satisfactory short-term liquidity but depends also on its profitability and efficiency in using assets. Early in our analysis, we need to determine the relative emphasis of each building block. Emphasis and analysis can later change as a result of evidence collected.

Decision Insight

Chips and Brokers The phrase *blue chips* refers to stock of big, profitable companies. The phrase comes from poker; where the most valuable chips are blue. The term *brokers* refers to those who execute orders to buy or sell stock. The term comes from wine retailers—individuals who broach (break) wine casks.

Information for Analysis

Some users, such as managers and regulatory authorities, are able to receive special financial reports prepared to meet their analysis needs. However, most users must rely on **general-purpose financial statements** that include the (1) income statement, (2) balance sheet, (3) statement of stockholders' equity (or statement of retained earnings), (4) statement of cash flows, and (5) notes to these statements.

Financial reporting refers to the communication of financial information useful for making investment, credit, and other business decisions. Financial reporting includes not only general-purpose financial statements but also information from SEC 10-K or other filings, press releases, shareholders' meetings, forecasts, management letters, auditors' reports, and Webcasts.

Management's Discussion and Analysis (MD&A) is one example of useful information outside traditional financial statements. **Best Buy**'s MD&A (available at **BestBuy.com**), for example, begins with an overview and strategic initiatives. It then discusses operating results followed by liquidity and capital resources—roughly equivalent to investing and financing. The final few parts discuss special financing arrangements, key accounting policies, interim results, and the next year's outlook. The MD&A is an excellent starting point in understanding a company's business activities.

Decision Insight

Analysis Online Many Websites offer free access and screening of companies by key numbers such as earnings, sales, and book value. For instance, **Standard & Poor's** has information for more than 10,000 stocks (**StandardandPoors.com**).

Standards for Comparisons

C3 Describe standards for comparisons in analysis.

When interpreting measures from financial statement analysis, we need to decide whether the measures indicate good, bad, or average performance. To make such judgments, we need standards (benchmarks) for comparisons that include the following:

- *Intracompany*—The company under analysis can provide standards for comparisons based on its own prior performance and relations between its financial items. **Best Buy**'s current net income, for instance, can be compared with its prior years' net income and in relation to its revenues or total assets.
- *Competitor*—One or more direct competitors of the company being analyzed can provide standards for comparisons. **Coca-Cola**'s profit margin, for instance, can be compared with **PepsiCo**'s profit margin.
- *Industry*—Industry statistics can provide standards of comparisons. Such statistics are available from services such as **Dun & Bradstreet**, **Standard & Poor's**, and **Moody's**.
- *Guidelines (rules of thumb)*—General standards of comparisons can develop from experience. Examples are the 2:1 level for the current ratio or 1:1 level for the acid-test ratio. Guidelines, or rules of thumb, must be carefully applied because context is crucial.

Point: Each chapter's *Reporting in Action* problems engage students in *intracompany* analysis, whereas *Comparative Analysis* problems require competitor analysis (Best Buy vs. RadioShack).

All of these comparison standards are useful when properly applied, yet measures taken from a selected competitor or group of competitors are often best. Intracompany and industry measures are also important. Guidelines or rules of thumb should be applied with care, and then only if they seem reasonable given past experience and industry norms.

Tools of Analysis

C4 Identify the tools of analysis.

Three of the most common tools of financial statement analysis are

1. **Horizontal analysis**—Comparison of a company's financial condition and performance across time.
2. **Vertical analysis**—Comparison of a company's financial condition and performance to a base amount.
3. **Ratio analysis**—Measurement of key relations between financial statement items.

The remainder of this chapter describes these analysis tools and how to apply them.

Quick Check   Answers—p. 592

1. Who are the intended users of general-purpose financial statements?
2. General-purpose financial statements consist of what information?
3. Which of the following is *least* useful as a basis for comparison when analyzing ratios?
   (*a*) Company results from a different economic setting. (*b*) Standards from past experience.
   (*c*) Rule-of-thumb standards. (*d*) Industry averages.
4. What is the preferred basis of comparison for ratio analysis?

Horizontal Analysis

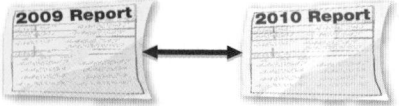

Analysis of any single financial number is of limited value. Instead, much of financial statement analysis involves identifying and describing relations between numbers, groups of numbers, and changes in those numbers. Horizontal analysis refers to examination of financial statement data *across time*. [The term *horizontal analysis* arises from the left-to-right (or right-to-left) movement of our eyes as we review comparative financial statements across time.]

Comparative Statements

P1 Explain and apply methods of horizontal analysis.

Comparing amounts for two or more successive periods often helps in analyzing financial statements. **Comparative financial statements** facilitate this comparison by showing financial amounts in side-by-side columns on a single statement, called a *comparative format*. Using figures from **Best Buy**'s financial statements, this section explains how to compute dollar changes and percent changes for comparative statements.

Computation of Dollar Changes and Percent Changes

Comparing financial statements over relatively short time periods—two to three years—is often done by analyzing changes in line items. A change analysis usually includes analyzing absolute dollar amount changes and percent changes. Both analyses are relevant because dollar changes can yield large percent changes inconsistent with their importance. For instance, a 50% change from a base figure of $100 is less important than the same percent change from a base amount of $100,000 in the same statement. Reference to dollar amounts is necessary to retain a proper perspective and to assess the importance of changes. We compute the *dollar change* for a financial statement item as follows:

Example: What is a more significant change, a 70% increase on a $1,000 expense or a 30% increase on a $400,000 expense? *Answer:* The 30% increase.

$$\text{Dollar change} = \text{Analysis period amount} - \text{Base period amount}$$

Analysis period is the point or period of time for the financial statements under analysis, and *base period* is the point or period of time for the financial statements used for comparison purposes. The prior year is commonly used as a base period. We compute the *percent change* by dividing the dollar change by the base period amount and then multiplying this quantity by 100 as follows:

$$\text{Percent change } (\%) = \frac{\text{Analysis period amount} - \text{Base period amount}}{\text{Base period amount}} \times 100$$

We can always compute a dollar change, but we must be aware of a few rules in working with percent changes. To illustrate, look at four separate cases in this chart:

Case	Analysis Period	Base Period	Change Analysis Dollar	Change Analysis Percent
A	$ 1,500	$(4,500)	$ 6,000	—
B	(1,000)	2,000	(3,000)	—
C	8,000	—	8,000	—
D	0	10,000	(10,000)	(100%)

When a negative amount appears in the base period and a positive amount in the analysis period (or vice versa), we cannot compute a meaningful percent change; see cases A and B. Also, when no value is in the base period, no percent change is computable; see case C. Finally, when an item has a value in the base period and zero in the analysis period, the decrease is 100 percent; see case D.

Example: When there is a value in the base period and zero in the analysis period, the decrease is 100%. Why isn't the reverse situation an increase of 100%? *Answer:* A 100% increase of zero is still zero.

It is common when using horizontal analysis to compare amounts to either average or median values from prior periods (average and median values smooth out erratic or unusual fluctuations).[1] We also commonly round percents and ratios to one or two decimal places, but practice on this matter is not uniform. Computations are as detailed as necessary, which is judged by whether rounding potentially affects users' decisions. Computations should not be excessively detailed so that important relations are lost among a mountain of decimal points and digits.

Comparative Balance Sheets

Comparative balance sheets consist of balance sheet amounts from two or more balance sheet dates arranged side by side. Its usefulness is often improved by showing each item's dollar change and percent change to highlight large changes.

---

[1] *Median* is the middle value in a group of numbers. For instance, if five prior years' incomes are (in 000s) $15, $19, $18, $20, and $22, the median value is $19. When there are two middle numbers, we can take their average. For instance, if four prior years' sales are (in 000s) $84, $91, $96, and $93, the median is $92 (computed as the average of $91 and $93).

Analysis of comparative financial statements begins by focusing on items that show large dollar or percent changes. We then try to identify the reasons for these changes and, if possible, determine whether they are favorable or unfavorable. We also follow up on items with small changes when we expected the changes to be large.

Exhibit 13.1 shows comparative balance sheets for **Best Buy**. A few items stand out. Many asset categories substantially increase, which is probably not surprising because Best Buy continues to grow. Much of the increase in current assets is from the 240.3% increase in receivables; but this is countered with a 65.4% decrease in cash and equivalents. Both are common outcomes of recessionary periods. The major long-term assets of property, equipment, and goodwill also increased. Of course, its sizeable total asset growth of 24.0% must be accompanied by future income to validate Best Buy's growth strategy.

EXHIBIT 13.1

Comparative Balance Sheets

BEST BUY Comparative Balance Sheets February 29, 2009 and March 1, 2008				
($ millions)	2009	2008	Dollar Change	Percent Change
Assets				
Cash and cash equivalents	$ 498	$ 1,438	$ (940)	(65.4)%
Short-term investments	11	64	(53)	(82.8)
Receivables, net	1,868	549	1,319	240.3
Merchandise inventories	4,753	4,708	45	1.0
Other current assets	1,062	583	479	82.2
Total current assets	8,192	7,342	850	11.6
Property and equipment	6,940	5,608	1,332	23.8
Less accumulated depreciation	2,766	2,302	464	20.2
Net property and equipment	4,174	3,306	868	26.3
Goodwill	2,203	1,088	1,115	102.5
Tradenames	173	97	76	78.4
Customer relationships	322	5	317	6340
Equity and other investments	395	605	(210)	(34.7)
Other long-term assets	367	315	52	16.5
Total assets	$15,826	$12,758	$3,068	24.0
Liabilities				
Accounts payable	$ 4,997	$ 4,297	$ 700	16.3%
Unredeemed gift card liabilities	479	531	(52)	(9.8)
Accrued compensation and related expenses	459	373	86	23.1
Accrued liabilities	1,382	975	407	41.7
Accrued income taxes	281	404	(123)	(30.4)
Short-term debt	783	156	627	401.9
Current portion of long-term debt	54	33	21	63.6
Total current liabilities	8,435	6,769	1,666	24.6
Long-term liabilities	1,109	838	271	32.3
Long-term debt	1,126	627	499	79.6
Minority interests	513	40	473	1182
Stockholders' Equity				
Common stock	41	41	0	0.0
Additional paid-in capital	205	8	197	2462
Retained earnings	4,714	3,933	781	19.9
Accumulated other comprehensive (loss) income	(317)	502	(819)	—
Total stockholders' equity	4,643	4,484	159	3.5
Total liabilities and stockholders' equity	$15,826	$12,758	$3,068	24.0

We likewise see substantial increases on the financing side, the most notable ones (in amount) being accounts payable and both short- and long-term debt totaling about $1,847 million. The increase in payables is probably related to the recessionary period covering this report, and the increase in debt is partly explained by the increase in long-term assets. Best Buy also reinvested much of its income as reflected in the $781 million increase in retained earnings. Again, we must monitor these increases in investing and financing activities to be sure they are reflected in increased operating performance.

Comparative Income Statements   Comparative income statements are prepared similarly to comparative balance sheets. Amounts for two or more periods are placed side by side, with additional columns for dollar and percent changes. Exhibit 13.2 shows Best Buy's comparative income statements.

EXHIBIT 13.2

Comparative Income Statements

BEST BUY Comparative Income Statements For Years Ended February 28, 2009 and March 1, 2008				
($ millions, except per share data)	2009	2008	Dollar Change	Percent Change
Revenues	$45,015	$40,023	$4,992	12.5%
Cost of goods sold	34,017	30,477	3,540	11.6
Gross profit	10,998	9,546	1,452	15.2
Selling, general, and administrative expenses	8,984	7,385	1,599	21.7
Restructuring charges	78	0	78	—
Goodwill and tradename impairment	66	0	66	—
Operating income	1,870	2,161	(291)	(13.5)
Other income (expense)	(170)	67	(237)	—
Earnings before tax, minority interests, and equity in income (loss) of affiliates	1,700	2,228	(528)	(23.7)
Income tax expense	674	815	(141)	(17.3)
Minority interests in earnings	(30)	(3)	(27)	(900.0)
Equity in income (loss) of affiliates	7	(3)	10	—
Net earnings	$ 1,003	$ 1,407	(404)	(28.7)
Basic earnings per share	$ 2.43	$ 3.20	$(0.77)	(24.1)
Diluted earnings per share	$ 2.39	$ 3.12	$(0.73)	(23.4)

Best Buy has substantial revenue growth of 12.5% in 2009. This finding helps support management's growth strategy as reflected in the comparative balance sheets. Best Buy also reveals some ability to control cost of sales, which increased 11.6%. Best Buy's net income decline of 28.7% on revenue growth of 12.5% is disappointing.

Point: Percent change can also be computed by dividing the current period by the prior period and subtracting 1.0. For example, the 12.5% revenue increase of Exhibit 13.2 is computed as: ($45,015/$40,023) − 1.

Trend Analysis

Trend analysis, also called *trend percent analysis* or *index number trend analysis,* is a form of horizontal analysis that can reveal patterns in data across successive periods. It involves computing trend percents for a series of financial numbers and is a variation on the use of percent changes. The difference is that trend analysis does not subtract the base period amount in the numerator. To compute trend percents, we do the following:

1. Select a *base period* and assign each item in the base period a weight of 100%.
2. Express financial numbers as a percent of their base period number.

Specifically, a *trend percent,* also called an *index number,* is computed as follows:

$$\text{Trend percent (\%)} = \frac{\text{Analysis period amount}}{\text{Base period amount}} \times 100$$

Point: *Index* refers to the comparison of the analysis period to the base period. Percents determined for each period are called *index numbers.*

To illustrate trend analysis, we use the **Best Buy** data shown in Exhibit 13.3.

EXHIBIT 13.3

Revenues and Expenses

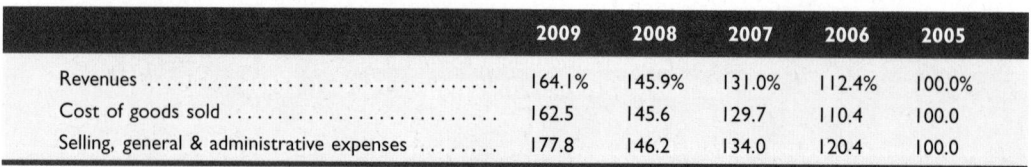

($ millions)	2009	2008	2007	2006	2005
Revenues	$45,015	$40,023	$35,934	$30,848	$27,433
Cost of goods sold	34,017	30,477	27,165	23,122	20,938
Selling, general & administrative expenses	8,984	7,385	6,770	6,082	5,053

These data are from Best Buy's *Selected Financial Data* section. The base period is 2005 and the trend percent is computed in each subsequent year by dividing that year's amount by its 2005 amount. For instance, the revenue trend percent for 2009 is 164.1%, computed as $45,015/$27,433. The trend percents—using the data from Exhibit 13.3—are shown in Exhibit 13.4.

EXHIBIT 13.4

Trend Percents for Revenues and Expenses

	2009	2008	2007	2006	2005
Revenues	164.1%	145.9%	131.0%	112.4%	100.0%
Cost of goods sold	162.5	145.6	129.7	110.4	100.0
Selling, general & administrative expenses	177.8	146.2	134.0	120.4	100.0

Point: Trend analysis expresses a percent of base, not a percent of change.

EXHIBIT 13.5

Trend Percent Lines for Revenues and Expenses of Best Buy

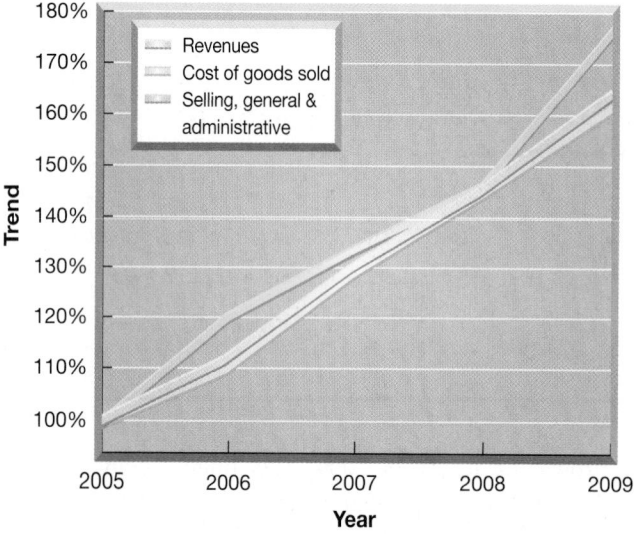

Graphical depictions often aid analysis of trend percents. Exhibit 13.5 shows the trend percents from Exhibit 13.4 in a *line graph,* which can help us identify trends and detect changes in direction or magnitude. It reveals that the trend line for revenues has consistently exceeded that for cost of goods sold since 2005. Moreover, the magnitude of that difference has persisted. This result bodes well for Best Buy because its cost of goods sold is by far its largest cost, and the company shows an ability to control these expenses as it expands. The line graphs also reveal a consistent increase in each of the accounts, which is typical of growth companies. The trend line for selling, general and administrative expenses is less encouraging because it exceeds the revenue trend line in each year. In sum, the good news is that management appears to have controlled the growth in cost of goods sold (to not exceed the growth in revenues), however, it must better control selling and administrative costs.

EXHIBIT 13.6

Trend Percent Lines—Best Buy and RadioShack

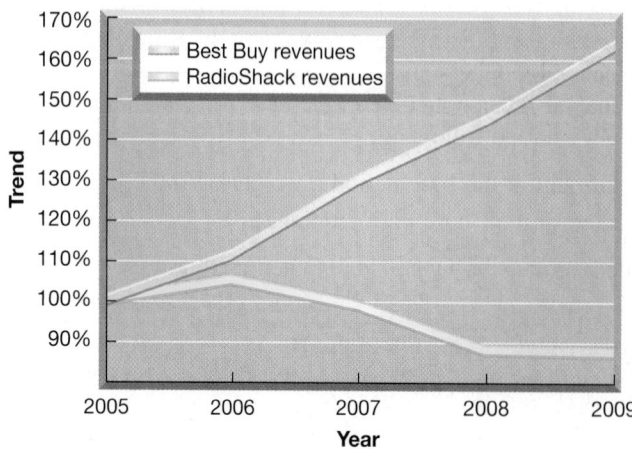

Exhibit 13.6 compares **Best Buy's** revenue trend line to that of **RadioShack** for this same period. Best Buy's revenues sharply increased over this time period while those of RadioShack were flat or declining. These data indicate that Best Buy's products and services have met with considerable consumer acceptance.

Trend analysis of financial statement items can include comparisons of relations between items on different financial statements. For instance, Exhibit 13.7

($ millions)	2009	2005	Trend Percent (2009 vs. 2005)
Revenues	$45,015	$27,433	164.1%
Total assets	15,826	10,294	153.7

EXHIBIT 13.7

Revenue and Asset Data for Best Buy

compares Best Buy's revenues and total assets. The rate of increase in total assets (153.7%) is less than the increase in revenues (164.1%) since 2005. Is this result favorable or not? It suggests that Best Buy was slightly more efficient in using its assets in 2009. Management has generated revenues sufficient to compensate for this asset growth.

Overall we must remember that an important role of financial statement analysis is identifying questions and areas of interest, which often direct us to important factors bearing on a company's future. Accordingly, financial statement analysis should be seen as a continuous process of refining our understanding and expectations of company performance and financial condition.

Decision Maker

Auditor   Your tests reveal a 3% increase in sales from $200,000 to $206,000 and a 4% decrease in expenses from $190,000 to $182,400. Both changes are within your "reasonableness" criterion of ±5%, and thus you don't pursue additional tests. The audit partner in charge questions your lack of follow-up and mentions the *joint relation* between sales and expenses. To what is the partner referring? [Answer—p. 592]

Vertical Analysis

Vertical analysis is a tool to evaluate individual financial statement items or a group of items in terms of a specific base amount. We usually define a key aggregate figure as the base, which for an income statement is usually revenue and for a balance sheet is usually total assets. This section explains vertical analysis and applies it to **Best Buy**. [The term *vertical analysis* arises from the up-down (or down-up) movement of our eyes as we review common-size financial statements. Vertical analysis is also called *common-size analysis*.]

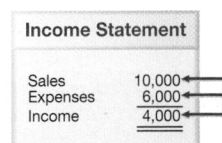

Income Statement

Sales	10,000
Expenses	6,000
Income	4,000

Common-Size Statements

The comparative statements in Exhibits 13.1 and 13.2 show the change in each item over time, but they do not emphasize the relative importance of each item. We use **common-size financial statements** to reveal changes in the relative importance of each financial statement item. All individual amounts in common-size statements are redefined in terms of common-size percents. A *common-size percent* is measured by dividing each individual financial statement amount under analysis by its base amount:

P2   Describe and apply methods of vertical analysis.

$$\text{Common-size percent } (\%) = \frac{\text{Analysis amount}}{\text{Base amount}} \times 100$$

Common-Size Balance Sheets   Common-size statements express each item as a percent of a *base amount,* which for a common-size balance sheet is usually total assets. The base amount is assigned a value of 100%. (This implies that the total amount of liabilities plus equity equals 100% since this amount equals total assets.) We then compute a common-size percent for each asset, liability, and equity item using total assets as the base amount. When we present a company's successive balance sheets in this way, changes in the mixture of assets, liabilities, and equity are apparent.

Exhibit 13.8 shows common-size comparative balance sheets for Best Buy. Some relations that stand out on both a magnitude and percentage basis include (1) an 8.2% decline in cash and equivalents as a percent of assets, (2) a 7.5% increase in receivables as a percent of assets, (3) a 6.9% decrease in inventories as a percent of assets, and (4) a 3.7% increase in short-term debt as a percent of assets. Observations (1), (2), and (4) are typical of companies in

Point: The *base* amount in common-size analysis is an *aggregate* amount from that period's financial statement.

Point: Common-size statements often are used to compare two or more companies in the same industry.

EXHIBIT 13.8

Common-Size Comparative
Balance Sheets

($ millions)	BEST BUY Common-Size Comparative Balance Sheets February 29, 2009 and March 1, 2009		Common-Size Percents*	
($ millions)	2009	2008	2009	2008
Assets				
Cash and cash equivalents	$ 498	$ 1,438	3.1%	11.3%
Short-term investments	11	64	0.1	0.5
Receivables, net	1,868	549	11.8	4.3
Merchandise inventories	4,753	4,708	30.0	36.9
Other current assets	1,062	583	6.7	4.6
Total current assets	8,192	7,342	51.8	57.5
Property and equipment	6,940	5,608	43.9	44.0
Less accumulated depreciation	2,766	2,302	17.5	18.0
Net property and equipment	4,174	3,306	26.4	25.9
Goodwill	2,203	1,088	13.9	8.5
Tradenames	173	97	1.1	0.8
Customer relationships	322	5	2.0	0.0
Equity and other investments	395	605	2.5	4.7
Other long-term assets	367	315	2.3	2.5
Total assets	$15,826	$12,758	100.0%	100.0%
Liabilities				
Accounts payable	$ 4,997	$ 4,297	31.6%	33.7%
Unredeemed gift card liabilities	479	531	3.0	4.2
Accrued compensation and related expenses	459	373	2.9	2.9
Accrued liabilities	1,382	975	8.7	7.6
Accrued income taxes	281	404	1.8	3.2
Short-term debt	783	156	4.9	1.2
Current portion of long-term debt	54	33	0.3	0.3
Total current liabilities	8,435	6,769	53.3	53.1
Long-term liabilities	1,109	838	7.0	6.6
Long-term debt	1,126	627	7.1	4.9
Minority interests	513	40	3.2	0.3
Stockholders' Equity				
Common stock	41	41	0.3	0.3
Additional paid-in capital	205	8	1.3	0.1
Retained earnings	4,714	3,933	29.8	30.8
Accumulated other comprehensive (loss) income	(317)	502	(2.0)	3.9
Total stockholders' equity	4,643	4,484	29.3	35.1
Total liabilities and stockholders' equity	$15,826	$12,758	100.0%	100.0%

* Percents are rounded to one decimal and thus may not exactly sum to totals and subtotals.

Point: Common-size statements are also useful in comparing firms that report in different currencies.

Global: International companies sometimes disclose "convenience" financial statements, which are statements translated in other languages and currencies. However, these statements rarely adjust for differences in accounting principles across countries.

recessionary periods. Observation (3) is consistent with companies reducing their inventories when facing an uncertain future. The concern, if any, is that Best Buy cannot sustain indefinitely a continuation of these financial trends.

Common-Size Income Statements Analysis also benefits from use of a common-size income statement. Revenues is usually the base amount, which is assigned a value of 100%. Each common-size income statement item appears as a percent of revenues. If we think of the 100% revenues amount as representing one sales dollar, the remaining items show how each revenue dollar is distributed among costs, expenses, and income.

Exhibit 13.9 shows common-size comparative income statements for each dollar of Best Buy's revenues. The past two years' common-size numbers are similar. The bad news is that Best Buy

BEST BUY Common-Size Comparative Income Statements For the Years Ended February 29, 2009, and March 1, 2008			Common-Size Percents*	
($ millions)	Feb. 29 2009	Mar. 1 2008	2009	2008
Revenues	$45,015	$40,023	100.0%	100.0%
Cost of goods sold	34,017	30,477	75.6	76.1
Gross profit	10,998	9,546	24.4	23.9
Selling, general and administrative expenses	8,984	7,385	20.0	18.5
Restructuring charges	78	—	0.2	0.0
Goodwill and tradename impairment	66	—	0.1	0.0
Operating income	1,870	2,161	4.2	5.4
Other income (expense)	(170)	67	(0.4)	0.2
Earnings before tax, minority interests, and equity in income (loss) of affiliates	1,700	2,228	3.8	5.6
Income tax expense	674	815	1.5	2.0
Minority interests in earnings	(30)	(3)	(0.1)	(0.0)
Equity in income (loss) of affiliates	7	(3)	0.0	(0.0)
Net earnings	$ 1,003	$ 1,407	2.2%	3.5%

EXHIBIT 13.9

Common-Size Comparative Income Statements

* Percents are rounded to one decimal and thus may not exactly sum to totals and subtotals.

has been squeezed out of 1.3 cents in earnings per revenue dollar—evidenced by the 3.5% to 2.2% decline in earnings as a percentage of revenues. This implies that management has been unable to effectively control costs and/or reap growth benefits in this recessionary period. The good news is that gross profit increased 0.5 cent per revenue dollar—evidenced by the 23.9% to 24.4% increase in gross profit as a percentage of revenues. This is a positive development given the price-competitive electronics market. Analysis here shows that common-size percents for successive income statements can uncover potentially important changes in a company's expenses. Evidence of no changes, especially when changes are expected, is also informative.

Common-Size Graphics

Two of the most common tools of common-size analysis are trend analysis of common-size statements and graphical analysis. The trend analysis of common-size statements is similar to that of comparative statements discussed under vertical analysis. It is not illustrated here because the only difference is the substitution of common-size percents for trend percents. Instead, this section discusses graphical analysis of common-size statements.

An income statement readily lends itself to common-size graphical analysis. This is so because revenues affect nearly every item in an income statement. Exhibit 13.10 shows **Best Buy**'s 2009 common-size income statement in graphical form. This pie chart highlights the contribution of each component of revenues for net earnings.

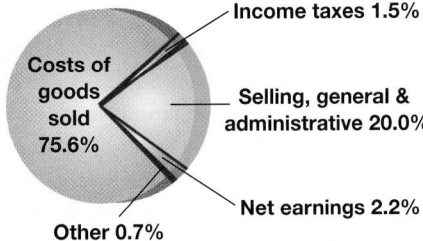

EXHIBIT 13.10

Common-Size Graphic of Income Statement

Exhibit 13.11 previews more complex graphical analyses available and the insights they provide. The data for this exhibit are taken from Best Buy's *Segments* footnote. Best Buy has two reportable segments: domestic and international.

EXHIBIT 13.11

Revenue and Operating Income Breakdown by Segment

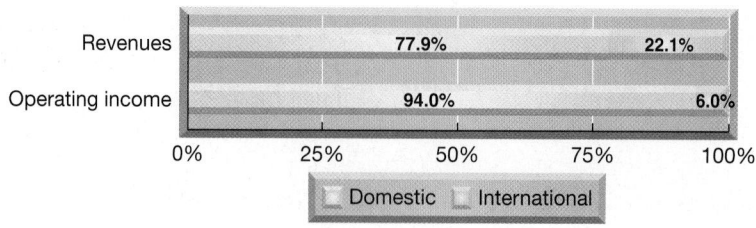

EXHIBIT 13.12

Common-Size Graphic of Asset Components

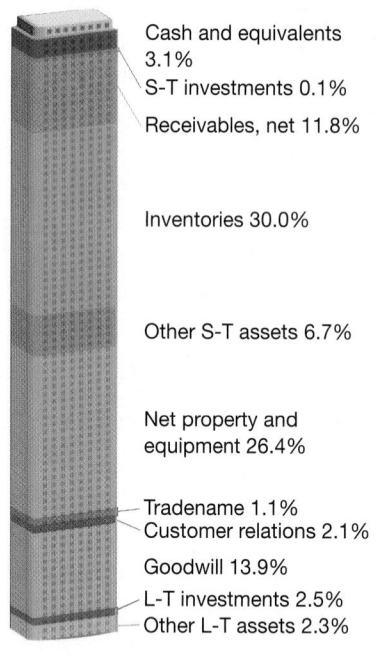

Cash and equivalents 3.1%

S-T investments 0.1%

Receivables, net 11.8%

Inventories 30.0%

Other S-T assets 6.7%

Net property and equipment 26.4%

Tradename 1.1%
Customer relations 2.1%

Goodwill 13.9%

L-T investments 2.5%
Other L-T assets 2.3%

The upper bar in Exhibit 13.11 shows the percent of revenues from each segment. The major revenue source is Domestic (77.9%). The lower bar shows the percent of operating income from each segment. Although International provides 22.1% of revenues, it provides only 6.0% of operating income. This type of information can help users in determining strategic analyses and actions.

Graphical analysis is also useful in identifying (1) sources of financing including the distribution among current liabilities, noncurrent liabilities, and equity capital and (2) focuses of investing activities, including the distribution among current and noncurrent assets. As illustrative, Exhibit 13.12 shows a common-size graphical display of Best Buy's assets. Common-size balance sheet analysis can be extended to examine the composition of these subgroups. For instance, in assessing liquidity of current assets, knowing what proportion of current assets consists of inventories is usually important, and not simply what proportion inventories are of total assets.

Common-size financial statements are also useful in comparing different companies. Exhibit 13.13 shows common-size graphics of **Best Buy**, **RadioShack**, and **GOME** on financing sources. This graphic highlights the lower percent of equity financing for Best Buy and GOME than for RadioShack. It also highlights the much larger noncurrent (debt) financing of RadioShack. Comparison of a company's common-size statements with competitors' or industry common-size statistics alerts us to differences in the structure or distribution of its financial statements but not to their dollar magnitude.

EXHIBIT 13.13

Common-Size Graphic of Financing Sources— Competitor Analysis

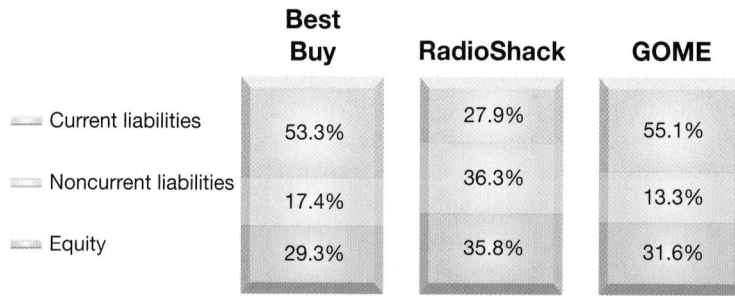

	Best Buy	RadioShack	GOME
Current liabilities	53.3%	27.9%	55.1%
Noncurrent liabilities	17.4%	36.3%	13.3%
Equity	29.3%	35.8%	31.6%

Quick Check

Answers—p. 592

5. Which of the following is true for common-size comparative statements? (*a*) Each item is expressed as a percent of a base amount. (*b*) Total assets often are assigned a value of 100%. (*c*) Amounts from successive periods are placed side by side. (*d*) All are true. (*e*) None is true.

6. What is the difference between the percents shown on a comparative income statement and those shown on a common-size comparative income statement?

7. Trend percents are (*a*) shown on comparative income statements and balance sheets, (*b*) shown on common-size comparative statements, or (*c*) also called *index numbers*.

Ratio Analysis

Ratios are among the more widely used tools of financial analysis because they provide clues to and symptoms of underlying conditions. A ratio can help us uncover conditions and trends difficult to detect by inspecting individual components making up the ratio. Ratios, like other analysis tools, are usually future oriented; that is, they are often adjusted for their probable future trend and magnitude, and their usefulness depends on skillful interpretation.

A ratio expresses a mathematical relation between two quantities. It can be expressed as a percent, rate, or proportion. For instance, a change in an account balance from $100 to $250 can be expressed as (1) 150% increase, (2) 2.5 times, or (3) 2.5 to 1 (or 2.5:1). Computation of a ratio is a simple arithmetic operation, but its interpretation is not. To be meaningful, a ratio must refer to an economically important relation. For example, a direct and crucial relation exists between an item's sales price and its cost. Accordingly, the ratio of cost of goods sold to sales is meaningful. In contrast, no obvious relation exists between freight costs and the balance of long-term investments.

This section describes an important set of financial ratios and its application. The selected ratios are organized into the four building blocks of financial statement analysis: (1) liquidity and efficiency, (2) solvency, (3) profitability, and (4) market prospects. All of these ratios were explained at relevant points in prior chapters. The purpose here is to organize and apply them under a summary framework. We use four common standards, in varying degrees, for comparisons: intracompany, competitor, industry, and guidelines.

P3 Define and apply ratio analysis.

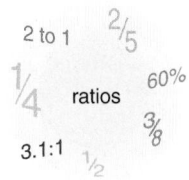

Point: Some sources for industry norms are *Annual Statement Studies* by Robert Morris Associates, *Industry Norms & Key Business Ratios* by Dun & Bradstreet, *Standard & Poor's Industry Surveys*, and Reuters.com/finance.

Liquidity and Efficiency

Liquidity refers to the availability of resources to meet short-term cash requirements. It is affected by the timing of cash inflows and outflows along with prospects for future performance. Analysis of liquidity is aimed at a company's funding requirements. *Efficiency* refers to how productive a company is in using its assets. Efficiency is usually measured relative to how much revenue is generated from a certain level of assets.

Both liquidity and efficiency are important and complementary. If a company fails to meet its current obligations, its continued existence is doubtful. Viewed in this light, all other measures of analysis are of secondary importance. Although accounting measurements assume the company's continued existence, our analysis must always assess the validity of this assumption using liquidity measures. Moreover, inefficient use of assets can cause liquidity problems. A lack of liquidity often precedes lower profitability and fewer opportunities. It can foretell a loss of owner control. To a company's creditors, lack of liquidity can yield delays in collecting interest and principal payments or the loss of amounts due them. A company's customers and suppliers of goods and services also are affected by short-term liquidity problems. Implications include a company's inability to execute contracts and potential damage to important customer and supplier relationships. This section describes and illustrates key ratios relevant to assessing liquidity and efficiency.

Working Capital and Current Ratio   The amount of current assets less current liabilities is called **working capital,** or *net working capital.* A company needs adequate working capital to meet current debts, to carry sufficient inventories, and to take advantage of cash discounts. A company that runs low on working capital is less likely to meet current obligations or to continue operating. When evaluating a company's working capital, we must not only look at the dollar amount of current assets less current liabilities, but also at their ratio. The *current ratio* is defined as follows (see Chapter 3 for additional explanation):

$$\text{Current ratio} = \frac{\text{Current assets}}{\text{Current liabilities}}$$

Drawing on information in Exhibit 13.1, **Best Buy**'s working capital and current ratio for both 2009 and 2008 are shown in Exhibit 13.14. **RadioShack** (2.81), **GOME** (1.23), and the Industry's current ratio of 1.2 is shown in the margin. Best Buy's 2009 ratio (0.97)

EXHIBIT 13.14

Best Buy's Working Capital and
Current Ratio

Current ratio
RadioShack* = 2.81
GOME† = 1.23
Industry = 1.2

($ millions)	2009	2008
Current assets	$ 8,192	$ 7,342
Current liabilities	8,435	6,769
Working capital	$ (243)	$ 573
Current ratio		
$8,192/$8,435	0.97 to 1	
$7,342/$6,769		1.08 to 1

*$1,792/$637.2
†$18.5/$15.1

is lower than any of the comparison ratios, but it does not appear in danger of defaulting on loan payments. A high current ratio suggests a strong liquidity position and an ability to meet current obligations. A company can, however, have a current ratio that is too high. An excessively high current ratio means that the company has invested too much in current assets compared to its current obligations. An excessive investment in current assets is not an efficient use of funds because current assets normally generate a low return on investment (compared with long-term assets).

Many users apply a guideline of 2:1 (or 1.5:1) for the current ratio in helping evaluate a company's debt-paying ability. A company with a 2:1 or higher current ratio is generally thought to be a good credit risk in the short run. Such a guideline or any analysis of the current ratio must recognize at least three additional factors: (1) type of business, (2) composition of current assets, and (3) turnover rate of current asset components.

Point: When a firm uses LIFO in a period of rising costs, the standard for an adequate current ratio usually is lower than if it used FIFO.

Type of business. A service company that grants little or no credit and carries few inventories can probably operate on a current ratio of less than 1:1 if its revenues generate enough cash to pay its current liabilities. On the other hand, a company selling high-priced clothing or furniture requires a higher ratio because of difficulties in judging customer demand and cash receipts. For instance, if demand falls, inventory may not generate as much cash as expected. Accordingly, analysis of the current ratio should include a comparison with ratios from successful companies in the same industry and from prior periods. We must also recognize that a company's accounting methods, especially choice of inventory method, affect the current ratio. For instance, when costs are rising, a company using LIFO tends to report a smaller amount of current assets than when using FIFO.

Composition of current assets. The composition of a company's current assets is important to an evaluation of short-term liquidity. For instance, cash, cash equivalents, and short-term investments are more liquid than accounts and notes receivable. Also, short-term receivables normally are more liquid than inventory. Cash, of course, can be used to immediately pay current debts. Items such as accounts receivable and inventory, however, normally must be converted into cash before payment is made. An excessive amount of receivables and inventory weakens a company's ability to pay current liabilities. The acid-test ratio (see below) can help with this assessment.

Turnover rate of assets. Asset turnover measures a company's efficiency in using its assets. One relevant measure of asset efficiency is the revenue generated. A measure of total asset turnover is revenues divided by total assets, but evaluation of turnover for individual assets is also first useful. We discuss both receivables turnover and inventory turnover on the next page.

 Decision Maker ▬▬▬▬▬▬▬▬▬▬▬▬▬▬▬▬▬▬▬▬

Banker   A company requests a one-year, $200,000 loan for expansion. This company's current ratio is 4:1, with current assets of $160,000. Key competitors carry a current ratio of about 1.9:1. Using this information, do you approve the loan application? Does your decision change if the application is for a 10-year loan? [Answer—p. 592]

Acid-Test Ratio   Quick assets are cash, short-term investments, and current receivables. These are the most liquid types of current assets. The *acid-test ratio,* also called *quick ratio,* and first introduced in Chapter 4, reflects on a company's short-term liquidity.

$$\text{Acid-test ratio} = \frac{\text{Cash} + \text{Short-term investments} + \text{Current receivables}}{\text{Current liabilities}}$$

($ millions)	2009	2008
Cash and equivalents	$ 498	$1,438
Short-term investments	11	64
Current receivables	1,868	549
Total quick assets	$2,377	$2,051
Current liabilities	$8,435	$6,769
Acid-test ratio		
$2,377/$8,435	0.28 to 1	
$2,051/$6,769		0.30 to 1

EXHIBIT 13.15

Acid-Test Ratio

Acid-test ratio
RadioShack* = 1.81
GOME† = 0.30
Industry = 0.5

*($815 + $99 + $242)/$637.2
†($3.1 + $0 + $1.4)/$15.1

Best Buy's acid-test ratio is computed in Exhibit 13.15. Best Buy's 2009 acid-test ratio (0.28) is lower than that for RadioShack (1.81) and GOME (0.30), and less than the 1:1 common guideline for an acceptable acid-test ratio. As with analysis of the current ratio, we need to consider other factors. For instance, the frequency with which a company converts its current assets into cash affects its working capital requirements. This implies that analysis of short-term liquidity should also include an analysis of receivables and inventories, which we consider next.

Global: Ratio analysis helps overcome currency translation problems, but it does *not* overcome differences in accounting principles.

Accounts Receivable Turnover   We can measure how frequently a company converts its receivables into cash by computing the *accounts receivable turnover*, which is defined as follows (see Chapter 7 for additional explanation):

$$\text{Accounts receivable turnover} = \frac{\text{Net sales}}{\text{Average accounts receivable, net}}$$

Short-term receivables from customers are often included in the denominator along with accounts receivable. Also, accounts receivable turnover is more precise if credit sales are used for the numerator, but external users generally use net sales (or net revenues) because information about credit sales is typically not reported. Best Buy's 2009 accounts receivable turnover is computed as follows ($ millions).

Point: Some users prefer using gross accounts receivable (before subtracting the allowance for doubtful accounts) to avoid the influence of a manager's bad debts estimate.

$$\frac{\$45,015}{(\$1,868 + \$549)/2} = 37.2 \text{ times}$$

Accounts receivable turnover
RadioShack = 17.0
GOME = 642.7

Best Buy's value of 37.2 is larger than RadioShack's 17.0 but much lower than GOME's 642.7. Accounts receivable turnover is high when accounts receivable are quickly collected. A high turnover is favorable because it means the company need not commit large amounts of funds to accounts receivable. However, an accounts receivable turnover can be too high; this can occur when credit terms are so restrictive that they negatively affect sales volume.

Point: Ending accounts receivable can be substituted for the average balance in computing accounts receivable turnover if the difference between ending and average receivables is small.

Inventory Turnover   How long a company holds inventory before selling it will affect working capital requirements. One measure of this effect is *inventory turnover*, also called *merchandise turnover* or *merchandise inventory turnover*, which is defined as follows (see Chapter 5 for additional explanation):

$$\text{Inventory turnover} = \frac{\text{Cost of goods sold}}{\text{Average inventory}}$$

Using Best Buy's cost of goods sold and inventories information, we compute its inventory turnover for 2009 as follows (if the beginning and ending inventories for the year do not represent the usual inventory amount, an average of quarterly or monthly inventories can be used).

Inventory turnover
RadioShack = 3.43
GOME = 7.62
Industry = 4.4

$$\frac{\$34,017}{(\$4,753 + \$4,708)/2} = 7.19 \text{ times}$$

Best Buy's inventory turnover of 7.19 is higher than RadioShack's 3.43 and the industry's 4.4, but lower than GOME's 7.62. A company with a high turnover requires a smaller investment in inventory than one producing the same sales with a lower turnover. Inventory turnover can be too high, however, if the inventory a company keeps is so small that it restricts sales volume.

Days' Sales Uncollected   Accounts receivable turnover provides insight into how frequently a company collects its accounts. Days' sales uncollected is one measure of this activity, which is defined as follows (Chapter 6 provides further explanation):

$$\text{Days' sales uncollected} = \frac{\text{Accounts receivable, net}}{\text{Net sales}} \times 365$$

Any short-term notes receivable from customers are normally included in the numerator. Best Buy's 2009 days' sales uncollected follows.

Day's sales uncollected
RadioShack = 20.90
GOME = 0.36

$$\frac{\$1,868}{\$45,015} \times 365 = 15.15 \text{ days}$$

RadioShack's days' sales uncollected of 20.90 days and GOME's 0.36 days are on either side of the 15.15 days for Best Buy. Days' sales uncollected is more meaningful if we know company credit terms. A rough guideline states that days' sales uncollected should not exceed $1\frac{1}{3}$ times the days in its (1) credit period, *if* discounts are not offered or (2) discount period, *if* favorable discounts are offered.

Days' Sales in Inventory   *Days' sales in inventory* is a useful measure in evaluating inventory liquidity. Days' sales in inventory is linked to inventory in a way that days' sales uncollected is linked to receivables. We compute days' sales in inventory as follows (Chapter 5 provides additional explanation).

$$\text{Days' sales in inventory} = \frac{\text{Ending inventory}}{\text{Cost of goods sold}} \times 365$$

Best Buy's days' sales in inventory for 2009 follows.

Days' sales in inventory
RadioShack = 100.9
GOME = 48.3

$$\frac{\$4,753}{\$34,017} \times 365 = 51.0 \text{ days}$$

Point: *Average collection period is estimated by dividing 365 by the accounts receivable turnover ratio. For example, 365 divided by an accounts receivable turnover of 6.1 indicates a 60-day average collection period.*

If the products in Best Buy's inventory are in demand by customers, this formula estimates that its inventory will be converted into receivables (or cash) in 51.0 days. If all of Best Buy's sales were credit sales, the conversion of inventory to receivables in 51.0 days *plus* the conversion of receivables to cash in 15.15 days implies that inventory will be converted to cash in about 66.15 days (51.0 + 15.15).

Total Asset Turnover *Total asset turnover* reflects a company's ability to use its assets to generate sales and is an important indication of operating efficiency. The definition of this ratio follows (Chapter 8 offers additional explanation).

$$\text{Total asset turnover} = \frac{\text{Net sales}}{\text{Average total assets}}$$

Best Buy's total asset turnover for 2009 follows and is greater than that for both RadioShack (1.98) and GOME (1.60).

$$\frac{\$45,015}{(\$15,826 + \$12,758)/2} = 3.15 \text{ times}$$

Total asset turnover
RadioShack = 1.98
GOME = 1.60

Quick Check
Answers—p. 592

8. Information from Paff Co. at Dec. 31, 2008, follows: cash, $820,000; accounts receivable, $240,000; inventories, $470,000; plant assets, $910,000; accounts payable, $350,000; and income taxes payable, $180,000. Compute its (a) current ratio and (b) acid-test ratio.

9. On Dec. 31, 2009, Paff Company (see question 8) had accounts receivable of $290,000 and inventories of $530,000. During 2009, net sales amounted to $2,500,000 and cost of goods sold was $750,000. Compute (a) accounts receivable turnover, (b) days' sales uncollected, (c) inventory turnover, and (d) days' sales in inventory.

Solvency

Solvency refers to a company's long-run financial viability and its ability to cover long-term obligations. All of a company's business activities—financing, investing, and operating—affect its solvency. Analysis of solvency is long term and uses less precise but more encompassing measures than liquidity. One of the most important components of solvency analysis is the composition of a company's capital structure. *Capital structure* refers to a company's financing sources. It ranges from relatively permanent equity financing to riskier or more temporary short-term financing. Assets represent security for financiers, ranging from loans secured by specific assets to the assets available as general security to unsecured creditors. This section describes the tools of solvency analysis. Our analysis focuses on a company's ability to both meet its obligations and provide security to its creditors *over the long run*. Indicators of this ability include *debt* and *equity* ratios, the relation between *pledged assets and secured liabilities*, and the company's capacity to earn sufficient income to *pay fixed interest charges*.

Debt and Equity Ratios One element of solvency analysis is to assess the portion of a company's assets contributed by its owners and the portion contributed by creditors. This relation is reflected in the debt ratio (also described in Chapter 2). The *debt ratio* expresses total liabilities as a percent of total assets. The **equity ratio** provides complementary information by expressing total equity as a percent of total assets. **Best Buy**'s debt and equity ratios follow.

($ millions)	2009	Ratios	
Total liabilities	$11,183	70.7%	[Debt ratio]
Total equity	4,643	29.3	[Equity ratio]
Total liabilities and equity	$15,826	100.0%	

Debt ratio :: Equity ratio
RadioShack = 64.2% :: 35.8%
GOME = 68.4% :: 31.6%

Best Buy's financial statements reveal more debt than equity. A company is considered less risky if its capital structure (equity and long-term debt) contains more equity. One risk factor is the required payment for interest and principal when debt is outstanding. Another factor is the greater the stockholder financing, the more losses a company can absorb through equity before the assets become inadequate to satisfy creditors' claims. From the stockholders' point of view, if a company

Point: Bank examiners from the FDIC and other regulatory agencies use debt and equity ratios to monitor compliance with regulatory capital requirements imposed on banks and S&Ls.

earns a return on borrowed capital that is higher than the cost of borrowing, the difference represents increased income to stockholders. The inclusion of debt is described as *financial leverage* because debt can have the effect of increasing the return to stockholders. Companies are said to be highly leveraged if a large portion of their assets is financed by debt.

Debt-to-Equity Ratio   The ratio of total liabilities to equity is another measure of solvency. We compute the ratio as follows (Chapter 10 offers additional explanation).

$$\text{Debt-to-equity ratio} = \frac{\text{Total liabilities}}{\text{Total equity}}$$

Best Buy's debt-to-equity ratio for 2009 is

$$\$11,183/\$4,643 = 2.41$$

Debt-to-equity
RadioShack = 1.79
GOME = 2.16
Industry = 1.09

Best Buy's 2.41 debt-to-equity ratio is greater than the 1.79 for RadioShack, the 2.16 for GOME, and the industry ratio of 1.09. Consistent with our inferences from the debt ratio, Best Buy's capital structure has more debt than equity, which increases risk. Recall that debt must be repaid with interest, while equity does not. These debt requirements can be burdensome when the industry and/or the economy experience a downturn. A larger debt-to-equity ratio also implies less opportunity to expand through use of debt financing.

Point: For analysis purposes, Minority Interest is usually included in equity.

Times Interest Earned   The amount of income before deductions for interest expense and income taxes is the amount available to pay interest expense. The following *times interest earned* ratio reflects the creditors' risk of loan repayments with interest (see Chapter 9 for additional explanation).

Point: The times interest earned ratio and the debt and equity ratios are of special interest to bank lending officers.

$$\text{Times interest earned} = \frac{\text{Income before interest expense and income taxes}}{\text{Interest expense}}$$

The larger this ratio, the less risky is the company for creditors. One guideline says that creditors are reasonably safe if the company earns its fixed interest expense two or more times each year. Best Buy's times interest earned ratio follows; its value suggests that its creditors have little risk of nonrepayment.

Times interest earned
RadioShack = 11.2
GOME = 8.0

$$\frac{\$1,003 + \$94 + \$674}{\$94} = 18.8$$

Decision Insight

Bears and Bulls   A *bear market* is a declining market. The phrase comes from bear-skin jobbers who often sold the skins before the bears were caught. The term *bear* was then used to describe investors who sold shares they did not own in anticipation of a price decline. A *bull market* is a rising market. This phrase comes from the once popular sport of bear and bull baiting. The term *bull* came to mean the opposite of *bear*.

Profitability

We are especially interested in a company's ability to use its assets efficiently to produce profits (and positive cash flows). *Profitability* refers to a company's ability to generate an adequate return on invested capital. Return is judged by assessing earnings relative to the level and sources of financing. Profitability is also relevant to solvency. This section describes key profitability measures and their importance to financial statement analysis.

Profit Margin   A company's operating efficiency and profitability can be expressed by two components. The first is *profit margin*, which reflects a company's ability to earn net income from sales (Chapter 3 offers additional explanation). It is measured by expressing net income as a percent of sales (*sales* and *revenues* are similar terms). **Best Buy**'s profit margin follows.

$$\text{Profit margin} = \frac{\text{Net income}}{\text{Net sales}} = \frac{\$1,003}{\$45,015} = 2.2\%$$

Profit margin
RadioShack = 4.6%
GOME = 2.4%

To evaluate profit margin, we must consider the industry. For instance, an appliance company might require a profit margin between 10% and 15%; whereas a retail supermarket might require a profit margin of 1% or 2%. Both profit margin and *total asset turnover* make up the two basic components of operating efficiency. These ratios reflect on management because managers are ultimately responsible for operating efficiency. The next section explains how we use both measures to analyze return on total assets.

Return on Total Assets *Return on total assets* is defined as follows.

$$\text{Return on total assets} = \frac{\text{Net income}}{\text{Average total assets}}$$

Best Buy's 2009 return on total assets is

$$\frac{\$1,003}{(\$15,826 + \$12,758)/2} = 7.0\%$$

Return on total assets
RadioShack = 9.0%
GOME = 3.7%
Industry = 3.2

Best Buy's 7.0% return on total assets is lower than that for many businesses and is less than RadioShack's return of 9.0% and the industry's 3.2% return. We also should evaluate any trend in the rate of return.

Point: Many analysts add back *Interest expense × (1 − Tax rate)* to net income in computing return on total assets.

The following equation shows the important relation between profit margin, total asset turnover, and return on total assets.

$$\textbf{Profit margin} \times \textbf{Total asset turnover} = \textbf{Return on total assets}$$

or

$$\frac{\text{Net income}}{\text{Net sales}} \times \frac{\text{Net sales}}{\text{Average total assets}} = \frac{\text{Net income}}{\text{Average total assets}}$$

Both profit margin and total asset turnover contribute to overall operating efficiency, as measured by return on total assets. If we apply this formula to Best Buy, we get

$$2.2\% \times 3.15 = 7.0\%$$

RadioShack: 4.6% × 1.98 = 9.0%
GOME: 2.4% × 1.60 = 3.8%
(with rounding)

This analysis shows that Best Buy's solid return on assets versus that of RadioShack and GOME is driven mainly by its higher total asset turnover.

Return on Common Stockholders' Equity Perhaps the most important goal in operating a company is to earn net income for its owner(s). *Return on common stockholders' equity* measures a company's success in reaching this goal and is defined as follows.

$$\text{Return on common stockholders' equity} = \frac{\text{Net income} - \text{Preferred dividends}}{\text{Average common stockholders' equity}}$$

Best Buy's 2009 return on common stockholders' equity is computed as follows:

$$\frac{\$1,003 - \$0}{(\$4,643 + \$4,484)/2} = 22.0\%$$

Return on common equity
RadioShack = 24.2%
GOME = 11.5%

The denominator in this computation is the book value of common equity (minority interest is often included in common equity here). In the numerator, the dividends on cumulative preferred stock are subtracted whether they are declared or are in arrears. If preferred stock is noncumulative, its dividends are subtracted only if declared.

Decision Insight

Wall Street   *Wall Street* is synonymous with financial markets, but its name comes from the street location of the original New York Stock Exchange. The street's name derives from stockades built by early settlers to protect New York from pirate attacks.

Market Prospects

Market measures are useful for analyzing corporations with publicly traded stock. These market measures use stock price, which reflects the market's (public's) expectations for the company. This includes expectations of both company return and risk—as the market perceives it.

Price-Earnings Ratio   Computation of the *price-earnings ratio* follows (Chapter 11 provides additional explanation).

$$\text{Price-earnings ratio} = \frac{\text{Market price per common share}}{\text{Earnings per share}}$$

Point: PE ratio can be viewed as an indicator of the market's expected growth and risk for a stock. High expected risk suggests a low PE ratio. High expected growth suggests a high PE ratio.

Predicted earnings per share for the next period is often used in the denominator of this computation. Reported earnings per share for the most recent period is also commonly used. In both cases, the ratio is used as an indicator of the future growth and risk of a company's earnings as perceived by the stock's buyers and sellers.

The market price of Best Buy's common stock at the start of fiscal year 2010 was $28.82. Using Best Buy's $2.43 basic earnings per share, we compute its price-earnings ratio as follows (some analysts compute this ratio using the median of the low and high stock price).

$$\frac{\$28.82}{\$2.43} = 11.9$$

PE (year-end)
RadioShack = 8.0

Point: Some investors avoid stocks with high PE ratios under the belief they are "overpriced." Alternatively, some investors *sell these stocks short*—hoping for price declines.

Best Buy's price-earnings ratio is greater than that for RadioShack, and is slightly higher than the norm for the recessionary period 2008–2009. Best Buy's middle-of-the-pack ratio likely reflects investors' expectations of continued growth but normal earnings.

Dividend Yield   *Dividend yield* is used to compare the dividend-paying performance of different investment alternatives. We compute dividend yield as follows (Chapter 11 offers additional explanation).

$$\text{Dividend yield} = \frac{\text{Annual cash dividends per share}}{\text{Market price per share}}$$

Best Buy's dividend yield, based on its fiscal year-end market price per share of $28.82 and its policy of $0.54 cash dividends per share, is computed as follows.

$$\frac{\$0.54}{\$28.82} = 1.9\%$$

Dividend yield
RadioShack = 2.1%

Some companies do not declare and pay dividends because they wish to reinvest the cash.

Summary of Ratios

Point: Corporate PE ratios and dividend yields are found in daily stock market quotations listed in *The Wall Street Journal, Investor's Business Daily*, or other publications and Web services.

Exhibit 13.16 summarizes the major financial statement analysis ratios illustrated in this chapter and throughout the book. This summary includes each ratio's title, its formula, and the purpose for which it is commonly used.

EXHIBIT 13.16

Financial Statement Analysis Ratios*

Ratio	Formula	Measure of
Liquidity and Efficiency		
Current ratio	$= \dfrac{\text{Current assets}}{\text{Current liabilities}}$	Short-term debt-paying ability
Acid-test ratio	$= \dfrac{\text{Cash} + \text{Short-term investments} + \text{Current receivables}}{\text{Current liabilities}}$	Immediate short-term debt-paying ability
Accounts receivable turnover	$= \dfrac{\text{Net sales}}{\text{Average accounts receivable, net}}$	Efficiency of collection
Inventory turnover	$= \dfrac{\text{Cost of goods sold}}{\text{Average inventory}}$	Efficiency of inventory management
Days' sales uncollected	$= \dfrac{\text{Accounts receivable, net}}{\text{Net sales}} \times 365$	Liquidity of receivables
Days' sales in inventory	$= \dfrac{\text{Ending inventory}}{\text{Cost of goods sold}} \times 365$	Liquidity of inventory
Total asset turnover	$= \dfrac{\text{Net sales}}{\text{Average total assets}}$	Efficiency of assets in producing sales
Solvency		
Debt ratio	$= \dfrac{\text{Total liabilities}}{\text{Total assets}}$	Creditor financing and leverage
Equity ratio	$= \dfrac{\text{Total equity}}{\text{Total assets}}$	Owner financing
Debt-to-equity ratio	$= \dfrac{\text{Total liabilities}}{\text{Total equity}}$	Debt versus equity financing
Times interest earned	$= \dfrac{\text{Income before interest expense and income taxes}}{\text{Interest expense}}$	Protection in meeting interest payments
Profitability		
Profit margin ratio	$= \dfrac{\text{Net income}}{\text{Net sales}}$	Net income in each sales dollar
Gross margin ratio	$= \dfrac{\text{Net sales} - \text{Cost of goods sold}}{\text{Net sales}}$	Gross margin in each sales dollar
Return on total assets	$= \dfrac{\text{Net income}}{\text{Average total assets}}$	Overall profitability of assets
Return on common stockholders' equity	$= \dfrac{\text{Net income} - \text{Preferred dividends}}{\text{Average common stockholders' equity}}$	Profitability of owner investment
Book value per common share	$= \dfrac{\text{Shareholders' equity applicable to common shares}}{\text{Number of common shares outstanding}}$	Liquidation at reported amounts
Basic earnings per share	$= \dfrac{\text{Net income} - \text{Preferred dividends}}{\text{Weighted-average common shares outstanding}}$	Net income per common share
Market Prospects		
Price-earnings ratio	$= \dfrac{\text{Market price per common share}}{\text{Earnings per share}}$	Market value relative to earnings
Dividend yield	$= \dfrac{\text{Annual cash dividends per share}}{\text{Market price per share}}$	Cash return per common

* Additional ratios also examined in previous chapters included credit risk ratio; plant asset useful life; plant asset age; days' cash expense coverage; cash
coverage of debt; free cash flow; cash flow on total assets; and payout ratio.

Decision Insight

Ticker Prices   *Ticker prices* refer to a band of moving data on a monitor carrying up-to-the-minute stock prices. The phrase comes from *ticker tape,* a 1-inch-wide strip of paper spewing stock prices from a printer that ticked as it ran. Most of today's investors have never seen actual ticker tape, but the phrase survives.

Quick Check   Answers—p. 592

10. Which ratio best reflects a company's ability to meet immediate interest payments? (*a*) Debt ratio. (*b*) Equity ratio. (*c*) Times interest earned.

11. Which ratio best measures a company's success in earning net income for its owner(s)? (*a*) Profit margin. (*b*) Return on common stockholders' equity. (*c*) Price-earnings ratio. (*d*) Dividend yield.

12. If a company has net sales of $8,500,000, net income of $945,000, and total asset turnover of 1.8 times, what is its return on total assets?

 **Global View**

The analysis and interpretation of financial statements is, of course, impacted by the accounting system in effect. This section discusses similarities and differences for our analysis of financial statements when prepared under U.S. GAAP vis-à-vis IFRS.

Horizontal and Vertical Analyses

Horizontal and vertical analyses help eliminate many differences between U.S. GAAP and IFRS when analyzing and interpreting financial statements. Financial numbers are converted to percentages that are, in the best case scenario, consistently applied across and within periods. This enables users to effectively compare companies across reporting regimes. However, when fundamental differences in reporting regimes impact financial statements, such as with certain recognition rule differences, the user must exercise caution when drawing conclusions. Some users will reformulate one set of numbers to be more consistent with the other system to enable comparative analysis. This reformulation process is covered in advanced courses. The important point is that horizontal and vertical analyses help strip away differences between the reporting regimes, but several key differences sometimes remain and require adjustment of the numbers. **GOME** reports the following partial vertical analysis to its shareholders as part of its MD&A report.

As a Percentage of Revenue	2008
Selling and distribution costs	9.78%
Administrative expenses	1.80
Other expenses	1.12
Total operating expenses	12.70%

Ratio Analysis

Ratio analysis of financial statement numbers has many of the advantages and disadvantages of horizontal and vertical analyses discussed above. Importantly, the ratios applied are fine, with some possible changes in interpretation depending on what is and what is not included in certain accounting measures across U.S. GAAP and IFRS. Still, we must take care in drawing inferences from a comparison of ratios across reporting regimes because what a number measures can differ across regimes. GOME offers the following example of its own ratio analysis applied to gross margin.

During the reporting period of 2008, the Group's consolidated gross profit margin reached 16.94%, representing an increase of 1.3 percentage points as compared to the 15.64% for the previous year. Consolidated gross profit margin is the sum of gross profit and other income as a percentage of revenue. [An] increase in gross profit margin and other income has contributed to the Group's year-on-year increase in its consolidated gross profit margin.

Decision Insight

SOX: Not Created Equal   SOX has several goals. Two of them are to ensure adequate accounting disclosure and to strengthen corporate governance. For disclosure purposes, companies must now provide details of related-party transactions and material off-balance-sheet agreements. This is motivated by several major frauds, including Enron. For corporate governance, the CEO and CFO must now certify the fairness of financial statements and the effectiveness of internal controls. Yet, concerns remain. A study reports that 23% of management and administrative employees observed activities that posed a conflict of interest in the past year (KPMG 2009). Another 12% witnessed the falsifying or manipulating of accounting information. The bottom line: All financial statements are not of equal quality.

Analysis Reporting

Decision Analysis

Understanding the purpose of financial statement analysis is crucial to the usefulness of any analysis. This understanding leads to efficiency of effort, effectiveness in application, and relevance in focus. The purpose of most financial statement analyses is to reduce uncertainty in business decisions through a rigorous and sound evaluation. A *financial statement analysis report* helps by directly addressing the building blocks of analysis and by identifying weaknesses in inference by requiring explanation: It forces us to organize our reasoning and to verify its flow and logic. A report also serves as a communication link with readers, and the writing process reinforces our judgments and vice versa. Finally, the report helps us (re)evaluate evidence and refine conclusions on key building blocks. A good analysis report usually consists of six sections:

A1 Summarize and report results of analysis.

1. **Executive summary**—brief focus on important analysis results and conclusions.
2. **Analysis overview**—background on the company, its industry, and its economic setting.
3. **Evidential matter**—financial statements and information used in the analysis, including ratios, trends, comparisons, statistics, and all analytical measures assembled; often organized under the building blocks of analysis.
4. **Assumptions**—identification of important assumptions regarding a company's industry and economic environment, and other important assumptions for estimates.
5. **Key factors**—list of important favorable and unfavorable factors, both quantitative and qualitative, for company performance; usually organized by areas of analysis.
6. **Inferences**—forecasts, estimates, interpretations, and conclusions drawing on all sections of the report.

We must remember that the user dictates relevance, meaning that the analysis report should include a brief table of contents to help readers focus on those areas most relevant to their decisions. All irrelevant matter must be eliminated. For example, decades-old details of obscure transactions and detailed miscues of the analysis are irrelevant. Ambiguities and qualifications to avoid responsibility or hedging inferences must be eliminated. Finally, writing is important. Mistakes in grammar and errors of fact compromise the report's credibility.

Decision Insight

Short Selling   *Short selling* refers to selling stock before you buy it. Here's an example: You borrow 100 shares of Nike stock, sell them at $40 each, and receive money from their sale. You then wait. You hope that Nike's stock price falls to, say, $35 each and you can replace the borrowed stock for less than you sold it for, reaping a profit of $5 each less any transaction costs.

Demonstration Problem

Use the following financial statements of Precision Co. to complete these requirements.

1. Prepare comparative income statements showing the percent increase or decrease for year 2009 in comparison to year 2008.

2. Prepare common-size comparative balance sheets for years 2009 and 2008.

3. Compute the following ratios as of December 31, 2009, or for the year ended December 31, 2009, and identify its building block category for financial statement analysis.

a. Current ratio
b. Acid-test ratio
c. Accounts receivable turnover
d. Days' sales uncollected
e. Inventory turnover
f. Debt ratio

g. Debt-to-equity ratio
h. Times interest earned
i. Profit margin ratio
j. Total asset turnover
k. Return on total assets
l. Return on common stockholders' equity

PRECISION COMPANY
Comparative Balance Sheets
December 31, 2009 and 2008

	2009	2008
Assets		
Current assets		
Cash	$ 79,000	$ 42,000
Short-term investments	65,000	96,000
Accounts receivable, net	120,000	100,000
Merchandise inventory	250,000	265,000
Total current assets	514,000	503,000
Plant assets		
Store equipment, net	400,000	350,000
Office equipment, net	45,000	50,000
Buildings, net	625,000	675,000
Land	100,000	100,000
Total plant assets	1,170,000	1,175,000
Total assets	$1,684,000	$1,678,000
Liabilities		
Current liabilities		
Accounts payable	$ 164,000	$ 190,000
Short-term notes payable	75,000	90,000
Taxes payable	26,000	12,000
Total current liabilities	265,000	292,000
Long-term liabilities		
Notes payable (secured by mortgage on buildings)	400,000	420,000
Total liabilities	665,000	712,000
Stockholders' Equity		
Common stock, $5 par value	475,000	475,000
Retained earnings	544,000	491,000
Total stockholders' equity	1,019,000	966,000
Total liabilities and equity	$1,684,000	$1,678,000

PRECISION COMPANY
Comparative Income Statements
For Years Ended December 31, 2009 and 2008

	2009	2008
Sales	$2,486,000	$2,075,000
Cost of goods sold	1,523,000	1,222,000
Gross profit	963,000	853,000
Operating expenses		
Advertising expense	145,000	100,000
Sales salaries expense	240,000	280,000
Office salaries expense	165,000	200,000
Insurance expense	100,000	45,000
Supplies expense	26,000	35,000
Depreciation expense	85,000	75,000
Miscellaneous expenses	17,000	15,000
Total operating expenses	778,000	750,000
Operating income	185,000	103,000
Interest expense	44,000	46,000
Income before taxes	141,000	57,000
Income taxes	47,000	19,000
Net income	$ 94,000	$ 38,000
Earnings per share	$ 0.99	$ 0.40

Planning the Solution

- Set up a four-column income statement; enter the 2009 and 2008 amounts in the first two columns and then enter the dollar change in the third column and the percent change from 2008 in the fourth column.

- Set up a four-column balance sheet; enter the 2009 and 2008 year-end amounts in the first two columns and then compute and enter the amount of each item as a percent of total assets.
- Compute the required ratios using the data provided. Use the average of beginning and ending amounts when appropriate (see Exhibit 13.16 for definitions).

Solution to Demonstration Problem

1.

PRECISION COMPANY
Comparative Income Statements
For Years Ended December 31, 2009 and 2008

	2009	2008	Increase (Decrease) in 2009 Amount	Increase (Decrease) in 2009 Percent
Sales	$2,486,000	$2,075,000	$411,000	19.8%
Cost of goods sold	1,523,000	1,222,000	301,000	24.6
Gross profit	963,000	853,000	110,000	12.9
Operating expenses				
Advertising expense	145,000	100,000	45,000	45.0
Sales salaries expense	240,000	280,000	(40,000)	(14.3)
Office salaries expense	165,000	200,000	(35,000)	(17.5)
Insurance expense	100,000	45,000	55,000	122.2
Supplies expense	26,000	35,000	(9,000)	(25.7)
Depreciation expense	85,000	75,000	10,000	13.3
Miscellaneous expenses	17,000	15,000	2,000	13.3
Total operating expenses	778,000	750,000	28,000	3.7
Operating income	185,000	103,000	82,000	79.6
Interest expense	44,000	46,000	(2,000)	(4.3)
Income before taxes	141,000	57,000	84,000	147.4
Income taxes	47,000	19,000	28,000	147.4
Net income	$ 94,000	$ 38,000	$ 56,000	147.4
Earnings per share	$ 0.99	$ 0.40	$ 0.59	147.5

2.

PRECISION COMPANY
Common-Size Comparative Balance Sheets
December 31, 2009 and 2008

	December 31 2009	December 31 2008	Common-Size Percents 2009*	Common-Size Percents 2008*
Assets				
Current assets				
Cash	$ 79,000	$ 42,000	4.7%	2.5%
Short-term investments	65,000	96,000	3.9	5.7
Accounts receivable, net	120,000	100,000	7.1	6.0
Merchandise inventory	250,000	265,000	14.8	15.8
Total current assets	514,000	503,000	30.5	30.0
Plant Assets				
Store equipment, net	400,000	350,000	23.8	20.9
Office equipment, net	45,000	50,000	2.7	3.0
Buildings, net	625,000	675,000	37.1	40.2
Land	100,000	100,000	5.9	6.0
Total plant assets	1,170,000	1,175,000	69.5	70.0
Total assets	$1,684,000	$1,678,000	100.0	100.0

[continued on next page]

[continued from previous page]

Liabilities				
Current liabilities				
Accounts payable	$ 164,000	$ 190,000	9.7%	11.3%
Short-term notes payable	75,000	90,000	4.5	5.4
Taxes payable	26,000	12,000	1.5	0.7
Total current liabilities	265,000	292,000	15.7	17.4
Long-term liabilities				
Notes payable (secured by mortgage on buildings)	400,000	420,000	23.8	25.0
Total liabilities	665,000	712,000	39.5	42.4
Stockholders' Equity				
Common stock, $5 par value	475,000	475,000	28.2	28.3
Retained earnings	544,000	491,000	32.3	29.3
Total stockholders' equity	1,019,000	966,000	60.5	57.6
Total liabilities and equity	$1,684,000	$1,678,000	100.0	100.0

* Columns do not always add to 100 due to rounding.

3. **Ratios for 2009:**

   a. Current ratio: $514,000/$265,000 = 1.9:1 (liquidity and efficiency)

   b. Acid-test ratio: ($79,000 + $65,000 + $120,000)/$265,000 = 1.0:1 (liquidity and efficiency)

   c. Average receivables: ($120,000 + $100,000)/2 = $110,000
   Accounts receivable turnover: $2,486,000/$110,000 = 22.6 times (liquidity and efficiency)

   d. Days' sales uncollected: ($120,000/$2,486,000) × 365 = 17.6 days (liquidity and efficiency)

   e. Average inventory: ($250,000 + $265,000)/2 = $257,500
   Inventory turnover: $1,523,000/$257,500 = 5.9 times (liquidity and efficiency)

   f. Debt ratio: $665,000/$1,684,000 = 39.5% (solvency)

   g. Debt-to-equity ratio: $665,000/$1,019,000 = 0.65 (solvency)

   h. Times interest earned: $185,000/$44,000 = 4.2 times (solvency)

   i. Profit margin ratio: $94,000/$2,486,000 = 3.8% (profitability)

   j. Average total assets: ($1,684,000 + $1,678,000)/2 = $1,681,000
   Total asset turnover: $2,486,000/$1,681,000 = 1.48 times (liquidity and efficiency)

   k. Return on total assets: $94,000/$1,681,000 = 5.6% or 3.8% × 1.48 = 5.6% (profitability)

   l. Average total common equity: ($1,019,000 + $966,000)/2 = $992,500
   Return on common stockholders' equity: $94,000/$992,500 = 9.5% (profitability)

APPENDIX

13A   Sustainable Income

A2 Explain the form and assess the content of a complete income statement.

When a company's revenue and expense transactions are from normal, continuing operations, a simple income statement is usually adequate. When a company's activities include income-related events not part of its normal, continuing operations, it must disclose information to help users understand these events and predict future performance. To meet these objectives, companies separate the income statement into continuing operations, discontinued segments, extraordinary items, comprehensive income, and earnings per share. For illustration, Exhibit 13A.1 shows such an income statement for ComUS. These

EXHIBIT 13A.1

Income Statement (all-inclusive) for a Corporation

ComUS Income Statement For Year Ended December 31, 2009		
Net sales		$8,478,000
Operating expenses		
Cost of goods sold	$5,950,000	
Depreciation expense	35,000	
Other selling, general, and administrative expenses	515,000	
Interest expense	20,000	
① Total operating expenses		(6,520,000)
Other gains (losses)		
Loss on plant relocation		(45,000)
Gain on sale of surplus land		72,000
Income from continuing operations before taxes		1,985,000
Income taxes expense		(595,500)
Income from continuing operations		1,389,500
Discontinued segment		
② Income from operating Division A (net of $180,000 taxes)	420,000	
Loss on disposal of Division A (net of $66,000 tax benefit)	(154,000)	266,000
Income before extraordinary items		1,655,500
Extraordinary items		
③ Gain on land expropriated by state (net of $85,200 taxes)	198,800	
Loss from earthquake damage (net of $270,000 tax benefit)	(630,000)	(431,200)
Net income		$1,224,300
Earnings per common share (200,000 outstanding shares)		
Income from continuing operations		$ 6.95
④ Discontinued operations		1.33
Income before extraordinary items		8.28
Extraordinary items		(2.16)
Net income (basic earnings per share)		$ 6.12

separate distinctions help us measure *sustainable income,* which is the income level most likely to continue into the future. Sustainable income is commonly used in PE ratios and other market-based measures of performance.

Continuing Operations

The first major section (①) shows the revenues, expenses, and income from continuing operations. Users especially rely on this information to predict future operations. Many users view this section as the most important. Earlier chapters explained the items comprising income from continuing operations.

Discontinued Segments

A **business segment** is a part of a company's operations that serves a particular line of business or class of customers. A segment has assets, liabilities, and financial results of operations that can be distinguished from those of other parts of the company. A company's gain or loss from selling or closing down a segment is separately reported. Section ② of Exhibit 13A.1 reports both (1) income from operating the discontinued segment for the current period prior to its disposal and (2) the loss from disposing of the segment's net assets. The income tax effects of each are reported separately from the income taxes expense in section ①.

Extraordinary Items

Section ③ reports **extraordinary gains and losses,** which are those that are *both unusual* and *infrequent.* An **unusual gain or loss** is abnormal or otherwise unrelated to the company's regular activities and environment. An **infrequent gain or loss** is not expected to recur given the company's operating environment. Reporting extraordinary items in a separate category helps users predict future performance, absent the effects of extraordinary items. Items usually considered extraordinary include (1) expropriation (taking away) of property by a foreign government, (2) condemning of property by a domestic government body, (3) prohibition against using an asset by a newly enacted law, and (4) losses and gains from an unusual and infrequent calamity ("act of God"). Items *not* considered extraordinary include (1) write-downs of inventories and write-offs of receivables, (2) gains and losses from disposing of segments, and (3) financial effects of labor strikes.

Gains and losses that are neither unusual nor infrequent are reported as part of continuing operations. Gains and losses that are *either* unusual *or* infrequent, but *not* both, are reported as part of continuing operations *but* after the normal revenues and expenses.

 Decision Maker ▬▬▬▬▬▬▬▬▬▬▬▬▬▬▬▬▬▬▬▬

Small Business Owner   You own an orange grove near Jacksonville, Florida. A bad frost destroys about one-half of your oranges. You are currently preparing an income statement for a bank loan. Can you claim the loss of oranges as extraordinary? [Answer—p. 592]

Earnings per Share

The final section ④ of the income statement in Exhibit 13A.1 reports earnings per share for each of the three subcategories of income (continuing operations, discontinued segments, and extraordinary items) when they exist. Earnings per share is discussed in Chapter 11.

Changes in Accounting Principles

Point: Changes in principles are sometimes required when new accounting standards are issued.

The *consistency concept* directs a company to apply the same accounting principles across periods. Yet a company can change from one acceptable accounting principle (such as FIFO, LIFO, or weighted-average) to another as long as the change improves the usefulness of information in its financial statements. A footnote would describe the accounting change and why it is an improvement.

Changes in accounting principles require retrospective application to prior periods' financial statements. *Retrospective application* involves applying a different accounting principle to prior periods as if that principle had always been used. Retrospective application enhances the consistency of financial information between periods, which improves the usefulness of information, especially with comparative analyses. (Prior to 2005, the cumulative effect of changes in accounting principles was recognized in net income in the period of the change.) Accounting standards also require that *a change in depreciation, amortization, or depletion method for long-term operating assets is accounted for as a change in accounting estimate*—that is, prospectively over current and future periods. This reflects the notion that an entity should change its depreciation, amortization, or depletion method only with changes in estimated asset benefits, the pattern of benefit usage, or information about those benefits.

Comprehensive Income

Comprehensive income is net income plus certain gains and losses that bypass the income statement. These items are recorded directly to equity. Specifically, comprehensive income equals the change in equity for the period, excluding investments from and distributions (dividends) to its stockholders. For **Best Buy**, it is computed as follows ($ millions):

Net income	$1,003
Accumulated other comprehensive income (loss)	(819)
Comprehensive income	$ 184

The most common items included in *accumulated other comprehensive income,* or *AOCI,* are unrealized gains and losses on available-for-sale securities and foreign currency translation adjustments. (Detailed computations for these items are in advanced courses.) Analysts disagree on how to treat these items. Some analysts believe that AOCI items should not be considered when predicting future performance, and some others believe AOCI items should be considered as they reflect on company and managerial performance. Whatever our position, we must be familiar with what AOCI items are as they are commonly reported in financial statements. Best Buy reports its comprehensive income in its statement of shareholders' equity (see Appendix A).

Quick Check
Answers—p. 592

13. Which of the following is an extraordinary item? (*a*) a settlement paid to a customer injured while using the company's product, (*b*) a loss to a plant from damages caused by a meteorite, or (*c*) a loss from selling old equipment.
14. Identify the four major sections of an income statement that are potentially reportable.
15. A company using FIFO for the past 15 years decides to switch to LIFO. The effect of this event on prior years' net income is (*a*) reported as if the new method had always been used; (*b*) ignored because it is a change in an accounting estimate; or (*c*) reported on the current year income statement.

Summary

C1 Explain the purpose of analysis. The purpose of financial statement analysis is to help users make better business decisions. Internal users want information to improve company efficiency and effectiveness in providing products and services. External users want information to make better and more informed decisions in pursuing their goals. The common goals of all users are to evaluate a company's (1) past and current performance, (2) current financial position, and (3) future performance and risk.

C2 Identify the building blocks of analysis. Financial statement analysis focuses on four "building blocks" of analysis: (1) liquidity and efficiency—ability to meet short-term obligations and efficiently generate revenues; (2) solvency—ability to generate future revenues and meet long-term obligations; (3) profitability—ability to provide financial rewards sufficient to attract and retain financing; and (4) market prospects—ability to generate positive market expectations.

C3 Describe standards for comparisons in analysis. Standards for comparisons include (1) intracompany—prior performance and relations between financial items for the company under analysis; (2) competitor—one or more direct competitors of the company; (3) industry—industry statistics; and (4) guidelines (rules of thumb)—general standards developed from past experiences and personal judgments.

C4 Identify the tools of analysis. The three most common tools of financial statement analysis are (1) horizontal analysis—comparing a company's financial condition and performance across time; (2) vertical analysis—comparing a company's financial condition and performance to a base amount such as revenues or total assets; and (3) ratio analysis—using and quantifying key relations among financial statement items.

A1 Summarize and report results of analysis. A financial statement analysis report is often organized around the building

blocks of analysis. A good report separates interpretations and conclusions of analysis from the information underlying them. An analysis report often consists of six sections: (1) executive summary, (2) analysis overview, (3) evidential matter, (4) assumptions, (5) key factors, and (6) inferences.

A2^A Explain the form and assess the content of a complete income statement. An income statement has four *potential* sections: (1) continuing operations, (2) discontinued segments, (3) extraordinary items, and (4) earnings per share.

P1 Explain and apply methods of horizontal analysis. Horizontal analysis is a tool to evaluate changes in data across time. Two important tools of horizontal analysis are comparative statements and trend analysis. Comparative statements show amounts for two or more successive periods, often with changes disclosed in both absolute and percent terms. Trend analysis is used to reveal important changes occurring from one period to the next.

P2 Describe and apply methods of vertical analysis. Vertical analysis is a tool to evaluate each financial statement item or group of items in terms of a base amount. Two tools of vertical analysis are common-size statements and graphical analyses. Each item in common-size statements is expressed as a percent of a base amount. For the balance sheet, the base amount is usually total assets, and for the income statement, it is usually sales.

P3 Define and apply ratio analysis. Ratio analysis provides clues to and symptoms of underlying conditions. Ratios, properly interpreted, identify areas requiring further investigation. A ratio expresses a mathematical relation between two quantities such as a percent, rate, or proportion. Ratios can be organized into the building blocks of analysis: (1) liquidity and efficiency, (2) solvency, (3) profitability, and (4) market prospects.

Guidance Answers to **Decision Maker**

Auditor The *joint relation* referred to is the combined increase in sales and the decrease in expenses yielding more than a 5% increase in income. Both *individual* accounts (sales and expenses) yield percent changes within the ±5% acceptable range. However, a joint analysis suggests a different picture. For example, consider a joint analysis using the profit margin ratio. The client's profit margin is 11.46% ($206,000 − $182,400/$206,000) for the current year compared with 5.0% ($200,000 − $190,000/$200,000) for the prior year—yielding a 129% increase in profit margin! This is what concerns the partner, and it suggests expanding audit tests to verify or refute the client's figures.

Banker Your decision on the loan application is positive for at least two reasons. First, the current ratio suggests a strong ability to meet short-term obligations. Second, current assets of $160,000 and a current ratio of 4:1 imply current liabilities of $40,000 (one-fourth of current assets) and a working capital excess of $120,000. This working capital excess is 60% of the loan amount. However, if the application is for a 10-year loan, our decision is less optimistic. The current ratio and working capital suggest a good safety margin, but indications of inefficiency in operations exist. In particular, a 4:1 current ratio is more than double its key competitors' ratio. This is characteristic of inefficient asset use.

Small Business Owner The frost loss is probably not extraordinary. Jacksonville experiences enough recurring frost damage to make it difficult to argue this event is both unusual and infrequent. Still, you want to highlight the frost loss and hope the bank views this uncommon event separately from continuing operations.

Guidance Answers to **Quick Checks**

1. General-purpose financial statements are intended for a variety of users interested in a company's financial condition and performance—users without the power to require specialized financial reports to meet their specific needs.

2. General-purpose financial statements include the income statement, balance sheet, statement of stockholders' (owner's) equity, and statement of cash flows plus the notes related to these statements.

3. *a*

4. Data from one or more direct competitors are usually preferred for comparative purposes.

5. *d*

6. Percents on comparative income statements show the increase or decrease in each item from one period to the next. On common-size comparative income statements, each item is shown as a percent of net sales for that period.

7. *c*

8. (*a*) ($820,000 + $240,000 + $470,000)/
   ($350,000 + $180,000) = 2.9 to 1.

(*b*) ($820,000 + $240,000)/($350,000 + $180,000) = 2:1.

9. (*a*) $2,500,000/[($290,000 + $240,000)/2] = 9.43 times.
   (*b*) ($290,000/$2,500,000) × 365 = 42 days.
   (*c*) $750,000/[($530,000 + $470,000)/2] = 1.5 times.
   (*d*) ($530,000/$750,000) × 365 = 258 days.

10. *c*

11. *b*

12. Profit margin × $\dfrac{\text{Total asset}}{\text{turnover}}$ = $\dfrac{\text{Return on}}{\text{total assets}}$

   $\dfrac{\$945,000}{\$8,500,000}$ × 1.8 = 20%

13. (*b*)

14. The four (potentially reportable) major sections are income from continuing operations, discontinued segments, extraordinary items, and earnings per share.

15. (*a*); known as retrospective application.

Key Terms

Business segment (p. 589)

Common-size financial statement (p. 571)

Comparative financial statements (p. 566)

Efficiency (p. 565)

Equity ratio (p. 579)

Extraordinary gains and losses (p. 589)

Financial reporting (p. 565)

Financial statement analysis (p. 564)

General-purpose financial statements (p. 565)

Horizontal analysis (p. 566)

Infrequent gain or loss (p. 590)

Liquidity (p. 565)

Market prospects (p. 565)

Profitability (p. 565)

Ratio analysis (p. 566)

Solvency (p. 565)

Unusual gain or loss (p. 589)

Vertical analysis (p. 566)

Working capital (p. 575)

Multiple Choice Quiz   Answers on p. 608   mhhe.com/wildFA5e

Additional Quiz Questions are available at the book's Website.

1. A company's sales in 2010 were $300,000 and in 2011 were $351,000. Using 2010 as the base year, the sales trend percent for 2011 is:
- **a.** 17%
- **b.** 85%
- **c.** 100%
- **d.** 117%
- **e.** 48%

Use the following information for questions 2 through 5.

GALLOWAY COMPANY
Balance Sheet
December 31, 2011

Assets

Cash	$ 86,000
Accounts receivable	76,000
Merchandise inventory	122,000
Prepaid insurance	12,000
Long-term investments	98,000
Plant assets, net	436,000
Total assets	$830,000

Liabilities and Equity

Current liabilities	$124,000
Long-term liabilities	90,000
Common stock	300,000
Retained earnings	316,000
Total liabilities and equity	$830,000

2. What is Galloway Company's current ratio?
- **a.** 0.69
- **b.** 1.31
- **c.** 3.88
- **d.** 6.69
- **e.** 2.39

3. What is Galloway Company's acid-test ratio?
- **a.** 2.39
- **b.** 0.69
- **c.** 1.31
- **d.** 6.69
- **e.** 3.88

4. What is Galloway Company's debt ratio?
- **a.** 25.78%
- **b.** 100.00%
- **c.** 74.22%
- **d.** 137.78%
- **e.** 34.74%

5. What is Galloway Company's equity ratio?
- **a.** 25.78%
- **b.** 100.00%
- **c.** 34.74%
- **d.** 74.22%
- **e.** 137.78%

Superscript letter ^{A} *denotes assignments based on Appendix 13A.*

Discussion Questions

1. What is the difference between comparative financial statements and common-size comparative statements?

2. Which items are usually assigned a 100% value on (*a*) a common-size balance sheet and (*b*) a common-size income statement?

3. Explain the difference between financial reporting and financial statements.

4. ♟ What three factors would influence your evaluation as to whether a company's current ratio is good or bad?

5. ♟ Suggest several reasons why a 2:1 current ratio might not be adequate for a particular company.

6. ♟ Why is working capital given special attention in the process of analyzing balance sheets?

7. ♟ What does the number of days' sales uncollected indicate?

8. ♟ What does a relatively high accounts receivable turnover indicate about a company's short-term liquidity?

9. ♟ Why is a company's capital structure, as measured by debt and equity ratios, important to financial statement analysts?

10. ♟ How does inventory turnover provide information about a company's short-term liquidity?

11. ♟ What ratios would you compute to evaluate management performance?

12. ♟ Why would a company's return on total assets be different from its return on common stockholders' equity?

13. Where on the income statement does a company report an unusual gain not expected to occur more often than once every two years or so?

14. Use **Best Buy**'s financial statements in Appendix A to compute its return on total assets for fiscal years ended February 28, 2009, and March 1, 2008. Total assets at March 3, 2007, were $13,570 (in millions).

15. Refer to **RadioShack**'s financial statements in Appendix A to compute its equity ratio as of December 31, 2008 and 2007.

16. Refer to **GOME**'s financial statements in Appendix A. Compute its debt ratio as of December 31, 2008, and December 31, 2007.

17. Refer to **Apple**'s financial statements in Appendix A. Compute its profit margin for the fiscal year ended September 27, 2008.

♟ *Denotes Discussion Questions that involve decision making.*

Available with Connect Accounting **connect**

QUICK STUDY

QS 13-1
Financial reporting   C1

Which of the following items (1) through (9) are part of financial reporting but are *not* included as part of general-purpose financial statements? (1) stock price information and analysis, (2) statement of cash flows, (3) management discussion and analysis of financial performance, (4) income statement, (5) company news releases, (6) balance sheet, (7) financial statement notes, (8) statement of shareholders' equity, (9) prospectus.

QS 13-2
Standard of comparison   C3

What are four possible standards of comparison used to analyze financial statement ratios? Which of these is generally considered to be the most useful? Which one is least likely to provide a good basis for comparison?

QS 13-3
Common-size and trend percents
P1   P2

Use the following information for Owens Corporation to determine (1) the 2010 and 2011 common-size percents for cost of goods sold using net sales as the base and (2) the 2010 and 2011 trend percents for net sales using 2010 as the base year.

($ thousands)	2011	2010
Net sales	$101,400	$58,100
Cost of goods sold	55,300	30,700

QS 13-4
Horizontal analysis
P1

Compute the annual dollar changes and percent changes for each of the following accounts.

	2011	2010
Short-term investments	$110,000	$80,000
Accounts receivable	22,000	25,000
Notes payable	30,000	0

QS 13-5
Building blocks of analysis
C2   C4   P3

Match the ratio to the building block of financial statement analysis to which it best relates.

A. Liquidity and efficiency   **C.** Profitability
B. Solvency   **D.** Market prospects

1. _____ Gross margin ratio   **6.** _____ Book value per common share
2. _____ Acid-test ratio   **7.** _____ Days' sales in inventory
3. _____ Equity ratio   **8.** _____ Accounts receivable turnover
4. _____ Return on total assets   **9.** _____ Debt-to-equity
5. _____ Dividend yield   **10.** _____ Times interest earned

---

QS 13-6
Identifying financial ratios
C4   P3

1. Which two short-term liquidity ratios measure how frequently a company collects its accounts?
2. What measure reflects the difference between current assets and current liabilities?
3. Which two ratios are key components in measuring a company's operating efficiency? Which ratio summarizes these two components?

For each ratio listed, identify whether the change in ratio value from 2010 to 2011 is usually regarded as favorable or unfavorable.

QS 13-7
Ratio interpretation
P3

Ratio	2011	2010	Ratio	2011	2010
1. Profit margin	10%	9%	5. Accounts receivable turnover	6.7	5.5
2. Debt ratio	43%	39%	6. Basic earnings per share	$1.25	$1.10
3. Gross margin	32%	44%	7. Inventory turnover	3.4	3.6
4. Acid-test ratio	1.20	1.05	8. Dividend yield	4%	3.2%

A review of the notes payable files discovers that three years ago the company reported the entire amount of a payment (principal and interest) on an installment note payable as interest expense. This mistake had a material effect on the amount of income in that year. How should the correction be reported in the current year financial statements?

QS 13-8ᴬ
Error adjustments
A2

Answer each of the following related to international accounting and analysis.

a. Identify an advantage to using horizontal and vertical analyses when examining companies reporting under different currencies.

b. Identify a limitation to using ratio analysis when examining companies reporting under different accounting systems such as IFRS versus U.S. GAAP.

QS 13-9
International ratio analysis

C4

connect Available with Connect Accounting

Compute trend percents for the following accounts, using 2007 as the base year. State whether the situation as revealed by the trends appears to be favorable or unfavorable for each account.

EXERCISES

Exercise 13-1
Computation and analysis of trend percents

P1

	2011	2010	2009	2008	2007
Sales	$282,700	$270,700	$252,500	$234,460	$150,000
Cost of goods sold	128,100	121,980	115,180	106,340	67,000
Accounts receivable	18,000	17,200	16,300	15,100	9,000

Common-size and trend percents for Danian Company's sales, cost of goods sold, and expenses follow. Determine whether net income increased, decreased, or remained unchanged in this three-year period.

Exercise 13-2
Determination of income effects from common-size and trend percents

P1 P2

	Common-Size Percents			Trend Percents		
	2010	2009	2008	2010	2009	2008
Sales	100.0%	100.0%	100.0%	104.9%	103.7%	100.0%
Cost of goods sold	67.7	61.2	58.4	102.5	108.6	100.0
Total expenses	14.4	13.9	14.2	106.5	101.5	100.0

Express the following comparative income statements in common-size percents and assess whether or not this company's situation has improved in the most recent year.

Exercise 13-3
Common-size percent computation and interpretation

P2

MULAN CORPORATION Comparative Income Statements For Years Ended December 31, 2011 and 2010		
	2011	2010
Sales	$657,386	$488,400
Cost of goods sold	427,301	286,202
Gross profit	230,085	202,198
Operating expenses	138,051	94,750
Net income	$ 92,034	$107,448

Exercise 13-4
Analysis of short-term
financial condition

A1   P3

Team Project: Assume
that the two companies apply
for a one-year loan from the
team. Identify additional
information the companies
must provide before the
team can make a loan
decision.

The following information is available for Orkay Company and Lowes Company, similar firms operating in the same industry. Write a half-page report comparing Orkay and Lowes using the available information. Your discussion should include their ability to meet current obligations and to use current assets efficiently.

	Orkay			Lowes		
	2010	2009	2008	2010	2009	2008
Current ratio	1.6	1.7	2.0	3.1	2.6	1.8
Acid-test ratio	0.9	1.0	1.1	2.7	2.4	1.5
Accounts receivable turnover	29.5	24.2	28.2	15.4	14.2	15.0
Merchandise inventory turnover	23.2	20.9	16.1	13.5	12.0	11.6
Working capital	$60,000	$48,000	$42,000	$121,000	$93,000	$68,000

Exercise 13-5
Analysis of efficiency and
financial leverage

A1   P3

Caren Company and Revlon Company are similar firms that operate in the same industry. Revlon began operations in 2009 and Caren in 2006. In 2011, both companies pay 7% interest on their debt to creditors. The following additional information is available.

	Caren Company			Revlon Company		
	2011	2010	2009	2011	2010	2009
Total asset turnover	3.0	2.7	2.9	1.6	1.4	1.1
Return on total assets	6.9%	6.5%	6.4%	4.3%	4.1%	3.1%
Profit margin ratio	2.3%	2.4%	2.2%	2.7%	2.9%	2.8%
Sales	$400,000	$370,000	$386,000	$200,000	$160,000	$100,000

Write a half-page report comparing Caren and Revlon using the available information. Your analysis should include their ability to use assets efficiently to produce profits. Also comment on their success in employing financial leverage in 2011.

Exercise 13-6
Common-size percents

P2

Nabisco Company's year-end balance sheets follow. Express the balance sheets in common-size percents. Round amounts to the nearest one-tenth of a percent. Analyze and comment on the results.

At December 31	2010	2009	2008
Assets			
Cash	$ 36,229	$ 42,780	$ 44,562
Accounts receivable, net	106,073	76,377	57,087
Merchandise inventory	137,408	98,929	62,038
Prepaid expenses	11,548	11,003	4,903
Plant assets, net	335,317	311,062	272,710
Total assets	$626,575	$540,151	$441,300
Liabilities and Equity			
Accounts payable	$157,577	$ 94,024	$ 57,087
Long-term notes payable secured by mortgages on plant assets	116,618	127,962	99,478
Common stock, $10 par value	163,500	163,500	163,500
Retained earnings	188,880	154,665	121,235
Total liabilities and equity	$626,575	$540,151	$441,300

Exercise 13-7
Liquidity analysis

P3

Refer to Nabisco Company's balance sheets in Exercise 13-6. Analyze its year-end short-term liquidity position at the end of 2010, 2009, and 2008 by computing (1) the current ratio and (2) the acid-test ratio. Comment on the ratio results. (Round ratio amounts to two decimals.)

Refer to the Nabisco Company information in Exercise 13-6. The company's income statements for the years ended December 31, 2010 and 2009, follow. Assume that all sales are on credit and then compute: (1) days' sales uncollected, (2) accounts receivable turnover, (3) inventory turnover, and (4) days' sales in inventory. Comment on the changes in the ratios from 2009 to 2010. (Round amounts to one decimal.)

Exercise 13-8
Liquidity analysis and interpretation

P3

For Year Ended December 31	2010		2009	
Sales		$685,000		$557,000
Cost of goods sold	$417,850		$356,265	
Other operating expenses	207,282		141,971	
Interest expense	8,175		8,960	
Income taxes	12,900		12,450	
Total costs and expenses		646,207		519,646
Net income		$ 38,793		$ 37,354
Earnings per share		$ 2.37		$ 2.28

Refer to the Nabisco Company information in Exercises 13-6 and 13-8. Compare the company's long-term risk and capital structure positions at the end of 2010 and 2009 by computing these ratios: (1) debt and equity ratios, (2) debt-to-equity ratio, and (3) times interest earned. Comment on these ratio results.

Exercise 13-9
Risk and capital structure analysis

P3

Refer to Nabisco Company's financial information in Exercises 13-6 and 13-8. Evaluate the company's efficiency and profitability by computing the following for 2010 and 2009: (1) profit margin ratio, (2) total asset turnover, and (3) return on total assets. Comment on these ratio results.

Exercise 13-10
Efficiency and profitability analysis P3

Refer to Nabisco Company's financial information in Exercises 13-6 and 13-8. Additional information about the company follows. To help evaluate the company's profitability, compute and interpret the following ratios for 2010 and 2009: (1) return on common stockholders' equity, (2) price-earnings ratio on December 31, and (3) dividend yield.

Exercise 13-11
Profitability analysis

P3

Common stock market price, December 31, 2010	$30.00
Common stock market price, December 31, 2009	28.00
Annual cash dividends per share in 2010	0.28
Annual cash dividends per share in 2009	0.24

In 2011, Simplon Merchandising, Inc., sold its interest in a chain of wholesale outlets, taking the company completely out of the wholesaling business. The company still operates its retail outlets. A listing of the major sections of an income statement follows:

A. Income (loss) from continuing operations

B. Income (loss) from operating, or gain (loss) from disposing, a discontinued segment

C. Extraordinary gain (loss)

Indicate where each of the following income-related items for this company appears on its 2011 income statement by writing the letter of the appropriate section in the blank beside each item.

Exercise 13-12ᴬ
Income statement categories

A2

Section	Item	Debit	Credit
_____	1. Net sales		$3,000,000
_____	2. Gain on state's condemnation of company property (net of tax)		330,000
_____	3. Cost of goods sold	$1,580,000	
_____	4. Income taxes expense	117,000	
_____	5. Depreciation expense	332,500	
_____	6. Gain on sale of wholesale business segment (net of tax)		875,000
_____	7. Loss from operating wholesale business segment (net of tax)	544,000	
_____	8. Salaries expense	740,000	

Exercise 13-13ᴬ

Income statement presentation

A2

Use the financial data for Simplon Merchandising, Inc., in Exercise 13-12 to prepare its income statement for calendar year 2011. (Ignore the earnings per share section.)

Exercise 13-14

Ratio analysis under different currencies

C3 P3

Nintendo Company, Ltd., reports the following financial information as of, or for the year ended, March 31, 2008. Nintendo reports its financial statements in both Japanese yen and U.S. dollars as shown (amounts in millions).

Current assets	¥1,646,834	$16,468.348
Total assets	1,802,490	18,024.903
Current liabilities	567,222	5,672.229
Net sales	1,672,423	16,724.230
Net income	257,342	2,573.426

1. Compute Nintendo's current ratio, net profit margin, and sales-to-total-assets using the financial information reported in (a) yen and (b) dollars.

2. What can we conclude from a review of the results for part 1?

Available with Connect Accounting **connect**

PROBLEM SET A   Selected comparative financial statements of Astalon Company follow.

Problem 13-1A

Ratios, common-size statements, and trend percents

P1 P2 P3

mhhe.com/wildFA5e

ASTALON COMPANY Comparative Income Statements For Years Ended December 31, 2010, 2009, and 2008			
	2010	**2009**	**2008**
Sales	$526,304	$403,192	$279,800
Cost of goods sold	316,835	255,624	179,072
Gross profit	209,469	147,568	100,728
Selling expenses	74,735	55,640	36,934
Administrative expenses	47,367	35,481	23,223
Total expenses	122,102	91,121	60,157
Income before taxes	87,367	56,447	40,571
Income taxes	16,250	11,572	8,236
Net income	$ 71,117	$ 44,875	$ 32,335

ASTALON COMPANY Comparative Balance Sheets December 31, 2010, 2009, and 2008			
	2010	**2009**	**2008**
Assets			
Current assets	$ 48,242	$ 38,514	$ 51,484
Long-term investments	0	800	3,620
Plant assets, net	92,405	97,259	58,047
Total assets	$140,647	$136,573	$113,151
Liabilities and Equity			
Current liabilities	$ 20,534	$ 20,349	$ 19,801
Common stock	69,000	69,000	51,000
Other paid-in capital	8,625	8,625	5,667
Retained earnings	42,488	38,599	36,683
Total liabilities and equity	$140,647	$136,573	$113,151

Required

1. Compute each year's current ratio. (Round ratio amounts to one decimal.)
2. Express the income statement data in common-size percents. (Round percents to two decimals.)
3. Express the balance sheet data in trend percents with 2008 as the base year. (Round percents to two decimals.)

Check (3) 2010, Total assets trend, 124.30%

Analysis Component

4. Comment on any significant relations revealed by the ratios and percents computed.

Selected comparative financial statements of Adobe Company follow.

Problem 13-2A
Calculation and analysis of trend percents

A1 P1

ADOBE COMPANY Comparative Income Statements For Years Ended December 31, 2010–2004							
($ thousands)	2010	2009	2008	2007	2006	2005	2004
Sales	$2,431	$2,129	$1,937	$1,776	$1,657	$1,541	$1,263
Cost of goods sold	1,747	1,421	1,223	1,070	994	930	741
Gross profit	684	708	714	706	663	611	522
Operating expenses	521	407	374	276	239	236	196
Net income	$ 163	$ 301	$ 340	$ 430	$ 424	$ 375	$ 326

ADOBE COMPANY Comparative Balance Sheets December 31, 2010–2004							
($ thousands)	2010	2009	2008	2007	2006	2005	2004
Assets							
Cash	$ 163	$ 216	$ 224	$ 229	$ 238	$ 235	$ 242
Accounts receivable, net	1,173	1,232	1,115	855	753	714	503
Merchandise inventory	4,244	3,090	2,699	2,275	2,043	1,735	1,258
Other current assets	109	98	60	108	91	93	48
Long-term investments	0	0	0	334	334	334	334
Plant assets, net	5,192	5,172	4,526	2,553	2,639	2,345	2,015
Total assets	$10,881	$9,808	$8,624	$6,354	$6,098	$5,456	$4,400
Liabilities and Equity							
Current liabilities	$ 2,734	$2,299	$1,509	$1,255	$1,089	$1,030	$ 664
Long-term liabilities	2,924	2,547	2,478	1,151	1,176	1,273	955
Common stock	1,980	1,980	1,980	1,760	1,760	1,540	1,540
Other paid-in capital	495	495	495	440	440	385	385
Retained earnings	2,748	2,487	2,162	1,748	1,633	1,228	856
Total liabilities and equity	$10,881	$9,808	$8,624	$6,354	$6,098	$5,456	$4,400

Required

1. Compute trend percents for all components of both statements using 2004 as the base year. (Round percents to one decimal.)

Check (1) 2010, Total assets trend, 247.3%

Analysis Component

2. Analyze and comment on the financial statements and trend percents from part 1.

Page Corporation began the month of May with $884,000 of current assets, a current ratio of 2.6:1, and an acid-test ratio of 1.5:1. During the month, it completed the following transactions (the company uses a perpetual inventory system).

Problem 13-3A
Transactions, working capital, and liquidity ratios

P3

mhhe.com/wildFA5e

May 2 Purchased $70,000 of merchandise inventory on credit.
    8 Sold merchandise inventory that cost $60,000 for $130,000 cash.
  10 Collected $30,000 cash on an account receivable.
  15 Paid $31,000 cash to settle an account payable.

Check   May 22: Current ratio, 2.23;
Acid-test ratio, 1.37

May 29: Current ratio, 2.00;
Working capital, $462,000

17   Wrote off a $5,000 bad debt against the Allowance for Doubtful Accounts account.
22   Declared a $1 per share cash dividend on its 67,000 shares of outstanding common stock.
26   Paid the dividend declared on May 22.
27   Borrowed $85,000 cash by giving the bank a 30-day, 10% note.
28   Borrowed $100,000 cash by signing a long-term secured note.
29   Used the $185,000 cash proceeds from the notes to buy new machinery.

Required

Prepare a table showing Page's (1) current ratio, (2) acid-test ratio, and (3) working capital, after each transaction. Round ratios to two decimals.

Problem 13-4A
Calculation of financial
statement ratios

P3

mhhe.com/wildFA5e

Selected year-end financial statements of Cadet Corporation follow. (All sales were on credit; selected balance sheet amounts at December 31, 2010, were inventory, $56,900; total assets, $219,400; common stock, $85,000; and retained earnings, $52,348.)

CADET CORPORATION
Income Statement
For Year Ended December 31, 2011

Sales	$456,600
Cost of goods sold	297,450
Gross profit	159,150
Operating expenses	99,400
Interest expense	3,900
Income before taxes	55,850
Income taxes	22,499
Net income	$ 33,351

CADET CORPORATION
Balance Sheet
December 31, 2011

Assets		Liabilities and Equity	
Cash	$ 20,000	Accounts payable	$ 21,500
Short-term investments	8,200	Accrued wages payable	4,400
Accounts receivable, net	29,400	Income taxes payable	3,700
Notes receivable (trade)*	7,000	Long-term note payable, secured	
Merchandise inventory	34,150	by mortgage on plant assets	67,400
Prepaid expenses	2,700	Common stock	85,000
Plant assets, net	147,300	Retained earnings	66,750
Total assets	$248,750	Total liabilities and equity	$248,750

* These are short-term notes receivable arising from customer (trade) sales.

Required

Check   Acid-test ratio, 2.2 to 1;
Inventory turnover, 6.5

Compute the following: (1) current ratio, (2) acid-test ratio, (3) days' sales uncollected, (4) inventory turnover, (5) days' sales in inventory, (6) debt-to-equity ratio, (7) times interest earned, (8) profit margin ratio, (9) total asset turnover, (10) return on total assets, and (11) return on common stockholders' equity.

Problem 13-5A
Comparative ratio
analysis   A1   P3

Summary information from the financial statements of two companies competing in the same industry follows.

	Karto Company	Bryan Company			Karto Company	Bryan Company
Data from the current year-end balance sheets				**Data from the current year's income statement**		
Assets				Sales	$790,000	$897,200
Cash	$ 19,500	$ 36,000		Cost of goods sold	588,100	634,500
Accounts receivable, net	36,400	53,400		Interest expense	7,600	19,000
Current notes receivable (trade)	9,400	7,600		Income tax expense	15,185	24,769
Merchandise inventory	84,740	134,500		Net income	$179,115	$218,931
Prepaid expenses	6,200	7,250		Basic earnings per share	$ 4.71	$ 5.58
Plant assets, net	350,000	307,400				
Total assets	$506,240	$546,150				
				Beginning-of-year balance sheet data		
Liabilities and Equity				Accounts receivable, net	$ 26,800	$ 51,200
Current liabilities	$ 63,340	$ 73,819		Current notes receivable (trade)	0	0
Long-term notes payable	82,485	99,000		Merchandise inventory	55,600	107,400
Common stock, $5 par value	190,000	196,000		Total assets	408,000	422,500
Retained earnings	170,415	177,331		Common stock, $5 par value	190,000	196,000
Total liabilities and equity	$506,240	$546,150		Retained earnings	124,300	95,600

Required

1. For both companies compute the (*a*) current ratio, (*b*) acid-test ratio, (*c*) accounts (including notes) receivable turnover, (*d*) inventory turnover, (*e*) days' sales in inventory, and (*f*) days' sales uncollected. Identify the company you consider to be the better short-term credit risk and explain why.

2. For both companies compute the (*a*) profit margin ratio, (*b*) total asset turnover, (*c*) return on total assets, and (*d*) return on common stockholders' equity. Assuming that each company paid cash dividends of $3.50 per share and each company's stock can be purchased at $85 per share, compute their (*e*) price-earnings ratios and (*f*) dividend yields. Identify which company's stock you would recommend as the better investment and explain why.

Check (1) Bryan: Accounts receivable turnover, 16.0; Inventory turnover, 5.2

(2) Karto: Profit margin, 22.7%; PE, 18.0

Selected account balances from the adjusted trial balance for Lindo Corporation as of its calendar year-end December 31, 2011, follow.

Problem 13-6A^A
Income statement computations and format

A2

	Debit	Credit
a. Interest revenue		$ 15,000
b. Depreciation expense—Equipment	$ 35,000	
c. Loss on sale of equipment	26,850	
d. Accounts payable		45,000
e. Other operating expenses	107,400	
f. Accumulated depreciation—Equipment		72,600
g. Gain from settlement of lawsuit		45,000
h. Accumulated depreciation—Buildings		175,500
i. Loss from operating a discontinued segment (pretax)	19,250	
j. Gain on insurance recovery of tornado damage (pretax and extraordinary)		30,120
k. Net sales		999,500
l. Depreciation expense—Buildings	53,000	
m. Correction of overstatement of prior year's sales (pretax)	17,000	
n. Gain on sale of discontinued segment's assets (pretax)		35,000
o. Loss from settlement of lawsuit	24,750	
p. Income taxes expense	?	
q. Cost of goods sold	483,500	

Required

Answer each of the following questions by providing supporting computations.

1. Assume that the company's income tax rate is 30% for all items. Identify the tax effects and after-tax amounts of the four items labeled pretax.

2. What is the amount of income from continuing operations before income taxes? What is the amount of the income taxes expense? What is the amount of income from continuing operations?

Check (3) $11,025

3. What is the total amount of after-tax income (loss) associated with the discontinued segment?

(4) $241,325

4. What is the amount of income (loss) before the extraordinary items?

(5) $262,409

5. What is the amount of net income for the year?

PROBLEM SET B

Selected comparative financial statement information of Danno Corporation follows.

Problem 13-1B

Ratios, common-size statements, and trend percents

P1 P2 P3

DANNO CORPORATION			
Comparative Income Statements			
For Years Ended December 31, 2010, 2009, and 2008			
	2010	**2009**	**2008**
Sales	$392,000	$300,304	$208,400
Cost of goods sold	235,984	190,092	133,376
Gross profit	156,016	110,212	75,024
Selling expenses	55,664	41,442	27,509
Administrative expenses	35,280	26,427	17,297
Total expenses	90,944	67,869	44,806
Income before taxes	65,072	42,343	30,218
Income taxes	12,103	8,680	6,134
Net income	$ 52,969	$ 33,663	$ 24,084

DANNO CORPORATION			
Comparative Balance Sheets			
December 31, 2010, 2009, and 2008			
	2010	**2009**	**2008**
Assets			
Current assets	$ 53,776	$ 42,494	$ 55,118
Long-term investments	0	400	4,110
Plant assets, net	99,871	106,303	64,382
Total assets	$153,647	$149,197	$123,610
Liabilities and Equity			
Current liabilities	$ 22,432	$ 22,230	$ 21,632
Common stock	70,000	70,000	52,000
Other paid-in capital	8,750	8,750	5,778
Retained earnings	52,465	48,217	44,200
Total liabilities and equity	$153,647	$149,197	$123,610

Required

1. Compute each year's current ratio. (Round ratio amounts to one decimal.)

2. Express the income statement data in common-size percents. (Round percents to two decimals.)

Check (3) 2010, Total assets trend, 124.30%

3. Express the balance sheet data in trend percents with 2008 as the base year. (Round percents to two decimals.)

Analysis Component

4. Comment on any significant relations revealed by the ratios and percents computed.

Selected comparative financial statements of Park Company follow.

Problem 13-2B
Calculation and analysis of trend percents

A1   P1

PARK COMPANY Comparative Income Statements For Years Ended December 31, 2010–2004							
($ thousands)	2010	2009	2008	2007	2006	2005	2004
Sales	$570	$620	$640	$690	$750	$780	$870
Cost of goods sold	286	300	304	324	350	360	390
Gross profit	284	320	336	366	400	420	480
Operating expenses	94	114	122	136	150	154	160
Net income	$190	$206	$214	$230	$250	$266	$320

PARK COMPANY Comparative Balance Sheets December 31, 2010–2004							
($ thousands)	2010	2009	2008	2007	2006	2005	2004
Assets							
Cash	$ 54	$ 56	$ 62	$ 64	$ 70	$ 72	$ 78
Accounts receivable, net	140	146	150	154	160	164	170
Merchandise inventory	176	182	188	190	196	200	218
Other current assets	44	44	46	48	48	50	50
Long-term investments	46	40	36	120	120	120	120
Plant assets, net	520	524	530	422	430	438	464
Total assets	$980	$992	$1,012	$998	$1,024	$1,044	$1,100
Liabilities and Equity							
Current liabilities	$158	$166	$ 196	$200	$ 220	$ 270	$ 290
Long-term liabilities	102	130	152	158	204	224	270
Common stock	180	180	180	180	180	180	180
Other paid-in capital	80	80	80	80	80	80	80
Retained earnings	460	436	404	380	340	290	280
Total liabilities and equity	$980	$992	$1,012	$998	$1,024	$1,044	$1,100

Required

1. Compute trend percents for all components of both statements using 2004 as the base year. (Round percents to one decimal.)

Check (1) 2010, Total assets trend, 89.1%

Analysis Component

2. Analyze and comment on the financial statements and trend percents from part 1.

Menardo Corporation began the month of June with $600,000 of current assets, a current ratio of 2.5:1, and an acid-test ratio of 1.4:1. During the month, it completed the following transactions (the company uses a perpetual inventory system).

Problem 13-3B
Transactions, working capital, and liquidity ratios

P3

Check June 3: Current ratio, 2.88; Acid-test ratio, 2.40

June 1 Sold merchandise inventory that cost $150,000 for $240,000 cash.
       3 Collected $176,000 cash on an account receivable.
       5 Purchased $300,000 of merchandise inventory on credit.
       7 Borrowed $200,000 cash by giving the bank a 60-day, 8% note.
      10 Borrowed $240,000 cash by signing a long-term secured note.
      12 Purchased machinery for $550,000 cash.
      15 Declared a $1 per share cash dividend on its 160,000 shares of outstanding common stock.
      19 Wrote off a $10,000 bad debt against the Allowance for Doubtful Accounts account.
      22 Paid $24,000 cash to settle an account payable.
      30 Paid the dividend declared on June 15.

June 30: Working capital, $(20,000); Current ratio, 0.97

Required

Prepare a table showing the company's (1) current ratio, (2) acid-test ratio, and (3) working capital after each transaction. Round ratios to two decimals.

Problem 13-4B
Calculation of financial
statement ratios

P3

Selected year-end financial statements of Steele Corporation follow. (All sales were on credit; selected balance sheet amounts at December 31, 2010, were inventory, $55,900; total assets, $249,400; common stock, $105,000; and retained earnings, $17,748.)

STEELE CORPORATION
Income Statement
For Year Ended December 31, 2011

Sales	$447,600
Cost of goods sold	298,150
Gross profit	149,450
Operating expenses	98,500
Interest expense	4,600
Income before taxes	46,350
Income taxes	18,672
Net income	$ 27,678

STEELE CORPORATION
Balance Sheet
December 31, 2011

Assets		Liabilities and Equity	
Cash	$ 8,000	Accounts payable	$ 25,500
Short-term investments	8,000	Accrued wages payable	3,000
Accounts receivable, net	28,800	Income taxes payable	4,000
Notes receivable (trade)*	8,000	Long-term note payable, secured	
Merchandise inventory	34,150	by mortgage on plant assets	63,400
Prepaid expenses	2,750	Common stock, $5 par value	105,000
Plant assets, net	150,300	Retained earnings	39,100
Total assets	$240,000	Total liabilities and equity	$240,000

* These are short-term notes receivable arising from customer (trade) sales.

Required

Check Acid-test ratio, 1.6 to 1;
Inventory turnover, 6.6

Compute the following: (1) current ratio, (2) acid-test ratio, (3) days' sales uncollected, (4) inventory turnover, (5) days' sales in inventory, (6) debt-to-equity ratio, (7) times interest earned, (8) profit margin ratio, (9) total asset turnover, (10) return on total assets, and (11) return on common stockholders' equity.

Problem 13-5B
Comparative
ratio analysis   A1   P3 ♟

Summary information from the financial statements of two companies competing in the same industry follows.

	Crisco Company	Silas Company			Crisco Company	Silas Company
Data from the current year-end balance sheets				**Data from the current year's income statement**		
Assets				Sales	$394,600	$668,500
Cash	$ 21,000	$ 37,500		Cost of goods sold	291,600	481,000
Accounts receivable, net	78,100	71,500		Interest expense	6,900	13,300
Current notes receivable (trade)	12,600	10,000		Income tax expense	6,700	14,300
Merchandise inventory	87,800	83,000		Net income	34,850	62,700
Prepaid expenses	10,700	11,100		Basic earnings per share	1.16	1.84
Plant assets, net	177,900	253,300				
Total assets	$388,100	$466,400				
				Beginning-of-year balance sheet data		
Liabilities and Equity				Accounts receivable, net	$ 73,200	$ 74,300
Current liabilities	$100,500	$ 98,000		Current notes receivable (trade)	0	0
Long-term notes payable	85,650	62,400		Merchandise inventory	106,100	81,500
Common stock, $5 par value	150,000	170,000		Total assets	384,400	444,000
Retained earnings	51,950	136,000		Common stock, $5 par value	150,000	170,000
Total liabilities and equity	$388,100	$466,400		Retained earnings	50,100	110,700

Required

1. For both companies compute the (*a*) current ratio, (*b*) acid-test ratio, (*c*) accounts (including notes) receivable turnover, (*d*) inventory turnover, (*e*) days' sales in inventory, and (*f*) days' sales uncollected. Identify the company you consider to be the better short-term credit risk and explain why.

2. For both companies compute the (*a*) profit margin ratio, (*b*) total asset turnover, (*c*) return on total assets, and (*d*) return on common stockholders' equity. Assuming that each company paid cash dividends of $1.10 per share and each company's stock can be purchased at $25 per share, compute their (*e*) price-earnings ratios and (*f*) dividend yields. Identify which company's stock you would recommend as the better investment and explain why.

Check (1) Crisco: Accounts receivable turnover, 4.8; Inventory turnover, 3.0

(2) Silas: Profit margin, 9.4%; PE, 13.6

Selected account balances from the adjusted trial balance for Harton Corp. as of its calendar year-end December 31, 2011, follow.

Problem 13-6B[A]
Income statement computations and format

A2

		Debit	Credit
a.	Accumulated depreciation—Buildings		$ 410,000
b.	Interest revenue		30,000
c.	Net sales		2,650,000
d.	Income taxes expense	$?	
e.	Loss on hurricane damage (pretax and extraordinary)	74,000	
f.	Accumulated depreciation—Equipment		230,000
g.	Other operating expenses	338,000	
h.	Depreciation expense—Equipment	110,000	
i.	Loss from settlement of lawsuit	46,000	
j.	Gain from settlement of lawsuit		78,000
k.	Loss on sale of equipment	34,000	
l.	Loss from operating a discontinued segment (pretax)	130,000	
m.	Depreciation expense—Buildings	166,000	
n.	Correction of overstatement of prior year's expense (pretax)		58,000
o.	Cost of goods sold	1,050,000	
p.	Loss on sale of discontinued segment's assets (pretax)	190,000	
q.	Accounts payable		142,000

Required

Answer each of the following questions by providing supporting computations.

1. Assume that the company's income tax rate is 25% for all items. Identify the tax effects and after-tax amounts of the four items labeled pretax.

2. What is the amount of income from continuing operations before income taxes? What is the amount of income taxes expense? What is the amount of income from continuing operations?

3. What is the total amount of after-tax income (loss) associated with the discontinued segment?

4. What is the amount of income (loss) before the extraordinary items?

5. What is the amount of net income for the year?

Check (3) $(240,000)

(4) $520,500

(5) $465,000

(This serial problem began in Chapter 1 and continues through most of the book. If previous chapter segments were not completed, the serial problem can begin at this point. It is helpful, but not necessary, to use the Working Papers that accompany the book.)

SERIAL PROBLEM

Success Systems

SP 13   Use the following selected data from Success Systems' income statement for the three months ended March 31, 2010, and from its March 31, 2010, balance sheet to complete the requirements below: computer services revenue, $25,160; net sales (of goods), $18,693; total sales and revenue, $43,853; cost of goods sold, $14,052; net income, $18,686; quick assets, $100,205; current assets, $105,209; total assets, $129,909; current liabilities, $875; total liabilities, $875; and total equity, $129,034.

Required

1. Compute the gross margin ratio (both with and without services revenue) and net profit margin ratio.

2. Compute the current ratio and acid-test ratio.

3. Compute the debt ratio and equity ratio.

4. What percent of its assets are current? What percent are long term?

BEYOND THE NUMBERS

REPORTING IN ACTION

A1 P1 P2

BTN 13-1   Refer to **Best Buy**'s financial statements in Appendix A to answer the following.

1. Using fiscal 2007 as the base year, compute trend percents for fiscal years 2007, 2008, and 2009 for revenues, cost of sales, selling general and administrative expenses, income taxes, and net income. (Round to the nearest whole percent.)

2. Compute common-size percents for fiscal years 2009 and 2008 for the following categories of assets: (*a*) total current assets, (*b*) property and equipment, net, and (*c*) goodwill. (Round to the nearest tenth of a percent.)

3. Comment on any notable changes across the years for the income statement trends computed in part 1 and the balance sheet percents computed in part 2.

Fast Forward

4. Access Best Buy's financial statements for fiscal years ending after February 28, 2009, from Best Buy's Website (BestBuy.com) or the SEC database (www.SEC.gov). Update your work for parts 1, 2, and 3 using the new information accessed.

COMPARATIVE ANALYSIS

C3 P2

BTN 13-2   Key figures for **Best Buy** and **RadioShack** follow.

($ millions)	Best Buy	RadioShack
Cash and equivalents	$ 498	$ 814.8
Accounts receivable, net	1,868	241.9
Inventories	4,753	636.3
Retained earnings	4,714	2,153.2
Cost of sales	34,017	2,301.8
Revenues	45,015	4,224.5
Total assets	15,826	2,283.5

Required

1. Compute common-size percents for each of the companies using the data provided. (Round percents to one decimal.)

2. Which company retains a higher portion of cumulative net income in the company?

3. Which company has a higher gross margin ratio on sales?

4. Which company holds a higher percent of its total assets as inventory?

ETHICS CHALLENGE

A1

BTN 13-3   As Beacon Company controller, you are responsible for informing the board of directors about its financial activities. At the board meeting, you present the following information.

	2011	2010	2009
Sales trend percent	147.0%	135.0%	100.0%
Selling expenses to sales	10.1%	14.0%	15.6%
Sales to plant assets ratio	3.8 to 1	3.6 to 1	3.3 to 1
Current ratio	2.9 to 1	2.7 to 1	2.4 to 1
Acid-test ratio	1.1 to 1	1.4 to 1	1.5 to 1
Inventory turnover	7.8 times	9.0 times	10.2 times
Accounts receivable turnover	7.0 times	7.7 times	8.5 times
Total asset turnover	2.9 times	2.9 times	3.3 times
Return on total assets	10.4%	11.0%	13.2%
Return on stockholders' equity	10.7%	11.5%	14.1%
Profit margin ratio	3.6%	3.8%	4.0%

After the meeting, the company's CEO holds a press conference with analysts in which she mentions the following ratios.

	2011	2010	2009
Sales trend percent	147.0%	135.0%	100.0%
Selling expenses to sales	10.1%	14.0%	15.6%
Sales to plant assets ratio	3.8 to 1	3.6 to 1	3.3 to 1
Current ratio	2.9 to 1	2.7 to 1	2.4 to 1

Required

1. Why do you think the CEO decided to report 4 ratios instead of the 11 prepared?

2. Comment on the possible consequences of the CEO's reporting of the ratios selected.

BTN 13-4 Each team is to select a different industry, and each team member is to select a different company in that industry and acquire its financial statements. Use those statements to analyze the company, including at least one ratio from each of the four building blocks of analysis. When necessary, use the financial press to determine the market price of its stock. Communicate with teammates via a meeting, e-mail, or telephone to discuss how different companies compare to each other and to industry norms. The team is to prepare a single one-page memorandum reporting on its analysis and the conclusions reached.

COMMUNICATING IN PRACTICE

C2 A1 P3

BTN 13-5 Access the February 20, 2009, filing of the December 31, 2008, 10-K report of **The Hershey Company** (ticker HSY) at **www.SEC.gov** and complete the following requirements.

TAKING IT TO THE NET

C4 P3

Required

Compute or identify the following profitability ratios of Hershey for its years ending December 31, 2008, *and* December 31, 2007. Interpret its profitability using the results obtained for these two years.

1. Profit margin ratio.

2. Gross profit ratio.

3. Return on total assets. (Total assets at year-end 2006 were $4,157,565,000.)

4. Return on common stockholders' equity. (Total shareholders' equity at year-end 2006 was $683,423,000.)

5. Basic net income per common share.

BTN 13-6 A team approach to learning financial statement analysis is often useful.

TEAMWORK IN ACTION

C2 P1 P2 P3

Required

1. Each team should write a description of horizontal and vertical analysis that all team members agree with and understand. Illustrate each description with an example.

2. *Each* member of the team is to select *one* of the following categories of ratio analysis. Explain what the ratios in that category measure. Choose one ratio from the category selected, present its formula, and explain what it measures.

    a. Liquidity and efficiency   **c.** Profitability

    b. Solvency   **d.** Market prospects

3. Each team member is to present his or her notes from part 2 to teammates. Team members are to confirm or correct other teammates' presentation.

Hint: Pairing within teams may be necessary for part 2. Use as an in-class activity or as an assignment. Consider presentations to the entire class using team rotation with transparencies.

BTN 13-7 Assume that David and Tom Gardner of **The Motley Fool** (**Fool.com**) have impressed you since you first heard of their rather improbable rise to prominence in financial circles. You learn of a staff opening at The Motley Fool and decide to apply for it. Your resume is successfully screened from the thousands received and you advance to the interview process. You learn that the interview consists of analyzing the following financial facts and answering analysis questions. (*Note:* The data are taken from a small merchandiser in outdoor recreational equipment.)

ENTREPRENEURIAL DECISION

A1 P1 P2 P3

	2010	2009	2008
Sales trend percents	137.0%	125.0%	100.0%
Selling expenses to sales	9.8%	13.7%	15.3%
Sales to plant assets ratio	3.5 to 1	3.3 to 1	3.0 to 1
Current ratio	2.6 to 1	2.4 to 1	2.1 to 1
Acid-test ratio	0.8 to 1	1.1 to 1	1.2 to 1
Merchandise inventory turnover	7.5 times	8.7 times	9.9 times
Accounts receivable turnover	6.7 times	7.4 times	8.2 times
Total asset turnover	2.6 times	2.6 times	3.0 times
Return on total assets	8.8%	9.4%	11.1%
Return on equity	9.75%	11.50%	12.25%
Profit margin ratio	3.3%	3.5%	3.7%

Required

Use these data to answer each of the following questions with explanations.

1. Is it becoming easier for the company to meet its current liabilities on time and to take advantage of any available cash discounts? Explain.
2. Is the company collecting its accounts receivable more rapidly? Explain.
3. Is the company's investment in accounts receivable decreasing? Explain.
4. Is the company's investment in plant assets increasing? Explain.
5. Is the owner's investment becoming more profitable? Explain.
6. Did the dollar amount of selling expenses decrease during the three-year period? Explain.

HITTING THE ROAD

C1 P3

BTN 13-8   You are to devise an investment strategy to enable you to accumulate $1,000,000 by age 65. Start by making some assumptions about your salary. Next compute the percent of your salary that you will be able to save each year. If you will receive any lump-sum monies, include those amounts in your calculations. Historically, stocks have delivered average annual returns of 10–11%. Given this history, you should probably not assume that you will earn above 10% on the money you invest. It is not necessary to specify exactly what types of assets you will buy for your investments; just assume a rate you expect to earn. Use the future value tables in Appendix B to calculate how your savings will grow. Experiment a bit with your figures to see how much less you have to save if you start at, for example, age 25 versus age 35 or 40. (For this assignment, do not include inflation in your calculations.)

GLOBAL DECISION

A1

BTN 13-9   GOME (www.GOME.com.hk), which is the leading chain retailer of consumer electronic products and household appliances in China, along with **Best Buy** and **RadioShack** are competitors in the global marketplace. Key figures for GOME follow (in RMB 000s).

Cash and equivalents	3,051,069
Accounts receivable, net	45,092
Inventories	5,473,497
Retained earnings	8,228,043
Cost of sales	41,381,223
Revenues	45,889,257
Total assets	27,495,104

Required

1. Compute common-sized percents for GOME using the data provided. (Round percents to one decimal.)
2. Compare the results with Best Buy and RadioShack from BTN 13-2.

ANSWERS TO MULTIPLE CHOICE QUIZ

1. d; ($351,000/$300,000) × 100 = 117%
2. e; ($86,000 + $76,000 + $122,000 + $12,000)/$124,000 = 2.39
3. c; ($86,000 + $76,000)/$124,000 = 1.31
4. a; ($124,000 + $90,000)/$830,000 = 25.78%
5. d; ($300,000 + $316,000)/$830,000 = 74.22%

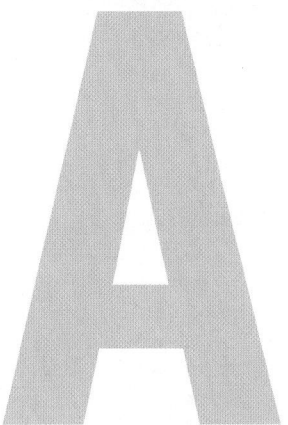

Financial Statement Information

This appendix includes financial information for (1) **Best Buy**, (2) **RadioShack**, (3) **GOME**, and (4) **Apple**. This information is taken from their annual 10-K reports filed with the SEC (GOME reports according to the Hong Kong Companies Ordinance as it trades on the Hong Kong Exchange.). An **annual report** is a summary of a company's financial results for the year along with its current financial condition and future plans. This report is directed to external users of financial information, but it also affects the actions and decisions of internal users.

A company often uses an annual report to showcase itself and its products. Many annual reports include photos, diagrams, and illustrations related to the company. The primary objective of annual reports, however, is the *financial section,* which communicates much information about a company, with most data drawn from the accounting information system. The layout of an annual report's financial section is fairly established and typically includes the following:

- Letter to Shareholders
- Financial History and Highlights
- Management Discussion and Analysis
- Management's Report on Financial Statements and on Internal Controls
- Report of Independent Accountants (Auditor's Report) and on Internal Controls
- Financial Statements
- Notes to Financial Statements
- List of Directors and Officers

This appendix provides the financial statements for Best Buy (plus selected notes), RadioShack, GOME, and Apple. The appendix is organized as follows:

- **Best Buy A-2** through **A-16**
- **RadioShack A-17** through **A-21**
- **GOME A-22** through **A-28**
- **Apple Computer A-29** through **A-33**

Many assignments at the end of each chapter refer to information in this appendix. We encourage readers to spend time with these assignments; they are especially useful in showing the relevance and diversity of financial accounting and reporting.

Special note: The SEC maintains the EDGAR (**E**lectronic **D**ata **G**athering, **A**nalysis, and **R**etrieval) database at www.sec.gov. (Over the next few years, the SEC will be moving to IDEA, short for Interactive Data Electronic Applications, which will eventually replace the EDGAR system.) The **Form 10-K** is the annual report form for most companies. It provides electronically accessible information. The **Form 10-KSB** is the annual report form filed by small businesses. It requires slightly less information than the Form 10-K. One of these forms must be filed within 90 days after the company's fiscal year-end. (Forms 10-K405, 10-KT, 10-KT405, and 10-KSB405 are slight variations of the usual form due to certain regulations or rules.)

Financial Report

Management's Report on the Consolidated Financial Statements

Our management is responsible for the preparation, integrity and objectivity of the accompanying consolidated financial statements and the related financial information. The consolidated financial statements have been prepared in conformity with GAAP and necessarily include certain amounts that are based on estimates and informed judgments. Our management also prepared the related financial information included in this Annual Report on Form 10-K and is responsible for its accuracy and consistency with the consolidated financial statements.

The accompanying consolidated financial statements have been audited by Deloitte & Touche LLP, an independent registered public accounting firm, which conducted its audits in accordance with the standards of the Public Company Accounting Oversight Board (U.S.). The independent registered public accounting firm's responsibility is to express an opinion as to the fairness with which such financial statements present our financial position, results of operations and cash flows in accordance with GAAP.

Management's Report on Internal Control Over Financial Reporting

Our management is responsible for establishing and maintaining adequate internal control over financial reporting as defined in Rule 13a-15(f) under the Exchange Act. Our internal control over financial reporting is designed under the supervision of our principal executive officer and principal financial officer, and effected by our Board, management and other personnel, to provide reasonable assurance regarding the reliability of financial reporting and the preparation of financial statements for external purposes in accordance with GAAP and include those policies and procedures that:

(1)   Pertain to the maintenance of records that in reasonable detail accurately and fairly reflect our transactions and the dispositions of our assets;

(2)   Provide reasonable assurance that our transactions are recorded as necessary to permit preparation of financial statements in accordance with GAAP, and that our receipts and expenditures are being made only in accordance with authorizations of our management and Board; and

(3)   Provide reasonable assurance regarding prevention or timely detection of unauthorized acquisition, use or disposition of our assets that could have a material effect on our financial statements.

Because of its inherent limitations, internal control over financial reporting may not prevent or detect misstatements. Therefore, even those systems determined to be effective can provide only reasonable assurance with respect to financial statement preparation and presentation.

Under the supervision and with the participation of our management, including our principal executive officer and principal financial officer, we assessed the effectiveness of our internal control over financial reporting as of February 28, 2009, using the criteria set forth by the Committee of Sponsoring Organizations of the Treadway Commission (COSO) in *Internal Control—Integrated Framework.* Based on our assessment, we have concluded that our internal control over financial reporting was effective as of February 28, 2009. During our assessment, we did not identify any material weaknesses in our internal control over financial reporting. We have excluded from our assessment the internal control over financial reporting at Best Buy Europe, which was acquired on June 28, 2008, and whose financial statements reflect total assets and total revenue constituting 26% and 7%, respectively, of our consolidated financial statement amounts as of and for the year ended February 28, 2009. We have also excluded from our assessment the internal control over financial reporting at Napster, which was acquired on October 25, 2008, and whose financial statements reflect total assets and total revenue that constitute less than 1% of our consolidated financial statement amounts as of and for the year ended February 28, 2009. Deloitte & Touche LLP, the independent registered public accounting firm that audited our consolidated financial statements for the year ended February 28, 2009, included in Item 8, *Financial Statements and Supplementary Data,* of this Annual Report on Form 10-K, has issued an unqualified attestation report on the effectiveness of our internal control over financial reporting as of February 28, 2009.

Bradbury H. Anderson
Vice Chairman and Chief Executive Officer
(principal executive officer)

James L. Muehlbauer
Executive Vice President—Finance
and Chief Financial Officer
(principal financial officer)

BEST BUY

Five-Year Financial Highlights

$ in millions, except per share amounts

Fiscal Year	2009	2008	2007	2006	2005
Consolidated Statements of Earnings Data					
Revenue	$45,015	$40,023	$35,934	$30,848	$27,433
Operating income	1,870	2,161	1,999	1,644	1,442
Earnings from continuing operations	1,003	1,407	1,377	1,140	934
Gain on disposal of discontinued operations, net of tax	—	—	—	—	50
Net earnings	1,003	1,407	1,377	1,140	984
Per Share Data					
Continuing operations	$2.39	$3.12	$2.79	$2.27	$1.86
Gain on disposal of discontinued operations	—	—	—	—	0.10
Net earnings	2.39	3.12	2.79	2.27	1.96
Cash dividends declared and paid	0.54	0.46	0.36	0.31	0.28
Common stock price:					
High	48.03	53.90	59.50	56.00	41.47
Low	16.42	41.85	43.51	31.93	29.25
Operating Statistics					
Comparable store sales (decline) gain	(1.3)%	2.9%	5.0%	4.9%	4.3%
Gross profit rate	24.4%	23.9%	24.4%	25.0%	23.7%
Selling, general and administrative expenses rate	20.0%	18.5%	18.8%	19.7%	18.4%
Operating income rate	4.2%	5.4%	5.6%	5.3%	5.3%
Year-End Data					
Current ratio	1.0	1.1	1.4	1.3	1.4
Total assets	$15,826	$12,758	$13,570	$11,864	$10,294
Debt, including current portion	1,963	816	650	596	600
Total shareholders' equity	4,643	4,484	6,201	5,257	4,449
Number of stores					
Domestic	1,107	971	873	774	694
International	2,835	343	304	167	144
Total	3,942	1,314	1,177	941	838
Retail square footage (000s)					
Domestic	40,924	37,511	34,092	30,874	28,513
International	13,331	11,069	9,419	4,652	4,057
Total	54,255	48,580	43,511	35,526	32,570

Fiscal 2007 included 53 weeks. All other periods presented included 52 weeks.

Consolidated Balance Sheets

$ in millions, except per share and share amounts

	February 28, 2009	March 1, 2008
Assets		
Current Assets		
Cash and cash equivalents	$ 498	$ 1,438
Short-term investments	11	64
Receivables	1,868	549
Merchandise inventories	4,753	4,708
Other current assets	1,062	583
Total current assets	8,192	7,342
Property and Equipment		
Land and buildings	755	732
Leasehold improvements	2,013	1,752
Fixtures and equipment	4,060	3,057
Property under capital lease	112	67
	6,940	5,608
Less accumulated depreciation	2,766	2,302
Net property and equipment	4,174	3,306
Goodwill	2,203	1,088
Tradenames	173	97
Customer Relationships	322	5
Equity and Other Investments	395	605
Other Assets	367	315
Total Assets	$15,826	$12,758
Liabilities and Shareholders' Equity		
Current Liabilities		
Accounts payable	$ 4,997	$ 4,297
Unredeemed gift card liabilities	479	531
Accrued compensation and related expenses	459	373
Accrued liabilities	1,382	975
Accrued income taxes	281	404
Short-term debt	783	156
Current portion of long-term debt	54	33
Total current liabilities	8,435	6,769
Long-Term Liabilities	1,109	838
Long-Term Debt	1,126	627
Minority Interests	513	40
Shareholders' Equity		
Preferred stock, $1.00 par value: Authorized—400,000 shares; Issued and outstanding—none	—	—
Common stock, $0.10 par value: Authorized—1.0 billion shares; Issued and outstanding—413,684,000 and 410,578,000 shares, respectively	41	41
Additional paid-in capital	205	8
Retained earnings	4,714	3,933
Accumulated other comprehensive (loss) income	(317)	502
Total shareholders' equity	4,643	4,484
Total Liabilities and Shareholders' Equity	$15,826	$12,758

See Notes to Consolidated Financial Statements.

BEST BUY

BEST BUY

Consolidated Statements of Earnings
$ in millions, except per share amounts

Fiscal Years Ended	February 28, 2009	March 1, 2008	March 3, 2007
Revenue	$45,015	$40,023	$35,934
Cost of goods sold	34,017	30,477	27,165
Gross profit	10,998	9,546	8,769
Selling, general and administrative expenses	8,984	7,385	6,770
Restructuring charges	78	—	—
Goodwill and tradename impairment	66	—	—
Operating income	1,870	2,161	1,999
Other income (expense)			
Investment income and other	35	129	162
Investment impairment	(111)	—	—
Interest expense	(94)	(62)	(31)
Earnings before income tax expense, minority interests and equity in income (loss) of affiliates	1,700	2,228	2,130
Income tax expense	674	815	752
Minority interests in earnings	(30)	(3)	(1)
Equity in income (loss) of affiliates	7	(3)	—
Net earnings	$1,003	$1,407	$1,377
Earnings per share			
Basic	$2.43	$3.20	$2.86
Diluted	$2.39	$3.12	$2.79
Weighted-average common shares outstanding (in millions)			
Basic	412.5	439.9	482.1
Diluted	422.9	452.9	496.2

See Notes to Consolidated Financial Statements.

Consolidated Statements of Cash Flows

$ in millions

Fiscal Years Ended	February 28, 2009	March 1, 2008	March 3, 2007
Operating Activities			
Net earnings	$1,003	$1,407	$1,377
Adjustments to reconcile net earnings to total cash provided by operating activities:			
Depreciation	730	580	509
Amortization of definite-lived intangible assets	63	1	—
Asset impairments	177	—	—
Restructuring charges	78	—	—
Stock-based compensation	110	105	121
Deferred income taxes	(43)	74	82
Minority interests	30	3	1
Excess tax benefits from stock-based compensation	(6)	(24)	(50)
Other, net	12	(7)	20
Changes in operating assets and liabilities, net of acquired assets and liabilities:			
Receivables	(419)	12	(70)
Merchandise inventories	258	(562)	(550)
Other assets	(175)	42	(47)
Accounts payable	139	221	320
Other liabilities	(75)	74	185
Income taxes	(5)	99	(136)
Total cash provided by operating activities	1,877	2,025	1,762
Investing Activities			
Additions to property and equipment, net of $42 and $80 non-cash capital expenditures in fiscal 2009 and 2008, respectively	(1,303)	(797)	(733)
Purchases of investments	(81)	(8,501)	(4,789)
Sales of investments	246	10,935	5,095
Acquisitions of businesses, net of cash acquired	(2,316)	(89)	(421)
Change in restricted assets	(97)	(85)	63
Other, net	(22)	1	5
Total cash (used in) provided by investing activities	(3,573)	1,464	(780)
Financing Activities			
Repurchase of common stock	—	(3,461)	(599)
Issuance of common stock under employee stock purchase plan and for the exercise of stock options	83	146	217
Dividends paid	(223)	(204)	(174)
Repayments of debt	(4,712)	(4,353)	(84)
Proceeds from issuance of debt	5,606	4,486	96
Excess tax benefits from stock-based compensation	6	24	50
Other, net	(23)	(16)	(19)
Total cash provided by (used in) financing activities	737	(3,378)	(513)
Effect of Exchange Rate Changes on Cash	19	122	(12)
(Decrease) increase in Cash and Cash Equivalents	(940)	233	457
Cash and Cash Equivalents at Beginning of Year	1,438	1,205	748
Cash and Cash Equivalents at End of Year	$498	$1,438	$1,205
Supplemental Disclosure of Cash Flow Information			
Income taxes paid	$766	$644	$804
Interest paid	83	49	14

See Notes to Consolidated Financial Statements.

BEST BUY

BEST BUY

Consolidated Statements of Changes in Shareholders' Equity

$ and shares in millions

	Common Shares	Common Stock	Additional Paid-In Capital	Retained Earnings	Accumulated Other Comprehensive Income (Loss)	Total
Balances at February 25, 2006	**485**	**$49**	**$643**	**$4,304**	**$261**	**$5,257**
Net earnings	—	—	—	1,377	—	1,377
Other comprehensive loss, net of tax:						
Foreign currency translation adjustments	—	—	—	—	(33)	(33)
Unrealized losses on available-for-sale investments	—	—	—	—	(12)	(12)
Total comprehensive income						1,332
Stock options exercised	7	1	167	—	—	168
Tax benefit from stock options exercised and employee stock purchase plan	—	—	47	—	—	47
Issuance of common stock under employee stock purchase plan	1	—	49	—	—	49
Stock-based compensation	—	—	121	—	—	121
Common stock dividends, $0.36 per share	—	—	—	(174)	—	(174)
Repurchase of common stock	(12)	(2)	(597)	—	—	(599)
Balances at March 3, 2007	**481**	**48**	**430**	**5,507**	**216**	**6,201**
Net earnings	—	—	—	1,407	—	1,407
Other comprehensive income (loss), net of tax:						
Foreign currency translation adjustments	—	—	—	—	311	311
Unrealized losses on available-for-sale investments	—	—	—	—	(25)	(25)
Total comprehensive income						1,693
Cumulative effect of adopting a new accounting standard	—	—	—	(13)	—	(13)
Stock options exercised	4	—	93	—	—	93
Tax benefit from stock options exercised and employee stock purchase plan	—	—	17	—	—	17
Issuance of common stock under employee stock purchase plan	1	—	53	—	—	53
Stock-based compensation	—	—	105	—	—	105
Common stock dividends, $0.46 per share	—	—	—	(204)	—	(204)
Repurchase of common stock	(75)	(7)	(690)	(2,764)	—	(3,461)
Balances at March 1, 2008	**411**	**41**	**8**	**3,933**	**502**	**4,484**
Net earnings	—	—	—	1,003	—	1,003
Other comprehensive (loss) income, net of tax:						
Foreign currency translation adjustments	—	—	—	—	(830)	(830)
Unrealized losses on available-for-sale investments	—	—	—	—	(19)	(19)
Reclassification adjustment for impairment loss on available-for-sale security included in net earnings	—	—	—	—	30	30
Total comprehensive income						184
Stock options exercised	2	—	34	—	—	34
Tax benefit from stock options exercised and employee stock purchase plan	—	—	4	—	—	4
Issuance of common stock under employee stock purchase plan	1	—	49	—	—	49
Stock-based compensation	—	—	110	—	—	110
Common stock dividends, $0.54 per share	—	—	—	(222)	—	(222)
Balances at February 28, 2009	**414**	**$41**	**$205**	**$4,714**	**$(317)**	**$4,643**

See Notes to Consolidated Financial Statements.

Best Buy—Selected Notes to Consolidated Financial Statements
$ in millions, except per share amounts or as otherwise noted

1. Summary of Significant Accounting Policies
Description of Business

Best Buy is a specialty retailer of consumer electronics, home office products, entertainment software, appliances and related services. We operate two reportable segments: Domestic and International. The Domestic segment is comprised of store, call center and online operations in all states, districts and territories of the U.S., operating under the brand names Best Buy, Best Buy Mobile, Geek Squad, Magnolia Audio Video, Napster, Pacific Sales and Speakeasy. U.S. Best Buy stores offer a wide variety of consumer electronics, home office products, entertainment software, appliances and related services. Best Buy Mobile offers a wide selection of mobile phones, accessories and related services. Geek Squad provides residential and commercial computer repair, support and installation services. Magnolia Audio Video stores offer high-end audio and video products and related services. Napster is an online provider of digital music. Pacific Sales stores offer high-end home-improvement products including appliances, consumer electronics and related services. Speakeasy provides broadband, voice, data and information technology services.

The International segment is comprised of: (i) all Canada store, call center and online operations, operating under the brand names Best Buy, Best Buy Mobile, Future Shop and Geek Squad, (ii) all Europe store, call center and online operations, operating under the brand names The Carphone Warehouse, The Phone House and Geek Squad, (iii) all China store, call center and online operations, operating under the brand names Best Buy, Geek Squad and Five Star and (iv) all Mexico store operations operating under the brand names Best Buy and Geek Squad. Our International segment offers products and services similar to those of our U.S. Best Buy stores. However, Best Buy Canada stores do not carry appliances and Best Buy China stores and Five Star stores do not carry entertainment software. Further, our store format and offerings in Europe are similar to our Best Buy Mobile format and offerings in the U.S., primarily offering mobile phones and related accessories and services.

Fiscal Year

Our fiscal year ends on the Saturday nearest the end of February. Fiscal 2009 and 2008 each included 52 weeks, and fiscal 2007 included 53 weeks.

Cash and Cash Equivalents

Cash primarily consists of cash on hand and bank deposits. Cash equivalents primarily consist of money market accounts and other highly liquid investments with an original maturity of three months or less when purchased. The amounts of cash equivalents at February 28, 2009, and March 1, 2008, were $159 and $871, respectively, and the weighted-average interest rates were 0.1% and 4.1%, respectively.

Outstanding checks in excess of funds on deposit (book overdrafts) totaled $146 and $159 at February 28, 2009, and March 1, 2008, respectively, and are reflected as accounts payable in our consolidated balance sheets.

Merchandise Inventories

Merchandise inventories are recorded at the lower of cost using either the average cost or first-in first-out method, or market. In-bound freight-related costs from our vendors are included as part of the net cost of merchandise inventories. Also included in the cost of inventory are certain vendor allowances that are not a reimbursement of specific, incremental and identifiable costs to promote a vendor's products. Other costs associated with acquiring, storing and transporting merchandise inventories to our retail stores are expensed as incurred and included in cost of goods sold.

Our inventory loss reserve represents anticipated physical inventory losses (e.g., theft) that have occurred since the last physical inventory date. Independent physical inventory counts are taken on a regular basis to ensure that the inventory reported in our consolidated financial statements is properly stated. During the interim period between physical inventory counts, we reserve for anticipated physical inventory losses on a location-by-location basis.

Our markdown reserve represents the excess of the carrying value, typically average cost, over the amount we expect to realize from the ultimate sale or other disposal of the inventory. Markdowns establish a new cost basis for our inventory. Subsequent changes in facts or circumstances do not result in the reversal of previously recorded markdowns or an increase in that newly established cost basis.

Property and Equipment

Property and equipment are recorded at cost. We compute depreciation using the straight-line method over the estimated useful lives of the assets. Leasehold improvements are depreciated over the shorter of their estimated useful lives or the period from the date the assets are placed in service to the end of the initial lease term. Leasehold improvements made significantly after the initial lease term are depreciated over the shorter of their estimated useful lives or the remaining lease term, including renewal periods, if reasonably assured. Accelerated depreciation methods are generally used for income tax purposes.

When property is fully depreciated, retired or otherwise disposed of, the cost and accumulated depreciation are removed from the accounts and any resulting gain or loss is reflected in the consolidated statement of earnings.

Repairs and maintenance costs are charged directly to expense as incurred. Major renewals or replacements that substantially extend the useful life of an asset are capitalized and depreciated.

$ in millions, except per share amounts or as otherwise noted

Estimated useful lives by major asset category are as follows:

Asset	Life (in years)
Buildings	25–50
Leasehold improvements	3–25
Fixtures and equipment	3–20
Property under capital lease	2–20

Impairment of Long-Lived Assets and Costs Associated with Exit Activities

We account for the impairment or disposal of long-lived assets in accordance with Statement of Financial Accounting Standards ("SFAS") No. 144, *Accounting for the Impairment or Disposal of Long-Lived Assets*, which requires long-lived assets, such as property and equipment, to be evaluated for impairment whenever events or changes in circumstances indicate the carrying value of an asset may not be recoverable. Factors considered important that could result in an impairment review include, but are not limited to, significant underperformance relative to historical or planned operating results, significant changes in the manner of use of the assets or significant changes in our business strategies. An impairment loss is recognized when the estimated undiscounted cash flows expected to result from the use of the asset plus net proceeds expected from disposition of the asset (if any) are less than the carrying value of the asset. When an impairment loss is recognized, the carrying amount of the asset is reduced to its estimated fair value based on quoted market prices or other valuation techniques.

Leases

We conduct the majority of our retail and distribution operations from leased locations. The leases require payment of real estate taxes, insurance and common area maintenance, in addition to rent. The terms of our lease agreements generally range from 10 to 20 years. Most of the leases contain renewal options and escalation clauses, and certain store leases require contingent rents based on factors such as specified percentages of revenue or the consumer price index. Other leases contain covenants related to the maintenance of financial ratios.

Goodwill and Intangible Assets

Goodwill

Goodwill is the excess of the purchase price over the fair value of identifiable net assets acquired in business combinations accounted for under the purchase method. We do not amortize goodwill but test it for impairment annually in the fiscal fourth quarter, or when indications of potential impairment exist. These indicators would include a significant change in operating performance, the business climate, legal factors, competition, or a planned sale or disposition of a significant portion of the business, among other factors. We test for goodwill impairment utilizing a fair value approach at the reporting unit level. A reporting unit is an operating segment, or a business unit one level below that operating segment, for which discrete financial information is prepared and regularly reviewed by segment management. We have deemed our reporting units to be one level below our operating segments, Domestic and International, which is the level at which segment management regularly reviews operating results and makes resource allocation decisions.

Tradenames

We have indefinite-lived intangible assets related to our Pacific Sales, Speakeasy and Napster tradenames which are included in our Domestic segment. We also have indefinite-lived intangible assets related to our Future Shop and Five Star tradenames and definite-lived intangible assets related to our The Carphone Warehouse and The Phone House tradenames, which are included in our International segment.

Our valuation of identifiable intangible assets acquired is based on information and assumptions available to us at the time of acquisition, using income and market approaches to determine fair value. We test our tradenames annually for impairment, or when indications of potential impairment exist.

Our tradenames were as follows:

	February 28, 2009	March 1, 2008
Indefinite-lived	$104	$97
Definite-lived	69	—
Total	$173	$97

Impairment Testing

The impairment test for goodwill involves comparing the fair value of a reporting unit to its carrying amount, including goodwill. If the carrying amount of the reporting unit exceeds its fair value, a second step is required to measure the goodwill impairment loss. The second step includes hypothetically valuing all the tangible and intangible assets of the reporting unit as if the reporting unit had been acquired in a business combination. Then, the implied fair value of the reporting unit's goodwill is compared to the carrying amount of that goodwill. If the carrying amount of the reporting unit's goodwill exceeds the implied fair value of the goodwill, we recognize an impairment loss in an amount equal to the excess, not to exceed the carrying amount. We determine the fair values calculated in an impairment test using free cash flow models involving assumptions that are based upon what we believe a hypothetical marketplace participant would use in estimating fair value on the measurement date. The key assumptions relate to margins, growth rates, capital expenditures, terminal values and weighted-average cost of capital rates. In developing these assumptions, we compare the resulting estimated enterprise value derived by the aggregate fair values of our reporting units to our market enterprise value plus an estimated control premium.

The impairment test for tradenames involves comparing the fair value to its carrying amount. We derive fair value based on a discounted cash flow model (e.g., relief from royalty approach) using assumptions about revenue growth rates, royalty rates, the appropriate discount rates relative to risk and estimates of terminal values.

$ in millions, except per share amounts or as otherwise noted

Lease Rights

Lease rights represent costs incurred to acquire the lease of a specific commercial property. Lease rights are recorded at cost and are amortized to rent expense over the remaining lease term, including renewal periods, if reasonably assured. Amortization periods range up to 18 years, beginning with the date we take possession of the property.

Investments

Debt Securities

Our short-term and long-term investments in debt securities are comprised of auction-rate securities and commercial paper. In accordance with SFAS No. 115, *Accounting for Certain Investments in Debt and Equity Securities,* and based on our ability to market and sell these instruments, we classify auction-rate securities and other investments in debt securities as available-for-sale and carry them at fair value. Auction-rate securities were intended to behave like short-term debt instruments because their interest rates reset periodically through an auction process, typically at intervals of 7, 28 and 35 days. Investments in these securities can be sold for cash at par value on the auction date if the auction is successful. Substantially all of our auction-rate securities are AAA/Aaa-rated and collateralized by student loans, which are guaranteed 95% to 100% by the U.S. government. We also hold auction-rate securities that are in the form of municipal revenue bonds, the vast majority of which are AAA/Aaa-rated and insured by bond insurers. We do not have any investments in securities that are collateralized by assets that include mortgages or subprime debt. Our intent with these investments is not to hold these securities to maturity, but to use the periodic auction feature to provide liquidity as needed.

Marketable Equity Securities

We also invest in marketable equity securities and classify them as available-for-sale. Investments in marketable equity securities are included in equity and other investments in our consolidated balance sheets, and are reported at fair value based on quoted market prices. All unrealized holding gains and losses are reflected net of tax in accumulated other comprehensive income in shareholders' equity.

Other Investments

We also have investments that are accounted for on either the cost method or the equity method that we include in equity and other investments in our consolidated balance sheets.

We review the key characteristics of our debt, marketable equity securities and other investments portfolio and their classification in accordance with GAAP on an annual basis, or when indications of potential impairment exist. If a decline in the fair value of a security is deemed by management to be other-than-temporary, we write down the cost basis of the investment to fair value, and the amount of the write-down is included in net earnings.

Income Taxes

We account for income taxes using the asset and liability method. Under this method, deferred tax assets and liabilities are recognized for the estimated future tax consequences attributable to differences between the financial statement carrying amounts of existing assets and liabilities and their respective tax bases, and operating loss and tax credit carryforwards. Deferred tax assets and liabilities are measured pursuant to tax laws using rates we expect to apply to taxable income in the years in which we expect those temporary differences to be recovered or settled. We recognize the effect of a change in income tax rates on deferred tax assets and liabilities in our consolidated statement of earnings in the period that includes the enactment date. We record a valuation allowance to reduce the carrying amounts of deferred tax assets if it is more likely than not that such assets will not be realized.

Long-Term Liabilities

The major components of long-term liabilities at February 28, 2009, and March 1, 2008, included long-term rent-related liabilities, unrecognized tax benefits recorded pursuant to FIN No. 48, deferred tax liabilities, advances received under vendor alliance programs, deferred compensation plan liabilities and self-insurance reserves.

Revenue Recognition

Our revenue arises primarily from sales of merchandise and services. We also record revenue from sales of service contracts and extended warranties, fees earned from private label and co-branded credit card agreements and amounts billed to customers for shipping and handling.

We recognize revenue when the sales price is fixed or determinable, collectibility is reasonably assured and the customer takes possession of the merchandise, or in the case of services, at the time the service is provided. Revenue is recognized for store sales when the customer receives and pays for the merchandise. For online sales, we estimate and defer revenue and the related product costs for shipments that are in-transit to the customer. Revenue is recognized at the time we estimate the customer receives the product. Customers typically receive goods within a few days of shipment. Such amounts were immaterial at February 28, 2009, and March 1, 2008.

Revenue from merchandise sales and services is reported net of estimated sales returns and excludes sales taxes. We estimate our sales returns reserve based on historical return rates. Our sales returns reserve was $94 and $101, at February 28, 2009, and March 1, 2008, respectively, and was recorded as a reduction of revenue.

We sell service contracts such as for phone or television service as well as extended warranties that typically have terms that range from three months to four years. In jurisdictions where we are deemed to be the obligor on the contract, service revenue is recognized in revenue ratably over the term of the service contract. In jurisdictions where we sell service contracts or extended warranties on behalf of an unrelated third party, where we are not deemed to be the obligor on the

$ in millions, except per share amounts or as otherwise noted

contract, commissions are recognized in revenue at the time of sale. Commissions from the sale of extended warranties represented 2.0%, 2.1% and 2.2% of revenue in fiscal 2009, 2008 and 2007, respectively.

Gift Cards

We sell gift cards to our customers in our retail stores, through our Web sites, and through selected third parties. We do not charge administrative fees on unused gift cards, and our gift cards do not have an expiration date. We recognize revenue from gift cards when: (i) the gift card is redeemed by the customer, or (ii) the likelihood of the gift card being redeemed by the customer is remote ("gift card breakage"), and we determine that we do not have a legal obligation to remit the value of unredeemed gift cards to the relevant jurisdictions. We determine our gift card breakage rate based upon historical redemption patterns. Based on our historical information, the likelihood of a gift card remaining unredeemed can be determined 24 months after the gift card is issued. At that time, we recognize breakage income for those cards for which the likelihood of redemption is deemed remote and we do not have a legal obligation to remit the value of such unredeemed gift cards to the relevant jurisdictions. Gift card breakage income is included in revenue in our consolidated statements of earnings.

Gift card breakage income was as follows in fiscal 2009, 2008 and 2007:

	2009	2008	2007
Gift card breakage income	$38	$34	$46

Cost of Goods Sold and Selling, General and Administrative Expenses

The following table illustrates the primary costs classified in each major expense category:

Cost of Goods Sold	SG&A
• Total cost of products sold including: — Freight expenses associated with moving merchandise inventories from our vendors to our distribution centers; — Vendor allowances that are not a reimbursement of specific, incremental and identifiable costs to promote a vendor's products; and — Cash discounts on payments to merchandise vendors; • Cost of services provided including: — Payroll and benefits costs for services employees; and — Cost of replacement parts and related freight expenses; • Physical inventory losses; • Markdowns; • Customer shipping and handling expenses; • Costs associated with operating our distribution network, including payroll and benefit costs, occupancy costs, and depreciation; and • Freight expenses associated with moving merchandise inventories from our distribution centers to our retail stores.	• Payroll and benefit costs for retail and corporate employees; • Occupancy costs of retail, services and corporate facilities; • Depreciation related to retail, services and corporate assets; • Advertising; • Vendor allowances that are a reimbursement of specific, incremental and identifiable costs to promote a vendor's products; • Tender costs, including bank charges and costs associated with credit and debit card interchange fees • Charitable contributions; • Outside service fees; • Long-lived asset impairment charges; and • Other administrative costs, such as supplies, and travel and lodging.

Advertising Costs

Advertising costs, which are included in SG&A, are expensed the first time the advertisement runs. Advertising costs consist primarily of print and television advertisements as well as promotional events. Net advertising expenses were $765, $684 and $692 in fiscal 2009, 2008 and 2007, respectively. Allowances received from vendors for advertising of $117, $156 and $140, in fiscal 2009, 2008 and 2007, respectively, were classified as reductions of advertising expenses.

$ in millions, except per share amounts or as otherwise noted

3. Investments

Investments were comprised of the following:

	February 28, 2009	March 1, 2008
Short-term investments		
Money market fund	$8	$—
Debt securities	—	64
Other investments	3	—
Total short-term investments	$11	$64
Equity and other investments		
Debt securities	$314	$417
Marketable equity securities	41	172
Other investments	40	16
Total equity and other investments	$395	$605

4. Fair Value Measurements

As discussed in Note 1, we adopted SFAS No. 157, subject to the deferral provisions of FSP No. 157-2, on March 2, 2008. This standard defines fair value, establishes a framework for measuring fair value and expands disclosure requirements about fair value measurements. SFAS No. 157 defines fair value as the price that would be received to sell an asset or paid to transfer a liability (an exit price) in the principal or most advantageous market for the asset or liability in an orderly transaction between market participants on the measurement date. The fair value hierarchy prescribed by SFAS No. 157 contains three levels as follows:

Level 1—Unadjusted quoted prices that are available in active markets for the identical assets or liabilities at the measurement date.

Level 2—Other observable inputs available at the measurement date, other than quoted prices included in Level 1, either directly or indirectly, including:

- Quoted prices for similar assets or liabilities in active markets;
- Quoted prices for identical or similar assets in non-active markets;
- Inputs other than quoted prices that are observable for the asset or liability; and
- Inputs that are derived principally from or corroborated by other observable market data.

Level 3—Unobservable inputs that cannot be corroborated by observable market data and reflect the use of significant management judgment. These values are generally determined using pricing models for which the assumptions utilize management's estimates of market participant assumptions.

Assets and Liabilities that are Measured at Fair Value on a Recurring Basis

The fair value hierarchy requires the use of observable market data when available. In instances in which the inputs used to measure fair value fall into different levels of the fair value hierarchy, the fair value measurement has been determined based on the lowest level input that is significant to the fair value measurement in its entirety. Our assessment of the significance of a particular item to the fair value measurement in its entirety requires judgment, including the consideration of inputs specific to the asset or liability. The following table sets forth by level within the fair value hierarchy, our financial assets and liabilities that were accounted for at fair value on a recurring basis at February 28, 2009, according to the valuation techniques we used to determine their fair values.

	Fair Value at February 28, 2009	Fair Value Measurements Using Inputs Considered as		
		Level 1	Level 2	Level 3
Assets				
Short-term investments				
Money market fund	$8	$—	$8	$—
Other current assets (restricted assets)				
U.S. Treasury bills	125	125	—	—
Equity and other investments				
Auction rate securities	314	—	—	314
Marketable equity securities	41	41	—	—
Other assets				
Assets that fund deferred compensation	64	64	—	—
Liabilities				
Long-term liabilities				
Deferred compensation	55	55	—	—

$ in millions, except per share amounts or as otherwise noted

5. Restructuring Charges

The composition of our restructuring charges in fiscal 2009 was as follows:

Termination benefits	$75
Facility closure costs	1
Property and equipment write-downs	2
	$78

The following table summarizes our restructuring activity in fiscal 2009 related to termination benefits and facility closure costs:

	Termination Benefits	Facility Closure Costs	Total
Balance at March 1, 2008	$—	$—	$—
Charges	75	1	76
Cash payments	(2)	—	(2)
Balance at February 28, 2009	$73	$1	$74

6. Debt

Short-Term Debt

Short-term debt consisted of the following:

	February 28, 2009		March 1, 2008	
	Principal Balance	Interest Rate	Principal Value	Interest Rate
JP Morgan credit facility	$162	0.7% to 1.5%	$120	3.6%
ARS revolving credit line	—	—	—	
Europe revolving credit facility	584	1.2% to 3.9%	—	
Canada revolving demand facility	2	4.0%	—	
China revolving demand facilities	35	4.6% to 5.0%	36	6.5% to 8.0%
Total short-term debt	$783		$156	

Long-Term Debt

Long-term debt consisted of the following:

	February 28, 2009	March 1, 2008
6.75% notes	$500	$—
Convertible debentures	402	402
Financing lease obligations, due 2010 to 2024, interest rates ranging from 3.0% to 8.1%	200	197
Capital lease obligations, due 2010 to 2035, interest rates ranging from 3.6% to 6.9%	65	51
Other debt, due 2010 to 2022, interest rates ranging from 2.6% to 8.8%	13	10
Total long-term debt	1,180	660
Less: current portion	(54)	(33)
Total long-term debt, less current portion	$1,126	$627

Other

The fair value of debt approximated $1,904 and $853 at February 28, 2009, and March 1, 2008, respectively, based on the ask prices quoted from external sources, compared with carrying values of $1,963 and $816, respectively.

At February 28, 2009, the future maturities of long-term debt, including capitalized leases, consisted of the following:

Fiscal Year	
2010	$54
2011	37
2012	431
2013	25
2014	524
Thereafter	109
Total long-term debt	$1,180

$ in millions, except per share amounts or as otherwise noted

7.   Shareholders' Equity
Repurchase of Common Stock

On June 26, 2007, our Board authorized a $5,500 share repurchase program that terminated and replaced our prior $1,500 share repurchase program authorized in June 2006. There is no expiration date governing the period over which we can make our share repurchases under the June 2007 share repurchase program. At February 28, 2009, $2,500 remains available for future purchases under the June 2007 share repurchase program. Repurchased shares have been retired and constitute authorized but unissued shares.

Comprehensive Income

Comprehensive income is computed as net earnings plus certain other items that are recorded directly to shareholders' equity. In addition to net earnings, the significant components of comprehensive income include foreign currency translation adjustments and unrealized gains and losses, net of tax, on available-for-sale marketable equity securities. Foreign currency translation adjustments do not include a provision for income tax expense when earnings from foreign operations are considered to be indefinitely reinvested outside the U.S. Comprehensive income was $184, $1,693 and $1,332 in fiscal 2009, 2008 and 2007, respectively.

The components of accumulated other comprehensive (loss) income, net of tax, were as follows:

	February 28, 2009	March 1, 2008
Foreign currency translation	$(303)	$527
Unrealized losses on available-for-sale investments	(14)	(25)
Total	$(317)	$502

8.   Leases

The future minimum lease payments under our capital, financing and operating leases by fiscal year (not including contingent rentals) at February 28, 2009, were as follows:

Fiscal Year	Capital Leases	Financing Leases	Operating Leases
2010	$28	$31	$1,097
2011	19	31	1,045
2012	8	31	964
2013	3	31	900
2014	2	29	846
Thereafter	24	107	3,748
Subtotal	84	260	$8,600
Less: imputed interest	(19)	(60)	
Present value of lease obligations	$65	$200	

9.   Benefit Plans

We sponsor retirement savings plans for employees meeting certain age and service requirements.

10.   Income Taxes

The following is a reconciliation of the federal statutory income tax rate to income tax expense in fiscal 2009, 2008 and 2007:

	2009	2008	2007
Federal income tax at the statutory rate	$595	$780	$747
State income taxes, net of federal benefit	49	67	38
Benefit from foreign operations	(30)	(25)	(36)
Non-taxable interest income	(3)	(17)	(34)
Other	16	10	37
Impairments	47	—	—
Income tax expense	$674	$815	$752
Effective income tax rate	39.6%	36.6%	35.3%

Income tax expense was comprised of the following in fiscal 2009, 2008 and 2007:

	2009	2008	2007
Current:			
Federal	$573	$609	$609
State	78	110	45
Foreign	66	22	16
	717	741	670
Deferred:			
Federal	(7)	47	51
State	1	(7)	19
Foreign	(37)	34	12
	(43)	74	82
Income tax expense	$674	$815	$752

$ in millions, except per share amounts or as otherwise noted

11. Segment and Geographic Information

Segment Information

We have organized our operations into two principal segments: Domestic and International. These segments are our primary areas of measurement and decision-making, as defined by SFAS No. 131, *Disclosures about Segments of an Enterprise and Related Information*. The Domestic reportable segment is comprised of all store, call center and online operations within the U.S. and its territories. The International reportable segment is comprised of all store, call center and online operations outside the U.S. and its territories. We rely on an internal management reporting process that provides segment information to the operating income level for purposes of making financial decisions and allocating resources. The accounting policies of the segments are the same as those described in Note 1, *Summary of Significant Accounting Policies*.

The following tables present our business segment information in fiscal 2009:

	2009
Revenue	
Domestic	$35,070
International	9,945
Total revenue	$45,015

	2009
Operating income	
Domestic	$1,758
International	112
Total operating income	1,870
Other income (expense)	
Investment income and other	35
Investment impairment	(111)
Interest expense	(94)
Earnings from operations before income tax expense, minority interests and equity in income (loss) of affiliates	$1,700
Assets	
Domestic	$9,059
International	6,767
Total assets	$15,826

12. Contingencies and Commitments

Contingencies

In December 2005, a purported class action lawsuit captioned, *Jasmen Holloway, et al. v. Best Buy Co., Inc.*, was filed in the U.S. District Court for the Northern District of California alleging we discriminate against women and minority individuals on the basis of gender, race, color and/or national origin with respect to our employment policies and practices. The action seeks an end to discriminatory policies and practices, an award of back and front pay, punitive damages and injunctive relief, including rightful place relief for all class members. At February 28, 2009, no accrual had been established as it was not possible to estimate the possible loss or range of loss because this matter had not advanced to a stage where we could make any such estimate. The Court has scheduled a class certification hearing. We believe the allegations are without merit and intend to defend this action vigorously.

We are involved in various other legal proceedings arising in the normal course of conducting business. We believe the amounts provided in our consolidated financial statements, as prescribed by GAAP, are adequate in light of the probable and estimable liabilities. The resolution of those other proceedings is not expected to have a material impact on our results of operations or financial condition.

Commitments

We engage Accenture LLP ("Accenture") to assist us with improving our operational capabilities and reducing our costs in the information systems, procurement and human resources areas. Our future contractual obligations to Accenture are expected to range from $76 to $262 per year through 2012, the end of the periods under contract. Prior to our engagement of Accenture, we incurred a significant portion of these costs as part of normal operations.

We had outstanding letters of credit and bankers' acceptances for purchase obligations with an aggregate fair value of $313 at February 28, 2009.

At February 28, 2009, we had commitments for the purchase and construction of facilities valued at approximately $34. Also, at February 28, 2009, we had entered into lease commitments for land and buildings for 211 future locations. These lease commitments with real estate developers provide for minimum rentals ranging from 2 to 19 years, which if consummated based on current cost estimates, will approximate $40 annually over the initial lease terms. These minimum rentals are reported in the future minimum lease payments included in Note 8, *Leases*.

RadioShack Financial Report

Appendix A   Financial Statement Information

RADIOSHACK

RADIOSHACK CORPORATION AND SUBSIDIARIES
Consolidated Statements of Income

| | Year Ended December 31, | | | | | |
| | 2008 | | 2007 | | 2006 | |
(In millions, except per share amounts)	Dollars	% of Revenues	Dollars	% of Revenues	Dollars	% of Revenues
Net sales and operating revenues	$ 4,224.5	100.0%	$ 4,251.7	100.0%	$ 4,777.5	100.0%
Cost of products sold (includes depreciation amounts of $11.2 million, $10.0 million and $10.7 million, respectively)	2,301.8	54.5	2,225.9	52.4	2,648.1	55.4
Gross profit	1,922.7	45.5	2,025.8	47.6	2,129.4	44.6
Operating expenses:						
Selling, general and administrative	1,509.8	35.7	1,538.5	36.2	1,810.7	37.9
Depreciation and amortization	88.1	2.1	102.7	2.4	117.5	2.5
Impairment of long-lived assets and other charges	2.8	0.1	2.7	--	44.3	0.9
Total operating expenses	1,600.7	37.9	1,643.9	38.6	1,972.5	41.3
Operating income	322.0	7.6	381.9	9.0	156.9	3.3
Interest income	14.6	0.3	22.6	0.5	7.4	0.1
Interest expense	(29.9)	(0.7)	(38.8)	(0.9)	(44.3)	(0.9)
Other (loss) income	(2.4)	--	0.9	--	(8.6)	(0.2)
Income before income taxes	304.3	7.2	366.6	8.6	111.4	2.3
Income tax expense	111.9	2.6	129.8	3.0	38.0	0.8
Net income	$ 192.4	4.6%	$ 236.8	5.6%	$ 73.4	1.5%
Net income per share:						
Basic	$ 1.49		$ 1.76		$ 0.54	
Diluted:	$ 1.49		$ 1.74		$ 0.54	
Shares used in computing net income per share:						
Basic	129.0		134.6		136.2	
Diluted	129.1		135.9		136.2	

The notes are an integral part of these consolidated financial statements.

RADIOSHACK CORPORATION AND SUBSIDIARIES
Consolidated Balance Sheets

	December 31,	
(In millions, except for share amounts)	2008	2007
Assets		
Current assets:		
Cash and cash equivalents	$ 814.8	$ 509.7
Accounts and notes receivable, net	241.9	256.0
Inventories	636.3	705.4
Other current assets	99.0	95.7
Total current assets	1,792.0	1,566.8
Property, plant and equipment, net	306.4	317.1
Other assets, net	185.1	105.7
Total assets	$ 2,283.5	$ 1,989.6
Liabilities and Stockholders' Equity		
Current liabilities:		
Short-term debt, including current maturities of long-term debt	$ 39.3	$ 61.2
Accounts payable	206.4	257.6
Accrued expenses and other current liabilities	367.3	393.5
Income taxes payable	24.2	35.7
Total current liabilities	637.2	748.0
Long-term debt, excluding current maturities	732.5	348.2
Other non-current liabilities	96.5	123.7
Total liabilities	1,466.2	1,219.9
Commitments and contingencies (see Note 12)		
Stockholders' equity:		
Preferred stock, no par value, 1,000,000 shares authorized:		
Series A junior participating, 300,000 shares designated and none issued	--	--
Common stock, $1 par value, 650,000,000 shares authorized;191,033,000 shares issued	191.0	191.0
Additional paid-in capital	106.0	108.4
Retained earnings	2,153.2	1,992.1
Treasury stock, at cost; 65,950,000 and 59,940,000 shares, respectively	(1,625.9)	(1,516.5)
Accumulated other comprehensive loss	(7.0)	(5.3)
Total stockholders' equity	817.3	769.7
Total liabilities and stockholders' equity	$ 2,283.5	$ 1,989.6

The notes are an integral part of these consolidated financial statements.

RADIOSHACK

RADIOSHACK CORPORATION AND SUBSIDIARIES
Consolidated Statements of Cash Flows

(In millions)	Year Ended December 31,		
	2008	2007	2006
Cash flows from operating activities:			
Net income	$ 192.4	$ 236.8	$ 73.4
Adjustments to reconcile net income to net cash			
provided by operating activities:			
Depreciation and amortization	99.3	112.7	128.2
Impairment of long-lived assets and other charges	2.8	2.7	44.3
Stock option compensation	10.2	10.7	12.0
Net change in liability for unrecognized tax benefits	4.6	(11.9)	--
Deferred income taxes	13.6	16.5	(32.7)
Other non-cash items	16.0	(9.0)	5.1
Provision for credit losses and bad debts	0.6	0.4	0.4
Changes in operating assets and liabilities:			
Accounts and notes receivable	15.2	(0.7)	61.8
Inventories	93.6	46.8	212.8
Other current assets	(8.7)	5.3	2.5
Accounts payable, accrued expenses, income taxes			
payable and other	(165.0)	(31.3)	(193.0)
Net cash provided by operating activities	274.6	379.0	314.8
Cash flows from investing activities:			
Additions to property, plant and equipment	(85.6)	(45.3)	(91.0)
Proceeds from sale of property, plant and equipment	0.9	1.5	11.1
Acquisition of Mexican subsidiary, net of cash acquired	(42.0)	--	--
Other investing activities	2.4	1.8	0.6
Net cash used in investing activities	(124.3)	(42.0)	(79.3)
Cash flows from financing activities:			
Purchases of treasury stock	(111.3)	(208.5)	--
Issuance of convertible notes	375.0	--	--
Convertible notes issuance costs	(9.4)	--	--
Purchase of convertible notes hedges	(86.3)	--	--
Sale of common stock warrants	39.9	--	--
Sale of treasury stock to employee benefit plans	--	--	10.5
Proceeds from exercise of stock options	--	81.3	1.7
Payments of dividends	(31.3)	(32.8)	(33.9)
Changes in short-term borrowings and outstanding			
checks in excess of cash balances, net	(16.8)	10.7	42.2
Repayments of borrowings	(5.0)	(150.0)	(8.0)
Net cash provided by (used in) financing activities	154.8	(299.3)	12.5
Net increase in cash and cash equivalents	305.1	37.7	248.0
Cash and cash equivalents, beginning of period	509.7	472.0	224.0
Cash and cash equivalents, end of period	$ 814.8	$ 509.7	$ 472.0
Supplemental cash flow information:			
Interest paid	$ 26.5	$ 42.6	$ 44.0
Income taxes paid	123.2	112.2	52.9

The notes are an integral part of these consolidated financial statements.

RADIOSHACK CORPORATION AND SUBSIDIARIES
Consolidated Statements of Stockholders' Equity and Comprehensive Income

(In millions)	Shares at December 31,			Dollars at December 31,		
	2008	2007	2006	2008	2007	2006
Common stock						
Beginning and end of year	191.0	191.0	191.0	$ 191.0	$ 191.0	$ 191.0
Treasury stock						
Beginning of year	(59.9)	(55.2)	(56.0)	$ (1,516.5)	$ (1,409.1)	$ (1,431.6)
Purchase of treasury stock	(6.1)	(8.7)	--	(111.3)	(208.5)	--
Issuance of common stock	0.1	0.5	0.6	1.9	12.8	18.6
Exercise of stock options and grant of stock awards	--	3.5	0.2	--	88.3	3.9
End of year	(65.9)	(59.9)	(55.2)	$ (1,625.9)	$ (1,516.5)	$ (1,409.1)
Additional paid-in capital						
Beginning of year				$ 108.4	$ 92.6	$ 87.7
Issuance of common stock				0.2	6.2	(5.7)
Exercise of stock options and grant of stock awards				--	(8.4)	(1.7)
Stock option compensation				10.2	10.7	12.0
Net stock-based compensation income tax benefits				--	7.3	0.3
Purchase of convertible notes hedges				(86.3)	--	--
Tax benefit from purchase of convertible notes hedges				33.6	--	--
Sale of common stock warrants				39.9	--	--
End of year				$ 106.0	$ 108.4	$ 92.6
Retained earnings						
Beginning of year				$ 1,992.1	$ 1,780.9	$ 1,741.4
Net income				192.4	236.8	73.4
Cash dividends declared				(31.3)	(32.8)	(33.9)
Adoption of FASB Interpretation No. 48				--	7.2	--
End of year				$ 2,153.2	$ 1,992.1	$ 1,780.9
Accumulated other comprehensive (loss) income						
Beginning of year				$ (5.3)	$ (1.6)	$ 0.3
Other comprehensive loss				(1.7)	(3.7)	(1.9)
End of year				$ (7.0)	$ (5.3)	$ (1.6)
Total stockholders' equity				$ 817.3	$ 769.7	$ 653.8
Comprehensive income						
Net income				$ 192.4	$ 236.8	$ 73.4
Other comprehensive loss, net of tax:						
Foreign currency translation adjustments				(2.5)	(4.0)	0.3
Pension adjustments, net of tax				0.8	0.4	(1.0)
Amortization of gain on cash flow hedge				--	(0.1)	(0.1)
Unrealized loss on securities				--	--	(1.1)
Other comprehensive loss				(1.7)	(3.7)	(1.9)
Comprehensive income				$ 190.7	$ 233.1	$ 71.5

The notes are an integral part of these consolidated financial statements.

RADIOSHACK

GOME Financial Report

GOME Electrical Appliances Holding Limited

Consolidated Income Statement

Year ended 31 December 2008

	2008 RMB'000	2007 RMB'000
Revenue	45,889,257	42,478,523
Cost of sales	(41,381,223)	(38,383,276)
Gross profit	4,508,034	4,095,247
Other income and gain	3,266,244	2,546,876
Selling and distribution costs	(4,487,131)	(3,547,907)
Administrative expenses	(828,028)	(686,740)
Other expenses	(515,357)	(604,768)
Profit from operating activities	1,943,762	1,802,708
Finance costs	(212,118)	(193,369)
Finance income	441,017	424,241
Loss on the derivative components of convertible bonds	(189,220)	(505,483)
Impairment of other investments	(449,592)	–
Profit before tax	1,533,849	1,528,097
Tax	(435,156)	(360,262)
Profit for the year	1,098,693	1,167,835
Attributable to:		
Equity holders of the parent	1,048,160	1,127,307
Minority interests	50,533	40,528
	1,098,693	1,167,835
Dividends		
Interim	344,486	254,193
Proposed final	–	328,629
	344,486	582,822
Dividend per share		
Interim	RMB2.7 fen	RMB7.8 fen
Proposed final	–	RMB9.9 fen
	RMB2.7 fen	RMB17.7 fen
Earnings per share attributable to ordinary equity holders of the parent		
Basic	RMB8.2 fen	RMB8.8 fen
Diluted	RMB8.2 fen	RMB8.8 fen

GOME

GOME Electrical Appliances Holding Limited

Consolidated Balance Sheet

31 December 2008

	2008 RMB'000	2007 RMB'000
ASSETS		
Non-current assets		
Property, plant and equipment	3,719,829	3,144,458
Investment properties	389,473	331,680
Goodwill	3,363,012	3,343,012
Other intangible assets	134,241	143,867
Other investments	108,810	–
Prepayments for acquisition of properties	270,160	138,300
Lease prepayments	355,089	342,744
Deferred tax assets	18,356	55,873
Other assets	653,423	–
	9,012,393	7,499,934
Current assets		
Hong Kong listed investments, at fair value	399	1,058
Investment deposits	30,000	30,000
Designated loan	3,600,000	1,500,000
Inventories	5,473,497	5,383,039
Trade and bills receivables	45,092	97,719
Prepayments, deposits and other receivables	1,384,355	2,211,998
Due from related parties	57,843	79,024
Other financial assets	–	150,000
Pledged deposits	4,840,456	6,614,725
Cash and cash equivalents	3,051,069	6,269,996
	18,482,711	22,337,559
TOTAL ASSETS	27,495,104	29,837,493

GOME Electrical Appliances Holding Limited

Consolidated Balance Sheet (continued)

31 December 2008

	2008 RMB'000	2007 RMB'000
EQUITY AND LIABILITIES		
Equity attributable to equity holders of the parent		
Issued capital	331,791	343,764
Reserves	8,228,043	9,630,586
Proposed final dividend	–	328,629
	8,559,834	10,302,979
Minority interests	140,201	89,689
Total equity	8,700,035	10,392,668
Non-current liabilities		
Deferred tax liabilities	78,269	80,431
Convertible bonds	3,569,553	3,184,303
	3,647,822	3,264,734
Current liabilities		
Interest-bearing bank loans	170,000	300,000
Trade and bills payables	12,917,958	13,556,545
Customers' deposits, other payables and accruals	1,530,141	1,939,695
Tax payable	529,148	383,851
	15,147,247	16,180,091
Total liabilities	18,795,069	19,444,825
TOTAL EQUITY AND LIABILITIES	27,495,104	29,837,493
NET CURRENT ASSETS	3,335,464	6,157,468
TOTAL ASSETS LESS CURRENT LIABILITIES	12,347,857	13,657,402

GOME

GOME Electrical Appliances Holding Limited

Consolidated Statement of Changes in Equity

Year ended 31 December 2008

	Attributable to equity holders of the parent												
	Issued capital RMB'000	Share premium RMB'000	Contributed surplus RMB'000	Capital reserve RMB'000	Asset revaluation reserve RMB'000	Other investment revaluation reserve RMB'000	Statutory reserves RMB'000 note 30(a)	Exchange reserve RMB'000	Retained earnings RMB'000	Proposed dividend RMB'000	Total RMB'000	Minority interests RMB'000	Total equity RMB'000
At 1 January 2008	343,764	8,263,293	657	(216,966)	–	–	568,329	(80,593)	1,095,866	328,629	10,302,979	89,689	10,392,668
Changes in fair value of other investments	–	–	–	–	–	(434,742)	–	–	–	–	(434,742)	–	(434,742)
Impairment of other investments	–	–	–	–	–	449,592	–	–	–	–	449,592	–	449,592
Revaluation surplus on property, plant and equipment	–	–	–	–	32,425	–	–	–	–	–	32,425	–	32,425
Related deferred tax liability arising from the revaluation of property, plant and equipment	–	–	–	–	(8,106)	–	–	–	–	–	(8,106)	–	(8,106)
Exchange realignment	–	–	–	–	–	–	–	(101,617)	–	–	(101,617)	–	(101,617)
Total income and expense for the year recognised directly in equity	–	–	–	–	24,319	14,850	–	(101,617)	–	–	(62,448)	–	(62,448)
Profit for the year	–	–	–	–	–	–	–	–	1,048,160	–	1,048,160	50,533	1,098,693
Total income and expense for the year	–	–	–	–	24,319	14,850	–	(101,617)	1,048,160	–	985,712	50,533	1,036,245
Repurchase and cancellation of shares	(11,973)	(2,055,584)	–	–	–	–	–	–	–	–	(2,067,557)	–	(2,067,557)
Dividend attributable to cancelled shares	–	–	–	–	–	–	–	–	12,025	(12,025)	–	–	–
Disposal of a jointly-controlled entity	–	–	–	–	–	–	(210)	–	–	–	(210)	(21)	(231)
Transfer to statutory reserves	–	–	–	–	–	–	192,958	–	(192,958)	–	–	–	–
Dividends paid	–	–	–	–	–	–	–	–	(344,486)	(316,604)	(661,090)	–	(661,090)
At 31 December 2008	331,791	6,207,709	657	(216,966)	24,319	14,850	761,077	(182,210)	1,618,607	–	8,559,834	140,201	8,700,035

GOME Electrical Appliances Holding Limited

Consolidated Cash Flow Statement

Year ended 31 December 2008

	2008 RMB'000	2007 RMB'000
CASH FLOWS FROM OPERATING ACTIVITIES		
Profit before tax	1,533,849	1,528,097
Adjustments for:		
Finance income	(441,017)	(424,241)
Finance costs	212,118	193,369
Loss on the derivative components of convertible bonds	189,220	505,483
Impairment of goodwill	8,000	–
Impairment of other investments	449,592	–
Impairment of property, plant and equipment	31,725	–
Fair value loss on property, plant and equipment	6,632	–
Fair value loss/(gain) on investment properties	34,441	(47,176)
Fair value loss/(gain) on Hong Kong listed investments	659	(150)
Depreciation	296,256	256,988
Loss on disposal of items of property, plant and equipment	13,763	13,104
Gain on disposal of a jointly-controlled entity	(3)	–
Amortisation of intangible assets	9,626	8,457
	2,344,861	2,033,931
Increase in lease prepayments	(12,345)	(279,970)
Increase in inventories	(90,458)	(466,578)
Decrease/(increase) in trade and bills receivables	52,627	(10,230)
Decrease/(increase) in prepayments, deposits and other receivables	1,007,795	(839,136)
Decrease in amounts due from related parties	21,181	110,439
Decrease in other financial assets	150,000	–
Decrease in pledged deposits	1,774,269	839,449
(Decrease)/increase in trade and bills payables	(638,587)	887,997
(Decrease)/increase in customers' deposits, other payables and accruals	(335,928)	547,003
Decrease in an amount due to a related party	–	(120,564)
Cash generated from operations	4,273,415	2,702,341
Interest received	260,645	390,864
Dividends paid	(661,090)	(364,311)
PRC income tax paid	(262,610)	(168,171)
Net cash inflow from operating activities	3,610,360	2,560,723

GOME

GOME Electrical Appliances Holding Limited

Consolidated Cash Flow Statement (continued)

Year ended 31 December 2008

	2008 RMB'000	2007 RMB'000
Net cash inflow from operating activities	**3,610,360**	2,560,723
CASH FLOWS FROM INVESTING ACTIVITIES		
Purchases of items of property, plant and equipment	**(1,179,635)**	(1,578,294)
Proceeds from disposal of items of property, plant and equipment	**15,042**	1,245
Acquisition of a subsidiary	**(8,000)**	(6,558)
Acquisition of minority interests	**–**	(13,158)
Acquisition of other investments	**(543,552)**	–
Payment of outstanding considerations for business combinations	**(45,000)**	–
Disposal of a jointly-controlled entity	**–**	(5,526)
Prepayment for acquisition of a subsidiary	**–**	(10,000)
Increase in a designated loan	**(2,100,000)**	(1,500,000)
Increase in other assets	**(653,423)**	–
Increase in investment deposits	**–**	(30,000)
Net cash outflow from investing activities	**(4,514,568)**	(3,142,291)
CASH FLOWS FROM FINANCING ACTIVITIES		
Proceeds from issue of shares	**–**	1,433,740
Share issue expenses	**–**	(1,434)
Repurchase of shares	**(2,067,557)**	–
Issue of convertible bonds	**–**	4,600,000
Transaction costs for issuing convertible bonds and warrants	**–**	(71,860)
New bank loans	**100,000**	400,000
Repayment of bank loans	**(230,000)**	(829,330)
Interest paid	**(16,088)**	(40,789)
Net cash (outflow)/inflow from financing activities	**(2,213,645)**	5,490,327
NET (DECREASE)/INCREASE IN CASH AND CASH EQUIVALENTS	**(3,117,853)**	4,908,759
Cash and cash equivalents at 1 January	**6,269,996**	1,451,837
Exchange differences	**(101,074)**	(90,600)
CASH AND CASH EQUIVALENTS AT 31 DECEMBER	**3,051,069**	6,269,996
ANALYSIS OF BALANCES OF CASH AND CASH EQUIVALENTS		
Cash and bank balances	**2,055,835**	2,529,443
Non-pledged time deposits with original maturity of less than three months when acquired	**995,234**	3,740,553
	3,051,069	6,269,996

GOME

Apple Financial Report

CONSOLIDATED BALANCE SHEETS

(In millions, except share amounts)

	September 27, 2008	September 29, 2007
ASSETS:		
Current assets:		
Cash and cash equivalents	$ 11,875	$ 9,352
Short-term investments	12,615	6,034
Accounts receivable, less allowances of $47 in each period	2,422	1,637
Inventories	509	346
Deferred tax assets	1,447	782
Other current assets	5,822	3,805
Total current assets	34,690	21,956
Property, plant, and equipment, net	2,455	1,832
Goodwill	207	38
Acquired intangible assets, net	285	299
Other assets	1,935	1,222
Total assets	$ 39,572	$ 25,347
LIABILITIES AND SHAREHOLDERS' EQUITY:		
Current liabilities:		
Accounts payable	$ 5,520	$ 4,970
Accrued expenses	8,572	4,310
Total current liabilities	14,092	9,280
Non-current liabilities	4,450	1,535
Total liabilities	18,542	10,815
Commitments and contingencies		
Shareholders' equity:		
Common stock, no par value; 1,800,000,000 shares authorized; 888,325,973 and 872,328,972 shares issued and outstanding, respectively	7,177	5,368
Retained earnings	13,845	9,101
Accumulated other comprehensive income	8	63
Total shareholders' equity	21,030	14,532
Total liabilities and shareholders' equity	$ 39,572	$ 25,347

See Notes to Consolidated Financial Statements.

CONSOLIDATED STATEMENTS OF OPERATIONS

(In millions, except share amounts which are reflected in thousands and per share amounts)

Three fiscal years ended September 27, 2008	2008	2007	2006
Net sales	$ 32,479	$ 24,006	$ 19,315
Cost of sales (1)	21,334	15,852	13,717
Gross margin	11,145	8,154	5,598
Operating expenses:			
Research and development (1)	1,109	782	712
Selling, general, and administrative (1)	3,761	2,963	2,433
Total operating expenses	4,870	3,745	3,145
Operating income	6,275	4,409	2,453
Other income and expense	620	599	365
Income before provision for income taxes	6,895	5,008	2,818
Provision for income taxes	2,061	1,512	829
Net income	$ 4,834	$ 3,496	$ 1,989
Earnings per common share:			
Basic	$ 5.48	$ 4.04	$ 2.36
Diluted	$ 5.36	$ 3.93	$ 2.27
Shares used in computing earnings per share:			
Basic	881,592	864,595	844,058
Diluted	902,139	889,292	877,526

(1)   Includes stock-based compensation expense as follows:

	2008	2007	2006
Cost of sales	$ 80	$ 35	$ 21
Research and development	$ 185	$ 77	$ 53
Selling, general, and administrative	$ 251	$ 130	$ 89

See Notes to Consolidated Financial Statements.

APPLE

CONSOLIDATED STATEMENTS OF SHAREHOLDERS' EQUITY

(In millions, except share amounts which are reflected in thousands)

	Common Stock		Deferred Stock Compensation	Retained Earnings	Accumulated Other Comprehensive Income	Total Shareholders' Equity
	Shares	Amount				
Balances as of September 24, 2005	835,019	$ 3,564	$ (61)	$ 3,925	$ —	$ 7,428
Components of comprehensive income:						
Net income	—	—	—	1,989	—	1,989
Change in foreign currency translation	—	—	—	—	19	19
Change in unrealized gain on available-for-sale securities, net of tax	—	—	—	—	4	4
Change in unrealized gain on derivative instruments, net of tax	—	—	—	—	(1)	(1)
Total comprehensive income						2,011
Common stock repurchased	(4,574)	(48)	—	(307)	—	(355)
Stock-based compensation		163	—	—	—	163
Deferred compensation	—	(61)	61	—	—	—
Common stock issued under stock plans	24,818	318	—	—	—	318
Tax benefit from employee stock plan awards	—	419	—	—	—	419
Balances as of September 30, 2006	855,263	4,355	—	5,607	22	9,984
Components of comprehensive income:						
Net income	—	—	—	3,496	—	3,496
Change in foreign currency translation	—	—	—	—	51	51
Change in unrealized loss on available-for-sale securities, net of tax	—	—	—	—	(7)	(7)
Change in unrealized gain on derivative instruments, net of tax	—	—	—	—	(3)	(3)
Total comprehensive income						3,537
Stock-based compensation	—	251	—	—	—	251
Common stock issued under stock plans, net of shares withheld for employee taxes	17,066	364	—	(2)	—	362
Tax benefit from employee stock plan awards	—	398	—	—	—	398
Balances as of September 29, 2007	872,329	5,368	—	9,101	63	14,532
Cumulative effect of change in accounting principle	—	45	—	11	—	56
Components of comprehensive income:						
Net income	—	—	—	4,834	—	4,834
Change in foreign currency translation	—	—	—	—	(11)	(11)
Change in unrealized loss on available-for-sale securities, net of tax	—	—	—	—	(63)	(63)
Change in unrealized gain on derivative instruments, net of tax	—	—	—	—	19	19
Total comprehensive income						4,779
Stock-based compensation	—	513	—	—	—	513
Common stock issued under stock plans, net of shares withheld for employee taxes	15,888	460	—	(101)	—	359
Issuance of common stock in connection with an asset acquisition	109	21	—	—	—	21
Tax benefit from employee stock plan awards	—	770	—	—	—	770
Balances as of September 27, 2008	888,326	$ 7,177	$ —	$ 13,845	$ 8	$ 21,030

See Notes to Consolidated Financial Statements.

CONSOLIDATED STATEMENTS OF CASH FLOWS

(In millions)

Three fiscal years ended September 27, 2008	2008	2007	2006
Cash and cash equivalents, beginning of the year	$ 9,352	$ 6,392	$ 3,491
Operating Activities:			
Net income	4,834	3,496	1,989
Adjustments to reconcile net income to cash generated by operating activities:			
Depreciation, amortization and accretion	473	317	225
Stock-based compensation expense	516	242	163
Provision for deferred income taxes	(368)	78	53
Loss on disposition of property, plant, and equipment	22	12	15
Changes in operating assets and liabilities:			
Accounts receivable, net	(785)	(385)	(357)
Inventories	(163)	(76)	(105)
Other current assets	(1,958)	(1,540)	(1,626)
Other assets	(492)	81	(1,040)
Accounts payable	596	1,494	1,611
Deferred revenue	5,642	1,139	319
Other liabilities	1,279	612	973
Cash generated by operating activities	9,596	5,470	2,220
Investing Activities:			
Purchases of short-term investments	(22,965)	(11,719)	(7,255)
Proceeds from maturities of short-term investments	11,804	6,483	7,226
Proceeds from sales of short-term investments	4,439	2,941	1,086
Purchases of long-term investments	(38)	(17)	(25)
Payments made in connection with business acquisitions, net of cash acquired	(220)	—	—
Payment for acquisition of property, plant, and equipment	(1,091)	(735)	(657)
Payment for acquisition of intangible assets	(108)	(251)	(28)
Other	(10)	49	10
Cash (used in)/generated by investing activities	(8,189)	(3,249)	357
Financing Activities:			
Proceeds from issuance of common stock	483	365	318
Excess tax benefits from stock-based compensation	757	377	361
Cash used to net share settle equity awards	(124)	(3)	(355)
Cash generated by financing activities	1,116	739	324
Increase in cash and cash equivalents	2,523	2,960	2,901
Cash and cash equivalents, end of the year	$ 11,875	$ 9,352	$ 6,392
Supplemental cash flow disclosures:			
Cash paid for income taxes, net	$ 1,267	$ 863	$ 194

See Notes to Consolidated Financial Statements.

APPLE

B

Applying Present and Future Values

CAP

Conceptual

C1 Describe the earning of interest and the concepts of present and future values. *(p. B-1)*

Procedural

P1 Apply present value concepts to a single amount by using interest tables. *(p. B-3)*

P2 Apply future value concepts to a single amount by using interest tables. *(p. B-4)*

P3 Apply present value concepts to an annuity by using interest tables. *(p. B-5)*

P4 Apply future value concepts to an annuity by using interest tables. *(p. B-6)*

The concepts of present and future values are important to modern business, including the preparation and analysis of financial statements. The purpose of this appendix is to explain, illustrate, and compute present and future values. This appendix applies these concepts with reference to both business and everyday activities.

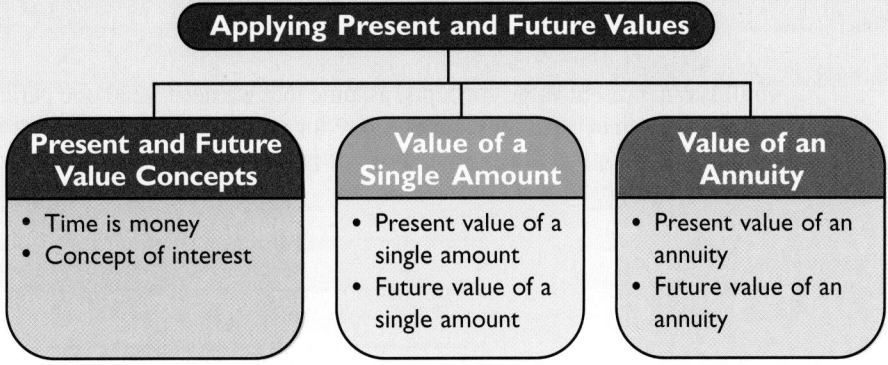

Present and Future Value Concepts

The old saying "Time is money" reflects the notion that as time passes, the values of our assets and liabilities change. This change is due to *interest,* which is a borrower's payment to the owner of an asset for its use. The most common example of interest is a savings account asset. As we keep a balance of cash in the account, it earns interest that the financial institution pays us. An example of a liability is a car loan. As we carry the balance of the loan, we accumulate interest costs on it. We must ultimately repay this loan with interest.

Present and future value computations enable us to measure or estimate the interest component of holding assets or liabilities over time. The present value computation is important when we want to know the value of future-day assets *today.* The future value computation is important when we want to know the value of present-day assets *at a future date.* The first section focuses on the present value of a single amount. The second section focuses on the future value of a single amount. Then both the present and future values of a series of amounts (called an *annuity*) are defined and explained.

C1   Describe the earning of interest and the concepts of present and future values.

Decision Insight

Keep That Job   Lottery winners often never work again. Kenny Dukes, a recent Georgia lottery winner, doesn't have that option. He is serving parole for burglary charges, and Georgia requires its parolees to be employed (or in school). For his lottery winnings, Dukes had to choose between $31 million in 30 annual payments or $16 million in one lump sum ($10.6 million after-tax); he chose the latter.

Present Value of a Single Amount

We graphically express the present value, called p, of a single future amount, called f, that is received or paid at a future date in Exhibit B.1.

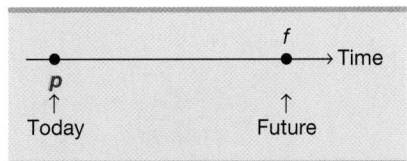

EXHIBIT B.1

Present Value of a Single Amount Diagram

The formula to compute the present value of a single amount is shown in Exhibit B.2, where p = present value; f = future value; i = rate of interest per period; and n = number of periods. (Interest is also called the *discount,* and an interest rate is also called the *discount rate.*)

EXHIBIT B.2

Present Value of a Single
Amount Formula

$$p = \frac{f}{(1 + i)^n}$$

To illustrate present value concepts, assume that we need $220 one period from today. We want to know how much we must invest now, for one period, at an interest rate of 10% to provide for this $220. For this illustration, the p, or present value, is the unknown amount—the specifics are shown graphically as follows:

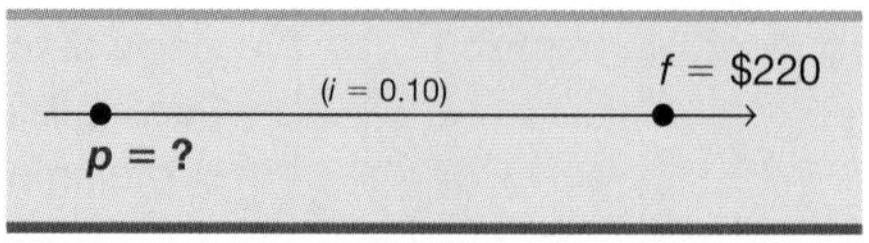

$(i = 0.10)$ $f = \$220$

$p = ?$

Conceptually, we know p must be less than $220. This is obvious from the answer to this question: Would we rather have $220 today or $220 at some future date? If we had $220 today, we could invest it and see it grow to something more than $220 in the future. Therefore, we would prefer the $220 today. This means that if we were promised $220 in the future, we would take less than $220 today. But how much less? To answer that question, we compute an estimate of the present value of the $220 to be received one period from now using the formula in Exhibit B.2 as follows:

$$p = \frac{f}{(1 + i)^n} = \frac{\$220}{(1 + 0.10)^1} = \$200$$

We interpret this result to say that given an interest rate of 10%, we are indifferent between $200 today or $220 at the end of one period.

We can also use this formula to compute the present value for *any number of periods.* To illustrate, consider a payment of $242 at the end of two periods at 10% interest. The present value of this $242 to be received two periods from now is computed as follows:

$$p = \frac{f}{(1 + i)^n} = \frac{\$242}{(1 + 0.10)^2} = \$200$$

I will pay your allowance at the end of the month. Do you want to wait or receive its present value today?

Together, these results tell us we are indifferent between $200 today, or $220 one period from today, or $242 two periods from today given a 10% interest rate per period.

The number of periods (n) in the present value formula does not have to be expressed in years. Any period of time such as a day, a month, a quarter, or a year can be used. Whatever period is used, the interest rate (i) must be compounded for the same period. This means that if a situation expresses n in months and i equals 12% per year, then i is transformed into interest earned per month (or 1%). In this case, interest is said to be *compounded monthly.*

A present value table helps us with present value computations. It gives us present values (factors) for a variety of both interest rates (i) and periods (n). Each present value in a present value table assumes that the future value (f) equals 1. When the future value (f) is different from 1, we simply multiply the present value (p) from the table by that future value to give us the estimate. The formula used to construct a table of present values for a single future amount of 1 is shown in Exhibit B.3.

EXHIBIT B.3

Present Value of 1 Formula

$$p = \frac{1}{(1 + i)^n}$$

This formula is identical to that in Exhibit B.2 except that *f* equals 1. Table B.1 at the end of this appendix is such a present value table. It is often called a **present value of 1 table**. A present value table involves three factors: *p*, *i*, and *n*. Knowing two of these three factors allows us to compute the third. (A fourth is *f*, but as already explained, we need only multiply the 1 used in the formula by *f*.) To illustrate the use of a present value table, consider three cases.

P1 Apply present value concepts to a single amount by using interest tables.

Case 1   (solve for *p* when knowing *i* and *n*). To show how we use a present value table, let's look again at how we estimate the present value of $220 (the *f* value) at the end of one period (*n* = 1) where the interest rate (*i*) is 10%. To solve this case, we go to the present value table (Table B.1) and look in the row for 1 period and in the column for 10% interest. Here we find a present value (*p*) of 0.9091 based on a future value of 1. This means, for instance, that $1 to be received one period from today at 10% interest is worth $0.9091 today. Since the future value in this case is not $1 but $220, we multiply the 0.9091 by $220 to get an answer of $200.

Case 2   (solve for *n* when knowing *p* and *i*). To illustrate, assume a $100,000 future value (*f*) that is worth $13,000 today (*p*) using an interest rate of 12% (*i*) but where *n* is unknown. In particular, we want to know how many periods (*n*) there are between the present value and the future value. To put this in context, it would fit a situation in which we want to retire with $100,000 but currently have only $13,000 that is earning a 12% return and we will be unable to save any additional money. How long will it be before we can retire? To answer this, we go to Table B.1 and look in the 12% interest column. Here we find a column of present values (*p*) based on a future value of 1. To use the present value table for this solution, we must divide $13,000 (*p*) by $100,000 (*f*), which equals 0.1300. This is necessary because *a present value table defines* f *equal to 1, and* p *as a fraction of 1*. We look for a value nearest to 0.1300 (*p*), which we find in the row for 18 periods (*n*). This means that the present value of $100,000 at the end of 18 periods at 12% interest is $13,000; alternatively stated, we must work 18 more years.

Case 3   (solve for *i* when knowing *p* and *n*). In this case, we have, say, a $120,000 future value (*f*) worth $60,000 today (*p*) when there are nine periods (*n*) between the present and future values, but the interest rate is unknown. As an example, suppose we want to retire with $120,000, but we have only $60,000 and we will be unable to save any additional money, yet we hope to retire in nine years. What interest rate must we earn to retire with $120,000 in nine years? To answer this, we go to the present value table (Table B.1) and look in the row for nine periods. To use the present value table, we must divide $60,000 (*p*) by $120,000 (*f*), which equals 0.5000. Recall that this step is necessary because a present value table defines *f* equal to 1 and *p* as a fraction of 1. We look for a value in the row for nine periods that is nearest to 0.5000 (*p*), which we find in the column for 8% interest (*i*). This means that the present value of $120,000 at the end of nine periods at 8% interest is $60,000 or, in our example, we must earn 8% annual interest to retire in nine years.

Quick Check   Answer—p. B-7

1. A company is considering an investment expected to yield $70,000 after six years. If this company demands an 8% return, how much is it willing to pay for this investment?

Future Value of a Single Amount

We must modify the formula for the present value of a single amount to obtain the formula for the future value of a single amount. In particular, we multiply both sides of the equation in Exhibit B.2 by $(1 + i)^n$ to get the result shown in Exhibit B.4.

$$f = p \times (1 + i)^n$$

EXHIBIT B.4

Future Value of a Single Amount Formula

The future value (*f*) is defined in terms of *p*, *i*, and *n*. We can use this formula to determine that $200 (*p*) invested for 1 (*n*) period at an interest rate of 10% (*i*) yields a future value of

$220 as follows:

$$f = p \times (1 + i)^n$$
$$= \$200 \times (1 + 0.10)^1$$
$$= \$220$$

P2 Apply future value concepts to a single amount by using interest tables.

This formula can also be used to compute the future value of an amount for *any number of periods* into the future. To illustrate, assume that $200 is invested for three periods at 10%. The future value of this $200 is $266.20, computed as follows:

$$f = p \times (1 + i)^n$$
$$= \$200 \times (1 + 0.10)^3$$
$$= \$266.20$$

A future value table makes it easier for us to compute future values (f) for many different combinations of interest rates (i) and time periods (n). Each future value in a future value table assumes the present value (p) is 1. As with a present value table, if the future amount is something other than 1, we simply multiply our answer by that amount. The formula used to construct a table of future values (factors) for a single amount of 1 is in Exhibit B.5.

EXHIBIT B.5

Future Value of 1 Formula

$$f = (1 + i)^n$$

Table B.2 at the end of this appendix shows a table of future values for a current amount of 1. This type of table is called a **future value of 1 table**.

There are some important relations between Tables B.1 and B.2. In Table B.2, for the row where $n = 0$, the future value is 1 for each interest rate. This is so because no interest is earned when time does not pass. We also see that Tables B.1 and B.2 report the same information but in a different manner. In particular, one table is simply the *inverse* of the other. To illustrate this inverse relation, let's say we invest $100 for a period of five years at 12% per year. How much do we expect to have after five years? We can answer this question using Table B.2 by finding the future value (f) of 1, for five periods from now, compounded at 12%. From that table we find $f = 1.7623$. If we start with $100, the amount it accumulates to after five years is $176.23 ($100 $\times$ 1.7623). We can alternatively use Table B.1. Here we find that the present value (p) of 1, discounted five periods at 12%, is 0.5674. Recall the inverse relation between present value and future value. This means that $p = 1/f$ (or equivalently, $f = 1/p$). We can compute the future value of $100 invested for five periods at 12% as follows: $f = \$100 \times (1/0.5674) = \$176.24$ (which equals the $176.23 just computed, except for a 1 cent rounding difference).

A future value table involves three factors: f, i, and n. Knowing two of these three factors allows us to compute the third. To illustrate, consider these three possible cases.

Case 1 (solve for f when knowing i and n). Our preceding example fits this case. We found that $100 invested for five periods at 12% interest accumulates to $176.24.

Case 2 (solve for n when knowing f and i). In this case, we have, say, $2,000 ($p$) and we want to know how many periods (n) it will take to accumulate to $3,000 ($f$) at 7% ($i$) interest. To answer this, we go to the future value table (Table B.2) and look in the 7% interest column. Here we find a column of future values (f) based on a present value of 1. To use a future value table, we must divide $3,000 ($f$) by $2,000 ($p$), which equals 1.500. This is necessary because *a future value table defines* p *equal to 1, and* f *as a multiple of 1*. We look for a value nearest to 1.50 (f), which we find in the row for six periods (n). This means that $2,000 invested for six periods at 7% interest accumulates to $3,000.

Case 3 (solve for i when knowing f and n). In this case, we have, say, $2,001 ($p$), and in nine years ($n$) we want to have $4,000 ($f$). What rate of interest must we earn to accomplish this? To answer that, we go to Table B.2 and search in the row for nine periods. To use a future value table, we must divide $4,000 ($f$) by $2,001 ($p$), which equals 1.9990. Recall that this is necessary because a future value table defines p equal to 1 and f as a multiple of 1. We look for a value nearest to 1.9990 (f), which we find in the column for 8% interest (i). This means that $2,001 invested for nine periods at 8% interest accumulates to $4,000.

2. Assume that you win a $150,000 cash sweepstakes. You decide to deposit this cash in an account earning 8% annual interest, and you plan to quit your job when the account equals $555,000. How many years will it be before you can quit working?

Present Value of an Annuity

An *annuity* is a series of equal payments occurring at equal intervals. One example is a series of three annual payments of $100 each. An *ordinary annuity* is defined as equal end-of-period payments at equal intervals. An ordinary annuity of $100 for three periods and its present value (p) are illustrated in Exhibit B.6.

P3 Apply present value concepts to an annuity by using interest tables.

EXHIBIT B.6

Present Value of an Ordinary Annuity Diagram

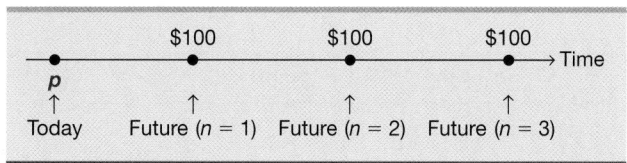

One way to compute the present value of an ordinary annuity is to find the present value of each payment using our present value formula from Exhibit B.3. We then add each of the three present values. To illustrate, let's look at three $100 payments at the end of each of the next three periods with an interest rate of 15%. Our present value computations are

$$p = \frac{\$100}{(1 + 0.15)^1} + \frac{\$100}{(1 + 0.15)^2} + \frac{\$100}{(1 + 0.15)^3} = \$228.32$$

This computation is identical to computing the present value of each payment (from Table B.1) and taking their sum or, alternatively, adding the values from Table B.1 for each of the three payments and multiplying their sum by the $100 annuity payment.

A more direct way is to use a present value of annuity table. Table B.3 at the end of this appendix is one such table. This table is called a **present value of an annuity of 1 table**. If we look at Table B.3 where $n = 3$ and $i = 15\%$, we see the present value is 2.2832. This means that the present value of an annuity of 1 for three periods, with a 15% interest rate, equals 2.2832.

A present value of an annuity formula is used to construct Table B.3. It can also be constructed by adding the amounts in a present value of 1 table. To illustrate, we use Tables B.1 and B.3 to confirm this relation for the prior example:

From Table B.1		From Table B.3	
$i = 15\%, n = 1$	0.8696		
$i = 15\%, n = 2$	0.7561		
$i = 15\%, n = 3$	0.6575		
Total	2.2832	$i = 15\%, n = 3$	2.2832

We can also use business calculators or spreadsheet programs to find the present value of an annuity.

Decision Insight

Better Lucky Than Good   "I don't have good luck—I'm blessed," proclaimed Andrew "Jack" Whittaker, 55, a sewage treatment contractor, after winning the largest ever undivided jackpot in a U.S. lottery. Whittaker had to choose between $315 million in 30 annual installments or $170 million in one lump sum ($112 million after-tax).

Quick Check   Answer—p. B-7

3. A company is considering an investment paying $10,000 every six months for three years. The first payment would be received in six months. If this company requires an 8% annual return, what is the maximum amount it is willing to pay for this investment?

Future Value of an Annuity

P4 Apply future value concepts to an annuity by using interest tables.

The future value of an *ordinary annuity* is the accumulated value of each annuity payment with interest as of the date of the final payment. To illustrate, let's consider the earlier annuity of three annual payments of $100. Exhibit B.7 shows the point in time for the future value (f). The first payment is made two periods prior to the point when future value is determined, and the final payment occurs on the future value date.

EXHIBIT B.7

Future Value of an Ordinary Annuity Diagram

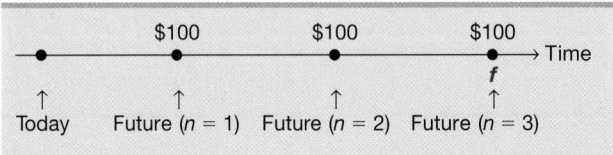

One way to compute the future value of an annuity is to use the formula to find the future value of *each* payment and add them. If we assume an interest rate of 15%, our calculation is

$$f = \$100 \times (1 + 0.15)^2 + \$100 \times (1 + 0.15)^1 + \$100 \times (1 + 0.15)^0 = \$347.25$$

This is identical to using Table B.2 and summing the future values of each payment, or adding the future values of the three payments of 1 and multiplying the sum by $100.

A more direct way is to use a table showing future values of annuities. Such a table is called a **future value of an annuity of 1 table**. Table B.4 at the end of this appendix is one such table. Note that in Table B.4 when $n = 1$, the future values equal 1 ($f = 1$) for all rates of interest. This is so because such an annuity consists of only one payment and the future value is determined on the date of that payment—no time passes between the payment and its future value. The future value of an annuity formula is used to construct Table B.4. We can also construct it by adding the amounts from a future value of 1 table. To illustrate, we use Tables B.2 and B.4 to confirm this relation for the prior example:

From Table B.2		From Table B.4	
$i = 15\%, n = 0$	1.0000		
$i = 15\%, n = 1$	1.1500		
$i = 15\%, n = 2$	1.3225		
Total	3.4725	$i = 15\%, n = 3$	3.4725

Note that the future value in Table B.2 is 1.0000 when $n = 0$, but the future value in Table B.4 is 1.0000 when $n = 1$. Is this a contradiction? No. When $n = 0$ in Table B.2, the future value is determined on the date when a single payment occurs. This means that no interest is earned because no time has passed, and the future value equals the payment. Table B.4 describes annuities with equal payments occurring at the end of each period. When $n = 1$, the annuity has one payment, and its future value equals 1 on the date of its final and only payment. Again, no time passes between the payment and its future value date.

Quick Check

Answer—p. B-7

4. A company invests $45,000 per year for five years at 12% annual interest. Compute the value of this annuity investment at the end of five years.

Summary

C1 **Describe the earning of interest and the concepts of present and future values.** Interest is payment by a borrower to the owner of an asset for its use. Present and future value computations are a way for us to estimate the interest component of holding assets or liabilities over a period of time.

P1 **Apply present value concepts to a single amount by using interest tables.** The present value of a single amount received at a future date is the amount that can be invested now at the specified interest rate to yield that future value.

P2 **Apply future value concepts to a single amount by using interest tables.** The future value of a single amount

invested at a specified rate of interest is the amount that would accumulate by the future date.

P3 **Apply present value concepts to an annuity by using interest tables.** The present value of an annuity is the amount that can be invested now at the specified interest rate to yield that series of equal periodic payments.

P4 **Apply future value concepts to an annuity by using interest tables.** The future value of an annuity invested at a specific rate of interest is the amount that would accumulate by the date of the final payment.

Guidance Answers to Quick Checks

1. $70,000 \times 0.6302 = \$44,114$ (use Table B.1, $i = 8\%$, $n = 6$).

2. $555,000/\$150,000 = 3.7000$; Table B.2 shows this value is not achieved until after 17 years at 8% interest.

3. $10,000 \times 5.2421 = \$52,421$ (use Table B.3, $i = 4\%$, $n = 6$).

4. $45,000 \times 6.3528 = \$285,876$ (use Table B.4, $i = 12\%$, $n = 5$).

connect Available with Connect Accounting

Assume that you must make future value estimates using the *future value of 1 table* (Table B.2). Which interest rate column do you use when working with the following rates?

1. 8% compounded quarterly

2. 12% compounded annually

3. 6% compounded semiannually

4. 12% compounded monthly

QUICK STUDY

QS B-1
Identifying interest
rates in tables

C1

Ken Francis is offered the possibility of investing $2,745 today and in return to receive $10,000 after 15 years. What is the annual rate of interest for this investment? (Use Table B.1.)

QS B-2
Interest rate
on an investment P1

Megan Brink is offered the possibility of investing $6,651 today at 6% interest per year in a desire to accumulate $10,000. How many years must Brink wait to accumulate $10,000? (Use Table B.1.)

QS B-3
Number of periods
of an investment P1

Flaherty is considering an investment that, if paid for immediately, is expected to return $140,000 five years from now. If Flaherty demands a 9% return, how much is she willing to pay for this investment?

QS B-4
Present value
of an amount P1

CII, Inc., invests $630,000 in a project expected to earn a 12% annual rate of return. The earnings will be reinvested in the project each year until the entire investment is liquidated 10 years later. What will the cash proceeds be when the project is liquidated?

QS B-5
Future value
of an amount P2

QS B-6 Present value of an annuity P3	Beene Distributing is considering a project that will return $150,000 annually at the end of each year for six years. If Beene demands an annual return of 7% and pays for the project immediately, how much is it willing to pay for the project?
QS B-7 Future value of an annuity P4	Claire Fitch is planning to begin an individual retirement program in which she will invest $1,500 at the end of each year. Fitch plans to retire after making 30 annual investments in the program earning a return of 10%. What is the value of the program on the date of the last payment?

Available with Connect Accounting **connect**

EXERCISES

Exercise B-1 Number of periods of an investment P2	Bill Thompson expects to invest $10,000 at 12% and, at the end of a certain period, receive $96,463. How many years will it be before Thompson receives the payment? (Use Table B.2.)
Exercise B-2 Interest rate on an investment P2	Ed Summers expects to invest $10,000 for 25 years, after which he wants to receive $108,347. What rate of interest must Summers earn? (Use Table B.2.)
Exercise B-3 Interest rate on an investment P3	Jones expects an immediate investment of $57,466 to return $10,000 annually for eight years, with the first payment to be received one year from now. What rate of interest must Jones earn? (Use Table B.3.)
Exercise B-4 Number of periods of an investment P3	Keith Riggins expects an investment of $82,014 to return $10,000 annually for several years. If Riggins earns a return of 10%, how many annual payments will he receive? (Use Table B.3.)
Exercise B-5 Interest rate on an investment P4	Algoe expects to invest $1,000 annually for 40 years to yield an accumulated value of $154,762 on the date of the last investment. For this to occur, what rate of interest must Algoe earn? (Use Table B.4.)
Exercise B-6 Number of periods of an investment P4	Kate Beckwith expects to invest $10,000 annually that will earn 8%. How many annual investments must Beckwith make to accumulate $303,243 on the date of the last investment? (Use Table B.4.)
Exercise B-7 Present value of an annuity P3	Sam Weber finances a new automobile by paying $6,500 cash and agreeing to make 40 monthly payments of $500 each, the first payment to be made one month after the purchase. The loan bears interest at an annual rate of 12%. What is the cost of the automobile?
Exercise B-8 Present value of bonds P1 P3	Spiller Corp. plans to issue 10%, 15-year, $500,000 par value bonds payable that pay interest semiannually on June 30 and December 31. The bonds are dated December 31, 2008, and are issued on that date. If the market rate of interest for the bonds is 8% on the date of issue, what will be the total cash proceeds from the bond issue?
Exercise B-9 Present value of an amount P1	McAdams Company expects to earn 10% per year on an investment that will pay $606,773 six years from now. Use Table B.1 to compute the present value of this investment. (Round the amount to the nearest dollar.)
Exercise B-10 Present value of an amount and of an annuity P1 P3	Compute the amount that can be borrowed under each of the following circumstances: **1.** A promise to repay $90,000 seven years from now at an interest rate of 6%. **2.** An agreement made on February 1, 2008, to make three separate payments of $20,000 on February 1 of 2009, 2010, and 2011. The annual interest rate is 10%.
Exercise B-11 Present value of an amount P1	On January 1, 2008, a company agrees to pay $20,000 in three years. If the annual interest rate is 10%, determine how much cash the company can borrow with this agreement.

Find the amount of money that can be borrowed today with each of the following separate debt agreements *a* through *f*. (Round amounts to the nearest dollar.)

Case	Single Future Payment	Number of Periods	Interest Rate
a.	$40,000	3	4%
b.	75,000	7	8
c.	52,000	9	10
d.	18,000	2	4
e.	63,000	8	6
f.	89,000	5	2

Exercise B-12
Present value
of an amount   P1

C&H Ski Club recently borrowed money and agrees to pay it back with a series of six annual payments of $5,000 each. C&H subsequently borrows more money and agrees to pay it back with a series of four annual payments of $7,500 each. The annual interest rate for both loans is 6%.

1. Use Table B.1 to find the present value of these two separate annuities. (Round amounts to the nearest dollar.)

2. Use Table B.3 to find the present value of these two separate annuities. (Round amounts to the nearest dollar.)

Exercise B-13
Present values of annuities

P3

Otto Co. borrows money on April 30, 2008, by promising to make four payments of $13,000 each on November 1, 2008; May 1, 2009; November 1, 2009; and May 1, 2010.

1. How much money is Otto able to borrow if the interest rate is 8%, compounded semiannually?

2. How much money is Otto able to borrow if the interest rate is 12%, compounded semiannually?

3. How much money is Otto able to borrow if the interest rate is 16%, compounded semiannually?

Exercise B-14
Present value with semiannual
compounding

C1 P3

Mark Welsch deposits $7,200 in an account that earns interest at an annual rate of 8%, compounded quarterly. The $7,200 plus earned interest must remain in the account 10 years before it can be withdrawn. How much money will be in the account at the end of 10 years?

Exercise B-15
Future value
of an amount   P2

Kelly Malone plans to have $50 withheld from her monthly paycheck and deposited in a savings account that earns 12% annually, compounded monthly. If Malone continues with her plan for two and one-half years, how much will be accumulated in the account on the date of the last deposit?

Exercise B-16
Future value
of an annuity   P4

Starr Company decides to establish a fund that it will use 10 years from now to replace an aging production facility. The company will make a $100,000 initial contribution to the fund and plans to make quarterly contributions of $50,000 beginning in three months. The fund earns 12%, compounded quarterly. What will be the value of the fund 10 years from now?

Exercise B-17
Future value of
an amount plus
an annuity   P2 P4

Catten, Inc., invests $163,170 today earning 7% per year for nine years. Use Table B.2 to compute the future value of the investment nine years from now. (Round the amount to the nearest dollar.)

Exercise B-18
Future value of
an amount   P2

For each of the following situations, identify (1) the case as either (*a*) a present or a future value and (*b*) a single amount or an annuity, (2) the table you would use in your computations (but do not solve the problem), and (3) the interest rate and time periods you would use.

a. You need to accumulate $10,000 for a trip you wish to take in four years. You are able to earn 8% compounded semiannually on your savings. You plan to make only one deposit and let the money accumulate for four years. How would you determine the amount of the one-time deposit?

b. Assume the same facts as in part (*a*) except that you will make semiannual deposits to your savings account.

c. You want to retire after working 40 years with savings in excess of $1,000,000. You expect to save $4,000 a year for 40 years and earn an annual rate of interest of 8%. Will you be able to retire with more than $1,000,000 in 40 years? Explain.

d. A sweepstakes agency names you a grand prize winner. You can take $225,000 immediately or elect to receive annual installments of $30,000 for 20 years. You can earn 10% annually on any investments you make. Which prize do you choose to receive?

Exercise B-19
Using present and future
value tables

C1 P1 P2 P3 P4

TABLE B.1

Present Value of 1

$$p = 1/(1 + i)^n$$

						Rate						
Periods	1%	2%	3%	4%	5%	6%	7%	8%	9%	10%	12%	15%
1	0.9901	0.9804	0.9709	0.9615	0.9524	0.9434	0.9346	0.9259	0.9174	0.9091	0.8929	0.8696
2	0.9803	0.9612	0.9426	0.9246	0.9070	0.8900	0.8734	0.8573	0.8417	0.8264	0.7972	0.7561
3	0.9706	0.9423	0.9151	0.8890	0.8638	0.8396	0.8163	0.7938	0.7722	0.7513	0.7118	0.6575
4	0.9610	0.9238	0.8885	0.8548	0.8227	0.7921	0.7629	0.7350	0.7084	0.6830	0.6355	0.5718
5	0.9515	0.9057	0.8626	0.8219	0.7835	0.7473	0.7130	0.6806	0.6499	0.6209	0.5674	0.4972
6	0.9420	0.8880	0.8375	0.7903	0.7462	0.7050	0.6663	0.6302	0.5963	0.5645	0.5066	0.4323
7	0.9327	0.8706	0.8131	0.7599	0.7107	0.6651	0.6227	0.5835	0.5470	0.5132	0.4523	0.3759
8	0.9235	0.8535	0.7894	0.7307	0.6768	0.6274	0.5820	0.5403	0.5019	0.4665	0.4039	0.3269
9	0.9143	0.8368	0.7664	0.7026	0.6446	0.5919	0.5439	0.5002	0.4604	0.4241	0.3606	0.2843
10	0.9053	0.8203	0.7441	0.6756	0.6139	0.5584	0.5083	0.4632	0.4224	0.3855	0.3220	0.2472
11	0.8963	0.8043	0.7224	0.6496	0.5847	0.5268	0.4751	0.4289	0.3875	0.3505	0.2875	0.2149
12	0.8874	0.7885	0.7014	0.6246	0.5568	0.4970	0.4440	0.3971	0.3555	0.3186	0.2567	0.1869
13	0.8787	0.7730	0.6810	0.6006	0.5303	0.4688	0.4150	0.3677	0.3262	0.2897	0.2292	0.1625
14	0.8700	0.7579	0.6611	0.5775	0.5051	0.4423	0.3878	0.3405	0.2992	0.2633	0.2046	0.1413
15	0.8613	0.7430	0.6419	0.5553	0.4810	0.4173	0.3624	0.3152	0.2745	0.2394	0.1827	0.1229
16	0.8528	0.7284	0.6232	0.5339	0.4581	0.3936	0.3387	0.2919	0.2519	0.2176	0.1631	0.1069
17	0.8444	0.7142	0.6050	0.5134	0.4363	0.3714	0.3166	0.2703	0.2311	0.1978	0.1456	0.0929
18	0.8360	0.7002	0.5874	0.4936	0.4155	0.3503	0.2959	0.2502	0.2120	0.1799	0.1300	0.0808
19	0.8277	0.6864	0.5703	0.4746	0.3957	0.3305	0.2765	0.2317	0.1945	0.1635	0.1161	0.0703
20	0.8195	0.6730	0.5537	0.4564	0.3769	0.3118	0.2584	0.2145	0.1784	0.1486	0.1037	0.0611
25	0.7798	0.6095	0.4776	0.3751	0.2953	0.2330	0.1842	0.1460	0.1160	0.0923	0.0588	0.0304
30	0.7419	0.5521	0.4120	0.3083	0.2314	0.1741	0.1314	0.0994	0.0754	0.0573	0.0334	0.0151
35	0.7059	0.5000	0.3554	0.2534	0.1813	0.1301	0.0937	0.0676	0.0490	0.0356	0.0189	0.0075
40	0.6717	0.4529	0.3066	0.2083	0.1420	0.0972	0.0668	0.0460	0.0318	0.0221	0.0107	0.0037

TABLE B.2

Future Value of 1

$$f = (1 + i)^n$$

						Rate						
Periods	1%	2%	3%	4%	5%	6%	7%	8%	9%	10%	12%	15%
0	1.0000	1.0000	1.0000	1.0000	1.0000	1.0000	1.0000	1.0000	1.0000	1.0000	1.0000	1.0000
1	1.0100	1.0200	1.0300	1.0400	1.0500	1.0600	1.0700	1.0800	1.0900	1.1000	1.1200	1.1500
2	1.0201	1.0404	1.0609	1.0816	1.1025	1.1236	1.1449	1.1664	1.1881	1.2100	1.2544	1.3225
3	1.0303	1.0612	1.0927	1.1249	1.1576	1.1910	1.2250	1.2597	1.2950	1.3310	1.4049	1.5209
4	1.0406	1.0824	1.1255	1.1699	1.2155	1.2625	1.3108	1.3605	1.4116	1.4641	1.5735	1.7490
5	1.0510	1.1041	1.1593	1.2167	1.2763	1.3382	1.4026	1.4693	1.5386	1.6105	1.7623	2.0114
6	1.0615	1.1262	1.1941	1.2653	1.3401	1.4185	1.5007	1.5869	1.6771	1.7716	1.9738	2.3131
7	1.0721	1.1487	1.2299	1.3159	1.4071	1.5036	1.6058	1.7138	1.8280	1.9487	2.2107	2.6600
8	1.0829	1.1717	1.2668	1.3686	1.4775	1.5938	1.7182	1.8509	1.9926	2.1436	2.4760	3.0590
9	1.0937	1.1951	1.3048	1.4233	1.5513	1.6895	1.8385	1.9990	2.1719	2.3579	2.7731	3.5179
10	1.1046	1.2190	1.3439	1.4802	1.6289	1.7908	1.9672	2.1589	2.3674	2.5937	3.1058	4.0456
11	1.1157	1.2434	1.3842	1.5395	1.7103	1.8983	2.1049	2.3316	2.5804	2.8531	3.4785	4.6524
12	1.1268	1.2682	1.4258	1.6010	1.7959	2.0122	2.2522	2.5182	2.8127	3.1384	3.8960	5.3503
13	1.1381	1.2936	1.4685	1.6651	1.8856	2.1329	2.4098	2.7196	3.0658	3.4523	4.3635	6.1528
14	1.1495	1.3195	1.5126	1.7317	1.9799	2.2609	2.5785	2.9372	3.3417	3.7975	4.8871	7.0757
15	1.1610	1.3459	1.5580	1.8009	2.0789	2.3966	2.7590	3.1722	3.6425	4.1772	5.4736	8.1371
16	1.1726	1.3728	1.6047	1.8730	2.1829	2.5404	2.9522	3.4259	3.9703	4.5950	6.1304	9.3576
17	1.1843	1.4002	1.6528	1.9479	2.2920	2.6928	3.1588	3.7000	4.3276	5.0545	6.8660	10.7613
18	1.1961	1.4282	1.7024	2.0258	2.4066	2.8543	3.3799	3.9960	4.7171	5.5599	7.6900	12.3755
19	1.2081	1.4568	1.7535	2.1068	2.5270	3.0256	3.6165	4.3157	5.1417	6.1159	8.6128	14.2318
20	1.2202	1.4859	1.8061	2.1911	2.6533	3.2071	3.8697	4.6610	5.6044	6.7275	9.6463	16.3665
25	1.2824	1.6406	2.0938	2.6658	3.3864	4.2919	5.4274	6.8485	8.6231	10.8347	17.0001	32.9190
30	1.3478	1.8114	2.4273	3.2434	4.3219	5.7435	7.6123	10.0627	13.2677	17.4494	29.9599	66.2118
35	1.4166	1.9999	2.8139	3.9461	5.5160	7.6861	10.6766	14.7853	20.4140	28.1024	52.7996	133.1755
40	1.4889	2.2080	3.2620	4.8010	7.0400	10.2857	14.9745	21.7245	31.4094	45.2593	93.0510	267.8635

$$p = \left[1 - \frac{1}{(1 + i)^n}\right]/i$$

TABLE B.3

Present Value of an Annuity of 1

						Rate						
Periods	1%	2%	3%	4%	5%	6%	7%	8%	9%	10%	12%	15%
1	0.9901	0.9804	0.9709	0.9615	0.9524	0.9434	0.9346	0.9259	0.9174	0.9091	0.8929	0.8696
2	1.9704	1.9416	1.9135	1.8861	1.8594	1.8334	1.8080	1.7833	1.7591	1.7355	1.6901	1.6257
3	2.9410	2.8839	2.8286	2.7751	2.7232	2.6730	2.6243	2.5771	2.5313	2.4869	2.4018	2.2832
4	3.9020	3.8077	3.7171	3.6299	3.5460	3.4651	3.3872	3.3121	3.2397	3.1699	3.0373	2.8550
5	4.8534	4.7135	4.5797	4.4518	4.3295	4.2124	4.1002	3.9927	3.8897	3.7908	3.6048	3.3522
6	5.7955	5.6014	5.4172	5.2421	5.0757	4.9173	4.7665	4.6229	4.4859	4.3553	4.1114	3.7845
7	6.7282	6.4720	6.2303	6.0021	5.7864	5.5824	5.3893	5.2064	5.0330	4.8684	4.5638	4.1604
8	7.6517	7.3255	7.0197	6.7327	6.4632	6.2098	5.9713	5.7466	5.5348	5.3349	4.9676	4.4873
9	8.5660	8.1622	7.7861	7.4353	7.1078	6.8017	6.5152	6.2469	5.9952	5.7590	5.3282	4.7716
10	9.4713	8.9826	8.5302	8.1109	7.7217	7.3601	7.0236	6.7101	6.4177	6.1446	5.6502	5.0188
11	10.3676	9.7868	9.2526	8.7605	8.3064	7.8869	7.4987	7.1390	6.8052	6.4951	5.9377	5.2337
12	11.2551	10.5753	9.9540	9.3851	8.8633	8.3838	7.9427	7.5361	7.1607	6.8137	6.1944	5.4206
13	12.1337	11.3484	10.6350	9.9856	9.3936	8.8527	8.3577	7.9038	7.4869	7.1034	6.4235	5.5831
14	13.0037	12.1062	11.2961	10.5631	9.8986	9.2950	8.7455	8.2442	7.7862	7.3667	6.6282	5.7245
15	13.8651	12.8493	11.9379	11.1184	10.3797	9.7122	9.1079	8.5595	8.0607	7.6061	6.8109	5.8474
16	14.7179	13.5777	12.5611	11.6523	10.8378	10.1059	9.4466	8.8514	8.3126	7.8237	6.9740	5.9542
17	15.5623	14.2919	13.1661	12.1657	11.2741	10.4773	9.7632	9.1216	8.5436	8.0216	7.1196	6.0472
18	16.3983	14.9920	13.7535	12.6593	11.6896	10.8276	10.0591	9.3719	8.7556	8.2014	7.2497	6.1280
19	17.2260	15.6785	14.3238	13.1339	12.0853	11.1581	10.3356	9.6036	8.9501	8.3649	7.3658	6.1982
20	18.0456	16.3514	14.8775	13.5903	12.4622	11.4699	10.5940	9.8181	9.1285	8.5136	7.4694	6.2593
25	22.0232	19.5235	17.4131	15.6221	14.0939	12.7834	11.6536	10.6748	9.8226	9.0770	7.8431	6.4641
30	25.8077	22.3965	19.6004	17.2920	15.3725	13.7648	12.4090	11.2578	10.2737	9.4269	8.0552	6.5660
35	29.4086	24.9986	21.4872	18.6646	16.3742	14.4982	12.9477	11.6546	10.5668	9.6442	8.1755	6.6166
40	32.8347	27.3555	23.1148	19.7928	17.1591	15.0463	13.3317	11.9246	10.7574	9.7791	8.2438	6.6418

$$f = [(1 + i)^n - 1]/i$$

TABLE B.4

Future Value of an Annuity of 1

						Rate						
Periods	1%	2%	3%	4%	5%	6%	7%	8%	9%	10%	12%	15%
1	1.0000	1.0000	1.0000	1.0000	1.0000	1.0000	1.0000	1.0000	1.0000	1.0000	1.0000	1.0000
2	2.0100	2.0200	2.0300	2.0400	2.0500	2.0600	2.0700	2.0800	2.0900	2.1000	2.1200	2.1500
3	3.0301	3.0604	3.0909	3.1216	3.1525	3.1836	3.2149	3.2464	3.2781	3.3100	3.3744	3.4725
4	4.0604	4.1216	4.1836	4.2465	4.3101	4.3746	4.4399	4.5061	4.5731	4.6410	4.7793	4.9934
5	5.1010	5.2040	5.3091	5.4163	5.5256	5.6371	5.7507	5.8666	5.9847	6.1051	6.3528	6.7424
6	6.1520	6.3081	6.4684	6.6330	6.8019	6.9753	7.1533	7.3359	7.5233	7.7156	8.1152	8.7537
7	7.2135	7.4343	7.6625	7.8983	8.1420	8.3938	8.6540	8.9228	9.2004	9.4872	10.0890	11.0668
8	8.2857	8.5830	8.8923	9.2142	9.5491	9.8975	10.2598	10.6366	11.0285	11.4359	12.2997	13.7268
9	9.3685	9.7546	10.1591	10.5828	11.0266	11.4913	11.9780	12.4876	13.0210	13.5795	14.7757	16.7858
10	10.4622	10.9497	11.4639	12.0061	12.5779	13.1808	13.8164	14.4866	15.1929	15.9374	17.5487	20.3037
11	11.5668	12.1687	12.8078	13.4864	14.2068	14.9716	15.7836	16.6455	17.5603	18.5312	20.6546	24.3493
12	12.6825	13.4121	14.1920	15.0258	15.9171	16.8699	17.8885	18.9771	20.1407	21.3843	24.1331	29.0017
13	13.8093	14.6803	15.6178	16.6268	17.7130	18.8821	20.1406	21.4953	22.9534	24.5227	28.0291	34.3519
14	14.9474	15.9739	17.0863	18.2919	19.5986	21.0151	22.5505	24.2149	26.0192	27.9750	32.3926	40.5047
15	16.0969	17.2934	18.5989	20.0236	21.5786	23.2760	25.1290	27.1521	29.3609	31.7725	37.2797	47.5804
16	17.2579	18.6393	20.1569	21.8245	23.6575	25.6725	27.8881	30.3243	33.0034	35.9497	42.7533	55.7175
17	18.4304	20.0121	21.7616	23.6975	25.8404	28.2129	30.8402	33.7502	36.9737	40.5447	48.8837	65.0751
18	19.6147	21.4123	23.4144	25.6454	28.1324	30.9057	33.9990	37.4502	41.3013	45.5992	55.7497	75.8364
19	20.8109	22.8406	25.1169	27.6712	30.5390	33.7600	37.3790	41.4463	46.0185	51.1591	63.4397	88.2118
20	22.0190	24.2974	26.8704	29.7781	33.0660	36.7856	40.9955	45.7620	51.1601	57.2750	72.0524	102.4436
25	28.2432	32.0303	36.4593	41.6459	47.7271	54.8645	63.2490	73.1059	84.7009	98.3471	133.3339	212.7930
30	34.7849	40.5681	47.5754	56.0849	66.4388	79.0582	94.4608	113.2832	136.3075	164.4940	241.3327	434.7451
35	41.6603	49.9945	60.4621	73.6522	90.3203	111.4348	138.2369	172.3168	215.7108	271.0244	431.6635	881.1702
40	48.8864	60.4020	75.4013	95.0255	120.7998	154.7620	199.6351	259.0565	337.8824	442.5926	767.0914	1,779.0903

Investments and International Operations

CAP

Conceptual

C1 Distinguish between debt and equity securities and between short-term and long-term investments. *(p. C-1)*

C2 Identify and describe the different classes of investments in securities. *(p. C-2)*

C3 Describe how to report equity securities with controlling influence. *(p. C-8)*

C4 *Appendix C-A*—Explain foreign exchange rates between currencies. *(p. C-16)*

Analytical

A1 Compute and analyze the components of return on total assets. *(p. C-11)*

LPC

Procedural

P1 Account for trading securities. *(p. C-4)*

P2 Account for held-to-maturity securities. *(p. C-5)*

P3 Account for available-for-sale securities. *(p. C-5)*

P4 Account for equity securities with significant influence. *(p. C-7)*

P5 *Appendix C-A*—Record transactions listed in a foreign currency. *(p. C-17)*

A Look at This Appendix

This appendix focuses on investments in securities. We explain how to identify, account for, and report investments in both debt and equity securities. We also explain accounting for transactions listed in a foreign currency.

This appendix's main focus is investments in securities. Many companies have investments, and many of these are in the form of debt and equity securities issued by other companies. We describe investments in these securities and how to account for them. An increasing number of companies also invest in international operations. We explain how to account for and report international transactions listed in foreign currencies.

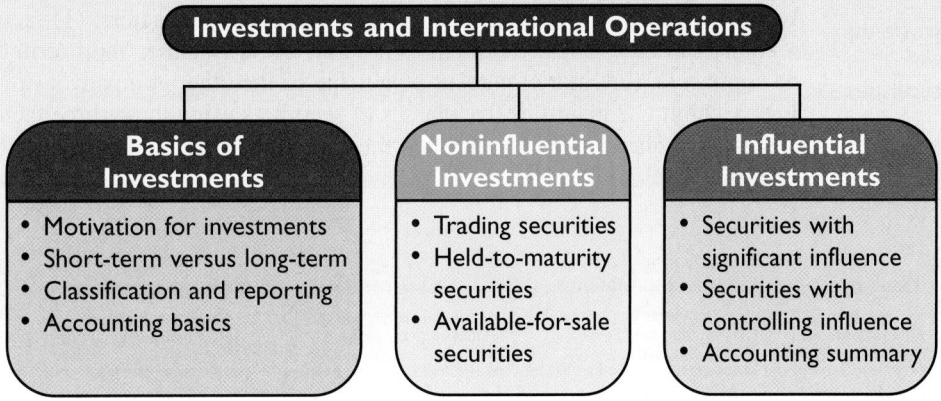

Basics of Investments

This section describes the motivation for investments, the distinction between short- and long-term investments, and the different classes of investments.

Motivation for Investments

Companies make investments for at least three reasons. First, companies transfer *excess cash* into investments to produce higher income. Second, some entities, such as mutual funds and pension funds, are set up to produce income from investments. Third, companies make investments for strategic reasons. Examples are investments in competitors, suppliers, and even customers. Exhibit C.1 shows short-term (S-T) and long-term (L-T) investments as a percent of total assets for several companies.

C1 Distinguish between debt and equity securities and between short-term and long-term investments.

EXHIBIT C.1

Investments of Selected Companies

Short-Term versus Long-Term

Cash equivalents are investments that are both readily converted to known amounts of cash and mature within three months. Many investments, however, mature between 3 and 12 months. These investments are **short-term investments,** also called *temporary investments* and *marketable securities*. Specifically, short-term investments are securities that (1) management intends to convert to cash within one year or the operating cycle, whichever is longer, and (2) are readily convertible to cash. Short-term investments are reported under current assets and serve a purpose similar to cash equivalents.

   Long-term investments in securities are defined as those securities that are not readily convertible to cash or are not intended to be converted into cash in the short term. Long-term investments can also include funds earmarked for a special purpose, such as bond sinking funds and investments in land or other assets not used in the company's operations. Long-term investments are reported in the noncurrent section of the balance sheet, often in its own separate line titled *Long-Term Investments*.

Investments in securities can include both debt and equity securities. *Debt securities* reflect a creditor relationship such as investments in notes, bonds, and certificates of deposit; they are issued by governments, companies, and individuals. *Equity securities* reflect an owner relationship such as shares of stock issued by companies.

Classification and Reporting

C2 Identify and describe the different classes of investments in securities.

Accounting for investments in securities depends on three factors: (1) security type, either debt or equity, (2) the company's intent to hold the security either short term or long term, and (3) the company's (investor's) percent ownership in the other company's (investee's) equity securities. Exhibit C.2 identifies five classes of securities using these three factors. It describes each of these five classes of securities and the usual reporting required under each class.

EXHIBIT C.2
Investments in Securities

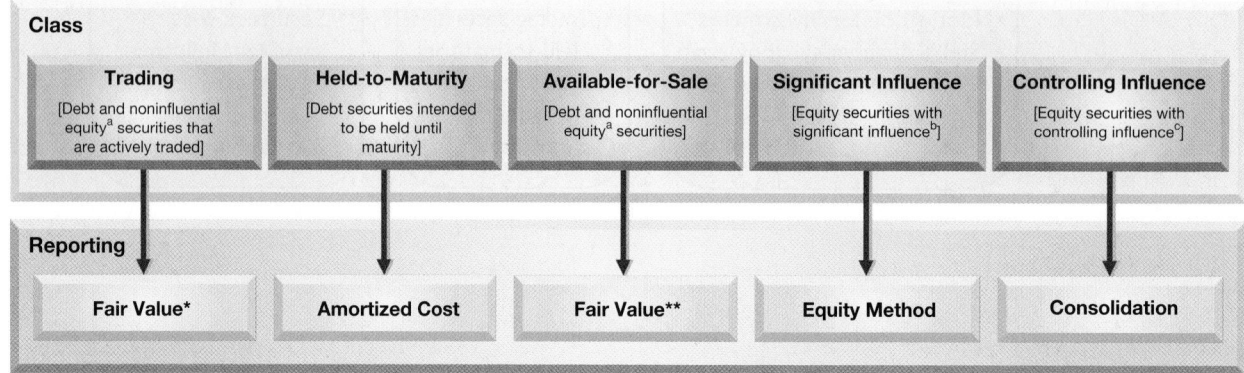

Class

Trading	Held-to-Maturity	Available-for-Sale	Significant Influence	Controlling Influence
[Debt and noninfluential equity[a] securities that are actively traded]	[Debt securities intended to be held until maturity]	[Debt and noninfluential equity[a] securities]	[Equity securities with significant influence[b]]	[Equity securities with controlling influence[c]]

Reporting

Fair Value*	Amortized Cost	Fair Value**	Equity Method	Consolidation

[a] Holding less than 20% of voting stock (equity securities only).   [b] Holding 20% or more, but not more than 50%, of voting stock.
[c] Holding more than 50% of voting stock.
* Unrealized gains and losses reported on the income statement.
** Unrealized gains and losses reported in the equity section of the balance sheet and in comprehensive income.

Accounting Basics for Debt Securities

This section explains the accounting basics for *debt securities,* including that for acquisition, disposition, and any interest.

Acquisition. Debt securities are recorded at cost when purchased. To illustrate, assume that Music City paid $29,500 plus a $500 brokerage fee on September 1, 2008, to buy Dell's 7%, two-year bonds payable with a $30,000 par value. The bonds pay interest semiannually on August 31 and February 28. Music City intends to hold the bonds until they mature on August 31, 2010; consequently, they are classified as held-to-maturity (HTM) securities. The entry to record this purchase follows. (If the maturity of the securities was short term, and management's intent was to hold them until they mature, then they would be classified as Short-Term Investments—HTM.)

Assets = Liabilities + Equity
+30,000
−30,000

2008			
Sept. 1	Long-Term Investments—HTM (Dell)	30,000	
	Cash		30,000
	Purchased bonds to be held to maturity.		

Interest earned. Interest revenue for investments in debt securities is recorded when earned. To illustrate, on December 31, 2008, at the end of its accounting period, Music City accrues interest receivable as follows.

Assets = Liabilities + Equity
+700   +700

Dec. 31	Interest Receivable	700	
	Interest Revenue		700
	Accrued interest earned ($30,000 × 7% × ¹⁄₁₂).		

The $700 reflects 4/6 of the semiannual cash receipt of interest—the portion Music City earned as of December 31. Relevant sections of Music City's financial statements at December 31, 2008, are shown in Exhibit C.3.

EXHIBIT C.3

Financial Statement Presentation of Debt Securities

On the income statement for year 2008:
Interest revenue .... $ 700
On the December 31, 2008, balance sheet:
Long-term investments—Held-to-maturity securities (at amortized cost) $30,000

On February 28, 2009, Music City records receipt of semiannual interest.

Feb. 28	Cash	1,050	
	Interest Receivable		700
	Interest Revenue		350
	Received six months' interest on Dell bonds.		

Assets = Liabilities + Equity
+1,050   +350
−700

Disposition.   When the bonds mature, the proceeds (not including the interest entry) are recorded as:

2010			
Aug. 31	Cash..	30,000	
	Long-Term Investments—HTM (Dell)		30,000
	Received cash from matured bonds.		

Assets = Liabilities + Equity
+30,000
−30,000

The cost of a debt security can be either higher or lower than its maturity value. When the investment is long term, the difference between cost and maturity value is amortized over the remaining life of the security. We assume for ease of computations that the cost of a long-term debt security equals its maturity value.

Example: What is cost per share? *Answer:* Cost per share is the total cost of acquisition, including broker fees, divided by number of shares acquired.

Accounting Basics for Equity Securities

This section explains the accounting basics for *equity* securities, including that for acquisition, dividends, and disposition.

Acquisition.   Equity securities are recorded at cost when acquired, including commissions or brokerage fees paid. To illustrate, assume that Music City purchases 1,000 shares of Intex common stock at par value for $86,000 on October 10, 2008. It records this purchase of available-for-sale (AFS) securities as follows.

Oct. 10	Long-Term Investments—AFS (Intex)	86,000	
	Cash		86,000
	Purchased 1,000 shares of Intex.		

Assets = Liabilities + Equity
+86,000
−86,000

Dividend earned.   Any cash dividends received are credited to Dividend Revenue and reported in the income statement. To illustrate, on November 2, Music City receives a $1,720 quarterly cash dividend on the Intex shares, which it records as:

Nov. 2	Cash	1,720	
	Dividend Revenue		1,720
	Received dividend of $1.72 per share.		

Assets = Liabilities + Equity
+1,720   +1,720

Disposition.   When the securities are sold, sale proceeds are compared with the cost, and any gain or loss is recorded. To illustrate, on December 20, Music City sells 500 of the Intex shares for $45,000 cash and records this sale as:

Assets = Liabilities + Equity		
+45,000	+2,000	
−43,000		

Dec. 20	Cash	45,000	
	Long-Term Investments—AFS (Intex)		43,000
	Gain on Sale of Long-Term Investments		2,000
	Sold 500 Intex shares ($86,000 × 500/1,000).		

Reporting of <u>Noninfluential</u> Investments

P1 Account for trading securities.

Companies must value and report most noninfluential investments at *fair value.* The exact reporting requirements depend on whether the investments are classified as (1) trading, (2) held-to-maturity, or (3) available-for-sale.

Trading Securities

Trading securities are *debt and equity securities* that the company intends to actively manage and trade for profit. Frequent purchases and sales are expected and are made to earn profits on short-term price changes. Trading securities are *always* reported as current assets.

Valuing and reporting trading securities.   The entire portfolio of trading securities is reported at its fair value; this requires a "fair value adjustment" from the cost of the portfolio. The term *portfolio* refers to a group of securities. Any **unrealized gain (or loss)** from a change in the fair value of the portfolio of trading securities is reported on the income statement. Most users believe accounting reports are more useful when changes in fair value for trading securities are reported in income.

Point: '*Unrealized gain (or loss)*' refers to a change in fair value that is not yet realized through actual sale.

Point: 'Fair Value Adjustment—Trading' is a *permanent account*, shown as a deduction or addition to 'Short-Term Investments—Trading.'

To illustrate, TechCom's portfolio of trading securities had a total cost of $11,500 and a fair value of $13,000 on December 31, 2008, the first year it held trading securities. The difference between the $11,500 cost and the $13,000 fair value reflects a $1,500 gain. It is an unrealized gain because it is not yet confirmed by actual sales. The fair value adjustment for trading securities is recorded with an adjusting entry at the end of each period to equal the difference between the portfolio's cost and its fair value. TechCom records this gain as follows.

Assets = Liabilities + Equity		
+1,500	+1,500	

Dec. 31	Fair Value Adjustment—Trading...................	1,500	
	Unrealized Gain—Income....................		1,500
	To reflect an unrealized gain in fair values		
	of trading securities.		

Example: If TechCom's trading securities have a cost of $14,800 and a fair value of $16,100 at Dec. 31, 2009, its adjusting entry is
Unrealized Loss—Income 200
    Fair Value Adj.—Trading ...   200
This is computed as: $1,500 Beg. Dr. bal. + $200 Cr. = $1,300 End. Dr. bal.

The Unrealized Gain (or Loss) is reported in the Other Revenues and Gains (or Expenses and Losses) section on the income statement. Unrealized Gain (or Loss)—Income is a *temporary* account that is closed to Income Summary at the end of each period. Fair Value Adjustment—Trading is a *permanent* account, which adjusts the reported value of the trading securities portfolio from its prior period fair value to the current period fair value. The total cost of the trading securities portfolio is maintained in one account, and the fair value adjustment is recorded in a separate account. For example, TechCom's investment in trading securities is reported in the current assets section of its balance sheet as follows.

Current Assets		
Short-term investments—Trading (at cost)	$11,500	
Fair value adjustment—Trading	1,500	
Short-term investments—Trading (at fair value)		$13,000
or simply		
Short-term investments—Trading (at fair value; cost is $11,500)		$13,000

Selling trading securities.   When individual trading securities are sold, the difference between the net proceeds (sale price less fees) and the cost of the individual trading securities that are sold is recognized as a gain or a loss. Any prior period fair value adjustment to the portfolio is *not* used to compute the gain or loss from sale of individual trading securities. For example, if TechCom sold some of its trading securities that had cost $1,000 for $1,200 cash on January 9, 2009, it would record the following.

Point: Reporting securities at fair value is referred to as *mark-to-market* accounting.

Jan. 9	Cash...	1,200	
	Short-Term Investments—Trading..............		1,000
	Gain on Sale of Short-Term Investments........		200
	Sold trading securities costing $1,000 for $1,200 cash.		

Assets = Liabilities + Equity
+1,200   +200
−1,000

A gain is reported in the Other Revenues and Gains section on the income statement, whereas a loss is shown in Other Expenses and Losses. When the period-end fair value adjustment for the portfolio of trading securities is computed, it excludes the cost and fair value of any securities sold.

Held-to-Maturity Securities

Held-to-maturity (HTM) securities are *debt* securities a company intends and is able to hold until maturity. They are reported in current assets if their maturity dates are within one year or the operating cycle, whichever is longer. HTM securities are reported in long-term assets when the maturity dates extend beyond one year or the operating cycle, whichever is longer. All HTM securities are recorded at cost when purchased, and interest revenue is recorded when earned.

P2 Account for held-to-maturity securities.

The portfolio of HTM securities is usually reported at (amortized) cost, which is explained in advanced courses. There is no fair value adjustment to the portfolio of HTM securities—neither to the short-term nor long-term portfolios. The basics of accounting for HTM securities were described earlier in this appendix.

Point: Only debt securities can be classified as *held-to-maturity*; equity securities have no maturity date.

Decision Maker

Money Manager   You expect interest rates to sharply fall within a few weeks and remain at this lower rate. What is your strategy for holding investments in fixed-rate bonds and notes? [Answer—p. C-19]

Available-for-Sale Securities

Available-for-sale (AFS) securities are *debt and equity securities* not classified as trading or held-to-maturity securities. AFS securities are purchased to yield interest, dividends, or increases in fair value. They are not actively managed like trading securities. If the intent is to sell AFS securities within the longer of one year or operating cycle, they are classified as short-term investments. Otherwise, they are classified as long-term.

P3 Account for available-for-sale securities.

Valuing and reporting available-for-sale securities.   As with trading securities, companies adjust the cost of the portfolio of AFS securities to reflect changes in fair value. This is done with a fair value adjustment to its total portfolio cost. However, any unrealized gain or loss for the portfolio of AFS securities is *not* reported on the income statement. Instead, it is reported in the equity section of the balance sheet (and is part of *comprehensive income,* explained later). To illustrate, assume that Music City had no prior period investments in available-for-sale securities other than those purchased in the current period. Exhibit C.4 shows both the cost and fair value of those investments on December 31, 2008, the end of its reporting period.

Example: If fair value in Exhibit C.4 is $70,000 (instead of $74,550), what entry is made? *Answer:*
Unreal. Loss—Equity 3,000
  Fair Value Adj.—AFS ...   3,000

EXHIBIT C.4

Cost and Fair Value of Available-for-Sale Securities

	Cost	Fair Value	Unrealized Gain (Loss)
Improv bonds	$30,000	$29,050	$ (950)
Intex common stock, 500 shares	43,000	45,500	2,500
Total..............................	$73,000	$74,550	**$1,550**

The year-end adjusting entry to record the fair value of these investments follows.

Dec. 31	Fair Value Adjustment—Available-for-Sale (LT).......	1,550	
	Unrealized Gain—Equity.....................		1,550
	To record adjustment to fair value of		
	available-for-sale securities.		

Point: 'Unrealized Loss—Equity' and 'Unrealized Gain—Equity' are *permanent* (balance sheet) equity *accounts.*

Exhibit C.5 shows the December 31, 2008, balance sheet presentation—it assumes these investments are long term, but they can also be short term. It is also common to combine the cost of investments with the balance in the Fair Value Adjustment account and report the net as a single amount.

EXHIBIT C.5

Balance Sheet Presentation of Available-for-Sale Securities

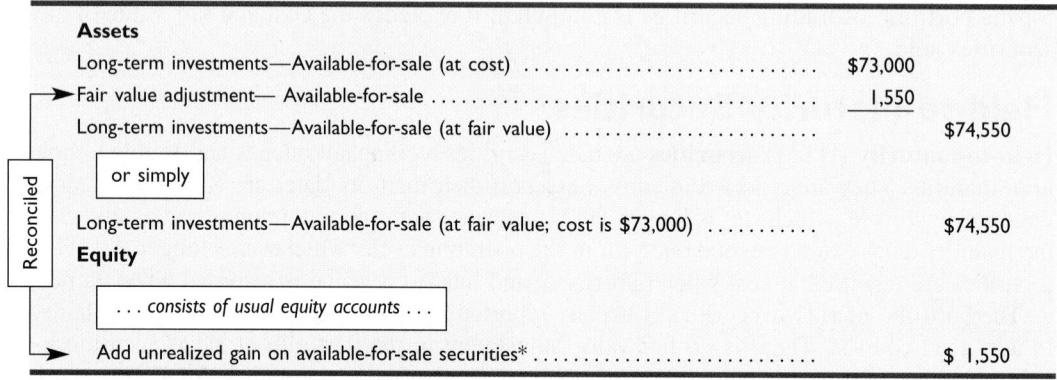

Assets

Long-term investments—Available-for-sale (at cost)	$73,000	
Fair value adjustment— Available-for-sale	1,550	
Long-term investments—Available-for-sale (at fair value)		$74,550

or simply

Long-term investments—Available-for-sale (at fair value; cost is $73,000)	$74,550

Equity

... consists of usual equity accounts ...

Add unrealized gain on available-for-sale securities*	$ 1,550

Reconciled

* Often included under the caption Accumulated Other Comprehensive Income.

Point: Income can be window-dressed upward by selling AFS securities with unrealized gains; income is reduced by selling those with unrealized losses.

Let's extend this illustration and assume that at the end of its next calendar year (December 31, 2009), Music City's portfolio of long-term AFS securities has an $81,000 cost and an $82,000 fair value. It records the adjustment to fair value as follows.

Dec. 31	Unrealized Gain—Equity.........................	550	
	Fair Value Adjustment—Available-for-Sale (LT)....		550
	To record adjustment to fair value of		
	available-for-sale securities.		

The effects of the 2008 and 2009 securities transactions are reflected in the following T-accounts.

Example: If cost is $83,000 and fair value is $82,000 at Dec. 31, 2009, it records the following adjustment:
Unreal. Gain—Equity ... 1,550
Unreal. Loss—Equity ... 1,000
   Mkt. Adj.—AFS 2,550

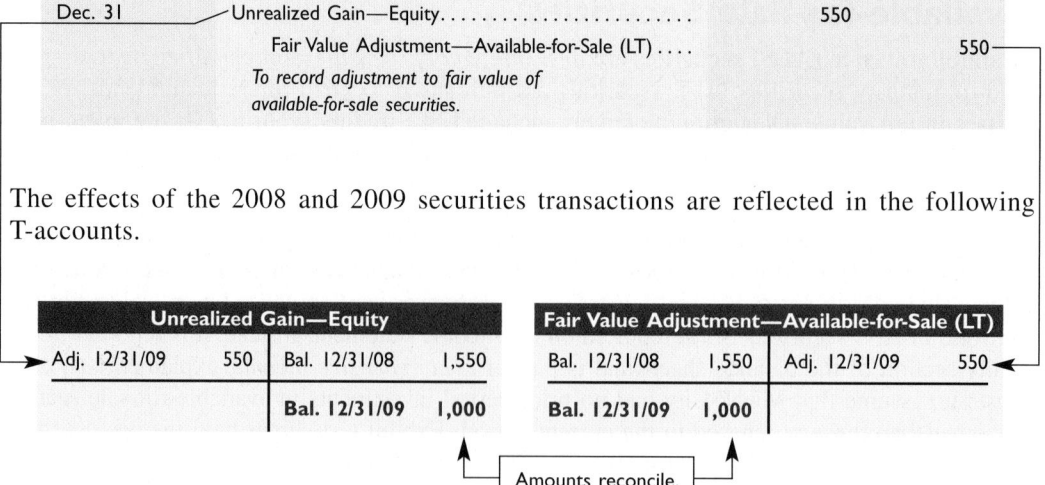

Unrealized Gain—Equity			
Adj. 12/31/09	550	Bal. 12/31/08	1,550
		Bal. 12/31/09	1,000

Fair Value Adjustment—Available-for-Sale (LT)			
Bal. 12/31/08	1,550	Adj. 12/31/09	550
Bal. 12/31/09	1,000		

Amounts reconcile.

Point: 'Fair Value Adjustment— Available-for-Sale' is a permanent account, shown as a deduction or addition to the Investment account.

Selling available-for-sale securities. Accounting for the sale of individual AFS securities is identical to that described for the sale of trading securities. When individual AFS securities are sold, the difference between the cost of the individual securities sold and the net proceeds (sale price less fees) is recognized as a gain or loss.

Quick Check   Answers—p. C-19

1. How are short-term held-to-maturity securities reported (valued) on the balance sheet?
2. How are trading securities reported (valued) on the balance sheet?
3. Where are unrealized gains and losses on available-for-sale securities reported?
4. Where are unrealized gains and losses on trading securities reported?

Alert   *Both U.S. GAAP and IFRS permit companies to use fair value in reporting financial assets (referred to as the fair value option). This option allows companies to report any financial asset at fair value and recognize value changes in income. This method was previously reserved only for trading securities, but is now an option for available-for-sale and held-to-maturity securities (and other 'financial assets and liabilities' such as accounts and notes receivable, accounts and notes payable, and bonds). U.S. standards also set a 3-level system to determine fair value:*
—Level 1: Use quoted market values
—Level 2: Use observable values from related assets or liabilities
—Level 3: Use unobservable values from estimates or assumptions
To date, a fairly small set of companies has chosen to broadly apply the fair value option—but, we continue to monitor its use...

Reporting of Influential Investments

Investment in Securities with Significant Influence

A long-term investment classified as **equity securities with significant influence** implies that the investor can exert significant influence over the investee. An investor that owns 20% or more (but not more than 50%) of a company's voting stock is usually presumed to have a significant influence over the investee. In some cases, however, the 20% test of significant influence is overruled by other, more persuasive, evidence. This evidence can either lower the 20% requirement or increase it. The **equity method** of accounting and reporting is used for long-term investments in equity securities with significant influence, which is explained in this section.

P4 Account for equity securities with significant influence.

Long-term investments in equity securities with significant influence are recorded at cost when acquired. To illustrate, Micron Co. records the purchase of 3,000 shares (30%) of Star Co. common stock at a total cost of $70,650 on January 1, 2008, as follows.

Jan. 1	Long-Term Investments—Star	70,650	
	Cash		70,650
	To record purchase of 3,000 Star shares.		

Assets = Liabilities + Equity
+70,650
−70,650

The investee's (Star) earnings increase both its net assets and the claim of the investor (Micron) on the investee's net assets. Thus, when the investee reports its earnings, the investor records its share of those earnings in its investment account. To illustrate, assume that Star reports net income of $20,000 for 2008. Micron then records its 30% share of those earnings as follows.

Dec. 31	Long-Term Investments—Star	6,000	
	Earnings from Long-Term Investment		6,000
	To record 30% equity in investee earnings.		

Assets = Liabilities + Equity
+6,000   +6,000

The debit reflects the increase in Micron's equity in Star. The credit reflects 30% of Star's net income. Earnings from Long-Term Investment is a *temporary* account (closed to Income Summary at each period-end) and is reported on the investor's (Micron's) income statement. If the investee incurs a net loss instead of a net income, the investor records its share of the loss and reduces (credits) its investment account. The investor closes this earnings or loss account to Income Summary.

The receipt of cash dividends is not revenue under the equity method because the investor has already recorded its share of the investee's earnings. Instead, cash dividends received by an investor from an investee are viewed as a conversion of one asset to another; that is, dividends reduce the balance of the investment account. To illustrate, Star declares and pays $10,000 in cash dividends on its common stock. Micron records its 30% share of these dividends received on January 9, 2009, as:

Assets = Liabilities + Equity
+3,000
−3,000

Jan. 9	Cash	3,000	
	Long-Term Investments—Star		3,000
	To record share of dividend paid by Star.		

The book value of an investment under the equity method equals the cost of the investment plus (minus) the investor's equity in the *undistributed* (*distributed*) earnings of the investee. Once Micron records these transactions, its Long-Term Investments account appears as in Exhibit C.6.

EXHIBIT C.6

Investment in Star Common Stock (Ledger Account)

Date	Explanation	Debit	Credit	Balance
2008				
Jan. I	Investment acquisition	70,650		70,650
Dec. 31	Share of earnings	6,000		76,650
2009				
Jan. 9	Share of dividend		3,000	73,650

Point: Security prices are sometimes listed in fractions. For example, a debt security with a price of $22\frac{1}{4}$, is the same as $22.25.

Micron's account balance on January 9, 2009, for its investment in Star is $73,650. This is the investment's cost *plus* Micron's equity in Star's earnings since its purchase *less* Micron's equity in Star's cash dividends since its purchase. When an investment in equity securities is sold, the gain or loss is computed by comparing proceeds from the sale with the book value of the investment on the date of sale. If Micron sells its Star stock for $80,000 on January 10, 2009, it records the sale as:

Assets = Liabilities + Equity
+80,000   +6,350
−73,650

Jan. 10	Cash	80,000	
	Long-Term Investments—Star		73,650
	Gain on Sale of Investment.		6,350
	Sold 3,000 shares of stock for $80,000.		

Investment in Securities with Controlling Influence

C3 Describe how to report equity securities with controlling influence.

A long-term investment classified as **equity securities with controlling influence** implies that the investor can exert a controlling influence over the investee. An investor who owns more than 50% of a company's voting stock has control over the investee. This investor can dominate all other shareholders in electing the corporation's board of directors and has control over the investee's management. In some cases, controlling influence can extend to situations of less than 50% ownership. Exhibit C.7 summarizes the accounting for investments in equity securities based on an investor's ownership in the stock.

EXHIBIT C.7

Accounting for Equity Investments by Percent of Ownership

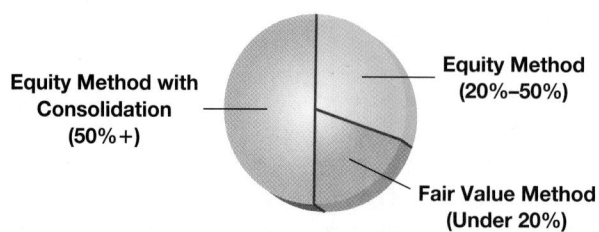

Equity Method with Consolidation (50%+)

Equity Method (20%–50%)

Fair Value Method (Under 20%)

The *equity method with consolidation* is used to account for long-term investments in equity securities with controlling influence. The investor reports *consolidated financial statements* when owning such securities. The controlling investor is called the **parent,** and the investee is called the **subsidiary.** Many companies are parents with subsidiaries. Examples are (1) **McGraw-Hill**, the parent of J.D. Power and Associates, Standard & Poor's, and Platt's; (2) **Gap, Inc.**, the parent of Gap, Old Navy, and Banana Republic; and (3) **Brunswick,** the parent of Mercury Marine, Sea Ray, and U.S. Marine. A company owning all the outstanding stock of a subsidiary can, if it desires, take over the subsidiary's assets, retire the subsidiary's stock, and merge the subsidiary into the parent. However, there often are financial, legal, and tax advantages if a business operates as a parent controlling one or more subsidiaries. When a company operates as a parent with subsidiaries, each entity maintains separate accounting records. From a legal viewpoint, the parent and each subsidiary are separate entities with all rights, duties, and responsibilities of individual companies.

Consolidated financial statements show the financial position, results of operations, and cash flows of all entities under the parent's control, including all subsidiaries. These statements are prepared as if the business were organized as one entity. The parent uses the equity method in its accounts, but the investment account is *not* reported on the parent's financial statements. Instead, the individual assets and liabilities of the parent and its subsidiaries are combined on one balance sheet. Their revenues and expenses also are combined on one income statement, and their cash flows are combined on one statement of cash flows. The procedures for preparing consolidated financial statements are in advanced courses.

IFRS

Unlike U.S. GAAP, IFRS requires uniform accounting policies be used throughout the group of consolidated subsidiaries. Also, unlike U.S. GAAP, IFRS offers no detailed guidance on valuation procedures.

Accounting Summary for Investments in Securities

Exhibit C.8 summarizes the usual accounting for investments in securities. Recall that many investment securities are classified as either short term or long term depending on management's intent and ability to convert them in the future. Understanding the accounting for these investments enables us to draw better conclusions from financial statements in making business decisions.

Classification	Accounting
Short-Term Investment in Securities	
Held-to-maturity (debt) securities	Cost (without any discount or premium amortization)
Trading (debt and equity) securities	**Fair value** (with fair value adjustment to income)
Available-for-sale (debt and equity) securities	**Fair value** (with fair value adjustment to equity)
Long-Term Investment in Securities	
Held-to-maturity (debt) securities	Cost (with any discount or premium amortization)
Available-for-sale (debt and equity) securities	**Fair value** (with fair value adjustment to equity)
Equity securities with significant influence	Equity method
Equity securities with controlling influence	Equity method (with consolidation)

EXHIBIT C.8

Accounting for Investments in Securities

Comprehensive Income   The term **comprehensive income** refers to all changes in equity for a period except those due to investments and distributions to owners. This means that it includes (1) the revenues, gains, expenses, and losses reported in net income *and* (2) the gains and losses that bypass net income but affect equity. An example of an item that bypasses net income is unrealized gains and losses on available-for-sale securities. These items make up *other comprehensive income* and are usually reported as a part of the statement of stockholders' equity. (Two other options are as a second separate income statement or as a combined income statement of comprehensive income; these less common options are described in advanced courses.) Most often this simply requires one additional column for Other Comprehensive Income in the usual columnar form of the statement of stockholders' equity (the details of this are left for advanced courses). The FASB encourages, but does *not* require, other comprehensive income items to be grouped under the caption *Accumulated Other Comprehensive Income* in the equity section of the balance sheet, which would include unrealized gains and losses on available-for-sale securities. For instructional benefits, we use actual account titles for these items in the equity section instead of this general, less precise caption.

Point: Some users believe that since AFS securities are not actively traded, reporting fair value changes in income would unnecessarily increase income variability and decrease usefulness.

Quick Check
Answers—p. C-19

5. Give at least two examples of assets classified as long-term investments.

6. What are the requirements for an equity security to be listed as a long-term investment?

7. Identify similarities and differences in accounting for long-term investments in debt securities that are held-to-maturity versus those available-for-sale.

8. What are the three possible classifications of long-term equity investments? Describe the criteria for each class and the method used to account for each.

 Global View

This section discusses similarities and differences for the accounting and reporting of investments when financial statements are prepared under U.S. GAAP vis-à-vis IFRS.

Accounting for Noninfluential Securities

The accounting for noninfluential securities is broadly similar between U.S. GAAP and IFRS. *Trading securities* are accounted for using fair values with unrealized gains and losses reported in net income as fair values change. *Available-for-sale securities* are accounted for using fair values with unrealized gains and losses reported in other comprehensive income as fair values change (and later in net income when realized). *Held-to-maturity securities* are accounted for using amortized cost. Similarly, companies have the option under both systems to apply the fair value option for available-for-sale and held-to-maturity securities. Also, both systems examine held-to-maturity securities for impairment. There are a couple of differences in terminology: (1) trading securities are commonly referred to as *financial assets at fair value through profit and loss,* and (2) available-for-sale securities are commonly referred to as *available-for-sale financial assets.* **GOME** provides the following descriptions about its noninfluential securities:

> **Financial assets at fair value through profit or loss** include financial assets held for trading and financial assets designated upon initial recognition as at fair value through profit or loss.
>
> **Available-for-sale financial assets** are measured at fair value, with gains or losses recognised as a separate component of equity until the investment is derecognised or until the investment is determined to be impaired.

Accounting for Influential Securities

The accounting for influential securities is broadly similar across U.S. GAAP and IFRS. Specifically, under the *equity method,* the share of investee's net income is reported in the investor's income in the same period the investee earns that income; also, the investment account equals the acquisition cost plus the share of investee income less the share of investee dividends (minus amortization of excess on purchase price above fair value of identifiable, limited-life assets). Under the *consolidation method,* investee and investor revenues and expenses are combined, absent intercompany transactions, and subtracting noncontrolling interests; nonintercompany assets and liabilities are similarly combined (eliminating the need for an investment account), and noncontrolling interests are subtracted from equity.

We should also note a couple items on terminology: (1) U.S. GAAP companies commonly refer to earnings from long-term investments as *equity in earnings of affiliates* whereas IFRS companies commonly use *equity in earnings of associated (or associate) companies,* (2) U.S. GAAP companies commonly refer to noncontrolling interests in consolidated subsidiaries as *minority interests* whereas IFRS companies commonly use *noncontrolling interests.*

Components of Return on Total Assets

Decision Analysis

A company's **return on total assets** (or simply *return on assets*) is important in assessing financial performance. The return on total assets can be separated into two components, profit margin and total asset turnover, for additional analyses. Exhibit C.9 shows how these two components determine return on total assets.

A1 Compute and analyze the components of return on total assets.

$$\text{Return on total assets} = \text{Profit margin} \times \text{Total asset turnover}$$

$$\frac{\text{Net income}}{\text{Average total assets}} = \frac{\text{Net income}}{\text{Net sales}} \times \frac{\text{Net sales}}{\text{Average total assets}}$$

EXHIBIT C.9

Components of Return on Total Assets

Profit margin reflects the percent of net income in each dollar of net sales. Total asset turnover reflects a company's ability to produce net sales from total assets. All companies desire a high return on total assets. By considering these two components, we can often discover strengths and weaknesses not revealed by return on total assets alone. This improves our ability to assess future performance and company strategy.

To illustrate, consider return on total assets and its components for **Gap Inc.** in Exhibit C.10.

Fiscal Year	Return on Total Assets	=	Profit Margin	×	Total Asset Turnover
2009	12.6%	=	6.66%	×	1.89
2008	10.2*	=	5.28	×	1.92
2007	9.0	=	4.9	×	1.84
2006	11.8*	=	6.9	×	1.70
2005	11.1	=	7.1	×	1.57

* Differences due to rounding.

EXHIBIT C.10

Gap's Components of Return on Total Assets

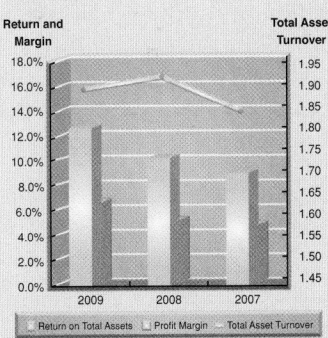

At least three findings emerge. First, Gap's return on total assets improved from 9.0% in 2007 to 12.6% in 2009. Second, total asset turnover has slightly improved over this period, from 1.84 to 1.89. Third, Gap's profit margin steadily increased over this period, from 4.9% in 2007 to 6.66% in 2009. These components reveal the dual role of profit margin and total asset turnover in determining return on total assets. They also reveal that the driver of Gap's recent improvement in return on total assets is not total asset turnover but profit margin.

Generally, if a company is to maintain or improve its return on total assets, it must meet any decline in either profit margin or total asset turnover with an increase in the other. If not, return on assets will decline. Companies consider these components in planning strategies. A component analysis can also reveal where a company is weak and where changes are needed, especially in a competitor analysis. If asset turnover is lower than the industry norm, for instance, a company should focus on raising asset turnover at least to the norm. The same applies to profit margin.

Decision Maker

Retailer You are an entrepreneur and owner of a retail sporting goods store. The store's recent annual performance reveals (industry norms in parentheses): return on total assets = 11% (11.2%); profit margin = 4.4% (3.5%); and total asset turnover = 2.5 (3.2). What does your analysis of these figures reveal?
[Answer—p. C-19]

Demonstration Problem—1

Garden Company completes the following selected transactions related to its short-term investments during 2008.

May 8   Purchased 300 shares of FedEx stock as a short-term investment in available-for-sale securities at $40 per share plus $975 in broker fees.

Sept. 2 Sold 100 shares of its investment in FedEx stock at $47 per share and held the remaining 200 shares; broker's commission was $225.

Oct. 2   Purchased 400 shares of Ajay stock for $60 per share plus $1,600 in commissions. The stock is held as a short-term investment in available-for-sale securities.

Required

1. Prepare journal entries for the above transactions of Garden Company for 2008.

2. Prepare an adjusting journal entry as of December 31, 2008, if the fair values of the equity securities held by Garden Company are $48 per share for FedEx and $55 per share for Ajay. (Year 2008 is the first year Garden Company acquired short-term investments.)

Solution to Demonstration Problem—1

1.

May 8	Short-Term Investments—AFS (FedEx).............	12,975	
	Cash..		12,975
	Purchased 300 shares of FedEx stock		
	(300 × $40) + $975.		
Sept. 2	Cash	4,475	
	Gain on Sale of Short-Term Investment		150
	Short-Term Investments—AFS (FedEx)		4,325
	Sold 100 shares of FedEx for $47 per share less		
	a $225 commission. The original cost is		
	($12,975 × 100/300).		
Oct. 2	Short-Term Investments—AFS (Ajay)	25,600	
	Cash.......................................		25,600
	Purchased 400 shares of Ajay for $60 per share		
	plus $1,600 in commissions.		

2. Computation of unrealized gain or loss follows.

Short-Term Investments in Available-for-Sale Securities	Shares	Cost per Share	Total Cost	Fair Value per Share	Total Fair Value	Unrealized Gain (Loss)
FedEx	200	$43.25	$ 8,650	$48.00	$ 9,600	
Ajay	400	64.00	25,600	55.00	22,000	
Totals			$34,250		$31,600	$(2,650)

The adjusting entry follows.

Dec. 31	Unrealized Loss—Equity........................	2,650	
	Fair Value Adjustment—Available-for-Sale (ST).....		2,650
	To reflect an unrealized loss in fair values		
	of available-for-sale securities.		

Demonstration Problem—2

The following transactions relate to Brown Company's long-term investments during 2008 and 2009. Brown did not own any long-term investments prior to 2008. Show (1) the appropriate journal entries and (2) the relevant portions of each year's balance sheet and income statement that reflect these transactions for both 2008 and 2009.

2008

Sept.	9	Purchased 1,000 shares of Packard, Inc., common stock for $80,000 cash. These shares represent 30% of Packard's outstanding shares.
Oct.	2	Purchased 2,000 shares of AT&T common stock for $60,000 cash. These shares represent less than a 1% ownership in AT&T.
	17	Purchased as a long-term investment 1,000 shares of Apple Computer common stock for $40,000 cash. These shares are less than 1% of Apple's outstanding shares.
Nov.	1	Received $5,000 cash dividend from Packard.
	30	Received $3,000 cash dividend from AT&T.
Dec.	15	Received $1,400 cash dividend from Apple.
	31	Packard's net income for this year is $70,000.
	31	Fair values for the investments in equity securities are Packard, $84,000; AT&T, $48,000; and Apple Computer, $45,000.
	31	For preparing financial statements, note the following post-closing account balances: Common Stock, $500,000, and Retained Earnings, $350,000.

2009

Jan.	1	Sold Packard, Inc., shares for $108,000 cash.
May	30	Received $3,100 cash dividend from AT&T.
June	15	Received $1,600 cash dividend from Apple.
Aug.	17	Sold the AT&T stock for $52,000 cash.
	19	Purchased 2,000 shares of Coca-Cola common stock for $50,000 cash as a long-term investment. The stock represents less than a 5% ownership in Coca-Cola.
Dec.	15	Received $1,800 cash dividend from Apple.
	31	Fair values of the investments in equity securities are Apple, $39,000, and Coca-Cola, $48,000.
	31	For preparing financial statements, note the following post-closing account balances: Common Stock, $500,000, and Retained Earnings, $410,000.

Planning the Solution

- Account for the investment in Packard under the equity method.
- Account for the investments in AT&T, Apple, and Coca-Cola as long-term investments in available-for-sale securities.
- Prepare the information for the two years' balance sheets by including the appropriate asset and equity accounts.

Solution to Demonstration Problem—2

1. Journal entries for 2008.

Sept. 9	Long-Term Investments—Packard		80,000	
	Cash			80,000
	Acquired 1,000 shares, representing a 30%			
	equity in Packard.			
Oct. 2	Long-Term Investments—AFS (AT&T)		60,000	
	Cash			60,000
	Acquired 2,000 shares as a long-term			
	investment in available-for-sale securities.			

[continued on next page]

[continued from previous page]

Oct. 17	Long-Term Investments—AFS (Apple).............	40,000	
	Cash		40,000
	Acquired 1,000 shares as a long-term		
	investment in available-for-sale securities.		
Nov. 1	Cash	5,000	
	Long-Term Investments—Packard		5,000
	Received dividend from Packard.		
Nov. 30	Cash	3,000	
	Dividend Revenue		3,000
	Received dividend from AT&T.		
Dec. 15	Cash	1,400	
	Dividend Revenue		1,400
	Received dividend from Apple.		
Dec. 31	Long-Term Investments—Packard	21,000	
	Earnings from Investment (Packard)...........		21,000
	To record 30% share of Packard's annual		
	earnings of $70,000.		
Dec. 31	Unrealized Loss—Equity........................	7,000	
	Fair Value Adjustment—Available-for-Sale (LT)* ...		7,000
	To record change in fair value of long-term		
	available-for-sale securities.		

* Fair value adjustment computations:

	Cost	Fair Value	Unrealized Gain (Loss)
AT&T	$ 60,000	$48,000	$(12,000)
Apple	40,000	45,000	5,000
Total	$100,000	$93,000	$ (7,000)

Required balance of the Fair Value Adjustment—Available-for-Sale (LT) account (credit)	$(7,000)
Existing balance	0
Necessary adjustment (credit)	$(7,000)

2. The December 31, 2008, selected balance sheet items appear as follows.

Assets
Long-term investments
Available-for-sale securities (at fair value; cost is $100,000) .... $ 93,000
Investment in equity securities   96,000
Total long-term investments   189,000
Stockholders' Equity
Common stock   500,000
Retained earnings   350,000
Unrealized loss—Equity ....   (7,000)

The relevant income statement items for the year ended December 31, 2008, follow.

Dividend revenue .... $ 4,400
Earnings from investment   21,000

1. Journal entries for 2009.

Jan. 1	Cash	108,000	
	Long-Term Investments—Packard		96,000
	Gain on Sale of Long-Term Investments		12,000
	Sold 1,000 shares for cash.		
May 30	Cash	3,100	
	Dividend Revenue		3,100
	Received dividend from AT&T.		
June 15	Cash	1,600	
	Dividend Revenue		1,600
	Received dividend from Apple.		
Aug. 17	Cash	52,000	
	Loss on Sale of Long-Term Investments	8,000	
	Long-Term Investments—AFS (AT&T).........		60,000
	Sold 2,000 shares for cash.		
Aug. 19	Long-Term Investments—AFS (Coca-Cola).........	50,000	
	Cash		50,000
	Acquired 2,000 shares as a long-term		
	investment in available-for-sale securities.		
Dec. 15	Cash	1,800	
	Dividend Revenue		1,800
	Received dividend from Apple.		
Dec. 31	Fair Value Adjustment—Available-for-Sale (LT)*.......	4,000	
	Unrealized Loss—Equity.....................		4,000
	To record change in fair value of long-term		
	available-for-sale securities.		

* Fair value adjustment computations:

	Cost	Fair Value	Unrealized Gain (Loss)
Apple	$40,000	$39,000	$(1,000)
Coca-Cola	50,000	48,000	(2,000)
Total	$90,000	$87,000	$(3,000)

Required balance of the Fair Value Adjustment—Available-for-Sale (LT) account (credit)	$(3,000)
Existing balance (credit)	(7,000)
Necessary adjustment (debit)	$ 4,000

2. The December 31, 2009, balance sheet items appear as follows.

Assets	
Long-term investments	
Available-for-sale securities (at fair value; cost is $90,000)	$ 87,000
Stockholders' Equity	
Common stock	500,000
Retained earnings	410,000
Unrealized loss—Equity	(3,000)

The relevant income statement items for the year ended December 31, 2009, follow.

Dividend revenue	$ 6,500
Gain on sale of long-term investments	12,000
Loss on sale of long-term investments	(8,000)

C-A Investments in International Operations

Many entities from small entrepreneurs to large corporations conduct business internationally. Some entities' operations occur in so many different countries that the companies are called **multinationals.** Many of us think of **Coca-Cola** and **McDonald's**, for example, as primarily U.S. companies, but most of their sales occur outside the United States. Exhibit C-A.1 shows the percent of international sales and income for selected U.S. companies. Managing and accounting for multinationals present challenges. This section describes some of these challenges and how to account for and report these activities.

Two major accounting challenges that arise when companies have international operations relate to transactions that involve more than one currency. The first is to account for sales and purchases listed in a foreign currency. The second is to prepare consolidated financial statements with international subsidiaries. For ease in this discussion, we use companies with a U.S. base of operations and assume the need to prepare financial statements in U.S. dollars. This means the *reporting currency* of these companies is the U.S. dollar.

EXHIBIT C-A.1

International Sales and Income as a Percent of Their Totals

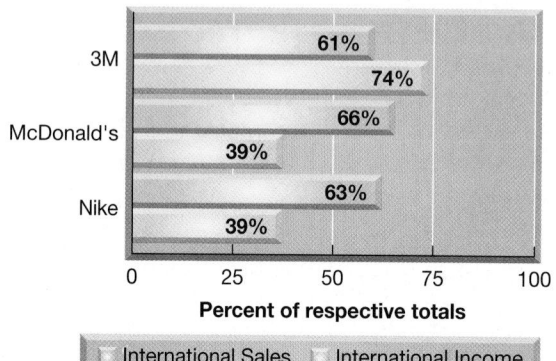

Percent of respective totals

☐ International Sales ☐ International Income

Point: Transactions *listed* or *stated* in a foreign currency are said to be *denominated* in that currency.

Exchange Rates between Currencies

C4 Explain foreign exchange rates between currencies.

Markets for the purchase and sale of foreign currencies exist all over the world. In these markets, U.S. dollars can be exchanged for Canadian dollars, British pounds, Japanese yen, Euros, or any other legal currencies. The price of one currency stated in terms of another currency is called a **foreign exchange rate.** Exhibit C-A.2 lists recent exchange rates for selected currencies. The exchange rate for British pounds and U.S. dollars is $1.8980, meaning 1 British pound could be purchased for $1.8980. On that same day, the exchange rate between Mexican pesos and U.S. dollars is $0.0925, or 1 Mexican peso can be purchased for $0.0925. Exchange rates fluctuate due to changing economic and political conditions, including the supply and demand for currencies and expectations about future events.

Point: To convert Currency, see XE.com

EXHIBIT C-A.2

Foreign Exchange Rates for Selected Currencies*

Source (unit)	Price in $U.S.	Source (unit)	Price in $U.S.
Britain (pound)	$1.8980	Canada (dollar)	$0.9793
Mexico (peso)	0.0925	Japan (yen)	0.0090
Taiwan (dollar)	0.0305	Europe (Euro)	1.2920

* Rates will vary over time based on economic, political, and other changes.

Decision Insight

Rush to Russia   Investors are still eager to buy Russian equities even in the face of rampant crime, corruption, and slow economic growth. Why? Many argue Russia remains a bargain-priced, if risky, bet on future growth. Some analysts argue that natural-resource-rich Russia is one of the least expensive emerging markets.

Sales and Purchases Listed in a Foreign Currency

When a U.S. company makes a credit sale to an international customer, accounting for the sale and the account receivable is straightforward if sales terms require the international customer's payment in U.S. dollars. If sale terms require (or allow) payment in a foreign currency, however, the U.S. company must account for the sale and the account receivable in a different manner.

P5 Record transactions listed in a foreign currency.

Sales in a Foreign Currency To illustrate, consider the case of the U.S.-based manufacturer Boston Company, which makes credit sales to London Outfitters, a British retail company. A sale occurs on December 12, 2008, for a price of £10,000 with payment due on February 10, 2009. Boston Company keeps its accounting records in U.S. dollars. To record the sale, Boston Company must translate the sales price from pounds to dollars. This is done using the exchange rate on the date of the sale. Assuming the exchange rate on December 12, 2008, is $1.80, Boston records this sale as follows.

Dec. 12	Accounts Receivable—London Outfitters...........	18,000	
	Sales*		18,000
	*To record a sale at £10,000, when the exchange rate equals $1.80. * (£10,000 × $1.80)*		

Assets = Liabilities + Equity
+18,000   +18,000

When Boston Company prepares its annual financial statements on December 31, 2008, the current exchange rate is $1.84. Thus, the current dollar value of Boston Company's receivable is $18,400 (10,000 × $1.84). This amount is $400 higher than the amount recorded on December 12. Accounting principles require a receivable to be reported in the balance sheet at its current dollar value. Thus, Boston Company must make the following entry to record the increase in the dollar value of this receivable at year-end.

Dec. 31	Accounts Receivable—London Outfitters...........	400	
	Foreign Exchange Gain		400
	To record the increased value of the British pound for the receivable.		

Assets = Liabilities + Equity
+400   +400

On February 10, 2009, Boston Company receives London Outfitters' payment of £10,000. It immediately exchanges the pounds for U.S. dollars. On this date, the exchange rate for pounds is $1.78. Thus, Boston Company receives only $17,800 (£10,000 × $1.78). It records the cash receipt and the loss associated with the decline in the exchange rate as follows.

Point: Foreign exchange gains are credits, and foreign exchange losses are debits.

Feb. 10	Cash..	17,800	
	Foreign Exchange Loss	600	
	Accounts Receivable—London Outfitters.......		18,400
	Received foreign currency payment of an account and converted it into dollars.		

Assets = Liabilities + Equity
+17,800   −600
−18,400

Gains and losses from foreign exchange transactions are accumulated in the Foreign Exchange Gain (or Loss) account. After year-end adjustments, the balance in the Foreign Exchange Gain (or Loss) account is reported on the income statement and closed to the Income Summary account.

Purchases in a Foreign Currency Accounting for credit purchases from an international seller is similar to the case of a credit sale to an international customer. In particular, if the U.S. company is required to make payment in a foreign currency, the account payable must be translated into dollars before the U.S. company can record it. If the exchange rate is different when preparing financial statements and when paying for the purchase, the U.S. company must recognize a foreign exchange gain or loss at those dates. To illustrate, assume NC Imports, a U.S. company, purchases products costing €20,000 (euros) from Hamburg Brewing on January 15, when the exchange rate is $1.20 per euro. NC records this transaction as follows.

Example: Assume that a U.S. company makes a credit purchase from a British company for £10,000 when the exchange rate is $1.62. At the balance sheet date, this rate is $1.72. Does this imply a gain or loss for the U.S. company? *Answer:* A loss.

Assets = Liabilities + Equity
+24,000   +24,000

Jan. 15	Inventory	24,000	
	Accounts Payable—Hamburg Brewing..........		24,000
	To record a €20,000 purchase when exchange rate is $1.20 (€20,000 × $1.20)		

NC Imports makes payment in full on February 14 when the exchange rate is $1.25 per euro, which is recorded as follows.

Assets = Liabilities + Equity
−25,000   −24,000   −1,000

Feb. 14	Accounts Payable—Hamburg Brewing..............	24,000	
	Foreign Exchange Loss	1,000	
	Cash.....................................		25,000
	To record cash payment towards €20,000 account when exchange rate is $1.25 (€20.000 × $1.25).		

Decision Insight

Global Greenback   What do changes in foreign exchange rates mean? A decline in the price of the U.S. dollar against other currencies usually yields increased international sales for U.S. companies, without hiking prices or cutting costs, and puts them on a stronger competitive footing abroad. At home, they can raise prices without fear that foreign rivals will undercut them.

Consolidated Statements with International Subsidiaries

A second challenge in accounting for international operations involves preparing consolidated financial statements when the parent company has one or more international subsidiaries. Consider a U.S.-based company that owns a controlling interest in a French subsidiary. The reporting currency of the U.S. parent is the dollar. The French subsidiary maintains its financial records in euros. Before preparing consolidated statements, the parent must translate financial statements of the French company into U.S. dollars. After this translation is complete (including that for accounting differences), it prepares consolidated statements the same as for domestic subsidiaries. Procedures for translating an international subsidiary's account balances depend on the nature of the subsidiary's operations. The process requires the parent company to select appropriate foreign exchange rates and to apply those rates to the foreign subsidiary's account balances. This is described in advanced courses.

Global: A weaker U.S. dollar often increases global sales for U.S. companies.

 ## Decision Maker

Entrepreneur   You are a U.S. home builder that purchases lumber from mills in both the U.S. and Canada. The price of the Canadian dollar in terms of the U.S. dollar jumps from US$0.70 to US$0.80. Are you now more or less likely to buy lumber from Canadian or U.S. mills? [Answer—p. C-19]

Summary

C1 Distinguish between debt and equity securities and between short-term and long-term investments. *Debt securities* reflect a creditor relationship and include investments in notes, bonds, and certificates of deposit. *Equity securities* reflect an owner relationship and include shares of stock issued by other companies. Short-term investments in securities are current assets that meet two criteria: (1) They are expected to be converted into cash within one year or the current operating cycle of the business, whichever is longer and (2) they are readily convertible to cash, or *marketable*. All other investments in securities are long term. Long-term investments also include assets not used in operations and those held for special purposes, such as land for expansion.

C2 Identify and describe the different classes of investments in securities. Investments in securities are classified into one of five groups: (1) trading securities, which are always short-term, (2) debt securities held-to-maturity, (3) debt and equity securities available-for-sale, (4) equity securities in which an investor has a significant influence over the investee, and (5) equity securities in which an investor has a controlling influence over the investee.

C3 Describe how to report equity securities with controlling influence. If an investor owns more than 50% of another company's voting stock and controls the investee, the investor's financial reports are prepared on a consolidated basis. These reports are prepared as if the company were organized as one entity.

C4^A **Explain foreign exchange rates between currencies.** A foreign exchange rate is the price of one currency stated in terms of another. An entity with transactions in a foreign currency when the exchange rate changes between the transaction dates and their settlement will experience exchange gains or losses.

A1 **Compute and analyze the components of return on total assets.** Return on total assets has two components: profit margin and total asset turnover. A decline in one component must be met with an increase in another if return on assets is to be maintained. Component analysis is helpful in assessing company performance compared to that of competitors and its own past.

P1 **Account for trading securities.** Investments are initially recorded at cost, and any dividend or interest from these investments is recorded in the income statement. Investments classified as trading securities are reported at fair value. Unrealized gains and losses on trading securities are reported in income. When investments are sold, the difference between the net proceeds from the sale and the cost of the securities is recognized as a gain or loss.

P2 **Account for held-to-maturity securities.** Debt securities held-to-maturity are reported at cost when purchased. Interest revenue is recorded as it accrues. The cost of long-term held-to-maturity securities is adjusted for the amortization of any difference between cost and maturity value.

P3 **Account for available-for-sale securities.** Debt and equity securities available-for-sale are recorded at cost when purchased. Available-for-sale securities are reported at their fair values on the balance sheet with unrealized gains or losses shown in the equity section. Gains and losses realized on the sale of these investments are reported in the income statement.

P4 **Account for equity securities with significant influence.** The equity method is used when an investor has a significant influence over an investee. This usually exists when an investor owns 20% or more of the investee's voting stock but not more than 50%. The equity method means an investor records its share of investee earnings with a debit to the investment account and a credit to a revenue account. Dividends received reduce the investment account balance.

P5^A **Record transactions listed in a foreign currency.** When a company makes a credit sale to a foreign customer and sales terms call for payment in a foreign currency, the company must translate the foreign currency into dollars to record the receivable. If the exchange rate changes before payment is received, exchange gains or losses are recognized in the year they occur. The same treatment is used when a company makes a credit purchase from a foreign supplier and is required to make payment in a foreign currency.

Guidance Answers to **Decision Maker**

Money Manager   If you have investments in fixed-rate bonds and notes when interest rates fall, the value of your investments increases. This is so because the bonds and notes you hold continue to pay the same (high) rate while the market is demanding a new lower interest rate. Your strategy is to continue holding your investments in bonds and notes, and, potentially, to increase these holdings through additional purchases.

Retailer   Your store's return on assets is 11%, which is similar to the industry norm of 11.2%. However, disaggregation of return on assets reveals that your store's profit margin of 4.4% is much higher than the norm of 3.5%, but your total asset turnover of 2.5 is much lower than the norm of 3.2. These results suggest that, as compared with competitors, you are less efficient in using assets.

You need to focus on increasing sales or reducing assets. You might consider reducing prices to increase sales, provided such a strategy does not reduce your return on assets. For instance, you could reduce your profit margin to 4% to increase sales. If total asset turnover increases to more than 2.75 when profit margin is lowered to 4%, your overall return on assets is improved.

Entrepreneur   You are now less likely to buy Canadian lumber because it takes more U.S. money to buy a Canadian dollar (and lumber). For instance, the purchase of lumber from a Canadian mill with a $1,000 (Canadian dollars) price would have cost the U.S. builder $700 (U.S. dollars, computed as C$1,000 × US$0.70) before the rate change, and $800 (U.S. dollars, computed as C$1,000 × US$0.80) after the rate change.

Guidance Answers to **Quick Checks**

1. Short-term held-to-maturity securities are reported at cost.
2. Trading securities are reported at fair value.
3. The equity section of the balance sheet (and in comprehensive income).
4. The income statement.
5. Long-term investments include (1) long-term funds earmarked for a special purpose, (2) debt and equity securities that do not meet current asset requirements, and (3) long-term assets not used in the regular operations of the business.
6. An equity investment is classified as long term if it is not marketable or, if marketable, it is not held as an available source of cash to meet the needs of current operations.

7. Debt securities held-to-maturity and debt securities available-for-sale are both recorded at cost. Also, interest on both is accrued as earned. However, only long-term securities held-to-maturity require amortization of the difference between cost and maturity value. In addition, only securities available-for-sale require a period-end adjustment to fair value.

8. Long-term equity investments are placed in one of three categories and accounted for as follows: (a) **available-for-sale** (non-influential, less than 20% of outstanding stock)—fair value; (b) **significant influence** (20% to 50% of outstanding stock)—equity method; and (c) **controlling influence** (holding more than 50% of outstanding stock)—equity method with consolidation.

Key Terms

Available-for-sale (AFS) securities (p. C-5)

Comprehensive income (p. C-9)

Consolidated financial statements (p. C-9)

Equity method (p. C-7)

Equity securities with controlling influence (p. C-8)

Equity securities with significant influence (p. C-7)

Foreign exchange rate (p. C-16)

Held-to-maturity (HTM) securities (p. C-5)

Long-term investments (p. C-1)

Multinational (p. C-16)

Parent (p. C-8)

Return on total assets (p. C-11)

Short-term investments (p. C-1)

Subsidiary (p. C-8)

Trading securities (p. C-4)

Unrealized gain (loss) (p. C-4)

Multiple Choice Quiz   Answers on p. C-36   mhhe.com/wildFA5e

Additional Quiz Questions are available at the book's Website.

1. A company purchased $30,000 of 5% bonds for investment purposes on May 1. The bonds pay interest on February 1 and August 1. The amount of interest revenue accrued at December 31 (the company's year-end) is:
- **a.** $1,500
- **b.** $1,375
- **c.** $1,000
- **d.** $625
- **e.** $300

2. Earlier this period, Amadeus Co. purchased its only available-for-sale investment in the stock of Bach Co. for $83,000. The period-end fair value of this stock is $84,500. Amadeus records a:
- **a.** Credit to Unrealized Gain—Equity for $1,500
- **b.** Debit to Unrealized Loss—Equity for $1,500
- **c.** Debit to Investment Revenue for $1,500
- **d.** Credit to Fair Value Adjustment—Available-for-Sale for $3,500
- **e.** Credit to Cash for $1,500

3. Mozart Co. owns 35% of Melody Inc. Melody pays $50,000 in cash dividends to its shareholders for the period. Mozart's entry to record the Melody dividend includes a:
- **a.** Credit to Investment Revenue for $50,000.
- **b.** Credit to Long-Term Investments for $17,500.

- **c.** Credit to Cash for $17,500.
- **d.** Debit to Long-Term Investments for $17,500.
- **e.** Debit to Cash for $50,000.

4. A company has net income of $300,000, net sales of $2,500,000, and total assets of $2,000,000. Its return on total assets equals:
- **a.** 6.7%
- **b.** 12.0%
- **c.** 8.3%
- **d.** 80.0%
- **e.** 15.0%

5. A company had net income of $80,000, net sales of $600,000, and total assets of $400,000. Its profit margin and total asset turnover are:

	Profit Margin	Total Asset Turnover
a.	1.5%	13.3
b.	13.3%	1.5
c.	13.3%	0.7
d.	7.0%	13.3
e.	10.0%	26.7

Superscript [A] *denotes assignments based on Appendix C-A.*

Discussion Questions

1. Under what two conditions should investments be classified as current assets?

2. On a balance sheet, what valuation must be reported for short-term investments in trading securities?

3. If a short-term investment in available-for-sale securities costs $6,780 and is sold for $7,500, how should the difference between these two amounts be recorded?

4. Identify the three classes of noninfluential and two classes of influential investments in securities.

5. Under what conditions should investments be classified as current assets? As long-term assets?

6. If a company purchases its only long-term investments in available-for-sale debt securities this period and their fair value is below cost at the balance sheet date, what entry is required to recognize this unrealized loss?

7. On a balance sheet, what valuation must be reported for debt securities classified as available-for-sale?

8. Under what circumstances are long-term investments in debt securities reported at cost and adjusted for amortization of any difference between cost and maturity value?

9. For investments in available-for-sale securities, how are unrealized (holding) gains and losses reported?

10. In accounting for investments in equity securities, when should the equity method be used?

11. Under what circumstances does a company prepare consolidated financial statements?

12.ᴬWhat are two major challenges in accounting for international operations?

13.ᴬAssume a U.S. company makes a credit sale to a foreign customer that is required to make payment in its foreign currency. In the current period, the exchange rate is $1.40 on the date of

the sale and is $1.30 on the date the customer pays the receivable. Will the U.S. company record an exchange gain or loss?

14.ᴬ⚐ If a U.S. company makes a credit sale to a foreign customer required to make payment in U.S. dollars, can the U.S. company have an exchange gain or loss on this sale?

15. ⚐ Refer to **Best Buy**'s statement of changes in shareholders' equity in Appendix A. What is the amount of foreign currency translation adjustment for the year ended February 28, 2009? Is this adjustment an unrealized gain or an unrealized loss?

16. Refer to **Apple**'s statement of stockholders' equity. What was the amount of its fiscal 2008 unrealized gain or loss on securities?

17. ⚐ Refer to the balance sheet of **GOME** in Appendix A. How can you tell that GOME uses the consolidated method of accounting?

18. ⚐ Refer to the financial statements of **RadioShack** in Appendix A. Compute its return on total assets for the year ended December 31, 2008.

⚐ **Denotes Discussion Questions that involve decision making.**

connect™ Available with Connect Accounting

On April 18, Rollo Co. made a short-term investment in 600 common shares of TXT Co. The purchase price is $84 per share and the broker's fee is $500. The intent is to actively manage these shares for profit. On May 30, Rollo Co. receives $0.75 per share from TXT in dividends. Prepare the April 18 and May 30 journal entries to record these transactions.

QUICK STUDY

QS C-1
Short-term equity
investments C2 P1 ⚐

Malox Co. purchased short-term investments in available-for-sale securities at a cost of $100,000 on November 25, 2009. At December 31, 2009, these securities had a fair value of $94,000. This is the first and only time the company has purchased such securities.

1. Prepare the December 31, 2009, year-end adjusting entry for the securities' portfolio.
2. For each account in the entry for part 1, explain how it is reported in financial statements.
3. Prepare the April 6, 2010, entry when Malox sells one-fourth of these securities for $27,000.

QS C-2
Available-for-sale securities

C2 P3

Prepare Vikon Company's journal entries to reflect the following transactions for the current year.

May 7   Purchases 200 shares of Felton stock as a short-term investment in available-for-sale securities at a cost of $100 per share plus $400 in broker fees.
June 6   Sells 200 shares of its investment in Felton stock at $112 per share. The broker's commission on this sale is $250.

QS C-3
Available-for-sale securities

C2 P3

Texar Company completes the following transactions during the current year.

May 9   Purchases 400 shares of Crayton stock as a short-term investment in available-for-sale securities at a cost of $30 per share plus $200 in broker fees.
June 2   Sells 200 shares of its investment in Crayton stock at $32 per share. The broker's commission on this sale is $120.
Dec. 31   The closing market price (fair value) of the Crayton stock is $28 per share.

Prepare the May 9 and June 2 journal entries and the December 31 adjusting entry. This is the first and only time the company purchased such securities.

QS C-4
Available-for-sale securities

C2 P3

Which of the following statements are true of long-term investments?
a. They are held as an investment of cash available for current operations.
b. They can include funds earmarked for a special purpose, such as bond sinking funds.

QS C-5
Identifying long-term investments

C1

c. They can include investments in trading securities.

d. They can include debt securities held-to-maturity.

e. They are always easily sold and therefore qualify as being marketable.

f. They can include debt and equity securities available-for-sale.

g. They can include bonds and stocks not intended to serve as a ready source of cash.

QS C-6
Describing investments
in securities

C1   C2   C3

Complete the following descriptions by filling in the blanks.

1. Equity securities giving an investor significant influence are accounted for using the ⎯⎯ ⎯⎯.

2. Trading securities are classified as ⎯⎯ assets.

3. Accrual of interest on bonds held as long-term investments requires a credit to ⎯⎯ ⎯⎯.

4. The controlling investor (more than 50% ownership) is called the ⎯⎯, and the investee company is called the ⎯⎯.

5. Available-for-sale debt securities are reported on the balance sheet at ⎯⎯ ⎯⎯.

QS C-7
Debt securities transactions

C2   P2

On February 1, 2011, Garzon purchased 6% bonds issued by Integal Utilities at a cost of $80,000, which is their par value. The bonds pay interest semiannually on July 31 and January 31. For 2011, prepare entries to record Garzon's July 31 receipt of interest and its December 31 year-end interest accrual.

QS C-8
Recording equity securities

C2   P3

On May 20, 2011, Chiu Co. paid $1,500,000 to acquire 25,000 common shares (10%) of BBE Corp. as a long-term investment. On August 5, 2012, Chiu sold one-half of these shares for $937,500. What valuation method should be used to account for this stock investment? Prepare entries to record both the acquisition and the sale of these shares.

QS C-9
Equity method transactions

C2   P4

Assume the same facts as in QS C-8 except that the stock acquired represents 40% of BBE Corp.'s outstanding stock. Also assume that BBE Corp. paid a $150,000 dividend on November 1, 2011, and reported a net income of $1,050,000 for 2011. Prepare the entries to record (a) the receipt of the dividend and (b) the December 31, 2011, year-end adjustment required for the investment account.

QS C-10
Recording fair value adjustment
for securities

P3

During the current year, Marketplace Consulting Group acquired long-term available-for-sale securities at an $85,000 cost. At its December 31 year-end, these securities had a fair value of $62,000. This is the first and only time the company purchased such securities.

1. Prepare the necessary year-end adjusting entry related to these securities.

2. Explain how each account used in part 1 is reported in the financial statements.

QS C-11
Return on total
assets   A1

The return on total assets is the focus of analysts, creditors, and other users of financial statements.

1. How is the return on total assets computed?

2. What does this important ratio reflect?

QS C-12
Component return
on total assets   A1

Return on total assets can be separated into two important components.

1. Write the formula to separate the return on total assets into its two basic components.

2. Explain how these components of the return on total assets are helpful to financial statement users for business decisions.

QS C-13ᴬ
Foreign currency transactions

P5

A U.S. company sells a product to a British company with the transaction listed in British pounds. On the date of the sale, the transaction total of $40,600 is billed as £20,000, reflecting an exchange rate of 2.03 (that is, $2.03 per pound). Prepare the entry to record (1) the sale and (2) the receipt of payment in pounds when the exchange rate is 1.95.

QS C-14ᴬ
Foreign currency transactions

P5

On March 1, 2011, a U.S. company made a credit sale requiring payment in 30 days from a Malaysian company, Hamac Sdn. Bhd., in 20,000 Malaysian ringgits. Assuming the exchange rate between Malaysian ringgits and U.S. dollars is $0.2963 on March 1 and $0.3005 on March 31, prepare the entries to record the sale on March 1 and the cash receipt on March 31.

The **Carrefour Group** reports the following description of its trading securities (titled "financial assets reported at fair value in the income statement").

QS C-15
International accounting for investments

P1

> These are financial assets held by the Group in order to make a short-term profit on the sale. These assets are valued at their fair value with variations in value recognized in the income statement.

Note 10 to Carrefour's 2008 financial statements reports €117 million in unrealized gains for 2008 and €63 million in unrealized losses for 2008, both included in the fair value of those financial assets held for trading. What amount of these unrealized gains and unrealized losses, if any, are reported in its 2008 income statement? Explain.

connect™ Available with Connect Accounting

Prepare journal entries to record the following transactions involving the short-term securities investments of Bolton Co., all of which occurred during year 2011.

EXERCISES

Exercise C-1
Accounting for transactions in short-term securities

C2 P1 P2 P3

a. On February 15, paid $170,000 cash to purchase ACC's 90-day short-term debt securities ($170,000 principal), dated February 15, that pay 8% interest (categorized as held-to-maturity securities).

b. On March 22, purchased 850 shares of Ross Company stock at $21 per share plus a $100 brokerage fee. These shares are categorized as trading securities.

c. On May 16, received a check from ACC in payment of the principal and 90 days' interest on the debt securities purchased in transaction *a*.

Check (c) Dr. Cash $173,400

d. On August 1, paid $70,000 cash to purchase Nita Co.'s 11% debt securities ($70,000 principal), dated July 30, 2011, and maturing January 30, 2012 (categorized as available-for-sale securities).

e. On September 1, received a $1.10 per share cash dividend on the Ross Company stock purchased in transaction *b*.

f. On October 8, sold 425 shares of Ross Co. stock for $31 per share, less a $150 brokerage fee.

(f) Dr. Cash $13,025

g. On October 30, received a check from Nita Co. for 90 days' interest on the debt securities purchased in transaction *d*.

Borchert Co. purchases various investments in trading securities at a cost of $76,000 on December 27, 2009. (This is its first and only purchase of such securities.) At December 31, 2009, these securities had a fair value of $85,000.

Exercise C-2
Accounting for trading securities

C1 P1

1. Prepare the December 31, 2009, year-end adjusting entry for the trading securities' portfolio.

2. Explain how each account in the entry of part 1 is reported in financial statements.

3. Prepare the January 3, 2010, entry when Borchert sells a portion of its trading securities (that had originally cost $38,000) for $40,250.

Check (3) Gain, $2,250

On December 31, 2011, Tagert Company held the following short-term investments in its portfolio of available-for-sale securities. Tagert had no short-term investments in its prior accounting periods. Prepare the December 31, 2011, adjusting entry to report these investments at fair value.

Exercise C-3
Adjusting available-for-sale securities to fair value

C2 P3

	Cost	Fair Value
Verrizano Corporation bonds payable	$ 81,400	$92,000
Porter Corporation notes payable	54,900	47,928
Laverne Company common stock	100,500	96,480

Check Unrealized loss, $392

Prepare journal entries to record the following transactions involving both the short-term and long-term investments of Corveau Corp., all of which occurred during calendar year 2011. Use the account Short-Term Investments for any transactions that you determine are short term.

Exercise C-4
Transactions in short-term and long-term investments

C1 C2

a. On February 15, paid $100,000 cash to purchase Anthem's 90-day short-term notes at par, which are dated February 15 and pay 6% interest (classified as held-to-maturity).

b. On March 22, bought 600 shares of Frain Industries common stock at $43 cash per share plus a $140 brokerage fee (classified as long-term available-for-sale securities).

c. On May 15, received a check from Anthem in payment of the principal and 90 days' interest on the notes purchased in transaction *a*.

d. On July 30, paid $30,000 cash to purchase Moto Electronics' 5% notes at par, dated July 30, 2011, and maturing on January 30, 2012 (classified as trading securities).

e. On September 1, received a $0.40 per share cash dividend on the Frain Industries common stock purchased in transaction *b*.

f. On October 8, sold 300 shares of Frain Industries common stock for $49 cash per share, less a $120 brokerage fee.

g. On October 30, received a check from Moto Electronics for three months' interest on the notes purchased in transaction *d*.

Exercise C-5
Fair value adjustment to available-for-sale securities

P3

On December 31, 2011, Loren Co. held the following short-term available-for-sale securities.

	Cost	Fair Value
Nintendo Co. common stock	$64,500	$70,305
Unilever bonds payable	25,800	23,994
Kellogg Co. notes payable	46,440	43,654
McDonald's Corp. common stock	87,075	82,721

Loren had no short-term investments prior to the current period. Prepare the December 31, 2011, year-end adjusting entry to record the fair value adjustment for these securities.

Exercise C-6
Fair value adjustment to available-for-sale securities

P3

Patica Co. began operations in 2010. The cost and fair values for its long-term investments portfolio in available-for-sale securities are shown below. Prepare Patica's December 31, 2011, adjusting entry to reflect any necessary fair value adjustment for these investments.

	Cost	Fair Value
December 31, 2010	$67,842	$61,736
December 31, 2011	73,479	77,888

Exercise C-7
Multi-year fair value adjustments to available-for-sale securities

P3

Basil Services began operations in 2007 and maintains long-term investments in available-for-sale securities. The year-end cost and fair values for its portfolio of these investments follow. Prepare journal entries to record each year-end fair value adjustment for these securities.

	Cost	Fair Value
December 31, 2007	$392,900	$381,113
December 31, 2008	447,906	474,780
December 31, 2009	609,152	720,627
December 31, 2010	919,820	818,640

Exercise C-8
Classifying investments in securities; recording fair values

C1 C2 P2 P3 P4

Information regarding Seaton Company's individual investments in securities during its calendar-year 2009, along with the December 31, 2009, fair values, follows.

a. Investment in Beeman Company bonds: $443,150 cost, $481,704 fair value. Seaton intends to hold these bonds until they mature in 2014.

b. Investment in Baybridge common stock: 29,500 shares; $352,304 cost; $382,954 fair value. Seaton owns 32% of Baybridge's voting stock and has a significant influence over Baybridge.

c. Investment in Carroll common stock: 12,000 shares; $181,692 cost; $195,864 fair value. This investment amounts to 3% of Carroll's outstanding shares, and Seaton's goal with this investment is to earn dividends over the next few years.

d. Investment in Newtech common stock: 3,500 shares; $101,038 cost; $99,320 fair value. Seaton's goal with this investment is to reap an increase in fair value of the stock over the next three to five years. Newtech has 30,000 common shares outstanding.

e. Investment in Flock common stock: 16,300 shares; $110,788 cost; $117,657 fair value. This stock is marketable and is held as an investment of cash available for operations.

Required

1. Identify whether each investment should be classified as a short-term or long-term investment. For each long-term investment, indicate in which of the long-term investment classifications it should be placed.

Check (2) Unrealized gain, $12,454

2. Prepare a journal entry dated December 31, 2009, to record the fair value adjustment of the long-term investments in available-for-sale securities. Seaton had no long-term investments prior to year 2009.

Prepare journal entries to record the following transactions and events of Kareen Company.

2009

Jan. 2 Purchased 55,000 shares of Altus Co. common stock for $374,000 cash plus a broker's fee of
         $2,650 cash. Altus has 137,500 shares of common stock outstanding and its policies will be
         significantly influenced by Kareen.
Sept. 1 Altus declared and paid a cash dividend of $3.05 per share.
Dec. 31 Altus announced that net income for the year is $1,106,900.

2010

June 1 Altus declared and paid a cash dividend of $3.30 per share.
Dec. 31 Altus announced that net income for the year is $1,240,900.
Dec. 31 Kareen sold 11,000 shares of Altus for $294,250 cash.

Exercise C-9
Securities transactions;
equity method
P4   C2

The following information is available from the financial statements of Interstate Industries. Compute
Interstate's return on total assets for 2009 and 2010. (Round returns to one-tenth of a percent.) Comment
on the company's efficiency in using its assets in 2009 and 2010.

Exercise C-10
Return on total assets
A1

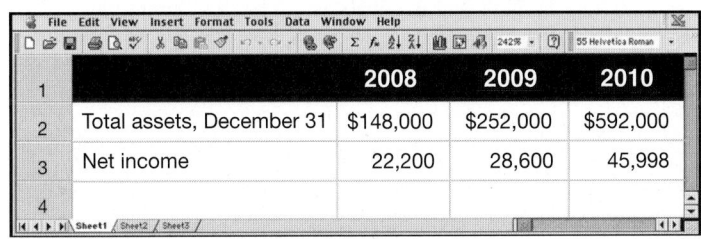

	2008	**2009**	**2010**
Total assets, December 31	$148,000	$252,000	$592,000
Net income	22,200	28,600	45,998

Leigh of New York sells its products to customers in the United States and the United Kingdom. On December
16, 2009, Leigh sold merchandise on credit to Berton Ltd. of London at a price of 20,000 pounds. The exchange rate on that day for £1 was $2.0325. On December 31, 2009, when Leigh prepared its financial state-
ments, the rate was £1 for $2.0292. Berton paid its bill in full on January 15, 2010, at which time the ex-
change rate was £1 for $2.0340. Leigh immediately exchanged the 20,000 pounds for U.S. dollars. Prepare
Leigh's journal entries on December 16, December 31, and January 15 (round to the nearest dollar).

Exercise C-11ᴬ
Foreign currency transactions
P5

On May 8, 2009, Jett Company (a U.S. company) made a credit sale to Munoz (a Mexican company).
The terms of the sale required Munoz to pay 850,000 pesos on February 10, 2010. Jett prepares quarterly
financial statements on March 31, June 30, September 30, and December 31. The exchange rates for
pesos during the time the receivable is outstanding follow.

Exercise C-12ᴬ
Computing foreign exchange
gains and losses on receivables
C4   P5

May 8, 2009	$0.0932
June 30, 2009	0.0941
September 30, 2009	0.0952
December 31, 2009	0.0935
February 10, 2010	0.0974

Compute the foreign exchange gain or loss that Jett should report on each of its quarterly income statements for the last three quarters of 2009 and the first quarter of 2010. Also compute the amount reported
on Jett's balance sheets at the end of each of its last three quarters of 2009.

The **Carrefour Group** reports the following description of its financial assets available-for-sale.

Exercise C-13
International accounting for
investments
C2   P3

> Assets available for sale are . . . valued at fair value. Unrealized . . . gains or losses are recorded as shareholders'
> equity until they are sold.

Note 10 to Carrefour's 2008 financial statements reports €6 million in *net* unrealized losses (net of
unrealized gains) for 2008, which is included in the fair value of its available-for-sale securities reported
on the balance sheet.

1. What amount of the €6 million net unrealized losses, if any, is reported in its 2008 income statement? Explain.

2. If the €6 million net unrealized losses are not reported in the income statement, in which statement
are they reported, if any? Explain.

Available with Connect Accounting **CONNECT™**

PROBLEM SET A

Problem C-1A

Recording transactions and fair value adjustments for trading securities

C2   P1

Protom Company, which began operations in 2009, invests its idle cash in trading securities. The following transactions are from its short-term investments in its trading securities.

2009

Jan. 20   Purchased 800 shares of Ford Motor Co. at $26 per share plus a $120 commission.
Feb. 9   Purchased 2,600 shares of Lucent at $39 per share plus a $578 commission.
Oct. 12   Purchased 800 shares of Z-Seven at $7.50 per share plus a $200 commission.

2010

Apr. 15   Sold 800 shares of Ford Motor Co. at $30 per share less a $300 commission.
July 5   Sold 800 shares of Z-Seven at $11 per share less a $103 commission.
July 22   Purchased 2,000 shares of Hunt Corp. at $39 per share plus a $444 commission.
Aug. 19   Purchased 1,600 shares of Donna Karan at $19.50 per share plus a $290 commission.

2011

Feb. 27   Purchased 3,500 shares of HCA at $31 per share plus a $420 commission.
Mar. 3   Sold 2,000 shares of Hunt at $35 per share less a $250 commission.
June 21   Sold 2,600 shares of Lucent at $36.75 per share less a $420 commission.
June 30   Purchased 1,300 shares of Black & Decker at $47.50 per share plus a $595 commission.
Nov. 1   Sold 1,600 shares of Donna Karan at $19.50 per share less a $309 commission.

Required

1. Prepare journal entries to record these short-term investment activities for the years shown. (Ignore any year-end adjusting entries.)

Check (2) Dr. Fair Value Adjustment—Trading $785

2. On December 31, 2011, prepare the adjusting entry to record any necessary fair value adjustment for the portfolio of trading securities when HCA's share price is $33 and Black & Decker's share price is $43.50. (Assume the Fair Value Adjustment—Trading account had an unadjusted balance of zero.)

Problem C-2A

Recording, adjusting, and reporting short-term available-for-sale securities

C2   P3

Freema Company had no short-term investments prior to year 2011. It had the following transactions involving short-term investments in available-for-sale securities during 2011.

Apr. 16   Purchased 8,000 shares of Gem Co. stock at $29.75 per share plus a $440 brokerage fee.
May   1   Paid $125,000 to buy 90-day U.S. Treasury bills (debt securities): $125,000 principal amount, 4% interest, securities dated May 1.
July   7   Purchased 4,000 shares of PepsiCo stock at $47.75 per share plus a $410 brokerage fee.
       20   Purchased 2,000 shares of Xerox stock at $19.75 per share plus a $490 brokerage fee.
Aug.   3   Received a check for principal and accrued interest on the U.S. Treasury bills that matured on July 29.
       15   Received a $0.90 per share cash dividend on the Gem Co. stock.
       28   Sold 4,000 shares of Gem Co. stock at $36.50 per share less a $250 brokerage fee.
Oct.   1   Received a $1.75 per share cash dividend on the PepsiCo shares.
Dec. 15   Received a $1.05 per share cash dividend on the remaining Gem Co. shares.
       31   Received a $1.30 per share cash dividend on the PepsiCo shares.

Required

1. Prepare journal entries to record the preceding transactions and events.

Check (2) Cost = $350,620

2. Prepare a table to compare the year-end cost and fair values of Freema's short-term investments in available-for-sale securities. The year-end fair values per share are: Gem Co., $32.00; PepsiCo, $45.00; and Xerox, $16.75.

(3) Dr. Unrealized Loss—Equity $9,120

3. Prepare an adjusting entry, if necessary, to record the year-end fair value adjustment for the portfolio of short-term investments in available-for-sale securities.

Analysis Component

4. Explain the balance sheet presentation of the fair value adjustment for Freema's short-term investments.

5. How do these short-term investments affect Freema's (a) income statement for year 2011 and (b) the equity section of its balance sheet at year-end 2011?

Tennant Security, which began operations in 2009, invests in long-term available-for-sale securities. Following is a series of transactions and events determining its long-term investment activity.

2009

Jan. 20   Purchased 1,200 shares of Johnson & Johnson at $20.50 per share plus a $240 commission.
Feb. 9   Purchased 1,000 shares of Sony at $46.20 per share plus a $220 commission.
June 12   Purchased 1,700 shares of Mattel at $28 per share plus a $195 commission.
Dec. 31   Per share fair values for stocks in the portfolio are Johnson & Johnson, $21.50; Mattel, $26.50; Sony, $38.

2010

Apr. 15   Sold 1,200 shares of Johnson & Johnson at $23.50 per share less a $525 commission.
July   5   Sold 1,700 shares of Mattel at $26.50 per share less a $235 commission.
July 22   Purchased 500 shares of Sara Lee at $22.50 per share plus a $420 commission.
Aug. 19   Purchased 900 shares of Eastman Kodak at $14 per share plus a $198 commission.
Dec. 31   Per share fair values for stocks in the portfolio are: Kodak, $16.25; Sara Lee, $20.00; Sony, $35.00.

2011

Feb. 27   Purchased 3,000 shares of Microsoft at $65 per share plus a $520 commission.
June 21   Sold 1,000 shares of Sony at $48.00 per share less an $880 commission.
June 30   Purchased 1,500 shares of Black & Decker at $38 per share plus a $435 commission.
Aug. 3   Sold 500 shares of Sara Lee at $16.25 per share less a $435 commission.
Nov. 1   Sold 900 shares of Eastman Kodak at $19.75 per share less a $625 commission.
Dec. 31   Per share fair values for stocks in the portfolio are: Black & Decker, $41; Microsoft, $67.

Required

1. Prepare journal entries to record these transactions and events and any year-end fair value adjustments to the portfolio of long-term available-for-sale securities.

2. Prepare a table that summarizes the (*a*) total cost, (*b*) total fair value adjustment, and (*c*) total fair value of the portfolio of long-term available-for-sale securities at each year-end.

3. Prepare a table that summarizes (*a*) the realized gains and losses and (*b*) the unrealized gains or losses for the portfolio of long-term available-for-sale securities at each year-end.

Problem C-3A
Recording, adjusting, and reporting long-term available-for-sale securities

C2 P3

Check   (2b) Fair value adjustment bal.: 12/31/09, $(10,205); 12/31/10; $(11,263)

(3b) Unrealized Gain at 12/31/2011, $9,545

Elevant Co.'s long-term available-for-sale portfolio at December 31, 2010, consists of the following.

Available-for-Sale Securities	Cost	Fair Value
40,000 shares of Company A common stock	$535,300	$500,000
7,000 shares of Company B common stock	159,380	151,000
17,500 shares of Company C common stock	662,600	640,938

Elevant enters into the following long-term investment transactions during year 2011.

Jan. 29   Sold 3,500 shares of Company B common stock for $79,100 less a brokerage fee of $1,400.
Apr. 17   Purchased 9,900 shares of Company W common stock for $197,500 plus a brokerage fee of $2,300. The shares represent a 30% ownership in Company W.
July   6   Purchased 4,200 shares of Company X common stock for $118,125 plus a brokerage fee of $1,650. The shares represent a 10% ownership in Company X.
Aug. 22   Purchased 50,000 shares of Company Y common stock for $375,000 plus a brokerage fee of $1,100. The shares represent a 51% ownership in Company Y.
Nov. 13   Purchased 8,300 shares of Company Z common stock for $261,596 plus a brokerage fee of $2,350. The shares represent a 5% ownership in Company Z.
Dec. 9   Sold 40,000 shares of Company A common stock for $515,000 less a brokerage fee of $4,000.

The fair values of its investments at December 31, 2011, are: B, $81,375; C, $610,312; W, $191,250; X, $110,250; Y, $531,250; and Z, $272,240.

Problem C-4A
Long-term investment transactions; unrealized and realized gains and losses

C2 C3 P3 P4

Required

1. Determine the amount Elevant should report on its December 31, 2011, balance sheet for its long-term investments in available-for-sale securities.

Check (2) Cr. Unrealized Loss—Equity, $13,508

2. Prepare any necessary December 31, 2011, adjusting entry to record the fair value adjustment for the long-term investments in available-for-sale securities.

3. What amount of gains or losses on transactions relating to long-term investments in available-for-sale securities should Elevant report on its December 31, 2011, income statement?

Problem C-5A
Accounting for long-term investments in securities; with and without significant influence

C2   P3   P4

Selk Steel Co., which began operations on January 4, 2009, had the following subsequent transactions and events in its long-term investments.

2009

Jan.   5   Selk purchased 50,000 shares (20% of total) of Wulf's common stock for $1,567,000.
Oct. 23   Wulf declared and paid a cash dividend of $3.20 per share.
Dec. 31   Wulf's net income for 2009 is $1,164,000, and the fair value of its stock at December 31 is $34 per share.

2010

Oct. 15   Wulf declared and paid a cash dividend of $2.50 per share.
Dec. 31   Wulf's net income for 2010 is $1,476,000, and the fair value of its stock at December 31 is $36.00 per share.

2011

Jan.   2   Selk sold all of its investment in Wulf for $1,895,500 cash.

Part 1

Assume that Selk has a significant influence over Wulf with its 20% share of stock.

Required

1. Prepare journal entries to record these transactions and events for Selk.

Check (2) Carrying value per share, $36.20

2. Compute the carrying (book) value per share of Selk's investment in Wulf common stock as reflected in the investment account on January 1, 2011.

3. Compute the net increase or decrease in Selk's equity from January 5, 2009, through January 2, 2011, resulting from its investment in Wulf.

Part 2

Assume that although Selk owns 20% of Wulf's outstanding stock, circumstances indicate that it does not have a significant influence over the investee and that it is classified as an available-for-sale security investment.

Required

(1) 1/2/2011 Dr. Unrealized Gain—Equity $233,000

1. Prepare journal entries to record the preceding transactions and events for Selk. Also prepare an entry dated January 2, 2011, to remove any balance related to the fair value adjustment.

2. Compute the cost per share of Selk's investment in Wulf common stock as reflected in the investment account on January 1, 2011.

(3) Net increase, $613,500

3. Compute the net increase or decrease in Selk's equity from January 5, 2009, through January 2, 2011, resulting from its investment in Wulf.

Problem C-6A[A]
Foreign currency transactions

C4   P5

Patriot Company, a U.S. corporation with customers in several foreign countries, had the following selected transactions for 2009 and 2010.

2009

Apr.   8   Sold merchandise to Salinas & Sons of Mexico for $27,456 cash. The exchange rate for pesos is $0.0932 on this day.
July 21   Sold merchandise on credit to Sumito Corp. in Japan. The price of 2.7 million yen is to be paid 120 days from the date of sale. The exchange rate for yen is $0.0082 on this day.

Oct. 14   Sold merchandise for 18,000 pounds to Smithers Ltd. of Great Britain, payment in full to be received in 90 days. The exchange rate for pounds is $2.0330 on this day.

Nov. 18   Received Sumito's payment in yen for its July 21 purchase and immediately exchanged the yen for dollars. The exchange rate for yen is $0.0079 on this day.

Dec. 20   Sold merchandise for 20,000 ringgits to Hamid Albar of Malaysia, payment in full to be received in 30 days. On this day, the exchange rate for ringgits is $0.2963.

Dec. 31   Recorded adjusting entries to recognize exchange gains or losses on Patriot's annual financial statements. Rates for exchanging foreign currencies on this day follow.

Pesos (Mexico)	$0.0937
Yen (Japan)	0.0075
Pounds (Britain)	2.0345
Ringgits (Malaysia)	0.2949

2010

Jan. 12   Received full payment in pounds from Smithers for the October 14 sale and immediately exchanged the pounds for dollars. The exchange rate for pounds is $2.0355 on this day.

Jan. 19   Received Hamid Albar's full payment in ringgits for the December 20 sale and immediately exchanged the ringgits for dollars. The exchange rate for ringgits is $0.2936 on this day.

Required

1. Prepare journal entries for the Patriot transactions and adjusting entries (round amounts to the nearest dollar).

2. Compute the foreign exchange gain or loss to be reported on Patriot's 2009 income statement.

Check (2) 2009 total foreign exchange loss, $811

Analysis Component

3. What actions might Patriot consider to reduce its risk of foreign exchange gains or losses?

Harter Company, which began operations in 2009, invests its idle cash in trading securities. The following transactions relate to its short-term investments in its trading securities.

PROBLEM SET B

Problem C-1B
Recording transactions and fair value adjustments for trading securities

C2   P1

2009

Mar. 10   Purchased 900 shares of Timex at $28.00 per share plus a $125 commission.
May   7   Purchased 2,500 shares of MTV at $37.00 per share plus a $578 commission.
Sept. 1   Purchased 780 shares of UPS at $7.00 per share plus a $200 commission.

2010

Apr. 26   Sold 2,500 shares of MTV at $35.50 per share less a $295 commission.
Apr. 27   Sold 780 shares of UPS at $10.50 per share less a $103 commission.
June   2   Purchased 1,600 shares of SPW at $34.00 per share plus a $444 commission.
June 14   Purchased 1,600 shares of Wal-Mart at $20.00 per share plus a $290 commission.

2011

Jan. 28   Purchased 3,400 shares of PepsiCo at $38.00 per share plus a $400 commission.
Jan. 31   Sold 1,600 shares of SPW at $29.00 per share less a $250 commission.
Aug. 22   Sold 900 shares of Timex at $26.25 per share less a $420 commission.
Sept. 3   Purchased 1,500 shares of Vodaphone at $47.50 per share plus a $600 commission.
Oct.   9   Sold 1,600 shares of Wal-Mart at $22.50 per share less a $309 commission.

Required

1. Prepare journal entries to record these short-term investment activities for the years shown. (Ignore any year-end adjusting entries.)

2. On December 31, 2011, prepare the adjusting entry to record any necessary fair value adjustment for the portfolio of trading securities when PepsiCo's share price is $36.00 and Vodaphone's share price is $44.00. (Assume the Fair Value Adjustment—Trading account had an unadjusted balance of zero.)

Problem C-2B
Recording, adjusting, and reporting short-term available-for-sale securities

C2   P3

SP Systems had no short-term investments prior to 2011. It had the following transactions involving short-term investments in available-for-sale securities during 2011.

Feb.   6   Purchased 6,000 shares of Nokia stock at $24.75 per share plus a $400 brokerage fee.
      15   Paid $250,000 to buy six-month U.S. Treasury bills (debt securities): $250,000 principal amount, 4% interest, securities dated February 15.
Apr.   7   Purchased 3,000 shares of Dell Co. stock at $49.25 per share plus a $370 brokerage fee.
June 2   Purchased 1,500 shares of Merck stock at $18.25 per share plus a $450 brokerage fee.
      30   Received a $0.19 per share cash dividend on the Nokia shares.
Aug. 11   Sold 1,500 shares of Nokia stock at $29.50 per share less a $490 brokerage fee.
      16   Received a check for principal and accrued interest on the U.S. Treasury bills purchased February 15.
      24   Received a $0.16 per share cash dividend on the Dell shares.
Nov. 9   Received a $0.20 per share cash dividend on the remaining Nokia shares.
Dec. 18   Received a $0.21 per share cash dividend on the Dell shares.

Required

1. Prepare journal entries to record the preceding transactions and events.

2. Prepare a table to compare the year-end cost and fair values of the short-term investments in available-for-sale securities. The year-end fair values per share are: Nokia, $23.50; Dell, $55.50; and Merck, $15.25.

3. Prepare an adjusting entry, if necessary, to record the year-end fair value adjustment for the portfolio of short-term investments in available-for-sale securities.

Analysis Component

4. Explain the balance sheet presentation of the fair value adjustment to SP's short-term investments.

5. How do these short-term investments affect (*a*) its income statement for year 2011 and (*b*) the equity section of its balance sheet at the 2011 year-end?

Problem C-3B
Recording, adjusting, and reporting long-term available-for-sale securities

C2   P3

Bleeker Enterprises, which began operations in 2009, invests in long-term available-for-sale securities. Following is a series of transactions and events involving its long-term investment activity.

2009

Mar. 10   Purchased 1,000 shares of Apple at $23.00 per share plus $240 commission.
Apr.   7   Purchased 1,300 shares of Ford at $46.20 per share plus $225 commission.
Sept. 1   Purchased 1,500 shares of Polaroid at $25.00 per share plus $195 commission.
Dec. 31   Per share fair values for stocks in the portfolio are: Apple, $24.00; Ford, $42.00; Polaroid, $27.00.

2010

Apr. 26   Sold 1,300 shares of Ford at $44.00 per share less a $250 commission.
June 2   Purchased 1,800 shares of Duracell at $19.25 per share plus a $235 commission.
June 14   Purchased 600 shares of Sears at $22.50 per share plus a $470 commission.
Nov. 27   Sold 1,500 shares of Polaroid at $29 per share less a $198 commission.
Dec. 31   Per share fair values for stocks in the portfolio are: Apple, $26.00; Duracell, $18.00; Sears, $25.00.

2011

Jan. 28   Purchased 2,000 shares of Coca-Cola Co. at $69 per share plus a $530 commission.
Aug. 22   Sold 1,000 shares of Apple at $20.00 per share less a $280 commission.
Sept. 3   Purchased 2,000 shares of Motorola at $36 per share plus a $435 commission.

Oct.   9   Sold 600 shares of Sears at $26.25 per share less a $435 commission.
Oct. 31   Sold 1,800 shares of Duracell at $15.00 per share less a $425 commission.
Dec. 31   Per share fair values for stocks in the portfolio are: Coca-Cola, $75.00; Motorola, $32.00.

Required

1. Prepare journal entries to record these transactions and events and any year-end fair value adjustments to the portfolio of long-term available-for-sale securities.

2. Prepare a table that summarizes the (*a*) total cost, (*b*) total fair value adjustment, and (*c*) total fair value for the portfolio of long-term available-for-sale securities at each year-end.

3. Prepare a table that summarizes (*a*) the realized gains and losses and (*b*) the unrealized gains or losses for the portfolio of long-term available-for-sale securities at each year-end.

Check   (2b) Fair value adjustment bal.: 12/31/09, $(2,120); 12/31/10, $1,305

(3b) Unrealized Gain at 12/31/2011, $3,035

Chavez's long-term available-for-sale portfolio at December 31, 2010, consists of the following.

Available-for-Sale Securities	Cost	Fair Value
55,000 shares of Company R common stock	$1,118,250	$1,198,000
17,000 shares of Company S common stock	600,600	586,500
22,000 shares of Company T common stock	294,590	303,600

Problem C-4B
Long-term investment transactions; unrealized and realized gains and losses

C2 C3 P3 P4

Chavez enters into the following long-term investment transactions during year 2011.

Jan. 13   Sold 4,250 shares of Company S stock for $145,500 less a brokerage fee of $650.
Mar. 24   Purchased 31,000 shares of Company U common stock for $565,750 plus a brokerage fee of $1,980. The shares represent a 62% ownership interest in Company U.
Apr.   5   Purchased 85,000 shares of Company V common stock for $267,750 plus a brokerage fee of $1,125. The shares represent a 10% ownership in Company V.
Sept. 2   Sold 22,000 shares of Company T common stock for $313,500 less a brokerage fee of $2,700.
Sept. 27   Purchased 5,000 shares of Company W common stock for $101,000 plus a brokerage fee of $350. The shares represent a 25% ownership interest in Company W.
Oct. 30   Purchased 10,000 shares of Company X common stock for $97,500 plus a brokerage fee of $300. The shares represent a 13% ownership interest in Company X.

The fair values of its investments at December 31, 2011, are: R, $1,136,250; S, $420,750; U, $545,600; V, $269,876; W, $109,378; and X, $91,250.

Required

1. Determine the amount Chavez should report on its December 31, 2011, balance sheet for its long-term investments in available-for-sale securities.

2. Prepare any necessary December 31, 2011, adjusting entry to record the fair value adjustment of the long-term investments in available-for-sale securities.

3. What amount of gains or losses on transactions relating to long-term investments in available-for-sale securities should Chavez report on its December 31, 2011, income statement?

Check   (2) Dr. Unrealized Gain— Equity, $74,660; Cr. Fair Value Adjustment—AFS (LT), $91,909

Devin Company, which began operations on January 3, 2009, had the following subsequent transactions and events in its long-term investments.

Problem C-5B
Accounting for long-term investments in securities; with and without significant influence

C2 P3 P4

2009

Jan.   5   Devin purchased 25,000 shares (25% of total) of Bloch's common stock for $401,000.
Aug.   1   Bloch declared and paid a cash dividend of $1.10 per share.
Dec. 31   Bloch's net income for 2009 is $164,000, and the fair value of its stock is $17.50 per share.

2010

Aug.   1   Bloch declared and paid a cash dividend of $1.30 per share.
Dec. 31   Bloch's net income for 2010 is $156,000, and the fair value of its stock is $19.25 per share.

2011

Jan.   8   Devin sold all of its investment in Bloch for $550,000 cash.

Part 1

Assume that Devin has a significant influence over Bloch with its 25% share.

Required

Check   (2) Carrying value per share, $16.84

1. Prepare journal entries to record these transactions and events for Devin.
2. Compute the carrying (book) value per share of Devin's investment in Bloch common stock as reflected in the investment account on January 7, 2011.
3. Compute the net increase or decrease in Devin's equity from January 5, 2009, through January 8, 2011, resulting from its investment in Bloch.

Part 2

Assume that although Devin owns 25% of Bloch's outstanding stock, circumstances indicate that it does not have a significant influence over the investee and that it is classified as an available-for-sale security investment.

Required

(1) 1/8/2011 Dr. Unrealized Gain—Equity $80,250

1. Prepare journal entries to record these transactions and events for Devin. Also prepare an entry dated January 8, 2011, to remove any balance related to the fair value adjustment.
2. Compute the cost per share of Devin's investment in Bloch common stock as reflected in the investment account on January 7, 2011.

(3) Net increase, $209,000

3. Compute the net increase or decrease in Devin's equity from January 5, 2009, through January 8, 2011, resulting from its investment in Bloch.

Problem C-6B[A]

Foreign currency transactions

C4 P5

Kitna, a U.S. corporation with customers in several foreign countries, had the following selected transactions for 2009 and 2010.

2009

May 26   Sold merchandise for 5.5 million yen to Fuji Company of Japan, payment in full to be received in 60 days. On this day, the exchange rate for yen is $0.0088.

June 1   Sold merchandise to Fordham Ltd. of Great Britain for $73,500 cash. The exchange rate for pounds is $2.0331 on this day.

July 25   Received Fuji's payment in yen for its May 26 purchase and immediately exchanged the yen for dollars. The exchange rate for yen is $0.0087 on this day.

Oct. 15   Sold merchandise on credit to Martinez Brothers of Mexico. The price of 425,000 pesos is to be paid 90 days from the date of sale. On this day, the exchange rate for pesos is $0.0932.

Dec. 6   Sold merchandise for 300,000 yuans to Chi-Ying Company of China, payment in full to be received in 30 days. The exchange rate for yuans is $0.1335 on this day.

Dec. 31   Recorded adjusting entries to recognize exchange gains or losses on Kitna's annual financial statements. Rates of exchanging foreign currencies on this day follow.

Yen (Japan)	$0.0089
Pounds (Britain)	2.0402
Pesos (Mexico)	0.0994
Yuans (China)	0.1351

2010

Jan. 5   Received Chi-Ying's full payment in yuans for the December 6 sale and immediately exchanged the yuans for dollars. The exchange rate for yuans is $0.1372 on this day.

Jan. 13   Received full payment in pesos from Martinez for the October 15 sale and immediately exchanged the pesos for dollars. The exchange rate for pesos is $0.0960 on this day.

Required

1. Prepare journal entries for the Kitna transactions and adjusting entries.

2. Compute the foreign exchange gain or loss to be reported on Kitna's 2009 income statement.

Check 2009 total foreign exchange gain, $2,565

Analysis Component

3. What actions might Kitna consider to reduce its risk of foreign exchange gains or losses?

SERIAL PROBLEM

Success Systems

(This serial problem began in Chapter 1 and continues through most of the book. If previous chapter segments were not completed, the serial problem can begin at this point. It is helpful, but not necessary, to use the Working Papers that accompany the book.)

SP C   While reviewing the March 31, 2010, balance sheet of Success Systems, Adriana Lopez notes that the business has built a large cash balance of $77,845. Its most recent bank money market statement shows that the funds are earning an annualized return of 0.75%. Lopez decides to make several investments with the desire to earn a higher return on the idle cash balance. Accordingly, in April 2010, Success Systems makes the following investments in trading securities:

April 16   Purchases 400 shares of Johnson & Johnson stock at $50 per share plus $300 commission.
April 30   Purchases 200 shares of Starbucks Corporation at $22 per share plus $250 commission.

On June 30, 2010, the per share market price (fair value) of the Johnson & Johnson shares is $55 and the Starbucks shares is $19.

Required

1. Prepare journal entries to record the April purchases of trading securities by Success Systems.

2. On June 30, 2010, prepare the adjusting entry to record any necessary fair value adjustment to its portfolio of trading securities.

BEYOND THE NUMBERS

BTN C-1   Refer to **Best Buy**'s financial statements in Appendix A to answer the following.

1. Are Best Buy's financial statements consolidated? How can you tell?

2. What is Best Buy's *comprehensive income* for the year ended February 28, 2009?

3. Does Best Buy have any foreign operations? How can you tell?

4. Compute Best Buy's return on total assets for the year ended February 28, 2009.

REPORTING IN ACTION

C3 C4 A1

Fast Forward

5. Access Best Buy's annual report for a fiscal year ending after February 28, 2009, from either its Website (**BestBuy.com**) or the SEC's database (**www.SEC.gov**). Recompute Best Buy's return on total assets for the years subsequent to February 28, 2009.

BTN C-2   Key figures for **Best Buy** and **RadioShack** follow.

COMPARATIVE ANALYSIS

A1

($ millions)	Best Buy Current Year	1 Year Prior	2 Years Prior	RadioShack Current Year	1 Year Prior	2 Years Prior
Net income	$ 1,003	$ 1,407	$ 1,377	$ 192.4	$ 236.8	$ 73.4
Net sales	45,015	40,023	35,934	4,224.5	4,251.7	4,777.5
Total assets	15,826	12,758	13,570	2,283.5	1,989.6	2,070.0

Required

1. Compute return on total assets for Best Buy and RadioShack for the two most recent years.

2. Separate the return on total assets computed in part 1 into its components for both companies and both years according to the formula in Exhibit C.9.

3. Which company has the highest total return on assets? The highest profit margin? The highest total asset turnover? What does this comparative analysis reveal? (Assume an industry average of 3.2% for return on assets.)

ETHICS CHALLENGE
C2 P2 P3

BTN C-3 Kaylee Wecker is the controller for Wildcat Company, which has numerous long-term investments in debt securities. Wildcat's investments are mainly in 10-year bonds. Wecker is preparing its year-end financial statements. In accounting for long-term debt securities, she knows that each long-term investment must be designated as a held-to-maturity or an available-for-sale security. Interest rates rose sharply this past year causing the portfolio's fair value to substantially decline. The company does not intend to hold the bonds for the entire 10 years. Wecker also earns a bonus each year, which is computed as a percent of net income.

Required

1. Will Wecker's bonus depend in any way on the classification of the debt securities? Explain.

2. What criteria must Wecker use to classify the securities as held-to-maturity or available-for-sale?

3. Is there likely any company oversight of Wecker's classification of the securities? Explain.

COMMUNICATING IN PRACTICE
C2 P4

BTN C-4 Assume that you are Jackson Company's accountant. Company owner Abel Terrio has reviewed the 2011 financial statements you prepared and questions the $6,000 loss reported on the sale of its investment in Blackhawk Co. common stock. Jackson acquired 50,000 shares of Blackhawk's common stock on December 31, 2009, at a cost of $500,000. This stock purchase represented a 40% interest in Blackhawk. The 2010 income statement reported that earnings from all investments were $126,000. On January 3, 2011, Jackson Company sold the Blackhawk stock for $575,000. Blackhawk did not pay any dividends during 2010 but reported a net income of $202,500 for that year. Terrio believes that because the Blackhawk stock purchase price was $500,000 and was sold for $575,000, the 2011 income statement should report a $75,000 gain on the sale.

Required

Draft a one-half page memorandum to Terrio explaining why the $6,000 loss on sale of Blackhawk stock is correctly reported.

TAKING IT TO THE NET
C1 C2

BTN C-5 Access the July 30, 2009, 10-K filing (for year-end June 30, 2009) of **Microsoft** (MSFT) at www.SEC.gov. Review its note 4, "Investments."

Required

1. How does the "cost-basis" total amount for its investments as of June 30, 2009, compare to the prior year-end amount?

2. Identify at least eight types of short-term investments held by Microsoft as of June 30, 2009.

3. What were Microsoft's unrealized gains and its unrealized losses from its investments for 2009?

4. Was the cost or fair value ("recorded basis") of the investments higher as of June 30, 2009?

BTN C-6   Each team member is to become an expert on a specific classification of long-term investments. This expertise will be used to facilitate other teammates' understanding of the concepts and procedures relevent to the classification chosen.

1. Each team member must select an area for expertise by choosing one of the following classifications of long-term investments.

   a. Held-to-maturity debt securities

   b. Available-for-sale debt and equity securities

   c. Equity securities with significant influence

   d. Equity securities with controlling influence

2. Learning teams are to disburse and expert teams are to be formed. Expert teams are made up of those who select the same area of expertise. The instructor will identify the location where each expert team will meet.

3. Expert teams will collaborate to develop a presentation based on the following requirements. Students must write the presentation in a format they can show to their learning teams in part (4).

Requirements for Expert Presentation

   a. Write a transaction for the acquisition of this type of investment security. The transaction description is to include all necessary data to reflect the chosen classification.

   b. Prepare the journal entry to record the acquisition.

   [*Note:* The expert team on equity securities with controlling influence will substitute requirements (*d*) and (*e*) with a discussion of the reporting of these investments.]

   c. Identify information necessary to complete the end-of-period adjustment for this investment.

   d. Assuming that this is the only investment owned, prepare any necessary year-end entries.

   e. Present the relevant balance sheet section(s).

4. Re-form learning teams. In rotation, experts are to present to their teams the presentations they developed in part 3. Experts are to encourage and respond to questions.

BTN C-7[A]   Assume that you acquire the Japanese rights to publish and print Wii "cheats" and gaming information from **Nintendo** for translation for the U.S. audience. Further, assume that on January 1, 2010, you agree to pay 12,000,000 yen per year for those rights. Quarterly payments are due March 31, June 30, September 30, and December 31 each year. On January 1, 2010, the yen is worth $0.00891.

Required

1. Prepare the journal entry to record the publishing rights purchased on January 1, 2010.

2. Prepare the journal entries to record the payments on March 31, June 30, September 30, and December 31, 2010. The value of the yen on those dates follows.

March 31	$0.00893
June 30	0.00901
September 30	0.00902
December 31	0.00897

3. How can you protect yourself from unanticipated gains and losses from currency translation if all of your payments are specified to be paid in yen?

BTN C-8[A]   Assume that you are planning a spring break trip to Europe. Identify three locations where you can find exchange rates for the dollar relative to the Euro or other currencies.

Appendix C   Investments and International Operations

**GLOBAL
DECISION**

A1

BTN C-9   GOME (www.GOME.com.hk), Best Buy, and RadioShack are competitors in the global marketplace. Following are selected data from each company.

Key Figure	GOME (RMB 000s)			Best Buy		RadioShack	
	Current Year	One Year Prior	Two Years Prior	Current Year	Prior Year	Current Year	Prior Year
Net income	1,098,693	1,167,835	942,624	—	—	—	—
Net sales	45,889,257	42,478,523	24,729,192	—	—	—	—
Total assets	27,495,104	29,837,493	21,176,229	—	—	—	—
Profit margin	?	?	—	2.23%	3.52%	4.55%	5.57%
Total asset turnover	?	?	—	3.15	3.04	1.98	2.09

Required

1. Compute GOME's return on total assets, and its components of profit margin and total asset turnover, for the most recent two years using the data provided.

2. Which of these three companies has the highest return on total assets? Highest profit margin? Highest total asset turnover? Interpret these results.

ANSWERS TO MULTIPLE CHOICE QUIZ

1. d; $30,000 × 5% × 5/12 = $625

2. a; Unrealized gain = $84,500 − $83,000 = $1,500

3. b; $50,000 × 35% = $17,500

4. e; $300,000/$2,000,000 = 15%

5. b; Profit margin = $80,000/$600,000 = 13.3%
Total asset turnover = $600,000/$400,000 = 1.5

Glossary

Accelerated depreciation method Method that produces larger depreciation charges in the early years of an asset's life and smaller charges in its later years. *(p. 338)*

Account Record within an accounting system in which increases and decreases are entered and stored in a specific asset, liability, equity, revenue, or expense. *(p. 51)*

Account balance Difference between total debits and total credits (including the beginning balance) for an account. *(p. 55)*

Account form balance sheet Balance sheet that lists assets on the left side and liabilities and equity on the right.

Account payable Liability created by buying goods or services on credit; backed by the buyer's general credit standing. *(p. 52)*

Accounting Information and measurement system that identifies, records, and communicates relevant information about a company's business activities. *(p. 4)*

Accounting cycle Recurring steps performed each accounting period, starting with analyzing transactions and continuing through the post-closing trial balance (or reversing entries). *(p. 112)*

Accounting equation Equality involving a company's assets, liabilities, and equity; Assets = Liabilities + Equity; also called *balance sheet equation*. *(p. 14)*

Accounting information system People, records, and methods that collect and process data from transactions and events, organize them in useful forms, and communicate results to decision makers. *(p. E-2)*

Accounting period Length of time covered by financial statements; also called *reporting period*. *(p. 94)*

Accounts payable ledger Subsidiary ledger listing individual creditor (supplier) accounts. *(p. E-7)*

Accounts receivable Amounts due from customers for credit sales; backed by the customer's general credit standing. *(p. 296)*

Accounts receivable ledger Subsidiary ledger listing individual customer accounts. *(p. E-7)*

Accounts receivable turnover Measure of both the quality and liquidity of accounts receivable; indicates how often receivables are received and collected during the period; computed by dividing net sales by average accounts receivable. *(p. 312)*

Accrual basis accounting Accounting system that recognizes revenues when earned and expenses when incurred; the basis for GAAP. *(p. 95)*

Accrued expenses Costs incurred in a period that are both unpaid and unrecorded; adjusting entries for recording accrued expenses involve increasing expenses and increasing liabilities. *(p. 102)*

Accrued revenues Revenues earned in a period that are both unrecorded and not yet received in cash (or other assets); adjusting entries for recording accrued revenues involve increasing assets and increasing revenues. *(p. 103)*

Accumulated depreciation Cumulative sum of all depreciation expense recorded for an asset. *(p. 100)*

Acid-test ratio Ratio used to assess a company's ability to settle its current debts with its most liquid assets; defined as quick assets (cash, short-term investments, and current receivables) divided by current liabilities. *(p. 172)*

Adjusted trial balance List of accounts and balances prepared after period-end adjustments are recorded and posted. *(p. 106)*

Adjusting entry Journal entry at the end of an accounting period to bring an asset or liability account to its proper amount and update the related expense or revenue account. *(p. 97)*

Aging of accounts receivable Process of classifying accounts receivable by how long they are past due for purposes of estimating uncollectible accounts. *(p. 304)*

Allowance for Doubtful Accounts Contra asset account with a balance approximating uncollectible accounts receivable; also called *Allowance for Uncollectible Accounts*. *(p. 301)*

Allowance method Procedure that (a) estimates and matches bad debts expense with its sales for the period and/or (b) reports accounts receivable at estimated realizable value. *(p. 301)*

Amortization Process of allocating the cost of an intangible asset to expense over its estimated useful life. *(p. 348)*

Annual financial statements Financial statements covering a one-year period; often based on a calendar year, but any consecutive 12-month (or 52-week) period is acceptable. *(p. 94)*

Annual report Summary of a company's financial results for the year with its current financial condition and future plans; directed to external users of financial information. *(p. A-1)*

Annuity Series of equal payments at equal intervals. *(p. 440)*

Appropriated retained earnings Retained earnings separately reported to inform stockholders of funding needs. *(p. 481)*

Asset book value (See *book value.*) *(p. 337)*

Assets Resources a business owns or controls that are expected to provide current and future benefits to the business. *(p. 14)*

Audit Analysis and report of an organization's accounting system, its records, and its reports using various tests. *(p. 11)*

Auditor An individual who checks the accuracy, fairness, and general acceptability of accounting records; an external auditor would attest to those checks. *(p. 13)*

Authorized stock Total amount of stock that a corporation's charter authorizes it to issue. *(p. 467)*

Available-for-sale (AFS) securities Investments in debt and equity securities that are not classified as trading securities or held-to-maturity securities. *(p. C-5)*

Average cost See *weighted average. (p. 210 & 226)*

Bad debts Accounts of customers who do not pay what they have promised to pay; an expense of selling on credit; also called *uncollectible accounts. (p. 300)*

Balance column account Account with debit and credit columns for recording entries and another column for showing the balance of the account after each entry. *(p. 58)*

Balance sheet Financial statement that lists types and dollar amounts of assets, liabilities, and equity at a specific date. *(p. 19)*

Balance sheet equation (See *accounting equation.) (p. 14)*

Bank reconciliation Report that explains the difference between the book (company) balance of cash and the cash balance reported on the bank statement. *(p. 265)*

Bank statement Bank report on the depositor's beginning and ending cash balances, and a listing of its changes, for a period. *(p. 264)*

Basic earnings per share Net income less any preferred dividends and then divided by weighted-average common shares outstanding. *(p. 483)*

Batch level activities Activities that are performed each time a batch of goods is handled or processed, regardless of how many units are in a batch; the amount of resources used depends on the number of batches run rather than on the number of units in the batch.

Batch processing Accumulating source documents for a period of time and then processing them all at once such as once a day, week, or month. *(p. E-16)*

Bearer bonds Bonds made payable to whoever holds them (the *bearer*); also called *unregistered bonds. (p. 434)*

Benchmarking Practice of comparing and analyzing company financial performance or position with other companies or standards.

Betterments Expenditures to make a plant asset more efficient or productive; also called *improvements. (p. 343)*

Bond Written promise to pay the bond's par (or face) value and interest at a stated contract rate; often issued in denominations of $1,000. *(p. 420)*

Bond certificate Document containing bond specifics such as issuer's name, bond par value, contract interest rate, and maturity date. *(p. 422)*

Bond indenture Contract between the bond issuer and the bondholders; identifies the parties' rights and obligations. *(p. 422)*

Bookkeeping (See *recordkeeping.) (p. 4)*

Book value Asset's acquisition costs less its accumulated depreciation (or depletion, or amortization); also sometimes used synonymously as the *carrying value* of an account. *(p. 100 & 337)*

Book value per common share Recorded amount of equity applicable to common shares divided by the number of common shares outstanding. *(p. 485)*

Book value per preferred share Equity applicable to preferred shares (equals its call price [or par value if it is not callable] plus any cumulative dividends in arrears) divided by the number of preferred shares outstanding. *(p. 485)*

Business An organization of one or more individuals selling products and/or services for profit. *(p. 11)*

Business entity assumption Principle that requires a business to be accounted for separately from its owner(s) and from any other entity. *(p. 11)*

Business segment Part of a company that can be separately identified by the products or services that it provides or by the geographic markets that it serves; also called *segment. (p. 589)*

C corporation Corporation that does not qualify for nor elect to be treated as a proprietorship or partnership for income tax purposes and therefore is subject to income taxes; also called *C corp. (p. D-4)*

Call price Amount that must be paid to call and retire a callable preferred stock or a callable bond. *(p. 477)*

Callable bonds Bonds that give the issuer the option to retire them at a stated amount prior to maturity. *(p. 435)*

Callable preferred stock Preferred stock that the issuing corporation, at its option, may retire by paying the call price plus any dividends in arrears. *(p. 477)*

Canceled checks Checks that the bank has paid and deducted from the depositor's account. *(p. 265)*

Capital expenditures Additional costs of plant assets that provide material benefits extending beyond the current period; also called *balance sheet expenditures. (p. 342)*

Capital leases Long-term leases in which the lessor transfers substantially all risk and rewards of ownership to the lessee. *(p. 445)*

Capital stock General term referring to a corporation's stock used in obtaining capital (owner financing). *(p. 467)*

Capitalize Record the cost as part of a permanent account and allocate it over later periods.

Carrying (book) value of bonds Net amount at which bonds are reported on the balance sheet; equals the par value of the bonds less any unamortized discount or plus any unamortized premium; also called *carrying amount* or *book value. (p. 424)*

Cash Includes currency, coins, and amounts on deposit in bank checking or savings accounts. *(p. 255)*

Cash basis accounting Accounting system that recognizes revenues when cash is received and records expenses when cash is paid. *(p. 95)*

Cash disbursements journal Special journal normally used to record all payments of cash; also called *cash payments journal. (p. E-14)*

Cash discount Reduction in the price of merchandise granted by a seller to a buyer when payment is made within the discount period. *(p. 159)*

Cash equivalents Short-term, investment assets that are readily convertible to a known cash amount or sufficiently close to their maturity date (usually within 90 days) so that market value is not sensitive to interest rate changes. *(p. 255)*

Cash flow on total assets Ratio of operating cash flows to average total assets; not sensitive to income recognition and measurement; partly reflects earnings quality. *(p. 529)*

Cash Over and Short Income statement account used to record cash overages and cash shortages arising from errors in cash receipts or payments. *(p. 257)*

Cash receipts journal Special journal normally used to record all receipts of cash. *(p. E-11)*

Change in an accounting estimate Change in an accounting estimate that results from new information, subsequent developments, or improved judgment that impacts current and future periods. *(p. 341 & 481)*

Chart of accounts List of accounts used by a company; includes an identification number for each account. *(p. 54)*

Check Document signed by a depositor instructing the bank to pay a specified amount to a designated recipient. *(p. 263)*

Check register Another name for a cash disbursements journal when the journal has a column for check numbers. *(p. 275 & E-14)*

Classified balance sheet Balance sheet that presents assets and liabilities in relevant subgroups, including current and noncurrent classifications. *(p. 113)*

Closing entries Entries recorded at the end of each accounting period to transfer end-of-period balances in revenue, gain, expense, loss, and dividend accounts to the retained earnings account. *(p. 108)*

Closing process Necessary end-of-period steps to prepare the accounts for recording the transactions of the next period. *(p. 108)*

Columnar journal Journal with more than one column. *(p. E-8)*

Committee of Sponsoring Organizations (COSO) An organization dedicated to improving the quality of financial reporting through several methods, including effective internal controls. *(p. 251)*

Common stock Corporation's basic ownership share; also generically called *capital stock*. *(p. 12, 53 & 466)*

Common-size financial statement Statement that expresses each amount as a percent of a base amount. In the balance sheet, total assets is usually the base and is expressed as 100%. In the income statement, net sales is usually the base. *(p. 571)*

Comparative financial statement Statement with data for two or more successive periods placed in side-by-side columns, often with changes shown in dollar amounts and percents. *(p. 566)*

Compatibility principle Information system principle that requires an accounting system to conform with a company's activities, personnel, and structure. *(p. E-3)*

Complex capital structure Capital structure that includes outstanding rights or options to purchase common stock, or securities that are convertible into common stock. *(p. 484)*

Components of accounting systems Five basic components of accounting systems are source documents, input devices, information processors, information storage, and output devices. *(p. E-3)*

Compound journal entry Journal entry that affects at least three accounts. *(p. 61)*

Comprehensive income Net change in equity for a period, excluding owner investments and distributions. *(p. C-9)*

Computer hardware Physical equipment in a computerized accounting information system.

Computer network Linkage giving different users and different computers access to common databases and programs. *(p. E-17)*

Computer software Programs that direct operations of computer hardware.

Conceptual framework System of interrelated objectives and fundamentals, disseminated by accounting regulators such as the FASB or IASB; intended to guide consistent standard setting and aid accounting practitioners. *(p. 9)*

Conservatism constraint Criterion that in the absence of certainty would encourage the accounting and disclosure of transactions and events to minimize income. *(p. 215)*

Consignee Receiver of goods owned by another who holds them for purposes of selling them for the owner. *(p. 204)*

Consignor Owner of goods who ships them to another party who will sell them for the owner. *(p. 204)*

Consistency principle Principle that prescribes use of the same accounting method(s) over time so that financial statements are comparable across periods. *(p. 213)*

Consolidated financial statements Financial statements that show all (combined) activities under the parent's control, including those of any subsidiaries. *(p. C-8)*

Contingent liability Obligation to make a future payment if, and only if, an uncertain future event occurs. *(p. 388)*

Contra account Account linked with another account and having an opposite normal balance; reported as a subtraction from the other account's balance. *(p. 99)*

Contract rate Interest rate specified in a bond indenture (or note); multiplied by the par value to determine the interest paid each period; also called *coupon rate, stated rate,* or *nominal rate. (p. 423)*

Contributed capital Total amount of cash and other assets received from stockholders in exchange for stock; also called *paid-in capital. (p. 14)*

Contributed capital in excess of par value Difference between the par value of stock and its issue price when issued at a price above par.

Control principle Information system principle that requires an accounting system to aid managers in controlling and monitoring business activities. *(p. E-2)*

Controlling account General ledger account, the balance of which (after posting) equals the sum of the balances in its related subsidiary ledger. *(p. E-7)*

Conversion costs Direct labor costs plus overhead costs incurred in producing a product or service; the costs to convert raw materials to finished goods; also called *manufacturing costs. (p. 604)*

Convertible bonds Bonds that bondholders can exchange for a set number of the issuer's shares. *(p. 435)*

Convertible preferred stock Preferred stock with an option to exchange it for common stock at a specified rate. *(p. 477)*

Copyright Right giving the owner the exclusive privilege to publish and sell musical, literary, or artistic work during the creator's life plus 70 years. *(p. 349)*

Corporation Business that is a separate legal entity under state or federal laws with owners called *shareholders* or *stockholders*. (p. 12 & 464)

Cost All normal and reasonable expenditures necessary to get an asset in place and ready for its intended use. (p. 333 & 335)

Cost-benefit constraint Criterion that only information with benefits of disclosure greater than the costs of providing it need be disclosed. (p. 12)

Cost-benefit principle Information system principle that requires the benefits from an activity in an accounting system to outweigh the costs of that activity. (p. E-3)

Cost of goods available for sale Consists of beginning inventory plus net purchases of a period. (p. 153)

Cost of goods sold Cost of inventory sold to customers during a period; also called *cost of sales*. (p. 156)

Cost principle Accounting principle that prescribes financial statement information to be based on actual costs incurred in business transactions. (p. 10)

Coupon bonds Bonds with interest coupons attached to their certificates; bondholders detach coupons when they mature and present them to a bank or broker for collection. (p. 434)

Credit Recorded on the right side; an entry that decreases asset and expense accounts, and increases liability, revenue, and most equity accounts; abbreviated Cr. (p. 55)

Credit memorandum Notification that the sender has credited the recipient's account in the sender's records. (p. 165)

Credit period Time period that can pass before a customer's payment is due. (p. 159)

Credit terms Description of the amounts and timing of payments that a buyer (debtor) agrees to make in the future. (p. 159)

Creditors Individuals or organizations entitled to receive payments. (p. 52)

Cumulative preferred stock Preferred stock on which undeclared dividends accumulate until paid; common stockholders cannot receive dividends until cumulative dividends are paid. (p. 476)

Current assets Cash and other assets expected to be sold, collected, or used within one year or the company's operating cycle, whichever is longer. (p. 113)

Current liabilities Obligations due to be paid or settled within one year or the company's operating cycle, whichever is longer. (p. 115 & 377)

Current portion of long-term debt Portion of long-term debt due within one year or the operating cycle, whichever is longer; reported under current liabilities. (p. 384)

Current ratio Ratio used to evaluate a company's ability to pay its short-term obligations, calculated by dividing current assets by current liabilities. (p. 117)

Date of declaration Date the directors vote to pay a dividend. (p. 471)

Date of payment Date the corporation makes the dividend payment. (p. 471)

Date of record Date directors specify for identifying stockholders to receive dividends. (p. 471)

Days' sales in inventory Estimate of number of days needed to convert inventory into receivables or cash; equals ending inventory divided by cost of goods sold and then multiplied by 365; also called *days' stock on hand*. (p. 218)

Days' sales uncollected Measure of the liquidity of receivables computed by dividing the current balance of receivables by the annual credit (or net) sales and then multiplying by 365; also called *days' sales in receivables*. (p. 270)

Debit Recorded on the left side; an entry that increases asset and expense accounts, and decreases liability, revenue, and most equity accounts; abbreviated Dr. (p. 55)

Debit memorandum Notification that the sender has debited the recipient's account in the sender's records. (p. 160)

Debt ratio Ratio of total liabilities to total assets; used to reflect risk associated with a company's debts. (p. 70)

Debt-to-equity ratio Defined as total liabilities divided by total equity; shows the proportion of a company financed by non-owners (creditors) in comparison with that financed by owners. (p. 435)

Debtors Individuals or organizations that owe money. (p. 51)

Declining-balance method Method that determines depreciation charge for the period by multiplying a depreciation rate (often twice the straight-line rate) by the asset's beginning-period book value. (p. 338)

Deferred income tax liability Corporation income taxes that are deferred until future years because of temporary differences between GAAP and tax rules. (p. 400)

Depletion Process of allocating the cost of natural resources to periods when they are consumed and sold. (p. 346)

Deposit ticket Lists items such as currency, coins, and checks deposited and their corresponding dollar amounts. (p. 263)

Deposits in transit Deposits recorded by the company but not yet recorded by its bank. (p. 266)

Depreciable cost Cost of a plant asset less its salvage value.

Depreciation Expense created by allocating the cost of plant and equipment to periods in which they are used; represents the expense of using the asset. (p. 99 & 335)

Diluted earnings per share Earnings per share calculation that requires dilutive securities be added to the denominator of the basic EPS calculation. (p. 484)

Dilutive securities Securities having the potential to increase common shares outstanding; examples are options, rights, convertible bonds, and convertible preferred stock. (p. 484)

Direct method Presentation of net cash from operating activities for the statement of cash flows that lists major operating cash receipts less major operating cash payments. (p. 516)

Direct write-off method Method that records the loss from an uncollectible account receivable at the time it is determined to be uncollectible; no attempt is made to estimate bad debts. (p. 300)

Discount on bonds payable Difference between a bond's par value and its lower issue price or carrying value; occurs when the contract rate is less than the market rate. (p. 423)

Discount on note payable Difference between the face value of a note payable and the (lesser) amount borrowed; reflects the added interest to be paid on the note over its life.

Discount on stock Difference between the par value of stock and its issue price when issued at a price below par value. *(p. 469)*

Discount period Time period in which a cash discount is available and the buyer can make a reduced payment. *(p. 159)*

Discount rate Expected rate of return on investments; also called *cost of capital, hurdle rate,* or *required rate of return.* *(p. B-2)*

Discounts lost Expenses resulting from not taking advantage of cash discounts on purchases. *(p. 276)*

Dividend in arrears Unpaid dividend on cumulative preferred stock; must be paid before any regular dividends on preferred stock and before any dividends on common stock. *(p. 476)*

Dividend yield Ratio of the annual amount of cash dividends distributed to common shareholders relative to the common stock's market value (price). *(p. 484)*

Dividends Corporation's distributions of assets to its owners. *(p. 14 & 53)*

Double-declining-balance (DDB) depreciation Depreciation equals beginning book value multiplied by 2 times the straight-line rate. *(p. 320)*

Double-entry accounting Accounting system in which each transaction affects at least two accounts and has at least one debit and one credit. *(p. 55)*

Double taxation Corporate income is taxed and then its later distribution through dividends is normally taxed again for shareholders.

Earnings (See *net income.*) *(p. 14)*

Earnings per share (EPS) Amount of income earned by each share of a company's outstanding common stock; also called *net income per share.* *(p. 483)*

Effective interest method Allocates interest expense over the bond life to yield a constant rate of interest; interest expense for a period is found by multiplying the balance of the liability at the beginning of the period by the bond market rate at issuance; also called *interest method.* *(p. 441)*

Efficiency Company's productivity in using its assets; usually measured relative to how much revenue a certain level of assets generates. *(p. 565)*

Electronic funds transfer (EFT) Use of electronic communication to transfer cash from one party to another. *(p. 263)*

Employee benefits Additional compensation paid to or on behalf of employees, such as premiums for medical, dental, life, and disability insurance, and contributions to pension plans. *(p. 385)*

Employee earnings report Record of an employee's net pay, gross pay, deductions, and year-to-date payroll information. *(p. 397)*

Enterprise resource planning (ERP) software Programs that manage a company's vital operations, which range from order taking to production to accounting. *(p. E-17)*

Entity Organization that, for accounting purposes, is separate from other organizations and individuals.

EOM Abbreviation for *end of month;* used to describe credit terms for credit transactions. *(p. 159)*

Equity Owner's claim on the assets of a business; equals the residual interest in an entity's assets after deducting liabilities; also called *net assets.* *(p. 14)*

Equity method Accounting method used for long-term investments when the investor has "significant influence" over the investee. *(p. C-7)*

Equity ratio Portion of total assets provided by equity, computed as total equity divided by total assets. *(p. 579)*

Equity securities with controlling influence Long-term investment when the investor is able to exert controlling influence over the investee; investors owning 50 percent or more of voting stock are presumed to exert controlling influence. *(p. C-8)*

Equity securities with significant influence Long-term investment when the investor is able to exert significant influence over the investee; investors owning 20 percent or more (but less than 50 percent) of voting stock are presumed to exert significant influence. *(p. C-7)*

Estimated liability Obligation of an uncertain amount that can be reasonably estimated. *(p. 385)*

Ethics Codes of conduct by which actions are judged as right or wrong, fair or unfair, honest or dishonest. *(p. 8)*

Events Happenings that both affect an organization's financial position and can be reliably measured. *(p. 15)*

Expanded accounting equation Assets = Liabilities + Equity; Equity equals [Contributed Capital + Retained Earnings + Revenues − Expenses] for a corporation where Dividends are subtracted from Retained Earnings. *(p. 14)*

Expense recognition principle (See Matching principle.) *(p. 11, 96)*

Expenses Outflows or using up of assets as part of operations of a business to generate sales. *(p. 14)*

External transactions Exchanges of economic value between one entity and another entity. *(p. 15)*

External users Persons using accounting information who are not directly involved in running the organization. *(p. 5)*

Extraordinary gains or losses Gains or losses reported separately from continuing operations because they are both unusual and infrequent. *(p. 589)*

Extraordinary repairs Major repairs that extend the useful life of a plant asset beyond prior expectations; treated as a capital expenditure. *(p. 343)*

Federal depository bank Bank authorized to accept deposits of amounts payable to the federal government. *(p. 395)*

Federal Insurance Contributions Act (FICA) Taxes Taxes assessed on both employers and employees; for Social Security and Medicare programs. *(p. 382)*

Federal Unemployment Taxes (FUTA) Payroll taxes on employers assessed by the federal government to support its unemployment insurance program. *(p. 384)*

Financial accounting Area of accounting mainly aimed at serving external users. *(p. 5)*

Financial Accounting Standards Board (FASB) Independent group of full-time members responsible for setting accounting rules. *(p. 9)*

Financial leverage Earning a higher return on equity by paying dividends on preferred stock or interest on debt at a rate lower than the return earned with the assets from issuing preferred stock or debt; also called *trading on the equity. (p. 491)*

Financial reporting Process of communicating information relevant to investors, creditors, and others in making investment, credit, and business decisions. *(p. 565)*

Financial statement analysis Application of analytical tools to general-purpose financial statements and related data for making business decisions. *(p. 564)*

Financial statements Includes the balance sheet, income statement, statement of stockholders' equity, and statement of cash flows. *(p. 19)*

Financing activities Transactions with owners and creditors that include obtaining cash from issuing long-term debt, repaying amounts borrowed, and obtaining cash from or distributing cash to owners. *(p. 512)*

First-in, first-out (FIFO) Method to assign cost to inventory that assumes items are sold in the order acquired; earliest items purchased are the first sold. *(p. 209)*

Fiscal year Consecutive 12-month (or 52-week) period chosen as the organization's annual accounting period. *(p. 95)*

Flexibility principle Information system principle that requires an accounting system be able to adapt to changes in the company, its operations, and needs of decision makers. *(p. E-3)*

FOB Abbreviation for *free on board;* the point when ownership of goods passes to the buyer; *FOB shipping point* (or *factory*) means the buyer pays shipping costs and accepts ownership of goods when the seller transfers goods to carrier; *FOB destination* means the seller pays shipping costs and buyer accepts ownership of goods at the buyer's place of business. *(p. 161)*

Foreign exchange rate Price of one currency stated in terms of another currency. *(p. C-14)*

Form 940 IRS form used to report an employer's federal unemployment taxes (FUTA) on an annual filing basis. *(p. 395)*

Form 941 IRS form filed to report FICA taxes owed and remitted. *(p. 393)*

Form 10-K (or 10-KSB) Annual report form filed with SEC by businesses (small businesses) with publicly-traded securities. *(p. A-1)*

Form W-2 Annual report by an employer to each employee showing the employee's wages subject to FICA and federal income taxes along with amounts withheld. *(p. 395)*

Form W-4 Withholding allowance certificate, filed with the employer, identifying the number of withholding allowances claimed. *(p. 397)*

Franchises Privileges granted by a company or government to sell a product or service under specified conditions. *(p. 349)*

Full disclosure principle Principle that prescribes financial statements (including notes) to report all relevant information about an entity's operations and financial condition. *(p. 11)*

GAAP (See *generally accepted accounting principles.*) *(p. 8)*

General and administrative expenses Expenses that support the operating activities of a business. *(p. 169)*

General journal All-purpose journal for recording the debits and credits of transactions and events. *(p. 51 & E-6)*

General ledger (See *ledger.*) *(p. 51)*

General partner Partner who assumes unlimited liability for the debts of the partnership; responsible for partnership management. *(p. D-3)*

General partnership Partnership in which all partners have mutual agency and unlimited liability for partnership debts. *(p. D-3)*

Generally accepted accounting principles (GAAP) Rules that specify acceptable accounting practices. *(p. 8)*

Generally accepted auditing standards (GAAS) Rules that specify acceptable auditing practices. *(p. 8)*

General-purpose financial statements Statements published periodically for use by a variety of interested parties; includes the income statement, balance sheet, statement of stockholders' equity (or statement of retained earnings), statement of cash flows, and notes to these statements. *(p. 565)*

Going-concern assumption Principle that requires financial statements to reflect the assumption that the business will continue operating. *(p. 11)*

Goodwill Amount by which a company's (or a segment's) value exceeds the value of its individual assets less its liabilities. *(p. 349)*

Gross margin (See *gross profit.*) *(p. 157)*

Gross margin ratio Gross margin (net sales minus cost of goods sold) divided by net sales; also called *gross profit ratio. (p. 172)*

Gross method Method of recording purchases at the full invoice price without deducting any cash discounts. *(p. 276)*

Gross pay Total compensation earned by an employee. *(p. 382)*

Gross profit Net sales minus cost of goods sold; also called *gross margin.* *(p. 156)*

Gross profit method Procedure to estimate inventory when the past gross profit rate is used to estimate cost of goods sold, which is then subtracted from the cost of goods available for sale. *(p. 229)*

Held-to-maturity (HTM) securities Debt securities that a company has the intent and ability to hold until they mature. *(p. C-5)*

Horizontal analysis Comparison of a company's financial condition and performance across time. *(p. 566)*

Impairment Diminishment of an asset value. *(p. 342 & 348)*

Imprest system Method to account for petty cash; maintains a constant balance in the fund, which equals cash plus petty cash receipts. *(p. 249)*

Inadequacy Condition in which the capacity of plant assets is too small to meet the company's production demands. *(p. 335)*

Income (See *net income.*) *(p. 14)*

Income statement Financial statement that subtracts expenses from revenues to yield a net income or loss over a specified period of time; also includes any gains or losses. *(p. 19)*

Income Summary Temporary account used only in the closing process to which the balances of revenue and expense accounts (including any gains or losses) are transferred; its balance is transferred to the retained earnings account. *(p. 109)*

Indefinite life Asset life that is not limited by legal, regulatory, contractural, competitive, economic, or other factors. *(p. 348)*

Indirect method Presentation that reports net income and then adjusts it by adding and subtracting items to yield net cash from operating activities on the statement of cash flows. *(p. 516)*

Information processor Component of an accounting system that interprets, transforms, and summarizes information for use in analysis and reporting. *(p. E-4)*

Information storage Component of an accounting system that keeps data in a form accessible to information processors. *(p. E-4)*

Infrequent gain or loss Gain or loss not expected to recur given the operating environment of the business. *(p. 590)*

Input device Means of capturing information from source documents that enables its transfer to information processors. *(p. E-4)*

Installment note Liability requiring a series of periodic payments to the lender. *(p. 430)*

Intangible assets Long-term assets (resources) used to produce or sell products or services; usually lack physical form and have uncertain benefits. *(p. 114 & 348)*

Interest Charge for using money (or other assets) loaned from one entity to another. *(p. 307)*

Interim financial statements Financial statements covering periods of less than one year; usually based on one-, three-, or six-month periods. *(p. 94 & 228)*

Internal controls or **Internal control system** All policies and procedures used to protect assets, ensure reliable accounting, promote efficient operations, and urge adherence to company policies. *(p. 250 & E-2)*

Internal transactions Activities within an organization that can affect the accounting equation. *(p. 15)*

Internal users Persons using accounting information who are directly involved in managing the organization. *(p. 6)*

International Accounting Standards Board (IASB) Group that identifies preferred accounting practices and encourages global acceptance; issues International Financial Reporting Standards (IFRS). *(p. 9)*

International Financial Reporting Standards (IFRS) IFRS is an abbreviation for International Financial Reporting Standards, which are set by the International Accounting Standards Board (IASB), headquartered in London; refers broadly to all pronouncements of the IASB. *(p. 9)*

Inventory Goods a company owns and expects to sell in its normal operations. *(p. 157)*

Inventory turnover Number of times a company's average inventory is sold during a period; computed by dividing cost of goods sold by average inventory; also called *merchandise turnover*. *(p. 217)*

Investing activities Transactions that involve purchasing and selling of long-term assets, includes making and collecting notes receivable and investments in other than cash equivalents. *(p. 512)*

Invoice Itemized record of goods prepared by the vendor that lists the customer's name, items sold, sales prices, and terms of sale. *(p. 273)*

Invoice approval Document containing a checklist of steps necessary for approving the recording and payment of an invoice; also called *check authorization*. *(p. 274)*

Journal Record in which transactions are entered before they are posted to ledger accounts; also called *book of original entry*. *(p. 56)*

Journalizing Process of recording transactions in a journal. *(p. 56)*

Known liabilities Obligations of a company with little uncertainty; set by agreements, contracts, or laws; also called *definitely determinable liabilities*. *(p. 378)*

Land improvements Assets that increase the benefits of land, have a limited useful life, and are depreciated. *(p. 334)*

Large stock dividend Stock dividend that is more than 25% of the previously outstanding shares. *(p. 472)*

Last-in, first-out (LIFO) Method to assign cost to inventory that assumes costs for the most recent items purchased are sold first and charged to cost of goods sold. *(p. 209)*

Lease Contract specifying the rental of property. *(p. 350 & 445)*

Leasehold Rights the lessor grants to the lessee under the terms of a lease. *(p. 350)*

Leasehold improvements Alterations or improvements to leased property such as partitions and storefronts. *(p. 350)*

Least-squares regression Statistical method for deriving an estimated line of cost behavior that is more precise than the high-low method and the scatter diagram.

Ledger Record containing all accounts (with amounts) for a business; also called *general ledger*. *(p. 51)*

Lessee Party to a lease who secures the right to possess and use the property from another party (the lessor). *(p. 350)*

Lessor Party to a lease who grants another party (the lessee) the right to possess and use its property. *(p. 350)*

Liabilities Creditors' claims on an organization's assets; involves a probable future payment of assets, products, or services that a company is obligated to make due to past transactions or events. *(p. 14)*

Licenses (See *franchises*.) *(p. 349)*

Limited liability Owner can lose no more than the amount invested.

Limited liability company Organization form that combines select features of a corporation and a limited partnership; provides limited liability to its members (owners), is free of business tax, and allows members to actively participate in management. *(p. D-4)*

Limited liability partnership Partnership in which a partner is not personally liable for malpractice or negligence unless that partner is responsible for providing the service that resulted in the claim. *(p. D-3)*

Limited life (See also *useful life*.) *(p. 348)*

Limited partners Partners who have no personal liability for partnership debts beyond the amounts they invested in the partnership. *(p. D-3)*

Limited partnership Partnership that has two classes of partners, limited partners and general partners. *(p. D-3)*

Liquid assets Resources such as cash that are easily converted into other assets or used to pay for goods, services, or liabilities. *(p. 255)*

Liquidating cash dividend Distribution of assets that returns part of the original investment to stockholders; deducted from contributed capital accounts. *(p. 472)*

Liquidation Process of going out of business; involves selling assets, paying liabilities, and distributing remainder to owners. *(p. D-11)*

Liquidity Availability of resources to meet short-term cash requirements. *(p. 255 & 565)*

List price Catalog (full) price of an item before any trade discount is deducted. *(p. 158)*

Long-term investments Long-term assets not used in operating activities such as notes receivable and investments in stocks and bonds. *(p. 114 & C-1)*

Long-term liabilities Obligations not due to be paid within one year or the operating cycle, whichever is longer. *(p. 115 & 397)*

Lower of cost or market (LCM) Required method to report inventory at market replacement cost when that market cost is lower than recorded cost. *(p. 213)*

Maker of the note Entity who signs a note and promises to pay it at maturity. *(p. 307)*

Managerial accounting Area of accounting mainly aimed at serving the decision-making needs of internal users; also called *management accounting*. *(p. 6)*

Manufacturer Company that uses labor and operating assets to convert raw materials to finished goods. *(p. 13)*

Market prospects Expectations (both good and bad) about a company's future performance as assessed by users and other interested parties. *(p. 565)*

Market rate Interest rate that borrowers are willing to pay and lenders are willing to accept for a specific lending agreement given the borrowers' risk level. *(p. 423)*

Market value per share Price at which stock is bought or sold. *(p. 467)*

Matching principle Prescribes expenses to be reported in the same period as the revenues that were earned as a result of the expenses. *(p. 11, 96 & 300)*

Materiality constraint Criterion that only information that would influence the decisions of a reasonable person need be disclosed. *(p. 12 & 301)*

Maturity date of a note Date when a note's principal and interest are due. *(p. 307)*

Measurement principle Accounting principle that prescribes transactions and events are measureable; commonly applied using historical costs, including variations that employ use of market measures such as replacement costs. *(p. 10)*

Merchandise (See *merchandise inventory.*) *(p. 156)*

Merchandise inventory Goods that a company owns and expects to sell to customers; also called *merchandise* or *inventory*. *(p. 157)*

Merchandiser Entity that earns net income by buying and selling merchandise. *(p. 157)*

Merit rating Rating assigned to an employer by a state based on the employer's record of employment. *(p. 384)*

Minimum legal capital Amount of assets defined by law that stockholders must (potentially) invest in a corporation; usually defined as par value of the stock; intended to protect creditors. *(p. 467)*

Modified Accelerated Cost Recovery System (MACRS) Depreciation system required by federal income tax law. *(p. 340)*

Monetary unit assumption Principle that assumes transactions and events can be expressed in money units. *(p. 11)*

Mortgage Legal loan agreement that protects a lender by giving the lender the right to be paid from the cash proceeds from the sale of a borrower's assets identified in the mortgage. *(p. 432)*

Multinational Company that operates in several countries. *(p. C-14)*

Multiple-step income statement Income statement format that shows subtotals between sales and net income, categorizes expenses, and often reports the details of net sales and expenses. *(p. 168)*

Mutual agency Legal relationship among partners whereby each partner is an agent of the partnership and is able to bind the partnership to contracts within the scope of the partnership's business. *(p. D-2)*

Natural business year Twelve-month period that ends when a company's sales activities are at their lowest point. *(p. 95)*

Natural resources Assets physically consumed when used; examples are timber, mineral deposits, and oil and gas fields; also called *wasting assets*. *(p. 346)*

Net assets (See *equity*.) *(p. 14)*

Net income Amount earned after subtracting all expenses necessary for and matched with sales for a period; also called *income, profit,* or *earnings*. *(p. 14)*

Net loss Excess of expenses over revenues for a period. *(p. 14)*

Net method Method of recording purchases at the full invoice price less any cash discounts. *(p. 276)*

Net pay Gross pay less all deductions; also called *take-home pay*. *(p. 382)*

Net realizable value Expected selling price (value) of an item minus the cost of making the sale. *(p. 204)*

Noncumulative preferred stock Preferred stock on which the right to receive dividends is lost for any period when dividends are not declared. *(p. 476)*

Noninterest-bearing note Note with no stated (contract) rate of interest; interest is implicitly included in the note's face value.

Nonparticipating preferred stock Preferred stock on which dividends are limited to a maximum amount each year. *(p. 476)*

Nonsufficient funds (NSF) check Maker's bank account has insufficient money to pay the check; also called *hot check*.

No-par value stock Stock class that has not been assigned a par (or stated) value by the corporate charter. *(p. 467)*

Not controllable costs Costs that a manager does not have the power to control or strongly influence.

Note (See *promissory note*.) *(p. 306)*

Note payable Liability expressed by a written promise to pay a definite sum of money on demand or on a specific future date(s). *(p. 52)*

Note receivable Asset consisting of a written promise to receive a definite sum of money on demand or on a specific future date(s). *(p. 51)*

Objectivity principle Principle that prescribes independent, unbiased evidence to support financial statement information. *(p. 10)*

Obsolescence Condition in which, because of new inventions and improvements, a plant asset can no longer be used to produce goods or services with a competitive advantage. *(p. 335)*

Off-balance-sheet financing Acquisition of assets by agreeing to liabilities not reported on the balance sheet. *(p. 445)*

Online processing Approach to inputting data from source documents as soon as the information is available. *(p. E-16)*

Operating activities Activities that involve the production or purchase of merchandise and the sale of goods or services to customers, including expenditures related to administering the business. *(p. 511)*

Operating cycle Normal time between paying cash for merchandise or employee services and receiving cash from customers. *(p. 113)*

Operating leases Short-term (or cancelable) leases in which the lessor retains risks and rewards of ownership. *(p. 445)*

Ordinary repairs Repairs to keep a plant asset in normal, good operating condition; treated as a revenue expenditure and immediately expensed. *(p. 343)*

Organization expenses (costs) Costs such as legal fees and promoter fees to bring an entity into existence. *(p. 465 & 470)*

Out-of-pocket cost Cost incurred or avoided as a result of management's decisions. *(p. 599)*

Output devices Means by which information is taken out of the accounting system and made available for use. *(p. E-5)*

Outsourcing Manager decision to buy a product or service from another entity; part of a *make-or-buy* decision; also called *make or buy.*

Outstanding checks Checks written and recorded by the depositor but not yet paid by the bank at the bank statement date. *(p. 266)*

Outstanding stock Corporation's stock held by its shareholders.

Owner investment Assets put into the business by the owner.

Owner's equity (See *equity* or *stockholders' equity.*)

Owner withdrawals (See *withdrawals.*) *(p. 53)*

Paid-in capital (See *contributed capital.*) *(p. 13 & 468)*

Paid-in capital in excess of par value Amount received from issuance of stock that is in excess of the stock's par value. *(p. 469)*

Par value Value assigned a share of stock by the corporate charter when the stock is authorized. *(p. 467)*

Par value of a bond Amount the bond issuer agrees to pay at maturity and the amount on which cash interest payments are based; also called *face amount* or *face value* of a bond. *(p. 420)*

Par value stock Class of stock assigned a par value by the corporate charter. *(p. 467)*

Parent Company that owns a controlling interest in a corporation (requires more than 50% of voting stock). *(p. C-8)*

Participating preferred stock Preferred stock that shares with common stockholders any dividends paid in excess of the percent stated on preferred stock. *(p. 476)*

Partner return on equity Partner net income divided by average partner equity for the period. *(p. D-14)*

Partnership Unincorporated association of two or more persons to pursue a business for profit as co-owners. *(p. 11 & D-2)*

Partnership contract Agreement among partners that sets terms under which the affairs of the partnership are conducted; also called *articles of partnership.* *(p. D-2)*

Partnership liquidation Dissolution of a partnership by (1) selling noncash assets and allocating any gain or loss according to partners' income-and-loss ratio, (2) paying liabilities, and (3) distributing any remaining cash according to partners' capital balances. *(p. D-12)*

Patent Exclusive right granted to its owner to produce and sell an item or to use a process for 20 years. *(p. 348)*

Payee of the note Entity to whom a note is made payable. *(p. 307)*

Payroll bank account Bank account used solely for paying employees; each pay period an amount equal to the total employees' net pay is deposited in it and the payroll checks are drawn on it. *(p. 397)*

Payroll deductions Amounts withheld from an employee's gross pay; also called *withholdings.* *(p. 382)*

Payroll register Record for a pay period that shows the pay period dates, regular and overtime hours worked, gross pay, net pay, and deductions. *(p. 395)*

Pension plan Contractual agreement between an employer and its employees for the employer to provide benefits to employees after they retire; expensed when incurred. *(p. 446)*

Periodic inventory system Method that records the cost of inventory purchased but does not continuously track the quantity available or sold to customers; records are updated at the end of each period to reflect the physical count and costs of goods available. *(p. 158 & 177)*

Permanent accounts Accounts that reflect activities related to one or more future periods; balance sheet accounts whose balances are not closed; also called *real accounts.* *(p. 108)*

Perpetual inventory system Method that maintains continuous records of the cost of inventory available and the cost of goods sold. *(p. 158)*

Petty cash Small amount of cash in a fund to pay minor expenses; accounted for using an imprest system. *(p. 260)*

Plant assets Tangible long-lived assets used to produce or sell products and services; also called *property, plant and equipment (PP&E)* or *fixed assets.* *(p. 99 & 332)*

Pledged assets to secured liabilities Ratio of the book value of a company's pledged assets to the book value of its secured liabilities.

Post-closing trial balance List of permanent accounts and their balances from the ledger after all closing entries are journalized and posted. *(p. 110)*

Posting Process of transferring journal entry information to the ledger; computerized systems automate this process. *(p. 56)*

Posting reference (PR) column A column in journals in which individual ledger account numbers are entered when entries are posted to those ledger accounts. *(p. 58)*

Preemptive right Stockholders' right to maintain their proportionate interest in a corporation with any additional shares issued. *(p. 466)*

Preferred stock Stock with a priority status over common stockholders in one or more ways, such as paying dividends or distributing assets. *(p. 475)*

Premium on bonds Difference between a bond's par value and its higher carrying value; occurs when the contract rate is higher than the market rate; also called *bond premium.* *(p. 426)*

Premium on stock (See *contributed capital in excess of par value.*) *(p. 469)*

Prepaid expenses Items paid for in advance of receiving their benefits; classified as assets. *(p. 97)*

Price-earnings (PE) ratio Ratio of a company's current market value per share to its earnings per share; also called *price-to-earnings.* *(p. 484)*

Principal of a note Amount that the signer of a note agrees to pay back when it matures, not including interest. *(p. 307)*

Principles of internal control Principles prescribing management to establish responsibility, maintain records, insure assets, separate recordkeeping from custody of assets, divide responsibility for related transactions, apply technological controls, and perform reviews. *(p. 251)*

Prior period adjustment Correction of an error in a prior year that is reported in the statement of retained earnings (or statement of stockholders' equity) net of any income tax effects. *(p. 481)*

Pro forma financial statements Statements that show the effects of proposed transactions and events as if they had occurred. *(p. 126)*

Profit (See *net income.*)

Profit margin Ratio of a company's net income to its net sales; the percent of income in each dollar of revenue; also called *net profit margin. (p. 116)*

Profitability Company's ability to generate an adequate return on invested capital. *(p. 565)*

Promissory note (or **note**) Written promise to pay a specified amount either on demand or at a definite future date; is a *note receivable* for the lender but a *note payable* for the lendee. *(p. 306)*

Proprietorship (See *sole proprietorship.*) *(p. 11)*

Proxy Legal document giving a stockholder's agent the power to exercise the stockholder's voting rights. *(p. 465)*

Purchase discount Term used by a purchaser to describe a cash discount granted to the purchaser for paying within the discount period. *(p. 159)*

Purchase order Document used by the purchasing department to place an order with a seller (vendor). *(p. 273)*

Purchase requisition Document listing merchandise needed by a department and requesting it be purchased. *(p. 273)*

Purchases journal Journal normally used to record all purchases on credit. *(p. E-13)*

Ratio analysis Determination of key relations between financial statement items as reflected in numerical measures. *(p. 566)*

Realizable value Expected proceeds from converting an asset into cash. *(p. 301)*

Receiving report Form used to report that ordered goods are received and to describe their quantity and condition. *(p. 274)*

Recordkeeping Part of accounting that involves recording transactions and events, either manually or electronically; also called *bookkeeping. (p. 4)*

Registered bonds Bonds owned by investors whose names and addresses are recorded by the issuer; interest payments are made to the registered owners. *(p. 434)*

Relevance principle Information system principle prescribing that its reports be useful, understandable, timely, and pertinent for decision making. *(p. E-2)*

Report form balance sheet Balance sheet that lists accounts vertically in the order of assets, liabilities, and equity. *(p. 18)*

Restricted retained earnings Retained earnings that are not available for dividends because of legal or contractual limitations. *(p. 481)*

Retail inventory method Method to estimate ending inventory based on the ratio of the amount of goods for sale at cost to the amount of goods for sale at retail. *(p. 228)*

Retailer Intermediary that buys products from manufacturers or wholesalers and sells them to consumers. *(p. 156)*

Retained earnings Cumulative income less cumulative losses and dividends. *(p. 14 & 468)*

Retained earnings deficit Debit (abnormal) balance in Retained Earnings; occurs when cumulative losses and dividends exceed cumulative income; also called *accumulated deficit. (p. 471)*

Return Monies received from an investment; often in percent form. *(p. 26)*

Return on assets (See *return on total assets*) *(p. 22)*

Return on total assets Ratio reflecting operating efficiency; defined as net income divided by average total assets for the period; also called *return on assets* or *return on investment. (p. C-11)*

Return on equity Ratio of net income to average equity for the period.

Revenue expenditures Expenditures reported on the current income statement as an expense because they do not provide benefits in future periods. *(p. 342)*

Revenue recognition principle The principle prescribing that revenue is recognized when earned. *(p. 11)*

Revenues Gross increase in equity from a company's business activities that earn income; also called *sales. (p. 14)*

Reverse stock split Occurs when a corporation calls in its stock and replaces each share with less than one new share; increases both market value per share and any par or stated value per share. *(p. 474)*

Reversing entries Optional entries recorded at the beginning of a period that prepare the accounts for the usual journal entries as if adjusting entries had not occurred in the prior period. *(p. 126)*

Risk Uncertainty about an expected return. *(p. 26)*

S corporation Corporation that meets special tax qualifications so as to be treated like a partnership for income tax purposes. *(p. D-4)*

Sales (See *revenues.*) *(p. 13)*

Sales discount Term used by a seller to describe a cash discount granted to buyers who pay within the discount period. *(p. 159)*

Sales journal Journal normally used to record sales of goods on credit. *(p. E-8)*

Salvage value Estimate of amount to be recovered at the end of an asset's useful life; also called *residual value* or *scrap value. (p. 335)*

Sarbanes-Oxley Act Created the *Public Company Accounting Oversight Board,* regulates analyst conflicts, impose coporate governance requirement, enhances accounting and control disclosures, impacts insider transactions and executive loans, establishes new types of criminal conduct, and expands penalties for violations of federal securities laws *(p. 12 & 250)*

Schedule of accounts payable List of the balances of all accounts in the accounts payable ledger and their total. *(p. E-14)*

Schedule of accounts receivable List of the balances for all accounts in the accounts receivable ledger and their total. *(p. E-9)*

Section 404 (of SOX) Section 404 of the Sarbanes-Oxley Act requires that management document and assess all internal control processes that impact financial reporting *(p. 251)*

Secured bonds Bonds that have specific assets of the issuer pledged as collateral. *(p. 434)*

Securities and Exchange Commission (SEC) Federal agency Congress has charged to set reporting rules for organizations that sell ownership shares to the public. *(p. 9)*

Segment return on assets Segment operating income divided by segment average (identifiable) assets for the period. *(p. E-18)*

Selling expenses Expenses of promoting sales, such as displaying and advertising merchandise, making sales, and delivering goods to customers. *(p. 169)*

Serial bonds Bonds consisting of separate amounts that mature at different dates. *(p. 434)*

Service company Organization that provides services instead of tangible products. *(p. 156)*

Shareholders Owners of a corporation; also called *stockholders. (p. 12)*

Shares Equity of a corporation divided into ownership units; also called *stock. (p. 12)*

Short-term investments Debt and equity securities that management expects to convert to cash within the next 3 to 12 months (or the operating cycle if longer); also called *temporary investments* or *marketable securities. (p. C-1)*

Short-term note payable Current obligation in the form of a written promissory note. *(p. 379)*

Shrinkage Inventory losses that occur as a result of theft or deterioration. *(p. 166)*

Signature card Includes the signatures of each person authorized to sign checks on the bank account. *(p. 263)*

Simple capital structure Capital structure that consists of only common stock and nonconvertible preferred stock; consists of no dilutive securities. *(p. 484)*

Single-step income statement Income statement format that includes cost of goods sold as an expense and shows only one subtotal for total expenses. *(p. 169)*

Sinking fund bonds Bonds that require the issuer to make deposits to a separate account; bondholders are repaid at maturity from that account. *(p. 434)*

Small stock dividend Stock dividend that is 25% or less of a corporation's previously outstanding shares. *(p. 472)*

Social responsibility Being accountable for the impact that one's actions might have on society. *(p. 8)*

Sole proprietorship Business owned by one person that is not organized as a corporation; also called *proprietorship. (p. 11)*

Solvency Company's long-run financial viability and its ability to cover long-term obligations. *(p. 565)*

Source documents Source of information for accounting entries that can be in either paper or electronic form; also called *business papers. (p. 50)*

Special journal Any journal used for recording and posting transactions of a similar type. *(p. E-6)*

Specific identification Method to assign cost to inventory when the purchase cost of each item in inventory is identified and used to compute cost of inventory. *(p. 207)*

Spreadsheet Computer program that organizes data by means of formulas and format; also called *electronic work sheet.*

State Unemployment Taxes (SUTA) State payroll taxes on employers to support its unemployment programs. *(p. 384)*

Stated value stock No-par stock assigned a stated value per share; this amount is recorded in the stock account when the stock is issued. *(p. 468)*

Statement of cash flows A financial statement that lists cash inflows (receipts) and cash outflows (payments) during a period; arranged by operating, investing, and financing. *(p. 19 & 510)*

Statement of partners' equity Financial statement that shows total capital balances at the beginning of the period, any additional investment by partners, the income or loss of the period, the partners' withdrawals, and the partners' ending capital balances; also called *statement of partners' capital. (p. D-7)*

Statement of retained earnings Report of changes in retained earnings over a period; adjusted for increases (net income), for decreases (dividends and net loss), and for any prior period adjustment. *(p. 19)*

Statement of shareholders' equity (See *statement of stockholders' equity;* also called *statement of owners' equity.*)

Statement of stockholders' equity Financial statement that lists the beginning and ending balances of each major equity account and describes all changes in those accounts. *(p. 482)*

Statements of Financial Accounting Standards (SFAS) FASB publications that establish U.S. GAAP. *(p. 9)*

Stock (See *shares.*) *(p. 12)*

Stock dividend Corporation's distribution of its own stock to its stockholders without the receipt of any payment. *(p. 472)*

Stock options Rights to purchase common stock at a fixed price over a specified period of time. *(p. 482)*

Stock split Occurs when a corporation calls in its stock and replaces each share with more than one new share; decreases both the market value per share and any par or stated value per share. *(p. 474)*

Stock subscription Investor's contractual commitment to purchase unissued shares at future dates and prices.

Stockholders' equity A corporation's equity; also called *shareholders' equity* or *corporate capital. (p. 468)*

Stockholders (See *shareholders.*) *(p. 12)*

Straight-line depreciation Method that allocates an equal portion of the depreciable cost of plant asset (cost minus salvage) to each accounting period in its useful life. *(p. 99 & 336)*

Straight-line bond amortization Method allocating an equal amount of bond interest expense to each period of the bond life. *(p. 424)*

Subsidiary Entity controlled by another entity (parent) in which the parent owns more than 50% of the subsidiary's voting stock. *(p. C-8)*

Subsidiary ledger List of individual sub-accounts and amounts with a common characteristic; linked to a controlling account in the general ledger. *(p. E-6)*

Supplementary records Information outside the usual accounting records; also called *supplemental records*. *(p. 162)*

Supply chain Linkages of services or goods extending from suppliers, to the company itself, and on to customers.

T-account Tool used to show the effects of transactions and events on individual accounts. *(p. 55)*

Temporary accounts Accounts used to record revenues, expenses, and dividends; they are closed at the end of each period; also called *nominal accounts*. *(p. 108)*

Term bonds Bonds scheduled for payment (maturity) at a single specified date. *(p. 434)*

Time period principle Assumption that an organization's activities can be divided into specific time periods such as months, quarters, or years. *(p. 11 & 94)*

Times interest earned Ratio of income before interest expense (and any income taxes) divided by interest expense; reflects risk of covering interest commitments when income varies. *(p. 390)*

Total asset turnover Measure of a company's ability to use its assets to generate sales; computed by dividing net sales by average total assets. *(p. 352)*

Trade discount Reduction from a list or catalog price that can vary for wholesalers, retailers, and consumers. *(p. 158)*

Trademark or trade (brand) name Symbol, name, phrase, or jingle identified with a company, product, or service. *(p. 349)*

Trading on the equity (See *financial leverage*.) *(p. 491)*

Trading securities Investments in debt and equity securities that the company intends to actively trade for profit. *(p. C-4)*

Transaction Exchange of economic consideration affecting an entity's financial position that can be reliably measured. *(p. 13)*

Treasury stock Corporation's own stock that it reacquired and still holds. *(p. 478)*

Trial balance List of accounts and their balances at a point in time; total debit balances equal total credit balances. *(p. 65)*

Unadjusted trial balance List of accounts and balances prepared before accounting adjustments are recorded and posted. *(p. 106)*

Unclassified balance sheet Balance sheet that broadly groups assets, liabilities, and equity accounts. *(p. 113)*

Unearned revenue Liability created when customers pay in advance for products or services; earned when the products or services are later delivered. *(p. 53 & 100)*

Unit contribution margin Amount a product's unit selling price exceeds its total unit variable cost.

Units-of-production depreciation Method that charges a varying amount to depreciation expense for each period of an asset's useful life depending on its usage. *(p. 337)*

Unlimited liability Legal relationship among general partners that makes each of them responsible for partnership debts if the other partners are unable to pay their shares. *(p. D-3)*

Unrealized gain (loss) Gain (loss) not yet realized by an actual transaction or event such as a sale. *(p. C-4)*

Unsecured bonds Bonds backed only by the issuer's credit standing; almost always riskier than secured bonds; also called *debentures*. *(p. 434)*

Unusual gain or loss Gain or loss that is abnormal or unrelated to the company's ordinary activities and environment. *(p. 589)*

Useful life Length of time an asset will be productively used in the operations of a business; also called *service life* or *limited life*. *(p. 335)*

Vendee Buyer of goods or services. *(p. 273)*

Vendor Seller of goods or services. *(p. 273)*

Vertical analysis Evaluation of each financial statement item or group of items in terms of a specific base amount. *(p. 566)*

Voucher Internal file used to store documents and information to control cash disbursements and to ensure that a transaction is properly authorized and recorded. *(p. 259)*

Voucher register Journal (referred to as *book of original entry*) in which all vouchers are recorded after they have been approved. *(p. 275)*

Voucher system Procedures and approvals designed to control cash disbursements and acceptance of obligations. *(p. 258)*

Wage bracket withholding table Table of the amounts of income tax withheld from employees' wages. *(p. 397)*

Warranty Agreement that obligates the seller to correct or replace a product or service when it fails to perform properly within a specified period. *(p. 402)*

Weighted average Method to assign inventory cost to sales; the cost of available-for-sale units is divided by the number of units available to determine per unit cost prior to each sale that is then multiplied by the units sold to yield the cost of that sale *(p. 210 & 226)*

Wholesaler Intermediary that buys products from manufacturers or other wholesalers and sells them to retailers or other wholesalers. *(p. 156)*

Withdrawals Payment of cash or other assets from a proprietorship or partnership to its owner or owners. *(p. 13)*

Work sheet Spreadsheet used to draft an unadjusted trial balance, adjusting entries, adjusted trial balance, and financial statements. *(p. 123)*

Working capital Current assets minus current liabilities at a point in time. *(p. 575)*

Working papers Analyses and other informal reports prepared by accountants and managers when organizing information for formal reports and financial statements. *(p. 123)*

Credits

Chapter 1
Page 1: AP Images/Paul Sakuma, FILE; page 8: ©Hiroko Masuike/Getty Images; page 10: ©Mel Curtis/Getty Images; page 11: ©Joe Robbins/Getty Images; page 15: ©Sam Sharpe/Corbis.

Chapter 2
Page 48: Courtesy of Spanx; page 52: Courtesy of Spanx; page 53: ©Jonathan Daniel/Getty Images; page 54: © 2007 NBAE.Photo by Joe Murphy/NBAE via Getty Images.

Chapter 3
Page 92: Courtesy of PopCap Games, Inc.; page 95: ©HENNY RAY ABRAMS/AFP/Getty Images; page 113: ©Brian Bahr/Getty Images.

Chapter 4
Page 154: ©Asia Kepka; page 161: ©Anne-Marie Weber/Getty Images/Taxi; page 165: ©Michael Newman/PhotoEdit.

Chapter 5
Page 202: Courtesy of Beauty Encounter, Photo: Larry Atil Content: Jacquelyn Tran; page 205: ©Sam Ogden/Photo Researchers, Inc.

Chapter 6
Page 248: ©Gustavo Caballero/Getty Images; page 252: ©Lawrence Lawry/ Getty Images/Photodisc; page 258: ©Bob Daemmrich/The Image Works.

Chapter 7
Page 294: AP Images/Nick Wass; page 298: AP images/Mark Lennihan; page 299: ©Car Culture/Corbis.

Chapter 8
Page 330: Courtesy of Sambazon.com; page 333: ©David M. Grossman/The Image Works; page 334: ©Lester Lefkowitz/ Getty Images/The Image Bank; page 336: © Ilene MacDonald/Alamy; page 341: ©George Tiedemann/GT Images/Corbis; page 346: ©Digital Vision/Getty Images; page 348: ©Scott Halleran/Getty Images.

Chapter 9
Page 374: Dennis Kleiman/Courtesy of Noodles & Company; page 379: ©Michael Loccisano/FilmMagic/Getty Images; page 381: ©JUPITERIMAGES/Thinkstock/Alamy; page 386: ©STEPHEN JAFFE/AFP/Getty Images; page 389: ©John Burcham/National Geographic/Getty Images.

Chapter 10
Page 418: Courtesy of Feed Granola Company; page 422: Courtesy of Dow Chemicals.

Chapter 11
Page 462: Courtesy of Inogen, Inc.; page 466: Courtesy of Green Bay Packers, Inc.

Chapter 12
Page 508: Courtesy of Jungle Jim's International Market; page 510: AP Images/Brian Kersey; page 516: ©Corbis Super RF/Alamy.

Chapter 13
Page 562: ©Dirck Halstead/Liaison/Getty Images; page 578: AP Images/Ben Margot; page 584: AP Images/Chuck Burton.

Appendix C
Page C-4: AP Images/Richard Drew.

Appendix D
Page D-3: ©David R. Frazier Photolibrary, Inc./Alamy; page D-5: ©Erik Freeland/Corbis; page D-8: ©Bill Bachmann/Alamy; page D-11: ©James Doberman/Getty Images/Iconica.

Appendix E
Page E-4: AP Images/Eric Risberg; page E-5: ©Royalty-Free/CORBIS; page E-7: ©Jody Dole/Getty Images/The Image Bank; page E-12: AP Images/Topeka Capital-Journal, David Eulitt; page E-16: ©Nick Koudis/Getty Images/PhotoDisc; page E-17: ©Sonda Dawes/The Image Works.

Index

A page number followed by an *e* indicates an exhibit on that page; an *n*, a footnote. A term with page number in **bold** indicates a definition.

Chart of Accounts

Following is a typical chart of accounts, which we use in various assignments. Every company has its own unique accounts and numbering system.

Assets

Current Assets

101 Cash
102 Petty cash
103 Cash equivalents
104 Short-term investments
105 Fair value adjustment, _____ securities (S-T)
106 Accounts receivable
107 Allowance for doubtful accounts
108 Legal fees receivable
109 Interest receivable
110 Rent receivable
111 Notes receivable
119 Merchandise inventory
120 _____ inventory
121 _____ inventory
124 Office supplies
125 Store supplies
126 _____ supplies
128 Prepaid insurance
129 Prepaid interest
131 Prepaid rent
132 Raw materials inventory
133 Goods in process inventory, _____
134 Goods in process inventory, _____
135 Finished goods inventory

Long-Term Investments

141 Long-term investments
142 Fair value adjustment, _____ securities (L-T)
144 Investment in _____
145 Bond sinking fund

Plant Assets

151 Automobiles
152 Accumulated depreciation—Automobiles
153 Trucks
154 Accumulated depreciation—Trucks
155 Boats
156 Accumulated depreciation—Boats
157 Professional library
158 Accumulated depreciation—Professional library
159 Law library
160 Accumulated depreciation—Law library
161 Furniture
162 Accumulated depreciation—Furniture
163 Office equipment
164 Accumulated depreciation—Office equipment
165 Store equipment
166 Accumulated depreciation—Store equipment
167 _____ equipment
168 Accumulated depreciation—_____ equipment
169 Machinery
170 Accumulated depreciation—Machinery
173 Building _____
174 Accumulated depreciation—Building _____
175 Building _____
176 Accumulated depreciation—Building _____
179 Land improvements _____
180 Accumulated depreciation—Land improvements _____
181 Land improvements _____
182 Accumulated depreciation—Land improvements _____
183 Land

Natural Resources

185 Mineral deposit
186 Accumulated depletion—Mineral deposit

Intangible Assets

191 Patents
192 Leasehold
193 Franchise
194 Copyrights
195 Leasehold improvements
196 Licenses
197 Accumulated amortization—_____

Liabilities

Current Liabilities

201 Accounts payable
202 Insurance payable
203 Interest payable
204 Legal fees payable
207 Office salaries payable
208 Rent payable
209 Salaries payable
210 Wages payable
211 Accrued payroll payable
214 Estimated warranty liability
215 Income taxes payable
216 Common dividend payable
217 Preferred dividend payable
218 State unemployment taxes payable
219 Employee federal income taxes payable
221 Employee medical insurance payable
222 Employee retirement program payable
223 Employee union dues payable
224 Federal unemployment taxes payable
225 FICA taxes payable
226 Estimated vacation pay liability

Unearned Revenues

230 Unearned consulting fees
231 Unearned legal fees
232 Unearned property management fees
233 Unearned _____ fees
234 Unearned _____ fees
235 Unearned janitorial revenue
236 Unearned _____ revenue
238 Unearned rent

Notes Payable

240 Short-term notes payable
241 Discount on short-term notes payable
245 Notes payable
251 Long-term notes payable
252 Discount on long-term notes payable

Long-Term Liabilities

253 Long-term lease liability
255 Bonds payable
256 Discount on bonds payable
257 Premium on bonds payable
258 Deferred income tax liability

Equity

Owner's Equity

301 _____, Capital
302 _____, Withdrawals
303 _____, Capital
304 _____, Withdrawals
305 _____, Capital
306 _____, Withdrawals

Paid-In Capital

307 Common stock, $ _____ par value
308 Common stock, no-par value
309 Common stock, $ _____ stated value
310 Common stock dividend distributable
311 Paid-in capital in excess of par value, Common stock
312 Paid-in capital in excess of stated value, No-par common stock
313 Paid-in capital from retirement of common stock
314 Paid-in capital, Treasury stock
315 Preferred stock
316 Paid-in capital in excess of par value, Preferred stock

Retained Earnings

318 Retained earnings
319 Cash dividends (or Dividends)
320 Stock dividends

Other Equity Accounts

321 Treasury stock, Common
322 Unrealized gain—Equity
323 Unrealized loss—Equity

Revenues

401 _____ fees earned
402 _____ fees earned
403 _____ services revenue
404 _____ services revenue
405 Commissions earned
406 Rent revenue (or Rent earned)
407 Dividends revenue (or Dividend earned)
408 Earnings from investment in _____
409 Interest revenue (or Interest earned)
410 Sinking fund earnings
413 Sales
414 Sales returns and allowances
415 Sales discounts

Cost of Sales

Cost of Goods Sold

502 Cost of goods sold
505 Purchases
506 Purchases returns and allowances
507 Purchases discounts
508 Transportation-in

Manufacturing

520 Raw materials purchases
521 Freight-in on raw materials
530 Factory payroll
531 Direct labor
540 Factory overhead
541 Indirect materials
542 Indirect labor
543 Factory insurance expired
544 Factory supervision
545 Factory supplies used
546 Factory utilities
547 Miscellaneous production costs
548 Property taxes on factory building
549 Property taxes on factory equipment
550 Rent on factory building
551 Repairs, factory equipment
552 Small tools written off
560 Depreciation of factory equipment
561 Depreciation of factory building

Standard Cost Variance

580 Direct material quantity variance
581 Direct material price variance
582 Direct labor quantity variance
583 Direct labor price variance
584 Factory overhead volume variance
585 Factory overhead controllable variance

Expenses

Amortization, Depletion, and Depreciation

601 Amortization expense—_____
602 Amortization expense—_____
603 Depletion expense—_____
604 Depreciation expense—Boats
605 Depreciation expense—Automobiles
606 Depreciation expense—Building _____
607 Depreciation expense—Building _____
608 Depreciation expense—Land improvements _____
609 Depreciation expense—Land improvements _____
610 Depreciation expense—Law library
611 Depreciation expense—Trucks
612 Depreciation expense—_____ equipment
613 Depreciation expense—_____ equipment
614 Depreciation expense—_____
615 Depreciation expense—_____

Employee-Related Expenses

620 Office salaries expense
621 Sales salaries expense
622 Salaries expense
623 _____ wages expense
624 Employees' benefits expense
625 Payroll taxes expense

Financial Expenses

630 Cash over and short
631 Discounts lost
632 Factoring fee expense
633 Interest expense

Insurance Expenses

635 Insurance expense—Delivery equipment
636 Insurance expense—Office equipment
637 Insurance expense—_____

Rental Expenses

640 Rent expense
641 Rent expense—Office space
642 Rent expense—Selling space
643 Press rental expense
644 Truck rental expense
645 _____ rental expense

Supplies Expenses

650 Office supplies expense
651 Store supplies expense
652 _____ supplies expense
653 _____ supplies expense

Miscellaneous Expenses

655 Advertising expense
656 Bad debts expense
657 Blueprinting expense
658 Boat expense
659 Collection expense
661 Concessions expense
662 Credit card expense
663 Delivery expense
664 Dumping expense
667 Equipment expense
668 Food and drinks expense
671 Gas and oil expense
672 General and administrative expense
673 Janitorial expense
674 Legal fees expense
676 Mileage expense
677 Miscellaneous expenses
678 Mower and tools expense
679 Operating expense
680 Organization expense
681 Permits expense
682 Postage expense
683 Property taxes expense
684 Repairs expense—_____
685 Repairs expense—_____
687 Selling expense
688 Telephone expense
689 Travel and entertainment expense
690 Utilities expense
691 Warranty expense
695 Income taxes expense

Gains and Losses

701 Gain on retirement of bonds
702 Gain on sale of machinery
703 Gain on sale of investments
704 Gain on sale of trucks
705 Gain on _____
706 Foreign exchange gain or loss
801 Loss on disposal of machinery
802 Loss on exchange of equipment
803 Loss on exchange of _____
804 Loss on sale of notes
805 Loss on retirement of bonds
806 Loss on sale of investments
807 Loss on sale of machinery
808 Loss on _____
809 Unrealized gain—Income
810 Unrealized loss—Income
811 Impairment gain
812 Impairment loss

Clearing Accounts

901 Income summary
902 Manufacturing summary

A Rose by Any Other Name

The same financial statement sometimes receives different titles. Following are some of the more common aliases.*

Balance Sheet	Statement of Financial Position
	Statement of Financial Condition
Income Statement	Statement of Income
	Operating Statement
	Statement of Operations
	Statement of Operating Activity
	Earnings Statement
	Statement of Earnings
	Profit and Loss (P&L) Statement
Statement of Cash Flows	Statement of Cash Flow
	Cash Flows Statement
	Statement of Changes in Cash Position
	Statement of Changes in Financial Position
Statement of Stockholders' Equity	Statement of Shareholders' Equity
	Statement of Changes in Shareholders' Equity
	Statement of Stockholders' Equity and Comprehensive Income
	Statement of Owners' Equity
	Statement of Changes in Capital Accounts

* The term **Consolidated** often precedes or follows these statement titles to reflect the combination of different entities, such as a parent company and its subsidiaries.

We thank Dr. Louella Moore from Arkansas State University for suggesting this listing.

SELECTED TRANSACTIONS AND RELATIONS

① Merchandising Transactions Summary

Merchandising Transactions		Merchandising Entries	Dr.	Cr.
Purchases	Purchasing merchandise for resale.	Merchandise Inventory	#	
		Cash or Accounts Payable		#
	Paying freight costs on purchases; FOB shipping point.	Merchandise Inventory	#	
		Cash		#
	Paying within discount period.	Accounts Payable	#	
		Merchandise Inventory		#
		Cash		#
	Recording purchase returns or allowances.	Cash or Accounts Payable	#	
		Merchandise Inventory		#
Sales	Selling merchandise.	Cash or Accounts Receivable	#	
		Sales		#
		Cost of Goods Sold	#	
		Merchandise Inventory		#
	Receiving payment within discount period.	Cash	#	
		Sales Discounts	#	
		Accounts Receivable		#
	Granting sales returns or allowances.	Sales Returns and Allowances	#	
		Cash or Accounts Receivable		#
		Merchandise Inventory	#	
		Cost of Goods Sold		#
	Paying freight costs on sales; FOB destination.	Delivery Expense	#	
		Cash		#

Merchandising Events		Adjusting and Closing Entries	Dr.	Cr.
Adjusting	Adjusting due to shrinkage (occurs when recorded amount larger than physical inventory).	Cost of Goods Sold	#	
		Merchandise Inventory		#
Closing	Closing temporary accounts with credit balances.	Sales	#	
		Income Summary		#
	Closing temporary accounts with debit balances.	Income Summary	#	
		Sales Returns and Allowances		#
		Sales Discounts		#
		Cost of Goods Sold		#
		Delivery Expense		#
		"Other Expenses"		#

② Merchandising Cash Flows

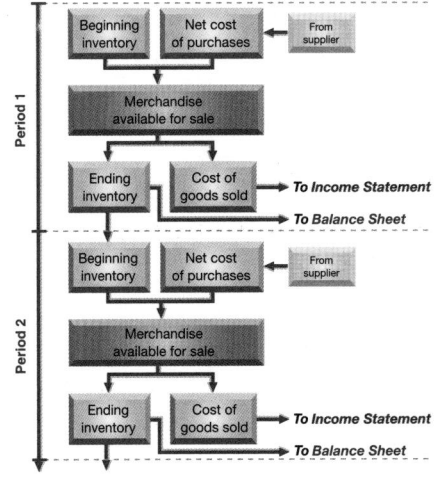

③ Credit Terms and Amounts

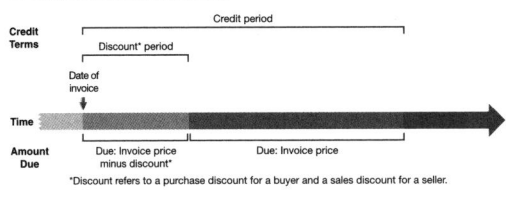

*Discount refers to a purchase discount for a buyer and a sales discount for a seller.

④ Bad Debts Estimation

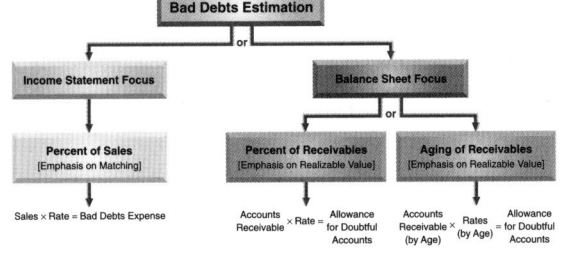

⑤ Bond Valuation

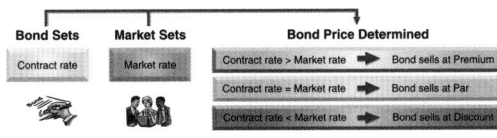

Bond Sets	Market Sets	Bond Price Determined
Contract rate	Market rate	Contract rate > Market rate ➡ Bond sells at Premium
		Contract rate = Market rate ➡ Bond sells at Par
		Contract rate < Market rate ➡ Bond sells at Discount

⑥ Stock Transactions Summary

Stock Transactions		Stock Entries	Dr.	Cr.
Issue Common Stock	Issue par value common stock at par (par stock recorded at par)	Cash	#	
		Common Stock		#
	Issue par value common stock at premium (par stock recorded at par).	Cash	#	
		Common Stock		#
		Paid-In Capital in Excess of Par Value, Common Stock		#
	Issue no-par value common stock (no-par stock recorded at amount received).	Cash	#	
		Common Stock		#
	Issue stated value common stock at stated value (stated stock recorded at stated value).	Cash	#	
		Common stock		#
	Issue stated value common stock at premium (stated stock recorded at stated value).	Cash	#	
		Common stock		#
		Paid-In Capital in Excess of Stated Value, Common Stock		#
Issue Preferred Stock	Issue par value preferred stock at par (par stock recorded at par).	Cash	#	
		Preferred Stock		#
	Issue par value preferred stock at premium (par stock recorded at par).	Cash	#	
		Preferred Stock		#
		Paid-In Capital in Excess of Par Value, Preferred Stock		#
Reacquire Common Stock	Reacquire its own common stock (treasury stock recorded at cost).	Treasury Stock, Common	#	
		Cash		#
Reissue Common Stock	Reissue its treasury stock at cost (treasury stock removed at cost).	Cash	#	
		Treasury Stock, Common		#
	Reissue its treasury stock above cost (treasury stock removed at cost).	Cash	#	
		Treasury Stock, Common		#
		Paid-In Capital, Treasury		#
	Reissue its treasury stock below cost (treasury stock removed at cost; if paid-in capital is insufficient to cover amount below cost, retained earnings is debited for remainder).	Cash	#	
		Paid-In Capital, Treasury		#
		Treasury Stock, Common		#
		Retained Earnings (if necessary) ...		#

⑦ Dividend Transactions

Account Effected	Type of Dividend		
	Cash Dividend	Stock Dividend	Stock Split
Cash	Decrease	—	—
Common Stock	—	Increase	—
Retained Earnings ..	Decrease	Decrease	—

⑧ Internal Control Principles

- Establish responsibilities.
- Maintain adequate records.
- Insure assets and bond key employees.
- Separate recordkeeping from custody of assets.
- Divide responsibility for related transactions.
- Apply technological controls.
- Perform regular and independent reviews.

FUNDAMENTALS

① Accounting Equation

Assets	=	Liabilities	+	Equity
↑ Debit for increases	↓ Credit for decreases	↓ Debit for decreases	↑ Credit for increases	↓ Debit for decreases	↑ Credit for increases

Contributed Capital*	+	Retained Earnings		
Common Stock	− Dividends	+ Revenues	− Expenses	
Dr. for decreases / Cr. for increases	Dr. for increases / Cr. for decreases	Dr. for decreases / Cr. for increases	Dr. for increases / Cr. for decreases	

▨ Indicates normal balance.
*Includes common stock and any preferred stock.

② Accounting Cycle

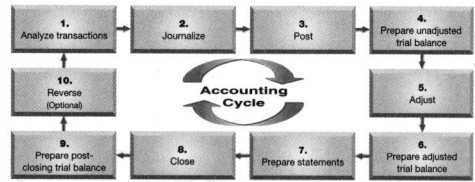

1. Analyze transactions
2. Journalize
3. Post
4. Prepare unadjusted trial balance
5. Adjust
6. Prepare adjusted trial balance
7. Prepare statements
8. Close
9. Prepare post-closing trial balance
10. Reverse (Optional)

Accounting Cycle

③ Adjustments and Entries

Type	Adjusting Entry
Prepaid Expenses	Dr. Expense Cr. Asset*
Unearned Revenues	Dr. Liability Cr. Revenue
Accrued Expenses	Dr. Expense Cr. Liability
Accrued Revenues	Dr. Asset Cr. Revenue

*For depreciation, credit Accumulated Depreciation (contra asset).

④ 4-Step Closing Process
1. Transfer revenue and gain account balances to Income Summary.
2. Transfer expense and loss account balances to Income Summary.
3. Transfer Income Summary balance to Retained Earnings.
4. Transfer Dividends balance to Retained Earnings.

⑤ Accounting Concepts

Characteristics	Assumptions	Principles	Constraints
Relevance	Business entity	Historical cost	Cost-benefit
Reliability	Going concern	Revenue recognition	Materiality
Comparability	Monetary unit	Expense recognition	Industry practice
Consistency	Periodicity	Full disclosure	Conservatism

⑥ Ownership of Inventory

	Ownership Transfers When Goods Passed To	Transportation Costs Paid By
FOB Shipping Point	Carrier	Buyer
FOB Destination	Buyer	Seller

⑦ Inventory Costing Methods

- Specific Identification
- First-In, First-Out (FIFO)
- Weighted-Average
- Last-In, First-Out (LIFO)

⑧ Depreciation and Depletion

Straight-Line: $\dfrac{\text{Cost} - \text{Salvage value}}{\text{Useful life in periods}} \times \text{Periods expired}$

Units-of-Production: $\dfrac{\text{Cost} - \text{Salvage value}}{\text{Useful life in units}} \times \text{Units produced}$

Declining-Balance: Rate* × Beginning-of-period book value
*Rate is often double the straight-line rate, or 2 × (1/Useful life)

Depletion: $\dfrac{\text{Cost} - \text{Salvage value}}{\text{Total capacity in units}} \times \text{Units extracted}$

⑨ Interest Computation
Interest = Principal (face) × Rate × Time

⑩ Accounting for Investment Securities

Classification*	Accounting
Short-Term Investment in Securities	
Held-to-maturity (debt) securities	Cost (without any discount or premium amortization)
Trading (debt and equity) securities	Fair value (with fair value adjustment to income)
Available-for-sale (debt and equity) securities	Fair value (with fair value adjustment to equity)
Long-Term Investment in Securities	
Held-to-maturity (debt) securities	Cost (with any discount or premium amortization)
Available-for-sale (debt and equity) securities	Fair value (with fair value adjustment to equity)
Equity securities with significant influence	Equity method
Equity securities with controlling influence	Equity method (with consolidation)

*A *fair value option* allows companies to report HTM and AFS securities much like trading securities.

ANALYSES

① Liquidity and Efficiency

Current ratio $= \dfrac{\text{Current assets}}{\text{Current liabilities}}$ — p. 117

Working capital = Current assets − Current liabilities — p. 575

Acid-test ratio $= \dfrac{\text{Cash} + \text{Short-term investments} + \text{Current receivables}}{\text{Current liabilities}}$ — p. 172

Accounts receivable turnover $= \dfrac{\text{Net sales}}{\text{Average accounts receivable, net}}$ — p. 312

Credit risk ratio $= \dfrac{\text{Allowance for doubtful accounts}}{\text{Accounts receivable, net}}$ — p. 312

Inventory turnover $= \dfrac{\text{Cost of goods sold}}{\text{Average inventory}}$ — p. 217

Days' sales uncollected $= \dfrac{\text{Accounts receivable, net}}{\text{Net sales}} \times 365^*$ — p. 270

Days' sales in inventory $= \dfrac{\text{Ending inventory}}{\text{Cost of goods sold}} \times 365^*$ — p. 218

Total asset turnover $= \dfrac{\text{Net sales}}{\text{Average total assets}}$ — p. 352

Plant asset useful life $= \dfrac{\text{Plant asset cost}}{\text{Depreciation expense}}$ — p. 352

Plant asset age $= \dfrac{\text{Accumulated depreciation}}{\text{Depreciation expense}}$ — p. 352

Days' cash expense coverage $= \dfrac{\text{Cash and cash equivalents}}{\text{Average daily cash expenses}}$ — p. 256

*360 days is also commonly used.

② Solvency

Debt ratio $= \dfrac{\text{Total liabilities}}{\text{Total assets}}$ Equity ratio $= \dfrac{\text{Total equity}}{\text{Total assets}}$ — pp. 70 & 579

Debt-to-equity $= \dfrac{\text{Total liabilities}}{\text{Total equity}}$ — p. 435

Times interest earned $= \dfrac{\text{Income before interest expense and income taxes}}{\text{Interest expense}}$ — p. 390

Cash coverage of growth $= \dfrac{\text{Cash flow from operations}}{\text{Cash outflow for plant assets}}$ — p. 529

Cash coverage of debt $= \dfrac{\text{Cash flow from operations}}{\text{Total noncurrent liabilities}}$ — p. 529

③ Profitability

Profit margin ratio $= \dfrac{\text{Net income}}{\text{Net sales}}$ — p. 116

Gross margin ratio $= \dfrac{\text{Net sales} - \text{Cost of goods sold}}{\text{Net sales}}$ — p. 172

Return on total assets $= \dfrac{\text{Net income}}{\text{Average total assets}}$ — p. 22

= Profit margin ratio × Total asset turnover — p. 581

Return on common stockholders' equity $= \dfrac{\text{Net income} - \text{Preferred dividends}}{\text{Average common stockholders' equity}}$ — p. 581

Book value per common share $= \dfrac{\text{Stockholders' equity applicable to common shares}}{\text{Number of common shares outstanding}}$ — p. 485

Basic earnings per share $= \dfrac{\text{Net income} - \text{Preferred dividends}}{\text{Weighted-average common shares outstanding}}$ — p. 483

Cash flow on total assets $= \dfrac{\text{Cash flow from operations}}{\text{Average total assets}}$ — p. 529

Payout ratio $= \dfrac{\text{Cash dividends declared on common stock}}{\text{Net income}}$ — p. 485

④ Market

Price-earnings ratio $= \dfrac{\text{Market value (price) per share}}{\text{Earnings per share}}$ — p. 484

Dividend yield $= \dfrac{\text{Annual cash dividends per share}}{\text{Market price per share}}$ — p. 484